SOCIOLOGICAL REALITIES

A Guide to the Study of Society

EDITED BY
*Irving Louis Horowitz &
Mary Symons Strong*

WITH THE ASSISTANCE OF
George A. Talbot

RUTGERS UNIVERSITY

A Trans-action Textbook

HARPER & ROW, PUBLISHERS
New York, Evanston, San Francisco, London

HM 51
.H637

111278

SOCIOLOGICAL REALITIES
A Guide to the Study of Society
Copyright © 1971 by *Trans*-action

Printed in the United States of America. All rights reserved. No part of this book may be used or reproduced in any manner whatsoever without written permission except in the case of brief quotations embodied in critical articles and reviews. For information address Harper & Row, Publishers, Inc., 49 East 33rd Street, New York, N.Y. 10016.

Standard Book Number: 06-042911-9
Library of Congress Catalog Card Number: 70-159575

COVER PHOTO: *Charles Gatewood*

Preface

Like the character in the Molière play who is surprised to find out that he has been speaking prose all his life, so too, there is a somewhat similar feeling in noting that *Trans-action* has been dealing in sociological terms, concepts, and ideas for its short life. And perhaps this is a central reason why we feel this volume is both unique and refreshing. It is unique because model building and theory construction are not imposed upon reality like a bit onto a horse. Rather, in the course of understanding small scale aspects of social reality, models and theories are made use of for the sole purpose of explaining things better and more efficiently. And such an approach is refreshing, particularly in a volume geared for use as a text, because students, like most people, are far more prone to be groping for a word or an idea with which to deal with experience, than to work out a systematic body of core concepts with which he or she is presumably responsible for ordering the society.

This is just another way of saying that sociology as an inductive science, based on experience, must proceed to build its theories rather than impose them. This is not to say that this volume is anti-theoretical; far from it. If anything, the ordering of sections and subsections into frameworks, that are easily identifiable as basic working units with which teachers of sociology are familiar, indicates that these articles are very much in the great mainstream of sociological literature—even to the extent of being readily linked to customary sectioning of the field. But what this volume does do, that few others, it seems to us have been able to do, is not to start with a great dualism of theory and actualities and then blend them and shove them onto each other with the triumphant glow of ideology that says: see, there is a connection between my beliefs and what happens, after all. What the readings do well, and what *Trans*-action has done well for eight years now, is show the organic connection between the life of society and the position of sociology—a connection that does not need to deny the unity of experience or the worth of any part of society.

This volume is remarkably comparative in character. Remarkable is an appropriate adjective, since this was not a foremost intention of the editors, but rather a serendipitous consequence of the way sociology has now evolved. The borders of sociology have finally broken through the domestic barrier. Survival techniques of Eskimo Indians and American blacks can now be seen as illustrating the same principles of adaptation. Deviant behavior in Sweden or in the United States can be seen to illustrate the same principles of stratification, the processes of modernization in Japan and Russia can be seen as responses to the same political demands for self-sufficiency and economic autonomy. In this sense, *Sociological Realities* is probably the first "jet age" text in the field. Just as man is a unitary phenomenon, so too is the world a unitary phenomenon. Throughout the book, one is struck by the unity in diversity, and the diversity which appears to highlight the same principles of everything from personal survival to national sovereignty.

This is not a manufactured product, processed and boiled down to meet imaginary student or teacher specification. Its organicism stems directly from the unity of imagination characterizing the authors over the years. Nor is it thrown together upon a moment's notice to respond to a new course sequence or new crisis of the moment—whether it be the war on poverty or the ecological crisis. It is neither of these false alternatives—neither a manufactured consensus nor an eclectic melange. The articles in this volume, and hopefully the editorial statements preceding each section, derive from a unity of purpose and a unity of conception that evolved over a decade of concentrated writing and editing. It is in this sense, the fulfillment of the promisory note offered in *The New Sociology* a decade earlier. It is the sociological imagination at work.

It is our genuine belief that this is neither a reader in the conventional sense nor a textbook in a conventional sense, but a new conception of the organic orientation of sociology through the writings of many and diverse people, who share common interests and a common sense of what is important and meaningful in the field of sociology at this time. It is also a unique product in the strong evidence of editorial direction invariably lacking in a reader which stems from many and diverse sources, and oftentimes, no less lacking in textbooks. In this sense the blend of internal editorial skills, combined with sociological statements, provide an authentic departure from any currently available literature in the field of sociology intended for college use.

Experience is the basis of sociology. It is therefore not surprising that *Trans*-action has placed a major emphasis on photography as a way of making statements graphically. Photography seems to be a natural way to illustrate the social sciences. Photographs are of people and social science is involved with behavior. Both record acts as the basis for their comment on society. This is not to say that photographers are ruthless empiricists capturing reality with their lenses, or that social scientists are pollsters satisfied with nose counting as an end. It isn't accidental, however, that the photographer's current concern for expressing reality—by showing the black borders of the film with the sprocket holes as if to say, "This is made from a real piece of film"—parallels the social scientist in his desire for hard data to back up his analysis.

The view of the world that placed a premium on observed reality led to the use of the camera obscura and eventually to the development of photography itself. Certainly, by the middle of the nineteenth century social and pictoral realism appeared in the works of sociologists like Henry Mayhew's *London Labour and the London Poor* (1861-62) and the works of photographers like Mathew Brady. Lewis Hine, trained in sociology, styled himself a social science photographer. His work became instrumental in child labor reforms of his day, and today stands as a landmark in the description of the life of the poor. That concern with people and affection for them and indignation about injustice done remains a part of the journalistic and documentary tradition. Some have attempted major photographic ethnographies; others have built up a way of presenting an intimate view of the life of people caught unawares; and still others have stood back from the scene and made dispassionate, analytic statement about society. In more than passing ways they share many goals the social scientists themselves have.

There are many people to whose assistance this book owes a great debt and to whom we can only express our gratitude collectively. We have in mind all those scholars, editors, and friends of *Trans*-action whose skills, wisdom, and imagination have contributed to the creation of a magazine in which the community of social scientists could report their research, recommend social policies based on their findings and concerns, and be listened to by a widening circle of *Trans*-action readers. We are particularly indebted to those authors of *Trans*-action articles that have been reprinted in this collection. In the eight years of the existence of *Trans*-action, these people have helped build a new culture of sociology and thus have put some real meat on the dry bones of contemporary sociology.

For their expert editorial judgment and pioneering work in social science editing we wish to acknowledge the work of our colleagues who have held the post of editor of *Trans*-action—Leonard Zweig, Warren Boroson, and Nelson W. Aldrich, Jr. The editorial quality of the articles over the years has been due also to many other editorial craftsmen on the magazine staff, among them William Krasner and Judith Fagan Burbank. Ann Novotny of Research Reports has acted as picture researcher. Hugh Edwards of the Chicago Art Institute and Jimmy Fox and Jerry Rosencrantz of Magnum have been especially helpful in putting us in touch with photographers.

With specific reference to *Sociological Realities,* which itself represents a considerable editorial undertaking, we must especially single out the contributions of the following people: Danielle Salti, for her painstaking work in preparing the indices and also for her careful examination of the entire manuscript; Frederick Roses and Mathew Greenwald, for assistance in compiling the bibliographies; Jean Gary, for her supervision of the various duties in assembling such a book, including article permissions and photographic rights. Also, many people at *Trans*-action were of inestimable help: Donald L. Steinbeigle, Mary E. Curtis, Harvey J. Kaye, Rayne Ayers, and Dee Maltese.

The artistic and photographic contributions of George A. Talbot to *Sociological Realities* is of such consequence that he is listed on the title page. This in itself bespeaks of our personal estimate of his efforts.

Irving Louis Horowitz
Mary Symons Strong

Rutgers University
New Brunswick, New Jersey
January 26, 1971

Contents

ONE THE CONDUCT OF CULTURE 1

Norms of Behavior

1. A Case of Ostracism—and Its Unusual Aftermath
   David W. Plath 6
2. Communal Brethren of the Great Plains
   John W. Bennett 12
3. The Decline and Fall of the Small Town
   William Simon & John H. Gagnon 18
4. Rural Russia Today
   Martin K. Whyte 28

Variation and Contrast

5. Time and Cool People
   John Horton 35
6. Kapluna Daughter: Living with Eskimos
   Jean L. Briggs 44
7. Two Tactics for Ethnic Survival—Eskimo and Indian
   Robert J. Dryfoos, Jr. 57
8. The Scandinavian Hangover
   Nils Christie 61

Social Change

9. The Japanese "Howdunit"
   Martin Bronfenbrenner 65
10. Modern India's Ancient Medicine
    Charles Leslie 70
11. Why All of Us May Be Hippies Someday
    Fred Davis 80

TWO SOCIAL ORGANIZATION & GROUPS 88

Groups and Associations

12. Conformity and Commitment
    Charles A. Kiesler 92
13. The Corner Gang Boys Get Married
    Walter B. Miller 96
14. Sanctuary or Prison—Responses to Life in a Mental Hospital
    Ailon Shiloh 98
15. The Making of a Black Muslim
    John R. Howard 106

Population and Urban Communities

16. Red Guard on Grant Avenue
    Stanford M. Lyman 113
17. Cleveland's Crisis Ghetto
    Walter Williams 127
18. Timing of our Lives
    Harley L. Browning 137

Bureaucracy

19. Beyond Bureaucracy
    Warren Bennis 143

20. The Power of the Powerless
    Trans-action Staff Report — 148
21. Who's Complaining?
    Julius Roth — 150

THREE SHAPING OF SOCIALIZATION — 155

Early Socialization

22. The Family as a Company of Players
    Annabelle B. Motz — 159
23. Psychological Miscarriage: An End to Mother Love
    Marian Gennaria Morris — 163
24. Psychosexual Development
    William Simon & John H. Gagnon — 169

Adult Socialization

25. Dynamic Young Fogies—Rebels on the Right
    Lawrence F. Schiff — 178
26. Young Intelligentsia in Revolt
    Richard Flacks — 184
27. Rebirth in the Airborne
    Melford S. Weiss — 194
28. The Fund of Sociability
    Robert S. Weiss — 198

Deviant Socialization

29. Hippies in College—From Teeny-Boppers to Drug Freaks
    Geoffrey Simmon & Grafton Trout — 206
30. The Culture of Civility
    Howard S. Becker & Irving Louis Horowitz — 209
31. The Respectable Criminal
    Donald R. Cressey — 216

FOUR SOCIAL STRATIFICATION & EQUALITY — 220

Class and Caste

32. Dead on Arrival
    David Sudnow — 225
    The Tipped Scales of American Justice
    Stuart S. Nagel — 233
34. Classical Music and the Status Game
    Joseph Bensman — 240
35. The Working Classes—Old and New
    Gerald Handel & Lee Rainwater — 246
36. The Politics of Protracted Conflict
    Anders Boserup — 248

Racial Cleavages

37. White Institutions and Black Rage
    David Boesel, Richard Berk, W. Eugene Groves, Bettye Eidson, Peter H. Rossi — 258
38. White Rites Versus Indian Rights
    A. D. Fisher — 266
39. Outsiders in Britain
    Peter I. Rose — 270

Social Mobility

40. America's New Officer Corps
    Charles H. Coates — 276
41. Seminole Girl
    Merwyn S. Garbarino — 280
42. Genteel Backlash: Chicago 1886
    Richard Sennett — 287

FIVE INSTITUTIONS — 297

The Family

43. "I Divorce Thee"
    Lawrence Rosen — 301
44. Sororities and the Husband Game
    John Finley Scott — 305
45. A Better Life: Notes from Puerto Rico
    Lloyd H. Rogler — 310

Religious Institutions

46. The Future of the Islamic Religion
    Guenter Lewy — 314
47. Religion Is Irrelevant in Sweden
    Richard F. Tomasson — 318
48. The Serpent-Handling Religions of West Virginia
    Nathan L. Gerrard — 325

Politics and Power

49. The Two Presidencies
    Aaron Wildavsky — 332
50. Black Powerlessness in Chicago
    Harold M. Baron with Harriet Stulman, Richard Rothstein, Rennard Davis — 340

Economic Life

51. Private Initiative in the "Great Society"
    Norton E. Long — 347
52. Rich Man's Qualifications for Poor Man's Jobs
    Ivar Berg — 353

SIX SYMBOLIC INTERACTION & HUMAN COMMUNICATION — 359

Patterns of Interaction

53. Healing by Negotiation
    Anselm Strauss — 364
54. Together in Isolation
    William W. Haythorn & Irwin Altman — 367
55. Open Occupancy—What Whites Say, What They Do
    Gordon H. DeFriese & W. Scott Ford, Jr. — 372

Conflict and Accommodation

56. Advocacy in the Ghetto
    Richard A. Cloward & Richard M. Elman — 376
57. Industrial Invasion of the Village Green
    Herbert G. Gutman — 385
58. Why Men Fight
    Charles C. Moskos, Jr. — 391

59. Does Military Deterrence Deter?
   Raoul Naroll … 402

Collective Behavior, Mass Communications, and Public Opinion

60. Murder, Juries, and the Press
   Rita James Simon … 409
61. Sniping—A New Pattern of Violence?
   Terry Ann Knopf … 411
62. Rumors in the Aftermath of the Detroit Riot
   Marilyn Rosenthal … 419

SEVEN POLITICAL PROTEST & SOCIAL MOVEMENTS … 429

Protest and Rebellion

63. Whitewash over Watts
   Robert Blauner … 432
64. Why a Rebellion at Columbia Was Inevitable
   Ellen Kay Trimberger … 440
65. Resistance in Czechoslovakia—An Underground in the Open
   Constantine C. Menges … 451
66. Algerian Peasant Revolt
   Eric R. Wolf … 457
67. The Wallace Whitelash
   Seymour Martin Lipset & Earl Raab … 471

EIGHT STYLE & SUBSTANCE IN SOCIOLOGY … 483

Social Science Methods and Viewpoints

68. Ecology and Environment
   Kenneth E. Boulding … 486
69. Science as a Frame of Reference
   Raymond W. Mack … 493
70. Intellectual Strategies and Research Tactics
   Raymond W. Mack … 495
71. The Convict as Researcher
   Hans Toch … 497
72. Evaluating Social Action Programs
   Peter Rossi … 501
73. Deception in Social Research
   Herbert C. Kelman … 504

Social Science and Public Policy

74. Black Families and the White House
   Lee Rainwater & William Yancey … 509
75. Social Science Yogis and Military Commissars
   Irving Louis Horowitz … 522
76. The Violence Commission
   Jerome H. Skolnick … 532

NOTES ON AUTHORS … 539
NAME INDEX … 543
SUBJECT INDEX … 546

1 Conduct of Culture

In his study of Charles Dickens, André Maurois asks why we need novels—those narratives of fictitious happenings. His answer is "Because our real life is passed in an incoherent universe. We long for a world subject to the laws of the spirit, an ordered world; through our senses we know only obscure forces, and beings with confused passions. From the novel we seek a universe which will help us, wherein we can seek emotions without exposing ourselves to the consequences of authentic emotions; find intelligible characters, and a Destiny on a human scale."

It is true that each individual does come to terms with "an incoherent universe" in part with the aid of his story tellers—mythmakers of old and novelists of modern times who either in oral or written form have attempted to make the "world subject to the laws of the spirit, an ordered world." But, in fact, man's lot is not so desperately confused as Maurois would have us believe. At birth, he falls heir to a vast heritage of organized ideas and values, which we call his culture—his group's accumulation of wisdom and expected ways of behavior, often so well organized as to be distilled into proverbs and adages and enacted into laws and constitutions. This culture presents him with a way of making sense of the myriad of people and phenomena in the world about him, and it does so with great coherence and quite insistently.

Some anthropologists have defined this culture as everything that man receives from previous generations as his social heritage. Edward Tylor, the nineteenth-century anthropologist, defined culture as "that complex whole which includes knowledge, belief, art, morals, law, custom, and any other capabilities and habits acquired by man as a member of society." By this definition, emphasis is placed on the broad distinction between the cultural heritage and the biological heritage of mankind, a distinction drawn by social scientists to make a case for the role of culture against the claims of biological and genetic determinists.

In the second half of the nineteenth century, there were, as a result of Charles Darwin's discoveries about the biological origins of man, strong tendencies to interpret all behavior biologically. Ideas from this era about the genetic causes of crime and poverty, for instance, have died hard, and some are still in circulation despite evidence refuting them. The countering notion is that the person acquires the culture by being a member of society, that he does not and cannot inherit it genetically. To propose that culture should be defined as all of man's social heritage—the sum total of what is passed on from generation to generation—is to stress the idea that culture is learned, not biologically inherited. That the culture has to be learned and relearned by each new generation is one of the important ideas of social science.

Groups and Culture

We have been talking about "cultural heritage" as if it were shared alike by all men. Man's culture is unique to man, but it is also as varied as the world is wide so that no man ever acquires or encompasses all of it. In fact, each man learns the culture that is peculiar to the group to which he belongs. He shares it with a particular group of people. As an example, no one could miss noticing that elements of the Japanese culture differ from the Hutterite culture of the great plains of Canada in the articles by David W. Plath, "A Case of Ostracism—and Its Unusual Aftermath," and John W. Bennett, "Communal Brethren of the Great Plains." Growing up in a small town in the Midwest is very different from being raised a peasant boy in Siberia. The articles by John H. Gagnon and William Simon, "The Decline and Fall

Ainu (the aboriginal residents of Japan's northern-most island) carving bears for the tourist trade while watching television.

of the Small Town" and Martin K. Whyte, "Rural Russia Today," illustrate this cultural variation.

At the same time, it should be noted that the organization of life into communes occurs in Japan as well as among the communal brethren of the Canadian prairie, the latter being a concept of group life brought by the Hutterites from the Russian Ukraine and Germany. Likewise, small town and rural life in America and Russia appear to stress similar kinds of conservative patterns of life. So we see that commonalities of cultures exist alongside great variation.

When anthropologists began to study the exotic societies discovered by the European explorers, Westerners were astonished to find customs practiced by other people strangely different from their own which they had considered almost God-given. They reacted variously with contempt, wonder, and a deepening curiosity. The concept of culture was offered to them as a way of understanding the new and mysterious variety of life patterns. When anthropologists undertook studies of these new peoples—they were principally small preliterate and peasant societies—and became acquainted with them as whole societies, they discovered that all of their parts interlocked and worked as a unit, that the relationship

Conduct of Culture

of one part to another had an internal logic. Thus exotic religious practices, for example, fitted into the other institutions of culture in meaningful ways. Cultures were seen as organized entities with all their parts contributing to a coherent pattern. From this viewpoint each culture could be considered unique and respected for its special qualities.

When we apply this viewpoint to a large industrial society, however, a difficulty arises, for it is almost impossible to study and catalogue every aspect of an immense nation such as the Soviet Union or the United States or Great Britain. If Americans, British, and Russians do not share in all aspects of the cultural heritage of their nations, they do, however, belong to other more restricted groups with whom they share beliefs, outlooks, and common ways of life. Such groups have been called subcultures. For example, young blacks in the United States are said to live in a "street culture" which has its own standards of behavior and admired roles to play as shown in the article by John Horton, "Time and Cool People." How much this so-called subculture of street-corner blacks has in common with other cultural groups in the United States remains a problem to be explored.

Coping

One way to view culture is to see it as a means by which man learns to survive. Like all living creatures, man was forced to secure food and to keep from being killed by wild animals and hostile conditions in his environment. His ability to solve the problems of survival—in all kinds of climates and terrains—testifies to his remarkable capacity to invent and transmit ways of coping with difficult problems. Adapting to many kinds of physical environments has been accomplished brilliantly by groups of people who have contrived ways and means for getting along and passed them on from generation to generation. To illustrate, an impressive adjustment by man to the forbiddingly cold climate of the Canadian Arctic is told by Jean L. Briggs in her article, "Kapluna Daughter: Living with Eskimos," in which an American anthropologist is "adopted" as a daughter by an Eskimo family who try to teach her their ways of living.

Man has been adaptive to all kinds of social conditions as well as physical environments. Robert J. Dryfoos, Jr. points out that Hudson Bay Eskimos have adapted more readily than Indians to their Euro-Canadian culture in his piece "Two Tactics for Ethnic Survival—Eskimo and Indian." Very few cultures die, although some are almost unrecognizably transformed, for though individuals die, cultures live on in others.

Over long stretches of history—probably two million years since our first man-ape ancestor put in his appearance—man has evolved biologically and culturally. His biological evolution has slowly changed his physical form, but it has not built in an instinctive biological apparatus to adjust to specific physical environments. Instead, man has learned painfully, step by step from experience, and taught what he knew to his children. This process is called social evolution, the idea of which is associated with the work of an early and great social scientist, Herbert Spencer.

With the accumulation of knowledge and skills, man has increased his ability to shape his own world and even to alter his physical surrounding, sometimes beneficially and other

INTRODUCTION

times, detrimentally to his physical and social survival. Looking again at the article by Bennett, "Communal Brethren of the Great Plains," we see that a tightly organized religious group made farming highly successful even under unpromising ecological circumstances. On the other hand, many of man's inventions create new and difficult problems and prove to be harmful to some members of society. Drinking alcohol in excess, for example, is one of many instances of the detrimental practices, beliefs, and customs that societies pass along to their members. Nils Christie presents, in "The Scandinavian Hangover," a comparison of Danish, Finnish, and United States methods of controlling consumption of alcohol at levels dangerous to their citizens. It should be evident after reading Christie's article that social evolution is not necessarily synonymous with progress, and not all discoveries and inventions are good for mankind.

Thanks to the Past

When we take the long view, the historical view, of culture we cannot help being impressed by what we owe to the past. The thought occurs to us—what if each man had to start from scratch? How long would it take modern man to invent fire and the wheel? If we were on our own, who would think of the musical scale, a knife, growing grain?

Sometimes, we wish we could shake off the dead hand of the past. A "design for living," as Clyde Kluckhohn phrased it, is prescribed for us by older generations, and sometimes it seems to shackle the new. Traditional ways of doing things become sacred, and people have vested interests in keeping them the same. Old ways hang on in all cultures even where so-called rational, scientific attitudes are present. In his article "Modern India's Ancient Medicine," Charles Leslie, an anthropologist, analyzes the efforts being made to revive medical practices based on ancient scientific texts, and shows how despair, growing out of rapid changes in culture, makes many Indian people long for traditional medicine while at the same time they despise the practitioners of it for their incompetence.

But change, even radical, revolutionary change in societies does occur. A sharp break with the past occurred in Japan, for example, about a hundred years ago when the traditional military rulers of Japan were ousted and replaced by the "Meiji statesmen," who shepherded the country through successful economic development. Martin Bronfenbrenner analyzes that century of Japanese modernization in "The Japanese 'Howdunit'."

Belonging to a culture means above all sharing rules and standards of behavior with other people. A person knows how he is expected to behave, if he is to remain a member in good standing. The "cognitive map" provided by his culture includes restrictions on what he ought and ought not do, and to what standards he should hold other people accountable.

Cultures differ very much in what they define as right and wrong. Having only one wife at a time is a keystone of

Conduct of Culture

Western morality, a norm that people of some other cultures do not abide by. Having several wives is not only moral, but seems the natural way of organizing households in many parts of the South Pacific, the Near East, and Africa.

In relation to such areas of behavior as sex and property, people may have very strict norms. At the same time, however, some rules of behavior are regarded less seriously. William Graham Sumner made a useful distinction between the folkways and mores of a culture. Folkways are those customary ways of doing things that are usually expected in everyday life, such as eating manners, ways of greeting people, and appropriate modes of dress. Violation of the folkways is not severely punished. More subtle ways of forcing people to toe the line are used—ridicule and gossip, for example, rather than arrest or ostracism. Most people find it difficult to be laughed at, to be thought uncouth or incompetent in the ways of the group, and they will put a good deal of effort into finding out what is expected of them and live up to the rules of the culture in most respects. But those who persist in violating the folkways can count on sliding through without being severely punished.

Mores, in contrast to folkways, are those standards that people regard as important for the welfare of the group. Violation of the mores cannot be tolerated because it is harmful to the survival of the shared values of the group. The group feels justified in punishing the offender. It is one thing to go barefoot in the city streets; it's quite another thing to go naked. The touchiness of our culture about the body and bodily functions, then, puts most of the norms governing them in the category of mores. When, for example, hippies break both the folkways of dress and hair styles and the mores of property, work, and sex, the public readily experiences contempt for them and tries to punish them.

In his article "Why All of Us May Be Hippies Someday" Fred Davis points out the "givens" of the culture being challenged by hippies—compulsive consumption, passive spectatorship, and frenetic use of time. The challenge of the hippies is a moral one and brings into bold relief the idea that a culture provides a moral order. The life that people build and maintain is based on agreement and relative adherence to moral rules and standards. We call this a normative order. As long as people live a collective life they will be guided by a moral consensus, however broadly or narrowly accepted the agreement on norms may be.

The term culture, then, refers to the beliefs, attitudes, values, and norms of conduct that prescribe the behavior expected of groups, communities, societies, nations, and even the world of mankind. Every man belongs to one or some of these cultures, lives by their values and meanings, and carves out a style of life that is his individual version of his cultural heritage reinterpreted and embodied in his person. The individual thus embodies his cultural heritage, and in turn, transforms that culture in the process of social organization, a theme to which we will turn in the next section.

A Case of Ostracism— and Its Unusual Aftermath

The origin of a Japanese commune

DAVID W. PLATH
with translations from
YOSHIE SUGIHARA

Shinkyō, in the village of Kasama about 35 miles from Osaka, Japan, has become widely known in recent years. For it is a communal society that has been successful, one that has—despite enormous hostility—endured and prospered.

Communal living—the sharing of resources, produce, and living experiences in a closely knit community—has been engaged in by many groups, for many reasons, all over the world and throughout history. Examples are the early Christian communities and the modern Communist collectives. What makes Shinkyō so unusual is that this communal society is non-ideological and non-missionary; in fact, its establishment was not even premeditated. Shinkyō began for negative reasons—because its founding members were ostracized.

In village Japan, organized ostracism is called *mura-hachibu,* or "village eight-parts." According to tradition, neighborly village social interaction consists of 10 parts, including the right to such near-necessities as disaster relief and the use of common land. When a family is ostracized, it will be deprived (at least in theory) of eight of these ten parts.

To have them restored, the head of the household must repent, persuade a village influential to stand as guarantor, and then make appropriate restitution. In Shinkyō, the offenders would not repent.

Shinkyō, and its success, were due in major part to the personality and work of its founder and dominant figure, Masutarō Ozaki.

The ostracism fell on four families at once, and they gave one another support; one alone would hardly have been able to stand up against its force. And they held together because of their trust, respect, and affection for Ozaki, who came to be called their *Sensei,* or revered leader.

Ozaki Sensei was born in 1900, at Kasama, the second son of a fairly prosperous farmer. Like most Kasama families, the Ozakis were ardent supporters of the Tenri church, one of the oldest and strongest of the more than 250 modern-era "new religions" of Japan. For several years, Ozaki himself served as a missionary, but then grew discouraged about Tenri's claims to healing powers—and disgusted by what he saw as the religion's milking of contributions from the poor and credulous. Eventually he refused to accept contributions for Tenri. Not long after, he destroyed the altar of his Osaka mission and persuaded four Kasama families (including his elder brother's) to do the same.

This was the official reason why Ozaki Sensei and the families were ostracized. Below the surface, however, was a covert power struggle between Ozaki and his childhood friend Iwazō Seki, then (1937) the foremost leader in Kasama. Seki reported Ozaki and the four families to the rural police—for criminal irreverence (the smashed altar) and abandoning a corpse (they had buried a man without religious rites, as directed in his will).

The police would not file charges. Thereupon the Seki faction called for *mura-hachibu.*

What happened next is best described by Mrs. Yoshie Sugihara, who joined Ozaki Sensei in the Shinkyō venture and later became his second wife. The following is translated and condensed from the fifth chapter of her book on the history of Shinkyō (Shunjusha Press, Tokyo, 1962):

On August 10, the Seki faction, having talked with the people of the Eastern section (which included Sensei's home), assembled them in the Mission, and summoned Sensei there. As they had planned, one after another the Seki faction roundly denounced him.

"You're a troublemaker who's disturbing the peace of the village."

"Have you managed to do anything but disrespectful work like burning up the gods?"

"Didn't you cheat an old man and hold a funeral that as much as threw away the corpse?"

"If these things are going to keep on and on we've got to consider what'll happen to the village. What in hell are you thinking of?"

In short they meant to close in on him, count up and review his "crimes" to date. They probably calculated that once he was faced by the power of the majority even the obstinate Ozaki would humble himself.

But Sensei wasn't bothered a bit. "If you mean the altar affair or that about Kunimatsu's burial," he said, "weren't they done only after everybody had talked them over and agreed to them? You talk about disrupting the village, but aren't those who go crying to the cops and secretly pull strings the real disturbers of the 'peace of the village'? They're right here among us. Do you want me to name names, or let it go at that?"

As Sensei spoke out so sharply and glared around, the gabbling assembly fell silent. Everybody had a guilty conscience. They hadn't foreseen that "Poke in the brush and the snakes come out"; they were completely flustered and didn't say another word.

Sensei said, "Well then, it's better that I hold off naming names for this meeting. I have nothing more to say, so it's best for you all to discuss it by yourselves." He hurried out, and not a single man tried to stop him.

But the gang was as persistent as could be. The next day, the 11th, a summons came for Hisajirō Yamanaka and Sei'ichi Mitani [members of the offending families]. First the gang surrounded Yamanaka and made him sit alone in the center.

"Break off with Ozaki!"

"If a good farmer like you tags along with a dangerous drifter like Ozaki," they said, "what do you think's going to happen in the future? We don't say you've done wrong, but break off with Ozaki today at this meeting and we'll see that you get a voice in village affairs." Such was their carrot-and-stick strategy. Knowing what had happened the day before with Ozaki Sensei, Yamanaka perceived the danger in the situation and was, as he put it, "scared silly." If he refused their demands here, what would come next? Considering how the gang operated, he could expect the worst.

But as Yamanaka himself told me later, "Before I thought about being hurt or helped or anything else I lost my temper at Seki and the rest of that gang, with their stinking proud attitude and their trying to force things their way; and I couldn't help what I did."

Yamanaka lifted his face and said to them, "He hasn't done a thing wrong. What he says is right. I won't leave him even if it kills me."

Next Mitani was called in and given exactly the same grilling. But Mitani also refused then and there, and said firmly that he would go along with Ozaki.

"We can't put up with people who've got the mad idea that they'll stick together to the death"—this was their reason for village ostracism. Of course we didn't have any way of knowing when and how it was decided; and there was no formal announcement. Nobody, not even a relative, was permitted to speak to any member of the four families; and a stiff rule was made that anybody who spoke even once would be fined 100 yen [equal to $100 at that time].

Becoming Nonpersons

The members of the four families were treated as if they didn't exist. They were stripped of all human rights. City people can't even imagine what a painful position you're put in when you suffer village ostracism.

NORMS OF BEHAVIOR   Photographs by David W. Plath

Mrs. Yoshie Sugihara, chronicler of Shinkyō.

The Shinkyō people have turned from farming to making *tatami*, the rice-straw mats that carpet Japanese dwellings.

Hemmed in by the ostracism, the four families had to resort to any means they could find in order just to keep alive during the war. [The war with China began on July 7, 1937.]

The influence of the China war gradually reached out. Recruits began to leave.

Saying farewell to a recruit was held to be a citizen's duty; neglecting it would be the same as treason. Eventually, unable to stand it, [members of the ostracized families] slipped out to discuss the situation with Sensei in Osaka.

"Out of respect for the red sash the right thing to do is to see off the recruit. Just go ahead and join the farewell party."

At a signal from firecrackers, the recruit, his family and kin, and the villagers assemble in the grounds of the community guardian shrine. The people just pass coldly by the four families, nobody says a word.

"This . . . it's a going-away present for the soldier. Couldn't you hand it to him for us?"

With a sour face Teijirō says, "We can't accept anything like this from people who've been ousted from the village."

Recruits continued to leave one after another, but eventually we couldn't take any more of it and we quit with the eighth one.

Instead we all eagerly poured our energy into our farm work.

The Eve. In Kasama this is the greatest event of the whole year, and a day for rest and relaxation.

Almost two months had passed in ostracism by the first of November 1937, when the Eve came around. By then all contact between the four families and the villagers had been completely cut off, starting with the farewell parties and extending to weddings, death-day anniversaries, and all other celebrations.

That day at Sensei's home we pounded ricecakes and prepared a feast just like anybody else. And the following day all the members of the four families, old and young, male and female, carried the feast and the ricecakes and fled to Hirao Saime. Hirao Saime is the boundary between Kasama and a place in Uda county called Hirao. The Yamanakas have a field there. In that field the families held their festival and "relaxation."

We had brought hoes and spades and rakes along with the feast. The innocent children had a good time eating the feast and the ricecakes; the old folks complained and sobbed regrets about "such an Eve"; and the men gritted their teeth, said nothing, and swung their hoes. We didn't care how much fun the villagers were having. We sowed radishes. Then we clasped hands firmly and vowed to each other that we would work together with all our might. And it was this that happened to become the first step toward our communal production and communal living.

Actually, having been ostracized, their ties with the villagers broken, freed from various rights and duties, the four families couldn't avoid strengthening their own bonds, like it or not, in order to make a living. For example they helped each other weed paddy, going from one's fields to another's. From time to time relatives of the four families came to us on the sly and asked us to tell them the reason for the ostracism. But we refused to discuss it, telling them as Sensei had instructed, "If that's what you want to know, instead of asking us you'd better go ask the village big shots."

When the Eve was past we entered the November harvest season. However, in the village they were saying they would not lend the community-owned ricehuller to the four families. The four families went right out, pooled their money in equal shares, and bought a huller and a thresher.

Once they had been refused the use of the huller even though they were members of the association, the four families requested repayment of their capital shares in the farmers' cooperative. The village went into an uproar. People came to offer compromises. The mayor came, the police came, and the head of the neighborhood association came. Finally even Iwazō Seki himself came. Sensei refused bluntly, telling them: "This isn't the kind of dispute you 'compromise.' We didn't start any fight so there's no issue over which we have to come to terms. We've simply been ostracized, and we're content to accept that. Instead of coming here you should go see those poor people in the village who are following the ostracism resolution without knowing anything about it, and ask them to tell you the origins of the reason for our being ostracized."

The Seki faction wouldn't agree to make public the reason for the ostracism. So the deliberate attempts to compromise and reconcile the parties could only end in separating them again. Sensei and the four families

David W. Plath (left) is shown here with Ozaki Sensei, founder and leader of the Shinkyō community. A fuller account of this case of ostracism appears in *Sensei and His People, The Building of a Japanese Commune* by Yoshie Sugihara and David W. Plath (Berkeley: University of California Press, 1969).

grew all the more strong in their desire to take up communal production.

When the autumn collective harvest was done, in December the four families turned to baking charcoal. At first each family dug its own oven, cut its own wood and made it into charcoal. We helped each other only with the baking. But efficiency was rotten this way. So from the second firing onward we collectivized thoroughly. That is, we baked everything in one oven on one hill.

Beginning the Communal Life

As the new year dawned we had a suggestion—from nobody in particular—that we build a meeting place where all of us could gather at ease. For one thing, we also could get Ozaki Sensei to live there. The site we chose was "Obatake," one of the Ozaki family's fields. It was one of those lonely edge-of-the-village places where at night the foxes and badgers come and go.

The house was not finished until November. Sensei's family and mine were already living communally in Osaka, and because of matters connected with my husband's job Sensei's wife and I decided to take turns for a while coming to the Obatake House. People gossiped about it viciously as "wife-swapping," but by that time we no longer were paying attention to what they said about us.

Once we had the Obatake House, everybody would come gather and talk things over both before going out on communal labor and again after the work was done. Not long after that we began to eat together, each of us bringing food from his home. Next we began to use the bath together.

Once we had a communal kitchen, the women and children also began to take their meals there. Eight of us already were living in the house—Sensei, his wife (or myself), his wife's parents and their two children, my child, and Ritarō's child. At meals we were joined by four Yamanakas (husband, wife, and two children); four Mitanis (same); and two Imanishis. We managed the meals by pooling our money and our own produce.

My job was to cook and to take care of clothing for the eight children. One day when I planned to wash the eight nemaki [sleeping kimono], my hand reached out and grabbed my own child's nemaki first. Once I noticed, I blinked in surprise. I'd had no bad intentions. Without thinking about it at all, sometime or other I'd gotten into the habit of doing it that way. But if somebody else were to see it, well, it would look like selfish concern for my own child. If they said I lack impartiality, what could I say? Warning myself that anything like this is absolutely out when you're working and living communally, I let go of my child's nemaki and began washing them in order from the end of the rack. Much ado about nothing, maybe, but after all we didn't have a single pattern to follow then for the communal way of life we were starting. Only after we hit against various problems in reality would we begin to catch on. We always had to remember to be on the alert for the chance that what seemed to be a trifle might turn into a major issue that could rock the whole basis of our common life. For me this was a great discovery.

Again, when I passed out the children's snacks, I was thinking to myself: "It would be good if my child got the best-looking piece." The children had no way of knowing what I had in mind; innocent beings that they are, they were just yelling for joy. I came to my senses, and once again I felt that a mother's instinct was actually repulsive and could lead to mistakes here.

All we had been thinking of was: what can we do to make communal labor more efficient and economical? and what can we do to make an effective comeback from ostracism? That was the goal of our daily struggles, though no doubt deep in everybody's heart there was a feeling all along that if we were to work communally we ought to be together as much as possible. Then we wouldn't be lonely and it would be equally convenient for all. That's why it wasn't unnatural at all that we began planning together to move and rebuild all the homes in a way that would be convenient for everybody and at the same time suitable for communal life.

As each wife set aside her field clothes and tied on a white apron, and tried her hand at cooking for a group without the meddlesome interference of a mother-in-law, she found a change, gain, and excitement that she hadn't expected. Once you tried it, it could even be fun.

As we were doing these things we definitely gave birth to what I'd call a new style of life. Slowly we had begun to change—especially the women—and to feel that we'd be far better off finding satisfaction in our daily communal life than fretting about family wealth, and so on, in a future that we couldn't count on anyway.

But surely there was no reason to expect that everything would go smoothly. I have to admit that the others could not (any more easily than I could) break away from bonds to dependents or from the instinctive selfishness you feel for kinsmen; and that there was an unseen suspiciousness and sense of competition at work among us. For example, the duty cook would bring her own child to stay with her in the kitchen, and even if she didn't go so far as to make anything special for the child she might leave her own serving untouched and give it to the child. We hadn't particularly talked about it, but it turned out that every one of us was doing the same thing. And we were jealously suspicious

Collective living in Shinkyō extends even to bathing. These lounging slippers are outside the communal bath.

about the partiality that other mothers might be showing towards their children. The children themselves caught on too, and each of them began to wait impatiently for his mother to take the kitchen duty. Under these conditions communal life would not work. Ignore them and we probably would end up separating again.

At this point Sensei suggested that the children trade off and sleep with somebody else's parents. At first glance it looked like a bright idea, but in fact a child who happened to wake in the night and realize that the person sleeping next to him was not his mother but "some auntie or other" would start bawling out loud and wouldn't quit. The temporary mother-for-the-night was really in a fix. But no matter how angry it made her, when she realized that her child probably was annoying some other mother too, she just had to set aside her feelings and do something to quiet the one with her. As these experiences accumulated, the idea of playing favorite with your child disappeared of its own accord.

In the early stages the men on cattle duty were just like the women on kitchen duty: Each favored his own pet ox, giving it extra feed or being more careful about cleaning its pen. But he couldn't avoid having a guilty conscience as he did it. The men say that one day when one of them spoke out about it and they realized that they all were worried about it, they had mixed feelings of strangeness and shame.

Then Sensei suggested that we sell off the four oxen in order to do away with these feelings. The four families agreed, sold the oxen and bought different ones in their place. That way the notion of which ox was whose no longer applied. For good or bad all of them had to be treated with equal care. This was how the oxen came to be our first common property.

Except for rice we brought everything under communal control, without partitions, and everybody was free to carry home as much as he needed. The need for anyone to carry food home gradually decreased as our communal cooking gradually was done on a more complete scale.

Sharing the Rice

But rice remained the exception. Since rice is the one thing you can readily change into cash it can't be pooled, we thought. Sensei said again and again: "If you all haven't the guts to go on helping each other in any and every way, then how about apologizing to the village right now and getting the ostracism removed?"

The four families said they'd die before they'd do that now anymore. "Well then," Sensei told them, "if you feel that way about apologizing to the village, a little thing like putting all your rice into one bin isn't anything at all, is it?" This took place a number of times, and in the end we eventually were able to bring rice, too, under communal control.

After that came the question of communal bathing. By farm village custom, the women would not enter the bath until all the men were finished. But it wasted time and was uneconomical on fuel, so we revised it and let anybody who was free, man or woman, use the bath. Before long the men also began to enter without embarrassment while women were in the tub, and in a very natural way we developed a practice of group bathing.

Common use of the chests and the clothing also began spontaneously. It wasn't that we had figured out how sensible it might be to rationalize our clothing habits. We merely set out with the idea that by putting things together it would be handy and there'd be no waste. For example, in the first chest we would put all the men's dress over-kimono, in the second chest the women's going-out kimono, in the third all of our everyday clothes—so it was easy to use them in common.

On New Year's Day of 1940 we moved into our new building while its walls were still only rough-plastered. We called it the Cookhouse.

The Cookhouse had four bedrooms on the second floor, and four bedrooms and two guest rooms downstairs. In addition it had a bath, washroom, pantry, kitchen, 20-by-30-foot wood-floored dining room, and a dirt-floored dining room. We even ran pipes to the kitchen, bath, and washroom. We heard that the villagers were spreading rumors that "if they could put in facilities like that, they must've gotten money from Russia."

But in fact the only reason why we had enough labor to build it was that we didn't celebrate Midsummer or New Year's, and we didn't take any days off.

And this was how from 1939 into 1940 we completed laying the main foundations for our communal life.

Ostracism as a technique of social control is not peculiar to Japan, although Japanese villages and small groups are notorious for favoring it. Well-documented cases are rare, however, and even more rare are cases in which the people ostracized proved capable of fighting back.

Shinkyō's development under Masutarō Ozaki calls up many parallels with American "backwoods utopias" of the 19th century, particularly with the Oneida community under John Humphrey Noyes. At the same time, its step-by-step collectivization process in the late 1930s is surprisingly similar to what was carried out in rural China in the early years of the Peoples' Republic.

In 1943 the Shinkyō people decided to move to Manchukuo. In August of 1945, the loss of the war obliged them to return to Kasama.

In the reconstruction years they took in some destitute acquaintances from Manchukuo, one of whom was skilled in making *tatami*, the rice-straw mats that carpet Japanese dwellings. Gradually Shinkyō turned from farming to tatami-manufacturing, and within a decade became one of the largest and most mechanized establishments in the country. Part of the profits have been put back into improving the plant, another part into creating a collective standard of living well above that of the ordinary Japanese villager. (For example, in 1965 eight of the founders went on a jet holiday to Taiwan and Hong Kong.) Still another part of the profits are given to various kinds of public service. Shinkyō has made massive donations for improving schools, roads, and other public facilities in Kasama—Seki is dead, and the ostracism has long been ended. For several years the Shinkyō people have regularly cared for two or three juvenile parolees, and this year they expect to open a center for the care of feeble-minded children.

Ozaki refuses to proselytize or propagandize, although the mass media frequently publicize him as a sort of peasant sage. He receives an average of three letters a day from people all over Japan wanting to join the community, but he responds to each by urging the sender to strive harder in his own situation. "People say it's utopia or Communism or a lot of other things," he said to me once. "But for us it's just the way of life we happened to develop together. If people can learn from it to get rid of some stupid old customs, well and good. But the lesson in Shinkyō is that if they really want reform, they need to start at home."

Another lesson is that *mura-hachibu* in village Japan is dying. Under postwar human-rights codes, it is illegal. Today discrimination must take a more subtle course. But even when *mura-hachibu* was strong, the history of Shinkyō indicates that it was not necessarily fatal. Confronted, with proper leadership and enough people willing to work together and determined not to submit, it actually provided a spur to new cooperative forms, and a better life. Without *mura-hachibu*, there would have been no Shinkyō.

January-February 1968

SUGGESTED READINGS

"The Japanese Rural Community: Norms, Sanctions, and Ostracism" by Robert J. Smith, *American Anthropologist*, Vol. 63, (1961). Summary and analysis of eight cases of ostracism.

"The Laws of the *Buraku*" by Minoru Kida, *Japan Quarterly*, Vol. 4, (1957). A Japanese essayist describes the operation of ostracism and other sanctions in a mountain village.

Local Government in Japan by Kurt Steiner (Stanford, Calif.: Stanford University Press, 1965). Chapter 10 includes a brief discussion of ostracism as it relates to local-group solidarity and to community involvement with outside political, legal and administrative institutions.

"The Fate of Utopia: Adaptive Tactics in Four Japanese Groups" by David W. Plath, *American Anthropologist*, Vol. 68 (1966). Discusses how members of Shinkyō and three other communal societies strive to routinize their dealings with the rest of Japanese society.

Communal Brethren of the Great Plains

Canada's Hutterites find religious and economic blessings from their combat against worldly temptations

JOHN W. BENNETT

"The conscious uniformity of clothes and possessions is based on the ideal that every man is alike in the sight of God."

Along with their religious cousins, the Amish, the Hutterian Brethren are the only sizable group of people in North America who are deliberately, and successfully, defying the trend to a "consumer culture" with its related personal anxieties and general cultural debasement. These people practice strict austerity and limitation of personal property. Commercials do not tempt them, since they own neither TV sets nor radios. Their children are encouraged to play with tractors instead of toys. Their women folk, not enslaved by fashion, make their own uniformly styled clothing. We shall be concerned only with the Hutterian Brethren, a Christian communal sect of 20,000 in 1970, living mostly in the northern Great Plains. The Amish are not really communal, and live as individual farm families.

The Hutterites are farmers, organized in colonies of 130 to 150 people on communal farms up to 16,000 acres in size. Their people are contented—few leave permanently for the outside world. Economically they are flourishing as the most successful farmer-adaptors to the ecology of the Great Plains area, and their population doubles about every 15 years. They have been able to support this increase through efficient farming methods and the use of modern equipment and also through frugality and limitation of personal luxuries and conveniences. The combination enables them to save enough money to continually buy land for new colonies.

Hutterites practice communal property ownership, which they call *community of goods*. This principle originated in the sixteenth century when their ancestors, fleeing into Moravia to avoid persecution in the Austrian Tyrol, symbolically pooled their possessions in a cloak spread on the ground. Unlike the Amish, they do not reject the advantages of modern technology for the community. They buy the most expensive farm machinery, and in their communal kitchens they have the most costly equipment, such as commercial refrigerators and electric meat saws.

But their apartment dwellings (about nine families to a row house) have few modern conveniences save electricity; most lack running water and nearly all lack flush toilets. Decoration is deliberately austere and uniform. The floors are of plain varnished wood; the walls are painted white and at the windows are plain white starched curtains. Furniture is sparse and mostly made in the colony shops. Few individual touches are found—perhaps an oddly-shaped, colorful pincushion or a fine old wall clock refinished by the man of the family and proudly pointed out to visitors.

This uniform austerity and emphasis on communal, rather than personal property and equipment, has a religious and social purpose. The Brethren believe that excessive interest in personal property is a form of idolatry, which comes between man and God. Also owning things different from, or better than, one's neighbors disrupts community morale.

In addition, there are economic reasons. Personal deprivation is the very foundation of their communal prosperity. The lack of plumbing in the family dwellings saves the average colony about $15,000. Communal refrigeration equipment is half as costly as buying refrigerators for each of the 20 families in a colony. Add one carryall station wagon instead of 20 family cars and the savings become even more impressive.

However, as Hutterian leaders are fully aware, it is no simple or easy matter to keep 17,000 people on such a Spartan routine when their colonies, as communes, enjoy prosperity and when the world on the "outside" is affluent. The principles on which this unique society operates are worth consideration by those of us still engaged in the "consumer culture" rat race.

Managed Democracy

The Hutterian system can be called a "managed democracy." Overall policy is made by councils for the *Leut,* or three main branches, of the sect. These meet frequently to set policy and review departures from custom, however trivial. Any changes they sanction are recorded in books called *Gemeinordenungen* and carefully consulted. The power structure operates on two levels; there are the farm enterprise managers and the elders. The elders have considerable charismatic power, especially the chief or "first minister"; the managers have power only over their respective enterprises. However, all these positions for men (and one for women—the colony's chief cook) are elective.

The basic administrative unit is the colony, which is kept below 150 members for both social and economic reasons. Above this level group decisions become unwieldy, there are not enough responsible positions to go round, and behavior is hard to control, especially among the young—for example, the young men may begin moonlighting for neighboring farmers in order to buy things they are not supposed to have.

Economic reasons are even more weighty. It takes between 8,000 and 16,000 acres to support 150 people, the exact amount depending on local moisture and soil conditions. This is about the largest acreage now available to the Brethren in most parts of the northern Great Plains. So when the colony reaches maximum size the question of splitting up is debated for a year or so and finally voted on by the whole group. This happens every 15 or 20 years. Then the colonists buy more land from 25 to 250 miles away; the land usually costs about $200,000 and is paid for from savings. This is called the "new farm." For a year or two, they put the new land into production and construct a few necessary buildings. Then lots are cast to see who shall live in the "daughter" colony. Ground rules call for a neat division down the age pyramid, so that the new community becomes, as far as possible, a duplicate of the old. The colonists are quite willing to go—they value the extra responsibility and the dedicated pioneer spirit found in a new colony under more deprived living conditions.

Hutterites are able to save large sums for new land partly by frugal living and partly because of efficient farming methods. The Brethren discovered, sooner than most American and Canadian farmers, that land on this continent has to be continuously productive in order to support an expanding population. Their emphasis on efficiency and technological know-how, so firmly resisted by the Amish, goes back to the founding of their sect. When they fled from Austria, Hutterites soon attracted the favorable attention of Moravian landowners. The lords invited them to act as stewards for their vast estates. They served without salaries in return for protection—a fine bargain for the protectors. Sixteenth century stewards were personnel officers and business managers combined. Thus the Hutterites learned a large number of skills including bookkeeping, farming techniques, and banking. They became construction engineers and surveyors; some set up craft industries and directed the training of apprentices in more than 45 different trades; a few were merchants and physicians.

Hutterian craftsmen made many ingenious gadgets and machines for their own use, and for the entertainment and interest of their masters. A few of these ancient devices still exist in the North American colonies, including several of the famous comb-cutting machines, using precision gears and saws. Hutterites preserve these interests; nearly every colony will have a yarn ball-winder, a sock-knitting machine, a noodle-maker—some of these made at the colony, others factory-made but improved by the colony mechanics. This extends to tools and farm machinery: colonies take pride in building cabs for combines and tractors, hay balestackers, forage wagons, automatic metal saws, and many other things. The Hutterian move toward farm machinery was undoubtedly facilitated by this traditional interest in machines and mechanical gadgets—something the Amish lack.

After being persecuted out of Moravia at the end of the sixteenth century the Hutterites learned another lesson which still stands then in good stead—from the standpoint of communal living. They found out that it does not pay to overproduce and become too wealthy. Catherine the Great invited them into Russia and promised them immunity from military service (which is against their basic beliefs). They settled in the Ukraine and prospered in that rich land. Colonies grew into large villages and many of them departed from the cherished *community of goods.* Others became impoverished. By 1870 when the Czar removed their immunity from the military draft, the Brethren were ready to move again. They determined to make the next migration a revival of their religious faith and communal traditions.

Eventually the Hutterites accepted the offer of American land agents and moved to the pleasant James valley in the southeastern corner of South Dakota. This was not the last move, nor did it end persecution. Harassment during World War I forced the Brethren to flee to Canada, where most of them remain.

Hutterites, whether in Canada, the Dakotas, Montana, or Washington, do not allow their colonies to become overly large or rich; communities with too much cash on hand will lend it to younger colonies not even members of their own "daughter" groups. Hutterian leaders leave nothing to chance in combatting worldly temptations. The executive officers, the managers and ministers, visit back and forth in order to keep an eye on behavior in the various communities. Any laxity—such as clandestine radios, too many electric razors for the men or ornaments on the girls, or too many ornaments on the bureaus—is supposed to be reported to the council. This intercolony surveillance also helps to keep the different groups at about the same living standard. No colony is allowed to lag behind its sisters to the point where jealousy arises and austerity begins to be felt as poverty.

Spending is strictly controlled. Business expenditures of more than $10 must have the consent of the farm manager. Major spending must be approved by the voting council of the adult men. Each family receives a small monthly cash allowance to buy necessities. Many items—such as fabric for clothing, clocks, or pocket knives—are bought and distributed by the elders. So are a few small luxuries, such as special treats of food and refreshment for weddings and religious holidays, including beer and wine. Each colony makes its own wine, and individual families are allowed a gallon a month. Inexpensive gifts are given to children at Christmas; but in general they are encouraged to play with farm equipment instead of toys, which trains them early.

The culture of austerity is also the culture of uniformity. A Hutterian friend explained to me the reason for the special old fashioned clothes they all wear: "It's just that we should all look different from outsiders, but like each other." This conscious uniformity of clothes and possessions is based on the ideal that every man is alike in the sight of God. Differentiation would mean the rise of idolatry and the dissolution of Christian brotherhood.

Silent Struggle in the Heart

The system sounds more severe than it actually is. Hutterian leaders usually show a sensible flexibility in enforcing these rules. The elders will tolerate small infractions so long as they do not spread or become too blatant. In nearly all colonies there are constant small violations of the property rules. Individuals may find some way of making a little extra cash by moonlighting on a neighboring farm or selling a bit of colony produce on the sly. Occasionally items acquired this way are eventually approved as desirable and bought and distributed to everyone. More often the offender is pressured into giving them up. The leaders have good reasons for doing this—whenever a colony breaks up (it happens occasionally) the first symptoms are always individual purchases of consumer goods, especially clothes.

Wisely, the Brethren do not treat the desire for personal property as a deadly sin. They recognize the intractable nature of the human spirit. As one author puts it, every Hutterite experiences a "silent struggle within the heart" when he sees the rich culture of the "outside," which he must reject. The Brethren also acknowledge the difficulty of individual privation in the midst of the collective wealth of the colony. But they glory in the fact that it can be maintained.

The obedience of the Brethren is really remarkable. Group interdependence and surveillance are not enough to account for it. There are other, deeper reasons. One of the weightiest is early social conditioning. Hutterian children are trained from infancy to accept the system and suppress their natural ambitions and material desires. The family raises each child

Men and women dine separately.

Ingenuity and Innovation

PHOTOGRAPHED BY JOHN W. BENNETT

Hutterites have always shown considerable skill in making machines and tools of all kinds. While old-fashioned items are becoming rarer, the typical colony has home-made metal saws, lathes, farm implements, wool carding machines, wool-winding gadgets for making balls of yarn, sock-knitting machines, and noodle-makers. Hutterites never rejected the idea of labor saving devices; this factor helps distinguish their culture from that of their cousins in Anabaptism, the Amish.

Using the last rays of daylight.

In the repair shop.

Hand-finished furniture

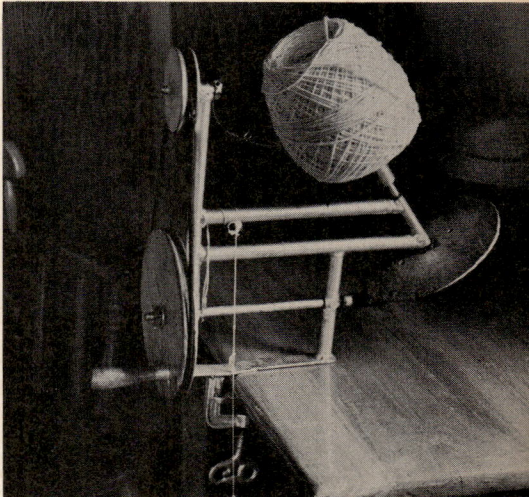

Gadget—a wool-ball winder.

Women house painters.

Noodle-making for the colony.

Anabaptists in North America—Mennonites, Amish, Hutterites

The Hutterian Brethren (about 20,000 in 1970) are one of the important surviving sects of the Anabaptists and the only one which did not stem from the Mennonites. The Anabaptist version of Christianity emerged in the sixteenth century, parallel with Protestantism, and has been called the "Radical Reformation." The "radical" element refers to the fact that the Anabaptists all have strong cooperative-communal leanings, and reject certain features of worldly political and economic organization.

Although the Anabaptist sects differ on a number of things, especially the degree of communalism, they all find agreement on the following basic doctrines:

- Adult baptism on confession of faith, a practice which was responsible for most of the persecution of Anabaptists by both Catholics and Protestants in the sixteenth and seventeenth centuries.
- Refusal to bear arms or serve in public office.
- Acceptance of the principles—if not always the literal practice—of the communal Apostolic Church of Jerusalem under Jesus, and as described especially in the Book of Acts. (The regular Baptist faith, which developed in England in the seventeenth century is similar to Anabaptism only in the first of these three doctrines.)

Persecution is an important element in Anabaptist historical memories and helps to keep alive their sense of distinctiveness. Hutterites have careful records of about 2,000 martyrs, including two young men who died of exposure and maltreatment in US military prisons as conscientious objectors in World War I.

The Mennonites are the best-known and by far the most numerous of all Anabaptist groups in the world (about a quarter of a million members). The name is derived from Menno Simons, a Dutch religious reformer who worked mainly in north Germany during the mid-sixteenth century but who later moved to Holland. Simons was attracted by the fundamentalist movements growing out of the translation of the Bible into the vernaculars, and he decided to accept a more literal interpretation of the organization of Christianity. It is this literalness which created the similarities between Anabaptist groups—there was no close contact between them, and no ecumenical conferences of any importance at any point in their history. The Mennonites became strong and numerous largely because they approached the pattern of regular Protestant sects in accepting the framework of the outside world—permitting their members to acquire higher education and to take jobs in almost any part of the secular system. Mennonites also accept, within their own ranks, about 10 sub-sects with varying degrees of orthodoxy.

The Old Order Amish are, essentially, the most orthodox and anti-worldly of all the Mennonite groups, although some Mennonites do not regard them as part of the Mennonite church. Amish have cooperative practices, but usually live on individual farmsteads and even have individual land ownership. They manifest their difference mainly by adhering to traditional, "horse-and-buggy" customs. While they are good farmers, their refusal to use machinery hampers them, and many Amish communities are in economic difficulty. They, like the Hutterites, have been the subject of repeated local and governmental persecution, usually stimulated by people who would like their land. The most recent Amish case occurred in Iowa in 1965, where local school board and law enforcement officials were persuaded to mount a campaign to force the young children into local schools—which would have the effect of breaking up the Amish community.

Hutterian Brethren are the most vigorously communal of all the Anabaptist groups and view themselves as the most orthodox and "correct." Nevertheless, there are no strong differences between Hutterian and Mennonite beliefs. Both use the same Lutheran translation of the Bible, and many of the same sermons, hymns, and catechistic works.

---

in its two or three room apartment until the age of three. The colony then takes over. From three to six he is in nursery school and then in German school, learning the Hutterian culture and traditions. The teachers may be his own aunts and uncles but kinship makes little difference; through playing out what anthropologists call a "cultural myth" kinfolk are able to ignore their relationship where the needs of the colony are concerned.

A public school teacher comes to each colony to instruct the children in secular education up to the eighth grade level. But these teachers find it difficult to get the students to compete for grades or in artistic work. Only with great difficulty can Hutterian youngsters produce anything really original, since they have been trained to avoid competition or individual differentiation. At 15 they return to their families and take up adult work responsibilities. They are baptized at 20.

The insulation of the child from the outside world is almost total up to the age of about 12, since children are taken into town only for important purposes like medical visits. This means that by the time the child does develop an awareness of "the outside," as Hutterites call it, he is already well-socialized in the system.

Temptations of the World

The leaders know that if young people were allowed to attend outside high schools the temptations of the world would undoubtedly prove too much. (This has been tried a few times with the predicted result.) Indeed, if they ever run out of land to support their expanding population (this threatens many areas), the Brethren might find it convenient to send some of their young people to high school in order to ease them out of the community.

Although Hutterian children are almost completely insulated from the outside world, adult Hutterites travel a lot. They visit other colonies and also travel long distances to find good buys on farm machinery and other equipment. They usually try to take along a few women and laborers so everyone has an opportunity to travel.

The people are also shielded from contamination by the mass media. A typical colony will subscribe to one or two newspapers, usually the local sheet and a German language Mennonite publication. Magazines are occasionally picked up from friends in town, but this kind of thing is closely watched. Television sets, radios, and movies are taboo. Every colony has a few young men who have managed to sneak into a theatre once or twice. But outside contacts of this type are not too serious a problem, especially in the more isolated rural areas. It is significant that the colonies in Manitoba near Winnipeg, have the most trouble with their young people.

In general, the Hutterites control their people and keep morale high through rewards and incentives. Most of them crave responsibility, though they are trained not to show any open sign of ambition. Because the colonies constantly subdivide, plenty of responsible positions become available. These are all elective but the system is subtly rigged to give all the available men a chance. In a study of about 25 interrelated colonies, only 3 percent of the males over 40 had never held one or more managerial jobs.

This satisfying rotation of responsibility may be one reason why so few Hutterites leave the colonies permanently. Total defection is rare. In the *Schmieden Leut,* one of the three branches of the sect, the population rose from 500 to 4,000 between 1900 and 1949. Of those born in this period only 98 men and seven women left the community permanently. Temporary departure is more common—possibly 5 percent of all Hutterian men leave the colonies for about a year.

Culture of Austerity

Commitment to the system is undoubtedly deep. The material deprivation suffered by the Brethren does not disenchant them. The Hutterites are not "poor," by any intelligent standard. Their culture of austerity is the exact opposite of the "culture of poverty" as defined by Oscar Lewis. In the outside world poverty is associated with hopelessness and lack of identification; feelings of alienation are accentuated by contrast with surrounding wealth. In the isolated Hutterian society austerity is consciously planned and sanctioned by religion. It is the basis both of collective economic success and spiritual welfare.

The Hutterian deprivation offers distinct compensations of a spiritual and emotional nature. Instead of running after gadgets the Brethren make their own. Instead of following fashions they refine and improve their traditional models, achieving gentle taste and beauty. True, they pay a certain emotional price for repressing some aspects of their individuality. Fears, anxieties, and little psychosomatic ailments plague them. But they suffer very little true mental illness.

(See *Personality in a Communal Society,* 1956, by Bert Kaplan and Thomas Plaut.) They are a remarkably healthy people. Inbreeding has produced a few undesirable genetic results, such as relatively high frequencies of minor bodily deformities, eye troubles, and the like, but it has also increased the intelligence of some of their members— most colonies contain people whose intellectual grasp of technology and economics is impressive, doubly so since they are all self-taught.

It is doubtful whether the Hutterites can provide a model for the reconstruction of personal living in the affluent society. They are a very special and very isolated people. They do, however, furnish certain inspirations. We may learn from them that there is valid satisfaction in cooperative effort and some suppression of individual rights. The Brethren suppress parts of their personalities, but they do so for a noble reason—the welfare and continuity of the group. The art of social living is almost lost in our urbanized society, with its broken families and increasing alienation. Despite the suppressive element in their society the Hutterites are interesting, vigorous human beings—unsophisticated and hickish perhaps, but full of wit and good conversation. They are more than adequate for their world.

Another summation of this unique way of life comes to me in the words of a Hutterian friend: "Some day they (the elders) will let us have radios, and if they do I am going to see to it that we make them ourselves."

December 1966

SUGGESTED READINGS

All Things Common: The Hutterian Way of Life by Victor Peters. (Minneapolis, Minn.: University of Minnesota Press, 1965.)

The Hutterite Way by Paul S. Gross (Saskatoon, Saskatchewan: Freeman Publishing Co., 1965.)

The Hutterites: South Dakota's Communal Farmers by Marvin P. Riley and J. R. Stewart (South Dakota State University, Rural Sociology Department, 1966.)

"Social Stratification in a 'Classless' Society" by Eva Rosenfeld, *American Sociological Review* (Vol. 16, Dec. 1951) is a study of how prestige distinctions arise in a commune which is ideologically opposed to stratification distinctions.

Two Paths to Utopia: The Hutterites and the Llano Colony by Paul Conklin (Lincoln, Neb.: University of Nebraska Press, 1964). In two contrasting monographs, Conklin writes interpretive essays describing the Hutterites (the largest and oldest communal Christian sect in the world) and the Llano colony (the last significant secular utopia in America).

A Season in Utopia: the Story of Brook Farm by Edith E. Curtis (New York: Thomas Nelson, 1961). Dismayed by the effects of the Industrial Revolution on social living in New England, a group of idealists founded Brook Farm. This experiment in group living began in Massachusetts in 1841 and disbanded in 1847.

Escape to Utopia, the Communal Movement in America by Everett Webber (New York: Hastings, 1959) is a chronical of a variety of American communal groups of the last century. Religious, economic, messianic and celibate communes are among those treated.

Kibbutz: Venture Into Utopia by Melford E. Spiro (New York: Schocken Books, 1963). An account of a collective settlement in Isreal.

The Decline and Fall of the Small Town

Its status quo way of life is an anachronism; can it possibly be saved from extinction?

WILLIAM SIMON
JOHN H. GAGNON

It is a fact of our twentieth century life that as the centers of economic, social, and political power have shifted from farm and countryside to city and suburb, those small communities that are not absorbed by some metropolitan complex come under threat (if not actual sentence) of decline and decay. But why do some small towns wither and not others? And is there long term hope for any?

Actually, this Darwinian life and death struggle of American small towns is not confined to modern times. During the nineteenth century the petering out of natural resources or the demand for them (gold in California, coal in parts of the Midwest) and the considerations that determined whether a railroad went through one area rather than another often determined whether a village would prosper or become a ghost town. Today, decisions about where to place highways, intersections, dams, or where to move an industry can have similar effects—revitalizing or building one community, sentencing another to senescence.

But in the nineteenth century decline or vitalization were considered to result from the natural workings of *laissez-faire*. The fittest survived. The economic success grew and the failure faded away—a process that was not to be interfered with and that made for progress. Today the state and federal governments are actively intervening to try to maintain the small town—which they perceive to be a useful way of life, a balancing force against the rise of megalopolis.

But is it enough to simply inject redevelopment funds into a community to assure its health? For that matter, what do we learn from using medical terms to describe a town's economic vitality—a robust community, a sick or moribund community? What really determines a town's viability? Is it different with each town?

This article attempts detailed analyses of three neighboring rural towns in southern Illinois, to determine why, despite many similarities in location, economic problems, and history, they developed differently after World War II.

The three communities—which we will call East Parrish, Clyde, and Spiresburg—are in an area distinctly "Southern" in many characteristics and values. It was originally settled in the first half of the nineteenth century by migrants from the southern hill country. They rapidly exhausted a land as inhospitable, if not more so, than what they had originally left. Its barren, clay-ridden soil did not, and will not in the future, support more than meager subsistence farming.

At the turn of the century coal was discovered in the area, and large-scale mining brought a new, unprecedented, and profoundly uncertain prosperity. Coal camps appeared, and rail lines connecting them to each other and to the outside world began to crisscross the region. Typical of the influence of the railroads, in a very few years entire town sites moved to the nearby rail lines.

The growing coal industry brought in a few Negroes and many immigrants, largely from Eastern Europe. Though farming continued, it increasingly became a part-time venture, and everything became tied to a highly unstable, single industry—coal. Typical of coal mining areas, a culture full of strong contrasts developed (as Herman Lantz described it in his *The People of Coaltown*). Side by side there was violence and resignation, Bible-belt religion and hard-drinking, serious gambling, and (at least historically) no small amount of whoring. All three communities are within 40 miles of what has, with full justification, become known as "Bloody Williamson County."

By the mid-1920's, the local coal boom reached its peak, and from then on, except for a brief period during World War II, went into continuous decline. East Parrish, the largest of the three towns, declined from almost 25,000 to its present 9,000. From 1950 to 1960 East Parrish declined by 21 percent, Clyde by 11 percent, and Spiresburg by 6 percent. People continue to leave in large numbers—primarily the younger, healthier, and better educated. Nor has there been (especially as far as mining is concerned) any

substantial leveling off of employment. Between 1950 and 1960 the number of persons employed in mining in East Parrish decreased by 71 percent, in Clyde by 72 percent, and in Spiresburg by 61 percent. And there were substantial, if smaller, declines in such things as railroad carloadings. All during the preceding decade the immediate area has been defined by government agencies as "chronically depressed" and "surplus labor."

By the early 1950's people in all three communities began to realize that the very survival of their towns was at stake. Responding to this realization, and prodded by federal and state governments and a nearby state university, community leaders became very adept at the rhetoric of community redevelopment.

But the consequences of both rhetoric and action have been markedly different among the three. East Parrish (population 9,000) has had virtually no change or improvement—nor does any appear even remotely likely. Clyde (population 7,000) has been able to check its decline somewhat and expects in the near future to derive the benefits of a federal water and land redevelopment project. Spiresburg, the smallest (population 3,000), has in the last six years attracted four new industries and thereby largely reconstituted its economic base.

East Parrish

East Parrish first recognized its problem openly in the early 1950's when the East Parrish Industrial Fund was created with working capital of $100,000 raised from over 2,000 public contributors. This fund was deposited in the local bank where it remained untouched for eight years. Its first expenditure was to rebuild a dress factory that had burned down. This factory, typical of industry attracted by such communities, is "labor-intensive," paying low wages and primarily employing women.

But while the basic fund was put to restricted use, the accumulated interest was more freely available. Much of it went to subsidize the local Chamber of Commerce; and this in turn strengthened the hold of the community conservatives over the Chamber.

Rarely was any money used in realistic scouting for new industry. As one member of the development board put it:

We didn't run around like some of the towns around here wining and dining company officials or taking junkets around the country looking for companies. And we weren't going to offer the moon to some of these companies. Industry that you get that way either won't stay or won't pay off. Sure, there are companies that we might have looked at, but they are out for what they can get. They don't want to pay taxes, want free water, gas, and free land. It is just like raping a community. And then they move on. If you can get them on this basis, so can another town get them from you on the same basis. Hell, they have no ties to the community; they could move tomorrow. Besides, our real problem is labor. For all the talk around here, most of the people really don't want to work—they're content on public assistance. And those that do want to work have been spoiled by the unions; they won't work for wages that the kind of industry that would come here would pay— they [the workers] think that they can only work for the $16 and $17 a day they used to make when the mines were running.

The next big economic event was the discovery of exploitable oil within the corporate limits of the community. However, the oil industry is highly automated. The oil ownership was concentrated among a very few, and additional employment was barely noticeable. To this day the endlessly see-sawing, black, squat pumps constantly remind the population of still another disappointment.

NORMS OF BEHAVIOR

19

Business as usual...

Photo Essay by
Barry Fitzgerald

"The only middle-class group whose children generally do not leave the small towns are the marginal retail merchants who often have little to bequeath except their businesses. The limits of recovery have been set by shopkeeper mentalities."

To date no federal funds have been requested—except for some public housing and clearance—and on at least two occasions they were rejected by community leaders when offered.

When we look at East Parrish's formal political structure one thing stands out: Since 1947, no mayor of the community succeeded himself (although two tried), and only two city commission members won re-election. This would suggest considerable political instability. Curiously, however, as one makes inquiries of community residents about community events during this period, one finds that essentially the same names appear. These names virtually never appear in contests for major political office (mayor or city commission), although roughly half of them have participated in one or more public commissions. Formal government apparently became the target for the expression of the frustrations of community residents, but rarely the framework within which serious solutions for community problems could be approached.

What, then, is the political life of East Parrish? Of the three communities, East Parrish is the only one with a strong tradition of working-class involvement in politics. This probably developed out of the high level of social solidarity characteristic of coal mining communities.

There is a basic cleavage going back for a number of decades between the miners (for whom the merchants remain those "bastards on Main Street") and the professional merchant group (for whom the miner remains the hillbilly

or hunkie to whom they once sold silk shirts at highly inflated prices). As the medical director of the United Mine Workers Association hospital remarked, it was still almost impossible to get a Main Street merchant to serve on the hospital board. One effect of this cleavage was a historic pattern of miner representation in city government. One mayor, deposed in a recent election, was employed as a miner concurrently with his occupancy of the mayor's office.

The effects of this traditional cleavage became intensified because the middle-class elite (if this term is at all applicable) is itself badly split. Among the merchants a split occurs between those whose operations serve a broad area is handled very informally through the township supermarket (there are 14 furniture stores in the community), and those whose business centers entirely upon local retail trade. One cost of this second cleavage has been the inability—despite successive attempts—to have Main Street broadened and repaved with state funds and turned over to state maintenance because the local retail merchants refuse to surrender angle parking.

Typical of self-centered communities, there is no local industrial elite—even in the heyday of the coal boom most operations were absentee owned.

With the decline of mining, its importance to the community and the number of people it employs, the effectiveness of the miners and their ability to organize has lessened. In addition, a relatively high proportion of miners or their families are on welfare. In towns like East Parrish, welfare

NORMS OF BEHAVIOR

is handled very informally through the township supervisor, a very political office. Further, people generally know who is on relief. Both these factors make welfare recipients feel very vulnerable, and this tends to undermine their political participation. Also, the more promising young people, potential political leaders, leave in large numbers.

This does not mean that working-class politics has eroded in East Parrish. There has been considerable miner participation. In 1959, for instance, three of four city commissioners were miners, and one of these was later appointed mayor upon the death of the incumbent. But it does mean that their effectiveness and independence has been undermined. Election rhetoric centers heavily on class politics—but the election of miners has not given rise to working-class programs. The miners in politics have been largely coopted by the "politicos" of the community.

Between the larger, more affluent merchants and the lower-class community a small but crucial group of professional, or near professional, politicians has developed—a a group whose basic constituency is greatly enhanced by a large number of dependent and chronic welfare recipients. As with government in an underdeveloped country, an amazing amount of money can be made by manipulating the local political structure, particularly in playing with taxes and land speculation, even where land itself is not worth much.

Significantly absent from political life are the community's hired professionals—schoolteachers and ministers.

...but no market in futures

"Resistance to change has many causes. Most important perhaps, community leaders do not really believe enough in the futures of their towns to be willing to commit their own children to them. The lower classes have little choice."

Local school systems, because they are small and split among several authorities, are highly vulnerable. Moreover, the staff in such school systems—either women tied to families that in turn are tied to the community, or men of rather low competence—are not likely to seek involvement. Ministers, at least Protestant ministers, move around a great deal and are at the mercy of lay leaders who are primarily drawn from the community conservatives. They tend to avoid speaking out on community issues because there is rarely a community issue that would not find competing factions within the same church, and it is a rare minister who, in the context of East Parrish's long history of community conflicts, would invite such a conflict into his church.

While churches seem to be nearly totally estranged from power and community decision-making in all three communities, in East Parrish the social and fraternal organizations have also tended to withdraw. A recent reform movement has taken control of city hall, and it reflects primarily the needs of local merchants. Ostensibly it is committed to industrial renewal, but little is expected to come of it. The professional politicians know all too well that they, despite this temporary setback, control access to county and state politicians, without whom little can be done.

As a result, the recent political history of East Parrish is one of apathy and distrust punctuated by episodes of scandal and conflict. Where decisions have to be made—such as providing a new library or even something as trivial as

NORMS OF BEHAVIOR

paying for a local production of an opera produced by a nearby university—they are made by a very small number of citizens operating in a completely nonpublic way. This nonpublic process—which turns out to be the only way to get something done because it does not invoke some form of community cleavage—only further feeds community paranoia and resentment. During our interview with one of the city fathers who showed us the drawings for a projected new library, he turned to his secretary and jokingly asked: "How much have we made on it so far?"

Clyde

Economically, Clyde, aside from its new dress factory, has seen no substantial change. Its biggest step forward came when a small group of community leaders, in the mid-1950's, created a tax-raising administration with special bond-issuing powers under some long obscure state law. About $250,000 were raised in taxes that went into a local water development based on a nearby lake. After considerable lobbying, the federal government took over the project. The leaders hope that this development will attract new industry, and lead to expanded development of Clyde and environs into a prosperous and pleasant recreation center and resort.

Politically, Clyde differs considerably from East Parrish. It has no real tradition of lower-class action. As a county seat, it has a higher proportion of middle-class people working for, or involved in, county and courthouse activities. This is also the reason why the main political focus in Clyde is on county, rather than civic, affairs. It does not even have the same "coal-camp" appearance of East Parrish. To the innocent urban eye it looks very much like any small town in Illinois; one has to go to the unincorporated fringe, or to a tavern in an obscure alley off the square, to see what almost 20 years of poverty will do to human beings. Of the three towns, only in Clyde does one hear frequent and almost compulsive talk of "white trash."

Also, probably because it is a county seat, a number of industry executives live there. The town's previous mayor was a retired railroad vice president; its present mayor is a retired coal company president—in manner and style very much resembling his famous brother who led the miner's union. One of the last major coal companies—the one reputed to be the most ruthlessly exploitative—maintains offices in Clyde. This small executive group has left its mark on the politics of Clyde.

If the politics of East Parrish resemble in a strange way the politics of France before DeGaulle, the politics of Clyde resemble the politics of DeGaulle. There have been a series of strong mayors who have not "sought" public office, but who have demanded that the community offer it to them. The present mayor in his first election cautioned supporters that, if campaign posters were put up, he would decline the office. These strong mayors have given the community its neat, clean appearance; they have also sapped the political vitality of the people.

The present upper-middle class, which might ordinarily have been expected to provide considerable leadership, will obviously bring little change. It has split into two elements. The more conservative element was described by one citizen:

> There is definitely a group of inheritors—doctors, lawyers, those running insurance agencies, stores, garages. For the most part a very unaggressive lot. . . . These people are in no great hurry to see things change.

One conservative spoke about his group this way:

> True, we might lack some spirit. For most of us, it is a matter of getting out of school and inheriting your father's business. This is what happened in my case. I'm not sure I really wanted to come back. . . . But, as I say, it is a life with many compensations.

To the extent that they take an interest in politics, they are Republican and concentrate on town affairs.

The other element mostly consists of the recently prosperous—including those who rose from Italian or Slavic coal mining families. They—with a few mavericks from the older elites—tend to dominate county politics which are largely Democratic. They are more concerned with the decline of the community than the older group, possibly because they are more vulnerable—yet they accept, with little quibble, the present structure of control.

Clyde has experienced none of the turbulence of East Parrish politics—but that is probably because it has not evinced as much interest as East Parrish—the interest caused by frustration. It developed no new community organizations, engaged in no campaigns to raise funds from community residents, and rarely did economic redevelopment become a political issue.

It is thus not unexpected that Clyde's major bid for renewal came not from some broad, popular campaign, but from an administrative unit of government; that it did not seek funds through public appeal, but through taxation. Despite the fact that, as one resident put it, "for years the merchants have been hanging on by their teeth hoping for a miracle to save them," and that the pressures of poverty are such that the state's attorney (the Illinois name for county prosecutor) complains that he "can only do a small part of what the state requires because I spend 90 percent of my time doing social work," this community feels it can afford to take the long view. But even at this point, the brightest estimate of the transformations to be wrought by the new lake development offers a promise for only a small section of the community.

The only public opposition, an angry typographer employed by the community's daily newspaper, can be seen on occasional Saturdays parading around the town square, carrying now familiar sandwich boards that decry the community's domination by a small and selfish group and that challenge the community to undertake its own program of revival. And just as this single, isolated figure is accepted with good humor but not much thought by the residents of Clyde, so there appears to be a somewhat thoughtless and casual acceptance of an unchanging drift.

Spiresburg

Spiresburg clearly has been the most successful of the three towns. In a sense, the crisis caused by the decline of the coal industry came to it first. Spiresburg lost its two major mines during the early years of the great depression and, while it retained a number of persons employed in mining, it served essentially as a dormitory for miners of the general area.

Like Clyde, it is a county seat and the core of the community is located around the courthouse. Also, like Clyde, Spiresburg is a second city in its county, subordinate in industry, retail, and service activity to a nearby town.

In these respects, as well as in general location, types of industry, natural resources and so on, it has some similarity to the other two. If anything, it has more disadvantages. It has not been nearly as successful as Clyde in attracting potentially prominent, capable, and educated people to live there. It is markedly smaller than either—less than half the population of Clyde, a third that of East Parrish. But it is the character and activity of the political and community leaders of Spiresburg that is most dramatically different.

They are a fairly well-integrated group of small merchants and independent professionals and semiprofessionals. Even schoolteachers and ministers, in contrast to Clyde and East Parrish, are included. Reading a roster of offices for social clubs, official and semiofficial boards, and local government offices for a period of years, one quickly detects an interweaving and reoccurrence of names that suggests nothing so much as a well-rehearsed square dance. To the middle class, high or low, a lot of sociability is most of what is required for access to community life. The pattern of integrated community leadership is so great that lower-class participation is all but impossible. (Its dormitory status, which meant a dispersal of its workers over the countryside, obviously weakened class solidarity, unlike East Parrish where residential and work populations overlapped.)

Social contacts among Spiresburg's upper group is the highest for all three communities—while social participation for its workers and reliefers is the lowest for all three. The frequent and easy contacts among influentials are facilitated by Spiresburg's size—it is small enough so that its community leadership can take a collective daily coffee break. While sitting in a restaurant in early afternoon for less than an hour with the mayor, the senior author met most of the town's leading merchants, a local insurance agent, the police chief, postmaster, state senator, optometrist, and the newspaper publisher.

In three of the cases of successful plant relocation in Spiresburg government aid was sought and utilized; in the fourth the community provided its own resources. The wages in all four plants are at best marginal, and there are few white collar or managerial positions.

However, the limits of Spiresburg's recovery have been set by the shopkeeper mentalities of its leadership. By these standards the town has recovered. But in Spiresburg's lower class there is a continuing, if ineffectual, discontent. And in the upper class the most promising young people leave, usually for college, and seldom return. Spiresburg's situation is best symbolized by the contrast between its four almost brand-new factories—on its outskirts—and its town square which looks today much as it must have about 1925.

The Issue of Leadership

From this comparison of the three towns it seems obvious that the quality of community leadership—particularly political leadership—is a crucial determinant of the course of development. The picture is amazingly consistent with that thesis. And it is also reflected in the feelings and attitudes of the citizens of each town.

The depressed spirit in East Parrish and Clyde, and the unrealistic attitudes toward their problems, is revealed by the answers people had to questions about events that had occurred recently. (For example, what was "the biggest thing that happened in the community during the last year?") The ones they emphasized were on the horizon rather than of immediate importance. Very prominent were a major interstate highway due to pass close to both towns and the federal lake resort project—both due for completion well in the future. Seventy-three percent of the citizens of Clyde, the town most directly involved, mentioned one or the other. Even though East Parrish was not as closely concerned, 27 percent also referred to them.

Similar results came from the more specific question that asked people to describe the "most important problem facing the community." Almost 80 percent of Clyde's respondents spoke of unemployment or poor business conditions, as did 66 percent from East Parrish. (The continuing political conflict in East Parrish, not present in Clyde, accounted for 17 percent, and so kept the score for economic depression from being even higher.) Spiresburg, too, registered a 47 percent vote for unemployment and poor business which indicated that its recovery was also far from complete. On the other hand, 36 percent of Spiresburg's respondents listed problems associated with growth—the taxing of existing community facilities or the financing of improvements—as being the "most important."

Would the picture get "better or worse in the next few months?" Fifty percent of East Parrish votes went for worse; in Clyde 26 percent felt this way; but in optimistic Spiresburg, only 12 percent.

How attached the respondents were to their communities and how they felt about them are described in the table.

Spiresburg is the easiest to single out. Its economic improvement has had an effect on (and perhaps also was affected by) the attitude of its citizens. A majority thought it no place for a young man just starting out (63 percent); but that is considerably lower than the 78 and 83 percent who felt that way about East Parrish and Clyde. They also show the highest community identification and commitment—68 percent selected it as their ideal community of residence; 84 percent felt their fellow residents "really care" about it.

The differences between the depressed communities, Clyde and East Parrish, were not great; but such as they were, they emphasized the greater magnitude of East Parrish's decline.

Change—But Don't Upset Anything

In these three towns different traditions and different political structures have led to three essentially different modes of adjustment to similar crises. What these modes do have in common however—despite a prevailing rhetoric of community renewal—is a deep-seated resistance to social change of any real significance. And in this respect they resemble hundreds of other declining communities too far from urban centers in an urban society.

This resistance to change has many causes. Most important perhaps, community leaders do not really believe enough in the futures of their towns to be willing to commit their own children to them. (The lower classes have little choice.) There was only one professional or semi-professional in all those we interviewed in all three communities who did not sometime boast about how well his children were doing somewhere else. The only middle-class group whose children, generally, did not leave, are the marginal retail merchants who often had little to bequeath except their businesses.

And it is precisely this element, notably in East Parrish, that is most committed to community renewal. The mayor of Spiresburg talked—as most people did—about the loss of young people to the community; each new plant was referred to as having taken care of the graduating class of the community high school of this year or that year. But the reference was not to the entire graduating class, only that part of it primarily, if not exclusively, lower class. That is, that portion not going on to college. The son of the mayor himself, obviously, had no future in a plant with few managerial or professional jobs.

Since the leaders are not really committed to the future of the towns—except in the most abstract way—there is little incentive to undertake community renewal that might rock their boats; and any genuine community renewal would have to rock it. The president of East Parrish's only bank was most explicit:

This community has lost population and it may have to lose more. But things have settled down quite nicely and everything operates smoothly. East Parrish has a pretty stable economy. Of course there are no new industries. But when I started this bank in 1943 there was a mine payroll of over one million dollars a month, now it is down to one hundred and fifty thousand. Then there were three banks with combined assets of about four million, now there is only one (his), but it has assets of over twelve million. . . . The town may get smaller instead of bigger. For a community, like a man, things have to balance out.

The town might die, but he was doing nicely. Things balanced out.

This banker was a leading member of the East Parrish Industrial fund; it is easy to see why it was so cautious about spending its $100,000 to attract new industry. Even in Spiresburg, though everyone was in favor of prosperity in general, some did not want too much—too much being defined as the point at which it might bring competition to established businesses and established allocations of power.

The present high level of integration of leadership in Spiresburg is sustained by systematic back-scratching. For example, the town's optometrist makes it perfectly clear that none of the town's four practicing physicians would dream of giving an eye examination. Unfortunately, economic back-scratching cannot survive where there is extensive economic and social growth, vital to community renewal. You can't have everything. Despite the rhetoric, the choice has been made.

PERCEPTION OF AND ATTACHMENT TO COMMUNITY

Items:	E. Parrish	Clyde	Spiresburg
Most of the important decisions in —— are made by a small group of people who are on "the inside."	82%*	72%*	78%*
There have been so many changes in —— that it is hardly the same town.	24	12	15
Most people in —— really care about what happens to the community.	68	62	84
—— is no place for a young man just starting out.	78	83	63
It is better to live in a small town than a big city.	80	88	90
Percent selecting present community in free choice of ideal community in which to live.	58	53	68

Percent agreeing.

Further, whether as rationalization or compensation, or because those who might think otherwise have already flown to the cities, a strongly anti-urban system of values has emerged. One community resident observed:

> When I or my wife want to take a walk we can do it without being robbed or assaulted. You can't say that in St. Louis or Chicago.

This is an overstatement, but not without some truth. However, he does not ask what the young people of the community ask continually: Where in town is there anything to walk to?

Since for most the money lies in the cities, those who stay must believe, or profess, a rejection of purely mercenary values. A young returnee to East Parrish commented:

> This is a friendly town. I known 'most everyone. When I walk down the street, everyone says hello. Here I am my own boss. I make less, but I also worry less. In St. Louis, at GM, everyone was worried that the guy at the next desk would get a promotion before you did—I could have stayed, they called from Flint and offered me a promotion. You have to grow up sometimes, a person has to learn to walk a straight road.

Or a young publisher in Clyde:

> You might say that we here in Clyde have learned to settle for second best. But I prefer to think that we just value things differently. . . . I have ten minutes from my house what the big city businessman has to travel hundreds of miles to get and then for only a few days a year.

The lessons are plain. First, superficial indicators are not the accurate predictors of community health they are often conceived to be. Whether a town will climb, slow its decline, or go under altogether is determined often very largely by the character and activity of its middle and upper-middle class political leadership.

But there is an even more important lesson hovering ominously in the background. The economic progress of each of the three Southern Illinois towns studied is different, and they have responded differently to crisis; but none represents a substantial—certainly not permanent—comeback in the face of increased urbanization.

Their approach to the future is one of improvisation. Their horizons must remain limited—for redevelopment is not only a promise but a threat to the ideologies of small town life. They must lose their best people and business concerns to the larger towns because of greater opportunities, education, and satisfactions there. Those who return will be failures—or be willing, for whatever reason, to settle for what represents second-best in our competitive society.

It is impossible for any similar small town to maintain a first-rate school system—and the children, and the future, must suffer for it. The fundamental character of the leadership of these communities will limit the nature and direction of growth—because they do not want to face real competition. If they had been willing and prepared to face it, they would have moved out long before. They cannot be expected to deliberately make their own worst fears come true.

The land and the economy of the United States will not support as many small towns as they did before. It is very difficult not to see the future as a long drawn-out struggle for community survival, lasting for half a century, in which some battles may be won but the war will be lost. A future in which most such towns will become isolated or decayed, in which the local amenities must deteriorate, and in which there will finally be left only the aged, the inept, the very young—and the local power elite.

March-April 1967

The ethnographic research for this article was part of a project of the National Opinion Research Center supported in part by the US Public Health Service and reported more fully in *Reports on Happiness* by Norman N. Bradburn and David Caplovitz (1965).

SUGGESTED READINGS

Small Town in a Mass Society: Class, Power, and Religion in a Rural Community by Arthur J. Vidich and Joseph Bensman (Princeton, N.J.: Princeton University Press, 1958). Particularly insightful in the consideration of community ideologies generated by residents of small towns.

The People of Coaltown by Herman R. Lantz (New York: Columbia University Press, 1958). Historical perspective and a consideration of pathological reactions to living in declining communities.

The Rulers and the Ruled: Political Power and Impotence in American Communities by Robert E. Agger, Daniel Goldrich, and Bert E. Swanson (New York: Wiley, 1964). An extended, complex attempt at a historical and comparative study of the political structures of communities.

The Talk in Vandalia by Joseph P. Lyford (Charlotte, N.C.: McNally & Loftin, 1964). A first-rate piece of social reportage providing immediate imagery of community self-perception.

"Death by Dieselization: A Case Study in the Reaction to Technological Change" by W. F. Cottrell, *American Sociological Review* (Vol. 16, June 1951). How a small western town reacted to the effects of technological progress.

Five Towns: A Compartive Community Study by Lois R. Dean (New York: Random House, 1967). Explores the relationship between political leadership and economic growth in five midwestern communities.

Who's Running this Town? by Ritchie P. Lowry (New York: Harper and Row, 1965). The problems of developing effective community leadership in the face of urbanization, mobility and the rise in education.

Plainville, U. S. A. by James West (pseud.) (New York: Columbia University Press, 1945).

Middletown by Robert S. Lynd and Helen M. Lynd (New York: Harcourt, Brace and Co., 1929).

Middletown in Transition by Robert S. Lynd and Helen M. Lynd (New York: Harcourt, Brace and Co., 1937).

Democracy in Jonesville by W. Lloyd Warner *et al.* (New York: Harper and Row, 1949).

Elmtown's Youth by August B. Hollingshead (New York: Wiley, 1949). The preceding are classic American community studies employing the social-anthropological method to uncover patterns in culture and social structure.

Rural Russia Today

Life on collective farms is shaped by traditional customs and beliefs; it is untouched by the progress that has been made in the cities

MARTIN K. WHYTE

History, in Marx's view, had little use for the countryside after the 1800s. Farms and villages were quite definitely *not* where the action was, and Marx consigned their inhabitants to a state of "rural idiocy." Soviet leaders have rarely been so dismissive, certainly not in their public rhetoric. From the earliest days of the new Russian state, its rulers have vowed to close the gap between town and country: in income, in educational and cultural opportunity, in the quality of life. Yet even today, more than half a century after the Revolution, the "farm problem" is generally conceded to be the major domestic issue in Russia.

Most American analysts of the "problem" have focused on the economic questions, on incentives, the demands of authorities, the adequacy of farm machinery and Soviet agricultural science. This has been the focus of most Soviet writers as well. Recently, however, one notes among Soviet academic, journalistic and literary people a growing concern with the more sociological and cultural aspects of the Russian countryside. There appears to be a dawning realization that the rural stagnation in which almost half the Soviet people still live is not something that can be remedied, or even understood, in economic terms alone.

In any paper on Soviet society, caveats are always in order but they are particularly important in my case. With the great variation throughout the Soviet Union in traditional cultures, prosperity of farms, climate and so forth, it is obviously not possible to make many generalizations that could cover the entire range—even if I could utilize village studies for every area, which I can't. Therefore I will try to describe what I have been able to learn from Soviet writings on the *kolkhozy,* the collective farms, as they exist today in several areas of the country—always with the understanding that some of my statements may have to be revised as more materials become available. Also, rather than try to describe the entire "life world" of the kolkhoznik, I will focus on areas of tradition and backwardness in rural life, and how these affect the supply and motivation of kolkhoz labor.

Survivals from the Past

Perhaps the most fascinating material contained in the recent studies of collective farms concerns the continuing importance of folk ceremonials and religious beliefs. Forty years after Stalin began his brutal collectivization campaigns, traditional holidays and ceremonials still seem to dominate rural social life in most areas, although there have been important changes. An example is the traditional Russian marriage ceremony. Formerly, getting married was a very involved process even in the Russian (that is, non-Muslim, non-Tartar) areas of the country. It meant detailed negotiations of matchmaking and then several days of elaborate ceremonies before and after the wedding itself. In Kalinin oblast (province) the matchmaking ceremony and the giving of dowries are still the rule today, although both have lost most of their economic significance. Other traditional elements, such as the viewing of the groom's house and the blocking of the bridal procession are also retained in many areas. Two Soviet anthropologists who studied the Kalinin oblast admit that the new "Komsomol wedding," which involves little more than the civil registration of the marriage and a reception with an orchestra in the kolkhoz club, has so far made little dent in the rural areas. Studies in the Tambov oblast and in the North Caucasus present a similar picture—marriage rituals changing, but still based on the traditional folk ceremonies.

Christenings and funerals also are carried out in traditional fashion in many Russian areas. In Viriatino we are told that christenings are the rule, although on the Rossiya farm in the Caucasus only 30 percent of the children are christened. Religious funerals are also still common, with elderly women reciting the scriptures from memory over the grave. And religious holidays are still widely celebrated. On the Rossiya farm in the Caucasus about half of the kolkholzniki questioned in one survey said they celebrated both Soviet and religious holidays, while another observer claims that in Viriatino even the young feel guilty about working on religious holidays.

It is difficult to judge how many people on collective farms feel a complete commitment to Christian beliefs. In 1953 ikons hung in virtually all the homes in Viriatino. But in the Ukrainian village of Terpenye only 47 percent of the homes contained ikons, while on the Rossiya farm in the Caucasus the figure was only 25 percent. In any case, even though those actually professing belief may be in a minority, the influence of religion may still be fairly strong. Religious holidays, for example, may still be observed by many or all peasants even when beliefs are absent. In Efim Dorosh's short story, "Country Diary," there is a peasant woman who, with the rest of the village, has stayed away from work on a religious holiday, despite the fact that she doesn't attend church and doesn't understand or remember what the holiday is. In academic studies, too, one often hears the complaint that, while religious views are strong only among the older people in the kolkhoz, the young people show little interest in agitating against religion.

Another important area of what the Soviets call "survivals" lies in family relations. Of course, here again important changes have taken place since the early 1800s; the powers of age over youth and of male over female, for instance, have both declined. Nevertheless, contrary to Soviet claims, there are still important economic factors that tend to strengthen family ties, thereby facilitating the passing on of traditional views. Most important here are the difficult economic position of the kolkhozniki and the low level of social services provided to them, which I will discuss later. Collective farmers still depend on their kin for help in domestic work, child care, house construction, loans and so on. It is general practice in many areas for all family members to turn over their earnings to the family head and even family members working away from the kolkhoz are expected to contribute part of their earnings. How the family's funds are spent is then determined internally, but in some families the male head still holds the purse strings tightly in his own hands, and younger members, who may be the major earners, will have to ask him for money whenever they have expenses.

Kinship Ties

Moreover, it is common even today for at least one child, usually a son, to remain with the parents to help support them in their old age. And in Kalinin oblast we are told that, while separate residence for married children is the rule, the new couple usually spends two or three years living with their parents while they accumulate enough money to set up their own household. Kinship ties through the male line are still apparently stronger than through the female line in both Russian and Moslem areas. One team of researchers describes a visit home to the kolkhoz by a young married couple who now live in the city. They stay with the husband's mother on their visit, and the wife's mother does not consider it proper to go to see her daughter until three days after their arrival. An-

Eve Arnold MAGNUM

Women on the kolkhoz work longer hours than the men: laboring for the state, tending private plots and taking care of husband and children.

other observer noted that in Uzbekistan it is fairly common for the husband's parents to live with a couple, but rare for the wife's parents to do so.

As one might expect, it is in some of the non-Russian parts of the country, particularly in the Moslem areas of Central Asia, that family relations have changed the least. A writer on Uzbek collective farmers states that of all types of survivals, traditional family relations are the strongest. The impulse to marry off children, especially daughters, at an early age is still strong, and many Uzbeks still consider 15 the ideal marriage age, some even preventing their daughters from finishing school. Practices such as polygyny, levirate marriage and the Moslem divorce procedure still occur occasionally, but are combatted, in some cases with jail sentences. And in some Uzbek families the daughter-in-law is still treated by her father-in-law like a "domestic semislave" (domashniaia polurabynia).

What are the factors underlying these survivals in religion, ceremonials and family relations? Generally speaking they are due to the long history of neglect of the social and economic welfare of the peasants which has made official modernizing philosophies seem distant and at times hostile. And, as mentioned, the economic insecurities of the peasants may result in a desire to strengthen kinship ties,

Robert Capa MAGNUM   Eve Arnold MAGNUM

Religious and folk beliefs persist because the State is indifferent to them as long as they don't interfere with productivity (to the right, a "State" christening).

particularly between parent and child, and this in turn may help the survival of traditional beliefs and behavior. Furthermore, the shortage of recreational facilities in the rural areas and the sobriety of the new Soviet ceremonials mean that there is little alternative to the folk celebrations in satisfying the people's need for play and relaxation.

But perhaps the major factor in the persistence of folk and religious traditions in the countryside is that, contrary to the impression given in many sources, these traditions have only been combatted intermittently and selectively. The kolkhoz has always been regarded as primarily an economic servant of the state, and not the creator of a new and higher form of social life. After collectivization had been completed, traditional customs were repressed for the most part only when they were thought to interfere with the economic tasks of the kolkhoz—e.g. holidays that broke up the working day, parents trying to keep their daughters cooped up in the home, and so forth. Only intermittently have the authorities conducted a whole-hearted attack on all religious views in the rural areas—partly no doubt to avoid alienating the peasants and partly simply because it didn't seem worth the effort. Only the exposure to the modern atmosphere of the city and work for a state enterprise could be expected to produce the new man. Thus,

NORMS OF BEHAVIOR

it seems to me that it would be a mistake to view the survivals I have been discussing as tenacious carry-overs from prerevolutionary times, which are being actively combatted at all times. Rather, a modus vivendi may exist for long periods of time, as long as the farm work gets done. But even the occasional bursts of antireligious propaganda are undermined by the social conditions created by past neglect—economic insecurity, lack of cultural and recreational facilities, and so on.

Soviet short story writers and social scientists agree that working conditions on the kolkhozy—the long hours and the prevalence of hand labor—are sore points to the kolkhozniks, and major reasons why many rural youths leave for the cities. A. S. Duchal's work and free-time studies, based on collective farms in four different regions, are particularly illuminating on this score. Duchal states that in the summer the average work week of the kolkhoznik, counting both work on the farm and on his own private plot, is 62.3 hours, but that it decreases to 32.5 hours a week in the winter. The average over the year, 47.4 hours per week, is still about eight hours above the average work week of urban workers and employees.

Russia's Rural Slums

In addition to the more arduous work conditions, the collective farmers have traditionally received much less for their labors than other workers, even workers on the state farms. For, on a state farm (or sovkhoz), workers are paid set wages as in a factory. Collective farmers, in contrast, have traditionally worked for units called labor days whose value is not fixed, but depends on the size of the harvests. In 1958, payments to collective farmers were 30 percent below the average for state farm workers, in 1959 the figure was 42 percent, in 1960 it was 39 percent and by 1965, 33 percent. The gap between collective farm pay and that of industrial workers is even larger—in 1965 the pay of collective farmers was only about half that of industrial workers. Consequently the collective farmer relies heavily on his private plot for income—he may spend 40 percent of his labor on his plot, and the plot may supplement his income by 30 to 50 percent. Even with private-plot incomes taken into account, however, the average per capita income of collective farm workers, according to recent figures, is still 19 percent below that of state farmers and about 33 percent below that of industrial workers.

The gap extends also into the realm of social welfare expenditures. The sociologist A. Aitov claims that the state spends about twice as much in social welfare payments (pensions, maternity stipends, etc.) on the average worker or employee as on the average peasant. And expenditures by the kolkhozy on their members don't come close to making up the difference, amounting to only eight rubles per capita in 1962. Paid services (tailors, bakers, barbers, cobblers and so forth) are also poorly provided in the countryside. One researcher states that in 1964 paid services made up 12 percent of the budgets of industrial workers, but only 3 percent of the budgets of kolkhozniks. And on the kolkhoz, two-thirds of these services were performed by private individuals, compared to one-fourth for urban residents.

To give just one more example of the rural lag, in 1965 there were only one million rural children in permanent preschool child care institutions, and only 150,000 of these on kolkhozy, compared to six million children in the cities. This is in spite of the fact that there were 18.4 million children under seven in rural areas and only 15.7 million in urban areas.

These figures give some picture of the disadvantages the kolkhoznik faces in terms of economic and social welfare, but the short stories and village studies yield information that statistics can't convey. Some villages, particularly in marshy areas, are so poorly connected to the outside world that they are virtually isolated for much of the year. And cultural and recreational facilities vary tremendously, depending on the prosperity of the farm. In the Moldavian village of Kopanka, the Lenin kolkhoz seems to be well supplied, with a club, a library and even an art gallery. But the short story writer A. Yashin describes the opposite side of the coin: "In the large village of Sushinovo there were, as yet, neither electricity nor radio, no library or club. In the last two years the travelling cinema had not visited the village once." Even when clubs and theaters are provided they may not be used during the time of greatest leisure—the winter—because they are not heated. For their water supply many kolkhozniks still depend on wells or streams; a standpipe in the street is a fairly advanced development. Peasant housing is still dominated by the two- or three-room house focused around the traditional Russian oven. And the costs of construction are still largely borne by individual peasants, although they can get loans from the farms.

In the last four or five years legislation has been passed which is designed to ease the situation of the peasant. Pensions have been introduced for peasants on a nationwide basis, and the current five-year plan calls for them to be brought into line with sovkhoz pensions. In 1966 legislation was passed "advising" collective farms to raise their levels of pay to correspond to sovkhoz levels. And by 1965 the prices charged for consumer goods in rural areas were supposed to be lowered to correspond to the urban price levels. Attention is also being given to the need to improve the recreational, cultural and educational facilities in the countryside. These are encouraging signs, but it will be some time before we can assess the effectiveness of these measures.

The reforms also suggest that the anomalous position of the kolkhoz within Soviet society is being altered. In theory the kolkhoz is an autonomous cooperative, managing its own affairs and providing for its own people except in the areas of health and education. In practice, this autonomy extends only to providing for the needs of its members, while in deciding what to produce and how much to deliver to the state there has been very little autonomy. But the economic goals imposed upon the farm by the state have been the main factor preventing the farm from adequately providing for its own—often there just isn't enough left. Now the state seems to be realizing that in order to maintain agricultural output, the kolkhoz must be given more of a hand in meeting its internal needs.

How Not to Keep Them Down on the Farm

The hardships of rural life weigh most heavily, perhaps, on the women and youth on the kolkhozy. Since the Revolution, as everyone knows, women have been brought out of the home and into the labor force. In one sense this has been an emancipation, as Soviet writers often note, but in many ways it has also meant additional burdens. Women who work on the farm tend to lack the training and experience to fill the most responsible positions and as a result they tend to be assigned the most manual labor. But besides their often tedious tasks for the collective, women also carry the bulk of the domestic chores and do most of the work on the private plots. Men as yet have not seen fit to share much of this load, and tend to confine their efforts to work on the farm. On the Rossiya farm in the North Caucasus, for example, one fifth of the men share in all types of domestic work (cleaning, cooking, child care, etc.), but often the men shove all of the child care duties onto their wives. Although women may spend less time on the average working for the farm than men, their extra duties result in a work day that is often much longer. The following figures from two of the village studies illustrate the point.

HOURS OF WORK PER DAY ON LENIN FARM, 1960

	On kolkhoz	On private plot	Total
Men	6.8	0.7	7.5
Women	7.5	4.7	12.2

HOURS OF WORK PER DAY ON ROSSIYA FARM, 1964

	On kolkhoz	On domestic work	Total
Men	8.87	1.22	10.09
Women	5.0	7.09	12.09

As a result of all this, various Soviet studies state that women get less sleep than men, are less active in community organizations, less often play musical instruments, are more religious, and miss out on much of the cultural and recreational life of the village—even in the winter. Thus kolkhoz women are seriously disadvantaged when compared with their male counterparts, not to mention urban women. Again, the shortage of facilities such as child care institutions and laundries, and the necessity to work on the plot in order to meet consumption needs can be seen at the root of the woman's plight.

Rural youth are also placed in a difficult position. If they decide to stay in the countryside they must accept the difficult working conditions and scarcity of amenities on the kolkhoz. Moreover, their abilities may not be fully utilized.

F. Il'iashenko states, "Some collective farms lack hands and therefore youth are employed at various unskilled jobs and the conditions for further study are not created."

Under these circumstances it is not surprising that in many areas relatively few youths do make the decision to stay on the farm. On the more prosperous collectives, such as the Rossiya farm in the Caucasus, youth exodus was a serious problem in the 1950s, but has decreased in recent years. However in the Smolensk oblast, where agricultural production has been particularly stagnant in recent years, the problem has reached crisis proportions. When a team of researchers interviewed rural secondary school students in that oblast in 1966, they found that on the average 72 percent planned to leave their native villages and live in the city. But the figure was 65 percent for eighth grade students, 83 percent for tenth grade students, and 96 percent for eleventh grade students: And the researchers imply that these figures actually understate the number of rural youths who will end up in the city. Aitov presents figures for students in a school in the Bashkir Autonomous Republic who were asked the same question in 1965. Of 46 students asked, only seven wanted to stay in the countryside after school, but in the last five years only four youths had actually stayed. In some areas, however, the picture is somewhat brighter. In one school in the Ves'egonskii region, in a period of nine years, over 50 percent of the graduates ended up staying in the countryside. Still, a short story by Anatoly Kuznetsov, who is now in self-imposed exile in London, reinforces the impression that returning to the village may be the exception and not the rule. In "At Home," Galya returns to her native village after completing secondary school in the city and is questioned suspiciously by the kolkhoz chairman, who thinks she wouldn't have wanted to return to work on the kolkhoz unless she had gotten into some kind of trouble in the city. To give yet another example, V. Fomin describes a Ukrainian village in which the residents hold their breaths when young men enter the army for fear they will not return home when they are discharged, but will escape to the cities.

The hardships of rural life are undoubtedly the major factor behind the exodus of rural youth, but I think we should also consider the fact that Soviet press and propaganda over the years have contributed to the low evaluation these young people have of the kolkhoz. For the city has always been depicted as the center of progress and glamor in Soviet society, the place where the new man was being created. The kolkhoz in contrast is seen as a transitional form, inferior to the factory in property relations, technology and organization of labor. This basic urban bias, reflected in past educational policy, may have reinforced dissatisfaction with village life.

The young people who do decide to leave are at a disadvantage compared with urban youth in getting education and jobs in the city. The main factor seems to be the inferior quality of rural schools. Great strides have been made in educating rural youth compared with the prerevolutionary years, and education is a major factor in the desire of youth to leave the kolkhoz. But the quality of education still lags far behind that in the cities. For instance in 1965 only 15 percent of the entrants into higher schools in Gorkii oblast were graduates of rural secondary schools. And in a study carried out by V. Shubkin in the Novosibirsk oblast in 1963, 76 percent of the secondary school graduates from families doing manual agricultural work wanted to continue their education, but only 10 percent succeeded—in other words the aspirations of two-thirds of the students with that background were thwarted. The success of students with other backgrounds, including rural nonmanual work, was uniformly much higher.

Efforts are being made to improve the quality of rural education, to orient rural education more to preparing students for agricultural work, and to give youth who decide to stay on the farm more responsible positions. And the exodus of youth has also resulted in increased concern for providing rural areas with cultural and recreational facilities. In some areas, farms are experimenting with guaranteeing youth higher pay than they could earn in the city, an experiment that doesn't set too well with older and more experienced farmers who lack such guarantees. But, again, it remains to be seen whether these measures will be effective in slowing the drain of youth, and in helping those rural youth who do decide to leave to compete with their urban counterparts.

Labor Shortage

The immigration of young people to the cities causes another basic problem of the kolkhozy—a shortage of labor during the busy agricultural seasons. Others besides youth have been leaving, even though it is more difficult for adult members to get away since they must get permission from the farm. Those adults who leave tend to have more skills and education than the average kolkhoznik. Thus in many areas the kolkhozy are not only being drained of their youth, but of some of their most qualified adults as well. As a result many farms have to rely largely on a relatively "old" and unskilled labor force for many tasks. In the busiest seasons pensioners and youth may have to be coaxed into pitching in. But on some farms the shortages may be still more severe. A fair number of farms apparently resort to hiring outside workers for the summer, and urban industrial firms are still counted on in many areas to bus some of their workers to nearby farms to help with the harvest—apparently a poor solution, since the workers chosen seem to be less than enthusiastic.

Here I think we can see one of those vicious circles which occurs in the process of development. The difficult conditions of kolkhoz labor prompt many of the most capable to leave for the cities. The productivity of those who are left is thus likely to be lower so that pay will be less. As wages go down, the labor shortage becomes more acute and those remaining have to work longer hours. Thus some of the conditions which lie behind the rural exodus are perpetuated.

It is hard to avoid the conclusion that the present state of Soviet rural life is the result of decades of neglect, although progress in some areas, such as health and education, has been impressive. Furthermore recent legislation on pensions and improved pay for collective farmers, and the increasing attention being given to providing cultural and recreational facilities in the countryside, may indicate a sincere desire to compensate for the decades of neglect—if only in order to get agricultural production moving again. Nevertheless, from the material I have presented it should be evident that past neglect has had such a pervasive influence on rural residents that selective reform efforts may not be sufficient—and in some cases may be self-defeating.

For instance, recent articles in the Soviet press stress the need to improve rural recreational facilities in order to make village life more attractive to the youth. But if farms try to invest in new facilities without substantial financial help from the state it will mean diverting funds away from payments for labor, which will not please those already working on the farm. A substantial investment in the improvement of rural education would help to develop young workers with skills needed by the farm, but unless this effort is accompanied by improvements in recreational facilities, working conditions and the like, the investment is likely to result in still larger numbers of rural youths wanting to escape to the cities. Even increasing the pay of kolkhozniks without improving the overall quality of rural life may have some negative side effects. Greater economic security might lead to the elimination of the custom of at least one child remaining on the farm, thus contributing to the labor supply problem. Also, some Soviet scholars are actually worried that if kolkhozniks are provided for too generously in wages and pensions, some family members who have been forced by economic necessity to work on the farm will drop out (primarily youth, women and the aged). In sum, it seems that only an across-the-board attempt to improve all areas of rural life holds much promise. Such an effort would demand much more financial assistance from the state than the farms are presently getting. And whether such a major effort will be forthcoming is uncertain, since for the state it would mean difficult decisions about diverting resources from other needs.

SUGGESTED READINGS   *January 1970*

The Peasants of Central Russia by S. P. Dunn and E. Dunn (New York: Holt, Rinehart and Winston, 1967) summarizes anthropological studies on Soviet villages in greater detail.

Central Asians Under Russian Rule by E. E. Bacon (Ithaca: Cornell University Press, 1966) details social life in a non-Russian area of the Soviet Union.

Collective Farming in Russia by R. D. Laird (Lawrence, Kansas: University of Kansas, 1958) describes the organizations and development of collective farms in the Soviet Union.

Photographs by Dudley Blake

Time and Cool People

Street life doesn't run by the clock; what counts is what's happening

JOHN HORTON

Street culture exists in every low income ghetto. It is shared by the hustling elements of the poor, whatever their nationality or color. In Los Angeles, members of such street groups sometimes call themselves "street people," "cool people," or simply "regulars." Whatever the label, they are known the world over by outsiders as hoods or hoodlums, persons who live on and off the street. They are recognizable by their own fashions in dress, hair, gestures, and speech. The particular fashion varies with time, place, and nationality. For example, in 1963 a really sharp Los Angeles street Negro would be "conked to the bone" (have processed hair) and "togged-out" in "continentals." Today "natural" hair and variations of mod clothes are coming in style.

Street people are known also by their activities—"duking" (fighting or at least looking tough), "hustling" (any way of making money outside the "legitimate" world of work), "gigging" (partying)—and by their apparent nonactivity, "hanging" on the corner. Their individual roles are defined concretely by their success or failure in these activities. One either knows "what's happening" on the street, or he is a "lame," "out of it," "not ready" (lacks his diploma in street knowledge), a "square."

There are, of course, many variations. Negroes, in particular, have contributed much to the street tongue which has diffused into both the more hip areas of the middle class and the broader society. Such expressions as "a lame," "taking care of righteous business," "getting down to the nitty-gritty," and "soul" can be retraced to Negro street life.

The more or less organized center of street life is the "set"—meaning both the peer group and the places where it hangs out. It is the stage and central market place for activity, where to find out what's happening. My set of Negro street types contained a revolving and sometimes disappearing (when the "heat," or police pressure, was on) population of about 45 members ranging in age from 18

VARIATION AND CONTRAST

to 25. These were the local "dudes," their term meaning not the fancy city slickers but simply "the boys," "fellas," the "cool people." They represented the hard core of street culture, the role models for younger teenagers. The dudes could be found when they were "laying dead"—hanging on the corner, or shooting pool and "jiving" ("goofing" or kidding around) in a local community project. Isolated from "the man" (in this context the man in power—the police, and by extension, the white man), they lived in a small section of Venice outside the central Los Angeles ghetto and were surrounded by a predominantly Mexican and Anglo population. They called their black "turf" "Ghost-town"—home of the "Ghostmen," their former gang. Whatever the origin of the word, Ghost-town was certainly the home of socially "invisible" men.

The Street Set

In 1965 and 1966 I had intensive interviews with 25 set members. My methods emerged in day to day observations. Identified as white, a lame, and square, I had to build up an image of being at least "legit" (not working

---

"Soul is getting down to the nitty-gritty, moving directly to what is basic—the opposite of hypocrisy, deceit, and phoniness."

---

for police). Without actually living in the area, this would have been impossible without the aid of a key fieldworker, in this case an outsider who could be accepted inside. This field worker, Cowboy, was a white dude of 25. He had run with "Paddy" (white), "Chicano" (Mexican), and "Blood" (Negro) sets since the age of 12 and was highly respected for having been president of a tough gang. He knew the street, how to duke, move with style, and speak the tongue. He made my entry possible. I was the underprivileged child who had to be taught slowly and sympathetically the common-sense features of street life.

Cowboy had the respect and I the toleration of several set leaders. After that, we simply waited for the opportunity to "rap." Although sometimes used synonymously with street conversation, "rap" is really a special way of talking—repartee. Street repartee at its best is a lively way of "running it down," or of "jiving" (attempting to put someone on), of trying "to blow another person's mind," forcing him "to loose his cool," to give in or give up something. For example, one needs to throw a lively rap when he is "putting the make on a broad."

Sometimes we taped individuals, sometimes "soul sessions." We asked for life histories, especially their stories about school, job, and family. We watched and asked about the details of daily surviving and attempted to construct street time schedules. We probed beyond the past and present into the future in two directions—individual plans for tomorrow and a lifetime, and individual dreams of a more decent world for whites and Negroes.

The set can be described by the social and attitudinal characteristics of its members. To the observer, these are expressed in certain realities of day to day living: not enough skill for good jobs, and the inevitable trouble brought by the problem of surviving. Of the 25 interviewed, only four had graduated from high school. Except for a younger set member who was still in school, all were dropouts, or perhaps more accurately kicked-outs. None was really able to use or write formal language. However, many were highly verbal, both facile and effective in their use of the street tongue. Perhaps the art of conversation is most highly developed here where there is much time to talk, perhaps too much—an advantage of the *lumpen-leisure* class.

Their incomes were difficult to estimate, as "bread" or "coins" (money) came in on a very irregular basis. Of the 17 for whom I have figures, half reported that they made less than $1,400 in the last year, and the rest claimed income from $2,000-4,000 annually. Two-thirds were living with and partially dependent on their parents, often a mother. The financial strain was intensified by the fact that although 15 of 17 were single, eight had one or more children living in the area. (Having children, legitimate or not, was not a stigma but proof of masculinity.)

At the time of the interview, two-thirds of them had some full- or part-time employment—unskilled and low-paid jobs. The overall pattern was one of sporadic and—from their viewpoint—often unsatisfactory work, followed by a period of unemployment compensation, and petty hustling whenever possible and whenever necessary.

When I asked the question, "When a dude needs bread, how does he get it?" the universal response was "the hustle." Hustling is, of course, illegitimate from society's viewpoint. Street people know it is illegal, but they view it in no way as immoral or wrong. It is justified by the necessity of surviving. As might be expected, the unemployed admitted that they hustled and went so far as to say that a dude could make it better on the street than on the job: "There is a lot of money on the street, and there are many ways of getting it," or simply, "This has always been my way of life." On the other hand, the employed, the part-time hustlers, usually said, "A dude could make it better on the job than on the street." Their reasons for disapproving of hustling were not moral. Hustling meant trouble. "I don't hustle because there's no security. You eventually get busted." Others said there was not enough money on the street or that it was too difficult to "run a game" on people.

Nevertheless, hustling is the central street activity. It is the economic foundation for everyday life. Hustling and the fruit of hustling set the rhythm of social activities.

What are the major forms of hustling in Ghost-town? The best hustles were conning, stealing, gambling, and selling dope. By gambling, these street people meant dice; by dope, peddling "pills" and "pot." Pills are "reds" and "whites"—barbiturates and benzedrine or dexedrine. Pot is, of course, marijuana—"grass" or "weed." To "con" means to put "the bump" on a "cat," to "run a game" on somebody, to work on his mind for goods and services.

The "woman game" was common. As one dude put it, "If I have a good lady and she's on County, there's always some money to get." In fact, there is a local expression for getting county money. When the checks come in for child support, it's "mother's day." So the hustler "burns" people for money, but he also "rips off" goods for money; he thieves, and petty thieving is always a familiar hustle. Pimping is often the hustler's dream of the good life, but it was almost unknown here among the small-time hustlers. That was the game of the real professional and required a higher level of organization and wealth.

Hustling means bread and security but also trouble, and trouble is a major theme in street life. The dudes had a "world of trouble" (a popular song about a hustler is "I'm in a World of Trouble")—with school, jobs, women, and the police. The intensity of street life could be gauged in part by the intensity of the "heat" (police trouble). The hotter the street, the fewer the people visible on the street. On some days the set was empty. One would soon learn that there had been a "bust" (an arrest). Freddy had run amok and thrown rocks at a police car. There had been a leadership struggle; "Big Moe" had been cut up, and the "fuzz" had descended. Life was a succession of being picked up on suspicion of assault, theft, possession, "suspicion of suspicion" (an expression used by a respondent in describing his life). This was an ordinary experience for the street dude and often did lead to serious trouble. Over half of those interviewed claimed they had felony convictions.

The Structure of Street Time

Keeping cool and out of trouble, hustling bread, and looking for something interesting and exciting to do created the structure of time on the street. The rhythm of time is expressed in the high and low points in the day and week of an unemployed dude. I stress the pattern of the unemployed and full-time hustler because he is on the street all day and night and is the prototype in my interviews. The sometimes employed will also know the pattern, and he will be able to hit the street whenever released from the bondage of jail, work, and the clock. Here I describe a typical time schedule gleaned through interviews and field observation.

Characteristically the street person gets up late, hits the street in the late morning or early afternoon, and works his way to the set. This is a place for relaxed social activity.

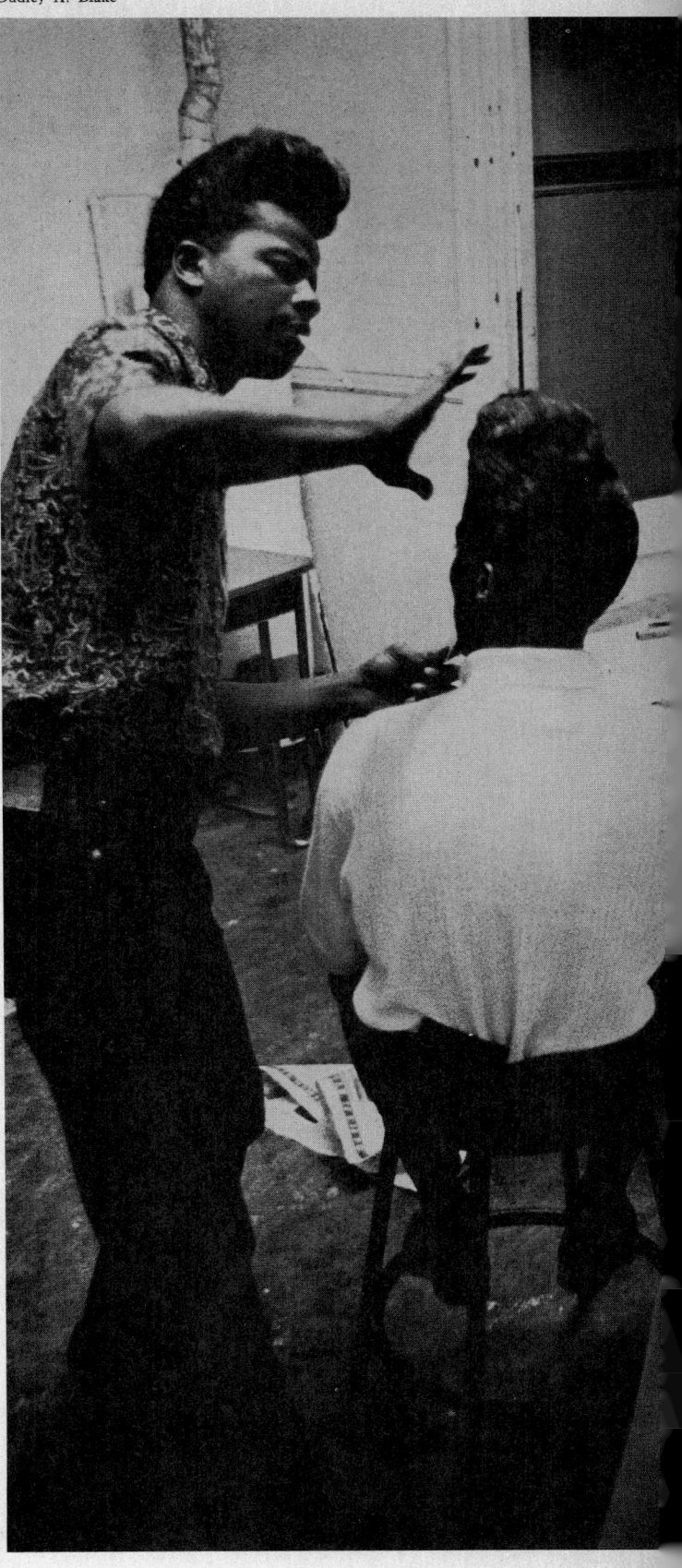

Dudley A. Blake

"Time may pick up when a few dudes drive down to Johnny's for a 'process' (hair straightening and styling)."

Hanging on the set with the boys is the major way of passing time and waiting until some necessary or desirable action occurs. Nevertheless, things do happen on the set. The dudes "rap" and "jive" (talk), gamble, and drink their "pluck" (usually a cheap, sweet wine). They find out what happened yesterday, what is happening today, and what will hopefully happen on the weekend—the perpetual search for the "gig," the party. Here peer socialization and reinforcement also take place. The younger dude feels a sense of pride when he can be on the set and throw a rap to an older dude. He is learning how to handle himself, show respect, take care of business, and establish his own "rep."

On the set, yesterday merges into today, and tomorrow is an emptiness to be filled in through the pursuit of bread and excitement. Bread makes possible the excitement—the high (getting loaded with wine, pills, or pot), the sharp clothes, the "broad," the fight, and all those good things which show that one knows what's happening and has "something going" for himself. The rhythm of time—of the day and of the week—is patterned by the flow of money and people.

Time is "dead" when money is tight, when people are occupied elsewhere—working or in school. Time is dead when one is in jail. One is "doing dead time" when nothing is happening, and he's got nothing going for himself.

Time is alive when and where there is action. It picks up in the evening when everyone moves on the street. During the regular school year it may pick up for an hour in the afternoon when the "broads" leave school and meet with the set at a corner taco joint. Time may pick up when a familiar car cruises by and a few dudes drive down to Johnny's for a "process" (hair straightening and styling). Time is low on Monday (as described in the popular song, "Stormy Monday"), Tuesday, Wednesday, when money is tight. Time is high on Friday nights when the "eagle flies" and the "gig" begins. On the street, time has a personal meaning only when something is happening, and something is most likely to happen at night—especially on Friday and Saturday nights. Then people are together, and there may be bread—bread to take and bread to use.

Human behavior is rational if it helps the individual to get what he wants whether it is success in school or happiness in the street. Street people sometimes get what they want. They act rationally in those situations where they are able to plan and choose because they have control, knowledge, and concern, irrationally where there are barriers to their wants and desires.

When the street dude lacks knowledge and power to manipulate time, he is indeed irrational. For the most part, he lacks the skills and power to plan a move up and out of the ghetto. He is "a lame" in the middle class world of school and work; he is not ready to operate effectively in unfamiliar organizations where his street strengths are his visible weaknesses. Though irrational in moving up and out of the street, he can be rational in day to day survival in the street. No one survives there unless he knows what's happening (that is, unless he knows what is available, where to get what he can without being burned or busted). More euphemistically, this is "taking advantage of opportunities," exactly what the rational member of the middle class does in his own setting.

To know what's happening is to know the goods and the bads, the securities, the opportunities, and the dangers of the street. Survival requires that a hustling dude know who is cool and uncool (who can be trusted); who is in power (the people who control narcotics, fences, etc.); who is the "duker" or the fighter (someone to be avoided or someone who can provide protection). When one knows what's happening he can operate in many scenes, providing that he can "hold his mud," keep cool, and out of trouble.

With his diploma in street knowledge, a dude can use time efficiently and with cunning in the pursuit of goods and services—in hustling to eat and yet have enough bread left over for the pleasures of pot, the chicks, and the gig. As one respondent put it, "The good hustler has the know-how, the ambition to better himself. He conditions his mind and must never put his guard too far down, to relax, or he'll be taken." This is street rationality. The problem is not a deficient sense of time but deficient knowledge and control to make a fantasy future and a really better life possible.

The petty hustler more fully realizes the middle class ideal of individualistic rationality than does the middle class itself. When rationality operates in hustling, it is often on an individual basis. In a world of complex organization, the hustler defines himself as an entrepreneur; and indeed, he is the last of the competitive entrepreneurs.

The degree of organization in hustling depends frequently on the kind of hustling. Regular pimping and pushing require many trusted contacts and organization. Regular stealing requires regular fences for hot goods. But in Ghosttown when the hustler moved, he usually moved alone and on a small scale. His success was on him. He could not depend on the support of some benevolent organization. Alone, without a sure way of running the same game twice, he must continually recalculate conditions and people and find new ways of taking or be taken himself. The phrase "free enterprise for the poor and socialism for the rich" applies only too well in the streets. The political conservative should applaud all that individual initiative.

Clock Time vs. Personal Time

Negro street time is built around the irrelevance of clock time, white man's time, and the relevance of street values and activities. Like anyone else, a street dude is on time by the standard clock whenever he wants to be, not on time when he does not want to be and does not have to be.

When the women in school hit the street at the lunch hour and he wants to throw them a rap, he will be there

The Variety of Time

Time in industrial society is clock time. It seems to be an external, objective regulator of human activities. But for the sociologist, time is not an object existing independent of man, dividing his day into precise units. Time is diverse; it is always social and subjective. A man's sense of time derives from his place in the social structure and his lived experience.

The diversity of time perspectives can be understood intellectually—but it is rarely tolerated socially. A dominant group reifies and objectifies its time; it views all other conceptions of time as subversive—as indeed they are.

Thus, today in the dominant middle class stereotype, standard American time is directed to the future; it is rational and impersonal. In contrast, time for the lower class is directed to the present, irrational and personal. Peasants, Mexican-Americans, Negroes, Indians, workers are "lazy"; they do not possess the American virtues of ambition and striving for success. Viewed solely from the dominant class norm of rationality, their presumed orientation to present time is seen only as an irrational deviation, something to be controlled and changed. It is at best an epiphenomenon produced in reaction to the "real, objective" phenomenon of middle class time.

Sociologists have not been completely exempt from this kind of reified thinking. When they universalize the middle class value of rational action and future time and turn it into a "neutral" social fact, they reinforce a negative stereotype: Lower classes are undependable in organized work situations (they seek immediate rewards and cannot defer gratification); in their political action, they are prone to accept immediate, violent, and extreme solutions to personal problems; their sense of time is dysfunctional to the stability of the economic and political orders. For example, Seymour Martin Lipset writes in a paper significantly entitled "Working Class Authoritarianism":

> This emphasis on the immediately perceivable and concern with the personal and concrete is part and parcel of the short time perspective and the inability to perceive the complex possibilities and consequences of action which often results in a general readiness to support extremist political and religious movements, and generally lower level of liberalism on noneconomic questions.

To examine time in relation to the maintenance or destruction of the dominant social order is an interesting political problem, but it is not a sociology of time; it is a middle class sociology of order or change in its time aspect. Surely, a meaningful sociology of time should take into account the social situation in which time operates and the actor's as well as the observer's perspective. The sociologist must at least entertain the idea that lower class time may be a phenomenon in and of itself, and quite functional to the life problems of that class.

Of course, there are dangers in seeking the viewpoint of a minority: The majority stereotypes might be reversed. For example, we might find out that no stereotype is more incorrect than that which depicts the lower classes as having no sense of future time. As Max Weber has observed, it is the powerful and not the powerless who are present-oriented. Dominant groups live by maintaining and expanding their present. Minority groups survive in this present, but their survival is nourished by a dream of the future. In "Ethnic Segregation and Caste" Weber says:

> The sense of dignity that characterizes positively privileged status groups is natural to their "being" which does not transcend itself, that is, to their beauty and excellence. Their kingdom is of this world. They live for the present by exploiting the great past. The sense of dignity of the negatively privileged strata naturally refers to a future lying beyond the present whether it is of this life or another. In other words it must be nurtured by a belief in a providential "mission" and by a belief in a specific honor before God.

It is time to re-examine the meaning of time, the reality of the middle class stereotype of itself, as well as the middle class stereotype of the lower class. In this article I explore the latter: the meaning of time among a group most often stereotyped as having an irrational, present sense of time—the sporadically unemployed young Negro street corner population. I choose the unemployed because they live outside of the constraints of industrial work time; Negroes because they speak some of the liveliest street language, including that of time; young males because the street culture of the unemployed and the hustler is young and masculine.

To understand the meaning of street time was to discover "what's happening" in the day-to-day and week-to-week activities of my respondents. Using the middle class stereotype of lower class time as a point of departure, I asked myself the following questions:

■ In what sense is street time personal (not run by the clock) and present oriented?
■ What kind of future orientation, if any, exists?
■ Are street activities really irrational in the sense that individuals do not use time efficiently in the business of living?

I have attempted to answer the questions in the language and from the experience of my respondents.

"Whatever 'respectable' society says helps him, he knows oppresses him. He has the autonomy which many middle class males might envy."

then and not one hour after they have left. But he may be kicked out of high school for truancy or lose his job for being late and unreliable. He learned at an early age that school and job were neither interesting nor salient to his way of life. A regular on the set will readily admit being crippled by a lack of formal education. Yet school was a "bum kick." It was not his school. The teachers put him down for his dress, hair, and manners. As a human being he has feelings of pride and autonomy, the very things most threatened in those institutional situations where he was or is the underdeveloped, unrespected, illiterate, and undeserving outsider. Thus whatever "respectable" society says will help him, he knows oppresses him, and he retreats to the streets for security and a larger degree of personal freedom. Here his control reaches a maximum, and he has the kind of autonomy which many middle class males might envy.

In the street, watches have a special and specific meaning. Watches are for pawning and not for telling time. When they are worn, they are decorations and ornaments of status. The street clock is informal, personal, and relaxed. It is not standardized nor easily synchronized to other clocks. In fact, a street dude may have almost infinite toleration for individual time schedules. To be on time is often meaningless, to be late an unconsciously accepted way of life. "I'll catch you later," or simply "later," are the street phrases that mean business will be taken care of, but not necessarily now.

Large areas of street life run on late time. For example, parties are not cut off by some built-in alarm clock of appointments and schedules. At least for the unemployed, standard time neither precedes nor follows the gig. Consequently, the action can take its course. It can last as long as interest is sustained and die by exhaustion or by the intrusion of some more interesting event. A gig may endure all night and well into another day. One of the reasons for the party assuming such time dimensions is purely economic. There are not enough cars and enough money for individual dates, so everyone converges in one place and takes care of as much business as possible there, that is, doing whatever is important at the time—sex, presentation of self, hustling.

Colored People's Time

Events starting late and lasting indefinitely are clearly street and class phenomena, not some special trait of Afro-Americans. Middle class Negroes who must deal with the organization and coordination of activities in church and elsewhere will jokingly and critically refer to a lack of standard time sense when they say that Mr. Jones arrived "CPT" (colored people's time). They have a word for it, because being late is a problem for people caught between two worlds and confronted with the task of meshing standard and street time. In contrast, the street dudes had no self-consciousness about being late; with few exceptions they had not heard the expression CPT. (When I questioned members of a middle class Negro fraternity, a sample matched by age to the street set, only three of the 25 interviewed could not define CPT. Some argued vehemently that CPT was the problem to be overcome.)

Personal time as expressed in parties and other street activities is not simply deficient knowledge and use of standard time. It is a positive adaption to generations of living whenever and wherever possible outside of the sound and control of the white man's clock. The personal clock is an adaptation to the chance and accidental character of events on the street and to the very positive value placed on emotion and feeling. (For a discussion of CPT which is close to some of the ideas presented here, see Jules Henry, "White People's Time, Colored People's Time," *Trans*-action, March/April 1965.)

Chance reinforces personal time. A dude must be ready on short notice to move "where the action is." His internal clock may not be running at all when he is hanging on the corner and waiting for something to do. It may suddenly speed up by chance: Someone cruises by in a car and brings a nice "stash" of "weed," a gig is organized and he looks forward to being well togged-out and throwing a rap to some "boss chick," or a lame appears and opens himself to a quick "con." Chance as a determinant of personal time can be called more accurately *uncertain predictability*. Street life is an aggregate of relatively independent events. A dude may not know exactly what or when something will happen, but from past experience he can predict a range of possibilities, and he will be ready, in position, and waiting.

In white middle class stereotypes and fears—and in reality—street action is highly expressive. A forthright yet stylized expression of emotion is positively evaluated and most useful. Street control and communication are based on personal power and the direct impingement of one individual on another. Where there is little property, status in the set is determined by personal qualities of mind and brawn.

The importance of emotion and expression appears again and again in street tongue and ideology. When asked, "How does a dude make a rep on the set?" over half of the sample mentioned "style," and all could discuss the concept. Style is difficult to define as it has so many referents. It means to carry one's self well, dress well, to show class. In the ideology of the street, it may be a way of behaving. One has style if he is able to dig people as they are. He doesn't put them down for what they do. He shows toleration. But a person with style must also show respect. That means respect for a person as he is, and since there is power in the street, respect for another's superior power. Yet one must show respect in such a way that he is able to look tough and inviolate, fearless, secure, "cool."

Style may also refer to the use of gestures in conversation or in dance. It may be expressed in the loose walk, the jivey or dancing walk, the slow cool walk, the way one "chops" or "makes it" down the street. It may be the loose, relaxed hand rap or hand slap, the swinger's greeting which is used also in the hip middle class teen sets. There are many refined variations of the hand rap. As a greeting, one may simply extend his hand, palm up. Another slaps it loosely with his finger. Or, one person may be standing with his hand behind and palm up. Another taps the hand in passing, and also pays his respect verbally with the conventional greeting "What's happening, Brother." Or, in conversation, the hand may be slapped when an individual has "scored," has been "digging," has made a point, has got through to the person.

Style is a comparatively neutral value compared to "soul." Soul can be many things—a type of food (good food is "soul food," a "bowl of soul"), music, a quality of mind, a total way of acting (in eating, drinking, dancing, walking, talking, relating to others, etc.). The person who acts with soul acts directly and honestly from his heart. He feels it and tells it "like it is." One respondent identified soul with ambition and drive. He said the person with soul, once he makes up his mind, goes directly to the goal, doesn't change his mind, doesn't wait and worry about messing up a little. Another said soul was getting down to the nitty-gritty, that is, moving directly to what is basic without guise and disguise. Thus soul is the opposite of hypocrisy, deceit, and phoniness, the opposite of "affective neutrality," and "instrumentality." Soul is simply whatever is considered beautiful, honest, and virtuous in men.

Most definitions tied soul directly to Negro experience. As one hustler put it, "It is the ability to survive. We've made it with so much less. Soul is the Negro who has the spirit to sing in slavery to overcome the monotony." With very few exceptions, the men interviewed argued that soul was what Negroes had and whites did not. Negroes were "soul brothers," warm and emotional—whites cold as ice. Like other oppressed minorities these street Negroes believed they had nothing except their soul and their humanity, and that this made them better than their oppressors.

The Personal Dream

Soul is anchored in a past and present of exploitation and deprivation, but are there any street values and activities which relate to the future? The regular in the street set has no providential mission; he lives personally and instrumentally in the present, yet he dreams about the day when

---

"No one survives on the street unless he knows what's happening and takes advantage of opportunities—exactly what the rational member of the middle class does in his own setting."

---

he will get himself together and move ahead to the rewards of a good job, money, and a family. Moreover, the personal dream coexists with a nascent political nationalism, the belief that Negroes can and will make it as Negroes. His present-future time is a combination of contradictions and developing possibilities. Here I will be content to document without weighing two aspects of his orientation: *fantasy personal future* and *fantasy collective future*. I use the word fantasy because street people have not yet the knowledge and means and perhaps the will to fulfill their dreams. It is hard enough to survive by the day.

When the members of the set were asked, "What do you really want out of life?" their responses were conventional, concrete, seemingly realistic, and—given their skills—rather hopeless. Two-thirds of the sample mentioned material aspirations—the finer things in life, a home, security, a family. For example, one said, in honest street language, "I want to get things for my kids and to make sure they have a father." Another said, jokingly, "a good future, a home, two or three girls living with me." Only one person didn't know, and the others deviated a little from the material response. They said such things as "for everyone to be on friendly terms—a better world . . . then I could get all I wish," "to be free," "to help people."

But if most of the set wanted money and security, they

wanted it on their own terms. As one put it, "I don't want to be in a middle class bag, but I would like a nice car, home, and food in the icebox." He wanted the things and the comforts of middle class life, but not the hypocrisy, the venality, the coldness, the being forced to do what one does not want to do. All that was in the middle class bag. Thus the home and the money may be ends in themselves, but also fronts, security for carrying on the usual street values. Street people believed that they already had something that was valuable and looked down upon the person who made it and moved away into the middle class world. For the observer, the myths are difficult to separate from the truths—here where the truths are so bitter. One can only say safely that street people dream of a high status, and they really do not know how to get it.

The Collective Future

The Negro dudes are political outsiders by the usual poll questions. They do not vote. They do not seek out civil rights demonstrations. They have very rudimentary knowledge of political organization. However, about the age of 18, when fighting and being tough are less important than before, street people begin to discuss their position in society. Verbally they care very much about the politics of race and the future of the Negro. The topic is always a ready catalyst for a soul session.

The political consciousness of the street can be summarized by noting those interview questions which attracted at least a 75 percent rate of agreement. The typical respondent was angry. He approves of the Watts incident, although from his isolated corner of the city he did not actively participate. He knows something about the history of discrimination and believes that if something isn't done soon America can expect violence: "What this country needs is a revolutionary change." He is more likely to praise the leadership of Malcolm X than Lyndon Johnson, and he is definitely opposed to the Vietnam war. The reason for his opposition is clear: Why fight for a country which is not mine, when the fight is here?

Thus his racial consciousness looks to the future and a world where he will not have to stand in the shadow of the white man. But his consciousness has neither clear plan nor political commitment. He has listened to the Muslims, and he is not a black nationalist. True, the Negro generally has more soul than the white. He thinks differently, his women may be different, yet integration is preferable to separatism. Or, more accurately, he doesn't quite understand what all these terms mean. His nationalism is real as a folk nationalism based on experience with other Negroes and isolation from whites.

The significance of a racial future in the day to day consciousness of street people cannot be assessed. It is a developing possibility dependent on unforeseen conditions beyond the scope of their skill and imagination. But bring up the topic of race and tomorrow, and the dreams come rushing in—dreams of superiority, dreams of destruction, dreams of human equality. These dreams of the future are salient. They are not the imagination of authoritarian personalities, except from the viewpoint of those who see spite lurking behind every demand for social change. They are certainly not the fantasies of the hipster living philosophically in the present without hope and ambition. One hustler summarized the Negro street concept of ambition and future time when he said:

> The Negro has more ambition than the whites. He's got farther to go. "The man" is already there. But we're on your trail, daddy. You still have smoke in our eyes, but we're catching up.

March-April 1967

SUGGESTED READINGS

Manchild in the Promised Land by Claude Brown (New York: The New American Library, 1966). An autobiographical account of street life in Harlem.

Street Corner Society by William Foote Whyte (Chicago: University of Chicago Press, 1943). A sociological account of street life among Italian-Americans in Boston.

The Voices of Time edited by J. T. Fraser (New York: George Braziller, 1965). Essays on man's views of time as expressed by the sciences and the humanities.

The Silent Language by Edward T. Hall (Greenwich, Conn.: Fawcett Publications, 1963). An anthropologist describes how time and other cultural concepts are communicated without the use of words.

The Gang by Frederic M. Thrasher (Chicago: University of Chicago Press, 1963). A seminal empirical study of the adolescent gang as a type of human group, and its relationship to problems of crime and urban politics.

The Vice Lords: Warriors of the Streets by R. Lincoln Keiser (New York: Holt, Rinehart and Winston, 1969). This recent ethnographic study of a Chicago street gang investigates its development, political system, roles and culture.

Deep Down in the Jungle: Negro narrative folklore from the streets of Philadelphia by Roger D. Abrahams (Chicago: Aldine, 1970).

Man, Time, and Society by Wilbert E. Moore (New York: Wiley, 1963). A survey of evidence for the sociocultural relativity of time, which is conceptualized as both a boundary condition and as the measure of persistence and change.

Sociocultural Causality, Space, Time by Pitirim Sorokin (New York: Russell and Russell, 1964). A pioneering theoretical work explaining some of the implications of time as an intervening variable in sociological statements of relationships.

Man and Time by J. B. Priestley (London: Aldus Books, 1964). Psychological time and chronological time explored through literature, history and science, developing new definitions for such concepts as past, present, future, before and after.

Black Experience: Soul edited by Lee Rainwater (Chicago: Aldine, 1970).

Kapluna Daughter—Living with Eskimos

JEAN L. BRIGGS

With photographs by the author

"It's very cold down there—*very cold*. If I were going to be at Back River this winter, I would like to adopt you and try to keep you alive."

My Eskimo visitor, Uunai, dramatized her words with shivers as we sat drinking tea in the warm nursing station in Gjoa Haven. It was only mid-August, but already the wind that intruded through the cracks in the window frame was bitter, and the ground was white with a dusting of new snow. Last winter's ice, great broken sheets of it, still clogged the harbor, so that the plane I was waiting for was unable to get through to us. I was on my way to spend a year and a half with the Utkuhikhalingmiut, a small group of Eskimos who lived in Chantrey Inlet at the mouth of the Back River on the northern rim of the American continent. They were the most remote group of Eskimos that I could find on the map of the Canadian Arctic, a people who in many ways lived much as they had in the days before *kaplunas* (white men) appeared in the north. They were nomadic; they lived in snowhouses in winter, in tents in summer; and their diet consisted very largely of fish—trout and whitefish—supplemented now and again by a few caribou.

Uunai's words presaged the most important influence on the course of my life at Back River, namely my adoption as a "daughter" in the household of an Utkuhikhalingmiut family. I want to describe an aspect of that relationship here, with the aim of illustrating some of the difficulties that a host community or family may encounter in its hospitable efforts to incorporate a foreigner.

From *Women in the Field* edited by Peggy Golde. © 1970 by Aldine Publishing Company. Reprinted by permission of the publisher.

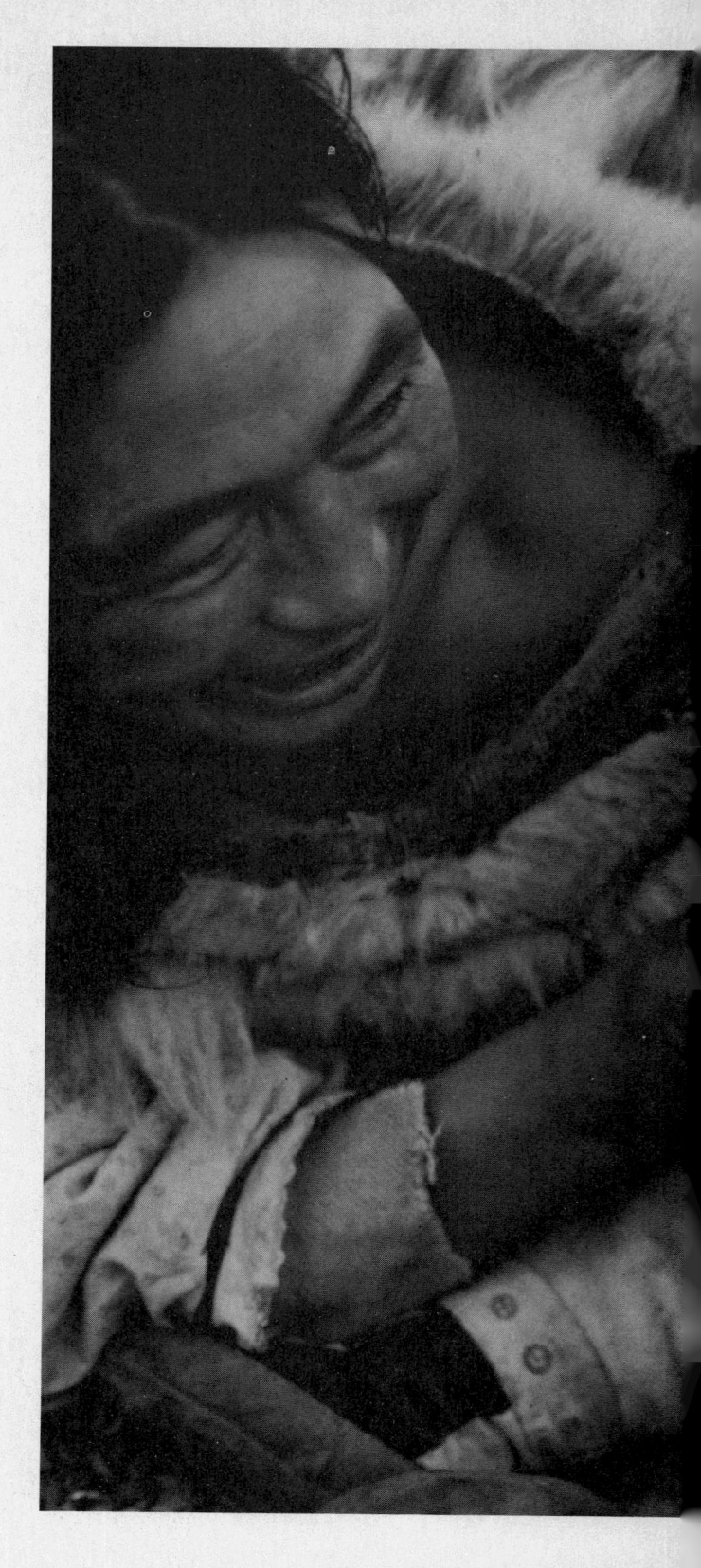

VARIATION AND CONTRAST

I arrived in Chantrey Inlet at the end of August 1963 on a plane that the Canadian government sent in once a year to collect the three or four schoolchildren who wished to go to Inuvik. I had with me letters of introduction from the Anglican deacon and his wife in Gjoa Haven. Nakliguhuktuq and Ikayuqtuq were Eskimos from the eastern Arctic who served as missionaries not only to the Anglican Eskimos in Gjoa Haven, but also to the Utkuhikhalingmiut. The letters—written in the syllabic script in which the Utkuhikhalingmiut, like most other Canadian Eskimos, are literate—noted that I would like to live with the Utkuhikhalingmiut for a year or so, learning the Eskimo language and skills: how to scrape skins and sew them, how to catch fish and preserve them or boil the oil out of them for use in lighting and heating the winter iglus. They asked the Eskimos to help me with words and fish and promised that in return I would help them with tea and kerosene. They told the people that I was kind and that they should not be shy and afraid of me—"She's a little bit shy herself"—and assured them that they need not feel (as they often do feel toward kaplunas) that they had to comply with my every wish. They said, finally, that I wished to be adopted into an Eskimo family and to live with them in their iglu as a daughter.

Choosing a Father

I had a number of reasons for wishing to be adopted, and there were several precedents for adoption as well: four other kaplunas of my acquaintance, both scholars and laymen, who had wintered with Eskimos had done so as "sons," sharing the iglus of their Eskimo families. Living in the iglu would be warmer than living alone, I thought (Ikayuqtuq and Nakliguhuktuq agreed); and I thought vaguely that it might be "safer" if one family had specific responsibility for me. The idea had romantic appeal too; I saw it as a fulfillment of a childhood wish to "be" an Eskimo, and I expected no rapport problems, since on two previous trips to the Alaskan Arctic I had identified strongly with the Eskimo villagers with whom I had lived. To be sure, there were also arguments against adoption: I had qualms concerning the loss of an "objective" position in the community, drains on my supplies that would result from contributing to the maintenance of a family household and loss of privacy with resultant difficulties in working. Still, when the moment of decision came, the balance lay in favor of adoption.

There were two suitable fathers among the Utkuhikhalingmiut (that is, two household heads who had wives alive and at home), and these two were both more than eager to adopt me. One, however—an intelligent, vigorous man named Inuttiaq—far outdid the other in the imagination and persistence with which he "courted" me as a daughter. Not only were he and his family extremely solicitous, but he was also a jolly and ingenious language teacher. Most gratifying of all, both he and his wife, Allaq, were astonishingly quick to understand my halting attempts to communicate. There was no question which family I preferred. Fortunately, Inuttiaq also occupied a much more central position among the Utkuhikhalingmiut than did Nilak, the other possible father. He had many more close kin and was also the Anglican lay leader of the group. I was convinced that both anthropology and I would benefit more if I were adopted by Inuttiaq.

Winter

From the moment that the adoption was settled, I was "Inuttiaq's daughter" in the camp. Inuttiaq and his relatives with much amusement drilled me in the use of kin terms appropriate to my position, just as they drilled his three-year-old daughter, who was learning to speak. They took charge of my material welfare and of my education in language and skills. Allaq also to some extent took charge of my daily activities, as it was proper that a mother should. She told me what the day's job for the women of the family was going to be: gathering birch twigs for fuel, scraping caribou hides in preparation for the making of winter clothing or skinning the fish bellies out of which oil was to be boiled. The decision to participate or not was left to me, but if I did join the women—and I usually did—she made sure that my share of the work was well within the limits of my ability and stamina. "We will be walking very far tomorrow to get birch twigs," she would say. "You will be too tired." If I went anyway, it was always silently arranged that my load should be the lightest, and if I wandered out of sight of the other women in my search for birch bushes, someone always followed behind—sent by Allaq, as I discovered months later—to make sure that I didn't get lost.

I felt increasingly comfortable with my family and found their solicitude immensely warming. At the same time, I dreaded the loss of privacy that the winter move into their iglu would bring. Curiously, the effect of the move when it came in October was the opposite of what I had expected. I basked in the protectiveness of Inuttiaq's household; and what solitude I needed I found on the river in the mornings, when I jigged for salmon trout through the ice with Inuttiaq, or, to my surprise, in the iglu itself in the afternoons, when the room was full of visitors and I retired into myself, lulled and shielded by the flow of quiet, incomprehensible speech.

Behaving

The family's continuing graciousness was very seductive. I came to expect the courtesies that I received and even to resent it a bit when they were not forthcoming, though at the same time I told myself that such feelings were shameful. However, as time passed and I became an established presence in the household, I was less and less often accorded special privileges, except insofar as my ineptitude made services necessary. Allaq still mended my skin boots for me and stretched them when they shrank in drying; my stitches were not small enough and my jaws not strong enough. She continued to fillet my fish when it was frozen nearly as hard as wood. But in other respects Allaq, and especially Inuttiaq—who was far less shy than his wife—more and more attempted to assimilate me into a proper adult parent-daughter relationship. I was expected to help with the household work to the best of my ability—to make tea or bannock and to fetch water—and I was expected to obey unquestioningly when Inuttiaq told me to do something or made a decision on my behalf.

Unfortunately, I found it impossible to learn to behave in every respect like an Utkuhikhalingmiut daughter. Inuttiaq lectured me in general terms on the subject of filial obedience, and once in a while I think he tried to shame me into good behavior by offering himself as a model of virtue—volunteering, for example, to make bannock for me if I were slow in making it for him—but to little avail. Sometimes I was genuinely blind and deaf to his lessons, unaccustomed as I was to Utkuhikhalingmiut subtlety. At other times I saw what was wanted but resisted for reasons I will describe in a moment. Inevitably, conflicts, covert but pervasive, developed, both regarding the performance of household chores and regarding the related matter of obedience to Inuttiaq.

Assumptions in Conflict

The causes of the conflicts were three. First was the fact that some feminine skills were hard for me to learn. Overtly my Utkahikhalingmiut parents were very tolerant of the lack of skill that they rightly attributed to kapluna ignorance and perhaps also to kapluna lack of intelligence, or *ihuma*. However, perhaps because of an assumption that kaplunas were unable to learn, if I was at all slow to understand Allaq's instructions and demonstrations, she easily gave up trying to teach me, preferring instead to continue to serve me. And though she stretched my boots and cut my fish in the most cheerful manner, after a while her added chores may well have been burdensome to her.

A second cause of the conflicts was that some of Inuttiaq's and Allaq's assumptions about the nature of parental and daughterly virtue were at variance with mine; in consequence not only did I have to learn new patterns, I also had to unlearn old ones. Hardest of all to learn was unquestioning obedience to paternal authority. Sometimes I could not help resisting, privately but intensely, when Inuttiaq told me to "make tea," to "go home," "to hurry up" or to "pray." I was irritated even by the fact that after the first weeks of gracious formality had passed he began to address me in the imperative form, which is often used in speaking to women, children and young people. Rationally I knew that I should have welcomed this sign of "acceptance," but I could not be pleased. My irritation was due partly to the fact that subordination threatened my accustomed—and highly valued—independence, but it was aggravated by a fear that the restrictions placed on me interfered with my work.

And herein lay the third cause of the conflicts: I found it hard sometimes to be simultaneously a docile and helpful daughter and a conscientious anthropologist. Though Allaq appeared to accept my domestic clumsiness as inevitable, she may have felt less tolerant on the occasions when it was not lack of skill that prevented me from helping her, but anxiety over the pocketful of trouser-smudged, disorganized field notes that cried out to be typed. A number of times, when I could have helped to gut fish or to carry in snow to repair the sleeping platform or floor or could have offered to fetch water or make tea, I sat and wrote instead or sorted vocabulary—tiny slips of paper spread precariously over my sleeping bag and lap. It was sometimes professional anxiety that prompted me to disobey Inuttiaq too; and I am sure that on such occasions, as on others, he must have found my insubordination not only "bad," but completely incomprehensible. My behavior at moving time is an example. My gear, minimal though it was by kapluna standards, placed a severe strain on Inuttiaq when we moved camp. Whereas the sleds of others were loaded to little more than knee height, the load on Inuttiaq's sled was shoulder-high. From his point of view it was only reasonable that he should instruct me to leave my heavy tape recorder and my metal box of field notes on the top of a small knoll, as the Utkuhikhalingmiut cached their own belongings, while we moved downstream, not to return until after the flood season. I, however, questioned whether the water might rise over the knoll, and Inuttiaq's silent scrutiny seemed to say that he considered my inquiry a reflection on his judgment.

I do not mean to create the impression that life in Inuttiaq's household during that first winter was continuous turmoil. There were many days, even weeks, when I, at least, felt the situation to be very peaceful and enjoyable. I was grateful for the warmth of my parents' company and care; it was good to feel that I belonged somewhere, that I was part of a family, even on a make-believe basis. But the rewards of my presence for Inuttiaq and his real family were of a different, and probably of a lesser, order. Because Inuttiaq's purchases in Gjoa Haven were supplemented by mine, our household was richer than others in store goods: tea, tobacco, flour, jam, dry milk, raisins and kerosene. But apart from these material benefits, and at first perhaps the novelty (and prestige?) of having a kapluna daughter, it is hard to see what Inuttiaq's family gained in return for the burden they carried. I played "Tavern in the Town" and "Santa Lucia" on my recorder; Inuttiaq enjoyed that and once in a while asked me to play for guests. I helped inefficiently in the mornings to remove the whitefish from the family nets and to drag them home, harnessed with Allaq to the sled. I assisted—erratically, as I have mentioned—with the other domestic chores; and in late winter, when the sun returned and Inuttiaq began again to jig for salmon trout, I usually fished with him. That is all that occurs to me, and a trivial contribution it must have been from my family's point of view.

Satan and Self-control

It was hard for me to know at the time, however, just what their reactions to me were, because the tensions that existed were nearly all covert. Hostility among Utkuhikhalingmiut is ignored or turned into a joke; at worst it becomes the subject of gossip behind the offender's back. I, too, did my best to smother my annoyance with frustration, but my attempts were not wholly successful. My training in self-control was less perfect than theirs, and at the same time the strains were greater than those I was accustomed to dealing with in my own world. Moreover, the most potentially gratifying of the outlets utilized by the Utkuhikhalingmiut—gossip—was not open to me as an anthropologist. I did my best to learn with the children when they were taught to turn annoyance into amusement, but laughter didn't come easily.

The Utkuhikhalingmiut are acutely sensitive to subtle indications of mood. They heard the coldness in my voice when I said, "I don't understand," noted the length of a solitary walk I took across the tundra or the fact that I went to bed early and read with my back turned to the others. Later, Inuttiaq might give me a lecture—phrased, as always, in the most general terms—about the fate of those who lose their tempers: Satan uses them for firewood. Or he might offer me an especially choice bit of fish—whether to shame me or to appease me I don't know. The contrast between my irritability and the surface equanimity of others gave me many uncomfortable moments, but I persuaded myself that the effects of my lapses were short-lived. When I laughed again and heard others laugh with me, or when they seemed to accept the generous gestures with which I tried to make amends, I was reassured that no damage had been done. I was wrong. But it was only when

I returned to Gjoa Haven on my way home a year later that I learned how severe the tensions had become between November and January of that first winter. Then the deacon's wife, Ikajuqtuq, told me of the report Inuttiaq had made of me in January when he went in to Gjoa Haven to trade: "She is not happy. She gets angry very easily, and I don't think she likes us anymore." Shortly after Inuttiaq's return from Gjoa Haven in January, conflict erupted into the open.

"The Iglus Are Cold"

The two weeks of Inuttiaq's absence in Gjoa Haven had been an especially trying period for me. I had looked forward to them as a much needed interlude in which to type and organize my swelling pile of penciled notes. When Inuttiaq was at home, it was often difficult to maintain the iglu temperature within the range of 27 to 31 degrees at which typing was feasible. If I tried to type during the daylight hours of the morning, when the outdoor work was done, my fingers and carbon paper froze as a result of Inuttiaq's drafty comings and goings at jobs that seemed to necessitate propping the door open. But in the sociable afternoon and evening hours the snow dome dripped in the heat and occasionally deposited lumps of slush into my typewriter, and the iglu steamed so that my work was lost in a wet fog as a result of Inuttiaq's demands for tea, boiled fox, bannock and soup in rapid succession. Many were the frustrated moments when I heartily wished him gone; but it was only when he *was* gone that I discovered how completely our comfort depended on his presence. "When the men are away the iglus are cold," the women said; and it was true. The morning drafts that had plagued me before were nothing compared with the chill that resulted when nobody came and went at all. It was partly, of course, that Inuttiaq had taken with him one of our two primus stoves and one of the two kerosene storm lanterns, which ordinarily heated the iglu. But Allaq's behavior during her husband's absence intensified the cold. She never boiled fish, rarely brewed tea and never lit the lamp to dry clothes—any of which activities would have warmed the iglu. She merely sat in her corner of the sleeping platform, blew on her hands and remarked that the iglu was cold. It was; it was 20 degrees colder than when Inuttiaq was at home. I fretted and fumed in silent frustration and determined that when he came back I would take drastic steps to improve my working conditions.

I broached the subject to Inuttiaq a few days after his return to camp. He listened attentively to my explanation. I told him that I had thought about going to live for a while in the empty wooden building that stood on a peninsula a few miles from camp. The government had built it as a nursing station, but it had never been used except by me as a cache for my useless belongings. It had a kerosene stove, which would make it luxuriously comfortable—unless the stove was as erratic as the one in the similar nursing station in Gjoa Haven, with which I had once had an unfortunate experience. Inuttiaq agreed that the stove was unpredictable. Instead, he suggested that he take me to the nursing station every morning and fetch me again at night, so that I would not freeze. As often before, he reassured me: "Because you are alone here, you are someone to be taken care of." And, as often before, his solicitude warmed me. "Taking me to the nursing station every day will be a lot of work for you," I said. The round trip took an hour and a half by dog sled, not counting the time and effort involved in harnessing and unharnessing the team. He agreed that it would be a lot of work. "Could you perhaps build me a small iglu?" I asked. It would take only an hour or two to build a tiny iglu near our own, which I could use as an "office"; then he need concern himself no further. Lulled by the assurance he had just given me of his desire to take care of me and by the knowledge that the request I made was not time-consuming, I was the more disagreeably startled when he replied with unusual vigor, "I build no iglus. I have to check the nets."

A Daughter's Tent

The rage of frustration seized me. He had not given me the true reason for his refusal. It only took two hours to check the nets every second or third day; on the other days, Inuttiaq did nothing at all except eat, drink, visit and repair an occasional tool. He was offended, but I could not imagine why. Whether Inuttiaq read my face I do not know, but he softened his refusal immediately: "Shall Ipuituq or Tutaq"—he named two of the younger men—"build an iglu for you?" Perhaps it would be demeaning for a man of Inuttiaq's status, a mature householder, to build an iglu for a mere daughter. There was something in Inuttiaq's reaction that I did not understand, and a cautioning voice told me to contain my ethnocentric judgment and my anger. I thought of the small double-walled tent that I had brought with me for emergency use. It was stored in the nursing station. "They say my tent is very warm in winter," I said. Inuttiaq smoked silently. After a while he asked, "Shall they build you an iglu tomorrow?" My voice shook with exasperation: "Who knows?" I turned my head, rummaging—for nothing—in my knapsack until the intensity of my feeling should subside.

Later, when Inuttiaq was smoking his last pipe in bed, I raised the subject again, my manner, I hoped, a successful facsimile of cheerfulness and firmness. "I would like to try the tent and see whether it's warm, as I have heard. We can bring it here, and then if it's not warm, I won't freeze; I'll come indoors." Allaq laughed, Inuttiaq accepted my suggestion, and I relaxed with relief, restored to real cheer by Inuttiaq's offer to fetch the tent from the nursing station the following day—if it stormed—so that he could not go on the trapping trip he had planned.

My cheer was premature. Two days later the tent had still not been fetched, though Inuttiaq had not gone trapping. I decided to walk to the nursing station. I had no intention of fetching the tent myself—it would have been impossible; but I needed a few hours alone, and vaguely I knew that the direction of my walk would be to Inuttiaq a sign, however futile, that I was in earnest about my tent.

But I did not dream that he would respond as charitably as he did. I had just arrived at the nursing station and was searching among my few books for a novel to comfort me in my frustration when I heard the squeak of sled runners on the snow outside and a familiar voice speaking to the dogs: "*Hoooo* [whoa]." Inuttiaq appeared in the doorway. I smiled. He smiled. "Will you want your tent?"

Gratitude and relief erased my anger as Inuttiaq picked up the tent and carried it to the sled. "You were walking," he said, in answer to my thanks. "I felt protective toward you."

It was a truce we had reached, however, not a peace, though I did not realize it at once. Since it was nearly dark when we reached camp, Inuttiaq laid the tent on top of the iglu for the night, to keep it from the dogs. Next morning I went with Inuttiaq to jig for trout up-river, and when we returned I thought that finally the time was ripe for setting up the tent. Not wanting to push Inuttiaq's benevolence too far, and remembering the force of his response to my query about iglu-building, I asked, "Shall I ask Ipuituq to help me put up my tent?" "Yes," said Inuttiaq. There was no warmth in his face; he did not smile, though he did tell me to keep my fur trousers on for warmth while I put up the tent. I obeyed, but the wind had risen while we drank our homecoming tea, so that even in fur trousers tent-raising was not feasible that day or the next.

When the wind died two days later, Inuttiaq and I went fishing again, most companionably. Relations seemed so amicable, in fact, that this time on our return I was emboldened to say directly, without mention of Ipuituq, "I would like to put up my tent."

Naïvely I thought that Inuttiaq would offer to help. He did not. His face was again unsmiling as he answered, "Put it up."

My anger was triggered again. "By myself?" I inquired rudely.

"Yes," said Inuttiaq, equally rudely.

"Thank you very much." I heard the coldness in my voice but did not try to soften it.

Inuttiaq, expressionless, looked at me for a moment then summoned two young men who were nearby and who came, with a cheer that was in marked contrast to his own manner, to help me set up the tent.

Although Inuttiaq thought it ridiculous anyway to set up a tent in winter, I think now that he was also personally affronted by my request. One clue to his reaction I find in a question that I hardly heard at the time: he had wanted to know, after the tent was up, whether I planned to sleep in it or only to work there, and I think he may have felt that my demand for a tent was a sign that I was dissatisfied with him as a father, with his concern for my welfare.

In any case, his behavior was a curious blend of opposites. He chose the site for my tent with care, correcting my own choice with a more practiced eye to prowling dogs and prevailing wind. He offered advice on heating the tent, and he filled my primus stove so that it would be ready for me to use when my two assistants and I had finished setting up the tent. And when I moved my writing things out of his iglu, he told me that if I liked, I might write instead of going fishing. "If I catch a fish, you will eat," he assured me. But he turned his back on the actual raising of the tent and went home to eat and drink tea.

Never in Anger

On the following day I saw his displeasure in another form. It was Sunday morning and storming; our entrance was buried under drifting snow. Since there could be no church service, Inuttiaq and Allaq had each, separately and in mumbling undertones, read a passage from the Bible. Then Inuttiaq began to read from the prayer book the story of creation, and he asked if I would like to learn. I agreed, the more eagerly because I feared that he had perceived my skepticism toward his religious beliefs and that this was another hidden source of conflict between us. He lectured me at length. The story of creation was followed by the story of Adam and Eve (whose sin was responsible for the division of mankind into kaplunas and Eskimos), and this story was in turn followed by an exposition of proper Christian behavior: the keeping of the Sabbath—and of one's temper. "God is loving," said Inuttiaq, "but only to believers. Satan is angry. People will go to heaven only if they do not get angry or answer back when they are scolded." He told me that one should not be attached to earthly belongings, as I was: "One should devote himself only to God's word." Most striking of all was the way Inuttiaq ended his sermon to me. "Nakliguhuktuq made me king of the Utkuhikhalingmiut," he said. "He wrote that to me. He told me that if people—including you—don't want to believe what I tell them and don't want to learn about Christianity, then I should write to him, and he will come quickly and scold them. If people don't want to believe Nakliguhuktuq either, then . . . a bigger leader, a kapluna, the king in Cambridge Bay [the government center for the central Arctic], will come in a plane with a big and well-made whip and will whip people. It will hurt a lot."

Much of this I had heard before, but this version was more dramatic than previous ones. It made me see more clearly than I had before something of Inuttiaq's view of kaplunas generally. I heard the hostility directed against myself as well, but again he had softened the latter by blending it with warmth, in the manner that I found so confusing. He knew that I believed in God, he said, because I helped people, I gave things to people—not just to one or two, which God doesn't want, but to everybody.

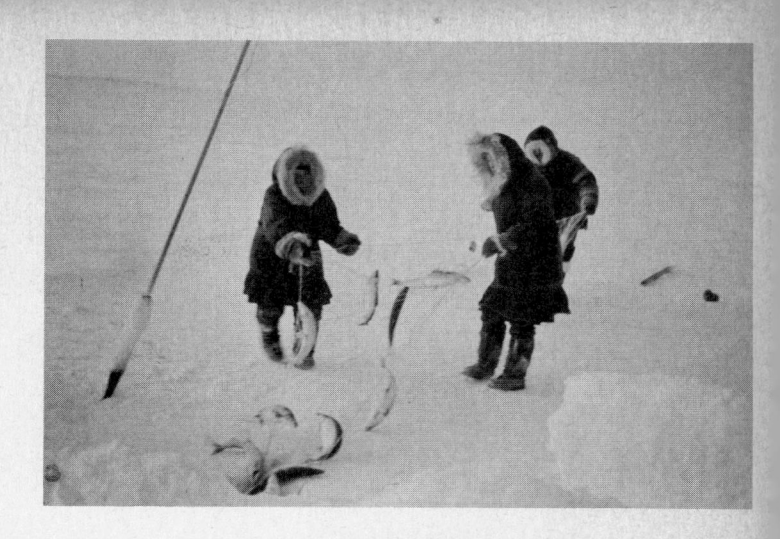

The rest of the winter passed more peacefully, at least on the surface. I spent much of the time working in my tent, and there was no more overt hostility. But I am no longer sure that my peace of mind was justified. In retrospect, it seems possible that the warm and solicitous acts my family continued to perform were neither rewards for improved behavior on my part nor evidence of a generous willingness to accept me in spite of my thorny qualities, but, rather, attempts to extract or blunt some of the thorns. If I knew I was cared for, I might not get angry so easily. I thought I heard similar logic in the admonition Inuttiaq once in a while gave his six-year-old daughter when she sulked: "Stop crying, you are loved." Another possible motive may have been a desire to shame me, by virtuous example, into reforming. Perhaps these kind acts even had the effect of nullifying Inuttiaq's and Allaq's own prickly feelings, permitting them to prove to themselves that—as Inuttiaq once said—they didn't get angry, only I did.

Incorrigible

But whatever the interpretation of these incidents, it is clear to me now that there existed more of an undercurrent of tension in my relationship with Inuttiaq and Allaq than I perceived at the time. I began to suspect its presence in the spring, when our iglu melted and I moved—at Inuttiaq's order—back into my own tent; Allaq almost never visited me, as she had done the first days after my arrival in Chantrey Inlet. More important, these winter tensions, I think, added their residue of hostility to a crisis situation that developed at the end of the summer. This introduced a new phase in my relations, not merely with Inuttiaq and Allaq, but with all the other Utkuhikhalingmiut as well —a phase in which I ceased to be treated as an educable child and was instead treated as an incorrigible offender, who had unfortunately to be endured but who could not be incorporated into the social life of the group.

The crisis was brought about by the visit to Chantrey Inlet of a party of kapluna sports fishermen. Every July and August in recent years Chantrey Inlet has been visited by sportsmen from the provinces and from the United States who charter bush planes from private sports airlines and fly up to the Arctic for a week's fishing. Every year the sportsmen ask permission to borrow the Eskimos' canoes, which were given to them by the Canadian government after the famine of 1958 and are indispensable to their economy. In 1958 the disappearance of the caribou herds from the Chantrey Inlet area forced the Eskimos to begin to rely much more completely on fish than they had formerly done. This meant accumulating and storing quantities of fish during seasons when they were plentiful, and to facilitate this, the government introduced fish nets and canoes. Originally there had been six canoes, one for each of the Utkuhikhalingmiut families, but by the time I arrived in Chantrey Inlet only two of these remained in usable condition.

In Anger

The first parties that came asked, through me, if they might borrow both canoes, and the Utkuhikhalingmiut, who for various reasons rarely, if ever, refuse such requests, acquiesced, at some cost to themselves. They sat stranded on the shore, unable to fish, unable to fetch the occasional bird that they shot on the water, unable to fetch a resupply of sugar for their tea from the cache on the nearby island and worst of all, perhaps, unable to visit the odd strangers who were camped out of sight across the river. Ultimately these kaplunas left and were replaced by another group, which asked to borrow only one canoe. But relief was short-lived; trolling up and down the unfamiliar river in the late twilight, the kaplunas were unfortunate enough to run the canoe on a rock and tear a large hole in the canvas, whereupon they returned the canoe and announced to the men through sign language that since that craft was unusable they were now obliged to borrow the other—Inuttiaq's. When I arrived on the scene, the kaplunas were attaching their outboard to the canoe as Inuttiaq and the other Utkuhikhalingmiut men watched.

I exploded. Unsmilingly and in a cold voice I told the kaplunas' guide some of the hardships that I foresaw if his men damaged the second canoe. Then, armed with the memory that Inuttiaq had earlier, before the arrival of this party of kaplunas, instructed me in vivid language never again to allow anyone to borrow his canoe, I told the kaplunas that the owner of that second canoe did not wish to lend it.

The kapluna guide was not unreasonable; he agreed at once that the loan of the boat was the owner's option: "It's his canoe, after all." Slightly mollified, I turned to Inuttiaq who stood nearby, expressionless like the other Utkuhikhalingmiut. "Do you want me to tell him you don't want to lend your canoe?" I asked in Eskimo. "He will not borrow it if you say you don't want to lend it."

Inuttiaq's expression dismayed me, but I didn't know how to read it. I knew only that it registered strong feeling, as did his voice, which was unusually loud: "Let him have his will!"

"We Wish She Would Leave"

That incident brought to a head months of uneasiness on the part of the Utkuhikhalingmiut concerning my volatility. I had spoken unbidden and in anger; that much the Eskimos knew. The words they couldn't understand, but it didn't matter; the intrusion and the anger itself were inexcusable. The punishment was so subtle a form of ostracism that I would have continued to think that my difficulties were all of my own imagining had I not come into possession of a letter that Allaq's father, Pala, had written to the deacon, Nakliguhuktuq, the day after the kaplunas left. Pala had intended to send it out on the plane that was daily expected to come and pick up the schoolchildren; he had kept it for a time, but then—fearing that when the plane finally came, he would forget the letter—he had given it to me to hold along with my own correspondence. The letter was in syllabics, of course; in an amoral spirit I decided to read it, to test my skill in reading Eskimo. I did not anticipate the contents: "Yiini [that was my name] lied to the kaplunas. She gets angry very easily. She ought not to be here studying Eskimos. She is very annoying; because she scolds and one is tempted to scold her. She gets angry easily. Because she is so annoying, we wish more and more that she would leave."

But it was not until October, when the autumn iglus were built, that the change in the Eskimos' feelings really became apparent. I was not at all sure that Inuttiaq would invite me to move in with his family again as he had done the year before, but I need not have worried; his hostility did not take such a crass form. However, the quality of life in the iglu was in striking contrast with the previous year. Whereas then Inuttiaq's iglu had been the social center of the camp, now family and visitors congregated next door, in Allaq's father's iglu. Inuttiaq and Allaq—the children too—spent the better part of every day at Pala's. Even in the early mornings, when the family awoke, and at night when we were preparing for bed, I was isolated. It was as though I were not there. If I made a remark to Inuttiaq or Allaq, the person addressed responded with his usual smile, but I had to initiate almost all communication. As a rule, if I did not speak, no one spoke to me. If I offered to fetch water or make tea (which I seldom did), my offer was usually accepted, but no one ever asked me to perform these services. The pointedness of this avoidance was driven home one day when we were cooking. I do not recall what was being made or who had initiated the cooking; I think it likely that I had done so, since the primus stood on the floor in front of me, instead of in its usual place near Allaq. Nevertheless, when the pressure began to run down, unnoticed by me, Inuttiaq turned not to me but to Allaq to order her to pump up the primus. And she had to get up and come over to my side of the iglu to pump up the stove! Had he spoken to me, I would only have had to lean over to do it. Too late I realized the dignity inherent in the Utkuhikhalingmiut pattern of authority, in which the woman is obedient to the man. I envied Allaq the satisfaction of knowing that she was appreciated because she did well and docilely what Inuttiaq told her to do.

One day, about a week after we had moved into the autumn iglus, Inuttiaq suggested that when we moved into winter iglus later on, I should be physically walled off to a degree. Often when Utkuhikhalingmiut build their permanent winter iglus, they attach to one side a small chamber, called a *hiqluaq*, in which to store the fish they net. The hiqluaq opens into the interior of the iglu by way of a hole just big enough to crawl through. Inuttiaq's idea was to build such a chamber for me to live in; after I left, he would use it in the orthodox manner, for fish storage.

But in spite of all these tensions, I was still treated with the most impeccable semblance of solicitude. I was amazed that it should be so—that although my company was anathema, nevertheless people still took care to give me plentiful amounts of the foods I liked best, to warn me away from thin ice and to caution me when my nose began to freeze. The Utkuhikhalingmiut saw themselves—and wanted me to see them—as virtuously solicitous, no matter what provocations I might give them to be otherwise. Allaq's sister expressed this ethos of concern explicitly in a letter to Ikayuqtuq in Gjoa Haven: "Because she is the only kapluna here and a woman as well, we have tried to

VARIATION AND CONTRAST

Karl Maslowski

The author

be good to her . . . and though she is sometimes very annoying . . . we still try to help her."

It was at the end of August that the incident with the kapluna fishermen occurred, and it was the end of November before I was finally able to explain myself to the Utkuhikhalingmiut. I had wanted from the beginning, of course, to confront them with an explanation of my behavior, but I had feared that such un-Eskimo directness would only shock them the more. Instead, I had written my version of the story to Ikayuqtuq, had told her about my attempt to protect the Utkuhikhalingmiut from the impositions of the kaplunas and had asked her if she could help to explain my behavior to the Eskimos. My letter went out to Gjoa Haven, along with Pala's, when the school plane came in September. Unfortunately there was no way in which Ikayuqtuq could reply until the strait froze in November, enabling the men to make the long trip out to Gjoa Haven to trade. But when Inuttiaq, accompanied as usual by Allaq's brother, Mannik, finally went out, they brought back from the deacon and his wife a response that surpassed my most sanguine expectations. Inuttiaq reported to his family: "Nakliguhuktuq says that the kaplunas almost shot us when Yiini wasn't there." The exaggeration was characteristic of Inuttiaq's lurid style of fantasy. He turned to me: "Did you write that to Nakliguhuktuq?" I denied it—and later, in Gjoa Haven, Nakliguhuktuq denied having made such a statement to Inuttiaq—but I did confirm the gist of Inuttiaq's report: that I had tried to protect the Eskimos. I described what it was that I had written to Ikayuqtuq, and I explained something of the reasons for my anger at the kaplunas.

Wall of Ice

The effect was magical. The wall of ice that had stood between me and the community suddenly disappeared. I became consultant on the moral qualities of fishing guides; people talked to me voluntarily, offered me vocabulary, included me in their jokes and in their anecdotes of the day's activities; and Inuttiaq informed me that the next day he and I were going fishing. Most heartwarming of all is the memory of an afternoon soon after the men had returned. The iglu was filled with visitors, and the hum of the primus on which tea was brewing mingled with the low voices of Inuttiaq and his guests. I knew every detail of the scene even as I bent over my writing, and I paid no attention until suddenly my mind caught on the sound of my name: "I consider Yiini a member of my family again." Was that what Inuttiaq had said? I looked up, inquiring. "I consider you a family member again," he repeated. His diction was clear, as it was only when he wanted to be sure that I understood. And he called me "daughter," as he had not done since August.

Not that I had suddenly become a wholly acceptable housemate; that could never be. I was not and could never become an Utkuhikhalingmiutaq, nor could I ever be a "daughter" to Inuttiaq and Allaq as they understood that role. Inuttiaq made this quite clear one day about this time when we were both sitting, silently working, in the iglu. "I think you're a leader in your country," he said suddenly. The remark had no obvious context; it must mean, I thought, that he had never reconciled himself to my intractable behavior. There was also the slightly wild look that I caught in his eye when I said I thought that I might someday return to Chantrey Inlet. The look vanished when Allaq explained that I meant to return after I had been to my own country, not merely to Gjoa Haven. "Yes," he said then, "We will adopt you again, or others may want to—Nilaak, perhaps, or Mannik, if he marries." And later, when we were talking about the possibility of other "learners" coming to Chantrey Inlet, Inuttiaq said, "We would be happier to have a woman come than a man—a woman like you, who doesn't want to be a wife. Maybe *you* are the only acceptable kapluna."

But it was the letters that Allaq and Inuttiaq wrote me when I left Chantrey Inlet in January that expressed most vividly and succinctly what it meant to them to have a kapluna daughter. They both said, "I didn't think I'd care when you left, but I did."

Stranger, Child, Simpleton

I observed three more or less distinct phases in the Utkuhikhalingmiut's view of me. During the first period I was a stranger and a guest, and I was treated with the formal courtesy and deference that the Utkuhikhalingmiut ordinarily accord to such persons. I was referred to as a kapluna, a white person, and addressed by my personal name —"Yiini" in the Eskimos' speech. Much of the time during this period the Eskimos must have been at a loss what to make of my behavior, and often when I did something that under other circumstances they might have defined as reprehensible—when I went to bed early, nursing a bad humor, or when I was silent in depression—they gave me the benefit of the doubt; they asked me if I were tired and considerately lessened my work load or withdrew so that I might "sleep."

Gradually, however, this first phase gave way to a second, in which my immediate family (though not others in the community) treated me in some respects as a daughter and a child. My parents replaced the name "Yiini" with the term "daughter" when speaking, and sometimes when referring to me; and my two small sisters called me "elder sister." Inuttiaq—though never Allaq—also began to use the imperative forms of speech that he used in addressing his other daughters and his wife. Even an appropriate age was invented for me: I had to be younger than Allaq—if only by one season—though all the evidence pointed to my being in fact slightly older than she was. Both parents directed my daily activities, and I was expected to obey them as a daughter should. When I did not, efforts were made to teach me better behavior through lecturing or shaming, the former a technique that was otherwise only used in teaching small children. My moodiness was no longer interpreted charitably, and efforts were made to educate me out of that behavior too.

Categorization of me as a "child" was probably determined by a combination of factors: I had introduced myself as one who wanted to "learn" from the Utkuhikhalingmiut, and I had asked to be adopted as a "daughter"; I was also obviously ignorant of Utkuhikhalingmiut proprieties and skills. The fact that I am a woman may also have facilitated my categorization as a child in several respects. For one thing, among the Utkuhikhalingmiut a woman's technical skill—skin-sewing—is very difficult to learn. I never mastered more than the most rudimentary, clumsy stitching; my work was so poor that when I mended my skin boots, Allaq considered it necessary to redo the job. Moreover, in order to be considered properly adult, a woman must have children, and I had none. For these reasons the role of an adult woman was virtually closed to me, whereas had I been a man, I might have earned an adult role as a fisherman and hunter, as some male kaplunas who have lived among Eskimos appear to have done. Finally, the fact that I am physically weaker than a man and thus unthreatening may have made it easier for the Utkuhikhalingmiut to view my ill temper, as I think they did, like that of a child. Had I been a man, I think they might have seen my temper as dangerous, even potentially lethal—anything but childish.

The third phase, in which I was treated as an incorrigible offender, replaced the "child" phase, I think, when it became apparent to the Utkuhikhalingmiut that I was uneducable. Inuttiaq no longer lectured me or used any other method to teach me. I was called "Yiini" again instead of "daughter," and daughterly services were no longer asked of me. In fact, nothing at all was demanded of me. Though my physical needs for warmth, food and protection from danger were still taken care of, socially I was simply "not there." There was one other person in the community who was similarly ostracized: a woman of about my age, who appeared to be of subnormal intelligence. Almost all of her personal qualities—her imperfect speech, clumsy gestures and domestic incompetence—were subject to comment behind her back, but hostility in her case, as in mine, centered on her volatility—the fact that she was easily upset and was unable to exercise proper restraint in the expression of her feelings. She too was considered uneducable, and I am sure that, like her, I was privately labeled simpleminded.

Hosts and Anthropologists

In more general terms the sequence of judgments passed on me seemed to be: strange; educable; uneducable in important ways. And each phase, each judgment, was associated with a role familiar to the Utkuhikhalingmiut: stranger; child; simpleton—each role being identifiable in terms of the way I was addressed, the kinds of behavior that were expected of me, the interpretations that were placed on my misbehavior and the methods that were used to control that misbehavior.

Although an anthropologist must have a recognized role or roles in order to make it possible to interact with him sensibly and predictably, nevertheless it will be evident from what I have described of my own case that the assignment of a role may create as many problems as it solves for both the anthropologist and his hosts. When Inuttiaq undertook to adopt me, I think he assumed that I would naturally behave as he was accustomed to having daughters behave. He knew, of course, that as a kapluna I was ignorant of the Eskimo skills that adult daughters have usually mastered, but it is easier to recognize cross-cultural differences in technology and language than differences in the structuring of interpersonal relations; one is far more inclined to think of the latter as given in "human nature."

He was wrong, of course, in assuming that my behavior would be that of an Utkuhikhalingmiut daughter. Consequently his first hypothesis was replaced by a second: that kaplunas don't (or Yiini doesn't) know how to behave correctly but can learn. For various reasons, none of which were, I think, recognized by Inuttiaq, I didn't learn easily. The first reason why learning must be difficult is that the intruder faces a double task. On the one hand he must discover what has to be learned—that is, what exactly is wrong with his "normal" behavior and what the proper behavior should be. And on the other hand he must overcome resistance to doing what is required—resistance caused by the interference of his old patterns of role behavior. Such interference may be expected to be particularly marked when the role to be learned bears the same name ("daughter") as a role one is accustomed to playing in one's own culture.

Learning will also be difficult and imperfect because the anthropologist is not completely committed to the role he is playing vis-à-vis his hosts. For one thing, he must try to learn all kinds of facts about the community, many of which it may be inappropriate for someone in his assumed native role to know. He must try to maintain sufficient distance from the culture he is studying and from himself so that he can record "objectively" and, hopefully, use his reactions to his experiences as sources of data. And he must try to record and participate simultaneously. The latter problem has been amply illustrated in my case as I have described it above.

It was because of these difficulties and others that Inuttiaq's second hypothesis—that I was educable—proved to a large extent wrong. And so he arrived at his third hypothesis (shared, as I have said, by the rest of the community), to the effect that I was a defective person: "bad" and "simpleminded."

This analysis of the relationship between my Eskimo family and me is, of course, far from complete. It is obvious that difficulties of conceptualization are only one of the problems that beset relationships of any kind. It is obvious also that most relationships—and the one described here is no exception—have strongly positive features as well, or they would cease to exist. Nevertheless, the account that I have presented here may serve as a basis for discussion of the general issues of anthropological role-playing.

June 1970

SUGGESTED READINGS

Land of the Good Shadows by Heluiz Washburne and Anauta (New York: John Day, 1940) is an account of Eskimos by an Eskimo woman.

Never in Anger: Portrait of an Eskimo Family by Jean L. Briggs (Cambridge, Mass.: Harvard Univ. Press, 1970).

Eskimos without Igloos: Social and Economic Development in Sugluk by Nelson Graburn (New York: Little, Brown and Co., 1969).

Hunters of the Northern Ice by Richard Nelson (Chicago: University of Chicago Press, 1969).

Book of the Eskimos by Peter Freuchen (Cleveland: World Pub. Co., 1961).

The Eskimos: Their Environment and Folkways by Edward M. Weyer (Hamden, Conn.: Archon Books, 1962).

Current Anthropology, (Vol. 6, Feb. 1965). An issue largely devoted to recent research on Eskimos and Eskimo culture change with a very good bibliography.

"Nanock of the North" by Robert Flaherty. An early, excellent documentary film on Eskimo life.

Dr. George Gerster RAPHO GUILLIMETTE

Two Tactics for Ethnic Survival—Eskimo & Indian

Hudson Bay Eskimos have adapted more readily than Indians to the Euro-Canadian culture, perhaps because their past has little nostalgic appeal

ROBERT J. DRYFOOS, JR.

On the isolated eastern shore of Hudson Bay, about 700 miles northwest of Montreal, lies the community of Great Whale River, Quebec. It cannot be reached by road. When the ice breaks up, in mid-May, the Hudson Bay Company boat makes its way bringing stock for the store. There is an aircraft landing strip, enabling weekly service from Montreal and twice weekly service from Moosonee, Ontario. But outside visitors are usually restricted to the federal or provincial authorities, police, doctors and dentists who serve the community.

At Great Whale River, subarctic temperatures of minus 50 degrees Fahrenheit are not uncommon during the short (six-hour) days of winter. Summer brings 18-hour days, balmy temperatures (up to 85), and swarms of flies and mosquitoes. The surrounding terrain is flat and sandy rising to low, rocky hills to the east and northeast. As the village lies only 100 miles south of the timber line, the trees are small and sparse. Berries grow in season, which is short. Life is hard. The community consists of about 450 Eskimos, 225 Indians and 100 Euro-Canadians. The latter include

VARIATION AND CONTRAST

Indian parents are still concerned that their children learn "the old ways" of the time when they were free, before the white man came.

teachers, medical personnel, Hudson Bay Company employees, representatives of both the federal Canadian government and the Quebec government, and missionaries of the Anglican and Catholic churches. The Indians are trappers and hunters, trapping beaver and mink in the winter, hunting bear and smaller game year around. Although they now use rifles and shot guns, the Indians still hunt in the bush country to the east as they did in earlier times. The Eskimos are more frequently employed by the government and the Hudson Bay Company. They still hunt seal, and they too have adopted the rifle and shot gun to wound the animals initially before they are harpooned and landed. They have also continued to hunt whale and they trap in the summer, though none of this could be considered their major endeavor. The authorities recognize the difficulties of life in Great Whale River, and most of the people are eligible for and receive welfare payments and child allotments.

While both the Eskimo and the Indians have become settled residents of the village and have largely adopted the material culture of the white man, each group has maintained its own individuality and continues to speak its own language. And although very few rituals, practices or beliefs persist among members of the two native groups, considerable knowledge of the old ways still survives.

Remembrance of things past is the focus of this study; particularly the curious contrast between the remembrances of the Eskimos and the Indians of Great Whale River. The Eskimo has very largely left the past behind with his entry into the modern world; he looks back, if at all, to see a life of hardship and insecurity which he has little wish to perpetuate. Not so the Indian. His past is tenacious, and the days before the coming of the white man are meaningful, valued and well remembered. It is as if the bush still calls to him, and the old life holds something of the fascination of a "lost horizons" for the town-dwelling Indian.

The fact that sharp differences in recall do exist between the two native groups emerged in the course of a seven-month field study I conducted during the summers of 1964 and 1965. Why these differing perceptions should exist simultaneously is an intriguing question, especially as the history of contact with modern culture has been almost identical for each group in regard to both duration and intensity. Explanations involve the complex interplay between past and present, and among the three ethnic groups living side by side.

During my two summers in Great Whale River I interviewed approximately half the members of each native group, in most cases more than once. To try to insure that "no response" to questions about the past resulted from lack of traditional knowledge and not from unwillingness to answer, I attempted to establish a cordial relationship with each person I interviewed, and came to know some quite well. I also established good rapport with my interpreters, some of whom I used throughout the two summers, and relied heavily on their judgement in determining the truthfulness of the replies.

Among the Eskimos, only 12 percent were able to give

information about former customs and beliefs, compared to 75 percent of the Indians. Not a single Eskimo under 35 could demonstrate any recall of the traditional ways; the average age for Eskimo informants was over 65. The average age for Indian informants was 42, and several Indian teen-agers as well as one child of 11 were able to give information about their past.

The amount and depth of knowledge retained shows a similar pattern. Members of both groups were asked for information about religion, rites of passage, rites of intensification, marriage and residence patterns, myths and legends, kinship, political organization and economic activities. The Indians were able to recall a total of about 85 such items, and almost invariably discussed them in considerable detail. The Eskimos recalled only 25 items, and could usually give only a skeletal version of the material they remembered.

In the traditional legends of both the Eskimos and the Indians there appears a great sea spirit which takes the form of a mermaid. Present-day experience with this mermaid is the closest to a survival of a traditional belief that I was able to discover. About 20 Indians reported that they, or someone they knew, had had some contact with the mermaid, whom they call Mentoxo—either seeing, hearing, or being affected in some way by this sea creature, in whose present existence they expressed belief. Only two Eskimos reported knowing of anyone who had encountered the Eskimo version of the mermaid, whom they call Tariup Inunga. (In most ethnographic literature this Eskimo spirit is known as Sedna, but none of the Eskimos at Great Whale River had ever heard this name, or were even able to pronounce it.) Several of the Indians who said they had confronted Mentoxo dated these events within very recent years, whereas the two Eskimo reports of Tariup Inunga occurred perhaps 40 or 50 years ago.

The vitality of the past among the Indians is easily explained on one level: most Indian fathers say it is desirable for their children to learn of traditional Indian customs, and take pains to tell them about the "way things were done, and what we believed before the white man came." Practically every Eskimo, on the other hand, has dispensed with such teaching, explaining that the "old days have little value for today's children." This is true not just in the area of custom and belief, but for practical skills as well. Most Indian parents say it is valuable for the young men to be able to engage in "real" Indian activities, and teach their sons the proper techniques for hunting in the bush. Only a few Eskimo parents want their children to learn how to hunt sea mammals; most adults dismiss the idea, saying it is "too difficult for people today," or "hunting does not pay enough."

The harsh physical environment and the problems of sheer survival in traditional times may provide one clue to both what and how much of the past is recalled today. Although life was difficult for both peoples, the Eskimos faced an environment that was more continuously threatening than did the Indians. Certainly this is how it is viewed in retrospect: many more Eskimos than Indians comment that the old days were "bad," or that "there was great hunger and starvation many years ago." The Eskimos, then, may well have been more apt to recognize the advantages of Euro-Canadian culture and to welcome a way

Eskimos are generally thought (by whites) to be better workers and more ambitious than Indians.

Peter Thomas BLACK STAR

of life offering security and comfort. The Indians, with their less oppressive past, may have adopted the material culture of the white man less wholeheartedly, and this may have carried over to ideological areas as well. For example, although both groups are Christians today, the Eskimos appear to have internalized the Christian faith to a greater extent than the Indians.

Traditionally, both Indian and Eskimo culture was loosely structured, but some of the available ethnographies indicate that Indian culture was the more highly structured of the two and I would hold that this is one reason for its greater persistence. Today, Indians continue to view themselves as comprising a "tribe" or society; knowledge of the past functions as an integrating mechanism and helps to provide a sense of identity as members of an enduring, albeit fragmenting, society. The Eskimos have never considered themselves members of a cohesive group, so identification with the past would have little meaning from this point of view.

The favored position enjoyed by the Eskimos today in the eyes of the dominant white community, and the comparatively inferior status of the Indians, may well be significant in explaining their different regard for the past. I interviewed about three-fourths of the Euro-Canadian population during my study, and learned that they greatly favor the Eskimos. In general, Eskimos are regarded as more industrious and honest, practical and pragmatic, while Indians are often characterized as "dreamers." Both the Eskimos and the Indians are well aware of these attitudes; the Indians also believe they have less chance of being hired for wage labor than the Eskimos, and that they do not have equal access to government funds. quite naturally, the Indians feel some resentment and hostility toward the white community as a result.

It is my belief that perpetuation of traditional knowledge serves the Indians as a relatively safe outlet for aggression against the whites. The passing on of stories, myths and beliefs of bygone days may also be seen as a nativistic movement, similar to the present-day mask-carving among the Onendaga, as suggested by Jean Hendry. The perpetuation of traditional knowledge may well serve to strengthen the Indians' image of themselves in the face of hostile white attitudes, especially vis-à-vis the Eskimos. Given their preferred status in relation to the Indians, the Eskimos would have no such reason to perpetuate the past, and might only alienate the dominant whites by doing so.

Shifting ecocultural patterns of the two groups may also suggest reasons for their differential recall of the past. Traditionally the Eskimos were oriented toward the sea, spending much of their time hunting seal and walrus on Hudson Bay. Today however, when an Eskimo leaves the village in the morning to hunt seal, he usually returns the same evening to a rather bustling village life. Hunting has become more and more a sideline activity, and at the urging of the white man during the last 20 to 25 years, the Eskimos have turned increasingly to various craft pursuits, especially soapstone-carving. (Soapstone-carving, formerly done only as a pleasant pastime during the long winter nights to ornament children's toys, was not a traditional economic activity of the Eskimos.) In other words, the Eskimo ecological orientation has shifted from the coast to the entirely novel one of the village; in this process, the traditional ties with the whole fabric of the past have been attenuated.

The ecocultural patterns of the Indian has not changed nearly so drastically, and he is still to some degree bush-oriented. The hunters and trappers of today must leave the village for extended periods to reach adequate game supplies—they cannot limit these activities to "off-business hours" as the Eskimos can. Indians are constantly reminded of their past by their present hunting and trapping patterns. Craft production is much less developed, though current efforts are being made to increase it. For the present, however, the Indians continue to think and talk largely in terms of their traditional bush orientation. The bush, and the old way of life that went with it, still linger as a powerfully nostalgic image to the Indians, even to those who never venture from the village now.

In summary, recollection of the past is meaningful to the Indians; it functions as a mechanism to make them "more Indian," to provide a sense of current identity. But the Eskimos have little interest in being "more Eskimo," and their past is being forgotten at an ever increasing rate.

January 1970

SUGGESTED READINGS

The Eskimos by Kaj Birket-Smith (London: Methuen, 1959) is a general book about Eskimos by a well-known authority.

Eskimo of the Canadian Arctic by Victor Valentine and Frank G. Vallee (Toronto: D. Van Nostrand, 1968) is a collection of Eskimo studies of traditional Eskimo culture and the Eskimos of the modern world.

"Indians of Canada" by Diamond Jenness (*Ottawa: National Museum of Canada Bulletin* No. 65, 1932) is a general survey of Canadian Indians.

An Eskimo Village in the Modern World by C. C. Hughes (Ithaca, N. Y.: Cornell University Press, 1960).

The Reduction of Intergroup Tension: A Survey of Research on Problems of Ethnic, Racial and Religious Group Relations by Robin M. Williams, Jr. (New York: Social Science Research Council, Bulletin No. 57, 1947).

"Toward a General Theory of Minority Groups" by R. A. Schermerhorn, *Phylon* (Vol. 25, Fall 1961).

The Nunamiut Eskimos by Nicholas Gubser (New Haven: Yale University Press, 1965).

In the Company of Man by Joseph B. Casabrande (New York: Harper, 1960). Twenty portraits by anthropologists in the field.

The Scandinavian Hangover

Danes drink most, but Finns get drunker. So which should be controlled—the drink or the drinker?

NILS CHRISTIE

The Scandinavian countries are sometimes seen as offering useful pre-tests of social welfare arrangements. Some of our arrangements work rather well, but some represent more muddles than models. The field of alcohol control within Scandinavia gives examples of both.

Let me first give some of the Scandinavian experience in regulating the *accessibility* of alcohol, then turn to some of our attempts to cope with the *problem drinker*. Diluted in alcohol, our social arrangements may be perceived as helpful experience for dealing with similar problems in the United States.

Denmark is very lenient about drinking. There is no state monopoly of liquor. Beer, wine, and brandy are widely available through approximately 20,000 stores, restaurants, and pubs.

Finland, Norway, and Sweden are immensely more restrictive. Finland holds a strict state monopoly on beer, wine and whisky. Finland in particular has a strict control of customers. All customers must show special identification cards, complete with photo and signature. They are closely examined to make sure that all drinkers are old enough and that none are known alcoholics. Sweden has a random spot-check system for identification (when an automatic lamp gives a signal, the buyer must produce identification). In Norway a seller will demand identification when, for any reason, he becomes suspicious. Both Norway and Sweden, like Finland, are strict about age limits and deny those with alcohol problems the right to buy.

To find out how to handle alcohol and its problems, we must try to set up a relationship between *accessibility, consumption,* and resulting *public nuisance*. Do countries (like Denmark) that allow easy access to alcohol also have more consumption per capita, more arrests, and more public drunkenness? Or is the opposite true—that making it difficult for the drinker to get the drink creates more alcoholic problems than its solves? It is also possible, of course, that such relationships are not clear—that national peculiarities or differences in cultural drinking patterns (for example, between drinking beer socially at home, or whisky alone in a bar) will have as much impact as the relative availability or consumption of alcohol itself.

What about consumption? As any prohibitionist might have predicted, Danes absorb the most alcohol—about 1.2 American gallons of pure alcohol per year; Finns consume the least, with about half that. Norwegians consume slightly less, per capita, than Swedes.

"The Scandinavian countries too have their 'drys,' similar to the WCTU and the Anti-saloon League in the United States." (Denmark)

When we turn from the use of alcohol to its abuse, the picture suddenly reverses. Denmark, the villain in the piece as viewed by a teetotaler, has only 4.6 arrests for drunkenness per 1,000 inhabitants 15 years old and over (1963), while Finland, the villain as viewed by the beverage industry, has nearly 10 times as many (44). Again, Sweden (17.0) and Norway (11.9) have intermediate positions.

Is Something Rotten in Denmark?

How to explain this anomaly? It can be partially explained by differences in the *types* of alcoholic drinks consumed as well as by differences in how they are consumed. For example, the average Dane drinks more beer than his fellows in the other three countries put together, and beer is known to produce a lower blood alcohol level per consumed unit than brandy—especially undiluted brandy. But the Danes also drink brandy—and their consumption is not so far below the Finns as to explain the gap (the average Dane drinks a little more than half as much brandy as the average Finn). Also, after all, Danish beer is not water.

Another possible explanation is that the Danes follow the continental Europeans in their drinking patterns—small, even, frequent imbibing extending throughout the year, while the Finns consume their entire year's quota on a few grand occasions. This explanation might hold true for older people, but it definitely does not hold true for the young. In a study of drinking patterns of 18-year-olds from the four Scandinavian capitals (over a four-month period) it was found that boys from Copenhagen drank most often and those from Helsinki least. But in terms of *quantity* consumed on each occasion, the records were equal. Helsinki youths drink no more on each occasion.

But they do seem to make more noise about it! A comparative study was made on self-reported crime among young males (this time only figures from Oslo and Helsinki were available). We find substantially more self-reporting of drunk and disturbing behavior at public places, and more contacts with police, in Helsinki than in Oslo—and this in spite of the fact that bootleg production of alcohol, and all it entails, is much more common among Oslo youths than among Finns. Self-reported drunken driving is about equal.

Ignoring national peculiarities, let me sum up: A strict system of legal and institutional control of accessibility of alcohol seems related to low alcohol consumption—but also to a high degree of public nuisance.

It probably works something like this: A drinking culture in which there are a lot of noisy drunks on the street, or other highly visible and offensive evidence of the bad effects of drinking, will eventually lead to a crackdown and tightening up, with tighter state control of liquor. This in turn may cut down on part of the visibility of the problem—with liquor harder to get, forbidden to minors and known alcoholics, there may be fewer drunks staggering openly out of state-owned and controlled bars, and somewhat less open revelry.

However, on the other hand as the American experiment with prohibition demonstrated, other forms of alcoholic problems may actually increase.

There is no simple cause and effect relationship. Interactions and interrelationships develop between the system of control, the amount of consumption, and the visible problems resulting from the use of alcohol.

Alcohol problems do not directly bring on a strict system of control. Rather, in political and social life, there are various pressure groups which act both as buffers and catalytic agents. The Scandinavian countries too have their "drys," similar to the WCTU and the Anti-saloon League in the United States. The parliaments in the four countries have the following percentages of teetotalers: Denmark 6.7 percent; Norway 30 percent; Sweden 36 percent; Finland 32.5 percent. The familiar pattern emerges: Denmark at one extreme of permissiveness, the other countries bunched toward the other extreme. Typically, the current prime ministers in Finland, Sweden, and Norway are teetotalers; the Danish prime minister is not.

In my country, Norway, teetotalers make up the largest non-party group in parliament. This, I believe, stems directly from, and represents a reaction against, our not-so-sober background. Most of the Scandinavian countries, from the Vikings on, have long and extreme drinking histories. In 1815 all Norwegian landowners, for instance, were given the right to distill liquor—and most took broad advantage of it. An extremely well-designed questionnaire study made in 1859 showed that more than one-third of the population were hardly, if at all, able to control their use of liquor. Observers described Norway as a thoroughly alcoholized country. Then the reaction set in. This was the time of the birth and very rapid growth of the abstinence movement. Temperance ideas from the United States found fertile ground, made common cause with other abstinence forces, and brought on a change in drinking habits. Even those who continued to drink—both users and abusers—were never the same again. We drink now, but with thorough feelings of guilt and anxiety.

The abstinence movement has, therefore, been successful so far. But the strength of the dry movement seems to be waning in Scandinavia, and this is probably related to the fact that the visibility of problems caused by alcohol is also declining. Norwegians are being arrested for drunkenness less frequently than they used to be. The steam is going out of the drive toward abstinence, and teetotalism is suffering.

Now that the rigidity of controls is declining, authorities feel freer to experiment with details of control. In Finland, beer and wine shops were opened in some rural areas in 1952; results were mixed, but generally good. Consumption went up among adult males, but declined among the young; and (reminiscent of American repeal) consumption of illegal or bootleg alcohol went down from 92 percent of the total to a bare 15 percent. In Sweden, abolition of strict rationing in 1955 (although associated with increases in all prices) led to a severe increase in consumption for heavy drinkers, but at the same time a slight decrease among "normal users." Both in Sweden and Finland the wine monopolies are trying hard, through advertising and price adjustments, to move consumption away from brandy and over to wine and beer.

Drunken Driving

Compared to America, the punishment for drunken driving in Scandinavia is severe. This is true also in Denmark, although the pattern of greatest leniency in Denmark, and greatest stringency in Finland is generally followed. (All four Scandinavian countries work closely together in law-enforcement, and Danish lawmakers are gravitating toward the joint Scandinavian standard.)

Norway has the lowest legal blood alcohol limit, while Denmark has none. Finland has the strictest penalties. If a driver's blood test measures above the legal minimum in Norway he will, typically, draw 21 days in prison and have his license suspended for one year on first offense (more on succeeding offenses). In Finland he would serve six months in prison (and can get up to three years—or, if a death is involved, up to seven) and lose his license for two to three years.

There is little chance that these laws will be changed—they have strong popular support. Poll after poll show that

"Why pay $6.00-$8.00 for a bottle of liquor when you can get a bottle of good wine for $1.00?" (Sweden)

the people approve of them. Only two groups have serious doubts about them—the drunken drivers themselves and the people who administer the laws. The drunk drivers stay prudently quiet; and the administrators are ambivalent, hampered by a feeling that there are many good things about our present practices.

For we feel that our present system curtails drinking in general, and drunk driving in particular. Many people don't drive to parties where they expect to find drink, or they don't drink when they get there. Those who do know that they run the risk of getting caught. More than 2000 persons were imprisoned in Norway in 1963 for drunk driving. That figure may not seem shocking to an American, used to crime on a large scale; but they are very shocking to a Norwegian (America has roughly 200 prisoners per 100,000 population; we have 44.) More people are imprisoned in Norway for drunk driving than for all crimes put together. A sizeable part of the Norwegian people at some time in their lives go through society's most severe ceremony of degradation—imprisonment with criminals.

The skid-row alcoholic is a more universally-defined problem case. He is a reject of society, with few family or social responsibilities, and so probably causes less real hardship to others than other alcoholics. But he is also extremely visible (especially perhaps in my country, which has a strong temperance movement and no slums). But the public demands for some sort of action are strong indeed. He stands out as an offense to the clean streets. He has no place to hide, no run-down building, no privileged areas reserved for chronic sickness and sin. At the same time the skid row person has to stay in the towns to have reliable access to his supply of alcohol.

This whole situation strongly tempts society to use *force*. But application of force means that law is brought into the picture, and law is very sensitive to problems of justice.

Here society is in trouble. Skid row activity is a disturbing one, but not one that can be defined as a very severe crime. And even severe crimes are treated with extreme leniency in Scandinavia as compared to the United States. The "just" punishment for skid row drunkenness should be a few days in prison. But strong forces within society feel the need to get rid of these persons for longer.

Hiding the Problem in Prison

So "compromises" help solve the problem for society. The skid row habitue cannot be *punished* by removal; but, (and here I cite a law professor in the debate that led up to our present law, passed in 1893): ". . . what cannot be inflicted as punishment, cannot be objected to when it is done to take care of a person. . . ." Later the terminology was modernized—incarcerations would not only "take care of" these poor people, but "treat" them as well. Special institutions should be created for them, and they would not be called prisoners, but inmates. So medicine became a justification for the kind of sentence that law itself could not justify. In practice, most skid row alcoholics serve in a very severe prison for a much longer period than the great majority of our ordinary prisoners do for ordinary crimes.

They are, naturally, extremely unhappy and see the whole situation as a great injustice. In a little study I once made, I asked both ordinary thieves and skid row alcoholics waiting for trial what they would do if they could act as judges of their own cases. The thieves came very close to the sentence they actually received some days later; but the skid row people declared themselves not guilty, or only deserving of a fine or a few days in jail. The discrepancy between their evaluation of a just sentence and the sentence they actually received was enormous. However, since their status is so low—and particularly so among puritans who place a high value on working—their plight is seldom of concern to anybody but some researchers who happen to get to know and like them.

What is interesting here is the way words, concepts, and even ideals have been taken out of one context (medicine) and used very efficiently within another one (a legal framework) to curb minorities who have little power to fight back. Skid-row alcoholics are not the only minorities that have been so curbed—nor is this practice confined to Scandinavia.

Another way that three of the four Scandinavian countries (characteristically, Denmark is excluded) have attempted to control alcoholism outside the usual control agencies is by a new device—a committee of *lay specialists* in alcohol problems who, presumably, would be more flexible than the regular agencies, and could help prevent and limit alcoholism by getting to the alcoholic before his public behavior made him a police problem.

In practice it has not worked out that way. These temperance boards seldom get into the act until after the police are already involved—in fact it is usually the police that call them in. In effect they have become, largely, just another arm of law-enforcement when they operate. Usually they are inactive.

A major trend in recent social and criminal policy is toward *combining* the different control disciplines. I doubt the fruitfulness of this approach—certainly when dealing with alcoholics. It may be that the quest for combination is futile—that law and medicine, like oil and water, cannot really mix. Perhaps law, which emphasizes internal control, and must therefore limit the knowledge it can use, and medicine, which must be free to seek unlimited knowledge and must therefore de-emphasize internal control, are basically antagonistic. This does not mean that they should not both be used in alcohol control—but that they should be used separately, each according to its peculiar strengths and insights, at different times in the process of control, rather than mixed together in a form that must eventually subvert both. Medicine—and social work and the other ameliorating disciplines—can study the nature of alcoholism and how to treat it. Law should dispense justice—with due regard for what justice is in each particular circumstance.

I do not believe that law, social work, or medicine should ever be attempting, or at least pretending, to be doing roughly the same things at the same time.

January-February 1967

SUGGESTED READINGS

Society, Culture, and Drinking Patterns edited by David J. Pittman and Charles R. Snyder (New York: Wiley, 1962). An anthology covering international patterns of social structure and culture and their relationship to alcohol.

Alcoholism in America by Harrison M. Trice (New York: McGraw-Hill, 1966). A social-psychological explanation of drinking in America and its implications, integrating both personality and group factors.

Human Deviance, Social Problems, and Social Control by Edwin M. Lemert (Englewood Cliffs, New Jersey: Prentice-Hall, 1967).

Social Welfare in Denmark by Orla Jensen (Copenhagen: Det Danske Selskab, 1961). An introduction to social control legislation and policy in a socialized political system.

The Japanese "Howdunit"

Japan has been an economic success; but can other underdeveloped nations follow its pattern?

MARTIN BRONFENBRENNER

The year 1968 was the 100th anniversary of Japan's Meiji Restoration. This "restoration" consisted of the ouster of the military government (or Shogunate) dominated by the Tokugawa family, and the ostensible transfer of power to the 15-year-old Emperor Mutsuhito. The Emperor took the title of Meiji (Enlightened Rule) and lived until 1912. His reign was called the Meiji Era; its 44 years constitute the glorious period of Japanese modernization. This article summarizes how the "Meiji Statesmen"—not the Meiji Emperor himself—accomplished their seeming miracle, and speculates about whether Japan's modernization can be emulated by the underdeveloped countries of today.

Japan is a unique success story of essentially capitalist economic development in a non-Caucasian country. The statistical researches of Kazushi Ohkawa and his associates indicate that Japan had an income growth rate of about 4.5 percent a year (3.5 percent per capita) for the 60-year period from 1878 to World War II. Now, 4.5 percent is not a remarkable rate for income growth for one, or five, or even ten years. The great accomplishment of the Japanese has been to keep it up, as an average, for two or three generations.

Meiji Japan developed *into*, not *out of*, the international economy. In fact, Western countries—using "unequal treaties"—forced a minimum-tariff policy upon Japan until 1899. Meiji Japan developed her own meager resources, with no outside financial aid. She first obtained large loans only after 1905. Meiji Japan moved in accordance with Adam Smith's "natural pattern" of development, from agriculture and handicrafts to light industry to heavy industry. This contrasts with the "forced-draft industrialization" so popular in underdeveloped countries today. Finally, by modern standards Meiji Japan progressed without major in-

A Japanese cannon that was used in the bombardment of Port Arthur in the Russo-Japanese war. *Underwood & Underwood*

flation. If we use as 100 an average price index of 1928-32, the price level rose only from 35.9 in 1878 to 68.9 at the end of the Meiji Era (and 136.8 in 1938). Under Count Matsukata's direction, the Meiji inflation—such as it was—was broken during the 1880s by a near-decade of substantial deflation.

Lest anyone think this achievement was an economist's Utopia, let me add right away that it was not. Japan's economic growth probably did not raise the low living standards of either the poor city workers, or the even poorer country peasants until after 1890. (Many poor people, however, raised their *own* standards by moving from the country to the city.) Nor—after the turn of the century—did this economic development avoid "dualism"—a concentration of the gains in a few classes or regions, the rest remaining backward. Finally, there are disputes as to whether the Meiji pattern of development led directly into military imperialism and World War II, and whether other countries could hope to repeat Japan's success today. I am myself "pro-Japanese" on the first point; I do not blame imperialism on Meiji Era development. At the same time, I am "anti-Japanese" on the second point; I do not think the Japanese model is especially helpful to today's Third World, for reasons I shall give later on.

Main Causes of Japan's Development

On a superficial level, it is probably safe to mention three main causes of Japanese economic development during the Meiji Era. One was the adaptation of Western technology to Japanese industry. (The development of a native technology in agriculture and handicrafts had come a century earlier.) Second was the fact that Japan had a major export—silk and silk fabrics—that financed nearly half of her necessary imports of both machinery and "know-how," without simultaneously introducing foreign control. Third was an internal "export surplus" of food, which—until about 1890—permitted peasants to migrate to the city and increase the industrial-labor force, without straining the country's international balance of payments.

As far as I know, no economist of the 1860s forecast that Japan would have an economic future more favorable than China's or India's. Yet hindsight suggests that economists should have done so, for Tokugawa Japan had a number of *initial advantages* overlooked at the time. Let me list seven of these. Combined, they are quite impressive.

1. Adam Smith has written, "Little else is required to carry a state to the highest degree of opulence from the lowest barbarism, but peace, easy taxes, and a tolerable administration of justice, all the rest being brought about in the natural course of things." Of these the greatest is peace, and the Tokugawa Shoguns gave Japan 250 years of it, broken only by frequent but minor peasant uprisings. (The Japanese *samurai* movies of violence are laid in pre-Tokugawa days.)

2. This peace—which included at least one aspect of "tolerable administration of justice," namely, the enforcement of contracts—permitted Japanese farmers to develop advanced labor-intensive techniques and handicraft side-employments—without fear of depredations by roving soldiers and bandits. And it had fostered the development of an economizing middle class of urban merchants and money lenders. These were native Japanese (not aliens, who might have been less safe). This middle class also had just the right degree of social mobility, being subject neither to frequent expropriations (like the Jews of Central Europe) nor to absorption into an idle landed aristocracy (as was happening in China). On the public side as well, peace permitted the Shogunate and the local lords *(daimyos)* to build up the best systems of "social overhead capital" to be found in mid-19th century Asia. This capital included harbors, roads, and even a rudimentary school system that used temple and shrine facilities. It should be mentioned, however, that the usefulness of this system was reduced somewhat by the Shoguns' suspicion of interregional trade and commerce, which might have made local *daimyos* too strong and wealthy, encouraging them to revolt against Tokugawa rule.

3. Stemming from her agricultural revolution, Tokugawa Japan had a large reservoir of skilled labor, both urban and rural—most underdeveloped countries boast only a few guilds of artists and artisans, superimposed upon unskilled masses of mere hands and backs. The rural skilled labor we have just touched upon. As for urban labor, it may come as a surprise to many Westerners that, in 1780 as today, the world's largest city was Tokyo (called Edo or Yedo in Tokugawa times), which had all the specialized labor one expects of such a metropolis.

4. Like many another race, the Japanese believed themselves specially favored by their gods. But unlike most peoples similarly deluded, the Japanese had a highly-developed tradition of cultural receptivity. They were willing and able both to learn even from "barbarians" and to adapt what they learned to their own uses. Japanese culture, as is well known, primarily derives from the Chinese, with Indian and Malaysian overtones. The same receptive attitude the Japanese had applied briefly to the West in the 16th century. This attitude was easily revived in the second half of the 19th century. Mogul India and Manchu China, overly conscious of their own superiority, learned nothing from the West—until too late.

5. To some extent, the difference between Japan's reaction to the West and Chinese and Indian reactions

was a matter of timing. The mid-19th century was late enough for the Japanese to know how India, Java, Siberia, and the Philippines had succumbed to Western power, and likewise, what was happening to China after the Opium War of 1840. The "reactive nationalism" of some Japanese feudal lords took the form of bull-headed resistance to the West, with armaments obsolete by two centuries or more. The Meiji statesmen, however, imposed economic development, military scholarship, and Westernization (*fukoku kyohei*, a rich country and a strong army) as their strategy for preserving Japanese independence. (This choice of strategy may have been the most important direct consequence of the Meiji restoration.)

6. More strictly economic in importance was the existence of a world silk market, with special conditions permitting early Japanese dominance over French, Italian, and Chinese rivals. Briefly, the opening of Japan to the West coincided with a Franco-Italian epidemic of a silkworm disease know as *pébrine* (on which Louis Pasteur carried out some of his crucial experiments). It also coincided with a 15-year civil war in China (the Taiping Rebellion), which disrupted that country's entire export trade. So great was the importance of silk for Meiji development that one wonders whether Japan could have done much better than 19th century China or India had silk-substitutes like rayon and nylon then been available to the West.

7. Finally, Japan had the advantages of the technological latecomer. The Japanese could absorb Western technology with few of the false starts and other development costs that the originating countries had already borne. This factor is often exaggerated, though. The Japanese task was not merely copying foreign industrial methods, but adapting them to their own

---

SUGGESTED READINGS

Short Economic History of Modern Japan, 1867-1937 by G. C. Allen (New York: Praeger, 1963)........

Japan's Emergence As a Modern State: Political & Economic Problems of the Meiji Period (New York: International Secretariat, Institute of Pacific Relations, 1940).

The Economic Development of Japan: Growth and Structural Change, 1868-1938 (Princeton: Princeton University Press, 1954).

Economic Development and the Labor Market in Japan by Koji Taira (New York: Columbia University Press, 1970). A recent analysis of the institutional aspects of the Japanese labor market and economic system.

Paternalism in the Japanese Economy by John W. Bennett and Iwao Ishino (Minneapolis, Minn.: University of Minnesota Press, 1963). Two anthropologists study non-Western practices of hiring, firing and employment in Japan.

The Japanese Factory by James Abegglen (Glencoe, Ill.: The Free Press, 1958). The forms of social responsibility and industrial decision-making and operations in Japan.

skills and to their own economy of high capital costs and low wage rates. This adaption process itself led to some costly false starts, mainly among Japanese firms that tried to imitate foreign methods too closely.

Meiji Development Policies

Meiji Japan did not simply sit back and enjoy these seven initial advantages. Through some combination of luck, statesmanship, and the traditional Japanese character, Japan avoided a great many of the mistakes that other countries—the standard "Developia" or "Faroffistan"—made later on. In this connection, I should list five policies—*special advantages*—as particularly important.

1. One was the "socialization of risk"—whereby the expensive "pilot-plant" operations of one industry after another (textile mills, shipyards, railroads, etc.) were borne by the public treasury. Private enterprise took over only later, after many of the basic adaptation problems had been solved. This, of course, is similar to what the United States did later in financing atomic-energy research, the development of artificial rubber, and satellite communications. And as in the American case, there have been protests in Japan that the government should have continued in control, or that corruption was involved in the "privatization" of some public pilot plants.

2. In their rush to modernize, the Japanese did not neglect the more humdrum varieties of social overhead capital—schools, hospitals, roads, and harbors, as well as the flashier railroads and universities. By the end of the Meiji Era, Japan had both a "Western" literacy rate, and at least one national university (Tokyo Imperial) of world stature.

3. From 1868 to 1940, the total of public capital formation, including all the plant and equipment involved in the works just mentioned, came to between 40 and 50 percent of total investments. With all this, the Japanese government refrained almost entirely from wasteful showpieces or monuments, such as have marred the record of Sukarno's Indonesia. (Incidentally, the private sector also refrained from such similar showpieces as luxury housing—the bane of some Latin American development programs.)

4. Restraint on private and public showpieces and monuments was only part of a Meiji stress on savings, and a discouragement of consumption that out-Franklined Poor Richard himself. In its extreme form of *bimbo-ron* (philosophy of poverty), the official line was that Japanese superiority to effete foreigners lay precisely in the national capacity to endure hardship. However seriously such notions were taken, potential high-consumption classes were continually held down, and what Veblen called "conspicuous consumption" was continuously inveighed against. A tax system rest-

ing primarily on land holdings slowed the economic rise of the peasantry, while labor militance and labor aristocracy of the trade-union variety were suppressed by harsh laws, vigorously enforced by a national police force. When lagging purchasing-power became a problem, an answer could be found in export markets.

5. In the first decade of the Meiji Era, the Japanese government, with only minor flare-ups of violence, was able to liquidate its *samurai* scholar-military aristocracy. The liquidation process was economic, not biological; not only did few *samurai* die resisting change, but many were successfully transformed into entrepreneurs, bringing their class prestige with them into the ranks of the money-grubbers. The government brought this about through an elaborate system of converting the rice stipends given to the *samurai* by the lords into lump-sum grants of central government bonds. The bonds themselves were a poor investment in the inflationary time of the 1870s, but they bore special privileges as business collateral, particularly in banking and finance. This unique combination of carrot and stick made the *samurai* a greater source of entrepreneurial talent than even the middle-class surviving from Tokugawa days.

A popular charge against Meiji Japanese economic development, however, has been that it led inexorably to imperialism, militarism, and finally to collapse in World War II. We can divide the argument into three points. The first relates to the Japanese population problem; the second, to the international struggle for markets and materials; and the third, to noneconomic explanations for Japanese military imperialism.

Japan did encourage population growth in order to keep up her labor supply, and incidentally to keep wage rates low. She also used her large and dense population as an excuse for overseas expansion. At the same time, though, she always retained a domestic frontier—the northern island of Hokkaido. And Japan's conquests were of populated areas with living standards lower than her own. Korea, Taiwan, and Manchuria could attract Japanese capital and Japanese supervisory personnel, but few Japanese workers or peasants relished the prospect of competing with lower-paid and equally hard-working Koreans and Chinese. The Empire, in other words, was poorly adapted to alleviate Japanese overpopulation.

Vladimir Lenin's explanation of imperialist wars is well known. These wars, he maintained, are waged by capitalist countries to obtain happy dumping-grounds for goods that their own exploited masses could not afford; or they are waged to obtain monopoly positions in underdeveloped countries where even cheaper labor and raw materials are available. (The second explanation fits resource-poor Japan better than the first, which is commonly stressed in America.)

There are two episodes in the history of Japanese expansion that Lenin's theory fits well. Both occurred during periods of world depression. The earlier episode was the Sino-Japanese War of 1894-95. This arose from a struggle between Japan and China for economic as well as political control of Korea, which was then valuable both as a market and a rice bowl. The second episode was the Manchurian Incident of 1931, which gave Japan a 15-year monopoly on that region's coal, iron, soybeans, and electric power. On the other hand, it is more difficult to fit Lenin's theory to the facts of Japan's two major expansionist efforts—the Russo-Japanese War of 1904-05, and the "China Incident" of 1937, which led to Pearl Harbor. Both of these efforts occurred in periods of general prosperity within Japan, with little or no economic distress to be alleviated by overseas adventure.

There are a few points to ponder in connection with any attempt to apply Lenin's theory of imperialist wars to the Japanese historical record. One is that, except in periods of world depression, Japan's home market absorbed more than 85 percent of Japan's gross national product—despite the low level of worker and peasant incomes. Second, the Japanese financial oligarchy, *Zaibatsu,* was always anti-militarist, even when it was engaged in economic expansion on the Asian continent. Finally, the Japanese army, dominated by ex-farm boys, not only repaid the Zaibatsu's distaste with interest, but tended to be anti-capitalist in its economic thinking.

■ Before blaming Japanese imperialism on Meiji Era

Emperor Mutsuhito CULVER PICTURES

economic development, one should at least consider three other explanations—all noneconomic. The most appealing is a crude, preventive-war explanation. Smaller and inherently weaker than China and Russia, Japan took advantage of her modernization to strengthen her position against danger from these powers, danger that has indeed materialized since World War II. Second, it may be important that Japan's first four military ventures (Sino-Japanese War, Russo-Japanese War, World War I, Manchurian Incident), however caused, paid off so handsomely—on a crude cost-benefit analysis—as to warp the national psychology temporarily in a militarist direction. And lastly, we should not overlook the "geographical fetishism," or "mapitis," that spurred many Western imperialistic ventures, and that seemed—to Japan also—necessary for Great Power status.

Japan as a Poor Model for Developing Nations

Similarly, I am skeptical that Meiji Japan furnishes a more useful model for today's Third World countries—Asian or non-Asian—than the British, American, German, or Russian models.

The main basis for this conclusion is that Meiji Japan had so many advantages that are largely absent in the developing countries of today. Thus, when we apply our list of Japan's seven *initial advantages* to the situation of any underdeveloped country one cares to mention, we find the great majority of these advantages are missing. One is the atmosphere of peace and domestic tranquility (maintained by one's own government, not imposed by foreign imperialists), symbolized in Japan by the 250 years of Pax Tokugawa. Then there is the ample supply of skilled and often literate labor that develops during such a period of peace. And the existence of a free market in advanced countries for an expansible export—in the Japanese case, silk. The same is true of the five *special advantages* that Japan had—most are absent in the underdeveloped countries of today. An example: Japan's stock of social capital, including an educational system.

Modern underdeveloped countries may have advantages that Japan did not have—such as one or more important natural resources, like fertile soil, coal, iron, lumber, petroleum. (Today Japan is deficient in almost everything but water power and electric power.) But natural resources are not enough for development as we know from numerous examples all over the world.

By and large, all of Japan's advantages were available from the outset of Meiji rule. In due course, Japan also developed an advantage outside the country itself—a sphere of influence near at hand, less developed than Japan herself, and endowed with resources that Japan lacked. Included in this sphere were Korea, Taiwan, and the southern half of Manchuria. The first two were already annexed at the death of the Meiji Emperor. For modern underdeveloped countries, parallel external opportunities seem lacking. When, for example, the Ibo tribe of Nigeria sought to make of that country's Northern Region an economic sphere of influence, the response was swift and bloody.

Another part of the success story of Meiji Japan was her ability to suppress the living standards of her masses without great expense—for the benefit of both the capitalist class and the national wealth of future generations. The acceptability of any such model is much less today, when savings and investment can be done by socialist governments themselves, and when both the U.S.S.R. and China have achieved noteworthy growth with almost no incentives for private investment. The bureaucrat seems (at least from the outside) both a cheaper and an equally efficient replacement for the capitalist entrepreneur. And he can be financed at less cost to the urban worker or the rural peasant.

What this means is that developing countries, whether or not they understand the Meiji Japanese economic miracle, seem to prefer heavy mixtures of the rival Soviet or Chinese recipes. It also means that when capitalist governments try to follow something like the Meiji Japanese model, a larger percentage of their potential resources must be drained away into military and police pursuits—to forestall revolutionary opposition. This drain alone keeps them from duplicating the Meiji achievement. The Republic of Korea, just across the Sea of Japan, is a case in point. Here, the maintenance of a regime not unlike military fascism has required keeping close to 10 percent of the country's labor force in the army and police, delaying development accordingly. The domestic Korean development effort, with this monetary and resource burden of keeping the masses quiet (and forestalling the invasion of Socialists across the border), seems crippled at the start, however much it strives to approach Meiji Era accomplishments. If it succeeds, massive foreign aid will have been required.

It is significant that, 100 years after the Meiji Restoration and with Japan's second economic miracle in progress, so much intellectual interest within Japan herself focuses *not* on what capitalist Japan did in the past, or even on what capitalist Japan is accomplishing today, but on Chinese revolutionary socialism and Scandinavian welfare-statism. What is true for Japan itself can hardly be false for the Third World—especially in Asian countries, where public opinion ties the Japanese development model more closely than I have tied it to imperialist wars and atomic destruction.

January 1969

A laboratory classroom at the Ayurvedic College at Poona.

Photographs by Charles Leslie

Modern India's Ancient Medicine

Alienation as sickness of the soul

CHARLES LESLIE

Vast stadiums with daringly cantilevered roofs; skyscraper hotels in cities with the most rudimentary sewerage systems; hydroelectric works and research institutes built without regard to their usefulness—these are some signs of an oft-described feature of many developing nations, symbolic modernization. These are the projects, one might say, that seem to have more expressive than instrumental value.

But there is in the developing world a less well-known counterpart to symbolic modernization that could be called *symbolic traditionalization*. This is the effort to garb the new and foreign in the guise of the antique and the indigenous. A striking example of this is going on today in the field of medicine in China and India where efforts are being made to revive medical practices based on ancient scientific texts. What is intriguing about this revivalism is not that it is happening—revivalism is another common feature of developing countries—but that it is happening in a domain of science and technology. Revivals are usually political or religious or aesthetic phenomena, or all three in combination. It is unexpected to find it in those human concerns where science and technology hold sway.

There is, however, a paradox in this development, a paradox that is both poignant and extremely interesting for the student of modernizing cultures. In South Asia, one of the consequences of symbolic traditionalization in the health field has been a significant degree of alienation from the Great Tradition itself, the ancient tradition of medicine that whole colleges, hospitals, and professional societies are devoted to trying to revive. In fact, there is feedback in the process: Alienation from tradition is both a cause of the development of these modern institutions (the hospitals, professional groups, etc.) that were set up to revive the Great Tradition and a consequence of the operation of these institutions.

The Authority of the Ancient

The Great Tradition of medicine in South Asia is contained in the Ayurveda. (The revival of ancient medical practice in Communist China probably involves processes similar to the ones I'm describing here, but unfortunately one can't study them firsthand.) The formulation of Ayurvedic medicine as a secular science and profession was approximately contemporary with the emergence of similar systems in ancient Greece and China.

The most authoritative texts comprising Ayurveda are the Caraka Samhita, which in its present form dates from the first century, the Susruta Samhita, from about the fourth century, and the Vagbhata, compiled about the eighth century. Legendary accounts hold that Ayurveda originated from Brahma and was given by Indra to Dhanvantari, the divine ruler of Benares. Although one branch of Ayurveda is devoted to illnesses caused by demons, its theories and therapeutic practices were as secular and scientific as those of ancient China and Greece. The other branches of the classical system were surgery, internal medicine, pediatrics, treatments for poisons, and so on.

The physiological and anatomical ideas of Ayurveda will appear familiar to those who know the history of Western science, at least since Aristotle. The universe is composed of five elements: earth, water, fire, wind, and ether. The elements have subtle and material forms, each element possessing five subtle and five material forms, and their arrangement in the human body is a microcosm of the universe. Health is maintained by the equilibrium of three humors: phlegm or mucus, bile or gall, and wind. Again, there are five kinds of wind, five fiery substances, and five watery substances concentrated in different parts of the body and circulating through it by means of different networks of vessels.

Illnesses are diagnosed as imbalances of one or more humors, but the degree and kind of imbalance in each case depend upon the humoral disposition of the individual, the season of the year, climatic conditions, astrological forces, and so forth. The point is that therapy was supposed to vary according to the contingencies of each illness. In addition to this profoundly individualized therapy, practitioners are supposed to gather the ingredients for their medications personally, at the proper time of year, and with particular precautions. And medications were to be prepared freshly each day, and individually for each patient. This is the opposite of the controlled and standardized procedures of the chemical and biological sciences that underlie modern medicine, not to mention the techniques of drug manufacturers and experimental clinical research.

Although all twice-born castes were qualified to seek training from a master physician, only Brahmins were to be taught the Nyaya, Vaisesika, and Sankhya philosophies that provided the metaphysical knowledge necessary for a complete grasp of the science. When the student joined the household of his teacher, he underwent an initiation rite that established a deep spiritual relationship between the two. He was supported by the master through his years of apprenticeship during which he memorized the medical texts and his master explained their significance. Though the knowledge was secular, it was treated in an elevated manner, and imparted in a relationship sanctioned by deep religious feeling. Heinrich Zimmer captured the spirit of Ayurvedic thought well:

> The science of longevity has no beginning nor origin. . . . Partaking in the law of nature which silently rules the life-process of all creatures, the laws of the medical code on health and longevity exist and are effective, whether or not they are . . . perceived by man's insight. . . . They inhere in the nature of life and living beings, reflecting their essence, which remains the same at all times.

This, briefly, is the classical system that provides the idealized past with which revivalists would re-establish contact. In their view, the traditional practice of Ayurvedic medicine degenerated, first under Muslim and then under British rule, becoming a mutilated remnant, a mockery of the original. Except for internal medicine, the few learned

By 1958, there were 100 Ayurvedic hospitals, 76 colleges with 8,500 students, and 115,000 registered practitioners throughout India. Of the colleges, 49 offered integrated courses and 27 taught pure Ayurveda. (Women wait at the family planning clinic at Poona.)

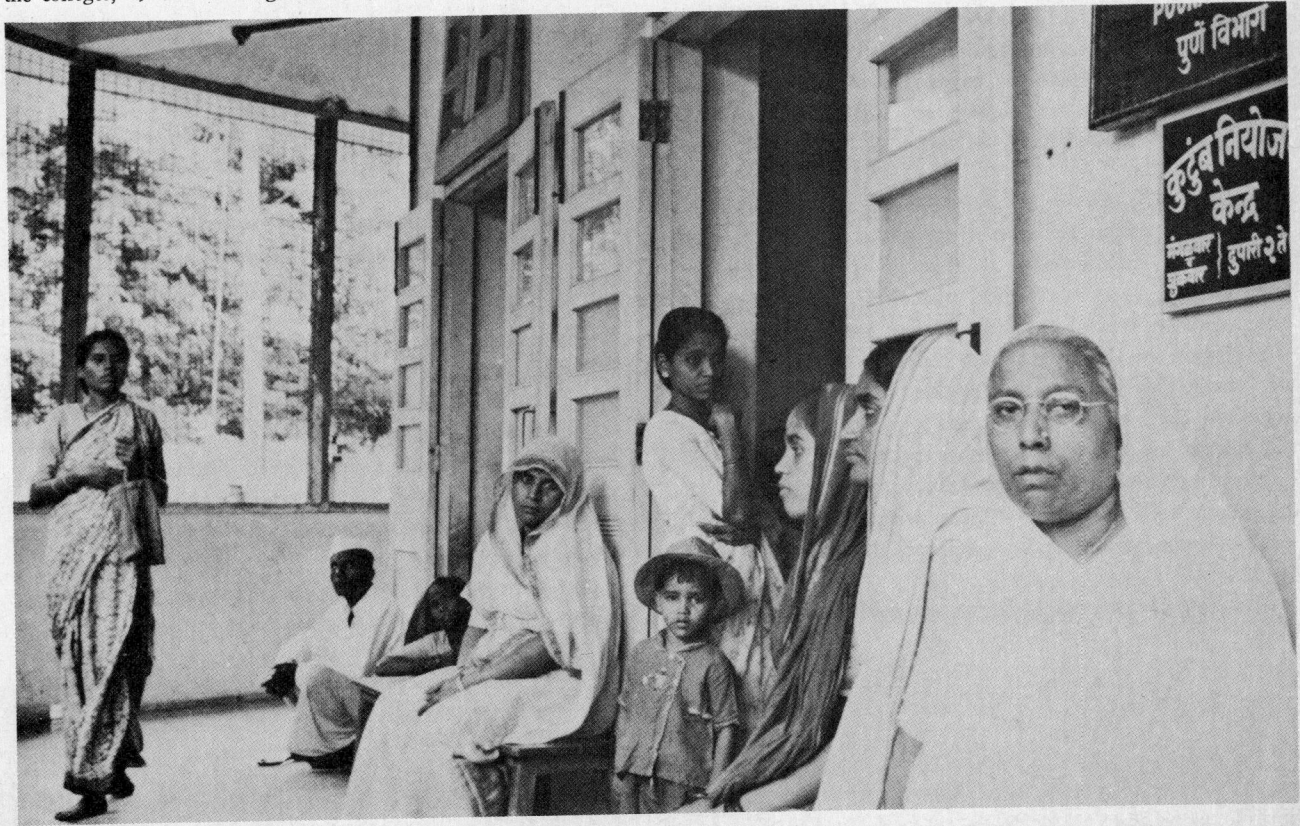

practitioners who remained had lost entirely the art of surgery and most arts of the other branches of Ayurveda. Like dry leaves on withered branches, their rote memorized texts were functionless. Abandoned to folk and quack practitioners, Ayurveda had become a brittle growth on dead superstitions.

The movement to revive Ayurveda began in the 19th century and has led to a dual system of professional medicine. Parallel sets of institutions devoted to indigenous and modern medicine exist throughout India and Ceylon. And these professionalized institutions—colleges, hospitals, associations of practitioners—stand in contrast to the extensive practice of folk medicine. In societies as complex as those of South Asia, these systems are elaborately interrelated, but my task here is to analyze the professional revival of Ayurveda as an example of symbolic traditionalization. To do so I must clarify this concept and a second term, alienation, which will be important for my analysis.

Symbolic traditionalization, like symbolic modernization, is an invidious phrase, implying spuriousness. Both terms focus attention on a self-deceptive substitution of appearance for reality. But symbolic modernization has greater visibility than historical significance, particularly to would-be critics of developing countries. In historical perspective, an oversized stadium, for example, may be a relatively harmless foible; but more than that, even now it might help create a climate of opinion conducive to modernization of a less symbolic character.

Symbolic traditionalization is altogether different. It is a symptom and an agent of profound social and cultural transformation. Its self-conscious forms are revivalistic, and the fact that revivalist movements have periodically swept through Western society from the Renaissance on—in contrast to the near absence of revivalism in antiquity—indicates that in our society revivalism and modernization are associated phenomena. That the association may be one of cause and effect is an impression that is only strengthened by the observation that the expansion of Europe set off waves of revivalism in non-Western societies as they respond to the modernizing influence of Western contact and domination.

Superficially, revivalism seems to be the opposite of ideologies based on the idea of progress. Revivalists criticize present circumstances as a break with the glorious past. They chafe over a radical historical discontinuity between themselves and a former golden age, and they seek to overcome the discontinuity by restoring traditions fallen into decay. By recovering what has been forgotten and neglected, they would regain access to lost sources of power and cultural creativity. In contrast, a pure form of the idea of progress interprets the difficulties and corruptions of the present as a result of continuity with past societies and sees power and creativity flowing from the possibilities inherent in the future.

The idea of progress is the most revolutionary idea in modern times. It shapes the conceptions of reality of many people. But Freud was right when he said that people can stand only a little reality, particularly if the maxim is revised to read, "People can stand only a little of the reality formulated in their world views." We are not threatened by reality so much as we are by our view of it.

My point is that because the idea of progress is central to our modern world view, the chief ideological problems of modernizing communities have been those of symbolic traditionalization, of rewriting history or reconceiving reality in the struggle to create a more tolerable future. Thus it comes about that revivalism is made an instrument of progress. It is a way of coping with alienation from modernity. Yet the instrument may not work, or it may serve its purpose only partially and for a limited time. So, for example, in one phase or dimension of the confrontation of modern knowledge and institutions with those of tradition, alienation stimulates revivalism; but in another phase, as we shall see, alienation becomes the counter-process and symptom of the failure of symbolic traditionalization.

Alienation: A Consequence of Historical Change

Alienation is a state of mind. It is a condition of the soul. It happens to people; they do not intend it. It is a consequence of historical change in which traditions become objectified so that people feel they live in a world they never made.

The model for studies of alienation is Marx's analysis of the consequences for workers of losing control of the tools and products of their labor. If we conceive of a society in which men's necessities and their desires perfectly coincide, we imagine a condition from which any change would create alienation. But there would be little chance for change, for who would be restless in paradise?

But in a far-from-perfect world, social change does happen and it may intensify existing forms of alienation and create new sources of estrangement. Specifically, in the capitalistic marketplace, as Marx put it, the progressive "objectification of social relations" and "the fetishism of commodities" result from the fact that "relations connecting the labor of one individual with that of the rest appear, not as direct social relations between individuals at work, but as what they really are, material relations between persons and social relations between things."

The specific form of alienation I want to describe is to be found in India; it results, as I hope to show, in large part from the objectification of Ayurvedic medical traditions. My account is based upon a survey throughout India and Ceylon in which I interviewed directors and faculty members in 27 schools of indigenous medicine, as well as government officials concerned with regulating and developing indigenous medical institutions. In addition, I visited Ayurvedic pharmaceutical companies and the headquarters of professional associations.

traditionalism in modern dress

The Gampaha Siddhayurveda College at Yakkala, Ceylon offers a four year course of study emphasizing traditional values.

"Ayurveda is not only a Science of curing physical ailments but *a way of noble living* as well." The students should carry "*a distinctive hall-mark of culture and refinement . . . as a sine quo non* of a true Ayurvedic Physician." (From the school memorandum) To inculcate this ideal the *guru* maintains the ancient tradition by not charging his students fees, and by giving them free room and board; "even the Diploma granted on leaving the Institution is conferred on them without any fee or charge." Also, by tradition the college is in a rural setting, religious rites are observed daily, and the students are expected to lead a celibate life. When the student leaves the school he establishes a Gampaha Siddhayurveda Branch, maintaining personal contact with his guru and using the medicinal preparations of the central institution.

Below, the preparation of medicinal wines.

Above, patients on a porch awaiting consultation.

Below, Pandit G.P. Wickremaratchi, the guru of the school.

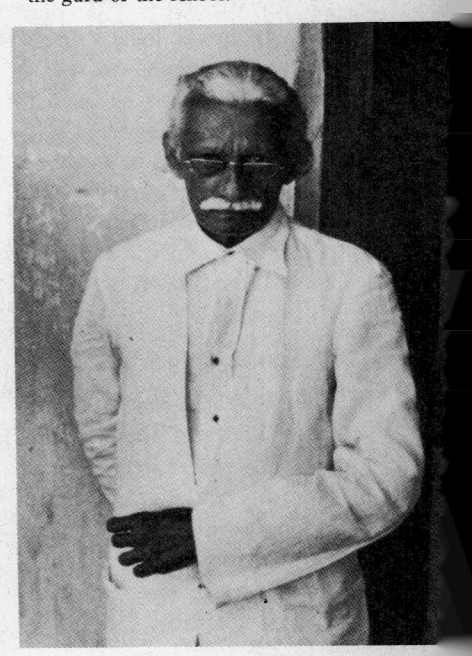

My field survey was made in 1962, before I had studied documents on the 19th and early 20th century movement to revive Indian medical science. Initially, I used the term alienation to describe the pervasive discontent among leading advocates of Hindu medicine, their low opinion of the institutions of indigenous medicine, and their lack of confidence in each other's integrity. My impression was that this condition had developed in recent years, for leaders of the Ayurvedic revival spoke frequently of the "missionary spirit" of the movement during the pre-Independence period, contrasting this spirit to the indifference and opportunism of contemporary students in Ayurvedic institutions. During British rule these leaders had nourished the hope that a sovereign government would patronize Ayurveda sufficiently for it to achieve a creative and prestigious role in the national culture. But after independence, government patronage continued to be guided by modern medical practitioners who saw to it that limited resources were allocated to the development of indigenous medicine. The hope and dedication of an earlier period seemed in

SOCIAL CHANGE

The Chopra committee on Indigenous Systems of Medicine was appointed by the Indian government in 1946. In response to an earlier committee's refusal to consider Ayurveda as part of the state supported medical system, it recommended the full professionalization of Indian medicine in combination with modern medicine.

bright contrast to the disappointment and opportunism of the present.

But when I looked into documents from early in the century, I found that my extrapolation of an historical pattern had been naive. I found that those I had talked to had been inclined to gild the past. The early materials contained abundant evidences of an alienation similar to what I encountered in 1962. This knowledge led me to conceive of what has been happening in this area of Indian life as dialectical: Alienation appears to be a source of medical revivalism and a counterprocess contributing to its failure.

Quacks and Purists

In the 18th and 19th centuries the most obvious disparity between Western and Ayurvedic knowledge was in anatomy and surgery. The preface to Kaviraj Kunja Lal's English translation of Susruta, published in Calcutta in 1911, contained an eloquent example of the turmoil of contradictory emotions felt by this Indian writer on comparing the ancient text with corresponding knowledge in modern medicine:

> To call it Descriptive Anatomy or Physiology, in the modern sense of the term is simply ridiculous. The absence of any reference to brain and spinal cord, to pancreas and heart, in a book of Anatomy and Physiology is unpardonable and in the Sarirasthana we feel this absence almost to despondency. Moreover, in the western medical science, Grey's Anatomy and Kirke's Physiology . . . in their bulk exceeds, each, more than a thousand of pages, and to present to the public, under the same name less than half a dozen pages, as the result of Indian wisdom, is certainly a very miserable contrast—a contrast that is calculated to inspire no admiration. . . . In order to save our venerable Rishis from this disastrous plight, we announce . . . that our beloved Science of Ayurveda is by no means an Encyclopaedic work, but distinctly possesses every characteristic that marks the Science of Biology.

Another writer on ancient surgery in the first decade of this century, Girindranath Mukhopadhyaya, complained that in a nation of people "who are proverbially conservative," the Ayurvedic physicians "are so conservative in their opinions that they cannot boldly advocate even the use of such drugs as are of unquestionable value in the treatment of diseases, as for example, the use of Quinine in Malaria." Mukhopadhyaya advocated the revival of Ayurveda, but he did so with a kind of cheerful cynicism. Again, on modern pharmaceuticals he observed:

> Opium, mercury, and arsenic were unknown to the ancient physicians, or if known, were not commonly used by them; but the modern kavirajes can hardly treat cases without these remedies. It will come to you as a surprise that many Ayurvedic physicians now use quinine in malaria, but though they do not admit it, we should not be astonished to find in some tantras or puranas later on, the properties of the drug described in the form of a dialogue between Siva and Parvati.

Similar accusations of deceit and of self-deception on the part of Ayurvedic practitioners were heard throughout the last half of the 19th century and are still commonly made by men concerned with Hindu medicine.

In response to these accusations, Ayurvedic pharmacies and schools were founded to rescue indigenous medicine from quacks, and to restore its vitality by relating it to modern skills and knowledge. For example, the Aryan Medical School was established in Bombay in 1896 so that "native medical science should be re-examined and revised in the light of Western science." By organizing instruction according to the categories and institutional routines of modern medicine, the hope was to upgrade Ayurveda. The founders of the Aryan Medical School asserted that:

> the class of native vaidyas and hakims have a sphere of their own in India. . . . But there is danger of the growth of irresponsible and incompetent men. The absence of instruction and tests leaves room for unfit men to get into the field. It is this danger which must be chiefly provided against.

This school was founded by a traditional practitioner, who moved to Bombay in the 1860's, and his son, who had earned a Licentiate degree in modern medicine.

Under the patronage of princely states, bourgeois philanthropists, and caste and religious associations, medical schools and charitable dispensaries were founded throughout India in the last decades of the 19th century. And everywhere the reasons were similar. The Maharaja of Mysore founded an Ayurvedic college in 1908, stating, "The fact that Hindu medicine is sometimes practiced by quacks and charlatans is . . . all the greater reason why it should be rescued from their hands and . . . provisions made for combining Ayurvedic teaching with sound European methods." By this time, the All-India Ayurvedic Congress had been organized to encourage the revival of indigenous medicine and agitate for state patronage. In 1910 this professional association established an academic branch to administer examinations on a nationwide basis to practitioners who had learned Ayurveda through apprenticeship with a master.

By founding pharmaceutical companies to manufacture and distribute Ayurvedic preparations in competition with English patent medicines, by founding modern schools to give instruction in indigenous medicine and professional associations at local and all-India levels, medical revivalists were acting as very modern entrepreneurs. But they were also challenging the practice of Ayurveda as they saw it. Their break with the present was justified and dignified by an ideological reversal. They were saying, in effect, "we must break with the present because the present has broken with the past. We are victims of history, heirs of a corrupted medical system. We must renew ourselves by rediscovering and reclaiming ancient medical wisdom, and this is best done by using modern knowledge and techniques."

In Marx's terms, they "awakened the dead" for "the purpose of glorifying the new struggles . . . of magnifying the given tasks in imagination." Modernity and tradition, so often at odds with one another, were joined in reciprocity. Here was the source of the missionary spirit that older leaders of the Ayurvedic revival recalled when I talked to them in 1962 and on subsequent visits to India.

From the time of World War I and the reforms in 1919 that gave Indians a larger role in governing India, the Ayurvedic revival was increasingly linked with nationalist politics. In 1921, the governments of Bengal and Madras appointed committees to recommend ways to encourage the revival of Indian medicine. In this year, too, Gandhi opened the new campus of an Ayurvedic college in Delhi. Several years later he laid the foundation stone for the hospital of the Ashtanga Ayurveda College in Calcutta, but other nationalist leaders supported the revival of Indian medicine to a much greater extent than Gandhi, and the Congress Party passed resolutions supporting its claims for state recognition.

The development of an Ayurvedic college at Poona illustrates the politicization of the medical revival in the postwar period. Students boycotted universities throughout India in 1920 as part of the noncooperation movement led by Gandhi. Political leaders in Poona founded a free university (to use contemporary lingo), which they named

The manufacture of Ayurvedic medicine (above) has become a big business for highly competitive Indian pharmaceutical companies.

While the pharmaceutical companies engaged in testing largely to aid their advertising, the medications of Ayurvedic medicine are being analyzed, tested, and prepared by Government-supported institutions (right, middle and bottom). They have recently set up a large institute at Lucknow exclusively for this purpose.

SOCIAL CHANGE

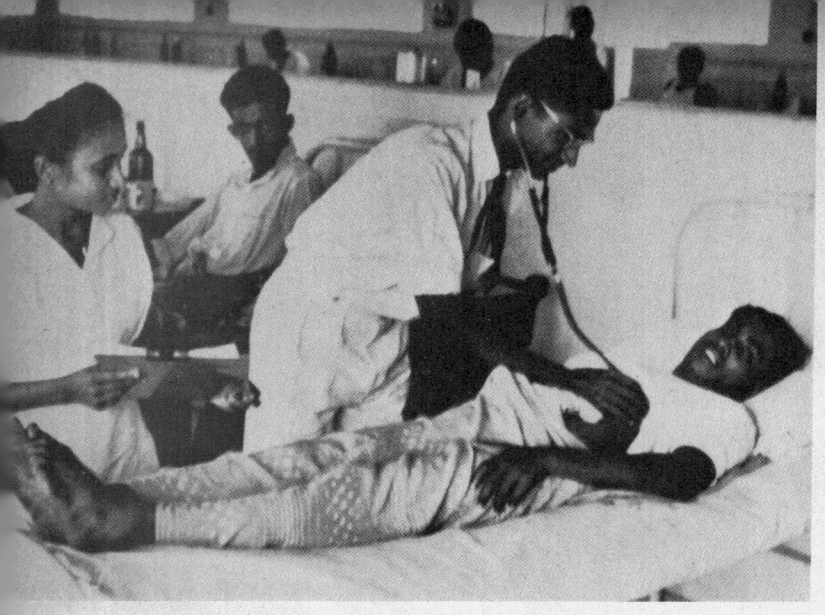

An intern examines a patient in the hospital of The Government College of Indigenous Medicine, Colombo, Ceylon

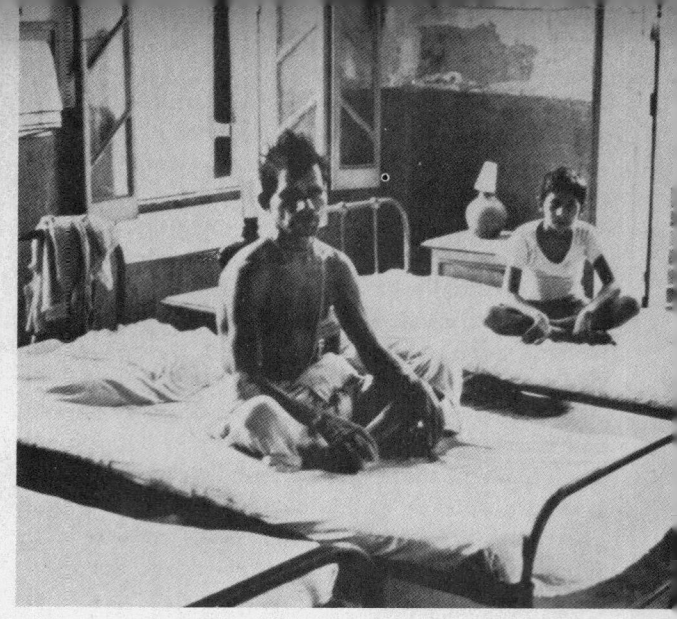

Patients at Vaidya Shastra Pitha, an Ayurvedic College and Hospital, Calcutta, West Bengal

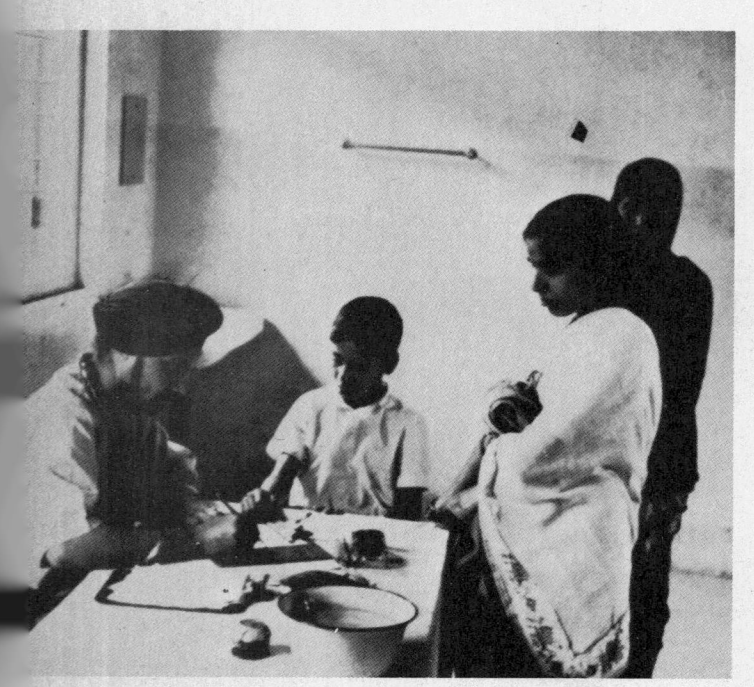

The Outpatient clinic at Poona Ayurvedic College, Maharashtra

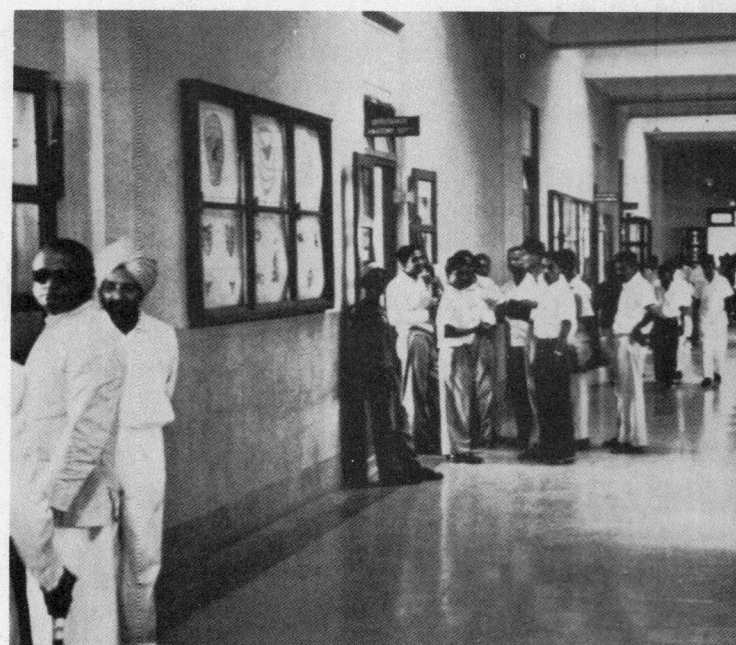

Students at the door of Graduate Center, at the Ayurvedic College of Jamnagar, Saurashtra.

departure from the ancient tradition

for the nationalist hero, Lokamanya Tilak. One of its courses of study was Ayurveda.

The British declared Tilak University an unlawful institution in 1932, and most of its students and staff members were jailed for participating in a second civil disobedience movement. A year later they were released and the corporate society that sponsored the University, which was still illegal, founded a new Ayurvedic college.

In 1937, a Congress Ministry assumed office and soon aided the Ayurvedic revival by creating a state Board of Indian Systems of Medicine with the power to register practitioners, regulate colleges, and hold examinations. The Ayurvedic college was recognized by the Board and, using the profits of a pharmaceutical company owned by the Society that founded the college, it expanded its facilities. In 1955, it achieved affiliation to Poona University and is

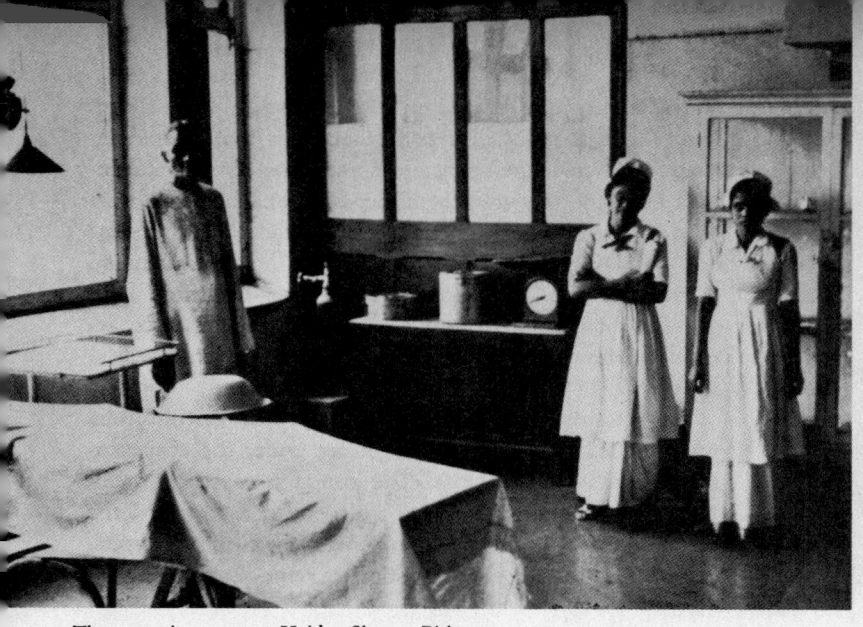

The operating room at Vaidya Shastra Pitha

A doctor and clerk with jars of fermenting medicinal tonics (sweet wines) at The Government College . . . Colombo

The founder of Vaidya Shastra Pitha

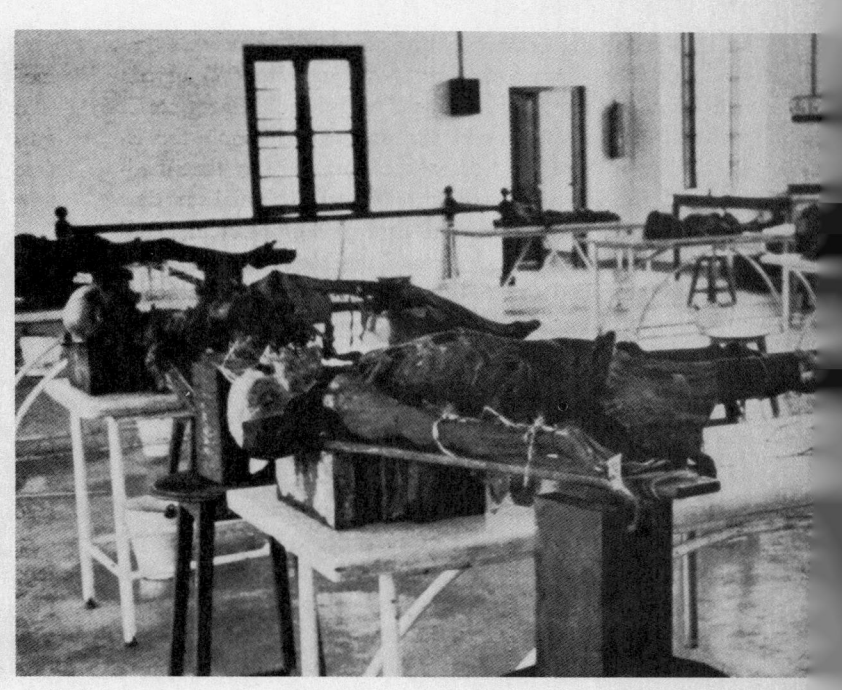

Dissection Hall of the Government Ayurvedic College in Trivandrum, Kerela

Although Ayurvedic institutions expanded rapidly, supported by many devoted people, and made a major contribution to Indian health, they are looked down upon. One critic, a Shuddha Ayurvedist, calls them "refugee camps for incompetent practitioners." Even their supporters have admitted that they are back doors to modern medical practice.

today one of the largest, best-run, and best-equipped Ayurvedic colleges in India.

The drive following World War I to gain state support for the medical revival was considerably aided by the Committee on Indigenous Systems of Medicine appointed in 1921 by the government of Madras. The committee, chaired by Sir Muhammad Usman, prepared a questionnaire in English, Sanskrit, Urdu, and the regional languages of South India, and distributed it throughout the country. In addition, a subcommittee toured India, visiting important centers of indigenous systems of medicine and conferring with leading exponents of these systems and other persons interested in their promotion.

The first question the committee raised was "whether the indigenous systems of medicine were scientific or not." The committee secretary wrote a monograph-length memoran-

SOCIAL CHANGE

dum arguing in a learned manner that Ayurveda was based upon viable scientific theories but that its practice had become deficient. To correct this condition, he contended, Ayurveda should incorporate the technology of modern medicine, particularly in surgery and diagnostics. The committee published the memorandum with its recommendations and other materials in two folio-sized volumes.

The Usman Committee Report was, in effect, a 625-page manifesto for modernizing the teaching and practice of indigenous medicine with state patronage and regulation. It recommended the creation of a Department of Indian Medicine in the Ministry of Medicine and Public Health, the registration of practitioners, establishment of colleges, hospitals and dispensaries, and scholarships for students to study combined courses of Indian and modern medicine. In short, the professionalization of indigenous medicine was to approximate that of modern medicine.

The recommendations of the Usman Committee were opposed by modern medical practitioners, who condemned them as obsolete science and misguided nationalism, and by traditional practitioners who considered them unorthodox. For more than a century the advocates of Ayurveda had been divided between those who would integrate it with modern medicine and the purists. Although the issues between them were complicated by the fact that modern medicine was associated with Western colonialism, they resembled issues at an earlier date in European arts and sciences between the Ancients and the Moderns. They centered on profound differences in men's views of authority and progress. The divergence is made transparently clear in the words of Pandit Hari Prapanna Sharma, who with sixteen co-signers, responded as follows to the Usman Committee:

> In reply to your questionnaire . . . the wording of the second question is enough to show that the Committee is not prepared to accept the third instrument of right knowledge (the teachings of authorities) . . . but would accept only two, i.e., perception and inference. . . . We are very much grieved at your words "How far your theory or theories stand the tests of modern scientific criticism"; we beg to say very modestly that the moderners cannot even comprehend our theories of causation and the modes of treatment. They are changing their ground almost every year by refuting the old theories, and experimenting, each according to his own whims, upon poor creatures, without any proportionate gain to anybody. Is it this that deserves the name of science? Our idea of science is that it should be a storehouse of incontrovertible, universal knowledge which holds good for all times—past, present and future. . . . The facts well-ascertained in our ancient books thousands of years ago have never been disputed, and can never lose their ground, being nothing short of absolute and universal truths.

Despite opposition from the modern medical profession and advocates of *Shuddha* or pure Ayurveda, new colleges were founded in Madras and other areas that offered instruction in modern science and medicine along with Indian medicine; government dispensaries and hospitals were opened; private institutions were allocated state funds; and laws were enacted to provide for the administration of various affairs connected with Indian medicine. Still, government-sponsored health education and services remained overwhelmingly dedicated to the modern medical system.

The first comprehensive health survey in British India was initiated in 1943 by a committee under the chairmanship of Sir Joseph Bhore. The committee's report, published in 1946, on the eve of independence, provided the guidelines for health planning over the next 15 years, except for the indigenous medical systems. Concerning indigenous medicine, the Bhore Committee acknowledged "the hold that these systems exercise not merely over the illiterate masses but over considerable sections of the intelligentsia," but refused "to venture into any discussion in regard to the place of these systems in organized State medical relief."

Ayurvedic revivalists were infuriated, and the central government, responding to resolutions passed by a conference of state Health Ministers, appointed a special Committee on Indigenous Systems of Medicine, with Colonel R. N. Chopra as the chairman. The Chopra Committee followed the spirit of the Usman Committee, reprinting the memorandum on the scientific adequacy but technological deficiency of Ayurveda by the secretary to the earlier committee. Again, though in greater detail, it recommended the full professionalization of Indian medicine in combination with modern medicine. But what is interesting for us is that by 1948, 25 years after the Usman Committee Report on the Madras government, the Chopra Committee recorded that there were in India 51 hospitals and 3,898 dispensaries of Ayurvedic and Unani medicine, 57 colleges with a current enrollment of 3,133 students and approximately 4,000 alumni. Of an estimated 200,000 practitioners, 51,700 had been registered by state boards of Indian medicine. Clearly, even as early as 1948, the Great Tradition medicine was well on its way to rather modern forms of institutionalization.

With independence, state aid to Ayurvedic institutions increased, new laws were passed to regulate these institutions and to register practitioners, several research institutes were established, and many new commissions, boards, committees, and councils were appointed. Even so, approximately 90 percent of the state funds committed to health were allocated to modern medical education and services. In the private sector, Ayurvedic pharmaceutical companies, professional associations and publications multiplied. By 1958, there were 100 Ayurvedic hospitals, 76 colleges with 8,500 students, and 115,000 registered practitioners throughout India. Of the colleges, 49 offered integrated courses and 27 taught pure Ayurveda. This was symbolic traditionalization on a very large scale. But how far had they come from the Great Tradition!

In the place of the practitioner who prepared special medications for each patient, sits the businessman, administering a company that competes in the marketplace with other pharmaceutical companies by advertising and new ways of packaging its products; and, in the place of Ayurvedic savants with loyal students who dedicated their lives to medical wisdom, sit the college administrators and officials in government agencies who look out for their careers and the careers of their friends as they administer institutions, disburse government funds, examine and register practitioners.

In contrast to the guru's household or the rustic school, there are institutions with laboratories and dissection halls. A Shuddha Ayurvedist and sharp-tongued critic of these institutions has called them "refugee camps for incompetent practitioners," while even their supporters have admitted that they are back doors to modern medical practice for students who failed to gain admission to modern medical colleges. For their part the students criticize their teachers. Graduates of these colleges look upon traditional Ayurvedic practitioners as quacks, while they in turn are looked down on by the graduates of modern medical colleges. On every hand, practitioners of Indian medicine complain of a lack of standards, and the educated public makes invidious comparisons between Ayurvedic institutions and the more disciplined, better-equipped, and more prestigious institutions of modern medicine.

Ayurvedic revivalists have built a professionalized infrastructure—the schools, hospitals, research institutes, associations, committees—but they have failed to achieve a corresponding professional morale. The integrationists cherish the ancient texts as much as the purist Shuddha Ayurvedists, so that like them, they find themselves in a world where the authority they cherish, the authority of the past, has been displaced by the idea and fact of progress. Their effort to interpret the ancient texts as storehouses of modern knowledge does not work. Authority has become the authority of the new, and for this inversion of their historical values there is no remedy—not, at least, in the realm of modern science.

And then there is the enormous accumulation of documents, the paper universe of legislative debates, committee reports, professional journals, histories, modern editions of ancient texts, and pamphlets and newspaper articles on Ayurvedic political controversies. Those who love Ayurveda might well find the anarchist slogan appropriate to their ends, "Incinerate the documents." With this accomplished, they could return to the wisdom and venerable practices they long for.

In conclusion, I'd like to pull together the themes of this article. A symbolic traditionalization of health practices has been under way in India for many years. The revivalism that spurred this movement was a response, a way of dealing with the alienation caused by an onrushing modernization. But the effort to restore Ayurveda contained within it an ambiguity that was to result in something that would sooner or later alienate its supporters from the very traditions they were trying to restore. That something, I contend, was what Marx called the "objectification" of human relationships and the "fetishism of commodities," which in our case means the whole complex of licensing, institutionalizing, and standardizing that Ayurveda has been subject to in our times.

Nevertheless, the institutions are there, and will remain in one form or another. The vast majority of Indian people, rich and poor, educated and ignorant, depend upon Ayurveda to meet some part of their medical needs. If I am correct, however, alienation has become a counterprocess to the further professionalization of Ayurveda, and the revival movement has stalled short of achieving a colleague-controlled professional ethic.

June 1969

SUGGESTED READINGS

Traditional Medicine in Modern China: Science, Nationalism, and the Tensions of Cultural Change by Ralph C. Croizier (Cambridge University Press, 1968) analyzes medical revivalism in the context of shifting climates of opinion and political contexts.

Understanding Science and Technology in India and Pakistan edited by Ward Morehouse (New York: University of the State of New York, Foreign Area Materials Center, Occasional Publication No. 8, 1967) is a collection of essays on needed research in South Asia, including research on health cultures.

The Modernity of Tradition: Political Development in India by Lloyd I. Rudolph and Susanne Hoeber Rudolph (Chicago: University of Chicago Press, 1967) refutes the assumption underlying most contemporary studies of modernization that modernity and tradition are radically contradictory.

Medical Innovation, A Diffusion Study by James S. Coleman, Elihu Katz and Herbert Menzel (Indianapolis, Ind.: Bobbs Merrill, 1966). The authors study the innovating process in the adoption of a specific drug by physicians.

The Passing of Traditional Society; Modernizing the Middle East by Daniel Lerner (Glencoe, Ill.: Free Press, 1958). The author analyzes the development of a modern communications elite in the middle east showing the importance of the mass media in the process of cultural change.

Sociology of Medicine by Rodney M. Coe (New York: McGraw-Hill, 1970) is a basic text in medical sociology with a wide scope and many references.

India: A World in Transition by Beatrice Pitney Lamb (New York: Praeger, 1966) is a comprehensive historical account of India.

Village India; Studies in the Little Community edited by McKim Marriott (Menaska, Wis.: American Anthropological Association, 1955). Seven anthropologists report on Indian villages in which they have lived, describing traditional society under transformation.

Behind Mud Walls by William H. Wiser and Charlotte Viall Wiser (Berkeley, Calif.: University of California Press, 1963). The Wisers present a humane account of a north Indian village in which they lived for five years during the twenties.

Why All of Us May Be Hippies Someday

FRED DAVIS

And thus in love we have declared the purpose of our hearts plainly, without flatterie, expecting love, and the same sincerity from you, without grumbling, or quarreling, being Creatures of your own image and mould, intending no other matter herein, but to observe the Law of righteous action, endeavoring to shut out of the Creation, the cursed thing, called Particular Propriety, which is the cause of all wars, bloud-shed, theft, and enslaving Laws, that hold the people under miserie.

Signed for and in behalf of all the poor oppressed people of England, and the whole world.

Gerrard Winstanley and others
June 1, 1649

This quotation is from the leader of the Diggers, a millenarian sect of communistic persuasion that arose in England at the time of Oliver Cromwell. Today in San Francisco's hippie community, the Haight-Ashbury district, a group of hippies naming themselves after this sect distributes free food to fellow hippies (and all other takers, for that matter) who congregate at about four o'clock every afternoon in the district's Panhandle, an eight-block strip of urban green, shaded by towering eucalyptus trees, that leads into Golden Gate Park to the west. On the corner of a nearby street, the "Hashbury" Diggers operate their Free Store where all—be they hip, straight, hostile, curious, or merely in need—can avail themselves (free of charge, no questions asked) of such used clothing, household articles, books, and second-hand furniture as find their way into the place on any particular day. The Diggers also maintained a large flat in the district where newly arrived or freshly dispossessed hippies could stay without charge for a night, a week, or however long they wished —until some months ago, when the flat was condemned by the San Francisco Health Department. Currently, the Diggers are rehabilitating a condemned skid-row hotel for the same purpose.

Not all of Haight-Ashbury's 7500 hippies are Diggers, although no formal qualifications bar them; nor, in one sense, are the several dozen Diggers hippies. What distinguishes the Diggers—an amorphous, shifting, and sometimes contentious amalgam of ex-political radicals, psychedelic mystics, Ghandians, and Brechtian avant-garde thespians—from the area's "ordinary" hippies is their ideological brio, articulateness, good works, and flair for the dramatic event. (Some are even rumored to be over 30.) In the eyes of many Hashbury hippies, therefore, the Diggers symbolize what is best, what is most persuasive and purposive, about the surrounding, more variegated hippie subculture—just as, for certain radical social critics of the American scene, the hippies are expressing, albeit elliptically, what is best about a seemingly ever-broader segment of American youth: its openness to new experience, puncturing of cant, rejection of bureaucratic regimentation, aversion to violence, and identification with the exploited and disadvantaged. That this is not the whole story barely needs saying. Along with the poetry and flowers, the melancholy smile at passing and ecstatic clasp at greeting, there is also the panicky incoherence of the bad LSD trip, the malnutrition, a startling rise in V.D. and hepatitis, a seemingly phobic reaction to elementary practices of hygiene and sanitation, and—perhaps most disturbing in the long run—a casualness about the comings and goings of human relationships that must verge on the grossly irresponsible.

But, then, social movements—particularly of this expressive-religious variety—are rarely of a piece, and it would be unfortunate if social scientists, rather than inquiring into the genesis, meaning, and future of the hippie movement, too soon joined ranks (as many are likely to, in any case) with solid burghers in an orgy of research into the "pathology" of it all: the ubiquitous drug use (mainly marihuana and LSD, often amphetamines, rarely heroin or other opiates), the easy attitudes toward sex ("If two people are attracted to each other, what better way of showing it than to make love?"), and the mocking hostility toward the middle-class values of pleasure-deferral, material success, and—ultimately—the whole mass-media-glamorized round of chic, deodorized, appliance-glutted suburban existence.

The Hip Scene Is the Message

Clearly, despite whatever real or imagined "pathology" middle-class spokesmen are ready to assign to the hippies, it is the middle-class scheme of life that young hippies are reacting against, even though in their ranks are to be found some youth of working-class origin who have never enjoyed the affluence that their peers now so heartily decry. To adulterate somewhat the slogan of Marshall McLuhan, one of the few non-orientalized intellectuals whom hippies bother to read at all, *the hip scene is the message,* not the elements whence it derives or the meanings that can be assigned to it verbally. (Interestingly, this fusion of disparate classes does not appear to include any significant number of the Negro youths who reside with their families in the integrated Haight-Ashbury district or in the adjoining Negro ghetto, the Fillmore district. By and large, Negroes view with bewilderment and ridicule the white hippies who flaunt, to the extent of begging on the streets, their rejection of what the Negroes have had scant opportunity to attain. What more revealing symbol of the Negro riots in our nation's cities than the carting off of looted TV sets, refrigerators, and washing machines? After all, aren't these things what America is all about?)

But granting that the hippie scene is a reaction to middle-class values, can the understanding of any social movement—particularly one that just in the process of its formation is so fecund of new art forms, new styles of dress and demeanor, and (most of all) new ethical bases for human relationships—ever be wholly reduced to its reactive aspect? As Ralph Ellison has eloquently observed in his critique of the standard sociological explanation of the American Negro's situation, a people's distinctive way of life is never solely a reaction to the dominant social forces that have oppressed, excluded, or alienated them from the larger society. The cumulative process of reaction and counterreaction, in its historical unfolding, creates its own ground for the emergence of new symbols, meanings, purposes, and social discoveries, none of which are ever wholly contained in embryo, as it were, in the conditions that elicited the reaction. It is, therefore, less with an eye toward explaining "how it came to be" than toward explaining what it may betoken of life in the future society that I now want to examine certain facets of the Hashbury hippie subculture. (Of course, very similar youth movements, subcultures, and settlements are found nowadays in many parts of the affluent Western world—Berkeley's Telegraph Avenue teeny-boppers; Los Angeles' Sunset Strippers; New York's East Village hippies; London's mods; Amsterdam's Provos; and the summer *Wandervögel* from all over Europe who chalk the pavement of Copenhagen's main shopping street, the Strøget, and sun themselves on the steps of Stockholm's Philharmonic Hall. What is culturally significant about the Haight-Ashbury hippies is, I would hazard,

Hippies reject the middle-class world and its values and choose instead expressiveness, "doing your own thing."

Haight-Ashbury has only one restaurant above the hot-dog stand level, but for a meal of white-bread sandwiches any sidewalk can become a cafe.

in general significant about these others as well, with—to be sure—certain qualifications. Indeed, a certain marvelous irony attaches itself to the fact that perhaps the only genuine cross-national culture found in the world today builds on the rag-tag of beards, bare feet, bedrolls, and beads, not on the cultural-exchange programs of governments and universities, or tourism, or—least of all—ladies' clubs' invocations for sympathetic understanding of one's foreign neighbors.)

What I wish to suggest here is that there is, as Max Weber would have put it, an *elective affinity* between prominent styles and themes in the hippie subculture and certain incipient problems of identity, work, and leisure that loom ominously as Western industrial society moves into an epoch of accelerated cybernation, staggering material abundance, and historically-unprecedented mass opportunities for creative leisure and enrichment of the human personality. This is not to say that the latter are the *hidden causes* or tangible *motivating forces* of the former. Rather, the point is that the hippies, in their collective, yet radical, break with the constraints of our present society, are—whether they know it or not (some clearly do intuit a connection)—already rehearsing *in vivo* a number of possible cultural solutions to central life problems posed by the emerging society of the future. While other students of contemporary youth culture could no doubt cite many additional emerging problems to which the hippie subculture is, willy-nilly, addressing itself (marriage and family organization, the character of friendship and personal loyalties, the forms of political participation), space and the kind of observations I have been able to make require that

I confine myself to three: the problems of *compulsive consumption,* of *passive spectatorship,* and of the *time-scale of experience.*

Compulsive Consumption

What working attitude is man to adopt toward the potential glut of consumer goods that the new technology will make available to virtually all members of the future society? Until now, modern capitalist society's traditional response to short-term conditions of overproduction has been to generate—through government manipulation of fiscal devices—greater purchasing power for discretionary consumption. At the same time, the aim has been to cultivate the acquisitive impulse—largely through mass advertising, annual styling changes, and planned obsolescence—so that, in the economist's terminology, a high level of aggregate demand could be sustained. Fortunately, given the great backlog of old material wants and the technologically-based creation of new wants, these means have, for the most part, worked comparatively well—both for advancing (albeit unequally) the mass standard of living and ensuring a reasonably high rate of return to capital.

But, as Walter Weisskopf, Robert Heilbroner, and other economists have wondered, will these means prove adequate for an automated future society in which the mere production of goods and services might easily outstrip man's desire for them, or his capacity to consume them in satisfying ways? Massive problems of air pollution, traffic congestion, and waste disposal aside, is there no psychological limit to the number of automobiles, TV sets, freezers, and dishwashers that even a zealous consumer can aspire to, much less make psychic room for in his life space? The specter that haunts post-industrial man is that of a near worker-less economy in which most men are constrained, through a variety of economic and political sanctions, to frantically purchase and assiduously use up the cornucopia of consumer goods that a robot-staffed factory system (but one still harnessed to capitalism's rationale of pecuniary profit) regurgitates upon the populace. As far back as the late 1940s sociologists like David Riesman were already pointing to the many moral paradoxes of work, leisure, and interpersonal relations posed by a then only nascent society of capitalist mass abundance. How much more perplexing the paradoxes if, using current technological trends, we extrapolate to the year 2000?

Hippies, originating mainly in the middle classes, have been nurtured at the boards of consumer abundance. Spared their parents' vivid memories of economic depression and material want, however, they now, with what to their elders seems like insulting abandon, declare unshamefacedly that the very quest for "the good things of life" and all that this entails—the latest model, the third car, the monthly credit payments, the right house in the right neighborhood —are a "bad bag." In phrases redolent of nearly all utopian thought of the past, they proclaim that happiness and a meaningful life are not to be found in things, but in the cultivation of the self and by an intensive exploration of inner sensibilities with like-minded others.

Extreme as this antimaterialistic stance may seem, and despite its probable tempering should hippie communities develop as a stable feature on the American landscape, it nonetheless points a way to a solution of the problem of material glut; to wit, the simple demonstration of the ability to live on less, thereby calming the acquisitive frenzy that would have to be sustained, and even accelerated, if the present scheme of capitalist production and distribution were to remain unchanged. Besides such establishments as the Diggers' Free Store, gleanings of this attitude are even evident in the street panhandling that so many hippies engage in. Unlike the street beggars of old, there is little that is obsequious or deferential about their manner. On the contrary, their approach is one of easy, sometimes condescending casualness, as if to say, "You've got more than enough to spare, I need it, so let's not make a degrading charity scene out of my asking you." The story is told in the Haight-Ashbury of the patronizing tourist who, upon being approached for a dime by a hippie girl in her late teens, took the occasion to deliver a small speech on how delighted he would be to give it to her— provided she first told him what she needed it for. Without blinking an eye she replied, "It's my menstrual period and that's how much a sanitary napkin costs."

Passive Spectatorship

As social historians are forever reminding us, modern man has—since the beginnings of the industrial revolution —become increasingly a spectator and less a participant. Less and less does he, for example, create or play music, engage in sports, dance or sing; instead he watches professionally-trained others, vastly more accomplished than himself, perform their acts while he, perhaps, indulges in Mitty-like fantasies of hidden graces and talents. Although this bald statement of the spectator thesis has been challenged in recent years by certain social researchers—statistics are cited of the growing numbers taking guitar lessons, buying fishing equipment, and painting on Sunday— there can be little doubt that "doing" kinds of expressive pursuits, particularly of the collective type, no longer bear the same *integral* relationship to daily life that they once did, or still do in primitive societies. The mere change in how they come to be perceived, from what one does in the ordinary course of life to one's "hobbies," is in itself of profound historical significance. Along with this, the virtuoso standards that once were the exclusive property of small aristocratic elites, rather than being undermined by the oft-cited revolutions in mass communications and mass education, have so diffused through the class structure as to even cause the gifted amateur *at play* to apologize for his efforts with some such remark as, "I only play at it." In short, the cult of professionalism, in the arts as elsewhere, has been institutionalized so intensively in Western society that the ordinary man's sense of expressive adequacy and competence has progressively atrophied. This is especially true of the college-educated, urban middle classes, which —newly exposed to the lofty aesthetic standards of high culture—stand in reverent, if passive, awe of them.

Again, the problem of excessive spectatorship has not proved particularly acute until now, inasmuch as most men have had other time-consuming demands to fill their lives with, chiefly work and family life, leavened by occasional vacations and mass-produced amusements. But what of the future when, according to such social prognosticators as Robert Theobald and Donald Michael, all (except a relatively small cadre of professionals and managers) will be faced with a surfeit of leisure time? Will the mere extension of passive spectatorship and the professional's monopoly of expressive pursuits be a satisfactory solution?

Here, too, hippies are opening up new avenues of collective response to life issues posed by a changing socio-technological environment. They are doing so by rejecting those virtuoso standards that stifle participation in high culture; by substituting an extravagantly eclectic (and, according to traditional aestheticians, reckless) admixture of materials, styles, and motifs from a great diversity of past and present human cultures; and, most of all, by insisting that every man can find immediate expressive fulfillment provided he lets the socially-suppressed spirit within him ascend into vibrant consciousness. The manifesto is: All men are artists, and who cares that some are better at it than others; we can all have fun! Hence, the deceptively crude antisophistication of hippie art forms, which are, perhaps, only an apparent reversion to primitivism. One has only to encounter the lurid *art nouveau* contortions of the hippie posters and their Beardsleyan exoticism, or the mad mélange of hippie street costume—Greek-sandaled feet peeking beneath harem pantaloons encased in a fringed American Indian suede jacket, topped by pastel floral decorations about the face—or the sitar-whining cacophony of the folk-rock band, to know immediately that one is in the presence of *expressiveness* for its own sake.

In more mundane ways, too, the same readiness to let go, to participate, to create and perform without script or forethought is everywhere evident in the Hashbury. Two youths seat themselves on the sidewalk or in a store entranceway; bent beer can in hand, one begins scratching a bongo-like rhythm on the pavement while the other tattoos a bell-like accompaniment by striking a stick on an empty bottle. Soon they are joined, one by one, by a tambourinist, a harmonica player, a penny-whistler or recorder player, and, of course, the ubiquitous guitarist. A small crowd collects and, at the fringes, some blanket-bedecked boys and girls begin twirling about in movements vaguely resembling a Hindu dance. The wailing, rhythmic beating and dancing, alternately rising to peaks of intensity and subsiding, may last for as little as five minutes or as long as an hour, players and dancers joining in and dropping out as whim moves them. At some point—almost any—a mood takes hold that "the happening is over"; participants and onlookers disperse as casually as they had collected.

Analogous scenes of "participation unbound" are to be observed almost every night of the week (twice on Sunday) at the hippies' Parnassus, the Fillmore Auditorium, where a succession of name folk-rock bands, each more deafening than the one before, follow one another in hour-long sessions. Here, amidst the electric guitars, the electric organs, and the constantly metamorphizing show of lights, one can see the gainly and the graceless, the sylph bodies and rude stompers, the crooked and straight—all, of whatever condition or talent, *dance* as the flickering of a strobe light reduces their figures in silhouette to egalitarian spastic bursts. The recognition dawns that this, at last, is dancing of utterly free form, devoid of fixed sequence or step, open to all and calling for no Friday after-school classes at Miss Martha's or expensive lessons from Arthur Murray. The sole requisite is to tune in, take heart, and let go. What follows must be "beautiful" (a favorite hippie word) because it is *you* who are doing and feeling, not another to whom you have surrendered the muse.

As with folk-rock dancing, so (theoretically, at least) with music, poetry, painting, pottery, and the other arts and crafts: expression over performance, impulse over product. Whether the "straight world" will in time heed this message of the hippies is, to be sure, problematical. Also, given the lavish financial rewards and prestige heaped upon more talented hippie artists by a youth-dominated entertainment market, it is conceivable that high standards of professional performance will develop here as well (listen to the more recent Beatles' recordings), thus engendering perhaps as great a participative gulf between artist and audience as already exists in the established arts. Despite the vagaries of forecasting, however, the hippies—as of now, at least—are responding to the incipient plenitude of leisure in ways far removed from the baleful visions of a Huxley or an Orwell.

The Time-Scale of Experience

In every society, certain activities are required to complete various tasks and to achieve various goals. These activities form a sequence—they may be of short duration and simple linkage (boiling an egg); long duration and complex linkage (preparing for a profession); or a variety of intermediate combinations (planting and harvesting a crop). And the activity sequences needed to complete valued tasks and to achieve valued goals in a society largely determine how the people in that society will subjectively experience *time*.

The distinctive temporal bent of industrial society has been toward the second of these arrangements, long duration and complex linkage. As regards the subjective experience of time, this has meant what the anthropologist Florence Kluckhohn has termed a strong "future orientation" on the part of Western man, a quality of sensibility that radically distinguishes him from his peasant and tribal forebears. The major activities that fill the better part of his life acquire their meaning less from the pleasure they may or may not give at the moment than from their perceived relevance to some imagined future state of being or affairs, be it salvation, career achievement, material success, or the realization of a more perfect social order. Deprived of the pursuit of these temporally distant, complexly modulated goals, we would feel that life, as the man in the street puts it, is without meaning.

This subjective conception of time and experience is, of course, admirably suited to the needs of post-18th century industrial society, needs that include a stable labor force; work discipline; slow and regular accumulation of capital with which to plan and launch new investments and to expand; and long, arduous years of training to provide certain people with the high levels of skill necessary in so many professions and technical fields. If Western man had proved unable to defer present gratifications for future rewards (that is, if he had not been a future-oriented being), nothing resembling our present civilization, as Freud noted, could have come to pass.

Yet, paradoxically, it is the advanced technology of computers and servo-mechanisms, not to overlook nuclear warfare, that industrial civilization has carried us to that is raising grave doubts concerning this temporal ordering of affairs, this optimistic, pleasure-deferring, and magically rationalistic faith in converting present effort to future payoff. Why prepare, if there will be so few satisfying jobs to prepare for? Why defer, if there will be a superabundance of inexpensively-produced goods to choose from? Why plan, if all plans can disintegrate into nuclear dust?

Premature or exaggerated as these questions may seem, they are being asked, especially by young people. And merely to ask them is to prompt a radical shift in time-perspective—from what *will be* to what *is*, from future promise to present fulfillment, from the mundane discounting of present feeling and mood to a sharpened awareness of their contours and their possibilities for instant alteration. Broadly, it is to invest present experience with a new cognitive status and importance: a lust to extract from the living moment its full sensory and emotional potential. For if the present is no longer to held hostage to the future, what other course than to ravish it at the very instant of its apprehension?

There is much about the hippie subculture that already betokens this alteration of time-perspective and concomitant reconstitution of the experienced self. Hippie argot—some of it new, much of it borrowed with slight connotative changes from the Negro, jazz, homosexual, and addict subcultures—is markedly skewed toward words and phrases in the active present tense: "happening," "where it's at," "turn on," "freak out," "grooving," "mind-blowing," "be-in," "cop out," "split," "drop acid" (take LSD), "put on," "uptight" (anxious and tense), "trip out" (experience the far-out effects of a hallucinogenic drug). The very concept of a happening signifies immediacy: Events are to be actively engaged in, improvised upon, and dramatically exploited for their own sake, with little thought about their origins, duration, or consequences. Thus, almost anything—from a massive be-in in Golden Gate Park to ingesting LSD to a casual street conversation to sitting solitarily under a tree—is approached with a heightened awareness of its happening potential. Similarly, the vogue among Hashbury hippies for astrology, tarot cards, I Ching, and other forms of thaumaturgic prophecy (a hippie conversation is as likely to begin with "What's your birthday?" as "What's your name?") seems to be an attempt to denude the future of its temporal integrity—its unknowability and slow unfoldingness—by fusing it indiscriminately with present dispositions and sensations. The hippie's structureless round-of-day ("hanging loose"), his disdain for appointments, schedules, and straight society's compulsive parceling out of minutes and hours, are all implicated in his intense reverence for the possibilities of the present and uninterest in the future. Few wear watches, and as a colleague who has made a close participant-observer study

This Digger store in New York—like those elsewhere—does not require customers to take trips to Washington, to confront the warmakers, or to Nirvana, to confront themselves. The stores are free in every way.

of one group of hippies remarked, "None of them ever seems to know what time it is."

It is, perhaps, from this vantage point that the widespread use of drugs by hippies acquires its cultural significance, above and beyond the fact that drugs are easily available in the subculture or that their use (especially LSD) has come to symbolize a distinctive badge of membership in that culture. Denied by our Protestant-Judaic heritage the psychological means for experiencing the moment intensively, for parlaying sensation and exoticizing mundane consciousness, the hippie uses drugs where untutored imagination fails. Drugs impart to the present—or so it is alleged by the hippie psychedelic religionists—an aura of aliveness, a sense of union with fellow man and nature, which—we have been taught—can be apprehended, if not in the afterlife that few modern men still believe in, then only after the deepest reflection and self-knowledge induced by protracted experience.

A topic of lively debate among hippie intellectuals is whether drugs represent but a transitory phase of the hippie subculture to be discarded once other, more self-generating, means are discovered by its members for extracting consummatory meaning from present time, or whether drugs are the *sine qua non* of the subculture. Whatever the case, the hippies' experiment with ways to recast our notions of time and experience is deserving of close attention.

The Hippies' Future

As of this writing, it is by no means certain that Haight-Ashbury's "new community," as hippie spokesmen like to call it, can survive much beyond early 1968. Although the "great summer invasion" of émigré hippies fell far short of the 100,000 to 500,000 forecast, the influx of youth from California's and the nation's metropolitan suburbs was, despite considerable turnover, large enough to place a severe strain on the new community's meager resources. "Crash pads" for the night were simply not available in sufficient quantity; the one daily meal of soup or stew served free by the Diggers could hardly appease youthful appetites; and even the lure of free love, which to young minds might be construed as a substitute for food, tarnished for many—boys outnumbered girls by at least three to one, if not more. Besides, summer is San Francisco's most inclement season, the city being shrouded in a chilling, wind-blown fog much of the time. The result was hundreds of youths leading a hand-to-mouth existence, wandering aimlessly on the streets, panhandling, munching stale doughnuts, sleeping in parks and autos and contracting virulent upper-respiratory infections. In this milieu cases of drug abuse, notably involving Methedrine and other "body-wrecking" amphetamines, have showed an alarming increase, beginning about mid-summer and continuing up to the present. And, while the city fathers were not at first nearly so repressive as many had feared, they barely lifted a finger to ameliorate the situation in the Haight-Ashbury.

Recently, however, with the upcoming city elections for Mayor and members of the Board of Supervisors, they have given evidence of taking a "firmer" attitude toward the hippies: Drug arrests are on the increase, many more minors in the area are being stopped for questioning and referral to juvenile authorities, and a leading Haight Street hippie cultural establishment, the Straight Theatre, has been denied a dance permit.

It has not, therefore, been solely the impact of sheer numbers that has subjected the new community to a difficult struggle for survival. A variety of forces, internal and external, appear to have conjoined to crush it. To begin with, there is the hippies' notorious, near-anarchic aversion to sustained and organized effort toward reaching some goal. Every man "does his own thing for as long as he likes" until another thing comes along to distract or delight him, whereupon the hippie ethos enjoins him to drop the first thing. (Shades of the early, utopian Karl Marx: ". . . in the communist society it [will be] possible for me to do this today and that tomorrow, to hunt in the morning, to fish in the afternoon, to raise cattle in the evening, to be a critic after dinner, just as I feel at the moment; without ever being a hunter, fisherman, herdsman, or critic." From *The German Ideology*.) Even with such groups as the Diggers, projects are abandoned almost as soon as they are begun. One of the more prominent examples: An ongoing pastoral idyll of summer cultural happenings, proclaimed with great fanfare in May by a group calling itself the Council for the Summer of Love, was abandoned in June when the Council's leader decided one morning to leave town. Add to this the stalling and ordinance-juggling of a city bureaucracy reluctant to grant hippies permits and licenses for their pet enterprises, and very little manages to get off the ground. With only a few notable exceptions, therefore, like the Haight-Ashbury Free Medical Clinic, which—though closed temporarily—managed through its volunteer staff to look after the medical needs of thousands of hippies during the summer, the new community badly failed to provide for the hordes of youth drawn by its paeans of freedom, love, and the new life. Perhaps there is some ultimate wisdom to "doing one's own thing"; it was, however, hardly a practical way to receive a flock of kinsmen.

Exacerbating the "uptightness" of the hippies is a swelling stream of encounters with the police and courts, ranging from panhandling misdemeanors to harboring runaway minors ("contributing to the delinquency of a minor") to, what is most unnerving for hip inhabitants, a growing pattern of sudden mass arrests for marihuana use and possession in which as many as 25 youths may be hauled off in a single raid on a flat. (Some hippies console themselves with the thought that if enough middle-class youths get "busted for grass," such a hue and cry will be generated in respectable quarters that the marihuana laws will soon be repealed or greatly liberalized.) And, as if the internal problems of the new community were not enough, apocalyptic rumors sprung up, in the wake of the Newark and Detroit riots, that "the Haight is going to be burned to the ground" along with the adjoining Fillmore Negro ghetto. There followed a series of ugly street incidents between blacks and whites—assaults, sexual attacks, window smashings—which palpably heightened racial tensions and fed the credibility of the rumors.

Finally, the area's traffic-choked main thoroughfare, Haight Street, acquired in the space of a few months so carnival and Dantesque an atmosphere as to defy description. Hippies, tourists, drug peddlers, Hell's Angels, drunks, speed freaks (people high on Methedrine), panhandlers, pamphleteers, street musicians, crackpot evangelists, photographers, TV camera crews, reporters (domestic and foreign), researchers, ambulatory schizophrenics, and hawkers of the underground press (at least four such papers are produced in the Haight-Ashbury alone) jostled, put-on, and taunted one another through a din worthy of the Tower of Babel. The street-milling was incessant, and all heads remained cocked for "something to happen" to crystallize the disarray. By early summer, so repugnant had this atmosphere become for the "old" hippies (those residing there before—the origins of Hashbury's new community barely go back two years) that many departed; those who remained did so in the rapidly fading hope that the area might revert to its normal state of abnormality following the expected post-Labor Day exodus of college and high-school hippies. And, while the exodus of summer hippies has indeed been considerable, the consensus among knowledgeable observers of the area is that it has not regained its former, less frenetic, and less disorganized ambience. The transformations wrought by the summer influx—the growing shift to Methedrine as *the* drug of choice, the more general drift toward a wholly drug-oriented subculture, the appearance of hoodlum and thrill-seeking elements, the sleazy tourist shops, the racial tensions—persist, only on a lesser scale.

But though Haight-Ashbury's hippie community may be destined to soon pass from the scene, the roots upon which it feeds run deep in our culture. These are not only of the long-term socio-historic kind I have touched on here, but of a distinctly contemporary character as well, the pain and moral duplicity of our Vietnam involvement being a prominent wellspring of hippie alienation. As the pressures mount on middle-class youth for ever greater scholastic achievement (soon a graduate degree may be mandatory for middle-class status, as a high-school diploma was in the 1940s), as the years of adolescent dependence are further prolonged, and as the accelerated pace of technological change aggravates the normal social tendency to intergenerational conflict, an increasing number of young people can be expected to drop out, or opt out, and drift into the hippie subculture. It is difficult to foresee how long they will remain there and what the consequences for later stages of their careers will be, inasmuch as insufficient time has passed for even a single age cohort of hippies to make the transition from early to middle adulthood. However, even among those youths who "remain in" conventional society in some formal sense, a very large number can be expected to hover so close to the margins of hippie subculture as to have their attitudes and outlooks substantially modified. Indeed, it is probably through some such muted, gradual, and indirect process of social conversion that the hippie subculture will make a lasting impact on American society, if it is to have any at all.

At the same time, the hippie rebellion gives partial, as yet ambiguous, evidence of a massiveness, a universality, and a density of existential texture, all of which promise to transcend the narrowly-segregated confines of age, occupation, and residence that characterized most bohemias of the past (Greenwich Village, Bloomsbury, the Left Bank). Some hippie visionaries already compare the movement to Christianity sweeping the Roman Empire. We cannot predict how far the movement can go toward enveloping the larger society, and whether as it develops it will—as have nearly all successful social movements—significantly compromise the visions that animate it with the practices of the reigning institutional system. Much depends on the state of future social discontent, particularly within the middle classes, and on the viable political options governments have for assuaging this discontent. Judging, however, from the social upheavals and mass violence of recent decades, such options are, perhaps inevitably, scarce indeed. Just possibly, then, by opting out and making their own kind of cultural waves, the hippies are telling us more than we can now imagine about our future selves.

December 1967

SUGGESTED READINGS

It's Happening by J. L. Simmons and Barry Winograd (Santa Barbara, Calif.: Marc-Laird Publications, 1966).

Looking Forward: The Abundant Society by Walter A. Weisskopf, Raghavan N. Iyer, and others (Santa Barbara, Calif.: Center for the Study of Democratic Institutions, 1966).

The Next Generation by Donald N. Michael (New York: Vintage Books–Random House, 1965).

The Future as History by Robert L. Heilbroner (New York: Grove Press, 1961).

The Pursuit of Loneliness by Philip E. Slater (Boston: Beacon Press, 1970) analyzes the current American character, and, in chapter 5, contrasts the established American culture with the new culture created by the hippies and the young.

The Making of a Counter Culture by Theodore Roszak (Garden City, N. Y.: Doubleday Anchor Books, 1969) investigates how the new culture rejects technology and intellectualism to emphasize the development of other aspects of human existence, for example, human communion.

FREAK CULTURE: Life Style and Politics by Daniel Foss, (New York: New Critics Press, 1971) shows that scarcity, consumption, hyperorganization and repression are characteristic of white middle-class America.

Social Organization & Groups 2

Sociology is the study of patterned relationships of people interacting in groups—from the smallest group of two people to large-scale associations, communities, and nations. The focus of the sociologist is not on the individual per se but rather on the ways in which human beings act as group members in recurring patterns. These patterns of interaction are called social organization. If the ways individuals interact were unpredictable and the ways groups are connected were haphazard, attempting to understand how society works would be impossible. We all know that predictable behavior by others in daily life can and even must be relied upon. Tomorrow's world will at least be recognizable—maybe the same to the point of boredom. The relations of individuals and groups are not haphazard. For example, the student expects his classmates to gather in the schoolroom at the appointed hour and the teacher to arrive sometime before or after the bell rings. Lectures and discussions are carried on in familiar forms, even though there is individuality of style according to the participants or the subject matter under consideration. People learn to act in anticipated ways and to expect others to do likewise. It certainly is not unheard of for a student to fall asleep during a dull lecture, but it would be strange and embarrassing for the professor to do so. Nevertheless, patterns for conducting classes change over time, sometimes slowly, sometimes rapidly.

By and large we take for granted that which is expected to happen and live our everyday existence accordingly. Common sense allows us to live comfortably in a secure world—until a disruption of routine occurs. When militant students interrupt a class with demonstrations and demands for a more relevant curriculum, for example, the neatly ordered world we are accustomed to and consider to be natural and right is challenged. The source of order is abruptly questioned. The old order may seem to stem from the nature of things, but a disruption exposes the true source of social organization as not in nature, but in man himself in his relations with other men. Human beings establish ties with others, cement the bonds between persons, strengthen the attachments within cohesive groups; when discontent sets in, they foster disharmony among members, support conflict between people, and eventually break up the patterned connections. At this point, one is most conscious that man himself is the creator of the social order and the creator of disruption. When he has disrupted this order, he has the task of re-creating it. Man himself is the builder of the society in which he lives. Using the culture he inherits from the past, he establishes organized and recurrent social relationships through interaction. Sociologists call these ordered patterns of behavior in collectivities social organization.

Patterned Interactions

When continuing social interaction takes place among the same people over a period of time, a structural form arises, which can be small or large, and which we refer to as a group or a society. Groups come in many shapes and sizes, and the sociologist has the task of sorting them out—from the nuclear family to the large-scale commune. This has been a preoccupation of the sociological enterprise since Auguste Comte first gave sociology its name in 1837.

An elementary definition of a group is two or more people in interaction. Mere aggregates of people are not groups, certainly not in a sociological sense. Customers waiting for an elevator in a department store, for example, or shopping in the women's clothing department, barely aware of each other and soon dispersed, are not groups by sociological definition. An aggregate of shoppers, of course, does have the potential for emerging into a full-fledged group. Should a group of office workers regularly use the elevator at noon to reach the restaurant for lunch, they might, over time, strike up acquaintances in pairs or larger groups. One task of the sociologist is to specify the conditions under which the transformation from aggregate to group takes place.

Some individuals also share common characteristics, like being car owners, mothers, or hockey fans. Like the aggregate of shoppers, such people are not necessarily group members, even though they have common social roles. All car owners in the state of Montana can be classified in a common social category of car owners, but since they all do not interact on that basis, they are not a social group. Clearly, some car owners, mothers, and hockey fans could change from socially unrelated aggregates into group members on the basis of their interests or roles. Some hockey fans meet at stadiums to watch games collectively where they are not all related as a group, but those who attend as members of a fan club have recurring relations with each other that transform them from a social category into a group. People who belong to social groups are involved in patterned interactions, share some similar beliefs and values, and accept rights and responsibilities of membership and exclude those people who do not.

It is important to realize that aggregates, although impermanent, may be just as volatile, if not more so, than structured groups. Hockey fans who came together in the Forum at Montreal became a raging mob when they recognized the presence of the then commissioner of hockey, Clarence Campbell, who earlier that week had suspended a favorite player of the *Canadiens*. The rioting that ensued, even though it involved almost everyone in the Forum, was still aggregate or "mob" behavior, rather than group behavior.

Personal Relations

Granted that social groups are different from unorganized aggregates of individuals and from people distinguished by belonging to the same social category, it is also perfectly apparent that the quality of interaction also varies greatly in different kinds of social groups. Charles Horton Cooley drew a distinction between primary and secondary groups. Primary groups are characterized by close and intimate relations, particularly where there are frequent face-to-face relations, such as those in the family, a friendship circle, or a closely knit work team. It is the kind of relationship that we call personal, because in it the person is regarded as an end in himself, not as a means to achieve something else. When we recognize, however, that the family is also an institution that society expects to carry out certain functions, then we must also recognize the strong possibility that family members do not always treat each other on a purely primary basis.

Group Ties

Secondary groups involve more impersonal relationships, are organized to seek some common outside interest or goal, and are established for limited purposes by members whose lives are only partially involved in the activities of the group. All large-scale organizations are secondary groups or associations, but small groups can also be impersonal and manipulative. The articles in the chapter on "Social Organization" present various kinds of social groups and various ways of analyzing them. The section called "Groups and Associations" illustrates the significance of group membership of various degrees of intensity and duration. In "Conformity and Commitment" Charles A. Kiesler shows under what conditions the group influences a member to modify his opinions to conform to theirs without openly exerting group pressure. The power of the group, the experiment in student discussion groups suggests, lies in the commitment of the individual to the goals of the group, but more especially to their expected length of association. In contrast, Walter B. Miller specifies the circumstances in which gang life no longer holds sufficient attraction for gang members to keep them attached to the group ("The Corner Gang Boys Get Married"). As earlier associations in groups loosen, the individual moves on to others, finding group membership an important part of his life. A sizeable number of mental patients in the institution studied by Ailon Shiloh ("Sanctuary or Prison—Responses to Life in a Mental Hospital") do not want to leave the mental hospital because it has become a home to them. Despite its limitations, its hardship, loneliness, and even fear, the hospital is an organized solution to their problem. No matter how weak the group ties, they are present and valued by those with few opportunities to establish others in the outside world. People respond to demands for personal sacrifice to belong to groups, as John R. Howard illustrates in his description of recruiting black families to the ascetic and dedicated life of the nation of Islam in "The Making of a Black Muslim."

Another way of looking at group relations is the social context in which they take place. The section on "Population and Urban Communities" focuses on the way groups relate to the larger community rather than on the social relations within groups. Cities abound with all kinds of groups, from informal social clubs and associations to highly structured businesses, educational and religious institutions, and political organizations. The study by Stanford M. Lyman, "Red Guard on Grant Avenue," relates the new militance of youth in San Francisco's Chinatown to the unbending traditional rule of the Chinese Six Companies and the majority political powers in the city.

The section on "Population and Urban Communities" also contains articles that present census data underscoring the

Social Organization & Groups

significance of numbers and social characteristics for the nature of groups and group relations. Using the midterm United States Census figures, Walter Williams in "Cleveland's Crisis Ghetto" found that ghetto conditions were getting worse, not better, in the 1960s. A sharp polarization of Cleveland's black citizens had occurred. While a substantial number had moved up the social scale and out of the central city, the group left behind in the worst part of the Hough ghetto was falling deeper into poverty and despair. The widening gap between the living conditions of the prosperous and the disadvantaged groups made the bondage of the hard-core poor all the more oppressive to bear. In another article on population problems, "Timing of our Lives," Harley Browning draws attention to the social consequences of early marriage and family formation for both third-world and industrialized countries.

Organizing People

The section on "Bureaucracy" looks at the special problems and prospects of the complex organizations that are widely prevalent in modern society. As people come together in large numbers to carry out tasks collectively, they face new and complex organizational problems. One solution is the development of bureaucracy, a form of social structure that aims to use people and resources efficiently. It accomplishes this by defining and dividing the tasks rationally, finding qualified people to perform them, establishing clear-cut lines of authority and responsibility from top to bottom, and rewarding people for doing their jobs well by guaranteeing security and advancement in their careers.

In "Beyond Bureaucracy" Warren Bennis contends that the type of bureaucratic organization that thrived in the highly competitive, undifferentiated, and stable environment of the Industrial Revolution is no longer suitable today and that new organizational forms are arising to adapt to the changing conditions. According to the bureaucratic ideal, policy is made at the top and the rest of the organization is the technical instrument that puts policy into practice, but the piece on "The Power of the Powerless" shows that bureaucracies seldom work that way because people in strategic lower positions can use delegated authority and information about the system to affect policy at the bottom. Another bureaucratic ideal is that there be a feedback mechanism flowing up to top officials, thus cutting down on errors. Julius Roth, in "Who's Complaining?" describes how this process breaks down externally and internally.

In short, organizations of groups originate in the desire to rationalize, channel, and systematize human wants. However, they may, and in many bureaucratic organizations do, end up being an additional form of irrationality, oppressive of the very people the organization ostensibly seeks to serve. This is a major reason why organizational life must be studied in the context of how people adapt to society, and how they evolve informal norms for dealing with structures that may become too cumbersome and too complex and hence beyond ordinary human control.

Conformity and Commitment

Commitment to a group changes members' opinions even without group pressure

CHARLES A. KIESLER

Should I go along with the group?

We have all confronted this question, consciously or not, in one form or another at some time in our multiple relationships with groups at work, in school, in social life, at play, even in the bosom of the family. Will we conform to go along with what others think is right?

People often talk of conformity in the abstract—and like sin in the abstract, they are usually against it. But men face *concrete* situations and decisions every day, often under considerable pressure. What do they do? When will a man change his attitudes and behavior to adjust? To what extent will he change them? What does conformity in this context actually mean? The word conformity implies one of three views of adaptive behavior:

■ The first view (the most popular) holds that conformity is an enduring personality characteristic—that organization men are essentially born, not made, so their seduction to conformity comes without strain.

■ The second view holds that conformist behavior is a kind of tactic—a superficial "going along with the crowd" because of necessity or temporary advantage—without essential change of private opinion.

■ The third is something of a middle ground, although closer to the second. It holds that a conforming individual may actually come to change his private as well as his public opinions and attitudes as a result of continued disagreement with the group; and that this change will last.

In the first view, the natural conformer will try to be like others in most things, finding his satisfactions and support not in personal uniqueness or integrity but in a group identification. There is a germ of truth in this belief. People do wish to be "correct" and in agreement. To some extent we all look to others to validate our opinions. We tend to pick up our cues on proper behavior and personal worth from others. This influence is pervasive and important. After all, the great majority of people conform in rules and customs or our civilization would be impossible.

However, there is little evidence that mankind tends to polarize around two distinct breeds, conformist and nonconformist. People vary in their dependence on, or independence of, the opinions and attitudes of others. They vary in their internal needs and in their perceptions. Thus conformity depends not only on personality and experience, but also on how we analyze our situations.

The second and third views shift emphasis from personality to the situation and how it is perceived.

The second type of conformer goes along with the crowd overtly—while keeping his real disagreement private from the group in question. He is not convinced—he merely pretends he is, whether for convenience or to serve some higher goal. For instance, if a subject in an experiment is told that he and the group would be given $50 if they agreed on some issue, agreement will usually come soon enough.

Does She or Doesn't She?

This second view of conformity is called *compliance*. Its forms and rationalizations are many. People may want to be tactful and considerate, and so pretend to believe things they do not; they may want to get something unpleasant over with as soon as possible; they may be animated by greed or malice; or, as with Galileo disavowing belief in the Copernican theory before church authorities (while, legend has it, muttering to himself, "It's true all the same"), they may simply consider that a certain amount of lip service is a necessary price for peace and the chance to go one's own way in most things. A complier, among friends, may express very different opinions from those he expresses before the group with which he complies.

There has been much research on compliance, most notably that of Solomon Asch and his associates. In Asch's experiments subjects were shown two lines and asked which was longer. When alone, they almost never made a mistake. But in the rigged company of others who insisted that the shorter was longer, one-third went along. Presumably they still believed their eyes, and only their public, but not their private, opinions conformed.

The third view, a logical next step after compliance, has most concerned my students and myself in the last several years. It states that not only the overt opinion, but the private one as well, can be changed as a result of disagreement. Certain consequences follow that would not follow from compliance alone and that do not depend on the presence of the group. If a person changes his opinion, his behavior and attitudes will be changed whether the group is around or not. And this change should last.

Of course, people do not change their opinions easily. They must be motivated to do it. Research has shown that one important motivation is approval—if someone feels that others generally agree with him and find him attractive, he is likely to adjust his opinions to theirs on some issue.

But prior research did not prepare us for a finding in our own work that is more important to us. Our experiments have shown that *commitment*—in this case the expectation by a person that he must continue working and associating with a particular group—is also a major factor in opinion change and conformity to that group's standards. (Elsewhere J. Sakumura and I have defined commitment as "a pledging or binding of the individual to behavorial acts." This is a perfectly reasonable, if somewhat limited, view of commitment, and could include more subjective meanings, such as dedication or resolve. We have evidence that commitment is not, in and of itself, a motivation to change or resistance to change; but the *effect* of commitment is to make particular cognitions, or perceptions, more resistant to change.)

Let us briefly review the complicated experimental procedure that led to this outcome.

The subjects, all volunteers, were told that they would be assigned to discussion groups designed to test how strangers can work together for common goals. Each was told he had to return for four successive one-hour sessions. However, some were told they would continue with the same groups for all sessions (were, in effect, committed to them) while others were told they would be switched later to different groups and had no anticipation of working with the same people all the time.

After a session each privately gave his "first impressions" of the others. He also discussed and ranked various objects by his preferences, including some modern paintings. Each subject was then given bogus information about how others rated him ("Perhaps you would like to see what others thought of you. . . .").

A NOTE ON THE STUDY

This article represents the culmination of a series of studies on consistency, conformity, and commitment. However, it deals primarily with two recent studies.

The first of these, conducted by myself and Lee H. Corbin in 1965, used 180 volunteers, sorted into six-man discussion groups as part of the requirements of an introductory psychology course. Subjects did not know each other personally. They were told of interest by the (fictitious) American Institute for Small Group Research in how strangers worked out certain tasks. They were supposed to rate 10 abstract paintings which, they were told, had previously been rated by experts; theoretically, the individuals and group that came closest to the experts would win cash prizes. Half were made to feel that they would continue with the same group through four sessions; the other half were made to understand that the composition of their groups could and might change and that in time each would have some choice about who would be included in his final group analysis. Half, therefore, felt they would be continuing on with the others, with the problems in adjustment and conformity that this might entail; and the other half should, theoretically, have felt more free of this continuing social pressure.

The second major study, conducted by myself, Mark Zanna, and James De Salvo at Yale and published in 1966, was quite similar in design and procedure. The subjects, however, were 198 high school boys who volunteered to take part in five- and six-man discussion groups. They had been recruited from newspaper advertisements and record shops and did not know one another.

The final study mentioned in this article, by myself, Sara Kiesler, and Michael Pallak, is still in process, and data analyses are not yet complete. Its findings, therefore, while very suggestive, are still tentative.

Thus some are told that others find them very attractive, average, or unattractive. All subjects are told that the others disagree with their rankings of the objects. Then each is asked to rerank the objects—" . . . just for the institute; the group will never see them."

Note that every relevant variable is manipulated: the anticipation of continuing with the group; the extent of disagreement; how attractive the group finds each one. The individuals were completely taken in, very serious about cooperating, and unaware that they were being manipulated. (After the experiment the subjects were informed of its purpose, and the manipulation was explained. We found them intrigued, interested, and not offended.)

Under such controlled and cooperative circumstances we could be precise about what factors produced our results and confident that the results could be reliably applied to others. Our studies also demonstrated that:
—the less others like us, the less we like them;
—the less we like them, the less they affect our opinions.
The more we impressed upon a subject that the group didn't like him, the more he indicated that he didn't like them either, and the less he changed his opinion to conform with what we told him theirs was. This much was predictable from other work. However, we found an important exception created by the factor of *commitment.* Results were not the same in those cases when the person was committed to continue associating with the same group.

A committed person—like the noncommitted—generally modified his own opinions when he felt there was a high expression of attraction from the others. They both also modified them, though somewhat less, when the attraction was moderate. *But at the extreme—when least attracted—the committed person (but not the uncommitted) changed his opinions almost as much as the highly attracted did!*

This fascinating finding is not easily accounted for in current psychological theory. The subject does not like the group; they apparently do not like him; yet they have large influence on him. It is passive influence—they do not overtly try to influence him at all, yet they do. Only the individual knows that he disagrees; the group, presumably, does not know he disagrees and would never know unless he brought it up himself. It is a safe position for him to be in, to disagree as much as he pleases privately without external consequence. Yet his opinion changes to meet what he has been told theirs is.

But this is true only if he must continue with the group. If he is not so committed the group does not influence him at all, and the relationship between attraction and opinion change proceeds in the predictable straight line.

Further, this opinion change is stable—it lasts. But the obvious suspicion that anyone capable of such change must be a well-oiled weathervane, swinging around to accommodate any new wind, is wrong.

The Deviate Ally

This was well illustrated when we told the committed but low-attracted person that he had an ally (a "deviate ally") who agreed with his original opinion in spite of the rest of the group. Previous studies have demonstrated that if a person who disagrees with a group finds he has even one ally, he will stick by his guns and hold out. But with the committed, low-attracted person it depended on *when* he found out about this ally. If he found out before he had changed his opinion, he stood fast, as expected—opinion change under these circumstances was near zero. But if he found out *after* he had accepted and expressed his new opinion, the ally had little effect. Moreover, he tended to resent this new-found "friend" and even to build

"The natural conformer will try to be like others in most things, finding his satisfactions and support not in personal uniqueness or integrity but in a group identification."

up an active dislike for him. Of those who found out about this ally early, before change, 58 percent liked him best in the group. But of those who discovered him late, after change, only 14 percent said they liked him best, and 13 percent said they liked him least.

Let us analyze the implications of this finding a little further. First, they definitely limit the concept that greater attraction must inevitably lead to greater private acceptance; they illustrate at least one significant condition under which it does not. Second, they illustrate how important commitment is for understanding the behavior of groups and of individuals within groups. Commitment obviously can make a difference in attitudes, conclusions, and behavior generally.

It must be reemphasized that commitment makes this difference only when there is very little (or even negative) attraction to the group—the person doesn't like them or the situation, and he doesn't want to keep on, but feels he must. Obviously, therefore, this change of attitude is not what the subject really prefers—it is used only when all other avenues of psychological escape are closed off.

How can we account for this reversal—which seems contrary not only to prior research but to "common sense" as well?

This process can loosely be described in the following way: If a person feels out of harmony with some others or with a group, he has certain alternative methods of response for self-protection or counterattack. He can reject the group—decide to have nothing to do with it, and break off as soon as possible. Or he can devalue it—say that its opinions, importance, and members are of no particular consequence, not worth agreeing with.

There is some evidence that people will act this way if they do not feel bound to continue with the others. But these alternatives are not available to someone who is committed. He must somehow make his peace with them—and with his own concept of himself as someone who acts from conviction.

Appeasement and Aggravation

This is not peace at any price. It is not bland and superficial conformity. As our findings indicate, the important peace is within the subject himself. Also, it takes the long view—it considers consequences for the whole length of the commitment. A person not committed to continue can afford to practice "appeasement"—to bend to immediate pressures in the hope that they will pass. The committed must be much more cautious.

Thus commitment does not only and always tend toward agreement and the easing of tensions. It can lead as well toward sharpened conflict *in the short term,* if this seems necessary for long-term benefits. People who must cooperate cannot forever sweep unpleasant things under the rug.

For instance, how should an individual react to someone else's unpleasant habits or overbearing manners? He can pretend to ignore them once or a very few times. But what if they must keep associating? He may face the same problem at each meeting—aggravated by time and apparent acceptance. This *would* be appeasement in its classical form.

I am now collaborating with Sara Kiesler and Michael Pallak on a series of experiments designed to answer such questions. Specifically, how will people react to a social faux pas made by another? Folklore—in fact, many of the precepts of formal etiquette—suggest we try to save the offender's "face" and "gloss things over" when he is annoying or embarrassing us.

Our data analyses are not yet complete. But so far we have found what we expected. The *un*committed will tend to ignore the faux pas in a private confrontation with the offender; but something very different occurs among people who must continue association. Committed subjects were quite blunt about privately calling the offender's attention to his acts, reproving him, trying to get him to change. They apparently feel compelled to face the problem *now,* rather than keep on suffering from it.

We often notice parallel behavior between husband and wife, people who could hardly be more closely committed. They may reprove each other for acts that each would tolerate without comment from strangers. We usually consider this a sign of breakdown of marriage ties. But could not, as our studies imply, something of the reverse also sometimes be true—a desire to clear away potential sources of friction to make for an easier and more sincere relationship?

It is unfortunate that the effects of commitment have not been given more study, and we can hope that more research will come soon. Any factor that can influence people to change convictions and attitudes is a major force in human behavior and must be reckoned with.

June 1967

SUGGESTED READINGS

An Anatomy for Conformity by Edward L. Walker and Roger W. Heyns (Englewood Cliffs, New Jersey: Prentice-Hall, Inc., 1962).

Conformity and Deviation edited by Irwin A. Berg and Bernard M. Bass (New York: Harper & Row, 1961).

The Presentation of Self in Everyday Life by Erving Goffman (Garden City, New York: Doubleday Anchor Books, 1959).

Social Behavior: Its Elementary Forms by George C. Homans (New York: Harcourt, Brace and World, 1961). An important theoretical statement of the processes behind activity within small groups.

Conformity by Charles A. and Sara B. Kiesler (Reading, Mass.: Addison-Wesley, 1969).

Attitude Change by Charles A. Kiesler, Barry E. Collins and Norman Miller (New York: Wiley, 1969).

The Psychology of Group Norms by Muzafer Sherif (New York: Harper and Row, 1966). An explanation of some of the elementary principles behind compliance among group members.

The Corner Gang Boys Get Married

WALTER B. MILLER

As in the case of many other forms of corner-boy behavior, the motives and circumstances attending marriage are closely related to the conditions and concerns of corner group life. During the steady-dating phase from about 14 to 19, marriages are rare. Then, as the boys approach the age of 20, a substantial proportion of the group suddenly takes the plunge —as if in response to a signal which says, "now is the time for group members to take a wife."

In the case of one gang, the Senior Outlaws of Midcity, the signal appeared to have been tripped off by the group worker himself. Shortly after he announced his own marriage plans to the group, the first of a flock of prospective bridegrooms rushed excitedly into the area clubroom shouting, "Man, I'm gonna do it!" This boy's wedding, in fact, occurred within two days of the worker's. A large proportion of these first-wave marriages took place within a few months of one another.

Furthermore, in many of these marriages, a baby was born within nine months of the wedding. This was not seen as unusual, and deviations from the pattern were remarked upon. The marriage of one boy was reported in these terms, "He got married and the baby didn't come for eleven months! Nobody (in the neighborhood) could believe it!" Another gang boy, who had just married his pregnant girl friend, boasted of the fact that by so doing he was obeying the group-issued signal for first-wave marriages—"They're *all* gettin' married!" A not yet married companion added quickly, "Sure, they forgot to buy safes."

The comment "they forgot to buy safes" indicates that the idea of the "forced marriage" was used by group members as an acceptable explanation of first-wave marriages. One "forgot" to use contraception, one's girl became pregnant, and one was then obliged to marry.

Accidental?

But was this forgetting accidental? And how binding was the obligation? The simple forced-marriage explanation has a number of flaws. In the first place, the boys were familiar with contraception and had been employing it for some years. Despite the fact that most youths were Catholic, they customarily used condoms which they called safes. Having a package of safes on one's person at all times was a badge of manhood. A 14-year-old about to leave for an overnight outing where girls would be present was teased by his groupmates for not including safes in his suitcase, and teased still more when he displayed some uncertainty as to their nature and use. He was later told very firmly by several group-mates, "Always carry safes on you!" Since group members were thus familiar with the use of condoms, it would seem unlikely that about half of them would forget such use at just about the same time.

Forced?

A second flaw concerns the assumption the impregnation forced marriage. Girls controlled few really effective devices to compel the fathers of their babies to marry them. The argument "my reputation will be ruined" had limited force, since a girl's reputation for sexual looseness had little real influence on her future chances. Nor would an argument based on providing a home for the baby be particularly persuasive, since males knew that babies could be and were accommodated quite readily within the female-based household. In particular, the paternally forced shotgun-wedding type of pressure was infrequently applied because for many of the girls, there was no one playing an active father role. Fathers who were in the picture generally did not see their daughters' nonmarital impregnation as a sufficient cause for taking active measures.

It would thus appear that the first-wave marriages, rather than being forced, in fact represented an essentially voluntary act on the part of the males. In view of the weakness of coercive sanctions, of the limited prestige conferred by fatherhood, and of the powerful gratifications of corner-group life —why this collective self-arranged rush into marriage?

Corner gang boys, in common with other young men in their own and other societies, are motivated to marry by a variety of factors: the desire to establish an independent residence, the desire to formalize an existing sexual attachment, and pressures by the girl. For Midcity corner boys, however, there was an additional set of highly influential factors —factors related to the special conditions and circumstances of gang membership.

As the boys approached the age of 20, they were subject to a variety of pressures to leave the physical, psychic and social status of adolescence and assume the status of young adult. The boys' corner gang and its particular way of life was defined, both by adults and the boys themselves, as appropriate to adolescence but inappropriate to adulthood. But making the transition from gang life to young adult life presented serious and difficult problems.

Membership in the gang demanded a high order of allegiance; making the grade according to gang standards and bases of prestige required the development of a particular set of demanding skills and qualities; involvement in gang life entailed a powerful emotional investment. Since many of the concerns and emphases of gang culture were directly geared to maintaining the cohesiveness of the group itself, it was necessary for the boys to reach for external levers to help them to break away from the gang. But the hold of gang values was such that these levers themselves had to accord with these same values and enable a boy to make the break without incurring group censure. Marriage was one such lever.

Marriage alone, however, could neither provide a fully satisfactory substitute for gang life nor a completely acceptable reason for leaving the corner group. Other events such as entry into the armed forces, leaving school for a job, or, in rare cases, entering a post high-school educational institution, often accompanied or served in lieu of marriage as devices for effecting separation. But marriage had certain special advantages as a method for arranging the break from the group and was supported on at least two levels: a less explicit psychic level and a more explicit social level.

The corner group served to provide its members a mechanism of restriction and limitation as well as a climate of nurturance. With the weakening of the solidarity of the gang in prospect, its members were induced to seek out new environments which provided similar elements of nurturance and control. While these elements could be and were found in the armed forces, correctional institutions and factories, the device most generally available and most frequently utilized was marriage.

The Ball and Chain

The postadolescent dissolution of the corner gang was the product of related factors—pressures to move out of the cultural phase of adolescence, the military draft, involvement in the world of jobs, and college entrance for a few. Within this complex marriage was neither cause nor effect; the simple explanation "those wedding bells are breaking up that old gang of mine" could just as well be phrased, "the break up of that old gang of mine is bringing on those wedding bells."

Females were viewed as agents of both restriction and nurturance; the boys attributed to their steadies or wives a consistent propensity to exert strong controls over their actions; while openly complaining about the "ball and chain," the boys in fact demanded that their wives assume many of the functions furnished first by their mothers and then by their gang.

The myth of the forced marriage provided a particularly useful public rationalization for lessening one's loyalty to and affiliation with the gang. Even if it had been consciously understood, explaining one's marriage as a desire to substitute it for gang controls and associations would have been inadmissible. It was, however, quite admissible to represent one's marriage as the product of forces over which one had no control. Knocking up a girl was understood and sympathetically regarded by all; representing one's entry into marriage as an inevitable consequence of pregnancy reduced the risk of being branded a willful traitor or deserter. Boys who followed the route of the forced marriage as a method of weakening corner group ties were often those who had been most deeply committed to the gang and its values.

Once married, the image of the old lady as an inflexible agent of control could be utilized as a device for limiting participation in corner group activities. One recently married corner boy said, "Sure. I'd like to go out drinkin' but the old lady would kill me! She'd drag me out by my ear if I went into the bar!" She was not, of course, strong enough to do this, but the legitimacy of the old lady's demand was recognized by the group.

Shortly after the marriage of the group worker, a member of a younger gang asked him why he had failed to appear on the corner the night before. Another boy very solemnly explained the worker's changed status in these terms: "He's a married man now! He don't haveta account to us no more. The only one he has to answer to is his wife!"

November 1963

SUGGESTED READINGS

"The Delinquent Gang as a Near Group" by Lewis Yablonsky, *Social Problems* (Vol. 7, Fall 1959). The gang is a nonautonomous human group with various prescribed and proscribed functions and activities.

Delinquent Boys: The Culture of the Gang by Albert K. Cohen (Glencoe, Ill.: The Free Press, 1955). Cohen claims that the frustrations of the working-class child, increased by middle-class pressures, create a hostile subculture of delinquency which must be understood to be remedied.

Delinquency and Opportunity by Richard A. Cloward and Lloyd E. Ohlin (Glencoe, Ill.: The Free Press, 1960). A theory of delinquent subculture hinging on the social-structural variable of differential for crime.

Social Class and Social Policy by Seymour M. Miller and Frank Riessman (New York: Basic Books, 1968). An optimistic collection of essays in social policy that treat the poor as a new working class.

Group Process and Gang Delinquency by James F. Short, Jr. and Fred L. Strodtbeck (Chicago: University of Chicago Press, 1965). An enlightening application of social-psychological group-process-analysis theory to the juvenile gang. The authors are also successful in delineating gang members' self-images.

"White Gangs" by Walter B. Miller (*Trans*-action, Vol. 6, September 1969). Gangs have not disappeared. They are where they always were—out on the corner.

Sanctuary or Prison—Responses to Life in a Mental Hospital

AILON SHILOH

It is unlikely that very many mental hospitals remain of the kind described 20 years ago by Ivan Belknap. At that time, hundreds of patients slept—winter and summer—on windswept porches or on bare concrete floors. All of the buildings were old, crowded, and hazardous. The food was tasteless to begin with and cold when served. The total daily budget per patient was 47 cents. On any day, patients had one chance in 280 of seeing a doctor. The basic therapy consisted of allowing the patients to sit on benches and stare at the blank walls.

That hospital represented the worst aspects of the custodial approach to treating the mentally ill, an approach requiring only that patients be kept alive and out of the way. While few hospitals would dare to provide that sort of barbaric custody nowadays, my own research in a large public mental hospital suggests that less obvious but no less pernicious aspects of the custodial approach are still central to mental hospitals today.

What does the custodial approach do to patients? Clifford W. Beers has caught it in an aphorism: "Madmen are too often man-made." Lucy Ozarin reached a similar conclusion: "After visiting 35 mental hospitals, the writer has formed the strong conviction that much of the pathological behavior of patients is a result of their hospital experience rather than a manifestation of their mental illness."

Many observers have tried to make sense of this phenomenon, but perhaps the best theoretical work on the meaning of the custodial approach has been that of Erving Goffman. In *Asylums,* Goffman used his research in a mental hospital to develop a theory of the world of the "total institution," a category that includes not only mental hospitals, but prison, the armed services, and so on. Goffman focused on the world of

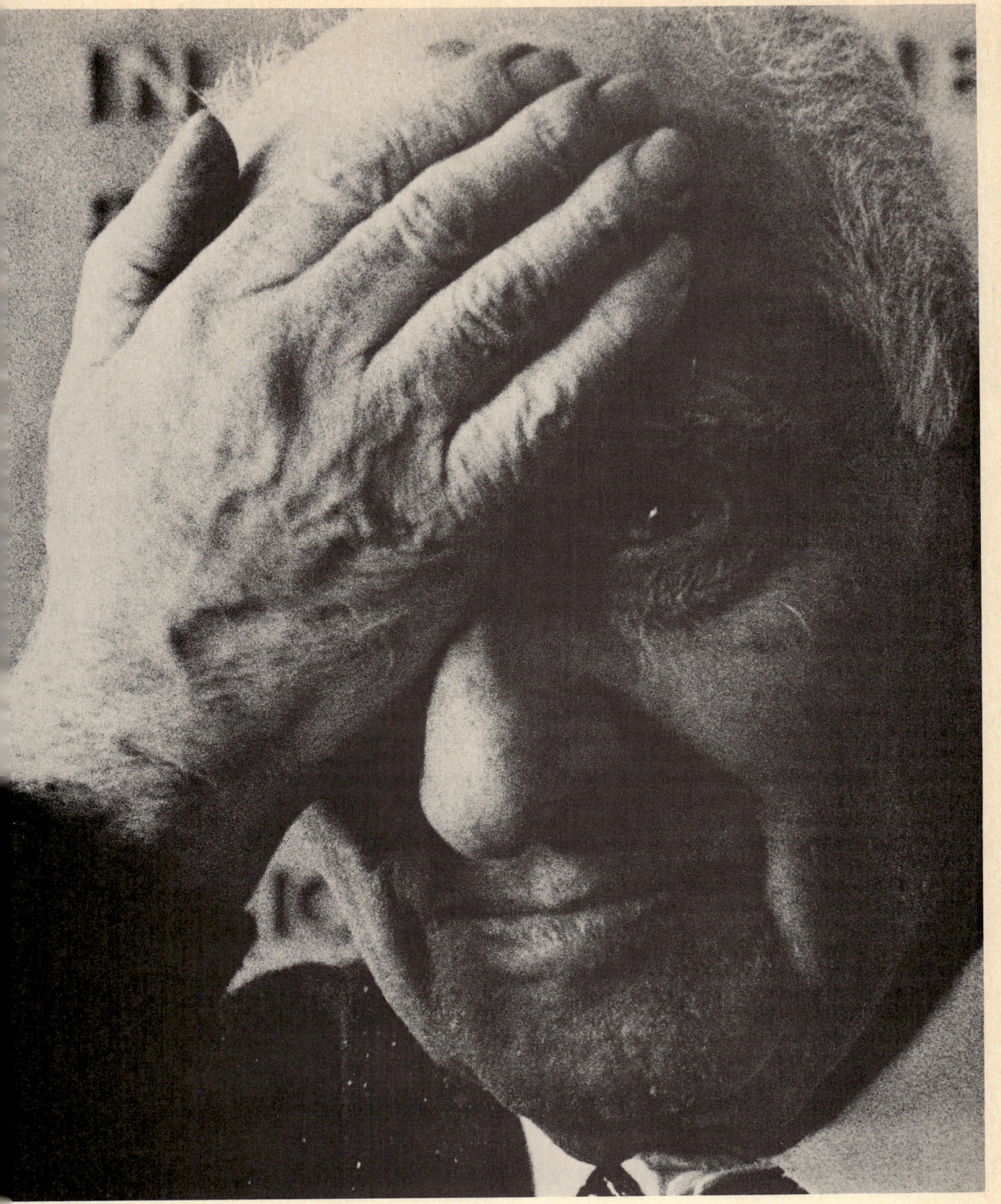

Ed Eckstein

GROUPS AND ASSOCIATIONS

A college student works with an elderly mental patient. Many mental patients—even those who could be rehabilitated for life outside an institution—find life in an institution so reassuring that they never want to leave.

the inmate and the ways in which he transforms his experience with the social world of the hospital into a "structure of the self."

Goffman's major research was a one-year field study of St. Elizabeth's Hospital in Washington, D.C. Since he wanted to give an anthropologist's detailed description of patient life, he did not employ measurements and controls—which, in addition, would have undermined his rapport with the patients and staff. I have employed much the same method in my study of a Veterans Administration hospital.

Goffman defined the total institution as a place of residence and work where a number of individuals in similar situations are cut off from the wider society and lead an enclosed, formally administered life. The key fact of the total institution is that many human needs of whole blocs of people are under bureaucratic control. In the total institution, there is a basic cleavage between the small managing groups (the staff, in the case of a hospital) and the large managed group (the inmates, or patients).

The staff is concerned with surveillance; the inmates with conformity. Each group sees the other in terms of narrow, hostile stereotypes. Their association is marked by misunderstanding and mistrust. Communications from inmates to staff are channeled and controlled by the lower staff with the knowledge and consent of the higher staff. Communications from staff to inmates are also restricted. Characteristically, inmates are excluded from knowing any decisions taken as to their fates, a fact that provides the staff with a further basis for distance from and control over the inmates.

All of these restrictions, Goffman believes, help maintain the mutually antagonistic stereotypes.

This split between staff and inmates is one major aspect of the total institution. Other considerations stressed by Goffman are the nature of the staff's work —their lack of motivation can lead to demoralization and to extreme boredom—and the relationship of the institution to the inmate's families, who are incompatible with the aims of the total institution. All of these factors are particularly important when the institution uses a custodial approach, when it may have no intention of releasing the inmates.

Goffman, having suggested the key features of the total institution, goes on to discuss the ways in which the inmates are "programmed." This process is fairly standardized. The new inmate is subjected to a series of abasements, degradations, humiliations, and profanations of his self. The institutional machinery examines, identifies, and codes him. He is stripped of his possessions and provided with institutional clothing. He is given tests of obedience and placed under a strict surveillance program to teach him how to behave in his new role.

Particularly during this initial period, the inmate's life is controlled from above by regulations, judgments, and sanctions. He must learn to follow the rules unthinkingly. If he does, he will be paid off in privileges —a better room, a little more privacy, a kind word from an attendant, an appointment with a physician. Also clearly communicated to the patients are the punishments for not following the rules. Not only are his privileges removed, but he may also suffer ridicule, beatings, threats, isolation, or difficulty of access to professional help.

Clearly, therapy is not the primary aim of the custodial mental hospital. And if that were not enough, Goffman also shows, the inmate must make a persistent, conscientious effort just to stay out of trouble. Yet this same effort provides the inmate with important—and sometimes critical—evidence that he still has some control over his environment.

How does the inmate adapt to the total institution? Goffman suggests that a person may choose at least three lines of adaptations:

■ He may drastically curtail his interaction with others —what Goffman calls the "situational withdrawal" or "regression line."

■ He may deliberately challenge the institution by refusing to cooperate—the "intransigent line."

■ He may fully accept the values and roles assigned him by the institution—the "colonization line."

Because the institution *is* total, Goffman believes that the intransigent line has to be temporary. He suggests that the regression line is also unsatisfactory: Too frequently it is irreversible.

Yet the staff may be embarrassed by inmates who take the colonization line. When an inmate admits having found a "home," and never having had it so good, staff members may sense that they are being used, or that their custodial role has become all too apparent.

Goffman believes that the colonization line appeals mostly to lower-class patients who have lived in orphanages, reformatories, or other total institutions; or who have grown up in authoritarian homes. These patient have been prepared for their roles as inmates in a total institution. Any attempt on the part of the staff to make the lives of such inmates more bearable may increase the likelihood that they will be colonized.

That is the theory, or at least a sketch of it.

Now, what of the people I studied in the Veterans Administration Hospital in Downey, Ill.?

Downey is 35 miles north of the Chicago Loop. The V.A. hospital there has 2487 beds. It is the largest of the 40 neuropsychiatric hospitals run by the V.A., and one of the largest mental institutions in the country. The hospital's annual budget is more than $13 million, or $15.37 per patient per day, which is about three times the average daily expenditure per patient in U.S. public mental hospitals.

At the time I studied the patients of Downey, 42 percent had been admitted with disabilities connected with their military service, and 58 percent had disabilities stemming from other sources.

In all, my study took five months. By the time it was completed I had interview data from 560 patients, more than half of the men in the open psychiatric wards of the hospital. My core interviewers were two female patients, both former army nurses. Three sets of interviews were given. First: 250 depth interviews about critical aspects of the hospital, for which both closed-end questions, and 10 prepared drawings, were used to elicit answers. Second: 210 guided interviews, with both open and closed questions, to go further into critical aspects of the hospital's operations and into the patient's perceptions of them. Third: 100 guided interviews, with open and closed questions, to find out what the patients thought about alternatives to remaining in the mental hospital.

There were two strikingly different kinds of patients in the hospital—this was the central finding from an analysis of the interviews. About 40 percent simply did not want to leave. In Goffman's terms, they had been colonized—or perhaps overcolonized. These inmates I call the *institutionalized*. Another 25 percent had hopes and expectations of being released. These—whose response does not quite match any of Goffman's categories—I call the *non*institutionalized.

The remaining one-third of the patients either did not fall into either of these categories or shared characteristics of both. In what follows, I shall concentrate on the first two categories, which encompass two-thirds of the interviewed sample.

Many patients could be placed in one of these categories almost as soon as the interview with them began. Institutionalized patients were passive and silent, given to rambling or disjointed answers, and quick to lapse into apathy or noncooperation. Many were frightened by the interview. "Is this material going to be used against me?" they asked. A more characteristic response was, "I'm going to leave the hospital when I decide to and no damn test is going to run me out!"

The Growth of the Custodial Ethic

If my findings at Downey and the theories of Goffman and other researchers apply generally, then a great deal of money is being spent in this country to *store* the mentally ill, as opposed to treating them and helping them return to society. This is what the custodial ethic really means. Where did it come from?

J. Sanbourne Bockoven maintains that the 1830's and 1840's were a golden age of *moral* treatment of mental patients—when they were treated with dignity and considered as guests, and when hospital discharge rates were at an all-time high. This moral treatment did not necessarily consist of any set of therapeutic measures. The assumption was that the recuperative powers of the patient would assert themselves and, if not obstructed, lead to his recovery. Hospitals were small, and the superintendents and staff shared their patients' daily life and living conditions.

But during the second half of the 19th century, the increasing population, particularly of immigrants, exerted such pressure upon mental hospitals that they grew rapidly in size. The physician became an administrator, remote from staff and patients. Attitudes toward patients were altered. As Milton Greenblatt, Richard H. York, and Esther Lucille Brown have written, "Physicians of colonial ancestry who were filled with compassion for the mentally ill who had a similar heritage were often revolted by the 'ignorant uncouth insane foreign paupers . . .'"

As these critical changes in attitudes and size were taking place, there was a general abandonment of moral treatment in favor of a concentration on the organic factors supposedly causing mental illness. At the same time, the philosophy of keeping patients in custody became dominant. The custodial approach thus arose with the arrival of patients who closely resemble those I have called the institutionalized, while moral treatment was reserved for those who match, less closely, those I have defined as *non*institutionalized.

As the Final Report of the Joint Commission on Mental Illness and Health put it, "By the beginning of the 20th century, the profile of the 'state asylum for the incurably insane' was stereotyped, both professionally and socially—it was an institution where hopeless cases were put away for good." This, of course, led to the sort of barbarities discussed in the opening of this article, for when patients are put away for good, it is for the good of society more than for the good of the patient.

Yet, as my investigation of Downey indicates, even after the reforms in the treatment of inmates that have come in the last 25 years, custodial attitudes have remained.

A.S.

*Non*institutionalized patients were far more articulate. They were interested in the study and pleased to have been included in it. Many *non*institutionalized patients dropped by my office sometime after their interviews to inquire about the findings. They gave full and coherent replies to questions and straightforward descriptions of the drawings.

Perhaps the class differences between the two groups throw some light on their opposite responses to the interviews. The institutionalized patients had, for the most part, been born and raised in poor urban centers. Their parents were often immigrants or first-generation Americans; their fathers were laborers or semi-skilled workers. These patients had rarely completed high school and usually held jobs with little security. They were usually single, separated, or divorced, and often lived away from their parents, brothers, sisters, and the like. Compared to the *non*institutionalized patients, they were older and had spent more time in hospitals.

The *non*institutionalized inmates had been raised in diverse settings, urban and rural. Their parents usually were second-generation Americans, at least, and upper-lower to middle class. Most of these inmates were high-school graduates; some had college experience. Most had good, secure jobs. Compared to the other patients, they were more likely to be married and less likely to have had marital problems. Those who unmarried or separated were more likely to be living with their nuclear families. These inmates were also younger, and had usually been in mental hospitals for periods totaling fewer than two years.

Patients' Attitudes Make the Difference

Particularly wide differences between the institutionalized and *non*institutionalized inmates showed up in their ages, occupations, family arrangements, and lengths of residence in mental hospitals. The medical diagnosis that had led to an inmate's hospitalization proved to be of limited significance in determining his general profile, which strengthens the view that these profiles themselves represent reactions to the *institution,* not aspects of mental illness. All in all, a patient's attitude toward his hospitalization most clearly demonstrated the difference between the institutionalized and the *non*institutionalized inmates.

Institutionalized patients considered themselves simply cut off from the outside. They viewed their friends and family in a distant, "I-it" relationship. Downey Hospital was "home" for them. These patients, however, did not seem to identify with the people in the sketches of hospital scenes that were shown to them.

"They" were mowing the lawn.

"He" was in the locked ward.

TV is good for "them."

For *non*institutionalized patients, their hospitalization was an unfortunate but temporary state. They were oriented toward the outside world and viewed outside friends and family in a close "I-thou" relationship. Downey was never referred to as "home." Further, *non*institutionalized patients rapidly identified with the person or situation in each sketch and used personal pronouns, "I," "me," "we," "us."

Institutionalized patients were well aware of the material comforts of the hospital—the good food, clean beds, warm rooms, the free television, movies, and live shows—but at the same time spoke of its essential loneliness and its negative emotional aspects. These patients spoke only occasionally of the hospital's therapeutic techniques or contributions to their mental health. Instead, they emphasized the punishment, the locked ward or electric-shock treatment, and the need to "keep out of the way" of the doctors and their staff.

Institutionalized patients seemed to see the hospital as a substitute for an old-age home, an old-soldier's home, a poorhouse. They were willing to endure the various disadvantages of the hospital only because they did not consider it a hospital.

The goal of the institutionalized inmates was security, and to achieve it there were recognized avenues of adaptation: to become occupied with certain minimal chores and thus ensure a secure role for oneself; to engage in all that was required of the patient, with a minimum of effort or participation; to just blend into the background and stay out of the way; or all of these at once.

The institutionalized patients could easily ignore the sports program. The staff was so busy that meetings between patient and doctor could be kept to a minimum, which often meant never. The workshops were useful places where one could be left alone by keeping "busy." Work details were perhaps unpleasant, but not too high a price to pay for the material returns. The day rooms and recreational facilities were a source of unlimited free pleasure. It was not wise to attract unfavorable attention—say, by sitting on the bed during the day—because of the possible punishment.

Leaving the hospital, or even going out on a pass, were not meaningful positive concepts for the institutionalized patients. Downey was their home, and it was large enough to provide for all of their needs.

*Non*institutionalized patients were also conscious of the material comforts of the hospital, but they tended to view them as the normal services of a modern hospital. They were more conscious of and more outspoken about the hospital's therapeutic techniques, and often evaluated specific programs or personnel. Like the institutionalized patients, they believed that the locked wards and electric-shock treatment were forms of punishment administered to recalcitrant patients.

*Non*institutionalized patients did not consider the hospital a substitute for an old-age home, an old-soldier's home, or a poorhouse, and they were critical of and most unwilling to endure the disadvantages of the hospital. To them the sports program was a possible aspect of their therapy, but the workshops and work details were onerous, untherapeutic chores. They, too, considered it unwise to attract unfavorable attention, and were resentful that it might be followed by punishment.

Leaving the hospital and going out on passes were quite meaningful to them: These events enabled them to renew their "normal" family and friendship ties. Downey, even with its day rooms and recreational program, by no means catered to all of their needs.

The responses to the guided interview in the second phase of the study also showed this essential dichotomy in the way the patients saw the mental institution.

The majority of the institutionalized patients were unable or unwilling to say who or what in Downey was most or least helpful to them. The *non*institutionalized patients *were* willing and able. They even volunteered criticism of specific aspects of the therapeutic program and showed clear awareness of the negative side of their experience in the hospital.

*Non*institutionalized patients, asked about the closed ward, replied promptly and clearly that they did not think that it helped them, and that they did not think all new patients should have to undergo such an experience. They questioned the therapeutic value of the closed ward and said it should be used only in extreme cases, and then only for short periods.

Institutionalized patients, on the other hand, thought that being in a closed ward had helped them; they saw nothing wrong with having all patients placed in a closed ward upon their entering the hospital; they accepted the idea that the closed ward had a useful purpose; and they did not believe that closed wards should be abolished.

Almost all of the patients, when asked about their friends in the hospital, replied that they were often lonely and had few or no close friends. This perceived, and apparently accepted, social isolation on the part of these patients could be a direct reflection of their adaptation to the local culture, or a continuation of their pre-hospitalization social behavior.

The respondents in this phase of the study were then asked if they wanted to leave the hospital and, if so, what they were doing about it. While all of the *non*institutionalized patients replied promptly and emphatically in the affirmative to the first question, institutionalized patients showed a greater range of responses. Some refused to acknowledge the question, ignored it, or were noncommital; others replied in the straight negative. The few institutionalized patients who said they wanted to leave nonetheless contemplated discharge only in the vague future, when the weather was better, or only if en route to another hospital or institution. Very few in either group showed any clear perception of a way that they, as patients, could appreciably hasten their hospital discharge.

Most of the *non*institutionalized patients, when asked what they liked about the hospital, were cautious or neutral, or even had nothing at all favorable to say. Those who had something good to say were almost always thinking of therapy. The institutionalized, however, spoke enthusiastically about the hospital's material comforts, recreational facilities, and the like. The *non*-

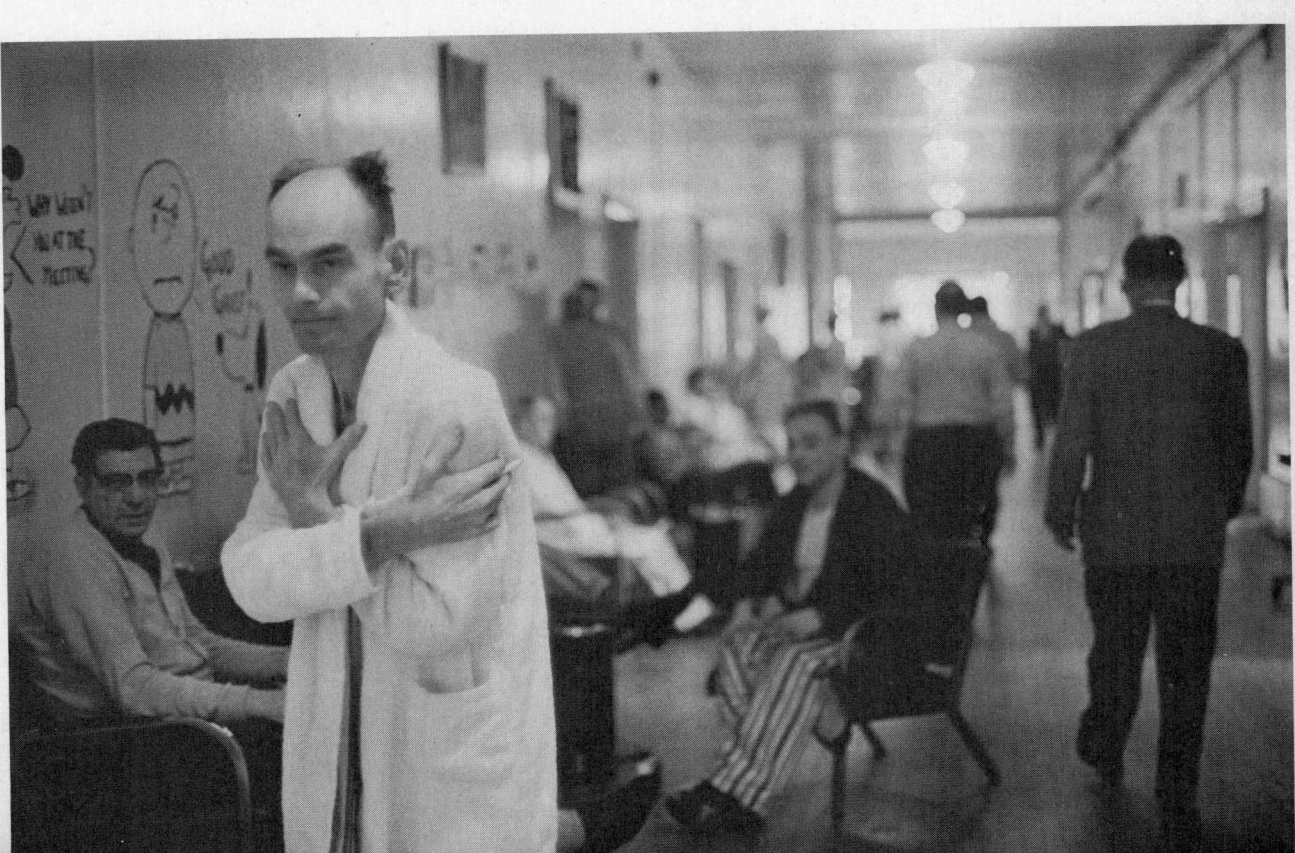

Pamela Harris McLeod

institutionalized were quite ready to air their complaints about Downey, while the institutionalized shied away from a question about what they disliked about the hospital.

If Patients Ran the Hospital

The patients were asked what changes they would make in the hospital if they were in charge. Most of the institutionalized patients were unable to see themselves in authority and found it difficult to answer the question. *Non*institutionalized patients were amused with the idea, but suggested corrections for the problems or complaints that they had previously mentioned.

What was their idea of a good doctor and a good nurse? Institutionalized patients found it difficult, or were reluctant, to provide answers; the *non*institutionalized patients volunteered a wide range of perceptions.

Yet the institutionalized patients, when asked what was their idea of a good patient, were more able to promptly volunteer criteria (essentially those of the total institution), while the *non*institutionalized patients were more uncertain and hesitant in their replies. The institutionalized inmates emphasized proper behavior; the *non*institutionalized spoke about cooperating with therapy.

Finally, the patients were asked what type of help they believed patients needed after leaving the hospital. Institutionalized patients were essentially finance-oriented; *non*institutionalized patients, again, were essentially therapy-oriented.

These basic differences between institutionalized and *non*institutionalized patients were further corroborated by the findings from the third phase of the study, in which 100 patients were asked a series of questions about other therapeutic solutions that the V.A. offers its mental patients.

Institutionalized patients, when asked the neutral question of how long they had been in this or other mental hospitals, replied, perhaps understandably, with vague remarks. *Non*institutionalized patients replied more promptly and specifically.

Institutionalized patients, asked if they considered it healthy to remain in a mental hospital for a long time, saw nothing essentially unhealthy in such a situation. *Non*institutionalized patients saw it as essentially undesirable, as interfering with therapy.

The inmates were then asked if there were some patients in the hospital who were not mentally ill. Across the board, patients from both groups said Yes. When asked who such patients were, it was the institutionalized patients who were better at identifying them. Asked if such patients could be discharged elsewhere, again the majority of the respondents, irrespective of their profile, replied Yes.

The essential difference between the institutionalized and the *non*institutionalized patients appeared clearest in the way they volunteered possible alternatives to remaining in Downey, places where patients in good mental health might go if discharged. *Non*institutionalized patients said such patients could go home; institutionalized patients said that they could go to other types of institutions.

The patients were asked about three V.A. alternatives to the hospital—nursing homes, foster homes, and group-placement homes. These questions highlighted a serious lack of communication between the V.A. and the patients. Few patients showed any clear awareness of these programs, and knew of them only in negative or questionable stereotypes. Using these stereotypes, *non*institutionalized patients had a qualified but positive perception of these homes as paths to ultimate discharge, while institutionalized patients were negative or doubtful.

The Downey program that permits trial visits home was better known to the patients, but again the dichotomy persisted. The *non*institutionalized patients were quite positive as to its therapeutic value, and the institutionalized patients were quite as skeptical and negative.

The night hospital and day hospital were then raised as other solutions to the inmates remaining fulltime patients. *Non*institutionalized inmates expressed general ignorance of such hospitals, but perceived their possible positive therapeutic role; institutionalized patients maintained a consistently more cautious and negative attitude. There did seem to be a tendency for the institutionalized patients to favor the night hospital, which provides full evening hospital privileges with a greater amount of freedom during the day.

*Non*institutionalized patients, asked their opinion of the large-sized mental hospital as a therapeutic aid, indicated an awareness that the patient can too easily become depersonalized and lost; the institutionalized patients praised the anonymity of the large hospital and its extensive recreation resources.

The Finite Approach to Hospitalization

The succeeding question concerned the "finite" approach to mental-hospital hospitalization—that, at first, patients be admitted into such a mental hospital only for a definite period of time, perhaps a week or month. This, of course, runs counter to the custodial ethic.

Institutionalized patients did not agree, and argued for continued indefinite hospitalization; *non*institutionalized patients were less certain in their replies, but thought the finite approach could be far more therapeutic than the indefinite hospitalization process, with its apparent aimlessness.

When asked whether they agreed that, instead of

going directly into the mental hospital, people should have the option of entering local mental-health clinics, neither institutionalized nor *non*institutionalized patients were enthusiastic. Institutionalized patients were likely to perceive the mental-health clinic as a possible block to hospitalization, while *non*institutionalized patients emphasized the general unavailability of such clinics. As with other solutions to remaining in the hospital, both kinds of patients had an unclear idea of what a mental-health clinic was or could do, and they were cautious to negative about it.

Finally, the patients in this last phase of the study were asked their views of how they themselves might fare once discharged from Downey. Institutionalized patients simply did not think they would ever be discharged, while *non*institutionalized patients were optimistic. But though the latter expected to be discharged, they were very uncertain as to when this might be. They expected to return home upon discharge, but were worried about their ability to return to a full role as an economic provider. Furthermore, *non*institutionalized patients did not show any clear knowledge of the resources within the hospital or community that might help them. They were as unaware of the help that they might get after they left the hospital as they were of the resources in therapy that were available within the hospital—another failure in communication between patients and staff.

Today, even the magnitude of the mental-health problem is unclear. In the United States, according to the National Association for Mental Health, at least one person in every ten—over 19 million people in all—manifests some form of mental or emotional illness that needs psychiatric treatment.

During 1962, over one and a half billion dollars was spent on the care and treatment of patients in state, county, and federal mental hospitals. Over one million people were treated. At any one time, there are more people hospitalized with mental illness than with all other diseases combined. Yet by no means do those hospitalized as mentally ill approximate the total population of the mentally ill.

What I have found at Downey—which is not contradicted by other, less extensive investigations of mental hospitals elsewhere—is that this well-funded and well-staffed institution is, in many ways, simply not functioning as a mental hospital.

Despite the essentially exploratory nature of my study, the remarkable finding has emerged that a sizable body of patients (perhaps 40 percent or more) do not want to leave the mental hospital. For a variety of reasons—social, economic, and even, perhaps, medical—the Downey V.A. mental hospital is home for them. Despite their perception of the mental hospital's limitations, of its hardship, loneliness, and even fear, the institutionalized patients still see Downey as the best solution to their problem. As one such patient put it, "It's still better than skid row."

For the institutionalized 40 percent, Downey is an old-soldiers' home with comfortable appointments, but with the constant danger of punishment for stepping out of line. The institutionalized *may* need an institution in order to function, but many of them are at Downey because they do not want to leave, not because they are mentally ill. And those who *are* mentally ill are not yearning after a cure that would require them to leave.

The *non*institutionalized 25 percent have the opposite problem with Downey. They want out, yet they cannot find the therapy they seek because the hospital is run for the institutionalized mass of patients. Unlike the institutionalized—who in many cases have no other place to go—the *non*institutionalized have a shelter outside the hospital to return to, but difficulty getting there.

What I question is the waste of public funds; the time and energy of the medical staff wasted on the reluctant institutionalized patients; and the tragic waste of the *non*institutionalized patients who are eager for a cure that seems a long time in coming. Downey and hospitals like it are not curing the institutionalized patients. Might not another home be found for them, to free the *non*institutionalized patients for treatment, and to make room for those others on the long waiting lists of mental hospitals—who might also be just as ready to be cured if room were made for them?

December 1968

SUGGESTED READINGS

Mind That Found Itself by Clifford W. Beers (Garden City, New York: Doubleday, 1948).

Human Problems of a State Mental Hospital by Ivan Belknap (New York: Blakiston Division, McGraw-Hill, 1956).

Moral Treatment in American Psychiatry by J. Sanbourne Bockoven (New York: Springer Publishing, 1963).

Asylums by Erving Goffman (Garden City, New York: Anchor Books, 1961).

From Custodial to Therapeutic Patient Care in Mental Hospitals by Milton Greenblatt (New York: Russell Sage Publishers, 1955).

Being Mentally Ill by Thomas Scheff (Chicago: Aldine, 1966). Scheff's focus on the significance of external and culture-bound, societal factors in defining mental illness leads to an analysis of the mentally-ill individual as a "residual deviant."

One Flew Over the Cuckoo's Nest by Ken Kesey (New York: Viking Press, 1969). Kesey's novel describes a struggle for survival in a mental hospital; a parable of life in a world of compulsion and conformity.

Social Class and Mental Illness by August B. Hollingshead (New York: Wiley, 1958). Different classes exhibit different types of mental illness, react to them differently, and receive different psychiatric treatment.

The Making of a Black Muslim

The nation of Islam recruits militants to an ascetic and dedicated life

JOHN R. HOWARD

You were black enough to get in here. You had the courage to stay. Now be man enough to follow the honorable Elijah Muhammad. You have tried the devil's way. Now try the way of the Messenger.

Minister William X, in a West Coast Black Muslim mosque

The Lost-Found Nation of Islam in the Wilderness of North America, commonly known as the Black Muslim movement, claims a small but fanatically devoted membership among the Negroes of our major cities. The way of the "Messenger" is rigorous for those who follow it. The man or woman who becames a Muslim accepts not only an ideology but an all-encompassing code that amounts to a way of life.

A good Muslim does a full day's work on an empty stomach. When he finally has his one meal of the day in the evening, it can include no pork, nor can he have drink before or a cigarette after; strict dietary rules are standard procedure, and liquor and smoking are forbidden under any circumstances. His recreation is likely to consist of reading the Koran or participating in a demanding round of temple-centered activities, running public meetings or aggressively proselytizing on the streets by selling the Muslim newspaper, *Muhammad Speaks*.

Despite allegations of Muslim violence (adverse publicity from the slaying of Malcolm X supports the erroneous notion that Muslims preach violence), the member's life is basically ascetic. Why then in a non-ascetic, hedonistically-oriented society do people become Muslims? What is the life of a Muslim like? These are questions I asked in research among West Coast members. Specifically, I wanted to know:

■ What perspective on life makes membership in such an organization attractive?

- Under what conditions does the potential recruit develop those perspectives?
- How does he happen to come to the door of the temple for his first meeting?
- The Black Muslims are a deviant organization even within the Negro community; the parents or friends of many members strongly objected to their joining. So how does the recruit handle pressures that might erode his allegiance to the organization and its beliefs?

Presenting my questions as an effort to "learn the truth" about the organization, I was able to conduct depth interviews with 19 West Coast recruits, following them through the process of their commitment to the Nation of Islam.

Two main points of appeal emerged—black nationalism and an emphasis on self-help. Some recruits were attracted primarily by the first, and some by the second. The 14 interviewees who joined the organization for its aggressive black nationalism will be called "Muslim militants." The remaining five, who were attracted more by its emphasis on hard work and rigid personal morality, may be aptly termed "Protestant Ethic Muslims."

Muslim Militants: Beating the Devil

Of the 14 Muslim militants, some came from the South, some from border states, and some from the North. All lived in California at the time of the interviews; some migrated to the state as adults, others were brought out by their families as children. They varied in age from 24 to 46, and in education from a few years of grade school to four years of college. Regardless of these substantial differences in background, there were certain broad similarities among them.

At some point, each one had experiences that led away from the institutionally-bound ties and commitments that lend stability to most people's lives. Nine had been engaged in semi-legal or criminal activities. Two had been in the military, not as a career but as a way of postponing the decision of what to do for a living. None had a stable marital history. All of them were acutely aware of being outsiders by the standards of the larger society—and all had come to focus on race bias as the factor which denied them more conventional alternatives.

Leroy X came to California in his late teens, just before World War II:

I grew up in Kansas City, Missouri, and Missouri was a segregated state. Negroes in Kansas City were always restricted to the menial jobs. I came out here in 1940 and tried to get a job as a waiter. I was a trained waiter, but they weren't hiring any Negroes as waiters in any of the downtown hotels or restaurants. The best I could do was busboy, and they fired me from that when they found out I wasn't Filipino.

Leroy X was drafted, and after a short but stormy career was given a discharge as being psychologically unfit.

I tried to get a job, but I couldn't so I started stealing. There was nothing else to do—I couldn't live on air. The peckerwoods didn't seem to give a damn whether I lived or died. They wouldn't hire me and didn't seem to worry how I was going to stay alive. I started stealing.

I could get you anything you wanted—a car, drugs, women, jewelry. Crime is a business like any other. I started off stealing myself. I wound up filling orders and getting rid of stuff. I did that for fifteen years. In between I did a little time. I did time for things I never thought of doing and went free for things I really did.

In my business you had no friends, only associates, and not very close ones at that.... I had plenty of money. I could get anything I wanted without working for it. It wasn't enough, though.

"The white man can blow up a church and kill four children, and the black man worries that an organization which tells you not to just take it is teaching hate."—Muhammad Kabah

---

Bernard X grew up in New York City:

As a kid ... you always have dreams—fantasies—of yourself doing something later—being a big name singer or something that makes you outstanding. But you never draw the connection between where you are and how you're going to get there. I had to—I can't say exactly when, 13, 14, 15, 16. I saw I was nowhere and had no way of getting anywhere.

Race feeling is always with you. You always know about The Man but I don't think it is real, really real, until you have to deal with it in terms of what you are going to do with your own life. That's when you feel it. If you just disliked him before—you begin to hate him when you see him blocking you in your life. I think then a sense of inevitability hits you and you see you're not going to make it out—up—away—anywhere—and you see The Man's part in the whole thing, that's when you begin to think thoughts about him.

Frederick 2X became involved fairly early in a criminal subculture. His father obtained a "poor man's divorce" by deserting the family. His mother had children by other men. Only a tenuous sense of belonging to a family existed. He was picked up by the police for various offenses several times before reaching his teens. The police patrolling his neighborhood eventually restricted him to a two-block area. There was, of course, no legal basis for this, but he was manhandled if seen outside that area by any policeman who knew him. He graduated in his late teens from "pot" to "shooting shit" and eventually spent time in Lexington.

William 2X, formerly a shoeshine boy, related the development of his perspective this way:

You know how they always talk about us running after white women. There have always been a lot of [white]

servicemen in this town—half of them would get around to asking me to get a woman for them. Some of them right out, some of them backing into it, laughing and joking and letting me know how much they were my friend, building up to asking me where they could find some woman. After a while I began to get them for them. I ran women—both black and white. . . . What I hated was they wanted me to do something for them [find women] and hated me for doing it. They figure "any nigger must know where to find it. . . ."

Things Begin to Add Up

Amos X grew up in an all-Negro town in Oklahoma and attended a Negro college. Because of this, he had almost no contact with whites during his formative years.

One of my aunts lived in Tulsa. I went to see her once when I was in college. I walked up to the front door of the house where she worked. She really got excited and told me if I came to see her anymore to come around to the back. But that didn't mean much to me at the time. It is only in looking back on it that all these things begin to add up.

After graduating from college, Amos joined the Marines. There he began to "see how they [the whites] really felt" about him; by the end of his tour, he had concluded that "the white man is the greatest liar, the greatest cheat, the greatest hypocrite on earth." Alienated and disillusioned, he turned to professional gambling. Then, in an attempt at a more conventional way of life, he married and took a job teaching school.

I taught English. Now I'm no expert in the slave masters' language, but I knew the way those kids talked after being in school eight and nine years was ridiculous. They said things like "mens" for "men." I drilled them and pretty soon some of them at least in class began to sound like they had been inside a school. Now the principal taught a senior class in English and his kids talked as bad as mine. When I began to straighten out his kids also he felt I was criticizing him. . . . That little black man was afraid of the [white] superintendent and all those teachers were afraid. They had a little more than other so-called Negroes and didn't give a damn about those black children they were teaching. Those were the wages of honesty. It's one thing to want to do an honest job and another thing to be able to. . . .

With the collapse of his career as a public school teacher and the break-up of his marriage, Amos went to California, where he was introduced to the Muslim movement.

I first heard about them [the Muslims] in 1961. There was a debate here between a Muslim and a Christian

"Most of the Protestant Ethic Muslims had joined the Nation because, at some point, they began to feel the need of organizational support for their personal systems of value."

Eve Arnold MAGNUM

minister. The Muslims said all the things about Christianity which I had been thinking but which I had never heard anyone say before. He tore the minister up.

Finding an organization that aggressively rejected the white man and the white man's religion, Amos found his own point of view crystallized. He joined without hesitation.

Norman Maghid first heard of the Muslims while he was in prison.

I ran into one of the Brothers selling the paper about two weeks after I got out and asked him about the meetings. Whether a guy could just go and walk in. He told me about the meetings so I made it around on a Wednesday evening. I wasn't even bugged when they searched me. When they asked me about taking out my letter [joining the organization] I took one out. They seemed to know what they were talking about. I never believed in nonviolence and love my enemies, especially when my enemies don't love me.

Muhammad Soule Kabah, born into a family of debt-ridden Texas sharecroppers, was recruited into the Nation of Islam after moving to California.

I read a series of articles in the Los Angeles *Herald Dispatch,* an exchange between Minister Henry and a Christian minister. It confirmed what my grandfather had told me about my African heritage, that I had nothing to be ashamed of, that there were six thousand books on mathematics in the Library of the University of Timbucktoo while Europeans were still wearing skins. Also my father had taught me never to kow-tow to whites. My own father had fallen away. My parents didn't want me to join the Nation. They said they taught hate. That's funny isn't it? The white man can blow up a church and kill four children and the black man worries that an organization which tells you not to just take it is teaching hate.

Protestant Ethic Muslims: Up by Black Bootstraps

The Protestant Ethic Muslims all came from backgrounds with a strong tradition of Negro self-help. In two cases, the recruit's parents had been followers of Marcus Garvey; another recruit explicitly endorsed the beliefs of Booker T. Washington; and the remaining two, coming from upwardly mobile families, were firm in the belief that Negroes could achieve higher status if they were willing to work for it.

When asked what had appealed to him about the Muslims, Norman X replied:

They thought that black people should do something for themselves. I was running this small place [a photog-

"Muslim doctrine assumes that there is a single ultimate system of truth. Elijah Muhammad and, by delegation, his ministers are in possession of this truth."

Eve Arnold MAGNUM

raphy shop] and trying to get by. I've stuck with this place even when it was paying me barely enough to eat. Things always improve and I don't have to go to the white man for anything.

Ernestine X stressed similar reasons for joining the Muslims.

You learned to stand up straight and do something for yourself. You learn to be a lady at all times—to keep your house clean—to teach your children good manners. There is not a girl in the M-G-T who does not know how to cook and sew. The children are very respectful; they speak only when they are spoken to. There is no such thing as letting your children talk back to you the way some people believe. The one thing they feel is the Negroes' downfall is men and sex for the women, and women and sex for the men, and they frown on sex completely unless you are married.

Despite their middle-class attitudes in many areas, Protestant Ethic Muslims denounced moderate, traditional civil rights organizations such as the NAACP, just as vigorously as the militant Muslims did. Norman X said that he had once belonged to the NAACP but had dropped out.

They spent most of their time planning the annual brotherhood dinner. Besides it was mostly whites—whites and the colored doctors and lawyers who wanted to be white. As far as most Negroes were concerned they might as well not have existed.

Lindsey X, who had owned and run his own upholstery shop for more than 30 years, viewed the conventional black bourgeoisie with equal resentment.

I never belonged to the NAACP. What they wanted never seemed real to me. I think Negroes should create jobs for themselves rather than going begging for them. That's why I never supported CORE.

In this respect Norman and Lindsey were in full accord with the more militant Amos X, who asserted:

They [the NAACP and CORE] help just one class of people. . . . Let something happen to a doctor and they are right there; but if something happens to Old Mose on the corner, you can't find them.

The interviews made it clear that most of the Protestant Ethic Muslims had joined the Nation because, at some point, they began to feel the need of organizational support for their personal systems of value. For Norman and Lindsey, it was an attempt to stop what they considered their own backsliding after coming to California. Both mentioned drinking to excess and indulging in what they regarded as a profligate way of life. Guilt feelings apparently led them to seek Muslim support in returning to more enterprising habits.

Commitment to Deviance

The Nation of Islam is a deviant organization. As such it is subject to public scorn and ridicule. Thus it faces the problem of consolidating the recruit's allegiance in an environment where substantial pressures operate to erode this allegiance. How does it deal with this problem?

The structural characteristics of the Nation tend to insulate the member from the hostility of the larger society and thus contribute to the organization's survival. To begin with, the ritual of joining the organization itself stresses commitment without questions.

At the end of the general address at a temple meeting, the minister asks those nonmembers present who are "interested in learning more about Islam" to step to the

---

"The NAACP spent most of their time planning the annual brotherhood dinner. Besides it was mostly whites—whites and the colored doctors and lawyers who wanted to be white. As far as most Negroes were concerned they might as well not have existed."—Norman X

---

back of the temple. There they are given three blank sheets of ordinary stationery and a form letter addressed to Elijah Muhammad in Chicago:

Dear Savior Allah, Our Deliverer:

I have attended the Teachings of Islam, two or three times, as taught by one of your ministers. I believe in it. I bear witness that there is no God but Thee. And, that Muhammad is Thy Servant and Apostle. I desire to reclaim my Own. Please give me my Original name. My slave name is as follows:

The applicant is instructed to copy this letter verbatim on each of the three sheets of paper, giving his own name and address unabbreviated at the bottom. If he fails to copy the letter perfectly, he must repeat the whole task. No explanation is given for any of these requirements.

Formal acceptance of his letter makes the new member a Muslim, but in name only. Real commitment to the Nation of Islam comes gradually—for example, the personal commitment expressed when a chain smoker gives up cigarettes in accordance with the Muslim rules even though he knows that he could smoke unobserved. "It's not that easy to do these things," Stanley X said of the various forms of abstinence practiced by Muslims. "It takes will and discipline and time, . . . but you're a much better person after you do." Calvin X told of periodic backsliding in the beginning, but added, "Once I got into the thing deep, then I stuck with it."

This commitment and the new regimen that goes with it have been credited with effecting dramatic personality changes in many members, freeing alcoholics from the bottle and drug addicts from the needle. It can be argued, however, that the organization does not change the member's fundamental orientation. To put it somewhat differently, given needs and impulses can be expressed in a variety of ways; thus, a man may give vent to his sadism by beating up strangers in an alley or by joining the police force and beating them up in the back room of the station.

"Getting into the thing deep" for a Muslim usually comes in three stages:
- Participation in organizational activities—selling the Muslim newspaper, dining at the Muslim restaurant, attending and helping run Muslim meetings.
- Isolation from non-Muslim social contacts—drifting away from former friends and associates because of divergent attitudes or simply because of the time consumed in Muslim activities.
- Assimilation of the ideology—marking full commitment, when a Muslim has so absorbed the organization's doctrines that he automatically uses them to guide his own behavior and to interpret what happens in the world around him.

The fact that the organization can provide a full social life furthers isolation from non-Muslims. Participation is not wholly a matter of drudgery, of tramping the streets to sell the paper and studying the ideology. The organization presents programs of entertainment for its members and the public. For example, in two West Coast cities a Negro theatrical troupe called the Touring Artists put on two plays, "Jubilee Day" and "Don't You Want to Be Free." Although there was a high element of humor in both plays, the basic themes—white brutality and hypocrisy and the necessity of developing Negro self-respect and courage—were consonant with the organization's perspective. Thus the organization makes it possible for a member to satisfy his need for diversion without going outside to do so. At the same time, it continually reaches him with its message through the didactic element in such entertainment.

Carl X's experiences were typical of the recruit's growing commitment to the Nation. When asked what his friends had thought when he first joined, he replied: "They thought I was crazy. They said, 'Man, how can you believe all that stuff?'" He then commented that he no longer saw much of them, and added:

When you start going to the temple four or five times a week and selling the newspaper you do not have time for people who are not doing these things. We drifted—the friends I had—we drifted apart. . . . All the friends I have now are in the Nation. Another Brother and I get together regularly and read the Koran and other books, then ask each other questions on them like, "What is Allah's greatest weapon? The truth. What is the devil's greatest weapon? The truth. The devil keeps it hidden from men. Allah reveals it to man." We read and talk about the things we read and try to sharpen our thinking. I couldn't do that with my old friends.

Spelled out, the "stuff" that Carl X had come to believe, the official Muslim ideology, is this:
- The so-called Negro, the American black man, is lost in ignorance. He is unaware of his own past history and the future role which history has destined him to play.
- Elijah Muhammad has come as the Messenger of Allah to awaken the American black man.
- The American black man finds himself now in a lowly state, but that was not always his condition.
- The Original Man, the first men to populate the earth, were non-white. They enjoyed a high level of culture and reached high peaks of achievement.
- A little over 6,000 years ago a black scientist named Yakub, after considerable work, produced a mutant, a new race, the white race.

"There was a debate between a Muslim and a Christian minister. The Muslim said all the things about Christianity which I had been thinking. He tore the minister up."—Amos X

- This new race was inferior mentally, physically, and morally to the black race. Their very whiteness, the very mark of their difference from the black race, was an indication of their physical degeneracy and moral depravity.
- Allah, in anger at Yakub's work, ordained that the white race should rule for a fixed amount of time and that the black man should suffer and by his suffering gain a greater appreciation of his own spiritual worth by comparing himself to the whites.
- The time of white dominance is drawing near its end. It is foreordained that this race shall perish, and with its destruction the havoc, terror, and brutality which it has spread throughout the world shall disappear.
- The major task facing the Nation of Islam is to awaken the American black man to his destiny, to acquaint him with the course of history.
- The Nation of Islam in pursuing this task must battle against false prophets, in particular those who call for integration. Integration is a plot of the white race to forestall its own doom. The black bourgeoisie, bought off by a few paltry favors and attempting to ingratiate themselves with the whites, seek to spread this pernicious doctrine among so-called Negroes.
- The Nation of Islam must encourage the American black man to begin now to assume his proper role by wresting economic control from the whites. The American black man must gain control over his own economic fortunes by going into business for himself and becoming economically strong.
- The Nation of Islam must encourage the so-called Negro to give up those habits which have been spread among them by the whites as part of the effort to keep them weak, diseased, and demoralized. The so-called Negro must give up such white-fostered dissolute habits as drinking, smoking, and eating improper foods. The so-called Negro must prepare himself in mind and body for the task of wresting control from the whites.
- The Nation of Islam must encourage the so-called Negro to seek now his own land within the continental United

States. This is due him and frees him from the pernicious influence of the whites.

The Problem of Defection

Commitment to the Nation can diminish as well as grow. Four of the members I interviewed later defected. Why?

These four cases can be explained in terms of a weak point in the structure of the Nation. The organization has no effective mechanisms for handling grievances among the rank and file. Its logic accounts for this. Muslim doctrine assumes that there is a single, ultimate system of truth. Elijah Muhammad and, by delegation, his ministers are in possession of this truth. Thus only Elijah Muhammad himself can say whether a minister is doing an adequate job. The result is the implicit view that there is nothing to be adjudicated between the hierarchy and its rank and file.

Grievances arise, however. The four defectors were, for various reasons, all dissatisfied with Minister Gerard X. Since there were no formal mechanisms within the organization for expressing their dissatisfaction, the only solution was to withdraw.

For most members, however, the pattern is one of steadily growing involvement. And once the ideology is fully absorbed, there is virtually no such thing as dispute or counter-evidence. If a civil rights bill is not passed, this proves the viciousness of whites in refusing to recognize Negro rights. If the same bill *is* passed, it merely proves the duplicity of whites in trying to hide their viciousness.

The ideology also provides a coherent theory of causation, provided one is willing to accept its basic assumptions. Norman X interpreted his victory over his wife in a court case as a sign of Allah's favor. Morris X used it to account for the day-to-day fortunes of his associates.

> Minister X had some trouble. He was sick for a long time. He almost died. I think Allah was punishing him. He didn't run the temple right. Now the Brothers make mistakes. Everyone does—but Minister X used to abuse them at the meetings. It was more a personal thing. He had a little power and it went to his head. Allah struck him down and I think he learned a little humility.

When a man reasons in this fashion, he has become a fully committed member of the Nation of Islam. His life revolves around temple-centered activities, his friends are all fellow Muslims, and he sees his own world—usually the world of an urban slum dweller—through the framework of a very powerful myth. He is still doing penance for the sins of Yakub, but the millennium is at hand. He has only to prepare.

The Nation of Islam does not in any real sense convert members. Rather it attracts Negroes who have already, through their own experiences in white America, developed a perspective congruent with that of the Muslim movement. The recruit comes to the door of the temple with the essence of his ideas already formed. The Black Muslims only give this disaffection a voice.

December 1966

SUGGESTED READINGS

Outsiders: Studies in the Sociology of Deviance, by Howard S. Becker (Glencoe, Ill.: Free Press of Glencoe, 1963). Provides a theoretical framework for analyzing behavior such as joining the Nation of Islam.

Black Nationalism: a Search for an Identity in America, by S. Essien-Udom (Chicago: University of Chicago Press, 1962). Valuable mainly in that it was done by an African.

The Black Muslims in America, by C. Eric Lincoln (Boston: Beacon Press, 1961). A standard work on the Nation of Islam.

The Social Psychology of Social Movements, by Hans Toch (Indianapolis: Bobbs-Merrill, 1965). An excellent treatment of a wide variety of political and non-political social movements.

Collective Dynamics by Kurt Lang and Gladys Lang (New York: Thomas Y. Crowell Co., 1961) has two fine chapters on social movements.

The Autobiography of Malcolm X by Malcolm X with the assistance of Alex Haley (New York: Grove Press, 1966).

Malcolm X Speaks by M. Little (New York: Grove Press, 1966) is a collection of speeches by Malcolm X taken mainly from the period after he split with the Muslims.

The Prophetic Minority by Jack Newfield (New York: New American Library of World Literature, Inc., 1966). An analysis of another movement and its members—the student Left.

"The Klan Revival" by James Vanderzanden, *American Sociological Review* (Vol. 65, March 1960). An analysis of the membership of the Ku Klux Klan.

The Trumpet Shall Sound: A Study of "Cargo" Cults in Melanesia by Peter Worsley (London: MacGibbon and Kee, 1957) studies millennial cults as they exist in New Guinea.

Social Mobility in Industrial Society by Seymour Lipset and Reinhart Bendix (Berkeley, Calif.: University of California Press, 1960). Points out how religion can be a mechanism of adaptation to strain.

Religion and Society in Tension by Charles Y. Glock and Rodney Stark (Chicago: Rand McNally, 1965) points out how religion appeals inordinately to the deprived.

The Religions of the Oppressed by Vittorio Lanternari (New York: Mentor Books, 1965) deals with the mechanisms by which religion serves the deprived.

The American Race Problem by Edward Reuter (New York: Thomas Y. Crowell, 1970).

Theory of Collective Behavior by Neil J. Smelser (New York: Free Press of Glencoe, 1963). Chapters 9 and 10 analyze social movements.

Collective Behavior by Ralph H. Turner and Lewis M. Killian (Englewood Cliffs, N.J.: Prentice Hall, 1957). An excellent general text on social movements and other forms of collective behavior.

Red Guard on Grant Avenue

STANFORD M. LYMAN

Visitors to San Francisco's historic Portsmouth Square on 7 May 1969 were startled to see the flag of the People's Republic of China flying over the plaza. The occasion had begun as a rally to commemorate the 50th anniversary of the May 4 movement in Peking, when Chinese students demonstrated to protest the ignominious treaties forced on a moribund Chinese Empire by Occidental imperialists. Now a half century later in San Francisco, a group of disaffected Chinatown youth took over the rally from its sponsors to protest against the community's poverty and neglect and to criticize its anachronistic and conservative power elite.

Calling themselves the Red Guards, the youths asserted their right to armed self-defense against the city police and called for the release of all Asians in city, state and federal prisons on the ground that they had had unfair trials. On a more immediate and practical level, the Red Guards announced plans for a remarkably unradical petition campaign to prevent the Chinese Playground from being converted into a garage and for a breakfast program to aid needy children in the Chinatown ghetto. If the platform of the Red Guards sounded vaguely familiar, a spokesman for the group made it plain: "The Black Panthers are the most revolutionary group in the country and we are patterned after them."

To most San Franciscans the rise of youthful rebellion in the Chinese quarter of the city must come as a surprise. For the past three decades Chinese-Americans have been stereotyped in the mass media as quiet, docile and filial, a people who are as unlikely to espouse radicalism as they are to permit delinquency among their juveniles. In the last few years, however, evidence has mounted to suggest a discrepancy between this somewhat saccharine imagery and reality. Not only is there an unmistakable increase in delinquent activity among Chinese young people, there is a growing restlessness among them as well. Chinatown's younger generation feels a gnawing frustration over hidebound local institutions, the powerlessness of youth and their own bleak prospects for the future. The politics as well as the "crimes" of Chinatown are coming to resemble those of the larger society, with alienation, race consciousness and restive rebelliousness animating a new generation's social and organizational energies.

A basic cause for the emergence of youthful rebellion among the Chinese is the increase in the youthful population itself. There are simply more Chinese youth in the ghetto now than there ever have been before, a fact that can be attributed to an increasing birth rate among the indigenous population and a sudden rise in immigration from Hong Kong and other Asian centers of Chinese settlement.

By 1890, eight years after a wave of sinophobia had prompted Congress to block any further immigration of Chinese to this country, there were approximately 102,620 residents here. The vast majority were laborers or small merchants lured here by the promise of the "Gold Mountain" in California and work on the railroads. But a more significant fact is that the vast majority were also men. Before the turn of the century there were about 27 men for every woman among the Chinese in America. What this meant for white perceptions of these newcomers is probably familiar enough. Forced into ghettos, their women and children left behind to care for and honor their parents, these men joined together in clan associations and secret societies to provide them with some sense of familiarity and solidarity; and they turned as well to the typical pleasures of lonely men—prostitutes, stupefaction (through opium) and gambling. Just as typically, in a society known for its hostile racial stereotypes, the Chinese came to be identified with these "vices" in the minds of many white Americans and to be regarded as bestial, immoral and dangerous. But the alarming imbalance in the sex ratio also meant that the Chinese communities in America were almost incapable of producing a second generation of American-born Chinese. It wasn't until 1950 that the American-born made up more than half the total Chinese population, and even this growth only came about through the small trickle of illegal entries made by Chinese women prior to 1943 and the much larger number who entered since that date, thanks to gradual but important relaxations of the immigration laws.

The most radical of these relaxations came with the Immigration Act of 1965 which repealed the entire system of quotas based on national origins and substituted an entry procedure based on skills and the reuniting of families. Under this law, according to District Immigration Director C. W. Fullilove, there will be approximately 1,200 Chinese entering San Francisco every year with the intention of staying there. Although not all of them will do so, this new influx of Chinese makes up a signficant proportion of San Francisco's burgeoning Chinese population, and many of them fall between what Fullilove calls "the problem ages" for Chinese youth, 16 to 19.

"The new influx of Chinese makes up a significant proportion of San Francisco's burgeoning Chinese population."

The Gold Mountain

Of course, sheer numbers alone do not account for the rise of rebelliousness among young Chinese in San Francisco. A more significant factor is that conditions of life in Chinatown are by no means pleasant, productive or promising. We must distinguish, however, from among the Chinese those who have escaped the ghetto, those who are American-born but who still inhabit Chinatown and the foreign-born youth who reluctantly find themselves imprisoned within a ghetto even less of their own making than it is of the others'. Among those who have escaped there are, first, the scholars, scientists, intellectuals and professionals—many of whom hail from regions other than southeastern China, the original home of the bulk of America's Chinese immigrants—who have found work and residence within the larger society. Enclosed in university, corporation, professional or government communities, these Chinese do not for the most part feel themselves to be a part of Chinatown; they go there only occasionally for a banquet or for a brief sense of their ethnic origins. A second group much larger than the first, although actually quite small in relation to the total number of Chinese, consists of those American-born Chinese who have successfully completed high school and college and gone on to enter the professions—most frequently pharmacy and engineering—the American middle class and, when they can evade or circumvent the still prevalent discrimination in housing, the finer neighborhoods or the suburbs. This "gold bourgeoisie"—to paraphrase E. Franklin Frazier—is also estranged from Chinatown. Proud of his own achievements, wary of any attempt to thrust him back into a confining ghetto existence and alternately angered, embarrassed or shamed by the presence of alienated, hostile and rebellious youth in Chinatown, the middle-class American Chinese holds tenaciously to his newly achieved material and social success.

Nevertheless, middle-class native-born Chinese are discovering that the American dream is not an unmixed blessing. The "Gold Mountain" of American bourgeois promise seems somehow less glittering now that its actual pinnacle has been reached. Chinese, like other descendants of immigrants in America, are discovering that the gold is alloyed more heavily than they had supposed with brass; but, like their second and third generation peers among the Jews and Japanese, they are not quite sure what to do about it. The price of success has been very great—not the least payments being the abandonment of language, culture and much of their ethnic identity. Among some there is a new search for cultural roots in Chinese history, a strong desire to recover the ancient arts and a renewed interest in speaking Chinese—at least at home. Others emphasize, perhaps with too much protestation, their happiness within the American middle class and carry on a conspicuous consumption of leisure to prove it. Finally, a few recognize their Chinatown roots and return there with a desire to aid somehow in the advancement of the Chinese ghetto-dwellers. Sometimes their offers of help are rejected with curses by the objects of their solicitude, but in any event the growing number of restive Chinatowners constitutes another challenge to the comfort of bourgeois Chinese.

In its most primordial sense the visible contrast between the style of life of the impoverished ghetto-dweller and that of the middle-class professional promotes guilt and shame. Somehow it seems wrong that one's ethnic compatriots should suffer while one enjoys the benefits of success. Yet middle-class Chinese are quite ready to attribute their success to their own diligence, proverbial habits of thrift and hard work and to their conscious avoidance of delinquent or other kinds of unruly behavior. Naturally, then, some middle-class Chinese are equally quick to charge the angry Chinatown youth with indolence, impropriety and impiety. But even as they preach the old virtues as a sure cure for the young people's personal and social ailments, some perceive that there is more to these problems than can be solved by the careful nurturing of Confucian or Protestant ethics. They see more clearly than the Americanized and less alienated Chinese of the fifties that poverty, cultural deprivation and discrimination are truly obdurate barriers to the advancement of the ghetto-dwellers of today. Moreover, there is an even more profound problem. Like other alienated youthful minorities, the youth of Chinatown appear to reject just that dream which inspired and activated the now bourgeois Chinese. For the middle-class Chinese, then, the peak of the "Gold Mountain" seems to have been reached just when those still down below started to shout up that the arduous climb isn't worth the effort.

Social Bandits and Primitive Rebels

Among Chinatown's rebellious groups there are two distinguishable types of youth—those who are American-born but have dropped out of school and form part of the under- or unemployed proletariat of the Chinese community; and those recently arrived immigrant youth who, speaking little or no English and having little to offer in the way of salable skills, find themselves unable to enter the city's occupational and social mainstream. Both native and foreign-born Chinese are included among the ranks of the quasi-criminal and quasi-political gangs that are accused of contributing to the mounting incidence of delinquency in the Chinese quarter. Culture, language and background have divided the native from the foreign-born Chinese in the past, and it is only recently that there is any sign of a common recognition between the two groups.

It is traditional to focus on Chinatown gangs as an unfortunate form of juvenile delinquency among a people otherwise noted for their social quiescence and honesty. A more fruitful approach however would adopt the perspective taken by E. J. Hobsbawm in his discussion of social bandits and primitive rebels. According to Hobsbawm, who has studied these phenomena in Europe, social banditry is a form of pre-ideological rebellion which arises among essentially agrarian, unskilled and unlettered peoples who are at great cultural distance from the official and oppressive power structure. It is led by those who enjoy a certain amount of local notoriety or awe. Often enough social banditry remains at a stage of petty criminality which is of concern, if at all, only to the local police. At a more refined stage, however, predatory gangs are formed which confine their criminal activities to attacks on strangers and officials and share any loot with local community members who, though not a party to the attacks, identify with and protect the robbers.

It is important to note that bandit gangs may adopt a populist or a conservative style. The former is symbolized by Robin Hood, who robbed the rich to feed the poor and attacked civic or state officialdom as intruders in the community's traditional way of life. In the conservative style, bandit gangs are co-opted as toughs and thugs to defend local satrapies and powerful petty interests. Social banditry may exist side by side with ideologically rebellious or revolutionary elements but is usually untouched by them except for particular reasons of strategy or tactics. Essentially, it is separated from ideological politics by its deep involvement with local ethnic rather than cosmopolitan class interests. However, it is not impossible for class and ethnic interests to merge and for the liberation of local groups to become enmeshed within the revolutionary aims of a radically politicized sector of a modern party state.

From the perspective of "primitive rebellion," Chinatown's gangs take on a greater significance for the understanding of loosely structured pluralistic societies like the United States. Gangs in Chinatown are by no means a new phenomenon, but their activities in the past describe mainly the early stages of social banditry. For the most part Chinatown's traditional social banditry has been of a particularly conservative type, identified with the recruitment of young toughs, thugs and bullies into the small criminal arm of Chinatown's secret societies. They formed the "flying squads" of mercenaries who "protected" brothels, guarded gambling establishments and enforced secret society monopolies over other vice institutions of Chinatown. From their numbers came assassins and strong-arm men who fought in the so-called tong wars that characterized Chinatown's internecine struggles of a half century ago and which still occasionally threaten to erupt today. But this form of social banditry was an exclusive and private affair of Chinatown. Insofar as Chinatown's violent altercations were circumscribed not only by the invisible wall around the ghetto but also by the limited interests of the contending parties for women, wealth and power, the community was isolated by its internal conflicts. Whether manifested in fearful acquiescence or active participation, the ghetto's residents were bound together in a deadly kind of "antagonistic cooperation."

Since 1943 a progressive cycle of rebellion among Chinatown's youth has metamorphosed from crime to politics, from individual acts of aggression to collective acts of rebellion and from nonideological modes of hostility to the beginnings of a movement of ideological proportions. From 1943 until 1949 juvenile crime in Chinatown was largely the activity of a small number of native-born boys about 15 years of age, hurt by unemployment, difficulties in home life or inadequate income. Their crimes were typical of the most individualized and inarticulate forms of primitive rebellion. Burglary, auto theft, robberies, larcenies, holdups and assault and battery constituted 103 of the 184 offenses for which Chinese male juveniles were referred to San Francisco's juvenile court in those years. There were also gangs of native-born youth, apparently sponsored by or under the protection of secret societies, who occasionally assaulted and robbed strangers in Chinatown, not a few of whom, incidentally, were Japanese-Americans recently returned from wartime internment camps and also organized into clubs, cliques and gangs.

Petty criminal gangs emerged more frequently among both the native and foreign-born youth in Chinatown from 1958 to 1964. In some cases these gangs were composed of young men sponsored in their criminal activities by secret societies. An example was the "cat" burglary ring broken up by police in 1958 and discovered to be a branch of the Hop Sing Tong. Three years later, two gangs, the "Lums" and the "Rabble Rousers," were reported to be engaged in auto thefts, extortion, street fights and petty larcenies. In January 1964 members of a San Francisco Chinatown gang were charged with the $10,000 burglary of a fish market in suburban Mountain View. A year later, the police broke up the "Bugs," a youthful criminal gang whose members dressed entirely in black, with bouffant hair style and raised-heel boots, and who, in committing 48 burglaries, made off with $7,500 in cash and $3,000 in merchandise in a period of six months. The "Bugs"—who capitalized on an otherwise stigmatizing aspect of their existence, their short stature—reemerged a year later despite an attempt by Chinatown's leaders to quell juvenile gangs by bringing in street workers from San Francisco's Youth for Service to channel the gang toward constructive activities. By the mid-1960s Chinatown's burglary gangs had begun to branch out and were working areas of the city outside the Chinese quarter.

The present stage of a more politicized rebellion may be dated from the emergence in May 1967 of Leway, Incorporated. In its history up to August 1969, the Leways experienced almost precisely the pattern of problems and response that typically give rise first to nonideological rebellion and then, under certain conditions, to the development of revolutionary ideology. Leway (standing for "legitimate way") began as a public-spirited self-help group among American-born Chinese teen-agers. Aged 17 to 22, these young men organized to unite Chinatown's youth, to combat juvenile delinquency and to improve conditions in the poverty-stricken Chinese ghetto through helping youths to help themselves. In its first months it gained the support of such Chinatown luminaries as Lim P. Lee, now San Francisco's postmaster and a former probation officer, and other prominent citizens. Through raffles, loans and gifts, these youths, many of whom could be classed as delinquents, raised $2,000 to rent a pool hall near the Chinatown-Filipino border area. And, with the help of the Chinese YMCA and Youth for Service, they outfitted it with five pool tables, seven pinball machines, some chairs and a television set. "This is a hangout for hoods," said its president, Denny Lai, to reporter Ken Wong. "Most of us cats are misfits, outcasts with a rap sheet. What we're trying to do is to keep the hoods off the streets, give them something to do instead of raising hell."

Leway was a local indigenous group seeking to employ its own methods and style to solve its own members' problems. And it was precisely this that caused its downfall. Police refused to believe in methods that eschewed official surveillance, sporadic shakedowns and the not always occasional beating of a youth "resisting arrest." Leway tried a dialogue with the police, but it broke down over the rights of the latter to enter, search and seize members at Leway's headquarters, a tiny piece of "territory" which the young Chinese had hoped to preserve from alien and hostile intrusion. Leway claimed it wanted only to be left alone by this official arm of a society which they saw as already hostile. "We are not trying to bother them [the police] . . . and we won't go out of our way to work with them either."

In addition to continuous harassment by white police, Leway failed to establish its legitimacy in Chinatown itself. The Chinese Chamber of Commerce refused it official recognition, and as a result Leway could not gain access to the local Economic Opportunity Council to obtain much-needed jobs for Chinatown youth. The Tsung Tsin Association, which owned the building where Leway had its headquarters, threatened to raise the rent or lease the premises to another renter. Finally, whether rightly or not, the members of Leway, together with other Chinatown youth groups, were blamed for the increasing violence in Chinatown. Throughout 1968–69 reports of violent assault on tourists and rival gangs were coming out of Chinatown. Police stepped up their intrusive surveillance and other heavy-handed tactics. Chinese youth charged them with brutality, but the police replied that they were only using proper procedures in the line of a now more hazardous duty. In late summer 1969 the combination of police harassment, rent hikes, Leway's failure to secure jobs for its chronically unemployed members and its general inability to establish itself as a legitimate way of getting Chinatown youth "straightened out" took its final toll. Leway House closed its doors. Dreams of establishing on-the-job training for the unskilled, new business ventures for the unemployed, a pleasant soda fountain for Leway adolescents and an education and recreation program for Chinatown teen-agers —all this was smashed. The bitterness stung deep in the hearts of Chinatown young people. "Leway stood for legitimate ways," a 15-year-old youth told reporter Bill Moore. "Helluva lot of good it did them." The closing of Leway destroyed many Chinatown young people's faith in the official culture and its public representatives.

The stage was set for the next phase in the development of rebellion. Out of the shambles of Leway came the Red Guards, composed of the so-called radical elements of the former organization. But now Leway's search for legitimacy has been turned on its head. The Red Guards flout the little red book *Quotations from Chairman Mao Tse-tung* as their credo, make nonnegotiable demands on the power structure of Chinatown and the metropolis and openly espouse a program of disruption, rebellion and occasionally, it seems, revolution.

Arthur Tress

Leway had been modeled after other San Francisco youthful gang reform groups, but the Red Guards have adopted the organizational form, rhetorical style and political mood of the Black Panthers. A few years ago this would have seemed highly improbable. In the 1960s there were frequent bloody clashes between gangs of Chinese and Negroes, and interracial incidents at Samuel Gompers School —a kind of incarceration unit for black and Oriental incorrigibles—had not encouraged friendly relations among

POPULATION AND URBAN COMMUNITIES

the two groups. Nevertheless it was just these contacts, combined with a growing awareness of Panther tactics and successes, and some not too secret proselytization by Panther leaders among the disaffected Leway members, that brought the young Chinese to adopt the black militant style. Whatever prejudices Chinese might harbor against Negroes, Black Panther rhetoric seemed perfectly to describe their own situation. After all, Leway had tried to be good, to play the game according to the white man's rules, and all it had gotten for its pains were a heap of abuse and a few cracked skulls. Now it was time to be realistic—"to stop jiving" and "to tell it like it is." Police were "pigs"; white men were "honkies"; officially developed reform programs were attempts to "shine" on credulous Chinese youth; and the goal to be attained was not integration, not material success, but power. "We're an organization made up mainly of street people and we're tired of asking the government for reforms," said Alex Hing, a 23-year-old Chinese who is the minister of information of the Red Guards. "We're going to attain power, so we don't have to beg any more."

Urban Populism

The Red Guards are a populist group among Chinatown's "primitive" rebels. They stand against not one but two power structures in their opposition to oppression and poverty—that of old Chinatown and that of the larger metropolis. Ideologically they are located somewhere between the inarticulate rumblings of rustic rebels and the full-scale ideology of unregenerate revolutionaries. They cry out for vengeance against the vague but powerful complex of Chinese and white elites that oppress them. They dream of a world in which they will have sufficient power to curb their exploiters' excesses; meanwhile they do the best they can to right local wrongs and to ingratiate themselves with the mass of their Chinatown compatriots. The free breakfasts for indigent youngsters, a copy of the Panthers' program, attracts popular support among Chinatown's poor at the same time that it shames Chinatown's elites for allowing the community's children to go hungry. The demand for the release of all imprisoned Asians seems to place the Red Guards squarely on the side of all those "little people" of Chinatown who feel themselves victimized by an alien and oppressive police system. However, their ethnic consciousness usually supersedes and sometimes clashes with their alleged attachment to a class-oriented ideology, as it did when the Red Guards accepted an invitation to guard a meeting of the Chinese Garment Contractors' Association against a threatened assault by Teamsters seeking to organize Chinatown's heavily exploited dressmakers. But it is precisely their parochial dedication to a sense of Chinese ethnicity that endears them to the less hardy of young Chinatowners who secretly share their dilemmas and dreams, as well as limits their political effectiveness.

Populist rebellion is not the only form of social politics in Chinatown. A conservative type of rebelliousness is illustrated in the evolution of the Hwa Ching and the Junior Hwa Ching. Hwa Ching emerged in 1967 as a loose association of mostly Hong Kong-born youth in Chinatown. Estimates of its size vary from 25 to 300, and this fact alone testifies to its low degree of cohesiveness and the sense of drift that characterizes its members. Until very recently Hwa Ching was represented in most public discussions by a "spokesman" (its looseness of organization prevented any greater clarification of title), George Woo, a former photographer who took on the task of bridging the communication gap between the largely Chinese-speaking youths and the officials of the metropolis. The aims of this association are difficult to ascertain exactly, partly because there was little agreement among its members and partly because spokesman Woo usually tended to a violently polemical speaking style in order to call attention to the situation of Chinatown's immigrants. Hwa Ching had less of a perfected program than a set of practical problems. Hong Kong youth were insufficiently educated and skilled to obtain any jobs other than Chinatown's dreary positions of waiter, busboy and sweated laborer; unequipped linguistically to enter the metropolis and, in the beginning, unwilling to accept confinement in a congested, poverty-stricken and despotically ruled ghetto.

Hwa Ching seemed to form itself around El Piccolo, an espresso coffeehouse opened in Chinatown in 1967 and operated by Dick and Alice Barkley. Alice Barkley, herself a Hong Kong-born Chinese, turned the coffeehouse into a haven for foreign-born Chinese youth. There they could meet in peace and with freedom to discuss, argue, complain and occasionally plan some joint activity. Reaction to their clubby fraternization at El Piccolo was mixed. Traditional Chinatowners accused the Barkleys of offering asylum to raffish criminal elements; a newly aroused college and university group of Chinese-Americans praised the establishment of a place for impoverished immigrants to congregate; and most San Franciscans didn't even know the Hwa Ching existed.

Early in 1968 Hwa Ching approached the Human Relations Commission, the Economic Development Council and the Chinese business elite to ask for their aid in establishing an educational program for alleviating the misery of Chinatown's immigrant youth. Their approach was unusually frank and plainly practical. They proposed the establishment of a comprehensive two-year educational program to provide Chinatown's young immigrants with a high school diploma and vocational training in auto repair, business machine operation, construction, sheet metal, electrical installation and plumbing. They closed with a statement that was unfortunately taken as a warning and a threat. "We've been hearing too many promises. The rise and fall of our hopes is tragic and ominous."

This first bid for help was unsuccessful. In late February, however, the Hwa Ching tried again and spoke to the Chinatown Advisory Board of the Human Relations Commission. This time Hwa Ching, represented by the fiery George Woo, was more modest in its request for a comprehensive program, but more militant in its presentation. Hwa Ching wanted $4,322 to build a clubhouse, but although Woo reiterated the same arguments as other Hwa Chings had presented in January, the tone was different. Describing his constituents, Woo said, "There is a hard core of delinquents in Chinatown who came from China. Their problems are the problems of all poor with the addition that they don't speak English." Then he added that "they're talking about getting guns and rioting.... I'm not threatening riots. The situation already exists, but if people in Chinatown don't feel threatened they won't do anything about it." The mention of guns and the warning of possible riots were too much for John Yehall Chin, a prominent Chinese businessman, principal of Saint Mary's Chinese Language School and member of the Human Relations Commission's Chinatown Advisory Board. In reply to the Hwa Ching's request he advised the commission, and indirectly the youths, "They have not shown that they are sorry or that they will change their ways. They have threatened the community. If you give in to this group, you are only going to have another hundred immigrants come in and have a whole new series of threats and demands." Although the commission expressed its interest, Hwa Ching's demand was rejected.

They tried again. In March the Hwa Ching's president, Stan Wong, presented the immigrant youths' case before the Chinese Six Companies, the oligarchy that controls Chinatown. Speaking in Cantonese, Wong repudiated the threat of riots made at the February meeting. "We made no threats," he said. "They were made by nonmembers. We need to help ourselves. We look to the future and are mindful of the immigrant youths who will be coming here later. We hope they do not have to go through what we've been through." Later he answered a question about possible Communist affiliation: "Hwa Ching is not involved with any political ideology." Although Commissioner Chin pointed out that the Hwa Ching had mended its ways, the Six Companies refused them help. Meanwhile the Human Relations Commission, under the direction of Chin, organized an Establishment-controlled Citizens for Youth in Chinatown. The Hwa Ching felt utterly rejected.

In their bitterness and anger, however, the Hwa Ching did not turn to populist revolt, as had the Leways. Instead they fragmented even more. Their loose coalition at El Piccolo ended when that establishment closed its doors in August 1968. The Hwa Ching had never in fact professed an ideology. What seemed to be one was more a product of the fervid imaginations of alarmed whites and of the fiery invective of George Woo than it was any coherent line of political or revolutionary thought. The Hwa Ching's practical needs were too immediate, their literacy in English too low and their limited but practical political experience in Hong Kong and Chinatown too real for them to accept an organization that used Mao's red book and which therefore ran for them the risks of political persecution and possible deportation. As Tom Tom, a 23-year-old immigrant who had been one of the earliest members of Hwa Ching, explained to a reporter, the immigrant youth were independent of the Leway and all other Chinatown groups, affected none of the hippie-Ché-Raoul-Panther styles and wanted little more than jobs, girls and to be left alone. The Hwa Ching found themselves oppressed by their supposed allies nearly as much as by their condition. Leway boys and other American-born Chinese called them "Chinabugs" and attacked them in gang rumbles; Negroes picked on the dimunitive Chinese until they learned to retaliate in numbers and with tactics; college students sought to tutor and to evangelize them with secular and sometimes political ideas but succeeded mostly in making them feel inferior and frightened by a kind of politics they abhorred.

By the middle of 1969 the Hwa Ching had split into three factions. One returned to the streets to fight, burglarize and assault all those available symbols and representatives of the seemingly monolithic power structure that had scorned them; two other factions apparently accepted co-optation into Chinatown's two most powerful though age-ridden secret societies—the Suey Sing and Hop Sing Tongs. There their anger could find outlet at the same time that their strength could be utilized for traditional aims. The secret societies could pay for the immigrant youths' basic needs and with the same expenditure buy the muscle to keep control of their own interests and institutions. And since the Tongs were part of the complex congeries of associations that make up Chinatown's power elite, it is not surprising that leaders of this same elite gave tacit approval to the Tongs' recruitment of what had appeared in early 1968 to be a serious threat to the old order. Unlike the Leway, which could not join the old order and may have been too Americanized to accept secret society patronage, the immigrant youth find in it a perhaps temporary expedient in their dilemma. Not being politicized, they can more readily join in the protection of old Chinatown. They have resumed a posture typical of earlier youthful generations' response to anger and poverty in Chinatown. They form the conservative wing of Chinatown's complex structure of conflict and rebellion.

In other areas and times of primitive rebellion, conservative and populist factions often fought each other as much as their professed enemies. Similarly, in Chinatown the young toughs who have become paid guards of the secret societies' and, occasionally, the Six Companies' meetings are not infrequently arrayed against the Leway–Red Guard gangs. And in this sense young Chinatown recapitulates a structure of conflict that characterized that of its earlier generations. Conservative-populist conflicts iso-

Gernot Newman

At the Chinese New Year parade, children march at left; while at right are representatives of the Chinese Six Companies whose leaders are shown here. They represent the pinnacle of the old order Establishment.

late the contending parties from outside groups and larger issues. The violent fights and smouldering feuds appear to noncomprehending outsiders to be exclusively Chinese in their nature and content. And this intramural conflict in turn circumscribes Chinatown and once again cuts it off from the metropolis.

Outside Ideologies

However, connections to the larger society of San Francisco in particular and the United States in general do exist. For the youth the most important one is the Intercollegiate Chinese for Social Action (ICSA). This group was formed at San Francisco State College from among the more socially concerned and politically aware Chinese-American students. For a while it managed the special program by which Chinese students from the ghetto were recruited to the college. But the long Third World strike at San Francisco State College in 1968–69 radicalized its members and propelled them into even greater contact with the Chinatown community. They became actively oriented toward conditions about which they had been only vaguely aware before. ICSA asserted aloud and with emphasis what had been but an open secret for decades—Chinatown was a racial ghetto—poverty-stricken, disease-ridden, overcrowded, underdeveloped and with a population growing in Malthusian proportions. To the remedy of all these defects they dedicated themselves and established offices not only in the college but in Chinatown itself. ICSA provides tutoring services to Chinatown's less educated youth and urges that San Francisco State College establish even more programs for community rehabilitation. The community-oriented Chinese college youth do not openly attack Leway or the Red Guards but remain in communication with them as well as with the erstwhile Hwa Ching. But, observes George Woo, now as an ICSA member, "We can also see the pitfalls in using too much of the blarney, as the Red Guards did. As a result, they alienated immigrant youths and the whole community in three months' time." By keeping open contacts among the native- and the foreign-born, among Hwa Ching and

Leway-Red Guards, among status conscious diploma-bearers and socially stigmatized delinquents and among the legitimated and the lowly, ICSA may yet be able to blunt the deadly edge of conflict and build a durable community for Chinatown.

What this means specifically is by no means clear even to the ICSA members themselves. "I'm still trying to figure out what I am supposed to be as a Chinese-American," complained a 21-year-old college student, echoing the inner nagging question of most of his compatriots. And George Woo replied, "I know how you feel. I don't identify with China either and I certainly don't identify with the petty American middle-class values of my aunts and uncles." ICSA emphasizes a two-way learning process between the lettered and the dropouts and calls for the formulation of a new ethic to replace the Confucian-Protestant ethos of Chinese America. As ICSA leader Mason Wong has said, "Our generation here will no longer accept the old and still prevalent Confucian doctrine of success coming only from hard work and humility." What that ethic will be is not yet known. However, the Chinese must still contend with the traditional social order that is Chinatown's Establishment.

The Old Order

Anyone at all conversant with San Francisco's Chinatown will have heard of the Chinese Six Companies. In a vague sense he might know about some of its activities, be able to point out its headquarters and note that it is a benevolent, protective and representational body of Chinese who enjoy unofficial but influential standing at City Hall. Beyond this he might know very little but the familiar litany that the Chinese take care of themselves, contribute little, if at all, to the welfare rolls or to the city's alarming rate of juvenile delinquency and, that while the Chinese were perhaps at one time a troublesome minority, they are now safely ensconced in their own quarter of the city where they enjoy a modicum of freedom to practice peculiar cultural expressions derived from a China that is no more. To him the Six Companies is one aspect of that cultural freedom.

Like many stereotypes that arise in racist societies, this one too contains some kernels of truth. The Chinese in San Francisco, like the Chinese in Calcutta, Singapore, Bangkok, Saigon, Manila and indeed in almost every large city to which Chinese have migrated, enjoy a measure of home rule that far exceeds that of any other minority group in the metropolis. During the colonial period in Southeast Asia, the British and Dutch formalized their practices of indirect rule into a specified system of titles. "Kapitan China" was the Dutch designation for the uniformed and bemedalled Chinese who represented his people in the colonial councils at Batavia, and the "Captain China" system prevailed in British Malaya and other colonies as well. For the colonial powers indirect rule was an

Gernot Newman

expedient way of maintaining sufficient control over restless and hostile native peoples in a precariously pluralistic society in order to extract their labor and the colony's natural resources without having to contend with all their tribal and customary ways and woes. For the subject peoples it meant that they could freely organize their lives in accordance with traditional practices, so long as they didn't interfere with the rather limited interests of the imperial powers. Outside the colonial area, Chinese immigrant elites also managed to establish a kind of cultural extraterritoriality and to achieve an added legitimation to their traditional control over their fellow migrants by winning unofficial but practically useful recognition from white civic elites. In Vancouver, and in New York City the Chinese Benevolent Association has obtained such perogatives; in San Francisco it is the Chinese Six Companies.

But to understand Chinatown's power structure fully, it is necessary to analyze the several kinds of traditional associations from which it is composed. First there are clan associations, or "family associations" as Occidental journalists and sociologists usually term them. Clan associations derive from the lineage communities so prevalent in Kwangtung and ideally unite all persons descended from a common male ancestor. Overseas, however, the more manageable lineage unit was replaced by a kinship network

wider than that which originally enclosed only a compact village. The clan association includes all who bear the same surname. In the early days of Chinese immigration, the clan associations became a special kind of immigrant aid society providing the newcomer with food, shelter, employment, protection and advice. Furthermore, the clan leaders reminded the immigrant of his obligations to parents and family in the home village and, in the absense of the village elders, assumed a role in loco parentis, settling disputes, arbitrating disagreements and in general containing intraclan differences within the kinship fold. Some clan associations exercised a monopoly over a trade or profession in Chinatown and effectively resisted encroachments on these monopolies by ambitious Chinese upstarts from other clans. Until the recent arrival of large numbers of immigrants from Hong Kong, the clan associations had been declining in power and authority as a result of the aging of their members and the acculturation of the American-born Chinese. However, even this new lifeblood is less acquiescent than the former sojourner members. Chinatown clan associations are now challenged to provide something more than a paltry benevolence in exchange for their petty despotism.

In addition to clans, however, there developed among overseas Chinese a functionally similar but structurally

Arthur Tress

The old benevolent societies are losing power as their members escape the ghetto, or simply grow old.

different type of association. The *hui kuan* united all those who spoke a common dialect, hailed from the same district in China or belonged to the same tribal or ethnic group. (It is a mistake to suppose, as many Occidentals do, that the peoples of China are culturally homogeneous. In the tiny area around Canton from which most of America's immigrants have come, there are numerous dialects which, while they have a common script, are almost mutually unintelligible when spoken.) In many ways the hui kuan were similar to those immigrant aid and benevolent societies established by Germans, Irish, Jews and other Europeans in America. In San Francisco and other cities in which Chinese dwelt, the hui kuan, like the clan association, maintained a headquarters and served as caravansary, hostelry, credit association and employment agency. In all these matters it exercised authoritarian control, and since most of the Chinese in America were debtors, directly or indirectly, to their hui kuan, its officers were not infrequently suspected of taking an excessive interest or a corrupt profit from their charges. The hui kuan, again similar to the clan, conducted arbitration and mediation hearings between disputing members, managed and collected the debts of its members and in addition charged them various fees for its services. An aging membership and the flight of the American-born bourgeoisie tended to undermine hui kuan authority, but the old businesses in Chinatown still affiliate with them and accept their mediation and arbitration services. They are especially important in the ownership and control of Chinatown property which they administer in a traditional way quite different from real estate management in the Occidental parts of the city.

The third major type of association in Chinatown is the secret society. Like the clan and the hui kuan, the secret society originated in China where for centuries it served as a principal agency for popular protest, violent rebellion and social banditry. The overseas migrants from Kwangtung included not a few members of the Triad Society, the most famous of China's clandestine associations. In nearly every significant overseas community of Chinese they established chapters of, or models based on that order. In the United States secret societies among the Chinese were set up by the early immigrants in the cities and also in those outlying areas where clans and hui kuan could not form a solid base. Inside Chinatown the secret societies soon took over control of gambling and prostitution, and it is with these activities rather than with their political or charitable activities that they are most often associated in the minds of non-Chinese in America. Clans, hui kuan and the several chapters of secret societies often fell out with one another over their competition for women, wealth and power inside Chinatown, and these so-called tong wars raged intermittently until a Chinatown Peace Association established a still perilous peace between the warring factions in the 1920s. The charitable works of secret societies were confined for the most part to giving mutual aid to their own members, the establishment of headquarters and hostelries and in recent years the building of clubhouses where their aged bachelor members might find hospitable fraternity. The political activities of the secret societies have consisted in their intermittent interest in the fortunes of China's several regimes, but they have not shown any particular interest in upsetting the national politics of the United States. Meanwhile the secret societies' most successful source of revenue in Chinatown—the control over gambling and prostitution—diminished as the Chinese bachelors aged and died and the American-born declined interest in these activities. The recruitment of the newly arrived and disaffected immigrant youth from Chinatown has undoubtedly done much to rejuvenate these societies, but it remains to be seen whether this will lengthen their life as institutions in America or change their function in accordance with new interests and current developments.

At the top of the community power structure of Chinatown is the Chinese Benevolent Association, commonly known as the Chinese Six Companies. It was formed in the late 1850s as a confederation of hui kuan—later it incorporated clans, guilds and, reluctantly, secret societies—in order to provide communitywide governance, to promote intracommunity harmony and to present at least the appearance of a common Chinese front to white society. Until the 1870s it functioned as an agency of international diplomacy and consular activity as well, since the Chinese Empire did not provide a specific overseas office for those duties. The Six Companies has been the principal spokesman for the Chinese to white America. It has protested against anti-Chinese legislation, helped fight discriminatory laws in the courts, petitioned federal, state and local governments in behalf of the Chinese and generally provided Chinatown with a modest respectability in the face of sinophobic stereotypy. One of its more recent efforts in defense of Chinese in America was a protest against Secretary of Transportation John Volpe's omission of the role that Chinese played in the building of the Transcontinental Railroad when he spoke at the centenary celebration of its completion.

Gradually the Six Companies established its legitimacy as rightful representatives of the Chinese in San Francisco. Composed of merchants and traders, the leaders of the Six Companies seemed to inspire assurance among civic leaders that the Chinese were not a threat to the city's economic base. Moreover, the anti-Chinese movement in America was largely a movement of small farmers and laborers against what they described as the unfair competition of Chinese laborers. Once labor agitation had succeeded in driving the Chinese workers out of the city's industries and into the confines of Chinatown—a mission largely accomplished by 1910—civic functionaries were quite prepared to negotiate with the Six Companies whatever agreements might have to be reached between the ghetto and the metropolis. For its part the Six Companies, although it protested against the excesses of ghettoization, must have realized the gain to be made in its own power by having the great majority of Chinese housed and employed in Chinatown. The final establishment of Chinatown as an unofficial but real quarter of the city consolidated and enhanced the power of the Six Companies over its denizens.

In effect the Six Companies' authority over Chinese in San Francisco was—until the advent of the American-born and the rise of intracommunity rebellion—an institutionalized version of the kind of control over Negroes in America exercised by Booker T. Washington and his "Tuskegee Machine" from 1890 until 1915. The slow growth of a second generation prevented an effective counteraction to its powers by an acculturated group demanding a new politics. To be sure, Chinatown's Six Companies had its W. E. B. DuBoises—men who opposed the despotic benevolence it exercised, the containment of Chinese in the ghetto that it tacitly espoused and the corruption in its offices. But they were too few in number to be effective, too readily co-opted into the controlled violence of Chinatown's secret societies or too easily frightened into silence by threats of financial loss, deportation or conviction of trumped-up crimes in the white man's courts, where Chinese interpreters could be bought and perjured witnesses were easily obtainable. When the American-born generation did reach maturity, many of its members went to college, entered the professions and departed from Chinatown. This caused the Six Companies some loss in its Chinese constituency,

Michael Alexander

but, since the Chinese-Americans *embourgeoisés* did not challenge the authority of the Six Companies, the loss did not undermine its control over Chinatown.

Legitimate and Illegitimate Rebellion

Today, in addition to the "illegitimate" rebellion of youth in Chinatown, there is a "legitimate" counteraction of adults against the communitywide authority of the Six Companies. This loyal opposition includes several intra-Chinatown associations composed of "respectable" members of the American-born and, occasionally, a foreign-born Chinese leader who opposes the associational oligarchy. Until 1956 the only significant organization among the American-born Chinese was the Chinese-American Citizens' Alliance, a group so small that in its early days, more than a half century ago, it was little more than a name promising assimilation. Since the mid-1950s, however, a new association has arisen—the Chinese-American Democratic Club (CADC). This organization of politically minded and socially conscious Chinese-Americans heralds a shift from communal-oriented traditionalism to civic-minded cosmopolitanism in Chinatown. Still another organization outside the domination of the Six Companies is the Concerned Chinese for Action and Change, a loose and informal association of middle-class Chinese-Americans who live outside the ghetto but who can be counted on to mass for support of more liberal social action in Chinatown. Third, the Chinatown-North Beach Area Youth Council, a product of the Economic Development Agency in Chinatown, seeks to link up the respectable middle-class Chinatowners with its less respectable youth groups. Finally, there is one aging Chinese, J. K. Choy, who almost alone has opposed the old order in Chinatown without effective reprisal. A Columbia-educated banker and a professed disciple of Fabianism, Choy has exposed the poverty and neglect hidden beneath the tinseled glitter of Chinatown's neon-lit ghetto. He organized a reading room and English classes for immigrants in the offices next to the branch bank which he oversees as general manager. When in October 1966 he advised the women employed in Chinatown's sweatshops to organize for better wages, shorter hours and improved conditions and offered a devastating criticism of the ghetto's poverty program, rumors were started in the community which resulted in a three-day run on the bank. Unlike the old Chinese boycotts, which were used so effectively in the early days of the economically isolated Chinatown, this attempt to destroy a Chinatown reformer failed because the bank was protected by its connections to the larger banking system of the state. The failure to silence Choy by traditional methods is a measure of the ghetto's growing interdependence with the nation and a testimony to the decreasing power of traditional sanctions available to intra-community elites.

In Chinatown the arena of battle between the new opposition and the old order has been for seats on the poverty board organized under the community action program of the Economic Opportunity Act of 1964. In April 1969, after three years of internecine in-fighting, the liberal opposition—largely composed of the members of the CADC—was finally able to depose the Six Companies' man on the board, Chairman Dapien Liang, and to replace him with a chairman more to its liking. The Six Companies charged that the poverty board was dominated by "left-wing militants" but was unable to secure its complete control over Chinatown's poverty program. However, the Chinatown program is budgeted so far only to the beginning of 1970. If the program is scrapped, the arena of conflict and opposition in Chinatown may shift on to some other plane.

Another challenge to the old order has been hurled recently by ICSA. In August 1969 a news reporter interviewed Foo Hum, tea merchant, mogul in the Chinese Six Companies and representative on the Chinatown antipoverty board, concerning Chinatown's social problems. In addition to denying that the community's problems were either exclusive or very grave, Hum refuted the assertion that they were attributable to newly arrived immigrants. Then he launched into an attack on the native-born youth, especially the Red Guards and the ICSA and was quoted in the press as saying, "The Red Guards and the Intercollegiate Chinese for Social Action—theirs are Communist activities. They should not be blamed on the new immigrants." ICSA promptly filed a slander suit against Hum for $100,000 general damages and $10,000 punitive damages. Hum, backed by a Six Companies legal defense fund of $10,000, refused to settle out of court to an offer made by Mason Wong, ICSA president, that the suit be dropped in return for Hum's writing a letter of apology and publishing it in all local papers, paying all legal fees that have arisen thus far and donating a token gift of money to ICSA.

The crust of Chinatown's cake of customary control may be beginning to crumble. The old order must contend not only with the mounting opposition of the community's respectable, professional and American-born younger and middle-aged adults, but also with the militant organization of Chinatown's disaffected youth. In addition, one cannot count on the new immigrants to bow to Chinatown's traditional power elite in the future as they have in the past.

It is by no means clear, however, what the outcome of this continuing power struggle will be. Chinatown's more liberal-minded leaders may defeat themselves by their ambiguous support of both progressive policies and a new racial consciousness. The former may call for a need to push for the introduction of unionization and other characteristic features of white America into Chinatown's anachronistic institutions. But the new ethnic consciousness, a consciousness that in its extreme forms opposes both the old order of transplanted Cathay and the middle-class ways of white America, may forbid cooperation with those institutions—progressive or not—that are dominated by Caucasians. It is in this possible paralysis that Chinatown's old order coalesces with its new rebels. Both seem to oppose the imposition of the metropolis upon the ghetto, but for quite different reasons. For the old elites any greater instrusion might undermine their exclusive and "extraterritorial" power; for the new rebels any intrusion might wrest away their newly discovered desire for ethnic self-determination. It would not be impossible for Chinatown's garment workers, as well as the community's other unprotected and impoverished denizens, to be caught helplessly in the vice of this excruciating cultural conflict.

Discrimination and National Oppression

Beyond the problems of the ghetto itself—some of which are typical of all poor ethnic enclaves in American cities, some of which are peculiarly Chinese—loom the attitude and action of the larger society. Chinatown's myth of social propriety, communal self-help, familial solidarity and a low crime rate was a carefully nurtured mystique, prepared to counteract the vicious stereotype of coolie laborers, immoral practices, murderous tong wars and inscrutable cunning that characterized the American white man's perspective. As a pervasive mystique coloring most reports of Chinatown for the past three decades, it has succeeded up to a point in its original purpose—to substitute a favorable stereotype for an unfavorable one. It had other latent functions as well, not the least of which was to protect the community's social and political structure from excessive scrutiny and destruction. So long as Chinatown could "contain" its problems, circumscribe its paragovernmental institutions with bourgeois or innocuously exotic descriptions and control its members, the community was safe, and the city adopted a relaxed attitude toward its own cosmopolitan character.

But Chinatown's safety rests also on America's foreign relations with China. The repeal of the exclusion laws in 1943 was a gesture of reconciliation toward the country's wartime ally in the war against Japan, just as the incarceration of the Japanese-Americans during that same war was a hostile move against those Americans who had the misfortune to be physically identifiable with America's enemy. Aware of the dangerously changeable character of America's friendliness toward her racially visible peoples,

Chinatown has presented a picture of cultural identity with nineteenth-century Cathay and of moral sympathy for the Nationalist Regime in Taiwan. This is not a false picture, for the political identity of the aged aliens is of very low intensity, but if it must be linked to old China it is most probably to the Republic founded by Sun Yat Sen and continued under Chiang Kai-shek. The American-born Chi-

Arthur Tress

nese are not "Zionists" to any degree and therefore feel themselves to be Americans politically and socially and do not identify with either China. Even the Red Guard's rhetorical usage of Mao's book is more a symbol of an American rebellion than the substance of Communist affiliation. And the new immigrants have shown a profound disinterest in associating even with the symbols of Maoism.

Nevertheless, the fires of fear and prejudice are still kindled in America. Not only are acts of prejudice and discrimination still visited upon Chinese-Americans in everyday life, at least one agency of the government itself is still not wholly satisfied with the loyalty of Chinese in America. On 17 April 1969 J. Edgar Hoover testified before a subcommittee of the House Committee on Appropriations that "the blatant, belligerent and illogical statements made by Red China's spokesmen during the past year leave no doubt that the United States is Communist China's No. 1 enemy." Hoover went on to warn the subcommittee of Communist Chinese intelligence activity "overt and covert, to obtain needed material, particularly in the scientific field." After hinting darkly that a Chinese-American who served a 60-day sentence in prison for making a false customs declaration about electronic parts being sent to Hong Kong might have been an agent of a Communist country, Hoover asserted, "We are being confronted with a growing amount of work in being alert for Chinese Americans and others in this country who would assist Red China in supplying needed material or promoting Red Chinese propaganda." "For one thing," he continued, "Red China has been flooding the country with its propaganda and there are over 300,000 Chinese in the United States, some of whom could be susceptible to recruitment either through ethnic ties or hostage situations because of relatives in Communist China." Hoover went on to say that "up to 20,000 Chinese immigrants can come into the United States each year and this provides a means to send illegal agents into our Nation." Hoover concluded his testimony on this point by asserting that "there are active Chinese Communist sympathizers in the Western Hemisphere in a position to aid in operations against the United States." Thus the Chinese in America were reminded that perhaps all their efforts at convincing white America that they were a peaceable, law-abiding, family-minded and docile people who contributed much and asked little in return had gone for naught. In time of crisis they too might suffer the same fate that overtook the highly acculturated Japanese-Americans a quarter century before—wholesale incarceration. When Hoover's remarks are coupled with the widespread report in 1966 that China's atomic bomb was "fathered" by Dr. Tsien Hwue-shen, an American-educated Chinese who was persecuted here for five years during the McCarthy era and then allowed to return to the country of his birth and citizenship, and with the fact that under Title II of the Emergency Detention Act of 1950 any person or group who is deemed to be a "threat to the internal security of the United States" may be incarcerated in the same detention camps in which the American Japanese were imprisoned, the safety of the Chinese in America from official persecution is by no means assured. The Chinese, of course, protested against Hoover's remarks, and one San Francisco paper labeled his testimony an irresponsible slur on "a large and substantial segment of American citizens." Meanwhile, Japanese-American, Chinese-American and several other kinds of organizations have joined together to attempt to get Congress to repeal the infamous Title II.

Race prejudice, as Herbert Blumer has reminded us, is a sense of group position. It arises out of the belief, supported and legitimated by various elites, that a racial group is both inferior and threatening. Such a belief may lie dormant beneath the facade of a long-term racial accommodation, made benign by a minority group's tacit agreement to live behind the invisible, but no less real for that, wall of a ghetto. Then when circumstances seem to call for new meanings and different explanations, the allegedly evil picture and supposedly threatening posture may be resuscitated to account for political difficulties or social problems that seem to defy explanation.

History, however, does not simply repeat itself. There is a new Chinatown and new sorts of Chinese in America. The old order holds its power precariously in the ghetto, and the new liberals and the now vocal radicals bid fair to supplant them and try new solutions to the old problems. Finally, the Japanese experience of 1942 may not be repeated either because the United States has learned that lesson too well or because too many Americans would not let it happen again.

April 1970

SUGGESTED READINGS

The Social Order of the Slum by Gerald D. Suttles (Chicago: University of Chicago Press, 1968). An outstanding work describing the distinct social organization and subcultures of four ethnic groups within Chicago's near-Westside.

The Urban Villagers by Herbert J. Gans (New York: The Free Press, 1962). A thoughtful analysis of an Italian working-class community in the light of both ethnicity and class considerations.

The Polish Peasant in Europe and America by William I. Thomas and Florian Znaniecki (New York: A. A. Knopf, 1927). Especially Volume II. This major early effort in sociology delineates some of the social and cultural changes undergone by Polish immigrants to the urban United States.

The Ghetto by Louis Wirth (Chicago: University of Chicago Press, 1966). As one of the leaders of the influential "Chicago School," Wirth made the definitive early statements on the quality of urban life.

The Death and Life of Great American Cities by Jane Jacobs (New York: Random House, 1961). An attack on urban planning policies in defense of neighborhoods as "what gives life and spirit to the city."

Cleveland's Crisis Ghetto

Census shows ghetto conditions getting worse

WALTER WILLIAMS

The riot in the Hough section of Cleveland, Ohio, occurred in July 1966. Not much more than a year earlier, in April 1965, the Bureau of the Census had conducted a special census for Cleveland that showed unexpected social and economic changes in the five years since 1960. What was most significant was a sharp economic polarization among the city's Negroes. A substantial number had moved up to a more affluent life; but the group in the worst part of the ghetto was at a level of poverty that was actually *below* the one recorded in 1960. Who rose and who stayed behind, and why?

What is most startling about the changes revealed by Cleveland's special census is their magnitude. These five years saw rapidly rising real income and falling unemployment for the city as a whole—but not for the very poor. The gap between haves and have-nots widened strikingly; and the most rapid widening was among Negroes—between those outside the slums who were rising, beginning finally to cash in on the American dream, and those still in the hard-core ghetto, on limited rations of income and hope.

In the special census nine neighborhoods at the bottom economically were grouped together and called the "Neigh-

"An unprovided-for family becomes a continuous symbol of a man's inability to fulfill the demands of his society—to be a man. So he opts out, and the sparse existence of the female-headed family has begun."

borhood." (See map.) The rest of the city, in which the prospering middle and upper classes are concentrated, was called the "Remainder of Cleveland." In Cleveland, however—as in the Inferno—there are different levels on the path downward, and one area of the Neighborhood is especially bad. This is the "Crisis Ghetto." It is predominantly Negro. Hough is part of it—on the edge.

The group that rose most swiftly in the period 1960-1965 were the Negroes who did not live in the Neighborhood. In 1960 they numbered 22,000. By 1965 their number had almost doubled. In all Cleveland they had achieved the greatest economic gains, showing that the door of opportunity, for some at least, was opening wider. (And also providing a convenient, but unwarranted, rationalization against help for the less fortunate—for if some Negroes could rise so quickly through their own efforts, why not all?)

At the opposite end of Cleveland's economic spectrum we find a grim picture. The number of Negro children in poor female-headed households increased sharply. By 1965 nearly two-thirds of these poor Negro youths in female families were in the Crisis Ghetto. Further, the Crisis Ghetto's average resident was in worse economic straits than in 1960. Unemployment was higher, income lower, and a larger percentage of the population was poor.

In relative terms the Crisis Ghetto was further away from the rest of the city than in 1960 in terms of major economic indices. For instance, the income gap between the Crisis Ghetto and the next economic stratum (the other five sections of the Neighborhood) had spread visibly. The range of median real incomes for the four sections of the Crisis Ghetto and the five sections in the rest of the neighborhood was as follows:

Range of Median Incomes	1960	1965
Crisis Ghetto	$3,170-4,900	$3,000-4,160
Rest of Neighborhood	$5,450-6,230	$5,460-6,500

Hence the top of the Crisis Ghetto income range is now $1,300 short of the next economic tier, in contrast to $550 in 1960. And that next tier itself had suffered in income terms over the five-year period relative to the Remainder of Cleveland.

Thus, at least in Cleveland, the census validated our fears of the emerging "two Americas." If this portrays what is happening in other cities, it is most disturbing.

The Crisis Ghetto's potential for generating earned income has declined a great deal since 1960. Those economic units with lowest earning potential—female-headed families and aged people—have increased in absolute numbers, while those with the greatest earning potential (younger male-headed families) have diminished sharply. The Crisis Ghetto has become a concentration point not merely for the poor, but for the hard-core poor—those with least hope or opportunity of being anything else.

The Widening Gap

The increasing distance between Cleveland's majority and its disadvantaged segment is frequently hidden in the overall economic indices of the city. Averaging the increasingly prosperous and the stable poor seems to give a "rise" to everybody. But the almost unchanged poverty rate between 1960 and 1965 masks within different groups large movements that have further split the population. Between 1960 and 1965, the poverty rate:

—declined markedly among male-headed families while it increased among female-headed families;

—fell for white people, but remained almost unchanged for Negroes;

—yet showed a much greater decline (almost 40 percent below the 1960 level) for non-Neighborhood Negroes than for any other group (the whites outside the Neighborhood experienced a 12 percent decrease);

—and rose sharply in the Crisis Ghetto while it fell in the Remainder of Cleveland.

Another important change was in the *kinds* of poor families and poor people in the Crisis Ghetto. Between 1960 and 1965, the number of poor people fell by roughly 14,000. But members of Negro female-headed families increased by almost 12,000 persons (all but the merest handful of whom were found in the Neighborhood) while persons in families headed by Negro males and white males and females decreased by 26,000. As a consequence of these population changes in the five-year period, members of Negro female-headed families increased from one-fifth to one-third of Cleveland's poor. And in 1965, 60 percent of these poor, Negro, female-headed family members lived in the Crisis Ghetto.

Changes in the structure of industry have hurt the Crisis Ghetto. As Louis Buckley notes in discussing the plight of the low-skilled city laborer:

> The changes in the demand for labor in our central cities have been in the direction of expansions of industries requiring well educated white collar workers and a relative decline in the industries employing blue collar unskilled and semi-skilled workers.

Many of these modern industries have fled to the suburbs. Unfortunately, public transportation has not followed, so ghetto residents have difficulty getting out to suburban jobs.

Further, an increasing percentage of the Crisis Ghetto's residents are in families whose heads have the least likelihood of increasing materially their earned income. In general, the two groups with the most limited economic potential are family units (our definition of unit includes single persons living alone) headed by women and by the aged. These groups rose significantly over the five-year period as a percentage of the Crisis Ghetto population. (See tables, page 131.) Not only do these two groups seem *least* likely to earn much more than at present—but they seem the *most* likely group to suffer an actual as well as a relative decline in earned income. In short, they have the lowest chance to improve their financial position, and the highest probability of declining. Once a unit in this limited potential group becomes poor, by definition, it is likely to remain so. This persistent poverty is the eroding evil. Real income in the Crisis Ghetto declined by 2 percent for male-headed families and 15 percent for female-headed

---

A NOTE ON THE STUDY

The special census of Cleveland of April 1965 described in this article is the *only* detailed census of a major city available at mid-decade. Further, comparable information from other cities will not be forthcoming in the near future. We do have a study of the same period for certain low-income areas in Los Angeles, including Watts, but not for the rest of the city. Thus, the Cleveland census is the only available study showing in detail the dynamics of change in a major American city since 1960—in this case, a city which had riots not much more than a year after the census was taken.

---

families between 1960 and 1965. At the end of the five-year period unemployment rates for both men (14.6 percent) and women (17.2 percent—up over one-third since 1960) were higher, standing at nearly three times the city's average; and the poverty level had risen from 36 to 40 percent. In 1965 the average Crisis Ghetto inhabitant was worse off than he had been in 1960, both absolutely and relative to others in the city. (The pattern of deterioration is shown in tables on page 131.)

These facts have major implications. On the one hand, those with economic strength or potential *can* flee the Crisis Ghetto. (True, if Negro, they may only be allowed to escape to a better Negro area.) But is is also clear that entrapment in the Crisis Ghetto springs directly from poverty. The price over the wall is primarily money, not skin color. However, once poverty has locked one into the Crisis Ghetto, the chances of being forced to remain—and the bad consequences of remaining—are greater than if one lived in any other area of the city.

Population Decline

The Crisis Ghetto population declined by about 20 percent during the five years (from 170,000 to 134,000 persons), and this exodus might seem to imply an explanation for the decline and the change. After all, if the more able, above-average people leave, averages should move down.

But exodus, by itself, cannot explain enough. Certainly the population decrease cannot be used to explain the absolute *increases* since 1960 of a few hundreds in the number of female-headed families, and of some 3,000 poor persons in such families. Yet that is what happened; and we have no pat explanation for it.

Nor does the population decrease necessarily counterbalance the possible adverse effects coming from the declining economic situation, particularly the rise in weak economic units as a part of the total population. These people seem likely to face the Crisis Ghetto over an extended period of time. What are the consequences?

The deleterious effects of a hard-core ghetto spread beyond the economy to the total environment—to schools, to street associations, to the preservation of life itself. This last point was driven home when three Washington medical schools threatened to pull out of the D.C. General Hospital because the meager budget provided almost medieval services. Even to be sick in the Crisis Ghetto is far more dangerous than in the suburbs. So, from birth to death the ghetto marks each person, and cuts his chances either to escape or survive. The Crisis Ghetto lacks the precise boundaries and imposed restrictions of the European ghettos of the past; but it is, nevertheless, an existing reality that limits and blights the lives of its inhabitants as effectively as did the old ghettos and pales.

Is this pattern confined to Cleveland? Only in Cleveland was a special census made for the city as a whole. But figures available for 1960-65 for South Los Angeles (which includes Watts and in an economic sense is like the Cleveland Neighborhood) also show a decrease in real income per family, a small increase in the percent of poor people, and a decrease in the male and increase in female unemployment rates (the Crisis Ghetto differs only in that it shows a very small male unemployment increase). Further, Negro female family members became a far more significant proportion of South Los Angeles poor (we do not have city-wide data) increasing from 37 percent to 48 percent. While the number of poor people in Negro female-headed households rose by 9,500 (roughly 25 percent) the number of poor among white male, white female, and Negro male-headed families all decreased.

At the national level poor Negro female-headed family members have increased both absolutely and as a proportion of the total poor population. For 1960 and 1966, the number of poor persons (in millions) for these categories was as follows: (Data furnished by Mollie Orshansky.)

	1960 Number in millions	1960 % of total poor	1966 Number in millions	1966 % of total poor
Negro female-headed family members	3.2	8%	3.8	12%
All other poor persons	35.7	92	28.9	88
Total poor persons	38.9	100	32.7	100

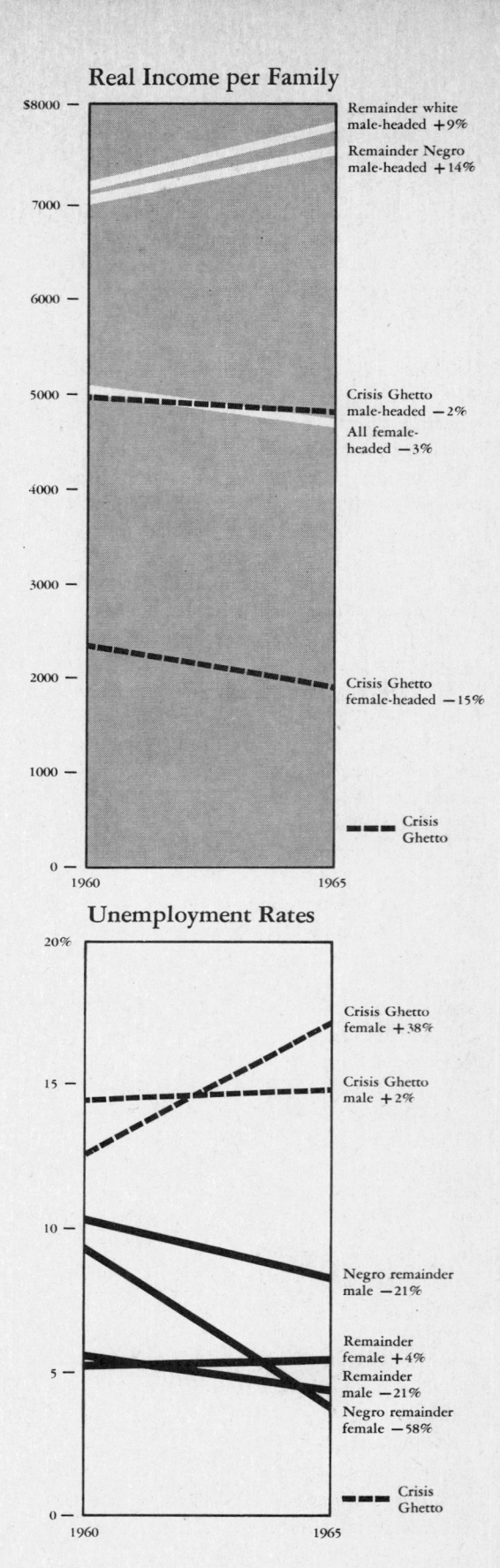

Real Income per Family

- Remainder white male-headed +9%
- Remainder Negro male-headed +14%
- Crisis Ghetto male-headed −2%
- All female-headed −3%
- Crisis Ghetto female-headed −15%
- ---- Crisis Ghetto

Unemployment Rates

- Crisis Ghetto female +38%
- Crisis Ghetto male +2%
- Negro remainder male −21%
- Remainder female +4%
- Remainder male −21%
- Negro remainder female −58%
- ---- Crisis Ghetto

the haves and the have-nots

"The years between 1960 and 1965 saw rapidly rising real income and falling unemployment for the city of Cleveland as a whole—but not for the very poor. The gap between the haves and the have-nots widened strikingly."

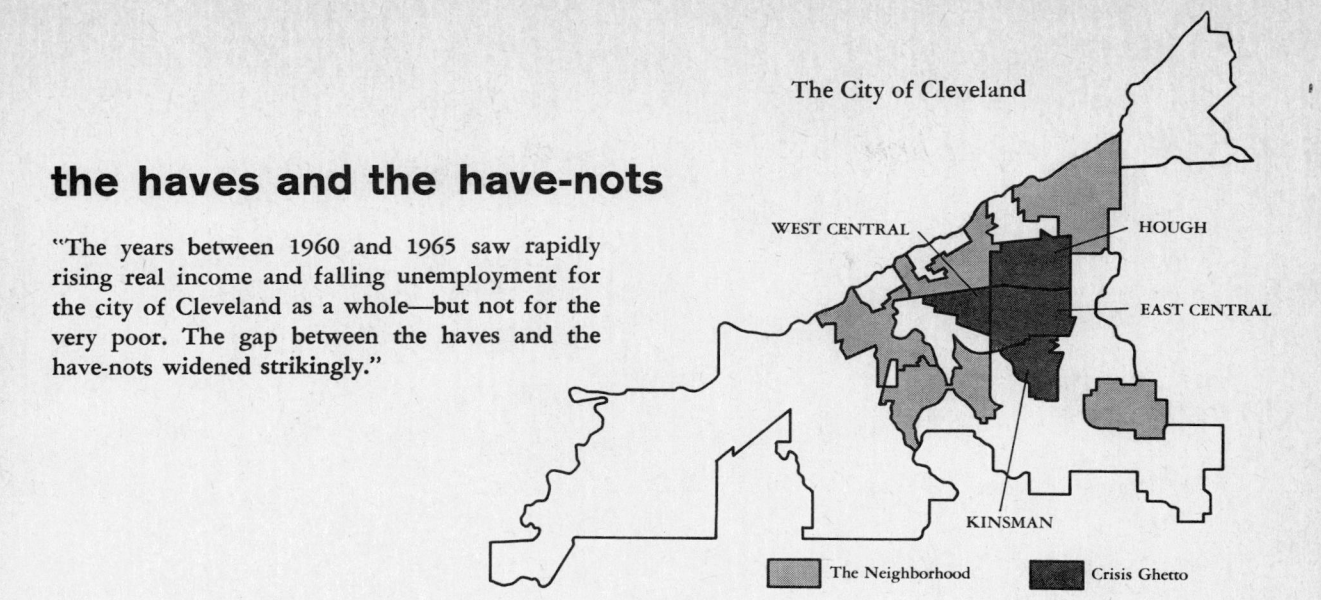

The City of Cleveland

WEST CENTRAL
HOUGH
EAST CENTRAL
KINSMAN

The Neighborhood | Crisis Ghetto

Percent of Cleveland Families in Poverty

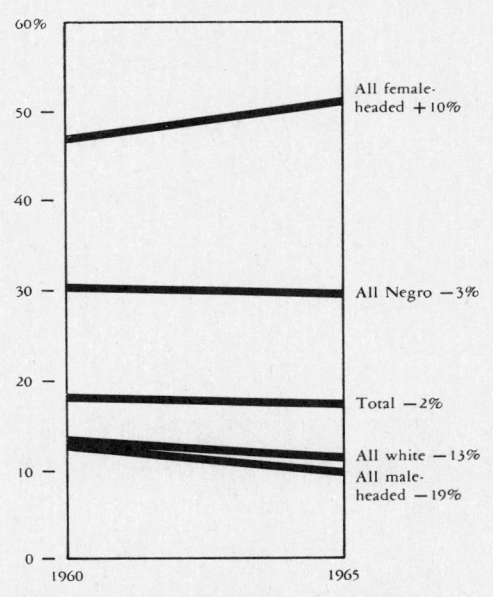

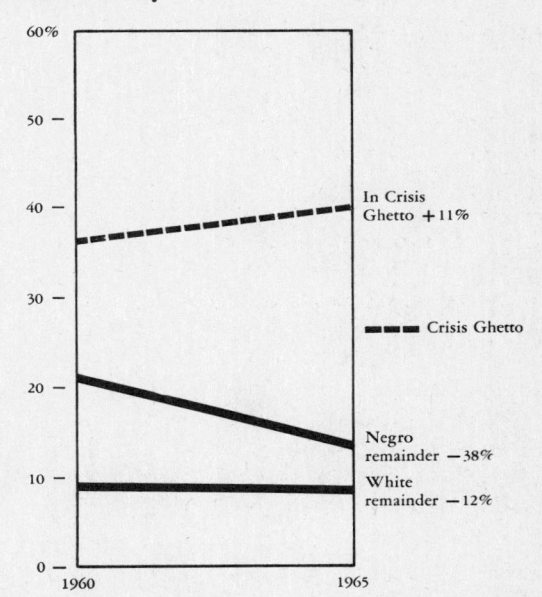

All female-headed +10%
All Negro −3%
Total −2%
All white −13%
All male-headed −19%

In Crisis Ghetto +11%
Crisis Ghetto
Negro remainder −38%
White remainder −12%

Limited Economic Potential Families

Crisis Ghetto +27%
Remainder +5%
Negro remainder −40%

1960
1965

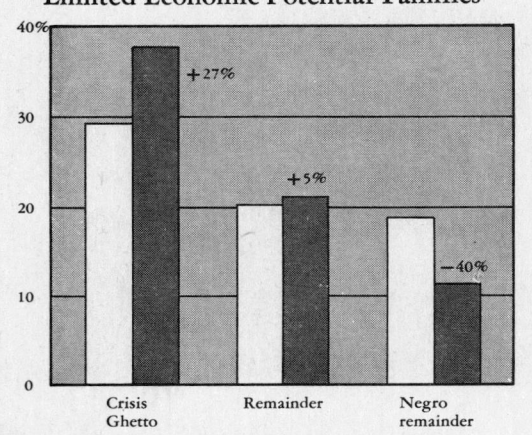

Poor Limited Economic Potential Families

Crisis Ghetto +37%
Remainder −2%
Negro remainder −49%

POPULATION AND URBAN COMMUNITIES

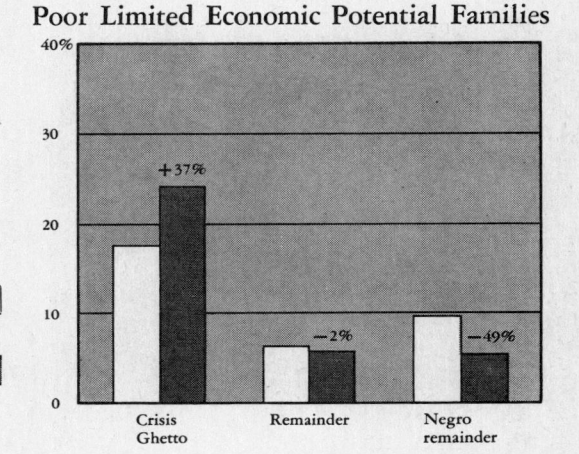

no exit?

Photographed by George Gardner

"Once poverty has locked one into the Crisis Ghetto, the chances of being forced to remain—and the bad consequences of remaining—are greater than if one lived in any other area of the city . . . the ghetto limits and blights the lives of its inhabitants."

The non-Neighborhood Negro has advanced greatly in the five years between the two censuses—more, as noted, than any other Cleveland group. Of course, this great improvement can be partly explained by residential segregation. The white on the rise goes to the suburbs—and out of the Cleveland census area—while his Negro counterpart must stay in the city. Still, there is no doubt that the Negroes escaping the Neighborhood are advancing as a group more rapidly than any within the city limits, and closing in on the Remainder of Cleveland whites. Even more striking than their increasing prosperity were their increasing numbers—from 22,000 to 41,000. They now account for 15 percent of the Negro population.

The Cleveland data indicate that economic discrimination has declined in Cleveland since 1960. Is this only in the upper and middle level jobs or has discrimination lessened across the board? I believe it may have lessened somewhat across the board; but this may not help the Crisis Ghetto Negroes unless direct action is taken to overcome their difficulties. Any decrease in overt economic discrimination, of course, is encouraging. However, it is absurd to think that this change *alone*—even if the reduction in discrimination had been far greater than I expect it was in Cleveland—will set right all the damage of the past. The liabilities of the Crisis Ghetto Negroes caused by past discrimination —poor education, lack of skills, poor health, police records—would still hold them back in the job market. In fact, the reduction in discrimination *alone* may exacerbate the split between the various strata of Cleveland Negroes.

Earlier discrimination possibly served as a lid for the advancement of *all* Negroes, squeezing them closer together in income and opportunity despite differences in skills and potentials. But once the lid was lifted, especially during boom years, the more skilled, educated, and able rose much more rapidly than the others. So the gap widened. Unless something is done the more able Negroes should continue

133

moving out

"Those with economic strength can flee the Crisis Ghetto. The more able Negroes should continue to widen their lead until they too become part of the symbols of success that make failure ever more visible and disturbing."

to widen their lead until they too become part of the symbols of success that have so far evaded the Crisis Ghetto Negroes and make failure ever more visible and disturbing.

At the opposite pole, though population in the Crisis Ghetto declined by one-fifth, Negro female-headed families increased by 8 percent, children in these families by 25 percent (16,900 to 21,000), and children in *poor* Negro female-headed families by 30 percent (13,100 to 17,000). Of the 21,000 children of female-headed families in the Crisis Ghetto, 17,000 are living below the poverty level. And it is this increasing group of female-headed families that suffered the largest real income decline of the five-year period, falling from $2,300 to $1,950 per family per year. That is, at the later survey date (1965), the average Crisis Ghetto female-headed family had an income *per week* of just over $37.50.

The implications of these statistics are appalling. There were 3,900 *more* poverty-stricken children in the ghetto in 1965 than 1960—in a population 36,000 less—and there is no reason to believe that this trend is not continuing or accelerating. These children can do least to improve their condition—yet they must have a tremendous influence on the future of the Neighborhood, and of all Cleveland.

Poor Negro children in female-headed families are the great tragedy of the Crisis Ghetto. They constitute 13 percent of all persons there, 30 percent of all the children. They make up over half of the members of the poor limited-potential families.

There has been tremendous movement in and out of the Crisis Ghetto—at least four out of every ten departed or died in the five years. But the option of movement is not a random phenomenon affecting all equally. It seems available at will to some and almost completely closed to others—and most tightly closed to adults with limited economic potential, and their children.

Although the percentage of people with limited economic potential in the Crisis Ghetto is about twice as large as the population in the Remainder of Cleveland, the percentage of poor among them—standing at nearly 25 percent—is about *five* times as large.

Recent prosperity has removed many from the rolls of the needy, but those remaining may be far more discontented than when most of their neighbors were also poor. "Relative deprivation" is a very real force. For example, the classic study of this phenomenon made during World War II showed that there was more jealousy and dissatisfaction in an Air Force fighter squadron noted for rapid promotions ("boy colonels") than in a military police unit with few promotions. This feeling of being ignored, discriminated against, and isolated, while all around others rise, may create a far more explosive situation than when many are in the same boat, as during the Depression.

The Cleveland Census reveals the city's contrasting prosperity and decay. Sharp differences emerge within the Negro population. The rapid income increase for non-Neighborhood Negroes probably indicates less economic discrimination. Also, while residential segregation remained strong, the white flight to the suburbs opened up some of the desirable Cleveland residential areas. For example, Lee Miles, an area with many expensive dwellings, changed from 28 to 72 percent Negro in five years (21,000 Negroes by 1965). Many strong economic units fled the ghetto.

As many fled to better circumstances, others became more ensnarled. And by 1965 the most disadvantaged group had grown to a very significant portion of the total Crisis Ghetto population. Particularly depressing is the increase of poor Negro young people in the economically weak female-headed homes—young people whose bondage becomes more oppressive as the rest of the city grows more prosperous.

Income and Incentive

What can be done? What can be our long term goals?

The ghetto male, frequently with limited skills, enters the job market with grave liabilities. Often the job does not pay him enough to support his family and has little prospect of leading to a living wage. The longer the man works, the longer he fails as a provider. His marriage will frequently deteriorate. As Elliot Liebow has suggested in *Tally's Corner,* the unprovided-for family becomes a continuous symbol of a man's inability to fulfill the demands of his society—to be a man. So he opts out, and the sparse existence of the female-headed family has begun.

Job and training programs for men in the Crisis Ghetto are thus a first order need. Employment that yields a living wage over time seems to be the best bet for *preventing* family break-up, and *re-establishing* stable families.

Many broken homes, however, are not going to be re-established. Consequently, the female-headed family, as the Cleveland data show so starkly, will face a particularly exposed financial position. The mother may well seek a relationship with a man that has some prospect of offering family stability and also additional income. Unfortunately, the "eligible" males are often the failures from prior marriages. The woman enters a tenuous relationship with the very unrealistic hope that it will work into a real family situation. The result is often another child.

Programs thus must be aimed at providing greater economic stability to the female-headed family. Job programs should be readily accessible for women as well as men. This means that major efforts for establishing day care centers are needed. Yet, work is not the answer for all these women. Also needed are better programs of income maintenance which will provide the family a reasonable income.

It is clear that our long run goals should be to prevent the breakup of families. But, many families are beyond the prevention of this sort. Further, the Negro mother has shown remarkable strength as a family head. Her great weakness has been in producing sufficient income, and the resultant poverty has had an adverse effect on the family. If these deficiencies can be overcome by work or transfer income, many of these mothers may be able to properly motivate their children. If freed from poverty, the inner strength of the matriarchal Negro family may begin to assert a positive effect upon the Crisis Ghetto.

Income increases from work and transfer payments are vital, but I believe that we must go beyond income programs to effect basic institutional changes in both the larger community that includes the Crisis Ghetto and the ghetto itself. A city must provide adequate education, health, and other services for all its residents. Further, direct community action must help Crisis Ghetto residents end the growing social decay in that area. As Richard A. Cloward and Lloyd E. Ohlin observed in *Delinquency and Opportunity,* the hard-core ghetto community must be structured to provide both social control and legitimate avenues of social ascent. That is, the neighborhood community—the Crisis Ghetto—must be a sound base of opportunity. The resident of the Crisis Ghetto must be able to form a realistic belief in a decent life.

We see the alternative in current trends. The poor in the Crisis Ghetto are falling further behind. Not only distance is building up between the two poles, but tension as well—as with electrodes approaching a sparking point.

If what is happening in Cleveland is also happening in other cities, we must multiply this tension, and the danger signals, by a large factor. If by inaction we consign the misery of the parents in the Crisis Ghettos to their children, the sickness of the central cities must fester and grow worse. Hough may be a pale prelude to other, greater Houghs—a short dramatic prologue, announcing that the tragedy has begun.

September 1967

SUGGESTED READINGS

Tally's Corner by Elliot Liebow (Boston: Little, Brown, & Co., 1967). An anthropological field study of Negro street-corner men which seems relevant to the study of family formation by females.

Negroes in the Cities by Karl E. Taeuber and Alma F. Taeuber (Chicago: Aldine, 1956). A wealth of statistical data on Negro migration patterns and racial segregation in large urban areas is presented.

The Moynihan Report and the Politics of Controversy by Lee Rainwater and William L. Yancey (Cambridge, Mass.: M.I.T. Press, 1967). A discussion of the Moynihan controversy, including the debate over poverty versus cultural inheritance.

Planning for a Nation of Cities edited by Sam Bass Warner Jr. (Cambridge, Mass.: M.I.T. Press, 1966). See particularly chapters on the expressive style and the problems of transition from country to city.

Why Families Move by Peter H. Rossi (Glencoe, Ill.: The Free Press, 1955). A study in the social psychology of urban residential mobility, exploring why people move, what they take into consideration and how mobility affects the social and economic life of areas.

Black Metropolis by St. Clair Drake and Horace B. Cayton (New York: Harper and Row, 1962). The effect of the urban North on Negro cultural and social life.

Poverty U.S.A. by Thomas Gladwin (Boston: Little, Brown, and Co., 1967). An anthropological examination of poverty and discrimination as linked and mutually supportive phenomena.

Behind Ghetto Walls by Lee Rainwater (Chicago: Aldine Publishing, 1970). An important new contribution in the study of the organization and disorganization of the slum.

Timing of Our Lives

HARLEY L. BROWNING

The social consequences of the biologically complete life

Only quite recently in his history has man been able to exercise any important and lasting influence on the control of his mortality. In Western Europe mortality declines have been documented for periods ranging up to several hundred years, but this accomplishment recently has been overshadowed by the spectacular drops in mortality in many developing countries. They are now accomplishing in a few decades what the European countries took many generations to achieve. In Mexico, to cite one remarkable example, male life expectancy at birth has nearly doubled within the span of a single generation (1930-1965). During this period, the life expectancy of Mexican men rose from 32 to 62 years.

Man's great leap forward in mortality control, which now permits so large a proportion of those born in advanced societies to pass through virtually all important stages in the life cycle, must surely be counted among his most impressive accomplishments. Yet, there has been no systematic effort to follow out all the ramifications of this relatively new condition. If a Mexican boy born in 1965 can expect to live twice as long as his father born in 1930, can he not also expect to pass through a life cycle markedly different in quality and content from that of his father?

One would think that a man who had little chance of living beyond 35 would want to cram all the important stages of his life into a brief period. Conversely, one might expect that if given twice the time in which to live out his life cycle, an individual might plan and space out the major events in his life such as education, marriage, birth of his children and beginning of his work career and so on—to gain the optimal advantage of all this additional time. But, in reality, little intelligent use is being made of the extension of life expectancy in terms of the spacing of key events in the life cycle.

Here, for purposes of exploring the possibilities opened up by recent advances in mortality control, I want first to document the astonishing increase in life expectancy of recent times. From there we can examine some of the implications that can be drawn from it and consider the potential consequences of increased longevity in altering the timing of events in the life cycle. Finally, I shall comment on the feasibility of planning changes in the life cycle to better utilize the advantages of reduced mortality rates. Since my purpose is to set forth a perspective for the linking of life expectancy and life cycle, I have not attempted systematically to provide data for all of my generalizations. Therefore, my conclusions must be taken as exploratory and tentative.

In the investigation of the relationship of changes in life expectancy to changes in the life cycle, it is worthwhile to consider two groupings of countries—the developed countries, where life expectancy has been increasing over a considerable period of time, and the developing countries, with their recent and very rapid increases.

For the developing countries, an important question for which we have little evidence as yet is how much people are aware at all social levels of the dramatic change in life expectancy. Perhaps it is not generally "perceived" because the change has not had time to manifest itself in the lifetime of many persons. The fact that in Mexico there is now so great a generational difference in life expectancy that the son may expect to live almost twice as long as his father surely will have considerable impact upon the family and other institutions. But we can only know these changes for certain as the son passes through his life span, well into the next century, a time when all of us will be dead.

Mexico is a striking case but by no means an isolated one. A number of other developing countries will achieve much the same record within a fifty-year period or less. Thus, for a substantial part of the world's population, the mortality experience of succeeding generations will differ markedly and to an extent unparalleled in any other historical period.

There are striking extremes between conditions in primitive and pre-industrial countries with unusually high death rates and the situation that many countries in Western Europe and Anglo-America either have already reached or are closely approaching. For instance, India between 1901 and 1911 represented the conditions of extremely high mortality under which mankind has lived during most of his time on this earth. A male child born in this period and locale had a life expectancy of slightly less than 23 years. Today such conditions are extremely rare. At the other extreme, a boy born in the United States in 1950, for example, could expect to live almost to age 74.

As is well-known, the greatest improvement in mortality control has come about through the reduction of deaths in infancy and early childhood. In India around 1901, nearly one-half of those born were lost by age five. By contrast, under the conditions prevailing in the United States in 1950, 98.5 per cent of male children were still living five years after birth.

For the purposes of relating life expectancy to life cycle, however, it is not the losses in the early years that are of the most importance. Death at any time, including the first few years of life, is of course a "waste," but the loss on "investment" at these ages for both parents and society is not nearly so great as for those persons who die at just about the time they are ready to assume adult responsibilities. This is when such significant events in the life cycle as higher education, work career, marriage and family take place. For this reason, the focus of this article is upon the fifty-year span from age 15 to 65. By age 15 the boy is in the process of becoming a man and is preparing himself either for college or entry into the labor force. Fifty years later, at age 65, the man is either retired or, if not, his productivity is beginning to decline noticeably in most cases.

But what are the consequences of these changes that have recently permitted a substantial part of the world's population for the first time to live what Jean Fourastie has called "a biologically complete life." What can be the meaning of death in a society where nearly everyone lives out his allotted threescore and ten years? Is death beyond the age of 65 or 70 really a "tragic" occurrence? The specter of early and unexpected death manifested itself symbolically in countless ways in societies with high mortality. Of France in the twelth century, Fourastie writes, "In traditional times, death was at the center of life, just as the cemetery was at the center of the village."

Not everyone believes that the great increase in life expectancy is entirely favorable in its consequences. Some argue that perhaps advanced societies now allow too high a proportion of those born into them to pass through to advanced ages. "Natural selection" no longer works effectively to eliminate the weak and the infirm. In other words, these people maintain that one consequence of improved mortality is that the biological "quality" of the population declines.

While we can grant that a number of individuals now survive to old age who are incapable of making any contribution to their society, the real question is how numerically important a group they are. My impression is that

A Mexican boy born today can expect to live to age 62, twice as long as his father born in 1930.

In most of the Third World, few could look forward to "a biologically complete life." Suddenly, many can.

their numbers have generally been exaggerated by some eugenicists. The cost of maintaining these relatively few individuals is far outweighed by the many benefits deriving from high survivorship. In any event, the strong ethical supports for the preservation of life under virtually all conditions are not likely to be dramatically altered within the next generation or so.

Whatever the problems occasioned by the great rise in natural increase, no one would want to give up the very real gains that derive from the control of mortality man now possesses. One of the most interesting features is the biological continuity of the nuclear family (parents and children) during the period when childbearing and childrearing take place. In most societies the crucial period, for men at least, is between ages 25 and 55. But only a little more than a third of the males born under very backward conditions survive from age 15 to age 55. By contrast, almost 94 percent in Europe and Anglo-America reach this age. The fact that until relatively recently it was highly probable that one or both parents would die before their children reached maturity had a profound effect upon family institutions. In "functional" terms, the survival of the society depended upon early marriages and early and frequent conceptions within those marriages. Andrew Collver has shown this very effectively in his comparative study of the family cycle in India and the United States:

> In the United States, the married couple, assured of a long span of life together, can take on long-term responsibilities for starting a new household, rearing children and setting aside some provisions for their old age. In India, by contrast, the existence of the nuclear family is too precarious for it to be entrusted entirely with these important functions. The joint household alone has a good prospect for continuity.

Not all societies with high mortality are also characterized by the importance of joint households. But all societies of the past in one way or another had to provide for children who were orphaned before they reached maturity. One largely uncelebrated consequence of greatly reduced mortality in Western countries, for example, has been the virtual disappearance of orphanages. In the United States, the number of complete orphans declined from 750,000 in 1920 to 66,000 in 1953. In this way a favorite theme of novelists a century or so ago has largely disappeared. Were Dickens writing today he would have to shift his attention from orphans to the children of divorced or separated parents. The psychological and economic consequences of whether homes are broken by divorce or separation rather than by the death of one or both parents obviously may be quite different.

I need not elaborate the obvious advantages of increased life expectancy both for the individual and his society in terms of advanced education and professional career. Under present conditions it is now possible for an individual realistically to plan his entire education and work life with little fear of dying before he can carry out his plans. In this respect, the developed countries have a considerable advantage over developing countries, for the former do not suffer many losses on their investments in the training and education of their youth. But under conditions that are still typical of a large number of countries, a third of those who have reached the age of 15 never reach age 45, the peak productive period of an educated person's life. In such countries, primary education for everyone may be desirable but a part of the investment will be lost for the substantial number who will die during their most productive period.

Another consequence, perhaps overlooked, of the improvement of life expectancy in advanced countries is the fact that while even the rich and powerful were likely to die at early ages in older societies, now everyone, including the poor, can expect to pass through most of the life span. Considerable attention in America is now concentrated on conditions of social inequality, and clearly very large differences exist for characteristics such as education, occupation, and income. But in a society where about eighty-five of every one hundred persons can expect to reach their 65th birthday, extreme differences in longevity among the social strata do not exist. This is not to say that mortality differentials do not exist; they do, but not nearly to the degree found for other major socioeconomic variables. For the poor, unfortunately, increased longevity may be at best a mixed blessing. Too frequently it can only mean a prolongation of ill health, joblessness, and dependency.

What is still not well-appreciated are the consequences of the prolongation of life for the spacing of key events in the life cycle. Obviously, wholesale transformation of the life cycle is impossible because most of the events of importance are to one degree or another associated with age. Retirement cannot precede first job. Nevertheless, the timing of such events or stages as education, beginning of work career, marriage and birth of first and last child is subject to changes that can have marked repercussions on both the individual and the society.

One of the difficulties of dealing with the life cycle is that it is rarely seen in its entirety. Specialists on child development concentrate only on the early years, while the period of adolescence has its own "youth culture" specialists, and so on.

But another important reason why changes in the life cycle itself have not received much attention is the lack of data. Ideally, life histories are required so that the timing of each event can be specified, but until quite recently the technical problems in gathering and especially in processing detailed life histories on a large scale were so great as to make the task unfeasible. Now, however, with the help of computers, many of these problems can be overcome.

Let's examine one particular instance—age at first marriage in the United States—in which one might expect increased life expectancy to have some effect either actual or potential on the life cycle. The data are reasonably good, at least for the last seventy years, and age at first marriage is an event subject to a fair amount of variation in its timing. More interestingly, age at first marriage can greatly affect the subsequent course of a person's life and is indicative of changes in social structure.

In the time period of concern to us, 1890-1960, the generational life expectancy in the United States at age 20 increased 13 years for males and 11 years for females. This is not so great an increase as is now occurring in developing countries but it is still an impressive gain. With an appreciable extension in his life expectancy, a person might reasonably be expected to alter the spacing of key events in his life cycle in order to take advantage of the greater "space" available. In particular, we might expect him to marry at a somewhat later age. But exactly the opposite has happened! Between 1890 and 1960 the median age at first marriage for males declined about four years, a very significant change. For females, the decline was only two years, but their age at first marriage in 1890 (22) already was quite low.

Isn't this strange? During the period of an important extension in life expectancy, a substantial decline in age at first marriage has occurred. Unquestionably, many factors go into an adequate explanation of this phenomenon. One of the reasons why age at first marriage was high around the turn of the century was the numbers of foreign-born, most of them from Europe where marriage at a later age was characteristic, even among the lower strata. Immigrants who arrived as single men had some difficulty finding wives and this delayed their first marriage. In addition, around the turn of the century, middle-class men were not expected to marry until they had completed their education, established themselves in their careers and accumulated sufficient assets to finance the marriage and a proper style of living.

The greatest drop in age at first marriage occurred between 1940 and 1960, especially for females. During this period a great many changes took place in society that worked to facilitate early marriages. "Going steady" throughout a good part of adolescence became accepted practice. Parents adopted more permissive attitudes toward early marriage and often helped young couples to get started. The reduced threat of military conscription after 1946 for married men with children was also a big factor along with a period of general prosperity and easy credit that enabled newlyweds to have a house, furnishings and car, all with a minimal down payment. And not only is marriage easier to get into, it is now easier to get out of; divorce no longer carries the stigma once attached to it.

Of course, many early marriages are not wholly voluntary and in a substantial number of cases the couple either would never have married or they would have married at a later age. David Goldberg has estimated, on the basis of a Detroit survey, that as high as 25 percent of white, first births are conceived outside of marriage, with a fifth of these being illegitimate. As he puts it:

> We have been accustomed to thinking of the sequence marriage, conception and birth. It is apparent that for a very substantial part of the population the current sequence is conception followed by birth, with marriage intervening, following birth or not occurring at all. This may represent a fundamental change in marriage and

fertility patterns, but historical patterns are lacking. An increase in illegitimate conceptions may be largely responsible for the decline in marriage age in the postwar period.

Unfortunately, there is no way to determine if the proportion of illegitimate conceptions has risen substantially since 1890.

The causes of early first marriage are not so important for the purposes of this article as their consequences for subsequent events of the life cycle. For one thing, age at first marriage is closely related to the stability of the marriage. The high dissolution of teenage marriages by divorce or other means is notorious. One may or may not consider this as "wastage" but there is no question about the costs of these unsuccessful unions to the couples involved, to their children and often to society in the form of greater welfare expenditures.

Not only has age at first marriage trended downward, especially since World War II, but family formation patterns have also changed. For the woman, the interval between first marriage and birth of her first child has diminished somewhat and the intervals between subsequent births also have been reduced. As a result, most women complete their childbearing period by the time they reach age 30.

Marriage, Work and Babies

The effects of these changes on the family cycle are as yet not very well understood. But the lowering of age at first marriage among men encompasses within the brief span of the early twenties many of the most important events of the life cycle—advanced education, marriage, first stages of work career and family formation. This is particularly true for the college-educated. Since at least four of every ten college-age males will have some college training, this is an important segment of the population. Each important stage of the life cycle requires commitment and involvement of the individual. If he crowds them together, he reduces both the time he can devote to each of them and his chances for success in any or all of them.

From our discussion of increased life expectancy and the timing of one particular aspect of the life cycle, age at first marriage, we might conclude that there is little relationship between the two. Man has been able to push back the threat of death both in developing and developed societies but he has not seen fit to make much use of this increased longevity. Must this be? Would not the "quality" of the populations in both developing and developed countries be improved by a wider spacing of key events in the life cycle? I believe a good argument can be made that it would.

First, take the situation in the developing countries. What would be the consequences of raising the age at marriage several years and of widening the interval between births? The demographic consequences would be very important, for, independent of any reduction of completed family size, these changes would substantially reduce fertility rates. Raising age at marriage would delay births as

The New York marriage registrar. With longer life, why do we cram the most significant events of our lives into our early twenties?

a short-run effect and in the long run it would lengthen the span of a generation. At a time when there is much concern to slow down the rate of population growth in most developing countries, this would be particularly effective when coupled with a concomitant reduction in completed family size.

A second effect of the raising of age at marriage and widening the spacing of births would be to allow these societies to better gear themselves to the requirements of a modernized and highly-trained population. A later age at marriage for women could permit more of them to enter the labor force. This in itself would probably result in lowered fertility. In most developing societies, the role and position of the woman *outside* of the home must be encouraged and strengthened.

Accommodating the Sex Drive

The case of the developed countries, particularly the United States, is somewhat different. I see very few advantages either for the individual, the couple or the society in the recent practice of squeezing the terminal stages of education, early work career and marriage and family formation into the period of the early twenties. There simply isn't time enough to do justice to all of these events. The negative effects are often felt most by the women. If a woman is married by age 20, completes her childbearing before 30 and sees her children leave home before she reaches 50, she is left with a long thirty years to fill in some manner. We know that many women have difficulty finding meaningful activities to occupy themselves. True, the shortening of generations will permit people the opportunity of watching their great-grandchildren grow up, but does this compensate for the earlier disadvantages of this arrangement? From the standpoint of the society, there are few if any advantages.

If an argument can be made that little intelligent use is being made of the extension of life expectancy in terms of timing key events in the life cycle, what can be done about it? In any direct way, probably very little. "Licensing" people to do certain things at certain ages is, to my mind, appropriate only in totalitarian societies. So far as I am aware, contemporary totalitarian societies have made relatively little effort to actively regulate the timing of events in the life cycle. The Chinese, for example, have only "suggested" that males defer marriage until age 30. But if the state is not to force people to do things at specified ages, at least it might educate them as to the advantages of proper spacing and also make them aware of the handicaps generated by early marriage and, particularly, early family formation. Both in developing and developed countries there probably is very little direct awareness of how spacing will affect one's life chances and how something might be done about it.

Obviously, if marriage is delayed, then something must be done to accommodate the sex drive. Fifty years ago the resolution of this problem was for men to frequent prostitutes while women had fainting spells, but neither alternative is likely to gain favor with today's generation. Perhaps Margaret Mead has once again come to our rescue with her proposal that two kinds of marriages be sanctioned, those with and those without children. Under her "individual" marriage young people could enter into and leave unions relatively freely as long as they did not have children. This, of course, would require effective contraception. Such a union would provide sexual satisfaction, companionship, and assuming the women is employed, two contributors to household expenses. This arrangement would not markedly interfere with the careers of either sex. Marriages with the purpose of having children would be made more difficult to enter into, but presumably many couples would pass from the individual into the family marriage. This suggestion, of course, will affront the conventional morality, but so do most features of social change.

October 1969

SUGGESTED READINGS

From Generation to Generation by S. N. Eisenstadt (Glencoe, Ill.: Free Press, 1956) sets forth the normative approach to the life cycle and its key events.

American Families by Paul Glick (New York: John Wiley, 1957) represents the demographic approach to the family life cycle.

Marriage and the Family: A Comprehensive Reader edited by Jeffrey K. Hadden and Marie L. Borgatta (Itasca, Illinois: F. E. Peacock, 1969) has a number of good articles on the family life cycle.

"Is a New Family Form Emerging in the Urban Fringe" by E. Gartly Jaco and Ivan Belknap, *American Sociological Review*, (Vol. 18, 1953) basically focuses on differing family patterns in differing environments—especially the suburbs.

"Familism and Suburbanization" by Wendell Bell, *Rural Sociology* (Vol. 21, 1956) treats the suburban family.

"Adjustment of Southern White Migrants to Northern Urban Norms" by Lewis M. Killian, *Social Forces* (Vol. 32, Oct-May 1953-54) discusses the adjustment of migrant families who settle in urban areas.

"The American Patrician Class: A field of Research" by Edward N. Saveth in *Kinship and Family Organization* edited by Bernard Farber (New York: John Wiley and Sons, 1966) studies the structure of the upper-class family.

And the Poor Get Children by Lee Rainwater (Chicago: Quadrangle Books, 1960) focuses on the lower-class family.

The Urban Villagers by Herbert Gans (New York: Free Press, 1962) studies Italian-American families living in Boston's West End.

Beyond Bureaucracy

Will organization men fit the new organizations?

WARREN BENNIS

Most of us spend all of our working day and a great deal of our non-working day in a unique and extremely durable social arrangement called "bureaucracy." I use the term "bureaucracy" descriptively, not as an epithet about those "guys in Washington" or as a metaphor *a la* Kafka's *Castle* which conjures up an image of red tape, or faceless and despairing masses standing in endless lines. Bureaucracy, as I shall use the term here, is a social invention, perfected during the industrial revolution to organize and direct the activities of the business firm.

It is my premise that the bureaucratic form of organization is becoming less and less effective; that it is hopelessly out of joint with contemporary realities; that new shapes, patterns, and models are emerging which promise drastic changes in the conduct of the corporation and of managerial practices in general. In the next 25 to 50 years we should witness, and participate in, the end of bureaucracy and the rise of new social systems better suited to twentieth century demands of industrialization. (Sociological evolutionists substantially agree that 25 to 50 years from now most people in the world will live in industrialized societies.)

Corsica, according to Gibbon, is much easier to deplore than to describe. The same holds true for bureaucracy. Basically, bureaucracy is a social invention which relies exclusively on the power to influence through rules, reason, and law. Max Weber, the German sociologist who developed the theory of bureaucracy around the turn of the century, once described bureaucracy as a social machine:

> Bureaucracy is like a modern judge who is a vending machine into which the pleadings are inserted together with the fee and which then disgorges the judgment together with its reasons mechanically derived from the code.

The bureaucratic "machine model" Weber outlined was developed as a reaction against the personal subjugation, nepotism, cruelty, emotional vicissitudes, and capricious judgment which passed for managerial practices in the early days of the industrial revolution. The true hope for man, it was thought, lay in his ability to rationalize, calculate, to use his head as well as his hands and heart. Thus, in the bureaucratic system social roles were institutionalized and reinforced by legal tradition rather than by the "cult of personality"; rationality and predictability were sought for in order to eliminate chaos and unanticipated consequences; emphasis was placed on technical competence rather than

Elliott Erwitt MAGNUM

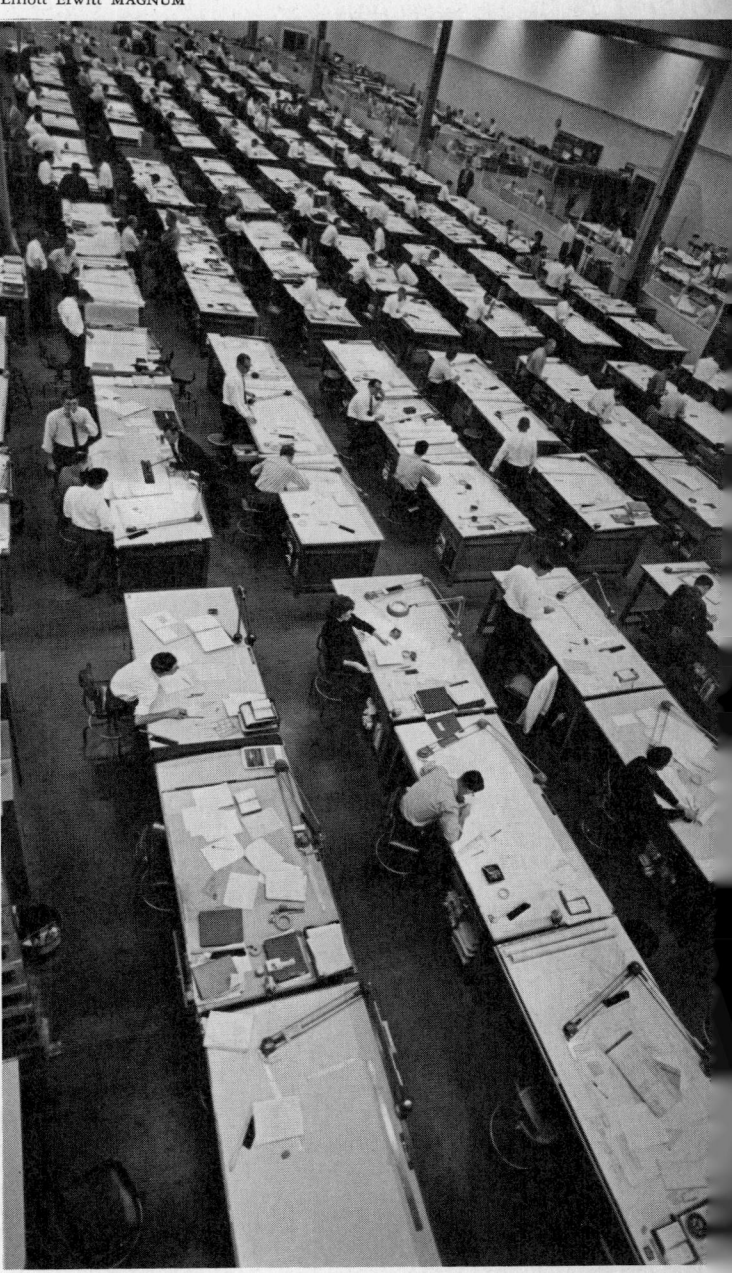

"It is horrible to think that the world could one day be filled with nothing but those little cogs, little men clinging to little jobs and striving towards bigger ones." (Max Weber)

arbitrary or "iron whims." These are oversimplifications, to be sure, but contemporary analysts of organizations would tend to agree with them. In fact, there is a general consensus that the anatomy of bureaucracy consists of the following "organs":

- a division of labor based on functional specialization.
- a well-defined hierarchy of authority.
- a system of rules covering the rights and duties of employees.
- a system of procedures for dealing with work situations.
- impersonality of interpersonal relations.
- promotion and selection based on technical competence.

It does not take great critical imagination to detect the flaws and problems in the bureaucratic model. We have all *experienced* them:

- bosses without (and underlings with) technical competence.
- arbitrary and zany rules.
- an underworld (or informal) organization which subverts or even replaces the formal apparatus.
- confusion and conflict among roles.
- cruel treatment of subordinates based not on rational or legal grounds but upon inhumanity.

The tremendous range of unanticipated consequences provides a gold mine of material for comics like Charlie Chaplin and Jacques Tati who capture with a smile or a shrug the absurdity of authority systems based on pseudologic and inappropriate rules.

Almost everybody, including many observers of organizational behavior, approaches bureaucracy with a chip on his shoulder. It has been attacked for many reasons: for theoretical confusion and contradictions; for moral and ethical reasons; on practical grounds such as its inefficiency; for methodological weaknesses; for containing too many implicit values and for containing too few. I have recently catalogued the criticisms of bureaucracy and they outnumber and outdo the ninety-five theses tacked on the church door at Wittenberg in attacking another bureaucracy. A small sample of these:

(1) Bureaucracy does not adequately allow for personal growth and the development of mature personalities.
(2) It develops conformity and "group-think."
(3) It does not take into account the "informal organization" and the emergent and unanticipated problems.
(4) Its systems of control and authority are hopelessly outdated.
(5) It has no adequate juridical process.
(6) It does not possess adequate means for resolving differences and conflicts between ranks, and most particularly, between functional groups.
(7) Communication (and innovative ideas) are thwarted or distorted due to hierarchical divisions.
(8) The full human resources of bureaucracy are not being utilized due to mistrust, fear of reprisals, etc.
(9) It cannot assimilate the influx of new technology or scientists entering the organization.

(10) It modifies personality structure so that people become and reflect the dull, gray, conditioned "organization man."

Max Weber, the developer of the theory of bureaucracy, came around to condemn the apparatus he helped immortalize. While he felt that bureaucracy was inescapable, he also thought it might strangle the spirit of capitalism or the entrepreneurial attitude, a theme which Schumpeter later developed. And in a debate on bureaucracy Weber once said, more in sorrow than in anger:

> It is horrible to think that the world could one day be filled with nothing but those little cogs, little men clinging to little jobs and striving towards bigger ones—a state of affairs which is to be seen once more, as in the Egyptian records, playing an ever-increasing part in the spirit of our present administrative system, and especially of its offspring, the students. This passion for bureaucracy . . . is enough to drive one to despair. It is as if in politics . . . we were deliberately to become men who need 'order' and nothing but order, who become nervous and cowardly if for one moment this order wavers, and helpless if they are torn away from their total incorporation in it. That the world should know no men but these: it is such an evolution that we are already caught up in, and the great question is therefore not how we can promote and hasten it, but what can we oppose to this machinery in order to keep a portion of mankind free from this parcelling-out of the soul, from this supreme mastery of the bureaucratic way of life.

In what ways has bureaucracy been modified over the years in order to cope more successfully with the problems that beset it? Before answering that, we have to say something about the nature of organizations, *all* organizations, from mass production leviathans all the way to service industries such as the university or hospital. Organizations are primarily complex, goal-seeking units. In order to survive they must also accomplish the secondary tasks of (1) maintaining their internal system and co-ordinating the "human side of enterprise"—a process of mutual compliance here called *reciprocity*—and (2) adapting to and shaping the external environment—here called *adaptability*. These two organizational dilemmas can help us to organize the pivotal ways in which the bureaucratic mechanism has been altered—and found wanting.

Reciprocity primarily covers the processes which can mediate conflict between the goals of management and the individual goals of the workers. Over the past several decades a number of interesting theoretical and practical resolutions have been made which truly allow for conflict and mediation of interest. They revise, if not transform, the very nature of the bureaucratic mechanism by explicit recognition of the inescapable tension between individual and organizational goals. These theories can be called, variously, *exchange, group, value, structural, situational*—depending on what variable of the situation one wishes to modify.

The *exchange* theories postulate that wages, incomes, and

services are given to the individual for an equal contribution to the organization in work. If the inducements are not adequate, men may withdraw and work elsewhere. This may be elaborated upon by regarding "payments" to individuals as including motivational units. That is to say, the organization provides a psychological anchor in times of rapid social change and a hedge against personal loss, as well as position, growth and mastery, success experience, and so forth—in exchange for energy, work, commitment.

Management tends to interpret motivation in economic terms. Man is logical; man acts in the manner which serves his self-interest; man is competitive. Elton Mayo and his associates were among the first to see human *affiliation* as a motivating force, to view industrial organization as a *social* system as well as an economic-technical system. A manager, they stated, should be judged in terms of his ability to sustain co-operation. In fact, once a cohesive, primary work group is seen as a motivating force, a managerial elite may become obsolete, and the work group itself becomes the decision maker. This allows decisions to be made at the most relevant point of the organization, where the data are most available.

Before this becomes possible, however, some theorists believe that the impersonal *value* system of bureaucracy must be modified. In this case the manager plays an important role as the instrument of change in interpersonal relations. He must instill values which permit and reinforce the expression of feeling, experimentalism, and norms of individuality, trust, and concern. Management, according to R. R. Blake, is successful insofar as it maximizes a "concern for people"—with "concern for production."

Others believe that a new conception of the *structure* of bureaucracy will create more relevant attitudes towards the function of management than formal role specifications now do. If the organization is seen as organic rather than mechanistic, as adapting spontaneously to its needs, then decisions will be made at the critical point and roles and jobs will devolve on the "natural" organizational incumbent. The shift would probably be from the individual level to cooperative group effort, from delegated to shared responsibility, from centralized to decentralized authority, from obedience to confidence, from antagonistic arbitration to problem-solving. Management centered upon problem-solving, that assumes or relaxes authority according to task demands, has most concerned some theorists who are as much interested in an organization's success and productivity as in its social system.

However, on all sides we find a growing belief that the effectiveness of bureaucracy should be evaluated by human *situation* as well as economic criteria. Social satisfaction and personal growth of employees must be considered as well as the productivity and profit of the organization. The criticism and revisions of the bureaucratic organization tend to concentrate on the internal system and its human components. But although it appears on the surface that the case against bureaucracy has to do with its ethical-moral posture and the social fabric, the real *coup de grace* has come from the environment.

Bureaucracy thrives in a highly competitive, undifferentiated and stable environment, such as the climate of its youth, the Industrial Revolution. A pyramidal structure of authority, with power concentrated in the hands of a few with the knowledge and resources to control an entire enterprise was, and is, an eminently suitable social arrangement for routinized tasks.

However, the environment has changed in just those ways which make the mechanism most problematic. Stability has vanished. As Ellis Johnson said, ". . . the once-reliable constants have now become galloping variables."

The factors accelerating change include:

■ the growth of science, research and development activities, and intellectual technology.

■ the increase of transactions with social institutions (and their importance in conducting the enterprise)—including government, distributors and consumers, shareholders, competitors, raw material and power suppliers, sources of employees (particularly managers), trade unions, and groups within the firms. There is also more interdependence between the economic and other facets of society, leading to greater complications of legislation and public regulation.

■ competition between firms diminishing as their fates intertwine and become positively correlated.

"Work groups will be transient and changing. . . . People will learn to develop quick and intense relationships on the job and to bear the loss of more enduring work relationships."

Burke Uzzle, MAGNUM

My argument so far, to summarize quickly, is that the first assault on bureaucracy arose from its incapacity to manage the tension between individual and management goals. However, this conflict is somewhat mediated by the growth of a new ethic of productivity which includes personal growth and/or satisfaction. The second and more major shock to bureaucracy is caused by the scientific and technological revolution. It is the requirement of *adaptability* to the environment which leads to the predicted demise of bureaucracy and to the collapse of management as we know it now.

A forecast falls somewhere between a prediction and a prophecy. It lacks the divine guidance of the latter and the empirical foundation of the former. On thin empirical ice, I want to set forth some of the conditions that will dictate organizational life in the next 25 to 50 years.

■ THE ENVIRONMENT. Those factors already mentioned will continue in force and increase. Rapid technological change and diversification will lead to interpenetration of the government—its legal and economic policies—with business. Partnerships between industry and government (like Telstar) will be typical. And because of the immensity and expense of the projects, there will be fewer identical units competing for the same buyers and sellers. Or, in reverse, imperfect competition leads to an oligopolistic and government-business controlled economy. The three main features of the environment will be (1) interdependence rather than competition, (2) turbulence rather than steadiness, and (3) large scale rather than small enterprises.

■ POPULATION CHARACTERISTICS. We are living in what Peter Drucker calls the "educated society," and I think this is the most distinctive characteristic of our times. Within fifteen years, two-thirds of our population living in metropolitan areas will have attended college. Adult education programs, especially the management development courses of such universities as M.I.T., Harvard, and Stanford, are expanding and adding intellectual breadth. All this, of course, is not just "nice," but necessary. For as Secretary of Labor Wirtz has pointed out, computers can do the work of most high school graduates—cheaper and more effectively. Fifty years ago education used to be regarded as "nonwork" and intellectuals on the payroll (and many of the staff) were considered "overhead." Today, the survival of the firm depends, more than ever before, on the proper exploitation of brain power.

One other characteristic of the population which will aid our understanding of organizations of the future is increasing job mobility. The lowered expense and ease of transportation, coupled with the real needs of a dynamic environment, will change drastically the idea of "owning" a job—or "having roots," for that matter. Participants will be shifted from job to job and even employer to employer with much less fuss than we are accustomed to.

■ WORK VALUES. The increased level of education and mobility will change the values we hold about work. People will be more intellectually committed to their jobs and will probably require more involvement, participation, and autonomy in their work. (This turn of events is due to a composite of the following factors: (1) positive correlation between a person's education and his need for autonomy; (2) job mobility places the educated in a position of greater influence in the system; (3) job requirements call for more responsibility and discretion.)

Also, people will tend to be more "other-directed" in their dealings with others. David McClelland's studies suggest that as industrialization increases, "other-directedness" increases; so we will tend to rely more heavily on temporary social arrangements, on our immediate and constantly-changing colleagues.

■ TASKS AND GOALS. The tasks of the firm will be more technical, complicated, and unprogrammed. They will rely more on the intellect than muscle. And they will be too complicated for one person to handle or for individual supervision. Essentially, they will call for the collaboration of specialists in a project or team form of organization.

Similarly there will be a complication of goals. "Increased profits" and "raised productivity" will sound like oversimplifications and cliches. Business will concern itself increasingly with its adaptive or innovative-creative capacity. In addition, *meta*-goals will have to be articulated and developed; that is, supra-goals which shape and provide the foundation for the goal structure. For example, one meta-goal might be a system for detecting new and changing goals; another could be a system for deciding priorities among goals.

Finally, there will be more conflict and contradiction among diverse standards of organizational effectiveness, just as in hospitals and universities today there is conflict between teaching and research. The reason for this is the increased number of professionals involved, who tend to identify as much with the supra-goals of their profession as with those of their immediate employer. University professors can be used as a case in point. More and more of their income comes from outside sources, such as private or public foundations and consultant work. They tend not to make good "company men" because they are divided in their loyalty to professional values and organizational demands.

■ ORGANIZATION. The social structure of organizations of the future will have some unique characteristics. The key word will be "temporary"; there will be adaptive, rapidly changing *temporary systems*. These will be "task forces" organized around problems-to-be-solved. The problems will be solved by groups of relative strangers who represent a set of diverse professional skills. The groups will be arranged on organic rather than mechanical models; they will evolve in response to a problem rather than to programmed role expectations. The "executive" thus becomes a coordinator or "linking pin" between various task forces. He must be a man who can speak the diverse languages of research, with skills to relay information and to mediate between groups. *People will be differentiated not vertically, according to rank and role, but flexibly and functionally according to skill and professional training.*

Adaptive, problem-solving, temporary systems of diverse specialists, linked together by co-ordinating and task evaluating specialists in an organic flux—this is the organizational form that will gradually replace bureaucracy as we know it. As no catchy phrase comes to mind, let us call this an *organic-adaptive* structure.

As an aside—what will happen to the rest of society, to the manual laborers, to the less educated, to those who desire to work under conditions of high authority, and so forth? Many such jobs will disappear; other jobs will be automated. However, there will be a corresponding growth in the service-type occupations, such as those in the "war on poverty" and the Peace Corps programs. In times of change, where there is a discrepancy between cultures, when industrialization and especially urbanization proceeds rapidly, the market for men with training and skill in human interaction increases. We might guess that approximately 40 percent of the population would be involved in jobs of this nature, 40 percent in technological jobs, with a 20 percent bureaucratic minority.

■ MOTIVATION. Our above discussion of "reciprocity" indicated the shortcomings of bureaucracy in maximizing employee effectiveness. The "organic-adaptive" structure should increase motivation, and thereby effectiveness, because it enhances satisfactions intrinsic to the task. There is a harmony between the educated individual's need for meaningful, satisfactory, and creative tasks and a flexible organizational structure.

Of course, where the reciprocity problem is ameliorated, there are corresponding tensions between the individual's involvement in his professional community and his involvement in his employing organization. Professionals are notoriously "disloyal" to organizational demands.

There will, however, also be reduced commitment to work groups, for these groups, as I have already mentioned, will be transient and changing. While skills in human interaction will become more important, due to the growing needs for collaboration in complex tasks, there will be a concomitant reduction in group cohesiveness. I would predict that in the organic-adaptive system people will have to learn to develop quick and intense relationships on the job, and learn to bear the loss of more enduring work relationships.

In general I do not agree with Clark Kerr, Harold Leavitt, and others in their emphasis on a "New Bohemianism" in which leisure—not work—becomes the emotional-creative sphere of life. They assume a technological slow-down and leveling-off, and a stabilizing of social mobility. This may happen in a society of the distant future. But long before then we will face the challenge of creating the new service-type organizations with an organic-adaptive structure.

Jobs in the next century should become more rather than less involving; man is a problem-solving animal and the tasks of the future guarantee a full agenda of problems. In addition, the adaptive process itself may become captivating to many. At the same time, I think that the future I described is not necessarily a "happy" one. Coping with rapid change, living in the temporary work systems, setting up (in quick-step time) meaningful relations—and then breaking them—all augur social strains and psychological tensions. Learning how to live with ambiguity and to be self-directing will be the task of education and the goal of maturity.

In these new organizations, participants will be called on to use their minds more than at any other time in history. Fantasy, imagination, and creativity will be legitimate in ways that today seem strange. Social structures will no longer be instruments of psychic repression but will increasingly promote play and freedom on behalf of curiosity and thought. I agree with Herbert Marcuse's thesis in *Eros and Civilization* that the necessity of repression and the suffering derived from it, decreases with the maturity of the civilization.

Not only will the problem of adaptability be overcome through the organic-adaptive structure, but the problem we started with, reciprocity, will be resolved. Bureaucracy, with its "surplus repression," was a monumental discovery for harnessing muscle power *via* guilt and instinctual renunciation. In today's world, it is a lifeless crutch that is no longer useful. For we now require structures of freedom to permit the expression of play and imagination and to exploit the new pleasure of work.

July-August 1965

SUGGESTED READINGS

Personality and Organization by Chris Argyris (New York: Harper, 1957). This book is concerned with the conflict between man and the organization he works in.

Changing Organizations by Warren G. Bennis (New York: Holt, Rinehart and Winston, 1966).

The Temporary Society by Warren G. Bennis and Phillip E. Slater (New York: Harper and Row, 1968) discusses spiralling change and the adaptive qualities of American society.

Reader in Bureaucracy edited by Robert Merton et al. (Glencoe, Ill.: Free Press, 1952) is a book of readings on bureaucracy which generally has a favorable orientation towards bureaucracy.

The Dynamics of Bureaucracy by Peter Blau (Chicago: University of Chicago Press, 1967) studies the interaction of workers in two government agencies.

Achieving Society by David McClelland (New York: Van Nostrand Reinhold, 1961), A study of personal motivation and its relationship to economic growth.

The Urban-Industrial Frontier edited by Davis Popenoe (New Brunswick, N.J.: Rutgers University Press, 1969) is a collection of essays dedicated to a description of the future.

The Power of the Powerless

"Take it up with my secretary"

TRANS-ACTION STAFF REPORT

Young men on the way up are very conscious of the power their superiors wield. They trim their actions to fit the predilections of the boss who controls hiring, firing, and promotion. The underlings, our rising young man assumes, can be safely ignored. Surely secretaries, receptionists, production workers can do him no harm; there is no need to placate them. This assumption is false and dangerous. Subordinates do have power, the kind of power that can mean success or failure for an executive's career. The potential boss ignores them at his peril. Let the following narratives act as cautionary tales.

■ At a busy city hospital a new resident physician finds that the rate of wound infection in his ward is shockingly high. The rate is high because sterility procedures in the ward have become sloppy, and so the resident sets up a program of reform. The whole phalanx of non-medical personnel—the nurses, the aides, the orderlies, the cleaning women—line up in opposition to the new procedures. The procedures are new; they involve more work; the need for them is not understood; they are resisted. The night nursing supervisor, who could protect a resident from the errors of his ignorance by offering the fruits of her years of experience, keeps silent. When the young doctor calls for a particular instrument, the aide (whom he brusquely scolded for inefficiency the day before) cannot seem to find it. The hospital pharmacy is frequently out of the drugs he orders. His lab reports are always late, because the messenger assigned to his ward seems to mislay his requests. As the doctor's relationship with the staff deteriorates, rumors of the situation reach the ears of the hospital administrator. The young doctor is called on the carpet. He is told that nurses and attendants are scarce but residents are not. He must mend his ways. The new procedures designed to reduce the incidence of wound infection are abandoned.

■ The newest member of a university department is inclined to stand on his dignity; his attitude toward the departmental secretary displays a conscious superiority. The secretary resents this and retaliates. She makes it difficult for him to get an appointment with her boss, the chairman of the department. She schedules his classes at inconvenient times. She is always late in typing his exams and letters. When the new professor needs the use of a conference room controlled by another department, the secretary tells him that he must write up a formal request and submit it through channels. She could have arranged this for him rapidly and informally because the secretary in the other department is a friend of hers. The official method takes twice as long. This professor is articulate about his wrongs and complains to the chairman. The chairman agrees that there is unwarranted interference here, and sets up a system of detailed regulations which should prevent discrimination by the secretary. The secretary abides by the letter of the rules; her inflexible performance is so inefficient that all members of the department complain. The chairman finds he is really much too busy to be involved with a petty matter like classroom scheduling and gradually returns this and other chores to his secretary. The needs of the department restore the secretary's discretionary role. The young professor learns how universities are run.

Both of these situations are familiar, and both are disquieting in the same way. Lower level personnel are exerting power; they are pushing back against their nominal superiors in the organizational chain of command. The secretary in the university has succeeded in forcing all the members of the department to accord her a dignity and respect out of proportion to her rank in academic society. Hospital staff have succeeded in preventing the introduction of new modes of treatment. Rank and file employees have proved that without their cooperation the boss cannot put his policies into effect.

What is the source of the power that these persons can exert? David Mechanic, associate professor of sociology at the University of Wisconsin, has developed a set of principles to explain subordinate power. If a subordinate can in some situations dominate the boss, the only possible explanation is that the boss is dependent on him. In any organization, the person who controls access to the basic necessities of work—information, people, and resources—has power. If subordinates have such control—and they often do—then higher level personnel must depend on them.

These examples can shed light on the factors involved in power at the lower levels. Typically, a powerful, low-ranking person has been in the organization longer than his superior has. The older, night nursing supervisor, for instance, has accumulated all sorts of information about hospital procedures and folkways which a new resident cannot know. As she offers this information, or as she witholds it, she can shape the young doctor's career. She knows the other personnel far better than the new resident can; she would know which ancillary employees are vital to the success of his reform scheme. She can smooth his way with these people—the keeper of the central supply room, for instance—or she can decline to do so. Because of his inexperience the new resident can be blocked from access to information, people, and resources by most of the lower level personnel on his ward.

The power of the lowly is proportional to the need for their skills and to the supply. In a large city hospital like the one we have described, nurses are scarce. The work is hard, and the pay is not attractive. The same hospital, because of the rich experience it provides, may have more applicants for residencies than it has places on the staff. In this situation the nurses' preferences become more important than those of the residents.

Low ranking personnel often gain and hold power because they are willing to perform dull but vital routine chores. By taking over the dull chores of scheduling classes, accounting for departmental funds, or arranging for parking permits, the university secretary comes to occupy a strategic position. The only way faculty members could reclaim some of the power they have handed over to her would be to do those jobs themselves; this they are quite unwilling to do. Allowing the secretary to exercise discretion in organizing her work relieves her superiors of the burden of close supervision; it also operates as a further source of secretarial power.

Power can be a by-product of a central position, and lower-level personnel often occupy such positions. Simply by being the person who sees the boss most often, or the person who sees the boss's mail before he does, a secretary can make many members of the organization dependent on her. A receptionist may be the only person in an organization who regularly deals with the public; therefore she bears heavy responsibility for the organization's public image.

Modern organizations are large, specialized, and complex. They are characterized by the extensive use of staff experts and by the delegation of responsibility. In order to free executives for policy decisions, the day-to-day workings of organizations must be delegated to lower level personnel. By this necessary act of delegation, the boss cedes some of his power to his subordinates. Let the young man just learning to climb the rungs of the organizational ladder beware of these reservoirs of power at the lower levels and model his conduct accordingly!

November-December 1964

SUGGESTED READINGS

"Sources of Power of Lower Participants in Complex Organizations" by David Mechanic (*Administrative Science Quarterly,* Vol. 7, December, 1962.)

"The Power to Resist Change Among Low Ranking Personnel" by David Mechanic (*Personnel Administration,* Vol. 26, July-August, 1963.)

A Comparative Analysis of Complex Organizations by Amitai Etzioni (New York: Free Press, 1961) gives excellent perspective for understanding organizations.

Explorations in Role Analysis by Neal Gross, Ward S. Mason and Alexander W. McEachern (New York: Wiley, 1958).

"An Analysis of Social Power" by Robert Bierstedt, *American Sociological Review* (Vol. 15, Dec. 1950).

"The Bases of Social Power" by John R. P. French and Bertram Raven in *Group Dynamics* ed. by Dorwin Cartwright and Alvin Zander (Evanston, Ill.: Row, Peterson, 1960).

Patterns of Industrial Bureaucracy by Alvin W. Gouldner (Glencoe, Ill.: Free Press, 1954).

The Strategy of Conflict by Thomas C. Schelling (Cambridge, Mass.: Harvard University Press, 1960). An entire discussion on the logic of bargaining.

Political Influence by Edward C. Banfield (New York: Free Press, 1961). An empirical study of decision-making on the societal level.

Who's Complaining?

The inhibitions of the dissatisfied consumer

JULIUS ROTH

The world is full of people who think they've gotten a raw deal—from the stores they patronize, from the professionals they have consulted, from their superiors at work. Customers are dissatisfied with shoddy goods; automobile owners are unhappy about a large bill for a lousy repair job; students and their parents resent a teacher's authoritarian treatment; hospital patients feel their nursing care is inadequate and their doctor's charges are unwarranted; citizens are fed up with bureaucratic red tape at government agencies; destitute persons resent the superior attitude of social workers; tenants are mad at their landlords; soldiers feel abused by their officers. But how many of them ever complain?

What each of these people does with his dissatisfaction depends on both the nature of the situation and the personality of the injured party. The way our services are organized is a most important factor. If you are dissatisfied with a given grocery store, you can readily switch to a competitor. However, if you're dissatisfied with the public school which your children attend, there is no competitor to switch to, and you can escape only by moving to another area (which may involve a great many other difficulties) or, if you can afford it, make use of a private school.

Between such extremes in "switchability" there are a variety of intermediate points. For example, you supposedly choose the physicians whose services you use. Actually, you almost always use a specialist because you were referred to him by another physician and you have little choice in the matter. If conditions in an apartment you rent are unsatisfactory, you can always move; but it is impractical and expensive to move often, so this solution to dissatisfaction has to be used sparingly.

The ways people handle their dissatisfactions might also be partially explained in terms of their personality structure. Robert Sommer has suggested the following scheme of psychological types to me:

■ THE ALIEN. The completely alienated person does not bother complaining to anyone or doing anything relevant about his dissatisfaction because he just doesn't care enough. When dissatisfied, his chief reaction is likely to be withdrawal from this situation whenever possible.

■ THE PASSIVE INDIVIDUAL. This person may feel wronged and have a good idea by whom he has been wronged, but is afraid to make any overt complaints. He merely mutters to himself.

■ THE DISCREET COMPLAINER. This person does a lot of open complaining, but usually not to anybody in a position of authority or anybody who could be expected to take any direct action on his complaints. He is more likely to complain to his fellow passenger on the bus, the bartender, to his wife, and so on, but not to the people who really frustrate him.

"High level executives may want feedback from customers so that they can consider appropriate changes, but local store managers or clerks are likely to feel personally threatened by these same complaints."

■ THE BRAVE MAN. This man complains to one or another level of authority with the hope of having changes made or getting some form of satisfaction. A subtype of the brave man is the brave smart man who knows just the right person to complain to in order to get things done.

One thing is sure: the "brave men" form only a small unit in the army of the dissatisfied. Bravery, in this usage, is not simply a dimension of personality, but rather the product of an interaction between personality and situation. What situations are likely to call the brave complainer into action? Sometimes there may be a simple, quantitative relationship. Customers are more likely to complain about a defective product when the amount of money involved is large than when it is small. Patients say that they complain about major lapses in medical service, but not about minor ones. But this quantitative distinction does not resolve the sociologically and psychologically important question: by what standard do people define an unsatisfactory incident as "large enough" to complain about?

Undoubtedly one basic factor in the definition is whether there are any penalties for complaining. Parents often fear retaliation against their children if they complain to teachers or school officials. They know that their child is helpless, a hostage in the hands of a potential enemy. Hospital patients are afraid that if they complain the nursing staff will retaliate with stricter enforcement of the rules, withdrawal of services, and an end to special favors. Soldiers anticipate, realistically, that there will be unofficial punishments for complaints against superiors. The sufferer must weigh the gravity of his dissatisfaction against the possibility of retaliation as he decides whether to complain or hold his tongue.

Ordinarily, making a complaint involves not one act but several; the complaint must be pursued through a number of steps. The parent of a school child may start out by complaining to a teacher and, if he receives no satisfaction, try complaining to the principal, and so on up the line. A customer may try complaining in person to a store manager, and if he is not satisfied with the results may then write a letter to the president of the company. At each stage in the complaint procedure, the aggrieved person must decide whether to continue his pursuit or to abandon it.

A complaint can be "brave" (i.e. effective) without being addressed directly to the person or organization who caused the dissatisfaction. Some complaints that are pursued in roundabout ways are as effective or more effective than those that take the direct route. One common method is to use a pressure group which can present the complaint more effectively than the sufferer can himself. A veteran who has a complaint against the Veterans Administration may be well advised to ask a veteran's organization to "carry the ball" for him. A citizen may get more action by complaining to his Congressman, rather than to the agency or official who caused the dissatisfaction.

Another indirect approach is to make use of regulatory or enforcement agencies. A customer may complain to the Federal Trade Commission, the Post Office Department, or the district attorney about a possible fraud; a hospital patient may complain to the local health department rather than directly to the hospital authorities. Another "official approach," but of a different kind, is the use of the courts to attempt to make a complaint effective. One may seek an injunction to prevent a certain practice or bring a lawsuit to force a change of procedure or the payment of damages for injury already incurred. This approach is used far more often as a threat than as an actual procedure. The brave complainer can choose any of these tactics, singly or in combination, in his pursuit of satisfaction.

In One Ear

So far we have been looking at complaint-provoking situations from the complainer's side. There is, of course, the other party to the situation—one who receives complaints or who is being complained against. People in positions of authority, or people who render services, vary in their awareness of the nature and extent of dissatisfaction. Some may even subscribe to the myth that if nobody complains, everybody is satisfied. Recipients will differ on what kinds of complaints they perceive as justified and/or important. They vary in the actions they take to rectify a justified complaint, and in the techniques they use to "cool out" the complainants they regard as unjustified or unimportant.

A brave complainer has a chance of success with persons or organizations that have some awareness of dissatisfaction, that have an ear for complaints. When the organization is complex, there may be some conflict about how a complaint is received and dealt with. The complainer's success will depend on which of several contending factions decides the issue on his case. When dealing with complex organizations, the complainer can be greatly assisted by having a hidden ally within the organization. For example, social workers in hospitals are, at least in part, in the business of conveying the complaints of patients and their families to physicians and staff and trying to get action on them.

If the aggrieved person is complaining about something in his own organization, his best bet is to have an outside agent working for him. Complaints by hospital patients, prisoners, or Welfare Department clients can usually be made most effectively by relatives or influential outsiders. My colleague, Elizabeth Eddy, has carried on some research in the public schools that indicates the importance of having a good complaint agent on tap. Middle class, suburban children get more considerate treatment from teachers and school officials largely because they have parents who are effective agents in dealing with the schools. Slum children may not have anyone to complain for them; either their parents have no interest in their schooling, or they don't know how to deal with people of higher social status and power, like teachers and school boards.

The alert complainer will be wary when he accepts help from these outside allies, however; they have a distressing tendency to switch sides. Members of the families of hospital patients—and this is particularly true in the case of mental hospitals—often accept the word of the hospital staff about what is good for their relative. Parents may decide that children's complaints about school are not justified, and that the school should be supported in its conflicts with their children. People in the institution often make a deliberate effort to enlist the aid of the middle man, and to convince him that the complainant's stance is unjustified. Some mental hospitals have a kind of public relations program consisting of written materials and conferences with physicians and social workers, all intended to convince family members that the complaints of the patient are simply symptoms of his illness. Family members are told that such "symptoms" cannot be taken at face value and they should take the hospital staff's word about what is best and even collaborate with them on a program of care and treatment. The aim of public schools in dealing with parent organizations and individual parents is much the same.

We are inclined to assume that most organizations want to know about complaints, because complaints give an indication of how customers or clients feel about them. And yet most organizations have rather elaborate mechanisms for warding off complaints. Why is this so? The trouble with the basic assumption is that it implies that all organizations, including business enterprises, are staffed entirely by people who have the central organizational goals at heart. This simply is not the case. High level executives may want feedback from customers so that they can consider appropriate changes, but local store managers or clerks are likely to feel personally threatened by these same complaints. Correction of mistakes and replacement of goods may lower commissions or lower local stores' profits; local personnel may well try to discourage and suppress complaints even though their actions, in the long run, damage the company's good-will and have an adverse effect on sales. Non-business organizations also have employees whose personal goals do not gibe with the organization's goals; complaints which might be useful feedback for the organization appear to individual staff members as an attack upon their competence or honesty, and thus something to be resisted rather than encouraged. The school principal may just as well *not* want to know what the public thinks of his school, because if the kind and the extent of the criticism were made known, his position might be in danger. If an organization is run by people who consider themselves experts—and most organizations nowadays are —they may well take the position that no one outside their specialty is competent to evaluate their work. Thus the complaints of the layman—who is presumed to be dissatisfied only because he doesn't know what is good for him—may properly be ignored.

Complaints can never be completely eliminated, but organizations can exert a great deal of control over complaints by restricting the way in which they can be made. In the Army all complaints must go through "channels"; given types of complaints must be presented to certain superior officers, and any attempt to skip a step results in a refusal to receive the complaint at all. In one school system, a patriotic organization took a Post Office box and invited all students and parents to report teachers who did not perform the proper patriotic ceremonies each morning; the school administration angrily announced that such irregular channels would not be recognized and that parents with a complaint about the actions of a teacher must take up the matter through prescribed channels: first with the teacher himself; then, if no satisfaction were obtained, with the principal; then with the superintendent; and finally with the school board. Organizations vary, of course, in the degree to which they can force their clientele to conform to prescribed channels.

The Compleat Complainer

My interest in the complaint process is not wholly theoretical; in addition to its psychological and sociological implications the issue has very live consequences for social action. After all, I became interested in dissatisfaction and complaints as a research issue only after many years of practical experience as a complainer. I like to complain, and I want to learn to do it better. I also think that complaining is socially necessary if authorities, businesses, and services are to be responsive rather than unreceptive or even abusive. And so I think it is worthwhile to ask: how do you encourage complaints? Here are some suggestions:

■ REDUCE RESTRAINTS. Since complaining inspires fear of retaliation, the power to retaliate must be reduced. This may mean, for example, that in mental hospitals and chronic disease hospitals the staff must be restricted in its discretionary controls over patients. Patients may be given more decision-making power about their own lives, more freedom to move about without special permission, direct access to goods and equipment, and to higher status treatment personnel. Thus the staff means of retaliation would be reduced and the inmates presumably would have less need to fear what might happen to them if they complain. Fear of retaliation might also be reduced if the complainer has a chance to escape (or be rescued) from a potentially threatening situation. Thus, if school children could be transferred more easily parents could make complaints without fearing excessive retaliation by classroom teacher or school principal.

■ PROVIDE COMPLAINT AGENTS. Some people are good at fighting for what they consider to be their rights. Some are not. In a chronic disease hospital we studied, for example, the great majority of patients are aged, disabled, diseased, destitute, and generally beaten down. They are not able to make a good case for themselves. Some have family or friends who act as their agents, but in the custodial type of institution most of them are there because they do not have any family or friends who are interested in them. Such people might benefit from the help of an outside agent, either a pressure group working on their behalf or perhaps an agent specifically appointed to look after their interests. Other groups may be at a distinct disadvantage for a variety of reasons—school children because of their age, prisoners because of their criminal status, consumers because of their lack of knowledge, destitute persons because of extreme dependence on welfare assistance. All such persons might benefit from an agent working on their behalf. In a custodial hospital, for example, such an agent should be someone who is completely independent of the hospital and the hospital system, but who is permitted to enter the hospital at any time, interview any of the personnel about the patient's treatment, examine any of the records, receive the complaints of the patients and present them to appropriate hospital personnel, and take legal action against the hospital or any of its staff when violations of the patient's rights are not properly redressed.

Citizens' committees or boards of various kinds may perform such an agent function, especially with respect to public or other non-profit institutions. Ideally, they should be units which regard themselves as representatives of the public and of the client population and not as arms of the institutional administration. They should be willing and ready to have complaints addressed to them outside the usual institutional channels and to require the organizational administrators to explain what they are going to do about the complaints or why they don't think anything should be done about them. Boards of trustees may seem suited for this function, but in fact they rarely perform it. Recently a patient from a Long Island nursing home escaped and made his way to the local newspaper office where he reported the abuse that the inmates received from the director of the institution, who held them there as virtual captives. The ensuing investigation revealed that none of the four members of the board of trustees had ever spoken to a single one of the inmates and that the board made only a few visits to the home in the course of the year, never getting past the director's office. Certainly such a group is utterly worthless as an agent for the inmates.

■ SEND IN AGITATORS. The agitator is useful for groups who are severely suppressed and threatened, and who often avoid complaining because of the severe punishments they are likely to receive in return. The term "outside agitator" is of course used as an epithet by members of an oppressing group. They fear and hate the outside agitator simply because they do not have any power over him. The Northern civil rights agitator who visits the South can be an aggressive ally simply because he does not have to fear economic reprisals or attacks upon his family. The critic of the public schools who has no children of his own can attack from a safe position and thus become a useful ally to parents who feel that they dare not criticize the schools.

■ GUARANTEE ANONYMITY. One might think up a scheme which would permit soldiers to bring their complaints to the attention of higher military levels or to controlling civilian agencies (for example, congressional committees) without being individually identified. In New York City, the mayor has a special office with a Post Office box and a phone number of its own. Citizens are encouraged to write or to call complaints about other city agencies which they feel have not been handled properly through the regular channels, or which they are afraid to put through regular channels. (After all, you can't file a complaint about police corruption with the police department.)

The most widely-known anonymous complaint system is the "suggestion box" used by some business concerns. My own acquaintance with it comes mainly from magazine cartoons. The theme of most of these cartoons is revealing. An employee is furtively looking around to see if someone is watching before dropping his slip of paper into the suggestion box. Another variant is the employee who has just put his paper into the box when a secret opening in the wall reveals the boss's face with the words, "I caught you, Smith." It is clear from these cartoons that the most important attribute of the suggestion box—when it is being properly used—is its anonymity.

■ OFFER GUIDE BOOKS. Complainers need to be shown how to play the system. Consumers need more inside dope about how business organizations work, patients need more inside dope about how hospitals and medical practitioners work, parents of school children must know more about how the school system works, the citizen should know more about how government agencies work. With such education, people would be in a better position to work the system—to know how to pose complaints and to whom. Who swings the weight in given kinds of organizations? What kind of arguments are usually most effective? What kind of persons from outside of the organization are most likely to bring action within the organization?

■ GIVE PRACTICAL HINTS. One simple suggestion I have, based on my own experience, is this—when you don't get satisfaction on a lower level of a large, complex organization, do not bother to work your way up the hierarchy. Each level is likely to protect the level immediately below. The thing to do is to jump straight to the top. If the local store manager won't give you satisfaction, write to the president of the company. Of course, the complaint comes back to the local store, but with a note to the manager that he better take care of this and see that the complaint doesn't come back to the president a second time.

■ MAKE THE PROCESS EASY. How many times have you been dissatisfied with service you have received and thought about complaining, but when faced with visiting stores or offices, making phone calls, wrapping and shipping unwanted goods, writing letters, finally said, "To hell with it. It isn't worth the trouble." This may well be the major reason why such a tiny proportion of cases of dissatisfaction are ever turned into effective complaints. If complaining is to be promoted, it must be made as simple as possible. What the customer, client, or subordinate regards as easy or convenient needs some exploration itself. In some cases it might consist of supplying simple forms with stamped self-addressed envelopes to encourage a customer or a client to report his experience. In some cases it may mean making someone who is responsible for receiving complaints readily and obviously available to the public or clientele, or even having interviewers solicit complaints at the convenience of the potential complainer. Where complaining must be done in person, it should be possible to do it in one place at one time—not by traipsing from person to person and office to office.

Easy-complaint procedures like these are rather rare. In most cases it is very difficult even to find out where, how, and to whom to make a complaint. Many organizations have no built-in way of receiving and processing complaints; when one does come in, it becomes somebody's annoying extra duty to deal with. Such difficulties are no accident. They simply reflect the fact that most people would just as soon not hear complaints about themselves or about their organizations.

July-August 1965

SUGGESTED READINGS

"Citizen Participation in Social Policy: The End of the Cycle?" by Jon Van Til and Sally Bould Van Til, *Social Problems* (Vol. 19, Winter 1970) discusses the character of citizen participation in an urban renewal project and a community action project.

Bureaucracy on Trial by William B. Boyer (Indianapolis, Ind.: Bobbs-Merrill, 1964) treats the advantages and disadvantages of the bureaucratic type of organization.

Communitas by Pericival Goodman and Paul Goodman (New York: Random House, 1947). The authors discuss the effects of city planning.

"Professional Autonomy and the Revolt of the Client" by Marie R. Haug and Marvin B. Sussman, *Social Problems* (Vol. 17, Fall 1969) discusses how professionals have been attacked by their clients and how they use cooptation in an attempt to preserve their autonomy.

"Professional Autonomy and the Role of the Layman" by Lee Braude, *Social Forces* (Vol. 39, May 1961). Using the interesting concepts of "license" and "mandate" this paper investigates how the lay public can encroach upon the autonomy of professionals.

Organizations by James March and H. Simon (New York: Wiley, 1958) includes a section on the sensitivity of an organization to different environments and pressures.

3 Shaping of Socialization

Each persons's fingerprints are different from everyone else's. Researchers are on the brink of perfecting the technology for identifying "voiceprints," which are also unique to each individual. It is conceivable that other inherited bodily characteristics of man separate him from the other billions inhabiting the earth. Every newborn infant, in some sense, possesses a unique physiological identity at birth. In the delivery rooms of the world, whether they be sterile hospital pavilions or simple grass huts, the birth cry announces the entrance of a unique young animal.

At birth the human animal is not a person at all, but an organism that has the remarkable potential for becoming a person in the raw materials of his body. He is not at all passive about demanding the care his body needs—the milk, the warmth, the feeling of closeness. But he is totally helpless in the sense that he cannot satisfy these needs without the help of others. The human animal is totally dependent on others to keep him alive as an organism and, perhaps more importantly, to develop his humanness. Relative to other animals, he has a longer period by far of development and learning in a dependent relationship. Human infants are always taken care of by others—parents, guardians, or parent substitutes supplied by society—and would perish if they were not.

How can we prove that a healthy young child could not survive alone and develop into a person? This is difficult to test. Nonetheless, it is significant to establish how much human nature is inborn or physiologically prepatterned and how much is the result of living with others in a society. The findings that babies reared in institutions without proper mothering display apathetic emotional responses and a high death rate, strongly suggest that the development of human nature requires interaction and communication with other human beings. In short, to become human is to become social.

Learning to be Human

Just how the individual acquires human nature is very complex and still under study by people in a number of scholarly disciplines. One thing sociologists have come to believe is that human nature is "learned" in interaction in a human group. This process has been labeled socialization. The processes and consequences of interaction are of primary interest to the discipline of sociology. Socialization is provided by many different groups. For the newborn baby, the first meaningful group is usualy a pair of nurturing parents who tend and love their unsocialized offspring. From daily and hourly attention to the infant and response by him to their care, the child learns to recognize the objects and people around him, to respond to the cues in the environment, and bit by bit to enter into communication with others. These acts of communication are the crucial aspects of the child's development, because by gradually agreeing on the distinctions between one object and another he learns to share the symbols of those around him. When the new human being uses the symbols of communication—the language of his social world—he has begun the first of a series of acts that distinguishes man from other creatures.

George Gardner

Language not only allows an increasingly subtle and complex interaction with others so that a person can become a member of the society and acquire its culture, but it also permits a person to think about himself so that a socially based conception of *self* emerges. To be able to respond to himself, to approve or disapprove of himself, means he can step outside of himself and regard himself as an object just as others are doing, employing the shared symbols of the language. This is how society "gets in" to the person and presses its standards and expectations upon him. He adopts ways of acting that win approval and reward; he thinks of himself as behaving or misbehaving, good or bad, according to the judgment of other people who are significant to him.

Society, then, is both the teacher of social roles and the judge of how well they are played. It has sanctions and it applies them, and most of the time people prefer to avoid the threat to their self-respect and reputation that lies in ridicule and gossip or the more severe sanctions of physical punishment and ostracism. It is easier, too, to want to behave and not feel, even secretly, in conflict with the rules.

Behaving

When a person accepts how society seems to want him to act, he is said to have internalized the norms. This is rarely done completely. In the first place, something about man's nature appears to set up resistance to complete conformity. There are areas of the individual's life that may never be totally socialized. Also, there is slippage between the conduct of the person and the norms of society, partly because the norms are imperfectly taught and partly because there is not complete agreement on what should be taught.

The articles in the section dealing with early socialization raise questions about how the person acquires a definition of himself, to what extent he conforms to society's expectations in some crucial areas of behavior, and in what ways socialization practices vary by class and ethnic and racial group. Annabelle B. Motz paints a picture of how the middle-class family conforms to society's rules and expectations and the price they pay in doing so in her article, "The Family as a Company of Players." Social arrangements harmful to the crucial early days of socialization of the newborn are described in "Psychological Miscarriage: An End to Mother Love" by Marian Gennaria Morris. People learn sexual behavior, William Simon and John Gagnon contend in their article on "Psychosexual Development," in the same way they learn other behavior—through scripts constructed and taught differently in various cultures and with variation according to sex and the social and economic status of the players in the psychosexual drama.

Socialization goes on throughout life. However, it is a debatable question just how strongly individual biological endowment and early childhood experience establish the general contours within which the personality will develop. On the whole it is true that basic traits of personality persist in recognizable form; friends meeting after some years of separation know each other—they can "pick up where they

Shaping of Socialization

left off" in their relationship. Nevertheless, maturation, learning, and critical life experiences have observable consequences for the individual throughout life.

Parents or Peers

Adolescence is one such critical period in which American young people search for their own identities by questioning the norms and values of their own particular families, peer groups, class, and communities and then set out on a course of their own. Usually we think of this period as involving a rejection of established rules and emancipation from parents and the older generation. And this is frequently the case. Surprisingly, it is just as true of some young political conservatives as it is of some young radicals—that they reject their parents' values during a stormy transitional break from boyhood to early manhood. Lawrence F. Schiff makes a distinction between boys whose political conversion to rightist beliefs takes place immediately following puberty from the dynamics and style of the converts in late adolescence in his article on "Dynamic Young Fogies—Rebels on the Right." Some similarities between the political socialization of both young conservatives and New Left university students can be noted in the findings of Richard Flacks in "Young Intelligentsia in Revolt," showing that some members of the new generation of rebels are in fact carrying on the political ideals of their parents rather than rejecting them. Where youth are gang members, the peer group often exercises the social function of control and nurturance equivalent to the family. Breaking up with the gang changes a boy's social status from adolescence to young adulthood just as rebelling from parents does in others, as Walter B. Miller indicates in "The Corner Gang Boys Get Married."

Socialization in a highly complex society involves the learning of work skills and professional roles that often cannot be taught in the home or the ordinary school system. Whereas in a simpler society children may learn from family or community members either with or without conscious instruction, in an industrial society more and more specialized job training is required, and the trainee has to not only learn new skills and attitudes but divest himself of unsuitable old ones. These processes could be thought of as desocialization and resocialization. The neophyte undergoes a regimen specifically designed to remake him into the occupational or professional image of the status he seeks to achieve. Entry into most skilled, technical, and professional occupations involves particular indoctrination procedures and is often followed by a formal initiation rite such as a graduation ceremony or a celebration where established members receive the newly qualified into the fold. Rites of passage, of course, are universal features of both simple and complex societies. Melford S. Weiss describes the "Rebirth in the Airborne" when paratroopers are initiated in various stages into the brotherhood of paratroopers with tests of courage and skill, and the use of superstition, magic, and ceremony—like the rites of many other tribes. Of course, some people fail to pass the entrance requirements of the course of instruction or the

Shaping of Socialization

final tests and drop out along the way or are washed out.

Socialization goes on as a person confronts new situations, adopts new roles, and drops others. The ordinary history of the nuclear family includes a series of roles and relationships —among them marriage, parenthood, the separation of adult children from home, loss of marriage partners through death or divorce, and retirement from a life-long occupation. Disturbance of social relationships comes inevitably with old age as the quality of family and friendship ties begin to change and break up. Robert S. Weiss points to the increasing loss of intimate relationships by aged persons in "The Fund of Sociability" and suggests that the feelings of loneliness, boredom, and worthlessness characteristic of many old people are normal reactions to lack of close relatives and friends, reactions that could be characteristic of any group in a similar situation. Weiss further hypothesizes that other relationships besides intimacy need fulfillment for an individual's sense of well-being and that the loss of them at various times of life can be traumatic.

Deviants

Those people who are socialized in a special subgroup and refuse to conform to the ways of the dominant society are often not accepted to full membership in society. If legal sanctions can be applied to them, they may be penalized, jailed, or segregated in some way. Or they may be discriminated against socially and kept from sharing equally in the benefits of employment and public services. In a multigroup nation like the United States, people have many backgrounds and life styles, but not all are considered legitimate ways of living by those exercising social control.

Tolerance of deviation from established norms is far greater in certain geographic locales and social circles. Howard S. Becker and Irving Louis Horowitz analyze the sources of the broad definition and acceptance of deviant behavior characteristics of San Francisco in their article, "The Culture of Civility." College campuses socialize some students in the use of drugs through instruction, experience, and social pressure in the same way they would learn the ropes of becoming a fraternity member. Geoffrey Simmon and Grafton Trout's article, "Hippies in College—From Teeny-Boppers to Drug Freaks," illustrates the principle that normal and abnormal behavior is acquired the same way. In fact, the line between normal and abnormal, criminal and noncriminal, acceptable and unacceptable is a difficult one to draw in a large, complex society. Violations of the law by fraudulent business and professional practices are widespread. Socialization into the ways of white-collar crime through example, teaching, and innovation are common in respectable social circles. In "The Respectable Criminal" Donald R. Cressey explains how embezzlement of funds by trusted clerks and bankers is typical of many activities that are rationalized as noncriminal by those who commit them.

The Family As a Company of Players

The management of impressions when the family "makes the scene"

ANNABELLE B. MOTZ

All the world's a stage, and we are all players.

Erving Goffman in his *The Presentation of Self in Everyday Life* views our everyday world as having both front stage and back. Like professionals, we try to give a careful and superior performance out front. Back stage we unzip, take off our masks, complain of the strain, think back over the last act, and prepare anxiously for the next.

Sometimes the "on stage" performances are solos; sometimes we act in teams or groups. The roles may be carefully planned, rehearsed, and executed; or they may be spontaneous or improvised. The presentation can be a hit; or it can flop badly.

Picture a theater starring the family. The "stars" are the husband, wife, and children. But the cast includes a wide range of persons in the community—fellow workers, friends, neighbors, delivery-men, shopkeepers, doctors, and everyone who passes by. Usually husband and wife are the leads; and the appeal, impact, and significance of their performances vary with the amount of time on stage, the times of day and week, the circumstances of each presentation, and the moods of the audience.

Backstage for the family members is generally to be found in their homes, as suggested by the expression, "a man's home is his castle." The front stage is where they act out their dramatic parts in schools, stores, places of employment, on the street, in the homes of other persons; or, as when entertaining guests, back in their own homes.

My aim is to analyze the performances of family members before the community audience—their *front stage* appearances. This behavior conforms to the rules and regulations that society places upon its members; perhaps the analysis of the family life drama will provide insights into the bases of the problems for which an increasing number of middle-class persons are seeking professional help.

Many years ago, Thorstein Veblen noted that although industrialization made it possible for the American worker to live better than at any previous time in history, it made him feel so insignificant that he sought ways to call attention to himself. In *The Theory of the Leisure Class,* Veblen showed that all strata of society practiced "conspicuous consumption"—the ability to use one's income for non-essential goods and services in ways readily visible to others.

A man's abilities were equated with his monetary worth and the obvious command he had in the market place to purchase commodities beyond bare necessities. Thus, a family that lives more comfortably than most must be a "success."

While conspicuous consumption was becoming an essential element of front stage performance, the ideal of the American as a completely rational person—governed and governing by reason rather than emotion—was being projected around the world. The writings of the first four decades of this century stress over and over again the importance of the individual and individual opinion. (The growth of unionism, the Social Security program, public opinion polling, and federal aid to education are a few

"Often the family acts as a team. The act may be rehearsed, but it must appear spontaneous." (A scene from *Life With Father*)

examples of the trend toward positive valuation of each human being—not to mention the impact of Freud and Dewey and their stress on individual worth.) The desirability of rule by majority and democratic debate and voting as the best means of reaching group decisions—all these glorified rationality.

As population, cities, and industry grew, so also did anonymity and complexity; and rationality in organizations (more properly known as bureaucratization) had to keep pace. The individual was exposed to more and more people he knew less and less. The face to face relationships of small towns and workshops declined. Job requirements, duties and loyalties, hiring and firing, had to "go by the book." Max Weber has described the bureaucratic organization: each job is explicitly defined, the rights of entry and exit from the organization can be found in the industry's manual, and the rights and duties of the worker and of the organization toward the worker are rationally defined; above all, the worker acts as a rational being on the job—he is never subject to emotional urges.

With the beams and bricks of "front" and rationality the middle-class theater is built; with matching props the stage is set.

There are two basic scenes. One revolves about family and close personal relationships. It takes place in a well-furnished house—very comfortable, very stylish, but not "vulgar." The actors are calm, controlled, reasonable.

The other scene typically takes place in a bureaucratic anteroom cluttered with physical props and with people treated like physical props. The actors do not want the audience to believe that they *are* props—so they attract attention to themselves and dramatize their individuality and worth by spending and buying far more than they need.

What does this mean in the daily life of the family stars?

Take first the leading lady, wife, and mother. She follows Veblen and dramatizes her husband's success by impressing any chance onlookers with her efficient house management. How does one run a house efficiently? All must be reasoned order. The wife-housekeeper plans what has to be done and does it simply and quickly. Kitchen, closets, and laundry display department store wares as attractively as the stores themselves. The house is always presentable, and so is she. Despite her obviously great labors, she does not seem to get flustered, over-fatigued, or too emotional. (What would her neighbors or even a passing door-to-door salesman think if they heard her screaming at the children?) With minimal household help she must appear the gracious hostess, fresh and serene—behind her a dirty kitchen magically cleaned, a meal effortlessly prepared, and husband and children well behaved and helpful.

Outside the home, too, she is composed and rational. She does not show resentment toward Johnny's teacher, who may irritate her or give Johnny poor marks. She does not yawn during interminable and dull PTA programs (what would they think of her and her family?). At citizen meetings she is the embodiment of civic-minded, responsible, property-ownership (even if the mortgage company actually owns the property). Her supermarket cart reflects her taste, affluence, efficiency, and concern. At church she exhibits no unchurchly feelings. She prays that her actions and facial expression will not give away the fact that her mind has wandered from the sermon; she hopes that as she greets people, whether interested in them or not, she will be able to say the "right" thing. Her clothes and car are extremely important props—the right make, style, finish; and they project her front stage character, giving the kind of impression she thinks she and the other members of the family want her to give.

Enter Father Center Stage

The male lead is husband, father, and man-of-affairs. He acts in ways that, he hopes, will help his status, and that of his family. At all times he must seem to be in relaxed control of difficult situations. This often takes some doing. For instance, he must be both unequal and equal to associates; that is, he is of course a good fellow and very democratic, but the way he greets and handles his superiors at work is distinctly, if subtly, different from the way he speaks to and handles inferiors. A superior who arrives unexpectedly must find him dynamically at work, worth every cent and more of his income; an inferior must also find him busy, demonstrating how worthy he is of superior status and respect. He must always be in control. Even when supposedly relaxing, swapping dirty jokes with his colleagues, he must be careful to avoid any that offend their biases. He has to get along; bigots, too, may be able to do him good or harm.

Sometimes he cannot give his real feelings release until he gets behind the wheel—and the savage jockeying which takes place during evening rush may reflect this simultaneous discharge by many drivers.

The scene shifts back to the home. The other stars greet him—enter loving wife and children. He may not yet be ready or able to re-establish complete emotional control—

SUGGESTED READINGS

The Presentation of Self in Everyday Life by Erving L. Goffman (Garden City, New York: Doubleday Anchor, 1959). A lucid, refreshing and significant perspective on social interaction as dramatic presentation.

Role Theory: Concepts and Research edited by Bruce J. Biddle and Edwin J. Thomas (New York: Wiley, 1966). A detailed introduction to the concepts, terminology, propositions and variables of role theory.

Explorations in Role Analysis by Neal Gross, Ward Mason and Alexander McEacheron (New York: Wiley, 1958). The authors have developed a useful schema for the analysis of role conflict and its resolution and a consistent language for role-behavior investigations.

"The Family as a Three-Person Group" by Fred L. Strodtbeck, *American Sociological Review* (Vol. 19, Feb. 1954). An interactionist treatment of the family as one form of small group.

after all, a man's home is his backstage—and the interplay of the sub-plots begins. If his wife goes on with her role, she will be the dutiful spouse, listening sympathetically, keeping the children and her temper quiet. If she should want to cut loose at the same time, collision will probably still be avoided because both have been trained to restrain themselves and present the right front as parents to their children—if not to each other.

Leisure is not rest. At home father acts out his community role of responsible family head. The back yard is kept up as a "private" garden; the garage as a showroom for tools on display. He must exhibit interest—but not too much enthusiasm—in a number of activities, some ostensibly recreational, retaining a nice balance between appearing a dutiful husband and a henpecked one. Reason must rule emotion.

The children of old vaudevillians literally were born and reared in the theater—were nursed between acts by mothers in spangles, trained as toddlers to respond to footlights as other children might to sunlight. The young in the middle-class family drama also learn to recognize cues and to perform.

Since "front" determines the direction and content of the drama, they are supposed to be little ladies and gentlemen. Proper performances from such tyros require much backstage rehearsal. Unfortunately, the middle-class backstage is progressively disappearing, and so the children too must be prepared to respond appropriately to the unexpected—whether an unwanted salesman at the door who must be discreetly lied to about mother's whereabouts or a wanted friend who must not be offended. They are taught rationality and democracy in family councils—where they are also taught what behavior is expected of them. Reason is rife; even when they get out of hand the parents "reason" with them. As Dorothy Barclay says when discussing household chores and the child, "Appealing to a sense of family loyalty and pride in maturity is the tack most parents take first in trying to overcome youngsters' objections (to household chores). Offering rewards come second, arguing and insisting third."

"Grown-up" and "good" children do family chores. They want the house to look "nice"; they don't tell family secrets when visitors are present, and even rush to close closet and bedroom doors when the doorbell rings unexpectedly.

The child, of course, carries the family play into school, describing it in "show and tell" performances and in his deportment and dress. Part of the role of responsible parenthood includes participation in PTA and teacher conferences, with the child an important player, even if offstage.

To the child, in fact, much of the main dynamic of the play takes place in the dim realm of offstage (not always the same as backstage)—his parents' sex activities, their real income and financial problems, and many other things, some of them strange and frightening, that "children are not old enough to understand."

They early learn the fundamental lessons of front stage: be prepared; know your lines. Who knows whether the neighbors' windows are open? The parents who answers a crying child with, "Calm down now, let's sit down and talk this over," is rehearsing him in stage presence, and in his character as middle-class child and eventually middle-class adult.

Often the family acts as a team. The act may be rehearsed, but it must appear spontaneous. Watch them file in and out of church on Sunday mornings. Even after more than an hour of sitting, the children seem fresh and starched. They do not laugh or shout as on the playground. The parents seem calm, in complete control. Conversations and postures are confined to those appropriate for a place of worship.

Audience reaction is essential to a play. At church others may say, "What nice children you have!" or, "We look forward to seeing you next Sunday." Taken at face value, these are sounds of audience approval and applause; the performers may bask in them. Silence or equivocal remarks may imply disapproval and cause anxiety. What did they really mean? What did we do wrong? Sometimes reaction is delayed, and the family will be uncertain of their impression. In any case, future performances will be affected.

Acting a role, keeping up a front, letting the impressions and expectations of other people influence our behavior, does result in a great deal of good. Organized society is possible only when there is some conformity to roles and rules. Also a person concerned with the impression others have of him feels that he is significant to them and they to him. When he polishes his car because a dirty one would embarrass him, when his wife straightens her makeup before answering the door, both exhibit a sense of their importance and personal dignity in human affairs. Those who must, or want to, serve as models or exemplars must be especially careful of speech and performance—they are always on stage. When people keep up appearances they are identifying themselves with a group and its standards. They need it; presumably it needs them.

Moreover, acting what seems a narrow role may actually broaden experience and open doors. To tend a lawn, or join a PTA, social club, or art group—"to keep up appearances"—may result in real knowledge and understanding about horticulture, education, or civic responsibility.

For the community, front produces the positive assets of social cohesion. Well-kept lawns, homes, cars, clean children and adults have definite aesthetic, financial, and sanitary value. People relate to one another, develop common experiences. People who faithfully play their parts exhibit personal and civic responsibility. The rules make life predictable and safe, confine ad-libs within acceptable limits, control violence and emotional tangents, and allow the show to go on and the day's work to be done. Thus, the challenging game of maintaining front relates unique personalities to one another and unites them in activity and into a nation.

So much for the good which preoccupation with front and staging accomplishes; what of the bad?

First, the inhibition of the free play of emotion must lead to frustration. Human energies need outlets. If onstage acting does not allow for release of tension, then the escape should take place backstage. But what if there is virtually no backstage? Perhaps then the releases will be found in the case histories of psychiatrists and other counselors. Communication between husband and wife may break down because of the contrast between the onstage image each has of the other as a perfect mate and the unmasked actuality backstage. Perhaps when masks crumble and crack, when people can no longer stand the strain of the front, then what we call nervous breakdown occurs.

Growing Up with Bad Reviews

And how does the preoccupation with front affect the growth and development of the child? How can a child absorb and pattern himself after models which are essentially unreal? A mother may "control" her emotions when a child spills milk on her freshly scrubbed floor, and "reason" with him about it; she may still retain control when he leaves the refrigerator open after repeated warnings; but then some minor thing—such as loud laughter over the funnies—may suddenly blow off the lid, and she will "let him have it, but good!" What can he learn from such treatment? To respect his mother's hard work at keeping the house clean? To close the refrigerator door? Not to laugh loudly when reading the comics? That mother is a crab? Or, she's always got it in for him? Whatever he has learned, it is doubtful it was what his mother wanted! Whatever it was it will probably not clarify his understanding of such family values as pride in work, reward for effort, consideration of other people, or how to meet problems. Too, since the family's status is vitally linked with the maintenance of fronts, any deviance by the child, unless promptly rectified, threatens family standing in the community. This places a tremendous burden on a child actor.

Moreover, a concentration on front rather than content must result in a leveling and deadening of values and feelings. If a man buys a particular hat primarily because of what others may think, then its intrinsic value as a hat—in fact, even his own judgment and feelings about it—become secondary. Whether the judgment of those whose approval he covets is good or bad is unimportant—just so they approve. Applause has taken the place of value.

A PTA lecture on "The Future of America" will call for the same attentive front from him as a scientist's speech on the "Effects of Nuclear Warfare on Human Survival." Reading a newspaper on a crowded bus, his expression undergoes little change whether he is reading about nuclear tests, advice to the lovelorn, or Elizabeth Taylor's marital problems. To his employer he presents essentially the same bland, non-argumentative, courteous front whether he has just been refused a much deserved pay raise or told to estimate the cost of light bulbs. He seems impartial, objective, rational—and by so doing he also seems to deny that there is any difference to him between the pay raise and the light bulbs, as well as to deny his feelings.

The Price of Admission

What price does the community pay for its role as audience?

The individual human talents and energies are alienated from assuming responsibility for the well-being and survival of the group. The exaggerated self-consciousness of individuals results in diluted and superficial concern with the community at a time when deep involvement, new visions, and real leadership are needed. Can the world afford to have over-zealous actors who work so hard on their lines that they forget what the play is all about?

It is probable that this picture will become more general in the near future and involve more and more people—assuming that the aging of the population continues, that the Cold War doesn't become hot and continues to need constant checks on loyalty and patriotism, that automation increases man's leisure at the same time as it keeps up or increases the production of consumer goods, and that improved advertising techniques make every home a miniature department store. The resulting conformity, loyalty, and patriotism may foster social solidarity. It may also cause alienation, immaturity, confusion, and much insecurity when new situations, for which old fronts are no longer appropriate, suddenly occur. Unless people start today to separate the important from the tinsel and to assume responsibility for community matters that are vital, individual actors will feel even more isolated; and the society may drift ever further from the philosophy that values every person.

Tomorrow's communities will need to provide new backstages, as the home, work place, and recreation center become more and more visible. Psychiatrists, counselors, confessors, and other professional listeners must provide outlets for actors who are exhausted and want to share their backstage thoughts. With increased leisure, business men will probably find it profitable to provide backstage settings in the form of resorts, rest homes, or retreats.

The state of the world is such today that unless the family and the community work together to evaluate and value the significant and direct their energies accordingly, the theater with its actors, front stage, backstage, and audience may end in farce and tragedy.

March-April 1965

Psychological Miscarriage: An End to Mother Love

Why some mothers hate, neglect, and abuse their babies

MARIAN GENNARIA MORRIS

Not long ago a mother in the Midwest, while giving her baby its bath, held its head underwater until it drowned. She said that there was something wrong with the child. Its smell was strange and unpleasant; it drooled; it seemed dull and listless. It reminded her of a retarded relative, and the thought of having to spend the rest of her life caring for such a person terrified her. Her husband was out of work, and she was pregnant again. She said she "felt the walls closing in." When, in her confused and ignorant way, she had asked her husband, a neighbor, and a doctor for help, she got promises, preachments, and evasions. So she drowned the baby.

This mother said she had felt "so all alone." But, unfortunately, she had plenty of company. Many thousands of American women do not love or want their babies. Although few actually kill their infants, the crippling effects of early maternal rejection on children can hardly be exaggerated—or glossed over. The number directly involved is large. The social harm, for everybody, is great. An idea of the size of the problem can be gained from the following figures, taken from federal, state, and local sources:

- 50-70,000 children neglected, battered, exploited annually;
- 150,000 children in foster homes for these reasons;
- over 300,000 children in foster care altogether;
- 8 to 10 percent of all school children in one twenty-county study in need of psychiatric examination and some type of treatment for their problems.

But even these figures can hardly begin to describe the violence, deprivation, and dehumanization involved.

Recently we concluded a study of thirty rejecting mothers and their children, who can serve as examples. Our findings are supported by a number of other studies of parents and their children who have various physical and psychological disorders. Although the poor are hardest hit by family and emotional problems it should be noted that the majority of these families were not poverty-stricken. Psychological miscarriage of motherhood attacks all classes and levels.

Twenty-one of the thirty mothers demonstrated clearly from the time of delivery that they could not properly mother or care for their babies—could not even meet their basic needs. Yet no one who had had contact with them—neither doctors, nurses, nor social workers—had apparently been able to help, effectively, any one of them, nor even seemed aware that severe problems existed.

The entire population of mothers was characterized by old troubles and hopelessness, stretching back to the previous generation—and in one-third of the cases, back to the third generation. Half the children were illegitimate, or conceived before marriage. Sixty percent of the families had been in juvenile, criminal or domestic courts at some earlier time. Two-thirds of the children were either first-borns, or first-borns of their sex—and lack of experience with children increased their mothers' insecurities.

All thirty children needed intensive psychiatric treatment. Only two of the thirty were "well" enough—from homes that were "stable" enough—for out-patient care to even be considered. The remaining twenty-eight were headed for institutions. Their prognoses are grave, their chances doubtful. They will cost us a great deal in the years to come, and their problems will be with us a long time. Some will never walk the streets as free men and women.

Actually, the children were so disturbed that they could not be diagnosed with great accuracy. For instance, it was impossible to tell how intelligent most really were because they were in such emotional turmoil that they could not function properly on tests, and seemed retarded. A fifth of them had been so beaten around the head that it is quite possible their brains were damaged. (One baby had been thrown across the room and allowed to stay where it fell.) Women who feel neglected and less than human in turn neglect their children and treat them as less than human.

Fear and Reality

In our supposedly interdependent society, we are close together in violence, but apathetic to each other's needs. But apathy to their needs constitutes a violence to women facing labor, delivery, and the early and bewildering adjustments of motherhood. And it is in these days and weeks that psychological miscarriage occurs.

During pregnancy, labor, and delivery the basic fears of childhood—mutilation, abandonment, and loss of love—are vividly revived for a woman, and with double force—for herself and the baby. Nor are these fears simply fantasies: mothers *are* frequently cut, torn, and injured, babies *are* born with congenital defects.

The entire pregnancy period, with its lowering of defenses, makes the mother more capable of loving and feeling for her baby. But whether she finds his needs pleasing or threatening depends on what happened to her in the past, and the support she gets in the present.

After delivery, still in physical and emotional stress, under great pressure, she must make the most important, difficult adjustments of all. She must "claim" her baby. That is, she must make it, emotionally, part of herself again; identify it with the qualities and values in herself and her life that she finds good, safe, reassuring, and rewarding. After all the dreams and fears of pregnancy, she now must face and cope with the reality—the baby and his needs. If she miscarries now and rejects the child as something bad that cannot be accepted, then the child cannot grow to be normal. Nor can its society be normal, since the mothers must hand down to each generation the values by which society survives.

In older days, when most women had their babies at home, these adjustments were made in familiar surroundings, with such family support as was available. Now they are made largely in the hospital. What actually happens to mothers in today's hospitals?

Childbirth, once a magnificent shared experience, has increasingly become a technical event. Administrative and physical needs get priority. Emotional needs and personalities tend to get in the way of efficiency. Administrators and medical personnel, like everyone else, respond most readily to those pressures which affect them. Since they are in charge, they pass them down to the patient, whether they help the patient or not.

The mothers of the poor in particular arrive faceless, knowing no one on the ward, with little personal, human contact from before birth until they leave. Increasingly, they arrive already in labor, so that the hospitals cannot turn them away. They also come at this late stage so that they can avoid the constant procession of doctors and the three and four-hour clinic waits, during which they are called "mother" because their names have been lost in the impersonal clinic protocols. In the wards, they may be referred to simply by their bed numbers.

Birth itself may be subordinated to the schedule: some doctors schedule their deliveries, and induce labor to keep them on time. Even "natural" labor may be slowed down or speeded up by drugs for convenience.

A Public Event

Mothers say that they are allowed little dignity or modesty. Doctors strange to them may, and do, examine them intimately, with little attempt at privacy. They say that without their permission they are often used as live lecture material, giving birth before interested audiences of young interns and students while the obstetrician meticulously describes each step and tissue. How apathetic we have become to the routine dehumanization of mothers is well illustrated by the story of an upper-middle-class woman I know. She was in labor, almost hidden by drapes preparatory to vaginal examination, light flooding her perineum (but not her face). Approached by a nurse and gloved physician she suddenly sat up in her short-tailed hospital gown and said, "I don't know who *you* are, doctor, but *I* am Mrs. Mullahy." Good for Mrs. Mullahy! She has a strong sense of personal identity, and is determined to preserve it.

"A mother enters the hospital prey to childhood insecurities, and stripped alike of defenses and clothes. Attitudes and cues from hospital personnel, and others, strongly affect her self-respect and her feelings about her baby's worth."
Eve Arnold MAGNUM

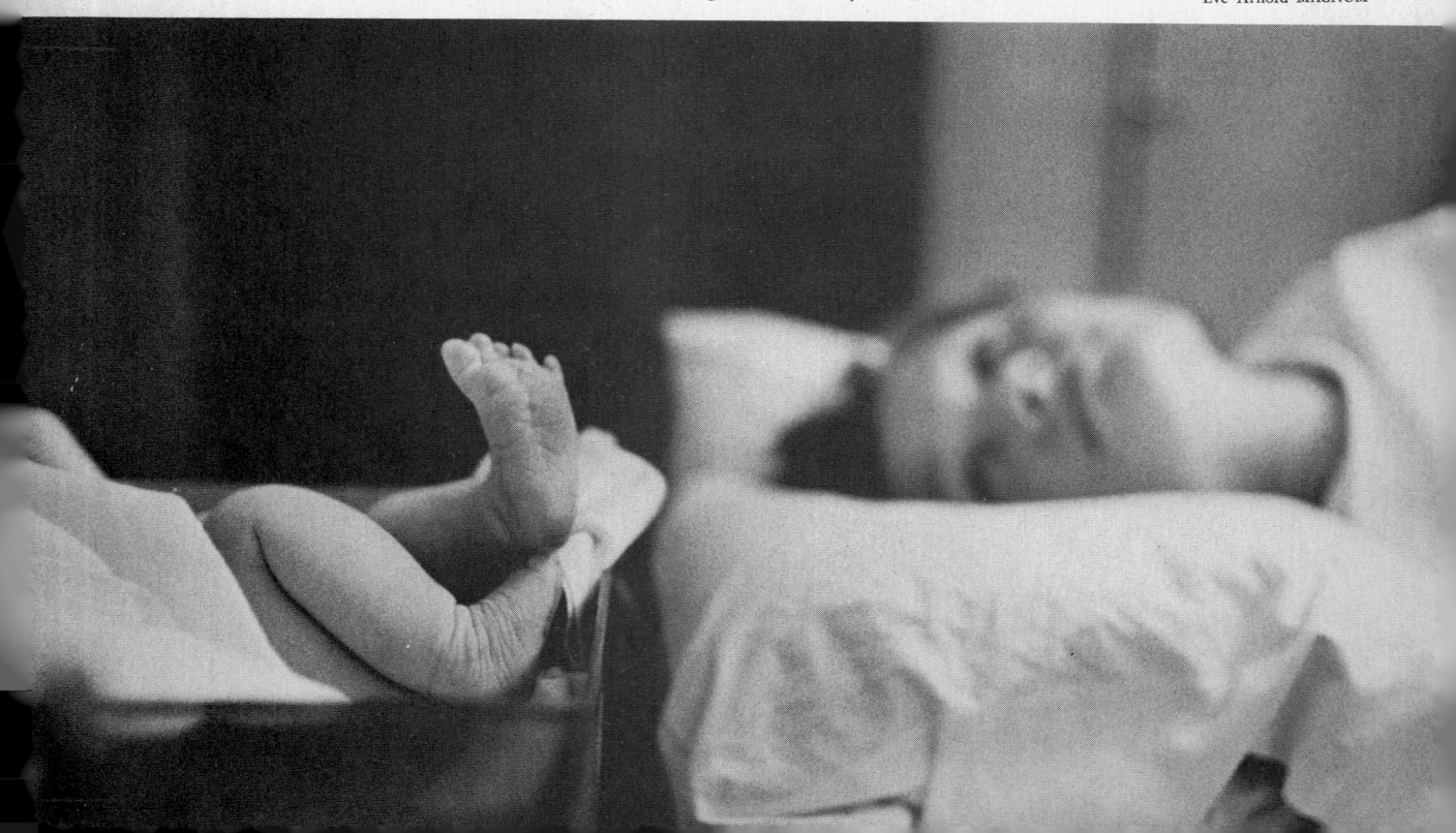

Mothers say they are isolated and humiliated. They say that in addition to their own anxieties they must worry about what their doctors think, and be careful to please and propitiate the staff members, who may have power of life and death over them and their babies.

They say that they are kept in stirrups for hours—shackled in what reduces them to something sub-human—yet afraid to complain.

Is it increasingly true, as mothers say, that babies are not presented to them for from four to twelve hours after birth? Social histories show that prompt presentation is necessary for the mental health of the mothers; studies of other mammals indicate that such delay interrupts mothering impulses and may bring on rejection of the young. Is this happening to human mothers and babies? How necessary, medically, is such a delay? Is it worth the price?

Many women become deeply depressed after childbirth. Is this at least partly a reaction to hospital experiences? Is it an early distress signal of psychological miscarriage? There is very little research that attempts to assess early maternal adaptation, and we need such research badly. Are the violent mothers, so brutal to their children, violent at least in part because of our faceless and impersonal birth practices? Clinical studies show that the less sense of identity and personal worth a mother has, the more easily she displaces her aggressions onto others—*any* others. Are we scapegoating our children?

Staking a Claim

To a mother, the birth of her baby is not a technical event. It starts in intimate contact with the father, and has deep roots in her feelings for and relationship with him, whether positive or negative. It reflects her personality, her state of maturity, the experiences of her most intimate anxieties and special hopes, and her associations with the adults who have had most influence on her. She enters the hospital prey to childhood insecurities, and stripped alike of defenses and clothes. Attitudes and cues from the hospital personnel, and from others, strongly affect her self-respect and her feelings about her own and her baby's worth.

It is difficult to observe most normal claiming behavior in a hospital. But some of it can be observed. Most mothers, for example, do find ways to make contact with their babies' bodies—touching and examining them all over delightedly, even to the tiny spaces between fingers and toes—cooing and listening to them, inhaling their odors, nuzzling and kissing them.

Socially, a major way to claim a child is to name it. Names suggest protective good magic; they establish identity and suggest personality; they emphasize masculinity or femininity; they affirm family continuity and the child's place in it.

Nevertheless, it is usually difficult to follow claiming behavior for two reasons. First, because hospital routines and tasks interfere. To the staff, the process of mothers becoming acquainted with infants is seen as merely cute, amusing, or inconvenient. Babies are presented briefly, pinned and blanketed tightly, making intimate fondling—for women who have carried these infants for months—difficult and sometimes even guilt-producing.

The second reason is related to the nature of normal motherhood. The well-adjusted mother is secure within herself, content to confine her communications mostly to her baby, rather than project them outward. As Tolstoy said of marriage, all happy ones tend to be happy in the same way, and relatively quiet. But the unhappy ones are different and dramatic—and it is by observing unhappy mothers that the pathological breakdown of maternal claiming can be most easily traced.

Let us consider a few examples:

Tim—Breakdown in Early Infancy

When Tim's mother first felt him move in her, and realized then that all evasion and doubt about her pregnancy was past, she blacked out (she said) and fell down a flight of stairs.

Tim was her second child. Her first pregnancy was difficult and lonely and, she had been told, both she and the baby had almost died during delivery. She suffered from migraine headaches, and was terrified of a second delivery.

For the first four months of Tim's life, she complained that he had virulent diarrhea and an ugly odor, and took him from doctor to doctor. Assured by each one that there was nothing wrong with the child (in the hospital the diarrhea cleared up in one day), she took this to mean that there was something wrong with *her*—so she sought another doctor. She took out thirteen different kinds of cancer insurance on Tim.

During an interview, she told a woman social worker that it was too bad that doctors could not look inside a baby and know he was *all* O.K.

The social worker decided to probe deeper: "You would have a hard time convincing me that you *deliberately* threw yourself down those stairs."

"Who, me? Why I told my mother all along that I would never *willingly* hurt a hair of one of my children's heads."

"But suppose you had, unwillingly. Would you blame someone else for doing it, under the circumstances?"

"No! I was sick and don't even know how it happened."

After that, the demon that had haunted her was in the open, and recovery began. She had felt that she was both criminal and victim, with the child as the instrument of her punishment. (Only a "good" mother deserves a good baby; a "bad" mother deserves a "bad"—damaged or sick—baby.) The implied criticisms of her mother and doctor had aggravated these feelings. She identified Tim not with the good in her but the "evil"—he was something faulty, something to be shunned.

Under treatment she learned to accept herself and regain her role of mother. She was not really the bad little girl her critical mother and doctor had implied; neither, therefore, was Tim bad—she could accept him. It was no longer dangerous to identify with her. She let Tim see her face; she held him comfortably for the first time; she did not mention his "ugly" smell; she stayed by his bed instead of restlessly patrolling the corridors. She referred to our hospital as the place she had "got him *at*," instead of the hospital, ninety miles away, where he had actually been born.

Jack—Effects on an Older Child

Shortly after Jack was born, his mother asked her obstetrician whether Jack's head was all right. Gently touching the forceps marks, he said, *"These* will clear up." Thinking that she had been told delicately that she had a defective child, she did not talk to Jack for five-and-a-half years—did not believe he could understand speech.

At five-and-a-half, approaching school, he had never spoken. A psychologist, thinking that the child was not essentially retarded, referred the mother to a child guidance clinic, where the social worker asked whether she had ever found out if the obstetrician had meant the *inside* of Jack's head. For the first time in all the years it occurred to her that there might have been a misunderstanding. Three months later Jack was talking—though many more months of treatment were still necessary before he could function adequately for his age.

Behind this, of course, was much more than a misunderstanding. Behind it was Jack's mother's feelings of guilt for having caused her own mother's death. Guilt went back many

Patterns of Rejection

There are several criteria that can be used to assess the adequacy of a mother's behavior during the early weeks of an infant's life. Mother-infant unity can be said to be *satisfactory* when a mother can:
find pleasure in her infant and in tasks for and with him;
understand his emotional states and comfort him;
read his cues for new experience, sense his fatigue points.

Examples: she can receive his eye contact with pleasure; can promote his new learnings through use of her face, hands and objects; does not overstimulate him for her own pleasure.

In contrast, there are specific signs that mothers give when they are *not adapting* to their infants:
See their infants as ugly or unattractive.
Perceive the odor of their infants as revolting.
Are disgusted by their drooling and sucking sounds.
Become upset by vomiting, but seem fascinated by it.
Are revolted by any of the infants' body fluids which touch them, or which they touch.
Show annoyance at having to clean up infants' stools.
Become preoccupied with the odor, consistency and numbers of infants' stools.
Let infants' heads dangle, without support or concern.
Hold infants away from their own bodies.
Pick up infants without warning by touch or speech.
Juggle and play with infants, roughly, after feeding, even though they often vomit at this behavior.
Think infants' natural motor activity is unnatural.
Worry about infants' relaxation following feeding.
Avoid eye contact with infants, or stare fixedly into their eyes.
Do not coo or talk with infants.
Think that their infants do not love them.
Believe their infants expose them as unlovable, unloving parents.

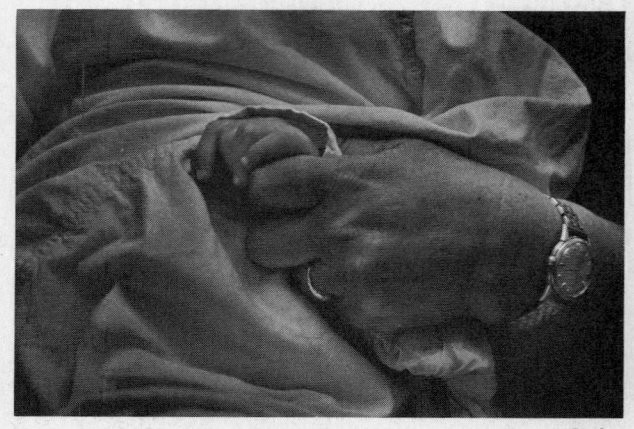

George Gardner

Think of their infants as judging them and their efforts as an adult would.
Perceive their infants' natural dependent needs as dangerous.
Fear death at appearance of mild diarrhea or cold.
Are convinced that infants have defects, in spite of repeated physical examinations which prove negative.
Often fear that infants have diseases connected with "eating": leukemia, or one of the other malignancies; diabetes; cystic fibrosis.
Constantly demand reassurance that no defect or disease exists, cannot believe relieving facts when they are given.
Demand that feared defects be found and relieved.
Cannot find in their infants any physical or psychological attribute which they value in themselves.
Cannot discriminate between infant signals of hunger, fatigue, need for soothing or stimulating speech, comforting body contact, or for eye contact.
Develop inappropriate responses to infant needs: over or under-feed; over or under-hold; tickle or bounce the baby when he is fatigued; talk too much, too little, and at the wrong time; force eye contact, or refuse it; leave infant alone in room; leave infant in noisy room and ignore him.
Develop paradoxical attitudes and behaviors.

Eve Arnold MAGNUM

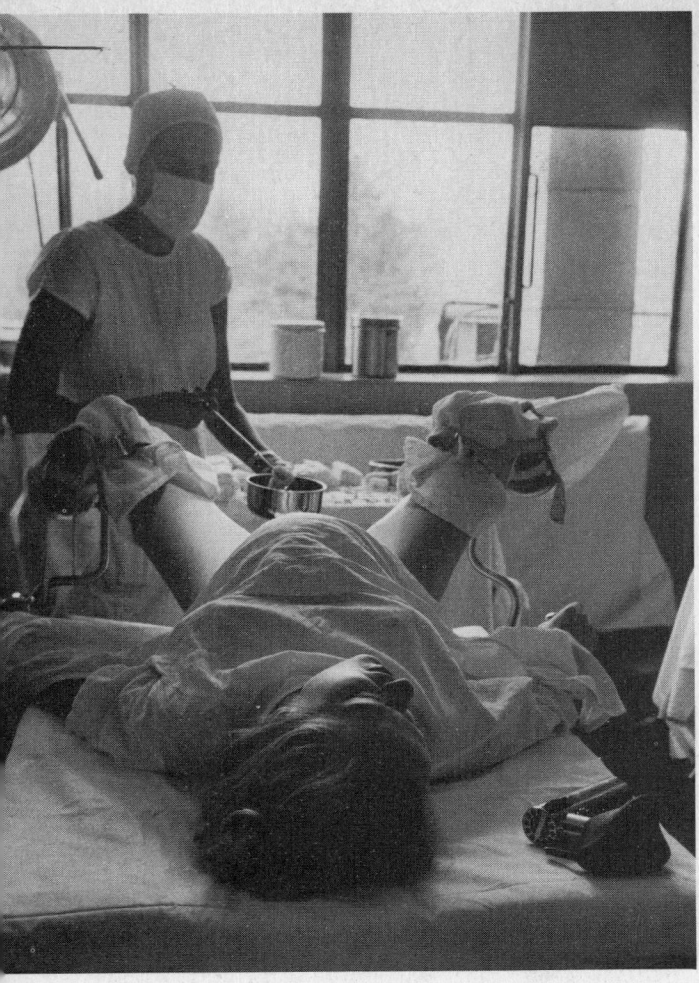

"Without their permission, mothers are often used as live lecture material, giving birth before interested audiences of young interns and students, while the obstetrician meticulously describes each step and tissue."

years. During an auto ride long ago, she had an accident in which her mother suffered a mild blow on the head. In the early months of pregnancy with Jack, she had found her mother dead in the tub. The cause was cancer, which had nothing to do with the bump. But deep down she could not believe this, and she developed the fear that Jack's head, too, was damaged—a fitting punishment for a woman who feared she had killed her mother. When her obstetrician seemed to confirm it, she did not question further.

For almost six years Jack was not so much an infant or child as a damaged head. Like her mother he was silent—from "brain injury." It was only under treatment that she accepted the possibility that she might have "misunderstood."

Babs—Hell Revisited

Babs was fourteen months old when she was flown to our hospital from South America, physically ill with diarrhea and dehydration, and emotionally badly withdrawn. In South America, her mother had trouble getting proper drugs and talking effectively with Spanish-speaking doctors—and when she had had to face Babs's pleading eyes with little relief to offer, she had gone into acute panic. She hadn't been able to comfort her child, but had drawn away and could hardly look at her or touch her. From this rejection Babs had in turn withdrawn, and a mutual vicious cycle of rebuff and retreat had come about.

The mother felt that she had lived through all this before in her own childhood. When she was five, she had had a little brother, aged three. Her sick mother often left him in her charge. ("He was *my* baby.") One day both ate sprayed peaches from a tree. Both came down with severe diarrhea. She survived. She remembers vividly seeing him in "his little white coffin."

The pregnancy period with Babs had been stormy, full of family crises; she felt guilty about "not feeding Babs right." She could not accept the reassurances of her obstetrician. After Babs was born she was over-meticulous about cleaning her after bowel movements.

During treatment she shook visibly when asked whether Babs resembled her in any way. But when asked: "Could you have been Jim's *real* mother when you were only five?" she relaxed, and grew radiant. Later she said: "I know *now* that I couldn't have known that the peaches were poisoned."

"Nor that Babs would get sick with diarrhea if you went to South America to live with your husband?"

"No. I know now that the *place* is not good for any of us. I didn't know that before."

In a few days she was admiring in Babs the very qualities she had said she admired in herself—her sense of fun, and her determination. The positive identification between them had been made.

Mothers as Patients

How can we prevent such psychological miscarriages—and how can we limit their ravages once they have already occurred?

The dynamics of maternal rejection are not completely known—we need far more research, far more detailed and orderly observation of early maternal behavior. Nevertheless, enough is known already about the symptoms (detailed in the box on page 11) for us to be able to work up a reliable profile of the kind of woman who is most likely to suffer damage, and to take steps to make sure that help is offered in time. After all, the ultimate cause of maladaptation is lack of human sympathy, contact, and support, even though the roots may go back for more than one generation. We must, therefore, offer that support. We may not be able completely to heal old, festering wounds, but we can palliate their worst effects, and keep them from infecting new babies.

Mothers in our study identified the periods of greatest

danger as just before and after delivery. It is then—and swiftly—that intervention by a psychiatric team should occur. What can be done?

■ We must have early recognition of trouble. Early signs of maternal maladaptation are evident in the mutual aversion of mother and child. But these signs have to be watched for—they cannot be ignored because of hospital routine that is "more important."

■ Let the mother have enough time to see and become acquainted with the hospital personnel with whom she will experience birth. Length of hospital stay is geared to technical requirements—five days for middle-class mothers, down (in some places) to twenty-four hours or less for the poor. Therefore, acquaintance should start before birth, at least with the physician, so that when delivery comes the mother will not be faced with a stranger in cap and gown, but a human being she already knows. Nurses and social workers should also be included. (The Hahnemann Medical College and Hospital in Philadelphia already assigns resident physicians to the pre-natal clinics to provide this continuity.)

■ Mothers of young infants suffer from geographical and psychological isolation. Services should work toward reducing both of these isolations. Ideally such services should come from a team, including not only the doctor and nurses, but a sympathetic pediatrician, psychiatric and medical social workers, of both sexes, who could also act as substitute parents. This help should be as available to the middle-class as to the poor (middle-class patients are sometimes denied hospital social services).

■ Help should carry over into home care. *Make sure that each mother has someone to care for her at home.* After their too brief hospital stay, poverty-stricken women, many without husband or family, are often more helpless and lost at home than in the hospital.

■ Mothers should not be left alone for long periods, whether under sedation or not. Schedules should and must be modified to allow them to have normal family support as long as possible. If they have none, substitutes—volunteers—should be found. Isolated mothers, cut off from support or even contact with their physicians, and treated as objects, much too often displace their loneliness, depression, resentment, bitterness, humiliation, rage, and pain onto their babies.

■ Get rid of the stirrups—and the practice of using them to hang mothers' legs in the air for hours! Find some other way to hold women on the delivery table until the last moments. Women often spend months recovering from backaches caused by stirrups.

■ Present the baby as soon as possible. The most frequent comment from mothers who remain conscious in the delivery room is, "The doctor gave him to me." This is psychologically very sound; when the father-image (doctor) presents the baby with the obvious approval of the mother-image (nurse), latent feelings of guilt about having a baby and about the acceptability of the baby—and of motherhood—are lulled and dispelled. Too often, however, the nurse is cast, or casts herself, in the role of unwilling, stingy, critical giver of the baby—in fact the whole institution lends itself to this. Presentation should precede and not depend on feeding; it should be made gladly and willingly; it should allow time and ease of access for the mother to examine her baby's body.

■ Doctors, nurses, and aides should understand and come to know pregnancy, labor, delivery, and early growth as a continuing process, rather than in bits and pieces, a series of techniques. They need to understand and see it from the mothers' viewpoint, as well as in terms of bottles, diapers, rooms, instruments, and procedures.

■ Reassure mothers about their infants. This includes understanding the real meanings of their questions. If a mother continually discounts good reports, rejection may be underway, and psychological miscarriage imminent.

■ First-born children, and the first-borns of each sex, are the ones most commonly rejected; their mothers need special care—as do the mothers of the poor and those without family, husband, or outside human supports.

None of these proposals are radical—even administratively. Most are quite simple, and could be done directly in the wards and the private rooms.

Overall, we need more research. We do not know enough about the earliest signals of psychological miscarriage; we have not trained ourselves, nor taken the trouble, to watch for these early signs. Nor do we know enough about the long-term effects of maladaptation. Are the older children completely lost? Is the process irreversible? Cannot something be done to bring them back to productive life?

There is nothing more important in a maternity pavilion, nor in a home, than the experiences with which life begins. We must stop the dehumanization of mothers. We must give all children a chance for life.

January-February 1966

SUGGESTED READINGS

No and Yes: On the Genesis of Human Communication by René Spitz (New York: International Universities Press, 1957). Explores the critical role of the mother in the infant socialization process.

Attachment and Loss by John Bowlby (New York: Basic Books, 1969). In a masterful manner, Bowlby has described the complex nature of a child's ties to his mother and the problems of separation anxiety and grief.

The Changing American Parent by Daniel R. Miller and Guy E. Swanson (New York: Wiley, 1958).

Two Worlds of Childhood: U.S. and USSR by Urie Bronfenbrenner (New York: Russell Sage Foundation, 1970). The author analyzes socialization practices in the United States and in Russia, and how these practices fit in with the general character of each society.

Dorka Raynor

Psychosexual Development

Men and women play the sexual drama according to a post-Freudian script

WILLIAM SIMON & JOHN GAGNON

Erik Erikson has observed that, prior to Sigmund Freud, "sexologists" tended to believe that sexual capacities appeared suddenly with the onset of adolescence. Sexuality followed those external evidences of physiological change that occurred concurrent with or just after puberty. Psychoanalysis changed all that. In Freud's view, libido—the generation of psychosexual energies—should be viewed as a fundamental element of human experience at least beginning with birth, and possibly before that. Libido, therefore, is essential, a biological constant to be coped with at all levels of individual, social, and cultural development. The truth of this received wisdom, that is, that sexual development is a continuous contest between biological drive and cultural restraint should be seriously questioned. Obviously sexuality has roots in biological processes, but so do many other capacities including many that involve physical and mental competence and vigor. There is, however, abundant evidence that the final states which these capacities attain escape the rigid impress of biology. This independence of biological constraint is rarely claimed for the area of sexuality, but we would like to argue that the sexual is precisely that realm where the sociocultural forms most completely dominate biological influences.

It is difficult to get data that might shed much light on the earliest aspects of these questions: Adults are hardly equipped with total recall and the pre-verbal or primitively verbal child does not have ability to report accurately on his own internal state. But it seems obvious—and it is a basic assumption of this paper—that with the beginnings of adolescence many new factors come into play, and to emphasize a straight-line developmental continuity with infant and childhood experiences may be seriously misleading. In particular, it is dangerous to assume that because some childhood behavior appears sexual to adults, it must be sexual. An infant or a child engaged in genital play (even if orgasm is observed) can in no sense be seen as experiencing the complex set of feelings that accompanies adult or even adolescent masturbation.

Therefore, the authors reject the unproven assumption that "powerful" psychosexual drives are fixed biological attributes. More importantly, we reject the even more dubious assumption that sexual capacities or experiences tend to translate immediately into a kind of universal "knowing" or innate wisdom—that sexuality has a magical ability, possessed by no other capacity, that allows biological drives to be expressed directly in psychosocial and social behaviors.

The prevailing image of sexuality—particularly that of the Freudian tradition—is that of an intense, high-pressure drive that forces a person to seek physical sexual gratification, a drive that expresses itself indirectly if it cannot be expressed directly. The available data suggest to us a different picture—one that shows either lower levels of intensity, or, at least, greater variability. We find that there are many social situations or life-roles in which reduced sex activity or even deliberate celibacy is undertaken with little evidence that the libido has shifted in compensation to some other sphere.

A part of the legacy of Freud is that we have all become remarkably adept at discovering "sexual" elements in nonsexual behavior and symbolism. What we suggest instead (following Kenneth Burke's three-decade-old insight) is the reverse—that sexual behavior can often express and serve nonsexual motives.

No Play Without A Script

We see sexual behavior therefore as *scripted* behavior, not the masked expression of a primordial drive. The individual can learn sexual behavior as he or she learns other behavior—through scripts that in this case give the self, other persons, and situations erotic abilities or content.

Desire, privacy, opportunity, and propinquity with an attractive member of the opposite sex are not, in themselves, enough; in ordinary circumstances, nothing sexual will occur unless one or both actors organize these elements into an appropriate script. The very concern with foreplay in sex suggests this. From one point of view, foreplay may be defined as merely progressive physical excitement generated by touching naturally erogenous zones. The authors have referred to this conception elsewhere as the "rubbing of two sticks together to make a fire" model. It would seem to be more valuable to see this activity as symbolically invested behavior through which the body is eroticized and through which mute, inarticulate motions and gestures are translated into a sociosexual drama.

A belief in the sociocultural dominance of sexual behavior finds support in cross-cultural research as well as in data restricted to the United States. Psychosexual development is universal—but it takes many forms and tempos. People in different cultures construct their scripts differently; and in our own society, different segments of the population act out different psychosexual dramas—something much less likely to occur if they were all reacting more or less blindly to the same superordinate urge. The most marked differences occur, of course, between male and female patterns of sexual behavior. Obviously, some of this is due to biological differences, including differences in hormonal functions at different ages. But the significance of social scripts predominate; the recent work of Masters and Johnson, for example, clearly points to far greater orgasmic capacities on the part of females than our culture would lead us to suspect. And within each sex—especially among men—different social and economic groups have different patterns.

Let us examine some of these variations, and see if we can decipher the scripts.

Childhood

Whether one agrees with Freud or not, it is obvious that we do not become sexual all at once. There is continuity with the past. Even infant experiences can strongly influence later sexual development.

But continuity is not causality. Childhood experiences (even those that appear sexual) will in all likelihood be influential not because they are intrinsically sexual, but because they can affect a number of developmental trends, *including* the sexual. What situations in infancy—or even early childhood—can be called psychosexual in any sense other than that of creating potentials?

The key term, therefore, must remain potentiation. In infancy, we can locate some of the experiences (or sensations) that will bring about a sense of the body and its capacities for pleasure and discomfort and those that will influence the child's ability to relate to others. It is possible, of course, that through these primitive experiences, ranges are being established—but they are very broad and overlapping. Moreover, if these are profound experiences to the child—and they may well be that—they are not expressions of biological necessity, but of the earliest forms of social learning.

In childhood, after infancy there is what appears to be

During the transition between childhood and adolescence many boys, "report arousal and orgasm while doing things not manifestly sexual —climbing trees, sliding down bannisters, or other activities that involve genital contact without defining them as sexual."

some real sex play. About half of all adults report that they did engage in some form of sex play as children; and the total who actually did may be half again as many. But, however the adult interprets it later, what did it mean to the child at the time? One suspects that, as in much of childhood role-playing, their sense of the adult meanings attributed to the behavior is fragmentary and ill-formed. Many of the adults recall that, at the time, they were concerned with being found out. But here, too, were they concerned because of the real content of sex play, or because of the mystery and the lure of the forbidden that so often enchant the child? The child may be assimilating outside information about sex for which, at the time, he has no real internal correlate or understanding.

A small number of persons do have sociosexual activity during preadolescence—most of it initiated by adults. But for the majority of these, little apparently follows from it. Without appropriate sexual scripts, the experience remains unassimilated—at least in adult terms. For some, it is clear, a severe reaction may follow from falling "victim" to the sexuality of an adult—but, again, does this reaction come from the sexual act itself or from the social response, the strong reactions of others? (There is some evidence that early sexual activity of this sort is associated with deviant adjustments in later life. But this, too, may not be the result of sexual experiences in themselves so much as the consequence of having fallen out of the social main stream and, therefore, of running greater risks of isolation and alienation.)

In short, relatively few become truly active sexually before adolescence. And when they do (for girls more often than boys), it is seldom immediately related to sexual feelings or gratifications but is a use of sex for nonsexual goals and purposes. The "seductive" Lolita is rare; but she is significant: She illustrates a more general pattern of psychosexual development—a commitment to the social relationships linked to sex before one can really grasp the social meaning of the physical relationships.

Of great importance are the values (or feelings, or images) that children pick up as being related to sex. Although we talk a lot about sexuality, as though trying to exorcise the demon of shame, learning about sex in our society is in large part learning about guilt; and learning how to manage sexuality commonly involves learning how to manage guilt. An important source of guilt in children comes from the imputation to them by adults of sexual appetites or abilities that they may not have, but that they learn, however imperfectly, to pretend they have. The gestural concomitants of sexual modesty are learned early. For instance, when do girls learn to sit or pick up objects with their knees together? When do they learn that the bust must be covered? However, since this behavior is learned unlinked to later adult sexual performances, what children must make of all this is very mysterious.

The learning of sex roles, or sex identities, involves many things that are remote from actual sexual experience, or that become involved with sexuality only after puberty. Masculinity or femininity, their meaning and postures, are rehearsed before adolescence in many nonsexual ways.

A number of scholars have pointed, for instance, to the importance of aggressive, deference, dependency, and dominance behavior in childhood. Jerome Kagan and Howard Moss have found that aggressive behavior in males and dependency in females are relatively stable aspects of development. But what is social role, and what is biology? They found that when aggressive behavior occurred among girls, it tended to appear most often among those from well-educated families that were more tolerant of deviation. Curiously, they also reported that "it was impossible to predict the character of adult sexuality in women from their pre-adolescent and early adolescent behavior," and that "erotic activity is more anxiety-arousing for females than for males," because "the traditional ego ideal for women dictates inhibition of sexual impulses."

The belief in the importance of early sex-role learning for boys can be viewed in two ways. First, it may directly indicate an early sexual capacity in male children. Or, second, early masculine identification may merely be an appropriate framework within which the sexual impulse (salient with puberty) and the socially available sexual scripts (or accepted patterns of sexual behavior) can most conveniently find expression. Our bias, of course, is toward the second.

But, as Kagan and Moss also noted, the sex role learned by the child does not reliably predict how he will act sexually as an adult. This finding also can be interpreted in the same two alternative ways. Where sexuality is viewed as a biological constant which struggles to express itself, the female sex role learning can be interpreted as the successful repression of sexual impulses. The other interpretation suggests that the difference lies not in learning how to handle a pre-existing sexuality, but in learning how to *be* sexual. Differences between men and women, therefore, will have consequences both for *what* is done sexually, as well as *when*.

Once again, we prefer the latter interpretation, and some recent work that we have done with lesbians supports it. We observed that many of the major elements of their sex lives—the start of actual genital sexual behavior, the onset and frequency of masturbation, the time of entry in sociosexual patterns, the number of partners, and the reports of feelings of sexual deprivation—were for these homosexual women almost identical with those of ordinary women. Since sexuality would seem to be more important for lesbians—after all, they sacrifice much in order to follow their own sexual pathways—this is surprising. We concluded that the primary factor was something both categories of women share—the sex-role learning that occurs before sexuality itself becomes significant.

Social class also appears significant, more for boys than girls. Sex-role learning may vary by class; lower-class boys are supposed to be more aggressive and put much greater emphasis on early heterosexuality. The middle and upper classes tend to tolerate more deviance from traditional attitudes regarding appropriate male sex-role performances.

Given all these circumstances, it seems rather naive to think of sexuality as a constant pressure, with a peculiar necessity all its own. For us, the crucial period of childhood has significance not because of sexual occurrences, but because of nonsexual developments that will provide the names and judgments for later encounters with sexuality.

Adolescence

The actual beginnings and endings of adolescence are vague. Generally, the beginning marks the first time society, as such, acknowledges that the individual has sexual capacity. Training in the postures and rhetoric of the sexual experience is now accelerated. Most important, the adolescent begins to regard those about him (particularly his peers, but also adults) as sexual actors and finds confirmation from others for this view.

For some, as noted, adolescent sexual experience begins before they are considered adolescents. Kinsey reports that a tenth of his female sample and a fifth of his male sample had experienced orgasm through masturbation by age 12. But still, for the vast majority, despite some casual play and exploration that post-Freudians might view as masked sexuality, sexual experience begins with adolescence. Even those who have had prior experience find that it acquires new meanings with adolescence. They now relate such meanings to both larger spheres of social life and greater senses of self. For example, it is not uncommon during the transition between childhood and adolescence for boys and, more rarely, girls to report arousal and orgasm while doing things not manifestly sexual—climbing trees, sliding down bannisters, or other activities that involve genital contact—without defining them as sexual. Often they do not even take it seriously enough to try to explore or repeat what was, in all likelihood, a pleasurable experience.

Adolescent sexual development, therefore, really represents the beginning of adult sexuality. It marks a definite break with what went on before. Not only will future experiences occur in new and more complex contexts, but they will be conceived of as explicitly sexual and thereby begin to complicate social relationships. The need to manage sexuality will rise not only from physical needs and desires, but also from the new implications of personal relationships. Playing, or associating, with members of the opposite sex now acquires different meanings.

At adolescence, changes in the developments of boys and girls diverge and must be considered separately. The one thing both share at this point is a reinforcement of their new status by a dramatic biological event—for girls, menstruation, and for boys, the discovery of the ability to ejaculate. But here they part. For boys, the beginning of a commitment to sexuality is primarily genital; within two years of puberty all but a relatively few have had the experience of orgasm, almost universally brought about by masturbation. The corresponding organizing event for girls is not genitally sexual but social: they have arrived at an age where they will learn role performances linked with proximity to marriage. In contrast to boys, only two-thirds of girls will report ever having masturbated (and, characteristically, the frequency is much less). For women, it is not until the late twenties that the incidence of orgasm from any source reaches that of boys at age 16. In fact, significantly, about half of the females who masturbate do so only after having experienced orgasm in some situation involving others. This contrast points to a basic distinction between the developmental processes for males and females: males move from privatized personal sexuality to sociosexuality; females do the reverse and at a later stage in the life cycle.

The Turned-On Boys

We have worked hard to demonstrate the dominance of social, psychological, and cultural influences over the biological; now, dealing with adolescent boys, we must briefly reverse course. There is much evidence that the early male sexual impulses—again, initially through masturbation—are linked to physiological changes, to high hormonal inputs during puberty. This produces an organism that, to put it simply, is more easily turned on. Male adolescents report frequent erections, often without apparent stimulation of any kind. Even so, though there is greater biological sensitization and hence masturbation is more likely, the meaning, organization, and continuance of this activity still tends to be subordinate to social and psychological factors.

Masturbation provokes guilt and anxiety among most adolescent boys. This is not likely to change in spite of more "enlightened" rhetoric and discourse on the subject (generally, we have shifted from stark warnings of mental, moral, and physical damage to vague counsels against nonsocial or "inappropriate" behavior). However, it may be that this very guilt and anxiety gives the sexual experience an intensity of feeling that is often attributed to sex itself.

Such guilt and anxiety do not follow simply from social disapproval. Rather, they seem to come from several sources, including the difficulty the boy has in presenting himself as a sexual being to his immediate family, particularly his parents. Another source is the fantasies or plans associated with masturbation—fantasies about doing sexual "things" to others or having others do sexual "things" to oneself; or having to learn and rehearse available but proscribed sexual scripts or patterns of behavior. And, of course, some guilt and anxiety center around the general disapproval of masturbation. After the early period of adolescence, in fact, most youths will not admit to their peers that they did or do it.

Nevertheless, masturbation is for most adolescent boys the major sexual activity, and they engage in it fairly frequently. It is an extremely positive and gratifying experience to them. Such an introduction to sexuality can lead to a capacity for detached sex activity—activity whose only sustaining motive is sexual. This may be the hallmark of male sexuality in our society.

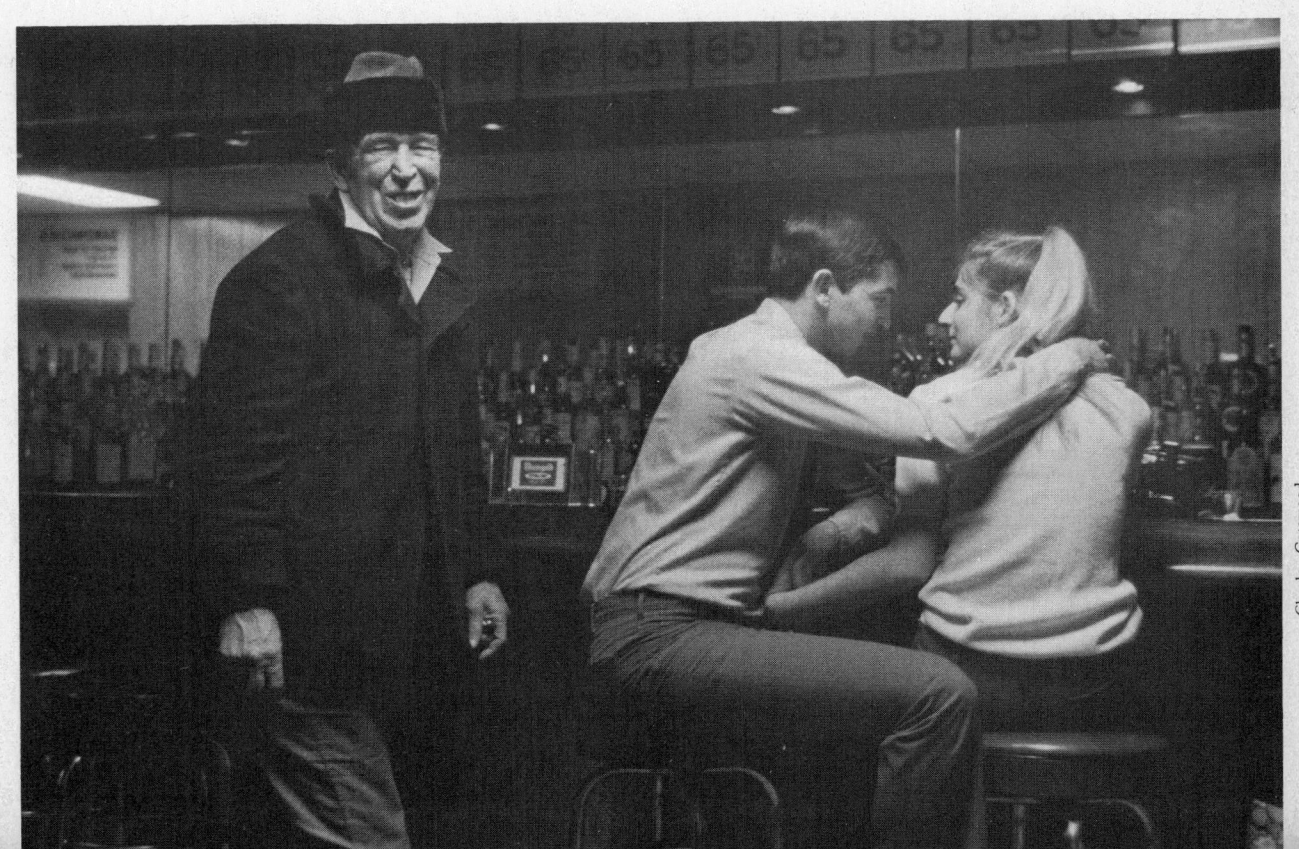

Of the three sources of guilt and anxiety mentioned, the first—how to manage both sexuality and an attachment to family members—probably cuts across class lines. But the others should show remarkable class differences. The second one, how to manage a fairly elaborate and exotic fantasy life during masturbation, should be confined most typically to the higher classes, who are more experienced and adept at dealing with symbols. (It is possible, in fact, that this behavior, which girls rarely engage in, plays a role in the processes by which middle-class boys catch up with girls in measures of achievement and creativity and, by the end of adolescence, move out in front. However, this is only a hypothesis.)

The ability to fantasize during masturbation implies certain broad consequences. One is a tendency to see large parts of the environment in an erotic light, as well as the ability to respond, sexually and perhaps poetically, to many visual and auditory stimuli. We might also expect both a capacity and need for fairly elaborate forms of sexual activity. Further, since masturbatory fantasies generally deal with relationships and acts leading to coitus, they should also reinforce a developing capacity for heterosociality.

The third source of guilt and anxiety—the alleged "unmanliness" of masturbation—should more directly concern the lower-class male adolescent. ("Manliness" has always been an important value for lower-class males.) In these groups, social life is more often segregated by sex, and there are, generally, fewer rewarding social experiences from other sources. The adolescent therefore moves into heterosexual—if not heterosocial—relationships sooner than his middle-class counterparts. Sexual segregation makes it easier for him than for the middle-class boy to learn that he does not have to love everything he desires, and therefore to come more naturally to casual, if not exploitative, relationships. The second condition—fewer social rewards that his fellows would respect—should lead to an exaggerated concern for proving masculinity by direct displays of physical prowess, aggression, and visible sexual success. And these three, of course, may be mutually reinforcing.

In a sense, the lower-class male is the first to reach "sexual maturity" as defined by the Freudians. That is, he is generally the first to become aggressively heterosexual and exclusively genital. This characteristic, in fact, is a distinguishing difference between lower-class males and those above them socially.

But one consequence is that although their sex lives are almost exclusively heterosexual, they remain homosocial. They have intercourse with females, but the standards and the audience they refer to are those of their male fellows.

SUGGESTED READINGS

Nature, Man, and Woman by Alan W. Watts (New York: Pantheon Books, 1958). Watts contrasts the Freudian perspective on sexual development with cultural patterns in the Far East, opposing Western concepts of "the ethical" to the Orient's approach to "the natural."

The Moral Judgment of the Child by Jean Piaget (Glencoe, Ill.: The Free Press, 1960).

The Development of Motives and Values in the Child by Leonard Berkowitz (New York: Basic Books, 1964). A review and integration of the socialization literature, focusing on the development of conscience and achievement motivation.

Men In Groups by Lionel Tiger (New York: Random House, 1969). A controversial interpretation of sex roles and "male bonding" from a biological-genetic perspective.

An Outline of Psychoanalysis by Sigmund Freud edited by James Strachey (New York: Norton, 1970).

The Sexual Scene edited by John Gagnon and William Simon, (Chicago: Aldine, 1970).

Middle-class boys shift predominantly to coitus at a significantly later time. They, too, need and tend to have homosocial elements in their sexual lives. But their fantasies, their ability to symbolize, and their social training in a world in which distinctions between masculinity and femininity are less sharply drawn, allow them to withdraw more easily from an all-male world. This difference between social classes obviously has important consequences for stable adult relationships.

One thing common in male experience during adolescence is that while it provides much opportunity for sexual commitment, in one form or another, there is little training in how to handle emotional relations with girls. The imagery and rhetoric of romantic love is all around us; we are immersed in it. But whereas much is undoubtedly absorbed by the adolescent, he is not likely to tie it closely to his sexuality. In fact, such a connection might be inhibiting, as indicated by the survival of the "bad-girl-who-does" and "good-girl-who-doesn't" distinction. This is important to keep in mind as we turn to the female side of the story.

With the Girls

In contrast to males, female sexual development during adolescence is so similar in all classes that it is easy to suspect that it is solely determined by biology. But, while girls do not have the same level of hormonal sensitization to sexuality at puberty as adolescent boys, there is little evidence of a biological or social inhibitor either. The "equipment" for sexual pleasure is clearly present by puberty, but tends not to be used by many females of any class. Masturbation rates are fairly low, and among those who do masturbate, fairly infrequent. Arousal from "sexual" materials or situations happens seldom, and exceedingly few girls report feeling sexually deprived during adolescence.

Basically, girls in our society are not encouraged to be sexual—and may be strongly discouraged from being so. Most of us accept the fact that while "bad boy" can mean many things, "bad girl" almost exclusively implies sexual delinquency. It is both difficult and dangerous for an adolescent girl to become too active sexually. As Joseph Rheingold puts it, where men need only fear sexual failure, women must fear both success and failure.

Does this long period of relative sexual inactivity among girls come from repression of an elemental drive, or merely from a failure to learn how to be sexual? The answers have important implications for their later sexual development. If it is repression, the path to a fuller sexuality must pass through processes of loss of inhibitions, during which the girl unlearns, in varying degrees, attitudes and values that block the expression of natural internal feelings. It also implies that the quest for ways to express directly sexual behavior and feelings that had been expressed nonsexually is secondary and of considerably less significance.

On the other hand, the "learning" answer suggests that women create or invent a capacity for sexual behavior, learning how and when to be aroused and how and when to respond. This approach implies greater flexibility; unlike the repression view, it makes sexuality both more and less than a basic force that may break loose at any time in strange or costly ways. The learning approach also lessens the power of sexuality altogether; all at once, particular kinds of sex activities need no longer be defined as either "healthy" or "sick." Lastly, subjectively, this approach appeals to the authors because it describes female sexuality in terms that seem less like a mere projection of male sexuality.

If sexual activity by adolescent girls assumes less specific forms than with boys, that does not mean that sexual learning and training do not occur. Curiously, though girls are, as a group, far less active sexually than boys, they receive far more training in self-consciously viewing themselves—and in viewing boys—as desirable mates. This is particularly true in recent years. Females begin early in adolescence to define attractiveness, at least partially, in sexual terms. We suspect that the use of sexual attractiveness for nonsexual purposes that marked our preadolescent "seductress" now begins to characterize many girls. Talcott Parsons' description of how the wife "uses" sex to bind the husband to the family, although harsh, may be quite accurate. More generally, in keeping with the childbearing and child-raising function of women, the development of a sexual role seems to involve a need to include in that role more than pleasure.

To round out the picture of the difference between the sexes, girls appear to be well-trained precisely in that area in which boys are poorly trained—that is, a belief in and a capacity for intense, emotionally-charged relationships and the language of romantic love. When girls during this period describe having been aroused sexually, they more often report it as a response to romantic, rather than erotic, words and actions.

In later adolescence, as dates, parties, and other sociosexual activities increase, boys—committed to sexuality and relatively untrained in the language and actions of romantic love—interact with girls, committed to romantic love and relatively untrained in sexuality. Dating and courtship may well be considered processes in which each sex trains the other in what each wants and expects. What data is available suggests that this exchange system does not always work very smoothly. Thus, ironically, it is not uncommon to find that the boy becomes emotionally involved with his partner and therefore lets up on trying to seduce her, at the same time that the girl comes to feel that the boy's affection is genuine and therefore that sexual intimacy is more permissible.

In our recent study of college students, we found that boys typically had intercourse with their first coital partners one to three times, while with girls it was ten or more. Clearly, for the majority of females first intercourse becomes possible only in stable relationships or in those with strong bonds.

"Woman, What Does She Want?"

The male experience does conform to the general Freudian expectation that there is a developmental move-

Many males elaborate exotic fantasy lives while masturbating, which may play "a role in the processes by which middle-class boys catch up with girls in measures of achievement and creativity."

Charles Gatewood

EARLY SOCIALIZATION

Working-class males get no peer admiration for marital sexual prowess but do for extracurricular endeavors pursued impersonally.

ment from a predominantly genital sexual commitment to a loving relationship with another person. But this movement is, in effect, reversed for females, with love or affection often a necessary precondition for intercourse. No wonder, therefore, that Freud had great difficulty understanding female sexuality—recall the concluding line in his great essay on women: "Woman, what does she want?" This "error"—the assumption that female sexuality is similar to or a mirror image of that of the male—may come from the fact that so many of those who constructed the theory were men. With Freud, in addition, we must remember the very concept of sexuality essential to most of nineteenth century Europe—it was an elemental beast that had to be curbed.

It has been noted that there are very few class differences in sexuality among females, far fewer than among males. One difference, however, is very relevant to this discussion —the age of first intercourse. This varies inversely with social class—that is, the higher the class, the later the age of first intercourse—a relationship that is also true of first marriage. The correlation between these two ages suggest the necessary social and emotional linkage between courtship and the entrance into sexual activity on the part of women. A second difference, perhaps only indirectly related to social class, has to do with educational achievement: here, a sharp border line seems to separate from all other women those who have or have had graduate or professional work. If sexual success may be measured by the percentage of sex acts that culminate in orgasm, graduate and professional women are the most sexually successful women in the nation.

Why? One possible interpretation derives from the work of Abraham Maslow: Women who get so far in higher education are more likely to be more aggressive, perhaps to have strong needs to dominate; both these characteristics are associated with heightened sexuality. Another, more general interpretation would be that in a society in which girls are expected primarily to become wives and mothers, going on to graduate school represents a kind of deviancy —a failure of, or alienation from, normal female social adjustment. In effect, then, it would be this flawed socialization—not biology—that produced both commitment toward advanced training and toward heightened sexuality.

For both males and females, increasingly greater involvement in the social aspects of sexuality—"socializing" with the opposite sex—may be one factor that marks the end of adolescence. We know little about this transition, especially among noncollege boys and girls; but our present feeling is that sexuality plays an important role in it. First, sociosexuality is important in family formation and also in learning the roles and obligations involved in being an adult. Second, and more fundamental, late adolescence is when a youth is seeking, and experimenting toward finding, his identity—who and what he is and will be; and sociosexual activity is the one aspect of this exploration that we associate particularly with late adolescence.

Young people are particularly vulnerable at this time. This may be partly due to the fact that society has difficulty protecting the adolescent from the consequences of sexual behavior that it pretends he is not engaged in. But, more importantly, it may be because, at all ages, we all have great problems in discussing our sexual feelings and experiences in personal terms. These, in turn, make it extremely difficult to get support from others for an adolescent's experiments toward trying to invent his sexual self. We suspect that success or failure in the discovery or management of sexual identity may have consequences in personal development far beyond merely the sexual sphere —perhaps in confidence and feelings of self-worth, belonging, competence, guilt, force of personality, and so on.

Adulthood

In our society, all but a few ultimately marry. Handling sexual commitments inside marriage makes up the larger part of adult experience. Again, we have too little data for firm findings. The data we do have come largely from studies of broken and troubled marriages, and we do not know to what extent sexual problems in such marriages exceed those of intact marriages. It is possible that, because we have assumed that sex is important in most people's lives, we have exaggerated its importance in holding marriages together. Also, it is quite possible that, once people are married, sexuality declines relatively, becoming less important than other gratifications (such as domesticity or parenthood); or it may be that these other gratifications can minimize the effect of sexual dissatisfaction. Further, it may be possible that individuals learn to get sexual gratification, or an equivalent, from activities that are nonsexual, or only partially sexual.

The sexual desires and commitments of males are the main determinants of the rate of sexual activity in our society. Men are most interested in intercourse in the early years of marriage—woman's interest peaks much later; nonetheless, coital rates decline steadily throughout marriage. This decline derives from many things, only one of which is decline in biological capacity. With many men, it is more difficult to relate sexually to a wife who is pregnant or a mother. Lower-class adult men receive less support and plaudits from their male friends for married sexual performance than they did as single adolescents; and we might also add the lower-class disadvantage of less training in the use of auxiliary or symbolic sexually stimulating materials. For middle-class men, the decline is not as steep, owing perhaps to their greater ability to find stimulation from auxiliary sources, such as literature, movies, music, and romantic or erotic conversation. It should be further noted that for about 30 percent of college-educated men, masturbation continues regularly during marriage, even when the wife is available. An additional (if unknown) proportion do not physically masturbate, but derive additional excitement from the fantasies that accompany intercourse.

But even middle-class sexual activity declines more rapidly than bodily changes can account for. Perhaps the ways males learn to be sexual in our society make it very difficult to keep it up at a high level with the same woman for a long time. However, this may not be vital in maintaining the family, or even in the man's personal sense of well-being, because, as previously suggested, sexual dissatisfaction may become less important as other satisfactions increase. Therefore, it need seldom result in crisis.

About half of all married men and a quarter of all married women will have intercourse outside of marriage at one time or another. For women, infidelity seems to have been on the increase since the turn of the century— at the same time that their rates of orgasm have been increasing. It is possible that the very nature of female sexuality is changing. Work being done now may give us new light on this. For men, there are strong social-class differences—the lower class accounts for most extramarital activity, especially during the early years of marriage. We have observed that it is difficult for a lower-class man to acquire the appreciation of his fellows for married intercourse; extramarital sex, of course, is another matter.

In general, we feel that far from sexual needs affecting other adult concerns, the reverse may be true: adult sexual activity may become that aspect of a person's life most often used to act out other needs. There are some data that suggest this. Men who have trouble handling authority relationships at work more often have dreams about homosexuality; some others, under heavy stress on the job, have been shown to have more frequent episodic homosexual experiences. Such phenomena as the rise of sadomasochistic practices and experiments in group sex may also be tied to nonsexual tensions, the use of sex for nonsexual purposes.

It is only fairly recently in the history of man that he has been able to begin to understand that his own time and place do not embody some eternal principle or necessity, but are only dots on a continuum. It is difficult for many to believe that man can change, and is changing, in important ways. This conservative view is evident even in contemporary behavioral science; and a conception of man as having relatively constant sexual needs has become part of it. In an ever-changing world, it is perhaps comforting to think that man's sexuality does not change very much, and therefore is relatively easily explained. We cannot accept this. Instead, we have attempted to offer a description of sexual development as a variable social invention—an invention that in itself explains little, and requires much continuing explanation.

March 1969

The article is reprinted in condensed form from *Handbook of Socialization Theory and Research* edited by David A. Goslin, Russell Sage Foundation, published by Rand McNally & Co. © 1969, all rights reserved by Rand McNally and Company.
The paper which formed the basis of this article was originally presented at the National Institute of Child Health and Human Development Conference on Social Aspects of Socialization in Washington, D.C., December 8, 1967. The research was supported by United States Public Health Service grant HD02257.

Dynamic Young Fogies—
Rebels on the Right

Adolescent conservatism can bring conformity or emancipation—it depends on the age of "conversion"

LAWRENCE F. SCHIFF

From the bearded poet to the motorcycle delinquent, American adolescents usually go through a period of uncertainty and search, of trying to break away from old controls and standards, and of trying to establish their own identities and personalities.

As psychiatrist Erik H. Erikson puts it, youth searches for "fidelity"—"something and somebody to be true to"—and "often tests extremes before settling on a considered course." This period in adolescence often involves the rejection of things as they are, or as society says they should be.

So it seems an amazing paradox that many young people today, in a small but apparently growing movement, have dedicated themselves to promoting *greater* conservatism, *more* tradition, and *more* devotion and adherence to the values not only of an older generation, but apparently even of an older century.

The conservative movement began in 1960 on the wave of enthusiasm generated by the abortive attempt to get the vice-presidential nomination for Barry Goldwater. The excitement, the spontaneous appearance of so many young conservatives, led to the formation of the Young Americans for Freedom—or YAF. Since then, fed by the rise of other non-affiliated but similarly oriented local college groups, the campus conservative movement has become a fairly successful and going concern. There is no doubt that, paradoxical or not, a small but sizable segment of our young people have found something in this movement to which they respond, and that seems to meet their internal and external demands.

In my study I found that about two-thirds of those interviewed had undergone such a strong change in belief and behavior in coming to conservatism that it could properly

"The young converts found in conservatism a way to bring internal needs and fears into the open in the form of ideas and actions."

be said that they had experienced a form of "conversion." (The other third had simply followed comfortably along the right-wing paths already set by their parents.) These converts, I discovered, had gone through crises and events that were very revealing about their development as adolescents and their total development as human beings.

Specifically, I have found that at the various stages of adolescence different kinds of persons were attracted by conservatism, for different reasons, and in response to different needs. It matters a great deal whether the conversion occurred *immediately following puberty* (between 12 and 17), or in *late adolescence* (beyond 17). There is some overlap; but the two groups are distinctive, each with its own dynamics and style.

The Obedient Rebels

The late converts—whom I call "the obedient rebels"—were the ones most representative of campus conservative activists. Typically they were from homes very much concerned with high status and achievement. In almost all cases their early experiences were dominated by a determined parent, or parents, with detailed and ambitious expectations for their children. All but one were eldest or only sons and the burden of parental ambition fell on them. The obedient rebels (at least in the early years and again after conversion) were usually considered the "good boys" of their families.

Each "rebelled"—sometimes because he felt he could not live up to or realize himself under such pressure—or departed to some degree from the path set out for him. But the revolt was not without peril. Suddenly he would be horrified to discover (on the campus, in the armed services, or among the lower-classes) that he was surrounded by "radicalism," "immorality," or personal hardship—something for which his comfortable background had not prepared him. He would reject the new environment totally and become converted to a conservatism not much different from the one he had left in the first place—but which, superficially at least, he had accepted on his own initiative and conviction.

Psychologically, in essence, his conversion was a reaction to the threat of genuine personality change—which allows great creative possibilities, but also involves dangers. In effect he had come to the pit of change, looked down into it, and turned back, rejecting all alternatives beyond the reaffirmation of obedience; if the non-convert conservatives had never left home, the obedient rebels had returned home.

The *early* adolescent converts, however, exhibited a strikingly different and even more interesting pattern—one signifying a very different way of coping with adolescence. Their conversions were made during, and as part of, the turbulent and formative center of adolescence, and were intertwined, warp and woof, with the demands, potentialities, problems, and limits of that period. The personality changes were reflected in the conversion experience itself.

Where the obedient rebel came to conversion as a result of shock and repulsion (a negative reaction), the early convert came as a result of attraction, or recognition, because he saw something that seemed to meet his needs (for positive reasons). The late convert came to escape from and to deny real change; the early convert came seeking answers and seeking change. His conversion was change itself.

The late convert identified with the overall posture and prestige of the new conservatism, rather than with its detailed content. He was concerned mostly with status, with position, with social identification, with respectability and role—not with passionate belief. As such he could accept its doctrine totally, without much quibble, since what counted was what it stood for, rather than what it was. But the early convert's acceptance of conservatism was specific, personal, immediate, discriminating, and emotional; and he was much more interested in content, as he understood it, than in form.

To understand the contrasts between early and late conversion it is best to go back to the beginnings, in boyhood, and follow the process through time.

As noted, the late converts typically came from families with great determination to see that their children rose in the world. They were under great pressure to achieve and conform—as the interviews revealed.

—Herron's father, a highly successful independent lawyer, early and ardently began to infuse his young son with the spirit of his "adherence to strict moral standards" . . .

—Finestock's immigrant father received a primary school education here and then in true Horatio Alger fashion, rose . . . to put together a fabulously successful business. He intended that his son would actualize his success. . . .

Under such pressure they bent; each in his own way, always covertly and at times involuntarily, they veered from the too high and too rigid parental blueprint.

—Herron . . . chafing under . . . his father's tutelage, began to channel his energies into activities only marginally related to the development of intellect or character. . . . Throughout his adolescence he managed to balance off his resentment against his father by avoiding overt disobedience, always maintaining the form but not the substance of his father's preachments.

—Finestock's father had "pulled strings" to get him into a first-rate college, but after two unhappy years there he flunked out.

Their conversions, when they came, were a reaction to the new standards to which their rebellion had exposed them. They rejected this new environment totally—and as individuals, rather than as a result of being solicited by other conservatives. While it may have set them apart for a time from most of their immediate fellows it did give them a reassuring image and identity, and it led them back toward their parents.

—Herron's conversion took place while he was stationed abroad in the Navy. Disturbed by the "slothfulness" and

"Commitment among adolescents tends to be 'all out.' Among the conservatives this takes the form of 'gung-ho' anti-Communism."

"self-indulgent habits" of the local citizenry, he had a sudden realization of "the consequences of not subscribing to a strict moral code."

—Manning reacted to his college's total climate. He found himself "appalled and amazed" about some of the college newspaper editorials . . . "disappointed" with the college's moral climate. . . .

Attack Toward the Rear

Conversion for the early adolescents presents a striking contrast. They did not turn from what they found in adolescence to go back to a childhood pattern. In fact, just the opposite—their adolescent conversions were a rejection of their beginnings.

Typically, the early convert came from a family where relationships were intense, and often stressful, unsettling, or full of strife:

—For O'Hara, childhood was . . . far from tranquil. His father (was) a man with a "quick temper" and "quick to criticize" . . . there were always "big arguments." "At one time I looked upon him as the oppressor of both me and my mother, and now I look on them both as in the same boat."

—Mann recalls himself as "a rather uncontrolled" kid, "disciplined from above. But inside I was rebellious . . . I was probably a pretty wretched kid."

—Arnold relates a persistent "inferiority complex. . . . I didn't conform to my mother's beliefs. . . . She kept repeating how no-good I was and how she wished I'd never been born. (This) had quite a dire effect on me."

Two of the young converts had alcoholic fathers; two others came from homes in which chronic instability kept things "wound up and involved."

In all of these cases, the child's emotional life was hyperactive and somewhat uncontrolled. Unlike the late converts, childhood experiences stimulated, rather than molded, character. They would not, or could not, silently conform. These early converts entered adolescence with still smoldering, unsettled infantile residues that had to be worked out some way.

Not surprisingly therefore, virtually all experienced during adolescence a sharp break with the past.

O'Hara: "I was flamboyant originally and a social guy, and then all of a sudden, snap! After sophomore year (high school) I became an introvent, a searcher. . . . I realized I didn't want to be anything like my father was —not his profession, not his personality—and that's just what I was going to be. . . . I wanted to go out on my own—I couldn't stand my dad."

Others went through a social dislocation that served as the break between childhood and what followed:

—Howard, after years of wandering . . . with his Army doctor father . . . at the onset of high school . . . settled into . . . an upper-middle-class suburban community where the family's style of living rose sharply. (He) felt "a little out of place for the first couple of years" . . . in "a rebellion against the accepted ideas I found around me."

—Mann was cut off from his Jewish past in New York City when he became a congressional page. . . . Assigned to the Republican side of the House, he became thoroughly involved in "contacts with those with another point of view."

Three boys came from working-class homes. They broke away from parental patterns and chose their own college-bound paths early—and alone. No brothers or sisters followed.

My mother wasn't even sure I should go to college. I just told her I was going.

Parental values—and even parental models—become irrelevant as each pursued his own road to self-realization.

Our society, with its lack of ritualized organization, does not make the path of growth easy for the young. Peter Blos (*On Adolescence,* The Free Press, 1962) points out: "Where tradition and custom offer no unchallenged influence over the individual, the adolescent has to achieve by personal resourcefulness the adaptation that institutionalization does not offer him. On the other hand, this lack of institutionalized pattern opens up the opportunity for individual development, for the creation of a unique, highly original, and personal variation on tradition."

Thus, finally, this breakaway, whatever handicaps it imposed, also allowed the early converts to work out their own highly individual fates without the inhibitions of family control or tradition. And their conversions played key roles in this working-out.

For some, separation from their families began with the pain of severe withdrawal—"a self-inflicted purgatory."

—O'Hara: "I don't remember those years—I try to forget—don't think about it that much." Through his second year in high school he alternated between the "good works" of a Catholic social action group and quasi-delinquency, then suddenly "realized that there was hypocrisy in my life" and literally "pulled out . . ." spending much of the next two years trying to "settle it by lying down and thinking about myself."

—For Griffith the marriage of his sister (who had served as a mother substitute) brought on a depressive state for several years. . . . Through high school he was "introverted, very, very quiet. . . . (the kids') middle-class outlooks repulsed me. . . ."

—For Arnold and Wilson the challenge of adjustment proved unmanageable and led to . . . enlistment in the armed forces. . . .

For other converts the transition was more benign, but just as decisive.

From this "purgatory," this searching, they found and embraced conservatism.

—(Griffith's) exposure to and developing enthusiasm about the writings of Ayn Rand and Goldwater conservatism crystallized soon after . . . the death of his father and a year of emotional turmoil for his widowed mother.
—O'Hara: "I wanted to spread out. I almost became a priest; but it's a much greater task to do it on your own. That's what I'm working on now." During two summers . . . away from home he made his first contacts with conservatism. "Things were so completely different . . . just remade me—my dad wasn't around—I made friends fast —everything else was forgotten."

For working-class converts the conversion came when they had replaced their family ties with outside middle-class and conservative models.

A NOTE ON THE STUDY

Forty-seven conservatives from nine college campuses (all but one in New England) were extensively interviewed and given a variety of tests. Geographically the sample included students from every region in the country; academically, from college drop-outs to Rhodes scholars; economically, from families with incomes from $5,000 to $75,000; politically, from moderate Republicans through John Birch enthusiasts to unreconstructed royalists; in religion from atheism to extreme orthodoxy.

About two-thirds of them, in becoming conservatives, had made such a strong break with their previous attitudes and behavior that it would be legitimate to call them "converts"; and it was on these that the study concentrated. The other conservatives were simply following along in footsteps already well worn by parents or community in expected and familiar ways. But the converts—whether by changing from indifference to commitment or by moving sharply to the right—had undergone changes and experiences important not only to their development as adolescents, but to their total life cycles.

A more detailed study of the obedient rebel-type converts has been published in the *Journal of Social Issues.*

In sum, these early conversions came about because they served to meet and answer the challenges of adolescence for these young men. They fit Blos's contention that: "Adolescence, not only in spite of, but rather because of, its emotional turmoil, often affords spontaneous recovery from debilitating childhood influences. . . ." and Erickson's suggestion that: "We look at adolescence not as an affliction, but as a normal phase of increased conflict characterized by a high growth potential."

Follow the Hero

Typically, the early convert had a "hero," who had great influence, both as recruiter and example.

There was a counselor there, a man who appealed to me. It turned out he had a ranch in Arizona, he was born on it and he was a conservative . . . that's where I first became interested . . . he was a cool guy and he seemed reasonable. . . . Naturally this transferred into the policies he put forth.

William F. Buckley, the popular and vocal editor of the *National Review,* is a key hero:

Well, my romance with him—first of all I think he has tremendous style—secondly he's a more complete man . . . he doesn't hedge—he says it, he's not afraid to say it. Lord, that is a tremendous quality in this age.

The archetypal heroes for the early convert, of course, are those that Ayn Rand creates—and Miss Rand herself. She, too, is "not afraid to say it." Her creations are heroic in the fullest and most uninhibited sense of the word. Existing outside of time, history, and social circumstance, they are unfettered men, free of any social or personal responsibilities or knowledge that might slow down their single-minded pursuit of their self-interest (which, as it happens, is also the greatest public good, since they are a unique breed of supermen whose genius is all that keeps the world moving). Miss Rand's unabashed "philosophy" is outside the conservative mainstream. It is avowedly atheistic and egotistical and is meant to shock the conventional, so it is taboo to the obedient rebels. But how many teen-agers, smarting under parental, social, and school controls which they find false and binding, would not thrill to the story of an architect who refused to compromise with his paying clients and blew up a building development because someone tampered with his design?

Unlike the "lone wolf" obedient rebel, the early convert is usually converted *by* somebody or *with* somebody—it is a social process. He becomes part of a group of similar persons who give support both to him and his belief. Conservatism is woven into the fabric of his relationships:

—Madding "got hold of the (John Birch) *Blue Book* and passed it on to my friends; nearly all were very much impressed. . . ."

—Riley joined his campus YAF chapter because "I liked the people in it."

The early adolescent undergoes a deep conversion. His whole "self-system" is involved. His personality and emotions have been expressed in the act, not just his public face.

—O'Hara (had) an experience of intense self examination which lasted through several "extremely turbulent years, psychologically and emotionally." He now sees conservatism as the only philosophy "congruent with my whole philosophy of life." For O'Hara to arrive at this point required a "personal experience of God" . . . "Inspiration first and examination later."

—Griffith found himself adopting political ideas that were the opposite of his father's. "I suppose there's some deep psychological basis."

—Mann's response to a suggestion of his mother that he would have to become a Democrat in order to be elected. . . . "She doesn't understand that this would mean changing me as a person."

Gung-ho Among the Conservatives

Commitment among adolescents tends to be "all out." Among the conservatives this takes the form of "gung-ho" anti-communism (a strange use of the old Chinese Communist slogan). With the older converts this was often directed most harshly at what they suspected were anti-anti-Communists in their midst—the enemy within—which may, psychologically, be an overt rejection of forbidden internal impulses. The early converts on the other hand seemed to have no such internal conflicts. The enemy was outside their ranks—distinct, identifiable, and real. "Gung-ho" meant to them what it did to Carlson's Raiders.

Conversion did, however, in other ways shed revealing lights on their deep inner needs and impulse life:

People are afraid of nuclear weapons (but) I don't fear the bomb . . . in a way I think it'd be an interesting experience . . . (I) would've enjoyed being a part of the Korean War. . . . I would've enjoyed shooting a few of those guys—they're our enemies.

The process of differentiating the self from the surrounding environment, a crucial part of self-realization, received dramatic form among the early converts. As Edgar Friedenberg describes it: "The oppositional, rebellious, and restive strivings, the stages of experimentation, the testing of the self by going to excess—all these have a positive usefulness . . . for self-definition." For several the conversion was a part of the means through which these strivings were expressed:

—Mann, aware of the unpopularity of his views, particularly back home, reacted with "a kind of strange and exaltative joy that someone was finding what I was saying especially incomprehensible."

—Griffith: "It's 'in' to be liberal. . . . Every once in a while, sitting at a table, everybody nods in agreement—and it's a little bit difficult to dissent. That's a very nice word, 'dissent,' and I think it should be preserved."

—Howard's original conservative thinking was formulated as a part of "a rebellion against the accepted ideas I found around me." He became, "by way of argument," a proponent of Herbert Hoover.

—O'Hara enjoys thinking of himself . . . as someone . . . able to "throw everything out."

Note the ease—indeed the relish and pride—in accepting the image of the self as iconoclast. They often seemed equally as concerned with what was "not me" within the spectrum of conservatism (a concern significantly different from that of the obedient rebels, who repudiated dissension within the ranks). What is distinctive is the emphasis on defining the self as in conflict with and yet as part of surrounding influences.

These young men are, more than most, "tuned in" on themselves—they have a heightened awareness of themselves.

—O'Hara reports feeling "as a man alone" after he "jumped out on my own, suddenly."

—Mann . . . thinks "everyone is basically insular . . . I am . . . everyone is distinct from everyone else deep inside. . . . There are many times when the most precious thing to me is to just sit down and think my own thoughts."

Important in this process of self-realization is the early convert's emphasis on the he-man self-image of conservatism—the rugged individualist, the combat soldier, Ayn Rand's hypermasculine heroes—an identification that might serve also to still any secret doubts about his own masculinity.

The early convert is at this stage still an unstable and incomplete human being—disengaged and aggrandized—a volatile configuration of conflicting strivings, tendencies, growth potentialities, and neurotic dangers. Since he is unfinished, only on rare occasions in the present sample did the political beliefs formed at conversion not undergo further important change.

Finally therefore, and most significantly, the early convert is engaged in a dynamic open-end process of alteration —similar, in this respect, to almost all other adolescents. He is on the "right track," but he is also traveling, and the end is neither in sight nor completely known. The obedient rebel has arrived; his beliefs and posture are round, firm, and fully packed. His conversion resulted in reduced tension and resolved conflict, and he will not again willingly risk uncertainty. Change is suspect and may be abhorrent. But to the early convert change is not at all unwelcome; he looks forward to it as another adventure. He delicately balances tentativeness and commitment:

> I feel that every student is essentially an observer in that he need not be committed to too many things. I have definitely not committed to conservative politics. . . . I'll give you my tendency, not my opinion. Opinion implies commitment.

In many cases he shows himself flexible, open to outside influences:

> Madding . . . is unsure if the economics course in which he is currently enrolled might not be "liberalizing me." . . . "Right now I'm just feeling my way along."

Actual changes take place:

> Howard began as a Randian disciple and then . . . "found I was looking for some 'new departure' in politics in the individualist direction, something not a revolt or return to the past."

In short and in summary, early conversion for these boys was a part of continuing development. It contributed substantially to self-definition; it helped integrate the entire personality; it helped the adolescent toward positive sexual identity, and the ability to have close relationships with other people. The conversion of the typical obedient rebel restored and bound him to his original role. The overall effect of the conversion of the young adolescent was emancipation.

But it is apparently true even of the young converts that, compared to the non-conservatives, they feel a need for all-inclusive answers, spelled out. Our society, according to Erik Erikson, requires of its youth many contradictory things, necessitating, therefore, "a distaste for ideological explicitness." The young conservatives need more than that: as convert Mann put it, "you must have a point of view . . . a basic premise . . . or everything is senseless."

Against the anti-hero of the modern novel with his existential despair, the analytic critic who debunks old traditions, and the disillusioned old radicals from the depression, the far right throws the heroic novel, the embattled and engaged young critic, and the refurbished old radical who has found another New Jerusalem—this one on the road back to Adam Smith. The new convert may not understand all of this, but it does give him something with sharp edges on which to shape himself, something more than the simple necessity to "get along." In this strident ideology and movement, he can find an object able to take on his fantasies and fears, to allow extreme possibilities to be tested, to provide space to work out problems, and room to grow or to regress.

The young converts found in conservatism a way to bring internal needs and fears into the open in the form of ideas and actions, there to communicate them, to shape them, to face them consciously and render them amenable to control. But the obedient rebels were more interested in restriction, in cutting off internal debate and conflict. It is paradoxical, therefore, but inevitable, that the obedient rebel demanded total and rigid conformity to conservative doctrine but was not emotionally involved in it very much; while the young converts cared passionately, but kept straying from orthodoxy.

Significantly then, the end for the young converts is not yet:

> O'Hara: "Where I go from here I don't know. Terms like 'truth' and 'right' and 'wrong' are fine . . . except in the sense that they've come to be pretty much meaningless. . . . But I think we can give them some meaning."

November 1966

SUGGESTED READINGS

They'd Rather Be Right, by Edward Cain. (New York: Macmillan, 1963). Factual, useful study of the current rightwing youth movement.

Youth: Change and Challenge, edited by Erik Erikson, based on Daedalus, Vol. 91, 1962 (New York: Anchor Books, 1965). Essays on current youth around the world.

The Vanishing Adolescent, by Edgar Z. Friedenberg. (Boston, Mass.: Beacon Press, 1959). Social criticism of American society's effect on adolescents, particularly of high school age.

Revolt on the Campus by M. Stanton Evans (Chicago: H. Regnery, 1961). A highly partisan and journalistic account of the origins, philosophy and activities of activist conservative college students.

Radical Libertarianism by Jerome Tuccille (Indianapolis, Indiana: Bobbs-Merrill, 1970). A theoretical description and analysis of the anarchistic branch of the conservative youth movement.

The Conflict of Generations by Lewis S. Feuer (New York: Basic Books, 1968). Historical survey and interpretation of student activism in terms of the Freudian concepts of symbolic patricide and unresolved Oedipal anxieties.

Growing Up Absurd by Paul Goodman (New York: Random House, 1960). Goodman delineates the relationship between society and the disaffected youngster, indicating some of the problems of youth in "the organized society."

The Uncommitted by Kenneth Keniston (New York: Harcourt, Brace and World, 1965).

Young Radicals by Kenneth Keniston (New York, Harcourt, Brace and World, 1968). Two kinds of youth, the alienated and the committed, both in that separate stage of life that intervenes between adolescence and adulthood.

Howard Harrison

Young Intelligentsia in Revolt

RICHARD FLACKS

Karl Marx expected that capitalist exploitation of industrial workers would lead them to oppose the culture of capitalism—that is, that workers would organize not only on behalf of their own interests but ultimately on behalf of human liberation. What now seems clear is that opposition to capitalist culture arose less in the working class than among tiny groups of artists and intellectuals. Obviously, such people were too few in number and too isolated from the productive process to have any historical significance in Marx's eyes. To the extent that he had any hope for a revolutionary contribution from them, it was that they would follow his example and join the working-class struggle, which of course few did.

What Marx could not anticipate, however, was that the antibourgeois intellectuals of his day were the first representatives of what has become in our time a mass intelligentsia, a group possessing many of the cultural and political characteristics of a class in Marx's sense. By intelligentsia I mean those engaged vocationally in the production, distribution, interpretation, criticism and inculcation of cultural values. Most of the occupations in which the intelligentsia work are located outside the capitalist sector of the economy, either as free professions or in nonprofit educational institutions or other public bureaucracies. If, as in the case of the mass media, they are coordinated by private corporations, the intelligentsia are often officially depicted as serving such values as pleasure, art and truth, rather than commercial values.

It is important to note that these occupations are among the most rapidly growing, numerically, of any in the society. This is due in part to increasing governmental investment in educational, scientific and social service activities, and in part to the increase in leisure time and the consequent demand for entertainment and recreation. But more fundamentally, it is a function of the need in advanced industrial society for people to do the work of planning, prediction, innovation and systematic training, and socialization that the system now requires for its survival and growth. In the past century, then, the intelligentsia has been transformed from a tiny group of marginal status to a fast-growing, increasingly organized mass playing a key role in the functioning of the system.

Several years ago, when some of us at the University of Chicago looked into the social backgrounds of New Left students, we found that our group of activists was distinct from other college students in the degree to which they aspired to be part of the intelligentsia. But we also found, after interviewing their parents, that there was a substantial continuity between basic values and aspirations of the two generations. Both the activists and their parents were hostile to the self-denying, competitive, status-oriented individualism of bourgeois culture, and both sought a way of life that emphasized self-expression, humanism, openness to experience and community. In addition, both the students and their parents were substantially disaffected from the political system—though the students, of course, were more thoroughly alienated than their parents. It seemed clear to us that the students, through their activism, were for the most part attempting to fulfill and extend an ideological and cultural tradition already present in their families, rather than rebelling against the values on which they had been raised.

The fact that there have been, in the United States and Europe, a number of previous examples of political and cultural movements, based in the intelligentsia, with parallel ideological overtones, suggests, as does the generational continuity within activists' families, that the current youth radicalism is an expression of a definite historical process. This process may be described as the effort by many in the ranks of the intelligentsia to articulate and implement values which would serve as alternatives to those prevailing in capitalist culture.

Intellectuals as a Class

Historically, the revolt against bourgeois culture has taken many, quite divergent, ideological forms, ranging from socialism on the left to romanticism on the right, and it was acted out in a variety of ways, from direct participation in revolutionary movements to withdrawal into bohemian communities. In the first years of this century, however, a characteristically American intellectual radicalism began to emerge, which differed in important respects from the perspectives that prevailed in Europe. Like the Europeans, the new radical American intellectuals expressed their disaffection in a variety of ways: muckraking journalism, literary and social criticism in little magazines, realistic novels, avant-garde poetry and painting, salon conversation, scholarly radicalism, progressive politics, labor-organizing, the socialist movement. But unlike their European counterparts, American intellectuals tended to have a relatively optimistic and rationalist perspective. They believed that social, political and personal reforms were possible, especially if science and reason were brought to bear on pressing problems.

Significantly, the revolt of American writers and intellectuals coincided with the rise of the feminist movement. One consequence of the impact of feminism on the perspective of American intellectuals was a tendency for the

Reprinted with permission of The Macmillan Company from *The New American Revolution* edited by Norman R. Miller and Roderick R. Aya. Copyright © 1971 by The Free Press, a Division of The Macmillan Company.

In the late 30s and 40s, middle-class families began living according to a new ethics of antiauthoritarianism and equality.

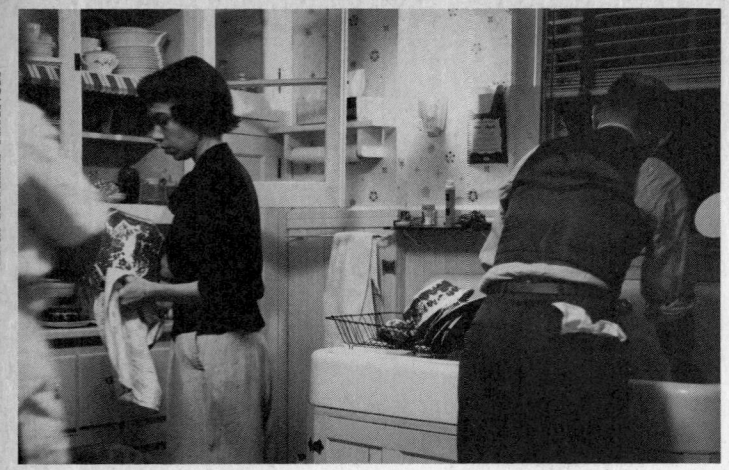

boundaries between private and public issues to become blurred or obliterated. Political reform in the larger society was linked to reform of family life and individual character, with the result that many intellectuals emphasized conscious, deliberate and scientific reform of the socializing institutions, the family and the school in order to create new values and character types and thereby to facilitate social change.

Optimism of the Intelligentsia

The specific hopes of the early twentieth century radical intellectuals were largely abortive. But their assault on Victorianism, the Protestant Ethic and business values had a wide impact. Progressive education, social work, child psychology, psychotherapy—a host of new professions emerged which had their original impulse in the desire to cure the effects of the dominant culture and which embodied implicit or explicit criticism of it. An important result of these new ideas, when combined with the rising status of women, was to create a new kind of middle-class family—less authoritarian, less hierarchical, more child-centered, more democratic, more self-conscious in its treatment of children. In these ways, the criticism of capitalist culture by tiny groups of European and American intellectuals became rooted in American life and incorporated into the value system of large numbers of middle-class Americans who attended the universities or were influenced by university-centered thought.

Now it is not the case, of course, that the rising intelligentsia was predominantly radical politically or unconventional culturally. Rather, what has been characteristic of this class politically is its very substantial optimism about the direction of the society and a whole-hearted acceptance of the legitimacy of the national political system, coupled with a strong hostility to those aspects of politics and culture identifiable as reactionary and regressive. What supported their optimism was their faith in three interrelated instruments of change.

First, they believed that the federal government could be molded into a force for social amelioration, economic progress and equality. This hope was, of course, crystallized during the New Deal and solidified during World War II and the immediate postwar period. Second, they believed that the new vocations, the service, helping and educational professions they had entered, would be significant in curing and preventing social and psychological pathology, extending the possibilities for democracy and upward mobility and raising the intellectual and cultural level of the people. Third, they tended to believe that the values they held were best implemented through self-conscious efforts to create families and a personal life style embodying democratic, humanistic, egalitarian principles, in contradiction to the authoritarian, repressed, Victorian, anti-intellectual and acquisitive style of life they perceived as characteristic of other middle-class people.

These beliefs emerged most strongly in the twenties and thirties, and it was possible to maintain them all during the New Deal period and the forties when it appeared that there was a real chance for the welfare state actually to be realized. Moreover, the horrors of fascism and Stalinism permitted many of the educated to feel that the United States, whatever its flaws, was the major defender of democratic values. Post–World War II prosperity greatly raised living standards and cultural possibilities for this group and also seemed to be creating the conditions for social equality. Thus, the parents of the present generation of student activists, despite their antipathy to traditional capitalist culture, maintained a generally complacent view of American society when they themselves were young and in the years when their children were growing up.

By the late fifties, however, some of this complacency undoubtedly began to break down. The Eisenhower years were a period of political stagnation and anti-Communist hysteria in which it became evident that the drive toward a welfare state and social equality might not be inherent in American political institutions. It also became clear that America's international role was incongruent with humanist, democratic values and beliefs. At a more fundamental level, many of the educated, as they reached middle age, began to have some doubts about the moral worth of their own occupations and about the degree to which they too had participated in the pursuit of status and material comfort. The late 1950s was a period of increasing social criticism much of which revolved around the collapse of meaning in vocation and about the moral callousness of the American middle class.

By 1960, then, the development of the American intelligentsia as a class had come to this. Demographically, it had grown over several decades from small pockets of isolated, independent intellectuals to a substantial stratum of the population, including many in new white-collar vocations. Culturally, it had begun to develop a family structure and value system at odds with the traditional capitalist, Protestant Ethic, middle-class culture. Political-

The civil rights movement in the South galvanized northern students to political action.

ly, it had passed through a period of optimistic reformism and seemed to be moving into a period of increasing disillusionment. The newest and largest generation of this stratum was thronging the nation's colleges, at just that point historically when the sustaining ideologies of industrial society—liberalism, socialism, communism—had reached exhaustion. At the same time, the cold war and anticommunism had ceased to be a workable framework for American international policy, and the colored population in the United States and around the world was breaking into active revolt.

Coming Together

In the decade since 1960, the offspring of the intelligentsia have become politicized and increasingly radicalized, despite the fact that, having been born to relatively high privilege and social advantage, they saw society opening ever wider vistas for personal success and enrichment. Why have they, in large numbers, refused to follow their fathers and mothers—adopting a stance of slightly uneasy acceptance of the prevailing social order while trying to establish a personal life on a somewhat different cultural basis?

In part, the disaffection of these youth is a direct consequence of the values and impulses their parents transmitted to them. The new generation had been raised in an atmosphere that encouraged personal autonomy and individuality. Implicitly and explicitly it had been taught to be skeptical about the intrinsic value of money-making and status and to be skeptical about the claims of established authority. It incorporated new definitions of sex roles. Having seen their parents share authority and functions more or less equally in the family, and having been taught to value aesthetic and intellectual activity, these were boys who did not understand masculinity to mean physical toughness and dominance, and girls who did not understand femininity to mean passivity and domesticity. Moreover, they were young people—young people for whom the established means of social control were bound to be relatively ineffective (and here they were particularly different from the older generation). Growing up with economic security in families of fairly secure status, the normal incentives of the system—status and income—were of relatively minor importance, and indeed many of their parents encouraged them to feel that such incentives ought to be disdained.

In retrospect, it seems inevitable that young people of this kind should come into some conflict with the established order. Because of their central values, they, like the earlier generations of intellectuals, would necessarily be social critics. Because of their material security, they, like earlier generations of high status youth, were likely to be experimental, risk-taking, open to immediate experience, relatively unrepressed. Because of their character structure, they would very likely come into conflict with arbitrary authority in school and other situations of imposed restriction. Because of their values and sex role identifications, they would find themselves out of harmony with the conventional youth culture with its frivolity, anti-intellectualism and stereotypic distinctions between the sexes.

Furthermore, their impulses to autonomy and individuality, their relative freedom from economic anxiety and their own parents' ambivalence toward the occupational structure would make it difficult for them to decide easily on a fixed vocational goal or life style, would make them aspire to construct their lives outside conventional career lines, would make them deeply critical of the compromise, corruption and unfreedom inherent in the occupations of their fathers—the very occupations for which they were being trained.

Much of this had happened before, but the situation of the young intelligentsia of the sixties differed radically from that of their precursors. First, their numbers were enormously greater than ever before. Second, they faced, not a scarcity of jobs, but an abundance of careers—yet the careers for which they were being trained no longer held the promise of social melioration and personal fulfillment that their parents had anticipated. Third, these youth sensed not only the narrowness and irrationality of the prevailing culture but the deeper fact that the dominant values of bourgeois society, appropriate in an age of scarcity and entrepreneurial activity, had become irrelevant to a society which was moving beyond scarcity and competitive capitalism. Thus, by the late fifties, more youth were feeling more intensely than ever before a sense of estrangement from capitalist culture—an estrangement which could not be assuaged by the promise of material security the system offered.

The cultural crisis these youth experienced provided the ground for their coming together. But the transformation of cultural alienation into political protest, and eventually into revolutionary action, was due to more immediate and concrete pressures. It was the emergence of the southern civil rights movement which, more than any other single event, led the young intelligentsia in the early sixties to see the relevance of political opposition and social change to their own problems. The nonviolent movement showed, for one thing, how small groups of committed youth could undertake action that could have major historical impact. It demonstrated how such action could flow directly from humanistic values. But above all, it confronted these white students with the fact that all of their opportunities for personal fulfillment were based on white upper-middle-class privilege and that continued passivity in the face of racism meant that one was in fact part of the oppressive apparatus of society, no matter what one's private attitudes might be.

Hopes of SDS

Participation in the civil rights struggle seemed, however, to offer a way out of this dilemma, and civil rights protest helped to open the consciousness of many students to other political issues. It made them aware that there was more to their problems than the fact that the culture offered little support for their personal aspirations; it also threatened their existence. But at the same time numbers of students became rapidly sensitive to the fact that the nuclear arms race, the cold war and the militarization of society were not simply facts of life but deliberate, therefore reversible, policies. It was not long before the protest tactics acquired in the civil rights movement began to be applied to the demand for peace.

When one reads today the Port Huron Statement (June 1962) and other documents of the early Students for a Democratic Society (SDS) and the New Left, one is struck by the degree to which the early New Left conceived of itself largely as a political reform movement rather than in clearly revolutionary terms. While it's true, as Todd Gitlin has suggested, that the early new radicals of the sixties were filled with "radical disappointment" with the American way of life, it is also the case that they retained a good deal of optimism about the possibilities for change in the context of American politics. In particular, it was hoped that the labor movement, the religious community, the liberal organizations, the intellectual community, the civil rights movement all could eventually unite around a broad-based program of radical reform.

The role of the student movement was seen by the early SDS leaders as providing the intellectual skills needed for such a new movement and, somewhat later, as important for producing people who would help to catalyze grass root activities in a variety of places. Direct action such as the sit-ins, freedom rides and other forms of protest and civil disobedience was seen, on the one hand, as a vital tactic for the winning of reform and, on the other hand, as a method by which the more established institutions such as the labor movement could be induced to move in the direction of more vigorous action. In this early phase of the student movement, SDS and other New Left leaders were little aware of the possibility that a mass movement of students on the campus could be created and engaged in collective struggles against university authority. Rather the New Left's role on the campus was seen primarily as one of breaking through the atmosphere of apathy, educating students about political issues, so that they could begin to take a role off the campus in whatever struggles were going on.

But the early reformism of the New Left was soon abandoned. The failure of the established agencies of reform to create a political opposition and to mobilize mass support for political alternatives was most decisive in preventing the new movement of the young intelligentsia from becoming absorbed by conventional politics, thereby following in the footsteps of previous movements of American intellectuals. This collapse of the so-called liberal establishment thus marked a new stage in the consciousness of the American intelligentsia—beyond cultural alienation, beyond social reform, beyond protest—toward active resistance and revolution.

The emergence of the student movement in the sixties, then, signifies a more fundamental social change and is not simply a species of "generational conflict." The convergence of certain social structural and cultural trends has produced a new class, the intelligentsia, and, despite the apparent material security of many in this class, its trajectory is toward revolutionary opposition to capitalism. This is because, first, capitalism cannot readily absorb the cultural aspirations of this group—aspirations that fundamentally have to do with the abolition of alienated labor and the achievement of democratic community. Second, the incorporation of this group is made more difficult by the concrete fact of racism and imperialism—facts which turn the vocations of the intelligentsia into cogs in the machinery of repression rather than means for self-fulfillment and general enlightenment. Third, the numerical size of this group and the concentration of much of it in universities make concerted oppositional political action extremely feasible. Finally, the liberal default has hastened the self-consciousness of students and other members of this class, exacerbated their alienation from the political system and made autonomous oppositional politics a more immediate imperative for them. Thus, a stratum, which under certain conditions might have accepted a modernizing role within the system, has instead responded to the events of this past decade by adopting an increasingly revolutionary posture.

In part, this development grows out of the antiauthoritarian impulses in the fundamental character structure of the individual members which provide much of the motivation and emotional fuel for the movement. But, as the history of the movement shows, there was an early readiness to consider whether established political alternatives were in fact viable. That such readiness has virtually disappeared is almost entirely due to the failure of the political system itself—a failure most manifest in the crises of race, poverty and urban life on the one hand and the international posture of the United States on the other.

Over the last decade the American government has consistently failed to enforce new or existing legislation guaranteeing civil rights. It has consistently failed to implement promised reforms leading to social and economic equality. It has demonstrated a stubborn unwillingness and/or incompetence in dealing with the deepening crises of urban life, and it has supported essentially repressive, rather than ameliorative, policies with respect to the black revolt.

Even more crucial in undermining the legitimacy of the system for young people was, of course, the war in Vietnam—the fact that the United States was unable to win the war; the fact that it dragged on endlessly to become the longest war in American history; the fact that the United States in Vietnam was involved in an effort to suppress a popular uprising; the fact that the United States in Vietnam committed an interminable series of atrocities and war crimes, especially involving the destruction of civilian life; the fact that the war was accompanied by a military draft and that alongside the draft a system involving the social tracking of all young males in America had grown up; the fact that the war in Vietnam was not simply an accident of policy but an essential ingredient of what became increasingly identified as a worldwide imperialist policy involving the suppression of popular revolution and the maintenance and extension of American political and corporate power throughout the Third World.

Moreover, alongside the growth of conventional and nuclear military power and the penetration of American institutions, including especially the universities, by military priorities, there grew up a paramilitary establishment which had attempted to control and manipulate organizations and events throughout the world and also at home. This development was perhaps best symbolized for students by the fact that the Central Intelligence Agency had subsidized the National Student Association and had extensive ties with American academics. Finally, the war continued and escalated despite vast expressions of popular discontent.

This, more than anything else, reinforced the New Left's disbelief in the efficacy of conventional political means of affecting policy. By the time of the Democratic Convention in 1968, a very large number of young people were convinced that only extreme action of a disruptive sort could have any substantial effect on major policy and that "working through the system" was a trap, rather than a means to effect change.

Obviously, many young people, fearing the consequences of a full-scale delegitimation of authority, continue to search for a more responsive political alternative within the system. But the stagnation of liberalism in these years along with the astonishing series of assassinations of spokesmen for its revitalization have made such hopes appear increasingly unrealistic. Thus the growth of revolutionary sentiment among the students proceeds apace. As the legitimacy of national authority declines, a process of delegitimation occurs for all in authoritative positions—for instance, university officials—and proposals for melioration and compromise are viewed with deepening suspicion. Political polarization intensifies, and those in the opposition feel, on the one hand, the imperative of confrontation as a means of further clarifying the situation and, on the other hand, that the entire structure of social control is being organized for the purpose of outright repression. And for American students confrontation is made more urgent by the moral pressure of the black liberation movement, which continuously tests the seriousness of their proclaimed revolutionary commitment.

New Front Line

The early New Left frequently criticized university life as well as the larger society, but it was also quite ambivalent toward the university as an institution. University authority was seen as paternalistic and as subservient to dominant interests in the society. University education was regarded as a contributor to student indifference towards social questions. At the same time, the Port Huron Statement and other early New Left writing viewed the university as a potential resource for movements for change, university intellectuals as potentially useful to such movements and the university as a relatively free place where political controversy could flourish provided it was catalyzed.

Prior to the fall of 1964, SDS leaders ignored the campus as a base of operation, persuading a considerable number of students to either leave school or to work off the campus in the efforts to organize the urban poor. In large measure, university reform campaigns were felt by the most committed activists to be both irrelevant and, in a certain sense, immoral, when people in the South were putting their bodies on the line. The Berkeley free speech movement of 1964 helped to change this perception of the campus. The police action at Berkeley, the first of numerous large-scale busts of student protestors, suggested that a campus struggle could be the front line. And the political impact of Berkeley in California, and indeed internationally, suggested that there was nothing parochial or irrelevant about an on-campus struggle. Moreover, these events coincided with the turning away of portions of the civil rights movement, especially the Student Nonviolent Coordinating Committee, from efforts to work with white students. Further, Berkeley coincided with the escalation of the war in Vietnam and with the discovery, only dimly realized before, that the universities were major resources in the development of the military potential of the United States.

Beginning in the fall of 1966 attacks on military research installations, on ROTC, on connections between the university and military agencies, on military recruitment and recruitment by defense corporations became the prime activity of SDS and other student groups for a number of

SUGGESTED READINGS

The New Radicalism in America by Christopher Lasch (New York: Random House, 1965) illuminates the development of radicalism among the American intelligentsia in the early twentieth century.

Campus Power Struggle edited by Howard S. Becker, (Chicago: Aldine, 1970).

Radicalism and the Revolt Against Reason: The Social Theories of Georg Sorel by Irving L. Horowitz (Carbondale, Illinois: Southern Illinois University Press, 1961). Parallels between Sorel and the New Left: combining radicalism with irrationalism, rejecting bourgeois society and intellect, and advocating violence as a healing agent in human affairs.

Movement and Revolution by Peter L. Berger and Richard J. Neuhaus (Garden City, New York: Doubleday, 1970). Self-proclaimed "radical" and "conservative" perspectives on today's revolutionary consciousness among the young.

Anti-Politics in America by John H. Bunzel (New York: Knopf, 1967). Traces the attempt to substitute "fundamental truth" for political conciliation and compromise in causes such as civil rights and pacifism.

Push Comes to Shove: The Escalation of Student Protest by Steven Kelman (Boston: Houghton-Mifflin, 1970). Kelman, Harvard '70, portrays the university as a subcultural "dream-world" and traces the resultant political activity.

The Elusive Revolution: Anatomy of a Student Revolt by Raymond Aron (New York: Praeger, 1969). Observations on the nihilistic and anarchistic trend in student uprisings, with the focus on turbulence in France in 1968.

Intellectual Origins of American Radicalism by Staughton Lynd (New York: Pantheon Books, 1968). A polemical, yet scholarly, review of the history of "moral absolutism" in 18th- and 19th-century America, as a foundation and context for contemporary radicalism.

---

months. Every major confrontation mobilized hundreds of students for highly committed direct action and many thousands more for supportive action. Typically the issues raised by the student movement on a campus were supported by as many as two-thirds of the student body, even though large numbers of students were unwilling to participate in disruptive actions as such. And as previously uncommitted students joined these actions, many were radicalized by the experience of participation in a community of struggle, by the intransigence and obtuseness of university administrators and by the violence of police repression of the protests. Institutional resistance was fostering student "class consciousness."

By the late sixties, the movement was no longer the exclusive property of those I've been calling the young intelligentsia. It was having a widening impact on students at nonelite campuses, in junior colleges and high schools, and on nonstudent youth in the streets and in the Armed Forces. To a great extent, the availability of larger numbers of young people for insurgent ideas and actions is rooted in the cultural crisis we alluded to at the outset of this paper. For all youth experience the breakdown of traditional culture, the irrelevance of ideologies based on scarcity. Vast numbers of youth in America today are in search of a less repressed, more human, more spontaneous life style.

The radicalization of youth is enhanced by the peculiar social position of high school and college students, who have achieved some degree of independence from family authority but are not yet subject to the discipline of work institutions. The high school and college situation is, on the one hand, extremely authoritarian but, on the other hand, functions to segregate young people, maintaining them in a peculiar limbo combining dependency with irresponsibility. The impact of the cultural crisis on the school situation is to make really vast numbers of young people ready for new and more liberating ideas, while they have the freedom and energy to spend time in examination and criticism of prevailing values and ideologies.

In addition, the situation of youth is exacerbated by the demands of the imperialist system for manpower and by the increasing bureaucratization of both education and vocation. More concretely, the draft is the reality that undermines the endless promises made to American youth. What the draft means is that one is not really free to pursue self-fulfillment, even though one has been taught that self-fulfillment is the highest goal and purpose of the system. Not only is that promise undermined by the necessity to serve in the army and die in the mud of some distant jungle, a fate reserved for relatively few young men, but the draft serves to facilitate control over the careers of all young men by serving explicitly as a means for tracking youth into occupations believed to be in the interest of the state. The result for school youth is postponement or avoidance of the military but subjugation to an educational system that reproduces many of the worst features of the larger society in terms of authoritarianism, competitiveness, individualism and dehumanization. The growth of a mass youth movement depended on the emergence of a group of young intelligentsia whose own socialization was particularly at odds with the dominant culture, but once such a circle of youth emerged, their expressions, both cultural and political, spread like wildfire.

Thus, the story of the student movement in the United States over the past decade has been one of continued self-transformation. Once student activism was characteristic of tiny groups of campus rebels, the offspring, as we have suggested, of the educated middle class, who faced severe value and vocational crisis, could find no moral way to assimilate into American society and so searched for a new basis for living in cultural avant-gardism and moralistic dedication to social reform. In the past decade, obviously, the movement has spread well beyond this original group. It has transformed itself from a nonideological movement for vague principles of social justice into a new radical movement in quest of a new social vision and a new framework for social criticism, and finally into a movement spearheaded by revolutionaries tending, more and more, to look to classical revolutionary doctrine as a guiding principle and to embody, more and more, classical models of revolutionary action as their own.

It is a movement that rejects and is at the same time entangled by its roots in what I have called the intelligentsia. Yet it has expressed most clearly the fundamental aspirations of the rising generation of that class for a new social order in which men can achieve autonomy and full participation in determining the conditions of their lives, in which hierarchy and domination are replaced by community and love, in which war, militarism and imperialism are obsolete and in which class and racial distinctions are abolished. It is a movement of surprising strength. It has touched the minds of millions and changed the lives of thousands of young people, both here and abroad. It has severely shaken the stability of the American empire and challenged the basic assumptions of its culture. But its most sensitive adherents have become increasingly despairing, as the movement has reached the limit of its possibilities. This despair is rooted first in the unresponsiveness of the political system to pressure for reform; second, in the narrow class base of the movement; third, in the seemingly overwhelming capacity of the authorities to manage social control. Out of this despair arises the sense that revolution is an urgent, if impossible, necessity, that the movement must transcend its social base, that it must make common cause with other enemies of the empire around the world.

Co-optation

Given this new consciousness, what can be said about the future of the movement? It seems to me that one can envision several possibilities. First, any student and youth movement has the potential of becoming a relatively insulated expression of generational revolt. This is not the explicit intention of very many spokesmen for the New Left, but it certainly appears to be the implicit expectation of many agencies of social control. A generational movement may be understood as a movement of cultural and social innovation whose impact has been contained within the framework of existing society. For agencies of social control, the ideal circumstance would be the opportunity to eliminate those elements in the movement that are most disruptive and destructive, while putting into effect some of the cultural, social and political innovations and reforms the movement advocates.

Accordingly, you put Yippies in jail but work out some means to legalize the use of marijuana. You put draft-resisters in jail or into exile while abolishing conscription. You expel SDS from the campus while admitting student representatives to the board of trustees. You deride and derogate the women's liberation movement while liberalizing abortion laws. You break up and harass hippie urban communities while providing fame and fortune to some rock music groups. This is all done with the aid of ideological perspectives that emphasize that what is going on is a generational revolt, that there is a generation gap, that the big problem is one of communication between the old and the young. The hope is that if reforms can be made that will liberalize the cultural and social atmosphere, particularly in relation to sex, drug use, art, music, censorship and so forth, the mass of youth will not become tempted by the message of the radical vanguard.

If the new political and cultural radicalism were to become channeled more fully in the direction of generational revolt, it would then be serving stabilizing and modernizing functions for the going system, and it would not be the first time that a radical movement in the United States ended up functioning this way. But from the point of view of New Left activists, such an outcome for the movement would represent profound failure, particularly if it meant, as it does now seem to mean, that the most active and militant of the participants of the movement would suffer, rather than benefit, from any social change that might be forthcoming.

There is a substantial likelihood, however, that the student movement and the New Left of the sixties will move in the direction we have just outlined. The most important fact supporting this outcome is that the movement has, in the ten years of its existence, failed very largely to break out of its isolation as a movement of the young, and particularly of the relatively advantaged young. There are reasons to think that this isolation could be broken in the near future, and we shall suggest some of these shortly, but it is important to recognize that most of the public understanding of what is happening has revolved around the generational problem, rather than the substantive political and social questions that the movement has raised. Most of the expressed sympathy for the movement on the part of the elders has been couched in terms of solving the problems of youth and liberalizing the cultural atmosphere, rather than in joining in the making of a social revolution.

At the same time, however, despite the very large-scale public discussion of the need for reform and innovation, the prevailing tendencies of the state and other dominant institutions do not seem to be primarily in this direction. Even such apparently unthreatening changes as liberalization of laws governing drug use, the 18-year-old vote, the involvement of students in direct participation in university government or the abolition of the draft meet very strong resistance and do not now seem to be on the agenda. Instead, what is in prospect is further tightening of drug laws, further restrictions and harassment of the communal outcroppings of the youth culture, further efforts at censorship, a continuation of the draft and a generally more hostile climate with respect to even the modest aspirations for change of most young people today. All of this, of course, could change in a relatively short period of time as those who are now young move into full citizenship and have the opportunity directly to influence public and institutional policies. But what happens in the intervening years is likely to be crucial.

Another reason for believing that the New Left has considerable capacity for resisting this kind of incorporation into the culture is that the movement is profoundly suspicious of and sensitive to the dangers of co-optation. Most movement participants are aware at one level or another that the classic American pattern for controlling revolutionary and quasi-revolutionary movements is to destroy or isolate the most militant sections while implementing, at least on paper, the programmatic thrust of the movement. This is what happened in the labor movement. It is what is happening in the black liberation movement, and it is certainly what is being advocated for the student movement. In this way the American political system has served to contain the revolutionary thrust of movements that develop within it, while keeping these movements fragmented, preventing their outreach into sectors of the population beyond those that form the original constituency of the movement.

As I say, new leftists wish to avoid at all costs the buying off of the movement through piecemeal reform. This is one reason why the movement is so hesitant to propose concrete reforms and to proclaim its interest in short-range goals. A greater danger, however, is that the movement has been unable to offset pressures, both internal and external, that maintain it as a movement of youth.

The future of the New Left depends now on its ability to break out of its isolation and to persuade the majority of Americans that their interests depend on the dismantling of imperialism and the replacement of capitalism with a fully democratized social order. The movement cannot afford to be encapsulated as a generational revolt. It cannot wait until the present young "take over." It cannot survive in a climate of repression and polarization unless large numbers of people are moving in a similar political direction. It cannot survive and ought not survive if it conceives itself to be an elite band of professional revolutionaries, aiming to "seize power" in the midst of social chaos and breakdown.

What are the structural conditions that might open up the possibility of the New Left transcending its present age and class base? Here are at least some:

☐ The class base of the movement is rapidly changing as the "youth culture" spreads to the high schools and junior colleges, to army bases and young workers. Along with this cultural diffusion, the mood of resistance spreads—protest is now endemic in high schools, it is evident in the armed forces, it is growing in the junior colleges.

☐ Inflation and high taxes have led to a decline in real wages. Current fiscal policies generate rising unemployment. A new period of labor militance may have already begun. This situation converges with the influx of postwar youth into the labor force, with the militant organization of black caucuses in unions, with intensifying organization and militance among public employees and with the first efforts by former student radicals to "reach" workers. It may be that in spite of the Wallace phenomenon, racism and the alleged conservatism of the American working class a new radicalism is about to become visible among factory, government and other workers.

☐ The impoverishment and disintegration of public services, the systematic destruction of the natural environment, urban squalor, the tax burden—all are deeply felt troubles which are directly traceable to the profit system and the military priority. The sense of crisis and frustration that these problems generate throughout society offers the ground for the formulation and promulgation of radical program, action and organization.

☐ Political repression, although obviously dangerous for the survival of radicalism, can have the effect of intensifying rather than weakening insurgency. This would be particularly true if repression is seen as an assault on whole categories of persons, rather than on handfuls of "outside agitators." So, for instance, many participants in the youth culture now connect their own harassment by the police with the Chicago Conspiracy trial and other government attacks on radicals. Repression at this writing seems more likely to stiffen the mood of resistance among young people than it is to end attacks on "law and order."

☐ By 1975 there will be well over 50 million adults born since 1940. Most of these will have achieved political consciousness in the past decade. This fact alone suggests a major transformation of the political landscape by the second half of the seventies.

☐ In the next five years the proportion of the labor force definable as "intelligentsia" will have substantially increased. Current Bureau of Labor Statistics manpower projections for "professional, technical and kindred workers" are for a 40 percent increase in this category between 1966 and 1975, reaching a total of about 13 million in 1975. If my analysis in this essay is correct, this group should be a major source of radicalism in the coming period. The situation of these workers is now dramatically changing from one of high opportunity to relative job scarcity due to current federal and state budgetary policies. Thus one can expect that the radicalization of the intelligentsia will continue to intensify in the years ahead.

One might suggest that these conditions provide the opportunity for a large-scale and successful "new politics" of liberal reform to assert itself. But the current exhaustion of political liberalism may well mean that a new "center-Left" coalition cannot be formed—that we have finally arrived in this country at the point where reformism is no longer viable.

An alternative possibility would be the emergence of a popular socialist party oriented to both "parliamentary" and "extraparliamentary" activity. Although this would certainly facilitate the transcendence of the New Left, there are as yet no signs that such a development is even incipient. In any case, the most important insight of the New Left is that political organization is not enough—the heart of revolution is the reconstruction of civil society and culture.

"The Long March"

It may well be that the singular mission of the new mass intelligentsia is to catalyze just such a transformation—to undertake what Rudi Dutschke called "the long march through the institutions of society." This march began in the universities. In coming years it may well continue through all significant cultural, educational, public service and professional institutions. It would have a double aim: to force these institutions to serve the people rather than the corporate system and the state and to engage cultural workers and professionals in struggles to control their work and govern the institutions that coordinate it and determine its use.

It is possible that such struggle by the intelligentsia could stimulate similar struggles in the primary economic institutions—to build a basis for workers' control and for the abolition of technologically unnecessary labor.

In addition to such institutional struggle, the reconstruction of civil society and culture requires the further development of self-organization of communities and especially of exploited and oppressed minorities. Such self-organization—of racial and ethnic minorities and of women—is necessary for any general cultural transformation. Struggle by communities for control of their own development and services prepares the basis for a decentralized and democratized civil society. It is obvious that all such developments have profound need for the services of professional, intellectual, cultural and scientific workers.

It is natural to assume that the development of political, civil and cultural struggle requires central, disciplined organization. My own feeling is that it requires something prior to, and perhaps instead of, the classical revolutionary party. What is really crucial is the organization of local "collectives," "affinity groups," "communes," "cells" of people who share a revolutionary perspective, a common locale of activity, a sense of fraternity, a willingness to bind their fates together. Each such group can be free to work out its priorities, projects and work style. What is necessary is that these groups generally conceive of themselves as catalysts of mass action rather than as utopian communities or elite terrorists. Most of the dramatic movements of the sixties occurred because small groups of friends undertook action that was catalytic or exemplary to larger masses. Most of the exciting cultural development in this period occurred in a similar way. Many of the problems the party is supposed to exist to solve can be coped with without centralization. Problems of communication can be handled by the underground media—which up to now have been the expression of a host of small collectives. National action projects can be coordinated by ad hoc coalitions and umbrella organizations. The generation of resources can be managed through movement banks and quasi foundations. There is no reason why collectives in different or similar milieus cannot meet together to exchange experience. If the purpose of a revolutionary movement is not to seize power but to educate the people to take it for themselves, then a maximally decentralized mode of work is appropriate. And in a period of tightening repression, a cellular rather than centralized mode of organization is obviously advantageous.

The revolution in advanced capitalist society is not a single insurrection. It is not a civil war of pitched battles fought by opposing armies. It is a long, continuing struggle—with political, social and cultural aspects inextricably intertwined. It is already underway. It is not simply a socialist revolution—if by that one means the establishment of a new form of state power that will introduce social planning and redistribute income. It is more than that. For it must be a revolution in which the power to make key decisions is placed in the hands of those whose lives are determined by those decisions. It is not, in short, a revolution aimed at seizing power but a revolution aimed at its dispersal.

It is possible that the New Left's current return to Old Left styles and models signifies that the kind of revolution of which I speak is premature, that the classes and groups that would be most active in producing it have not achieved full consciousness. We are not yet in an age of "postscarcity," and consequently the revolutionary visions appropriate to that age will have a difficult time establishing their reality. Perhaps, then, the New Left of the sixties is not destined to be the catalyst of the new revolution. I am personally convinced, however, that whatever the immediate destiny of the movement might be, the social and cultural changes that produced it and were accelerated by it are irreversible and cannot be contained within a capitalist framework. Once the material basis for human liberation exists, men will struggle against the institutions that stand in its way. The rise of the student movement in the United States and other industrial societies is a crucial demonstration of the truth of this proposition. For it is a sign that a revolutionary class consciousness appropriate to the era of monopoly capital, advanced technology and dying imperialism is in existence.

June 1970

…obert Capa MAGNUM

Rebirth in the Airborne

Paratrooper initiations include superstition, magic, and ceremony—like the rites of many other tribes

MELFORD S. WEISS

When an American paratrooper first learns to jump, he does more than step out of an airplane. He steps into a new way of life. Furthermore, his training even takes note of this major transition in his life in a formal ceremonial manner. This training period—marked by pomp and circumstance, superstition and ritual—is what anthropologists refer to as a *rite of passage*.

Rites of passage are universal features of complex as well as simple societies. They mark critical changes in man's life cycle, such as birth, death, and initiation. The paratrooper training program can best be understood as an initiation, a form of entry into an elite group. The process is interwoven with magical and symbolic ritual practices. In one training unit, for example, each time the trainees enter the airplane, the jumpmaster draws a line on the ground in front of the entrance hatch with the toe of his boot. Each prospective jumper then stomps upon the line before entering the airplane in order to ensure a safe landing. Whether or not they actually believe in the practice (many do not) is of decidedly less importance than the fact that this ritual serves to bind the group together.

A paratooper's training ends in a ceremonial climax. At the close of training it is customary in some military units to reenact the jumping procedure in a fashion symbolic of rebirth. Newly-qualified paratroopers are invited to a "prop blast" at the noncommissioned officers' club. There a wooden model of an airplane has been hastily rigged. The new initiates line up in jump formation inside the plane. They jump and land facing the jumpmaster, their instructor. He hands each a loving cup full of "blast juice." This must be quaffed within the count of "1000, 2000, 3000," the time between an actual jump from a plane and the opening of the chute. Failure to drain it to the dregs within the allotted span is called a "malfunction," the term for chute failure. The process must be repeated, perhaps three or four times, till success is achieved. Then the initiate is ritually one with his fellows.

Initiation Rites

Rites of passage vary in different cultures, but according to Arnold Van Gennep a typical rite has three stages:
— *separation* from the former group or state;
— *transition* to the new;
— and, finally, *incorporation*.

In birth and death rites, for example, separation is emphasized most: "The Lord giveth, the Lord has taken away." In the case of paratrooper training the transitional phase is most important. The paratrooper rite described here is a composite of training programs of many groups from World War II to the present time.

The paratrooper school is inside a compound surrounded by barbed wire and guarded by sentries. In this compound the trainee is fed, trained, and occasionally entertained. He is allowed to go out in the evening but usually does so in the company of other troopers. Fraternization with the non-paratrooper world is not encouraged, but separation from the former civilian environment is only partial.

The transitional phase usually lasts three weeks. During the last week the candidate makes five practice jumps which mark stages in his progress toward final acceptance. Not all the jumps are equally important—the first and fifth are most significant.

Paratrooper training is officially a secular affair. But certain superstitious practices which are interwoven show that, in the broadest sense, it is also a religious rite. From the beginning of the transition period the trainees are subjected to continuous periods of anxiety. Since they are all volunteers with a strong emotional investment in success, these stresses serve to bind them more closely to one another and to the group they seek to enter. So do the "magical" devices they learn to use to relieve anxiety. These include the wearing of charms and fetishes, such as a girl friend's picture above the heart, a pair of sweat socks worn on a previous successful jump, or a replica of the "trooper wings" placed inside a boot.

Use of "sympathetic magic" is fostered by the paratrooper mythology to which the trainee is exposed during this stage. The following examples of paratrooper tales illustrate elements of both *mana* (a spiritual force independent of persons or spirits which explains success, excellence, and potency when these qualities are not otherwise explainable) and *taboo* (a prohibition based upon the assumption that disastrous consequences can be averted if certain acts are not performed):

- "He was a jinx and was always present at any accident. I would never jump with him in my line. I once touched him before I was about to jump and pretended to be sick in order to avoid jumping that day. Nobody laughed at me when I told them the real reason."
- A master jumper told this story: "When I was a youngster, I felt that should I ever lose my original set of wings I could never jump again. They had a natural magic about them which protected me. When I went home I put them in the bottom drawer of my mother's dresser. I knew they would be safe there!"
- Legend maintains that the paratrooper compound is off limits, and one myth relates the unhappy story of the intoxicated soldier from another unit who tried to sneak into the compound and was found next morning with his face severely scratched. The soldier claimed that he was attacked by a small bird and then passed out. But paratroopers claim that the bird was in fact the "screaming eagle," the totemic symbol of the 101st Airborne Division.

During the transition period myth and magic help the trainee to identify with paratroopers in general and share their *esprit de corps*. This becomes a formidable force as airborne units are made up entirely of volunteers. Thus a man becomes a paratrooper by choice and remains one all his military life unless he disobeys a direct order to jump. As in the case of other select military units, paratroopers are bound to one another by pride in a common history and system of training. They consider themselves superior to all other such groups—not only in their military virtues, but in their vices as well. A paratrooper is supposed to be able to outdrink, outbrawl, and outwhore any other member of the armed forces.

The Jumpout Dropout

Systems of initiation depend for their success upon how much the candidate wants to belong to the group. Sometimes, in the case of paratrooper training, he may not want to badly enough. A young man may decide he does not care to spend his active life plunging out of airplanes with nothing but the silkworm's art for support. Since all trainees are volunteers, this is technically no disgrace. All he has to do is request reassignment.

But because of the problem of preserving group morale the dropout is usually eliminated with almost indecent haste. Many instructors feel that to let him hang around will spread the "rot," and other failures or jumping accidents may result. When a would-be dropout says he wants out at the end of a training day, he is more than likely to be called to the orderly room during the next morning's formation. By the time the other trainees return from their midday meal he will have left the training area forever, usually to spend a month's KP duty in some non-elite holding company. For example one dropout said:

> I was scared and I knew it. I dared not let the others know, but I did not think I could hide it very long. We were listening to a master jumper telling us about his first jump and my stomach got queasy and I was sick. I told my sergeant I wanted out. I left the very next day.

If a trainee should quit during the training day, particularly with a public fuss, more brusque tactics may be used. One would-be paratrooper reports:

> I was fed up with this bastard. I made a scene and cursed the Army and shouted that you can shove the paratroopers. I yelled, "I quit." My training NCO rapidly approached me, ripped the patch from my shoulder, and cut the laces of my jump boots.

In some primitive societies those who fail the tests of manhood may be killed outright. The ripping of the patch and the cutting of the laces serves the same function symbolically. It signifies the separation of the dropout from his companions and thus binds the group more closely together, as does the knowledge that the failure is headed for KP or some other nonstatus duty.

As noted before, the transitional phase of paratrooper training has substages. These occur mainly after the first and fifth (last) practice jump. After the first there is no ceremony, but there is a change in the relationship between the trainees and the seasoned paratroopers. As soon as the jumping experience has been shared, the trainee begins to be treated with at least a modicum of respect by his instructors. Conversation in the barracks becomes less guarded. Before any mention of "spilling silk" or "flying a streamer" was avoided. Now jokes about jumping accidents and chute failures are freely bandied about.

The fifth jump is marked by a definite ritual. After the first four the trainee rolls his own chute. After the last he hands it to the platoon sergeant, who rolls it for him and places it in the supply truck. Then the NCO shakes his pupil's hand, congratulates him, and in some cases invites him to use his, the sergeant's, given name. This reversal of roles marks acceptance into the group. The same evening this is confirmed at a party at the enlisted men's club, usually off limits to officers. The paratroopers-to-be, including officer candidates, are invited to join in the drinking and usually do.

The whole transitional period in paratrooper training closely parallels initiation rites in both Western and non-Western societies. During this stage the initiate learns the formulas, gestures, and chants of the brotherhood. These include a paratrooper prayer and a paratrooper song. The latter is a gruesome chant in which the paratrooper verbalizes, jokingly, his fear of sudden and gory death. It is sung to the tune of "The Battle Hymn of the Republic":

Is everybody ready? cried the Sergeant, looking up.
Our hero feebly answered yes, as they stood him up.
He leapt right out into the blast, his static line unhooked.
O he ain't gonna jump no more!

There was blood upon the risers, there were brains upon the chute,
His intestines were a dangling from his paratrooper boots;
They picked him up still in his chute and poured him from his boots;
O he ain't gonna jump no more!

Chorus: Glory gory what a helluva way to die!
Glory gory what a helluva way to die!
Glory gory what a helluva way to die!
Oh he ain't gonna jump no more!

Wings and a Three-Day Pass

After transition comes incorporation in two stages—an official ceremony and the unofficial "prop blast" described earlier. The official ceremony is a colorful affair in the tradition of most military rituals. It marks the end of the rigorous training and is a welcome climax to weeks of agonizing tension. It takes place the day after the final (fifth) practice jump. The men in the training unit line up in alphabetical order; uniforms are smartly pressed, faces agonizingly clean shaven, and hair close cropped. They stand at attention while the post band plays the national anthem, followed by "Ruffles and Flourishes." The division flag flies just beneath Old Glory.

The men bow their heads as the post chaplain reads from the Bible. After a congratulatory speech the training commandant presents each man with his diploma. The division commandant passes through the ranks, reviews the troops, and pins "wings" to each man's chest. The chaplain delivers the closing benediction. The band continues to play military music as the men now assemble by training platoon and proudly march by the reviewing stand. As the soldiers reach the stand, they are saluted by the senior officers, and the new troopers return the salute. The men are then dismissed and given a three-day pass.

Many features of this ceremony have symbolic significance. The new paratrooper is being initiated into a special brotherhood within the military forces of an American, predominantly Christian, society. The chaplain's benediction gives the ceremony "divine sanction" and links it, however tenuously, with the prevailing Christian religion. The "American heritage" is reflected by the American flag and the national anthem. The polished boots, clean shaves, and close haircuts set up the image of the "clean-cut, all-American boy." The rest of the rite is military, with calculated differences. The marching, the salute, the respect for rank, and the three-day pass remind the paratrooper that he is a member of the armed forces. But the jump-school graduation certificate and the "wings" belong only to paratroopers and serve as permanent marks of that status.

The brotherhood of all troopers is symbolized by the formation itself. While the platoon is the standard military unit, on this one day the men line up in alphabetical order. This wipes out platoon distinctions and incorporates all the men in a pan-paratrooper sodality. Being saluted first by their superiors, against military protocol, shows the "troopers" that they now occupy a coveted status in the military.

Although the training NCO's are not required to attend, they are present throughout the ceremony. At the close they rush to congratulate the new members and welcome them into the brotherhood. The new status of the members has now been recognized and sanctioned by military society. With the evening's "prop blast" and its symbolic reenactment of the jumping process, the rite of passage is complete. The initiate is now wholly separated from his past life and "reborn" into a new, select brotherhood and a new way of life.

May 1967

SUGGESTED READINGS

Essays in the Ritual of Social Relations edited by Max Gluckman (Manchester, England: Manchester University Press, 1962). See "Les Rites de Passage" by Gluckman.

The Rites of Passage by Arnold Van Gennep (London, England: Routledge & Kegan Paul, 1960).

Reader in Comparative Religion by William A. Lessa and Evon Z. Vogt (New York City: Harper & Row, second edition, 1965).

Religion in Primitive Society by Edward Norbeck (New York: Harper & Row, 1961).

"The Military Academy as an Assimilating Institution" by Sanford Dornbusch, *Social Forces* (Vol. 33, May 1955) illustrates the process by which the Coast Guard Academy builds loyalty and commitment among its recruits.

The Andaman Islanders by A. R. Radcliffe-Brown (Glencoe, Ill.: Free Press, 1948). A leading anthropologist illustrates how primitive people are brought into their society.

Thought Reform and the Psychology of Totalism by Robert Jay Lifton (New York: Norton, 1961). Another way of bringing a person into a group is through the coercive process of brainwashing. In this book a psychiatrist describes brainwashing as employed by the Chinese on American *POW*'s during the Korean War.

Symbolic Wounds by Bruno Bettelheim (New York: Collier Books, 1962) treats another method of bringing a person into a group— the puberty rite.

The Fund of Sociability

Relationships with other people are essential and their loss can be traumatic

ROBERT S. WEISS

Why do people require relationships with one another? What needs are being expressed? We recognize constantly, sometimes with surprise, how important relationships are to us. Newly divorced individuals are distressed by loneliness, even as they congratulate themselves on having ended a conflict-laden marriage. Individuals who work alone, such as writers, complain of isolation, even as they prize their autonomy. Travelers on shipboard, separated from their network of friends, may find themselves greeting with enthusiasm an acquaintance from their home town who, in other circumstances, they might have barely acknowledged. In all these ways social needs express themselves. What can be their nature?

In trying to find answers to this question, people have

generally taken two lines of argument. One, associated with some schools of sociology, has been to assert that relationships which are close, so close they may be called primary, provide the individual with his understandings of reality, his moral values, his goals, even his sense of self. Relationships are important because through them the society organizes the individual's thinking and acting. Essentially, the society teaches its members what they want.

The second view, associated more with psychology than with sociology, has been that people have a number of needs or requirements which only relationships can satisfy, and that without appropriate relationships the individual will suffer. These needs are intrinsic to the individual, and are not formed by the society in which he lives. They may include needs for recognition, for affection, for power, for prestige, for belonging, and many more.

How can we move from these fairly general theoretical positions to a testable formulation of why people require relationships? Perhaps the simplest hypothesis we can phrase, one which would seem to be an implication of the first view but not of the second, is that of the "fund of sociability." According to this idea individuals require a certain amount of interaction with others, which they may find in various ways. They may with equal satisfaction have a few intense relationships or have a large number of relationships of lesser intensity. They would experience stress only if the total amount of relating to others was too little or too great.

The "fund of sociability" idea seemed to us to be a useful starting point in our effort to learn more regarding the assumptions, content, and functions of social ties. The research strategy that seemed to us a promising way to test this hypothesis was to seek out a group of individuals, all of whom had lost an important relationship but who also had the opportunity for unlimited sociability. It might then be seen whether increased sociability in some way compensated for the loss of the relationship.

For about a year, a colleague and I attended meetings of the Boston chapter of Parents Without Partners, a national organization of people who have children but who are living alone because of separation, divorce, or the death of their spouse. By listening to discussions of their past and current problems, and also from interviews with a good many members and former members, we hoped to be able to specify the nature of the losses sustained by these men and women with the end of their marriages, and the way in which membership in Parents Without Partners was useful to them.

We found that most members had joined simply because they were lonely, although there may well have been other reasons, including concern for their children or the desire to help others. The loneliness resulted directly from the absence of the marital relationship, rather than from such secondary factors as change in social role.

According to the "fund of sociability" hypothesis, we should expect to find members reporting that they had been lonely and restless after the dissolution of the marriage, but that interaction with others in Parents Without Partners had made up some part of that loss. We found, however, that although Parents Without Partners offered its members help with a host of difficulties, the sociability of belonging did not particularly diminish the sense of loneliness. Dating helped a good deal, but friendship did not. Although many members, particularly among the women, specifically mentioned friendship as the main contribution they received from Parents Without Partners, and these friendships sometimes became very close and very important to the participants, they did not compensate for the loss of the marriage. Friends and activities (discussion groups were perhaps the best) made the loneliness easier to manage, but they did not end it or even appreciably dimish it. One woman said, "Sometimes I have the girls over, and we talk about how hard it is. Misery loves company, you know."

Simple Sociability Not Satisfactory

Clearly the social needs satisfied in marriage, and, apparently, in dating, were not satisfied by simple sociability, no matter how much of it there was. But this raised the question of whether friendship was simply inadequate to supply the kind of interaction required, or whether friendship supplied something quite different, something that might not be found in marriage.

It seemed to us that friendship did offer something distinct from what marriage provides. But how to test this? We needed to find people who were married, but without friends. If friendships met social needs distinct from those met by marriage, then people without friends should be in distress, even though married. However, if friendship provided only a kind of time-filling sociability, then married people without friends should get along almost as well as married people with friends.

We began with a pilot study of six couples who had moved to the Boston suburbs from at least two states away. Our respondents were all middle-class and they had moved to Boston because of the husband's job.

Soon after the move, all but two of the wives were seriously unhappy; they were feeling a sense of social isolation similar in intensity (albeit shorter in duration) to the sense of emotional isolation that seemed to follow the dissolution of a marriage in others. The problem appeared to be that the housebound wife had no one with whom she could share the concerns of her daily life. Husbands could not really discuss with interest the dilemmas of child care nor the burdens of housework, and though they sometimes tried, they simply could not function properly as a friend. They might even compound the difficulty by saying they couldn't understand what was happening to their wives, and sometimes be downright unsympathetic because of what they felt were their own more serious problems of proving themselves on the new job. They were not troubled by the lack of people with whom they could share common interests, because at work they found men to talk to about the things that concerned them; the job, politics, sports, the local driving patterns, and the like. Two of the men with whom we worked listed for us the people they talked with during the day, and the number was impressive.

Meanwhile, the newcomer wives were likely to become painfully bored. In the absence of anyone with whom they could share their interests, they found housework and child care increasingly unrewarding. One wife who had been socially active and had considered herself reasonably happy in her former home began to drink heavily. Another wanted her husband to give up the promotion that had brought him to the Boston area, and to return to her parents' home town.

Of the two wives who did not seem to suffer from newcomer blues, the first was a woman who had no children and who immediately solved the problem of social isolation by going to work. The other was married to a man who in a previous move had bought a house in an old and settled neighborhood where friendships were well-established. To escape social isolation, she began taking night-school classes, and as her husband said when he talked with us, he hardly saw her except when they passed each other in the driveway. This time the husband moved into a new development where other homes were also owned by newcomers to the region, and spent his first weekend making friends with the new neighbors.

It now appeared clear to us that just as friendships do not provide the functions ordinarily provided by marriage, neither does marriage provide the functions ordinarily provided by friendship. Our current work on the nature of marriage suggests that marriages may vary in this, but nevertheless we believe that even in the most companionate of marriages, some important interests will not be shared within the marriage, and for women in the social group of the newcomer sample and even to a greater degree among poorer women the concerns of managing a family are not shared with the husband.

At this point, the hypothesis of a "fund of sociability" could be confidently rejected. It was clear that there were different kinds of relationships, providing different functions. The question then arose, how many relationships seemed to be necessary, and what functions did they seem to provide?

On the basis of further work with Parents Without Partners, we have been led to develop a theory that might be characterized as "the functional specificity of relationships." We believe that individuals have needs which can only be met within relationships, that relationships tend to become relatively specialized in the needs for which they provide, and as a result individuals require a number of different relationships for well-being.

Although there are many variations in the way people organize their lives, one can in general say that relations with kin seem to be reliable as sources of help, but not as sources of companionship; friends offer companionship, but not intimacy; and marriage or a near-marital relationship offers intimacy, but rarely friendship. We are not sure why this specialization develops. Undoubtedly, much has to do with underlying cultural definitions of the relationship. If wholehearted commitment between friends is difficult—and this seems the case in adult American life—then it will be possible for friends to share interests, but extremely difficult for them to develop the level of trust which would permit emotional intimacy.

The marriage relationship may be an exception to the generalization that relationships are specialized in function. In marriage each spouse provides for the other a degree of emotional integration, and also provides collaboration in managing the mechanics of life. But even here there may be conflicts between the way of relating to one another that is associated with the one function, and that associated with the other. In terms of the collaborative relationship, for example, it may be reasonable for a wife to criticize her husband's capacity to earn, but since she is also a source of emotional integration, her criticism can be devastating.

The specialization of relationship is probably always incomplete. Undoubtedly every friendship involves some emotional exchange and has the potential for more. Yet going beyond the understood assumptions of the relationship can endanger it. When it happens, for example, that one partner in a friendship seeks to move the relationship to one in which there is an assumption of unbounded trust, the more usual assumptions of the friendship may be temporarily flooded out. The consequence is likely to be uneasiness when the friends later find it necessary to return to the old basis. Generally there is so much resistance to changes of definition of a relationship that if a person loses the relationship that provided a particular function—as through the death of a spouse—he will be able only temporarily to alter his remaining relationships to fill the gap. Among members of Parents Without Partners, for example, we found a good deal of bitterness that stemmed from the failure of their friends to respond to their new relational needs.

Five Categories of Relationships

On the basis of our material we believe we can identify five categories of relational functions, each for the most part provided by a different relationship. All these functions seem to us to be necessary for well-being.

1) *Intimacy,* for want of a better term, is used to characterize the provision of an effective emotional integration in which individuals can express their feelings freely and without self-consciousness. It seems to us that this function of relationships prevents the individual from experiencing the sense of emotional isolation that is expressed in the term "loneliness." For a relationship to provide intimacy,

Only in marriage or a near-marital relationship can be found the intimacy that enables people to express their feelings freely and without self-consciousness, a comforting defense to loneliness and an essential ingredient for a healthy personality.

there must be trust, effective understanding, and ready access. Marriage provides such a relationship and so, often, does dating, at least for a time. Occasionally a woman may establish a relationship of this kind with a close friend, her mother, or a sister. And under some circumstances a man may establish a relationship of this sort with a friend.

It may be noted, parenthetically, that the relationship between sexual involvement and emotional intimacy, when the individuals concerned are potentially appropriate sexual partners, is quite complex and may well vary by social group and by circumstance. Certainly sex and intimacy are not necessarily associated. Still, rather fragmentary evidence suggests that in the groups we have worked with, individuals who are potentially appropriate partners may find it difficult to maintain a non-sexual emotionally intimate relationship. Where individuals are not appropriate sexual partners there is no apparent difficulty in maintaining such a relationship.

2) *Social integration* is provided by relationships in which participants share concerns, either because of similar situations ("we are in the same boat") or because they are striving for similar objectives (as in relationships among colleagues). Such relationships allow a good deal of sharing of experience, information, and ideas. They provide the basis for exchange of favors, and sometimes for more substantial help (though not for help continued over time). Among women this function is usually provided by friendships; among men, by relations with colleagues, as well as by friendships. The absence of this relationship may be experienced as a sense of social isolation and will, we suspect, be accompanied by feelings of boredom.

3) *Opportunity for nurturant behavior* is provided by relationships in which the adult takes responsibility for the well-being of a child. Our impression, based on experience with Parents Without Partners, is that men seem able to act as foster fathers to children not their own, but that it is much more difficult for women to act as foster mothers. The conditions for the expression of nurturance—and the nature of nurturance—may be different in men and women. We suspect that absence of this function may be signaled by a sense that one's life is unfulfilled, meaningless, and empty of purpose.

4) *Reassurance of worth* is provided by relationships that attest to an individual's competence in some role. Colleague relationships, and the social support and mutual respect they imply, can do this for some men, particularly

those whose work is difficult or valued. Successful family life may function in this way for other men, competence or worth here depending not on particular skills, but on the ability to support and defend a family. Women who work may also find their employment a source of reassurance of worth. Women who do not work must look to relationships with husbands, children, and acquaintances for recognition of their competence in making and managing a home. The loss of any system from which recognition of work, value, or competence may be gained will, we believe, result in decreased self-esteem.

5) *Assistance* through the provision of services or the making available of resources, although a primary theme in kin relationships, may be provided by a number of other relationships as well, including friendships and relationships with neighbors. However it seems to be only among close kin that one may expect assistance that is not limited in time and extent. It is the importance of this function for the poor that leads to the development of relational patterns in which kin ties are of primary importance. We suspect that the absence of any relationship providing the assurance of assistance if needed would be reflected in a sense of anxiety and vulnerability.

In addition, there seems to be a sixth function which can be provided by relationships that some people find important. This function might be characterized as *guidance,* and may be provided by mental-health professionals such as social workers or psychiatrists, or by ministers and priests, among others.

Undoubtedly there are individual differences in capacity to withstand the absence of one or another of the functions without giving way to restlessness and to the development of such symptoms as loneliness and boredom. On the basis of accounts of individuals who have successfully weathered long periods of isolation, one might suspect that individuals who have more rigid character structures might be better able to forego the

"The aged are vulnerable to . . . loneliness, boredom, and worthlessness, and a sense that they are no longer of critical importance to anyone else."

Richard Bellak

ADULT SOCIALIZATION

absence of some relational functions. One device that seems to have helped these men and women was to establish a detailed daily routine from which they did not deviate.

It is difficult at this point to say that any one of the relational functions is more important than another. The absence of intimacy can clearly be disorganizing for many individuals, and for most it would be accompanied by painful loneliness, but we are not able at this time to say that it is a more serious deficit than the absence of opportunity for nurturance. I have known childless couples to be as downcast by difficulties in adopting a baby as a lonely person might be by difficulties in finding love. It seems as though the absence of any relational function will create some form of dissatisfaction, accompanied by restlessness and occasional spells of acute distress.

This theory, like any theory of human nature, has implications for the way in which we might deal with individuals in difficult situations. We might consider two possible areas of application of these ideas: to the problem of relational loss, and to the problem of aging.

There are many forms of relational loss. There is the loss of friends that comes with moving from one area to another, the loss of colleagues that accompanies retirement, the loss of newly adult children from home, the loss of a spouse through death or divorce. Each of these losses would seem to have two aspects: first, the trauma that accompanies the damage to the individual's life organization; and, second, the deficit in the individual's life that is a result of the continuing absence of the functions once provided by the now-lost relationship. When individuals move from one area to another, the trauma aspect may be nothing more than sadness at leaving old friends and old associations, and not especially serious. The primary problem of relocation is that of deficit in the wife's relationships, the absence of new friends in the new situation. In conjugal bereavement, the loss by death of a spouse, the pain of loss is ordinarily very great and, for a good while, the trauma of the loss will be the primary source of distress. Yet even when this has been resolved, the life of the widow or widower is apt to continue to be unsatisfactory because of problems of relational deficit. It can be helpful to a widow or widower to recognize these two consequences of loss and to acknowledge that loneliness may be an unavoidable response to an unsatisfying situation rather than an inability to resolve the disruption of loss. Being able to identify what is wrong makes it easier to find remedies.

To turn to aging, the theory alerts us to the disturbances of social relationships that come with time. These include departure of children, retirement, possibly the loss of spouse, and, as a result of all the preceding, painful and sometimes bewildering reorientation of central life concerns.

When their children leave, the older couple may find a

freedom they have not known for decades, but they also lose their opportunity for nurturance. They may continue to help their now-grown children, and they may be able periodically to indulge their grandchildren, but they probably will never again have the sense of being essential to someone else, which is at least one of the functions small children seem to provide for their parents.

Retirement Removes Important Basis for Self-Esteem

Retirement varies in its implications, but for many men, as Eugene A. Friedmann and Robert J. Havighurst have shown, it removes from their lives an important basis for self-esteem. The parallel, for a woman, would be the loss of a home to keep up. This too can occur in time, but usually at a considerably later point in a woman's life than retirement occurs in a man's. It must be said, though, that the loss of children from the home may constitute a partial retirement for women.

With bereavement, the aged person may have no access to intimacy, and despite remaining relationships with grown children, other relatives, and friends, may begin to experience chronic loneliness. The absence of an intimate tie, we suspect, makes it difficult for an individual to maintain an even emotional balance. Since his emotional responses are not communicated and responded to, they go unchecked, uncorrected by another's perceptions. The result may be distortions either in the direction of pathological distrust or in the direction of depression which are difficult to interrupt.

The aged will lose friends through death, including old friends with whom so much is shared that the relationships are irreplaceable. But they also may give up friends because the interests and concerns that were central to the friendship no longer have meaning for them. Losing her husband may change a woman's life so much that she may no longer have anything in common with her married friends. Retirement may make irrelevant a man's relationships with former colleagues. And at the same time these bases for former friendships are lost, the afflictions of age—sickness, limited income, dependence—may produce new central life concerns which can be shared by few others. The aged who become seriously ill, or crippled, or have a chronic condition that requires frequent medical care, cannot share with anyone their feelings about these physical problems, even though they may well find them the central concerns of their lives. Small wonder, then, if an aged person who is ill seeks out a doctor just to talk about his condition, even at the risk of being thought a hypochondriac.

The aged, therefore, are vulnerable to relational losses that bring in their wake feelings of loneliness, boredom, and worthlessness, and a sense that they are no longer of critical importance to anyone else. These feelings, taken together, have sometimes been characterized as a psychological syndrome that accompanies age. A simpler explanation is that these feelings are normal reactions to relational deficits, reactions that would be found in any group similarly afflicted.

This appraisal suggests that the social and emotional distresses that accompany age can be remedied, but only by relationships that supply the required functions. It gives us a guide to the sort of relationships that may help and the sort that probably will not. For the retired, activities that clearly benefit others, or display competence in an important or valued way, may substitute for employment; but a make-work task, a hobby, or just keeping busy will not.

The appraisal also suggests that relational losses can be repaired. Should loss take place, and this is almost inevitable with age, then the view taken here suggests that it would be better to advise such people that they attempt to establish new relationships that will provide the same functions, rather than "gracefully" accept constriction.

But this recommendation could be made universally. Beyond a certain point we cannot limit our relations with others without incurring serious loss. Just as it is bad advice to tell a widow to live for the children, or to tell someone who is aged to accept the inevitable losses, it is bad advice to tell a young person to forego intimacy for a time while he concentrates on his studies.

July-August 1969

SUGGESTED READINGS

Kinship in an Urban Setting by Bert Adams (Chicago: Markham, 1968). This is an analysis of survey data dealing with the functioning of kin relationships for a sample of married adults living in Greensboro, North Carolina.

Husbands and Wives by Robert O. Blood, Jr. and Donald M. Wolfe (New York: Free Press, 1960). This is a report of a survey of married pairs living in Detroit which describes in detail how the couples manage their joint enterprises of home and family, and in somewhat less detail how the couples maintain the more emotional aspects of their relationship.

Family and Social Network by Elizabeth Bott (London: Tavistock, 1957) is a study of some different organizations of marital and social relationships which can serve to provide the same set of relational functions.

Sourcebook in Marriage and the Family by Marvin B. Sussman (New York: Houghton Mifflin, 1963) is an excellent collection of articles on various aspects of dating, marital relationships, parent-child relationships, and relationships with other kin.

The Meaning of Work and Retirement, Eugene Friedman and Robert J. Havighurst (Chicago: University of Chicago Press, 1954) is a collection of studies describing the meaning of work in various occupations.

The Sociology of Georg Simmel edited by Kurt H. Wolff (New York: The Free Press, 1950). Part I, chapter III, "Sociability." A classic theoretical statement of the forms of human sociability.

Dennis H. Wrong, "The Oversocialized Conception of Man in Modern Sociology," *American Sociological Review* (Vol. 26, April 1961)

The Art of Loving by Erich Fromm (New York: Harper and Row, 1956). A discourse on love in all its aspects, aimed at enhancing the reader's capacity for a broad-based, mature and courageous kind of love.

Hippies in College—From Teeny-boppers to Drug Freaks

GEOFFREY SIMMON
GRAFTON TROUT

Though it isn't generally recognized, hippies living—more or less permanently—in urban hippie colonies such as the Hashbury and the East Village differ very much from their campus confreres. The confusion of the two is not surprising, since the mass media have focused almost exclusively on the city hippies. In addition, much of the hippie style derives from city hippies and rapidly diffuses to the campus scenes.

But while college students with long hair, bare feet and brightly colored beads frequently vacation in the Hashburys of our cities, few wish to settle there. Many return to campuses somewhat disillusioned with the drug abuse (especially of speed drugs like methedrine) and with the increasing violence of the bad scene of the city. Furthermore, the college hippie wants to turn on and tune in, but not to drop out, at least not completely.

In our two-year study of the hippie community at a midwestern multiversity, we focused mainly on the process by which college hippies are recruited and socialized. We believe that by finding out how one becomes a hippie, we might contribute something new to the more usual discussions of who becomes a hippie and why. Though personality traits or family experience may predispose a teenager toward becoming a hippie, it is clear that one has to learn how to be hip in association with others. Hippies are made, not born.

A study of hippies, however, cannot be conducted in the usual manner of interviewing and observation. Hippies have little respect for sociology, which they equate with the establishment and, particularly, with the university. To them, it is the stereotype classifications of middle-class conformists that keep people from being themselves—from doing their own thing. They have little enthusiasm for cooperating with social researchers who, they believe, will simply attempt to fit them into other classifications. Furthermore, the hippies' use of drugs makes access difficult, since the social scientist might seem to be a more sophisticated cover for the Feds, or local narcotics-squad agents. This particular study was made possible by the younger author's association with the hippie community as an undergraduate and a graduate student. His participant observation was supplemented by some 50 interviews conducted both individually and in groups at parties he gave. While he encountered considerable skepticism regarding the usefulness of the research, the people interviewed were generally cooperative and frank. His inside knowledge of the hippie community, and his acceptance in it, minimized the possibility of their attempts to put him on or to blow his mind.

Activism vs. Hedonism

Early in the research, it became clear that campus hippies differ not only from city hippies, but differ among themselves as well. Indeed, many individuals shift from one type of hippie to another as they move through the socialization process within the hippie community. While the campus hippies appear to be similar in dress, coiffure, grooming, and in many aspects of their behavior, two categories are readily distinguishable—by their orientation toward political activism and personal hedonism.

One group, known as politicals on many campuses, can be distinguished by their dedication to the achievement of rather well-defined political goals (which may, of course, differ from campus to campus, depending on the current local causes). These are the leaders and followers of the new student Left. They devote a great deal of time and energy to organizing protest demonstrations and confronting the establishment—in this case, usually embodied by the university administration. The politicals on the campus we studied used a private cafeteria near the campus as their headquarters. They deprecated the introspective hedonism and political individualism of the second group, known as skuzzies on the campus we studied but called groddies, grotties, grubbies, heads or freaks on other campuses. The skuzzies had taken over the coffee shop in the student union as their headquarters. While they frequently would give verbal and bodily support to the politicals during a crisis, the skuzzies were committed more to doing their own thing, which did not include the hard, collectively-organized work of political protest and the weekly publication of the local underground newspaper.

The leaders of the skuzzie group are not so easily identified as those of the political group. This is because of the difference in the degree of structuring of the two groups. The political leaders not only are more visible as a result of campus publicity, but also hold official positions, such as chairmanships of steering committees and editorial positions on the underground newspaper. The skuzzies, on the other hand, lack any such formal organization. The skuzzies' leader is distinguished chiefly by his more advanced age and higher class standing, and by his ability to function with a certain degree of social and academic success while continuing to participate in the hippie community. He provides the model of how to turn on without dropping out.

Two further categories are needed to complete the classification of participants in the hippie community. The term *teeny-boppers* was applied most frequently to the hippie equivalent of the pledge class. These were the incoming freshmen, in the initial stage of developing hippie associations and learning how to be hip. Finally, a group of long-standing and unusually far-out hippies was also encountered in this research. There was no local name applied to this group, so we will call them *hippie deviants* for purposes of discussion later.

Most of the hippies interviewed were freshmen and sophomores, although the leaders were upperclassmen or (especially among the politicals) graduate students. There was a surprising number of National Merit Scholars and scholarship students. Although most had no preference for an academic major, the most common majors were in social sciences—a curious contradiction, considering their attitude toward the social scientific study of themselves. There was a disproportionate number of Jewish students but only two Negroes. Most of the participants came from middle- to upper-middle-income families living in urban or suburban areas. Few were the products of broken homes.

While in high school, the potential hippie achieved status primarily through academic success. Few were athletes or student-body officials then. Few identified strongly with their high schools. Upon entering college, the bright and successful high-school upperclassman becomes one of thousands of freshmen, most of whom have nonintellectual orientations. While many students try to shrink the multiversity to human scale by joining clubs and fraternities and sororities, this does not work for the sort of students we have described, since these organizations emphasize just what the potential hippies don't have—social spirit.

Now, many students have awaited college as an opportunity to find other students of similar interests and to begin actively seeking out the likely groups of such students. Among the most visible of these groups today are the hippies, especially the politicals. The politicals are involved in activities that appear to be intellectual and important. Best of all, *the politicals are easily accessible*. Teeny-boppers need no formal introduction. There is no rite of passage, such as smoking pot or tripping with LSD. All they have to do is carry signs, go to committee meetings, and drink coffee at the politicals' cafeteria. To the potential hippie, the politicals offer an opportunity to shrink the university, to regain status as an intellectual, and to acquire some sort of cause or direction.

The political leaders include self-avowed communists, socialists, Maoists, and Trotskyites. But although the political teeny-boppers wear the buttons and carry the signs, the majority do not share the convictions of the leaders. Often they don't even know what these convictions really are.

A key characteristic of the politicals is their selective adherence to the hedonistic hang-loose ethic. Though they often voice approval of the skuzzies' casual acceptance of drugs, they do not share their practice. Since the politicals believe in immediate social reform, any activity not dedicated to this end is considered a dangerous waste of time and is therefore discouraged among their teeny-bopper followers. Status is confronted on the teeny-boppers through political buttons, armbands, and committee positions. If anyone shows too much skuzziness, he is drummed out of the ranks with the same dispatch applied to lax wardheelers in any political machine.

Since the politicals do not engage in or encourage what most would call hippie behavior, it may be asked if they are really hippies. The skuzzies don't think so, although the political teeny-boppers believe they are. The politicals' rationale for their deviation from hippie norms is what the skuzzies call paranoia. The following is an example:

Interviewer: "Do you like drugs?"
Political: "Yes, if you mean pot and acid."
Interviewer: "Do you turn on with any of the local heads?"
Political: "Are you out of your mind? I'm currently involved in . . . [an impressive array of New Left activities]. I guess you know I'm being tailed by the Feds and my phone is tapped. They're looking for any excuse to bust me. If I got within smelling distance of any pot they would bust me *so fast*. Not only to break me, but to attach the addict label to my cause."

The skuzzies don't accept this excuse. They have been around long enough to recognize that the politicals are not really hemmed in. Still, the teeny-boppers like the story for the excitement and importance it lends to what they are doing.

Becoming a Skuzzie

But as the teeny-bopper grows older, he is likely to give up on the politicals. The teeny-bopper gradually becomes aware of the meaning of the deviant political philosophies of the political leaders and becomes uncomfortable. Furthermore, and perhaps more important, the teeny-bopper's enthusiasm for constant political effort diminishes. His head is full of tales about what the skuzzies are doing—experimenting with life without the pressure of political activity. He is fascinated by drugs. Hedonism conquers political altruism and activism. He comes to the decision that the politicals are not really so hip. Their chief concern is political evangelism—"dumping"—and not "hanging loose."

It takes only two terms to transform a political teeny-bopper into a skuzzie teeny-bopper. Once in the student union with the skuzzies, he normally fights with his parents, drops out of school (either officially or effectively), and lives off his allowance.

As a political, the teeny-bopper's grades were, probably, better than average. During his transition from political to skuzzie, his grades usually fall. If he drops out of school and then eventually comes back, they return to better than average.

Still, few teeny-boppers remain in the hippie culture long enough to obtain the seniority needed to become hard-core skuzzies. The two distinguishing characteristics of the hard-core skuzzie are his advanced age and his more conservative adherence to hippie norms. The hard-core skuzzie is older than the teeny-bopper, but not as old as the hard-core political.

The teeny-bopper skuzzies live the free hippie life with great abandon—a life usually far skuzzier than that of the hard-core skuzzies. Like the scene along fraternity row, where the freshman and the sophomore brothers are a bit more pleasure-oriented than the juniors and seniors, the younger skuzzies do most of the sexual and drug experimenting. Just as the younger Greeks drink more, the younger skuzzies smoke more pot. And the older, hard-core skuzzies are also cooler, more individualistic, than their followers in another way: They get better grades.

Thus the hard-core skuzzies do not actively lead their followers. Instead, they serve as models and as living proof that the skuzzie life does not produce useless bums.

The skuzzie life usually lasts about a year and a half. The skuzzie tries to find himself through drugs, drinking, sex, and very little work. After that, he usually discovers that it is difficult to find himself and feed himself at the same time. Or, after finding a mate, he may decide that he no longer believes in free sex and communal living. At this point, he may drop out of the skuzzie system and even get a haircut.

The other path out of the skuzzie system leads on to hippie deviance. The deviants should not be confused with the hardest-core skuzzies. The skuzzies hang loose, but not too loose. They justify the hippie way of life on Establishment terms. The deviants consist of promiscuous girls, homosexuals, and heavy drug users. Of all the hippie types around the campus, the deviants are the most likely to migrate to the city.

The other campus hippies, no matter how liberal or accepting they are supposed to be, apparently have little use for the drug addict or for completely promiscuous sex of either variety. The hippie deviants mark the outer boundary of hippieness. Nevertheless, the rest of the campus hippies tolerate the deviants. Because they move around a great deal and develop connections with city hippies, the deviants can get drugs more easily than anyone else.

Even as we write about the campus hippies, certain changes seem to be under way. Several years ago, it might have been sufficient to describe the hippies as an emergent deviant subculture generated by people of a certain type sharing a common problem in the new environment of the multiversity. This subculture, having been institutionalized on most large campuses, would presumably then continue to provide a ready-made solution for the problems of the same type of people who originally created that solution.

But something more has happened. The hippies have been publicized and, to an important degree, shaped by the mass media. Knowledge of how to play the game, if not actual participation, begins in high school. With this anticipatory socialization, the freshman may have already taken on some of the hippie values and behavior when he arrives on campus.

Thus, the process of assimilation and socialization has speeded up. This may undermine the role of the politicals as gatekeepers for the hippie subculture, robbing them of the recruits who have carried their posters and sat in their sit-ins for a year or so before freaking out to the life of hedonism and hanging loose. Future generations of hippies may have turned on years before freshman orientation, and therefore may never tune in to political activism.

In addition, the great moral cause of civil rights has been increasingly taken away from the committed white college student, and the student Left is, on many campuses, in disarray. This moral unemployment of the student Left may work against the politicals and in favor of the drug freaks. The hang-loose ethic, the psychedelic experience, and the quest for self-knowledge become increasingly attractive as attempts at positive political action become less meaningful and more difficult.

The extent and the impact of the hippie subculture—amplified as it is by new drugs, new music, new sexual morality and a new kind of war—may be, in some respects, unprecedented. We must guard against the easy assumption that, because each student generation develops some sort of deviant subsociety, each of these is basically the same. Changes in American society may provide a more permanent niche for certain aspects of the present, hippie version of campus bohemianism. Whether the eventual standard bearers will be the confirmed drug dropouts, the currently more restrained college skuzzies, or the precollege artificial-flower children who flock to New York's turned-on Macdougal Street every weekend from their comfortable homes in the suburbs, the possibility is clear: We may well be in the presence not of just the latest wrinkle in youthful rebellion, but of an emergent social movement.

December 1967

SUGGESTED READINGS

Socialization after Childhood by Orville G. Brim and Stanton Wheeler (New York: John Wiley and Sons, 1966) comprises two essays on socialization focusing on personality development and the importance of social facts.

Students under Stress by David Mechanic (Glencoe, Ill.: Free Press, 1962). This book focuses on 22 graduate students reacting to Ph.D. preliminary examinations. It deals with how they handle the anxieties of preparing, taking and reacting to this stressful requirement.

"The Condemnation and Persecution of Hippies" by Michael E. Brown, (*Trans*-action, Vol. 6, Sept. 1969).

Michael Alexander

The Culture of Civility

Deviance and Democracy in "The City"

HOWARD S. BECKER & IRVING LOUIS HOROWITZ

Deviants of many kinds live well in San Francisco—natives and tourists alike make that observation. The city's apparently casual and easygoing response to "sex, dope and cheap thrills" (to crib the suppressed full title of Janis Joplin's famous album—itself a San Francisco product) astounds visitors from other parts of the country who can scarcely credit either what they see happening or the way natives stroll by those same events unconcerned.

■ Walking in the Tenderloin on a summer evening, a block from the Hilton, you hear a black whore cursing at a policeman: "I wasn't either blocking the sidewalk! Why don't you motherfucking fuzz mind your own goddamn business!" The visiting New Yorker expects to see her arrested, if not shot, but the cop smiles good-naturedly and moves on, having got her back into the doorway where she is supposed to be.

■ You enter one of the famous rock ballrooms and, as you stand getting used to the noise and lights, someone puts a lit joint of marijuana in your hand. The tourist looks for someplace to hide, not wishing to be caught in the mass arrest he expects to follow. No need to worry. The police will not come in, knowing that if they do they will have to arrest people and create disorder.

■ Candidates for the city's Board of Supervisors make their pitch for the homosexual vote, estimated by some at 90,000. They will not be run out of town; the candidates' remarks are dutifully reported in the daily paper, as are the evaluations of them by representatives of SIR, the Society for Individual Rights.

■ The media report (tongue in cheek) the annual Halloween Drag Ball, for which hundreds of homosexuals turn out at one of the city's major hotels in full regalia, unharassed by police.

■ One sees long-haired, bearded hippies all over the city, not just in a few preserves set aside for them. Straight citizens do not remark their presence, either by gawking, hostility or flight.

■ Nudie movies, frank enough to satisfy anyone's curiosity, are exhibited in what must be the largest number of specialty movie houses per capita in the country. Periodic police attempts to close them down (one of the few occasions when repression has been attempted) fail.

DEVIANT SOCIALIZATION 209

The items can be multiplied indefinitely, and their multiplicity demands explanation. Most cities in the United States refuse to let deviants indulge themselves publicly, let alone tolerate candidates who seek their bloc votes. Quite the contrary. Other cities, New York and Chicago being good examples, would see events like these as signs of serious trouble, omens of a real breakdown in law enforcement and deviance control, the forerunner of saturnalia and barbarian take-over. Because its politicians and police allow and can live with activities that would freak out their opposite numbers elsewhere, San Francisco is a natural experiment in the consequences of tolerating deviance. We can see from its example what results when we ignore the warnings of the custodians of conventional morality. We can see too what lessons can be learned about the conditions under which problems that perhaps lie deeper than matters of morals or life style can be solved to the satisfaction of all the parties to them.

A Culture of Civility

We can summarize this low-key approach to deviance in the phrase "a culture of civility." What are its components, and how does it maintain itself?

San Francisco prides itself on its sophistication, on being the most European of American cities, on its picturesque cosmopolitanism. The picturesque quality, indeed the quaintness, rests in part on physical beauty. As the filling of the Bay and the destruction of the skyline by high-rise buildings proceeds to destroy that beauty, the city has come to depend even more on the presence of undigested ethnic minorities. It is as though San Francisco did not wish its Italians, Chinese or Russians to assimilate and become standard Americans, preferring instead to maintain a panoply of ethnic differences: religious, cultural and culinary (especially culinary). A sophisticated, livable city, on this view, contains people, colonies and societies of all kinds. Their differences create a mosaic of life styles, the very difference of whose sight and smell give pleasure.

Like ethnic minorities, deviant minorities create enclaves whose differences add to the pleasure of city life. Natives enjoy the presence of hippies and take tourists to see their areas, just as they take them to see the gay area of Polk Street. Deviance, like difference, is a civic resource, enjoyed by tourist and resident alike.

To enjoy deviance instead of fearing it requires a surrender of some common sense notions about the world. Most people assume, when they see someone engaging in proscribed activity, that there is worse to come. "Anyone who would do that [take dope, dress in women's clothes, sell his body or whatever] would do anything" is the major premise of the syllogism. "If you break one law or convention, who knows where you'll stop." Common sense ignores the contrary cases around us everywhere: professional criminals often flourish a legionnaire's patriotism; housewives who are in every other respect conventional sometimes shoplift; homosexuals may be good family providers; some people, who habitually use the rings from poptop cans to work the parking meter, would not dream of taking dope, and vice versa. "Deviance," like conforming behavior, is highly selective. San Francisco's culture of civility, accepting that premise, assumes that if I know that you steal or take dope or peddle your ass, that is all I *know*. There may be more to know; then again, there may be nothing. The deviant may be perfectly decent in every other respect. We are often enjoined, in a generalization of therapeutic doctrine, to treat other people as individuals; that prescription comes nearer to being filled in San Francisco than in most places in the United States.

Because of that tolerance, deviants find it possible to live somewhat more openly in San Francisco than elsewhere. People do not try so hard to catch them at their deviant activities and are less likely to punish them when caught. Because they live more openly, what they do is more visible to straight members of the community. An established canon of social psychology tells us that we find it harder to maintain negative stereotypes when our personal experience belies them. We see more clearly and believe more deeply that hippies or homosexuals are not dangerous when we confront them on the street day after day or live alongside them and realize that beard plus long hair does not equal a drug-crazed maniac, that limp wrist plus lisp does not equal child-molester.

When such notions become embodied in a culture of civility, the citizenry begins to sense that "everyone" feels that way. We cannot say at what critical point a population senses that sophistication about deviance is the norm, rather than a liberal fad. But San Francisco clearly has that critical mass. To come on as an anti-deviant, in a way that would probably win friends and influence voters in more parochial areas, risks being greeted by laughter and ridicule in San Francisco. Conservatives who believe in law and order are thus inclined to keep their beliefs to themselves. The more people keep moralistic notions to themselves, the more everyone believes that tolerance is widespread. The culture maintains itself by convincing the populace that it is indeed the culture.

It gets help from public pronouncements of civic officials, who enunciate what will be taken as the collective sentiment of the city. San Francisco officials occasionally angle for the conservative vote that disapproves licentiousness. But they more frequently take the side of liberty, if not license. When the police, several years ago, felt compelled to close the first of the "topless joints," the judge threw the case out. He reasoned that Supreme Court decisions required him to take into account contemporary community standards. In his judgment San Francisco was not a prudish community; the case was dismissed. The city's major paper, the *Chronicle,* approved. Few protested.

Similarly, when California's leading Yahoo, Superintendent of Public Instruction Max Rafferty, threatened to revoke the teaching credentials of any San Francisco teacher who used the obscene materials listed in the standard high school curriculum (Eldridge Cleaver's *Soul on Ice* and LeRoi Jones' *Dutchman*), the City did not remove the offending books from its curriculum. Instead, it successfully sued to have Rafferty enjoined from interfering in its operation.

In short, San Franciscans know that they are supposed to be sophisticated and let that knowledge guide their public actions, whatever their private feelings. According to another well-known law of social psychology, their private feelings often come to resemble their public actions, and they learn to delight in what frightens citizens of less civil cities.

We do not suggest that all kinds of deviation are tolerated endlessly. The police try, in San Francisco as elsewhere, to stamp out some vices and keep a ceiling on others. Some deviance frightens San Franciscans too, because it seems to portend worse to come (most recently, users and purveyors of methedrine—"speed merchants" and "speed freaks"—whose drug use is popularly thought to result in violence and crime). But the line is drawn much farther over on the side of "toleration" in San Francisco than elsewhere. A vastly wider range of activities is publicly acceptable. Despite the wide range of visible freakiness, the citizenry takes it all in stride, without the fear and madness that permeates the conventional sectors of cities like Detroit, Chicago, New York, Washington, D.C. and similar centers of undaunted virtue.

Madames and Unionists

How does a culture of civility arise? Here we can only speculate, and then fragmentarily, since so few cities in the United States have one that we cannot make the comparisons that might uncover the crucial conditions. San Francisco's history suggests a number of possibilities.

It has, for one thing, a Latin heritage. Always a major seaport, it has long tolerated the vice that caters to sailors typical of such ports. It grew at the time of the gold rush in an explosive way that burst through conventional social controls. It ceded to its ethnic minorities, particularly the Chinese, the right to engage in prostitution, gambling and other activities. Wickedness and high living form part of the prized past every "tourist" city constructs for itself; some minor downtown streets in San Francisco, for instance, are named for famous madames of the gold rush era.

Perhaps more important, a major potential source of repressive action—the working class—is in San Francisco more libertarian and politically sophisticated than one might expect. Harry Bridges' longshoremen act as bellwethers. It should be remembered that San Francisco is one of the few major American cities ever to experience a general strike. The event still reverberates, and working people who might support repression of others know by personal experience that the policeman may not be their friend. Trade unionism has a left-wing, honest base which gives the city a working-class democracy and even eccentricity, rather than the customary pattern of authoritarianism.

Finally, San Francisco is a town of single people. Whatever actual proportion of the adult population is married, the city's culture is oriented toward and organized for single people. As a consequence, citizens worry less about what public deviance will do to their children, for they don't have any and don't intend to, or they move from the city when they do. (Since there are, of course, plenty of families in the city, it may be more accurate to say that there are fewer white middle-class families, that being the stratum that would, if family-based, provide the greatest number of complaints about deviance. Black, chicano and oriental populations ordinarily have enough to worry about without becoming guardians of public morality.)

The Place to Live

San Francisco is known across the country as a haven for deviants. Good homosexuals hope to go to San Francisco to stay when they die, if not before. Indeed, one of the problems of deviant communities in San Francisco is coping with the periodic influx of a new generation of bohemians who have heard that it is the place to be: the beatnik migration

More Americans prefer San Francisco to any other city in the United States, according to a recent Gallup poll, and so do most Europeans.

Fred Lyon RAPHO GUILLIMETTE

of the late fifties and the hippie hordes of 1967. But those problems should not obscure what is more important: that there are stable communities of some size there to be disrupted. It is the stable homosexual community that promises politicians 90,000 votes and the stable bohemian communities of several vintages that provide both personnel and customers for some important local industries (developing, recording and distributing rock music is now a business of sizeable proportions).

Stable communities are stable because their members have found enough of what they want to stay where they are for a while. If where they were proved totally unsatisfying, they presumably would move elsewhere, unless restrained. But no one forces deviants to live in San Francisco. They stay there because it offers them, via the culture of civility, a place to live where they are not shunned as fearsome or disgusting, where agents of control (police and others) do not regard them as unfortunate excrescences to be excised at the first opportunity. Because they have a place to stay that does not harass them, they sink roots like more conventional citizens: find jobs, buy houses, make friends, vote and take part in political activities and all the other things that solid citizens do.

Sinking roots stabilizes deviants' lives, as it does the lives of conventional citizens. They find less need to act in the erratic ways deviants often behave elsewhere, less need to fulfill the prophecy that because they are deviant in one respect they will be deviant in other, more dangerous ways. San Francisco employers know that homosexuals make good employees. Why not? They are not likely to be blackmailed by enterprising hustlers. The police seldom haul them off to jail for little reason or beat them because they feel like pushing some "queers" around. Homosexuals fear none of this in San Francisco, or fear it much less than in most places, and so are less given to the overcompensatory "camping" that gets their fellows into trouble elsewhere.

Police and others do not harass deviants because they have found, though they may deny it for public relations purposes, that looking the other way is sometimes a good policy. It is easier, when a Be-In is going on, to turn your back on the sight of open marijuana smoking than it is to charge into the crowd and try to arrest people who will destroy the evidence before you get there, give you a hard time, make a fool of you and earn you a bad press—and have no conviction to show for it. At the same time, when you turn your back, nothing worse is likely to happen: no muggings, no thefts, no rapes, no riots. Police, more calculating than they seem, often choose to reach just this kind of accommodation with stable deviant communities.

The accommodation works in circular fashion. When deviants can live decent lives, they find it possible to behave decently. Furthermore, they acquire the kind of stake they are often denied elsewhere in the present and future structure of the community. That stake constrains them to behave in ways that will not outrage nondeviants, for they

Michael Alexander

do not want to lose what they have. They thus curb their activities according to what they think the community will stand for.

The community in turn, and especially the police, will put up with more than they might otherwise, because they understand that nothing else is forthcoming, and because they find that what they are confronted with is not so bad after all. If homosexuals have a Halloween Drag Ball, the community discovers it can treat it as a good-natured joke; those who are offended discover that they needn't go near the Hilton while it is happening.

No doubt neither party to such a bargain gets quite what he would like. Straight members of the community presumably would prefer not to have whores walking the downtown streets, would prefer not to have gay bars operating openly. Deviants of all kinds presumably would prefer not to have to make any concessions to straight sensibilities. Each gives up something and gets something, and to that degree the arrangement becomes stable, the stability itself something both prize.

Deviance and Democracy

What we have just described verges on the idyllic, Peace and Harmony in Camelot forever. Such a dream of perfection does not exist in San Francisco, though more deviants there have more of the advantages of such a bargain, perhaps, than in any other city in the United States. Nor is it clear that the system we described, even in its perfect form, would be such an idyll.

In San Francisco, as everywhere, the forces of decency and respectability draw the line somewhere and can be every bit as forceful and ruthless the other side of that line as the forces of decency and respectability anywhere else. When the Haight-Ashbury got "out of hand" with the overcrowded transiency of 1967, the city moved in the police Tactical Squad, the City Health Department and all the other bureaucratic weapons usually used to roust deviants. They did it again with the growth of violence in that area associated with the use and sale of methedrine. In general, the city has responded with great toughness to those deviants it believes will not be satisfied with something "reasonable." In particular, political dissent has sometimes been met with force, though San Francisco police have never indulged themselves on any large scale such as that which made Chicago police internationally detested.

The system has beauty only for those deviants who do not mind giving up some portion of their liberty, and then only if the portion they are willing to give up is the same as what the community wants given up. This no doubt is the reason an accommodative system works well with those whose deviant desires are narrowly circumscribed, and may have less utility with those whose wants can be accommodated only at the expense of others who will not easily give up their privileges. In fact, current political difficulties clearly result from the breakdown of accommodation.

Gernot Newman

These considerations indicate the more general importance of San Francisco's experiment in tolerating and accommodating to the minor forms of deviance encompassed in sex, dope and cheap thrills. How can a complex and differentiated society deal with variety and dissent and simultaneously with its own urges for centralized control? An accommodative relationship to difference, in which it is allowed to persist while it pays some minimal dues to the whole, is what San Francisco recommends to us, suggesting that the amount of the dues and the breadth of the license be set where both parties will, for the time being, stand still for it. The resulting working arrangement will be at least temporarily stable and provide for all concerned a tranquility that permits one to go about his business unharmed that many will find attractive.

But is this no more than a clever trick, a way of buying off deviant populations with minor freedoms while still keeping them enslaved? Beneath the rhetoric, the analysis is the same. The more radical statement adds only that the people who accept such a bargain ought not to, presumably because they have, if they only knew it, deeper and more important interests and desires which remain unsatisfied in the accommodative arrangement. So, of course, do those who hold them in check. Perhaps that is the ultimate lesson of San Francisco: the price of civilization, civility and living together peacefully is not getting everything you want.

Limits of Accommodation

It is tempting to think that an accommodation based on civility and mutual interest provides a model for settling the conflicts now wracking our urban areas. Our analysis suggests that this is a possibility, but no more than that. Peace can occur through accommodation, the example of the potheads and pimps tells us, only under certain not so easily attained conditions. Those conditions may not be present in the ethnic and political problems our major cities, San Francisco among them, are now experiencing.

Accommodation requires, as a first condition, that the

parties involved prize peace and stability enough to give up some of what they want so that others may have their desires satisfied as well. But people take that point of view only when the accommodation leaves them enough of a share to want no more. Some urban groups no longer believe that they are getting that necessary minimum, either because they have learned to interpret their situation in a new light or because they have lost some advantages they once had.

Members of black communities may be no worse off than ever, but they are considerably worse off than whites and know it. For a variety of historical reasons, and as a matter of simple justice, some of them no longer regard the little they have as sufficient reason to keep the peace. All the discussion about how many blacks feel this way (is it 10 percent or 50 percent?) and how strongly they feel it (are they willing to fight?) is irrelevant to the main point: enough feel strongly enough to make a lot of trouble for the white community, thus changing the balance of costs to the whites and insisting on a new division of rights as the price of stability.

Some members of white communities probably are objectively worse off and may resent it sufficiently to give up peace and stability in an effort to raise the costs to others and thus minimize their losses. Many whites in civil service positions, in the skilled trades and in similar protected occupational positions have lost or are in danger of losing competitive job advantages as governments act to do something about the injustice that afflicts black communities. Without a general expansion of the economy, which is *not* what blacks demand, injustices inflicted on blacks can be remedied only by taking something away from more favorably situated whites. It may be possible to improve the education of poor black children, for instance, only by taking away some of the privileges of white teachers. It may be possible to give black youths a chance at apprenticeships in skilled trades only by removing the privileged access to those positions of the sons of present white union members. When whites lose those privileges, they may feel strongly enough to fracture the consensus of civility.

The deviant communities of San Francisco show us cases in which the parties involved agree in a way that leaves each enough. But that may only be possible when the interests to be accommodated involve morals and life styles. When those interests include substantial economic prizes, major forms of privilege and real political power, it may be that nothing less than a real-life assessment of relative intensities of desire and ability to inflict costs on others will suffice. That assessment takes place in the marketplace of conflict.

This suggests a second, more procedural condition for the achievement of urban peace through accommodation and civility. Mechanisms and procedures must exist by which the conflicting desires and resources for bargaining can be brought together to produce a temporarily stable working arrangement. The accommodations of enforcement officials and deviants typically occur in a host of minor bargaining situations. Hassles are settled by the people immediately involved, and settled "on their own merits"— which is to say, in a way that respects the strength of everyone's feelings and the amount of trouble each is prepared to make to have his way. The culture of civility works well because the myriad of separate local bargains respect and reflect what most of the involved parties want or are willing to settle for.

We do not allow ourselves this extreme degree of decentralized decision-making with respect to many important problems (though many critics have suggested we should). Instead, we allow federal, state or city bureaucracies to make general policies that inhibit local accommodation. While government might well intervene when circumstances make bargaining positions unequal, we know now that it is not ordinarily well equipped to reach accommodative agreements that will work at the grass roots. Unable to know what the people who inhabit local areas will want and settle for, officials turn to technocrats for solutions.

Thus, when we confront the problem of slums and urban renewal, we send for the planner and the bulldozer. But the lives of urban residents are not determined by the number or newness of buildings. The character of their relationships with one another and with the outside world does that. Planners and technocrats typically ignore those relationships, and their influence in shaping what people want, in constructing solutions. They define "slums" impersonally, using such impersonal criteria as density or deterioration, and fail to see how awakened group consciousness can turn a "slum" into a "ghetto," and a rise in moral repute turn a "ghetto" into a "neighborhood."

Too often, the search for "model cities" implies not so much a model as an ideology—a rationalistic vision of human interaction that implies a people whose consistency of behavior can nowhere be found. We already have "model cities": Brasilia at the bureaucratic end and Levittown at the residential end. And in both instances, the force of human impulses had to break through the web of

Bruce Davidson MAGNUM

Michael Alexander

formal models to make these places inhabitable. In Brasilia the rise of shantytown dwellings outside the federal buildings made the place "a city," whereas the Levittowners had to break the middle-class mode and pass through a generation of conformity before they could produce a decent living arrangement. To design a city in conformity to "community standards"—which turn out to be little more than the prejudices of building inspectors, housing designers and absentee landlords—only reinforces patterns of frustration, violence and antagonism that now characterize so many of America's large cities. To think that the dismal failure of large housing projects will be resolved by their dismal replacement of small housing projects is nonsense. Minibuildings are no more of a solution than maxibuildings are the problem.

In any event, centralized planning operating in this way does not produce a mechanism through which the mutual desires, claims and threats of interested groups can sort themselves out and allow a *modus vivendi,* if one exists, to uncover itself. The centralized body makes bargains for everyone under its influence, without knowing their circumstances or wants, and so makes it impossible for the people involved to reach a stable accommodation. But centralized planning still remains a major solution proffered for urban problems of every kind.

Accommodations reached through the mechanism of old-fashioned city political machines work little better, for contemporary machines typically fail to encompass all the people whose interests are at stake. Richard Daley demonstrated that when the Chicago ghetto, supposedly solidly under his control, exploded and revealed some people his famed consensus had not included. Lyndon Johnson made the same discovery with respect to opponents of the Vietnam War. Insofar as centralized decision-making does not work, and interested parties are not allowed to make bargains at the local level, accommodative stability cannot occur.

So the example of San Francisco's handling of moral deviance may not provide the blueprint one would like for settling urban problems generally. Its requirements include a day-to-day working agreement among parties on the value of compromise and a procedure by which their immediate interests can be openly communicated and effectively adjusted. Those requirements are difficult to meet. Yet it may be that they are capable of being met in more places than we think, that even some of the knottier racial and political problems contain possibilities of accommodation, no more visible to us than the casual tolerance of deviance in San Francisco was thinkable to some of our prudish forebearers.

April 1970

The Respectable Criminal

Why some of our best friends are crooks

DONALD R. CRESSEY

Spring has returned, and with it two of the major themes of strategy in American life—how to win a baseball pennant and how to beat the income tax collector. Because as a sociologist I'm professionally interested in why people cheat, I'll leave theories about baseball to others.

At this time of year many of us toy with the idea of income tax evasion. Some succumb to the temptation. Those who do are not poor, culturally deprived slum dwellers. They do not like to think of themselves as "criminals." Tax evaders, along with people who pad their insurance claims, embezzle from their employers, or conspire with others to fix the price of goods usually have steady jobs and wear white collars to work. They are, nevertheless, committing what we call "respectable crimes." As recurrent newspaper headlines remind us, these are widespread forms of criminal behavior in our society. To develop a truly comprehensive theory of criminality we must learn more about why such men become violators of the law.

My own interest in "respectable crime" goes back to my days as a graduate student at Indiana University after World War II. My major professor, Edwin H. Sutherland, was conducting a study of the crimes committed by the 70 largest non-financial corporations in the U.S. He invented the concept of white-collar crime and encouraged criminologists, administrators of criminal justice, and laymen to re-examine the generalizations they had traditionally made about crime and criminals.

Sutherland's examination of the laws on certain kinds of business practices—such as restraint of trade, infringement of patents, false and misleading advertising, unfair labor practices—convinced him that these were indeed criminal laws. Violation of these laws is, accordingly, a crime; crimes of this sort must be included in any generalization about crimes and criminals. Sutherland found that the 70 largest corporations had about 980 decisions recorded against them for violation of four laws—an average of about 14 for each corporation. At the time of the study, the most popular criminological theories tended to link criminal behavior to social and personal pathologies of various kinds. Theoreticians emphasized poverty, poor education, broken homes, and psychological characteristics of criminals. The white-collar criminals that Sutherland had discovered, like the high officials of G.E. and Westinghouse who were convicted of conspiracy to fix prices in 1962, were persons of respectability and high social status who had committed crimes in connection with business. They did not fit the theoretical description. It followed that the theory would have to be revised to account for this type of criminality.

Sutherland's position was confused by the fact that he studied corporations, rather than individual white-collar criminals. I tried to correct this defect by making a study of embezzlers. It was my impression that embezzlers are white-collar criminals whose backgrounds are not likely to contain the social and personal pathologies which popular notions and traditional theory ascribe to criminals. Actually I doubt that these characteristics are in fact present in the background of *most* criminals. On the basis of my study, I *know* that they are almost never present in the background of embezzlers.

The Natural History of Embezzling

When I turned, as a first step, to the existing literature for an explanation of embezzling, I found that there was a basic confusion about the nature of this crime. Most books about embezzling are written by accountants—guides to businessmen to help them avoid embezzling in their own firms. Their major thesis is that weak internal controls and poor auditing systems cause defalcations by failing to eliminate the possibility of committing the crime.

While I must agree that a detailed check on all business transactions would prevent defalcations, I doubt whether these crimes can be "explained" by the absence of such checks. In the first place, even the most "foolproof" accounting procedures can never eliminate cheating entirely. The versatility of embezzlers is astounding, and greatly underestimated. In the second place, modern society presupposes business transactions based upon a considerable amount of trust. No matter what accounting system is used, an element of trust remains. A brief review of the history of embezzlement as a crime will make this point clear.

When commerce was beginning to expand in the 16th century, the legal rule regarding financial relations between master, servants, and third persons was simply this: (a) property received from the master remained in his possession, the servant having "mere charge or custody" of it; but (b) property received from a third person for the master *was* in the *servant's* possession, and he was not guilty of a felony if he converted it for his own use. As business expanded and "servants" became in fact clerks and cashiers, the situations in which the master retained possession were expanded. It became the rule that if a clerk placed money in a cash drawer, it thereby came into the possession of the master; if the servant subsequently took the money from the cash drawer to keep, this act was larceny. But until 1799, if a clerk received money from one of his employer's customers and *put it directly into his own pocket,* he had committed no crime; the money had not yet come into his employer's possession. Later that same year the first general embezzlement statute was passed in England. The new law covered "servants" but it did not cover "agents"; when in 1812 a stockbroker took money given to him to invest and converted it for his own uses, the court held that the general embezzlement law did not cover this act. New legislation to cover brokers, agents, etc., was passed almost immediately. Clearly, the common law of fraud and larceny had been sufficient for a relatively simple economy where there was no need to trust servants with business transactions. But with the growth of business firms in the 19th century, embezzlement statutes had to be invented to cover the new offenses which arose with the new economic structure.

Dependence upon trusted employees, agents, brokers, and factors has increased steadily since the passage of these first statutes. To argue that criminal violation of financial trust can be prevented by rigid accounting methods is to overlook the pertinent point: if strict controls were imposed on all trusted persons, embezzlement could be prevented, but very little business could be conducted. To remove "the temptation, the opportunity, and even the suggestion to violate the solemn trust which has been placed in officers and employees," as one accountant-author suggests, would eliminate both "solemn trust" and large numbers of business transactions.

Writers who are not accountants have an alternative explanation of embezzling; they blame it on the weakness, moral depravity, natural dishonesty, weak moral fibre, etc., of the violator. The trouble with explanations of this sort is that they are always after-the-fact. Such hidden variables can be said to cause almost any kind of behavior. They usually become evident only after a person has proved that he is "bad" by stealing from his employer. The notion that an evil result must have something evil as a cause is a fallacy.

In my own attempt to explain this kind of crime, I spent about a year at the Illinois State Penitentiary at Joliet interviewing embezzlers. I then moved to California and talked to some more embezzlers in the California State Institution for Men at Chino. I was also able to gather a considerable number of cases from other studies. But I was disturbed because my sample of embezzlers included very few bankers; this was because bank embezzlement is a federal offense and most of my interviews had been conducted in state prisons. So I spent a summer working in the United States Penitentiary in Terre Haute, Indiana. From these interviews I developed a generalization which I think can be applied to all the embezzlers I talked to. I see no good reason to believe that it does not apply to all embezzlers, although I realize that one should not generalize beyond his data.

The Compleat Cheater

What I came up with was the idea that embezzlement involves three essential kinds of psychological processes:
- the feeling that a personal financial problem is unshareable;
- the knowledge of how to solve the problem in secret, by violating a position of financial trust;
- the ability to find a formula which describes the act of embezzling in words which do not conflict with the image of oneself as a trusted person.

A man has an *unshareable financial problem* if it appears to him that he cannot turn to ordinary, legitimate sources for funds. To an outsider, the situation may not seem so dire; what matters is the psychological perspective of the potential embezzler. Recently I found an example of this state of mind in a newspaper letter to Ann Landers. The writer was a bookkeeper who had taken $75 from petty cash to pay some long-overdue personal bills. "I could have gone to my boss and received a loan for this amount with no trouble, but I had too much pride. My husband makes a small salary, and I was ashamed to admit we were having a difficult time financially." The writer, who signed herself "Ashamed," was paying the money back, but was terrified that she might succumb to the temptation again.

After I first formulated this unshareable problem notion, I tested it by asking a group of fifty embezzlers about an imaginary financial problem. I asked them to suppose that for some reason their fire insurance policy had lapsed and then, through no fault of their own, there was a short circuit in the wiring, or lightning struck, and their home burned down. The family lost everything they owned in the fire. My question was, "Do you think that in a situation like this you would have been tempted to embezzle to get the money you would need?" Sixty percent of the cases indicated clearly that this situation did not seem to them unshareable, and that therefore they would not embezzle. The reasoning is clear in responses like these:

Case 42. I don't believe I would. I think that in a case like that folks would have sympathized with me and helped me out. There would be outside aid. But in my own case, they didn't know about it and so they couldn't help.

Case 57. Well, I don't doubt that I would if I couldn't borrow the money or something of the sort. There are people or relatives that have money. I've never got along with them, but if it was a necessity like that I would go to them. I'd do anything to give my wife and children what they needed. (He indicated earlier that he had been too proud to go to his relatives for help at the time when he had embezzled.)

The second part of my generalization, the *realization* that the problem could be solved in secret by violating a trust, is a problem in the psychological perception of the opportunity to embezzle. Let me give just one statement, made by an embezzler (and former accountant), about the opportunity and techniques of embezzlement:

> In my case, I would have to say that I learned all of it in school and in my ordinary accounting experience. In school they teach you in your advanced years how to detect embezzlements, and you sort of absorb it. . . . It is just like a doctor performing abortions . . . I did not use any techniques which any ordinary accountant in my position could not have used; they are known by all accountants, just like the abortion technique is known by all doctors.

The third process in my generalization, *verbalization*, is the crux of the problem. I am convinced that the *words* that the potential embezzler uses in his conversation with himself are actually the most important elements in the process which gets him into trouble, or keeps him out of trouble. If he sees a possibility for embezzlement, it is because he has defined the relationship between the unshareable problem and an illegal solution in language that lets him look on trust violation as something other than trust violation. If he cannot do this, he does not become an embezzler.

To illustrate, let us suppose a man who is a pillar of the community, a respected, honest employee, a man with a background no more criminal than that of most of us. This man finds himself with an unshareable problem, and an objective opportunity to steal money from his company. The chances are very good that if in that situation I walked up to him and said, "Jack, steal the money from your boss," he would look at me in horror, as if I had suggested that he could solve his problem by going down and sticking a pistol into the face of the local cigar store owner. Honest and trusted men "just don't do such things." However, honest and trusted men do "borrow," and if he tells himself that he is borrowing the money he can continue to believe that he is an honest citizen, even as he is stealing the boss blind. Since he wants to remain an honest citizen, the "borrowing" verbalization becomes the key to his dishonest conduct.

I do not wish to overemphasize the idea of "borrowing." There are many verbalizations used, some of them quite complex. The "borrowing" verbalization is simply an example of a vocabulary that can adjust two contradictory roles—the role of an honest man and the role of a crook. I call the use of such a vocabulary a rationalization, which is different from the way psychoanalysts use the term. Let me give an illustration of rationalization that does *not* involve a dishonest role:

Suppose a Dean who is swamped with work in his university is invited to speak at a seminar of businessmen. He might at first feel he should decline the invitation, on the ground that he doesn't have the time, or he has to get the budget in, or he has to finish writing his book. But then suppose he says to himself, "A Dean should get out of the ivory tower now and then," or "Theoretical knowledge is no good unless it is passed on to practical men." *Now* he can accept the invitation, and does.

Vocabularies of motive are not something invented by embezzlers (or anyone else) on the spur of the moment. Before they can be taken over by an individual, these verbalizations exist as group definitions in which the behavior in question, even crime, is in a sense *appropriate*. There are any number of popular ideologies that sanction crime in our culture: "Honesty is the best policy, but business is business"; "It is all right to steal a loaf of bread when you are starving"; "All people steal when they get in a tight spot"; Once these verbalizations have been assimilated and internalized by individuals, they take a form such as: "I'm only going to use the money temporarily, so I am borrowing, not stealing," or "I have tried to live an honest life but I've had nothing but troubles, so to hell with it."

If my generalization about the psychological elements of embezzling is valid, it should have ramifications for crime prevention. Some change in prevention techniques is clearly necessary, for the embezzlement rate in the United States is on the rise. Increasingly complex business organizations need larger proportions of "trusted employees." Business procedures are becoming so involved that the whole fabric of an enterprise depends more and more upon men who have been given independent control over some segment of the enterprise. At the same time, studies of professional and technical workers indicate that many are dissatisfied with their jobs. These disgruntled employees are potential embezzlers.

It follows from my generalization that embezzling can be effectively blocked either at the unshareable problem point or at the verbalization point.

■ Trust violation rates might be reduced by eliminating some of the unshareable problems among employees. This means development of company programs so that employees have fewer financial problems and/or feel that they can share their financial problems with their employer. Wherever a company program solves a financial problem, or makes it shareable, embezzlement will not occur.

■ Companies could introduce educational programs that emphasize how trust violators commonly use verbalizations. These programs would make it increasingly difficult for trusted employees to think of themselves as "borrowers" rather than "thieves" when they take the boss's money. It is highly probable that our current practices in this regard actually encourage embezzlement. We tend to emphasize the notion that embezzlers are people who are the victims of "wine, women, and wagering." Because this lore is so popular, a person with an unshareable problem who is not gambling, drinking, or running around with women can easily think of himself as a nonembezzler who is simply "borrowing." What I am proposing is an educational program in which we say over and over again that a person who "pilfers" or "taps the till" or "borrows" or who is guilty of "defalcation," "peculation," or some other nice term is, in fact, a crook. And if the trusted employee rejects the notion of himself as a crook (and as a "respectable" type, he must), he will also reject the possibility of embezzling.

Crime as Business Policy

The generalization I have developed here was made to fit only one crime—embezzling. But I suspect that the verbalization section of the generalization will fit other types of respectable crime as well. There is a study of crimes among New England shoe manufacturers that supports this notion. In the eight New England communities studied, there were wide variations in the number of shoe firms violating labor relations laws. In Haverhill, Massachusetts, for example, 7 percent of the shoe firms violated these laws, while in Auburn, Maine, 44 percent violated them. The author, Robert E. Lane, concluded that one of the reasons for the differences among the towns was differences in "attitudes toward the law, the government, and the morality of illegality." Those shoe manufacturers who associated with men whose attitudes favored violation were more likely to break the law; those manufacturers who were isolated from these attitudes were less likely to break the law. This influence on attitudes was evident even in the reading habits of these men; those who had violated the law had immersed themselves in a segment of the daily press so hostile to government that violation of the law seemed quite appropriate to them. Here, even the newspapers were providing verbalizations that made crime "all right." Lane predicted, on the basis of such observations, that managers of companies located in bigger cities, with a cosmopolitan press, diversified social life, and greater tolerance for heterodoxy, would accept legal restrictions on how they conducted their businesses more readily than would small town management. This prediction was borne out; firms located in small towns violated the laws much more frequently than did similar firms located in larger cities. The small town atmosphere provided a rationale to justify this particular crime; (government shouldn't tell a man how to run his business; "that man" in Washington is no good anyway; labor unions are corrupt). The bigger cities did not provide this justification. Another study, by Marshall B. Clinard, analyzed O.P.A. violations during World War II and concluded that businessmen violated the regulations simply because they did not "believe in" them.

The G.E. and Westinghouse officials must have had a formula that made their conspiracy to fix the price of electrical equipment something other than a crime. Perhaps it was a generalized dislike of government regulation of business; perhaps they had convinced themselves that no one really abides by the Sherman Anti-trust Act anyway and that, like the prohibition amendment, it could be transgressed without any stigma of criminality. And surely all the income tax evaders do not see themselves as stealing money from the U.S. Treasury—to them the government may seem so rich that "they'll never miss it" or the intricate tax laws may seem a kind of game that allows an advantage to the shrewd player.

But whether the stakes are high or low, whether the financial game is played by an individual or a conspiring group, an aura of personal respectability does not erase (though it may temporarily obscure), the act of a criminal.

March-April 1965

READINGS–WHITE COLLAR CRIME

The Thief in the White Collar by Norman Jaspan and Hillel Black (New York: Lippincott, 1960). An analysis of the nature and causes of embezzling.

White Collar Criminal: The Offender in Business and the Professions edited by Gilbert Geis (New York: Atherton Press, 1968) is a useful collection of 32 articles. Sutherland and Ross are represented as well as some British social scientists.

White Collar Crime by Edwin H. Sutherland (New York: Holt, Reinhart and Winston, 1949). The seminal work in the field, this book has had an extremely important impact on criminological thought.

"Techniques of Neutralization" by Gresham M. Sykes and David Matza, *American Journal of Sociology* (Vol. 22, Dec. 1957). An interesting and important article that describes different techniques that juvenile delinquents use to rationalize their illegal and immoral behavior.

Other People's Money by Donald R. Cressey (Glencoe, Ill.: Free Press, 1953). A social psychological study of embezzling with interesting sections on the techniques embezzlers use to rationalize their acts.

"Social Structure and Anomie" in *Social Theory and Social Structure,* by Robert K. Merton (New York: The Free Press, 1957). Classic essay on the social structural sources of deviant behavior.

The Sane Society by Erich Fromm (New York: Rinehart, 1955). Details the disorganization in contemporary society and its impact on the individual personality.

Theft of a Nation by Donald R. Cressey (New York: Harper & Row, 1969). Organized crime in America.

Deviance: The Interactionist Perspective edited by Earl Rubington and Martin S. Weinberg (New York: Macmillan, 1968).

The Crime Problem, by Walter C. Reckless (New York: Appleton-Century-Crofts, 1961).

Crime and Society by Gresham M. Sykes (New York: Random House, 1956).

Crime, Correction and Society by Elmer H. Johnson (Homewood, Illinois: Dorsey Press, 1968).

The Sociology of Punishment and Correction edited by Norman Johnson, Leonard Savitz and Martin E. Wolfgang (New York: Wiley, 1962).

Principles of Criminology by Edwin H. Sutherland & Donald R. Cressey (Philadelphia: Lippincott, 1966).

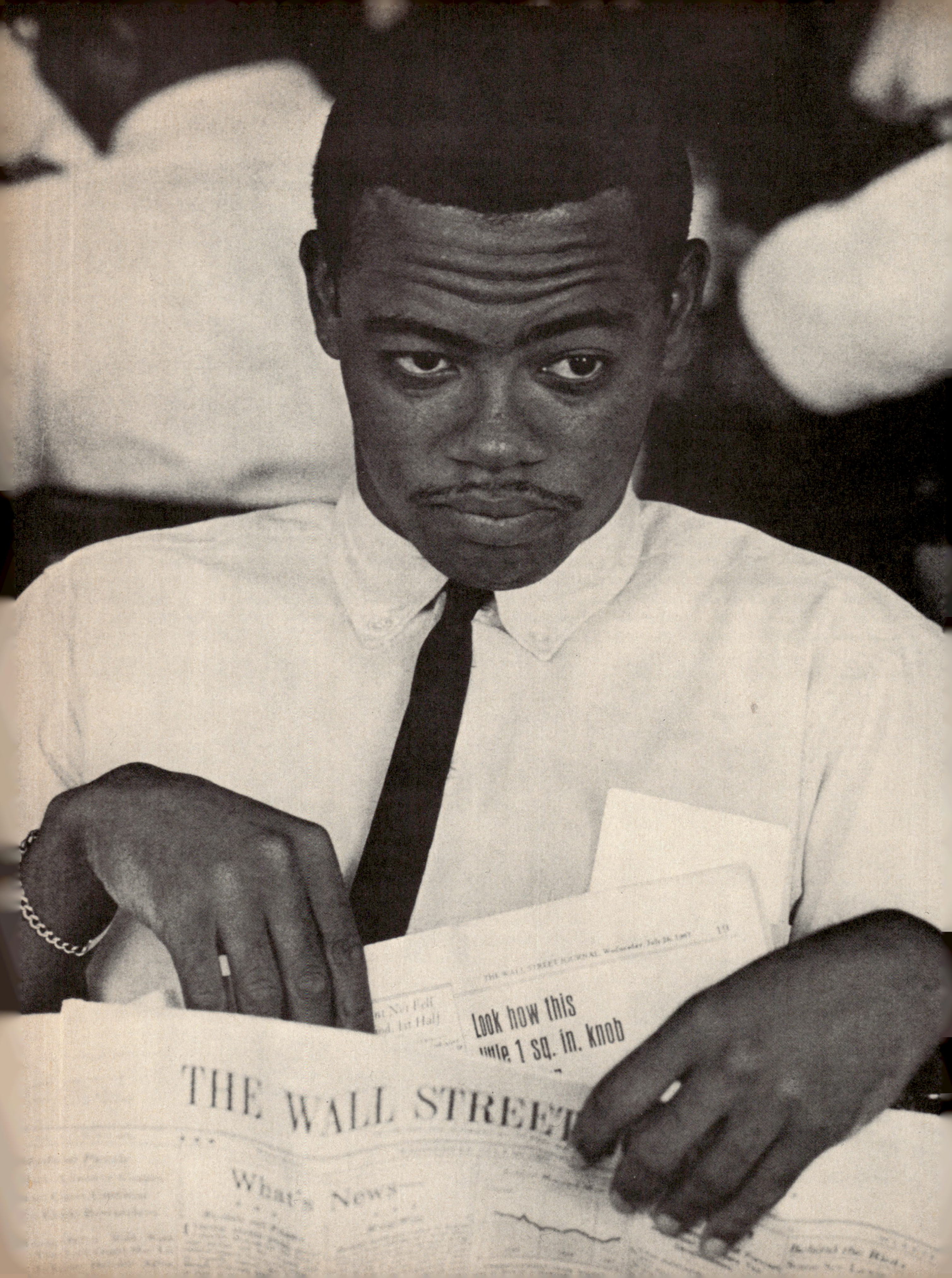
Look how this
little 1 sq. in. knob
THE WALL STREET
What's News

4 Social Stratification & Equality

In all societies distinctions are made between one individual and another based on social, economic, or biological differences. People recognize others as their equals, superiors, or inferiors, and they rank individuals and groups in a hierarchy of distinctions they consider important. Although the American democratic way is supposed to embody the Jeffersonian assertion that "all men are created equal," few of us accept all other Americans as social equals. Most of us learn at quite an early age to recognize the material and behavioral signs that set off people of prestige, power, wealth, and influence from those of lower rank. As much as we might decry the injustice of judging people on unworthy, surface criteria rather than on qualities of character alone, we see the class, racial, and ethnic structures of society constantly in evidence. As a consequence we recognize that individuals higher on the scale have access to greater amounts of the desirable goods of the system. Indeed, the vocabulary of social status is among the richest in the language: VIP, big shot, snob, average guy, GI Joe, Main Street America, and Skid Row bum. People therefore understand that differences exist in opportunities and in objectives, and as a result they rank people accordingly.

In addition to the vocabulary of status, we recognize patterns of behavior that are responsive and peculiar to status difference. People are respectful, even obsequious, around influential people, and these people in turn can be observed treating those of lower standing discourteously and rudely. Friction occurs when social inferiors respond in an unexpectedly cool or hostile manner. Although Americans do not literally prostrate themselves before their superiors as do Muslims before the Sultan of Sokoto, they acknowledge by their daily behavior that social positions are precisely ranked in modern industrial society and that deference and privileges are due according to the attributes deemed important.

Even at death, people of various social positions are treated in different ways which are not related to medical diagnosis. Nurses and interns in emergency wards of two hospitals studied by David Sudnow in "Dead on Arrival" tailor their resuscitation efforts on behalf of dying patients to the person's assumed social value. They mobilize special procedures for saving middle-class persons whereas the down-and-outer is treated routinely. "If one anticipates a critical heart attack, he had best keep himself well-dressed and his breath clear," advises a hospital employee. Similarly, in "The Tipped Scales of American Justice" Stuart S. Nagel investigates the proposition that "there can be no equal justice where the kind of trial a man gets depends on the amount of money he has." Nagel finds that there are disparities in criminal procedure treatment for the poor, blacks, and the less educated that result in their receiving unequal treatment when charged with serious crimes of felonious assault and grand larceny.

These two articles contain evidence that there are perceptions by others that some people are less worthy than others and that different attitudes and actions are legitimately expressed toward them.

What is it about human society that causes this social ranking process? Is it possible to have a society of equals—the classless society dreamed about by those who hold an equalitarian ideal? The study of social stratification considers these questions in its analysis of the structure of historical and modern societies. It seeks to understand the basis of power and privilege and the concomitant powerlessness and subservience of various groups.

Social class is a concept for explaining the emergence of stratified societies of many different forms. Karl Marx focused on the class structure of the nineteenth-century industrial nation as the perspective for explaining the rise of capitalism and the likelihood of revolutionary change. Class refers to a social group having the same economic position in society who act in a roughly similar way with important consequences for the society as a whole. The upper, middle, and lower class, for instance, have been viewed as resulting from the economic organization of societies and the division of labor. More recently emphasis has been placed on occupation as a basis for class position rather than the ownership of property solely. It seems self-evident that economic assets are highly significant in the system of stratification. Our expression is "money talks." One question to pose is how groups got into the position of controlling economic resources and perpetuating control over them.

Does wealth alone secure upper-class position? Some perspectives on the class structure suggest there are important noneconomic factors in class formation. Part of the ability of the privileged to perpetuate their position lies outside simply being rich. According to Max Weber—like Marx, a German sociologist of the late nineteenth century—social class also depends on status position which may be inherited or ascribed, according to the values of a particular society. People can gain high status through their professional accomplishments; in other words, they can achieve status even though their material wealth is not equivalent to their achievement in their occupation. For instance, one way to secure high status in a religious society is to become a priest and make a career in the church hierarchy. Joseph Bensman in "Classical Music and the Status Game" pictures the social life of classical musicians as an example of how circles of celebrities become status groups and gain a recognized high place in society.

Status and Power

As with artists, life style is significant for the definition of other social classes. Members of the working class, for instance, may have taken on some surface similarities to those of the middle class by their spending patterns for hard goods, but they have retained a basic working-class outlook in behavior and attitudes in most areas of their lives, according to Gerald Handel and Lee Rainwater in "The Working Classes—Old and New."

Power is another dimension of stratification that contributes to the hierarchical ranking of groups in society. Power is the capacity to control the action of others, to make them do things or not do things, even against their wishes. The three dimensions of stratification—economic class, social status, and power—are interrelated and support one another in a ratio of importance that probably varies from society to society.

Because the state possesses the legal monopoly of force in most countries, we might assume that power is possessed only by political groups and government. This is not the case. There is a close intertwining of political institutions and

Social Stratification & Equality

the agencies of government—its army, police force, legal, and administrative officials—with the social-class structure and the status hierarchy. Ander Boserup examines in "The Politics of Protracted Conflict" the interlocking relationship of power holders in Northern Ireland and how the landed aristocracy, the local industrial and commercial classes, and the foreign-controlled economic interests exploit the Catholic-Protestant religious divisions to uphold the political system. In matters of governing states and conserving or changing modern social institutions, all three dimensions come into play, but the facts of class and power are on the whole more significant than those of status.

Class and Caste

The class, status, and power mix distinguishes societies from each other. In some, class and status lines are very sharply drawn, whereas others have somewhat fluid boundaries. Most industrial societies are characterized by relatively open class systems in which some individual members can change their status through upward or downward mobility. In closed stratification systems, individual mobility is much more limited. Individual achievement is recognized and rewarded in open societies, whereas in closed societies for the most part the characteristics inherited from the family or group at birth establish a person's position in life.

These two types of stratified societies are usually referred to as class and caste systems. India comes immediately to mind as an example of a caste system, whereas the United States, Canada, and Great Britain are nations usually regarded as open societies. The articles that follow, however, draw attention to castelike features within such societies.

While what are called "open societies" allow some individuals to move up in position through achievement, they prevent others from doing so on account of birth, such as race, religion, and foreign origin. Black Americans, for example, are blocked from full participation in the social and economic life of the United States. An article by David Boesel and his research associates "White Institutions and Black Rage"—which was based on studies in fifteen northern cities done for the Kerner Commission studying riots in American cities—describes the organized means used by white society to keep blacks in an undercaste. North American Indians are also treated as a distinct population and excluded from participation in the so-called open society. A. D. Fisher, "White Rites Versus Indian Rights," shows how expanded educational opportunities for Canadian Indians fail to provide appropriate training for cultural values and to confine them, on the basis of race, to the lowest rungs of society. In "Outsiders in Britain" Peter I. Rose shows that colored immigrants to England from the Commonwealth face hostility and discrimination on two counts—their racial differences and their alien customs.

Despite some castelike penalties against minorities, most modern industrial societies have fluid and vaguely defined class and status lines for many of their citizens. Chances for upward mobility coupled with an equalitarian ideology exist alongside definite differences in inherited status, income, life chances, and life styles. In American society, occupation is a major determinant of status, since it contributes not only a particular income level, but also makes possible a standard of living, a life style, and a group of fellow workers and neighbors that in time affect status. For an occupational struc-

Social Stratification & Equality

ture requiring training and skills, access to education and the desire to achieve are necessary for an individual to succeed in a job. By spending time in college rather than working at an early age, an individual's total life income from his occupation is greatly increased.

Class position of a family is correlated with the financial ability to postpone earnings during late adolescence and early adulthood, the differential quality of public education available, the family stress on achievement, and other factors. Lack of mobility may cut off avenues for advancement for many workers permanently. In an article on "America's New Officers Corps" Charles H. Coates shows that military careers have become one of the primary avenues to upward mobility for the less privileged. At the same time, education of limited groups, the less privileged, can estrange them from their own people and fail to fit them into a viable new way of life. "Seminole Girl" by Merwyn S. Garbarino is the autobiography of an Indian woman whose goal to help her own people was thwarted rather than helped by her college education.

Equality and Justice

In societies heavily dominated by the caste system, a stable and secure place is provided for everyone, since the important relationships between people and groups are clearly defined. But in achievement-oriented societies both upward and downward mobility occur and require adjustment that many men find difficult to make. Measured against the full range of opportunities available, some individuals and groups are unable to make the grade. The pressure to maintain status and the fear of failure in a competitive social order cause some groups, like the lower-middle classes and working class to lash out against other vulnerable groups—a phenomenon known as "backlash." In his article on the Haymarket riot, "Genteel Backlash: Chicago 1886," Richard Sennett describes such a group of forgotten men.

In the raging controversies concerning the foundations of stratification—that is, whether social stratification is fixed in human nature, or simply a consequence of a special social system like feudalism or capitalism—what must be appreciated is that patterns of stratification do, in fact, change, and that tendencies either toward or away from greater social equality arise in certain socioeconomic systems. Too often in the past, theorists have spoken of stratification and egalitarianism as a choice between the inevitable and the impossible. Sociology has intended to eschew such reification and polarization. Rather, it has shown how changes over time have tended either to advance or retard the cause of equity and justice for all men. While it is true that every program of revolutionary change falls drastically short of the egalitarian and antistratification goals it sets for itself, it is nonetheless the case that men have inched closer to goals of being treated as equals and away from assumptions that differences in class, caste, and race are automatic grounds for divisions between men according to wealth and property. In short, whatever the biological grounds of difference among men, the work of students of social stratification has undermined the idea that such difference is itself grounds for justifying conditions of superiority and inferiority. In this way, studies in social stratification have contributed to the advancement of modern theories of democracy.

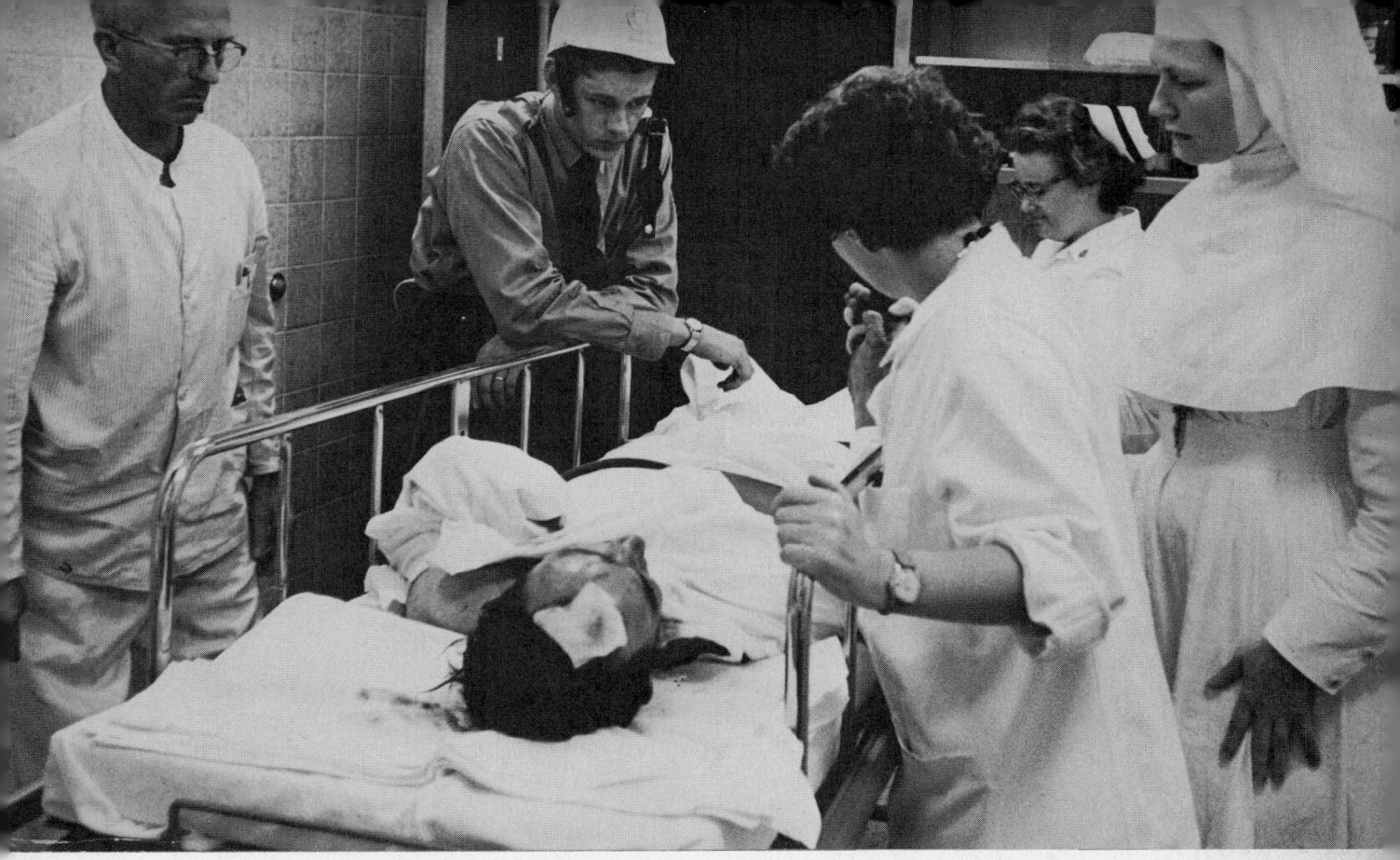

Michel Lambeth

Dead on Arrival

Resuscitation efforts—and the uses of a corpse—may depend on social factors, not medical diagnosis

DAVID SUDNOW

In County Hospital's emergency ward, the most frequent variety of death is what is known as the "DOA" type. Approximately 40 such cases are processed through this division of the hospital each month. The designation "DOA" is somewhat ambiguous insofar as many persons are not physiologically *dead on arrival*, but are nonetheless classified as having been such. A person who dies within several hours after having been brought to the hospital might, if upon arrival he was initially announced by the ambulance driver to be dead, retain such a classification at the time he is so pronounced by the physician.

When an ambulance driver suspects that the person he is carrying is dead, he signals the emergency ward with a special siren alarm as he approaches the entrance driveway. As he wheels his stretcher past the clerk's desk, he restates his suspicion with the remark, "possible," a shorthand reference for "possible DOA." (The use of the term *possi-*

ble is required by law, which insists, primarily for insurance purposes, that any diagnosis unless made by a certified physician be so qualified.) The clerk records the arrival in a log book and pages a physician, informing him in code of the arrival. Often a page is not needed, as physicians on duty hear the siren alarm, expect the arrival, and wait at the entranceway. The patient is rapidly wheeled to the far end of the ward corridor and into the nearest available foyer or room, supposedly out of sight of other patients and possible onlookers from the waiting room. The physician arrives, makes his examination, and pronounces the patient dead or not. If the patient is dead, a nurse phones the coroner's office, which is legally responsible for the removal and investigation of all DOA cases.

Neither the hospital nor the physician has medical responsibility in such cases. In many instances of clear death, ambulance drivers use the hospital as a depository because

CLASS AND CASTE

it has the advantages of being both closer and less bureaucratically complicated a place than the downtown coroner's office for disposing of a body. Here, the hospital stands as a temporary holding station, rendering the community service of legitimate and free pronouncements of death for any comers. In circumstances of near-death, it functions more traditionally as a medical institution, mobilizing life-saving procedures for those for whom they are still of potential value, at least as judged by the emergency room's staff of residents and interns. The boundaries between near-death and sure death are not, however, as we shall shortly see, altogether clearly defined.

In nearly all DOA cases the pronouncing physician (commonly that physician who is the first to answer the clerk's page or spot the incoming ambulance) shows in his general demeanor and approach to the task little more than passing interest in the event's possible occurrence and the patient's biographical and medical circumstances. He responds to the clerk's call, conducts his examination, and leaves the room once he has made the necessary official gesture to an attending nurse. (The term "kaput," murmured in differing degrees of audibility depending upon the hour and his state of awakeness, is a frequently employed announcement.) It happened on numerous occasions, especially during the midnight-to-eight shift, that a physician was interrupted during a coffee break to pronounce a DOA and returned to his colleagues in the canteen with, as an account of his absence, some version of "Oh, it was nothing but a DOA."

It is interesting to note that, while the special siren alarm is intended to mobilize quick response on the part of the emergency room staff, it occasionally operates in the opposite fashion. Some emergency room staff came to regard the fact of a DOA as decided in advance; they exhibited a degree of nonchalance in answering the siren or page, taking it that the "possible DOA" most likely is "D." In so doing they in effect gave authorization to the ambulance driver to make such assessments. Given that time lapse which sometimes occurs between that point at which the doctor knows of the arrival and the time he gets to the patient's side, it is not inconceivable that in several instances patients who might have been revived died during this interim. This is particularly likely in that, apparently, a matter of moments may differentiate the revivable state from the irreversible one.

Who Are the 'Dead'?

Two persons in similar physical condition may be differentially designated dead or not. For example, a young child was brought into the emergency room with no registering heartbeat, respirations, or pulse—the standard "signs of death"—and was, through a rather dramatic stimulation procedure involving the coordinated work of a large team of doctors and nurses, revived for a period of eleven hours. On the same evening, shortly after the child's arrival, an elderly person who presented the same physical signs, with —as one physician later stated in conversation—no discernible differences from the child in skin color, warmth, etc., arrived in the emergency room and was almost immediately pronounced dead, with no attempts at stimulation instituted. A nurse remarked, later in the evening: "They (the doctors) would never have done that to the old lady (attempt heart stimulation) even though I've seen it work on them too." During the period when emergency resuscitation equipment was being readied for the child, an intern instituted mouth-to-mouth resuscitation. This same intern was shortly relieved by oxygen machinery, and when the woman arrived, he was the one who pronounced her dead. He reported shortly afterwards that he could never bring himself to put his mouth to "an old lady's like that."

It is therefore important to note that the category DOA is not totally homogeneous with respect to actual physiological condition. The same is generally true of all deaths, the determination of *death* involving, as it does, a critical decision, at least in its earlier stages.

There is currently a movement in progress in some medical and lay circles to undercut the traditional distinction between "biological" and "clinical" death, and procedures are being developed and their use encouraged for treating any "clinically dead" person as potentially revivable.

A NOTE ON THE STUDY

David Sudnow collected his data on the social organization of hospitals—the major setting of dying in our society—by intensive observation at two major medical institutions, which he calls "County" and "Cohen" hospitals. He spent nearly the entire work week for nine months at County Hospital, a large charitable establishment in a West Coast urban center, and five months at Cohen, a private general hospital in the Midwest, for comparative study. The two institutions were of similar large size, but differed in the social class compositions of their patient populations. County was a lower class establishment and Cohen Hospital middle class. Sudnow reports:

In both settings, in the role of a "nonparticipant observer," I have sought to get close to occasions of "dying" and "death," record what transpires in the behavior of staff members of the institutions on such occasions, and analyze some of the general features of that behavior. My central effort has been to locate "death" and "dying" as organizationally relevant events, conceive of their handling as governed by the practically organized work considerations of hospital personnel and ward social organization, and sketch out certain themes which appear to bring together a set of observed facts about social practices relating to "dying" and "death."

The study was done for a doctoral dissertation in sociology at the University of California, Berkeley. This article is adapted from the "Death, Uses of a Corpse, and Social Worth" and "Overview" sections of the resulting book, *Passing On: The Social Organization of Dying,* © 1967. Reprinted by permission of Prentice-Hall, Inc., Englewood Cliffs, New Jersey.

Should such a movement gain widespread momentum (and it, unlike late 19th-century arguments for life after death, is legitimated by modern medical thinking and technology), it would foreseeably have considerable consequence for certain aspects of hospital social structure, requiring perhaps that much more continuous and intensive care be given "dying" and "dead" patients than is presently accorded them, at least at County. (At Cohen Hospital, where the care of the "tentatively dead" is always very intensive, such developments would more likely be encouraged than at County.)

Currently at County there seems to be a rather strong relationship between the age, social background, and the perceived moral character of patients and the amount of effort that is made to attempt revival when "clinical death signs" are detected (and, for that matter, the amount of effort given to forestalling their appearance in the first place). As one compares practices in this regard at different hospitals, the general relationship seems to hold; although at the private, wealthier institutions like Cohen the overall amount of attention given to "initially dead" patients is greater. At County efforts at revival are admittedly superficial, with the exception of the very young or occasionally wealthier patient who by some accident ends up at County's emergency room. No instances have been witnessed at County where, for example, external heart massage was given a patient whose heart was stethoscopically inaudible, if that patient was over 40 years of age. At Cohen Hospital, on the other hand, heart massage is a normal routine at that point, and more drastic measures, such as the injection of Adrenalin directly into the heart, are not uncommon. While these practices are undertaken for many patients at Cohen if "tentative death" is discovered early (and it typically is because of the attention "dying" patients are given), at County they are reserved for a very special class of cases.

Generally speaking, the older the patient the more likely is his tentative death taken to constitute pronounceable death. Suppose a 20-year-old arrives in the emergency room and is presumed to be dead because of the ambulance driver's assessment. Before that patient will be pronounced dead by a physician, extended listening to his heartbeat will occur, occasionally efforts at stimulation will be made, oxygen administered, and often stimulative medication given. Less time will elapse between initial detection of an inaudible heartbeat and nonpalpitating pulse and the pronouncement of death if the person is 40 years old, and still less if he is 70. As best as can be detected, there appeared to be no obvious difference between men and women in this regard, nor between white and Negro patients. Very old patients who are initially considered to be dead solely on the basis of the ambulance driver's assessment of that possibility were seen to be put in an empty room to wait several moments before a physician arrived. The driver's announcement of a "possible" places a frame of interpretation around the event, so that the physician expects to find a dead person and attends the person under the general auspices of that expectation. When a young person is brought in as a "possible," the driver tries to convey some more alarming sense to his arrival by turning the siren up very loud and keeping it going after he has already stopped, so that by the time he has actually entered the wing, personnel, expecting "something special," act quickly and accordingly. When it is a younger person that the driver is delivering, his general manner is more frantic. The speed with which he wheels his stretcher in and the degree of excitement in his voice as he describes his charge to the desk clerk are generally more heightened than with the typical elderly DOA. One can observe a

---

"The older the person, the less thorough the examination; frequently elderly people are pronounced dead on the basis of only a stethoscopic examination of the heart."

---

direct relationship between the loudness and length of the siren alarm and the considered "social value" of the person being transported.

The older the person, the less thorough is the examination he is given; frequently, elderly people are pronounced dead on the basis of only a stethoscopic examination of the heart. The younger the person, the more likely will an examination preceding an announcement of death entail an inspection of the eyes, attempt to find a pulse, touching of the body for coldness, etc. When a younger person is brought to the hospital and announced by the driver as a "possible" but is nonetheless observed to be breathing slightly, or have an audible heart beat, there is a fast mobilization of effort to stimulate increased breathing and a more rapid heartbeat. If an older person is brought in in a similar condition there will be a rapid mobilization of similar efforts; however, the time which will elapse between that point at which breathing noticeably ceases and the heart audibly stops beating and when the pronouncement of death is made will differ according to his age.

Emergency Care and Social Worth

One's location in the age structure of the society is not the only factor that will influence the degree of care he gets when his death is considered possibly to have occurred. At County Hospital a notable additional set of considerations relating to the patient's presumed "moral character" is made to apply.

The smell of alcohol on the breath of a "possible" is nearly always noticed by the examining physician, who announces to his fellow workers that the person is a drunk. This seems to constitute a feature he regards as warranting less than strenuous effort to attempt revival. The alcoholic patient is treated by hospital physicians, not only when the status of his body as alive or dead is at stake, but throughout the whole course of medical treatment, as one for whom the concern to treat can properly operate somewhat weakly. There is a high proportion of alcoholic patients at County, and their treatment very often involves an earlier admission of "terminality" and a consequently more marked suspension of curative treatment than is observed in the treatment of nonalcoholic patients. In one case, the decision whether or not to administer additional blood needed by an alcoholic man bleeding badly from a stomach ulcer was decided negatively, and that decision was announced as based on the fact of his alcoholism. The intern in charge of treating the patient was asked by a nurse, "Should we order more blood for this afternoon?" and the doctor answered, "I can't see any sense in pumping it into him because even if we can stop the bleeding, he'll turn around and start drinking again and next week he'll be back needing more blood." In the DOA circumstance, alcoholic patients have been known to be pronounced dead on the basis of a stethoscopic examination of the heart alone, even though such persons were of such an age that were they not alcoholics they would likely have received much more intensive consideration before being so decided upon. Among other categories of persons whose deaths will be more quickly adjudged, and whose "dying" more readily noticed and used as a rationale for apathetic care, are the suicide victim, the dope addict, the known prostitute, the

---

"If one anticipates a critical heart attack, he had best keep himself well-dressed and his breath clean if there is a likelihood he will be brought into County as a 'possible.'"

---

assailant in a crime of violence, the vagrant, the known wife-beater, and, generally, those persons whose moral characters are considered reproachable.

Within a limited temporal perspective at least, but one which is not necessarily to be regarded as trivial, the likelihood of "dying" and even of being "dead" can be said to be partially a function of one's place in the social structure, and not simply in the sense that the wealthier get better care, or at least not in the usual sense of that fact. If one anticipates having a critical heart attack, he had best keep himself well-dressed and his breath clean if there is a likelihood he will be brought into County as a "possible."

The DOA deaths of famous persons are reportedly attended with considerably prolonged and intensive resuscitation efforts. In President Kennedy's death, for example, *The New York Times* (Nov. 23, 1963) quoted an attending physician as saying:

Medically, it was apparent the President was not alive when he was brought in. There was no spontaneous respiration. He had dilated, fixed pupils. It was obviously a lethal head wound. Technically, however, by using vigorous resuscitation, intravenous tubes and all the usual supportive measures, we were able to raise the semblance of a heart beat.

The Uses of a Corpse

There are a series of practical consequences of pronouncing a patient dead in the hospital setting. His body may properly be stripped of clothing, jewelry, and the like, wrapped up for discharge, the family notified of the death, and the coroner informed in the case of DOA deaths. In the emergency unit there is a special set of procedures which can be said to be partially definitive of death. DOA cases are very interestingly "used" in many American hospitals. The inflow of dead bodies, or what can properly be taken to be dead bodies, is regarded as a collection of "guinea pigs," in the sense that procedures can be performed upon those bodies for the sake of teaching and research.

In any "teaching hospital" (in the case of County, I use that term in a weak sense, that is, a hospital which employs interns and residents; in other settings a "teaching hospital" may mean systematic, institutionalized instruction) the environment of medical events is regarded not merely as a collection of treatable cases, but as a collection of experience-relevant information. It is a continually enforced way of looking at the cases one treats to regard them under the auspices of a concern for experience with "such cases." That concern can legitimately warrant the institution of a variety of procedures, tests, and inquiries which lie outside and may even on occasion conflict with the strict interests of treatment; they fall within the interests of "learning medicine," gaining experience with such cases, and acquiring technical skills.

A principle for organizing medical care activities in the teaching hospital generally—and perhaps more so in the county hospital, where patients' social value is often not highly regarded—is the relevance of any particular activity to the acquisition of skills of general import. Physicians feel that among the greatest values of such institutions is the ease with which medical attention can be selectively organized to maximize the general benefits to knowledge and technical proficiency which working with a given case expectably affords. The notion of the "interesting case" is, at County, not simply a casual notion but an enforced principle for the allocation of attention. The private physician is in a more committed relation to each and every one of his patients; and while he may regard this or that case as more or less interesting, he ideally cannot legitimate his varying interest in his patients' conditions as a basis for devoting varying amounts of attention to them. (His reward for treating the uninteresting case is, of course, the fee, and physicians are known to give more attention to those of their patients who shall be paying more.)

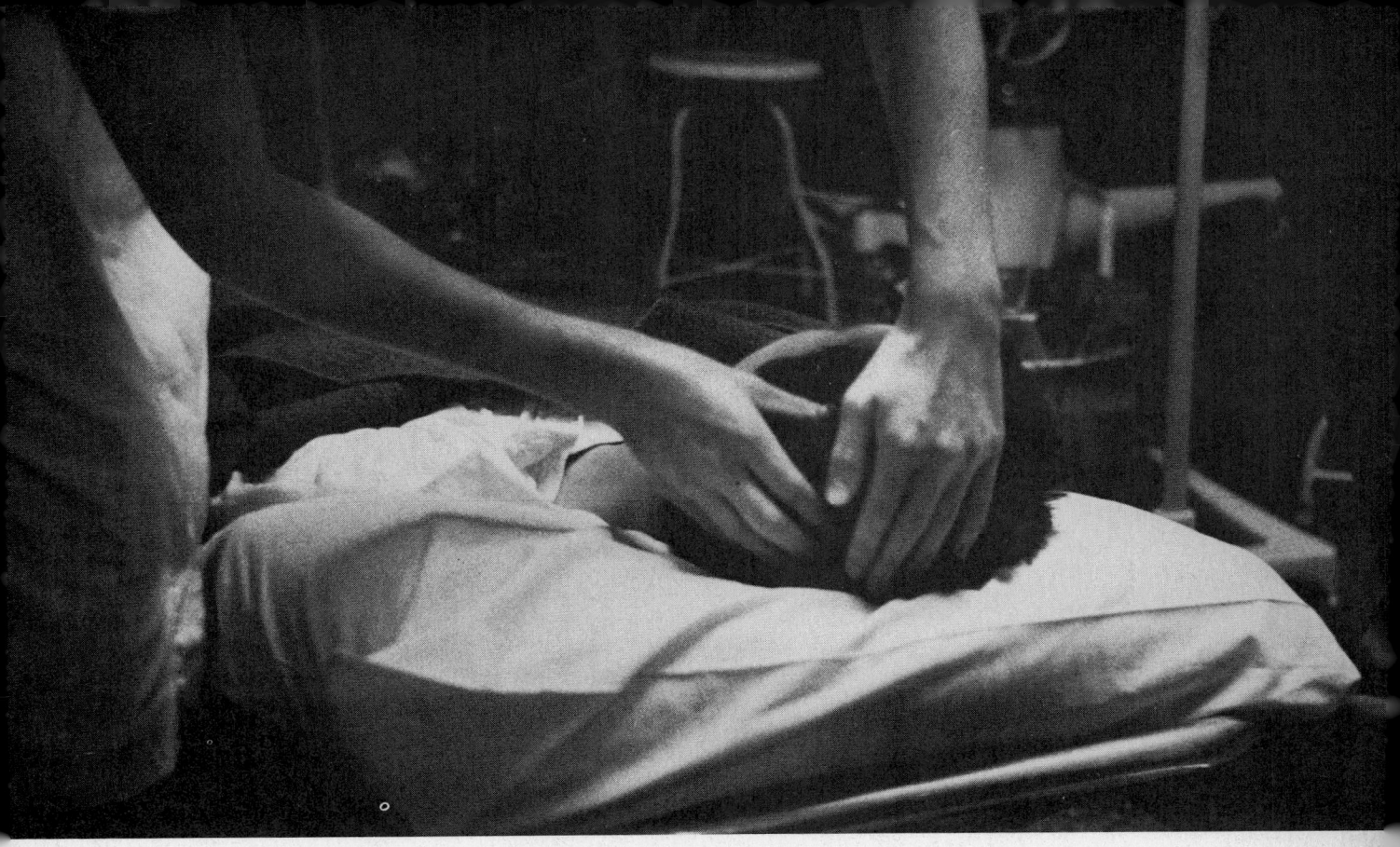

Apparently the attention a patient receives at a hospital may depend on the unusualness of his problems.

At County Hospital a case's degree of interest is a crucial fact, and one which is invoked to legitimate the way a physician does and should allocate his attention. In surgery, for instance, I found many examples. If on a given morning in one operating room a "rare" procedure was scheduled and in another a "usual" procedure planned, there would be no special difficulty in getting personnel to witness and partake in the rare procedure, whereas work in the usual case was considered as merely work, regardless of such considerations as the relative fatality rate of each procedure or the patient's physical condition. It is not uncommon to find interns at County who are scrubbed for an appendectomy taking turns going next door to watch a skin graft or chest surgery. At Cohen such house staff interchanging was not permitted. Interns and residents were assigned to a particular surgical suite and required to stay throughout the course of a procedure. On the medical wards, on the basis of general observation, it seems that one could obtain a high order correlation between the amount of time doctors spent discussing and examining patients and the degree of unusualness of their medical problems.

I introduce this general feature to point to the predominant orientation at County to such matters as "getting practice" and the general organizational principle that provides for the propriety of using cases as the basis for this practice. Not only are live patients objects of practice, so are dead ones.

There is a rule in the emergency unit that with every DOA a doctor should attempt to insert an "endo-tracheal" tube down the throat, but only after the patient is pronounced dead. The reason for this rule (on which new interns are instructed as part of their training in emergency medicine) is that the tube is extremely difficult to insert, requires great yet careful force, and, insofar as it may entail great pain, the procedure cannot be "practiced" on live patients. The body must be positioned with the neck at such an angle that the large tube will go down the proper channel. In some circumstances when it is necessary to establish a rapid "airway" (an open breathing canal), the endo-tracheal tube can apparently be an effective substitute for the tracheotomy incision. The DOA's body in its transit from the scene of the death to the morgue constitutes an ideal captive experimental opportunity. The procedure is not done on all deceased patients, the reason apparently being that it is part of the training one receives in the emergency unit and is to be learned there. Nor is it done on all DOA cases, for some doctors, it seems, are uncomfortable in handling a dead body whose charge as a live one they never had, and handling it in the way such a procedure requires. It is important to note that when it is done, it is done most frequently and most intensively with those persons who are regarded as lowly situated in the moral social structure.

No instances were observed where a young child was used as an object for such a practice nor where a well-dressed, middle-aged, middle-class adult was similarly used. On one occasion a woman supposed to have ingested a fatal amount of laundry bleach was brought to the emergency unit, and after she died, several physicians took turns trying to insert an endo-tracheal tube, after which one of them suggested that the stomach be pumped to examine its contents to try to see what effects the bleach had on the gastric secretions. A lavage was set up and the stomach contents removed. A chief resident left the room and gathered together a group of interns with the explanation that they ought to look at this woman because of the apparent results of such ingestion. In effect, the doctors conducted their own autopsy investigation without making any incisions.

The Interest Doctors Take

On several similar occasions physicians explained that with these kinds of cases they didn't really feel as if they were prying in handling the body, but that they often did in the case of an ordinary death—a "natural death" of a morally proper person. Suicide victims are frequently the objects of curiosity, and while there is a high degree of distaste in working with such patients and their bodies (particularly among the nursing staff; some nurses will not touch a suicide victim's dead body), "practice" by doctors is apparently not as distasteful. A woman was brought into the emergency unit with a self-inflicted gunshot wound which ran from her sternum downward and backward,

---

"The DOA's body in its transit from the scene of the death to the morgue constitutes an ideal captive experimental opportunity for teaching and research."

---

passing out through a kidney. She had apparently bent over a rifle and pulled the trigger. Upon her "arrival" in the emergency unit she was quite alive and talkative, and though in great pain and very fearful, was able to conduct something of a conversation. She was told that she would need immediate surgery and was taken off to the operating room; following her were a group of physicians, all of whom were interested in seeing the damage done in the path of the bullet. (One doctor said aloud, quite near her stretcher, "I can't get my heart into saving her, so we might as well have some fun out of it.") During the operation the doctors regarded her body much as they do one during an autopsy. After the critical damage was repaired and they had reason to feel the woman would survive, they engaged in numerous surgical side ventures, exploring muscular tissue in areas of the back through which the bullet had passed but where no damage had been done that required repair other than the tying off of bleeders and suturing. One of the operating surgeons performed a side operation, incising an area of skin surrounding the entry wound on the chest, to examine, he announced to colleagues, the structure of the tissue through which the bullet passed. He explicitly announced his project to be motivated by curiosity; one of the physicians spoke of the procedure as an "autopsy on a live patient," about which there was a little laughter.

In another case, a man was wounded in the forehead by a bullet, and after the damage was repaired in the wound, which resembled a usual frontal lobotomy, an exploration was made of an area adjacent to the path of the bullet, on the forehead proper, below the hair line. During this exploration the operating surgeon asked a nurse to ask Dr. X to come in, and when Dr. X arrived, the two of them, under the gaze of a large group of interns and nurses, made a further incision, which an intern described to me as unnecessary in the treatment of the man, and which left a noticeable scar down the side of the temple. The purpose of this venture was to explore the structure of that part of the face. This area of the skull, that below the hair line, cannot be examined during an autopsy because of a contract between local morticians and the Department of Pathology to leave those areas of the body which will be viewed free of surgical incisions. The doctors justified the additional incision by pointing to the "fact" that since he would have a "nice scar as it was, a little bit more wouldn't be so serious."

During autopsies themselves, bodies are routinely used to gain experience in surgical techniques, and many incisions, explorations, and the like are conducted that are not essential to the key task of uncovering the "cause" of the death. Frequently specialists-in-training come to autopsies though they have no interest in the patient's death; they await the completion of the legal part of the procedure, at which point the body is turned over to them for practice. Mock surgical procedures are staged on the body, often with co-workers simulating actual conditions, tying off blood vessels which obviously need not be tied, and suturing internally.

When a patient died in the emergency unit, whether or not he had been brought in under the designation DOA, there occasionally occurred various mock surgical procedures on his body. In one case a woman was treated for a chicken bone lodged in her throat. Rapidly after her arrival via ambulance a tracheotomy incision was made in the attempt to establish an unobstructed source of air, but the procedure was not successful and she died as the incision was being made. Several interns were called upon to practice their stitching by closing the wound as they would on a live patient. There was a low peak in the activity of the ward, and a chief surgical resident used the occasion to supervise teaching them various techniques for closing such an incision. In another case the body of a man who died after being crushed by an automobile was employed for instruction and practice in the use of various fracture setting techniques. In still another instance several interns and residents attempted to suture a dead man's dangling finger in place on his mangled hand.

The Routine of Dying

What has been developed here is a "procedural definition of death," a definition based upon the activities which that phenomenon can be said to *consist of*. While in some respects this was a study of "dying" and "death," it might be better summarized as a study of the activities of managing dying and death as meaningful events for hospital staff members. My attention has been exclusively given to the description of staff behavior occurring in the course of doing those things which daily ward routines were felt to require.

It was in the course of these routines—handling bodies, taking demographic information on incoming and outgoing patients, doing diagnosis, prognosis, medical experimentation, and teaching—that certain patients came to be recognized as persons legitimately accorded special treatments—the "dying" and "death" treatments. In the hospital world these treatments—organized to fit institutionalized daily ward routines built up to afford mass treatments on an efficiency basis, to obtain "experience," avoid dirty work, and maximize the possibilities that the intern will manage to get some sleep—give "dying" and "death" their concrete senses for hospital personnel. Whatever else a "dying" or "dead" patient might mean in other contexts, in the hospital I investigated, the sense of such states of affairs was given by the work requirements associated with the patients so described. For a "dying" patient to be on the ward meant that soon there would be a body to be cleansed, wrapped, pronounced dead, and discharged, and a family to be told. These activities and the work requirements they entailed provided the situational frame of interpretation around such states.

At least one question that has not been directly addressed is that which would ask why hospital personnel feel treatments must be organized on a mass basis. Its answer, I believe, is to be found in a historical analysis of the development of the medical ideology toward the nonpaying patient and in the peculiarly impersonal environment of the charity institution I examined. I decided at the outset of my investigation to leave unexplained general matters of ideology about patient care and to proceed from there to learn something about the ways in which existing practices were organized and what these practices entailed as regarded the occurrence of "dying" and "death."

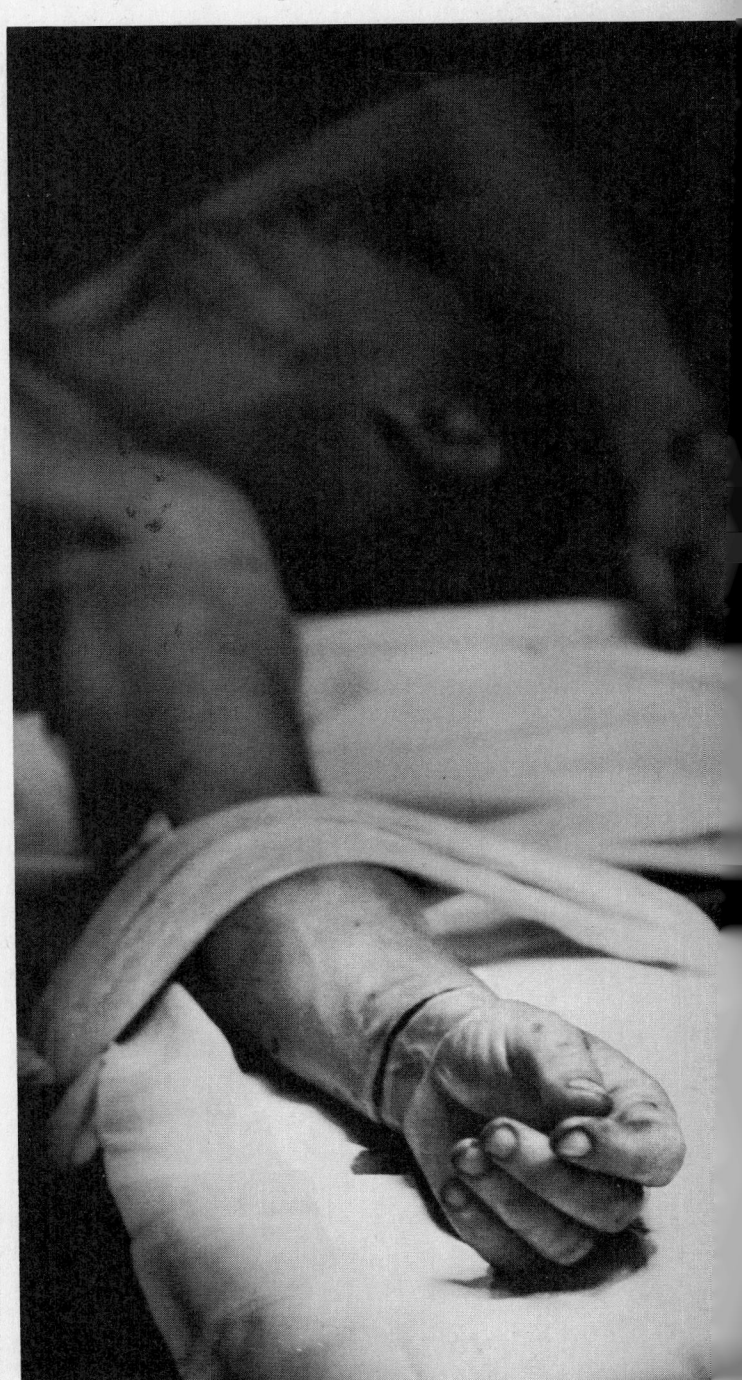

While hospital personnel managed, on the whole, to sustain a detached regard for the event of death, it occurred, on occasion, that routinely employed procedures and attitudes became altered and upset. The successful daily management of "dying" and "dead" bodies seemed to require that patients have a relatively constant character as social types. So long as the patient whose death was anticipated or had occurred was an elderly, poor, and morally proper person, the occasion of his "dying" and "death" was treated with little notice and in accord with ordinarily enforced routines of "death care." On critical occasions, however—when, for example, a child died or a successful, middle-class person was brought into the emergency unit as a DOA—ordinarily employed procedures of treatment were not instituted, and special measures were felt to be necessary. Nowhere was this disruption clearer than with the deaths of children. Nurses have been known to break down in tears when a child died, and in such cases, particularly, "dying" and "death" temporarily cease to have their firmly grounded, organizationally routinized meanings, activities, and consequences. When an intoxicated or suicidal or "criminal" patient was treated, these persons' moral characters intruded as prevalent considerations in the way in which they were regarded, providing a special frame of interpretation around the way care was organized over and above that which the category "patient" established. In key instances, patients' external attributes operated to alter the institutional routine in significant ways, causing vehemence, disgust, horror, or empathetic dismay, and—particularly in the case of children's deaths—a radical though short-lived movement entirely out of role on the part of staff members. No matter how routinized an institution's methods for handling its daily tasks, those routines remain vulnerable at certain key points. No matter how nonchalantly staff members managed to wrap patients' bodies for discharge to the morgue, taper off in the administration of drugs and care to the "dying," pronounce deaths, and return to other tasks, special circumstances caused these routines to be upset—either made more difficult to carry off, more interestedly attended, or substantially revised.

Nontypical Emotions

In regarding these special cases—those persons deemed particularly obnoxious or particularly worthy—perhaps insight may be gained into the requirements for usual, orderly ward activities. On those occasions when a nontypical death caused staff members to step outside their regularly maintained attitudes of indifference and efficiency, one could glimpse a capacity for emotional involvement which ordinary work activities did not provide proper occasions for displaying. The maintenance of appropriate impersonality in the hospital requires an enforced standardization to the types of events and persons which personnel confront. This work of *affect* management is aided by staff-held theories of proper fate, proper deaths, proper persons, and notions regarding the appropriate role of medicine and surgery in prolonging life and delaying death. These theories are invoked on a daily basis to support the patterns of care given the dying, the tentatively dead, and the decidedly dead, but they can be employed only as long as the patient in question can be construed to fit the categories for which the theories are relevant. I made every effort to construct classifications of patients so as to provide for the propriety of treating them in organizationally routine ways, but occasionally there was a case which resisted that classification. The death of a child, a young adult, or the deaths of those persons who were regarded as morally imperfect stirred a noticeably atypical degree of moral sentiment.

This class of atypical deaths, those occurring for atypical persons or in atypical ways, became set off as the specially noteworthy events of hospital life, the cases which staff members recounted for long periods of time and built into stories that were frequently retold when death was made a specific topic of conversation. In selecting certain cases to invest with special meaning, staff members demonstrated that despite their work involvements in matters of life and death and their routinely casual attitude toward such events, death nonetheless was an event which could call forth grief and empathy.

"Dying" and "death" are categories that have very broad currency, being variously used in many settings throughout the society. I have examined only one setting, only one locus of meanings and associated activities. The use of the categories in the hospital is to be regarded as hospital specific, although in other domains their usages may share features in common with those found in the hospital. While clinical death occurs, in American society at least, chiefly within the hospital setting, that setting provides only one of a variety of socially organized worlds within which its meaningful character is provided. What "dying" and "death" procedurally entail among staff physicians within the hospital would seem to share little in common with those activities anticipatorily organized by and consequential for the patient himself and members of his family—those for whom doing autopsies, handling the census of a hospital ward, cleaning up dead bodies, and the rest are not relevant considerations. My restricted interest in death in the hospital requires that the formulation of the notions "dying" and "death" given here be clearly confined in generality to this highly instrumental domain of technical activity.

November 1967

SUGGESTED READINGS

Awareness of Dying by Barney Glaser and Anselm Strauss (Chicago: Aldine, 1965).

Death, Property and the Ancestors by John Goody (Stanford: Stanford University Press, 1962).

The Meaning of Death by Herman Feifel (New York: McGraw-Hill, 1959).

Where Medicine Fails edited by Anselm Strauss (Chicago: Aldine Press, 1970).

The Troubled Calling: Crisis in the Medical Establishment by Selig Greenberg (New York: Macmillan, 1965). Examines the alienation between patient and doctor and some of the social and economic factors involved.

Patients, Physicians, and Illness edited by E. Gartley Jaco (Glencoe, Ill.: The Free Press, 1958).

The Cancer Ward by Aleksandar I. Solzhenitsyn (New York: Dial Press, 1968). Contemporary Russian fiction depicting the personal, social and political antagonisms in a hospital.

The Tipped Scales Of American Justice

*All citizens are equal in court,
but some are less equal than others*

STUART S. NAGEL

The Fourteenth Amendment to the Constitution of the United States asserts that no state or local government shall "deny any person within its jurisdiction the equal protection of the laws." The due process clause of the Fifth Amendment by judicial interpretation provides a similar restraint on the federal government. Other clauses in the Bill of Rights guarantee the right to a lawyer, a grand jury indictment, a speedy trial, and a trial by jury. Do all defendants in American courts get the full benefit of these guarantees?

Many criminologists, lawyers, and other observers say that they do not. The equality before the law guaranteed by the Fourteenth Amendment often turns out in practice to be much like the equality proclaimed on George Orwell's *Animal Farm*—all men are equal, but some groups are more equal than others. Justice, some observers say, may have a blindfold, but it may also have a price, a complexion, a location, and even age and sex; and those with enough money, the right complexion, in the right court, and even sometimes of the right age and the right sex, can often get better treatment. The "least equal" in America are generally those the Fourteenth Amendment was apparently designed specifically to protect—the Negro, the poor, and the ignorant.

The Supreme Court, in an opinion in 1956, stated that "there can be no equal justice where the kind of trial a man gets depends on the amount of money he has." The Attorney General's Committee on Poverty and the Administration of Federal Criminal Justice, headed by Professor Francis A. Allen, then of the University of Michigan Law School, in its 1963 report documented the charge that the poor suffer in the courts because of their poverty. The committee recommended reforms in the bail system, in legal representation, in appeals, and at other steps in the long ladder from arrest to release or conviction.

These propositions would seem to be further supported by common sense. Bail, lawyers, appeals, parole, frequently require money and professional help which are in short supply among the poor. Policemen, prosecutors, judges, and jailors are all human products of our times and nation and, therefore, like the rest of us, are capable of error, prejudice, and "taking the easy way." Our trials are based on the adversary system, in which two more or less evenly matched sides are supposed to meet in the cockpit of a courtroom, under rules designed to insure fair play, and contend until the side with the stronger case wins. How can the indigent, the ignorant, and the victims of discrimination hope to be strong adversaries?

In answer to this question, many prosecutors, law enforcement officers, and editorial writers contend that discrimination in the administration of justice is minor and relatively unimportant. What they believe is much more important—and more damaging—is that safeguards for defendants have already thrown the scales of justice out of balance, and more safeguards could make it almost impossible to get convictions.

Perhaps the picture is muddled partly because not enough broad reliable research has been done on the American system of justice, based on a large, nationwide sample. What has been needed was an analysis of a lot of data taken at all stages of criminal procedure, from all over the country, and including both federal and state cases. This article is based on such an analysis with a concentration on grand larceny and felonious assault cases.

How Safe are Safeguards

Disparities in justice may appear at any stage of the criminal process—and most groups suffer both apparent advantages and disadvantages from them. For instance, in larceny cases non-indigent defendants are more apt to get probation or suspended sentences than indigent ones, but are also more apt to draw longer sentences if they don't get probation, possibly because of the larger amounts of money which they steal. Also, one defendant's handicap may be another's special privilege. An adult male who does not get a grand jury hearing is possibly being denied a fundamental right; a woman or juvenile who doesn't get one is possibly being given special, informal treatment.

Let us examine these stages briefly, and see what safeguards at each level can mean to an accused.

■ PRELIMINARY HEARING. The preliminary hearing is the first stage on which data are available. The main purpose of a preliminary hearing is to allow the presiding official (police magistrate, justice of the peace, or judge) to decide whether there is enough evidence against the accused to justify further action. If he decides there is not, then an innocent person may be spared considerable humiliation, expense, delay, and inconvenience. The hearing is preliminary to the prosecutor's formal accusation or to a grand jury indictment, which it can prevent. The preliminary hearing also has other advantages for an accused: (1) it deters the use of the third-degree; (2) it allows counsel to appear and plead for the accused, particularly with regard to bail; (3) and it reveals the fact that the accused has been arrested and detained, so that *habeas corpus* (which can bring about immediate release), right to a copy of the complaint, and other guarantees can be secured. In short, the preliminary hearing is a safeguard for the rights of the accused; and its denial is a limitation to those rights.

Of the 1,168 state cases coming from counties that have provisions for preliminary hearings and on which information was available, the accused received no preliminary hearing in 434. In 357 of these he waived his right to a preliminary hearing—possibly without realizing its importance; the rest were recorded as "no preliminary hearing, reason unknown." Information as to the preliminary hearing was not available in the federal data.

■ BAIL. The next important protection for a defendant is the right, or the ability, to be released on bail. Bail reduces his hardship, especially if he is innocent, and gives him a better chance to investigate and prepare his case. Of the 1,552 state cases on which information is available, 44 percent (689) were not released on bail. Of these, 562 were eventually found guilty, 71 found not guilty, and information was not available for 56. Of the 71 not con-

victed, 20 had stayed in jail for two months or less, 13 for over three months, and we have no information for 38. Five of those not convicted, nor released on bail, in effect served jail terms of six months or more although found guilty of nothing.

■ DEFENSE COUNSEL. Lawyers generally concede that few persons (including lawyers) are capable of properly preparing and arguing their own cases—especially when confined. Having a lawyer, preferably of your own choice, is therefore a fundamental right.

All the state cases were felonies, punishable by more than a year in prison. Yet 183 of the 1,561 cases had no lawyer at all, and only 13 of these were recorded as having waived counsel. (Under the Supreme Court ruling in the famous case of *Gideon versus Wainright*, decided in 1963, all indigent state defendants must hereafter be assigned counsel for any felony. The 1962 data for this study, however, precedes Gideon.) In federal court, all defendants must have counsel of some kind, and the cases were divided according to whether the lawyer was the defendant's own. At least 390 of the 1,151 federal defendants did not have a lawyer of their own choosing.

A lawyer is considered essential for investigation, negotiation with the prosecutor, examination of witnesses, and the presentation of legal and factual arguments to judge and jury. A court-appointed lawyer is better than none, and often better than some, but he can easily suffer from lack of experience, sympathy, enthusiasm, and especially finances and time, since he will probably be appointed late, and may have to take much expense money out of his own pocket.

■ GRAND JURY. What percentage of cases went before a grand jury? Like the preliminary hearing (and the trial) the grand jury process is designed mainly to protect and to minimize the harm done to the innocent. The alternative is to let the prosecutor alone judge whether the accused should be held for trial. The state data did not separate those indicted by a grand jury from those who were not. Of the 915 federal cases involving either grand jury or the prosecutor alone, 344 involved only the prosecutor—although of these only half the defendants formally waived the right to a grand jury hearing.

■ DELAY. The American Law Institute Code of Criminal Procedure provides that if a defendant is held for more than three months without trial due to no fault of his own, then he must be set free without danger of rearrest for the same crime, except for extremely extenuating circumstances. A long delay before trial, especially in jail, can penalize the innocent or over-punish the guilty, as well as make witnesses less available and reliable.

The federal data unfortunately do not distinguish between those who await trial in jail and those who can afford to wait at home. Nevertheless it does reveal that, inside or out, there was, for almost half the cases, more than two months delay from arrest until release or trial (whichever came first). In the state cases, of the 405 *not* released on bail, 162 were kept in jail more than two months. (Two months was chosen as the watershed for all cases, half being delayed less, and half more.)

■ TRIAL BY JURY. Generally, there is less chance that twelve jurors will agree unanimously on conviction than one judge (especially a so-called "hanging judge"). Therefore a defendant usually has a greater chance of acquittal before a jury. In addition, if he is a member of a disadvantaged group (uneducated, working-class, or Negro) he stands a much better chance of encountering somebody like himself on a jury than on the bench.

On the other hand, our data show that seeking a jury trial may mean greater delay. It may also mean that if the defendant is found guilty, he is less likely to get probation than if he only had a bench trial. (The stiffer penalties for those convicted by juries may reflect the possibility that the more severe cases come before juries.) But on balance, the chance at a trial by "a jury of his peers" is a strong safeguard of the rights of a defendant.

Nevertheless, in the state data, 63 percent of those cases going to trial did so without a jury; 48 percent of federal trials were held without juries.

■ CONVICTION AND SENTENCING. About four of every five tried defendants, state and local, are found, or plead, guilty. The approximately 20 percent found not guilty, of course, had been put to the expense and anxiety of criminal proceedings. Of those considered guilty, 83 percent pleaded guilty—25 percent to lesser offenses than the original charge, possibly after negotiating with the prosecutor. Almost half the defendants found guilty were given suspended sentences or probation. Slightly more than half of those convicted and sentenced received sentences of more than one year.

The Unequal Defendants

These are the major stages in standard criminal procedure. And it is within this framework that disparities because of poverty, race, sex, age, and residence must be understood. The question is not whether the "average" accused person gets complete justice but whether some people and some groups suffer (or benefit) more or less than others—and if so, how and why.

Let us examine some of these disparities.

■ ECONOMIC CLASS. In the state data, "indigent" is defined, generally, to mean not able to afford one's own lawyer—a legalistic rather than a sociological definition. The poor, then, must usually have court-appointed lawyers, or none. In the federal cases, where indigency is not specified, the poor may be defined as those with assigned counsel.

In the pre-sentencing stages, 34 percent of indigents up for felonious assault in state courts did not get preliminary hearings—compared to 21 percent of non-indigents. This was also true, if not as markedly, in state grand larceny cases. Bail, since it requires the ability to raise money, shows the greatest disparity between those who have money and those who do not. About three-quarters of all indigent state cases did not raise bail and stayed locked up, with all this means in unearned punishment and inability to prepare for trial, while 79 percent of non-indigent assault cases, and 69 percent of larceny, did raise bail and got out.

In *having a lawyer,* an interesting reversal occurs; In most states one must be poor to have assigned lawyers, the rich hire their own, and it is the middle group that may be the most apt to be undefended. (Since the *Gideon* decision, as noted, merely having a lawyer is perhaps no longer a major disparity; what *kind* of lawyer, of course, is something else.)

In the state cases, the indigent were delayed in jail awaiting trial more than the non-indigent. This, obviously, is related to their relative inability to raise bail. In the federal figures delay is measured irrespective of whether or not the defendant is in jail—and here the indigent have *shorter* waits. A court-appointed lawyer would be inclined, apparently, to put in less time and trouble on his case than a private lawyer, and not be as apt to ask for delays; he might also want to get his bail-less client out of jail as soon as possible, and so be less likely to delay the trial.

The federal data show that the indigent are much less likely to have a grand jury indictment than the non-indigent. Perhaps they lack knowledge and are more easily persuaded to waive this right. Perhaps also this ignorance, coupled with appointed attorneys' desires to be rid of their cases, accounts for their relatively high frequency of bench, rather than jury trials. The state indigents also have proportionately fewer jury trials—but here the difference between them and the non-indigent is much less, perhaps because state juries are usually presumed to be of a lower class than federal juries, and middle-class defendants may show less preference for them.

About 90 percent of all indigents studied were found guilty. Though the percentage of non-indigents found guilty was also high, it was consistently lower (averaging about 80 percent). The greatest disparity was in the federal cases, where all indigents had court-appointed lawyers, and this may indicate that poorer representation had something to do with the higher rate of conviction. The poor also tend to feel more helpless, and may be more easily persuaded to plead guilty.

Not only are the indigent found guilty more often, but they are much less likely to be recommended for probation by the probation officer, or be granted probation or suspended sentences by the judge. Of the defendants on whom we had data in this study, a sizeable majority of indigents stayed in jail both before and after trial, unlike non-indigents.

The federal data show that this is true also of those with *no* prior record: 27 percent of the indigent with no prior record were *not* recommended for probation against 16 percent of the non-indigent; 23 percent indigent did *not* receive suspended sentences or probation against 15 percent non-indigent. Among those of both groups with "some" prior record the spread is even greater.

Why these class disparities? They reflect, at least partly, inferior legal help. But even when the lawyer works hard and well, the indigent faces the handicap that he is, and looks, lower class, while those who determine his destiny—probation officer and judge—are middle-class. Therefore, apart from the other disabilities of the poor, class bias among judicial personnel may work against them.

■ SEX. Are women discriminated against in criminal proceedings as in other walks of life? The findings are much less definite for sex than for poverty, partly because the sample was too small. (Women simply do not commit as many larcenies—and especially assaults—as men.) What differences do emerge seem to be in favor of women, especially in sentencing. It is apparently assumed that women cannot—or, chivalrously, should not—endure as much as men. On the other hand, it is possible that women can be persuaded to give up their rights more easily, and that procedures with them tend to be less formal.

Men are much less likely to be released on bail they can afford than women. In trial, women are more likely to be found innocent, and if guilty more likely to be put on probation or given suspended sentences. Studies in women's prisons have shown that women develop fewer defenses against the pains of incarceration than men and perhaps suffer more, and it is possible that judges and juries know or sense this. Or perhaps they simply find the idea of women in prison, away from their families, offensive.

■ RACE. Most Negroes are poor. A great many poor people are Negroes. So the figures about indigency and race must overlap. But they are not identical, and the differences are important. Generally, the poor suffer even more discrimination than Negroes in criminal justice; and Negroes may suffer more from lack of money than from race.

For instance, a Negro is more likely to get a preliminary hearing than a poor man. He is not as likely as the white

NOTES ON THE STUDY

This article is based on raw data gathered by the American Bar Foundation from state trial court dockets for 1962, in a balanced sample of 194 counties located in all 50 states—a grand total of 11,258 cases of all kinds. The raw data for the federal cases was obtained by the Administrative Office of the United States Courts, and was not a sample, but the complete universe of the 36,265 federal criminal cases decided in 1963. Cases from the District of Columbia and from American territories were excluded, however, in order to confine the data to the 50 states.

The type of crime has a substantial influence on treatment of the criminal, especially at the bail and sentencing stages. So this article concentrates on the two most representative crimes—*larceny,* the most frequently reported crime against property, and *assault,* the most frequently reported against persons. These crimes are also very widespread, being committed by many different kinds of people all over the country. When cases in which the defendant was charged with more than one crime were eliminated, the final sample consisted of 846 assault and 1,103 grand larceny for the states, and for federal offenses, 196 assault and 785 interstate larceny cases. All cases were felonies (except for 51 federal cases of non-aggravated assault).

Felonious assault is generally defined as assault with intent to kill, or to do great bodily harm. Often, studies have shown, the chief difference between it and homicide is that the victim manages to survive.

Grand larceny can be roughly defined as stealing money or property worth more than $50 or $100 (depending on the state) without force or the threat of force.

defendant to be released on bail, but much more likely to be released than the indigent defendant. Since many Negro defendants are also indigent, the Negro is slightly more likely to have a lawyer than a white defendant, given the indigency prerequisite for receiving a court-appointed lawyer. When the Negro has a lawyer, his lawyer is much more likely to be court-appointed than the lawyers of white defendants. In the federal larceny cases, 52 percent of the Negroes did not have their own lawyers as contrasted to 25 percent of the whites.

Like the indigent, the Negro awaiting trial with his court-appointed lawyer tends to have *less* delay than the white defendant. In fact, being subjected to delay seems to be a sign of high status rather than discrimination. Delay while released on bail may be desired by the defendant because it can benefit the guilty defendant by prolonging his freedom and weakening the memories of witnesses.

The Negro is much less likely than the white to have a grand jury indictment in either federal assault or larceny cases. If he goes to trial he is even more unlikely to have a jury trial. Indeed, 86 percent of the Negroes in federal assault cases failed to receive a jury trial, contrasted to a 26 percent figure for white defendants. It appears that the constitutional rights of a grand jury indictment and of trial by jury are mainly for white men. Perhaps Negroes believe white juries to be more discriminatory than white judges. But it is also possible that Negroes commit the less severe larcenies and assaults, and so do not as often require grand or petit juries.

Negroes, compared to whites, are particularly discriminated against when it comes to probation or suspended sentences. This is evident in the assault convictions, but is more dramatic for larceny; 74 percent of guilty Negroes were imprisoned in state larceny cases, against only 49 percent of guilty whites; in federal larceny cases the score is 54 percent to 40 percent. With prior record held constant, the disparity still holds up.

Why the difference in treatment between Negro assault and Negro larceny? Are not crimes against the person usually considered more reprehensible than those against property? The answer possibly is that larcenies by Negros are more often (than assaults) committed against white men, who are more likely to be worth robbing; but assaults occur most frequently within one's community, in this case against other Negroes. Disparities in sentencing may therefore be double, determined not only by the color of the skin of the criminal, but of his victim too.

It is interesting to note that there is a greater race disparity in federal probation *recommendations* than in probations *granted*. This may be because probation officers deal more subjectively with people, while judges (who are also better educated) tend to put more emphasis on objective factors, like the nature of the crime and the law.

On the other hand, of those actually imprisoned, the Negro defendants (particularly in larceny cases) tended to receive lighter sentences. This may be because, like the indigent defendants, they tend to steal smaller amounts; but it is probably also because the mild white offender is more likely to escape imprisonment altogether.

Generally, and surprisingly, discrimination against the Negro in criminal proceedings was only slightly greater in the South than in the North. It was, however, consistently greater in the South at all stages, pre-trial, trial, and sentencing. Discrimination in the South, predictably, was also greater at the state level than the federal level, possibly because federal judges are more independent of local pressures than state judges.

■ AGE. Younger defendants (below 21 in the state data, 22 in federal) generally are less likely to receive the safeguards the older defendants do, but are more likely to get lighter sentences.

Thus 66 percent of the young did not have their own lawyers in federal assault cases compared to 36 percent of the older defendants. They are less likely to face either grand or trial juries. There is, however, no substantial difference in preliminary hearing or bail. Much of the lack of formal procedure may actually be an advantage, reflecting a protective attitude by the courts toward the young (as toward women), and the belief that informality of procedure diminishes the "criminal" stigma, and leads more easily into rehabilitation. This is, of course, the rationale behind separate juvenile courts. The lack of a personal lawyer probably also reflects some poverty—people 21 and under seldom have much money of their own.

Young defendants are more likely to be recommended for probation, more likely to get it (or suspended sentences), and those few who do go to prison generally receive shorter sentences. (The one exception—longer sentences for youthful federal larcenists who are imprisoned—is probably unrepresentative because of the small sample, or perhaps because only the most hardened cases actually go to federal prison.) Younger people, of course, usually have shorter prior records, and this could count for some of the disparity; but the main reason is probably the belief that the young (again like women) are not as responsible, are more easily rehabilitated, and suffer more hardship in prison.

■ URBAN VS. RURAL, SOUTH VS. NORTH. The sample does not distinguish between *defendants* from the North or the South, the city or the farm—but it does distinguish between *courts* in different locales. Which were the fairest? The answer might sometimes surprise those who automatically accept the stereotype of Northern-urban civil-libertarianism, as opposed to Southern-rural anti-civil-libertarianism.

In the state data, an urban county was defined as one with more than 100,000 population; the federal data used a similar but more sophisticated definition. For both, "South" meant the original eleven states of the Confederacy. The six border states were considered neutral, and the "North" encompassed all the rest. As it developed, most cases (especially the larcenies) were tried in urban courts. Generally, North-South differences in treatment were greater than urban-rural differences.

In preliminary hearing and bail, urban-rural differences were small and inconclusive, but North-South differences were large and consistent—and not to the credit of the North. Thus 38 percent of Northern assaults had no preliminary hearing in spite of laws providing for them, compared to only 10 percent in the South. The South is more traditional toward law and custom, perhaps. The bail difference may also be due to the fact that more Northern defendants were classified as indigents.

Not having any lawyer at all was disproportionately rural and Southern; of the eleven Southern states, eight did not have laws providing for compensated counsel. (*Gideon vs. Wainwright* originated in a Southern state, Florida, and the South will now have to change its ways.) But in the federal cases, where assigned counsel was available, the rural and Southern defendants were *more* apt to have their own hired lawyers than in the cities and the North. That more defendants were labeled indigent in the North, and lawyers cost more there, may be an explanation.

The urban and Northern courts are more congested; defendants wait longer for trial. In the state assault cases, 56 percent of urban defendants sat in jail for more than two months, contrasted to 31 percent of rural defendants, and there is a similar 25 percent spread for federal larceny cases. Much has been written about congestion and delay in urban civil cases, but delay in criminal cases also needs attention, especially in the Northern cities.

In assault cases, jury trials and grand jury indictments are more common in the South than in the North; in larceny cases, however, it is the other way around. (The findings are similar in rural and urban courts, although not as consistent.) Urban and Northern courts are more likely to *imprison* for *assault*; the rural and Southern, for *larceny*. Perhaps these disparities reflect the "frontier" morality still lingering in the open country and the South, in which a man is expected to be prepared to personally defend his honor (and therefore assault is not so terrible) but a crime against property is something else again.

In the congested cities and the North, perhaps, crimes against the person seem more terrible, whereas property tends to be considered corporate and impersonal. Moreover, people in settled areas are more conditioned to rely on professional police, not personal defense and retribution. No great differences exist North and South, urban and rural, in percentages of convictions. But there is a good deal of difference in length of sentences. Rural and Southern courts are harsher, at least at the state level—66 percent of Southern state larceny sentences were for more than a year, contrasted to 35 percent in the North. Assault shows about the same spread. Rural-urban differences are parallel,

Disparities in Criminal Procedure Treatment

	DISADVANTAGED GROUPS (Indigents, Negroes, & Less Educated)	PATERNALIZED GROUPS (Juveniles & Females)	INDUSTRIALIZED GROUPS (Northern & Urban Defendants)
SAFEGUARDS FOR THE INNOCENT	Unfavorable, especially as to bail, but favorable as to being provided with a lawyer.	Unfavorable for juveniles especially as to jury trial, but unclear for females.	Unfavorable as to preliminary hearing and delay, but favorable as to providing lawyers. Mixed as to jury trial depending on the crime.
ASSAULT SENTENCING	Unfavorable, especially as to the probation officer decision.	Favorable, especially at the federal level.	Unfavorable as to whether to grant probation, but favorable as to length of imprisonment.
LARCENY SENTENCING	Unfavorable (more so than assault) as to whether to imprison, but favorable as to length of imprisonment.	Favorable, especially at the federal level.	Relatively favorable treatment.

(Based on 1,949 state cases and 981 federal cases from all 50 states for the years 1962-63 in which the defendant was charged with a single charge of assault or of larceny.)

if less marked. Southern states make the greatest use of capital punishment.

■ FEDERAL VERSUS STATE. Because of different constitutions and judicial interpretations, federal defendants have greater access to the grand jury and to counsel (when the data was collected) than state defendants. Delays are much shorter at the federal level. Shorter delays mean less need for bail, and the grand jury hearing diminishes the importance of the preliminary hearing. A slightly higher percent of federal trials are tried before juries.

Both federal and state trials end in guilty findings (or pleas) about 80 percent of the time; both find assault defendants guilty less often than larceny defendants. Probation and suspended sentences are more common in federal court—but, perhaps because the milder cases are already winnowed out, federal assault sentences are longer.

As detailed earlier, disparities unfavorable to Negroes are slightly greater in the states. Juveniles are more likely to be deprived of safeguards at the federal than the state level—but also given lighter sentences. In the broad outline, however, the same disparity patterns show up in both.

At risk of oversimplification, the major findings of this study are summarized in the accompanying chart.

Significant disparities in the administration of justice do exist. Some groups are more likely than others to receive preliminary hearings, release on bail, better lawyers, grand jury proceedings, jury trials, acquittals, shorter sentences.

Some of these differences are justifiable. The severity of the crime and the prior record, should affect the sentence (though not due process). Women and juveniles should perhaps be given more consideration. Some crimes may have greater importance in one place than another, and minor adjustments made accordingly. Nevertheless, the majority of disparities discussed in this article are probably not socially justifiable and run contrary to our democratic philosophy and to those laws which are supposed to guarantee due process and equal treatment.

Correcting the Balance

What can be done about it? Remedies vary with the specific disorder. But these discriminations in the courts partly reflect the same discriminations in our society. The indigent would not get different treatment if there were no indigent; Negroes would not be discriminated against as Negroes if there were no race prejudice. If general American performance matched American oratory and promise, equality in the courts would come quickly enough. Thus the problem of criminal procedure disparities is inherently tied to attempts to remove distinctions that are considered undesirable between the city and the country and the North and the South, and to attempts to further emancipate women, as well as to decrease the numbers of the indigent and the uneducated, and to eliminate general racial discrimination.

Meanwhile, what is being done with regard to a more piecemeal attack on specific disparities?

Partly as the result of the recommendations of such groups as the Attorney General's Committee on Poverty and the Administration of Federal Criminal Justice, the Vera Foundation in New York City, and the National Bail Conference, the federal courts have been releasing many more people considered trustworthy *without bail,* pending trial. There is some evidence that state courts are starting to follow suit. Illinois now has a law requiring that most defendants waiting trial be released if they can afford a 10 percent down payment on the bail bond—the interest usually charged by commercial bondsmen. Philadelphia, New York, and St. Louis have followed the Vera recommendation to set up bodies that investigate defendants and advise judges whether they are good risks for release without bail. The fact is that judges have almost always had the authority to forego bail for trustworthy defendants—but few have been willing to use it with what little information they could pick up from the bench. In these cities at least they are using it now, and with increasing frequency.

Since *Gideon versus Wainwright,* all felony defendants can probably be assured of *some* kind of representation. In addition, a large scale campaign to provide *competent* counsel has been started by the National Legal Aid and Defender Association, and the American Bar Association. The Administrative Office of the U.S. Courts is currently conducting an educational program to encourage more rational sentencing practices and a statistical program to show more clearly just what those practices are. Though the evidence is very spotty, there does seem to be a general trend, especially in the large cities, toward better trained and better educated policemen, probation officers, and court officials. The civil rights movement, by focusing publicity on disparities, is also bringing change.

Bringing the facts to light can expedite needed change. The disparities exist partly because the facts have been denied, ignored, disbelieved, or simply unknown to a large public. The facts are available, and they keep accumulating. We may reasonably hope that when a similar study is done five or ten years from now it will show less disparity in the administration of criminal justice.

May-June 1966

SUGGESTED READINGS

Law and Order: The Scales of Justice edited by Abraham S. Blumberg (Chicago: Aldine, 1971).

Law and Order: Modern Criminals edited by James F. Short, Jr. (Chicago: Aldine, 1970).

Civil Justice and the Poor by Jerome E. Carlin, Jay Howard and Sheldon L. Messinger (New York: Russell Sage, 1968). Good discussion of the special legal problems facing the poor.

Crime and Justice in Society edited by Richard Quinney (Boston: Little, Brown, and Co., 1969). Two recent volumes of readings in various aspects of American justice.

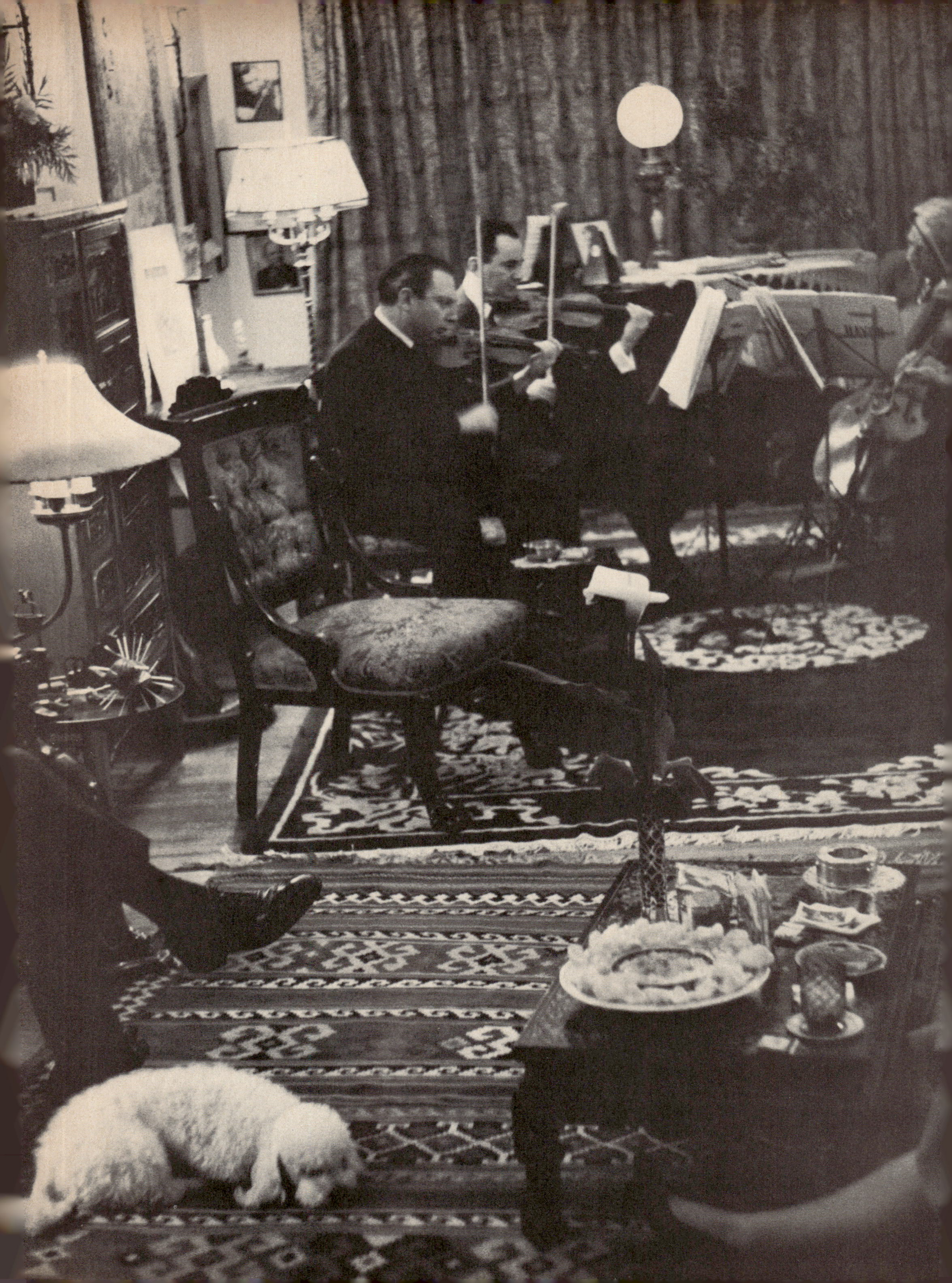

Classical Music and the Status Game

A celebrity exchange among the super-elite bridges the gap between occupational and social prestige groups

JOSEPH BENSMAN

The classical musician dealing with the layman alternates between exhibitionism and embarrassment at being regarded as a freak. Both feelings stem from the same cause—he is ill at ease with the "civilian population." He can most easily relate to them by showing esoteric knowledge of his craft. Like the psychiatrist, the astronaut, the atomic scientist, or any other professional in a world of specialists whose work is inaccessible to others, the classical musician finds that the role he plays with laymen is almost always his professional one.

Discomfort with outsiders and the desire to seek out others like himself is often typical of the member of what I call a "status community." Such a community is composed of people who make adherence to a certain complex of values and practices the organizing principle of their lives. The professional musician, for example, having made his choice of a career, has committed himself to the relative superiority of the value of music and musical pursuits.

Musicians tend to concentrate their social contacts on those who have chosen the same way of life. Many of them draw their friends almost exclusively from fellow professionals or devoted amateurs. They frequently marry other musicians and raise children who become seriously interested in music. They entertain each other—playing for pleasure when not performing, rehearsing, or practicing professionally. They frequently attend concerts or listen to records or FM radio. Many of them have their own students to whom they transmit the tastes and values of the musical community as well as their own technical expertise.

"Musicians entertain each other—playing for pleasure when not performing." (Isaac Stern and friends at home.)

Their social contacts with nonmusicians are usually limited to family members and old friends from their premusical days. Contacts with neighbors, officials, and the rest of the "civilian population" are necessary but minimal. The musician may, however, have a nonmusical hobby—such as gardening, painting, or craftsmanship in household repairs—in which he takes particular delight as proof of his nonprofessional humanity. (The reverse situation frequently is found among other types of professional people, such as doctors or engineers, who may cultivate music as evidence of their broader interests.)

The musician, then, lives very much within the confines of his status community. Such communities have in fact replaced the territorial communities of earlier times as the fundamental units of society. The modern city dweller organizes his life around his vocation or profession, his clubs and voluntary organizations, his hobbies and leisure-time activities—not around the physical limits of his block or borough. The geographical limits that used to constitute local or "natural" boundaries have become irrelevant, and people have formed psychological communities in their place. The New York musician is more at home in the concert halls of Salzburg, Moscow, and London than in the apartment of his next-door neighbor.

A vast number of these status communities exist in urban society. Each is based on a relatively narrow set of values, internally consistent but often in conflict with those of rival communities. Taken together they present an enormous array of life styles for the city dweller to choose from.

It is precisely because of these often unrelated ad hoc status communities that the breakdown of a simple overall societal structure does not result in widespread social and personal disorganization. People organize their lives around the office, the club, or the union, confining their contacts to people with similar interests and thus preventing themselves from having to deal with an apparent infinity of social relations. The complexity of the metropolitan culture lies in the number of its diverse status communities, and not necessarily in complexity of life for particular individuals. Many people are so firmly encased in their own status communities that they are effectively isolated from the kaleidoscopic urban life going on around them. The professional musician, for example, may not know how the stock market is doing, who is running for city councilman in his district, or exactly why the workers at a plant he passes every day are on strike. Furthermore, he may not care.

Validation from the Audience

How do these status communities develop and gain a recognized place in the social order? This process is closely related to the formation of status-giving audiences.

The status-giving audience for professional musicians consists partly of their fellow musicians, but most of its members are laymen. This group serves as the ultimate validator of the professional's claims to status. It confers prestige by accepting his claims to prestige. Its members join the opera guild, support the symphony drive, attend concerts, and buy recordings. In doing so, they implicitly affirm that the musician's product is a valuable one, and that its producer is entitled to certain recognition.

This prestige system operates the other way as well. In allying themselves with the musical performers and accepting their emphasis on aesthetic values, the lay members of the classical music audience borrow a certain amount of prestige from their performing idols. They are recognized in their own circles of acquaintance as people with knowledge of and taste in the arts. As lovers of classical music, they bear society's official badge of cultivation. They adopt the whole gamut of symbols, culture, speech, dress, and consumption styles that become characteristic of a status-giving audience. This process perhaps goes furthest and is most evident among the teenage audience that grants prestige and support to pop musicians, but there are elements of it among the classical music audience as well.

Training and Folklore

What are the characteristics of the status community that classical music lovers support? Relative isolation from the rest of the world combined with the relative density of social relationships within the musical community results in a rather inbred culture. What is it like, and what does it take to be admitted?

First, it takes years to become thoroughly familiar with the technology, skills, rhetoric, and technical symbolic systems upon which music is based. This knowledge is necessary for full-fledged entry into the musical community.

Further, it takes years to assimilate the folklore of this farflung group. Most professional musicians know hundreds of others. Taken together, they have moved through a great variety of musical organizations and have intimate knowledge of the people and events associated with each. This common experience—the source of countless anecdotes and endless speculation on the talents and careers of other performers—provides even previously unacquainted musicians with a solid basis for conversation. It is through such networks of personal interchange that, for example, a member of the New York Philharmonic may have a working knowledge of the Cleveland Orchestra, the London Philharmonic, the Philadelphia Orchestra, or the Vienna or Berlin Philharmonic, as well as of the soloists who perform with these orchestras. This is why the musical community in London may be closer and more familiar to the New York musician than the events in his immediate neighborhood.

Through his union, or guild, the musician has a vast fund of technical information related to his salary and modes of payment. He is alert to special legal arrangements in this area. He wants to know about the organization that pays his salary, the hours, wages, vacations, rehearsal time and pay, and about the financial arrangements which make these possible. If he plays the tympani in a symphony orchestra he finds out not only the approximate fee he will receive in a similar group, but what he can expect performing in the pit during a Broadway musical.

A string player may object to the salaries paid the woodwind, the brass, or tympani players, since theirs are substantially higher per note than his own. These latter musicians feel that they deserve the higher pay, however, since they tend to play more solos and participate more in smaller intraorchestral ensembles, where mistakes are more noticeable. They believe they should be paid for quality, not quantity.

Some instrumentalists appear to be able to bargain more effectively than others as individuals. They are paid far above the union minimum scale.

Conductors and Critics

Musicians' major institutional enemies are conductors and critics. The performances of individual conductors always provoke comment. The conductor who can't maintain a beat, who loses his place, who "hams it up," who abuses his orchestra or a particular instrumentalist, or who loses control of his orchestra or of his temper will be the sources of countless anecdotes that circulate through the international music community.

The musician regards the conductor as an arbitrary, capricious martinet whose knowledge of music is eclipsed by his egotism, megalomania, and flair for histrionics—qualities he can indulge to the fullest when he ascends the podium.

The nature of the conductor's position invites these responses, for the conductor is required to control, direct, and discipline simultaneously, in a public setting, as many as a hundred or more specialists, each of whom in his own specialty feels he is more competent than the conductor. Each will resent the discipline to which he is subjected, especially if it is administered unskillfully.

The instrumentalists tend to feel that the conductor gets the credit for a good performance, the performers the blame for a bad one. The conductor, of course, is better paid and is a celebrity. Thus the musician often perceives him as a social climber and a traitor to the art of music.

The conductor, on the other hand, is likely to feel that his instrumentalists are lazy, incompetent, and obstreperous. He may regard them as children who resist the discipline necessary to create an ensemble. If a firm hand is not used, he may reason, they can wreck the orchestra and destroy his own reputation. Both conductors and instrumentalists can cite instances of this having occurred.

Another institutional enemy of the musician is the critic. He is more the enemy of the soloist than of the orchestra member, but both regard him with caution. Whether or not they respect his judgment, they must respect his power. He has vast influence over the lay audience; he can wreck the career of a soloist, a conductor, or an entire orchestra. Musicians regard him as arbitrary and capricious to the extent they think, as they sometimes do, that he is bent on destroying a performer, conductor, or ensemble. Such professional paranoia is least common among members of the orchestra because they see each review as part of a campaign, with the cumulative effects being greater than a single battle. To the soloist, however, a bad and possibly unjust review or one based on an "off night" can be a Waterloo.

Musicians often view critics as frustrated performers whose failure as musicians has led them to merely talk and write about music and to compensate for their own inadequacies by attacking those musicians who have not given up. The musician sees criticism as an act of resentment against creation and creators. Nevertheless, the critic's opinions will be warmly applauded when he castigates the work of a rival performer or group.

The critic is usually considered superior to the music historian or musicologist, unless the latter happens to be working on specific problems of performance or on unearthing valuable lost manuscripts.

Musical Rivalries

Major performing groups (and likely individual performers) select one or more special rivals almost in the way that college football teams do. For the rivalry to be meaningful, the two contestants must be almost equally matched. Each performer or performing group has distinctive characteristics which form the basis for competitive evaluations, both favorable and unfavorable.

Thus, regardless of the music played, the Philadelphia Orchestra is viewed either as having the richest singing tones in its string section—or as being overblown, overcolored, and excessively romantic.

The New York Philharmonic is regarded as a source of great individual performers—or as a collection of disruptive individualists who are often under rehearsed, over performed, and directed by too many different (and not always competent) conductors, all of whom they seem bent on destroying.

The Cleveland Orchestra is viewed by other musicians as being one of the most disciplined groups in the world, but one whose tempos often exceed the score or the intentions of the composer.

The Boston Symphony is sometimes viewed as the most balanced orchestra, and occasionally as a most dull and academic one.

Among soloists, similar distinctions are made. Some are known for tone (and oversentimentalizing the music); others for virtuosity (and playing too fast, loud, and inaccurately). Some are authentic (and too cold and academic); others are poetic (and too mannered or personal in their styles).

Prestige Systems in the Community

These stereotypes suggest that there is a great deal of categorical thinking within the musical community. It is so large and its culture so varied that some sort of pecking order is necessary for identification and placement. How do musicians divide up their world and assign their fellows to more or less prestigious pigeonholes?

Conductors, soloists, and opera stars are at the pinnacle of the prestige structure. This is true for conductors despite the institutional hostility that performers have for them. Stars and soloists derive their prestige partly from the unique skills and personal qualities that convert a highly talented professional into a star. There appears to be relatively little envy of great performers by able performers who are not stars.

Among soloists, size of fee is likely to help determine prestige. Victory in such competitions as the Leventritt, Chopin, or Tchaikowsky music festivals bestows prestige, as well as the possibility of performing fees sufficient to

"The modern city dweller organizes his life around his vocation or profession. The New York musician is more at home in the concert halls of Salzburg, Moscow, and London than in the apartment of his next-door neighbor."

sustain a successful career. Ownership of a valued instrument—a Stradivarius, Guarnieri, or Amati—confers prestige on the string player.

Conductors, soloists, ensembles, composers, and even critics and musicologists may receive prestige by the type of music they are identified with. One conductor's reputation may rest on his advocacy and interpretation of new or experimental music. Another may be known as the foremost conductor of Beethoven, Mahler, or French Impressionist music. The same applies to soloists and smaller ensembles. A soloist or ensemble may revive a previously forgotten master such as Alkan or Telemann or rank as the foremost interpreter of a composer, style, or composition. Ensembles may specialize in Baroque or Renaissance music or in minor works by great masters. Some critics are able to write more intelligently or knowingly than others about a particular composer. A musicologist or a critic may be responsible for resurrecting a forgotten mode, and a composer may similarly adapt a neglected style.

If the musician, as lobbyist, succeeds in establishing a reputation for such specialization or leadership in stylistic movements, he acquires the prestige of the musical style, composer, or type of music, often independently of his own technical or performing skill.

Prestige is also based on the type of performing group. In general, small permanent ensembles such as trios and string quartets bestow more prestige to their members than larger ensembles. We might regard this as an extension of the prestige continuum of the soloist, the conductor, and the star. Anonymity, in the sense of being lost in the welter of sound created by a large performing group, diminishes prestige. The rating of "share-of-total" performance intersects with the rating of the performing group.

The great American symphony orchestras have high prestige, as do about a dozen chamber groups. Rivalries about the exact prestige ratings of these ensembles operate at all levels.

Types of instruments are also a basis of prestige. The strings and piano are high prestige instruments, followed generally by the woodwinds (especially the oboe), with lower prestige assigned to the brasses and percussion. Within these instrumental groups, desk or chair is important, and the position of concertmaster is highly prestigious.

Age is important both with respect to position in the orchestra and the prominence of the soloist. The musician who achieves a high position at an uncommonly early age receives special prestige. The child prodigy, for example, has unusual opportunities in music. Likewise, since musical performance also involves physical skills and equipment that deteriorate as the performer ages, unusual prestige accrues to individuals who retain their performing skills long after the age of expected decline.

Recording opportunities are also a source of prestige for both the soloist and the ensemble. Within the symphony orchestra, recordings are frequently played by less than the full orchestra. An invitation to perform as a member of the reduced orchestra (the "Mozart Orchestra," for example) or as a soloist within the ensemble is a prestigeful event.

Accompanists have lower prestige than featured performers. This includes orchestral accompaniment of a ballet, opera, or musical, as well as of a soloist. But the prestige of the accompanist is directly related to that of the soloist. An accompanist to an outstanding soloist may have even higher prestige than a soloist of middle rank.

With some exceptions, music teachers have relatively low rank. The teacher who is also a performer receives the prestige of his performing role (which helps him in recruiting top students) and not of his teaching role. The teacher of soloists and outstanding performers receives part of the prestige of his students. The teacher affiliated with a conservatory or music school receives the prestige of the school (if he has no higher source of prestige). The student or aspiring soloist will receive prestige from affiliation with a teacher of high rank and distinction.

The teacher who does nothing but teach and who has not previously made a reputation as a performer is the low man on the prestige scale. This is a source of anxiety and chagrin to music teachers' guilds, as well as a reason for their existence.

We suspect the composer's prestige (except that of well-known "star" composers) depends more on who performs his work and how he makes a living than on his function as a writer of music or the particular qualities of his compositions.

The many-sided quality of prestige within the musical community reflects its division into smaller subcommunities, each of which is highly specialized and has its own internal system of prestige. Sopranos, bassoonists, and percussion experts all have their own criteria of excellence for ranking the members of their own specialties.

Moreover, every type of musical expression has its own culture. This is true because the individual musician moves from organization to organization within the same type, and music fans frequently attach themselves to a particular genre, such as chamber music or the opera.

Some musical communities are entirely separated from the groups described above. Folk, popular, jazz, and ethnic music are each the basis of separate status communities which have their distinctive cultures and systems of social honor. The classical musician is usually a layman in his relationship to these other musical communities.

Celebrity Exchange

In a society consisting of many and varied status communities, each community will have its stars, its own special elite. The mass media makes celebrities out of these stars, making them visible not only to the people of their own group but to each other and to the public at large. These celebrities then form a super-elite.

A labor leader who can halt the routine functioning of a vast segment of the economy by calling a strike becomes a public personality. In the same way a temperamental opera star or a piano virtuoso becomes visible outside the community of music lovers through television reportage, guest appearances at civic events, and news and gossip coverage in the national and international press. An orchestra conductor or a comedian may become a social lion, the friend of kings, queens, and presidents.

All the traditional ways of ascribing status—wealth, education, talent, ethnic background, family background, and the rest—become of secondary importance to stardom, leadership, elitehood. The heads of wealthy old families entertain and are entertained by society prostitutes, ex-junk dealers, former bootleggers, band leaders, ethnic politicians, and Hollywood film personalities. If they are stars in their own status areas, the sons of immigrants and the descendants of slaves can become social equals with the traditional upper classes.

A massive trading of social status takes place within such a system. The parvenu movie idol or sports hero or political figure starts to receive invitations from members of the old upper classes. They can offer him a certain social legitimacy to go with his new wealth and power. But he can offer them something too: the rewards of publicity and recognition, and the feeling—not to be underestimated in a society geared to the image of the jet set—of being "where the action is."

This sort of mutual social backscratching among the leaders of different status communities is what binds their communities together in a workable system of exchange. And it is just this star system that provides a basis for pluralism without anarchy. Musicians trade status with labor leaders, painters with politicians, and professors with presidents, but each is still firmly anchored in his own status group.

As part of this exchange, the very wealthy serve on the boards of various specialized institutions. They contribute financial support to these organizations as well as lending the prestige, influence, and authority of their respective spheres of prominence. In return they receive social recognition and personal satisfaction. Entertainers assist in fund raising by guest appearances, by allowing their names to be used, and by appearing as officers in voluntary organizations whose major purposes lie outside their special field. In politics the status community leader becomes an important source for dramatizing support for a candidate, issue, or policy.

The coordination, integration, or coalescence of the elite communities is by no means perfect or complete, however. There is no single super-elite, no unity of all status and power leadership. The vast complexity of urban society prevents such unity. The number of status communities that produce candidates for the super-elite is too large. As a result, there remain many different elites and many different combinations or alliances into which they may fall. The exchange system works, but not with the precision or the predictability of a finely tuned machine.

A huge number of more or less temporary alliances or subcommunities exist among the elites. They are not organized in any specific or formal way, but depend on the mutual selection of various stars and leaders. These subcommunities may have overlapping memberships. Some may be based on membership in only a few status communities; others will be drawn from different value and institutional spheres. An individual may be a member of a number of subcommunities, and be excluded for personal or other reasons from others.

Some will be organized for specific purposes—to support a given organization, policy, or person—and may dissolve or change membership and character in a relatively short period of time. They may compete for attention, may divide on major issues, or may be unrelated to each other.

As a result, it would be difficult to support the charge that the elite community is an organized, unified conspiracy. Individual elite subcommunities may, of course, be organized for specific purposes and therefore appear to contain elements of a "conspiracy." But their purposes are often purely social or cultural. They appear to be a conspiracy because they are temporary alliances of "men at the top" which exclude men at the middle or the bottom from all roles but those of complying or serving. Resentment is natural and human.

These patterns of organization among the elite subcommunities explain in part how it is possible to coordinate a society so complex that most of its members can live in only one or a few of a vast number of status groups.

I have concentrated on sketching the inner workings of one such group—the classical music community—to give a closer look at one of the many building blocks of the prestige system in a competitive mass society.

September 1967

SUGGESTED READINGS

Philadelphia Gentlemen by E. Digby Baltzell (Glencoe, Ill.: The Free Press, 1958). How 19th-century tycoons supported various exclusive institutions which have today produced a distinctive, national, upper-class way of life.

Boys in White by Howard S. Becker, Blanche Geer, Everett Hughes and Anselm Strauss (Chicago: University of Chicago Press, 1961). Traces the development of a student culture in medical school.

The Academic Marketplace by Theodore Caplow and Reece J. McGee (New York: Basic Books, 1958). An empirical study of faculty recruitment, appointments and dismissals, this work arrives at some distressing conclusions concerning intercampus politics.

Prescription for Leadership by Steven J. Miller (Chicago: Aldine 1970). Analysis of the establishment and maintenance of an elite within the medical profession.

Professionalization edited by Howard M. Vollmer and Donald L. Mills (Englewood Cliffs, N. J.: Prentice-Hall, 1968). An excellent reader in the area.

The Working Classes—Old and New

GERALD HANDEL &
LEE RAINWATER

In 1959 the United States Department of Labor heralded the near achievement of a classless society in the United States in a report that stated: "The wage-earner's way of life is well-nigh indistinguishable from that of his salaried co-citizens." This was welcome news not only to the Labor Department but to the business community. *Business Week* summarized the report in an article entitled "Worker Loses His Class Identity."

The Labor Department report, written by economists, raises an issue which concerns sociologists seeking to understand the structure of American society. Has the rise in working class income in the postwar years and the movement of working-class people into suburbs been sufficient to transform working-class people into middle class—or at least to set in motion a strong process of transformation?

The Labor Department says yes, and states, without much documentation: "The adoption of middle-class attitudes, the change in what workers have come to expect . . . points to this great revolution in class relations."

We interviewed a sample of 298 working-class couples and 101 lower middle-class couples—husbands and wives being interviewed separately—distributed in five cities: Camden, New Jersey; Gary, Indiana; Chicago; Louisville; and Denver. They lived in apartments, in new and old city houses, and in new and old houses in the suburbs.

Three general conclusions emerged:

• Certain behaviors and attitudes increasingly found in the working class have a surface similarity to those in the middle class, but they have a different meaning for the working class than they do for the middle class. They are caused by increased opportunity rather than by any change in basic working-class outlook and are occurring primarily in education and housing.

• In family life and social participation, the working class seems to be dividing into two main groups, traditional and modern. In these areas the modern group comes closer to lower middle-class values and behaviors.

• As consumers, the working class resembles the middle class in spending for hard goods but not in other ways. This reflects persisting differences in working class and middle class life styles.

The pattern is complex, and reflects the interplay of many factors. Below are indications how these generalizations apply to specific life areas.

Education

Where once the working class could see little value in higher education, it is now commonplace for working-class parents to want a college education for their children. Yet as we probe deeper it becomes clear that college education has quite different meanings for working-class and middle-class people. For instance, working-class parents seldom aspire to a college education for their daughters. They are likely to regard a daughter's stay in college as wasted unless she completes the course and uses it in a job—school teaching is the occupation usually mentioned. Education is conceived quite narrowly as vocational training—a kind of entry card to employment.

While people in the lower middle class do not slight the importance of vocational preparation, they conceive education more broadly. They are likely to believe that education is valuable even if not put to direct use. They might regard a year or two of college for a girl valuable for making her a more "refined" person rather than a total waste of time and money. Middle-class parents look on schooling not only as preparation for a job but as a means of enabling children to get more out of life. They also expect the school to teach their children how to get along with other people.

A Home in the Suburbs

Like the middle class, working-class people have been moving to new tract housing, both in suburbs and inside city limits. The attitudes that prompt these moves show certain differences from those of the middle class, though there are also similarities. The working-class couple is more often motivated by a desire to flee from subordination to a landlord. Living in an apartment carries to them something of the same meaning as working for a boss. The landlord can and often will tell them to keep their children from playing in the halls of the building, not to run water after 10 p.m. or not to be noisy. Owning one's own home means to the working class an escape from restriction.

To the middle-class suburbanite, owning a house is an assertion of his rightful place in society. He is not fleeing from exploitation by property-owners; he is a property-owner, one in a neighborhood of similar responsible persons, and he has the house and deed to prove it.

The increasing respect for education by the working class and the increased interest in home owning involve attitudes and behavior that superficially resemble those of the middle class but have a quite different significance.

Traditional and Modern

In family behavior the changes are more varied. The modern working-class pattern has more similarities to the middle class than it has with the traditional working class. The essential change is the increased importance given to the immediate family at the expense of the broad, extended family.

In the old-fashioned traditional working class, family relationships intertwine with economic relationships. Very often a young man will choose an occupation in which his father or some other close relative is already working. He will be taken on in the same factory or join a closely controlled union. In the modern working class, this link between family and occupation is broken. A young man is more likely to work where and at what he likes, or can get, regardless of family.

Living near parents, brothers and sisters, or other close relatives is highly valued in the traditional working class. Numerous studies have shown that working people are more likely than middle class to have most of their social activities with relatives. If they do not live near relatives, they may very well spend their vacations visiting them. In contrast, the modern working-class couple is more likely to have unrelated couples as friends, and social activities with these friends are more important to them than activities with relatives.

In the traditional working-class family, the wife thinks of herself as someone who does *for* her family. Her self-conception as a wife centers around cooking, laundry and cleaning house. She considers the kitchen the most important room in her home.

But the modern working-class wife bases her self-regard on what she does *with* her family. Her image is broadened from servant of the family to sharer in family affairs. She considers the living room the most important room because that is the one where the family relaxes together.

Less for Services

The prosperity of the postwar years has resulted in increased working-class purchases of houses, automobiles and other durable items. At the same time, however, the American economy as a whole has shown a rapid increase in spending for services in which the working class has not shared proportionately. There are several aspects of working-class life style that account for their low output for services.

Even though a larger percentage of working-class children are going to college, the proportion is still lower than in the middle class. Further, the children are far more likely to go to publicly supported junior colleges or state universities, where fees are lower, than to private schools. Expenditures for educational services, therefore, claim a smaller percentage of the working-class income.

Working-class men do a tremendous amount of their own home repairs and improvements. Expenditures for carpenters, plumbers, electricians and painters are likely to be less than in middle-class families.

For similar reasons, expenses for car repairs and car washings are also generally less.

Working-class men buy fewer suits and spend less on dry cleaning.

Working-class families are more likely to buy an automatic washer—or to use coin-operated laundromats—than to use a commercial laundry or diaper service.

They will more probably spend their vacations either at home or visiting relatives. Their hotel, motel and transportation expenses will be lower than those for middle-class people.

They do not eat in restaurants as often, though some working-class women say they wish they could. Their meals away from home are more often picnics in the park, dinner with relatives, or stops at a drive-in.

In all of these areas, working-class attitudes and life style keep down expenditures for services. The great growth in the service sector of the economy is a middle-class phenomenon.

Is the working class becoming part of the middle class? There is no flat yes or no answer that will cover all aspects of life. In different areas, change proceeds at different rates, with different consequences—and all the factors are not yet known. But the obliteration of class lines heralded by the Labor Department report is a great exaggeration.

November 1963

SUGGESTED READINGS

Blue Collar Life by Arthur B. Shostak (New York: Random House, 1969).

Blue Collar Man by Theodore V. Purcell (Cambridge, Mass.: Harvard University Press, 1960). An empirical study describing the dual loyalty — to both employer and union — found among packing-house workers.

Blue Collar World edited by Arthur B. Shostak and William Gomberg (Englewood Cliffs, N. J.: Prentice-Hall, 1964). A collection of readings organized around the question, "Is there a style of life peculiar to blue-collar men, and what are its characteristics?"

Blue Collar Marriage by Mirra Komarovsky and Jane H. Phillips (New York: Random House, 1964). An analysis of the day-to-day activities, satisfactions and difficulties that make up the working-class marriage.

Working Class Suburb by Bennett Berger (Berkeley, Calif.: University of California Press, 1960). Berger discovered that auto workers retained their working-class values and activities when they moved to a middle-class suburban environment.

The Anatomy of Work: Labor, Leisure, and the Implications of Automation by Georges Friedmann (Glencoe, Ill.: The Free Press, 1961). The effects of new industrial technology on the worker, especially the problems of job enhancement and plentiful leisure time.

The Politics of Protracted Conflict

Religious divisions have always played a dominant role in Ulster, but they are not the fundamental issues.

ANDERS BOSERUP

The recent eruption of civil warfare in Northern Ireland has been analysed and reanalysed in many ways. But the implicit assumption of most of these efforts is that the conflict between Catholics and Protestants is merely a local idiosyncrasy of a typical western democracy, and that the outbreaks of violence are little more than passing convulsions of an otherwise well-integrated system.

My starting point here is the opposite. I assume as a working hypothesis that in a protracted conflict the antagonistic relationship is itself the basis of the social system within which it occurs, and, further, that it determines the nature of the antagonists as social entities. In the case of Ulster, the key factors of the conflict that shapes the social system are, I believe, the inherent weakness of her postcolonial institutions and ruling class, and the consequent need for privileges, sectarianism and discrimination to uphold the political system.

Elite Weakness and Sectarianism

The parliament at Stormont is, on a number of essential points, more like a provincial council than a national parliament. It has little freedom to fashion Ulster's policies, and particularly her economic policy, according to her needs. Finance and credit are heavily dependent upon conditions in Britain, and most taxes and duties are Reserved Revenue, controlled by the parliament of the United Kingdom. Policies in these areas are evidently determined primarily with British needs in mind.

Ulster's domestic market is very small, and her main trading area, Britain, which takes an estimated 55 percent of her GNP (foreign countries taking another 15 percent), is completely outside the control of Stormont and cannot even be regulated by tariffs or monetary policy. The main tools at the disposal of the government for promoting local enterprise appear to be direct subsidies and, to a much lesser extent, its long-term influence upon transport and production costs.

A rapidly growing part of the industry consists of subsidiaries of British firms. The largest Belfast paper is British-owned. All matters of foreign policy and defense policy are conducted from Westminster. The fatal political weakness of a country with no regular army was vividly demonstrated when the government recently had to rely upon British troops. Other means of social control, such as the courts, the educational and electoral systems, are also either operated directly from Britain or are mere copies of similar British institutions, only slightly adapted, if at all, to the particular requirements of the Irish scene. (There are some notable exceptions of a purely repressive kind: the Special Powers Act, the antiquated franchise system, the volunteer corps of the B-Specials and so forth.)

Nor does there seem to be much by way of a powerful ruling elite. One often hears of the landed aristocracy of Ulster, but it is clear that whatever power the proprietors of the large estates might have retained after the Land Purchase Acts around the turn of the century enabled tenants to buy out the land they occupied, are sure to have been lost as a result of the steadily declining share of agriculture in Ulster's economy. In 1966 agriculture contributed only 9.4 percent to the GNP. The aristocracy of Ulster is more likely to derive social prestige from its ownership of land than the more tangible economic and political power it formerly had.

This class is, however, closely intertwined with the present industrial elite. It was responsible for the early industrialization of Ulster, first by creating the linen and later the shipbuilding industries. These are still among the main manufactures of Ulster, with shipbuilding accounting for 10 percent of all industrial employees and the textile industries for 23 percent. Corresponding figures for the United Kingdom as a whole are 3 and 6 percent, respectively. It also seems reasonable to assume that this "traditional elite" holds the better part of the many small family-owned companies which are a characteristic feature of Ulster's economy.

It is not clear to what extent the modern commercial and industrial elite associated with the rapidly expanding new corporate industries in Ulster has economic interests that diverge significantly from those of this traditional family-based elite. This is an important issue to investigate, since there appear to have been profound divisions within the leadership of the Unionist party in recent years. Certainly, the fact that the traditional elite provides most of Ulster's top politicians should not be taken too literally, as it might well reflect more on the traditions of Unionist politics than on any real distribution of power. Moreover, Unionist economic policies, which provide large subsidies to new industries while traditional ones are given insufficient assistance to keep them alive, hardly suggest a predominance of the traditional interests.

In discussing possible outcomes of the present crisis a clear picture of the composition of the ruling groups in Ulster as well as their relation to the middle and lower-middle class becomes crucial, but for the present it suffices

Photographs by Leif Skoogfors

to note that even though a new owning and managerial elite may have developed in Northern Ireland most new industries are "foreign" as far as Ulster is concerned.

Third World Parallels

A situation similar to that in Northern Ireland seems to have arisen in many new countries after they gained formal independence. In these countries, too, there is little by way of a local bourgeoisie, and where one exists the basis of its former power, the landed estates, is now of decreasing importance. Economic resources are largely foreign-controlled; and the political, educational and legal institutions, instead of having evolved gradually from the power struggles of opposing domestic classes, are often mere replicas of the corresponding institutions in the mother country. For this reason they only imperfectly represent and protect the national interest groups and their mutual power relations.

One way of coping with the resulting political instability is the military takeover, familiar in Latin America and now rapidly spreading over Africa, Asia and southern Europe. The thesis I am advocating is that the maintenance of discrimination and the promotion of sectarianism is just another way of adapting to what is essentially the same problem: an oligarchic rule with insufficient backing and insufficient means of social control.

In their study of Ghana during the Nkrumah era, Bob Fitch and Mary Oppenheimer provide an illustration of a situation which is apparently analogous to that in Ulster. When in 1956 the Convention People's party was forced to go to the polls, it had already lost its popular appeal and completely lacked any significant power base. As a result, it revived and exploited local and tribal disputes during its electoral campaign, this despite its official and loudly proclaimed opposition to tribalism.

The two main parties in Ulster, the Unionist party and the Nationalists, are formed on exclusively religious lines, and only the relatively small Labour and Liberal parties are to any significant extent interdenominational. Both Unionists and Nationalists have come to assemble under their respective banners all the diverging opinions and interests within each religious community, and as a consequence they are incapable of putting forward any clear social or economic program. (A recent Unionist declaration of principle, for instance, contains only the vaguest and most uncontroversial generalities about furthering economic progress and social welfare.) Instead, the parties have to revive the sectarian issue at each successive election. Religious divisions have always played a dominant role in Ulster, of

CLASS AND CASTE 249

Leif Skoogfors

course, but this does not mean that they constitute the fundamental issues, only that party leaders on either side know that religious prejudices, especially where there exists a substratum of economic competition, are most easily exploited.

The disappearance of class distinction as a significant factor in politics appears to be a fairly general feature in ethnic conflicts. Ulster is but one illustration of it; in Belgian Flanders the dominant Social-Christian party similarly groups all social classes, as does the Democratic party in the American Deep South.

It is of course not enough to show that there might be a need for the rulers to foster sectarianism and grant privileges in return for political support. One must consider in more detail the way it's done, the relative importance of attitudes and purely material factors in maintaining cohesion, the institutional framework that makes an exchange possible and the rationalizations by which the system is made morally acceptable to its perpetrators.

We shall return to this presently, but first we shall have to briefly clarify the relation between, on the one hand, the theory here advocated and, on the other hand, two theories of the origins of ethnic conflict, that of race prejudice and of intolerance.

Race Prejudice

The race prejudice theory has been developed by the Marxists. It holds that racialism arose with capitalism, is inseparable from it and was (and is) a device for creating a readily exploitable subhuman class. Further, by fostering divisions among the workers it also serves as a means of subordinating the major proletarian struggle to artificially intensified minor cultural conflicts. The prejudice of the victimized groups (against their oppressors or against other victimized groups) is held to be a secondary defensive or adaptive reaction. There is considerable supportive evidence for this theory if it is taken in a broad historical sense.

I would suggest, though on admittedly insufficient evidence, that a straightforward interpretation of religious conflict in Northern Ireland in terms of the economic interests, the exploitation of Catholics by Protestants or the exploitation of both by domestic (Northern Irish) or foreign (British) capital can at best supply only part of the explanation. It is plain, and on the whole undisputed, that the exploitation of Ireland by Britain in past centuries, its relegation to a status of supplier of cheap labor and food to the British market, has been the key determinant of the whole economic, social and political development in the south as well as in the north and that the origin of the communal strife must be understood in that light. At present, however, these factors are clearly of diminishing importance. One illustration is the fact that it is precisely the new industries in Ulster and the subsidiaries of foreign firms that are least prone to practice discrimination.

The kind of theory I am urging here owes much to the Marxist analysis of classes and of the function of ethnic conflict in a more general sense. Indeed, my analysis presupposes a sort of class perspective on society, since its very base is the assumption that "objectively" diverging interests of one kind or another are temporarily bridged by sectarian strife. Ethnic conflict, in this view, cannot exist in isolation and necessarily interacts across one or several other lines of conflict. It is only by considering these conflicts that the perpetuation or the breakup of a given ethnic confrontation can be discussed. For my purposes, the ruling class (whether foreign or domestic) is not necessarily characterized by its ownership of the means of production. That is normally an accessory factor, the specific importance of which must be determined in each particular case. The class concept used here defines classes by their relation to the exercise of authority.

Intolerance

The intolerance theory simply holds that it is normal for societies to be intolerant of culturally divergent groups which, like the Jews, refuse to be assimilated. The feelings aroused and the persecution of the minority group become particularly violent, of course, if the group is believed to threaten the status quo or to be in collusion with an external enemy and if its members hold positions of some power within the society. Thus intolerance—which is often reciprocated—serves both to protect the in-group and to enhance its social solidarity.

This theory too has obvious applicability to Northern Ireland.

Among the Protestant lower-middle and working class in particular, stories abound of Catholic atrocities perpetrated on Protestants, often in outlandish places, and since they circulate within a fairly closed group their truthfulness, it seems, is never effectively challenged. The pages of the *Ulster Protestant,* the Orange Order weekly, provide many examples of the way in which world events are normally interpreted as instances of the great struggle of Roman Catholicism against the reformed churches. I have found in discussions with Protestant workers that these facts and interpretations are often held to be unquestionably true and demonstrable; they are not simply convenient rationalizations.

When one turns to the subject of all these stories, the Catholics themselves, he finds little of the militancy and religious fanaticism often ascribed to them, certainly if surveys or journals and papers are to be trusted. Most Catholics appear to have reconciled themselves to the existence of the Border, a reconciliation in which the better material conditions available in Ulster as compared with the Republic probably plays no small part.

Among the upper-middle class Protestants, however, these strongly distorted views of Catholicism are not found, or not to that extent. In this group it is more common to simply deny that any discrimination exists or to claim that it is on its way to disappearing or, finally, to refer to "the tendency, which is worldwide, for people to prefer to give jobs to their own 'sort.'"

To sum up: the question is not which theory is true in an absolute sense, since all three we have considered here are perfectly compatible. The question is simply which theory will give the most economical and complete picture of those aspects of the situation with which we are most concerned. A theory of the economic interests behind prejudice would provide the best long-term projections of intergroup relations and reveal some of the constraints on short-term developments as well. The theory of intolerance is useless from the point of view of application because it is entirely static, unless supplemented with a theory of how perceptions change. But the theory of political cohesion here advocated would provide the simplest guide to the short-term strategic considerations of the parties concerned and to the feasibility and effects of various political measures. This latter approach is therefore at least a convenient starting point.

Pillars of Protestant Rule

The key to understanding the political setup in Ulster is the institution of the Loyal Orange Lodge, the Orange Order and the way they have come to group wholly divergent class interests under the Protestant loyalist banner. Historically the order arose in the countryside as a peasant organization to protect Protestant tenants' interests against Catholic competition. As were other secret societies of the time (the Oakboys, the Hearts of Steel), it seems to have been largely directed against the landowners, even though it was formed on a sectarian basis. James Connolly, in his *Labour in Irish History,* quotes Archbishop Whatley to show that Irish politics and divisions turned primarily around questions of property and only nominally around questions of religion. Says Whatley: "Many instances have

Leif Skoogfors

come to my knowledge of the most furious Orangemen stripping their estates of a Protestant tenantry who had been there for generations and letting their land to Roman Catholics . . . at an advance of a shilling an acre."

It wasn't until the end of the eighteenth century that the Orange Order was used for the first time to uphold the social order, in this instance by crushing Wolfe Tone's United Irishmen, a secret society with a program not too different from that of the French revolutionaries. Tone had achieved considerable support among the urban middle-class Catholic tenants in the north and, to a lesser degree, among the Protestant tenants as well. The Orange Order, however, by "defending the British Crown, shoulder to shoulder with the royal troops" evidently left peasants divided and largely along religious lines. The political alliance of the lodges with the Protestant landowners probably dates back to this period. Even up to the time of partition at the beginning of this century the cement of the Orange Order and other Protestant societies was not a simple community of interests in opposition to the Catholic peasantry of Ulster. Rather, they were held together by a serious divergence of interests between predominantly Protestant Ulster with its relatively advanced industry and cash crops on the one hand, and on the other, predominantly Catholic Munster, Leinster and Connaught with an almost nonexistent industry and a vital need for protective customs barriers if any was to develop.

The specific "success" of Orangeism therefore appears to have two components: its transmission to, and survival in the growing urban environment of Ulster, particularly its integration of a section of the Protestant industrial workers; and secondly, its survival after partition had, I should think, largely undermined its raison d'être.

The traditional values and the intense religious feelings of the peasantry that became the Belfast lower-middle class and working class were maintained in this new environment by the Orange Lodges which established themselves in the towns and became "congregationally-based urban centers of political and cultural life." In this they were parallels of the Working Men's Clubs and Friendly Societies in England. They came to comprise the political, leisure and religious activities of their members, in keeping with the precepts of the Presbyterian, Calvinist or Wesleyan faiths.

According to Peter Gibbon's essay on Ulster in the *New Left Review,* the lodges finally came to serve more directly the interests of their members as a result of "the capture by the landed and business elite of two senior Orange institutions, the Apprentice Boys of Derry and the Royal Black Preceptory. . . . The local lodges had previously

Leif Skoogfors

maintained a cultural continuity for the Protestant urban poor without providing them with a direct political expression or link with the ruling groups. Through the intervention of the officers of the Apprentice Boys and the Preceptory, Protestants could now find access to housing, employment and social promotion, and the historical separation of differentiated education and residence was confirmed. In return, all that was demanded of the poor was their political allegiance."

The Divisions of Labor

Although several of the trade-unions in Northern Ireland are effectively segregated according to religion by virtue of the different occupations held by the two communities, the unions have nevertheless often taken a stand against sectarianism. They are one of the very few institutions that have provided a place of meeting and common action for Protestants and Catholics. To be sure, Protestants were (and are) mainly found in the craft industries, and as such they were in opposition to the unskilled Catholics. But when the latter were organized by the turn of the century into the new mass unions by Larkin and Connolly, there was initially some success in getting some support among the lower-paid Protestant workers. At the dockers' strike in Belfast in 1907, Green and Orange banners were paraded side by side. Yet as Connolly changed his stand on the nationality issue and took part in the Easter rising in 1916, which was later to result in the partition of Ireland, the unity of the northern industrial workers was effectively broken for a long time to come. Connolly had himself anticipated this: "The effect of such exclusion [i.e. partition] upon labour in Ireland will be . . . disastrous. All hopes of uniting the workers, irrespective of religion or old political battle cries, will be shattered, and through North and South the issue of Home Rule will still be used to cover the iniquities of the capitalist and landlord class. I am not speaking without due knowledge of the sentiments of the organized labour movement in Ireland when I say that we would much rather see the Home Rule Bill defeated than see it carried with Ulster or any part of Ulster left out."

It was the common opposition to home rule that finally fused all these diverse elements and interests into the "Orange Bloc," politically represented by the Unionist party, held together by the Orange Lodges and ideologically unified by Protestantism or, more precisely, by opposition to "Romanism." Unionist and Protestant, Nationalist and Catholic had become synonyms.

In his *The Irish Question*, Nicholas Mansergh describes as follows the development since independence came to the south in 1920: "The Unionists have remained in office in Northern Ireland for more than forty years. No government in Europe, is the boast, has been so stable. In this respect, therefore, the calculations of 1920 (regarding the appropriate size of Ulster if it were to retain a Unionist majority) have proved well founded. In a province where political parties are founded on differences in creed, . . . a floating vote does not exist. A party that has a majority retains it, for at the least threat of disaffection, the old party cry is raised and every issue of political or social reform is subordinated to the chill hand of sectarian prejudice. As a result the Unionist majorities at successive elections have remained virtually unchanged. . . . The forms of democracy remain, but its spirit can scarcely flourish in a political atmosphere so frozen that up to 70 percent of the seats have been uncontested at a general election."

However obvious, it must be said that in describing Unionism as the main perpetrator of sectarianism in Northern Ireland I am trying to expose the key factors, not to distribute the blame. The Nationalist party which one observer calls "The miserable Catholic obverse of the Unionist party—miniature and mirror of it" similarly survives largely through its constant appeals to sectarianism and antiquated divisions. Nevertheless, the difference is important, not only because the Nationalists never have been and never will become the ruling party, but mainly because they control only a third of the Catholic electorate, as compared with the Unionists who have the support of some 80 percent of Protestants. The Catholic equivalent of the Orange Order, the Ancient Order of Hibernians, never succeeded in gaining a firm foothold in Belfast, partly because of the strength of the predominantly Catholic unions, partly because there was no substantial Catholic middle class and no ruling group with which to link up.

Scarecrows in the Mirror

The main political function of the Nationalist party has undoubtedly been that of a convenient scarecrow to keep the Unionists together. In addition to the Protestant party, lodges and religion itself, it is the fourth pillar of Protestant rule. It does not seem unlikely that if the Catholics in the Nationalist party had not also felt embattled (this time, however, within Ulster, not Ireland as a whole) and had not also exploited the Border question as a means of keeping together its diverse followers, it would have been much more difficult for the Unionists to avoid fragmentation, as the experience of Tone in the late eighteenth

For Ulster's Protestants, the Orange Order became the focus of political, leisure and religious activity.

century and of Larkin and Connolly in the twentieth had shown. Thus the two parties and their associated organizations stand in a perfect polar relation to one another: they are made of the same sectarian cement, they are one another's opposites and yet neither could exist in isolation.

Precipitants of Crisis

It is presumably an impossible task to determine in detail why a particular historical event like the eruption in Ulster in 1968 took place at that moment rather than at any other. Nevertheless we shall try to point to a few factors that appear to have been particularly important.

A proper place to start what might otherwise become an infinite regression is at the increasingly audible protests of the Catholic professional strata in the mid-sixties. One organization, perhaps not the only one, was the Campaign for Social Justice, a small group which tried to attract the attention of British politicians and newspapers by issuing pamphlets and writing personal letters to them. The solidly upper-middle-class basis of the Campaign is unmistakably clear from any of its publications, the composition of its committee or the type of discrimination it was apparently most concerned about. A very large part of the material published by the Campaign deals with discrimination against Catholics in top positions within the civil service, on public boards and so forth; another major topic is gerrymandering.

Why that particular type of political activity emerged in the mid-sixties must, I believe, be seen within the general context of the economic development of Northern Ireland since the war. It is a widespread but untenable myth that the economy of Ulster has by and large been stagnating. There was a temporary depression in the late fifties—as in so many other parts of Europe—but during the sixties production has been growing rather faster than in Britain. As already pointed out, this growth must be seen against the backdrop of a rapid decline in the most important labor-intensive industries. As a result, the new jobs in the subsidized foreign industries that were coming into being more or less balanced the new vacancies in the declining sectors. Unemployment has changed fairly little during the last decades.

Thus the lower classes, and particularly the unskilled Catholic workers and the small farmers, have probably not witnessed much improvement in their position over the years, and the increase in wealth must have accrued primarily to the upper-middle class, the managerial groups and the professional strata. Moreover, as the new foreign employers tended to discriminate less than the old domestic Protestant ones, it seems that the very top echelon among the Catholics has been enjoying fast improving opportunities in the private sector during the sixties when the growth of the foreign industries gathered momentum. In comparison with this, their limited opportunities in public positions and political roles gained a new saliency.

The political means at the disposal of this Catholic elite were, however, rather limited. Our own survey in 1966 showed a widespread passivity among the Catholic poor and little or no expectation that the future would bring any improvement over the present. Besides, as the nature of its activities showed, the Campaign did not really think of rallying support in this direction but concentrated upon influencing opinion in Britain and elsewhere.

This could probably have gone on forever but for the change of government in Britain at the end of 1965. Prior to the election Wilson had pledged a Labour government "to do everything in its power . . . etc." Whether or not anything was done, I do not know. Nor does it matter, for it is clear that the Campaign and its likes now had an audience in Britain, the mere existence of which would force the government of Northern Ireland either to liberalize or at least to pretend that it was in the process of doing so. Once again, true intentions are largely immaterial, for as we have said already, and as we shall discuss further, liberalization is the only policy the Unionist party cannot survive. Consequently, the mere rumor of reform would create a reaction from the Protestant middle and working class in the form of Paisleyism, a movement which in the spring of 1966 had still appeared like the rumble of a distant drum. According to a survey, by the end of 1967, 20 percent of the Protestant middle class and almost 40 percent of the Protestant working class found that they "usually agreed with what the Reverend Ian Paisley said."

I have said nothing so far about the Catholic students at Queens University, Belfast, who are an important part of the civil rights movement. Gibbon points out the particular role of the students in Northern Ireland: "It is important to emphasize that Queen's University, Belfast, is one of the very few unsegregated institutions of any description in Ulster. This meant that it provided a natural base from which an attack on sectarianism could be launched. Moreover, Queen's University is decisively not a regulative institution of entry into the Ulster ruling class. The children of this group are sent to English schools and thence to Sandhurst, Oxbridge or Trinity College, Dublin. Queen's students, on the other hand, are overwhelmingly middle and petit-bourgeois. . . . Accession to the university potentially separated them from their political and religious backgrounds. . . . The preconditions for political radicalism thus existed." One must also note the coincidence between the student revolts in Paris and elsewhere in the spring of 1968 and Ulster's hot summer the same year. Once again, to quote Metternich, France sneezed and Europe caught cold.

Social misery in itself has apparently never bred revolt, and I would think that the rise of the civil rights movement in Ulster and its capture of a section of the Catholic working class were partly the result of the fluid situation as the Protestants polarized the conflict and partly a simple reaction of fear, as in some of the recent riotings.

One must now ask how permanent are the factors responsible for the "recent disorders," as the government calls them. Three points may be noted: first, that the push by the Catholic elite can hardly be stopped now, but second, that it plays a secondary role in itself and can achieve nothing without first provoking a real or imagined pressure from Britain and finally, that the Protestant backlash is constantly available. From a political point of view an essential factor is the combination of a popular base with the strategic guidance available to the civil rights movement in the coalition of students from Queen's University with the Catholic poor of Derry. Together, there is at least the prospect of a political movement; separate, the former are powerless and the latter an amorphous group, merely reacting in self-defense.

Liberal Reforms

Turning now to a consideration of the prospects for the future and the available political options, let us begin by considering the likelihood of effective liberal reforms in Ulster being carried through.

Successive governments have pledged themselves—in more or less vague terms—to various measures of political reform aimed at admitting Catholics as full members of the society. From what has been said so far, however, it should be plain that in my view such reforms are simply not possible within the present political system in Ulster. This is so because any substantial reduction of the difference of opportunities offered to Protestants and Catholics would destroy Unionist cohesion at its base: the Unionist party would break up long before reforms had become effective. A parliamentary majority cannot exist to carry them through. Considered within the sole frame of Northern Ireland, that is, as a voluntary act by its government, reforms would be stopped at this point, if not long before.

It was precisely the prospect that the previous government would actually carry out the reforms it had promised which led to its fall. To ask whether the present prime minister, or his successor, is personally more or less in favor of granting equal rights to Catholics is completely irrelevant, as it counts for nothing in determining the policies actually being implemented. The forces that count are the centrifugal forces in the Protestant coalition and the real or imagined pressure from Britain.

A considerably less ambitious program for pacification is the co-optation of the Catholic middle class. Paul Baran and Paul Sweezy refer to this policy as "tokenism" when describing the increased social opportunities now available to middle-class Negroes in the United States. In their view this social promotion reaches only an infinitesimal part of the Negro community and merely serves to detach its political and intellectual elite from its masses, the continued exploitation of which is thus assured.

Leaving aside the question of the practicability of such a policy in the United States, we can assert that it would not be practicable in Northern Ireland. This is so for two reasons: the first is that the abyss in social distance between the "black bourgeoisie" and the overwhelming majority of the Negroes in the black ghettos of the United States is not matched by a comparable distance between upper- and lower-class Catholics in Northern Ireland. Co-optation might conceivably work in the United States (in the sense of being acceptable to the whites) because the recruitment to the black bourgeoisie from below is small and could be stopped if need be. But in Northern Ireland upward mobility within the Catholic community could probably not be prevented because there the middle rungs of the social ladder are not so depleted. Furthermore, middle-class Catholics are much more numerous in relative terms than are middle-class Negroes in the United States. Opening up for the top stratum of the Catholics would therefore mean admitting many more than the system might be willing to absorb.

The other reason, which alone would be sufficient, lies in the different functions which discrimination serves in the two countries. If we assume unquestioningly (since it is at any rate immaterial to the issue at hand) that Baran and Sweezy are right in claiming that unskilled Negro masses are needed for economic reasons, the only problem in the United States would be to prevent excessive upward mobility. In Ulster, however, I hold that the function of discrimination is a political one. It is the maintenance of the social distance as such which matters, and this social distance has to be maintained in all strata. Co-optation of middle-class Catholics while excluding the rest would not silence Catholic grievances, and it would alienate the politically important Protestant middle class by depriving them of both status and material benefits (the latter being probably more imaginary than real).

The Fascist Danger

Tokenism in another sense, namely the granting of concessions (such as an extension of the franchise for local elections) that do not significantly affect the real distribution of power between the communities, could perhaps be carried through (and even that is by no means certain)—provided their token character is absolutely plain to everyone concerned. Such measures can of course do no more than postpone events, but it seems likely that actually granting a few such token reforms and promising more substantial ones (which, as we have seen, would not be carried out) could for some time create enough confusion among Catholics, dividing them over strategy, that the present system could survive a little longer.

None of this means that effective liberal reform is impossible in Northern Ireland, only that it would have to be imposed from outside. To do so would be to destroy the Unionist party and the Protestant bloc in general, and as this would become clear long before the process was completed, it seems unlikely that forced liberalization would be carried through to its end unless this particular consequence had been foreseen and was actually accepted as a necessary cost or actively pursued as a goal in itself.

The first group to split off will, of course, be precisely that one which is already threatening to do so, the group around the Reverend Paisley. Its violent opposition would entail a very definite danger of an armed Protestant uprising and a political turn towards fascism or something similar. This fascist danger would provide an opportunity, and a very reasonable motive perhaps, for shelving any reform program.

A Thought Experiment

I have claimed—or rather it has been understood throughout—that the religious conflict in Ulster is an artificial conflict in the sense that the relationship between the two communities is no longer a necessarily antagonistic one, and only the social institutions make it remain so. I have further claimed that contrary to appearances not so long ago, the institutions by which sectarianism is maintained in Ulster are in fact extremely vulnerable and are probably now verging on collapse. It should follow from this that it might not be so difficult to assist "the forces of history" a little.

Let us therefore consider what kind of approach Britain might adopt on the assumption (entirely gratuitous) that she has no particular interests in Ulster save that of finding a long-term solution to the problem. Those skeptics who learn from history, and from Irish history in particular, may take the following as merely a mental exercise.

The one institution that has dismally failed in the past is Stormont parliamentarianism. Only one proposal by the opposition has ever been accepted by the majority, and it had to do with wild-bird life. It is also clear that a parliament where one party has a permanent absolute majority and votes never shift from one party to another is worse than no parliament at all, because it merely provides a democratic varnish to the dictatorship of the majority. If either condition is relaxed there will be some motivation for the majority to anticipate future needs and seek the cooperation of the minority.

Another obvious observation is that it is hardly a durable solution to patch over the conflict, but on the contrary that if one recognizes it, formalizes it and establishes an institutional frame within which it can be fought as a clear-cut power struggle, then one is likely to defuse the powder keg. A well-known example of this is the ritualization of the class struggle which has been achieved by means of the organized wage negotiations.

One may therefore consider replacing the Senate and the House of Commons at Stormont with a new bicameral parliament, one elected by Catholics and one by Protestants, and requiring a majority in both houses for certain types of legislation. An example might be the location of highways for which a delay in decision is bearable, yet costly to all involved. This constitutional device alone, which reproduces the fictitious equality of the parties to a wage negotiation, would force the representatives of the two communities into dialogue and mutual concessions.

To give Catholics a real say in matters concerning them, and to give Protestants a reasonably larger share of the total budgetary resources, each house would need to have a separate budget which it can dispose of on its own. This might cover the most sensitive areas like subsidies to housing, schools, hospitals and new industry. It would again force the two houses into a minimum of cooperation, or coordination at least, of their programs; but the more important effect to be sought is the redirection of some of the grievances "inwards" towards one's own community.

The separation of Catholics and Protestants into two communities that vote for separate parliaments would have as a major benefit the immediate breakup of the Unionist and Nationalist parties because there would no longer be any electoral advantage in remaining as a bloc. Protestants may go on discriminating in favor of Protestants, but this would no longer be a cement to Orangeism. Political fragmentation in turn would lead to the manifestation of the divergent interests of classes and other political groupings and result in a more fluctuating electorate and a greater likelihood of political alliances crossing the religious barrier on particular issues.

There is a large body of legislation that cannot be dealt with in these ways and would have to come before a joint session of the two houses. Although this would probably have a Protestant majority (a Labour and Catholic majority is also quite conceivable), the Catholics would have to be listened to, because their cooperation would be needed in other contexts.

The executive would obviously need the confidence of both houses; and this would create a pressure from above, not only on the parliaments, but also on the electorate towards less sectarian attitudes, once more, presumably, a complete reversal of the present situation. Finally, the Protestant fears of being "outbreeded" would become less tenable in a system where the minority had veto-rights.

This "homeopathic" approach to "solving" ethnic conflict *of this particular nature* is very far from the "All-Irish Worker's Republic" which some demand, but it is also far from the "Protestant Country for a Protestant People" of others. It is probably as impossible of execution as either of these. The aim of this discussion is not of course to present a blueprint for anything. Many other types of reforms would have similar effects, and some, no doubt, would be easier to operate in practice. Besides, such proposals optimistically assume that disinterested, yet powerful outside actors exist. The aim in bringing up this proposal is simply to point out that the problems may not be incapable of solution if the simplistic dichotomy between integration and polarization is dropped, and one realizes that in real situations where a number of different conflicts interact with one another, these two concepts are more complementary than contradictory.

T. Michael O'Sullivan

Future Prospects

So far there is little evidence to suggest that any of the principal actors has any particular interest in doing much about the situation in Northern Ireland except restore "law and order." Probably this applies even to the Catholic middle class which, having seen the considerable forces it unleashed both on the Protestant Right and on the Catholic Left, might not be hard to convince that tolerating the present situation is preferable to both available alternatives.

Nevertheless, we have seen that the forces that press for change and bring the conflict to the surface are likely to continue to operate in the foreseeable future. One reason for this is that the activation of the conflict does not require any mass movement by the Catholic middle class but can be provoked by quite small groups within it. Hence we should expect a long period with governmental instability —each successive government balancing uneasily between the need to show the outsider its willingness for reform while appearing to Ulstermen to be firmly conservative— and with a succession of violent outbursts, interspersed with periods of "armistice" in which the Catholics wait for promised reforms to become effective. As the credibility of the reform programs declines over the years, periods of relative quiet may come to result increasingly from sheer police repression.

Whether or not that day will come when international, and particularly British, opinion will be ripe for accepting a "temporary" regime based on physical force is impossible to tell, but it should be clear that there can be no simple peaceful settlement under the present conditions; for if there appeared to be, if the Catholics appeared to have accepted their inferior position, the Protestants would have to reactivate the conflict in order to maintain their unity. Such is, according to this analysis, the delicate balance upon which the social structure of Northern Ireland is based.

White Institutions & Black Rage

Representatives of white society's outposts in the ghetto present the face of racism

DAVID BOESEL, RICHARD BERK, W. EUGENE GROVES,
BETTYE EIDSON & PETER H. ROSSI

Five summers of black rebellion have made it clear that the United States is facing a crisis of proportions not seen since the Great Depression. And one of the root causes of this crisis, it has also become clear, is the performance of white institutions, especially those institutions in the ghetto. Some of these institutions—police and retail stores, for example—have done much to antagonize Negroes; others, such as welfare departments and black political organizations, have tried to help and have failed.

Why have these white institutions helped engender black rage? One way to find out might be to study the attitudes of the men working for them—to discover what their personnel think about the racial crisis itself, about their own responsibilities, about the work they are doing. Therefore, at the request of the National Advisory Commission on Civil Disorders (the riot commission), we at Johns Hopkins University visited 15 Northern cities and questioned men and women working for six different institutional groups: major employers, retail merchants, teachers, welfare workers, political workers (all Negro), and policemen. All of the people we questioned, except the employers, work right in the ghetto, and are rank-and-file employees—the cop on the beat, the social caseworker, and so on.

Employers' Social Responsibility

The "employers" we questioned were the managers or personnel officers of the ten institutions in each city that employed the most people, as well as an additional 20 managers or personnel officers of the next 100 institutions. As such, they represented the most economically progressive institutions in America. And in their employment policies we could see how some of America's dominant corporate institutions impinge on the everyday lives of urban Negroes.

Businessmen are in business to make a profit. Seldom do they run their enterprises for social objectives. But since it is fashionable these days, most of the managers and personnel officers we interviewed (86 percent, in fact) accepted the proposition that they "have a social responsibility to make strong efforts to provide employment for Negroes and other minority groups." This assertion, however, is contradicted by unemployment in the Negro community today, as well as by the hiring policies of the firms themselves.

Businessmen, as a whole, do not exhibit openly racist attitudes. Their position might best be described as one of "optimistic denial"—the gentlemanly white racism evident in a tacit, but often unwitting, acceptance of institutional practices that subordinate or exclude Negroes. One aspect of this optimistic denial is a nonrecognition of the seriousness of the problems that face black people. Only 21 percent of our sample thought that unemployment was a very serious problem in the nations' cities, yet 26 percent considered air pollution very serious and 31 percent considered traffic very serious. The employers' perspective is based upon their limited experience with blacks, and that experience does not give them a realistic picture of the plight of Negroes in this country. Employers don't even think that racial discrimination has much to do with the Negroes' plight; a majority (57 percent) felt that Negroes are treated at least as well as other people of the same income, and an additional 6 percent felt that Negroes are treated *better* than any other part of the population.

This optimistic denial on the part of employers ("things really aren't that bad for Negroes") is often combined with a negative image of Negroes as employees. Half of those employers interviewed (51 percent) said that Negroes are likely to have higher rates of absenteeism than whites, so that hiring many of them would probably upset production schedules. Almost a third thought that, because Negro crime rates are generally higher than white crime rates, hiring many Negroes could lead to increased theft and vandalism in their companies. About a fifth (22 percent) thought that hiring Negroes might bring "agitators and troublemakers" into their companies, and another one-fifth feared that production costs might rise because Negroes supposedly do not take orders well.

The employer's views may reflect not only traditional white prejudices, but also some occasional experience he himself has had with Negroes. Such experiences, however, may stem as much from the employer's own practices and misconceptions as from imputed cultural habits of Negroes. As Elliott Liebow observed in his study of Negro street-corner men *(Tally's Corner)*, blacks have learned to cope with life by treating menial, low-status, degrading jobs in the same way that the jobs treat them—with benign nonconcern.

Most of the employers believe that Negroes lack the preparation for anything but menial jobs. A full 83 percent said that few Negroes are qualified for professional jobs, and 69 percent thought that few are qualified for skilled positions. When it comes to unskilled jobs, of course, only 23 percent of the employers held this view.

The employers seem to share a widespread assumption—one frequently used as a cover for racism—that for historical and environmental reasons Negroes have been disabled to such an extent as to make them uncompetitive in a highly competitive society. And while it is certainly true that black people have suffered from a lack of educational and other opportunities, this line of thinking—especially among whites—has a tendency to blame the past and the ghetto environment for what is perceived as Negro incompetence, thus diverting attention from *present* institutional practices. So, many employers have developed a rhetoric of concern about upgrading the so-called "hard-core unemployed" in lieu of changing their employment policies.

To a considerable extent our respondents' assessment of Negro job qualifications reflects company policy, for the criteria used in hiring skilled and professional workers tend to exclude Negroes. The criteria are (1) previous experience and (2) recommendations. It is evident that because Negroes are unlikely to have *had* previous experience in positions from which they have long been excluded, and because they are unlikely to have had much contact with people in the best position to recommend them, the criteria for "qualification" make it probable that employers will consider most Negroes unqualified.

Negroes Get the Worst Jobs

In short, the employers' aversion to taking risks (at least with people), reinforced by the pressure of labor unions and more general discriminatory patterns in society, means that Negroes usually get the worst jobs.

Thus, although Negroes make up 20 percent of the unskilled workers in these large corporations, they fill only a median of one percent of the professional positions and only 2 percent of the skilled positions. Moreover, the few Negroes in the higher positions are unevenly distributed among the corporations. Thirty-two percent of the companies don't report Negroes in professional positions, and 24 percent do not report any in skilled positions. If these companies are set aside, in the remaining companies the median percentage of Negroes in the two positions rises to 3 percent and 6 percent respectively. Further, in these remaining companies an even larger percentage (8 percent in both cases) of *current* positions are being filled by Negroes—which indicates, among other things, that a breakthrough has been accomplished in some companies, while in others Negro employment in the upper levels remains minimal or nonexistent.

Even among those companies that hire blacks for skilled jobs, a Negro applicant's chances of getting the job are only one-fourth as good as those of his white counterpart. For professional positions, the chances are more nearly equal: Negro applicants are about three-fourths as likely to get these jobs as are white applicants. It seems that Negroes have come closest to breaking in at the top (though across all firms only about 4 percent of the applicants for professional positions are Negro). The real stumbling-block to equal employment opportunities seems to be at the skilled level, and here it may be that union policies—and especially those of the craft unions—augment the employers' resistance to hiring Negroes for and promoting Negroes to skilled positions.

What do urban Negroes themselves think of employers' hiring practices? A survey of the same 15 cities by Angus Campbell and Howard Schuman, for the riot commission, indicates that one-third (34 percent) of the Negro men interviewed reported having been refused jobs because of racial discrimination, and 72 percent believed that some or many other black applicants are turned down for the same reason. Almost as many (68 percent) think that some or many black people miss out on promotions because of prejudice. And even when companies do hire Negroes (presumably in professional positions), this is interpreted as tokenism: 77 percent of the black respondents thought that Negroes are hired by big companies for show purposes.

The companies we studied, which have little contact with the ghetto, are very different from the other institutions in our survey, whose contact with the ghetto is direct and immediate. The corporations are also up-to-date, well-financed, and innovative, while the white institutions inside the ghetto are outdated, underfinanced, and overloaded. In historical terms, the institutions in the ghetto represent another era of thought and organization.

Ghetto Merchants

The slum merchants illustrate the tendency of ghetto institutions to hark back to earlier forms. While large corporations cooperate with one another and with the government to exert substantial control over their market, the ghetto merchant still functions in the realm of traditional laissez-faire. He is likely to be a small operator, economically marginal and with almost no ability to control his market. His main advantage over the more efficient, modern retailer is his restricted competition, for the ghetto provides a captive market. The difficulty that many blacks have in getting transportation out of the ghetto, combined with a lack of experience in comparative shopping, seems to give the local merchant a competitive aid he sorely needs to survive against the lower prices and better goods sold in other areas of the city.

The merchants in our study also illustrate the free-enterprise character of ghetto merchandising. They run very small operations—grocery stores, restaurants, clothing and liquor stores, and so on, averaging a little over three employees per business. Almost half of them (45 percent) find it difficult to "keep up with their competition" (competition mainly *within* the ghetto). Since there are almost no requirements for becoming a merchant, this group is the most heterogeneous of all those studied. They have the widest age range (from 17 through 80), the highest percentage of immigrants (15 percent), and the lowest educational levels (only 16 percent finished college).

Again in contrast to the large corporations, the ghetto merchant must live with the harsh day-to-day realities of violence and poverty. His attitudes toward Negroes, different in degree from those of the employers, are at least partly a function of his objective evaluations of his customers.

Running a business in a ghetto means facing special kinds of "overhead." Theft is an especially worrisome problem for the merchants; respondents mentioned it more frequently than any other problem. There is, of course, some basis in fact for their concern. According to the riot commission, inventory losses—ordinarily under 2 percent of sales—may be twice as great in high-crime areas (most of which are in ghettos). And for these small businesses such losses may cut substantially into a slender margin of profit.

Thus it is not surprising that, of all the occupational groups interviewed in this study, the retail merchants were among the most likely to consider Negroes violent and criminal. For example, 61 percent said that Negroes are more likely to steal than whites, and 50 percent believed that Negroes are more likely to pass bad checks. No wonder, then, that black customers may encounter unusual surveillance and suspicion when they shop.

Less understandable is the ghetto merchant's apparent ignorance of the plight of ghetto blacks. Thus, 75 percent believe that blacks get medical treatment that is equal to or better than what whites get. A majority think that Negroes are not discriminated against with regard to treatment by the police, recreation facilities and so forth. Logically enough, 51 percent of the merchants feel that Negroes are making too many demands. This percentage is the second-highest measured (the police were the least sympathetic). So the merchants (like all other groups in the survey except the black politicians) are inclined to emphasize perceived defects in the black community as a major problem in their dealings with Negroes.

The shaky economic position of the merchants, their suspicion of their Negro customers, and the high "overhead" of doing business in the ghetto (because of theft, vandalism, bad credit risks) lead many merchants to sell inferior merchandise at higher prices—and to resort to other strategems for getting money out of their customers. To elicit responses from the merchants on such delicate matters, we drew up a series of very indirect questions. The responses we obtained, though they no doubt understate the extent to which ghetto merchants provide a poor dollar value per unit of goods, are nevertheless revealing. For example, we asked the merchants to recommend various ways of "keeping up with business competition." Some 44 percent said that you should offer extra services; over a third (36 percent) said you should raise prices to cover unusually high overhead; and the same number (36 percent) said that you should buy "bargain" goods at lower prices, then sell them at regular prices. (To a small merchant, "bargain goods" ordinarily means "seconds," or slightly spoiled merchandise, because he doesn't do enough volume to gain real discounts from a wholesaler.) A smaller but still significant segment (12 percent) said that one should "bargain the selling price with each customer and take whatever breaks you can get."

The Campbell-Schuman study indicates that 56 percent of the Negroes interviewed felt that they had been overcharged in neighborhood stores (24 percent said often); 42 percent felt that they had been sold spoiled or inferior goods (13 percent said often). Given the number of ghetto stores a customer may visit every week, these data are entirely compatible with ours. Since one-third of the merchants indicated that they were not averse to buying "bargain" goods for sale in their stores, it is understandable that 42 percent of the Negroes in these areas should say that at one time or another they have been sold inferior merchandise.

It is also understandable that during the recent civil disorders many Negroes, unable to affect merchants by routine methods, struck directly at the stores, looting and burning them.

Teachers in the Ghetto

Just as ghetto merchants are in a backwater of the economy, ghetto schools are in a backwater of the educational system, experimental efforts in some cities notwithstanding.

Negroes, of course, are most likely to be served by outmoded and inadequate schools, a fact that the Coleman Report has documented in considerable detail. In metropolitan regions of the Northeast, for example, 40 percent of the Negro pupils at the secondary level attended schools in buildings over 40 years old, but only 15 percent of the whites did; the average number of pupils per room was 35 for Negroes but 28 for whites.

The teachers covered in our survey (half of whom were Negro) taught in ghetto schools at all levels. Surprisingly, 88 percent said that they were satisfied with their jobs. Their rate of leaving, however, was not consistent with this. Half of the teachers had been in their present schools for no more than four years. Breaking the figures down year by year, we find that the largest percentage (17 percent) had been there only one year. In addition, the teachers' rate of leaving increased dramatically after they had taught for five years.

While the teachers thought that education was a major problem for the cities and especially for the ghettos, they did not think that ghetto schools were a source of the difficulty. A solid majority, comparing their own schools with others in the city, thought that theirs were average, above average, or superior in seven out of eight categories. The high quality of the teaching staff, so rated by 84 percent of the respondents, was rivaled only by the high quality of the textbooks (again 84 percent). The one doubtful area, according to the teachers, was the physical plant, which seemed to them to be just barely competitive; in this respect, 44 percent considered their own schools below average or inferior.

The teachers have less confidence in their students than in themselves or their schools. On the one hand, they strongly reject the view that in ghetto schools education is sacrificed to the sheer need for order: 85 percent said it was not true that pupils in their schools were uneducable, and that teachers could do little more than maintain discipline. On the other hand, the teachers as a group could not agree that their students were as educable as they might be. There was little consensus on whether their pupils were "about average" in interest and ability: 28 percent thought that their pupils were; 41 percent thought it was partially true that they were; and 31 percent thought it was not true. But the teachers had less difficulty agreeing that their students were *not* "above average in ability and . . . generally co-operative with teachers." Agreeing on this were 59 percent of the teachers, with another 33 percent in the middle.

The real problem with education in the ghetto, as the teachers see it, is the ghetto itself. The teachers have their own version of the "Negro disability" thesis: the "cultural deprivation" theory holds that the reason for bad education in the ghetto is the student's environment rather than the schools. (See "How Teachers Learn to Help Children Fail," Fuchs, *Trans*-action, September, 1968.) Asked to name the major problems facing their schools, the teachers most frequently mentioned community apathy; the second most-mentioned problem, a derivation of the first, was an alleged lack of preparation and motivation in the students. Fifty-nine percent of the teachers agreed to some extent that "many communities provide such a terrible environment for the pupils that education doesn't do much good in the end."

Such views are no doubt detrimental to education in the ghetto, for they imply a decided fatalism as far as teaching is concerned. If the students are deficient—improperly motivated, distracted, and so on—and if the cause of this deficiency lies in the ghetto rather than in the schools themselves, then there is little reason for a teacher to exert herself to set high standards for her students.

There is considerable question, however, whether the students in ghetto schools are as distracted as the teachers think. Events in the last few years indicate that the schools, especially the high schools and the junior high schools, are one of the strongest focuses of the current black rebellion. The student strike at Detroit's Northern High School in 1966, for example, was cohesive and well-organized. A boycott by some 2,300 students, directed against a repressive school administration, lasted over two weeks and resulted in the dismissal of the principal and the formation of a committee, including students, to investigate school conditions. The ferment in the ghetto schools across the country is also leading to the formation of permanent and independent black students' groups, such as the Modern Strivers in Washington, D.C.'s Eastern High, intent on promoting black solidarity and bringing about changes in the educational system. In light of such developments, there is reason to think that the teachers in the survey have overestimated the corrosive effects of the ghetto environment on students—and underestimated the schools' responsibility for the state of education in the ghetto.

Social Workers and the Welfare Establishment

Public welfare is another area in which old ideas have been perpetuated beyond their time. The roots of the present welfare-department structure lie in the New Deal legislation of the 1930s. The public assistance provisions of the Social Security Act were designed to give aid to the helpless and the noncompetitive: the aged, the blind, the "permanently and totally" disabled, and dependent children. The assumption was that the recipient, because of personal disabilities or inadequacies, could not make his way in life without outside help.

The New Deal also provided work (e.g., the W.P.A.) for the able-bodied who were assumed to be unemployed only temporarily. But as the Depression gave way to the war years and to the return of prosperity, the massive work programs for the able-bodied poor were discontinued, leaving only those programs that were premised on the notion of personal disability. To a considerable extent today's Negro poor have had to rely on the latter. Chief among these programs, of course, is Aid for Dependent Children, which has become a mainstay of welfare. And because of racial discrimination, especially in education and employment, a large part of the Negro population also experiences poverty as a permanent state.

While most of the social workers in our survey showed considerable sympathy with the Negro cause, they too felt that the root of the problem lay in weaknesses in the Negro community; and they saw their primary task as making up the supposed deficiency. A hefty majority of the respondents (78 percent) thought that a large part of their responsibility was to "teach the poor how to live"—rather than to provide the means for them to live as they like. Assuming disability, welfare has fostered dependency.

The social workers, however, are unique among the groups surveyed in that they are quite critical of their own institution. The average welfare worker is not entirely at one with the establishment for which she works. She is likely to be a college graduate who regards her job as transitional. And her lack of expertise has its advantages as well as its disadvantages, for it means that she can take a more straightforward view of the situations she is confronted with. She is not committed to bureaucracy as a way of life.

The disparity between the welfare establishment and the average welfare worker is evident in the latter's complaints about her job. The complaints she voices the most deal *not* with her clients, but with the welfare department itself and the problems of working within its present structure—the difficulty of getting things done, the red tape, the lack of adequate funds, and so on. Of the five most-mentioned difficulties of welfare work, three dealt with such intra-agency problems; the other two dealt with the living conditions of the poor.

There is a good deal of evidence to support the social worker's complaints. She complains, for example, that welfare agencies are understaffed. The survey indicates that an average caseload is 177 people, each client being visited about once a month for about 50 minutes. Even the most conscientious of caseworkers must be overwhelmed by such client-to-worker ratios.

As in the case of the schools, welfare has engendered a countervailing force among the very people it is supposed to serve. Welfare clients have become increasingly hostile to the traditional structure and philosophy of welfare departments and have formed themselves into an outspoken movement. The welfare-rights movement at this stage has aims: to obtain a more nearly adequate living base for the clients, and to overload the system with demands, thus either forcing significant changes or clearing the way for new and more appropriate institutions.

Black Political Party Workers

Usually when segments of major social institutions become incapable of functioning adequately, the people whom the institutions are supposed to serve have recourse to politics. In the ghetto, however, the political machinery is no better off than the other institutions. Around the turn of

Some politicians like this committeeman deal with Negro constituents' problems, but "the black community has no illusions about the ability of routine politics to meet its needs."

the century Negroes began to carve out small niches for themselves in the politics of such cities as Chicago and New York. Had Negro political organizations developed along the same lines as those of white ethnic groups, they might today provide valuable leverage for the ghetto population. But this has not happened. For one thing, the decline of the big-city machine, and its replacement in many cities by "nonpolitical" reform governments supported by a growing middle class, began to close off a route traditionally open to minority groups. Second, black politicians have never been regarded as fullfledged political brokers by racist whites, and consequently the possibility of a Negro's becoming a powerful politician in a predominantly white city has been foreclosed (the recent election of Carl Stokes as Mayor of Cleveland and Richard D. Hatcher, Mayor of Gary, Indiana, would be exceptions). Whites have tended to put aside their differences when confronting Negro political efforts; to regard Negro demands, no matter how routine, as racial issues; and hence to severely limit the concessions made to black people.

Today the sphere of Negro politics is cramped and closely circumscribed. As Kenneth B. Clark has observed, most of the Negroes who have reached high public office have done so *not* within the context of Negro politics, but through competition in the larger society. In most cities Negro political organizations are outmoded and inadequate. Even if, as seems probable, more and more Negro mayors are elected, they will have to work within the antiquated structure of urban government, with sharply limited resources. Unless things change, the first Negro mayor of Newark, for example, will preside over a bankrupt city.

Our survey of Negro political workers in the 15 cities documents the inadequacy of Negro politics—and the inadequacy of the larger system of urban politics. The political workers, understandably, strongly sympathize with the aspirations of other black people. As ghetto politicians, they deal with the demands and frustrations of other blacks day after day. Of all the groups surveyed, they were the most closely in touch with life in the ghetto. Most of them work in the middle and lower levels of municipal politics; they talk with about 75 voters each week. These political workers are, of course, acutely aware of the precipitous rise in the demands made by the black community. Most (93 percent) agreed that in the last few years people in their districts have become more determined to get what they want. The strongest impetus of this new determination comes from the younger blacks: 92 percent of the political workers agreed that "young people have become more militant." Only a slight majority, however (56 percent), said the same of middle-aged people.

Against the pressure of rising Negro demands, urban political organizations formed in other times and on other assumptions, attentive to other interests, and constrained by severely limited resources, find themselves unable to respond satisfactorily. A majority of the political workers, in evaluating a variety of services available to people in their districts, thought that all except two—telephone service and the fire department—were either poor or fair. Worst of the lot, according to the political workers, were recreation, police protection, and building inspection.

In view of these respondents, the black community has no illusions about the ability of routine politics to meet its needs. While only 38 percent of the political workers thought that the people in their districts regarded their councilmen as friends fighting for them, 51 percent said that the people considered their councilmen "part of the city government which must be asked continually and repeatedly in order to get things done." (Since the political workers were probably talking about their fellow party members, their responses may have been more favorable than frank. A relatively high percentage of "don't know" responses supports this point.)

Almost all the Negro politicians said that they received various requests from the voters for help. Asked whether they could respond to these requests "almost always, usually, or just sometimes," the largest percentage (36 percent) chose "sometimes"—which, in context, is a way of saying "seldom." Another 31 percent said they "usually" could respond to such requests, and 19 percent said "almost always." Logically enough, 60 percent of the political workers agreed that in the last few years "people have become more fed up with the system, and are becoming unwilling to work with politicians." In effect, this is an admission that they as political workers, and the system of urban politics to which they devote themselves, are failing.

When economic and social institutions fail to provide the life-chances that a substantial part of a population wants, and when political institutions fail to provide a remedy, the aspirations of the people begin to spill over into forms of activity that the dominant society regards either as unacceptable or illegitimate—crime, vandalism, noncooperation, and various forms of political protest.

Robert M. Fogelson and Robert D. Hill, in the *Supplemental Studies* for the riot commission, have reported that 50 percent to 90 percent of the Negro males in ten cities studied had arrest records. Clearly, when the majority of men in a given population are defined as criminals—at least by the police—something more than "deviant" behaviour is involved. In effect, ghetto residents—and especially the youth—and the police are in a state of subdued warfare. On the one hand, the cities are experiencing a massive and as yet inchoate social rising of the Negro population. On the other hand, the police—devoted to the racial status quo and inclined to overlook the niceties of mere law in their quest for law and order—have found a variety of means, both conventional and otherwise, for countering the aims of Negroes. In doing so, they are not only adhering to the norms of their institution, but also furthering their personal goals as well. The average policeman, recruited from a lower- or middle-class white background, frequently of "ethnic" origins, comes from a group whose social position is marginal and who feel most threatened by Negro advances.

The high arrest rate in the Negro community thus mirrors both the push of Negroes and the determined resistance of the police. As the conflict intensifies, the police are more and more losing authority in the eyes of black people; the young Negroes are especially defiant. Any type of contact between police and black people can quickly lead to a situation in which the policeman gives an order and

Stop and frisk. "Many departments have adopted patrol practices which . . . 'replaced harassment by individual patrolmen with harassment by entire departments.'"

the Negro either defies it or fails to show sufficient respect in obeying it. This in turn can lead to the Negro's arrest on a disorderly conduct charge or on a variety of other charges. (Disorderly conduct accounted for about 17 percent of the arrests in the Fogelson-Hill study.)

Police Harassment Techniques

The police often resort to harassment as a means of keeping the Negro community off-balance. The riot commission noted that:

> Because youths commit a large and increasing proportion of crime, police are under growing pressure from their supervisors—and from the community—to deal with them forcefully. "Harassment of youths" may therefore be viewed by some police departments—and members even of the Negro community—as a proper crime prevention technique.

The Commission added that "many departments have adopted patrol practices which, in the words of one commentator, have 'replaced harassment by individual patrolmen with harassment by entire departments.'"

Among the most common of the cops' harassment techniques are breaking up street-corner groups and stop-and-frisk tactics. Our study found that 63 percent of the ghetto police reported that they "frequently" were called upon to disperse loitering groups. About a third say they "frequently" stop and frisk people. Obviously then, the law enforcer sometimes interferes with individuals and groups who consider their activities quite legitimate and necessary. Black people in the ghetto—in the absence of adequate parks, playgrounds, jobs, and recreation facilities, and unwilling to sit in sweltering and overcrowded houses with rats and bugs—are likely to make the streets their front yards. But this territory is often made uninhabitable by the police.

Nearly a third of the white policemen in our study thought that most of the residents of their precinct (largely Negro) were not industrious. Even more striking about the attitudes of the white police working in these neighborhoods is that many of them deny the fact of Negro inequality: 20 percent say the Negro is treated better than any other part of the population, and 14 percent say he is treated equally. As for their own treatment of Negroes, the Campbell-Schuman survey reported that 43 percent of the black men, who are on the streets more than the women, thought that police use insulting language in their neighborhoods. Only 17 percent of the white males held this belief. Of the Negro men, 20 percent reported that the police insulted them personally and 28 percent said they knew someone to whom this had happened; only 9 percent and 12 percent, respectively, of the whites reported the same. Similarly, many more blacks than whites thought that the police frisked and searched people without good reason (42 percent compared to 12 percent); and that the police roughed up people unnecessarily (37 percent as compared to 10 percent). Such reports of police misconduct were most frequent among the younger Negroes, who, after all, are on the receiving end most often.

The policeman's isolation in the ghetto is evident in a number of findings. We asked the police how many people —of various types—they knew well enough in the ghetto to greet when they saw them. Eighty-nine percent of the police said they knew six or more shopowners, managers, and clerks well enough to speak with, but only 38 percent said they knew this many teenage or youth leaders. At the same time, 39 percent said that most young adults, and 51 percent said that most adolescents, regard the police as enemies. And only 16 percent of the white policemen (37 percent of the blacks) either "often" or "sometimes" attended meetings in the neighborhood.

The police have wound up face to face with the social consequences of the problems in the ghetto created by the failure of other white institutions—though, as has been observed, they themselves have contributed to those problems in no small degree. The distant and gentlemanly white racism of employers, the discrimination of white parents who object to having their children go to school with Negroes, the disgruntlement of white taxpayers who deride the present welfare system as a sinkhole of public funds but are unwilling to see it replaced by anything more effective—the consequences of these and other forms of white racism have confronted the police with a massive control problem of the kind most evident in the riots.

In our survey, we found that the police were inclined to see the riots as the long range result of faults in the Negro community—disrespect for law, crime, broken families, etc.—rather than as responses to the stance of the white community. Indeed, nearly one-third of the white police saw the riots as the result of what they considered the basic violence and disrespect of Negroes in general, while only one-fourth attributed the riots to the failure of white institutions. More than three-fourths also regarded the riots as the immediate result of agitators and criminals—a suggestion contradicted by all the evidence accumulated by the riot commission. The police, then, share with the other groups—excepting the black politicians—a tendency to emphasize perceived defects in the black community as an explanation for the difficulties that they encounter in the ghetto.

The state of siege evident in many police departments is but an exaggerated version of a trend in the larger white society. It is the understandable, but unfortunate, response of people who are angry and confused about the widespread disruption of traditional racial patterns and who feel threatened by these changes. There is, of course, some basis for this feeling, because the Negro movement poses challenges of power and interest to many groups. To the extent that the movement is successful, the merchants, for example, will either have to reform their practices or go out of business—and for many it may be too late for reform. White suburbanites will have to cough up funds for the city, which provides most of them with employment. Police departments will have to be thoroughly restructured.

The broad social rising of Negroes is beginning to have a substantial effect upon all white institutions in the ghetto, as the situation of the merchants, the schools, and the welfare establishment illustrates. Ten years ago, these institutions (and the police, who have been affected differently) could operate pretty much unchecked by any countervailing power in the ghetto. Today, both their excesses and their inadequacies have run up against an increasingly militant black population, many of whom support violence as a means of redress. The evidence suggests that unless these institutions are transformed, the black community will make it increasingly difficult for them to function at all.

March 1970

Members of the Group for Research on Social Policy at Johns Hopkins University are David Boesel, Richard Berk, W. Eugene Groves, Bettye K. Eidson, and Peter H. Rossi, chairman of the department of social relations at Johns Hopkins University and director of the Group for Research on Social Policy, under whose auspices this article was written.

The article is based on *Between White and Black: A Study of American Institutions in the Ghetto,* prepared for the National Advisory Commission on Civil Disorders, June 1968.

SUGGESTED READINGS

Report of the National Advisory Commission on Civil Disorders (New York: Bantam Books, 1968).

Supplemental Studies for the National Advisory Commission on Civil Disorders by Robert M. Fogelson and Robert D. Hill (Washington: U.S. Government Printing Office, 1968). Sociological studies of racial attitudes in 15 large cities, of white institutions in the ghettos of those cities, and of the characteristics of arrestees in major riots.

Dark Ghetto: Dilemmas of Social Power by Kenneth B. Clark (New York: Harper Torchbooks, 1965). One of the best studies of the ghetto and its relation to white society.

Ghetto Revolts edited by Peter H. Rossi (Chicago: Aldine, 1970).

A Time to Burn?: An Evaluation of the Present Crisis in Race Relations by Louis H. Masotti, Jeffrey K. Hadden, Kenneth F. Seminatore and Jerome R. Corsi (Chicago, Ill.: Rand McNally and Co., 1969) investigates black-white relations and the interaction with social structure and values in the past and present.

The Circle of Discrimination: An Economic and Social Study of the Black Man in New York by Herman D. Bloch (New York: New York University Press, 1969). A study of black-white relations which focuses on the history of the blacks in the trade union movement and on the economic consequences of prejudice against blacks.

An American Dilemma by Gunnar Myrdal (New York: Harper and Brothers, 1944). A valuable study in the field of American black-white relations.

Soul on Ice by Eldridge Cleaver (New York: Dell Publishing Company, 1968). A collection of essays and letters written when Cleaver was in Folsom State Prison.

The Power Structure by Arnold M. Rose (New York: Oxford University Press, 1967). A reaction to the Floyd Hunter *(Community Power Structure)* and C. Wright Mills *(Power Elite)* picture of power arrangements in the United States. Rose offers an alternative conception of the power structure.

White Rites Versus Indian Rights

Expanded educational opportunities for Indians may not be opportunities at all

A. D. FISHER

The lyrics of a song in the top ten last summer put the matter unequivocally. "Education's the thing," wails the lead singer of a black group called The Winstons, "if you want to compete. Without it, life just ain't very sweet." Almost everyone in North America, I suspect, would say "Amen" to that. The belief in increasing educational opportunities as the avenue to social progress has become an article of faith, and "going to school" an assurance of secular salvation akin to "good works" and "saving grace" in other times and other religions.

That for many sectors of North American society this belief flies in the face of observable facts should surprise no one. Yet it is a fact that the propitiation of the gods of learning simply isn't working for vast numbers of Americans and Canadians, especially the poor, the black and the Indian. Indeed, for those with whom I am most concerned in this essay, the Indian people of Canada, it can be demonstrated that education has been very nearly a total disaster.

Despite a considerable expansion of the number of schools and in the number of years of schooling available to Canadian Indian children, the unemployment rate among them has increased. Between the years 1959-60 and 1962-63, the welfare costs among Alberta's Indian population jumped from $294,625 to $683,080, and a sizeable portion of the latter figure went to unemployed but "educated" Indians. The incidence of unemployment among Indians with education is even more graphically illustrated by comparing the average unemployment of the total Indian population (43 percent) to that of Alberta Indian students who terminated their education in 1964-65 (64 percent).

While these figures clearly indicate that the Canadian Indian fails to use whatever education he receives once his schooling is over, other studies show that he also fails to take advantage of the schooling available to him. For example, in 1965 a study was made of junior high school dropouts at the Blackfoot Indian Reserve, Gleichen-Cluny, Alberta. It was determined that 86 of 168 students, or 51 percent, had dropped out of school in the years since 1961 and of these dropouts, 95 percent left school before they had completed grade nine. Something quite obviously happened to these children between grades five and nine.

Numerous hypotheses have been advanced to explain the phenomenon of the school dropout by persons of lower socioeconomic class; however none has been wholly satisfactory. This essay is an attempt to account for the phenomenon in a more fruitful manner, by redefining the dropout situation, and by applying this definition to the specific case of dropouts among Canadian Indians.

It will be useful to list some hypotheses used to explain dropping out, not because they are the most important or the most misleading, but because they illustrate the direction of concern among various students of education. Seymour Rubenfeld, in his 1965 study, *Family of Outcasts,* offers the hypothesis that the dropout as well as the juvenile delinquent gets that way because of an incomplete socialization that results in a self-discontent which is then externalized and "lived out" through deviant behavior, some of which is in relation to the school.

Lucius F. Cervantes' *The Dropout: Causes and Cures* presents the dropout as suffering from the failure of his primary group, his family. The result of this failure is the inability to achieve success in primary interpersonal relationships, which produces personality disorganization. This causes an end to interpersonal communication and makes personal satisfaction unattainable. For these reasons the individual leaves school.

Richard Cloward and Lloyd Ohlin, in the immensely influential *Delinquency and Opportunity,* focus on what might be called "objective status discontent." This implies that the deviant or delinquent individual is alienated from his environment and the legitimate means to success in that environment (e.g. "education") because these institutions are, quite objectively, alienating. Because of this alienation, however, the individual turns to illegitimate means to nurture success. Another author utilizing the theme of alienation is John F. Bryde, who sees the Indian student of South Dakota as literally being outside of and between both Indian and white-man cultures. As such, he is alienated from both the goals of education and his Indian identity, which leads to his scholastic failure and "dropping out."

Finally, Murray and Rosalie Wax's study of the same Sioux Indian students that Bryde discussed, indicates that one of the major causes of dropping out is what can be called "institutional intolerance." The Waxes argue that the school situation at Pine Ridge, South Dakota, is characterized by a lack of communication between the school functionaries and those they serve. There is "social distance" between students and teachers and considerable individual isolation, even within the same school.

These explanations appear to be suitable for the particular cases they describe. Almost all of them, however, concentrate upon one variable, the student or ex-student. They fail to consider the institutional and cultural variable, the school. It is the latter that I shall focus on in this essay.

In Euro-Canadian society the school is a "primary institution," in the sense that it is basic and widespread. All Euro-Canadian children are expected to attend school for extensive periods of time and to profit from the experience. It is, in fact and in theory, the major socialization device of the industrialized, urbanized segment of the Canadian population. As such it consumes a tremendous amount of time, substantial amounts of money and a great deal of energy.

In this paper, then, I define "the school," all formal education from kindergarten to grade twelve or thirteen, as a rite of passage, or rather a series of rites signifying separation from, transition through and incorporation into culturally recognized statuses and roles. Within the larger chronological rite there are also numerous other rites and ceremonials indicating partial transitions and new role relationships.

The School as Ritual

This redefinition of the school as a rite of passage is likely to provoke some disagreement. Anthropologists and laymen alike choose to think of ritual and rites of passage as essentially magico-religious activities, and of schools as being only partially or minimally engaged in this type of activity. This is not altogether so. Not all ritual must be magico-religious, nor are schools as institutions, or what goes on in schools, completely free from magico-religious significance. It is quite difficult to categorize ritual activity clearly as to religious content. Further, ritual activity ranges from the purely magical and religious through the pseudo-rational to rational routine, albeit it is up to the observer to ascertain its rationality. Clearly, in any case, there are numerous calendrical and other rites and ceremonies in the public school that signify changes in the student's social life. Thus, the whole educational structure can be envisioned as a long-term ritual marking various changes in the social lives of the individuals. It is difficult for an outside observer to assess their magico-religious or secular content.

Nevertheless, it would be very hard to argue that the majority of Canadian students, parents and teachers see "education" in a wholly rational light. In a recent study, a noted American educator pointed out that despite scientific knowledge to the contrary the vast majority of public school classrooms in the United States operate on the two-thirds theory (*Trans*-action, 1967): two-thirds of the time someone is talking, two-thirds of the time it is the teacher who is talking, two-thirds of the time the teacher is talking she is lecturing or commenting upon the behavior of children in the classroom. If this is the case in the United States, then Canadian schools, generally, operate on the three-quarters theory, and schools catering to Indians operate on the seven-eighths theory. The involvement of the school in teaching moral-ethical behavior, the continuing belief in "disciplining the mind" through rigid curricula and repetitive testing, the various rites of prayer and of patriotism, indeed, the whole defensive ethos of the school point to the pseudorational nature of the school.

More succinctly, one can look at "the school" as a series of "ideological rituals," using "ideological" here in Mannheim's sense, as a means to protect and perfect the existing social system, in contrast to the "utopian" striving for revolutionary change. In this sense the public school in North America is indeed an ideological rite of passage. Educators have long thought the institution of the public school as the common ground that allows immigrant and indigenous groups the wherewithal for intelligent self-government, common mores and economic perfection and advancement within the ideological system of North American "democratic" society.

Rites of Passage

There is little doubt that the characteristic form of North American public education is typical of North American society. It exemplifies and reflects the values of that society, and prepares students for urban, industrialized middle-class society. Finally the whole ritual culminates in a pseudoreligious ceremonial known as "Convocation" or "Commencement" in which it tells the ex-student, "Now do it." Those who "can do it" have been certified for that society. From kindergarten or grade one when the child learns who his "helpers" in the school and neighborhood are, to grade twelve or thirteen when each student is ranked and evaluated on the formalized "external" or Departmental examinations, he passes through a multitude of statuses and plays many roles. The result of the whole process is the development of a particular sort of individual, that is if the process is successful.

But, what would happen if we were to take this ceremonial system out of its context, North American middle-class society, and place it in a wholly or partly alien context such as an Indian reserve? The answer is that unless there were community support for it, it would fail. Let me stress this point. It would be the rite of passage, the rituals recognized and enjoined by middle-class society that would fail; *not the Indian student.*

Since 1944 there has been little doubt among scholars that students of North American Indian ancestry have intelligence adequate for most activities, exclusive of school. Robert Havighurst's well-known 1957 article demonstrates that Indian children perform ". . . about as well . . ." as white children on performance tests of intelligence. More recently, in Charles Ray, Joan Ryan, and Seymour Parker's 1962 study of Alaskan secondary-school dropouts, the authors state:

> The conclusion to be derived from the data is that intelligence *per se* cannot be considered a major contributing factor to dropouts and that achievement levels are not markedly different.

As this essay is focused primarily on dropouts with Eskimo, Aleut, or Tlingit ethnic backgrounds as contrasted with white children, it appears to indicate that the cause of dropout is elsewhere than intelligence. But where are we to find it?

Thinking in Two Tongues

California Achievement Test scores in Alberta and South Dakota among Plains Cree, Blackfoot and Sioux Indians indicate that the young Indian starts out *ahead* of his white peers, but then gradually tails off in achievement. Fourth-grade Indians who had averaged 4.3 on achievement tests while their white counterparts scored only 4.1, had by the eighth grade been surpassed by the white students who achieved an 8.1 average while Indian students had one of 7.7. Test scores consistently decline between grades five and seven. Furthermore, a parallel phenomenon in retardation of grade placement in relationship to age has been indicated in a study of Kwakiutl Indians on Gilford Island, British Columbia. The number of students at the expected grade-level decreased sharply from 4 at grade one to 1 by grade five and 0 by grade six. At the same time, the numebr of students *below* the expected grade-level increased from 2 at grade one to 4 at grade five. Similar studies done by the Waxes on South Dakota Sioux also reveal that between the fifth and seventh grade the number of students of appropriate grade-age decreases. Thus, where the majority of fifth-grade students are in the 10- to 11-year category, the majority of sixth-grade students are in the 12- to 13-year range. From these patterns of slumping achievement-test scores and increasing age-grade level retardation, it appears that some sort of difficulty arises in the relationship between "the school" and the pre-pubescent/pubescent Indian. Admittedly, some Indian students drop out later than others but it would appear that in most cases of prolonged schooling it is the enforcement of the School Act that made the difference. The Blackfoot and Blood Indians of southern Alberta, for example, are under considerable compulsion to stay in school. If they do not "fit" the existing academic program, they are enrolled in "pre-employment" courses or in special programs such as "upgrading." It is therefore quite difficult for these students to leave school. The younger student often "solves" this problem by becoming a "troublemaker" in school (sassing teachers, being truant, refusing to work, etc.) or by becoming "delinquent" outside school (drinking and sexual escapades, fighting and theft). Of these Blackfoot "early dropouts," ages thirteen to sixteen (which is the school-leaving age) 75 percent of the fifteen-year-olds and 70 percent of the sixteen-year-olds were considered "delinquent." Among the older students, ages seventeen, eighteen and nineteen, the amount of delinquent behavior was radically reduced. Apparently, then, when a Blackfoot student passes the school-leaving age, he can choose to stay or to go, and he generally chooses to go.

Another difference leading to local variation in the school-leaving age may be the attitudes of Indians about what is appropriate for them in the school. What the Indian expects to get out of school, what it means to him and what he believes himself to be are really the critical issues. Even though the specific answers to these questions may vary with different tribes, the result of these answers is the same: early dropout and unused education.

Indian expectations of school are conditioned by what the young Indian learns in the environment of his home community. Because what he learns at home often differs widely from what he learns at school, the Indian student is frequently forced to separate the two learning experiences. George Spindler once heard a "successful" Blood Indian say:

> I have to think about some things in my own language and some things in English. Well, for instance, if I think about horses, or about the Sun Dance, or about my brother-in-law, I have to think in my own language. If I think about buying a pickup truck or selling some beef or my son's grades in school I have to think in English.

The languages of Blackfoot and English are kept entirely apart; the former is for thinking about basic cultural elements, while the latter is used for school work. The Indian student grows up in a particular society with its own particular role transitions and in the presence of or absence of appropriate ritual recognition of these changes. Since the expectations about ritual and about role transitions held by any society and recognized as legitimate for that society are peculiar to that society, and to part-societies, at any time the school, as a rite of passage, may become inappropriate to members of a particular society that differs from North American middle-class society. This is what seems to happen to the Indian student.

Identity and Work

Young Blood Indians have certain very specific ideas about what they are and what they are going to be. Among a stratified sample of forty young Bloods the most popular choices of a career or vocation were as follows: ranching, auto-mechanic, carpenter, bronc rider, haying, and farming. All of these occupations can be learned and practiced right on the Blood Reserve. They chose these occupations for two important reasons: knowledge and experience or, in other words, experiential knowledge that they already held. Among the Blackfoot dropouts and "stay-ins" a very similar pattern emerged. They, too, chose occupations that were familiar to them, even if they pertained little to their academic life. And this pattern emerges elsewhere in only slightly different form.

In Harry Wolcott's "Blackfish Village" Kwakiutl study he mentions in passing the response by students to the essay topic, "What I Would Like to Be Doing Ten Years from Now." Almost all the students thought they would be in and around their village. Two of the older girls guessed they would be married and in the village. Farther north, in Alaska, the Ray, Ryan and Parker study notes that the three primary reasons given for dropping out of secondary school are "needed at home," "marriage" and "wanted to work." Of the secondary reasons, to help at "home," "marriage" and "homesick" were most important. These reasons appear to indicate that the Alaskan dropout was opting out of formal education to return home to what he or she knows. As the authors indicate, "The majority of dropouts saw little relationship between what they were learning in school and jobs that were available to them."

Turning inland from British Columbia and Alaska we note the same phenomenon among the Metis of the Lac La Biche area (Kikino, Owl River, Mission), among the Blackfoot dropouts of Gleichen and Cluny and among the young Blood of southwestern Alberta. In each case the Indian student on the one hand expects to be doing what is now done in the context of his community, and on the other hand sees only a vague, if any, correlation between the demands of formal education in the context of the school and that which he expects to do.

A final point in this regard is made in the Waxes' study of the Pine Ridge Sioux. They state that education and being a good Sioux Indian are two separate processes, if becoming a good Indian is a process at all. They say that the full-bloods think that:

> ... education harms no one, but on the other hand it has almost nothing to do with being a good person. ... [They] do not seem to be aware that their offspring are regarded as unsocialized, amoral or backward by their teachers. That a child could be educated to the point where he would become critical of his kin or attempt to dissociate himself from them is still beyond their comprehension.

In conclusion, these studies show that the expanded educational opportunities for Canadian Indians are not really opportunities at all. For what the school offers is an irrelevant set of values and training. Moreover, the school often comes into direct conflict with certain moral and cultural values of the student. Thus, it is the educational system that fails the student and not the student who fails the system. In trying to be a good and successful Indian, the Indian student must often be a bad and unsuccessful student.

November 1969

SUGGESTED READINGS

Structures and Function in Primitive Society by A. R. Radcliffe-Brown (New York: Free Press, 1965).

The Adolescent Society by James S. Coleman (New York: Free Press, 1962).

A Kwakiutl Village and School by Harry Wolcott (New York: Holt, Rinehart and Winston, 1967).

Formal Education in an American Indian Community by Murray Wax, Rosalie Wax and Robert Dumont Jr. (Atlanta, Ga.: Emory University, 1964) expands on some of the basic problems in fitting an educational system to the needs of the American Indian.

Man's Rise to Civilization by Peter Farb (New York: E. P. Dutton and Co., 1968).

Indians of North America by Harold E. Driver (Chicago: Univ. of Chicago Press, [2nd edition] 1969).

Outsiders in Britain

Colored immigrants from the Commonwealth face two barriers—their racial differences and alien customs

PETER I. ROSE

Ian Berry MAGNUM

Until very recently, Great Britain might well have been called a "white little island." As recently as 1950 there were fewer than 50,000 Negroes in the country (compared to over 15 million in the United States at the same time), and the combined figures for all other non-whites probably came to even less. During the past decade the situation has changed dramatically. Close to a million colored immigrants from Commonwealth nations have entered Britain (over one-half from the West Indies, some 165,000 from India, and approximately 100,000 from Pakistan). Their reception has been considerably less than cordial and, for the first time, the UK has a color problem.

Although Britain played an instrumental role in the African slave trade, few slaves were taken there, and of those who were, many were freed upon arrival and the rest (or their descendants) were freed by the Mansfield Judgment of 1772 which proclaimed the holding of slaves illegal. Compared to "whites," the number of Africans and Asians remained infinitesimal during the whole of the nineteenth century and half of the twentieth.

In 1950 the majority were dockers (longshoremen) and seamen who lived in the port towns of Bristol, Cardiff, Liverpool, and London, or students attending English or Scottish schools or universities. In addition, some West Indian workers were to be found in various parts of the country (London, Birmingham, and the West Midlands), workers who had come—or whose families had come—during the First World War or the Second. There were also some Africans, a few Indians, and even fewer Pakistanis. Far more British West Indians emigrated to the United States than to the United Kingdom—until the McCarran Act of 1952 sealed American ports of entry to those from the islands. It was then that Southampton replaced New York as the gateway to opportunity, at least in the dreams of the colored immigrants.

Population pressures and depressed living conditions in their homelands, the desire for social advancement (the world-wide "revolution of rising expectations"), the emergence of a welfare state guaranteeing at least a minimum standard of living to all, and the attraction of economic opportunities in England combined to encourage emigration.

The rapid influx brought with it a growing concern that, with unrestricted immigration, the flow would become a torrent; and that soon black and brown immigrants (perjoratively called "spades" and "wogs") would seriously threaten the fabric of British society. Anxiety over the problems created by the presence of newcomers prompted the Conservative government to enact the Commonwealth Immigration Law of 1962, a decidedly racialistic piece of legislation, which limited the number and "types" of persons allowed to enter the country. Fenner Brockway has recently written that while "it is true that the Act itself

"The Indians and Pakistanis—with their different clothes, spicy foods, and seemingly strange religious customs—are ready butts for racial jokes and taunts."

"Once Commonwealth immigrants reach the promised land they find themselves relegated to the shabbiest neighborhoods and oldest parts of the cities; they find employment primarily in those areas with little prestige and low wages."

makes no mention of race or colour; there is no need for it to do so because the categories to be admitted to this country cover most white applicants and its provisions for exclusion apply almost entirely to coloured applicants." In fact, he continues, "when during the discussion of the Bill in Parliament it was admitted that immigration from Southern Ireland, the Republic of Eire, could not be controlled, the measure patently became discriminatory against the nonwhite peoples of the Commonwealth, particularly those of the West Indies, Pakistan, and India." Against his wishes, Lord Brockway's own Labor party, once in power, supported and tightened the very law it had so vehemently opposed.

Although the act effectively curtailed the inflow, it did not offset resentment in many sections of the country. On the contrary, during the 1960's racialism has shown a decided upsurge, and the "immigration problem" has become one of Britain's most pressing political issues.

During the election campaign of the fall of 1964, for example, it was not uncommon to see the slogan, IF YOU WANT A NIGGER NEIGHBOUR, VOTE LABOUR, in those areas which have large numbers of immigrants. The seat in Smethwick, a constituency of Birmingham, was won by an outspoken Conservative advocate of segregation, Peter Griffiths. (He lost his seat in the Labor "sweep" in the general election of 1966, an election in which other issues played a far more significant role than that of race.) And race was an issue in at least five other constituencies. Its actual impact on voting patterns is difficult to assess since, by the time of the general election, both parties favored the restriction of immigration while both officially deplored using racialism as an overt political plank. Moreover a study of the election conducted by the Institute of Race Relations in London suggests that neither party's followers hold a monopoly on prejudice; that "Tories" and "Socialists" are not unlike in their resentment of immigrants in their midst—though their rationalizations may differ.

In by-elections held during the winter, the issue of immigration kept surfacing in various parts of the country. And in the spring of 1965, chapters of the Ku Klux Klan were being formed in several Midland cities and a number of crosses had been set aflame.

During the very same week in August 1965, when in the United States President Johnson signed a bill dramatically reversing a 50-year policy of discriminatory quotas against foreigners seeking entry, the Wilson government reduced the number of permits to be issued to potential Commonwealth immigrants to Britain from 20,000 to 8,500; and these are to be awarded only to those with specialized skills (such as physicians and ancillary medical personnel) or those with jobs awaiting them. Referring to these new restrictions and other reversals wrought by the Labor party, one spokesman for the immigrants reported that "there is a new mood amongst Britain's coloured people today—a mood of humiliation, of bitterness and anger." And another commented: "They want our doctors. They want our nurses. They want our scientists and technologists. But they don't want our ordinary people."

While similar to their predecessors in discriminating against those wishing to come, the Labor party has been somewhat more forward-looking about those already there. In the spring of 1965 it succeeded in getting some antiracialist legislation through Parliament, modeled on the

RACIAL CLEAVAGES 271

public accommodation sections of the American Civil Rights Bill of 1964. In addition, on November 8, 1965, Parliament passed a law making incitement to racial unrest a crime. But it has done little to alleviate the basic malaise. Tensions continue to mount and an end to Britain's interracial difficulties is nowhere in sight. In some ways, one feels they have hardly begun.

American Pluralism and British Insularity

There is a tendency on this side of the Atlantic to draw comparisons between race relations there and here. Certain parallels can be drawn; but they cannot be pushed too far.

During much of American history immigrants (especially from the poorer nations of Europe) were strangers whose very presence grated against those who had already settled —including many recent arrivals. Each group, in making its own way, looked with rising anxiety at those who seemed different and menacing to their hard-won status.

Yet, for most of those who left Europe for the US, the "American dream" in time proved to be more than a mere slogan. Although they suffered greatly from economic exploitation and social discrimination, expanding opportunities and a fundamental social fluidity made it possible for one group after the other to begin the slow climb, taking their places as representatives of the new America. The melting pot was proclaimed as an ideal. Though it was always more of a dream than a blueprint for social action, significant portions of the society believed in it—or pretended to.

Unlike their American counterparts, those who immigrated to Great Britain always retained more than an ethnic spirit of cultural pluralism as we know it does not typify British life. No one there talks glowingly about an "orchestration of diversity" or of a "multiplicity in a unity." And no one there would say, with John Dewey, "The hyphen connects instead of separates." While "tolerance" for those who differ is *au courant* in Britain, there is also the sentiment that they are really there on sufferance.

Even those who will boast of the "melting pot" history of Britain—citing Angles, Saxons, Danes, and the like as their proud forebears—will simultaneously indicate that the admixture was concocted long, long ago and that today there is really but one dominant culture and that is decidedly English.

Such insular views (in contrast to our ostensibly pluralistic ethos) have particular relevance today, when Britain is faced with a substantial number of persons who not only differ in terms of social organization and culture (though it must be said that many West Indians are very "British") but are considerably darker than the "ruddy" Britishers. That the colored immigrants are British subjects and often the legatees of colonial exploitation means little to the majority of whites in the UK. Few feel they "owe" those from Commonwealth countries anything, and more than a few proclaim, often with self-righteous indignation, that the "blacks" and "wogs" and the rest should remember how the British brought them the benefits of civilization. Though in varied guises, prejudice is widespread.

The White Man's Burden

Three hypotheses have been advanced to explain this rising antipathy and distrust. The first, called the "color-class" hypothesis, was suggested by the anthropologist Kenneth Little. It states that, because of their past, British citizens have been imbued with a colonial mentality. Although they have had little personal contact with colored people, they tend to identify them with the lowest, most backward, and uncivilized elements in the Commonwealth. They tend to think in black-and-white terms.

And it is true that the "white man's burden" is a phrase that is once again being echoed in Britain. Benevolent paternalism is still in the air (especially evident in the comments of welfare workers who talk about "their people," who say, "only *we* really know what's good for *them*"). One is reminded of the recent statement by Nicholas Deakin of the Institute of Race Relations that one of the most paradoxical characteristics of the British, both individually and collectively, is their capacity for considering themselves tolerant, even while displaying prejudice!

The second hypothesis suggests that the visibility and cultural distinctiveness of colored immigrants make them archetypal "strangers" in a society in which xenophobia has long been a latent feature of social life, in which, as Ruth Glass says, "social segregation is the accepted norm."

The third hypothesis, discussed by various writers including A. H. Richmond, offers the view that both prejudice

Henri Cartier-Bresson MAGNUM

distinctiveness; to a large degree they continued to be outsiders. Harold Isaacs made this point quite clearly recently:

> Jews who migrated from Eastern Europe two or three generations ago became "British" but this never made them "Englishmen." . . . By contrast, the "American" identity implies an inclusiveness that would make "Americans" out of all the different kinds of people who have arrived on American soil. The ideal holds any imposed separateness to be the right of any group or person, limited only by the common rights of all.

Although literally more a "nation of nations" than the United States (consisting as it does of four countries—England, Scotland, Wales, and Northern Ireland), the United Kingdom is not a "mosaic of minorities." In fact, the very word "minority" is rarely used in the UK. The and discrimination in Britain, as elsewhere, are related to insecurity, a fear of losing hard-won ground by those most vulnerable—the old elites and, especially, the rising working classes. Recent surveys indicate that the working classes, who feel they have the most to lose, are most vehement in their opposition to integration. The argument that employment is at an all-time high does not appear to allay fears. These people (or their parents) have known harsh times; they cannot discount more of them in the future. For them, any added competition is threatening.

Actually these theses are not at all mutually exclusive. No single factor can possibly account for all contingencies. The real explanation, probably, incorporates all three of the elements cited by the British social scientists: racial prejudice, fear of strangers, and status-anxiety.

That is, stereotypes of dark persons (aggravated greatly by textbook treatment of British colonial history and by the glorification of the writings of Kipling and others), coupled with a fear of strangers (or, at the least, conformity to the norm of social exclusiveness), plus a real or imagined socio-economic threat, all combine to produce the existing attitudes toward immigrants.

Exactly how many people feel this way is hard to assess. There have been very few comprehensive studies of white attitudes. A lack of systematic research has also hampered understanding of the experiences of immigrants. But from what there is, several generalizations may be made.

First, and perhaps foremost, is the evidence that, contrary to the views of many white Britons, there are *many* colored communities which not only vary markedly in history and character but also have little to do with one another. And as Nicholas Deakin has indicated, "The various immigrant communities have few points of contact; differences of language and culture seal them off from each other as most are sealed off from the host community." It is erroneous to speak or write of *the* immigrant. Each group—whether West Indian or African or Indian or Pakistani or Cypriot or Maltese—brings a piece of its homeland to Britain and maintains it. In *this* sense all of Britain's colored immigrants are more akin to our European immigrants and, especially, to Puerto Ricans, than to the American Negroes to whom they are invariably—and erroneously—compared.

W. E. B. DuBois once said that there was nothing so American, so indigenous as the American Negro. After 300 years of enculturation, the Negro in the United States may remain alienated, but he is not a foreigner. He has internalized the attitudes of his society, including—in many instances—those which have kept him in servitude. He has internalized his group's disgrace. Such is not the case with Britain's colored immigrants.

Like those who left Europe for America and are still migrating from Puerto Rico to New York, the "Commonwealth immigrants" are voluntarily seeking their fortunes in a New World of which they know little but have heard much. London is their *El Dorado*. Yet, once they reach the promised land they find themselves relegated to the shabbiest neighborhoods and oldest parts of the cities; they find employment primarily in those areas which carry little prestige and low wages (such as urban transport); and they find themselves closed off from most contacts with whites by the color barrier in most private and many public places.

In almost all cases—whether for those, like the West Indians, who wish to integrate and stay, or those, like the Indians and Pakistanis, who wish only to accommodate themselves temporarily, make money, and then go back home—the colored immigrants are finding the new environment far more difficult than they had foreseen. Since Britain is even less receptive to its immigrants than was America, it is no wonder that, isolated and scorned, they turn inward and seek out compatriots. Shut off from the mainstream by limited skills and economic discrimination, finding it difficult to adjust to the physical and social climate, they become increasingly dependent upon those who share their status and accept them—sometimes reluctantly—as kith and kin. Many barriers separate the immigrant communities from others—and even from each other. The result has been the growth of ghetto-like enclaves which aggravate tensions and lend credence to the widely held stereotypes about "clannish foreigners."

Some stereotypes carry a kernel of truth. The newcomers are highly visible. They behave differently from those nurtured on British standards and values. The varied groups of colored immigrants fulfill many of the images others hold of them. West Indians, for example, are more permissive in social and sexual relationships; they are more apt to entertain at times when Englishmen feel one should be in bed asleep; they do prefer brighter clothing and decor.

The Indians and Pakistanis, with their different clothes, spicy foods, seemingly strange religious customs and poor English, are also ready butts for racial jokes and taunts. More serious, because of overcrowded housing and the high proportion of young single men, venereal disease rates have increased. So have the numbers of persons living on drugs and off immoral earnings. While these matters may be explained in terms of anomie and alienation, culture shock, and poverty, they do exist—not only in the minds of critics of the "coloureds" but among the immigrants themselves.

Persecution or Pluralism?

What to do? Everyone seems to have an opinion.

■ At one extreme is a small but active group of latter-day "Know Nothings" who are haranguing their countrymen to KEEP BRITAIN WHITE and SEND THE BLACKS BACK. Their intention is to make life as uncomfortable as possible for the immigrants in an effort to get them to leave the country. Their support, among the lower middle and urban working classes, appears to be growing.

■ The majority of citizens (and many members of the government) believe that restrictions on further immigration should be stepped up, but concede that something must also be done for those already there. With a clangor familiar to students of early American history, some demand that the newcomers divest themselves of their foreign and exotic ways—their clothing styles, sexual mores, patterns of entertainment, ways of living—and become like everybody else. This is Anglo-conformity in its purest form. The more "tolerant" wish only that the immigrant should keep his proper place and social distance. Given British society, its heavy emphasis on deference, order, privacy, and the repression of personal feelings, this is understandable. Whether it is socially desirable is something else. Some, including many immigrants, think it is not.

■ As might be expected, a form of pluralism is also offered. Those who advocate pluralism are most often academic liberals, left-wing "laborites," and articulate spokesmen for the newly emerging immigrants who want to mobilize immigrant groups into an effective coalition or, at least, increase their participation in communal life. Unlike America, there is little indication in today's Britain of ethnic bloc voting as a political device to gain representation, nor of a widespread civil rights movement.

There is a stirring, however. The first sign is the establishment of CARD, the Committee Against Racial Discrimination, a loose coalition of immigrant leaders. Like some civil rights leaders in the United States, CARD's members favor a combined program of pride and protest—a demand for equality but not at the expense of losing their cultural identities. They are advocating change through forceful anti-racialist legislation, adequate education, meaningful community organization, and, if necessary, demonstrations by both white and colored. In addition they request that adequate information be provided immigrants about their legal rights, and adequate preparation for the kinds of problems they (like any newcomers) are likely to face. They want specialized services to ease the transition (reminiscent of our own settlement house movement 50 years ago). The teaching of English as a foreign language (for Indians, Pakistanis, and Cypriots, for example) is encouraged. So is the use of textbooks which promote the ideal of "multi-racial" living.

Of special significance is the desire to encourage immigrants to retain those features of daily life which provide a link between home and Great Britain. Too often, it is argued, too heavy an emphasis is placed on requiring the outsider to rid himself of his culture. While pluralism is not the norm in Britain, much could be gained, it is said, by accepting and even benefitting from cultural diversity.

Social scientists who have studied the problem are in disagreement as to how to help everyone adjust to an unprecedented situation. None support the idea of sending immigrants back "home." There are those who lean toward assimilation (though they recognize the special difficulties of Hindu Indians and Moslem Pakistanis); and there are those who advocate accommodation—or what Milton Gordon would term "structural pluralism."

Some, such as Philip Mason, director of the Institute of Race Relations in London, appear to opt for something in between. In a recent issue of *New Society,* Mason answers the question "What do we mean by integration?" saying:

Let there be calypsos and steel bands; let Pakistanis meet for a *mash 'ara* (their equivalent to an *Eisteddfod*). But let no one be denied entry to one group on the sole ground that he belongs to another. It is no use expecting people to refrain from grading each other against some scale of reference—but in a healthy society there will be more than one scale, and good workmanship or success at cricket will redeem some damaging disqualification such as birth outside Britain. It will follow that an individual may be well adapted to the majority group and widely accepted by them, in fact as an individual almost completely assimilated, and yet that he will in certain circumstances return to his group and there take part in activities in which he reconstructs his own background.

While it is likely that many (perhaps most) immigrants would welcome such a plan for enjoying the best of both worlds, it is unlikely that others will so readily accept it. In fact, it can be argued, without a substantial change in the social (and political) climate and a significant alteration in the national ethos, tensions will continue to mount and gaps between the white Britishers and "the outsiders" will widen.

On the other hand, it should be pointed out that, *should it choose to do so,* the British government might be able to effect changes in a way that, until recently, has been extremely difficult in the United States. Here, owing to the apportionment of authority at the federal and state and local levels, each of which has particularly strong vested interests to uphold, each has worked out its own plans for social reform—or resistance to it. There, the centralized control of the Parliament and the organs of government, whose direct or indirect administrative and financial influence extends to every constituency, could be used to initiate programs to reduce discrimination and aid in the adjustment of newcomers on all fronts.

Whether it will take such initiative is difficult to predict. But should it not, colored immigrants to Britain will remain second class—in name and in fact.

March 1967

SUGGESTED READINGS

Ethnic Stratification: A Comparative Approach by Tamotsu Shibutani and Kian M. Kwan (New York: Macmillan, 1965) is a useful textbook on intergroup relations.

Social Change in the Industrial Revolution by Neil J. Smelser (Chicago, Ill.: University of Chicago Press, 1959). An account of the industrialization of England that is well supported empirically and especially theoretically.

America's New Officer Corps

Is the military elite losing its "class"?

CHARLES H. COATES

"It is increasingly possible to rise above one's social origins in a military career—perhaps much more easily than in a managerial career in civilian business or industry."

At the end of January the Department of Defense released a startling set of Vietnam casualty figures. Since the beginning of American troop involvement in the fighting, 1,545 officers and enlisted men had been killed, 8,952 had been wounded, 149 were missing, and 26 were detained in captivity. These Vietnam casualty figures—incurred in "peacetime"—dramatize a recurrent problem for the armed services—the training and retention of qualified officers not only to serve in the field, but to run the lives of almost 3 million uniformed men and women and to administer a defense budget of more than $60 billion.

On October 31, 1965, there were 337,359 officers in the Army, Navy, Air Force, and Marines; 1,309 of them having the rank of general or admiral. The next generation of admirals and generals are among today's middle and lower rank officers—but whenever the Vietnam conflict ends many of them will choose not to make the military a career. Out of the thousands of lieutenants, captains, majors, and equivalent Naval ranks, what kind of men will stay in the service for most of their lives, and (discounting the possibility of death on the battlefield) hope to emerge later in their careers with stars on their collars?

Traditionally, the "military elite" has come from the business and professional classes. As C. Wright Mills says of the old guard generals and admirals in his book, *The Power Elite*:

On the whole, the high officers of the Army and Navy have been men of the upper-middle rather than the truly higher or definitely lower classes. Only a very small percentage of them are working-class in origin. They have been the sons of professional men, of business men, of farmers, of public officials and of military men. They are overwhelmingly Protestant, mainly Episcopalians or Presbyterians. Few have served in the ranks.

But Mills adds an important qualification to this picture, the seed of a trend away from the class-bound "military elite":

Social origins and early backgrounds are less important to the character of the professional military man than to any other high social type. The training of the future Admiral or General begins early and is thus deeply set, and the military world which he encounters is so all-encompassing that his way of life is firmly centered within it. To the extent that these conditions exist, whether he is the son of a carpenter or a millionaire is that much less important.

The suggestion is plain that it is increasingly possible to rise above one's social origins in a military career—perhaps much more easily than in a managerial career in civilian business or industry.

Morris Janowitz made a much more comprehensive analysis of the social origins of the military elite in his 1960 book, *The Professional Soldier*. Janowitz noted, significantly, that "no profession resists inquiry into its social origins as stubbornly as does the military. To inquire about social background, especially about religion, is resented as impolite." But he was, nevertheless, able to show a developing trend away from an officer corps reserved for the sons of the upper-middle class, toward an officer corps which includes a cross-section of all American social classes. In his words, "The recruitment into the officer corps since the end of World War II seems, on the one hand, to involve a much greater reliance on the sons of professional soldiers and, on the other hand, the opening of greater opportunity for the sons of the lower-middle and working classes." Janowitz concluded that "there is considerable justification for the belief that the military establishment is becoming an avenue of social mobility for those of lower social origins."

The Mobile Military Man

The Mills and Janowitz studies applied only to the high-ranking "military elite." But, in 1958, Rufus C. Browning made a study of the social backgrounds of all ranks and found that, throughout the Army, men of lower socio-economic origins generally favored a continuing military career more than did men from more privileged social backgrounds.

The 1958 Browning study also reinforced earlier findings that, although officers generally come from higher social strata than do enlisted men, both groups come from all socio-economic levels, and the officer corps is not restricted to men of high status backgrounds. Browning showed, too, that men from rural backgrounds have more favorable attitudes toward a military career than those who were reared in cities, a finding which seems to confirm the traditional image of the military man.

From 1962 to 1964, a period of increasing American involvement in Vietnam, the author and his associate, Paul L. Doerr, attempted to develop a clearer intergenerational portrait of military officers to see if the trend toward an officer corps drawn from a broader social base was continuing. Information on their socio-cultural backgrounds was gathered from 650 retired military officers and 663 cadets of the class of 1966 at the Air Force Academy who will graduate this June as second lieutenants. The material fell into five main categories: (1) father's occupation, (2) father's education, (3) individual's own education, (4) rural vs. urban background, and (5) religious background.

FATHER'S OCCUPATION. Retired officers and academy cadets had similar percentages of fathers in the "Worker" group (Table 1). But in the next category on the occupational scale, the picture changed sharply: only 6.7 percent of the cadets had fathers who were farmers, in contrast to 18.6 percent of the retired officers. This difference was made up in the business and professional categories, where the cadets' fathers outnumber the fathers of the retired officers 51.6 percent to 40 percent.

The overall picture was that both retired officers (51.4 percent) and the cadets (36.8 percent) had social origins which are substantially working class and middle class.

Table 1. Father's Occupation

Father's Occupation	Retired Officers %	Air Force Academy Cadets, Class of 1966 %
Worker	25.7 ⎫	22.7 ⎫
Farmer	18.6 ⎬ (51.4)	6.7 ⎬ (36.8)
White Collar	7.1 ⎭	7.4 ⎭
Business	13.7 ⎫	5.0 ⎫
Professional &	⎬ (40.0)	⎬ (51.6)
Managerial	26.3 ⎭	46.6 ⎭
Other	7.4	9.5
Unknown	1.2	2.1
TOTAL	100.0	100.0
NUMBER	(650)	(663)

EDUCATION. The majority of fathers of both the retired officers and the active duty officers in Browning's 1958 study had only a high school education or less. Taking father's educational level as a measure of socio-cultural background, it appeared that the older groups came mainly from working and lower-middle social strata (67.2 percent of retired and 64.9 percent of active), whereas cadets came mostly from the middle strata of American society (56 percent).

Concerning the education of the retired officers and cadets, themselves, both groups reached educational levels much higher than those of their fathers. Of the retired officers, 54 percent were college graduates, and it can be assumed that most of the cadets will become college graduates. The implication, widely corroborated in other fields, is also true of the military—education is an excellent means of rising on the social ladder.

Table 2. Urban vs. Rural Background

Size of Community	Retired Officers %	Air Force Academy Cadets, Class of 1966 %
Over 400,000	13.4	24.0
Over 100,000 (or a suburb of a city this size)	8.1	14.0
25,000 to 100,000	12.8	19.0
2,500 to 25,000	22.2	26.9
(Total Urban)	(56.5)	(83.9)
Farm and Rural (Towns under 2,500)	35.4	10.1
Unknown	8.1	6.0
TOTAL	100.0	100.0
NUMBER	(650)	(663)

RURAL VS. URBAN BACKGROUND. Contrary to Browning's 1958 finding that career military men came predominantly from rural backgrounds, this research indicated (Table 2) that retired officers were predominantly of urban origin (56.5 percent) and that the cadets were very highly urban (83.9 percent). The explanation of this increasingly urban

Table 3. Differences between Acceptors and Rejectors of the Military Career

	ACCEPTORS	REJECTORS
AGE/RANK	Junior officers in their late twenties.	Junior officers in their early twenties.
MARITAL STATUS	Large majority married (78%) with emphasis on the small family.	Over half married (53%) with a tendency toward medium-sized and sometimes large families.
RURAL/URBAN BACKGROUND	Majority (60%) from towns of 100,000 or less—small cities, small towns, and rural areas.	High percentage (43%) from the large metropolitan centers with distinctly urban cultural environments.
RELIGION	Predominantly Protestant (67%) 28% Catholic and 1% Jewish.	Mostly Protestant (61%); 25% Catholic and 6% Jewish.
EDUCATION	Great majority college graduates (81%), representing a substantial gain over their parents educationally.	Again, 81% college graduates, but with parents also well above average educationally.
SOCIO-ECONOMIC BACKGROUND	Predominantly lower-middle and working class (53%); fathers generally laborers, mechanics, farmers, salesmen.	High percentage from upper classes (43%); fathers mostly business and professional men.
REASONS GIVEN FOR ACCEPTANCE/REJECTION	1) Opportunities for leadership and responsibility 2) Educational opportunities 3) Travel opportunities 4) Desire to serve the United States 5) Desire to help preserve the American way of life.	1) Ability not used to the fullest 2) Military pay deficient 3) Comparative attractiveness of civilian life 4) Housing below acceptable standards 5) Too frequent family separations

picture probably is related to the continuing trend toward city-dwelling in the nation as a whole.

RELIGIOUS DENOMINATION. An interesting shift in the relative percentages of Protestants and Catholics in the military showed up between generations. The Protestant percentage dropped about 8 percent (79.4 percent for retired to 71.5 percent for cadets) and a corresponding increase occurred among the Catholics (from 14.9 percent to 26.0 percent). Jewish percentages were comparatively small in both cases (2.8 percent and 1.5 percent). It seems that the military profession, traditionally and still predominantly Protestant, is becoming less so with an increasing influx of Catholics.

The Military Way Up

In sum, the inter-generational study confirmed the work of Mills, Janowitz, and Browning in one highly significant respect. It showed that military officers consistently rise above their fathers in the social world, and so points to the inescapable conclusion that *a military career is an excellent means of upward social mobility.*

But does this finding apply to the young officers currently in the military? And does it mean that those from lower socio-economic strata can expect to rise above their origins by remaining in the service as career officers? The author and his associate recently made a comparative study of 282 junior grade career officers and 203 men of similar age and rank who had left the service after one tour of duty. There was one outstanding difference between the Acceptor and Rejector groups drawn from all of the services: *those who accepted the military career tended to come from lower socio-economic strata than did those who rejected further service.* The striking implication was that young men from less privileged social backgrounds are finding opportunities for increased social status in the military career more attractive than in civilian careers.

The major finding of the acceptance-rejection study, especially when placed in the context of earlier socio-cultural studies of the military profession, is unmistakable. The military career has become a unique avenue to upward mobility for young men from the less privileged social classes. Many have already taken this path to higher status, and it seems reasonable to assume that many more will do so in the future.

What are the implications of this study for the military establishment, and for the overall civilian society? Does it really make any difference that military life is more attractive to working class youths than to those from the middle and upper classes? Indeed it does, since within the modern military establishment the barriers to vertical mobility and career success, based on class distinctions, are disappearing more rapidly than in many other segments of society.

March-April 1966

SUGGESTED READINGS

The American Myth of Success: From Horatio Alger to Norman Vincent Peale by Richard Weiss (New York: Basic Books, 1969).

The Social Context of Ambition by Ralph H. Turner (San Francisco, Calif.: Chandler, 1964). Investigates the origin, development and process of ambition through a study of seniors in one Beverly Hills and nine Los Angeles high schools.

The Professional Soldier: A Social and Political Portrait by Morris Janowitz (Glencoe, Ill.: Free Press, 1960). A classic study of the military profession.

Origins of American Scientist by Robert H. Knapp (Chicago: Univ. of Chicago Press, 1952). A study of what factors have led college students into the scientific professions.

The American Military edited by Martin Oppenheimer (Chicago: Aldine, 1971).

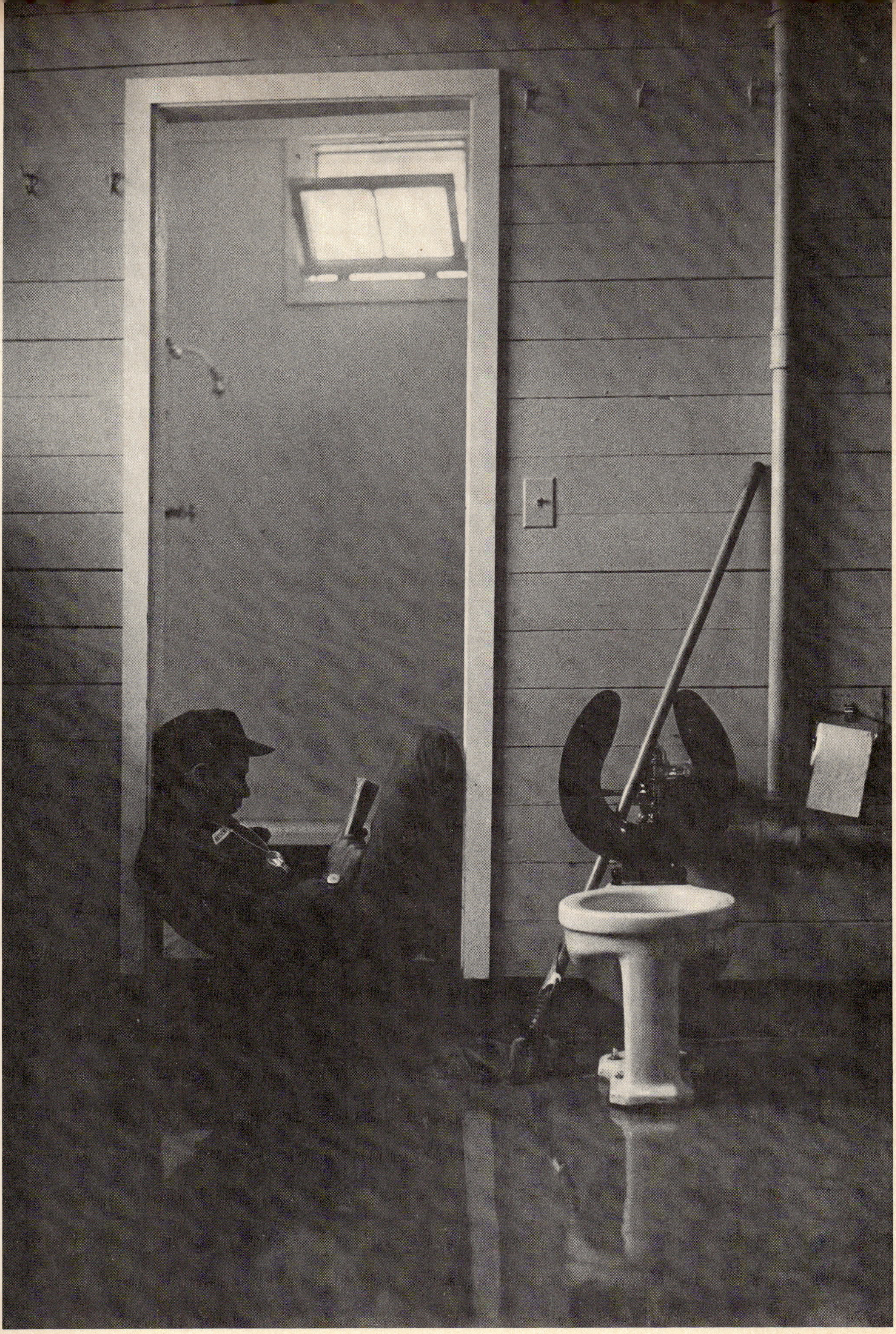

Seminole Girl

The autobiography of a young woman between two worlds

MERWYN S. GARBARINO

ONE HUNDRED and thirty miles of circuitous road and 250 years of history separate the city of Miami from the four federal reservations that lock the Seminole Indians into the Florida swamplands known as Big Cypress Swamp. A new road is under construction that will trim in half the traveling distance between the city and the reservations scattered along the present winding U.S. Highway 41 or Tamiami Trail as it is called by the Indians. But the new road will only draw the two communities closer on the speedometer; it will not alter the vastly different lifeways it links; it may only make more apparent the historical inequities that brought the two areas into existence.

The Seminoles are harsh examples of what happened to American Indians caught in the expansion process that saw the United States swell from a federation of 13 colonies to a nation blanketing more than half a continent. The peoples who came to be known as "Seminole," which means "wild" or "undomesticated," were Indians who fled south from the guns and plows of the whites. Some were Yamassee who were driven from the Carolinas in 1715. Others were Hitchiti-speaking Oconee who moved down the Apalachicola River to settle in Spanish-held Florida. These two groups were joined by others escaping soldiers or settlers or other Indians demanding their lands.

The loose confederation of Seminoles was tripled by a large influx of Creeks after the Creek War of 1813–14. Although the Creeks were linguistically related to the Hitchiti, the primary factor uniting the diverse groups was the hatred and fear they felt toward their common foe, the young United States. But this common bond was enough to regroup the broken political units into a single body that absorbed not only Indians, but renegade whites and Negroes escaping slavery.

In 1817–18, the United States sent Andrew Jackson to Florida, ostensibly to recover runaway slaves. This resulted in the First Seminole War, one of the three Seminole Wars that were among the bloodiest ever fought by American forces against Indians. The war also led to the annexation of Florida by the U.S. in 1821 because Spain was in no position to fight for it.

At the time of annexation, the Indians held extensive farm and pasture lands that the Spaniards had not wanted for themselves. American settlers, however, wanted them very much. Insatiable, they forced the Seminoles ever southward, until finally they demanded that the Indians relocate to the area of the Louisiana Purchase which is now Oklahoma. Some Indians went westward, but a number under the leadership of Osceola fought bitterly. When Osceola was captured under a flag of truce, some of his warriors fled into the Everglades where they could not be flushed out. To this day they haven't recognized the treaty that drove their fellow tribesmen to the West.

In 1911, Florida reservation land was set aside by an executive order. The Seminoles, however, were not pressured at that time into moving on to the federal territory. South Florida was a real wilderness; Miami was little more than a town, and lavish coastal resorts were unforeseen. Literally no one but the alligators, snakes, birds and the Indians wanted the land they lived on. The climate is one of wet summers and dry winters, and the area is often struck by hurricanes from the Caribbean. Annual rainfall is in excess of 60 inches and without drainage, the prairie is almost always under water. Brush fires in the dry season destroy valuable hardwood trees on the hummocks which are the low-lying hills undulating through the swampland. Fire also destroys the highly flammable drained peat and for the same reason, there is an absence of pines in many areas suitable for their growth. Elsewhere however, there are moderately to heavily wooded places, and sometimes great flocks of white egrets alight in the branches of the trees, looking like puffs of white blossoms. Except for the hummocks, the horizon is flat, a vista of sky and water, broken only by the occasional wooded clumps.

Most inhabitants of this waste and water live on elevated platforms under thatched roofs held in place by poles. Unemployment is an ever-present problem helped somewhat by seasonal agricultural work or by crafts such as the gaily colored garments, dolls, basketry and carvings made for the tourists who are now visiting their homeland on a year 'round basis. Lands are leased to commercial vegetable farmers and deer can still be hunted. So subsistence living is still possible for the "wild" Seminoles.

SOMEWHERE along the Tamiami Trail, Nellie Greene —a pseudonym of course—was born a Seminole, raised in a chickee, and learned the ways of her people. Her father was a frog hunter and could neither read nor write; her mother was a good Seminole mother who later had troubles with tuberculosis and drinking. No one Nellie knew had much more education than her father and mother. Yet, despite the ignorance and illiteracy on the reservation, Nellie Greene wanted and was encouraged to get a good education. As it does for most Indians in the United

States, this meant leaving her "backward" people, mixing with whites who at best patronized her.

I first met Nellie Greene when she had graduated from college and was living in an apartment in Miami where she worked as a bank clerk. I knew her background from having spent three summers in the middle sixties, thanks to the National Science Foundation, on the Seminole reservations of Florida. In September of 1966 Nellie wrote me that she had been offered a job as manager in the grocery store back on the reservation. If she didn't take it, a white person would, for she was the only native with the necessary knowledge of bookkeeping. She had accepted the job, she said, but since she had once told me (in Miami) that she could never give up the kind of life she had grown accustomed to there, I was curious to find out why she had returned to the reservation.

She herself said that she took the job to help her people, but she added that it had not been an easy decision; in fact it had been quite a struggle. I could have guessed that this was so; many Indian tribes that offer educational grants to their younger members do so only with the stipulation that the recipients later return to the reservation. The stipulation is a measure of the difficulty in getting their educated members to come back to the tribe. In any event, I wanted to hear Nellie Greene tell her own story. I went to see her, and this is what she told me.

Nellie Greene's Story

I was born in a Miami hospital on February 6, 1943. At that time my parents were living on the (Tamiami) Trail, and my daddy was making his living frog hunting. He owned an air boat and everything that goes along with frog hunting. It was during the war, and at that time I guess it was hard to get gas. When it was time for me to be born, my father had to borrow gas from a farmer to get to Miami. But the tail light was broken, so my father took a flashlight and put a red cloth over it and tied it on to the truck and went to the hospital. My daddy often told me about that.

I had an older sister and an older brother. We lived in a chickee until 1961 when my daddy bought a CBS (a cement block structure, "hurricane proof" according to state standards) at Big Cypress, and we moved into it. When I was little, my daddy had to be out in the Everglades a lot, so he would take all of us out to a hummock, and we would make camp there and stay there while he went off to hunt for frogs. When he got back, he'd take the frog legs into the hotels and sell them. Then he would bring back something for each of us. When he would ask us what we wanted, I always asked for chocolate candy.

About all I remember of the Everglades is that it was a custom when you got up to take a bath or go swimming early in the morning. My mother says they always had to chase me because I didn't like to get wet in winter when it was cold. We were there four or five years, and then we moved near the Agency at Dania (renamed Hollywood in 1966). I had never been to school until then. We were taught at home, the traditional things: to share with each other and with children of other families, to eat after the others—father and grandfather first, then mothers and kids. But lots of times us kids would climb up on our father's knees while they were eating. They didn't say anything, and they'd give us something. It just wasn't the custom for families to eat the way we do today, everybody sitting together around the table.

Folktales, too, we learned; they were like education for us, you know. The stories told about someone doing something bad, and then something bad happened to him. That was the way of teaching right and wrong.

When we were growing up we broke away from some family customs. My parents spanked us, for instance, not my mother's brother, who would have been the right person to punish his sister's children—one of the old ways. But they were not close to my mother's family because my daddy was a frog hunter, and we wandered around with him. My parents were chosen for each other by their families. I guess they learned to love each other in some ways, but I have heard my mother say that it is not the same kind of love she would have had if she had chosen her own husband. It was respect, and that was the custom of the Indians.

Most parents here show so little affection. Even if they love their kids, maybe they don't think they should show love. I know a lot of parents who really care, but they don't tell their kids how they feel. We always knew how our parents felt about us. They showed us affection. Sometimes I hear kids say, "My mother doesn't care whether I go to school or not." These kids have seen how others get care from their parents, like the white children at school. And that kind of concern doesn't show up here. A lot of parents don't even think of telling their children that they want them to succeed. They don't communicate with their children. You never see an Indian mother here kiss and hug children going to school. But white parents do that, and when Indian children see this in town or on TV, it makes them think that Indian parents just don't care. Kids are just left to go to school or not as they wish. Often the mothers have already left to work in the fields before the school bus comes. So no one sees whether children even go to school.

I felt loved. My parents never neglected us. We have never gone without food or clothes or a home. I have always adored my mother. She has made her mistakes, but I still feel the same about her as when I was a child.

We moved to Big Cypress around 1951 or 1952. I had been in first grade at Dania. I remember I didn't understand English at all when I started first grade. I learned it then. We moved around between Big Cypress and Dania, visiting, or because my father was doing odd jobs here and there.

SOCIAL MOBILITY

Both my parents wanted me to go to school because they had wanted to go to school when they were kids. I can remember my mother telling me that she and her sister wanted to go to school. But the clan elders—their uncles—wouldn't let them. The uncles said they would whip the two girls if they went.

One of my father's greatest desires was to go to school when he was a boy. He said that he used to sneak papers and pencils into the camp so that he could write the things he saw on the cardboard boxes that the groceries came in, and figures and words on canned goods. He thought he would learn to read and write by copying these things. My daddy adds columns of figures from left to right, and he subtracts the same way. His answers will be correct, but I don't know how. Almost everything he knows he learned on his own. He can understand English, but he stutters when he talks. He has a difficult time finding the right word when he speaks English, but he understands it.

When my parents said no, they meant no. That was important to me. They could be counted on. The other thing that was important in my childhood schooling was that my daddy always looked at my report card when I brought it home from school. He didn't really know what it meant, and he couldn't read, but he always looked at my report card and made me feel that he cared how I did in school. Other parents didn't do this. In fact, most of the kids never showed their parents their report cards. But my daddy made me feel that it was important to him. I told him what the marks stood for. It was rewarding for me because he took the time.

"Nothing for Me to Do"

Public school was hard compared to what I'd had before, day school on the reservation and a year at Sequoyah Government School. I almost flunked eighth grade at the public school, and it was a miracle that I passed. I just didn't know a lot of things, mathematics and stuff. I survived it somehow. I don't know how, but I did. The man who was head of the department of education at the Agency was the only person outside of my family who helped me and encouraged me to get an education. He understood and really helped me with many things I didn't know about. For a long time the white public school for the Big Cypress area would not let Indian children attend. A boy and I were the first Big Cypress Indians to graduate from that school. He is now in the armed forces.

After I graduated from high school I went to business college, because in high school I didn't take courses that would prepare me for the university. I realized that there was nothing for me to do. I had no training. All I could do was go back to the reservation. I thought maybe I'd go to Haskell Institute, but my mother was in a TB hospital, and I didn't want to go too far away. I did want to go on to school and find some job and work. So the director of education said maybe he could work something out for me so I could go to school down here. I thought bookkeeping would be good because I had had that in high school and loved it. So I enrolled in the business college, but my English was so bad that I had an awful time. I had to take three extra months of English courses. But that helped me. I never did understand why my English was so bad—whether it was my fault or the English I had in high school. I thought I got by in high school; they never told me that my English was so inferior, but it was not good enough for college. It was *terrible* having to attend special classes.

"I Learned How to Dress"

At college the hardest thing was not loneliness but schoolwork itself. I had a roommate from Brighton (one of the three reservations), so I had someone to talk to. The landlady was awfully suspicious at first. We were Indians, you know. She would go through our apartment, and if we hadn't done the dishes, she washed them. We didn't like that. But then she learned to trust us.

College was so fast for me. Everyone knew so much more. It was as though I had never been to school before. As soon as I got home, I started studying. I read assignments both before and after the lectures. I read them before so I could understand what the professor was saying, and I read them again afterwards because he talked so fast. I was never sure I understood.

In college they dressed differently from high school, and I didn't know anything about that. I learned how to dress. For the first six weeks, though, I never went anywhere. I stayed home and studied. It was hard—real hard. (I can imagine what a real university would be like.) And it was so different. If you didn't turn in your work, that was just your tough luck. No one kept at me the way they did in high school. They didn't say, "OK, I'll give you another week."

Gradually I started making friends. I guess some of them thought I was different. One boy asked me what part of India I was from. He didn't even know there were Indians in Florida. I said, "I'm an American." Things like that are kind of hard. I couldn't see my family often, but in a way that was helpful because I had to learn to adjust to my new environment. Nobody could help me but myself.

Well, I graduated and went down to the bank. The president of the bank had called the agency and said he would like to employ a qualified Indian girl. So I went down there and they gave me a test, and I was interviewed. And then they told me to come in the following Monday. That's how I went to work. I finished college May 29, and I went to work June 1. I worked there for three years.

In the fall of 1966, my father and the president of the Tribal Board asked me to come back to Big Cypress to manage a new economic enterprise there. It seemed like a dream come true, because I could not go back to live at Big Cypress without a job there. But it was not an easy decision. I liked my bank work. You might say I had fallen in love with banking. But all my life I had wanted to do something to help my people, and I could do that only by leaving my bank job in Miami. Being the person I am, I had to go back. I would have felt guilty if I had a chance to help and I didn't. But I told my daddy that I couldn't give him an answer right away, and I knew he was upset because he had expected me to jump at the chance to come back. He did understand though, that I had to think about it. He knew when I went to live off the reservation that I had had a pretty hard time, getting used to a job, getting used to people. He knew I had accomplished a lot, and it wasn't easy for me to give it up. But that's how I felt. I had to think. At one time it seemed to me that I could never go back to reservation life.

But then really, through it all, I always wished there was something, even the smallest thing, that I could do for my people. Maybe I'm helping now. But I can see that I may get tired of it in a year, or even less. But right now I'm glad to help build up the store. If it didn't work out, if the store failed, and I thought I hadn't even tried, I would really feel bad. The basic thing about my feeling is that my brothers and sisters and nieces and nephews can build later on in the future only through the foundation their parents and I build. Maybe Indian parents don't always show their affection, but they have taught us that, even though we have a problem, we are still supposed to help one another. And that is what I am trying to do. Even when we were kids, if we had something and other kids didn't, we must share what we had with the others. Kids grow up the way their parents train them.

By the age of nine, girls were expected to take complete care of younger children. I too had to take care of my little brother and sister. I grew up fast. That's just what parents expected. Now teen-agers don't want to do that, so they get angry and take off. Headstart and nurseries help the working mothers because older children don't tend the little ones any more. The old ways are changing, and I hope to help some of the people, particularly girls about my age, change to something good.

There are people on the reservation who don't seem to like me. Maybe they are jealous, but I don't know why. I know they resent me somehow. When I used to come in from school or from work back to the reservation, I could tell some people felt like this. I don't think that I have ever, ever, even in the smallest way, tried to prove myself better or more knowing than other people. I have two close friends here, so I don't feel too lonely; but other people my age do not make friends with me. I miss my sister, and I miss my roommate from Miami. My two friends here are good friends. I can tell them anything I want. I can talk to them. That's important, that I can talk to them. That's what I look for in a friend, not their education, but for enjoyment of the same things, and understanding. But there are only two of them. I have not been able to find other friends.

The old people think I know everything because I've been to school. They think it is a good thing for us to go to school. But the old people don't have the kind of experience which allows them to understand our problems. They think that it is easy somehow to come back here. They think there is nothing else. They do not understand that there are things I miss on the outside. They do not understand enough to be friends. They are kind, and they are glad that I am educated, but they do not understand my problems. They do not understand loneliness.

It was hard for me to get used again to the way people talk. They have nothing interesting to talk about. They are satisfied to have a TV or radio, but they don't know anything about good books or good movies or the news. There is almost no one I have to talk to about things like that. Here people don't know what discussion is. That's something I found really hard. They gossip: they talk about people, not ideas.

And it was hard getting used to what people think about time. You know, when you live in the city and work, everything is according to time. You race yourself to death, really. But I got used to that and put myself on a schedule. But here, when you want something done, people take their time. They don't come to work when they should, and I just don't want to push them. I would expect it of the older people, but the younger generation should realize how important time is. When you go to school, you just eat and study and go to school, and not worry too much about time; but on a job, you must keep pace. You are being paid for a certain performance. If you do not do what you are supposed to, you do not get paid. But how do I get that across to my people?

"I Don't Know Why..."

I was lonely when I first came back here. I was ready to pack up and go back to Miami. People hardly talked to me —just a few words. I don't know why. I've known these people all my life. I don't know why they didn't know me after just three years. I couldn't carry on a conversation with anyone except my own family. I was working all day at the store, and then I had nothing to do but clean the house, or go fishing alone, or with someone from my family.

Coming back to the reservation to live did not seem to be physically hard. At first I lived in a house with a girl friend because I did not want to stay with my family. I wanted to be sure of my independence. I think this hurt my father. But later, when more of my friend's family moved back to the reservation, I decided it was too crowded with her and went back to live in my old home with my father and family. My father's CBS is clean and comfortable. It is as nice as an apartment in Miami.

My idea was that, being raised on the reservation and knowing the problems here, I could hope that the Indian girls would come to me and ask about what they could do after they finished high school: what they could do on the reservation, what jobs they could get off the reservation. I hoped they would discuss their problems with me, what their goals should be. I'd be more than happy to talk with them. But I can't go to them and tell them what to do. Just because I've worked outside for three years doesn't give me the right to plan for other people. But I thought I had something to offer the girls here, if only they would come for advice.

"They Say I'm Mean..."

I would like to see the financial records at the store so well kept that an accountant could come in at any time and check the books, and they would be in perfect order. It is difficult because only Louise and I can run the store, and if either of us gets sick, the other one has to be at the store from 7 AM to 9 PM, or else close the store. At first I had to be very patient with Louise and explain everything to her. She had no training at all. Sometimes I started to get mad when I explained and explained, but then I'd remember that she can't help it. People do not know some of the things I know, and I must not get irritated. But if things go wrong, I am responsible, and it is a big responsibility. The younger people are not exactly lazy; they just don't know how to work. I want them to work and be on time. If they need time off, they should tell me, not just go away or not appear on some days.

So some of them start calling me bossy. But that is my responsibility. I tried to talk to them and tell them why I wanted them to come to work on time, but still they didn't. I want them to realize that they have to work to earn their money. It is not a gift. They were supposed to do something in return for their wages. They are interested in boys at their age, and that's why they aren't good workers. But still, the National Youth Corps, operating in Big Cypress, gives kids some idea of how it is to work, to have a job. If I don't make them do the job, they're really not earning their money. That is one thing I had to face. I know that they are going to say I'm mean and bossy. I expect that. But if I'm in charge, they're going to do what they're supposed to do. That's the way I look at it. Everybody talks here. I know that, but I've been away, and I can take it.

I think people my own age are jealous. It is not shyness. Before I left, they were all friendly to me. I came back, and they all look at me, but when I go to talk to them, they just turn around, and it is so hard for me.

They answer me, but they don't answer like they used to, and talk to me. That has been my main problem. It is hard for someone to come back, but if he is strong enough, you know, he can go ahead and take that. Maybe some day people will understand. There is no reason to come back if you really think you are better than the people. They are wrong if that is what they believe about me. There is not enough money here, and if I didn't really care about the people, then I would have no reason to return.

I am worried about my mother, and I want to stay where I can help her (my parents are now divorced). It is best to come back and act like the other people, dress like they dress, try to be a part of them again. So even if a person didn't have kinfolk here, if he wanted to help, he could. But he must not show off or try to appear better.

If I didn't have a family here, it would be almost like going to live with strangers. I have to work now. It has become a part of my life. People here just don't understand that. I can't just sit around or visit and do nothing. If there were no work here, I could not live here. It would be so hard for me to live the way the women here do, sewing all the time or working in the fields, but if I had to take care of my family and there was nothing else to do, I guess I would stay here for that. My aunt has taught me to do the traditional sewing, and how to make the dolls, so I could earn money doing that; but I wouldn't do it unless I had to stay here to take care of my family.

I think the reason almost all the educated Indians are girls is because a woman's life here on the reservation is harder than the man's. The women have to take all the responsibility for everything. To go to school and get a job is really easier for a woman than staying on the reservation. The men on the reservation can just lay around all day and go hunting. They can work for a little while on the plantations if they need a little money. But the women have to worry about the children. If the women go away and get jobs, then the men have to take responsibility.

A woman and a man should have about the same amount of education when they marry. That means there is no one at Big Cypress I can marry. The boys my age here do not have anything in common with me. If a girl marries an outsider, she has to move away, because the Tribal Council has voted that no white man can live on the reservation. A woman probably would miss the closeness of her family on the reservation. I would want to come back and visit, but I think I could marry out and make it successful. I would expect to meet and know his family. I would like to live near our families, if possible. I will always feel close to my family.

"I Think About the City . . ."

Sometimes I think about the city and all the things to do there. Then I remember my mother and how she is weak and needs someone who will watch over her and help her. You know my mother drinks a lot. She is sick, and the doctors want her to stop; but she herself cannot control her drinking. Well, I guess us kids have shut our eyes, hoping things will get better by themselves. I know you have not heard this before, and I wish I was not the one to tell you this sad story, but my move back to the reservation was partly brought on because of this. She has been to a sanitarium where they help people like her. It has helped her already to know that I want to see her get help and be a better person. I am having a chickee built for her, and I must stay here until she is well enough to manage alone.

ECONOMIC *opportunity has been severely limited on the reservation until recently. Employment for field hands or driving farm machinery has been available on ranches in the area, but the income is seasonal. Both men and women work at crafts. The products are sold either privately or through the Arts and Crafts Store at the tribal agency on the coast but the income is inadequate by itself. Some of the men and one or two Indian women own cattle, but none of these sources of income would appeal to a person with higher education. Until the opening of the grocery store, there was no job on the reservation which really required literacy, let alone a diploma.*

Examining these possibilities and the words of Nellie Greene, what would entice an educated Indian to come back to work and live on the reservation? A good paying job; a high status as an educated or skilled person; to be back in a familiar, friendly community; a desire to be with his family and to help them. Perhaps for the rare individual, an earnest wish to try to help his own people. But income from a job on the reservation must allow a standard of living not too much lower than that previously enjoyed as a member of outer society. Nellie never gave any consideration to returning to the reservation until there was the possibility of a job that challenged her skills and promised a comparable income. The salary she receives from managing the store is close to what she had made at the bank in Miami. In Miami, however, she worked 40 hours a week, while on the reservation she works nearly 60 hours a week for approximately the same pay, because there are no trained personnel to share the responsibility. Given the isolation of Big Cypress, there is not enough time, after she has put in her hours at the store, to go anywhere off the reservation. It is not merely a question of total pay; it is a problem of access to a way of life unattainable on the reservation. Economic opportunity alone is not sufficient.

It is quite apparent from Nellie's interviews and from observation of the interaction between Nellie and other Indians, both in the store and elsewhere on the reservation, that her status is very low. Her position appears to vary: from some slight recognition that her training places her in a category by herself, to distinct jealousy, to ap-

parent puzzlement on the part of some of the old folks as to just what her place in the society is. Through the whole gamut of reaction to Nellie, only her proud family considers her status a high one.

The primary reason Nellie gave for returning to the reservation was to help her people, but the reservation inhabitants did not indicate that they viewed her activities or presence as beneficial to them. Older Indians, both male and female, stated that it was "right" that she returned because Indians should stay together, not because she might help her people or set an example to inspire young Indians who might otherwise be tempted to drop out of school. Younger people regard her as bossy and trying to act "white." She does not even have the status of a marriageable female. There is no Indian man on the reservation with the sort of background that would make him a desirable marriage partner, from her standpoint; in their traditional view of an ideal wife, she does not display the qualities preferred by the men. At the same time, there is a council ordinance which prohibits white men from living on the reservation, and therefore marriage to a white man would mean that she would have to leave the reservation to live. There is no recognized status of "career woman," educated Indian, or marriageable girl, or any traditional status for her.

Obviously, with an inferior status, it is unlikely that a person would perceive the community as a friendly, familiar environment. From the point of view of the reservation people, who have had contacts with her, she is no longer truly "Indian," but rather someone who has taken over so much of the Anglo-American ways as to have lost her identity as an Indian woman. Nearly all of Nellie's close acquaintances are living off the reservation. The only two girls she considers friends on the reservation are, like herself, young women with more than average contact with outside society, although with less formal education.

Nellie may have rationalized her decision to return by stressing her determination to help the people, but her personal concern for her mother probably influenced her decision to return more than she herself realized. Nellie was the only person in the family who had the ability, knowledge and willingness to see that her mother received the proper supervision and help.

THE BUREAU of Indian Affairs is attempting to increase the economic opportunities on the reservations, but I believe their efforts at holding back the "brain drain" of educated Indians will not be effective. Retraining the reservation people who do not have an education is certainly desirable. But, as the story of Nellie Greene points out, it takes more than good pay and rewarding work to keep the educated Indians down on the reservations. If the educated Indian expects to find status with his people, he is going to be disappointed. White people outside are apt to pay more attention to an educated Seminole than his own Indian society will. If the Indian returns from college and expects to find warm personal relationships with persons of his own or opposite sex, he is going to find little empathy, some distrust and jealousy because of his training and experiences outside the reservation. For Nellie Greene there was a personal goal, helping her sick mother. She was lucky to find a job that required her skills as an educated person, and which paid her as well as the bank at Miami. Her other goal, to help her own people, was thwarted rather than helped by her college education.

February 1970

SUGGESTED READINGS

AMERICAN INDIANS TODAY

The American Indian Today by Stuart Levine and Nancy Lurie (De Land, Fla.: Everett Edwards, 1968) is a collection of contemporary problems facing Indians.

The Indian, America's Unfinished Business edited by William Brophy and Sophie D. Aberle (Norman, Oklahoma: University of Oklahoma Press, 1966) is part of the University of Oklahoma's American Indian Series and treats the Indian and his problems from a more statistical point of view and very sympathetically.

The Changing Indian edited by Oliver La Farge (Norman, Oklahoma: University of Oklahoma Press, 1942). The report of a symposium on Indian affairs; includes discussions of health, land ownership, employment patterns, population, culture, native languages, religion and education.

The New Indians by Stanley Steiner (New York: Harper and Row, 1967). Journalistic report of American exploitation of Indians and their reactions, especially the rise of the "red power" movement and civil rights agitation.

Laughing Boy by Oliver La Forge (Boston: Houghton-Mifflin, 1929). This novelistic account of Navaho life explores moral and religious questions in the light of their subjective meaning to contemporary Indians.

Sociocultural and Psychological Processes in Menomini Acculturation by George D. Spindler (Berkeley, Calif.: University of California Press, 1955). An empirical anthropological study that seeks to determine how closely in the course of acculturation a tribe of Indians approaches American middle-class life on a number of variables.

MARGINAL MEN

The Marginal Man by Everett Stonequist (New York: Russell Sage Foundation, 1962). Stonequist indicates some of the positive consequences of anomie for creativity.

The Crisis of the Negro Intellectual by Harold Cruse (New York: Morrow, 1967). A historical survey of the dilemma of the American Negro intellectual as a spokesman for the masses.

Automobile Workers and the American Dream by Ely Chinoy (New York: Random House, 1955). The adaptive behavior of men for whom the American dream is an unattainable myth.

"Cultural Contradictions and Sex Roles" by Mirra Komarovsky, *American Journal of Sociology* (Vol. 52, 1946). A treatment of the role conflicts of college-educated women.

The Des Plaines Street Police Station, Chicago, May 4, 1886, after the Haymarket riot (from a painting of the period).

Genteel Backlash: Chicago 1886

The Haymarket riot wouldn't be the last time that Chicago's police went out of control

RICHARD SENNETT

A bomb exploded in Chicago's Haymarket Square on May 4, 1886, killing seven people and setting off what may have been the first police riot in that city's history. The neighborhood in which this violence broke out was hardly what one would call a high crime area today. The quiet residential district adjacent to the Haymarket was considered so nondescript, so ordinary, that it had never even been given a special name. Richer and poorer neighborhoods had names; Union Park, as I shall call it here, was anonymous, like most other middle- and lower middle-class communities in the industrial cities of nineteenth century America.

The people of Union Park were the forgotten men of that era, neither poor enough to be rebels like the Socialist workingmen who assembled that day in Haymarket Square, nor affluent enough to count in the affairs of the city. For a quarter of the century, from 1865 to 1890, Union Park epitomized that tawdry respectability of native-born, lower middle-class Americans that Dreiser was to capture in *Sister Carrie,* or that Farrell would later rediscover in the bourgeois life of Catholic Chicago.

The beginnings of Union Park, when Chicago was a commercial town rather than a diverse manufacturing city, were much grander. In the 1830s and 1840s it was a fashionable western suburb, separated by open land from the bustle of the business district and the noisome unhealthy river at the heart of the city. Then, in the years after the Civil War, a change in the pattern of commercial land investment, the filling in of a swamp on the edge of Lake Michigan by Potter Palmer and the growth of a manufacturing district to the south of Union Park led fashionable people to desert the old suburb for newer, more magnificent residences along the lake shore of Chicago. In their place, in the 1870s, came people of much lesser means,

This article is from *Nineteenth-Century Cities: Essay in the New Urban History* edited by Stephan Thernstrom and Richard Sennett (New Haven and London: Yale University Press, 1969). Copyright © 1969 by Yale University.

seeking a respectable place to live where rents and land were becoming cheap. Union Park for these new people was a neighborhood where they could enjoy the prestige of a once-fashionable address, and even pretend to be a little grander than they were. "The social Brooklyn of Chicago," Mayor Harrison called it; "a place where modest women become immodest in their pretentions," wrote another contemporary observer. For 25 years the old holdings were gradually divided up into little plots, and native-born Americans—who were the bulk of the migrants to the cities of the Midwest before the 1880s—rented small brick houses or a half floor in one of the converted mansions.

It was here, in this modest, cheerless community, that a series of unexpected events took place in the late 1880s, beginning with the bloody encounter between police and workingmen in nearby Haymarket Square. That riot was followed 18 months later by a series of highly expert robberies in the community, a crime wave that culminated in the murder of a leading Union Park resident. The striking feature of all this violence lay not in the events themselves but in the reaction of shopkeepers, store clerks, accountants and highly skilled laborers to the disorder suddenly rampant among their sedate homes. Their reaction to the violence was impassioned to an extent that in retrospect seems unwarranted by events; the character of their reaction will, however, seem familiar to students of urban backlash in our own time. The forgotten men of Union Park responded to violence by holding a whole class—the poor, and especially the immigrant poor—responsible for the course of these violent eruptions. For a modern observer, the puzzle is what made them react this way.

The Haymarket Bombing

> Certain people, mostly foreigners of brief residence among us, whose ideas of government were derived from their experience in despotic Germany, sought by means of violence and murder to inaugurate a carnival of crime. *F. H. Head, official orator at the unveiling of the Haymarket Square Statue for policemen slain in the riot, reported in the* Chicago Daily Tribune, *May 31, 1889.*

Chicago's haymarket constituted the dividing line between the residences and neighborhood stores of Union Park and the warehouses of the growing central city. Haymarket Square itself was enclosed by large buildings and the Des Plaines Street Police Station was just off the Square. It was hardly a place to engage in clandestine activity, but, for a peaceful meeting, the Square was an ideal forum, since it could accommodate roughly 20,000 people.

The common notion of what happened on May 4, 1886, is that a group of labor unionists assembled in Haymarket Square to listen to speeches and that, when the police moved in to break up the meeting, someone in the crowd threw a bomb, killing and wounding many policemen and bystanders. This account is true as far as it goes, but explains little of what determined the event's effect on the community and city in the aftermath.

The people who came to the meeting were the elite of the working class, those who belonged to the most skilled crafts; they were hardly the "dregs" of society. The crowd itself was small, although it had been supposed that events in Chicago during the preceding days would have drawn a large gathering. On May 3, demonstrations had been organized in the southwestern part of the city against the McCormick Works, where a lockout of some union members had occurred. The police had responded with brutal force to disperse the crowd. Later that same night, at a number of prescheduled union meetings, it was resolved to hold a mass meeting at some neutral place in the city.

A small group of Socialist union leaders, led by August Spies and Albert Parsons, decided the time was ripe for a mass uprising of laboring men; the moment seemed perfect for an expression of labor solidarity, when large numbers of people might be expected to rally to the cause as Spies and Parsons understood it—the growth of Socialist power. Haymarket Square was the obvious choice for a neutral site.

REVENGE!
Workingmen, to Arms!!!

Your masters sent out their bloodhounds — the police —; they killed six of your brothers at McCormicks this afternoon. They killed the poor wretches, because they, like you, had the courage to disobey the supreme will of your bosses. They killed them, because they dared ask for the shortening of the hours of toil. They killed them to show you, "Free American Citizens!", that you must be satisfied and contended with whatever your bosses condescend to allow you, or you will get killed!

You have for years endured the most abject humiliations; you have for years suffered unmeasurable iniquities; you have worked yourself to death; you have endured the pangs of want and hunger; your Children you have sacrificed to the factory-lords — in short: You have been miserable and obedient slave all these years: Why? To satisfy the insatiable greed, to fill the coffers of your lazy thieving master? When you ask them now to lessen your burden, he sends his bloodhounds out to shoot you, kill you!

If you are men, if you are the sons of your grand sires, who have shed their blood to free you, then you will rise in your might, Hercules, and destroy the hideous monster that seeks to destroy you. To arms we call you, to arms!

Your Brothers.

Rache! Rache!
Arbeiter, zu den Waffen!

Arbeitendes Volk, heute Nachmittag morbeten die Bluthunde Eurer Ausbeuter 6 Eurer Brüder draußen bei McCormick's. Warum morbeten sie dieselben? Weil sie den Muth hatten, mit dem Loos unzufrieden zu sein, welches Eure Ausbeuter ihnen beschieden haben. Sie forderten Brod, man antwortete ihnen mit Blei, eingedenk der Thatsache, daß man damit das Volk am wirksamsten zum Schweigen bringen kann! Viele, viele Jahre habt Ihr alle Demüthigungen ohne Widerspruch ertragen, habt Euch vom frühen Morgen bis zum späten Abend geschunden, habt Entbehrungen jeder Art ertragen, habt Eure Kinder selbst geopfert — Alles, um die Schatzkammern Eurer Herren zu füllen, Alles für sie! Und jetzt, wo Ihr vor sie hintretet, und sie ersucht, Eure Bürde etwas zu erleichtern, da hetzen sie zum Dank für Eure Opfer ihre Bluthunde, die Polizei, auf Euch, um Euch mit Bleikugeln von Eurer Unzufriedenheit zu kuriren Sklaven, wir fragen und beschwören Euch bei Allem, was Euch heilig und werth ist, jagt diesen scheußlichen Mord, den man heute an Euren Brüdern begieng, und vielleicht morgen an Euch begehen wird. Arbeitendes Volk, Herkules, Du bist am Scheidewege angelangt. Wofür entscheidest Du Dich? Für Sklaverei und Hunger, oder für Freiheit und Brod? Entscheidest Du Dich für das Letztere, dann säume keinen Augenblick; dann, Volk, zu den Waffen! Vernichtung den menschlichen Bestien, die sich Deine Herrscher nennen! Rücksichtslose Vernichtung ihnen — das muß Deine Losung sein! Denk' der Helden, deren Blut den Weg zum Fortschritt, zur Freiheit und zur Menschlichkeit gedüngt — und strebe, ihre würdig zu werden!

Eure Brüder.

Despite the call to arms posted by the Socialists (right) the turnout at the Haymarket was meager. But following the riot, police Captain Schaak (opposite) kept "respectable" people's fears alive with lurid stories of other "anarchist" plots.

Posters were printed in the early hours of the next day and spread throughout the city.

When Parsons and Spies mounted the speakers' rostrum the next night in Haymarket Square, they must have been appalled. Instead of vast crowds of militants, there were only a thousand or so people in the Square, and as speaker after speaker took his turn the crowd dwindled steadily. The audience was silent and unmoved as the explanations of the workers' role in socialism were expounded, though there was respect for the speakers of the kind one would feel for a friend whose opinions grew out of a different sphere of life. Yet as the meeting was about to die out, a phalanx of policemen suddenly appeared on the scene to disperse the crowd.

Why the police intruded is the beginning of the puzzle we have to understand. Their reaction was totally inappropriate to the character of what was occurring before their eyes; they ought rather to have breathed a sigh of relief that the meeting was such a peaceful fiasco. But, as the civil riots of a later chapter in Chicago's history show, it is sometimes more difficult for the police to "cool off" than it is for the demonstrators. In any event, just as the Haymarket meeting was falling apart, the police moved in to disperse it by force, and thus brought back to life the temporary spirit of unity and of outrage against the violence at McCormick Works that had drawn the crowd and orators together.

The knots of men moved back from the lines of police advancing toward the speaker's stand, so that the police gained the area in front of the rostrum without incident. Then, suddenly, someone in the crowd threw a powerful bomb into the midst of the policemen, and pandemonium broke loose. The wounded police and people in the crowd dragged themselves or were carried into the hallways of buildings in the eastern end of Union Park; drugstores, like Ebert's at Madison and Halstead and Barker's on West Madison, suddenly became hospitals with bleeding men stretched out on the floors, while police combed the residences and grounds of Union Park looking for wounded members of the crowd who had managed to find shelter under stoops or in sheds from the police guns booming in the Square.

As the news spread, small riots with aimless energy broke out in the southwestern part of the city, but they were soon dispersed. By the morning of May 5, the working-class quarters were quiet, though the police were not.

PROCLAMATION
TO THE PEOPLE OF CHICAGO:
MAYOR'S OFFICE, Chicago, May 5, 1886.

WHEREAS, Great excitement exists among the people of this good city, growing out of the **LABOR TROUBLES**, which excitement is intensified by the open defiance of the guardians of the peace by a body of lawless men, who, under the pretense of aiding the laboring men, are really endeavoring to destroy all law. And Whereas, last night these men, by the use of weapons never resorted to in **CIVILIZED LANDS, EXCEPT IN TIMES OF WAR or for REVOLUTIONARY PURPOSES, CAUSED GREAT BLOODSHED AMONG CITIZENS AND AMONG OFFICERS** of the **MUNICIPALITY** who were simply in the performance of their duties. And Whereas, the **CITY AUTHORITIES PROPOSE TO PROTECT LIFE AND PROPERTY AT ALL HAZARDS**, and in doing so will be compelled to break up all unlawful or dangerous gatherings; and

WHEREAS, Even when men propose to meet for lawful purposes, bad men will attempt to mingle with them, armed with cowardly missiles, for the purpose of bringing about bloodshed, thus endangering innocent persons;

THEREFORE, I, Carter H. Harrison, MAYOR OF THE CITY OF CHICAGO, DO HEREBY PROCLAIM THAT GATHERINGS OF PEOPLE IN CROWDS OR PROCESSIONS IN THE STREETS and PUBLIC PLACES OF THE CITY ARE DANGEROUS AND CANNOT BE PERMITTED, AND ORDERS HAVE BEEN ISSUED TO THE POLICE TO PREVENT ALL SUCH GATHERINGS and TO BREAK UP and DISPERSE ALL CROWDS, TO PREVENT INJURY TO INNOCENT PERSONS.

I urge all law-abiding people to quietly attend to their own affairs, and not to meet in crowds. If the police order any gatherings to disperse, and they be not obeyed, all persons so disobeying will be treated as law-breakers, and will surely incur the penalty of their disobedience.

I further assure the good people of Chicago that I believe the police can protect their lives and property and the good name of Chicago, and WILL do so.

CARTER H. HARRISON, Mayor.

The intersection of Washington Boulevard and Ogden Avenue as seen from Union Park in the nineties.

They, and the middle-class people of Chicago, especially those living in Union Park, were in a fever, a fever compounded of fear, a desire for vengeance, and simple bewilderment.

It is this reaction that must be explored to gauge the true impact of the Haymarket incident on the Union Park community. The first characteristic of this reaction was how swiftly an interpretation, communally shared, was formed; the middle-class people of Union Park, and elsewhere in Chicago, were immediately moved by the incident to draw a clearly defined picture of what had happened, and they held onto their interpretation tenaciously. Today it is easy to recognize, from the location of the meeting next to a police station, from the apathy of the crowd, from the sequence of events that preceded the bombing, that the Haymarket incident was not a planned sequence of disorder or a riot by an enraged mob, but rather the work of an isolated man, someone who might have thrown the bomb no matter who was there. But the day after the bombing, these objective considerations were not the reality "respectable" people perceived. Middle-class people of Chicago believed instead that "the immigrant anarchists" were spilling out of the slums to kill the police, in order to destroy the security of the middle classes themselves. "Respectable" people felt some kind of need to believe in the enormity of the threat, and in this way the community quickly arrived at a common interpretation of what had happened.

The enormity of the threat was itself the second characteristic of their reaction. The color red, which was taken as a revolutionary incitement, was "cut out of street advertisements and replaced with a less suggestive color." On the day after the riot a coroner's jury returned a verdict that all prisoners in the hands of the police were guilty of murder, because Socialism as such led to murderous anarchy, and anyone who attended the meeting must have been a Socialist. Yet this same jury observed that it was "troublesome" that none of those detained could be determined to have thrown the bomb. Anarchism itself was generalized to a more sweeping scope by its identification with foreign birth; the "agitators" were poor foreigners, and this fact could explain their lawlessness. For example, the *Tribune* reported that on the day after the Haymarket Riot police closed two saloons

> that were the headquarters of the foreign-speaking population, which flaunts and marches under the red flag, and heretofore they were the centers of a great throng of men who did little but drink beer and attend the meetings in the halls above.

On May 5 and 6, the police were engaged in a strenuous effort to determine where the "anarchist" groups lived, so that the population as a whole might be controlled. On May 7, and this was the view to prevail henceforth, they announced that the residences of most anarchists must be in the southwestern portion of the city, the immigrant, working-class area.

In Union Park the assigning of the responsible parties to the general category of "foreigner" excited even more panic. The *Tribune* of May 7 reported that the community was gripped by a fear that lawless marauders would again erupt out of the proletarian sector of the city and terrorize people in the neighborhood of the riot. These fears were sustained by two events in the next week.

First were reports of the deaths, day after day, of policemen and innocent bystanders who had been seriously wounded by the bomb on May 4, coupled with a massive newspaper campaign to raise money for the families of the victims. Second, and by far more important, fear of renewed bombing was kept alive by the fantasies of a Captain Schaack of the Chicago police who day by day discovered and foiled anarchist plots, plans to bomb churches and homes, attempts on the lives of eminent citizens. Such were the scare stories with which the middle-class people of Chicago horrified themselves for weeks.

The same deep communal force that immediately led the people of Union Park to interpret an objectively confused event in a very similar and very simplistic fashion also led them to use increasingly horrific metaphors to describe the nature of the threat and challenge. But as events a year later were to show, this force also prevented the men of Union Park from being able to deal effectively with the future violence.

Crime in the Streets

On Thursday, February 9, 1888, the *Chicago Tribune* gave its lead space to the following story:

> Amos J. Snell, a millionaire who lived at the corner of Washington Boulevard and Ada Street, was shot to death by two burglars who entered his house and made off with $1,600 worth of county warrants and $5,000 in checks. The murder was committed at about 2 A.M. and discovered by a servant at about 6:30 A.M.

Snell had been a resident of the area since 1867, when he built a home in Union Park and bought up many blocks of desirable real estate around it.

The murder of Snell climaxed a tense situation in Union Park that had existed since the beginning of the year 1888. Since New Year's Day, "between forty and fifty burglaries have been committed within a radius of half a mile from the intersection of Adams and Ashland Avenues," the editor of the *Tribune* wrote the day after Snell's death. Though the police counted half this number, it appears that the burglars had a simple and systematic scheme: to loot any household goods, such as furs, silver plate, jewelry or bonds left in unlocked drawers. Occasionally some of the property was recovered, and occasionally a thief was arrested who seemed to have been involved, but the operation itself was remarkably smooth and successful.

How did people in Union Park react to these burglaries, and what did they do to try to stop them? The reaction of the community was much like their reaction to the Haymarket bombing: they felt caught up at once in a "reign of terror," as the *Tribune* said, "that was none of their doing —they didn't know when the danger would strike again or who would be hurt. Most of all, they didn't know how to stop it." Once again, community fear was escalated to a general, sweeping and impersonal terror.

Before the Snell murder, the citizens of the community had tried two means of foiling the robbers, and so of quieting the fears of their families. One was to make reports to the police, reports which the editor of the *Tribune* claimed the police did not heed. The citizens then resorted to fortifying their homes, to hiring elderly men as private guards but the thieves were professional enough to deal with this: "somehow or other the burglars evaded all the precautions that were taken to prevent their nocturnal visits."

The Neighborhood as Garrison State

The Snell murder brought public discussion of the robberies, and how to stop them, to a high pitch. Especially in Union Park, the vicinity of Snell's residence, the community was "so aroused that the people talked of little else than vigilance committees and frequent holdings of court . . . as a panacea for the lawless era that had come upon them." Gradually, the small-town vigilante idea gave way to a new attitude toward the police, and how the police should operate in a large city. "It is no use," said one member of the Grant Club, the West Side club to which Snell himself had belonged, "to attempt to run a cosmopolitan city as you would run a New England village." He meant that the police had up to that time concentrated on closing down gambling houses and beer parlors as a major part of their effort to keep the town "respectable" and "proper." Thus they didn't deal effectively with serious crimes like robbery and murder because they spent too much time trying to clean up petty offenses; the main thing was to keep the criminal elements confined to their own quarters in the city. In all these discussions, the fact of being burglarized had been forgotten. The search turned to a means of separatism, of protection against the threatening "otherness" of the populace outside the community.

Such views were striking, considering the position of Union Park. The community's own physical character, in its parks and playgrounds, was nonurban, designed in the traditions of Olmstead and Vaux; the people, as was pointed out repeatedly in the newspaper account, were themselves among the most respectable and staid, if not the most fashionable in the city. Yet here were the most respectable among the respectable arguing for abandoning the enforcement of a common morality throughout the city. The petty criminals outside the community's borders ought to be left in peace, but out of sight. Union Park existed in a milieu too cosmopolitan for every act of the lower classes to be controlled; the police ought to abandon attempts to be the guardians of all morality and instead concentrate on assuring the basic security of the citizens against outbursts of major crime.

What Union Park wanted instead, and what it got, was a garrison of police to make the community riotproof and crimeproof. For the police did indeed abandon the search for the killers, and concentrated on holding the security of Union Park, like an area under siege. In this way, the original totally suburban tone of the parks and mansions was transformed; this respectable neighborhood felt its own existence to be so threatened that only rigid barriers, enforced by a semimilitary state of curfew and surveillance, would permit it to continue functioning.

The characteristics of their reaction to violence could only lead to such a voluntary isolation: everyone "knew" immediately what was wrong; and what was wrong was overwhelming: it was nothing less than the power of the "foreigner," the outsider who had suddenly become dominant in the city. Isolation, through garrisons and police patrols, was the only solution.

Union Park held onto its middle-class character until the middle of the 1890s; there was no immediate desertion by respectable people of the area in the wake of the violence: where else in a great city, asked one citizen, was it safe to go? Everywhere the same terror was possible.

The contrast between the limited character of civil disturbance and the immediate perception of that disturbance as the harbinger of an unnameable threat coming from a generalized enemy is a theme that binds together much research on urban disorders.

Until a few years ago, riots were taken to be the expression of irrational and directionless aggression. "Irrationality of crowds" and similar explanations of crowd behavior as an innate disorder were first given a cogent interpretation in the industrial era in the writings of Le Bon, for whom the irrational brutality of crowds was a sign of how the "psychology" of the individual becomes transformed when the individual acts in concert with other people. This image of crowds was as congenial to many of the syndicalists on the Left as it was to the fears of bourgeois people like those in Union Park. The difficulty with the image is that, for the nineteenth century at least and for the Haymarket Riots certainly, it does not seem to fit the facts of crowd behavior.

Nevertheless, expecting "seething passions" to erupt hysterically, the middle-class people of Chicago and their po-

The close-knit nuclear family offered a warm, sheltering retreat from the confusing and risky world of burgeoning industrial capitalism.

lice were somehow blind to a spectacle they should have enjoyed, that of the workers' increasing boredom with the inflammatory talk of their supposed leaders. The expectations of a seething rabble had somehow to be fulfilled, and so the police themselves took the first step. After the shooting was over, the respectable people of Chicago became inflamed. This blind passion in the name of defending the city from blind passion is the phenomenon that needs to be explained. A similar contradiction occurred in the series of robberies 18 months later as well. As in the riot, the facts of the rationality of the enemy and his limited purpose, although acknowledged, were not absorbed; he was felt to be something else—a nameless, elusive terror, all-threatening—and the people reacted with a passion equal to his.

This mystifying condition, familiar now in the voices heard from the "New Right," is what I should like to explain, not through a sweeping theory that binds the past to the present, but through a theory that explains this peculiar reaction in terms of strains in the family life of the Union Park people. What I would like to explore—and I certainly do not pretend to prove it—is how, in an early industrial city, the fears of the foreign masses held by a middle-class group may have reflected something other than the actual state of interaction between bourgeoisie and proletariat. These fears may have reflected instead the impact of family life on the way the people like those in Union Park understood their places in the city society.

If it is true that in the character one ascribes to one's enemy lies a description of something in one's own experience, the nature of the fear of lower-class foreigners among Union Park families might tell something about the Union Park community itself. The Union Park men, during the time of the riot and robberies, accused their chosen enemies of being lawless anarchists whose base passions pushed them outside the bounds of acceptable behavior, which finally, sent them emotionally out of control. If the poor were reasonable, if they were temperate, ran the argument, these violent things would not have come to pass.

What about the Union Park people themselves, then? Were they masters of themselves? A study I have recently completed on the family patterns of the Union Park people during the decades of the 1870s and 1880s may throw some light on the question of stability and purposefulness in their lives: it is the dimension of stability in these family patterns, I believe, that shaped their reaction to violence in their city.

A Close and Happy Home?

In 1880, on a 40-square-block territory of Union Park, there lived 12,000 individuals in approximately 3,000 family units. The latter were of three kinship types: single-member families, where one person lived alone without any other kin; nuclear families, consisting of a husband and wife and their unmarried children; and extended families, where to the nuclear unit was added some other relative—a brother or sister of the parents, a member of a third generation, or a son or daughter who was married and lived with his spouse in the parental home. The most common form of the extended family in Union Park was that containing "collateral kin," that is, unmarried relatives of the same generation as the husband or wife.

The dominant form of family life in Union Park was nuclear, for 80 percent of the population lived in such homes, with 10 percent of the population living alone in single-member families, and the remaining 10 percent living in extended family situations. A father and mother living alone with their growing children in an apartment or house was the pervasive household condition. There were few widowed parents living with their children in either nuclear or extended homes, and though the census manuscripts on which my study of the year 1880 is based were inexact at this point, there appeared to be few groups of related families living in the same neighborhood but in separate dwellings.

Family Sizes

The size of the Union Park family was small. Most families had one or two children; it was rare for a family to have more. And, the size of poorer families was in its contours similar to the size of the wealthier ones: few families were larger than six members.

Over the course of time internal conditions of family structure and of family size tended to lead to similar family histories. Nuclear families had characteristic histories similar to the experience of smaller families having from two to four kin members in the 1870s and 1880s. Extended families, on the other hand, had histories similar to the experience of the minority of families with four to six kin members during these decades. What made this process subtle was that nuclear families did not tend to be smaller, or extended larger. Family size and family kinship structure seemed rather to be independent structures with parallel internal differences in functioning.

Why and how this was so can be understood by assessing the patterns of the generations of the dominant group.

The nuclear, small-size families during the year 1880 were very cohesive in relations between husbands and wives, parents and children. Whether rich or poor—and about 25 percent of the community fell into a working class category—the young men and women from such homes rarely broke away to live on their own until they themselves were ready to marry and found families, usually when the man was in his early thirties. The families of Union Park, observers of the time noted, were extremely self-contained, did little entertaining, and rarely left the home even to enjoy such modest pleasures as a church social or, for the men, a beer at the local tavern. The small family, containing only parents and their immediate children, resisted the diverse influences either of other relatives or extensive community contacts. These intensive families would seem to epitomize stability among the people of Union Park.

Mobility and Family Stability

Nevertheless, my study of intergenerational mobility in work and residence from 1872 to 1890 did reveal a complicated, but highly significant pattern of insecurity in the dominant intensive families as compared to the smaller group of less intensive families.

The first insecurity of these families was in the rate of desertion. While divorce was rare—it was an act carrying a terrible stigma a hundred years ago—practical divorce in the form of desertion did occur. In Union Park, the rate of desertion was twice as high as that of *poorer* communities—in nearly one out of ten families husband or wife had deserted. A more subtle pattern of insecurity was at work as well.

In the nuclear-family homes and in the smaller families the fathers were stable job holders, as a group, over the course of the 18 years studied; roughly the same proportions of unskilled, skilled and white-collar workers of various kinds composed the labor force of these nuclear fathers in 1890 as in 1872. Given the enormous growth of Chicago's industrial production, its banking and financial capital, retail trade volume, as well as the increase of the population (100 percent increase each ten years) and the greatly increasing proportion of white-collar pursuits during this time, such stability in job distribution is truly puzzling.

But equally puzzling is the fact that this pattern of job holding among the fathers of intensive families was not shared by the fathers in extended families or fathers of larger families living in Union Park. For, unlike their neighbors, fathers of these more complex and extensive families were mobile up into exclusively bureaucratic, white-collar pursuits—so much so that by 1890 virtually none of these fathers worked with their hands. They gradually concentrated in executive and other lesser managerial pursuits and decreased their numbers in shopkeeping, toward which, stereotypically, they are supposed to gravitate.

Even more striking were the differences between fathers and sons in each of these family groups. The sons in the dominant family homes were, unlike their fathers, very unstable in their patterns of job holding. As many moved down into manual pursuits over the course of the 18 years as moved up into the white-collar occupations. One is tempted to explain this simply as a regression toward the mean of higher status groups in time. But the sons of extended and large families did not move in this mixed direction. Rather, they followed the footsteps of their fathers into good white-collar positions, with almost total elimination of manual labor in their ranks as well. This pattern occurred in small-family sons versus large-family sons and in nuclear-family sons versus extended-family sons. The difference in the groups of sons was especially striking in that the starting points of the sons in the occupational work force had virtually the *same* distribution in all types of families. Stephan Thernstrom has pointed out that economic aid between generations of workers is more likely to manifest itself at the outset of a young person's career than when the older generation has retired and the young have become the principal breadwinners. But the fact is that in Union Park, both extended-family and nuclear-family sons, both large- and small-family sons, began to work in virtually the same pursuits as their fathers, then became distinctively different in their patterns of achievement. This strongly suggests that something *beyond* monetary help was at work in these families to produce divergences in the work experiences of the different groups of sons.

The residence patterns of the generations of the intensive and less intensive families also bears on the issues of stability and instability in the lives of the people of Union Park. Up to the time of violence in the Union Park area, the residence patterns of the two kinds of families, in both the parents' and the sons' generations, were rather similar. In the wake of the violence, however, it appears that within the parents' generation there was significant movement back into the Union Park area, whereas for the half decade preceding the disturbances there was a general movement out to other parts of Chicago. It is in the generation of the sons that differences between the two family groups appeared. In the wake of the violence, the sons of large families and of extended families continued the exodus from Union Park that began in the early 1880s. The sons from intensive families did not; in the years following the violence they stopped migrating beyond the boundaries of the community they had known as children, and instead kept closer to their first homes.

Family Background and Making It

These observations have an obvious bearing on an important debate over what form of bourgeois family life best nurtures the kind of children who can cope with the immensely dynamic and risky world of the industrial city. Talcott Parsons has argued that the small nuclear family is a kinship form well adapted to the industrial order; the lack of extensive kin obligations and a wide kin circle in this family type means, Parsons has contended, that the kinship unit does not serve as a binding private world of its own, but rather frees the individual to participate in "universalized" bureaucratic structures that are urban-wide and dynamic.

The cultural historian Phillippe Aries, in *Centuries of Childhood,* has challenged this theory by amassing a body of historical evidence to show that the extended kinship relationships in large families, at least during an earlier era, were actually less sheltering, more likely to push the individual out into the world where he would have to act like a full man on his own at an early age, than the intense, intimate conditions of the nineteenth-century home. In intensive homes, the young person spent a long time in a state of dependence under the protection and guidance of his elders. Consequently, argues Aries, the capacity of the young adult from small nuclear homes to deal with the world about him was blunted, for he passed from a period of total shelter to a state in which he was expected to be entirely competent on his own.

The data I collected on Union Park clearly are in line with the argument made by Aries. The young from homes of small scale or from homes where the structure of the family was nuclear and "privatistic," in Aries' phrase, had an ineptness in the work world, and a rootedness to the place of their childhood not found to the same degree among the more complex, or larger-family situations. (I have no desire to argue the moral virtues of this rootedness to community or failure to "make it" in the city; these simply happened to be the conditions that existed.) But the conditions that faced Union Park families in a new kind of city, a city at once disorganized and anarchic, set the stability of the family against adaptation to city life. For it is clear that the nineteenth-century, privatistic, sheltering homes Aries depicts, homes that Frank Lloyd Wright describes in his *Autobiography* of his early years in Chicago, homes that observers of the time pointed to as a basic element in the composition of the "dull respectability" of Union Park, could themselves have easily served as a refuge from the confusing, dynamic city that was taking shape all around the confines of Union Park.

And what is more natural than that middle-class people should try to hold onto the status position they had in such a disrupting, growing milieu, make few entrepreneurial ventures outside their established jobs, and withdraw into the comfort and intimacy of their families. Here is the source of that job "freeze" to be seen in the mobility patterns of fathers in intense-family situations; the bourgeois intensive family in this way became a shelter from the work pressures of the industrial city, a place where men tried to institute some control and establish some comforting intimacies in the shape of their lives, while withdrawing to the sidelines as the new opportunities of the city industries opened up. Such an interpretation of these middle-class families complements Richard Hofstadter's interpretation of middle-class political attitudes in the latter part of the nineteenth century. He characterizes the middle-class as feeling that the new industrial order had passed them by and left them powerless. It is this peculiar feeling of social helplessness on the part of the fathers that explains what use they made of their family lives.

But the late nineteenth century was also the world of Horatio Alger, of "luck and pluck"; it was no time for withdrawal. The idea of seizing opportunities, the idea of instability of job tenure for the sake of rising higher and higher, constituted, as John Cawelti has described it, the commonly agreed-upon notion among respectable people of the road to success. One should be mobile in work, then, for this was the meaning of "opportunity" and "free enterprise," but in fact the overwhelming dislocations of the giant cities seem to have urged many men to retreat into the circle of their own families, to try simply to hold onto jobs they knew they could perform.

Conditions of privacy and comfort in the home weakened the desire to get ahead in the world, to conquer it; since the fathers of the intensive families were retreating from the confusions of city life, their preparation of their sons for work in Chicago became ambiguous, in that they wanted, surely, success for their sons, yet shielded the young, and did not themselves serve as models of successful adaptation. The result of these ambiguities can be seen directly in the work experience of the sons, when contrasted to the group of sons from families which, by virtue either of family form or size, were more complex or less intense. Overlaid on these family patterns was a relatively high rate of hidden marital breakdown in Union Park—one in every ten homes—while the expectation was, again, that such breakdowns must not occur, that they were a disgrace.

Because the goals of these middle-class people were bred of contradictory desires to escape from and succeed in the city, the possibility of a wholly satisfying pattern of achievement for them was denied. The family purposes were innately contradictory. A family impulse in one direction inevitably defeated another image of what was wanted. This meant that the sources of defeat were nameless for the families involved; surely these families were not aware of the web of self-contradictions in which in retrospect they seem to have been enmeshed; they knew only that things never seemed to work out to the end planned, that they suffered defeats in a systematic way. It is this specific kind of frustration that would lead to a sense of being overwhelmed, which, in this community's family system, led easily to a hysterical belief in hidden, unknown threats ready to strike at a man at almost any time.

What I would like to suggest is that this complex pattern of self-defeat explains the character of the Union Park reaction to violence. For the dread of the unknown that the middle classes projected onto their supposed enemies among the poor expressed exactly the condition of self-instituted defeat that was the central feature of the family system in Union Park. And this dread was overwhelming precisely because men's own contradictory responses to living in such a city were overwhelming. They had defined a set of conditions for their lives that inevitably left them out of control. The fact that in Union Park there was a desire to destroy the "immigrant anarchists" or to garrison the neighborhood against them, as a result of the incidents of violence, was important in that it offered an outlet for personal defeats, not just for anger against lawbreakers. This response to violence refused to center on particular people, but rather followed the "path of hysterical reaction," in Freud's phrase, and centered on an abstract class of evildoers. The fear of being suddenly overwhelmed from the outside was really a sign that one was in fact in one's own life being continually overwhelmed by the unintended consequences of what one did.

The terrible fear of attack from the unbridled masses was also related to the fear of falling into deep poverty that grew up in urban middle-class families of this time. To judge from a wide range of novels in the latter half of the nineteenth century there was a dread among respectable people of suddenly and uncontrollably falling into abject poverty; the Sidwells in Thackeray's *Vanity Fair* plummet from wealth to disorganized penury in a short space of time; In Edith Wharton's *Age of Innocence,* Lily Bart's father is similarly struck down by the symbol of entrepreneurial chance in the industrial city, the stock market. This feeling of threat from the impersonal, unpredictable workings of the city economy was much like the sense of threat that existed in the Union Park families, because the dangers encountered in both cases were not a person or persons one could grapple with, but an abstract condition, poverty, or family disorder that was unintended, impersonal and swift to come if the family should once falter. Yet what one *should* do was framed in such a self-contradictory way that it seemed that oneself and one's family were always on the edge of survival. In this way, the growth of the new industrial city, with its uncertainties and immense wastes in human poverty, not all victims of which were easily dismissed as personal failures, could surely produce in the minds of middle-class citizens who were uneasy about their own class position and lived out from the center of town, the feeling that some terrible force from below symbolized by the poor, the foreigner, was about to strike out and destroy them unless they did something drastic.

The reaction among most of the families to the eruption of violence bears out this interpretation of events. With the exception of the upwardly mobile, extended-family sons, most family members did not try to flee the community as a response to the threats of riot and the organized wave of crime. There was a renewed feeling of community solidarity in the face of violence, a solidarity created by fear and a common dread of those below.

The relations between family life and the perception of violence in this Chicago community could be formed into the following general propositions. These were middle-class families enormously confused in what they wanted for themselves in the city, both in terms of their achievements in the society at large and in terms of their emotional needs for shelter and intimacy. Their schema of values and life goals was in fact formed around the issues of stability and instability as goals in a self-contradictory way. The result of this inner contradiction was a feeling of frustration, of not really being satisfied, in the activities of family members to achieve *either* patterns of stability or mobility for themselves. The self-defeat involved in this process naturally led these families to feel themselves threatened by overwhelming, nameless forces they could not control, regardless of what they did. The outbreak of violence was a catalyst for them, giving them in the figure of the "other," the stranger, the foreigner, a generalized agent of disorder and disruption.

It is this process that explains logically why the people of Union Park so quickly found a communally acceptable villain responsible for violence, despite all the ambiguities perceived in the actual outbreaks of the disorders themselves. This is why the villain so quickly identified, was a generalized, nonspecific human force, the embodiment of the unknown, the outside, the foreign. This is why the people of Union Park clung so tenaciously to their interpretation, seemed so willing to be terrorized and distraught.

Then and Now

If the complex processes of family and social mobility in Union Park are of any use in understanding the great fear of disorder among respectable, middle-class urbanites of our own time, their import is surely disturbing. For the nature of the disease that produced this reaction to violence among the industrial middle classes was not simply a matter of "ignorance" or failure to understand the problems of the poor; the fear was the consequence, rather, of structural processes in the lives of the Union Park families themselves. Thus for attitudes of people like the Union Park dwellers to change, and a more tolerant view of those below to be achieved, nothing so simple as more education about poor people, or to put the matter in contemporary terms, more knowledge about Negroes, would have sufficed. The whole fabric of the city, in its impact on staid white-collar workers, would have to have been changed. The complexity and the diversity of the city itself would need to have been stilled for events to take another course. But were the disorder of the city absent, the principal characteristic of the industrial city as we know it would also have been absent. These cities were powerful agents of change, precisely because they replaced the controlled social space of village and farm life with a kind of human settlement too dense and too various to be controlled.

And it comes to mind that the New Right fears of the present time are as deeply endemic to the structure of complex city life as was the violent reaction to violence in Union Park. Perhaps, out of patterns of self-defeat in the modern middle classes, it is bootless to expect rightwing, middle-class repression to abate simply through resolves of goodwill, "education about Negroes," or a change of heart. The experience of bourgeois people of Chicago 100 years ago may finally make us a great deal more pessimistic about the chances for reason and tolerance to survive in a complex and pluralistic urban society.

January 1970

5 Institutions

Over time societies develop shared outlooks, beliefs, and norms that they wish to preserve for themselves and future generations. In fact, a society is by definition an historic working-out of human arrangements, which give a group, large or small, simple or complex, a common past, present, and future. Men develop ideals and goals, tools and techniques, and modes of acceptable human relations that provide for the continuation of the life of the group. They also discover what is harmful to the group's welfare and make rules to protect the group from harm. These are taught to their children and enforced in the community.

There is no set of instincts that guides man into some predetermined pattern of living. He creates his own patterns. It is hard to conceive of facing the world without the rich and varied alternatives of how to act that we are offered, no, nudged into adopting, from the cradle to the grave. Most problems of daily life have solutions that minimize an individual's need to invent new ones or make difficult personal decisions. We call these solutions the traditional or institutionalized ways of doing things.

Beyond Individual Death

Institutions are man-made ways of solving some problems that all individuals and societies face. If there were only one way to solve problems, the institutions of various societies would all be alike. But man in his ingenuity can conceive of alternative and even contradictory sets of values and patterns of life. So we have all kinds of customs and practices created by the people of the world to handle all the various situations they face.

Institutions that are common to all societies are the family, religion, government, education, and the economy. Each one includes a patterned system of social relations that has evolved to carry out some important objectives of the society. Social institutions are organized around critical issues of survival and bear responsibility for supporting the important values of the group. They share the responsibility of social survival beyond individual death. If any institution fails to perform well, group members are alarmed and take steps to defend, repair, or change the practices at fault. Often the persons who appear to break institutional norms are brought into line by sanctions of some level of severity. The most severe punishment is meted out to people who break norms connected with sexual behavior and family life, and the use of property and political power. When conventional practices such as the form of the wedding ceremony or the upkeep of property according to local expectations are not abided by, people may disapprove but they will not insist on compliance with the usual customs or folkways. But when the group thinks matters of morals have crossed over into matters of survival, they will not let such behavior go unrestrained or unpunished. The most cherished group ways are enacted into law and enforced by the state.

The family is the basic unit of every culture. All cultures have beliefs and practices regulating family life, since the survival of the group depends on the procreation and rearing of a new generation to replace the old. Norms for sexual behavior and child rearing always exist, but methods for meeting the needs of the community to regulate sexual behavior and family life are infinitely varied. In other words,

Charles Gatewood

some form of the family is found in virtually all societies, although its importance as a separate unit within a larger network of relatives, kin, and other significant associates varies greatly all the way from a central and dominating place to a minimal one. When speaking of the institution of the family, then, the place of the individual family in the larger whole known as a kinship system and the functions the individual family fulfills in different societies or in the various parts of any complex society are crucial elements to distinguish. For instance, the method of selecting marriage partners is greatly affected by whether the form of the family is a small, nuclear group made up of husband, wife, and children or an extended family made up of several family units and others related by marriage and blood ties.

Not only is the choice of a mate patterned according to a prevailing family structure, but so also are the transfer of goods and property at the time of marriage, the place of residence, the rearing of children, and the conjugal relations between man and wife. In most Moslem countries, for example, the legal powers of the husband to divorce his wife unilaterally are absolute, although they have been somewhat modified in revisions of family law in Algeria, Tunisia, and Egypt. In an article on the divorce practices of Morocco, "I Divorce Thee," Lawrence Rosen describes how the marriage contract is made and broken and how a modern urban Moroccan woman and her family can restrict her husband's seemingly unlimited legal privileges through the use of their nonlegal economic and social advantages over him.

In the middle-class American family, parents often play an active part in putting children into situations where they will choose mates of appropriate social characteristics. The university campus at one time was a middle-class preserve where parents could send their offspring with some assurance that freedom of choice in selecting a spouse would not be poorly exercised. In "Sororities and the Husband Game" John Finley Scott shows how mothers try to keep control of their daughters' social contacts on campuses where the growing diversity of students' backgrounds means the status of prospective bridegrooms can no longer be guaranteed.

Family Roles

The functions of the modern middle-class family have been so truncated that most of the significant educational, religious, economic, political, health, and welfare responsibilities have been taken over by other institutions. Left with emotional and affectional relations as its prime functions, the family concentrates on its own interpersonal relations within the family group, and parents often find their own children's behavior and activities of uppermost concern.

Although the particular patterns of the family as an institution in any society seem to be slow to change, institutions cannot maintain their forms indefinitely if they impose com-

Institutions

peting or contradictory demands. Movement from one social class to another, for example, often requires redefinition of family roles. In "A Better Life: Notes from Puerto Rico," Lloyd H. Rogler details the change from the usual role of a lower-class Puerto Rican *macho* "he-man" to a reliable and faithful middle-class husband and provider for the sake of upward mobility.

Religious institutions have at their base the awe and wonder men feel as they face the mysteries of nature—birth, life, and death. In all societies people have agonized over the meaning of these events and shared reverent feelings concerning those elements that are beyond the ordinary and really are not subject to the usual kinds of explanations. Toward the ultimates of life, a sense of sacredness arises that separates them from the profane.

The institutionalization of religious practices has resulted in two counter trends in belief and participation by communicants. On the one hand the organization and large numbers involved in world religious bodies have established their social and political power; on the other hand, growing secularization in modern societies and within religious structures themselves have undercut the importance of religious adherence in people's lives. In "The Future of the Islamic Religion" Guenter Lewy assesses the important political role of the Moslems in the Middle East, but in "Religion Is Irrelevant in Sweden," Richard F. Tomasson finds that although Swedes abide by the religious ceremonies of baptism, marriage, and burial, the established church is no longer a significant influence on their daily lives. In contrast, the emotionalism of the Holiness churches and serpent-handling rituals serves a meaningful purpose in the lives of fundamentalists in southern Appalachia according to Nathan L. Gerrard's "The Serpent-Handling Religions of West Virginia."

Political institutions express the organization of power and authority in society. The legal structure gives the judge on the bench, for example, the authority to conduct a trial involving a life-or-death outcome for the defendant. As long as his authority is considered legitimate, the judge carries out the traditional legal procedures without serious challenge to his basic right to do so. However, once this legitimacy is questioned and the political institutions are thought unfair or repressive, as in the trial of the Chicago 7 or various trials of the Black Panthers, a struggle ensues for a change in the basis of legitimate authority. It becomes apparent, then, that those who occupy a lower position in the social and economic hierarchy, can exert pressure to force changes by those who hold power.

The formal and informal power and authority of political office holders and the constraints on their capabilities to carry out their will are expressed in various ways in different societies. Aaron Wildavsky in his article "The Two Presidencies" shows that the power of the president of the United States is greatest when directing military and foreign policy and much less when controlling domestic affairs.

Some groups are excluded from such powerful positions as high political offices and policy-making roles in enterprises that control human and material resources or influence the shape of public and private policy. Harold M. Baron and his associates' study of Chicago Negroes in policy-making positions, "Black Powerlessness in Chicago," shows that they hold not only a minimal number of high positions in government, business, labor unions, universities, and professional firms, but that the actual power vested in Negro policy-makers is even less than the nominal posts they hold. Clearly, certain basic features of the socioeconomic system, leadership characteristics, and historical development of a nation shape the nature of its power relationships.

Comparing institutions of nations like Cuba, the much less developed countries of Asia, Latin America, and Africa

Institutions

and highly industrialized states like the United States, Canada, Great Britain, Japan, and the Soviet Union, it is noticeable that political and economic activities are much less separated from family and religious affairs in some than others. It is characteristic of the development of capitalism and industrialism in the West, for instance, that economic processes of production and distribution take place in an impersonal market not strongly tied to kinship and religious structures. At the same time, in preindustrial societies it is next to impossible to distinguish economic activities from religious and political ones. The freeing of economic institutions from the influence of other institutions lessens the amount of moral guidance that religious and family institutions can bring to bear on business and commercial enterprise and allows economic forces to become powerful, even dominant, in a country. But even where economic organization is the most differentiated—with advanced technology, and complex occupational, corporate, and financial structures—the interaction between economic and noneconomic activities remains. Motivations to work, for example, are instilled early in the family and reinforced by religious support of the work ethic. The tremendous productivity of an advanced technology may, however, make goods so abundant that people in the future will find that working for a living no longer is the central occupation of their lives.

The articles in the section on economic institutions illustrates some of the important interrelations of economic and other activities. Norton E. Long in "Private Initiative in the 'Great Society'" raises questions about distributing public goods like schooling, police, and recreational facilities so that people with less economic power get a fair share of them. Ivar Berg in "Rich Men's Qualifications for Poor Man's Jobs" documents the thesis that private employers demand too much education for jobs they offer because of their mistaken belief that higher education necessarily means better performance on the job.

Allegiance

Institutions give expression to sentiments. They are the physical embodiment of culture. Institutions relieve the individual of every responsibility for every event. They provide a sort of legal as well as organizational scaffolding for delimiting the rights and responsibilities of people. If men were uniformly accountable for every social breakdown and every social dislocation, we would be in a permanent state of conflict without possibility of resolution. Institutions provide a benchmark for progress, or at least, of measuring changes over time. They also provide a means whereby people can relate to objects other than other people. Institutions provide a sense of security, a framework for collective response to challenges that simply cannot be met at the individual level. The allegiance that a person tenders to an institution is not simply arbitrary, not simply a matter of inherited sloth, but more pointedly, an allegiance that is earned by the ability of institutions to reward their members and participants. And while it is true that institutions take on a life of their own, even when they become dysfunctional and fail in their human purpose, they do in the long pull of time represent the highest achievement of man as a social animal, living in a state of collective goals, defined by meaningful publics.

"I Divorce Thee"   LAWRENCE ROSEN

There is probably no better example of a stereotype that springs from wish-fulfillment than the widespread notion that Moslem men have only to intone "I divorce thee" three times in order to be rid of the harridan that plagues their married years. To be sure, it's getting a lot easier these days, almost everywhere in the West, to get a divorce; but for sheer simplicity and ease the Moslem practice seems unbeatable.

Unfortunately, like many stereotypes of the nonwestern world, this one too is a mixture of half-truth and complete misunderstanding. It is true that in most Moslem countries men still retain the right to repudiate their spouses unilaterally. But it is equally true that there is a host of social, economic and indeed legal means through which a woman and her family may effectively check her husband's ability to do anything with his seemingly unlimited legal powers. In a modern Islamic nation like Morocco the law codes alone offer only the narrowest view of husband-wife relations in such a society. One must look closely at a number of social and economic factors associated with divorce to get a more sophisticated view.

Moreover, a study of this sort reveals various social and legal problems that are of considerable importance to several aspects of contemporary sociological theory. For if it is indeed true, as we shall argue, that Moroccan society is not composed of a series of fixed groupings whose members relate to one another on the basis of very narrowly defined roles such as "husband" and "wife," then it becomes necessary to consider the situational contexts of these relationships and the ways in which contractual ties and personal manipulations may modify relationships that would seem to be defined simply on the basis of status.

Morocco presents a good example of the interplay of social and legal factors associated with divorce in the contemporary Moslem world. As embodied in the Code of Personal Status adopted two years after national independence in 1956, the Moroccan laws of divorce reflect fewer significant changes from the traditional rules of the Malikite school of Islamic law than do the codes of, say, Algeria, Tunisia or even Egypt, which were heavily influenced by French and Swiss legal codes. The Moroccan husband's rights of divorce remain very considerable. Indeed, the first time a man repudiates his wife, the courts will not only uphold his right to do so, they will also sanction his power to call her back to his bed and board at any time during a three-month period. If the three months go by without a reconciliation—and any pregnancy on the woman's part will be attributed to the husband—the divorce will be declared final. If, however, the husband exercises the right to call his wife back, and then for some reason thinks better of the idea, he can repudiate her a second time. But if he changes his mind again, he must have the wife's consent in order to bring her back. Moreover, the husband will have to give her some gift as a sign of their reconciliation. If, finally, the husband repudiates his wife for a third time, the law will not permit them to take up residence together once again even if both parties desire it. Only after the expiration of the waiting period and the formation and dissolution of a marriage with another man would the woman be eligible to remarry her first husband.

A Bird in Hand

One Moroccan characterized the differences between these three forms of divorce as being similar to the situation of a man who holds a small bird in his hand. To repudiate a woman for the first time would be like releasing the bird with a string attached to one of its legs: provided the bird does not get three months distant the captor can reel it back whenever he chooses. In a second repudiation, however, the bird has been released completely unfettered and will only return to its master if properly enticed. And after a third repudiation the bird will fly away altogether to seek a new and more congenial source of sustenance.

In each of these cases, then, the legal powers of the husband are indeed absolute, but there are several other forms of divorce in which the initiative actually lies with the wife and the officials of the local court. If, for example, a woman can prove to the court that her husband has failed to fulfill one of the defining duties of the marital contract—if, say, he fails to support her or mistreats her excessively—she can petition the court for a judicial decree of separation. In another instance the woman may secure a divorce by getting her husband to agree to accept some form of remuneration for releasing her. Acceptance of such an arrangement by the husband carries with it an inherent and irrevocable repudiation. Clearly such an arrangement places a great deal of power—verging at times on extortion—in the hands of the husband, but the bride and her family may have hedged against such an eventuality when the marital contract itself was drawn up.

At the time a marital contract is agreed upon, representatives for the woman may have certain stipulations written into the document which are intended to strengthen the position of the woman and her family against the husband. Among the most common stipulations not directly concerned with property are, for example, the understanding that the woman need never move more than a specified distance away from her family of origin, or that her husband may never take an additional wife without first granting her a divorce. The woman's family may even stipulate that the marriage will actually be subject to termination at the pleasure of the wife herself. Court officials rationalize this apparent breach of the Koranic law (which grants the power of repudiation to the husband alone) by saying that the woman has actually contracted a situation similar to that in which she gains release from her husband through some form of remuneration. But here the "payment" is with the words the husband himself agreed to have placed in the contract rather than with a sum of money, custody of a child or some other form of consideration.

The most common stipulation found in marital contracts, however, refers to the payment of the brideprice. In Islamic law and custom every marriage requires as its fundamental defining act the payment to the bride or her marital guardian of a sum of money or goods whose value may vary from that of a simple token to any sum agreed upon by the representatives of the bride and groom. However, not all of the brideprice need actually be paid at the time the marriage itself is contracted. Rather, a portion of the brideprice may remain to be paid at the time of any subsequent divorce or at any time the woman herself chooses to demand it. Clearly this condition gives a woman considerable leverage in curbing her husband's right to summarily dismiss her. Any man who has contracted a marriage with this provision in it will think twice before arbitrarily exercising his right of divorce or indeed of provoking his wife in any way that might move her to demand the outstanding portion of her brideprice.

The extent to which a man may find himself obliged to acquiesce in the inclusion of such contractual provisions as these is, for the most part, a function of the relative power of each of the parties concerned, particularly economic power. If a man is attempting to marry up socially or economically, and if at the same time the bride's family suspects that the prospective husband may mistreat his wife or try to make life for her so miserable that she will pay any sum to secure her freedom, the family of the bride may leave part of the brideprice unpaid or require certain other rights for the bride. In some parts of the countryside whole communities customarily use the deferred brideprice clause as a means of insuring some degree of marital stability. There will often be considerable haggling over the terms of a marital contract and the sums involved. The outcome will vary according to such considerations as the intangible prestige value of one's descent, the present market in potential mates and the conflicting motives of various members of both families.

Sources of Power

There are several other factors associated with the laws of brideprice payments and divorce that may give women and their families considerable power to modify the husband's legal privileges. In recent years, there has been a substantial increase in brideprices paid in Morocco, particularly by members of the urban upper classes. Where ten years ago a well-to-do man may have paid several hundred dollars as a brideprice, a man of comparable circumstances today may have to spend as much as $1,000. People sometimes speak of this as brideprice competition, and there is little doubt that brideprice payments may be one way to establish social standing in a heterogeneous and highly mobile society lacking in any all-pervasive system of group stratification. But insofar as only the closest friends and relatives will know exactly what sums or conditions are involved, there is reason to suspect that the competition is, in point of fact, not for brideprices per se but for the dowries associated with each brideprice payment.

Upon receipt of a brideprice for his daughter or marital ward, a man will add a substantial sum of his own and use the combined amount to purchase a dowry for the bride. This dowry itself is called, quite significantly, "the furnishings of the household." It is these goods, whether actual furnishings, items of personal jewelry or raw wool, which will be considered the personal property of the woman and will leave the marriage with her in the event of divorce or widowhood. In addition to their security value these goods, rather than the brideprice itself, are made clearly visible to the entire community as well as to those who later visit the couple's home. Indeed, on the day a bride moves to her husband's home the goods comprising her dowry are paraded around the streets of the city to the accompaniment of oboists and drummers, chanting relatives and screaming children. Poorer families carry the goods in their hands and on their heads while wealthier people will lay out the entire dowry—down to the last fragile teacup— on the beds of several pickup trucks. It is for these goods, which represent both the status of the bride and a real source of her personal security, for which the competition directly expressed in brideprices is being carried on. The mother of the bride is usually the most insistent that her daughter's dowry should be as substantial as possible. She will nag her husband to increase the brideprice demanded, while he, seeking both respite from the nagging and a vehicle for emphasizing his own social standing, will increase the brideprice accordingly.

In addition to setting up an index of relative social status, it is also important to note that the law automatically assumes that all of the "household furnishings" except for the most personal possessions of the husband (such as his clothing and tools) are the sole property of the woman and may be taken away by her when she leaves. Since the woman's family generally doesn't allow the precise content of the dowry itself to be entered into the marriage contract, this legal fiction gives the wife a potentially powerful lever to use against her husband. Indeed, insofar as they can do so without creating an unbearable strain on the marriage itself, Moroccan women frequently try to pressure their husbands into buying them as many things as possible in order to insure themselves against a sudden divorce. Everyone is well aware that the more a man has to lose financially by divorce, the less likely he will be to exercise his legal powers arbitrarily. And if such a divorce means not only the loss of those goods bought during the marriage and any outstanding portion of the brideprice, but also means incurring a whole new set of social and financial debts associated with the collection of a new brideprice, a man will certainly hesitate before making use of his power of instant repudiation. The extent, then, to which a husband may be put at an economic disadvantage by a wife who is herself at a clear legal disadvantage will be a function of the relative power of the persons involved, particularly their respective financial positions.

In addition to the legal prerogatives and economic pressures affecting marital relations, there is a host of ways in which different social ties may be utilized by the parties involved. We have already seen how the bride's mother may cajole and conspire to elicit from her husband the largest dowry possible for her daughter, and how a husband may be reluctant to divorce his wife because of the degree of personal independence he may have to give up in seeking help with a new brideprice from his relatives and acquaintances. Similarly a wife who wants to get her husband to abandon his plan to divorce her may turn to commonly shared friends and relatives, neighbors or some individual "in whose presence her husband feels shame." For example, if a husband and wife are first paternal cousins, which is quite common in Moslem societies, the wife may utilize the position of her father as the husband's uncle rather than simply as his father-in-law to constrain the husband to act as a nephew properly should. Or by galvanizing the opinion of neighbors or threatening a public court action a woman may hope to induce her husband to give her more substantial support, abstain from occasional beatings or spend less of his time at a nearby café. Again the success of her endeavors will vary tremendously with the social, economic and legal positions of all those involved. What remains constant in this system, however, is neither the forms of behavior associated with certain relationships nor the groupings that are crystallized at any given moment to accomplish an ad hoc task but simply the ways in which persons can indeed relate to one another without overstepping "the bounds of permissible leeway" as they pursue their individually and pointedly defined goals.

Mohamed's Case

As an example of the subtle interplay of social, legal and economic factors associated with divorce in Morocco, take the case of a young friend of mine who was experiencing some difficulty with his wife. Mohamed was a clerk in the local administrator's office who had married a girl from his home town of Fez and settled down to live with her in his father's house. Almost from the start, however, his wife and mother began fighting with one another as each tried to maintain the greater degree of influence over Mohamed's actions. The situation created great strains among the members of Mohamed's own family and between all of them and his wife's kinsmen. Mohamed finally decided to move away altogether in the hope that setting up house for himself in a nearby town would solve the basic problem. But his wife continued to nag him and demand his complete attentiveness to her every wish. Mohamed tried go-betweens from his wife's family and from neighbors, but in each case his wife's agreement to behave herself was quickly followed by a renewal of her bossy and nagging attitude. Mohamed was hesitant to divorce her since he would then have to pay a very substantial sum remaining from the brideprice and begin all over again to collect money for a new wife of the standing he deemed appropriate for a man of his background and position. He thought that having children might make her more tractable but was equally afraid that if this did not settle the problem and he still had to divorce her he would then have the additional burden of long-term child support. Quite literally, he said, he could neither live with his wife nor without her. He finally decided that since it was an independent identity of her own and an ability to have a say in her own future that was at the root of his wife's problem the only workable solution was to allow her to finish enough of her education so that she could find some work outside of their home. Although he had the power and even the desire to repudiate his wife forthwith, Mohamed recognized that he was effectively constrained from doing so by the social and financial implications of such an act.

Nonlegal Powers

In more general terms, then, Mohamed's marital difficulties point up several important aspects of the law and practice of divorce in Morocco. Unlike many other societies in the world, in which an individual's actions are almost wholly determined by the ways he is expected to behave towards his various kinds of relatives, in Morocco a person is usually free to manipulate these relationships in a wide variety of ways. One can play on the different interests of family members, the control one has over the family's property, the aid one can expect from having done favors for non-kinsmen, and indeed the implications of the existing laws to establish a position of relative power vis-à-vis the other people in one's family. Because so many different interests can be brought to bear in the arrangement or dissolution of a marriage, even the strong legal position of a husband may be undercut by the economic and social forces available to his wife and her family.

During the course of a marriage a woman and her family will, therefore, try to balance their social and legal obligations with the demands that can be made on a husband in the hope of giving the wife the greatest degree of security possible under the circumstances. And the husband and his family, in turn, will seek to use their properties and relationships to maintain the husband's ability to exercise his legal powers without incurring a significant loss of money or personal independence. When divorce does occur, then, it is less because of a division of loyalties between one's family and one's spouse than because of the numerous tensions that develop from this constant personal struggle for economic, social or legal superiority.

The Moroccan government is itself aware of the fact that these tensions are at the root of the country's high divorce rate and it has tried to take certain legal steps to ease the situation. The law does, therefore, recognize the woman's right to demand that her husband find living quarters for the couple outside his parent's home and in an area sufficiently well populated with respectable people to enable the woman to call upon the necessary witnesses to substantiate any case she might bring alleging misconduct on the part of her husband. With full recognition that husbands may act without due consideration, in moments of great stress, the law also denies the husband the right to divorce his wife three times all at once. And, recognizing that fear of financial loss is the greatest dissuader of hasty action, the law also requires the husband make a "conciliatory payment" of unspecified amount to his wife upon divorcing her. But insofar as local courts generally fix this sum at roughly one-third of the registered brideprice with a ceiling of less than $100, it is clear that this relatively insignificant sum has not greatly affected divorce rates, though it may have increased the frequency with which a husband and wife use this payment in maneuvering for positions of greater strength in a marital dispute.

Consideration of the laws of divorce alone, then, give only a partial and truncated view of the nature of divorce as it is actually practiced in an Islamic state like Morocco. A woman's legal rights, though limited, can be supplemented with significant economic and social powers. This is so because of the maleability of various relationships each of which contains wide behavioral alternatives that can be developed into divers patterns.

But to say this means that we will have to reconsider certain features of contemporary sociological theory. For it would appear that one's inherent positions in this society do not define the whole person or the whole range of one's possible associations. Rather, one constantly uses both the ideal forms of behavior associated with any inherent position and the wide range of ambiguous behavior permitted within such role relations to establish ties centered on the individual and capable of being developed into a host of distinctive and often ephemeral associations. One cannot, as some present-day students of nonwestern legal processes do, argue with Sir Henry Maine that in such societies "all the relations of Persons are summed up in the relations of Family." The norm of behavior is not so rigidly fixed nor the sanctions on that behavior so narrowly confined that one cannot arrange certain ties with more distant kinsmen or outsiders in such a way as to place one in closer alliance with these persons than with the members of one's own immediate family. And one can also utilize these same contractual ties and manipulated alliances of kinsmen and others to strenghten one's own position in situations where one's legal rights may actually be rather limited.

Although the legal rights of women in many Islamic countries have been substantially increased in recent years, a true picture of the actual relations between husbands and wives—as well as an appreciation of the repercussions any changes in the law might have—requires a careful consideration of the social and economic means through which these legal powers are sustained, amended, or significantly undermined. The Moroccan case thus reflects not only the law and practice of divorce in one modern Islamic state but the dynamic interplay of family law and social structure characteristic of a number of the developing nations.

June 1970

Sororities and the Husband Game

Can they still guarantee catching the "right kind" of man?

JOHN FINLEY SCOTT

Marriages, like births, deaths, or initiations at puberty, are re-arrangements of structure that are constantly recurring in any society; they are moments of the continuing social process regulated by custom; there are institutionalized ways of dealing with such events.

A. R. Radcliffe-Brown
African Systems of Kinship and Marriage

In many simple societies, the "institutionalized ways" of controlling marriage run to diverse schemes and devices. Often they include special living quarters designed to make it easy for marriageable girls to attract a husband: the Bontok people of the Philippines keep their girls in a special house, called the *olag,* where lovers call, sex play is free, and marriage is supposed to result. The Ekoi of Nigeria, who like their women fat, send them away to be specially fattened for marriage. Other peoples, such as the Yao of central Africa and the aborigines of the Canary Islands, send their daughters away to "convents" where old women teach them the special skills and mysteries that a young wife needs to know.

Accounts of such practices have long been a standard topic of anthropology lectures in universities, for their exotic appeal keeps the students, large numbers of whom are sorority girls, interested and alert. The control of marriage in simple societies strikes these girls as quite different from the freedom that they believe prevails in America. This is ironic, for the American college sorority is a pretty good counterpart in complex societies of the fatting houses and convents of the primitives.

Whatever system they use, parents in all societies have more in mind than just getting their daughters married; they want them married to the *right* man. The criteria for defining the right man vary tremendously, but virtually all parents view some potential mates with approval, some with disapproval, and some with downright horror. Many ethnic groups, including many in America, are *endogamous,* that is, they desire marriage of their young only to those within the group. In *shtetl* society, the Jewish villages of eastern Europe, marriages were arranged by a *shatchen,* a matchmaker, who paired off the girls and boys with due regard to the status, family connections, wealth, and personal attractions of the participants. But this society was strictly endogamous—only marriage within the group was allowed. Another rule of endogamy relates to social rank or class, for most parents are anxious that their children marry at least at the same level as themselves. Often they hope the children, and especially the daughters, will marry at a higher level. Parents of the *shtetl,* for example, valued *hypergamy* —the marriage of daughters to a man of higher status— and a father who could afford it would offer substantial sums to acquire a scholarly husband (the most highly prized kind) for his daughter.

The marriage problem, from the point of view of parents and of various ethnic groups and social classes, is always one of making sure that girls are available for marriage with the right man while at the same time guarding against marriage with the wrong man.

The University Convent

The American middle class has a particular place where it sends its daughters so they will be easily accessible to the boys—the college campus. Even for the families who worry about the bad habits a nice girl can pick up at college, it has become so much a symbol of middle-class status that the risk must be taken, the girl must be sent. American middle-class society has created an institution on the campus that, like the fatting house, makes the girls more attractive; like the Canary Island convent, teaches skills that middle-class wives need to know; like the *shtetl,* provides matchmakers; and without going so far as to buy husbands of high rank, manages to dissuade the girls from making alliances with lower-class boys. That institution is the college sorority.

A sorority is a private association which provides separate dormitory facilities with a distinctive Greek letter name for selected female college students. Membership is by invitation only, and requires recommendation by former members. Sororities are not simply the feminine counterpart of the college fraternity. They differ from fraternities because marriage is a more important determinant of social position for women than for men in American society, and because standards of conduct associated with marriage correspondingly bear stronger sanctions for women than for men. Sororities have much more "alumnae" involvement than fraternities, and fraternities adapt to local conditions and different living arrangements better than sororities. The college-age sorority "actives" decide only the minor details involved in recruitment, membership, and ac-

"The sorority is not the servant of youthful interests; on the contrary, it is an organized agency for controlling those interests. College-age 'actives' decide only the minor details; parent-age alumnae control the important choices."

tivities; parent-age alumnae control the important choices. The prototypical sorority is not the servant of youthful interests; on the contrary, it is an organized agency for controlling those interests. Through the sorority, the elders of family, class, ethnic, and religious communities can continue to exert remote control over the marital arrangements of their young girls.

The need for remote control arises from the nature of the educational system in an industrial society. In simple societies, where children are taught the culture at home, the family controls the socialization of children almost completely. In more complex societies, education becomes the province of special agents and competes with the family. The conflict between the family and outside agencies increases as children move through the educational system and is sharpest when the children reach college age. College curricula are even more challenging to family value systems than high school courses, and children frequently go away to college, out of reach of direct family influence. Sometimes a family can find a college that does not challenge family values in any way: devout Catholic parents can send their daughters to Catholic colleges; parents who want to be sure that daughter meets only "Ivy League" men can send her to one of the "Seven Sisters"—the women's equivalent of the Ivy League, made up of Radcliffe, Barnard, Smith, Vassar, Wellesley, Mt. Holyoke, and Bryn Mawr—if she can get in.

The solution of controlled admissions is applicable only to a small proportion of college-age girls, however. There are nowhere near the number of separate, sectarian colleges in the country that would be needed to segregate all the college-age girls safely, each with her own kind. Private colleges catering mostly to a specific class can still preserve a girl from meeting her social or economic inferiors, but the fees at such places are steep. It costs more to maintain a girl in the Vassar dormitories than to pay her sorority bills at a land-grant school. And even if her family is willing to pay the fees, the academic pace at the elite schools is much too fast for most girls. Most college girls attend large, tax-supported universities where the tuition is relatively low and where admissions policies let in students from many strata and diverse ethnic backgrounds. It is on the campuses of the free, open, and competitive state universities of the country that the sorority system flourishes.

When a family lets its daughter loose on a large campus with a heterogenous population, there are opportunities to be met and dangers to guard against. The great opportunity is to meet a good man to marry, at the age when the girls are most attractive and the men most amenable. For the girls, the pressure of time is urgent; though they are often told otherwise, their attractions are in fact primarily physical, and they fade with time. One need only compare the relative handicaps in the marital sweepstakes of a 38-year old single male lawyer and a single, female teacher of the same age to realize the urgency of the quest.

The great danger of the public campus is that young girls, however properly reared, are likely to fall in love, and—in our middle-class society at least—love leads to marriage. Love is a potentially random factor, with no regard for class boundaries. There seems to be no good way of preventing young girls from falling in love. The only practical way to control love is to control the type of men the girl is likely to encounter; she cannot fall dangerously in love with a man she has never met. Since kinship groups are unable to keep "undesirable" boys off the public campus entirely, they have to settle for control of counter-institutions within the university. An effective counter-institution will protect a girl from the corroding influences of the university environment.

There are roughly three basic functions which a sorority can perform in the interest of kinship groups:
- It can ward off the wrong kind of men.
- It can facilitate moving-up for middle-status girls.
- It can solve the "Brahmin problem"—the difficulty of proper marriage that afflicts high-status girls.

Kinship groups define the "wrong kind of man" in a variety of ways. Those who use an ethnic definition support sororities that draw an ethnic membership line; the best examples are the Jewish sororities, because among all the ethnic groups with endogamous standards (in America at any rate), only the Jews so far have sent large numbers of daughters away to college. But endogamy along class lines is even more pervasive. It is the most basic mission of the sorority to prevent a girl from marrying out of her group (exogamy) or beneath her class (hypogamy). As one of the founders of a national sorority artlessly put it in an essay titled "The Mission of the Sorority":

> There is a danger, and a very grave danger, that four years' residence in a dormitory will tend to destroy right ideals of home life and substitute in their stead a belief in the freedom that comes from community living . . . culture, broad, liberalizing, humanizing culture, we cannot get too much of, unless while acquiring it we are weaned from home and friends, from ties of blood and kindred.

A sorority discourages this dangerous weaning process by introducing the sisters only to selected boys; each sorority, for example, has dating relations with one or more fraternities, matched rather nicely to the sorority on the basis of ethnicity and/or class. (A particular sorority, for example, will have dating arrangements not with all the fraternities on campus, but only with those whose brothers are a class-match for their sisters.) The sorority's frantically busy schedule of parties, teas, meetings, skits, and exchanges keeps the sisters so occupied that they have neither time nor opportunity to meet men outside the channels the sorority provides.

Marrying Up

The second sorority function, that of facilitating hypergamy, is probably even more of an attraction to parents than the simpler preservation of endogamy. American society is not so much oriented to the preservation of the *status quo* as to the pursuit of upward mobility.

In industrial societies, children are taught that if they study hard they can get the kind of job that entitles them to a place in the higher ranks. This incentive actually is appropriate only for boys, but the emphasis on using the most efficient available means to enter the higher levels will not be lost on the girls. And the most efficient means for a girl—marriage—is particularly attractive because it requires so much less effort than the mobility through hard work that is open to boys. To the extent that we do socialize the sexes in different ways, we are more likely to train daughters in the ways of attracting men than to motivate them to do hard, competitive work. The difference in motivation holds even if the girls have the intelligence and talent required for status climbing on their own. For lower-class girls on the make, membership in a sorority can greatly improve the chances of meeting (and subsequently marrying) higher-status boys.

Now we come to the third function of the sorority—solving the Brahmin problem. The fact that hypergamy is encouraged in our society creates difficulties for girls whose parents are already in the upper strata. In a hypergamous system, high status *men* have a strong advantage; they can offer their status to a prospective bride as part of the marriage bargain, and the advantages of high status are often sufficient to offset many personal drawbacks. But a *woman's* high status has very little exchange value because she does not confer it on her husband.

This difficulty of high status women in a hypergamous society we may call the Brahmin problem. Girls of Brahmin caste in India and Southern white women of good family have the problem in common. In order to avoid the horrors of hypogamy, high status women must compete for high status men against women from all classes. Furthermore, high status women are handicapped in their battle by a certain type of vanity engendered by their class. They expect their wooers to court them in the style to which their fathers have accustomed them; this usually involves more formal dating, gift-giving, escorting, taxiing, etc., than many college swains can afford. If upper-stratum men are allowed to find out that the favors of lower class women are available for a much smaller investment of time, money, and emotion, they may well refuse to court upper-status girls.

In theory, there are all kinds of ways for upper-stratum families to deal with surplus daughters. They can strangle them at birth (female infanticide); they can marry several to each available male (polygyny); they can offer money to any suitable male willing to take one off their hands (dowries, groom-service fees). All these solutions have in fact been used in one society or another, but for various reasons none is acceptable in our society. Spinsterhood still works, but marriage is so popular and so well rewarded that everybody hopes to avoid staying single.

The industrial solution to the Brahmin problem is to corner the market, or more specifically to shunt the eligible bachelors into a special marriage market where the upper stratum women are in complete control of the bride-supply. The best place to set up this protected marriage-market is where many suitable men can be found at the age when they are most willing to marry—in short, the college campus. The kind of male collegians who can be shunted more readily into the specialized marriage-market that sororities run, are those who are somewhat uncertain of their own status and who aspire to move into higher strata. These boys are anxious to bolster a shaky self-image by dating obviously high-class sorority girls. The fraternities are full of them.

How does a sorority go about fulfilling its three functions? The first item of business is making sure that the girls join. This is not as simple as it seems, because the values that sororities maintain are more important to the older generation than to college-age girls. Although the sorority image is one of membership denied to the "wrong kind" of girls, it is also true that sororities have quite a problem of recruiting the "right kind." Some are pressured into pledging by their parents. Many are recruited straight out of high school, before they know much about what really goes on at college. High school recruiters present sorority life to potential rushees as one of unending gaiety; life outside the sorority is painted as bleak and dateless.

A membership composed of the "right kind" of girls is produced by the requirement that each pledge must have the recommendation of, in most cases, two or more alumnae of the sorority. Membership is often passed on from mother to daughter—this is the "legacy," whom sorority actives have to invite whether they like her or not. The sort of headstrong, innovative, or "sassy" girl who is likely to organize a campaign inside the sorority against prevailing standards is unlikely to receive alumnae recommendations. This is why sorority girls are so complacent about alumnae dominance, and why professors find them so bland and uninteresting as students. Alumnae dominance extends beyond recruitment, into the daily life of the house. Rules, regulations, and policy explanations come to the house from the national association. National headquarters is given to explaining unpopular policy by any available strategem; a favorite device (not limited to the sorority) is to interpret all non-conformity as sexual, so that the girl who rebels against wearing girdle, high heels, and stockings to dinner two or three times a week stands implicitly accused of promiscuity. This sort of argument, based on the shrewdness of many generations, shames into conformity many a girl who otherwise might rebel against the code imposed by her elders. The actives in positions of control (house manager, pledge trainer or captain) are themselves closely supervised by alumnae. Once the right girls are initiated, the organization has mechanisms that make it very difficult for a girl to withdraw. Withdrawal can mean difficulty in finding alternative living quarters, loss of prepaid room and board fees, and stigmatization.

Sororities keep their members, and particularly their flighty pledges, in line primarily by filling up all their time with house activities. Pledges are required to study at the house, and they build the big papier-mache floats (in collaboration with selected fraternity boys) that are a traditional display of "Greek Row" for the homecoming game.

Time is encompassed completely; activities are planned long in advance, and there is almost no energy or time available for meeting inappropriate men.

The girls are taught—if they do not already know—the behavior appropriate to the upper strata. They learn how to dress with expensive restraint, how to make appropriate conversation, how to drink like a lady. There is some variety here among sororities of different rank; members of sororities at the bottom of the social ladder prove their gentility by rigid conformity in dress and manner to the stereotype of the sorority girl, while members of top houses feel socially secure even when casually dressed. If you are born rich you can afford to wear Levi's and sweatshirts.

Preliminary Events

The sorority facilitates dating mainly by exchanging parties, picnics, and other frolics with the fraternities in its set. But to augment this the "fixer-uppers" (the American counterpart of the *shatchen*) arrange dates with selected boys; their efforts raise the sorority dating rate above the independent level by removing most of the inconvenience and anxiety from the contracting of dates.

Dating, in itself, is not sufficient to accomplish the

GLOSSARY OF MARRIAGE TERMS

Endogamy: A rule or practice of marriage within a particular group.

Exogamy: A practice or rule of marriage only between persons who are *not* members of a well-defined group, such as one based on family or locality.

Hypergamy: The movement of a woman, through marriage, to status *higher* than that to which she was born.

Hypogamy: The movement of a woman, through marriage, to a status *lower* than that to which she was born.

Polygyny: The marriage of one husband to two or more wives. It is not the same as *polygamy,* which simply means a plurality of mates irrespective of sex.

---

sorority's purposes. Dating must lead to pinning, pinning to engagement, engagement to marriage. In sorority culture, all dating is viewed as a movement toward marriage. Casual, spontaneous dating is frowned upon; formal courtship is still encouraged. Sorority ritual reinforces the progression from dating to marriage. At the vital point in the process, where dating must be turned into engagement, the sorority shores up the structure by the pinning ritual, performed after dinner in the presence of all the sorority sisters (who are required to stay for the ceremony) and attended, in its classic form, by a choir of fraternity boys singing outside. The commitment is so public that it is difficult for either partner to withdraw. Since engagement is already heavily reinforced outside the sorority, pinning ceremonies are more elaborate than engagements.

The social columns of college newspapers faithfully record the successes of the sorority system as it stands today. Sorority girls get engaged faster than "independents," and they appear to be marrying more highly ranked men. But what predictions can we make about the system's future?

All social institutions change from time to time, in response to changing conditions. In the mountain villages of the Philippines, the steady attacks of school and mission on the immorality of the *olag* have almost demolished it. Sororities, too, are affected by changes in the surrounding environment. Originally they were places where the few female college students took refuge from the jeers and catcalls of men who thought that nice girls didn't belong on campus. They assumed their present, endogamy-conserving form with the flourishing of the great land-grant universities in the first half of this century.

On the Break

The question about the future of the sorority system is whether it can adapt to the most recent changes in the forms of higher education. At present, neither fraternities nor sororities are in the pink of health. On some campuses there are chapter houses which have been reduced to taking in non-affiliated boarders to pay the costs of running the property. New sorority chapters are formed, for the most part, on new or low-prestige campuses (where status-anxiety is rife); at schools of high prestige fewer girls rush each year and the weaker houses are disbanding.

University administrations are no longer as hospitable to the Greeks as they once were. Most are building extensive dormitories that compete effectively with the housing offered by sororities; many have adopted regulations intended to minimize the influence of the Greeks on campus activities. The campus environment is changing rapidly: academic standards are rising, admission is increasingly competitive and both male and female students are more interested in academic achievement; the proportion of graduate students seriously training for a profession is increasing; campus culture is often so obviously pluralist that the Greek claim to monopolize social activity is unconvincing.

The sorority as it currently stands is ill-adapted to cope with the new surroundings. Sorority houses were built to provide a setting for lawn parties, dances, and dress-up occasions, and not to facilitate study; crowding and noise are severe, and most forms of privacy do not exist. The sorority songs that have to be gone through at rushing and chapter meetings today all seem to have been written in 1915 and are mortifying to sing today. The arcane rituals, so fascinating to high school girls, grow tedious and sophomoric to college seniors.

But the worst blow of all to the sorority system comes from the effect of increased academic pressure on the dating habits of college men. A student competing for grades in a professional school, or even in a difficult undergraduate major, simply has not the time (as he might have had in, say, 1925) to get involved in the sorority forms of courtship. Since these days almost all the "right kind" of men *are* involved in demanding training, the traditions of the sorority are becoming actually inimical to hypergamous marriage. Increasingly, then, sororities do not solve the Brahmin problem but make it worse.

One can imagine a sorority designed to facilitate marriage to men who have no time for elaborate courtship. In such a sorority, the girls—to start with small matters—would improve their telephone arrangements, for the fraternity boy in quest of a date today must call several times to get through the busy signals, interminable paging, and lost messages to the girl he wants. They might arrange a private line with prompt answering and faithfully recorded messages, with an unlisted number given only to busy male students with a promising future. They would even accept dates for the same night as the invitation, rather than, as at present, necessarily five to ten days in advance, for the only thing a first-year law student can schedule that far ahead nowadays is his studies. Emphasis on fraternity boys would have to go, for living in a fraternity and pursuing a promising (and therefore competitive) major field of study are rapidly becoming mutually exclusive. The big formal dances would go (the fraternity boys dislike them now); the football floats would go; the pushcart races would go. The girls would reach the hearts of their men not through helping them wash their sports cars but through typing their term papers.

But it is inconceivable that the proud traditions of the sororities that compose the National Panhellenic Council could ever be bent to fit the new design. Their structure is too fixed to fit the changing college and their function is rapidly being lost. The sorority cannot sustain itself on students alone. When parents learn that membership does not benefit their daughters, the sorority as we know it will pass into history.

September 1965

SUGGESTED READINGS

The Family, A Dynamic Interpretation by Willard Waller, revised by Reuben Hill (New York: Dryden Press, 1951) has a good section on the courtship process.

Mate-selection; a Study of Complementary Needs by Robert Winch (New York: Harper, 1958) tests the hypothesis that the selection of marriage partners is based on complementary personal and emotional needs.

Family: Organization and Interaction by Bernard Farber (San Francisco, Calif.: Chandler Publishing Co., 1964).

Sourcebook in Marriage and the Family by Marvin R. Sussman (New York: Houghton Mifflin, 1968) is an interesting collection of readings with a broad scope.

A Better Life: Notes from Puerto Rico

This family wants to move up. What makes it different?

LLOYD H. ROGLER

All of the husbands and wives interviewed during a recent study of families in the *caseríos*—large housing projects in Puerto Rico—dreamed of buying a small house in the suburbs. They often described that dream house. But only one family had ever actually done anything about that dream—the Vilás.

Luis and Rosa Vilá have made a down payment on a house located in a mushrooming middle-class development on the outskirts of San Juan. Physically, the house is not a notable improvement over their present apartment, which is centrally located, has three bedrooms, living-dining room, kitchen, porches at front and back, and adequate closets. It is freshly painted and Mrs. Vilá keeps it immaculate.

By their own admission, the Vilás have never before lived in such physical comfort and the monthly rental is only $17.00. But nevertheless they are not happy. According to Mrs. Vilá:

> The neighbors are low-class, bad people. . . . They drink too much. . . . The neighbors upstairs throw scrub water and garbage out the window. . . . The husbands and wives insult each other. Some married women are having affairs with other men. I have a neighbor who is always kissing her boy friend in public. . . . They gossip a lot. . . . They have stolen some plants which I put outside to grow. . . . One of my neighbors belonged to the can-can gang (a group of notorious shoplifters).

Most of all, the Vilás do not believe it is a good neighborhood in which to raise children. "Hoodlums" frequently accost their daughters and "tell them nice things with bad intent." The Vilás do not mingle with their neighbors or allow their daughters to play outside. They yearn to assume a respectable position among persons and families who count socially.

The Vilás are no better off than the other families we studied. Luis Vilá, a self-employed, semiskilled upholsterer, earns $160 per month.

Clearly, Luis' family does not enjoy an advantage in income. If income does not propel them toward the middle class, what does?

Rosa Vilá is 36 years old, with a sixth grade education. She was born and raised on a farm, in a wooden shack with a corrugated zinc roof and an outdoor latrine and shower. Her father was a sharecropper, raising tobacco and several tropical fruits and vegetables. He went through the fourth grade, was barely able to read, and could not write. Her mother was illiterate. When Rosa was 14 years old, the parents came to San Juan with their ten children. Shortly afterward, her father abandoned them, lived with a mistress, and then returned to the farm.

Rosa's mother became a seamstress doing piecework at home, and Rosa left school to help sew blouses. The human misery which they experienced is deeply etched in Rosa's memory. She recalls how her mother lost control, became very nervous, had to be taken to the psychiatric hospital, and died without regaining her mental health. "After this," Rosa says, "I decided to marry a hard-working and reliable man, even though he might be poor. I wanted a man who would take care of me—who would provide for my family."

Rosa Vilá came to San Juan; but San Juan reached out to Luis Vilá. The farm on which he was born and raised was swallowed up by the city. Streets, homes, apartment houses and a church now cover it.

As a boy he had worked with his father and helped supplement the family income with bootlegging. Both parents were illiterate. Luis completed the eighth grade. Now he regrets not having gone through high school. "My only serious complaint against my father is that he did not let me remain in school after the eighth grade. We had too much work on the farm." Otherwise he admired his father extravagantly. Emotionally he still feels closer to him than to any member of his parental family. He remembers him as a man of impeccable morality, of service to his community, clean and orderly, and not mercenary. He sees these attributes also in himself. "Most of all, my father was a very hard worker and a responsible man. I am that way too."

After he left the farm he labored on a truck which carried heavy supplies to construction sites. He clerked in a warehouse, greased cars, and was helper to an auto mechanic. Four years ago he got a job installing seat covers in cars, and capitalized on this to learn the rudimentary skills he now employs in his own business.

Because his father's earnings from agriculture were supplemented by the bootlegging and the family was able to live moderately well, Luis believes his parents belonged to the middle class. Although by most social and economic standards he himself would be considered lower class, he sees himself as middle class. The move from caserío to private home will, to him, confirm that vision.

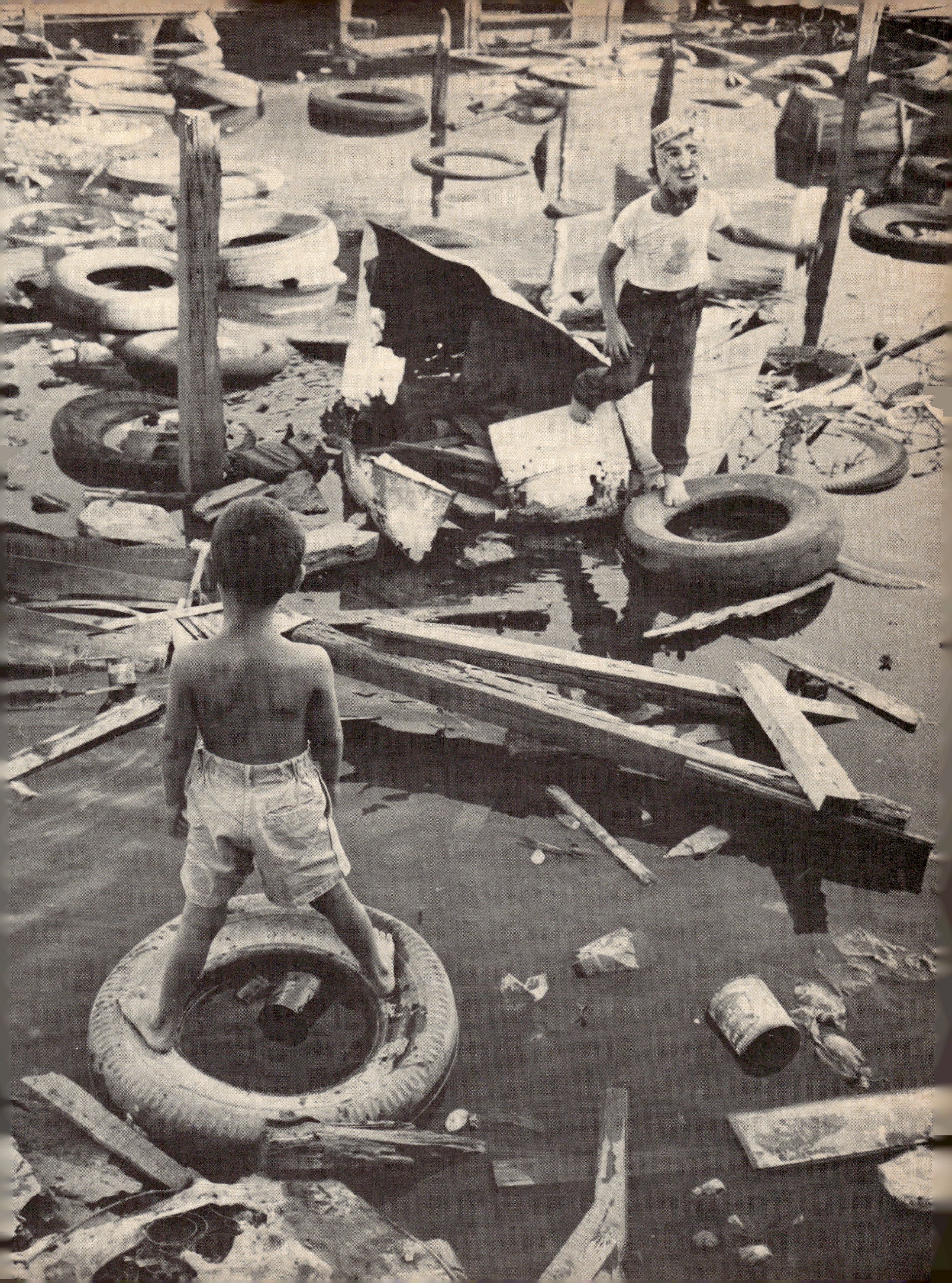

The move will also represent a triumph for Rosa and the children—a 17-year-old boy and two daughters, 14 and 12. During the first years of marriage Luis was not as committed to their welfare as he is now. Although even then a hard worker, he was a casual husband and father, typical of the other husbands in our study. He was a thorough *macho*—the traditional he-man of Puerto Rican society. The husband who is a macho follows the dictum that "the woman belongs in the home, the man in the street." In the street the man proves his masculinity by sexual accomplishments; he continually describes them with great emphasis on his vigor and potency. A macho is physically strong and courageous; he does not retreat from a fight, display cowardice, or fear pain; if he is married, he does not allow his wife to govern him. In the early years of marriage, evening always found Luis in the local *cafetines*. Much of his income was spent on drinking and "women of the happy life." By Rosa's account, he had affairs with about 50 women: "Even when I was pregnant he was chasing women."

After several years of marriage, Rosa returned from a visit to her relatives to be told by a neighbor that Luis had a girl friend. She was upset and angry but did not discuss it with him. She began to have violent attacks which frightened him. He reports that during an attack, "she hurls herself on the floor and is almost unconscious for half-an-hour. She gestures wildly and her mouth is out of shape." One of our staff psychiatrists diagnoses Rosa's attacks as hysterical hyperkinetic seizures. To the Vilás, however, the attacks have supernatural meaning. During them Rosa has revelations from the world of spirits. Luis believes it was the spirits who informed Rosa of his extramarital affair:

My wife is a spiritualistic medium. She has revealed secrets that only I knew. At that time she told me that the spirits told her that I had a girl friend. She told me where and when I had been meeting the girl. She even told me what the girl looked like and the color of her skin. I believe that spirits can communicate through persons who have mental faculties.

Not only were Rosa's spirits potent enough to detect Luis's infidelities, but even his much-admired father has spoken to him through Rosa's mouth:

My father speaks through my wife to give me advice. He tells me to be kind to the children and not to lose my temper with them. He tells me to advise them, not to spank them. He tells me that I have a complete family, a good family, and a very good wife. He tells me that I ought not to make my wife suffer, to think things over.

As a result, nine years ago Luis quit being a macho and has been a model husband ever since.

Typically the lower-class Puerto Rican husband maintains close control over his earnings. The husbands spend freely without rendering an account, and the wives, ruled by the norm that they must accept things as they are, seldom question what they get for household expenses. But the Vilás decide together what is to be purchased, from groceries and furniture to the new house. The expenditures serve to benefit the family as a whole.

Typically also, lower-class Puerto Rican parents seldom discuss sex with their children, fearing disrespect and promiscuous behavior. But the Vilás have agreed that their daughters should get sex instruction from Rosa. Rosa tells them the details of sexual intercourse, but reminds them of the importance of chastity before marriage. Luis and Rosa also differ from other couples in their beliefs about child rearing. They seldom use physical punishment, preferring to reprimand, discuss the nature of the wrong, and in the extreme case, confine to a bedroom. Recently however, Luis lost his temper and slapped their son for dating a girl with a bad reputation. Rosa shared Luis' concern that their son might be forced to marry the girl. She did not openly dispute Luis's use of physical punishment, but afterward she talked to him in private, suggesting that the boy should be handled *a la buena* (with gentle persuasion). Luis agrees that this method is more effective.

After the third child was born, Rosa had herself sterilized because, "We did not want to have any more children. . . . We want to give our children the best. I knew that if we would have any more children we would not be able to give them the education they should have because we do not have much money." Both parents would like to have the children finish high school and attend college although they know that their eldest child, the son, is not interested in school and that their youngest daughter is not very intelligent. However, they have high hopes that the elder daughter will receive two years of college education. Despite the reservations the Vilás have about their oldest and youngest children, they spend many hours with all three, helping with homework. The strong involvement of the Vilás in the details of their children's education is most unusual. When other parents were questioned, most announced lofty educational aspirations for their offspring, but few are familiar with their children's educational experiences. Recently, Luis joined the Parent-Teachers Association in which few slum or caserío parents participate.

Luis Vilá brought to his marriage habits of hard work, a conviction that he belongs in the middle class, and a willingness to acquire higher skills. His mental health, drive and vigor have enabled him to capitalize on his relatively limited resources. Rosa's desire for a stable family and a reliable and hard-working husband is so intense that she is not only willing to sacrifice, scheme and fight for them, but a strong threat to them could throw her into attacks.

The Vilás started with a few advantages, not the least being the example and influence of Luis' much revered father. At present Luis has no particular advantage in education, occupation or earnings over his neighbors; but the values, activities and family relations of the Vilás separate them from the other families in ways that compel them to rise.

Their way has not been easy. Probably their greatest victory and lift upward occurred when Luis quit being the self-indulgent, Latin macho "he-man" to become the sober, faithful provider Rosa dreamed about. And this might very well have not been possible without a little timely help from the supernatural.

March-April 1965

SUGGESTED READINGS

The Newcomers by Oscar Handlin (Cambridge, Mass.: Harvard University Press, 1959). The adjustments of blacks and Puerto Ricans to life in New York City.

The Children of Sanchez by Oscar Lewis (New York: Random House, 1961). An autobiographical account of a poverty stricken Mexican family, the Sanchez children, through extensive interviews, reveals the story of their lives.

The Puerto Ricans by Christopher Rand (New York: Oxford University Press, 1958). A sympathetic study of Puerto Rican immigrants in their homes and at their jobs.

The Puerto Rican Journey by C. Wright Mills, Clarence Senior and Rose K. Goldsen (New York: Harper, 1950). This report covers the reasons for the Puerto Ricans' migration to New York City. It focuses on economic and social conditions in New York and in Puerto Rico.

Spanish Harlem by Patricia C. Sexton (New York: Harper and Row, 1965).

Blue-Collar Marriage by Mirra Komarovsky (New York: Random House, 1964). An analysis of the working class family.

Family and Kinship in East London by Michael Young and Peter Willmott (Glencoe, Ill.: Free Press, 1957).

Studies in Marriage and the Family by Robert R. Bell (New York: Thomas Y. Crowell, 1968) is a small but interesting collection. It covers a wide range and has useful bibliography.

The Family edited by Norman Bell and Ezra Vogel (Glencoe, Ill.: Free Press, 1960) is a good reader in the field.

Social Structure by George P. Murdock (New York: Macmillan, 1949) gives a comparative picture of the family institution.

"Intermarriage and the Social Structure" by R. K. Merton, *Psychiatry* (Vol. 4, 1941).

"Strain and Harmony in American-Japanese War bride Marriages" by Anselm L. Strauss, *Marriage and Family Living* (Vol. 16, May 1954).

"The Sociology of Parent-Youth Conflict" by Kingsley Davis, *American Sociological Review* (Vol. 15, 1941).

Mate-Selection: A Study of Complimentary Needs by Robert F. Winch (New York: Harper, 1958) advances the theory that marriage partners are selected on the basis of ability to meet the others needs.

Premarital Sex in a Changing Society by Robert Bell (Englewood Cliffs, New Jersey: Prentice Hall, 1966).

Sanity, Madness and the Family by R. D. Laing (New York: Pelican, 1970). Laing is a psychologist primarily interested in meaning, sanity and insanity.

Husbands and Wives: The Dynamics of Married Living by Robert O. Blood and Donald M. Wolfe (Glencoe, Ill.: Free Press, 1960) is a useful basic text.

Negro Family in the United States by E. Franklin Frazier (Chicago, Ill.: University of Chicago Press, 1939).

The Future of the Islamic Religion

GUENTER LEWY

The history of Islam begins in Arabia with Mohammed's move from Mecca to Medina in the year 622 of the Christian era. Within less than a century the Arabs had swept through North Africa into Spain and France and had reached the banks of the Indus River. A great new civilization had been born.

Today there are about 350,000,000 Muslims in the world—embracing one-seventh of the earth's population. Modern Islam presents a wide spectrum of religious and political ideology, ranging from the ultra-orthodox to the modernistic-secularistic. It is a not-to-be-ignored factor in the politics of the Near East and North Africa, as well as in Pakistan and Indonesia. In these pages I want to discuss the Muslim religion as a political force in the history of the Islamic states, and to venture some comments about the future of Islam in the modern world.

There are two important themes in the history of the Islamic states. The major theme is submission to political authority. The minor theme is rebellion against an unjust ruler. Both themes spring directly from the teachings of the Muslim religion.

When Mohammed organized his followers into a permanent community, it existed in order to perpetuate the new religion. This first community was a theocracy, at once religious and political. God and His revealed law were the supreme authority; Mohammed, His apostle, was the Lord's viceregent on earth.

When the prophet died in A.D. 632, the community elected Abu-Bekr, Mohammed's faithful friend, as their new leader. He was called the successor (caliph) of the Prophet. His political power was as complete as that of Mohammed. The first caliph nominated his successor, Omar, and the Arabian community of Medina accepted and confirmed this nomination. The third and fourth caliphs were also elected, but violence had begun playing a considerable role in the succession. Of the four caliphs following Mohammed, only the first died a natural death; the other three were murdered.

The fifth caliph nominated his son as his successor, thus founding a dynasty (the Umayyads) and formally introducing the hereditary principle. This precedent

Elliott Erwitt MAGNUM

was followed for the next 400 years. By the time the Abbasid dynasty in Baghdad replaced the Umayyads in the year 750, hereditary autocratic rule had become firmly established, a practice leaning heavily upon the ancient Persian concept of kingship by divine right. Whereas early tradition had considered the caliphate an elective office, the traditional number of electors now was reduced to one, a change that amounted to an implicit acceptance of the hereditary principle: The predecessor appointed his successor. But the myth of election continued to exist, drawing strength from the oath of allegiance paid to the new prince in the capital and throughout the growing Islamic empire.

Islamic constitutional doctrine developed, during the first two centuries of Islam, as a rationalization of the existing practice. The doctrine involved a kind of social contract. It held that the ultimate source of political authority was God, who had provided for a ruler to command the people and thus ensure peace and protect the faithful. By accepting this office, the caliph promised to exercise his powers within the limits of the law. He confirmed this promise in a contract *(bay'a)* with the representatives of the community. If he violated this contract, the people were absolved of allegiance and could elect another ruler.

The doctrine of a contract between ruler and ruled made no provision, short of complete revolution, for removing a bad caliph. So if the doctrine were to serve the interests of the ruling class, it needed modification; it had to be stated in ways that stressed the duty of obedience, rather than the right to rebel. The occasional religious saying affirming the duty of Muslims to rebel against a ruler was checked—by the deliberate introduction of far more numerous sayings that branded the creation of disorder without adequate justification a mortal sin. All earthly authority was seen as ordained by God, and if a tyrant ruled he was simply God's punishment for man's sin.

The enormous Arab empire that the first caliphs had built did not last. Even the caliphate was swept aside by anyone who could take and keep power in the many smaller Arab states that succeeded the empire.

Adjusting theory to current reality (a pattern throughout Islamic history), the religious teachers now held that anyone in effective possession of power had to be obeyed—no matter how he had acquired power or how impious or barbaric his conduct. The Islamic community was intact, it was argued, as long as the secular government recognized the Koran and the traditions of Mohammed; consulted the religious teachers; and created conditions so that individual Muslims could obey the holy law. For centuries thereafter, the dominant theme of the Muslim countries was political quietism, supported and encouraged by religious arguments.

But the minor theme of rebellion against sinful leaders never died out. Thus members of the Khawarij sect viewed themselves as saints under a moral obligation to revolt against sinful government and its supporters. Under the Umayyad caliphs, these "Puritans of Islam" spread terror among their opponents, often killing male Muslims along with women and children. And the Shi'ite Muslims, of non-Arabic descent, pressed for an order in which all Muslims would be equal and Arab birth would not carry special privileges.

Indeed, throughout the first 1100 years of its existence, Islamic political life had its share of rebellions. The orthodox doctrine stressing the duty of obedience was always beset by heresies and sects that taught the duty of revolt against impious or oppressive authority. These seemingly contradictory doctrines are, of course, related. Muslim political theories and political institutions failed to assure a peaceful resolution of social and economic issues; they did not provide for an orderly succession of rulers. Regional and tribal loyalties remained strong. In this situation, rebellions and military mutinies were frequent. In Algiers, for example, between 1671 and 1818 some 14 of the 30 rulers achieved power through a military rebellion or by assassinating their predecessors. These rivalries, internal wars, and rebellions signaled the failure of Islamic political institutions—and at the same time ensured the survival of Islam itself. The rebellions, often inspired by religious motives, acted as a safety valve that helped renovate political authority even as it attacked a particular ruler.

Islam Confronts the West

The centuries-long tradition of autocratic rule and political quietism, interrupted from time to time by futile rebellions, lasted in the Islamic world until the French Revolution. The new slogans of liberty, equality, and popular sovereignty were easy to accept because they were expressed in non-Christian terms: Carried by European soldiers and traders into the Middle East, these slogans breached the walls of that ancient citadel of autocracy. Almost immediately began the Westernization that is still in progress more than 170 years later, and that has created the turbulence that can be observed today throughout the Islamic world, from North Africa to Pakistan and Indonesia.

Islamic intellectuals reacted to this new reality in different ways. If we take an overall view of the last 100 years, we can distinguish four main groups:
—MODERNISTS—who aim at integrating Western democracy into a rejuvenated Islam;
—TRADITIONALISTS—religious teachers for the most part, who see no need for basic doctrinal change and are willing to go along with any existing form of government;

—FUNDAMENTALISTS—who want to return to the theocratic foundation of early Islam; and

—SECULAR NATIONALISTS—who may still appeal to the Islamic emotions of the masses but who seek modernization and a new secular foundation for the legitimacy of government.

The modernists, many of them Western-educated, argue that Islam and democracy are compatible. They point to the *bay'a,* the ancient doctrine of a contract between the ruler and the ruled, and they make much of the Prophet's having consulted important members of the aristocracy of Medina.

But this attempt to plant modern political ideals in the Islamic tradition is based on a failure to understand both democracy and Islam completely. The political practices of a tribal society do *not* fit the complexities of the 20th century. The democratic idea of elected, representative bodies legislating in spiritual matters offends the very basis of Islam. This attempt to reconcile democracy and Islam, to be sure, has served the need of some Muslim intellectuals to restate their faith in terms of the fashionable ideology of the day, and it has fostered pride in the Muslim past. It has not, however, provided guidance in solving the political problems of modern nation-building.

The traditionalists have been the least perturbed by the political and intellectual challenge of the West. Most of the religious teachers, the *ulama,* have cooperated with the newest Arab nation-states and with their secular rulers. They have adjusted themselves to the powerful currents of nationalism, even though orthodox Islam recognizes neither geographical nor ethnic boundaries. In Egypt, the *ulama* even condemned the Muslim Brotherhood because it used force in opposing the secular government of Naguib and Nasser. The *ulama* of Pakistan have gracefully accepted the country's failure to achieve an Islamic constitution, although they and their allies had worked for one for many years. The prestige of the *ulama,* especially in the rural areas, is still high, but they have almost no influence on the thinking of those elite groups that hold the reins of government.

The third type of response to the revolutionary impact of Western thinking has been fundamentalism. Most recently fundamentalism has been expressed in the movement of the Muslim Brotherhood, an organization founded in 1928 by an Egyptian elementary-school teacher. The Brotherhood wants the establishment of an Islamic state, governed if possible by a caliph, which will carry out the rules and injunctions of the Koran and the tradition. Adultery, usury, drinking, and gambling will be vigorously suppressed; marriage and the begetting of children will be encouraged. The Brotherhood regards narrow nationalism as a "hideous pestilence"; it advocates, instead, the union of all Islamic countries and the driving out of any European influences through a holy war. The Brotherhood also seeks the eventual conquest and conversion of all the rest of the world. The legitimacy of secular governments that neglect the teachings of Islam is denied by the Brotherhood, which exhorts its followers to fight such governments by all available means.

The fourth category of contemporary Islamic political thought is secular nationalism, which rejects religion as a basis for political action. The secular nationalist view was propounded in 1950 by Khalid Muhammad Khalid. Openly acknowledging his intellectual debt to Voltaire, Rousseau, and Thomas Paine, Khalid called the Islamic priesthood a reactionary, totalitarian body that had dragged the people into "an abyss of servility and subjection." Theocratic government, whether in Christianity or Islam, had always been the worst possible type of tyranny, Khalid insisted.

Khalid's ideas are very similar to the theoretical basis of Egypt's politics under Naguib and Nasser. The officers who overthrew the monarchy in 1952, General Naguib has said, did not want to turn their backs on the Islamic faith. But they felt that the messages preached by the Prophet had to be interpreted in the light of the great changes since those early days. "There is nothing in the Koran," Naguib has written, "that calls for theocratic government." President Nasser's allusions to Islam are primarily a matter of foreign policy, and not ideology. The basis of Nasser's claim to legitimacy is secular.

The Islamic Future

In the years since World War II, Islam—which had been waning as a political force before the war—seemed to revive. Confidence in the West was shaken by the war, which seemed to have brought Western democracy to the brink of destruction. The increased political pressure of the Western powers, the presence of foreign troops, and finally the creation of Israel all increased nationalist sentiment.

Since the masses were still predominantly Muslim, and since the nationalist leaders sought to mobilize these masses, nationalism was increasingly tied to religion. In the Near East, Islam was described as the product of the Arab national genius. On the Indian subcontinent, Islam saw a powerful resurgence through the creation of Pakistan. The hold of religion on the Muslim masses has, of course, benefited the cause of fundamentalist extremism. By the end of World War II, the Muslim Brotherhood had at least a million followers in Egypt and several other Near Eastern countries, and—despite harassment and repression—the movement continues to show strength.

Now that the old value system is crumbling under the impact of technology and mass communications, fundamentalism seems to offer salvation and meaning in life by striving to resurrect an idealized past. The submerged masses still have no stake in the modern world and are disappointed by the failure of the new governments to bring a real improvement in their lot. To them, a militant, messianic radicalism glorifying passion and struggle has considerable appeal. Since 1945, several secular nationalist leaders in Egypt, Iran, and Pakistan have been assassinated by fundamentalist extremists; in 1965, a plot against President Nasser was uncovered and his assassination foiled. Clearly, even though Islam is often expressed merely as ritual, it is still a force to be reckoned with.

Yet it is doubtful that fundamentalism and other forms of neo-orthodoxy truly have a future. The forces of secularization increasingly undermine religion. Urbanization and industrialization break up tribal life and weaken the traditional family. The state almost everywhere is in the hands of secular nationalists, who may still use traditional symbols and an Islamic vocabulary, but who increasingly adhere to a secular path. Religious leaders, unable to confront the problems of a country challenged by Western technology and power, ever more lose their prestige and influence to the new secular leadership. Islam is neither persecuted nor abolished; it is simply being bypassed as no longer relevant.

The struggle for independence from the colonial powers weakened political authority and the legitimacy of the state. At that time, the task of the patriot was to defy the alien state and subvert it. Today the most urgent job is to reverse this trend, to build political cohesion and a stable government that can deal with the problems of nation-building and social change, as well as to find a new basis for legitimacy. The constitutions of most Islamic countries still provide that Islam be the religion of the state and that the head of state be a Muslim, but such provisions are of largely deferential character. They cannot guarantee national integration or legitimize political power. Sovereignty can no longer be derived from religious tradition. To be considered legitimate, political authority must confront the problems created by the uprooting of the old structure of society.

Many governments in today's Islamic world quite consciously stress the tie between modernization and legitimacy. At the same time they often dismiss the Western democratic idea of rival parties competing for the allegiance of the voters as unsuitable for regimes struggling to accomplish rapid social change. An Egyptian, writing about Nasser's Arab Socialist Union (the regime's official agent for mobilizing mass support), stressed that this movement was not an ordinary political party but represented the whole people. "The people," he continued, "are not limited by partisan principles but are gathered together around their national goals to achieve the mission of Arab nationalism and to stimulate their efforts for the sound political, social, and economic construction of the nation." Strong-man regimes like those of Nasser, or Ayub Khan of Pakistan, are facilitated by the traditional subordination of the individual to the state or community in Muslim political practice, and by the Islamic respect for power.

Still, power and force alone are not enough to inspire loyalty. Hence the appeal to nationalism, social reform, and modernization, accompanied by a religious ceremonial in order to bolster legitimacy. Islam has been quite adaptive in the past and it may well adjust itself to this new situation as well. It may in time become what much of Christianity has already become: A body of private religious beliefs, fulfilling the psychological needs of some individuals and contributing to a sense of national heritage, but without practical implication for the conduct of the state. Though such a kind of Islam may be radically different from anything history has known so far, it would be presumptuous to maintain that such a religion should no longer be called Islamic.

March 1968

SUGGESTED READINGS

The Caliphate by Thomas W. Arnold (New York: Barnes and Noble, 1966, revised edition). The classic study of the institution of the caliphate—written in 1924 and brought up to date by Sylvia G. Haim, a leading authority on the history of ideas in the Arab world.

Mohammedanism: An Historical Survey by Hamilton A. R. Gibb (New York: Oxford University Press, Galaxy Books, 1962, second revised edition). The best brief general introduction to Islam and its contemporary situation, written by the present dean of Islamic studies.

The Politics of Social Change in the Middle East and North Africa by Manfred Halpern (Princeton, N.J.: Princeton University Press, 1963). A sophisticated analysis of the political ramifications of modernization in the major centers of the Islamic world.

Nationalism and Revolution in the Arab World by Sharabi Hisham (Princeton, N.J.: D. van Nostrand, 1966). A concise overview of recent political developments in the Arab world, together with documentary materials illustrating the author's discussion of political ideology, constitutional structures, and coups d'etat.

People and Politics in the Middle East edited by Michael Curtis (New Brunswick, N.J.: Transaction Books, 1971). A unique confrontation between Arab, Israeli and Western viewpoints on the Arab-Israeli conflict.

The Sacred Canopy by Peter L. Berger (Garden City, N.Y.: Doubleday Anchor Book, 1969) presents a sociological and historical approach to secularization.

A Rumour of Angels by Peter L. Berger (Garden City, N.Y.: Doubleday, 1969) is an account of the place of religion in modern society.

Religion Is Irrelevant in Sweden

Swedes believe in God and have a state church but pay little attention to either

RICHARD F. TOMASSON

In 1544, the Swedish riksdag declared the Evangelical-Lutheran religion to be the official religion of the state. At the same time, it warned that anyone who opposed the state church would be "banished and regarded as a heretic and heathen." Yet today Sweden is a land of liberal sexuality and the welfare state—as secular as any Western industrial country.

On an average Sunday, church attendance in Sweden is only 4 or 5 percent of the population. The number of clergymen is no more than it was two centuries ago, when the population was less than a quarter of what it is now. Compared with the United States, where church news and services are regularly carried by newspapers, radio, and television, religion is a scarce commodity in the Swedish mass media.

Still, there is little hostility among the Swedish people toward religion or toward the clergy. The school system is the only one in Western Europe which has established a universal policy of *objective* teaching of religion at all levels. About 90 percent of the Swedes continue to be baptized, confirmed, married, and buried by the church. And the majority claim they would join the church if it were disestablished—which is likely to happen in the 1970s. Thus, there is neither widespread participation in nor hostility toward the church. The prevailing attitude in Sweden is indifference.

Why is traditional religion so irrelevant throughout most of Swedish society, while in other Western countries—even in much of nearby Norway—it continues to command substantial support from the people? Before trying to answer this intriguing question, let us first get a clearer picture of religion in modern Sweden—by examining what the Swedes feel and think about religion, and how religion influences them.

All Swedes—except for some 33,000 Catholics, 15,000 Jews, and a small number who have resigned from the church—are formal members of the Church of Sweden. This is more than 98 percent of the population. About 5 percent of the population also belongs to various "free churches"—Protestant sects emphasizing salvation, strict morality, and freedom of religion.

Attendance at Sunday mass in the state church has declined from 17 percent of the population in 1900 to 3.3 percent in 1962. Those who belong to the free churches are more likely to attend Sunday services and therefore they bring the overall attendance figure to about 5 percent. Finland and Denmark have equally low patterns of Sunday church attendance. Attendance is probably lower in these three Scandinavian societies than in any other Western country. For Great Britain, average Sunday attendance is around 15 percent; for the United States, attendance is between 46 and 49 percent.

Sweden has 13 dioceses, and there is a significant variation in their residents' attendance at Church of Sweden services on Sunday. The urban dioceses of Stockholm have the lowest attendance—1.1 percent. The diocese of Luleå—the most northern, rural, and most unevenly developed area in Sweden—has the highest: 6.3 percent, which is over twice the average attendance throughout Sweden (3.1 percent). Other surveys have indicated substantially higher attendance records generally, but they included attendance at ceremonies such as baptisms, weddings, and burials, the great majority of which are conducted under church auspices. Of course, church attendance is also considerably higher at Christmas and Easter. As might be expected, attendance is greater among the more traditional segments of the population: rural people, women, and the old, than among urban people, men, and the young.

The relationship between a Swede's social class and his church attendance is interesting. Table 1 shows the percentage of Swedes by class who attended religious services at least twice the month before the survey—a measure of the religiously committed. It is clear that the middle class participates more in organized religion than the working class and the upper class. Moreover, there are marked differences by class in participation in the Church of Sweden and in the free churches. The working class is the *least* likely to participate in the Church of Sweden. The upper class is the *least* likely to participate in the free churches.

Despite these low attendance records, the majority of Swedes say they believe in God—if not an orthodox Christian God, at least a deity who "oversees the world." In 1956, a study found that 52 percent of Swedish men 18 to 55, and 72 percent of Swedish women 18 to 55, believed in such a God. (See Table 2.) In the United States, by contrast, over 95 percent of the people say they believe in God. When these

THE MAJORITY OF SWEDES SAY Table 2
THEY BELIEVE IN GOD

Religious beliefs of Swedish men and women, 18-55 (1956)

Percentage who	Men	Women
"believe in a God who oversees the world"	52%	72%
"believe in a God who intervenes in my own life"	37	57
"believe that believers will go to heaven"	22	35
"try to be a real Christian"	26	36

Number: 1000 men
1000 women
Source: Svenska Institutet för Opinionsundersökningar.

Swedes were asked whether they believed in a "God who intervenes in my own life," the percentage answering Yes declined to 37 for men and 57 for women. Asked whether they thought that "believers will go to heaven," the percentages dropped to 22 for men and 36 for women. Asked "Do you try to be a real Christian?" only 26 percent of the men and 36 percent of the women answered Yes.

In Sweden, it seems, the word Christian means a person who is of the community of believers, not someone who behaves in a morally approved way, as it may mean in the Anglo-American societies. Herbert Tingsten, a leading editor and political scientist, once said the great majority of Swedish Christians are Christians in name only, and went on:

"They say they believe in God, yet do not accept the doctrines that distinguish Christianity. They want to keep education in Christianity in the schools yet do not go to Church. Baptism, confirmation, marriage and burial—these are the contacts these people have, not with religion (for there is no reason to have such contact!), but only with the Church. The holy sacraments provide a setting for festive occasions. A necessity for this state of affairs is that they do not listen, do not understand, or at least do not pay any attention to what is said. They inquire as little into the meaning of these things as they ponder electricity on a journey by tram. This we all know, and this we all say—but the convention is so well established that it is considered a trifle unbecoming to say so publicly."

An individual's answer to the question whether he tries to be a real Christian or not is probably a good clue to how much he subscribes to orthodox Christian

THE MIDDLE-CLASS ATTENDS CHURCH MOST Table 1

Active participants in the Church of Sweden and the free churches, by social class (1955-56)

Attended church at least twice in previous month	Church of Sweden	Free Church	Total
Social group 1 (professionals, executives, university graduates)	10%	2%	12%
Social group 2 (white-collar workers, small-business men, etc.)	10	8	18
Social group 3 (workers)	6	7	13

Number: 2579
Source: Berndt Gustafsson, *Kristen I 50-talets Sverige* (Stockholm: Svenska Kyrkans Diakonistyrelses Bokförlag, 1958).

In recent decades there has been a marked decline in religious belief in Sweden, especially among the young. Less than 25 percent of Swedes between 18 and 35 years old admit to "trying to be a real Christian."

beliefs. Among Swedes, there is a remarkable variation by age in answers to this question. (See Table 3.) Some 35 percent of Swedes, age 12 to 15, say Yes. Then among Swedes 18 to 25, there is a decline to a low point of 18 percent saying Yes. (For men between these ages, the figure is only 15 percent.) The per-

THE GENERATION GAP IN TRYING TO BE A REAL CHRISTIAN   Table 3

Answers to "Do you try to be a real Christian" by age, entire population (1955-56)

	Yes	Uncertain Don't know	No	Number
12-15	35%	41%	24%	289
16-17	20	36	44	91
18-25	18	20	62	320
26-35	24	27	49	366
36-45	31	27	42	375
46-55	38	24	38	356
56-	70	19	11	641

Source: Gustafsson, *Kristen I 50-talets Sverige*, op. cit., p. 27.

centage increases consistently with age—70 percent of Swedes 56 and over answer Yes.

These figures, even in the absence of data for other societies, certainly indicate a low acceptance of orthodox Christian belief among the Swedes. While there is evidence that religious beliefs increase with age, in Sweden the variation between the young and old is so great that another explanation is needed—namely, that in recent decades there has been a marked decline in religious belief. It is unlikely that when the 18-25 cohort reaches 56 and over, 70 percent of *them* will say they try to be real Christians. A study of the attitudes of over 2000 Swedish youth 12-24 done this year reveals that almost half unequivocally deny the existence of a deity. Results to the question "Do you believe there is a God?" were as follows:

22 percent Yes, absolutely; 31 percent Maybe, uncertain; 46 percent, there is not.

In Stockholm 63 percent deny the existence of a God.

A sizable minority of Swedes continue to believe in a life after death, although substantially fewer than in most Western societies. In a 1960 poll, 40 percent of a national sample answered Yes to such a question. This percentage can be compared with those of seven other Western countries in which sample polls were taken at about the same time. The percentages believing in a life after death, in rank order were:

74 percent United States, 71 percent Norway, 68 percent Canada, 63 percent Netherlands, 56 percent Great Britain, 55 percent Switzerland, 40 percent Sweden and, 38 percent West Germany. A Swedish report of this international study pointed out that in no other country were there so many uncertain answers as in Sweden: 37 percent gave Don't Know answers, and only 23 percent actually disclaimed belief in a life after death.

In 1964, a cross-section of Swedes 16 and over were asked how often they "pray to God." The results: 13 percent "daily," 13 percent "quite often," 27 percent "more rarely," 46 percent "never." By contrast, only 8 percent of a 1953 American sample claimed that they never prayed.

An important observation about religious belief in Sweden is the absence of much opinion that sees religion as the sole basis of morality. The same people who were asked about praying made these comments about the relation between religion and morality:

■ 16 percent "There is no other basis for morality than religion."
■ 27 percent "For me personally religion is the only basis for morality, but I still believe that men can find another basis for moral behavior."
■ 41 percent "Morality does not need to be based on religion."
■ 16 percent "Do not agree with any of the above statements."

In the United States, on the other hand, religion is conventionally viewed not only as the basis of morality, but as the basis of the "American way of life" and of democracy. Similarly in England—more comparable with Sweden in having an established church—morality and democracy are conventionally viewed as being rooted in religion. The substantially enhanced role for Christian education called for by the English Education Act of 1944 was facilitated by "the association of the Christian religion with the cause of democracy...." Basic to the framers of the law was the conviction that "education must have a religious base...." By contrast, Christian education as a school subject in Sweden must, by law, be "objective" and must not propagandize for any particular religion or view of morality—although this is commonly not adhered to in practice. A substantial majority of Swedes accept this "objectivity," as is indicated by the 1964 study. Given various alternatives on Christian education, the Swedes chose as follows:

■ 25 percent "Christian education should not only give students knowledge but also influence them toward the Christian faith."
■ 66 percent "Christian education should only give students knowledge about religion, but should not attempt to influence them in questions of faith."
■ 4 percent "Any special Christian education is not needed in the schools."
■ 4 percent "None of these agree with my opinion."
■ 1 percent No answer.

In spite of their relatively low level of church attendance and of orthodox Christian belief, Swedes, as mentioned, are not unfriendly to religion in general. In one 1961 study, asked whether "men in our time need religion," 82 percent of a national sample answered Yes. In 1962 a Swedish newspaper sponsored a study of what Swedes regard as important problems. Answers to a question about whether Swedes need a "greater interest in religion" were: 30 percent "very important," 42 percent "quite important," 24 percent "not at all important," 4 percent "can't say."

Nor are most Swedes disturbed by the relation between church and state. In 1957, a national sample of Swedes were asked how they would vote if there were a referendum on the separation of church and state. The results: 18 percent would vote for it, 51 percent would vote against it and 34 percent were undecided.

Yet some pious people, particularly high-church Lutherans, favor such a separation. They argue that the church would be free from government pressures and could become a community of authentic believers. On the other hand, some opinion not sympathetic to the church favors the present relationship precisely because it makes the church subject to some control by the government, the most important being the government's potential power in the appointment of clergy and the control of the budget. An example of this power was seen in the 1950s when the government exerted pressure on the church to allow women to be ordained. High-church opinion bitterly opposed the measure, but with government support it passed the Church Assembly.

Conflicting Opinions on Church & State

Within the church, and outside of it, there are a number of conflicting opinions about the most desirable relationship between state and church and just how this might be realized. Indeed, it has been clear for a number of years that there has been intense disagreement within the church over such issues.

One indication of how favorably the Swedish people regard the church is that the great majority would request church membership if such membership were no longer automatic. A 1958 study of Swedes over 15 found that, if the church were disestablished, 72 percent would join, 19 percent would not join and 9 percent were undecided. In 1961, a sample of Swedes were asked how well they thought the "state churches and the state church clergy were perfroming their duties." Their verdict was that the churches and clergy were doing tolerably well. Results: 25 percent very well, 53 percent fairly well, 9 percent not especially well, 3 percent poorly and 10 percent can't say.

Comparing the clergy with other occupations, Swedes apparently rank clergymen lower in their usefulness to society than Americans do. Indeed, on this count, Swedes ranked the clergy lower than dentists and business executives. On the other hand, Swedes rank clergymen *higher* in intellectual ability than Americans do. The fact is that the clergy of the state church are graduates of the same prestigious universities as other professionals, and have the status of "akademiker"; whereas the great majority of American clergymen come from little-known denominational institutions. These findings come from a study of American and Swedish university students, who were asked to rank clergymen, and seven other occupational groups, according to usefulness to society, intellectual ability, and prestige. The Swedes and the Americans gave clergymen the same prestige ranking.

The indifference of Swedes toward religion and toward their state church certainly seems clear from all the statistics. But what can be said for the other side of the relationship? How much influence does religion in general, the state church, or the clergy have on the people of Sweden?

It does not take much study of contemporary Sweden to conclude that influence from religious sources is minimal. The church has no illusions about the magnitude of her influence. In fact, the Swedish contributor to a recent symposium sponsored by the World Council of Churches aptly entitled his contribution, "Where the Church no Longer Shapes the Common Life."

The clergy and the church are neutral in political questions. It is almost inconceivable for a clergyman to officially support any political party or position, even though there are fewer sanctions against his participation as a private individual than in many other societies. In recent decades, the church has had little influence on public policy of any kind. It is even difficult for the church to speak out on questions of morality without being subject to a barrage of criticism, particularly when it takes a conservative position. In 1964, when the bishops deplored the "privatizing" of sexual life and reasserted their 1951 view that premarital intercourse was sinful, they received sharp criticism in a number of Liberal and Social Democratic papers. The headline of a critical editorial in one Stockholm paper was "What do the Bishops Know about Love?"

In Swedish politics, religious beliefs or affiliations are irrelevant—except to the extent that some of the names of the Liberal Party lists are chosen for their free-church affiliations. No religious party has ever been able to elect a representative to the riksdag; the most recent attempt was made by the Christian Democratic Assembly, formed in 1964 and largely supported by Pentacostals and other fundamentalist groups.

Members of the government, or political leaders, virtually never invoke God or any religious sanction in any context. During a television interview in the early 1960s, Gunnar Heckscher, the leader of the Conservative Party from 1961 to 1964, even admitted being an atheist though he claimed to be sympathetic to the Christian tradition. Even though the Conservative Party is the party of those most strongly involved in the Church of Sweden, this surprising admission caused Heckscher no apparent difficulties!

Various studies have shown that Swedes who are religious engage in less premarital sexual behavior than the less religious, and are generally more conservative in their attitudes toward sex. It is also clear that those with a strong involvement in the state church (predominantly the upper and middle classes) tend to support the Conservative Party, while those strongly committed to the free churches (predominantly the middle class and workers) tend to support the Liberal Party or the very small Christian Democratic Assembly.

When it comes to religion, then, it seems that Swedes behave in much the same manner as a persnickety dinner guest. Swedes are content to accept invitations to the church meal, but after allowing the table to be set and sampling a few hors d'oeuvres, they invariably snub their noses at the entrée.

A Look at the History of the Church

Perhaps a look into the history of the church in Sweden will give us some insight into this curious situation.

Christianity came late to Sweden. An established Catholic Church had existed there only four centuries before the Reformation of the 16th century. As in England and Denmark, the Reformation in Sweden occurred through the decision of a king, Gustav Vasa (reigned 1523-60). He revolted against the Catholic Church, at least at first, for wholly political and economic reasons. He wanted to create a strong, centralized, and secure nation-state. To do that, he had to reduce the Catholic Church's economic position. In 1527 he gained the consent of the riksdag to reduce the church's land holdings; at his death in 1560, the church's lands had been totally confiscated.

Actually, the first step in the Reformation in Sweden came in 1527 when the riksdag proclaimed that the word of God should "be preached pure"—a step that supported Lutheran doctrine, but was not strong enough to disturb non-Lutherans. The new law emphasized the authority of scripture over the Church. In 1536, a Church Assembly helped the Reformation in a number of ways: It made the Swedish mass and manual obligatory throughout Sweden, and it gave the clergy the right to marry. An autonomous national church had in fact appeared, and orthodoxy was officially established in 1544.

The desire for orthodoxy dominated Swedish religious and political thought until the 18th century, and remained a powerful force until after the mid-19th century. Vestiges of it continued up to the Religious Freedom Law of 1951, which dispensed with the rule that all cabinet ministers and civil servants had to be members of the Church of Sweden. For the population in general, this law made it possible to leave the Swedish church without having to enter another religious congregation.

In 1634, the concept of the religious unity of the state—that the state and the church were one and the same—was first incorporated in the Swedish Constitution. This concept was reaffirmed in all successive Constitutions, including the most recent one that was adopted in 1809. This is in striking contrast to England and Holland, where tolerance toward other Christians began to develop in the 17th century.

Just as the 17th century marks the establishment of religious orthodoxy in Sweden, so the 18th century marks its decline. Two forces contributed to the breakdown of this orthodoxy. One was the skepticism and rationalism of the Enlightenment. The other, interesting enough, was almost the opposite. It was a movement called pietism, which originated in Germany in the 17th century and later spread to Sweden. Pietism was essentially a reaction to formalism and intellectualism, and it stressed the need for Bible study and personal religious experience.

Pietists in Sweden quickly became the targets of much repressive legislation. The most far-reaching was a government edict of 1726, which forbade any assembly for worship, public or private, without the presence of a parish clergyman. (The exception: private prayers.) The penalties for violation were fines, imprisonment, or banishment from the country. This law infringing as it did on religious activities, prompted many Swedes, including non-Pietists, to become hostile to the established church. The law was even criticized from *within* the church.

The Enlightenment contributed to the breakdown of orthodoxy by influencing the church to become more rational and quite secular. Gustav III, who attained the throne after a coup d'état in 1771, was a full-fledged Enlightenment king. In 1781 he gave foreign Christians the right to form their own congregations, to build their own churches, and to have their children trained by their own clergy. The next year similar rights were given to Jews. For the remaining Swedes, however, the compulsions to attend church and take communion remained intact, as did other rules governing religious activity.

Meanwhile, a great deal of freedom was growing within the church itself. By Calvinist standards, there was an absence of puritanism and narrow moralistic concerns. The clergy was well educated, and placed a good deal of value on scholarship. The better-educated among them led upper-class styles of life. Many tilled their own farms, and made contributions to agricultural science. Traditionally, the clergy functioned as teachers, doctors, and parish politicians, and even took care of the population registers, in effect acting as Anglo-American county clerks—a function they have carried down to the present. With all of their activities, it is

The Swedes leaving this church are among a tiny minority—only 4 or 5 percent of the total population—which attends church on Sunday.

not surprising that to many of them the care of souls was of quite secondary importance.

At the higher levels, the Swedish church had become very much secularized by the first half of the 19th century. Thus, becoming a bishop was considered a natural niche for leading cultural figures, regardless of their religious beliefs or training in theology. Esaias Tegnér, a professor and poet of the time, upon his appointment as a bishop, wrote to a friend that "A pagan I am and shall remain."

Partly as a reaction to such secularization, the church began returning to a greater orthodoxy and social conservatism in the 1840s. Up to the middle of the 1880s and—to some extent—even later, the church held reactionary ideologies that rationalized and defended the existing benevolent and hierarchial order against liberalism at first, and against socialism later. Two or three decades of internal conflict ensued, during which the church provided the major support for the values of traditional Swedish society. The already hostile views of the Social Democrats, and some of the Liberals, toward the church and religion were therefore further aggravated. Thus, while modern notions of religious freedom and tolerance, equality and popular democracy were sweeping Western Europe and the New World in the 19th century, the Swedish church was defending the old order. The fact that the church so completely committed itself to reactionary values during this period is crucial to understanding the secularization of the working class and the educated middle class.

It was not until the first decade of the 20th century that a rapprochement began between the church and the Social Democrats and other popular movements—the union, the free churches, and the temperance societies. But it may already have been too late for the church to expect to ever again exert a powerful influence over the Swedish people.

Our review of Swedish religious history has shown the changes that have taken place in the relationship between the church and the common people. But what is the official relationship of the church and the state?

Since the 1809 constitution that reaffirmed their union, relations between the church and state have been marked by three major developments.
- the legalizing of religious freedom.
- the institution of a Church Assembly to replace the riksdag in dealing with matters of internal concern to the church.
- the transfer of a number of the church's educational and political duties to the civil community.

A proposal to allow church members to resign was first introduced into the riksdag in 1824. In 1860, a modified version of this proposal was approved. It was not until nearly a century later, however, with the passage of the Religious Freedom Law in 1951, that it became possible for someone to leave the church without entering another religious congregation. Yet since 1952 only about 40,000 Swedes have left the church.

In the parliamentary reforms of 1866, the clergy lost formal representation in the riksdag. In exchange, the riksdag established a Church Assembly with the authority to veto government decisions regarding church law and the prerogatives of the clergy. At the same time, the riksdag gave the church and clergy greater authority over still more of their internal affairs. In 1949 the Church Assembly, for the first time, came to consist of a majority of laymen. Today, the Swedish church has more autonomy from the government than does the state church in either Norway or Denmark—but not so much as in Finland.

Over the years, the distinction between ecclesiastical and civil authority has been sharpened. Legislation passed in 1862 took away many of the secular functions of the church and clergy and gave them to the civil community. Subsequent legislation has removed the clergy's duties in social welfare and education, including teaching religion in the schools.

In sum, the great amount of secularism in Sweden can perhaps be explained in the following way:

Religion has never become a major source of cleavage among Swedes. This is contrary to the situation in the United States, England, and the Netherlands, where a variety of religions has thrived, with a lot of religious disagreement among them. Such differences seem to stimulate religious concerns.

As mentioned, during the crucial period of early modernization—particularly during the last two decades of the 19th century—the church solidly aligned itself with the old order and its traditional values. State Church Lutheranism, with its emphasis on absolute doctrinal authority and its essentially medieval view of society, was inherently less receptive to egalitarianism and tolerance than Calvinism and the more individualistic forms of Protestantism. This alienated the growing segments of society oriented toward modern values as it did elsewhere in Europe, but the division was particularly sharp in Sweden.

Sweden had a relatively late but extraordinarily successful modernization. With modernization came a new respect for science and empiricism, which thoroughly discredited 19th-century society, with its traditional and idealistic values. The state church simply failed to keep pace with the rapid changes of the 20th century and undoubtedly it did not realize how costly its abdication would turn out to be.

December 1968

SUGGESTED READINGS

Religion and the Rise of Scepticism by Franklin Baumer (New York: Harcourt Brace, 1960) investigates the conflict between religion and scepticism in the Western world for four centuries.

Sociology Looks at Religion by J. Milton Yinger (New York: Macmillan, 1963) is a useful introduction to the sociology of religion.

At the Scrabble Creek service, a woman "speaks in tongues." James Holland

The Serpent-Handling Religions of West Virginia

In surprising ways, the personalities of the serpent-handlers differed from those of members of a conventional church

NATHAN L. GERRARD

"... And these signs shall follow them that believe; In my name shall they cast out devils; they shall speak with new tongues; They shall take up serpents; and if they drink any deadly thing, it shall not hurt them; they shall lay hands on the sick, and they shall recover." *Mark 16:17-18*

In Southern Appalachia, two dozen or three dozen fundamentalist congregations take this passage literally and "take up serpents." They use copperheads, water moccasins, and rattlesnakes in their religious services.

The serpent-handling ritual was inaugurated between 1900 and 1910, probably by George Went Hensley. Hensley began evangelizing in rural Grasshopper Valley, Tenn., then traveled widely throughout the South, particularly in Kentucky, spreading his religion. He died in Florida at 70—of snakebite. To date, the press has reported about 20 such deaths among the serpent-handlers. One other death was recorded last year, in Kentucky.

For seven years, my wife and I have been studying a number of West Virginia serpent-handlers, primarily in order to discover what effect this unusual form of religious practice has on their lives. Although serpent-han-

RELIGION 325

dling is outlawed by the state legislatures of Kentucky, Virginia, and Tennessee and by municipal ordinances in North Carolina, it is still legal in West Virginia. One center is the Scrabble Creek Church of All Nations in Fayette County, about 37 miles from Charleston. Another center is the Church of Jesus in Jolo, McDowell County, one of the most poverty-stricken areas of the state. Serpent-handling is also practiced sporadically elsewhere in West Virginia, where it is usually led by visitors from Scrabble Creek or Jolo.

The Jolo church attracts people from both Virginia and Kentucky, in addition to those from West Virginia. Members of the Scrabble Creek church speak with awe of the Jolo services, where people pick up large handfuls of poisonous snakes, fling them to the ground, pick them up again, and thrust them under their shirts or blouses, dancing ecstatically. We attended one church service in Scrabble Creek where visitors from Jolo covered their heads with clusters of snakes and wore them as crowns.

Serpent-handling was introduced to Scrabble Creek in 1941 by a coal miner from Harlan, Ky. The practice really began to take hold in 1946, when the present leader of the Scrabble Creek church, then a member of the Church of God, first took up serpents. The four or five original serpent-handlers in Fayette County met at one another's homes until given the use of an abandoned one-room school house in Big Creek. In 1959, when their number had swelled several times over, they moved to a larger church in Scrabble Creek.

Snakebites, Saints, and Scoffers

During the course of our seven-year study, about a dozen members of the church received snakebites. (My wife and I were present on two of these occasions.) Although there were no deaths, each incident was widely and unfavorably publicized in the area. For their part, the serpent-handlers say the Lord causes a snake to strike in order to refute scoffers' claims that the snakes' fangs have been pulled. They see each recovery from snakebite as a miracle wrought by the Lord—and each death as a sign that the Lord "really had to show the scoffers how dangerous it is to obey His commandments." Since adherents believe that death brings one to the throne of God, some express an eagerness to die when He decides they are ready. Those who have been bitten and who have recovered seem to receive special deference from other members of the church.

The ritual of serpent-handling takes only 15 or 20 minutes in religious sessions that are seldom shorter than four hours. The rest of the service includes singing Christian hymns, ecstatic dancing, testifying, extemporaneous and impassioned sermons, faith-healing, "speaking in tongues," and foot-washing. These latter rituals are a part of the firmly-rooted Holiness move- ment, which encompasses thousands of churches in the Southern Appalachian region. The Holiness churches started in the 19th century as part of a perfectionist movement.

The social and psychological functions served by the Scrabble Creek church are probably very much the same as those served by the more conventional Holiness churches. Thus, the extreme danger of the Scrabble Creek rituals probably helps to validate the members' claims to holiness. After all, the claim that one is a living saint is pretentious even in a sacred society—and it is particularly difficult to maintain in a secular society. That the serpent-handler regularly risks his life for his religion is seen as evidence of his saintliness. As the serpent-handler stresses over and over, "I'm afraid of snakes like anybody else, but when God anoints me, I handle them with joy." The fact that he is usually not bitten, or if bitten usually recovers, is cited as further evidence of his claim to holiness.

After we had observed the Scrabble Creek serpent-handlers for some time, we decided to give them psychological tests. We enlisted the aid of Auke Tellegen, department of psychology, University of Minnesota, and three of his clinical associates: James Butcher, William Schofield, and Anne Wirt. They interpreted the Minnesota Multiphasic Personality Inventory that we administered to 50 serpent-handlers (46 were completed)—and also to 90 members of a conventional-denomination church 20 miles from Scrabble Creek. What we wanted to find out was how these two groups differed.

What we found were important personality differences not only between the serpent-handlers and the conventional church members, but also between the older and the younger generations within the conventional group. We believe that these differences are due, ultimately, to differences in social class: The serpent-handlers come from the nonmobile working class (average annual income: $3000), whereas members of the conventional church are upwardly mobile working-class people (average annual income: $5000) with their eyes on the future.

But first, let us consider the similarities between the two groups. Most of the people who live in the south central part of West Virginia, serpent-handlers or not, have similar backgrounds. The area is rural, nonfarm, with only about one-tenth of the population living in settlements of more than 2500. Until recently, the dominant industry was coal-mining, but in the last 15 years mining operations have been drastically curtailed. The result has been widespread unemployment. Scrabble Creek is in that part of Appalachia that has been officially declared a "depressed area"—which means that current unemployment rates there often equal those of the depression.

There are few foreign-born in this part of West Virginia. Most of the residents are of Scottish-Irish or Pennsylvania Dutch descent, and their ancestors came to the New World so long ago that there are no memories of an Old World past.

Generally, public schools in the area are below national standards. Few people over 50 have had more than six or seven years of elementary education.

Religion has always been important here. One or two generations ago, the immediate ancestors of both serpent-handlers and conventional-church members lived in the same mining communities and followed roughly the same religious practices. Today there is much "backsliding," and the majority seldom attend church regularly. But there is still a great deal of talk about religion, and there are few professed atheists.

Hypochondria and the Holy Spirit

Though the people of both churches are native-born Protestants with fundamentalist religious beliefs, little education, and precarious employment, the two groups seem to handle their common problems in very different ways. One of the first differences we noticed was in the way the older members of both churches responded to illness and old age. Because the members of both churches had been impoverished and medically neglected during childhood and young adulthood, and because they had earned their livelihoods in hazardous and health-destroying ways, they were old before their time. They suffered from a wide variety of physical ailments. Yet while the older members of the conventional church seemed to dwell morbidly on their physical disabilities, the aged serpent-handlers seemed able to cheerfully ignore their ailments.

The serpent-handlers, in fact, went to the opposite extreme. Far from being pessimistic hypochondriacs like the conventional-church members, the serpent-handlers were so intent on placing their fate in God's benevolent hands that they usually failed to take even the normal precautions in caring for their health. Three old serpent-handlers we knew in Scrabble Creek were suffering from serious cardiac conditions. But when the Holy Spirit moved them, they danced ecstatically and violently. And they did this without any apparent harm.

No matter how ill the old serpent-handlers are, unless they are actually prostrate in their beds they manage to attend and enjoy church services lasting four to six hours, two or three times a week. Some have to travel long distances over the mountains to get to church. When the long sessions are over, they appear refreshed rather than weary.

One evening an elderly woman was carried into the serpent-handling church in a wheelchair. She had had a severe stroke and was almost completely paralyzed. Wheeled to the front of the church, she watched everything throughout the long services. During one particularly frenzied singing and dancing session, the fingers of her right hand tapped lightly against the arm of the chair. This was the only movement she was able to make, but obviously she was enjoying the service. When friends leaned over and offered to take her home, she made it clear she was not ready to go. She stayed until the end, and gave the impression of smiling when she was finally wheeled out. Others in the church apparently felt pleased rather than depressed by her presence.

Both old members of the conventional denomination and old serpent-handlers undoubtedly are frequently visited by the thought of death. Both rely on religion for solace, but the serpent-handlers evidently are more successful. The old serpent-handlers are not frightened by the prospect of death. This is true not only of those members who handle poisonous snakes in religious services, but also of the minority who do *not* handle serpents.

One 80-year-old member of the Scrabble Creek church—who did not handle serpents—testified in our presence: "I am not afraid to meet my Maker in Heaven. I am ready. If somebody was to wave a gun in my face, I would not turn away. I am in God's hands."

Another old church member, a serpent-handler, was dying from silicosis. When we visited him in the hospital he appeared serene, although he must have known that he would not live out the week.

The assertion of some modern theologians that whatever meaning and relevance God once may have had has been lost for modern man does not apply to the old serpent-handlers. To them, God is real. In fact, they often see Him during vivid hallucinations. He watches over the faithful. Misfortune and even death do not shake their faith, for misfortune is interpreted, in accordance with God's inscrutable will, as a hidden good.

Surprisingly, the contrast between the optimistic old serpent-handlers and the pessimistic elders of the conventional church all but disappeared when we shifted to the younger members of the two groups. Both groups of young people, on the psychological tests, came out as remarkably well adjusted. They showed none of the neurotic and depressive tendencies of the older conventional-church members. And this cheerful attitude prevailed despite the fact that many of them, at least among the young serpent-handlers, had much to be depressed about.

The young members of the conventional church are much better off, socially and economically, than the young serpent-handlers. The parents of the young conventional-church members can usually provide the luxuries that most young Americans regard as necessities. Many conventional-church youths are active in extracurricular activities in high school or are attending college.

A songfest (above) among the serpent-handlers—to the accompaniment of electric guitars, accordions, banjos, and tambourines. Any member of the congregation (below) may rise to lead a prayer or give a short sermon.

they shall take up serpents...

PHOTOGRAPHED BY
JAMES HOLLAND

Until the snakes come out, services at the Scrabble Creek Church of All Nations in West Virginia are much like services at thousands of other pentecostal and holiness churches, with joyous singing and testifying, washing of feet and impassioned sermons. These churches take their inspiration from the Acts of the Apostles, which describes the ecstasy of the disciples when they received the Holy Spirit for the first time, at Pentecost. So joyous were the disciples that bystanders jeered, "These men are full of new wine." The Apostle Peter explained that they were full of the Holy Spirit instead. The two dozen or three dozen congregations that include serpent-handling in their rites don't worship snakes, members explain, and use them only to express their faith.

INSTITUTIONS

The rattler will be out of his box (above, and right) for only 15 minutes of the four-hour service. The serpent-handling churches use rattlesnakes, water moccasins, and copperheads—all native to the area. The snakes have both fangs and poison and their bite can kill. Yet during the services they are passed from hand to hand and even tossed across the room. Below, two generations of serpent-handlers.

The young serpent-handlers, in contrast, are shunned and stigmatized as "snakes." Most young members of the conventional denomination who are in high school intend to go on to college, and they will undoubtedly attain a higher socioeconomic status than their parents have attained. But most of the young serpent-handlers are not attending school. Many are unemployed. None attend or plan to attend college, and they often appear quite depressed about their economic prospects.

The young serpent-handlers spend a great deal of time wandering aimlessly up and down the roads of the hollows, and undoubtedly are bored when not attending church. Their conversation is sometimes marked by humor, with undertones of cynicism and bitterness. We are convinced that what prevents many of them from becoming delinquent or demoralized is their wholehearted participation in religious practices that provide an acceptable outlet for their excess energy, and strengthen their self-esteem by giving them the opportunity to achieve "holiness."

Now, how does all this relate to the class differences between the serpent-handlers and the conventional-church group? The answer is that what allows the serpent-handlers to cope so well with their problems—what allows the older members to rise above the worries of illness and approaching death, and the younger members to remain relatively well-adjusted despite their grim economic prospects—is a certain approach to life that is typical of them as members of the stationary working class. The key to this approach is hedonism.

Hopelessness and Hedonism

The psychological tests showed that the young serpent-handlers, like their elders, were more impulsive and spontaneous than the members of the conventional church. This may account for the strong appeal of the Holiness churches to those members of the stationary working class who prefer religious hedonism to reckless hedonism, with its high incidence of drunkenness and illegitimacy. Religious hedonism is compatible with a

Scrabble Creek's serpent, a four-foot diamondback rattlesnake, travels in a plywood box painted with appropriate biblical citations.

puritan morality—and it compensates for its constraints.

The feeling that one cannot plan for the future, expressed in religious terms as "being in God's hands," fosters the widespread conviction among members of the stationary working class that opportunities for pleasure must be exploited immediately. After all, they may never occur again. This attitude is markedly different from that of the upwardly mobile working class, whose members are willing to postpone immediate pleasures for the sake of long-term goals.

Hedonism in the stationary working class is fostered in childhood by parental practices that, while demanding obedience in the home, permit the child license outside the home. Later, during adulthood, this orientation toward enjoying the present and ignoring the future is reinforced by irregular employment and the other insecurities of stationary working-class life. In terms of middle-class values, hedonism is self-defeating. But from a psychiatric point of view, for those who actually have little control of their position in the social and economic structure of modern society, it may very well aid acceptance of the situation. This is particularly true when it takes a religious form of expression. Certainly, hedonism and the associated trait of spontaneity seen in the old serpent-handlers form a very appropriate attitude toward life among old people who can no longer plan for the future.

In addition to being more hedonistic than members of the conventional church, the serpent-handlers are also more exhibitionistic. This exhibitionism and the related need for self-revelation are, of course, directly related to the religious practices of the serpent-handling church. But frankness, both about others and themselves, is typical of stationary working-class people in general. To a large extent, this explains the appeal of the Holiness churches. Ordinarily, their members have little to lose from frankness, since their status pretensions are less than those of the upwardly mobile working class, who are continually trying to present favorable images of themselves.

Because the young members of the conventional denomination are upwardly mobile, they tend to regard their elders as "old-fashioned," "stick-in-the-muds," and "ignorant." Naturally, this lack of respect from their children and grandchildren further depresses the sagging morale of the older conventional-church members. They respond resentfully to the tendency of the young "to think they know more than their elders." The result is a vicious circle of increasing alienation and depression among the older members of the conventional denomination.

Respect for Age

There appears to be much less psychological incompatibility between the old and the young serpent-handlers. This is partly because the old serpent-handlers manage to retain a youthful spontaneity in their approach to life. Then too, the young serpent-handlers do not take a superior attitude toward their elders. They admire their elders for their greater knowledge of the Bible, which both old and young accept as literally true. And they also admire their elders for their handling of serpents. The younger church members, who handle snakes much less often than the older members do, are much more likely to confess an ordinary, everyday fear of snakes—a fear that persists until overcome by strong religious emotion.

Furthermore, the young serpent-handlers do not expect to achieve higher socioeconomic status than their elders. In fact, several young men said they would be satisfied if they could accomplish as much. From the point of view of the stationary working class, many of the older serpent-handlers are quite well-off. They sometimes draw two pensions, one from Social Security and one from the United Mine Workers.

Religious serpent-handling, then—and all the other emotionalism of the Holiness churches that goes with it—serves a definite function in the lives of its adherents. It is a safety valve for many of the frustrations of life in present-day Appalachia. For the old, the serpent-handling religion helps soften the inevitability of poor health, illness, and death. For the young, with their poor educations and poor hopes of finding sound jobs, its promise of holiness is one of the few meaningful goals in a future dominated by the apparent inevitability of lifelong poverty and idleness.

May 1968

SUGGESTED READINGS

They Shall Take Up Serpents by Weston LaBarre (Minneapolis: University of Minnesota Press, 1962). A psychological interpretation of serpent-handling and its history.

"Ordeal by Serpents, Fire and Strychnine" by Berthold Schwarz, *Psychiatric Quarterly*, 1960, 405-429. The author personally observed more than 200 instances of serpent-handling.

The Small Sects in America by Elmert T. Clark (New York: Abingdon Press, 1959). An excellent account of the holiness movement, of which the serpent-handling sect is an offshoot.

Life and Religion in Southern Appalachia by W. D. Weatherford and Earl D. C. Brewer (New York: Friendship Press, 1962). The role of religion in the life of the rural poor in Appalachia.

The True Believer by Eric Hoffer (New York: Harper, 1951). This book explores the psychology and the sociology of the fanatic believer in a cause or movement.

Social Class in American Protestantism by N. J. Demerath III (Chicago: Rand McNally and Company, 1965). Chapters 1 and 2 contain a comparison of the chruch and the sect in American Protestantism.

"Sectarianism and Religious Sociation" by Peter L. Berger, *American Journal of Sociology* (Vol. 64, July 1958) analyzes the difference between sect and church.

"The Church-Sect Typology and Socio-Economic Status" by Russell R. Dynes, *American Sociological Review* (Vol. 20, Oct. 1955) relates sect membership to economic position.

Millhands and Preachers by Liston Pope (New Haven, Conn.: Yale University Press, 1942) is a study of the interaction between church, mill workers and mill owners during a labor dispute.

The Two Presidencies

Presidential power is greatest when directing military and foreign policy

AARON WILDAVSKY

SUGGESTED READINGS

The Common Defense by Samuel P. Huntington (New York: Columbia University Press, 1963). The best study of presidential participation in the making of defense policy.

Congress and the Presidency by Nelson W. Polsby (Englewood Cliffs, New Jersey: Prentice-Hall, 1965). A fine short study of executive-legislative relationships.

From Max Weber: Essays in Sociology edited by H. H. Gerth and C. Wright Mills (New York: Oxford University Press, 1946). Note Chapter VIII. Weber wrote the seminal essay on the nature and functions of the bureaucratic type of social organization.

The American Presidency by Clinton Rossiter (New York: Harcourt, Brace and World, 1956). Rossiter discusses the nature of the role of president, its powers and limitations, and modifications made to it by recent incumbents.

The Functions of the Executive by Chester I. Barnard (Cambridge, Mass.: Harvard University Press, 1938). An important essay on the problems of organization and authority, one of the first to deal with informal relations within the formal structure of an organization.

Studies in Leadership edited by Alvin W. Gouldner (New York: Harper and Row, 1950). In this anthology Gouldner tries to develop a typology of leadership within different situations; includes discussions of the tactics of leadership and ethical problems.

Leadership in Administration, A Sociological Interpretation by Phillip Selznick (Evanston, Ill.: Row, Peterson, 1957). Selznick traces the metamorphosis from organization to institution through the unifying force of leadership: "The executive becomes a statesman as he makes the transition from administrative management to institutional leadership."

The Organization Man by William H. Whyte (New York: Simon and Schuster, 1962). A popular account of the impact that life within large, formal organizations has on the values and activities of its executives.

The United States has one President, but it has two presidencies; one presidency is for domestic affairs, and the other is concerned with defense and foreign policy. Since World War II, Presidents have had much greater success in controlling the nation's defense and foreign policies than in dominating its domestic policies. Even Lyndon Johnson has seen his early record of victories in domestic legislation diminish as his concern with foreign affairs grows.

What powers does the President have to control defense and foreign policies and so completely overwhelm those who might wish to thwart him?

The President's normal problem with domestic policy is to get congressional support for the programs he prefers. In foreign affairs, in contrast, he can almost always get support for policies that he believes will protect the nation —but his problem is to find a viable policy.

Whoever they are, whether they begin by caring about foreign policy like Eisenhower and Kennedy or about domestic policies like Truman and Johnson, Presidents soon discover they have more policy preferences in domestic matters than in foreign policy. The Republican and Democratic parties possess a traditional roster of policies, which can easily be adopted by a new President—for example, he can be either for or against Medicare and aid to education. Since existing domestic policy usually changes in only small steps, Presidents find it relatively simple to make minor adjustments. However, although any President knows he supports foreign aid and NATO, the world outside changes much more rapidly than the nation inside—Presidents and their parties have no prior policies on Argentina and the Congo. The world has become a highly intractable place with a whirl of forces we cannot or do not know how to alter.

The Record of Presidential Control

It takes great crises, such as Roosevelt's hundred days in the midst of the depression, or the extraordinary majorities that Barry Goldwater's candidacy willed to Lyndon Johnson, for Presidents to succeed in controlling domestic policy. From the end of the 1930's to the present (what may roughly be called the modern era), Presidents have often been frustrated in their domestic programs. From 1938, when conservatives regrouped their forces, to the time of his death, Franklin Roosevelt did not get a single piece of significant domestic legislation passed. Truman lost out on most of his intense domestic preferences, except perhaps for housing. Since Eisenhower did not ask for much domestic legislation, he did not meet consistent defeat, yet he failed in his general policy of curtailing governmental commitments. Kennedy, of course, faced great difficulties with domestic legislation.

In the realm of foreign policy there has not been a single major issue on which Presidents, when they were serious and determined, have failed. The list of their victories is impressive: entry into the United Nations, the Marshall

Plan, NATO, the Truman Doctrine, the decisions to stay out of Indochina in 1954 and to intervene in Vietnam in the 1960's, aid to Poland and Yugoslavia, the test-ban treaty, and many more. Serious setbacks to the President in controlling foreign policy are extraordinary and unusual.

Table I, compiled from the Congressional Quarterly Service tabulation of presidential initiative and congressional response from 1948 through 1964, shows that Presidents have significantly better records in foreign and defense matters than in domestic policies. When refugees and immigration—which Congress considers primarily a domestic concern—are removed from the general foreign policy area, it is clear that Presidents prevail about 70 percent of the time in defense and foreign policy, compared with 40 percent in the domestic sphere.

World Events and Presidential Resources

Power in politics is control over governmental decisions. How does the President manage his control of foreign and defense policy? The answer does not reside in the greater constitutional power in foreign affairs that Presidents have possessed since the founding of the Republic. The answer lies in the changes that have taken place since 1945.

The number of nations with which the United States has diplomatic relations has increased from 53 in 1939 to 113 in 1966. But sheer numbers do not tell enough; the world has also become a much more dangerous place. However remote it may seem at times, our government must always be aware of the possibility of nuclear war.

TABLE I—Congressional Action on Presidential Proposals From 1948-1964.

Policy Area	Congressional Action % Pass	% Fail	Number of Proposals
Domestic policy (natural resources, labor, agriculture, taxes, etc.)	40.2	59.8	2499
Defense policy (defense, disarmament, manpower, misc.)	73.3	26.7	90
Foreign policy	58.5	41.5	655
Immigration, refugees	13.2	86.0	129
Treaties, general foreign relations, State Department, foreign aid	70.8	29.2	445

Source: Congressional Quarterly Service, *Congress and the Nation,* 1945-1964 (Washington, 1965)

Yet the mere existence of great powers with effective thermonuclear weapons would not, in and of itself, vastly increase our rate of interaction with most other nations. We see events in Assam or Burundi as important because they are also part of a larger worldwide contest, called the cold war, in which great powers are rivals for the control or support of other nations. Moreover, the reaction against the blatant isolationism of the 1930's has led to a concern with foreign policy that is worldwide in scope. We are interested in what happens everywhere because we see these events as connected with larger interests involving, at the worst, the possibility of ultimate destruction.

Given the overriding fact that the world is dangerous and that small causes are perceived to have potentially great

---

"In the realm of foreign policy there has not been a single major issue on which Presidents, when they were serious and determined, have failed."

---

effects in an unstable world, it follows that Presidents must be interested in relatively "small" matters. So they give Azerbaijan or Lebanon or Vietnam huge amounts of their time. Arthur Schlesinger, Jr., wrote of Kennedy that "in the first two months of his administration he probably spent more time on Laos than on anything else." Few failures in domestic policy, Presidents soon realize, could have as disastrous consequences as any one of dozens of mistakes in the international arena.

The result is that foreign policy concerns tend to drive out domestic policy. Except for occasional questions of domestic prosperity and for civil rights, foreign affairs have consistently higher priority for Presidents. Once, when trying to talk to President Kennedy about natural resources, Secretary of the Interior Stewart Udall remarked, "He's imprisoned by Berlin."

The importance of foreign affairs to Presidents is intensified by the increasing speed of events in the international arena. The event and its consequences follow closely on top of one another. The blunder at the Bay of Pigs is swiftly followed by the near catastrophe of the Cuban missile crisis. Presidents can no longer count on passing along their most difficult problems to their successors. They must expect to face the consequences of their actions—or failure to act—while still in office.

Domestic policy-making is usually based on experimental adjustments to an existing situation. Only a few decisions, such as those involving large dams, irretrievably commit future generations. Decisions in foreign affairs, however, are often perceived to be irreversible. This is expressed, for example, in the fear of escalation or the various "spiral" or "domino" theories of international conflict.

If decisions are perceived to be both important and irreversible, there is every reason for Presidents to devote a great deal of resources to them. Presidents have to be oriented toward the future in the use of their resources. They serve a fixed term in office, and they cannot automatically count on support from the populace, Congress, or the administrative apparatus. They have to be careful, therefore, to husband their resources for pressing future needs. But because the consequences of events in foreign affairs are potentially more grave, faster to manifest themselves, and

"... and there's a bad crevasse just past this ridge ..."
Copyright 1961, St. Louis Post-Dispatch reproduced by courtesy of William H. Mauldin & WIL-JO ASSOCIATES, INC.

less easily reversible than in domestic affairs, Presidents are more willing to use up their resources.

The Power to Act

Their formal powers to commit resources in foreign affairs and defense are vast. Particularly important is their power as Commander-in-Chief to move troops. Faced with situations like the invasion of South Korea or the emplacement of missiles in Cuba, fast action is required. Presidents possess both the formal power to act and the knowledge that elites and the general public expect them to act. Once they have committed American forces, it is difficult for Congress or anyone else to alter the course of events. The Dominican venture is a recent case in point.

Presidential discretion in foreign affairs also makes it difficult (though not impossible) for Congress to restrict their actions. Presidents can use executive agreements instead of treaties, enter into tacit agreements instead of written ones, and otherwise help create *de facto* situations not easily reversed. Presidents also have far greater ability than anyone else to obtain information on developments abroad through the Departments of State and Defense. The need for secrecy in some aspects of foreign and defense policy further restricts the ability of others to compete with Presidents. These things are all well known. What is not so generally appreciated is the growing presidential ability to *use* information to achieve goals.

In the past Presidents were amateurs in military strategy. They could not even get much useful advice outside of the military. As late as the 1930's the number of people outside the military establishment who were professionally engaged in the study of defense policy could be numbered on the fingers. Today there are hundreds of such men. The rise of the defense intellectuals has given the President of the United States enhanced ability to control defense policy. He is no longer dependent on the military for advice. He can choose among defense intellectuals from the research corporations and the academies for alternative sources of advice. He can install these men in his own office. He can play them off against each other or use them to extend spheres of coordination.

Even with these advisers, however, Presidents and Secretaries of Defense might still be too bewildered by the complexity of nuclear situations to take action—unless they had an understanding of the doctrine and concepts of deterrence. But knowledge of doctrine about deterrence has been widely diffused; it can be picked up by any intelligent person who will read books or listen to enough hours of conversation. Whether or not the doctrine is good is a separate question; the point is that civilians can feel they understand what is going on in defense policy. Perhaps the most extraordinary feature of presidential action during the Cuban missile crisis was the degree to which the Commander-in-Chief of the Armed Forces insisted on controlling even the smallest moves. From the positioning of ships to the methods of boarding, to the precise words and actions to be taken by individual soldiers and sailors, the President and his civilian advisers were in control.

Although Presidents have rivals for power in foreign affairs, the rivals do not usually succeed. Presidents prevail not only because they may have superior resources but because their potential opponents are weak, divided, or believe that they should not control foreign policy. Let us consider the potential rivals—the general citizenry, special interest groups, the Congress, the military, the so-called military-industrial complex, and the State Department.

Competitors for Control of Policy

■ THE PUBLIC. The general public is much more dependent on Presidents in foreign affairs than in domestic matters. While many people know about the impact of social security and Medicare, few know about politics in Malawi. So it is not surprising that people expect the President to act in foreign affairs and reward him with their confidence. Gallup Polls consistently show that presidential popularity rises after he takes action in a crisis—whether the action is disastrous as in the Bay of Pigs or successful as in the Cuban missile crisis. Decisive action, such as the bombing of oil fields near Haiphong, resulted in a sharp (though temporary) increase in Johnson's popularity.

The Vietnam situation illustrates another problem of

public opinion in foreign affairs: it is extremely difficult to get operational policy directions from the general public. It took a long time before any sizable public interest in the subject developed. Nothing short of the large scale involvement of American troops under fire probably could have brought about the current high level of concern. Yet this relatively well developed popular opinion is difficult to interpret. While a majority appear to support President Johnson's policy, it appears that they could easily be persuaded to withdraw from Vietnam if the administration changed its line. Although a sizable majority would support various initiatives to end the war, they would seemingly be appalled if this action led to Communist encroachments elsewhere in Southeast Asia. (See "The President, the Polls, and Vietnam" by Seymour Martin Lipset, *Trans*-action, Sept/Oct 1966.)

Although Presidents lead opinion in foreign affairs, they know they will be held accountable for the consequences of their actions. President Johnson has maintained a large commitment in Vietnam. His popularity shoots up now and again in the midst of some imposing action. But the fact that a body of citizens do not like the war comes back to damage his overall popularity. We will support your initiatives, the people seem to say, but we will reserve the right to punish you (or your party) if we do not like the results.

■ SPECIAL INTEREST GROUPS. Opinions are easier to gauge in domestic affairs because, for one thing, there is a stable structure of interest groups that covers virtually all matters of concern. The farm, labor, business, conservation, veteran, civil rights, and other interest groups provide cues when a proposed policy affects them. Thus people who identify with these groups may adopt their views. But in foreign policy matters the interest group structure is weak, unstable, and thin rather than dense. In many matters affecting Africa and Asia, for example, it is hard to think of well-known interest groups. While ephemeral groups arise from time to time to support or protest particular policies, they usually disappear when the immediate problem is resolved. In contrast, longer-lasting elite groups like the Foreign Policy Association and Council on Foreign Relations are composed of people of diverse views; refusal to take strong positions on controversial matters is a condition of their continued viability.

The strongest interest groups are probably the ethnic associations whose members have strong ties with a homeland, as in Poland or Cuba, so they are rarely activated simultaneously on any specific issue. They are most effective when most narrowly and intensely focused—as in the fierce pressure from Jews to recognize the state of Israel. But their relatively small numbers limits their significance to Presidents in the vastly more important general foreign policy picture—as continued aid to the Arab countries shows. Moreover, some ethnic groups may conflict on significant issues such as American acceptance of the Oder-Neisse line separating Poland from what is now East Germany.

■ THE CONGRESS. Congressmen also exercise power in foreign affairs. Yet they are ordinarily not serious competitors with the President because they follow a self-denying ordinance. They do not think it is their job to determine the nation's defense policies. Lewis A. Dexter's extensive interviews with members of the Senate Armed Services Committee, who might be expected to want a voice in defense policy, reveal that they do not desire for men like themselves to run the nation's defense establishment. Aside from a few specific conflicts among the armed services which allow both the possibility and desirabliity of direct intervention, the Armed Services Committee constitutes a sort of real estate committee dealing with the regional economic consequences of the location of military facilities.

The congressional appropriations power is potentially a significant resource, but circumstances since the end of World War II have tended to reduce its effectiveness. The appropriations committees and Congress itself might make their will felt by refusing to allot funds unless basic policies were altered. But this has not happened. While Congress makes its traditional small cuts in the military budget, Presidents have mostly found themselves warding off congressional attempts to increase specific items still further.

Most of the time, the administration's refusal to spend has not been seriously challenged. However, there have been occasions when individual legislators or committees have been influential. Senator Henry Jackson in his campaign (with the aid of colleagues on the Joint Committee on Atomic Energy) was able to gain acceptance for the Polaris weapons system and Senator Arthur H. Vandenberg played a part in determining the shape of the Marshall Plan and so on. The few congressmen who are expert in defense policy act, as Samuel P. Huntington says, largely as lobbyists with the executive branch. It is apparently more fruitful for these congressional experts to use their resources in order to get a hearing from the executive than to work on other congressmen.

When an issue involves the actual use or threat of violence, it takes a great deal to convince congressmen not to follow the President's lead. James Robinson's tabulation of foreign and defense policy issues from the late 1930's to 1961 (Table II) shows dominant influence by Congress in only one case out of seven—the 1954 decision not to intervene with armed force in Indochina. In that instance President Eisenhower deliberately sounded out congressional opinion and, finding it negative, decided not to intervene —against the advice of Admiral Radford, chairman of the Joint Chiefs of Staff. This attempt to abandon responsibility did not succeed, as the years of American involvement demonstrate.

■ THE MILITARY. The outstanding feature of the military's participation in making defense policy is their amazing weakness. Whether the policy decisions involve the size of the armed forces, the choice of weapons systems, the total defense budget, or its division into components, the military have not prevailed. Let us take budgetary decisions as representative of the key choices to be made in defense policy. Since the end of World War II the military has not been able to achieve significant (billion dollar) increases in appropriations by their own efforts. Under Truman and Eisenhower defense budgets were determined by what Huntington calls the remainder method: the two Presidents estimated revenues, decided what they could spend on domestic matters, and the remainder was assigned to defense. The usual controversy was between some military and congressional groups supporting much larger expenditures while the President and his executive allies refused. A typical case, involving the desire of the Air Force to increase the number of groups of planes is described by Huntington in *The Common Defense*:

> The FY [fiscal year] 1949 budget provided 48 groups. After the Czech coup, the Administration yielded and backed an Air Force of 55 groups in its spring rearmament program. Congress added additional funds to aid Air Force expansion to 70 groups. The Administration refused to utilize them, however, and in the gathering economy wave of the summer and fall of 1948, the Air Force goal was cut back again to 48 groups. In 1949 the House of Representatives picked up the challenge and appropriated funds for 58 groups. The President impounded the money. In June, 1950, the Air Force had 48 groups.

The great increases in the defense budget were due far more to Stalin and modern technology than to the military. The Korean War resulted in an increase from 12 to 44 billions and much of the rest followed Sputnik and the huge costs of missile programs. Thus modern technology and international conflict put an end to the one major effort to subordinate foreign affairs to domestic policies through the budget.

It could be argued that the President merely ratifies the decisions made by the military and their allies. If the military and/or Congress were united and insistent on defense policy, it would certainly be difficult for Presidents to resist these forces. But it is precisely the disunity of the military that has characterized the entire postwar period. Indeed, the military have not been united on any major matter of defense policy. The apparent unity of the Joint Chiefs of Staff turns out to be illusory. The vast majority of their recommendations appear to be unanimous and are accepted by the Secretary of Defense and the President. But this facade of unity can only be achieved by methods that vitiate the impact of the recommendations. Genuine disagreements are hidden by vague language that commits no one to anything. Mutually contradictory plans are strung together so everyone appears to get something, but nothing is decided. Since it is impossible to agree on really important matters, all sorts of trivia are brought in to make a record of agreement. While it may be true, as Admiral Denfield, a former Chief of Naval Operations, said, that "On nine-tenths of the

TABLE II—Congressional Involvement in Foreign and Defense Policy Decisions

Issue	Congressional Involvement (High, Low, None)	Initiator (Congress or Executive)	Predominant Influence (Congress or Executive)	Legislation or Resolution (Yes or No)	Violence at Stake (Yes or No)	Decision Time (Long or Short)
Neutrality Legislation, the 1930's	High	Exec	Cong	Yes	No	Long
Lend-Lease, 1941	High	Exec	Exec	Yes	Yes	Long
Aid to Russia, 1941	Low	Exec	Exec	No	No	Long
Repeal of Chinese Exclusion, 1943	High	Cong	Cong	Yes	No	Long
Fulbright Resolution, 1943	High	Cong	Cong	Yes	No	Long
Building the Atomic Bomb, 1944	Low	Exec	Exec	Yes	Yes	Long
Foreign Services Act of 1946	High	Exec	Exec	Yes	No	Long
Truman Doctrine, 1947	High	Exec	Exec	Yes	No	Long
The Marshall Plan, 1947-48	High	Exec	Exec	Yes	No	Long
Berlin Airlift, 1948	None	Exec	Exec	No	Yes	Long
Vandenberg Resolution, 1948	High	Exec	Cong	Yes	No	Long
North Atlantic Treaty, 1947-49	High	Exec	Exec	Yes	No	Long
Korean Decision, 1950	None	Exec	Exec	No	Yes	Short
Japanese Peace Treaty, 1952	High	Exec	Exec	Yes	No	Long
Bohlen Nomination, 1953	High	Exec	Exec	Yes	No	Long
Indo-China, 1954	High	Exec	Cong	No	Yes	Short
Formosan Resolution, 1955	High	Exec	Exec	Yes	Yes	Long
International Finance Corporation, 1956	Low	Exec	Exec	Yes	No	Long
Foreign Aid, 1957	High	Exec	Exec	Yes	No	Long
Reciprocal Trade Agreements, 1958	High	Exec	Exec	Yes	No	Long
Monroney Resolution, 1958	High	Cong	Cong	Yes	No	Long
Cuban Decision, 1961	Low	Exec	Exec	No	Yes	Long

Source: James A. Robinson, *Congress and Foreign Policy-Making* (Homewood, Illinois, 1962)

BULLDOGGER

Reproduced by courtesy of William H. Mauldin & WILL-JO ASSOCIATES, INC.

matters that come before them the Joint Chiefs of Staff reach agreement themselves," the vastly more important truth is that "normally the *only* disputes are on strategic concepts, the size and composition of forces, and budget matters."

■ MILITARY-INDUSTRIAL. But what about the fabled military-industrial complex? If the military alone is divided and weak, perhaps the giant industrial firms that are so dependent on defense contracts play a large part in making policy.

First, there is an important distinction between the questions "Who will get a given contract?" and "What will our defense policy be?" It is apparent that different answers may be given to these quite different questions. There are literally tens of thousands of defense contractors. They may compete vigorously for business. In the course of this competition, they may wine and dine military officers, use retired generals, seek intervention by their congressmen, place ads in trade journals, and even contribute to political campaigns. The famous TFX controversy—should General Dynamics or Boeing get the expensive contract?—is a larger than life example of the pressures brought to bear in search of lucrative contracts.

But neither the TFX case nor the usual vigorous competition for contracts is involved with the making of substantive defense policy. Vital questions like the size of the defense budget, the choice of strategic programs, massive retaliation vs. a counter-city strategy, and the like were far beyond the policy aims of any company. Industrial firms, then, do not control such decisions, nor is there much evidence that they actually try. No doubt a precipitous and drastic rush to disarmament would meet with opposition from industrial firms among other interests. However, there has never been a time when any significant element in the government considered a disarmament policy to be feasible.

It may appear that industrial firms had no special reason to concern themselves with the government's stance on defense because they agree with the national consensus on resisting communism, maintaining a large defense establishment, and rejecting isolationism. However, this hypothesis about the climate of opinion explains everything and nothing. For every policy that is adopted or rejected can be explained away on the grounds that the cold war climate of opinion dictated what happened. Did the United States fail to intervene with armed force in Vietnam in 1954? That must be because the climate of opinion was against it. Did the United States send troops to Vietnam in the 1960's? That must be because the cold war climate demanded it. If the United States builds more missiles, negotiates a test-ban treaty, intervenes in the Dominican Republic, fails to intervene in a dozen other situations, all these actions fit the hypothesis by definition. The argument is reminiscent of those who defined the Soviet Union as permanently hostile and therefore interpreted increases of Soviet troops as menacing and decreases of troop strength as equally sinister.

If the growth of the military establishment is not directly equated with increasing military control of defense policy, the extraordinary weakness of the professional soldier still requires explanation. Huntington has written about how major military leaders were seduced in the Truman and Eisenhower years into believing that they should bow to the judgment of civilians that the economy could not stand much larger military expenditures. Once the size of the military pie was accepted as a fixed constraint, the military services were compelled to put their major energies into quarreling with one another over who should get the larger share. Given the natural rivalries of the military and their traditional acceptance of civilian rule, the President and his advisers—who could claim responsibility for the broader picture of reconciling defense and domestic policies—had the upper hand. There are, however, additional explanations to be considered.

The dominant role of the congressional appropriations committee is to be guardian of the treasury. This is manifested in the pride of its members in cutting the President's budget. Thus it was difficult to get this crucial committee to recommend even a few hundred million increase in defense; it was practically impossible to get them to consider the several billion jump that might really have made a difference. A related budgetary matter concerned the planning, programming, and budgeting system introduced by Secretary of Defense McNamara. For if the defense budget contained major categories that crisscrossed the services, only the Secretary of Defense could put it together. Whatever the other debatable consequences of program budgeting, its major consequence was to grant power to the secretary and his civilian advisers.

The subordination of the military through program budgeting is just one symptom of a more general weakness of the military. In the past decade the military has suffered a lack of intellectual skills appropriate to the nuclear age. For no one has (and no one wants) direct experience with nuclear war. So the usual military talk about being the only people to have combat experience is not very impressive. Instead, the imaginative creation of possible future wars—in order to avoid them—requires people with a high capacity for abstract thought combined with the ability to manipulate symbols using quantitative methods. West Point has not produced many such men.

■ THE STATE DEPARTMENT. Modern Presidents expect the State Department to carry out their policies. John F. Kennedy felt that State was "in some particular sense 'his' department." If a Secretary of State forgets this, as was apparently the case with James Byrnes under Truman, a President may find another man. But the State Department, especially the Foreign Service, is also a highly professional organization with a life and momentum of its own. If a President does not push hard, he may find his preferences somehow dissipated in time. Arthur Schlesinger fills his book on Kennedy with laments about the bureaucratic inertia and recalcitrance of the State Department.

> "The outstanding feature of the military's participation in making defense policy is their amazing weakness.... The great increases in the defense budget were due far more to Stalin and modern technology than to the military."

Yet Schlesinger's own account suggests that State could not ordinarily resist the President. At one point, he writes of "the President, himself, increasingly the day-to-day director of American foreign policy." On the next page, we learn that "Kennedy dealt personally with almost every aspect of policy around the globe. He knew more about certain areas than the senior officials at State and probably called as many issues to their attention as they did to his." The President insisted on his way in Laos. He pushed through his policy on the Congo against strong opposition with the State Department. Had Kennedy wanted to get a great deal more initiative out of the State Department, as Schlesinger insists, he could have replaced the Secretary of State, a man who did not command special support in the Democratic party or in Congress. It may be that Kennedy wanted too strongly to run his own foreign policy. Dean Rusk may have known far better than Schlesinger that the one thing Kennedy did not want was a man who might rival him in the field of foreign affairs.

Schlesinger comes closest to the truth when he writes that "the White House could always win any battle it chose over the [Foreign] Service; but the prestige and proficiency of the Service limited the number of battles any White House would find it profitable to fight." When the President knew what he wanted, he got it. When he was doubtful and perplexed, he sought good advice and frequently did not get that. But there is no evidence that the people on his staff came up with better ideas .The real problem may have been a lack of good ideas anywhere. Kennedy undoubtedly encouraged his staff to prod the State Department. But the President was sufficiently cautious not to push so hard that he got his way when he was not certain what that way should be. In this context Kennedy appears to have played his staff off against elements in the State Department.

The growth of a special White House staff to help Presidents in foreign affairs expresses their need for assistance, their refusal to rely completely on the regular executive agencies, and their ability to find competent men. The deployment of this staff must remain a presidential prerogative, however, if its members are to serve Presidents and not their opponents. Whenever critics do not like existing foreign and defense policies, they are likely to complain that the White House staff is screening out divergent views from the President's attention. Naturally, the critics recommend introducing many more different viewpoints. If the critics could maneuver the President into counting hands all day ("on the one hand and on the other"), they would make it impossible for him to act. Such a viewpoint is also congenial to those who believe that action rather than inaction is the greatest present danger in foreign policy. But Presidents resolutely refuse to become prisoners of their advisers by using them as other people would like. Presidents remain in control of their staff as well as of major foreign policy decisions.

How Complete Is the Control?

Some analysts say that the success of Presidents in controlling foreign policy decisions is largely illusory. It is achieved, they say, by anticipating the reactions of others, and eliminating proposals that would run into severe opposition. There is some truth in this objection. In politics, where transactions are based on a high degree of mutual interdependence, what others may do has to be taken into account. But basing presidential success in foreign and defense policy on anticipated reactions suggests a static situation which does not exist. For if Presidents propose only those policies that would get support in Congress, and Congress opposes them only when it knows that it can muster overwhelming strength, there would never be any conflict. Indeed, there might never be any action.

How can "anticipated reaction" explain the conflict over policies like the Marshall Plan and the test-ban treaty in which severe opposition was overcome only by strenuous efforts? Furthermore, why doesn't "anticipated reaction" work in domestic affairs? One would have to argue that for some reason presidential perception of what would be successful is consistently confused on domestic issues and most always accurate on major foreign policy issues. But the role of "anticipated reactions" should be greater in the more familiar domestic situations, which provide a backlog of experience for forecasting, than in foreign policy with many novel situations such as the Suez crisis or the Rhodesian affair.

Are there significant historical examples which might refute the thesis of presidential control of foreign policy? Foreign aid may be a case in point. For many years, Presidents have struggled to get foreign aid appropriations because of hostility from public and congressional opinion. Yet several billion dollars a year are appropriated regularly despite the evident unpopularity of the program. In the aid programs to Communist countries like Poland and Yugoslavia, the Congress attaches all sorts of restrictions to the aid, but Presidents find ways of getting around them.

What about the example of recognition of Communist China? The sentiment of the country always has been against recognizing Red China or admitting it to the United Nations. But have Presidents wanted to recognize Red China and been hamstrung by opposition? The answer, I suggest, is a qualified "no." By the time recognition of Red China might have become a serious issue for the Truman administration, the war in Korea effectively precluded its consideration. There is no evidence that President Eisenhower or Secretary Dulles ever thought it wise to recognize Red China or help admit her to the United Nations. The Kennedy administration viewed the matter as not of major importance and, considering the opposition, moved cautiously in suggesting change. Then came the war in Vietnam. If the advantages for foreign policy had been perceived to be much higher, then Kennedy or Johnson might have proposed changing American policy toward recognition of Red China.

One possible exception, in the case of Red China, however, does not seem sufficient to invalidate the general thesis that Presidents do considerably better in getting their way in foreign and defense policy than in domestic policies.

The World Influence

The forces impelling Presidents to be concerned with the widest range of foreign and defense policies also affect the ways in which they calculate their power stakes. As Kennedy used to say, "Domestic policy . . . can only defeat us; foreign policy can kill us."

It no longer makes sense for Presidents to "play politics" with foreign and defense policies. In the past, Presidents might have thought that they could gain by prolonged delay or by not acting at all. The problem might disappear or be passed on to their successors. Presidents must now expect to pay the high costs themselves if the world situation deteriorates. The advantages of pursuing a policy that is viable in the world, that will not blow up on Presidents or their fellow citizens, far outweigh any temporary political disadvantages accrued in supporting an initially unpopular policy. Compared with domestic affairs, Presidents engaged in world politics are immensely more concerned with meeting problems on their own terms. Who supports and opposes a policy, though a matter of considerable interest, does not assume the crucial importance that it does in domestic affairs. The best policy Presidents can find is also the best politics.

The fact that there are numerous foreign and defense policy situations competing for a President's attention means that it is worthwhile to organize political activity in order to affect his agenda. For if a President pays more attention to certain problems he may develop different preferences; he may seek and receive different advice; his new calculations may lead him to devote greater resources to seeking a solution. Interested congressmen may exert influence not by directly determining a presidential decision, but indirectly by making it costly for a President to avoid reconsidering the basis for his action. For example, citizen groups, such as those concerned with a change in China policy, may have an impact simply by keeping their proposals on the public agenda. A President may be compelled to reconsider a problem even though he could not overtly be forced to alter the prevailing policy.

In foreign affairs we may be approaching the stage where knowledge is power. There is a tremendous receptivity to good ideas in Washington. Most anyone who can present a convincing rationale for dealing with a hard world finds a ready audience. The best way to convince Presidents to follow a desired policy is to show that it might work. A man like McNamara thrives because he performs; he comes up with answers he can defend. It is, to be sure, extremely difficult to devise good policies or to predict their consequences accurately. Nor is it easy to convince others that a given policy is superior to other alternatives. But it is the way to influence with Presidents. For if they are convinced that the current policy is best, the likelihood of gaining sufficient force to compel a change is quite small. The man who can build better foreign policies will find Presidents beating a path to his door.

December 1966

Black Powerlessness in Chicago

HAROLD M. BARON

With Harriet Stulman, Richard Rothstein, and Rennard Davis

Until recently, the three principal targets of the civil-rights movement in the North were discrimination and inferior conditions in (1) housing for Negroes, (2) jobs for Negroes, and (3) the education of Negroes. But after failing to bring about major changes, many Negroes realized that one reason the status quo in housing, jobs, and education continues is that *the black community lacks control over decision-making.* Negroes remain second-class citizens partly because of the discrimination of individual whites, but mainly because of the way whites control the major institutions of our society. And therefore the fourth major goal of Negro organizations and the civil-rights movement has become the acquisition of power.

It was because of this concern with power for black people that, more than two years ago, the Chicago Urban League—a social-welfare organization dedicated to changing institutions so as to achieve full racial equality—started to study the decision-making apparatus in Cook County, Ill., and particularly how it affects or ignores Negro citizens. (Cook County takes in the city of Chicago, and two-thirds of the population of the surrounding suburban ring included in the Chicago Standard Metropolitan Statistical area.) Among the questions we posed were:

■ What is the extent of Negro exclusion from policy-making positions in Chicago?

■ Where Negroes *are* in policy-making positions, what type of positions are these, and where are Negroes in greatest number and authority?

- Do Negroes in policy-making positions represent the interests of the Negro community? and
- How might an increase in the percentage of Negro policy-makers affect socio-economic conditions for Negroes in general?

What we found was that in 1965 some 20 percent of the people in Cook County were Negro, and 28 percent of the people in Chicago were Negro. Yet the representation of Negroes in policy-making positions was minimal. Of the top 10,997 policy-making positions in the major Cook County institutions included in our study, Negroes occupied only 285—or 2.6 percent.

In government (see Table 1), out of a total of 1088 policy-making positions Negroes held just 58. This 5 percent is about one-fourth of the percentage of Negroes in the total county population. Of the 364 elective posts in the survey, however, Negroes occupied 29, or 8 percent, indicating that the franchise has helped give Negroes representation. Yet Negroes had the most positions, percentagewise, on appointed supervisory boards, such as the Board of Education and the Chicago Housing Authority. There they occupied 10 of the 77 policy-making positions, or about 13 percent.

Negroes were better represented on appointed supervisory boards and in elected (nonjudicial) offices than they were in local administrative positions, or in important federal jobs based in Chicago. Thus, Negroes held 12 percent of the nonjudicial elected posts in Chicago's government, but only a little over 1 percent of the appointive policy-making positions in the city administration. The same anomaly appears at the federal level. There is one Negro out of the 13 U.S. Congressmen from Cook County (8 percent), but Negroes held only one out of 31 Presidential appointments (3 percent), and eight of the 368 top federal civil-service posts (2 percent).

Nonetheless, Negroes have—proportionately—two-and-half-times as many important posts in the public sector as they have in the private sector. As Table 2 indicates, Negroes are virtually barred from policy-making positions in the large organizations that dominate the private institutions in the Chicago area. Out of a total of 9909 positions, Negroes fill a mere 227. This 2 percent representation is only one-tenth of the proportionate Negro population.

The whitest form of policy-making in Chicago is in the control of economic enterprises. Out of 6838 positions identified in business corporations, Negroes held only 42 (six-tenths of 1 percent). Thirty-five of these were in insurance, where Negroes occupy 6 percent of the 533 posts. But all 35 were in two all-Negro insurance firms. The other seven positions were in four smaller banks. In banks in general, Negroes occupied three-tenths of 1 percent of the policy posts. There were no Negro policy-makers at all in manufacturing, communications, transportation, utilities, and trade corporations.

Out of the 372 companies we studied, the Negro-owned insurance companies were the only ones dominated by blacks (see Table 3). And if we had used the same stringent criteria for banks and insurance companies that we used for nonfinancial institutions, there would have been no black policy-makers in the business sector at all.

Now, amazingly enough, Chicago has proportionately more Negro-controlled businesses, larger than neighborhood operations, than any other major city in the North. Therefore, similar surveys in other Northern metropolitan areas would turn up an even smaller percentage of Negro policy-makers in the business world.

The legal profession, represented by corporate law firms, had no Negroes at high policy levels. We are convinced that the same situation would be found in other professions, such as advertising and engineering.

The very prestigious universities—the University of Chicago, Northwestern University, Loyola University, DePaul University, Roosevelt University, the Illinois Institute of Technology, and the University of Illinois (the only public university of the seven)—had a negligible 1 percent Negro representation. Most of

THE EXCLUSION OF NEGROES FROM GOVERNMENT
Policy-Making Positions in the
Cook County Public Sector (1965) (Table 1)

	Policy-Making Positions	Positions Held by Negroes	Percent
1. Elected Officials			
U.S. House of Representatives	13	1	8
State Legislature	120	10	8
Cook County—nonjudicial	34	3	9
Chicago—nonjudicial	59	7	12
Cook County—judicial	138	8	6
Total:	364	29	8
2. Appointive Supervisory Boards			
Total:	77	10	13
3. Local Administrative Positions			
City of Chicago	156	2	1
Chicago Board of Education	72	7	9
Metropolitan Sanitary District	7	0	0
Cook County Government	13	1	8
Total:	248	10	4
4. Federal Government			
Civil Service	368	8	2
Presidential Appointments	31	1	3
Total:	399	9	2
Grand Total:	1088	58	5

THE EXCLUSION OF NEGROES FROM PRIVATE INSTITUTIONS
Policy-Making Positions in the Cook County Private Sector (1965) (Table 2)

	Policy-Making Positions	Positions Held by Negroes	Percent
1. Business Corporations			
Banks	2258	7	*
Insurance	533	35	6
Nonfinancial Corporations	4047	0	0
Total:	6838	42	*
2. Legal Profession			
Total:	757	0	0
3. Universities**			
Total:	380	5	1
4. Voluntary Organizations			
Business & Professional	324	3	1
Welfare & Religious	791	69	9
Total	1115	72	6
5. Labor Unions			
Internationals	94	15	16
District Councils	211	20	9
Locals	514	73	14
Total:	819	108	13
Grand Total:	9909	227	2
Grand Total for Public & Private Sectors:	10997	285	2

* Below 1 percent.
** Includes the University of Illinois, which is a public body.

these universities had few Negro students, faculty members, or administrators. Five of the seven had no Negro policy-makers. The University of Illinois had one. Roosevelt University, the sole institution that had a number of Negroes at the top, was the newest, and the one with the *least* public support. When this university was founded, its leaders had made a forthright stand on racial questions and a firm commitment to liberal principles.

We included these major universities in our survey because other institutions—public and private—have been placing increasingly greater value on them. Every year hundreds of millions of dollars in endowment and operating funds are given to the Chicago-area schools. After all, their research activities, and their training of skilled personnel, are considered a key to the region's economic growth. One indication of the tremendous influence these universities have is that they have determined the nature of urban renewal more than any other institutional group in Chicago (aside from the city government). Without a doubt, the universities have real—not nominal—power. And perhaps it is a reflection of this real power that only five out of 380 policy-making positions in these universities are held by Negroes.

The exclusion of Negroes from the private sector carries over to its voluntary organizations: Negroes are found in only 1 percent of the posts there. It is in the voluntary associations that it is easiest to make symbolic concessions to the black community by giving token representation, yet even here Negroes were underrepresented—which highlights the fundamental norms of the entire sector.

The sectors and individual groups in the Chicago area with the highest Negro representation were those with a Negro constituency—elective offices, supervisory boards, labor unions, and religious and welfare organizations. These four groups accounted for 216 of the posts held by Negroes, or 75 percent, although these four groups have only 19 percent of all the policy-making positions we studied. Labor unions had a larger percentage—13 percent—than any other institution in the private sector. In welfare and religious organizations, whose constituents were often largely Negro, Negroes occupied 8 percent of the positions, the same percentage of the elected public offices they held.

Now, either the black constituency elected the Negroes directly (in the case of elective offices and trade unions); or the Negroes were appointed to posts in an operation whose clients were largely Negro (principal of a Negro school, for example); or Negroes were given token representation on bodies that had a broad public purpose (like religious organizations).

THE EXCLUSION OF NEGROES FROM PRIVATE ESTABLISHMENTS
Percentage of Negro Policy-Makers in the Cook County Private Sector by Establishment (1965) (Table 3)

	Total Establishments	None	1-5%	6-15%	16-50%	51%+
1. Business Corporations						
Banks	102	98	0	4	0	0
Insurance	30	28	0	0	0	2
Nonfinancial Corporations	240	240	0	0	0	0
2. Legal Professions	54	54	0	0	0	0
3. Universities*	7	5	0	2	0	0
4. Voluntary Organizations						
Business & Professional	5	3	2	0	0	0
Welfare & Religious	14	2	4	7	1	0
5. Labor Unions						
Internationals	4	0	1	1	2	0
District Councils	23	13	0	5	5	0
Locals	33	14	2	8	7	2
Total:	512	457	9	27	15	4

* Includes the University of Illinois, which is a public body.

By "token representation," we mean—following James Q. Wilson—that "he is a man chosen because a Negro is 'needed' in order to legitimate [but not direct] whatever decisions are made by the agency."

Of the three ways a black constituency had of getting itself represented, the most important was the first. The statistics clearly show the importance of the Negro vote. The elected political offices and the elected trade-union offices account for only 11 percent of all the policy-making positions in Cook County. Yet almost half of all the Negro policy-makers were found in these two areas—137 out of 285.

Nonetheless, even in the major areas where Negro representation was the greatest—labor unions, elective offices, supervisory boards, and religious and welfare organizations—many institutions still excluded Negroes from positions of authority.

There are, of course, few Negroes in the building-trade unions, most of which bar Negroes from membership. Only two out of the 12 building-trade-union organizations we studied had even one Negro in a decisive slot. These two Negroes made up a mere one and a half percent of the policy-making positions in the building-trade unions.

The greatest degree of black representation was found in the former C.I.O. industrial unions. Only one-fourth of these units in the survey totally excluded Negroes from leadership. In almost half, the percentage of Negro policy-makers was over 15 percent—which is above token levels.

The former A.F. of L. unions (not including those in the building trades) had a higher rate of exclusion than those of the C.I.O. Two-fifths of these A.F. of L. unions had no Negroes at all in policy-making posts. But one-third of this group had leaderships that were 15 percent or more Negro. And the only two black-controlled locals large enough to be included in this study were in A.F. of L. unions.

In elective offices, the Negro vote certainly does give Negroes some representation—though far below their proportionate number. In public administration, however, where advancement to policy-making offices comes through appointment and influence, Negroes are all but excluded from decisive posts, at both the federal and local levels. Although a very high percentage of all Negro professionals are in public service, they do not reach the top.

The only major governmental operation that had a goodly number of Negroes at the upper level of the bureaucratic hierarchy was the public-school system. Nine percent of the top positions were occupied by Negroes. This unique situation is the result of some fairly recent appointments, made as concessions after an intense civil-rights campaign directed at the Chicago Board of Education. In this instance, one can

Ben Fernandez

Whites in a Polish neighborhood of Chicago demonstrating against Negroes. The authors say that institutional racism is more potent than the racism of individual whites.

consider these civil-rights actions as a proxy for Negro votes. Still, this high-level representation in the Chicago school hierarchy did not seem to reflect any uniform policy of including Negroes in management. At the level of principalship that was not included as a policy-making position in this study, only 3 percent of the positions were occupied by blacks.

The voluntary welfare and religious associations that were sufficiently important to be included in the study usually had at least a few Negro policy-makers.

Negroes & Mobsters

The exclusion of Negroes from important posts in Chicago is not limited to legitimate spheres of activity. Thirty years ago, gambling was one of the few areas in which Negroes held tangible power in Chicago. Today, Negroes have lost even this.

Although the Syndicate, with its billion-dollar-a-year Chicago operation, was not included in our formal survey, it is worthwhile noting the Chicago Crime Commission's data on this powerful, influential organization. There were no Negroes among the top 13 leaders in the Syndicate; and while five Negroes were on the Crime Commission's 1967 list of 216 major and minor syndicate members, only one is reputed to have even minor authority. As the *Wall Street Journal* has noted, in the rackets as in legitimate business, Negroes are effectively barred from the executive suite.

Only two out of 14 bodies had no Negroes in policy positions (see Table 3), while four organizations had token representation—below 5 percent. None had a Negro majority in the key posts. Only the Chicago Urban League (with 43 percent) had Negroes in more than 15 percent of its policy slots. If individual religious denominations had been among the organizations counted in the survey, there would have been some black-dominated groups. As it was, Negro representation in the United Protestant Federation, which *was* included, came largely from the traditionally Negro denominations. It is of interest to note that, in recent years, Protestant groups have provided some of the few instances in which Negroes have been elected to important offices by a constituency that was overwhelmingly white.

Not only were Negroes grossly underrepresented in Chicago's policy-making posts, but even where represented they had less power than white policy-makers. The fact is that *the number of posts held by Negroes tended to be inversely related to the power vested in these positions—the more powerful the post, the fewer the black policy-makers.*

As we have seen, Negroes were virtually excluded from policy-making in the single most powerful institutional sector—the business world. In *all* sectors, they were generally placed in positions in which the authority was delegated from a higher administrator, or divided among a board. Rarely were Negroes in positions of ultimate authority, either as chief executive or as top board officer.

When Negroes ran for a board or for a judicial office on a slate, their number had been limited by the political parties apportioning out the nominations. The percentage of Negroes on such boards or (especially) in judicial offices tended to run lower than the number of Negroes in legislative posts, for which Negroes run individually.

It is also true that no Negro has *ever* been elected to one of the key city-wide or county-wide executive positions, such as Mayor, City Clerk, or President of the Cook County Board. These are the positions with the greatest power and patronage.

In welfare agencies, where Negroes have token representation, they are virtually excluded from the key posts of executive director. Only five of the 135 directors of medium and of large welfare agencies were Negro.

Now, it was in the trade-union sector that the highest percentage of Negroes had policy posts—13 percent. We asked several experts on the Chicago trade-union movement to list the number of Negroes among the 100 most powerful trade unionists in the area. Among the 100 people they named, the number of Negroes ranged from two to five. This did not surprise us, for it was compatible with our general knowledge of the number of Negroes with truly powerful posts in other sectors.

A Rule of Thumb on Negro Power

All in all, then, we would suggest the following rule of thumb: *The actual power vested in Negro policy-makers is about one-third as great as the percentage of the posts they hold.*

Thus when Negroes elected other Negroes to office, these officers tended to represent small constituencies. For example, the greatest number of Negroes in legislative posts came from relatively small districts that happen to have black majorities. Indeed, according to Cook County tradition, Negroes simply do not hold legislative posts in city, state, or federal government *unless* they represent a district that is mostly black. No district with Negroes in the minority had a Negro representative, even when Negroes constituted the single largest ethnic group. And some districts with a Negro majority had a *white* representative.

Then too, the smaller the district, the more likely it would be homogeneous, and the greater the chances of its having a black majority that could return a Negro to office. In the Chicago area, consequently, Negroes were best represented on the City Council, which is based on 50 relatively small wards, each representing about 70,000 people; Negroes were represented most poorly in the U.S. House of Representatives, for which there are only nine rather large districts in Chicago, each representing about 500,000 people.

Most of the government policy-making posts that Negroes had been appointed to were in operations that had a large Negro clientele, if not a majority—as in the case of the Chicago public schools; or in operations that had largely Negro personnel, as in the case of the post office. On the appointed supervisory

The Methodology of the Study

In studying the exclusion of Negroes from the decision-making structure in Chicago, our working assumption was that the men who hold power are those who have been elevated to policy-making positions in powerful institutions, like banks, law firms, and unions. This approach differed from the more popular methodologies of studying community power— thus, we did not try to identify the top decision-makers, and we did not assume that a power élite was at work.

To identify policy-making posts, we relied on these assumptions:

■ In each major area of metropolitan life, certain enterprises have a disproportionate amount of power—because of their control over human and material resources, or because of their responsibility for making public policy.
■ Individuals who occupy policy-making posts in these key enterprises have a disproportionate amount of power *within* these institutions.
■ Policy decisions are made at every level of a bureaucracy. But certain posts within a bureaucracy will structure the range of decision-making for all other posts. Posts that have this responsibility we call "policy-making," and these are the posts we studied.

Under stable conditions, policy-making is the most important way in which power is exercised. In any firm or government department, policy-makers are relatively few. They are the ones who set the major goals and orientation, while the more numerous *management* is responsible for their implementation.

Just as our definition of "policy-making position" was restrictive, so was our definition of "power." In our study, power means the ability to make and enforce decisions for an institution, for a community, or for society at large— and the ability to determine in whose interest these decisions are made.

Our study began with a census of those Negroes occupying public or private policy-making positions. First we identified Cook County's major institutional areas—that is, related types of formally organized activities, such as local government, religious organizations, and business firms. In those areas where we could *not* be exhaustive in our research, we selected one or more representative groups. Corporate law firms, for example, were chosen to represent business-oriented professions and services.

Within each institutional area, we developed criteria to determine how large an individual enterprise or organization had to be before it has significant potential influence and power over other organizations. Next, we determined which positions within these powerful enterprises or organizations had policy-making authority. Finally, we conducted interviews with knowledgeable informants to learn which of the policy-making positions were held by Negroes.

In our study, the chairman of the board of the largest industrial firm was given the same statistical weight as the vice-president of the smallest bank included in the survey. While differentiating between them would have been useful for a study of the total process of decision-making in the Chicago area, our aim was to document only the inclusion or exclusion of Negroes. If there is any methodological bias in our study, then, it operates in favor of employing less strict criteria in determining important positions in order to include at least a few Negroes.

Our census was based on information for the year 1965. Since then, although there have been some shifts in the number and percentage of Negroes in particular organizations, the pattern of power traced remains fundamentally the same.

---

boards, in fact, those with as many as two Negro members were the Chicago Board of Education and the Board of Health, both of which serve very large numbers of Negroes.

This limiting of Negro policy-makers to Negro constituencies was quite as evident in the private sector. Three of the four banks with Negroes in policy-making posts were in Negro neighborhoods; and two were the smallest of the 102 banks we studied, and the other two were not much larger. The two insurance firms had mainly Negro clients, and were among the smallest of the 30 studied. In the voluntary organizations, the more they served Negroes, the higher the percentage of Negroes on their boards (although representation was by no means proportionate). Thus, the five Negro executive directors of welfare organizations we studied headed all-Negro constituencies: Three directed moderate-sized neighborhood settlements in the ghetto; one directed a virtually all-Negro hospital; and one directed an interracial agency that has traditionally had a Negro executive.

Still another way of limiting the power of Negro policy-makers, we discovered, was by "processing" them. Public and private institutions, as indicated, tend to have a token representation of Negroes. And many Negroes in these positions have totally identified with the traditional values and goals of the institution, regardless of what they mean to the mass of Negroes. Some of these Negro policy-makers, because of their small numbers and lack of an independent source of power, are neutralized. Others, if they are firm in representing the needs and outlook of the black community, are isolated. The two Negro members of the Chicago Board of Education represented these extremes. Mrs. Wendell Green, a longtime Board member and the elderly widow of a former judge, had been the most diehard supporter of Benjamin Willis, the former Schools Superintendent, through all of his fights against the civil-rights movement. The other Negro—Warren Bacon, a business executive—sympathized with the campaign against inferior, segregated housing and, as a result, has been largely isolated on the Board. He was rarely consulted on critical questions. His vote was usually cast with a small minority, and sometimes alone.

The fact is that the norms and traditions of *any* organization or enterprise limit the amount of power held by black policy-makers. It is no longer bold to assert that the major institutions and organizations of our society have an operational bias that is racist, even though their *official* policies may be the opposite. The Negro policy-maker in one of these institutions (or in a small black-controlled organization dependent upon these institutions, such as the head of a trade-union local) has a certain degree of conflict. If he goes along with the institution, from which he gains power and prestige, he ends up by implementing operations that restrict his minority group. Edward Banfield and James Q. Wilson have neatly pinpointed this dilemma in the political sphere:

> "Not only are few Negroes elected to office, but those who are elected generally find it necessary to be politicians first and Negroes second. If they are to stay in office, they must soft-pedal the racial issues that are of the most concern to Negroes as Negroes."

This pattern is seen in the failure of William Dawson, Cook County's one Negro Congressman, to obtain many Presidential appointments or top federal civil-service posts for Negroes. Theoretically he is in a more strategic position to influence government operations than any other Chicago-based Congressman, since he has 23 years' seniority and holds the important chairmanship of the Government Operations Committee. Yet in 1965 Negroes held only 2 percent of the top federal jobs in Chicago.

Any examination of the real power of Negroes in Chicago requires an examination of the strongest single organization in the Negro community—the Democratic Party. Wilson's study, *Negro Politics,* points out that the strength and cohesiveness of the Negro Democratic organization is largely dependent upon the strength of the total Cook County Democratic organization. The Negro organization is a "sub-machine" within the larger machine that dominates the city. The Negro sub-machine, however, has basically settled for lesser patronage positions and political favors, rather than using its considerable strength to try to make or change policy. Therefore, this Negro organization avoids controversial questions and seeks to avoid differences with the central organization on such vital issues as urban renewal and the schools.

In short, then, not only are Negroes underrepresented in the major policy-making positions in Cook County, but even where represented their actual power is restricted, or their representatives fail to work for the long-term interests of their constituency. It is therefore safe to estimate that Negroes really hold less than 1 percent of the effective power in the Chicago metropolitan area. Realistically, the power structure of Chicago is hardly less white than that of Mississippi.

From these figures it is clear that, at this time, Negroes in the Chicago area lack the power to make changes in the areas of housing, jobs, and education.

The basic subjugation of the black community, however, would not end if there were simply more Negroes in policy-making posts. We have seen the prevalence of tokenism, of whites' choosing Negro leaders who are conservative, of their boxing in Negro leaders who are proved to be liberal, of their giving these leaders less actual power than they give themselves.

Our analysis suggests that the best way to increase both the number *and* the power of Negro policy-makers is through unifying the black constituency. Access to policy-making positions could come through both the development of large, black-controlled organizations, and through getting Negroes into white-dominated organizations. If the constituency lacks its own clear set of goals and policies, however, things will surely remain the same. For success depends not just upon formal unity, but upon the nature of the goals set by the black community. In this situation, the overcoming of black powerlessness seems to require the development of a self-conscious community that has the means to determine its own interests, and the cohesiveness to command the loyalty of its representatives. We can safely predict that more and more Negroes will be moved into policy-making positions. The fundamental conflict, therefore, will take place between their co-optation into the established institutions and their accountability to a black constituency.

November 1968

SUGGESTED READINGS

Black Metropolis: A Study of Negro Life in a Northern Metropolis by St. Clair Drake and Horace Cayton, revised edition (New York & Evanston: Harper and Row, 1962). The best study on an urban black community. It contains much relevant material on the exercise of leadership within the community.

Black Power, the Politics of Liberation in America by Stokely Carmichael and Charles V. Hamilton (New York: Random House, 1968). A joint work by an activist and a scholar, and an argument for power through self-determination.

Black Bourgeoisie by E. Franklin Frazier (Glencoe, Ill.: The Free Press, 1957). A short, impressionistic work emphasizing the Negro's lack of significant power or wealth despite pretenses to the contrary by the black middle-class.

The Power Elite by C. Wright Mills (New York: Oxford University Press, 1956). A provocative interpretation of the very rich, the military and the political directorate as converging and cooperative elements of power in our society.

Community Power and Political Theory by Nelson W. Polsby (New Haven: Yale University Press, 1963). Polsby's pluralistic theory of community power disputes Mills' contention that the urban upper classes hold disproportionate political influence.

Community Power Structure by Floyd Hunter (Chapel Hill, North Carolina: University of North Carolina Press, 1953). Hunter concludes that in Atlanta, Georgia, local politics are controlled by the dominant economic influences of the area.

Who Governs? by Robert A. Dahl (New Haven: Yale University Press, 1963). Examines the distribution of political resources and how they are used; Dahl concludes that the exercise of political power is a much more diffuse phenomenon than is reported by Hunter.

Private Initiative in the 'Great Society'

One thing we must do, says a political scientist, is 'level up' while preventing 'leveling down'

NORTON E. LONG

America puts a very high value on achievement. It also puts a very high value on equality. The trouble is that, as with rivals in a Western film, there is constant tension between these values—and often open conflict.

How do we solve, or resolve, this tension? In the past, we kept the areas in which equality dominated separate from those in which achievement (or accumulation) dominated. Citizens were given formal equality in law and government, especially in voting privileges, and accepted inequality in the economy. Everyone's vote was supposed to be equal, but the well-to-do could buy more Buicks, or factories, as rewards for more achievement.

This contrast between the formal equality in the political institutions and the actual inequality in the economy led Marxists and many others to call bourgeois democracy a fraud. Focusing on this disparity, Anatole France made the famous comment:

"The law, in its majestic equality, forbids the rich as well as the poor to sleep under bridges, to beg in the streets, and to steal bread."

But today this picture has been radically altered—by the tremendous increase in the availability and importance of public goods and services (such as schools, li-

Enrico Natali

Urban whites, such as these at a patriotic parade in Detroit, have become an unpublicized part of the central city. They do not face the color problem of their neighboring blacks, says the author, but their chances of getting better jobs, improved housing, and decent schools are often just as poor.

ECONOMIC LIFE

braries, police and fire protection, parks, sanitation). Indeed, one of the main problems of our economy may be how to ensure that achievement is encouraged when so many of the things that men value are supposed to be equally available to all. There is a corollary problem: how to keep an unfair share of the public goods, especially good schooling, from going to the wealthy simply because they do have more economic power.

These considerations go to the heart of policy-making, for—from one point of view—all governments, national and local, are really so many devices and institutions for mobilizing and allocating resources, for determining who gives what and gets what and when. So, in its own way, is the market place of private industry. What mix of governmental and private initiatives is most desirable, therefore, depends upon what we want them to accomplish. And how successful our system is depends upon how nearly we achieve our goals of allocation.

Suburbs, the Reward for Achievement

How will achievement be rewarded and encouraged in a society dominated by equality, where public goods are becoming more and more important? So far, the preferred strategy has been suburbanization. In his own suburb the achiever can get a larger return for his money through better schools and services, and more control over his local government, which tends to be composed of people pretty much like himself. He comes into the central city for work, and occasionally for shopping or entertainment, but otherwise lets its stew in its own social problems.

The metropolitan areas, with their many local governments, have become like so many competing residential hotels, with varying qualities of service and different classes of paying guests; and many local politicians have come to act like hotel keepers—competing for the desirable trade, while trying to make sure that undesirables and deadbeats go elsewhere. Even if the politicians rise a notch above this, property-tax considerations will make them act like real-estate men, trying to keep up the value—and raise the income—of the property.

So the metropolitan area has become a patchwork of independent governments offering a wide variety of goods and permissible uses of land. If you pay your money, and are not from an undesirable minority, you can take your choice.

To some people, this state of affairs appears perfectly sensible. It seems to reflect the pluralism of our society; it seems to rescue some measure of quality, variety, and individuality from mass homogenization. But to others it reverberates with the crack of civic doom: It means the fragmentation of the community, political absenteeism, social irresponsibility, tax dodging, and the ghettoization of the poor and colored. Both views have a measure of truth. And they must be reconciled if equality, quality, and achievement are all to remain in our society.

Nationally, it has become possible and even expedient to pass civil-rights legislation, to try to provide equal opportunity, full employment, and open housing, and to make a pass at ending poverty. But many of those who support these national measures also practice local segregation, and therefore unequal rights to public goods. And this segregation obstructs justice. Housing has come to determine education, education to determine jobs, and jobs income. Income, in turn, is the key to housing, and so on around the tightening circle. For Negroes this democracy of the buck—the "free competitive market"—is nullified by that other capitalist ideal, the right to discriminate.

Fragmentation means unrepresentative local governments. Now, the federal government must work through these local governments, and with private enterprise. Consequently, national legislative ideals are easily gutted by the "realism" of local politics and economics. In urban renewal the poor have been *unhoused* by federal subsidies, and the banks *rehoused* with federal subsidies. Since the mayors act as municipal realtors, they try to use federal aid to get more taxes from their real estate (hence, new bank sites) and to get rid of nonpaying tenants (slum dwellers). Why shouldn't they? Federal bureaucrats and congressmen who want to survive in the political game go along. What is often viewed as cynicism is simply the inevitable result of the way the game is structured and played.

Governments can be organized to reflect narrow and selfish interests, but they can also be compelled to aspire to greatness. At present the nation's metropolises, stricken with fiscal anemia, plagued by social absenteeism, and obstructed by the country-club suburb with its toy government, have necessarily become organized on a dog-eat-dog, devil-take-the-hindmost basis. These metropolitan areas contain the overwhelming bulk of the nation's wealth and human talent—but they do not have the structure, the legal power, or even the coordinated theory needed to mobilize this immense strength and wealth behind a meaningful conception of human community. A Great Society will be forever impossible with this metropolitan disorganization, which substitutes the competition of municipal real-estate operators for responsible politics.

As an essential first step, we must create a single political organization for each of our 200-odd metropolitan areas. No smaller divisions have enough means and potential leaders to tackle the full array of local problems facing us. The radical shakeup needed to provide housing, education, and jobs to all requires local leaders who will face these problems. And they must have enough stature, enough of a following, and enough law and money behind them. The federal government cannot achieve major local changes by fiat. The paratroopers at Little Rock and the marshals at Old Miss could coerce, but not persuade. Without the willing cooperation of local leaders, the federal government is almost like an army of occupation. We must have a national system of able local governments to complement a federal government that responds to the national will. The fragmented metropolis we have now is a shattered mirror, utterly incapable of reflecting great or unified national purpose.

It is not enough to put a governmental superstructure, or regional "authority," on top of our divided local governments. Thus Metropolitan Toronto has an overall success in its public-works program that is worthy of Robert Moses—but it has yet to get beyond bricks and mortar to the more important human problems. New York City, big enough for greatness, verges on bankruptcy—until recently, at least, from a lack of purpose and direction. Metropolitan governments *without access to the ample fiscal resources within them* become hardly more than outsized special districts. Great leaders rise where there are great problems, *and* the means and power to solve them. The United States has settlements with untold richness in human talent and material resources. So far they are no more than census statistics with traffic problems, crime, slums, downtown-business districts, and heaps of buildings—without identity, purpose, or direction.

But, again, if fragmentation is a danger, so is homogenization. Metropolitan areas are the only units smaller than states that are nonetheless large enough to have the resources necessary for good government and equal opportunity. But they can also become so many shambling New Yorks, where quality is lost in sodden, equalized mediocrity. Equality of opportunity doesn't have to lead to this—but it can. We can level down as well as up, and wipe out our diversity.

What we must do is look to our principles and priorities. It was inevitable that, when public goods became more and more important in our lives, a powerful drive should develop to maintain the same inequalities in the public sector that there are in the private sector.

In suburbia, middle-class Americans can forget about the city, the author points out. They travel into the central city for work, occasionally for shopping or entertainment, but otherwise let it stew in its own social problems.   Inga Morath MAGNUM

After all, if parents can buy better food and toys for their children, why should they not also be able to buy safer streets and, especially, better schooling?

But public goods are *not* simply another form of private goods. All children may not be entitled to the best clothes or bicycles, but they *are* entitled to an equal chance at a better life. And this is the nub of the matter: Schools have become gatekeepers to jobs, careers, and opportunities. And when suburbanites demand superior schools for their children, they are demanding superior opportunities and lives for them as well.

Like the English, we have been trying to move from a plutocracy to a meritocracy through education, so that the most able—no matter what their backgrounds—can rise in the social scale. But what this has meant, by and large, is something like scholarships for poor bright boys to go to Oxford and Harvard. The impact of such programs on the opportunities in general is less than spectacular. It does take some of the curse off crass plutocracy, and—despite the anguish of old grads—places some limitation on the ability of the well-heeled to buy success for their children. But it is not enough.

Education in the metropolitan areas is crucial for their future. A Great Society must make full use of its human resources—and it can do this only by improving both education and motivation. It is urgent that we de-ghettoize and improve the metropolitan area's central city. But this, too, cannot be enough—because the central city simply does not have the resources, human and fiscal, to meet its problems. A central city is radically different from a metropolitan area, and the two can never be the same (unless the white middle class should flee the entire metropolitan area—an utterly unlikely possibility). There must be a better, and more democratic, way to achieve quality education than by concentrating it in élite neighborhoods and élite schools. A school system based on the resources of an entire metropolitan area might, like a great state university, be able to achieve quality, and diversity as well.

After quality education has been achieved, what then? Education becomes a cruel farce if there are no jobs for the graduates. The mockery and tragedy of much education in arts, music, and other fields comes from the lack of opportunity for adult careers, even when there is no discrimination. Broad avocational interests are fine, but they are not substitutes for jobs.

Now, the number and kinds of jobs are generally limited to what is available within the narrow limits of the private sector. Both the private *and* public sectors must be studied carefully to see whether they can provide jobs and careers for everyone; and, of equal importance, whether this employment makes meaningful use of talent. We need "spiritual" full employment, as well as physical. All of this will require a new system of national, state, and local cooperation and priorities.

The fact is that desirable social goals are often most effectively advanced by both private and public means. Even the Communist countries have begun to recognize the extraordinary advantages of individual and group initiatives, and the deadening routine of hide-bound bureaucracy. Centralized bureaucracies of any kind can become deadly. It is even possible that the state university system of California, one of the outstanding accomplishments of our states, may degenerate into a paper-shuffling civil service as low in morale and originality as the New York City school system. This eventuality is built into the dynamics of centralized administration. The space program and the armed forces have found that they can get much work—and, more important, much-needed new thinking—done for them by the unfettered energies of independent organizations. On the other hand, the Tennessee Valley Authority has provided a public yardstick for private initiative in this country—T.V.A.'s electricity rates can be compared with those of private companies. In this connection, private colleges and universities are providing a yardstick for their state-run counterparts.

The old socialist-capitalist dichotomy of public versus private enterprise is giving way to a realization that we need, and have, a variety of means for achieving desired ends. The profit system is one of the best systems ever evolved for getting unstructured cooperation between people, and it is an essential device for determining costs even in socialist systems. The public responsibility, then, becomes one of creating a general program of goals, and goal supports, that will allow the fullest use of whatever means are best for their attainment. Space is being explored through private, public, and academic cooperation; full employment could be achieved through the same model.

Full employment and the fuller use of talent means not only more jobs for people, but new roles—roles

---

SUGGESTED READINGS

A Great Society? by Bertram M. Gross (New York: Basic Books, 1968). A set of essays originally prepared for a seminar at Syracuse on the possible contents of and directions for a great society.

TVA and the Grass Roots by Phillip Selznick (New York: Harper and Row, 1966). This sociologically-informed history of the Tennessee Valley Authority traces the interplay of federal planning and local pressures that forced the program to revise some of its goals.

The New Industrial State by John Kenneth Galbraith (Boston: Houghton-Mifflin, 1967). Analyzes the roles of the state, industry and the individual within the "techno-structure" of today's American society.

The Unheavenly City by Edward C. Banfield (Boston: Little, Brown and Co., 1970). Banfield's wide-ranging urban analysis argues that the problems in American cities stem from class, not race, and condemns conventional urban renewal and welfare programs.

The Polity by Norton E. Long (Chicago: Rand-McNally, 1961). Hardheaded observations and analyses of urban political process.

According to the author, there is a contrast between the formal equality of our political institutions and the actual inequality in our capitalistic economy. And that inequality is felt most among the urban poor, especially Negroes, he says.

that give people more identity, more meaningful stakes in society. Not least among the needed roles are those of vital neighborhood "actors" and leaders, who can transform neighborhoods into living subcommunities. For instance, the "participant democracy" envisaged by the poverty program would provide such roles, and reduce the pervasive feelings of powerlessness and alienation among slum dwellers. Organized pressure, under competent leaders, has been a historic method for giving people a stake in society and improving their lot.

Under the old Homesteading Act, it was national policy to give farms to those who would make use of the property. This settled the frontier. On the urban frontier we need a similar device—to turn those with no stake in the community into property owners with an equity and interest in their neighborhoods. The Veterans Administration program gave servicemen housing with no down payments and with long-term mortgages. We can do the same in our slums for those who will maintain their own housing and neighborhoods, whether they own homes or cooperative apartments.

For low-income people, ownership is one of the most powerful socializers. The excess costs of maintenance in public housing could be reduced if tenants became owners, and ownership had been earned in a fashion similar to the way the homesteaders earned their farms. Enough new property-owners could transform the gray areas. These men, too, would be the potential neighborhood leaders through whom the "human renewal" that is supposed to accompany urban renewal can become more than an empty phrase.

In the next 20 years, Chicago will add to its population a city the size of Detroit, almost all of it outside

ECONOMIC LIFE 351

the present city limits. From the burgeoning tangle of new and of old jurisdictions, spawned by urban developers, a new urban nation is rising from the old. While most of our attention and funds go into a belated attempt to do something about our central cities, only minor concern and resources are devoted to trying to make sense out of the new America. A few—but only a few—new approaches, like the projected Oakland East and the already building Reston, show how these planned communities could be properly developed.

The poor cannot break the vicious circle of poor housing and poor schools by themselves. New towns, planned communities, are another important way to see that segregation and poverty do not wall them away from the quality public goods.

We are interested in leveling up, and preventing leveling down. We know that segregation promotes the perpetuation of the culture of poverty. This means, at the least, that the poor must have an opportunity to live with the more prosperous in such a way that good neighborhoods will be kept up, that the poor will be enriched, and that nobody will be impoverished.

This leveling up cannot be done piecemeal, with segregated classes, races, or political groups. It cannot be done if every man is left to seek security for himself—this produces only segregation by flight, and racially unbalanced neighborhoods. In our new towns, we need to work out a pattern that will allow the middle class to enjoy good neighborhoods and good schools *without* segregation. If the poor and the black are also to have access to these goods, they must be spread around so as not to seriously jeopardize current standards. For this, we cannot rely either on the real-estate market or the fragmented local political jurisdictions. Only in the well-organized metropolitan areas can a Great Society fully employ the human resources of an urban civilization; only with federal funds and insurance can large-scale new town and tract developments be encouraged and controlled.

And beyond this—and before this—we must have a coherent idea of what the Great Society should be, and do—what our goals are, and how we may best mobilize the means and talents to achieve them.

November 1968

George Gardner

Rich Man's Qualifications for Poor Man's Jobs

Are employers demanding too much education for the jobs they offer?

IVAR BERG

It is now a well-known fact that America offers more and more jobs to skilled workers while the increase in unskilled jobs has slowed down. Newspaper articles regularly remind us that we have a shortage of computer programmers, and, at the same time, too many unskilled laborers. The conventional solution is to correct the shortcomings of the labor force by educating more of the unemployed. Apart from its practical difficulties, this solution begs the important question: Are academic credentials important for *doing* the job—or just for *getting* it?

My studies of manpower use indicate that although in recent years requirements for many jobs have been upgraded because of technological and other changes, in many cases education requirements have been raised arbitrarily. In short, *many employers demand too much education for the jobs they offer.*

Education has become the most popular solution to America's social and economic ills. Our faith in education as *the* cure for unemployment, partly reflects our inclination as a society to diagnose problems in individualistic terms. Both current and classical economic theories merely reinforce these attitudes; both assume that the labor supply can be significantly changed by investments in education and health. Meanwhile private employers, on the other side of the law of supply and demand, are held to be merely reacting to the imperatives that generate the need for better educated manpower.

Certainly the government cannot force private employers to hire people who have limited educations. Throughout our history and supported by our economic theory, we have limited the government's power to deal with private employers. According to law and the sentiments that support it, the rights of property owners and the protection of their property are essential functions of government, and cannot or should not be tampered with. In received economic doctrine, business stands apart as an independent variable. As such, business activity controls the demand for labor, and the best way the government has to reduce unemployment is by stimulating business growth.

Some of the methods the government uses to do this are direct subsidies, depreciation allowances, zoning regulations, fair-trade laws, tax holidays, and credit guarantees. In return for these benefits, governments at all levels ultimately expect more jobs will be generated and more people employed. But when the market for labor does not work out according to theory, when employer demand does not increase to match the number of job seekers, attention shifts to the supply of labor. The educational, emotional, social, and even moral shortcomings of those who stand outside the boundaries of the social system have to be eliminated, we are told—and education seems to be the best way of doing it.

Unfortunately, economists and public planners usually assume that the education that employers require for the jobs they offer is altogether beneficial to the firm. Higher education, it is thought, means better performance on the job. A close look at the data, however, shows that here reality does not usually correspond with theory.

In recent years, the number of higher-level jobs has not increased as much as personnel directors lead us to believe. The big increase, rather, has been in middle-level jobs—for high-school graduates and college dropouts. This becomes clear when the percentages of jobs requiring the three different levels of education are compared with the percentages of the labor force that roughly match these categories. The comparison of census data with the U.S. Employment Service's descriptions of 4,000 different jobs also shows that (1) high-education jobs have expanded somewhat faster for men than for women; (2) those jobs in the middle have expanded faster for women than for men; and (3) that highly educated people are employed in jobs that require *less* education than these people actually have.

The fact is that our highly educated people are competing with lesser educated people for the jobs in the middle. In Monroe County, N.Y. (which includes Buffalo), the National Industrial Conference Board has graphically demonstrated this fact. Educational requirements for most jobs, the board has reported, vary with the academic calendar: Thus, requirements rise as the end of the school year approaches and new graduates flood the market. Employers whose job openings fall in the middle category believe that by employing people with higher-than-necessary educations they are benefiting from the increasing educational achievements of the work force. Yet the data suggest that there is a "shortage" of high-school graduates and of people with post high school educations short of college degrees while there is a "surplus" of college graduates, especially females.

The economic and sociological theories that pour out of university computers have given more and more support to the idea that we, as a society, have more options in dealing with the supply side of employment —with the characteristics of the work force—than with demand.

These studies try to relate education to higher salaries; they assume that the income a person earns is a valid measure of his job performance. The salaries of better-educated people, however, may not be closely related to the work they do. Female college graduates are often employed as secretaries; many teachers and social workers earn less than plumbers and others who belong to effective unions. What these rate-of-return studies lack is productivity data isolated according to job and the specific person performing the job.

In any event, it is circular reasoning to relate wage and salary data to educational achievements. Education is often, after all, the most important criterion for a person's getting a job in the first place! The argument that salaries may be used to measure the value of education and to measure the "value added" to the firm by employees of different educational backgrounds, may simply confirm what it sets out to prove. In jobs for which educational requirements have not been thoughtfully studied, the argument is not an argument at all, but a self-fulfilling prophecy.

Despite the many attempts to relate a person's achievements to the wages he receives, researchers usually find that the traits, aptitudes, and educational achievements of workers vary as greatly *within* job categories as they do *between* them. That is, people in job A differ as much from one another as they differ from people in job B. Only a small percentage of the labor force—those in the highest and those in the lowest job levels—are exceptions. And once workers become members of the labor force, personal virtues at even the lower job levels do not account for wage differences—intelligent, well-educated, low-level workers don't necessarily earn more than others at the bottom of the ladder. Marcia Freedman's study of employment patterns for Columbia's Conservation of Human Resources project, indicates that, although many rungs of the organizational ladder are linked to differences in pay, these rungs are not closely related to differences in the employees' skills and training.

Educational requirements continue to go up, yet most employers have made no effort to find out whether people with better educations make better workers than people with inferior educations. Using data collected from private firms, the military, the federal civil service, and public-educational systems, and some collected from scratch, I have concentrated on this one basic question.

Business managers, supported by government leaders and academics interested in employment problems, have well-developed ideas about the value of a worker's educational achievement. They assert that with each increment of education—especially those associated with a certificate, diploma, or degree—the worker's attitude is better, his trainability is greater, his capacity for adaptation is more developed, and his prospects for promotions are rosier. At the same time, those workers with more modest educations, and especially those who drop out of school, are held to be less intelligent, less adaptable, less self-disciplined, less personable, and less articulate.

The findings in my studies do not support these assertions.

A comparison of 4,000 insurance agents in a major company in the Greater New York area showed that an employee's productivity—measured by the dollar value of the policies he sold—did not vary in any systematic way with his years of formal education. In other words, those salesmen with less education brought as much money into the company as their better educated peers. When an employee's experience was taken into account, it was clear that those with *less* education and *more* experience sold the most policies. Thus, even an employer whose success in business depends on the social and psychological intangibles of a customer-client relationship may not benefit from having highly educated employees. Other factors such as the influence of colleagues and family obligations were more significant in explaining the productivity of agents.

In another insurance agency, the job performances of 200 young female clerks were gauged from the number of merit-salary increases they had received. Researchers discovered that there were *no* differences in the performance records of these women that could easily be attributed to differences in their educational backgrounds. Once again, focusing on the educational achievements of job applicants actually diverted attention from characteristics that are really relevant to job performance.

At a major weekly news magazine, the variation in educational achievement among over 100 employees was greater than among the insurance clerks. The magazine hired female college graduates, as well as high-school graduates, for clerical-secretarial positions. While the employers argued that the girls needed their college degrees to qualify for future editorial jobs, most editorial positions were *not* filled by former secretaries, whether college graduates or not, but by college graduates who directly entered into those positions. And although the personnel director was skeptical of supervisors' evaluations of the secretaries, the supervisors determined the salary increases, and as many selective merit-pay increases were awarded to the lesser-educated secretaries as to the better-educated secretaries.

Executives of a larger well-known chemical company in New York told me that the best technicians in their research laboratory were those with the highest educational achievement. Therefore, in screening job applicants, they gave greater weight to a person's educational background than to his other characteristics. Yet, statistical analysis of relevant data revealed that the rate of turnover in the firm was positively associated with the employees' educational achievement. And a close look at the "reasons for leaving" given by the departing technicians showed that they intended to continue their educations. Furthermore, lesser-educated technicians earned higher performance evaluations than did their better-educated peers. Understandably, the employer was shocked by these findings.

Over Educated Are Less Productive

The New York State Department of Labor's 1964 survey of employers suggests that technicians often possess educational achievements far beyond what employers themselves think is ideal for effective performance. Thousands of companies reported their minimal educational requirements to the Labor Department, along with their ideal requirements and the actual educators of the technicians they employed. In many industries and in respect to most types of technicians, the workers were better educated than they were required to be; in 10 out of 16 technical categories they were even better educated than their employers dared hope, exceeding the "ideal" requirements set down by the employers.

Upper- and middle-level employees are not the only ones who are overqualified for their jobs. Nor is the

More highly educated women piece workers produce less and have higher turnover rates than women with less education. "Many employers demand too much education for the jobs they offer."

George Gardner

ECONOMIC LIFE

phenomenon only to be observed in metropolitan New York. In a study of eight Mississippi trouser plants, researchers found that the more education an employee had, the less productive she was. Several hundred female operators were paid by "piece work" and their wages therefore were a valid test of workers' productivity. Furthermore this study showed that educational achievement was positively associated with turnover: The better-educated employee was more likely to quit her job.

Education's negative relationship to jobs can be measured not only by the productivity and turnover of personnel, but also by worker satisfaction. It may be argued that dissatisfaction among workers leads to a desirable measure of labor mobility, but the funds a company spends to improve employee morale and make managerial personnel more sensitive to the needs of their subordinates strongly suggest that employers are aware of the harm caused by worker dissatisfaction. Roper Associates once took a representative sample of 3,000 blue-collar workers in 16 industries in all parts of the United States. Among workers in lower-skilled jobs, dissatisfaction was found to increase as their educational achievements increased.

These studies of private firms suggest that many better-educated workers are assigned to jobs requiring low skills and that among the results are high turnover rates, low productivity, and worker dissatisfaction. Nonetheless, the disadvantages of "overeducation" are best illustrated by employment practices of public-school systems.

Educated Teachers Opt Out

Many school districts, to encourage their teachers to be highly educated, base teachers' salaries upon the number of credits they earn toward higher degrees. However, data from the National Opinion Research Center and the National Science Foundation's 1962 study of 4,000 teachers show that, like employees elsewhere, teachers become restless as their educational achievements rise. Elementary and secondary school teachers who have master's degrees are less likely to stay in their jobs than teachers with bachelor's degrees. And in a similar study done by Columbia Teachers College, it was evident that teachers with master's degrees were likely to have held jobs in more than one school system.

Thus, for school systems to tie pay increases to extra credits seems to be self-defeating. Teachers who earn extra credits apparently feel that their educational achievements reach a point beyond which they are overtrained for their jobs, and they then want to get administrative jobs or leave education for better paying jobs in industry. The school districts are, in a sense, encouraging teachers not to teach. This practice impedes the upgrading of teacher qualifications in another way. Thanks to the extra-credit system, schools of education have a steady supply of students and therefore are under little pressure to furnish better and more relevant courses.

For the most part, though, employers in the public sector do not suffer from problems of unrealistic educational requirements. For a variety of reasons, they do not enjoy favored positions in the labor market and consequently have not been able to raise educational requirements nearly so fast as the private employer has. But for this reason alone, the experiences of government agencies are significant. How well do their employees with low-education backgrounds perform their jobs?

The pressure on the armed forces to make do with "what they get" has forced them to study their experiences with personnel. Their investigations clearly show that a person's educational achievement is not a good clue to his performance. Indeed, general tests developed for technical, military classifications and aptitude tests designed to screen individual candidates for training programs have turned out to be far better indicators of a person's performance.

In a 1948 study of Air Force personnel, high-school graduates were compared with nongraduates in their performance on the Army Classification Tests and on 13 tests that later became part of the Airman Classification Battery. The military's conclusion: "High-school graduates were not uniformly and markedly superior to non-graduates. . . . High-school graduation, unless supplemented by other screening measures such as tests or the careful review of the actual high-school record, does not insure that a basic trainee will be of high potential usefulness to the Air Force."

In 1963, the Air Force studied 4,458 graduates of eight technical courses. Comparing their performances in such courses as Reciprocating Engine Mechanic, Weather Observer, Accounting, and Finance Specialist with the education they received before entering the service, the Air Force found that a high-school diploma only modestly predicted the grades the airmen got in the Air Force courses. In other Air Force studies, aptitude tests were consistently found to correlate well with a person's proficiency and performance, while educational achievement rarely accounted for more than 4 percent of the variations.

These Air Force data do not conclude that education is unimportant, or that formal learning experiences are irrelevant. Rather, it points out the folly of confusing a man's driver's license with his driving ability. Just as different communities have different safety standards, so schools and school systems employ different kinds of teachers and practices. It should surprise no one that a person's credentials, by themselves, predict his performance so poorly.

Army and Navy studies confirm the Air Force findings. When 415 electronic technicians' scores on 17 concrete tasks were analyzed in conjunction with their age, pay grades, and education, education was found to be negatively associated with performance. When the Navy updated this study, the outcome was the same. For high performance in repairing complicated electronic testing equipment, experience proved more significant than formal education.

Perhaps the military's most impressive data came from its experiments with "salvage" programs, in which illiterates and men who earn low scores on military classification tests are given remedial training. According to research reports, these efforts have been uniformly successful—as many graduates of these programs develop into useful servicemen as the average, normal members of groups with which they have been regularly compared.

Naval Manpower Salvage

In a 1955 study done for the Navy, educational achievements were not found to be related to the performance of 1,370 recruits who attended "recruit preparatory training" courses. Neither were educational achievements related to the grades the recruits received from their company commanders and their instructors, nor to their success or failure in completing recruit training. In some instances, the low-scoring candidates with modest educational backgrounds performed at higher levels than better-educated men with high General Classification Test scores. The military recently expanded its "salvage" program with Project 100,000, and preliminary results tend to confirm the fact that training on the job is more important than educational credentials.

Military findings also parallel civilian studies of turnover rates. Reenlistment in the Navy is nearly twice as high among those men who have completed fewer than 12 years of school. But reenlistment in the military, of course, is related to the fact that the civilian economy does not particularly favor ex-servicemen who have modest educational achievements.

Wartime employment trends make the same point. During World War II, when demand for labor was high, both public and private employers adapted their recruiting and training to the labor supply. Productivity soared while a wide range of people mastered skills almost entirely without regard to their personal characteristics or previous circumstances. Labor's rapid adjustment on the job was considered surprising; after the war, it was also considered to be expensive. Labor costs, it was argued, had gone up during the war, and unit productivity figures were cited as evidence. These figures, however, may have been misleading. Since the majority of wartime laborers were employed in industries with "cost-plus" contracts—where the government agreed to reimburse the contractor for all costs, plus a certain percentage of profit—such arrangements may have reduced the employer's incentives to control costs. The important lesson from the war period seems to be that people quickly adjust to work requirements once they are on the job.

A 5 percent sample of 180,000 men in the federal civil service shows that while the number of promotions a person gets is associated with his years of education, the link is far from complete. Education has a greater bearing on a person's rank at *entry* into the civil service than on his prospects for a promotion. Except for grades 11-15, in accounting for the promotion rates of civil servants, length of service and age are far more significant than education. A closer look at one government agency will perhaps clarify these points.

Few organizations in the United States have had to adapt to major technological changes as much as the Federal Aviation Agency has. Responsible among other things for the direction and control of all flights in the United States, it operates the control-tower facilities at all public airports. With the advent of jet-powered flights, the F.A.A. had to handle very quickly the horrendous technical problems posed by faster aircraft and more flights. Since no civilian employer requires the services needed by the F.A.A. in this area, the agency must train its own technicians and control-tower people. The agency inventively confronted the challenge by hiring and training many new people and promoting those trained personnel it already had. Working with the background data on 507 men—all the air-traffic controllers who had attained grade 14 or above—it would seem that, at this high level, education would surely prove its worth.

On the Job Training for Tower Controllers

Yet in fact these men had received very little formal education, and almost no technical managerial training except for the rigorous on-the-job training given by the F.A.A. itself. Of the 507 men in the sample, 211, or 42 percent, had no education or training beyond high school. An additional 48, or 10 percent, were high-school graduates who had had executive-training courses. Thus, more than half of the men had had no academic training beyond high school. There were, however, no patterns in the differences among the men in grades 13 or 15 with respect to education. That is, education and training were *not* related to the higher grade.

The F.A.A.'s amazing safety record and the honors and awards given to the tower controllers are good indicators of the men's performance. The F.A.A.'s Executive Selection and Inventory System records 21 different kinds of honors or awards. Only one-third of the men have never received any award at all. Half of the 77 percent who have been honored have been honored more than once. And a relatively high percentage of those with no education beyond high school received four or more awards; those with a B.A. degree were least likely to receive these many honors. Other breakdowns of the data confirm that education is not a factor in the daily performance of one of the truly demanding decision-making jobs in America.

The findings reported in these pages raise serious questions about the usefulness of raising educational requirements for jobs. They suggest that the use of formal education as a sovereign screening device for jobs adequately performed by people of lower educational achievements may result in serious costs—high turnover, employee dissatisfactions, and poorer performance. Programs calculated to improve employees' educations probably aim at the wrong targets, while programs calculated to reward better-educated people are likely to miss their targets. It would be more useful to aim at employers' policies and practices that block organizational mobility and seal off entry jobs.

There Are More Job Openings in the Middle

Given the facts that there are more job openings in the middle, and that many people are overqualified for the jobs they do have, policies aimed at upgrading the educational achievements of the low-income population seem at best naïve. It would make better sense to upgrade people in the middle to higher jobs and upgrade those in lower-level jobs to middle positions, providing each group with an education appropriate to their age, needs, and ambitions. The competition for lower-level jobs would then be reduced, and large numbers of drop-outs could move into them. (Only after young people, accustomed to a good income, develop middle-class aspirations are they apparently interested in pursuing the balance of their educations.) Current attempts to upgrade the labor supply also seem questionable in light of what psychologists and sociologists have to say. Changing people's attitudes, self-images, and achievements is either enormously time-consuming—sometimes requiring half a generation—or it is impossible. At any rate, it is always risky.

If the much-maligned attitudes of low-income Americans were changed without establishing a full-employment economy, we might simply be adding fuel to the smoldering hatreds of the more ambitious, more frustrated groups in our urban ghettos. And if we wish to do something about the supposed shortcomings in the low-income Negro families, it will clearly require changes in those welfare arrangements that now contribute to family dissolution. The point is that rather than concentrate on the supply of labor, we must reconsider our reluctance to alter the *demand* for labor. We must have more realistic employment requirements.

Unfortunately, attempts to change people through education have been supported by liberal-intellectuals who place great value upon education and look appreciatively upon the economic benefits accruing to better-educated Americans. Indeed, one of the few elements of consensus in present-day American politics may well be the reduction of the gap between the conservative and liberal estimate of the worth of education.

Obviously, the myths perpetuated about society's need for highly-educated citizens work to the disadvantage of less-educated people, particularly nonwhites who are handicapped whatever the state of the economy. Information obtained by economist Dale Hiestand of Columbia does not increase one's confidence that educational programs designed to help disadvantaged people over 14 years old will prove dramatically beneficial. Hiestand's studies show that even though the best-educated nonwhites tend to have more job mobility, they are more likely to enter occupations that are *vacated* by whites than to compete with whites for *new* jobs. Since the competition for middle-education jobs is already very intense, it will be difficult to leapfrog Negroes into jobs not yet vacated by whites, or into new jobs that whites are likely to monopolize.

Now, nothing in the foregoing analysis should be construed as suggesting that education is a waste of time. Many jobs, as was stated at the outset, have changed, and the need for education undoubtedly grows quite aside from the monetary benefits individuals derive from their educations. But I think it is fundamentally subversive of education and of democratic values not to see that, in relation to jobs, education has its limits.

As the burden of evidence in this article suggests, the crucial employment issue is not the "quality of the work force." It is the overall level of employment and the demand for labor in a less than full-employment economy.

March 1969

SUGGESTED READINGS

The Rise of the Meritocracy by Michael Young (New York: Random House, 1958) shows how the criteria for success in our occupational structure has changed and how it will continue to change through the year 2033.

Making the Grade: The Academic Side of Life by Howard S. Becker, Blanche Geer and Everett C. Hughes (New York: Wiley, 1968) is a study of the grading system in our colleges and its effects upon student and teacher. The authors recommend dispensing with grades.

"Creaming the Poor" by S. M. Miller, Pamela Roby and Alwine A. de Vos van Steenwijk, *Trans*-action (Vol. 7, June 1970) reveals how antipoverty programs are ineffective in helping the real poor and more efficient in helping those who do not need help as much.

Symbolic Interaction & Human Communication

Communication refers to the processes by which a set of meanings is transmitted from one person to another or from one group to another. It is accomplished through the use of an endless variety of signs, gestures, sights, and sounds. The means of communication can be as subtle as the tilt of the head or as blatant as a screaming fire alarm. The process of communication always involves a sender, a message, and a receiver, who reacts to the message. If there is no response at the receiving end of the message, there is a failure of communication.

When receiving a communicated message, a human being is capable of being more than a passive instrument that is affected by a stimulus and responds in some predictable way, as the leg jerks when the kneecap is tapped in the right place. A human being reflects and reacts to symbols. A person responds reflexively to some kinds of stimuli, to be sure, and he can be conditioned to certain kinds of learned responses, just as Pavlov's famous dog was conditioned to salivate upon hearing a bell ring. Animals can be conditioned in rather complex ways and, as any pet owner knows, a dog or cat is "almost human" in its behavior—wagging its tail, purring and rubbing against its master's legs. But animals are incapable of responding to symbols, that is, of establishing and using an arbitrary system of signs that stand for objects, events, and relationships that are not in their immediate environment. It is man's particular characteristic—one highly related to his intelligence—that he has created a system of symbols to stand for the world he lives in. He does not need to be presented with the stimuli or the outward sign to talk about things that are absent. He has created a language that is a shared system of sounds and sights that stand for what he wishes to communicate with others or contemplate in his own mind. Some of the symbols have reference to the outside world such as "cats and dogs"; others stand for, say, a Cheshire cat or Pooh Bear and Piglet, who have to be seen in drawings or read about to be known, since they do not exist in the flesh. These are symbols that represent man's imaginary creations. Man also devises symbols to represent other symbols as in the logical and mathematical signs that are used as purely symbolic operations. In fact, man knows his world solely through the symbolic system of language that names, identifies, and classifies his experience; his language is his reality—unnamed things just don't exist until he can think about and talk about them.

This symbolic system—including the spoken and written language, the language of gestures, and the most abstract symbols of symbols—comes out of human interaction. Possession of a language is not instinctive; it must be learned anew by each human being who is born into a human community whose language emerges from its shared experience in a specific setting.

Communicating

The process of interaction is carried on through the communication of meaning between people or groups of people using language or some other kinds of meaningful symbols. This is called symbolic interaction and can occur because people have substantial agreement on a set of meanings and values associated with a symbol. Thus, the v-sign made with the two forefingers spread apart is not a specific shape or

Barry Fitzgerald

form that stands for a single event or activity. At first, the sign stood for victory in World War II. That meaning withered away, but the sign has been replenished with the complex, and changing, set of meanings and values of the peace movement. It includes the feelings of solidarity of people in the movement, of sharing in a history of defiance, and of hopes for accomplishing its goals. "Peace, Brother" puts into words a further elaboration of the meaning of the v-sign, extended to include opposition not only to war, but to oppression of all kinds and support for all groups working for liberation.

Social interaction refers to the processes involved when men associate with each other and exert reciprocal influence through talking, gesturing, and so on. Two people in conversation is a good example of interaction. Each person directs verbal messages and gestures at the other and at the same time receives the messages and gestures of the other. Each is simultaneously trying to anticipate the response of the person with whom he is conversing and modifying the content and form of his verbal behavior on the basis of these anticipations. Often, one will anticipate so eagerly that he interrupts the other person. All the while each is "taking account" of the other person, interpreting and organizing his ideas on the basis of how he defines the person and in what social context the interaction is taking place.

Men in interaction, whether in one-to-one relationships or larger groups, are taking part in a dynamic process that involves them in interpretation and meaningful response to the verbal and bodily action of others. Group and community life have no existence outside the relationships between people and, although there are patterned and habitual ways of behaving that can be thought of as social structure, the life of society must be engaged in daily, renewed by the hour and by the minute. These social processes consist of an unending series of interactions, some forms of which appear as either cooperation, competition, or conflict, and mixtures of these.

Settings

The reading selections of the first two parts of Chapter VI illustrate how men interact in small and large groups; they also point up the various forms that interaction takes. Anselm Strauss in "Healing by Negotiation" pictures the hospital as a place in which doctors, nurses, aides, orderlies, and patients bargain and negotiate for the conditions under which they give and receive medical care. It is evident that hospitals, like most large organizations and institutions where people work together, are settings for the ongoing interaction of people who create informal structures offsetting or even subverting the official rules and regulations of the organization.

Another element of importance in the shaping of interaction is the setting in which it takes place. What happens to the relationships between pairs of persons who are isolated from all other people for considerable lengths of time, such as Arctic explorers or astronauts? William Haythorn and Irwin Altman conducted a series of experiments with pairs of men kept in complete isolation and report in "Together in Isolation" that the amount of strain resulting from isolation is related to personality types. Gordon H. De Friese and W. Scott Ford, Jr. in "Open Occupancy—What Whites Say, What They Do," draw attention to the difference between public and private behavior where acts subject to scrutiny are different from those shielded from public censure.

Conflict is endemic in society as long as men struggle over scarce resources and different values or priorities of values.

Symbolic Interaction & Human Communication

Individual men and groups of men try to further their interests and goals and, in so doing, attempt to change the social order to reflect their own values. When society is viewed as a static social order that is harmed by clashes of interests and values, then conflict is something to be prevented. Violence, in that view, rends the fabric of society, and the damage may be irreparable. A perspective that views change as only a threat to social order fails to see that social relationships are in constant flux and that disorganization is followed by realignments and reorganization.

The selections on social conflict include analyses of various settings in which men and groups are studied during the process of pressing their claims for more power, money, and status; adjustment of claims, accommodation, cooperation with others, stalemate, and defeat are all possible consequences of such action.

Worth consideration is the view that conflict has positive rather than negative functions for the group or the larger society. For members of a depressed class, shaking up the established order by direct action is one way to try to improve their position. Two articles on militant action by deprived American minorities analyze the problems faced by groups with few resources and power when they organize to fight for their rights. The welfare poor and slum dwellers are shown as learning not only their legal rights and economic power but how to demand them in Richard A. Cloward and Richard M. Elman's "Advocacy in the Ghetto." Townspeople of Paterson, New Jersey, supported mill workers when they organized to oppose the manufacturers' exploitation and domination of the town in the early period of American industrialization that is described in Herbert G. Gutman's "Industrial Invasion of the Village Green."

International conflict results in changes in the power and fortunes of nation-states. With conflict in the form of warfare between countries so apparently destructive of human lives and wealth, we are not apt to view war as justifiable, much less beneficial. Is it a contradiction to see positive aspects of conflict within countries at the same time as we see only negative aspects of international warfare? Through cross-cultural comparisons of preparedness and aggressiveness in warfare by primitive tribes Raoul Naroll's "Does Military Deterrence Deter?" makes a case against military deterrence as an effective way to achieve peace. But international conflict has not stopped and nations train and send men to kill and be killed in combat. Is it formal military training and discipline, esprit de corps, patriotism, loyalty to buddies, or self-preservation that keeps soldiers on the battlefront exposed to injury and death? Charles C. Moskos, Jr. reports from direct observation on "Why Men Fight in Vietnam."

Mass Media

While face-to-face communication and participation in groups are the basic relationships that attach people to the society, an increasing amount of communication does not flow between persons but rather from a mass-communications source to the person. In the United States, people spend approximately three and a half hours a day watching television or listening to the radio. The mass media—television, radio, newspapers, motion pictures, and books—distribute information and entertainment in written, pictorial, and oral form to a vast, varied, and anonymous audience daily. People react to these messages on the basis of their personal experience and place in society and share their reactions with family

Symbolic Interaction & Human Communication

members, friends, and work associates, but they cannot interact (with few exceptions) with the distant, impersonal broadcaster, even though they may "talk back" to the screen or argue with the newspaper headlines.

Information and Influence

As purveyors of information and influence on public opinion and public affairs, the mass media of communication possess enormous power to affect the societies in which they function. As they operate in various parts of the world today, they are widely viewed by governments and other influential sectors of society as important sources of social control. As we know them in the United States, most of the mass media seem to be more effective in reinforcing existing attitudes, beliefs, and habits than in working for significant social changes. At the same time, though, fads and fashions in consumption items and popular tastes are rapidly spread by the media. And there are many unknown long-run effects and potentialities of the electronic media in particular, which are in the early stages of technological development and public control.

Some of the effects of the mass media on opinion and behavior are reported in the articles by Simon, Knopf, and Rosenthal. Rita James Simon conducts an experiment to assess whether jury members are influenced by newspaper stories on the case they are considering and comes to surprising conclusions in "Murder, Juries and the Press." The problem of news distortion and misrepresentation is dealt with by Terry Ann Knopf in "Sniping—A New Pattern of Violence?." What happens when the usual sources of information are cut off, as in a newspaper strike? The relationship between information or lack of information to the development of social unrest is considered by Marilyn Rosenthal in "Rumors in the Aftermath of the Detroit Riot."

It is often said that modern society reveals a breakdown in the pattern of communication—i.e., that there is a "lack of communication." In point of fact, there is a communication overload, too much information, that often degenerates into too much misinformation. The problems now seem to be of overloading rather than insufficiencies. As a result, new problems have emerged: the reliability of information, the relationship between information heard from friends vis-à-vis reported information in the media, the substance of information as distinct from its packaging. What is so amazing is how face-to-face relationships or primary relationships have managed to retain their integrity and their primacy in spite of (or maybe because of) the communications overload of the modern epoch. It might well be that fundamental interaction between people will become more significant rather than less so, in the face of sophisticated means for conveying the story of people and products. In any event, communication as an act, and the symbols by which men determine the significance of an act, continue to form the base of society.

George Gardner

Charles Harbutt MAGNUM

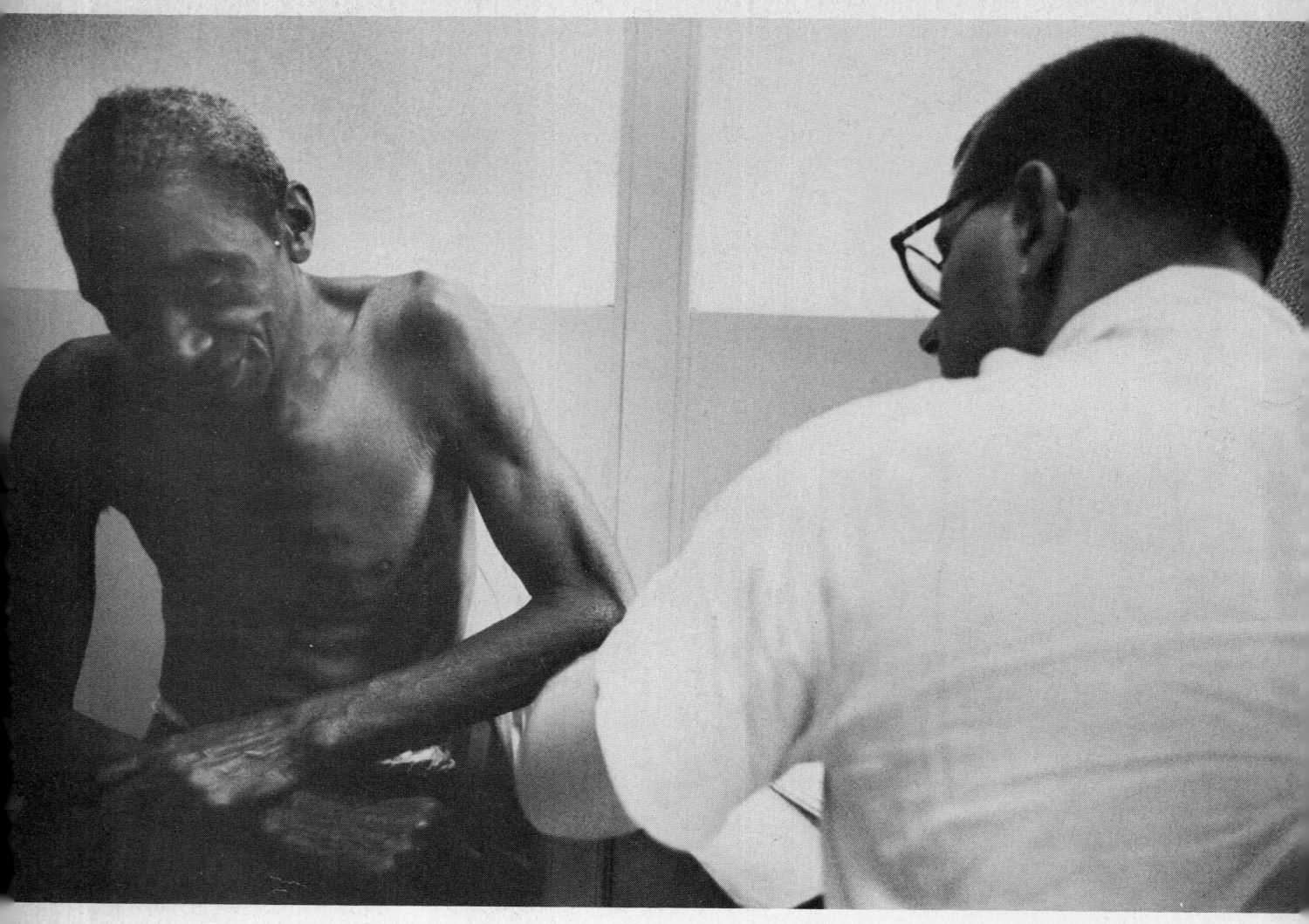

Healing by Negotiation

ANSELM STRAUSS

A hospital seems to reflect the laboratory precision of the sciences that contribute to it. Its corridors, beds, facilities and wards are geometrically arranged; its meals exactly scheduled; its nursing personnel uniformed and starched. Everything seems clearly organized, ordered, structured, marching like wound-up tin soldiers straight toward the common humanitarian goal—relief of the sick.

This appearance is deceptive. Although the various professionals and nonprofessionals who worked in the hospital we studied (the psychiatric division of Michael Reese Hospital in Chicago) were supposed to be engaged in a common enterprise, they had different responsibilities, different amounts of power, different backgrounds, different training, different beliefs, different experiences and different personal or professional reasons for being there. Operating from such diverse sources, often working toward separate specific goals, the hospital could only be kept running by continuous, often secret, occasionally unconscious, processes of negotiation and adjustment—by check and countercheck—which sometimes broke down into polite guerrilla warfare. Relationships and situations were continually arranged and rearranged.

The rules and regulations of the hospital were supposed to impose overriding order; but hardly anyone knew all of them—much less what situations or persons they applied to, and with what force. One head nurse told us, "I wish they would write them all down somewhere"—but she said it with a smile.

The staff therefore interpreted scripture to suit their own needs and purposes. Nurses frequently appointed themselves defenders of the hospital against inappropriate demands of certain physicians. The doctors, on to the game, sometimes accused them of more interest in their own personal welfare and comfort than of that of the patients.

When they felt it desirable or necessary, these same nurses—in fact, all staff—broke or stretched regulations. The motives were not always selfish—usually, the staff honestly wanted to get things done without bureaucratic impediment. The administration well understood this and took a tolerant attitude.

The ground actually covered by clearly enunciated and enforced rules was very small—and these rules mostly formalized long-existing understandings. Only a few very general regulations covered even the proper placement of new patients in the wards.

Grounds for Negotiation

There was a common purpose—to return patients to the outside world in better shape. Symbolically, this goal held the organization together.

But as soon as a specific case was confronted, disagreement might flare up; contentions about treatment, placement, procedure and regulations might immediately arise. The common goal could even serve as a club with which contenders could beat each other—"If he had the real interest of the patient at heart he would agree with me."

Conflict and negotiation were not accidental: they were built into the structure of beliefs and relationships. Where should a new patient be placed? Some thought he would get better sooner in one ward, some another, and each worked toward placing him best.

Different staff levels hold different ideas of what getting better means. Both aides and nurses, working immediately with patients, tend to judge progress by visible behavior, while the psychiatrist considers behavior merely symptomatic of underlying disorder. Frequently the staff finds the patient getting better while the psychiatrist does not.

Modes and Methods

If placement involves negotiation, so does treatment. A psychiatrist who is neurologically trained, who inclines more toward physiology, will prescribe more drugs, more convulsive shock therapy, and spend much less time with each patient than one who uses psychotherapeutic methods. The nurses and aides may take either side in this controversy, or neither. If they do not agree with the psychiatrist they may argue with him, subvert him, or go over his head to an administrator. To get what he wants done, the psychiatrist has to negotiate. Even if the nurses and aides obey direct orders, they still may not cooperate. The psychiatrist cannot be there to give or enforce every order; he cannot anticipate every situation. Nurses and aides need not be openly disobedient to defeat a psychiatrist; they need only refuse to take initiative. Aides often simply do not see things psychiatrically; they prefer to judge patients by common sense standards—or even as moral problems.

Diversity of purpose affects the institution's division of labor—not only what tasks each person is expected to do, but how he maneuvers to get them done, and why. Very little of this can be predetermined and programmed by top administration; whether an individual achieves his goal depends on what cooperation he can get, and what he is prepared to pay for it.

Further, the usual philosophy of treatment emphasizes that each case, and each patient, is unique. Treatment must be individually tailored. Rules handed down from the top can only cover small patches of whole cloth; the rest must be negotiated.

The Resistant Nonprofessionals

For policy reasons the aides are often told that they are vital to the process of helping patients get better. Generally, however, the doctors consider their contribution inconsequential.

The aides definitely do not agree. Our inquiry left no doubt that most aides consider themselves the principal cause of patient improvement.

The aides believe that they have more frequent and intimate contact with patients than anyone, and therefore know and understand them better. "I always know more than the doctors and nurses. We're with the patients almost eight hours, while the doctors and nurses hardly come in. The nurse reads the chart and passes the medicine." Even the best nurses may be so busy administrating that they scarcely leave the office; the doctors may spend so little time with patients that they must call on aides and nurses for information about the patient's behavior.

Aides can understand a physician's special competence for giving shock or other medical treatment; but they cannot see any fundamental difference between the talking they do with the patients during the day and, the talk between the psychiatrist and his case during psychotherapy.

With this viewpoint it is obvious that however often they attend staff meetings, however carefully psychiatrists instruct them, they will always respond by understanding patients in their own way.

Like anyone else, nonprofessionals want to control their conditions of work. They bargain: stake their claims, back up a trifle, stake counter claims, push their chess pieces back and forth on the board. Among the prizes: Where will one work? With whom? Under what superior? With what kinds of patients?

The patients too do not simply get what they want when they want it; they must negotiate and bargain. Unless they themselves are nurses or physicians, they bargain, as laymen —a status which has a few advantages, mostly in private psychiatric hospitals, but has the great disadvantage of physical dependency and lack of inside knowledge, influence and authority.

Most visibly they bargain for privileges—more freedom to roam the grounds, for instance. Like any respectable tenant they become concerned with living conditions, and keeping up the tone of the neighborhood. They negotiate with each other and the staff about noise, orderliness and cleanliness in the ward, and whether violent, trouble-making patients can't be better controlled or moved. Sometimes patients are even as jealous of ward order as the nurses.

But patients also bargain about the kind and duration of treatment—which wards, what drugs and how much, which psychiatrist, and how long before they leave.

Any psychiatrist or nurse who takes the trouble to study and follow a patient's negotiations will achieve unexpected insight into that patient's illness. Apparently random or unconscious behavior becomes clear. Patients search, bargain, and beg for precious understanding of their own sickness and problems. As their disorders wax or wane, the tempo and focus of their negotiations, like faithful graph traces, also alter.

Specialty of the House

Some psychiatrists in Michael Reese Hospital have established long-term understandings with certain head nurses, who know, almost without words, what is expected of them. A neurologist-psychiatrist generally tries to get his patients into the two wards where most electric shock treatment is done—and his nurses take it from there. We called this specialty of the house—as opposed to à la carte—treatment.

Once the negotiated arrangements are relatively stabilized, certain responses become almost automatic. Woe to the psychiatrist whose ideas of treatment are very troublesome to established routine and understandings, and who gets stubborn about it. He may suddenly find himself surrounded, perhaps hopelessly enmeshed, by an increasingly tight web of negotiation woven back and forth among nurses, administrators and aides. When the furor in the ward is the greatest, the negotiation is most visible. Unless he has very powerful administrative support, he will sooner or later have to sue for peace.

The dynamics which bring about the necessity for negotiation in a mental hospital are not confined to it, any more than the psychological dynamics which bring the patients in begin or end at the hospital door.

In any organization possessing one or more of the following characteristics a negotiated order will probably be found:

- Personal are trained for several different occupations.
- One or more occupational groups has individuals trained in different approaches, disciplines or traditions.
- These in turn lead to differing philosophies, with different values and different methods, requiring adjustments between groups.
- If at least some of the staff are professionals, they are likely to be mobile, and have outside professional interests—that is, their careers carry them into and out of the organization, at different times and at different rates.

What organizations besides hospitals have such characteristics? Universities, corporations, military services, government agencies—and many other large groups.

September-October 1964

SUGGESTED READINGS

Presentation of Self in Everyday Life by Erving Goffman (Edinburgh: Edinburgh University Press, 1958). Goffman is interested in how people attempt to manage the impression they make on others.

Stigma: Notes on the Management of Spoiled Identity by Erving Goffman (Englewood Cliffs, N.J.: Prentice-Hall, 1963). What happens to people who are labeled "not normal" by society.

Defining the Situation by Peter McHugh (New York: Bobbs-Merrill Co., 1963). How people define situations and what happens when the definition fails.

"Functions of a Bureaucratic Ideology" by Elliot A. Krause, *Social Problems* (Vol. 16, Fall 1968). The ideology of "citizen participation" is viewed as a strategy of motivating people to work for an organization.

Interaction Process Analysis by Robert Bales (Cambridge, Mass.: Addison-Wesley, 1950). A classic work on the sociology of small groups.

The Prison: Studies in Institutional Organization and Change edited by Donald R. Cressey (New York: Holt, Rinehart and Winston, 1961). Especially "On the Characteristics of Total Institutions" by Erving Goffman. Goffman describes the systematic invasion of privacy and resocialization that follows when an individual becomes totally immersed within one undifferentiated institutional realm.

The Society of Captives by Gresham M. Sykes (New York: Atheneum Press, 1965). Sykes describes the social structure, functions and values of prison personnel and inmates, two antagonistic groups whose polarization spotlights the issue of social control.

"Control over Policy by Attendants in a Mental Hospital" by Thomas J. Scheff, *Journal of Health and Human Behavior* (Vol. 2, Summer 1961).

"The Corruption of Authority and Rehabilitation" by Gresham M. Sykes in *Complex Organizations* edited by Amitai Etzioni (New York: Holt, Rinehart and Winston, 1961).

"Power-Dependence Relationships" by Richard M. Emerson, *American Sociological Review* (Vol. 27, Feb. 1962).

"The Laws of Power in a Large Mental Hospital" by Elaine and John Cumming, *Psychiatry* (Vol. 19, Nov. 1956).

"Professional Autonomy and the Revolt of the Client" by Marie R. Haug and Marvin B. Sussman, *Social Problems* (Vol. 17, Fall 1969) discusses how professionals have been attacked by their clients and how they use cooptation in an attempt to preserve their autonomy.

Together in Isolation

Can the strains of isolation be reduced by careful psychological pairing?

WILLIAM W. HAYTHORN
IRWIN ALTMAN

When Admiral Richard E. Byrd "wintered over" at an advanced weather station close to the South Pole in 1934-1935, he decided to go it alone because he felt that two could hardly be cooped up together for five months without seriously threatening each other's existence. He understood very well that he would face stresses of complete isolation. But isolation *with* another man—with all the personal conflicts and irritations that would inevitably result—seemed worse to Byrd.

The terrors of isolation are well known to explorers, prospectors, wardens, lighthousekeepers—and, more recently, submariners, Arctic weather and radar station operators, and astronauts. Our earliest prisons were built so that the sinner might have solitude in which to meditate on and repent his sins; but they produced more suicides and psychotics than repentant sinners. "Cabin fever" and "going stir-crazy" are still potent expressions for the effects of loneliness.

A variety of psychological strains—apart from any physical dangers—are created when small groups are isolated from their fellows and confined to limited spaces, such as undersea stations and space capsules. Chief among these strains are *stimulus reduction, social isolation,* and *interpersonal conflict.*

■ Research on *stimulus reduction* shows that man needs a minimum level of stimulation—and variety of stimuli—to survive and retain his faculties. People confined to dark, quiet chambers—the traditional "solitary confinement" of the prisoner, or the sound-proof room used for training astronauts—often display bizarre stress and anxiety symptoms, including hallucinations, delusions, apathy, and the fear of losing sanity. Their performance deteriorates. In fact, recent evidence suggests that important changes may actually occur in the nervous system that will persist for some time after the isolate comes back to the normal world. Men in lonely military stations have shown similar reactions, if to a lesser degree. Men simply may not be built to adapt well to a closed-in world with too little stimulus or variety.

■ *Social isolation* creates other problems. Man is a social animal. He needs other people; he gets emotional support from them; he understands and tests reality, and his feelings and beliefs, in large part through his interactions with them. Confined to a small group, his opportunity to get what he needs are strongly limited, and this can lead to frustration, dissatisfaction, and increased irritability. Without the normal ability to judge himself and his performance through the reactions of others, the accuracy and stability of his performance must fall, his emotional responses become less appropriate, and he may even become confused about what he really believes.

■ In isolation, *interpersonal conflict* becomes exaggerated —and there is less chance to go outside to blow off steam or escape from the difficulties of adjustment. In these circumstances irritations are likely to accumulate to the point of explosion. Such frictions are reported in histories of isolated groups almost without exception. In many instances, such conflicts have resulted in breaking up the group—even murder. Taken together, existing research and other evidence indicates that explorers of the future— in space and underseas—face socio-psychological hazards that may equal the physical threats of new environments.

Who Is the Good Adjustor?

From the available literature, mostly anecdotal descriptions of what presumably took place in such environments as Arctic stations, we get some general descriptions of the persons who adjust well to isolation—and of those who do not. In temperament the poor adjustor to isolation is anxious, restless, individualistic. He wants a lot of activity and an ever-changing environment. He is intolerant of whatever he doesn't like. But the good adjustor *is* tolerant—of others, of authority, of tedium. He is more conformist, much less likely to do something considered against regulations, improper, or illegal.

But "good adjustor," of course, is a relative term; all men suffer in isolation. Even a good adjustor cannot be locked into a space capsule with just anybody—or even with just any other good adjustor. So what kinds of people can get along together with the least amount of open friction in isolation? What kinds can accomplish most work when locked up together? What kinds simply sentence one another to mutual tedium?

The literature on group composition, though not addressed specifically to isolated groups, sheds some light on interpersonal stresses and adjustments. It indicates that compatibility and team coordination can be strongly affected by proper choices of group members. A large variety of group characteristics have been examined, but for two-man teams they can be generally classified as:

—*competitive,* in which both cannot be mutually satisfied, as when both seek to dominate;

—*congruent,* in which both have similar needs, which can be satisfied from the same source, as when both like classical music, similar foods, or the same topics of conversation—or when both want to achieve a common goal;

—*complementary,* in which the needs are different, but mutually satisfied in the same situation, as when one likes to lead and one to be led, one is dependent and one likes to help others.

But ordinary group behavior is not necessarily the same as isolated group behavior. Specifically, what happens when pairs of men are locked together around the clock that would not happen if they were merely fellow workers or roommates who went their own ways at night? To answer this question the literature was not enough; a controlled experiment was necessary.

Eighteen pairs of men—young sailors in boot training —were selected to meet certain conditions of compatibility, in order to determine how much of the stress of isolation could be relieved by properly matching personalities. They were tested and rated in four personality dimensions:

■ Need for *achievement.* This was defined as the desire or need to accomplish some overall goal—a task-orientation, or work-orientation.

■ Need for *dominance:* the need or desire for control over others, for individual prominence—a self-orientation.

■ Need for *affiliation:* the need and desire for affection, and association with others.

■ Need for *dogmatism:* the need to believe that one's own opinions and ideas are the only important ones; an inability to tolerate dissent; ethnocentric personality.

They were then matched in such a way that in one-third of the pairs both men were high in each of these dimensions, in one-third both were low, and in the final third one was high and one low.

Each pair in the experimental group was confined to a small room (12 feet by 12 feet) and isolated from outside contacts for 10 days. They were given a certain amount of work to do on a fixed schedule, but they were free to talk, read, play cards and checkers for several hours each day. They were not free to communicate in any way with the outside. They had no mail, radios, watches, or calendars.

The control group, composed of similar pairs, followed the same work schedule in identical rooms—but they slept in their regular Navy barracks, ate at the base mess, and were allowed to leave work for short breaks. In the evening they could use base recreation facilities.

The findings of the experiment will be presented in several categories:

- *Territoriality*—the degree and intensity of the tendency to stake out certain areas, positions, and pieces of furniture as being exclusively one's own and off limits to others.
- *Disclosure*—the intimacy with which each person confided in his partner and the extent of the confidence.
- *Performance*—how well each personality type, in each condition of matching and environment did his tasks.
- *Personality interaction and social behavior*—how well the different pairings got along with each other.

This Land Is My Land

Many animals show a possessiveness about specific objects and places that has been called "territoriality." Early in the spring, for instance, male robins stake out individual areas to receive mates and will fight any other males that try to enter. Very little scientific evidence on territoriality exists for humans, but many parallels have been marked, and a few anthropological and social-psychological studies suggest that it operates in men. For instance, delinquent gangs fight to protect their "turf." Anthropologist Jules Henry in *Culture Against Man* describes a dreadful scene in a home for aged paupers in which the inmates, stripped of possessions and dignity, still fought to protect their final refuge of identification—their beds.

Possessiveness about pieces of furniture and equipment has been cited as one cause of friction in isolated groups. Through one-way glass we observed our experimental isolated pairs and control pairs to see how true this was, and whether and to what extent it really affected both the isolation and the clash of personalities.

We predicted that the isolates would be much more particular about staking claims to specific beds, chairs, and sides of the table than the non-isolated. This turned out to be true. Isolates established preferences for their beds quickly and definitely, with little intrusion into each other's sleeping space. This separation eased a little with time but not very much. Since beds are highly personal objects with fixed geographic locations, but chairs are non-personal and movable, territoriality about chairs and place at table developed more slowly, but it was definite after a few days.

The reverse pattern held for the non-isolates: they established early preferences for chairs and place at table, which declined with time, and relatively little personal preferences for bunks at first, but this increased with time.

Getting to Know You

We had anticipated that the isolated pairs would, over time, confide much more personal information to each other than those who left every evening and that this would increasingly include intimate information—in other words, both greater breadth *and* depth of disclosure. Literature about isolated groups had suggested that people use each other as sources of stimulation—and that they might use disclosure to speed up acquaintanceship.

"Admiral Richard E. Byrd understood that he would face stresses of complete isolation, but isolation with another man—with all the personal conflicts and irritations that would inevitably result—seemed worse to Byrd."

Results, obtained from questionnaires, were pretty much as predicted. Isolated pairs gave each other more personal information of every kind, both intimate and non-intimate, than non-isolates. In contrast, the controls confided in each other about as much as they usually did with men in their regular training company, but much less than with their best friends. Confidences by isolates to their roommates, both intimate and general, were considerably greater than they gave to the usual barracks acquaintance. While less than "best friends," they could be considered the equivalent of relations with close friends.

It appeared that such extremely close contact and dependency produced pressures to learn about each other rapidly—a situation that does not necessarily lead to permanence (much like a fragile "summer romance," with too little time spent in "courtship"). The results showed that more intimate information is exchanged only after a certain amount of less intimate information has been sampled—as though the total information about a person is padded around a central core like the layers of an onion, and the social penetration process consists of cutting a wedge through the layers. Isolates did not achieve broad exchange at these deeper levels.

Were these greater exchanges due merely to the greater amount of time spent together? Not entirely. Observers reported that during free periods isolates generally talked, socialized, and played together more than non-isolates. They were rated as being more friendly, showing more social initiative, than the controls. There were exceptions, of course (as discussed below), and the pattern did vary somewhat with time. But, generally, the isolates seemed to be trying harder to get to know each other, realizing perhaps that they had little alternative.

Records were also kept of the extent to which the men engaged in solitary or joint activities. Isolated pairs at first, as noted, did many things together, but gradually drew apart, spending more time in solitary activities such as reading or lying on their bunks. It appeared as though isolates began to draw a "cocoon" around themselves as the pattern of isolation became firmly fixed, withdrawing into their own territories and dealing with each other less and less. This same "cocooning" has been reported in groups kept isolated by nature. The non-isolates, in contrast, started out spending more and more of their time alone, but this declined in the last days as joint activity increased.

Toil and Trouble

Questionnaire responses and performance scores on various tasks indicated that the isolated pairs experienced greater stress than the non-isolated—but nonetheless performed better. It has been known for many years that moderate levels of stress generally result in better performance. Nobody worked hard in the Garden of Eden.

But nobody can get much work done in the middle of combat either. Isolated pairs had far more trouble and personal conflict than controls. Two pairs were unable to complete the 10 days in the room, though it was comfortable enough, air-conditioned, and in no way physically threatening. Two other pairs showed great hostility—including extreme verbal abuse and some actual fighting. In one pair it reached such a pitch that the experimenters—who monitored the rooms day and night—had to step in to keep it from getting worse or being repeated. These results reflect closely not only the effects of isolation but the interactions of the personalities involved, exaggerated and made more dramatic by isolation.

As noted, one of the chief interests of the study was to determine the effects of the various combinations of different personalities. The characteristics—need for dominance, dogmatism, affiliation, and achievement—had been chosen because they had proved useful in previous studies of small groups. For every personality characteristic, at least one combination was incompatible. Two dominant men in the same room would be obviously incompatible. Those with different ways of thinking would not agree on how to face mutual problems; those with different needs for affiliation would expect contrasting things from each other, leading to a tense "climate" (the cool, laconic, independent man would obviously irk and be irked by the gregarious, loud, dependent one); and dissimilar needs to achieve could easily convince one man that the other was lazy, and the other that the first was an "eager beaver" "bucking" for promotion.

Of the four groups that had the most trouble, including the severe arguments and fighting, three pairs were both high in dominance, and two were strongly contrasting in their need for achievement—proving the hypothesis that

"The terrors of isolation are well known to explorers, prospectors, wardens, lighthousekeepers—and, more recently, submariners and astronauts." (Full-scale model for the three-man Apollo spacecraft)

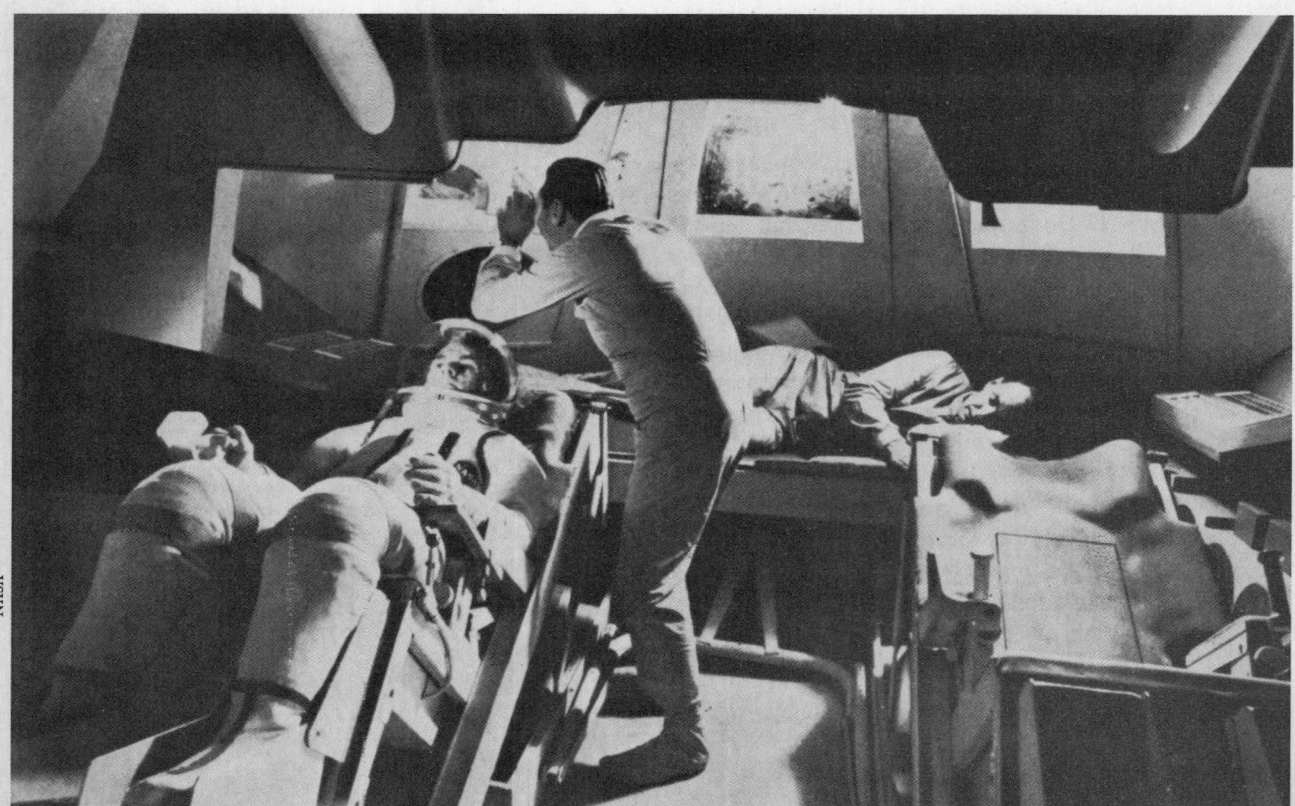

putting together in isolation two domineering men, or one who was a driving "go-getter" and one who was not, would very likely lead to trouble. Territoriality was much more strongly marked in these incompatibles than in other isolated pairs.

However, "in isolation" is an important qualifier. Among the controls, who went home every evening, though there was obvious tension, fighting did not break out, and incompatibles actually performed better than the compatible —once more demonstrating the idea that a certain amount of tension is desirable for good performance.

While these two incompatible combinations showed similarity in conflict and territoriality, they also showed a fundamental difference. The high dominance pairs worked, played (and argued) together a lot—they could be termed active, competitive, and volatile, and their arguments were part of this picture. But those incompatible in achievement, when duty or circumstance did not force them into confrontation, tended to withdraw and avoid each other when they could.

The dogmatic isolates (who believed that only their opinions were worth considering) also had a lot of active social interchange, including arguments—but they were not so concerned with private territories.

But the isolated pairs with contrasting needs for affiliation were the most consistently passive and withdrawn of the lot, staking out private preserves to which they could retreat from each other. In this way they resembled closely those pairs with incompatible achievement needs. Generally, they had relatively subdued, quiet and private relationships, where members bore one another in relative silence, at a distance, and from their own territories. Their method of adjustment to incompatibility was social withdrawal—movement *away* from one another. This is in strong contrast with dominance incompatibility, which led to a noisy, volatile, aggressive relationship—movement *against* one another.

The Self and the Social

Perhaps these differences and similarities in personality adjustments and clashes can be better understood if we take the analysis a step further. Dominance and dogmatism are *egocentric* qualities—they reflect primary concern for the self—whether in relation to other persons (dominance) or to ideas and/or things (dogmatism). Need for affiliation and need for achievement are *sociocentric* qualities—they reflect concern for joint relationships between the self and others (affiliation) and as members of a group striving for a common goal outside the self (achievement).

The high dominance pair is competitive because each is trying to get the other to do what he wants. The highly dogmatic person regards his view as the only important one, whether in personal beliefs or in organization and performance of mutual tasks; and his partner is not likely to take this arrogance quietly.

Those with high need for affiliation, on the other hand, satisfy themselves *by* satisfying others, working to set up close and friendly relationships; and, similarly, a man with a strong need to achieve will work closely and enthusiastically with another who is in pursuit of the same goal. Thus self-fulfillment is achieved through joint effort, helping each other. In both need for affiliation and achievement the focus is more on what a person does *for others* than it is with either dominance or dogmatism. Where the pair is incompatible for affiliation or achievement—that is, a high affiliator or achiever combined with a low one—they are incongruent rather than competitive or conflicting. They are frustrated more by the situation than the person—by what the other *doesn't* do rather than by what he does. Eager to cooperate, they depend on parallel eagerness. Faced by apathy, non-cooperation, or unfriendliness, they retreat and try to go their own ways. On the other hand the dominant or dogmatic do not really want cooperation (though they may use the word)—they want acquiescence.

This study demonstates clearly that the stresses of isolation are considerably affected by the relations between personality types. Good adjustment may decrease or modify stress in constructive ways; bad adjustment may increase, exaggerate, or complicate it, sometimes in destructive ways.

Should interpersonal conflict therefore be avoided in today's space capsules, Antarctic stations, and sea labs? No. It can enliven an existence of otherwise deadly and crippling monotony. It can produce better performance. The questions we now have to answer are: How much stress? What kinds? How to assure that proper matches are made?

January-February 1967

SUGGESTED READINGS

Sensory Restriction: Effects on Behavior by D. P. Schultz (New York: Academic Press, 1965).

Isolation: Clinical and Experimental Approaches by C. A. Brownfield (New York: Random House, 1965).

Theory and Experiment in Social Communication by Leon Festinger, Stanley Schachter and Kurt Back (Ann Arbor, Michigan: Research Center for Group Dynamics, University of Michigan, 1950).

The Social Psychology of Groups by John W. Thibaut and Harold H. Kelley (New York: John Wiley and Sons, 1959).

The Machiavellians by Stanley S. Guterman (Lincoln: University of Nebraska, 1970). A social psychological study of moral character and organizational milieu.

Hidden Society by Vilhelm Aubert (Totowa, New Jersey: Bedminster, 1965). Articles on social groups which are isolated from the rest of society, i.e. the underground, a remote ship, a love relationship.

Paths of Loneliness by Margaret Wood (New York: Columbia University Press, 1953) discusses loneliness and separation felt by an increasing proportion of our society.

Open Occupancy—What Whites Say, What They Do

In predicting how people will act, their attitudes are good clues—but so are social pressures

GORDON H. DeFRIESE
W. SCOTT FORD JR.

In recent years, the issue of "open occupancy" has become a source of fierce social conflict, particularly in urban areas where there are shortages of adequate housing for certain minority groups. Not only is this an important contemporary social issue, but it is an arena of behavior that involves some of the fundamental issues of social psychology—such as the question of an individual's readiness to translate his attitude into overt action.

Thus, suppose a white man says he is not prejudiced against Negroes. Would he also be willing to have Negroes of his same social class move into his neighborhood—and willing to let his anti-Negro neighbors *know* how he feels? Suppose we were aware of what his feelings about Negroes were, and also aware of what power social pressure had over him. Could we then accurately predict what he would say if asked to let his anti-Negro neighbors know about his feelings?

These questions can be rephrased as follows:

■ How are the attitudes that whites express about open occupancy related to their willingness to take clear, public stands for—or against—neighborhood desegregation?

■ How do social pressures affect a white person's willingness to do so?

Prior studies suggest that whatever people say they believe is strongly related to what they actually do. But there is no one-to-one relationship: You almost always find discrepancies.

In 1958, Melvin L. DeFleur and Frank R. Westie conducted a study that bears directly on the question of attitude versus action (*American Sociological Review*). They tried to find out how willing a number of college students were to be photographed with members of another race.

First, the students were given a verbal test that measured their general attitudes toward Negroes. Then they were asked to sign a series of "releases," indicating that they were willing to be photographed with Negroes—and that they would allow these photographs to be widely publicized. The researchers found that many of the students were inconsistent: One-third of those who had evinced liberal attitudes balked at signing the releases.

Next, each of the students was asked why he had signed, or refused to sign, the releases. From their answers, it appeared that most of the students were greatly influenced by social pressure—by whether they thought certain groups that they respected (parents, friends) would approve or disapprove of their signing. DeFleur and Westie concluded that this indirect pressure from reference groups is what intervenes between attitude and behavior—and brings about discrepancies.

Lawrence S. Linn used the DeFleur-Westie technique in a 1965 study (*Social Forces*), and found that over 50 percent of his subjects diverged in their attitudes toward Negroes and the way they behaved toward Negroes. In post-test interviews, his subjects told him they couldn't adjust their actions to their attitudes because of social and cultural pressures around them.

Yet, in one important way, Linn's findings differed from those of DeFleur and Westie. DeFleur and Westie concluded that social constraints intervened between attitudes and behavior—attitudes → social pressure → behavior. But Linn concluded that social and cultural influences are actually part of the background environment, and don't intervene *directly* in decision-making—social pressure → attitudes → behavior. In other words, social pressures help form attitudes, which influence behavior. Their effect, therefore, is indirect.

We ourselves agree with Linn—that when a person forms his attitudes, he "internalizes" the sentiments and values of other people who are important to him. But we also believe that social pressures *do* intervene directly between attitude and behavior. In short, social pressure → attitudes → social pressure → behavior. When people are in situations where they must make choices between conflicting demands, "what others will think or do" becomes a direct and important variable.

From the body of theory and research on attitudes and reference groups, we have formulated this proposition: In theory, a direct relationship exists between a person's expressed attitude and his likely behavior. But discrepancies do occur, and they are due to social constraints, which intervene between attitude and action and disturb the direct relationship.

For our study on open occupancy, we devised these hypotheses:
■ There is a direct relationship between the intensity of a person's verbal attitude toward Negroes and the way he behaves in regard to open occupancy.
■ There is a direct relationship between a person's response to open occupancy and the influence exerted by individuals and groups important to him.
■ These two variables—prior attitudes and influential groups—are better clues to a person's future behavior when measured together than when measured separately.

To Sign or Not to Sign?

To test these hypotheses, we interviewed some 400 whites in an urban area where housing values ranged between $10,000 and $15,000. There was an urgent need for Negro housing in that price range. But the study area was in a border state, and we knew of no Negroes who had bought or rented homes in middle- or upper-class white neighborhoods. Local real-estate agents resisted such sales or rentals, and many whites were afraid that their property values were threatened. Open occupancy had become an issue of bitter controversy.

From our individual subjects, we tried to learn three things:
■ What is his attitude toward Negroes?
■ Will he sign a statement indicating his willingness to endorse, or participate in, an interracial-housing policy for his neighborhood and town?
■ What groups might influence his attitudes and behavior—and how?

All the subjects took a test that measured their attitudes toward Negroes in general. Then they received two documents, each with a place for a signature. The first read:

"I, the undersigned, do hereby make public the declaration that I have *no objection* to having Negro families of social and economic characteristics similar to my own live in my neighborhood, and I *would*, in fact, uphold such practices within the community.

The second document read:

"I, the undersigned, do hereby make public the declaration that I *do object* to having Negro families live in my neighborhood, regardless of their social and economic characteristics, and I would *not,* in fact, uphold such practices within the community."

The subjects could sign either or neither. Of course, we put no pressure on them. But we told them that if they did sign, we would feel free to use these signatures in any way we wish, including *publicizing them through the news media.* Signing either document, therefore, was a real, meaningful, overt expression of a subject's stand on open occupancy.

After the subjects had either signed or not signed one of the documents, we gave them a list of groups that might have influenced them in their decision—immediate family, co-workers, neighbors, close relatives, and close friends. We then asked our subjects to indicate how much influence each group might have had on their decision to sign or not to sign ("great," "small," "no importance"). We also asked them to identify any other people or group *not* listed that might have influenced their decision. Finally, we asked them how they thought each of these groups felt about open occupancy, and how much these groups agreed with one another. (A subject's estimate of a group's attitudes might not be precisely accurate, of course, but we considered this less important than the fact that he *thought* his estimate was accurate. When people think something is true, it *is* true, for them, and they act accordingly.)

TABLE I—How Attitudes Indicate Behavior—Responses to the Open Occupancy Documents

Attitude Scale Scores	Signed document for open housing	Did not sign	Signed document against open housing
0.00 to 0.99 (least prejudice)	1	1	1
1.00 to 1.99	8	36	5
2.00 to 2.99	5	50	7
3.00 to 3.99	1	47	30
4.00 to 4.99	0	31	23
5.00 to 5.99	0	6	10
6.00 to 7.00 (most prejudice)	0	0	0
Totals	15	171	76
Median Attitude Scale Scores	1.90	3.02	3.80

All the interviews were conducted over a single weekend—the short time-schedule was arranged to keep rumors from spreading that might affect the findings. Then too, we were afraid that, by interviewing people about open occupancy in a former slave-owning state with continuing problems of integration, there might be nasty incidents. Fortunately, no serious trouble arose. Some subjects, however, flatly refused to cooperate; some didn't supply important parts of the attitude tests; some had problems in communicating. Still, we obtained 262 fully completed, cooperatively obtained interviews.

Table I illustrates the relationship, in our study, between prejudice and overt behavior. Generally, the least prejudiced were the most likely to sign the first document; the most prejudiced were the most likely to sign the second document; those falling in between were most likely to sign neither.

Had we known in advance what a subject's attitude toward Negroes was, we could have increased the accuracy of predicting which document he would sign, or whether he would sign at all, by about 10 percent above chance. And if we consider only those subjects who signed one document—not those who signed neither—advance knowledge of *their* attitudes would have enabled us to increase our accuracy of prediction by as much as 40 percent above chance. Obviously, on the open-occupancy issue there is a definite connection between expressed attitude and overt behavior.

Table II indicates how much importance the subjects attributed to the influence of outside groups in trying to decide whether or not to sign either document. By and large, if we had known beforehand the importance our subjects attributed to social pressures, we could *not* have increased our accuracy of prediction very much beyond what knowledge of their attitudes had already provided. It might seem, then, that the influence of reference groups is minor: People responded to the question of open occupancy according to their own internal attitudes. However, the rest of the data allows another interpretation.

We had asked our subjects whether the groups that might influence them were "for," "against," or "neutral" about open occupancy (or whether they didn't know). We found that what a subject *thought* the reference groups thought about open occupancy was *as good* a predictor of how he would act as the attitudes he had expressed. Apparently our subjects were unwilling to acknowledge, or unconscious of, the power these outside groups had on their actions.

The Group Influence

Next, let's consider how a subject's views about the degree of consensus within his reference groups may have influenced his signing or not signing one of the documents. Clearly, social pressure from a group thought to be unanimous in outlook should be strongest. And here we found that we could predict which document a subject would sign, or whether he would not sign either, just as easily by measuring his belief about the amount of consensus in influence groups as by measuring his attitudes. There was a direct relationship between the subject's views on open occupancy and his conception of what his reference groups' views were.

Now, the third hypothesis was that attitudes and the influence of others, working together, would show a greater total effect on behavior than these two factors measured separately. This turned out to be true only when *all* choices (signing the first, signing the second, or signing neither) were considered. When only the signers of either the first or second document were considered, attitudes and influence groups together were *not* better predictors than each taken separately. This may be because these people had the strongest opinions and resolve, and were the most inner-directed, so their attitudes were far more decisive than social pressures. In fact, the reference groups these people have may have been chosen according to their agreement with the subjects' own views.

That the behavior of those willing to take a stand could be predicted as easily from their attitudes or

TABLE II—How Reference Groups Indicate Behavior— Responses to the Open Occupancy Documents

Attributed importance of reference groups (Index values*)	Signed document for open housing	Did not sign	Signed document against open housing
0-5 (little importance)	10	82	30
6-10	3	38	14
11-15	2	23	12
16-20	0	10	5
21-25	0	9	6
26-30 (great importance)	0	9	9
Totals	15	171	76

* For each reference group of "Great Importance," respondent was given 6 points; for each of "Some Importance," 3 points; and for each of "No Importance," no points were given. Maximum index value = 30 points.

reference groups *taken singly* is, of course, significant. True, it is much simpler to learn people's attitudes than to learn what groups influence them, how much, and why, and then work out a combination of the two factors. But on an issue as touchy as open occupancy, the majority may well be unable or unwilling to state their preferences openly. In this study (Tables I and II), the number who signed neither paper was nearly twice as high as the number who signed either of the documents. There were over 11 times as many who signed neither as there were who took the unpopular course of signing the first document. And for this large, cautious group (and, therefore, for all groups put together), expressed attitude *plus* the pressure of influence groups is a better predictor of ultimate behavior than either factor alone.

Certainly, the nonsigner—the disengaged in general—warrants more attention from researchers. In this study, he was not strongly committed for or against open occupancy. In amount of prejudice against Negroes, he ranged between signers of the first document and signers of the second. Still, we will have a much better idea of how he will behave if we know what groups influence him than if we know only the attitudes he expresses. Outside pressures have a tremendous power over him, and when the winds of passion and social change rise, he leans with them.

All in all, our data confirm the hypothesis that a person's attitudes, and the social pressures on him, are better clues to his future behavior when measured together than when measured separately. These data certainly do not suggest that measuring attitudes alone is useless in this respect: Knowledge of a person's attitudes is important in our effort to make valid predictions about human behavior. But what our findings do suggest is that there are also definite advantages in measuring the force of social pressures when trying to predict how people will respond to significant social issues.

April 1968

SUGGESTED READINGS

Strangers Next Door: Ethnic Relations in American Communities by Robin M. Williams, Jr. (Englewood Cliffs, N.J.: Prentice-Hall, 1964). Reports the results of several community studies of discrimination and prejudice. Empirical results, theoretical discussions, and policy recommendations are included.

Studies in Housing and Minority Groups edited by Nathan Glazer and Davis McEntire (Berkeley: University of California Press, 1960). Presents research reports on discrimination in housing prepared for the Commission on Race and Housing.

Social Change and Prejudice by Bruno Bettelheim and Morris Janowitz (New York: The Free Press, 1964). Essentially an evaluation and extension of their first work, *The Dynamics of Prejudice;* includes a discussion of the changing manifestations of prejudice.

Interracial Housing by Morton Deutch and Mary E. Collins (Minneapolis: University of Minnesota Press, 1951). In housing projects where Negroes and whites were integrated, the authors found a reduction in prejudice and an increase in harmonious inter-group relations.

Advocacy in the Ghetto

Social workers fight the "welfare establishment" to secure legal rights of the poor

RICHARD A. CLOWARD
RICHARD M. ELMAN

There are 500,000 people in New York City living on welfare payments, but until November 1965 no delegation of public dependents had been received in the office of a Commissioner of Welfare for more than 30 years. (The last time was in the days of the Worker's Alliance, a union of recipients and public welfare workers.) Three decades had gone by since welfare recipients had presented their needs and their grievances directly to the man in charge. This is the story of events that led up to that meeeting—a story of how social workers turned into advocates in order to secure their clients' rights from the welfare bureaucracy and of how recipients themselves began to organize for action. It suggests a pattern that can be used elsewhere in the country to deal with the daily problems of living under the welfare state.

In November 1962 a social worker from Mobilization for Youth and one assistant moved into an unoccupied storefront at 199 Stanton Street on New York's Lower East Side. It was located in an apartment building which did not then rent to Negroes, Puerto Ricans, or persons on welfare.

Across the street was a *bodega*. Another grocery, down the block, was the principal numbers racket drop for the area. MFY put some chairs and couches in the brightly painted waiting room in the front of the store. Then a sign was painted on the front window: CENTRO DE SERVICIO AL VECINDARIO . . . NEIGHBORHOOD SERVICE CENTER. On the door was lettered: WALK IN! Many Stanton Street residents, 14 percent of whom are on public assistance, accepted the invitation. They were invited to describe their problems. The MFY workers soon found that the lengthy verbal charge sheet made by people against the hostile environment in which they were forced to live, could be distilled into a grievance against "welfare."

It soon became clear to branch director Joseph Kreisler that unresolved problems with public welfare were a crucial factor in the instability of life along Stanton Street. If people didn't have enough welfare they weren't able to pay their bills at the grocer. If they didn't get their welfare

INTERACTION AND COMMUNICATION

checks on time, they would be in trouble with their landlords. If welfare didn't provide money for school clothing, they would have to keep their children home from school and would have difficulties with the authorities. This day-to-day relationship with the welfare bureaucracy was making people bitter and angry and punitive toward one another.

But, if the pattern seemed clear to Kreisler and his supervisor, Sherman Barr, those who complained most bitterly were not able to pinpoint the sources of their misery quite so precisely. As one man put it, "I feel that the City of New York has abandoned me." Others told of harrowing experiences with welfare officials as if such dealings were the way that things should be. Since they had never been led to expect any better treatment from such an agency, they had no awareness of their rights under the law.

It became necessary, therefore, for the MFY workers to assure people that they did have rights, and to demonstrate that their rights could be upheld and defended without recriminations. Such a determination by the workers often required a dogmatic conviction about injustice. One of them put it this way:

When I think that Mrs. Cortez hasn't gotten any money for her rat allowance I sometimes want to throw up my hands and say: What difference does it make? Why should people in this day and age have rat allowances? (A New York City welfare policy allows slum families extra allowances toward their utility bills to offset the cost of keeping their lights burning all night as a deterrence against rats.) But when I realize that it isn't just the rat allowance . . . that it's a total system of oppressiveness and disrespect for people, why then I've got to get her that rat allowance. I've got to help her get as many things as possible.

Few of the workers were at first so dogmatic. Kreisler, for example, was a veteran of the public welfare systems of New York and Maine, familiar with the savagery of some welfare policies and the Pecksniffian quality of others (such as a New York City regulation which makes it mandatory to mail clients' checks out late before a weekend so that they will not have the money to spend on drink). But even he had his "eyes opened" by the volume of abuses that were recorded by workers through the testimony of their clients.

Bucking the Bureaucracy

In its first six months of operation, 199 Stanton Street received more than 200 families from an immediate three or-four block radius who attested to their antagonistic relationship with the Department of Welfare. Through the neighborhood grapevine many soon learned to come directly to Stanton Street after an affront at one of the local welfare centers. In addition, of the non-welfare families who came during those first six months, nearly two-thirds listed "insufficient income" as their principal problem, which meant, in many cases, that they were not getting welfare benefits even though they were eligible. At 199 Stanton Street the social workers discovered that the problems of their clients were so tied to the bureaucratic workings of the city that they could keep their storefront open profitably only from 9 to 5 on weekdays, the normal working hours of public agencies.

This came as a distinct surprise to supervisory personnel at MFY. They had originally hoped to bring their workers more intimately in touch with the day-to-day affairs of their clients departing from traditional psycho-therapeutic methods and offering instead specific and practical advice on problems of health, housing, welfare, education, and employment. But even here, they saw their chief function as liaisons between clients and agencies; they did not yet realize that even these concrete activities would fail to resolve issues between the poor and the welfare state. Many workers soon found, however, that they had to do something more than refer, advise, and counsel if they were to get results. They were being called upon to take sides in a pervasive dispute between their clients and an agency of the welfare state. When they refused to do so, their clients abandoned them. A new practice soon evolved which came to be known as *advocacy*.

An advocate in this context is one who intervenes between an agency of government and his client to secure an entitlement or right which has thus far been obscured or denied. To act effectively, the advocate must have sufficient knowledge of the law and of the public agency's administrative procedures to recognize injustice when it occurs and then seek a solution in harmony with his client's interests. In practice, the Stanton Street advocates often found that they had to instruct the representatives of welfare agencies in the law and how it should be interpreted. One of the advocate's most demanding tasks was to serve notice on his opposite number within the welfare bureaucracy that he was prepared to move a notch further up the hierarchy if justice was not tendered on the present level.

Thus the advocates listened to endless tales of woe. They counted up scores of welfare budgets to detect possible underbudgeting. They placed telephone calls to a great number of functionaries and sometimes accompanied clients when they went to see these people in person. They argued and they cajoled. They framed rebuttals to cases put forward by welfare, but they also charged negligence.

They attacked as well as defended. When, for example, a Stanton Street woman was charged with child neglect, the alert worker was able to show that she had been consistently under-budgeted for more than a year, making her efforts at successful child-rearing virtually impossible. When another client was evicted for non-payment of rent, the worker attempted to force welfare to make the payment —because he could show that it had failed repeatedly in its legal obligation to do so.

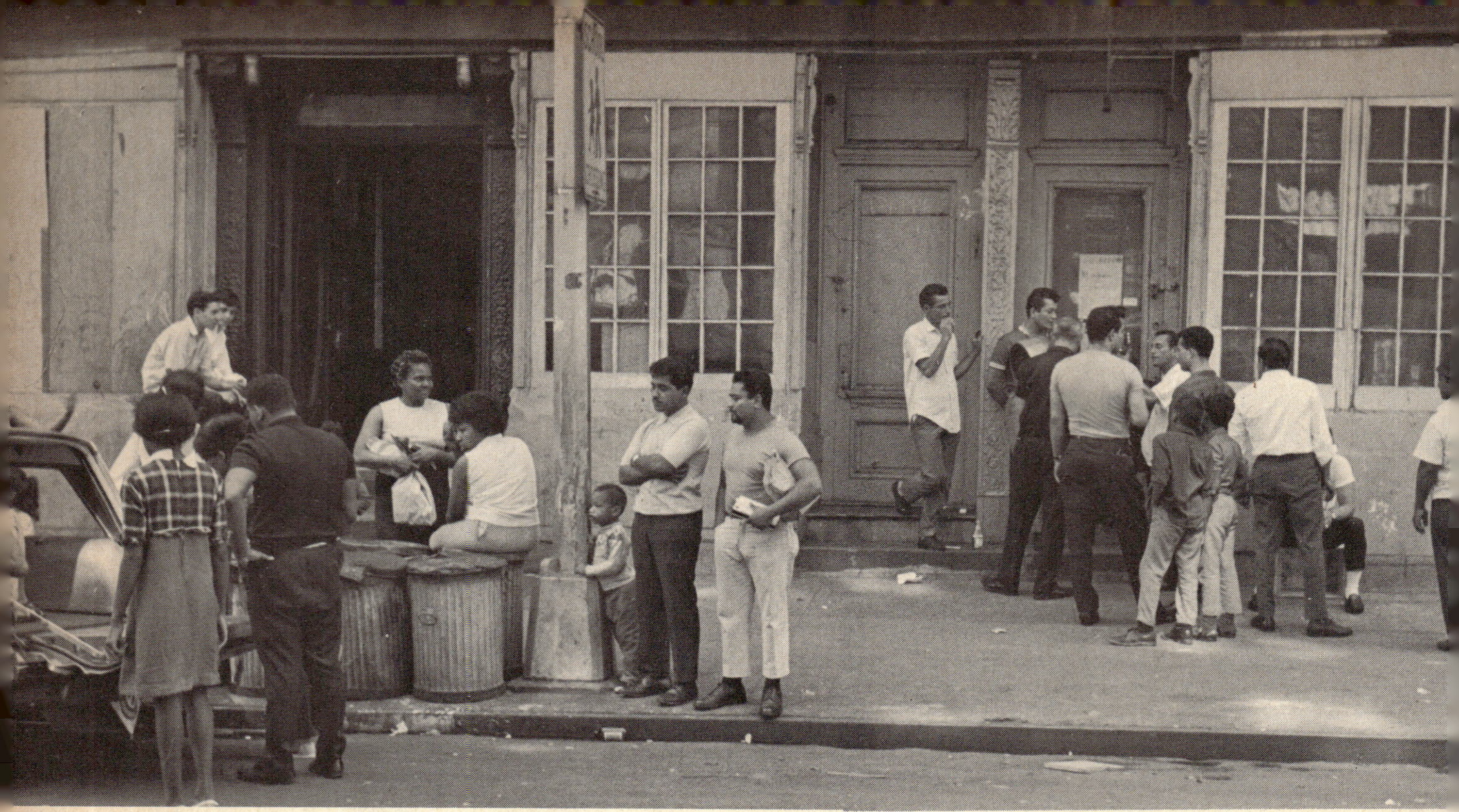

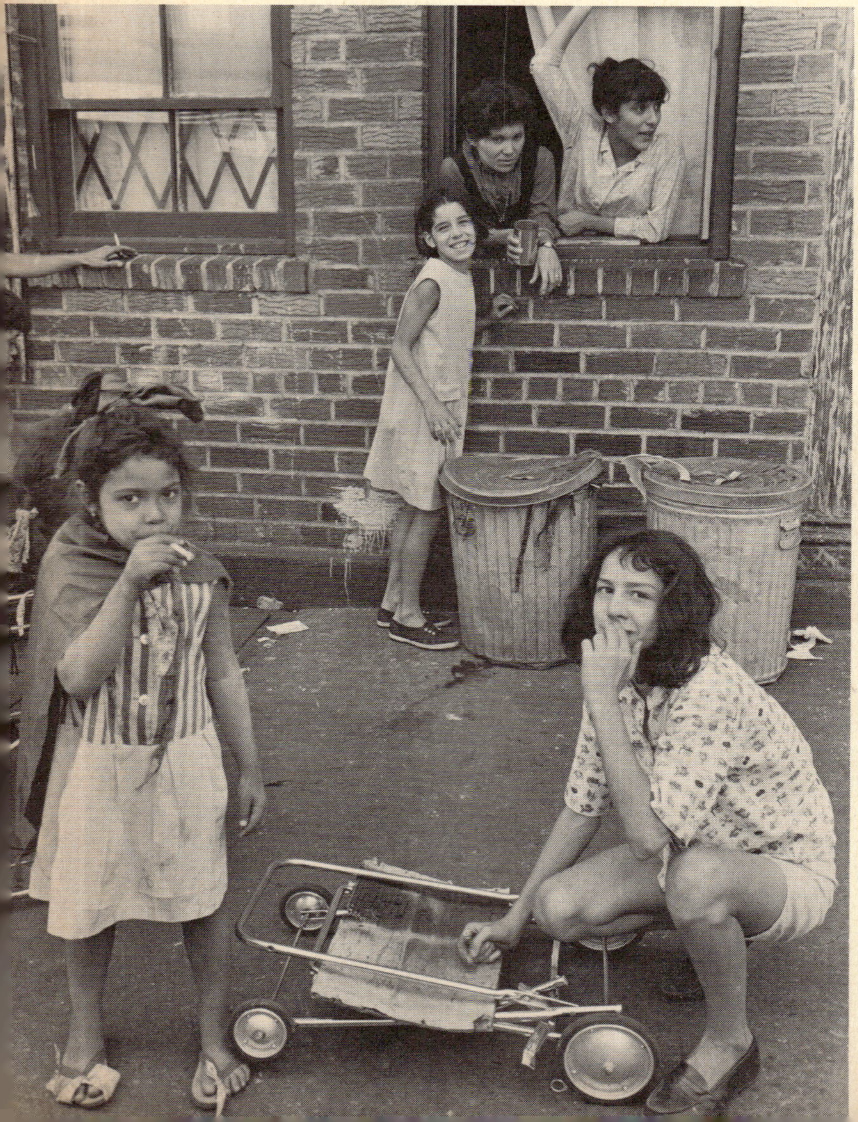

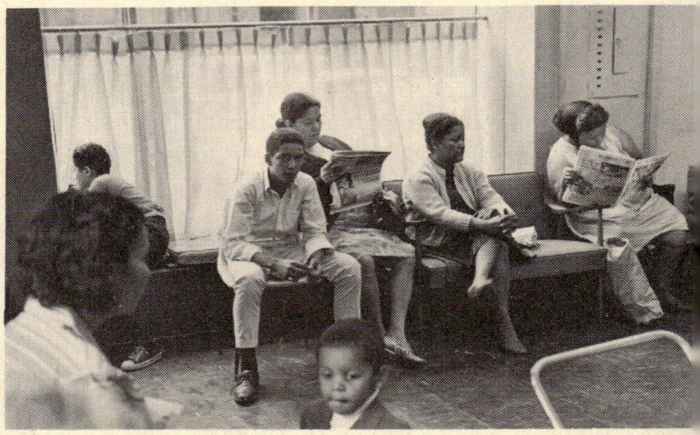

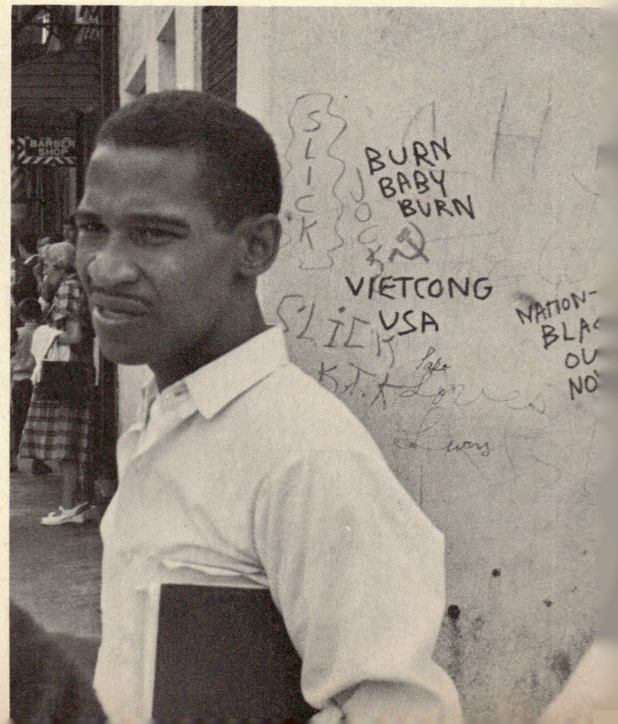
BURN
BABY
BURN
VIETCONG
USA

the scene on Stanton Street

Photographed by Charles Gatewood

"The storefront on Stanton Street has been in existence four years, and its work has increased ten-fold. If people don't have enough welfare they aren't able to pay their bills at the grocer. If they don't get their welfare checks on time, they will be in trouble with their landlords. If welfare doesn't provide money for school clothing, they will have to keep their children home from school and will have difficulties with the authorities."

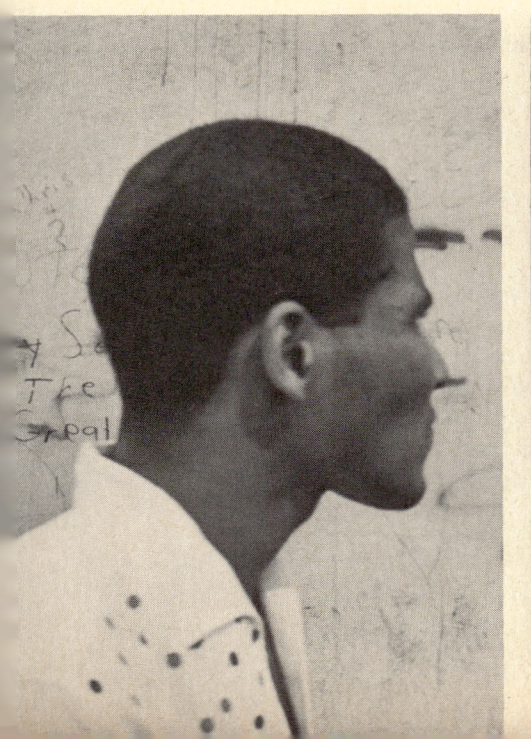

But, whether their threats were applied with politeness or out of anger, out of careful manipulation or a blustering disregard for the sensibilities of their opposite numbers, the primary force of such advocacy was in serving notice upon the low-level employee that he would be held responsible for his actions to his supervisor and on up the line. Thus advocacy was the bludgeon by which this city agency was made responsive to a portion of its Lower East Side constituency. At 199 Stanton Street the workers came to serve as surrogates for their clients with the bureaucratically arranged world outside the welfare ghetto.

This often militant advocacy was always carried on with a calculated informality. Young people were not discouraged from idling about the place, any client was free to come and go as he pleased; parties were held on holidays; neighborhood people were employed as janitors, clericals, and translators. Many of the professional workers and "case-aides" were either Negro or Puerto Rican, and there was little attention given to any differentiation of duties according to professional status. Moreover, the center managed to keep up an active and informative interviewing referral practice when clients came in with requests for other kinds of service. When a client came for help with welfare it was always possible for him to receive a loan or even a small outright gift of cash to tide him over while his case was being adjudicated. An effort was also made to keep a supply of clean used clothing on hand for those whose requests from welfare might take more than a few hours to resolve.

However, even though as much as $600 was given out in some months in small grants, the major reason that people were drawn to the center was that the workers took sides. They were willing to put themselves out to uphold their clients' rights under the welfare state. One Puerto Rican mother put it this way: "When you go alone to welfare they treat you like dirt. When you go with a social worker it's different."

Litigation—Not Indignation

After a year it became clear to the administration of MFY that the indignation of the social worker was not sufficient protection against the injustices of the social welfare state. So the agency established a free legal service to take referrals from neighborhood centers such as the storefront on Stanton Street. These attorneys applied themselves to eviction proceedings in public and private housing; they dealt with consumer frauds and other specialized areas of practice among the poor. But they also began to challenge decisions concerning welfare clients where the facts were at issue, or where actions had been taken in seeming violation of the intent of the law.

As a case in point, one might cite the New York State Welfare Abuses Act, passed in 1962 as a compromise measure to satisfy demands that New York bar public assistance to applicants from out of state. It was clearly stipulated by the legislators that only persons who could be shown to have come to New York for the express purpose of collecting relief could be lawfully denied such a benefit. In actual practice, however, the new resident's mere appearance at a welfare center to apply for relief was often taken as sufficient justification to deny him benefits.

By 1964 four attorneys were employed full time at MFY on cases brought to their attention by the social workers. It was because these lawyers threatened litigation that the local Department of Welfare center no longer invoked the Welfare Abuses Act as a matter of course. It was fear of litigation which prompted the department to abandon its policy of after-midnight intrusions on the residences of AFDC mothers to detect the presence of males—a policy which

---

"I trust the lawyers more than anybody because they would make a living even if there were no poor people."—A mother on welfare

---

seemed a clear-cut violation of the normal guarantees of privacy. The workers at Stanton Street were encouraged to bring those cases to the attention of MFY attorneys through which the legality of administrative acts could be contested in open hearings, so that precedents could be established.

Nevertheless, the lawyers also spent a good deal of their time advising workers and clients about how to adopt lawful and proper strategies to exploit those rights which did seem vested. Working closely with the social workers, the lawyers contested capricious eligibility rulings and attempted to reinstate eligibles whose benefits had been arbitrarily terminated. At times they argued the merits of the case. At other times they argued that the law had been perverted by bad administrative policies. The lawyers were prepared to represent the clients at the formal appeals tribunals of the state Department of Social Welfare, but they found that a majority of client grievances did not need to come before such "fair hearings." Often, just a telephone call from an MFY attorney expressing interest in a particular case served to persuade a functionary that he was acting without respect to a person's rights.

Because of welfare's desire to avoid establishing precedents and hence to settle out of court, the MFY legal service was able to litigate only a small percentage of the cases it was called in on, but its impact upon the legal vacuum within the welfare ghetto was impressive. Even after the addition of this free legal service, the workers at Stanton Street continued to be confronted with the bulk of cases requiring immediate advocacy; but they could now defend their clients' rights reinforced by the legal expertise of Edward Sparer (the first MFY legal director) and his associates. Moreover, they were able to increase their sophistication about welfare law through their continuing association with the attorneys, and they passed on some of this education to their opposite numbers in the welfare bureaucracy.

Even the clients benefited educationally from the program. Many had never before had any contacts with attorneys, except, perhaps, as their adversaries. Now these attorneys were representing them in adversary proceedings against the Department of Welfare, and they became aware of the power which proper representation bestows upon the private citizen. As one AFDC mother stated: "I trust the lawyers more than anybody because they would make a living if there were no poor people." When a bitter and prolonged strike afflicted the Department of Welfare in the winter of 1964-65, some MFY workers and clients from Stanton Street demonstrated in support of the welfare workers to signify that their complaints were against laws and policies, not individuals.

By the summer of 1963 MFY had established three other neighborhood centers along the Lower East Side. The agency's supervisory staff decided to solicit even more clients by publicizing its services through handbills, posters, and mass meetings. Some workers had also begun to seek out clients in distress, among other ways by reading newspaper accounts in the Spanish-language press. The strategy of the centers was now fixed. They were given a definite set of priorities for intervention with city agencies, of which welfare was to be the pre-eminent target.

This increasing attention to the advocacy tactic meant that the workers had to contend with increasing antagonism from the welfare department. The commissioner was angered, for example, by the threats of aggressive court action against welfare. The lower-echelon functionaries were angered by their harassment by MFY and would often respond with open hostility to calls from Stanton Street employees. "When I go to welfare," one Stanton Street worker declared, "I don't wait around for the stall. If I don't get treated with respect, I start hollering for the supervisor." Another said: "Any way you cut it they are the enemy." Perhaps this explains what one welfare worker meant when she described MFY's staff as "rude, angry, and non-professional." The accusation was also continually being made that some MFY workers lacked information about public-welfare policies in taking on their advocacy positions. But, since many Stanton Street workers were former welfare employees, it seems more reasonable to suppose that they were merely placing more liberal interpretations upon existing welfare regulations. Where, for example, some welfare caseworkers might use improvidence to justify not making an additional grant for a client, the Stanton Street workers would insist upon the person's legal right to such an entitlement beyond his supposed characterological defect.

One veteran employee with more than 30 years in the Department of Welfare was critical of the MFY policy of giving money to people on some occasions rather than forcing welfare to make these payments. However, though she found some of MFY's advocacy tactics "a little hard to bear," she was generally appreciative of the effects. "If we were doing our job," she said, "you wouldn't need any neighborhood centers . . . and if there were more neighborhood centers like this in the city of New York," she added, "we might have to begin to do a better job. . . . I learned what my workers were doing with some clients from the neighborhood service center. I might never have known otherwise." When this same person subsequently retired from the Department of Welfare, she was hired as a consultant by MFY to help cut through the knotty complex of rules and regulations by which people on Stanton Street were being governed. "What this proves to me," said one MFY staff member, "is that you have to work 30 years in the department to be able to get people what they are entitled to . . . and they expect our clients to just walk in and apply. . . ."

Such comments reflected the increasing hostility between welfare and the workers on Stanton Street. The workers also showed a tendency to exhibit hostility toward and impatience with their clients, who by now had transferred some of their previous dependency on welfare to the storefront on Stanton Street. "Can't these people do anything themselves?" was a phrase frequently heard among the workers.

Many of the workers seemed to be developing a resentment at having to perform rudimentary "non-professional" services on behalf of their clients over and over again, and some of the clients were also restless, spurred on, in part, by their activities in various MYF social-action programs. Presently the program heads, Barr and Kreisler, began to wonder whether, if the clients were given staff support and encouragement, they could begin to take over some of these practical efforts to deal with the welfare system. They reasoned, for example, that if 50 clients all needed the same items of clothing it might be more effective to make one request on behalf of 50 rather than 50 individual requests. They reasoned, too, that this strategy might coerce welfare into making certain of its grants more automatic, or, rather, less discretionary.

So, after three years, the center on Stanton Street decided to hire a "community organizer" to bring people together around their most commonly held interest—public welfare.

Organizing on Stanton Street

In the hot summer months Stanton Street people rarely go away on vacations. They start worrying about the cold months ahead. They know if they do not begin to bother their welfare workers about clothing for the winter, their requests may never be fulfilled. Thus, in the late summer of 1965, they came to make their usual requests to the advocate at 199 Stanton Street. Would the workers talk to welfare? Would they tell them what they needed? To their surprise they were advised to go next door and speak to the Committee of Welfare Families.

The Committee of Welfare Families was hardly more than a name at the time, although the concept of com-

The Welfare Marches

The first harbinger of a national welfare recipients' movement occurred in Ohio this year. Concerned groups throughout Ohio, loosely federated in a body known as the Regional Committee for Adequate Welfare, decided last spring to stage a 155-mile "walk for decent welfare," starting in Cleveland and ending on the steps of the state capitol in Columbus.

At the same time, a new national organization, the Poverty/Rights Action Center, was formed in Washington under the aegis of George Wiley, a former associate director of the Congress of Racial Equality. Upon learning of the welfare march in Ohio, the Poverty/Rights Action Center began to establish contact with welfare-recipient groups throughout the country, asking them to send delegates to the Ohio march and, if possible, to stage a demonstration in their home cities to coincide with the climax rally in Columbus.

Ohio's "walk for decent welfare" began on June 20, with the endorsement of a broad coalition of groups in Ohio—including professional, religious, and civic organizations. Approximately 35 persons, mostly welfare mothers and children, walked the entire 155 miles. In a number of cities they passed through, several hundred persons joined them for short distances. However, the 10-day walk through Ohio was largely eclipsed in the press by the more dramatic civil-rights march in Mississippi following the shooting of James Meredith. Nevertheless, on June 30, 2,000 persons congregated at East High School in Columbus to make the last leg of the march to the steps of the state capitol.

On that same day in New York City, a similar rally was in progress. Stimulated by the organizing success of the Committee of Welfare Families on the Lower East Side, welfare-recipient groups had begun to emerge in other sections of the city. In the late spring, a Citywide Coordinating Committee of Welfare Groups had been formed under the leadership of an executive committee of eight welfare recipients. The New York rally at City Hall drew 2,000 participants—mostly welfare recipients, but including social workers, clergymen, and members of the public welfare unions. They were met by the commissioner of welfare and the deputy mayor, and a session to negotiate greviances was conducted.

Similar but smaller demonstrations were held in approximately 18 other cities, including Boston, New Haven, Trenton, Philadelphia, Baltimore, Louisville, Chicago, Monterey.

Speaking at the Ohio rally, Dick Gregory said that this event "was not a civil rights movement, but a human rights movement" (for half of America's welfare poor are white). George Wiley described the nationwide demonstrations as the "first concerted action of a new movement."

In early August the Poverty/Rights Action Center convened a meeting in Chicago of 100 leaders of welfare recipient groups from 35 cities. For the first time, welfare groups began to have the feeling of being a national movement. It was agreed that the Poverty/Rights Action Center would continue to act as the coordinating agent for the welfare movement, and a national advisory committee to the Center was established.

As the summer ended, welfare groups in various cities opened new demonstrations, some of them employing tactics of direct action. On September 12, for example, New York welfare groups staged a mass demonstration at the Welfare Department, and when their demands for increased clothing allowances were not met, a sit-in was staged. Three days later, after constant picketing and mass rallies, 25 weary welfare mothers who had been sitting-in were finally arrested. Similar arrests have occurred in other cities, including Syracuse and Hartford. Out of these struggles, welfare recipient groups are developing confidence, are overcoming their deep-seated fear of the welfare system, and are producing militant leaders.

It remains to be seen whether a new movement can indeed be formed by the most despised sector of American society—its welfare poor. But it should at least be noted that there are powerful incentives for people to join such a movement. For one thing, ghetto people are becoming progressively more aware of the extent to which their rights as citizens are violated in the welfare state, notably by public welfare agencies. Resentment is growing against midnight raids and other forms of illegal search and seizure, not to speak of the violations of privacy which are standard practices in our welfare state. In part, the embryonic welfare recipients' movement has as its goal liberation from such governmental tyranny.

The possibility of increased governmental benefits can also be a powerful incentive for organizing. Studies have shown that welfare recipients are regularly denied many hundreds of millions of dollars in cash benefits (for clothing and household furnishings, among other things) to which they are entitled under law. The unlawful denial of benefits is, in fact, one of the most conspicuous features of the American welfare system. As a result of the failure to inform clients of their entitlements and of the intimidating and shaming practices designed to discourage people from applying for benefits, these vast entitlements go unused. Mass organization can compel the welfare system to live by its own regulations, thereby releasing large amounts of money to the poor. A movement that can benefit people in so immediate and practical a way may have a chance of gaining adherents.

If a movement of welfare recipients should, in fact, take form and gather strength, the ghetto and the slum will have yielded up a new political force. And it is conceivable that such a force could eventually be turned to the objective of procuring federal legislation for new programs of income redistribution (such as a guaranteed minimum income) to replace a welfare system that perpetuates poverty while it strips men of their fundamental rights as citizens.

Cloward and Elman

munity action was certainly not novel to people on Stanton Street. Many of the initial membership cadre had already participated in rent strikes and civil rights demonstrations, but, where these were activities of short duration, the committee hoped to be an ongoing organization. Aside from a few of the local women, who had been most active previously, there was an MFY attorney and social-work organizer, Ezra Birnbaum. Birnbaum went to great efforts to make the group appear to be like any other voluntary membership organization, but, in fact, the women continually referred to him as their "social worker."

The Coat Check

When clients went to see Birnbaum and the neighborhood women who were working with him, they were told that the group would bring together Negroes and Puerto Ricans who had common problems with welfare. If they wanted to be part of the group, they were asked to make surveys of their winter clothing needs and then bring them to the committee, which would attempt to act as the bargaining agents for all of them. Within a month over 90 families had agreed to the procedure, and the first tentative strategies were proposed.

"We chose the winter clothing issue," Birnbaum has since pointed out, "because it was something that genuinely concerned people . . . because they had so many small children . . . and because the injustice was so blatant. Many people hadn't gotten coats in six or seven years. Here was an issue we could exploit which would genuinely benefit our people. . . ."

The winter clothing issue also went to the heart of the perennially nagging question of what constituted a welfare entitlement. Every welfare family is budgeted a very small sum semi-monthly with which to augment clothing supplies. Invariably this sum is used for ordinary living expenses because grants for food are so low. In addition, it was department policy to allow special grants of approximately $150 a year per family for winter clothing, but these grants were usually not given out unless requested, and, even then, the family usually got less than the full amount. In October 1965, individual workers at all the welfare centers serving residents of the MFY area began to receive neat, concise letters from their clients. It was clear that they had all been prepared by one agency and mailed out simultaneously, but, since they were written as individual requests, it was not immediately clear to welfare what was behind this sudden flurry of letters which read:

> I would like to request winter clothing for my children and myself. I would appreciate it if you would grant this request as quickly as possible, as the weather is cold at this time. My family is in need of the following items of winter clothing. . . .

There followed individual itemized requests for coats, children's snowsuits, coveralls, boots, scarves, woolen skirts. All these requests had been certified by the committee as being in accord with current welfare schedules. When, after a few weeks, the welfare caseworkers did not reply, a follow-up letter was sent, with copies to supervisory personnel at welfare. When this effort also netted scant results, the committee as a group wrote to Commissioner Louchheim:

> We, as members of the Committee of Welfare Families of the Lower East Side, have written letters to our investigators requesting winter clothing. . . . The first 21 letters were mailed between October 12th and October 15th. Of these, only 9 have received any money at all, and none of these nine have been given enough money to keep their families warm this winter. *More important, the other 12 families have received no money at all!*
>
> We feel that we are being neglected—especially since many of our investigators haven't even been in touch with us to find out about the seriousness of the situation.
>
> Winter is here; our children are cold. Many of us are unable to keep clinic appointments because we do not have proper clothing. Many of our children have caught colds which can lead to other serious illnesses. Some of our children haven't been to school since the weather turned cold.
>
> In most years, many of us have had to wait until December, January, or even later to buy our winter clothing. This year, we're not willing to wait that long and see our children have to wear thin summer clothing when it gets below freezing. That is why we asked Mobilization for Youth to help us this year.
>
> Commissioner Louchheim—we feel we have waited long enough to receive our winter clothing. . . . We need your help in securing winter clothing for all our members before the weather gets any colder.
>
> We request that our meeting with you be held within the next 3 days.

The committee waited three days. When the commissioner did not respond to their letter, they were prepared to picket at his office but were prevailed upon by MFY to send a telegram instead:

> You received letter from us on Monday November 15 requesting meeting with you to discuss our members needs for winter clothing. We received no reply. Our children are cold. Winter is here. Our investigators have not answered our letters or have not given us enough money to keep children warm. We need your help before weather gets colder. We will be at your office to meet with you Tuesday November 23 1:30 p.m.

That same day the commissioner replied by telegram (after attempting to telephone) that he would be able to meet with the committee on Friday, November 26, at 1:30 p.m. In the meantime he would endeavor to get information on each of the cases specified in the documents attached to the committee's original ultimatum.

The meeting which took place between the welfare commissioner and the Committee of Welfare Families was, in the commissioner's own words, the first such meeting between a commissioner and a New York City client group in over 30 years. All of the welfare recipients had been well briefed by Birnbaum on what they would say to the commissioner, but, in fact, protest proved to be unnecessary. The commissioner quickly agreed that all members of the committee who were entitled to winter clothing would receive it, and he further formalized the bargaining status of the committee of Lower East Side families by outlining a formal grievance procedure. Clients were to continue to make their requests either by mail or in person through their workers at the various welfare centers. He would thenceforth instruct all workers to acknowledge the receipt of these requests immediately and in writing. If, within 10 days, no reply was received to an individual client's request, the committee was free to contact predesignated liaison personnel at each of the welfare centers serving the neighborhood, who would be empowered to act so that their grievances could be corrected.

Facing New Issues

The hard-pressed membership of the Committee of Welfare Families was quick to interpret their meeting with the commissioner as a victory. By agreeing to consult with them as a group about their needs, he had implicitly recognized for perhaps the first time in their careers as welfare clients that they had a legitimate corporate interest in helping to determine the rules of their own dependency. In the days that followed many of these families began to receive generous checks from the Department of Welfare to purchase winter clothing.

There were further meetings arranged with the designated liaison personnel at the various welfare centers to arrange bargaining procedures. The women were delighted that they could dictate just who and how many of their number could be in attendance at these formal procedures. Thus, when the department tried to insist that only members of the committee could meet with welfare officials, the women held firm in their insistance that the committee could designate anybody it chose to represent it at these meetings, and the Department of Welfare was forced to give in on this point. And, as most of the Lower East Side families began to have their winter clothing needs satisfied, the women decided to take up other issues such as budgeting. They requested that all members ask for budgets from their caseworkers if they did not already have them and, if they did have them, to bring them to the committee where they could be properly scrutinized.

The committee also began to elect officers. It designated sub-committees to investigate various new problem areas having to do with their welfare dependency. The leadership attended briefing sessions with MFY's attorneys in an effort to acquire a better understanding of their legal rights. Gradually, as the natural leadership potentials of some of the women emerged more clearly, MFY's paid organizer began to function more as an adviser than as a leader. One of the women gave this explanation for the process:

> Some of us know we are going to be on welfare the rest of our lives. They know it and we know it. So it's about time to act like we know it. It's about time we started acting like human beings.

For the unemployed or under-employed men who have still not been organized, Stanton Street's workers have much work to do in beginning to provide them with the entitlements which they have thus far been denied. "It wouldn't be so bad living here," one of these men told us, "if you were rich. We're not rich. All we have is the welfare. That means freezing in the winter and boiling in the summer. It means living on credit when we can't afford it. It means lying. It means doing without. . . . When I come home in the evening my wife has been at Bellevue which is uptown and maybe at Church Street, all the way across town, and I'm wondering where she got the money for the carfare. . . ."

The storefront on Stanton Street has been in existence a little less than four years, and its work has increased tenfold, with two offices added. It is still too early to evaluate its permanent contributions to life in the community. Its powers have been limited. It has not yet been able to change substantially the terms of economic dependency when it still seems to be the consensus among most legislators and their constituents that such dependency is to be discouraged, abhored, and punished.

Many more people from Stanton Street are on welfare than before. The storefront's clients are better clothed, better housed, and better fed than they were four years ago. Many now have telephones, quite a few have washing machines and television sets.

Are they better people? Are they worse? Such questions seem like the supreme irrelevancy. For if they are not better for their improved economic circumstances, the society is better for their actions against it. Democracy cannot be said to exist where government is allowed to oppress its citizens so blatantly.

December 1966

SUGGESTED READINGS

The Poorhouse State by Richard M. Elman (New York: Pantheon, 1966). Welfare as a program of condescension and humiliation; how it feels to be indigent in American society.

Maximum Feasible Misunderstanding by Daniel P. Moynihan (New York: The Free Press, 1970). Moynihan seeks out the intellectual and social assumptions of the war on poverty and analyzes the link between ideas about society and the actual actions of government programs.

"Will the War on Poverty Change America?" by S. Michael Miller and Martin Rein, *Trans*-action (Vol. II, July/Aug. 1965). Improving opportunities for the poor requires changes in the institutions which shape them.

Community Control and the Black Demand for Participation in American Cities by Alan A. Altshuler (New York: Pegasus, 1970). The Negro drive for enfranchisement as seen in such controversies as school decentralization.

Industrial Society and Social Welfare by Harold L. Wilensky and Charles M. Lebeaux (New York: The Free Press, 1965).

Ombudsmen for American Government? edited by Stanley V. Anderson (Englewoods Cliffs, N. J.: Prentice-Hall, 1968). A history of the ombudsman principle and an investigation of some of the problems and prospects of its domestic application in the solution of urban inequities.

Industrial Invasion
Of the Village Green

Strange allies fought 19th century manufacturers for domination of America's small cities

HERBERT G. GUTMAN

Apart from the dislocations of the Civil War, the economic and social history of the United States in the second half of the last century—both the glory and the agony—is in large part the histories of the booming and changing industrial cities.

No place felt the radical and far-reaching effects of the post-1850 industrial boom more than the mill towns of the East. Peaceful villages, proud of their green spaces and leisurely ways, saw great factories and towering smokestacks rise to dominate their skylines and atmospheres in a few short years. Their populations often doubled and even tripled in a single decade as propertyless workers, many of them immigrants, jammed together in what soon became tenements, slums, and shacks. Their economies came under the domination of hard-driving manufacturers, many from out of town, who were used to playing rough with competition and opposition and were careless or contemptuous of the old ways.

Historians—conservative or liberal, the chroniclers of business as well as of labor and the city—exhibit rare agreement about what life in those mill towns was like. From the *start,* they imply, the industrialists had the social and political power and prestige to match their economic force, and controlled the towns. Local politics zigged and zagged according to their interests. Other property owners—especially small businessmen and professionals—identified with them, applauded their innovations and successes, and made common cause; and the factory workers almost inevitably found themselves totally alienated from the general community, practically helpless before their all-powerful employers. Stated in another fashion, from the beginning there existed a close relationship between economic class, social status, and power, and that control over "things"—most especially industrial property and machinery—was transformed quickly and with relative ease into legitimate authority so that industrialists could do little wrong.

This picture is distorted. These historians have accepted much too uncritically a misleading generalization. They have made too much of the early New England textile towns as later "models" or have drawn inaccurate parallels with large cities. As a result they have tended to bypass the actual histories of the mill towns they describe. Detailed study of the history of almost any victorian American mill town reveals these errors.

Throughout their early years for at least a generation the large impersonal corporations, the new factories with their new methods, and the wage earners, remained unusual and even alien elements in the industrial town. They disrupted tradition, challenged the accepted and respected modes of thought, and threatened the old ruling groups. How then could the mill owners *from the first* have dominated the social and political structures?

Conservatism is not always automatic obeisance to wealth; it is more often resistance to change and challenge. The industrialists had great economic power and influence over *things;* but in my studies I have found that often they

"Mill town economies came under the domination of hard-driving manufacturers who were used to playing rough with competition and opposition and were careless or contemptuous of the old ways." (Officers, Dexter, Lambert & Co., Paterson, New Jersey.)

CONFLICT AND ACCOMMODATION

could not even control the public decisions and judgments that directly affected their own economic welfare. The nonindustrial property owners often opposed them; they did not dominate the government; and the professional groups and middle-classes frequently criticized them and rejected their leadership. Even the apparently resourceless workers were able to find friends and support where their employers could not, in spite of the lack of strong unions.

Take as an example the industrial city of Paterson, New Jersey, with its highly suggestive official motto, *Spe et Labore* (With Hope and Labor). Its development provides clear examples of the early, frustrated search for status and unchallenged authority by big mill and factory owners.

"Paterson was regarded by New Yorkers, only fourteen miles away, as an 'up-country hamlet, chiefly noted for fine waterfall and valuable waterpower.'"

THE SILKEN THREAD OF POWER

The history of an industrial town can often be divided into two almost distinct stories: what happened in the more isolated village before the large factories came, and what happened after. Until 1850 Paterson's growth was fitful and relatively slow, its industry (mostly cotton textiles) not very efficient. As late as 1838 it was regarded by New Yorkers, only fourteen miles away, as an "up-country hamlet, chiefly noted for its fine waterfall and valuable waterpower."

But its closeness to a market and to a port, that "valuable waterpower," and the skilled machinists and machine shops that the cotton mills had attracted, made it very attractive to industry in the booming years before, during, and just after the Civil War.

By the early 1870's Paterson was a major American industrial city, producing one-fourth of the nation's locomotives, and much of the ironwork used in the great public buildings and bridges in New York and Pennsylvania. It led the country in silk textile production, and its jute, flax, and mosquito net mills were the largest of their kinds in the nation. Since most of these mills were founded after 1850 and the others had had their greatest growth in the same period, the older inhabitants of Paterson saw a new city they hardly recognized spring up around them between 1850 and 1870. The first locomotive shop was founded in 1836; by 1873 three large locomotive works employed 3000 men. A machine shop which had ten workers in 1845 employed 1100 in 1873. The textile factories, taking advantage of the water power, cheap mills, and help left behind by the declining cotton industry, rose even faster. In 1860 four silk mills employed 590 workers; just sixteen years later fourteen silk factories employed 8000.

Although small spinning and weaving shops started in the 1840's, the great stimulus to the textile industry came from outside the city in the 1860's when New York and Boston textile manufacturers and importers moved their mills to Paterson or built new ones there. A Coventry Englishman brought his silk mill from New York in 1860. Two years later, the nation's leading importer of tailor trimmings moved there from Boston. In 1868, a great New York silk importer came to Paterson. Eighty-one years after its founding in Northern Ireland, Barbour Brothers opened a linen factory that quickly became one of Paterson's great mills. From the start, these men of wealth constructed large mills, introduced power machinery, and made other significant innovations. One even imported an entire English factory. A new industrial leadership alien to the older city, these men represented a power unknown in earlier years. And they transformed the city.

In 1846 Paterson had 11,000 inhabitants; by 1870 it had 33,000. More than a third of these—a group larger than the whole 1846 population—were European immigrants, including skilled silk workers from France, Germany, and England. Large numbers of unskilled Irish laborers came, too. The booming city offered employment to whole families. Iron factories hired only men, and textile mills relied mainly on female and child labor. Two-thirds of the silk workers in 1876 were women, and one of every four workers under 16 years of age. Small business also prospered: from 1859 to 1870 the number of grocers more than doubled, and saloonkeepers increased from 46 to 270.

The social dislocations were severe, but prosperity was general—until the depression of 1873-1878.

The decline then was almost as extreme as the rise had been. The economy was crippled. "Among all classes (in 1873) there is a feeling of gloom and intense anxiety in regard to the future." In three years these fears had been realized, and a silk worker reported that "Paterson is in a deplorable condition." The production of locomotives fell off by five-sixths. Wages paid locomotive workers in 1873 amounted to $1,850,000; by 1877 they had fallen to $165,000. The unemployed overtaxed all available charities and even paraded in the streets demanding public works. In 1876 a *New York Sun* reporter called Paterson an industrial ghost town, and compared it to a Southern city after Lee's surrender.

Generally, historians contend that the depression of 1873-78, because of the great suffering and insecurity it caused, broke the back of labor's independence and immeasurably strengthened employers. Again, this narrow economic interpretation ignores the total reality. The workers were not the only ones put to the test. The city government, the middle class, and the older inhabitants also faced grave problems. So did the new industrialists. Trying to meet the economic crises resulting from declining markets, declining profits, and strikes, they needed support and help at critical times from the community and its leaders. Did they always get it?

Four conflicts involving the mill owners occurred between 1877 and 1880—two textile strikes and two libel suits against a newspaper editor. They tell the story pretty well. They reveal much about the actual prestige and political influence the owners had at that time.

Revolt of the Ribbon Weavers

In June of 1877, immigrant silk-ribbon weavers struck because of a 20 percent wage cut and an irksome contract. At its height the strike was Patterson's largest up to then: it idled 2000 workers and closed down the mills.

The workers had no union to speak of; they had endured forty-four months of depression. They showed great staying power, but in practical economic terms they had very little to bargain with. Yet after ten weeks the employers accepted a compromise which rescinded the wage cut and ended the strike. Why?

Local people refused to give their approval and support to the mill owners. Elected city officials either supported the strikers, or, even more significantly, refused to bow to pressures and "commands" from owners.

A few examples: small shopkeepers gave credit and raised money for the strikers; the daily newspapers, though critical of the strikers too, urged the employers to use "conscience as well as capital." The courts remained independent. Weavers on trial for disorderly conduct went free or received small fines. When a manufacturer successfully prosecuted two weavers for violating contracts, city officials, including the mayor, persuaded a local judge to postpone forty similar trials indefinitely.

Republican Mayor Benjamin Buckley and the Democratic-controlled board of aldermen gave the manufacturers their greatest trouble. The aldermen were mostly self-made men: skilled workmen of independent means, retail shopkeepers, and professionals, their number included neither factory workers nor large manufacturers. Mayor Buckley personified the pre-corporate American dream. Born in England in 1808, he had come to Paterson as a young man, worked first in a cotton factory, and then achieved much. By 1877, he owned a small spindle factory, headed a local bank, and thrived in Republican politics, serving several terms in the state legislature before winning the 1875 mayoralty election.

Buckley believed his primary duty was to maintain order, and he used his small police force with great skill and tact, but only to stop open conflict. He would not suppress the strikers or their leaders. This infuriated the industrialists, who insisted that the mayor's inaction allowed a few agitators to dominate hundreds of workers. The Paterson Board of Trade, controlled by the largest mill owners, charged

"Paterson produced one-fourth of the nation's locomotives and much ironwork used in the great public buildings and bridges in New York and Pennsylvania."

that "the laws of the land are treated with contempt and trampled upon by a despotic mob" led by immigrant radicals and "Communists." (This in 1877.) They tried to pressure the city authorities to enlarge the police force and declare a state of emergency that would severely hamper the strikers. A manufacturer warned that unless the authorities put down these troublemakers, the city would be left "with nothing . . . but the insignificant industries of an unimportant town." One urged that strike leaders be "taken out and shot"; another offered to finance a private militia.

Mayor Buckley refused all these demands. He charged that the Board of Trade did "great injury to the credit of the city," and commended "the good sense of the working people." All elected city officials, Republican and Democratic, were property owners, but they remained independent, and rejected the claim that the Board of Trade was "best able to judge what the city needed to protect it." The Democratic-controlled Board of Aldermen unanimously commended Republican Mayor Buckley's "wise and judicious course" and added insult to injury by passing a resolution urging immediate prosecution of mill owners who violated local fire-escape ordinances. No wonder iron manufacturer Watts Cooke lamented: "All the classes of the community are coming to lean towards and sympathize with the men rather than the employers."

After the strike the manufacturers turned away from politics and raised a private militia. The Board of Trade listened approvingly to a member who found "more virtue in one well-drilled soldier than in ten policemen, or in one bullet than in ten clubs in putting down a riot." Money was quickly collected and 120 militiamen quickly recruited. But for ten years after the strike the ratio of *policemen* to population remained the same. Clearly it was easier to get up money for a private militia than to "reform" the stubborn city government. And the fact that the mill owners were forced to raise this militia was a measure of their local weakness, not of their strength.

The Adams Company Strike

A year after the ribbon weaver's strike was settled, 550 more unorganized textile workers, mostly women and children, reacted to their third wage cut in a year by striking the factories of Robert and Henry Adams, the largest manufacturers of mosquito netting in the country.

More unequal adversaries could hardly be imagined. The Adams brothers had brought a small factory from New York in 1857, and in twenty years had added several large and efficient mills to it, so that by 1878 they were practically dominating their industry, exporting huge quantities of mosquito netting to Africa and Asia. Yet after a strike of nine months, they conceded defeat. The senior partner, Robert Adams, bitterly quit the firm and left Paterson.

It was he, not the strikers, who had fought the lonely and friendless battle. No one publicly protested his repeated threats to move the mills. The press stayed neutral. With only one exception, he got no encouragement from other manufacturers, retail businessmen, or professionals. He even was forced to fire some of his own foremen for defending the strikers.

On the other hand, strikers received much support. Some took jobs in other mills. Strike funds were collected from other workers—and especially from shopkeepers and merchants. Concerts and picnics were given in their honor and to their benefit. Street demonstrations supported them; more than one-eighth of all Patersonians signed petitions attacking the Adams brothers.

"Two-thirds of the silk workers in 1876 were women, and one of every four workers was under sixteen years of age."

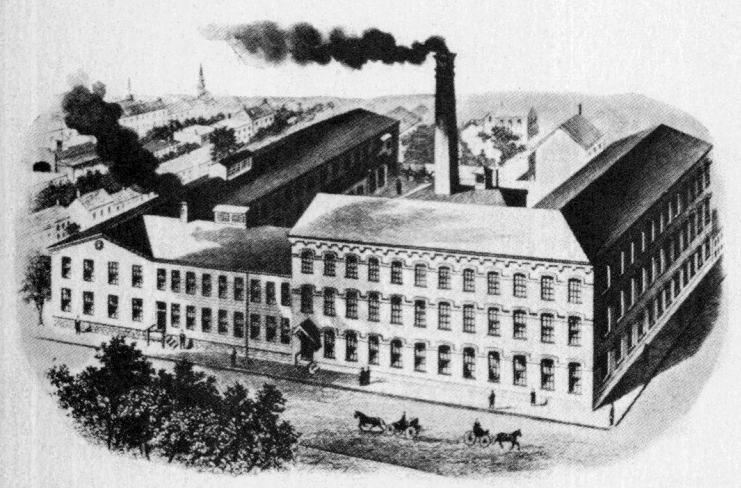

An outspoken Irish Socialist, Joseph P. McDonnell, came to Paterson from New York to support the strikers and to successfully organize them. He found a socialist weekly, the Paterson *Labor Standard*. The front pages quoted Karl Marx, and called Robert Adams "Lucifer" and his mills "a penitentiary." But the back pages carried advertisements from forty-five retail enterprises, which kept it going.

When Adams recruited new workers from nearby towns, they were met at the rail depot or in the streets by as many as 2000 strikers and sympathizers, and persuaded to go back. The strikers had full use of the streets. The city authorities arrested a few workers when tempers flared, but quickly released them and did not restrain them so long as they stayed peaceful. By carefully discriminating between peaceful coercion and "violence," the authorities effectively (even if unintentionally) strengthened the strikers. Adams had only his firm's money with which to fight, and it was limited. His power was checked, his impotence revealed, and he was forced to surrender and leave the city.

The Libel Trials—I

Socialist Joseph P. McDonnell, though only thirty-two years old when he came to Paterson, already had a long and active career in political agitation. He had edited Irish nationalist newspapers, engaged in Fenian "conspiracies," represented Ireland at the 1872 Hague Congress of the First International (siding with the Marxists), helped organize several huge London labor demonstrations and served four prison terms before coming to the United States. In this country he indignantly exposed the steerage conditions of his passage, edited a New York Socialist weekly, and traveled the East denouncing capitalism and organizing weak Socialist-led trade unions. According to the usual historical stereotypes, he should have been a pariah to almost all Patersonians and easy game for his opponents. But even though he did have trouble and went to prison, he and his newspaper nevertheless soon won acceptance and popularity.

His legal difficulties started with the first issue of the *Labor Standard* and lasted for eighteen months. He called some loyal Adams workers "scabs"; they filed a formal complaint and he was indicted, convicted, and fined $500 and costs. He narrowly averted a second libel indictment a few months later. But in the fall of 1879 he was indicted again, this time for publishing a bitter letter by a brickyard worker, denouncing working and living conditions in a Passaic River brickyard. Both he and the worker were found guilty and sent to the Passic County Jail for three months.

Did these convictions illustrate the power of "capital" and the supineness of judges before it? Not entirely, if at all.

At his first trial McDonnell was still a newcomer and radical and controversial; nevertheless his lawyer was an old Patersonian, wealthy in real estate, father of the state's first ten-hour law and important banking reforms, organizer of the city's waterworks, and a prominent Republican for

INTERACTION AND COMMUNICATION

twenty years before standing as Greenback candidate for New Jersey governor. Predictably, the prosecutor castigated McDonnell as a "woman libeler," a threat to established order, and a "foreign emissary" sent by English manufactures to "breed discontent" in America. Nevertheless, the jury stayed deadlocked for three days and nights and only unusual pressure from the judge brought in a conviction. Even then, another judge, himself originally a Lancashire worker and then the owner of a small bobbin pin factory, convinced the presiding judge to go easy, and the $500 fine was a great deal less than the $2000 and two years in prison that could have been assessed.

Workers crowded the courtroom to cheer McDonnell, and after conviction quickly raised the fine and costs, hoisted their hero aloft, and carried him triumphantly through the streets. Storekeepers and merchants contributed handsomely to a defense fund. The trial occurred during the bitter 1878 Congressional election, and the prosecutor suddenly found himself surrounded by hostile voters. Workers, supported by sympathetic shopkeepers, jammed the Democratic meetings, and demonstrated against him or walked out when he tried to speak. Politicians got the point. A Republican argued that only free speech and a free press could preserve American liberty. The Democrats defended the right to strike and one declaimed: "Away with the government of the aristocracy! Away with legislators only from the wealthy classes! We have had enough of them!" A nearby non-Socialist newspaper concluded: "In Paterson he (McDonnell) is stronger than his accusers. Today he has the sympathy of the people."

The Libel Trials—II

The second trial—and the imprisonment—were, paradoxically, even greater triumphs for McDonnell. Outside the courtroom, no one publicly attacked him. The decision was severely criticized. The judge justified the prison sentence only because he felt that a fine would, again, be paid by others. McDonnell's support was overwhelming and bipartisan. His lawyers were the son of a former Democratic mayor, and Socrates Tuttle, Paterson's most respected attorney and Republican ex-Mayor. Tuttle called the trial an attack on a free press and on the right of workers to protest. Two former silk factory foremen, one German and the other English, led McDonnell's sympathizers and got help from a Baptist and a Methodist clergyman, the latter active in Republican politics and Paterson's most popular preacher. Several aldermen, former aldermen, and county freeholders visited him in prison. Even a nephew of Robert Adams, McDonnell's 1878 adversary, gave the Socialist $20 and visited him in jail. Garrett A. Hobart, a rising corporation lawyer, president of the New Jersey State Senate and chairman of the Republican State Committee, (later to be Vice President of the United States), sent ten dollars for McDonnell's defense, offered "to do his best," and tried to get the state libel law changed. (During the 1896 national election, McDonnell's paper still carried Karl Marx's

THE ATTEMPT TO CRUSH LABOR.

The Memorable Blood-Money Bill.

"Joseph McDonnell, with a long career in political agitation, edited his newspaper and organized a national campaign of protest from his prison cell."

words on its masthead. Though a strong foe of McKinley conservatism, the *Labor Standard* said of Hobart: "a rare specimen of manhood in the class in which he moves . . . to know him is to like him whether you agree with his opinions or not.")

McDonnell's jail experience is one of the most unusual in American penal history. Warden Buckley, the former mayor's son, did his best to assure the comfort and freedom for his guest. McDonnell edited his newspaper and organized a national campaign of protest from his cell. He received his visitors (and their children) daily in the warden's office—one day he entertained twenty-one visitors. His meals came from outside the jail, and saloon and boarding house keepers overstocked him with cigars, wines, and liquors. Others brought fresh fruit, cakes, and puddings. Shamrocks came on St. Patrick's Day, and two fancy dinners on his birthday. Released ten days early, McDonnell had the warden's personal commendation for good behavior.

On his release, 15,000 persons greeted him in Paterson's greatest demonstration. He went on to found the New Jersey Federation of Trades and Labor Unions in 1883, and to push for protective labor legislation. Less than six years after coming to Paterson, and four years after release from prison, a Democratic governor appointed him New Jersey's first Deputy Inspector of Factories and Workshops. The prosecutor who had convicted him advertised his legal services in McDonnell's paper; the City of Paterson brought space for its official announcements. The paper survived and prospered until his death in 1903.

A NATIONAL PATTERN

Was this general pattern of events confined to Paterson? Not at all. It was, instead, typical of the history of many factory towns during that period. The examples are common: the merchant mayor of an Illinois mining town disarmed Pinkerton police imported to guard an operator's properties; Ohio Valley newspapers condemned iron manufacturers for arming strikebreakers; northern Pennsylvania merchants housed striking, evicted coal miners.

The pattern had recognizable and common elements. Poorly organized and unorganized workers displayed surprising staying power and received much sympathy from non-workers. Local politicians often rejected or at least modified pressures from industrialists. Most surprising, and most significant, were the attitudes of the non-industrial property owners. They enjoyed "traditional" prestige and power; they believed in competitive free enterprise and used it for their own enrichment; nevertheless they responded equivocally or critically to the practices of the new industrialists.

How can these facts, so contrary to the usual historical interpretations, be explained? First, we must rid ourselves of some misconceptions. One, that the new industrialist and his power achieved standing and acceptance quickly and easily in the local communities; in most cases they did not. Two, that all urban property owners share common attitudes, interests, and prejudices. Grocers—or even local bankers—are not the same as factory owners. Because Andrew Carnegie applauded Herbert Spencer, it does not mean that all urban property owners cheered along, too. Three, we cannot equate the patterns in mill towns with those occurring in large cities, states, or even the nation. Congress gave huge land grants to railroads and state governors frequently supplied militia to "settle" strikes; but paradoxically, it does not necessarily follow that mill owners commanded equivalent power and prestige in their own towns.

What then is the explanation?

■ It must be emphasized again that in nineteenth century America power and standing had meaning almost entirely within a given community—at least as far as that community was concerned. The new industrialist—especially if he came from elsewhere—was an outsider and a disruptive one. He found a more or less static city which thrived on small and personal workshops and an intimate and personal way of life. It was not ideal, but it was settled and familiar. He brought in radical new ways of making things and using people. Where he violated community traditions or made extreme or new demands—such as the special use of a police force or the suppression of a newspaper—he often provoked opposition.

■ In the smaller towns change—and power—were more visible and vulnerable than in the large, complex cities.

Since relationships tended to be personal, the middle class and the older residents could themselves see and understand what was happening to the town and the workers instead of accepting second-hand information through the opaque filter of *laissez-faire* economic thought or pseudo-Darwinian ideology.

■ In the factory town, the worker had more economic and political power than in the metropolis. A larger percentage of grocers, saloon-keepers, and other shopkeepers depended on him and knew it; his vote meant much more in Paterson than it would have in New York, and the politicians knew that, too.

■ Strangely, the rapid growth of the mill town, which the industrialists had themselves brought about, weakened their chances for civic and police control. A number of studies of the mobility patterns of Paterson men show that the more ambitious and able workers found expanding opportunities outside the factories in small retail business, politics, and the police force—the very areas in which the industrialists demanded cooperation or control. Conservative in many ways, these men had a "stake" in the new society. But they still had memories, roots, and relatives among the workers. They had, in fact, often suffered from the same employers they were now called on to protect. During strikes and other crises the industrialists could not expect unswerving loyalty or approval from them; nor did they get it.

Wealth does talk; and eventually it will be heard. The factories and their owners dug deeper and deeper into the lives of the mill towns and became more and more accepted and powerful. Yesterday's innovators became today's watchdogs of tradition. The old middle class, and those who remembered and revered the old, pre-corporate towns, lost influence and died off; they were replaced by others closer to the corporate image. The city governments became more bureaucratic, less responsive to "popular" pressures.

But the notion that the 19th century factory owners moved into overnight control of the industrial towns is a myth that must be discarded in order to understand the real nature of these twentieth century changes.

May—June 1966

SUGGESTED READINGS—INDUSTRIALIZATION

Planning for a Nation of Cities edited by Sam Bass Warner (Cambridge, Mass.: M.I.T. Press, 1966). A collection of essays based on the urban situation and the quality of life in our cities.

The Jungle by Upton Sinclair (New York: New American Library, 1964). The trials and radicalization of an immigrant to Chicago.

Sister Carrie by Theodore Dreiser (New York: Holt, Rinehart and Winston, 1957). One of Dreiser's best novels based in Chicago during a period of especially rapid growth.

The Magnificent Ambersons by Booth Tarkington (Magnolia, Mass.: Peter Smith Pub. Co., 1960).

We Shall Be All: A History of the Industrial Workers of the World by Melvyn Dubofsky (Chicago, Ill.: Quadrangle Books, 1969). An outstanding history of a 19th-century American labor movement leader, Big Bill Haywood led a textile strike in Paterson, New Jersey.

Why Men Fight

American combat soldiers in Vietnam

CHARLES C. MOSKOS, JR.

Few stories to come out of the Vietnam War are so poignant as the story of Company A of the 196th Light Infantry Brigade, Third Battalion. As told by Associated Press reporters Horst Fass and Peter Arnett in a cable dated August 26, 1969, Company A had been pushing for five days through enemy-held territory in an effort to recover the bodies of eight Americans killed in a helicopter crash 31 miles south of Da Nang. Now, its strength halved to 60 men, its platoon leaders dead or wounded, Company A was ordered to move down a jungle rocky slope of Nuilon Mountain. They refused. Most of the men were 19 to 20 years old, draftees, and many of them had only a short time to go before being rotated back to the States. They were ordered to move out and they refused.

The rest of the story is unimportant; as far as the military command is concerned the whole story is unimportant. But for many Americans, Company A's refusal to fight that day must have raised terrible questions—perhaps above all questions about one's own personal courage, but questions too about how and why American soldiers continue to expose themselves to death and pain in a war that few civilians any longer believe in.

The most popular notion of how men are brought to kill and be killed in combat has to do with the presumed national character of the soldiers. Different national armies perform better or worse according to the putative martial spirit of their respective citizenries. Italians make "poor" soldiers, Germans "good" ones. Another view has it that combat performance is basically a consequence of the operation of the formal military organization—the strict discipline, military training, unit esprit de corps and so forth. This viewpoint is, naturally enough, found in traditional military thought; but the importance of military socialization is similarly emphasized—albeit from different premises—by antimilitarists concerned with the perversions that military life allegedly inflicts on men's minds. Another interpretation—often the hallmark of political rhetoric—holds that combat performance depends on the soldier's conscious allegiance to the stated purposes of the war. Whether motivated by patriotism or a belief that he is fighting for a just cause, the effective soldier is ultimately an ideologically inspired soldier.

Yet another explanation of combat motivation developed out of the social science studies of World War II. This interpretation deemphasizes cultural, formal socialization and ideological factors and focuses attention instead on the crucial role of face-to-face or "primary" groups. The motivation of the individual combat soldier rests on his solidarity and social intimacy with fellow soldiers at small-group levels. This viewpoint was characteristic of the studies that Samuel Stouffer and his associates reported in *The American Soldier,* as well as of the analysis of the *Wehrmacht* by Edward Shils and Morris Janowitz. The re-discovery of the importance of primary groups by social scientists was paralleled in the accounts given by novelists and other writers about combat behavior such as Norman Mailer, James Jones, J. Glenn Gray and S. L. A. Marshall. In a few of the more extreme elaborations of this theory, primary relations among men in combat were viewed as so intense that they overrode not only preexisting civilian values and formal military goals, but even the individual's own sense of self-preservation.

My own research among American soldiers in Vietnam has led me to question the dominant influence of the primary group in combat motivation on at least two counts. First, the self-serving aspects of primary relations in combat units must be more fully appreciated. War is a Hobbesian world and, in combat, life is truly short, nasty and brutish. But, to carry Hobbes a step farther, primary group processes in combat are a kind of rudimentary social contract, a contract that is entered into because of its advantages to oneself. Second, although the American soldier has a deep aversion to overt political symbols and patriotic appeals, this fact should not obscure his even deeper commitments to other values that serve to maintain the soldier under dangerous conditions. These values—misguided or not—must be taken into account in explaining the generally creditable combat performance American soldiers have given. Put most formally, I would argue that combat motivation arises out of the linkages between individual self-concern and the shared beliefs of soldiers as these are shaped by the immediate combat situation.

The Combat Situation

To convey the immediacy of the combat situation is hard enough for the novelist, not to say the sociologist. But to understand the fighting soldier's attitudes and behavior, it is vital to comprehend the extreme physical conditions under which he must try to live. It is only in the immediate context of battle that one can grasp the nature of the group processes developed in combat squads. For within the network of his relations with fellow squad members, the combat soldier is also fighting a very private war, a war he desperately hopes to leave alive and unscathed.

The concept of relative deprivation—interpreting an individual's evaluation of his situation by knowing the group he compares himself with—has been one of the most fruitful in social inquiry. We should not, however, forget that there are some conditions of life in which deprivation is absolute. In combat, a man's social horizon is narrowly determined by his immediate life chances in the most literal sense. The fighting solider, as an absolutely deprived person, responds pragmatically to maximize any and all short-run opportunities to improve his chances of survival. For the soldier the decisions of state that brought him into combat are irrelevant, meaningless.

Under fire, the soldier not only faces an imminent danger of his own death and wounding; he also witnesses the killing and suffering of his buddies. And always there are the routine physical stresses of combat life—the weight of the pack, tasteless food, diarrhea, lack of water, leeches, mosquitos, rain, torrid heat, mud and loss of sleep. In an actual firefight with the enemy, the scene is generally one of terrible chaos and confusion. Deadening fear intermingles with acts of bravery and, strangely enough, even moments of exhilaration and comedy. If prisoners are taken, they may be subjected to atrocities in the rage of battle or its immediate aftermath. The soldier's distaste for endangering civilians is overcome by his fear that any Vietnamese, of any age or sex, could very well want him dead. Where the opportunity arises, he will often loot. War souvenirs are frequently collected, either to be kept or later sold to rear-echelon servicemen.

As Stendahl and Tolstoy noted long ago, once the fight is over, the soldier still has little idea of what has been accomplished in a strategic sense. His view of the war is limited to his own observations and subsequent talks with others in the same platoon or company. The often-noted reluctance of soldiers to discuss their war experiences when back home doesn't hold true in the field. They talk constantly, repetitiously, of the battles and skirmishes they have been through. They talk about them not just to talk, but more importantly to nail down tactics that may save their lives in future encounters with the enemy.

DEROS and Agape

For the individual soldier, the paramount factor affecting combat motivation is the operation of the rotation system. Under current assignment policies Army personnel serve a 12-month tour of duty in Vietnam. Barring his being killed or severely wounded, then, every soldier knows exactly when he will leave Vietnam. His whole being centers on reaching his personal "DEROS" (Date Expected Return Overseas). It is impossible to overstate the soldier's constant concern with how much more time—down to the day—he must remain in Vietnam.

Within the combat unit, the rotation system has many consequences for social cohesion and individual motivation. The rapid turnover of personnel hinders the development of primary group ties, even as it rotates out of the unit men who have attained fighting experience. It also, however, mitigates those strains (noted in World War II in *The American Soldier*) that occur when new replacements are confronted by seasoned combat veterans. Yet because of the tactical nature of patrols and the somewhat random likelihood of encountering the enemy, a new arrival may soon experience more actual combat than some of the men in the same company who are nearing the end of their tour in Vietnam. Whatever its effects on the long-term combat effectiveness of the American forces as a whole however, the rotation system does largely account for the generally high morale of the combat soldier.

During his one-year stint in Vietnam, the fighting soldier finds his attitude undergoing definite changes. Although attitudes depend a good deal on individual personality and combat exposure, they usually follow a set course. Upon arrival at his unit and for several weeks thereafter, the soldier is excited to be in the war zone and looks forward to engaging the enemy. After the first serious encounter, however, he loses his enthusiasm for combat. He becomes highly respectful of the enemy's fighting abilities and begins to fear and scorn the South Vietnamese. He grows skeptical of victory statements from headquarters and of the official reports of enemy casualties. From about the third to the eighth month of his tour, the soldier operates on a kind of plateau of moderate commitment to his combat role.

Toward the ninth and tenth months, the soldier begins to regard himself as an "old soldier," and it is usually at this point that he is generally most effective in combat. As he approaches the end of his tour in Vietnam, however, he begins noticeably to withdraw his efficiency. He now becomes reluctant to engage in offensive combat operations; and increasingly, he hears and repeats stories of men killed the day they were to rotate back home.

It is significant, though, that "short-timer's fever" is implicitly recognized by the others, and demands on short-timers are informally reduced. The final disengagement period of the combat soldier is considered a kind of earned prerogative which those earlier in the rotation cycle hope eventually to enjoy.

Overall, the rotation system reinforces a perspective which is essentially private and self-concerned. Somewhat remarkably, for example, I found little difference in the attitudes of combat soldiers in Vietnam over a two-year interval. The consistency was largely due, I believe, to the fact that each soldier goes through a similar rotation experience. The end of the war is marked by the date a man leaves Vietnam, and not by its eventual outcome—whether victory, defeat or stalemate. Even discussion of broader military strategy and the progress of the war—except when directly impinging on one's unit—appears irrelevant to the combat soldier: "*My* war is over when I go home."

When the soldier feels concern over the fate of others, it is for those he personally knows in his own outfit. His concern does not extend to those who have preceded him or will eventually replace him. Rather, the attitude is typically, "I've done my time; let the others do theirs." Or, as put in the soldier's vernacular, he is waiting to make the final entry on his "FIGMO" chart—"Fuck it, got my order [to return to the United States]." Whatever incipient identification there might be with abstract comrades-in-arms is flooded out by the private view of the war fostered by the rotation system.

Conventionally, the primary group is described as a network of interpersonal relationships in which the group's maintenance is valued for its own sake rather than as a mechanism that serves one's own interests. And, as has been noted, social science descriptions of combat motivation

Research in the Combat Zone

The information for this article is based on my observations of American soldiers in combat made during two separate stays in South Vietnam. During the first field trip in 1965, I spent two weeks with a weapons squad in a rifle platoon of a paratrooper unit. The second field trip in 1967 included a six-day stay with an infantry rifle squad, and shorter periods with several other combat squads. Although identified as a university professor and sociologist, I had little difficulty gaining access to the troops because of my official status as an accredited correspondent. I entered combat units by simply requesting permission from the local headquarters to move into a squad. Once there, I experienced the same living conditions as the squad members. The novelty of my presence soon dissipated as I became a regular participant in the day-to-day activities of the squad.

The soldiers with whom I was staying were performing combat missions of a patrolling nature, the most typical type of combat operation in Vietnam. Patrols are normally small-unit operations involving squads (9-12 men) or platoons (30-40 men). Such small units made up patrols whose usual mission was to locate enemy forces which could then be subjected to ground, artillery or air attack. Patrols normally last one or several days and are manned by lower-ranking enlisted men, noncommissioned officers leading squads and lieutenants heading platoons.

In the vast majority of instances these patrols turn out to be a "walk in the sun," meeting only sporadic or no enemy resistance. Even when enemy contact is not made, however, patrols suffer casualties from land mines and booby traps. But it is primarily on those occasions when enemy forces are encountered that casualty rates are extremely high. Upon return to the permanent base camp, members of the patrol are able to enjoy a modicum of physical comfort. They live in large tents, eat hot food, get their mail more or less regularly, see movies, and can purchase beer, cigarettes and toilet articles at field Post Exchanges. They spend the bulk of their time in camp on guard duty and maintaining equipment.

In both the 1965 and 1967 field trips, I collected data through informal observations and personal interviewing of combat soldiers. During the second field trip I also conducted 34 standardized interviews with the men of the particular squads with whom I was staying. Some of the information contained in these 34 interviews is amenable to tabular ordering. Yet even when given in tabular form the data are not to be conceived as self-contained, but rather as supportive of more broadly based observations. The attitudes expressed by the formally interviewed soldiers constantly reappeared in conversations I had with numerous other combat soldiers in both 1965 and 1967. Again and again, I was struck by the common reactions of soldiers to the combat experience and their participation in the war. By myself being in the combat situation, I could conduct lengthy interviews on an intimate basis. I assert with some confidence that the findings reflect a set of beliefs widely shared by American combat soldiers throughout Vietnam during the period of the field work.

A prefatory comment is needed on the social origins of the men I interviewed. The 34 soldiers had the following civilian backgrounds prior to entering the service: ten were high-school dropouts, only two of whom were ever regularly employed; 21 were high-school graduates, six directly entering the service after finishing school; and three were college dropouts. None were college graduates. Eighteen of the 34 men had full-time employment before entering the service, 12 in blue-collar jobs and six in white-collar employment. About two-thirds of the soldiers were from working-class backgrounds with the remainder being from the lower-middle class.

As for other social background characteristics: eight were black; one was a Navajo; another was from Guam; the other 20 men were white including three Mexican-Americans and one Puerto Rican. Only seven of the squad members were married (three after entering the service). All the men, except two sergeants, were in their late teens and early twenties, the average age being 20 years. Again excepting the sergeants, all were on their initial enlistments. Twenty of the men were draftees and 14 were Regular Army volunteers. Importantly, except for occasional sardonic comments directed toward the regulars by the draftees, the behavior and attitudes of the soldiers toward the war were very similar regardless of how they entered the service.

in World War II placed particular emphasis on the importance of groupings governed by intimate face-to-face relations. Roger Little's observations of a rifle company during the Korean War differed somewhat by pointing to the two-man or "buddy system" as the basic unit of cohesion rather than the squad or platoon.

My observations in Vietnam, however, indicate that the concept of primary groups has limitations in explaining combat motivation even beyond that suggested by Little. The fact is that if the individual soldier is realistically to improve his survival chances, he must *necessarily* develop and take part in primary relationships. Under the grim conditions of ground warfare, an individual's survival is directly dependent upon the support —moral, physical and technical—he can expect from his fellow soldiers. He gets such support to the degree that he reciprocates to the others in his unit. In other words, primary relations are at their core mutually pragmatic efforts to minimize personal risk.

Interpreting the solidarity of combat squads as an outcome of individual self-interest can be corroborated by two illustrations. The first deals with the behavior of the man on "point" in a patrolling operation. The point man is usually placed well in front of the main body, in the most exposed position. Soldiers naturally dread this dangerous assignment, but a good point man is a safeguard for the entire patrol. What happens, as often as not, is that men on point behave in a noticeably careless manner in order to avoid being regularly assigned to the job. At the same time, of course, the point man tries not to be so incautious as to put himself completely at the mercy of an encountered enemy force. In plain language, soldiers do not typically perform at their best when on point; personal safety overrides group interest.

The paramountcy of individual self-interest in combat units is also indicated by the letters soldiers write. Squad members who have returned to the United States seldom write to those remaining behind. In most cases, nothing more is heard from a soldier after he leaves the unit. Perhaps even more revealing, those still in the combat area seldom write their former buddies. Despite protestations of life-long friendship during the shared combat period, the rupture of communication

Phillip Jones-Griffith MAGNUM

All Vietnamese are seen by G.I.s as potential enemies, certainly not as allies.

is entirely mutual, once a soldier is out of danger. The soldier writes almost exclusively to those he expects to see when he leaves the service: his family and relatives, girl friends, and civilian male friends.

Do these contrasting interpretations of the network of social relations in combat units—the primary groups of World War II, the two-man relationships of the Korean War, and the essentially individualistic soldier in Vietnam described here—result from conceptual differences on the part of the commentators, or do they reflect substantive differences in the social cohesion of the American soldiers being described? If substantive differences do obtain, particularly between World War II and the wars in Korea and Vietnam, much of this variation could be accounted for by the disruptive effects on unit solidarity caused by the introduction of the rotation system in the latter two wars.

Latent Ideology

Even if we could decide whether combat primary groups are essentially entities *sui generis* or outcomes of pragmatic self-interest, there remain other difficulties in understanding the part they play in maintaining organizational effectiveness. For it has been amply demonstrated in many contexts that primary groups can hinder as well as serve to attain the formal goals of the larger organization. Thus, to describe effective combat motivation principally in terms of primary group ties leaves unanswered the question of why various armies—independent of training and equipment—perform differently in times of war. Indeed, because of the very ubiquity of primary groups in military organizations, we must look for supplementary factors to explain variations in combat motivation.

I propose that primary groups maintain the soldier in his combat role only when he has an underlying commitment to the worth of the larger social system for which he is fighting. This commitment need not be formally articulated, nor even perhaps consciously recognized. But the soldier must at some level accept, if not the specific purposes of the war, then at least the broader rectitude of the society of which he is a member. Although American combat soldiers do not espouse overtly ideological sentiments and are extremely reluctant to voice patriotic rhetoric, this should not obscure the existence of more latent beliefs in the legitimacy, and even superiority, of the American way of life. I have used the term "latent ideology" to describe the social and cultural sources of those beliefs about the war held by American soldiers. Latent ideology, in this context, refers to those widely shared sentiments of soldiers which, though not overtly political, nor even necessarily substantively political, nevertheless have concrete consequences for combat motivation.

Students of political behavior have too often been uninterested in answers that do not measure up to their own standards of expressiveness. When a person responds in a way that seems either ideologically confused or apathetic, he is considered to have no political ideology. But since any individual's involvement in any polity is usually peripheral, it is quite likely that his political attitudes will be organized quite differently from those of ideologists or political theorists. Yet when one focuses on underlying value orientations, we find a set of attitudes having a definite coherence—especially within the context of that individual's life situation.

Quite consistently, the American combat soldier displays a profound skepticism of political and ideological appeals. Somewhat paradoxically, then, anti-ideology itself is a recurrent and integral part of the soldier's belief

397

Most soldiers think of being in Vietnam as simply a matter of bad luck or their own stupidity; they don't blame U.S. policy.

system. They dismiss patriotic slogans or exhortations to defend democracy with "What a crock," "Be serious, man," or "Who's kidding who?" In particular, they have little belief that they are protecting an outpost of democracy in South Vietnam. United States Command Information pronouncements stressing defense of South Vietnam as an outpost of the "Free World" are almost as dubiously received as those of Radio Hanoi which accuse Americans of imperialist aggression. As one soldier put it, "Maybe we're supposed to be here and maybe not. But you don't have time to think about things like that. You worry about getting zapped and dry socks tomorrow. The other stuff is a joke."

In this same vein, when the soldier responds to the question of why he is in Vietnam, his answers are couched in a quite individualistic frame of reference. He sees little connection between his presence in Vietnam and the national policies that brought him there. Twenty-seven of the 34 combat soldiers I interviewed defined their presence in the war in terms of personal misfortune. Typical responses were: "My outfit was sent over here and me with it," "My tough luck in getting drafted," "I happened to be at the wrong place at the wrong time," "I was fool enough to join this man's army," and "My own stupidity for listening to the recruiting sergeant." Only five soldiers mentioned broader policy implications—to stop Communist aggression. Two soldiers stated they requested assignment to Vietnam because they wanted to be "where the action is."

Because of the combat soldier's overwhelming propensity to see the war in private and personal terms, I had to ask them specifically what they thought the United States was doing in Vietnam. When the question was phrased in this manner, the soldiers most often said they were in Vietnam "to stop Communism." This was about the only ideological slogan these American combat soldiers could be brought to utter; 19 of the 34 interviewed soldiers saw stopping Communism as the purpose of the war. But when they expressed this view it was almost always in terms of defending the United States, not the "Free World" in general and certainly not South Vietnam. They said: "The only way we'll keep them out of the States is to kill them here," "Let's get it over now, before they're too strong to stop," "They have to be stopped somewhere," "Better to zap this country than let them do the same to us."

Fifteen of the soldiers gave responses other than stopping Communism. Three gave frankly cynical explanations of the war by stating that domestic prosperity in the United States depended on a war economy. Two soldiers held that the American intervention was a serious mistake initially; but that it was now too late to back out because of America's reputation. One man even gave a Malthusian interpretation, arguing that war was needed to limit population growth. Nine of the soldiers could give no reason for the war even after extensive discussion. Within this group, one heard responses such as: "I only wish I knew" "Maybe Johnson knows, but I sure don't" and "I've been wondering about that ever since I got here."

I asked each of the 19 soldiers who mentioned stopping Communism as the purpose of the war what was so bad about Communism that it must be stopped at the risk of his own life. The first reaction to such a question was usually perplexity or rueful shrugging. After thinking about it, and with some prodding, 12 of the men expressed their distaste for communism by stressing its authoritarian aspects in social relations. They saw Communism as a system of excessive social regimentation which allows the individual no autonomy in the pursuit of his own happiness. Typical descriptions of Communism were: "That's when you can't do what you want to do," "Somebody's always telling you what to do," or "You're told where you work, what you eat, and when you shit." As one man wryly put it, "Communism is something like the army."

While the most frequently mentioned features of Communism concerned individual liberty, other descriptions were also given. Three soldiers mentioned the atheistic and antichurch aspects of Communism; two specifically talked of the absence of political parties and democratic political institutions; and one man said Communism was good in theory, but could never work in practice because human beings were "too selfish." Only one soldier mentioned the issues of public versus private property ownership.

I should stress once again that the soldiers managed to offer reasons for the war or descriptions of communism only after extended discussion and questioning. When left to themselves, they rarely discussed the goals of America's military intervention in Vietnam, the nature of Communist systems, or other political issues.

Americanism

To say that the American soldier is not overtly ideological is not to deny the existence of salient values that do contribute to his motivation in combat. Despite the soldier's lack of ideological concern and his pronounced embarrassment in the face of patriotic rhetoric, he nevertheless displays an elemental American nationalism in the belief that the United States is the best country in the world. Even though he hates being in the war, the combat soldier typically believes—with a kind of joyless patriotism—that he is fighting for his American homeland. When the soldier does articulate the purposes of the war, the view is expressed that if Communist aggression is not stopped in Southeast Asia, it will be only a matter of time before the United States itself is in jeopardy. The so-called domino theory is just as persuasive among combat soldiers as it is among the general public back home.

The soldier definitely does *not* see himself fighting for South Vietnam. Quite the contrary, he thinks South Vietnam is a worthless country, and its people contemptible. The low regard in which the Vietnamese—"slopes" or "gooks"—are held is constantly present in the derogatory comments on the avarice of those who pander to G.I.s, the treachery of all Vietnamese, and the numbers of Vietnamese young men in the cities who are not in the armed forces. Anti-Vietnamese sentiment is most glaringly apparent in the hostility toward the ARVN (Army of the Republic of Vietnam, pronounced "Arvin") who are their supposed military allies. Disparaging remarks about "Arvin's" fighting qualities are endemic.

A variety of factors underlie the soldier's fundamental pro-Americanism, not the least of them being his im-

G.I.s quickly learn to despise their South Vietnamese allies as parasites, profiteers and cowards; not an army worth fighting for.

mediate reliance on fellow Americans for mutual support in a country where virtually all indigenous people are seen as actual or potential threats to his physical safety. He also has deep concern for his family and loved ones back home. These considerations, however, are true of any army fighting in a foreign land. It is on another level, then, that I tried to uncover those aspects of American society that were most relevant and important to the combat soldier.

To obtain such a general picture of the soldier's conception of his homeland, I asked the following question, "Tell me in your own words, what makes America different from other countries?" The overriding feature in the soldier's perception of America is the creature comforts that American life can offer. Twenty-two of the soldiers described the United States by its high-paying jobs, automobiles, consumer goods and leisure activities. No other description of America came close to being mentioned as often as the high—and apparently uniquely American—material standard of living. Thus, only four of the soldiers emphasized America's democratic political institutions; three mentioned religious and spiritual values; two spoke of the general characteristics of the American people; and one said America was where the individual advanced on his own worth; another talked of America's natural and physical beauties; and one black soldier described America as racist. Put in another way, it is the materialistic—and I do not use the word pejoratively—aspects of life in America that are most salient to combat soldiers.

The Big PX

The soldier's belief in the superiority of the American way of life is further reinforced by the contrast with the Vietnamese standard of living. The combat soldier cannot help making invidious comparisons between the life he led in the United States—even if he is working class—and what he sees in Vietnam. Although it is more pronounced in the Orient, it must be remembered that Americans abroad—whether military or civilian—usually find themselves in locales that compare unfavorably with the material affluence of the United States. Indeed, should American soldiers ever be stationed in a country with a markedly higher standard of living than that of the United States, I believe they would be severely shaken in their belief in the merits of American society.

Moreover, the fighting soldier, by the very fact of being in combat, leads an existence that is not only more dangerous than civilian life, but more primitive and physically harsh. The soldier's somewhat romanticized view of life back home is buttressed by his direct observation of the Vietnamese scene, but also by his own immediate lower standard of living. It has often been noted that front-line soldiers bitterly contrast their plight with the physical amenities enjoyed by their fellow countrymen, both rear-echelon soldiers as well as civilians back home. While this is superficially true, the attitudes of American combat soldiers toward their compatriots are actually somewhat more ambivalent. For at the same time the soldier is begrudging the civilian his physical comforts, it is these very comforts for which he fights. Similarly, they envy rather than disapprove of those rear-echelon personnel who engage in sub rosa profiteering.

The materialistic ethic is reflected in another characteristic of American servicemen. Even among front-line combat soldiers, one sees an extraordinary amount of valuable paraphernalia. Transistor radios are practically *de rigueur*. Cameras and other photographic accessories are widely evident and used. Even the traditional letter-writing home is becoming displaced by tape recordings. It seems more than coincidental that American soldiers commonly refer to the United States as "The Land of the Big PX."

Another factor that plays a part in combat motivation is the notion of masculinity and physical toughness that pervades the soldier's outlook toward warfare. Being a combat soldier is a man's job. Front-line soldiers often cast aspersions on the virility of rear-echelon personnel ("titless WAC's"). A soldier who has not experienced combat is called a "cherry" (i.e. virgin). Likewise, paratroopers express disdain for "legs," as nonairborne soldiers are called. This he-man attitude is also found in the countless joking references to the movie roles of John Wayne and Lee Marvin. These definitions of masculinity are, of course, general in America and the military organization seeks to capitalize on them with such perennial recruiting slogans as "The Marine Corps Builds Men" and "Join the Army and Be a Man."

Needless to say, however, the exaggerated masculine ethic is much less evident among soldiers after their units have been bloodied. As the realities of combat are faced, more prosaic definitions of manly honor emerge. (Also, there is more frequent expression of the male role in manifestly sexual rather than combative terms, for example, the repeatedly heard "I'm a lover not a fighter.") That is, notions of masculinity serve to create initial motivation to enter combat, but recede once the life-and-death facts of warfare are confronted. Moreover, once the unit is tempered by combat, definitions of manly honor are not seen to encompass individual heroics. Quite the opposite, the very word "hero" is used to describe negatively any soldier who recklessly jeopardizes the unit's welfare. Men try to avoid going out on patrols with individuals who are overly anxious to make contact with the enemy. Much like the slacker at the other end of the spectrum, the "hero" is also seen as one who endangers the safety of others. As is the case with virtually all combat behavior, the ultimate standard rests on keeping alive.

The Fighting Man's Peace Demonstrator

On both of my trips to Vietnam I repeatedly heard combat soldiers—almost to a man—vehemently denounce peace demonstrators back in the United States. At first glance such an attitude might be surprising. After all, peaceniks and soldiers both fervently want the troops brought home. In fact, however, the troops I interviewed expressed overt political sentiments only when the antiwar demonstrations came up in the talk. Significantly, the soldier perceived the peace demonstrations as being directed against himself personally and not against the war. "Did I vote to come here? Why blame the G.I.?" There was also a widespread feeling that if peace demonstrators were in Vietnam they would change their minds. As one man stated: "How can they know what's happening if they're sitting on their asses in the States. Bring them here and we'd shape them up quick enough." Or as one of the more philosophically inclined put it, "I'd feel the same way if I were back home. But once you're here and your buddies are getting zapped, you have to see things different."

Much of the soldier's dislike of peace demonstrators is an outcome of class hostility. To many combat soldiers—themselves largely working class—peace demonstrators are socially privileged college students. I heard many remarks such as the following: "I'm fighting for those candy-asses just because I don't have an old man to support me." "I'm stuck here and those rich draft dodgers are having a ball raising hell." "You'd think they'd have more sense with all that smart education."

The peace demonstrators, moreover, were seen as undercutting and demeaning the losses and hardships already suffered by American soldiers. Something of this sort undoubtedly contributed to the noticeable hawklike sentiments of combat soldiers. "If we get out now, then every G.I. died for nothing. Is this why I've been putting my ass on the line?" Here we seem to have an illustration of a more general social phenomenon: the tendency in human beings to justify to themselves sacrifices they have already made. Sacrifice itself can create legitimacy for an organization over a short period of time. It is only after some point when sacrifices suddenly seem too much, that the whole enterprise comes under critical reevaluation. But sharp questioning of past and future sacrifices does not generally occur among combat soldiers in Vietnam. I believe this is because the 12-month rotation system removes the soldier from the combat theater while his personal stake remains high and before he might begin to question the whole operation. The rotation system, in other words, not only maintains individual morale but also fosters a collective commitment to justify American sacrifices.

The soldier's hostility toward peace demonstrators is reinforced by his negative reactions to the substance of certain antiwar arguments. For while the combat soldier is constantly concerned with his own and his fellow American's safety, as well as being a fundamental believer in the American way of life and profoundly apolitical to boot, the radical element of the peace movement mourns the suffering of the Vietnamese, is vehement in its anti-Americanism, and is self-consciously ideological. At almost every point, the militant peace movement articulates sentiments in direct opposition to the basic values of the American soldier. Statements bemoaning civilian Vietnamese casualties are interpreted as wishes for greater American losses. Assertions of the United States' immorality for its interventionism run contrary to the soldier's elemental belief in the rectitude of the American nation. Arguments demonstrating that the Viet Cong are legitimate revolutionaries have no credence both because of the soldier's ignorance of Vietnamese history and—more importantly—because the Viet Cong are out to kill him. As one man summed it up:

"I don't know who are the good guys or the bad guys, us or the V.C. But anybody who shoots at me ain't my friend. Those college punks are going to answer to a lot of us when we get back."

It must be stressed, however, that the soldier's dislike of peace demonstrators is reactive and does not imply any preexisting support for the war. Paradoxically, then, the more militant peace demonstrations have probably created a level of support for the war among combat soldiers that would otherwise be absent. This is not to say that the soldier is immune to antiwar arguments. But the kind of arguments that would be persuasive among soldiers (e.g. Vietnam is not worth American blood, South Vietnam is manipulating the United States, the corruptness of the Saigon regime and ineptitude of the ARVN make for needless U.S. casualties) are not the ones usually voiced by radical peace groups. *The combat soldier is against peace-demonstrators rather than for the war.* For it should also be known that he has scant affection for "support-the-boys" campaigns in the United States. Again, the attitude that "they don't know what it's all about" applies. As one soldier succinctly put it—and his words spoke for most: "The only support I want is out."

November 1969

SUGGESTED READINGS

The American Soldier: Combat and Its Aftermath by Samuel A. Stouffer (Princeton, N.J.: Princeton University Press, 1949).

Up Front by Bill Mauldin (New York: Holt, Rinehart and Winston, 1945) contains the tragicomical cartoons of World War II's "Willie and Joe" along with a perceptive discussion of combat from the viewpoint of the average G.I.

The Warriors by J. Glenn Gray (New York: Harcourt, Brace, 1959) is a philosopher's recollections of the experiences of warfare.

Men Against Fire by S. L. A. Marshall (New York: William Morrow, 1947) contains after-battle interviewing to assess combat tactics.

The American Military edited by Martin Oppenheimer (Chicago: Aldine, 1971).

The Territorial Imperative by Robert Ardrey (New York: Atheneum, 1966).
On Aggression by Konrad Lorenz (New York: Harcourt, Brace and World, 1966).
Man and Aggression edited by M. F. Ashley Montagu (New York: Oxford University Press, 1968). Lorenz, an ethologist, and Montagu and Ardrey, anthropologists, debate the animal origins of man's aggressiveness — anthropomorphism or scientific extrapolation?

Roots of Aggression edited by Leonard Berkowitz (New York: Atheneum, 1969). Recent explorations of the frustration-aggression hypothesis, and other social-psychological explanations of human stress-seeking.

War: The Anthropology of Armed Conflict and Aggression edited by Morton Fried, Marvin Harris and Robert Murphy (Garden City, New York: Natural History Press, 1968).

The Professional Soldier by Morris Janowitz (New York: The Free Press, 1960). The impact of technology and changes in warfare on both the organization and ideology of the armed services. Extensive and systematic role analysis of the man in uniform.

Does Military Deterrence Deter?

From warclub to warhead—primitive combat patterns shed light on current prospects for peace

RAOUL NAROLL

In a time when Polaris submarines patrol the seas and Minuteman missiles are poised for flight at the flick of a switch, it sometimes seems as if modern military technology had created an entirely new, uniquely terrifying human situation in which past experience provides no answers to our present dilemma. How could such problems as the "balance of terror" or the credibility of the Strategic Air Command possibly be solved by considerations of military antiquities such as the fire-and-movement tactics of the Iroquois Indians or the exchanges of hostages among the Hottentots? But the waging of war goes back a long way in human culture. The techniques change, but the underlying human propensities for war—and for peace—remain constant.

It is known that primitive tribes—although lacking the destructive capability of civilized peoples—have a wider variety of military practices and warlike attitudes. A knowledge of how and why primitive peoples made war may shed light on the prospects for war or peace in our own time.

When we sort out all the arguments men make about war and peace—in UN debates, around the Geneva conference tables, in the editorial columns—most of them these days turn out to be variations on four basic theories about the causes and prevention of war:

- the arms race,
- deterrence,
- cultural exchange,
- cultural selectivity.

Each theme has its intellectual proponents who see it as the key to understanding the origins and solutions of the problem of war.

THE ARMS-RACE. This is a favorite theme for many academic authors, the Society of Friends, Ban-the-Bomb petitioners, and White House picketers of various descriptions. The theory holds, simply, that wars are caused by armaments. In an arms race each side strives without limit for military superiority. Neither can be satisfied with simple parity, because an underestimated rival may at any time achieve a technological breakthrough that will give *him* superiority. The psychological climate generated in an arms race is such that each side is likely to interpret the rival's capability as intent: "We are simply protecting ourselves in case of attack, but *they* are arming for war." An arms race thus becomes a circular, self-generating phenomenon of ever-increasing danger. To those who see the problem this way, there are only two possible alternatives—disarmament or annihilation.

"The tactic of first firing on the enemy from a distance and then moving in for hand-to-hand combat is a characteristic that distinguishes primitive from civilized tactics" (Armed combat in New Guinea)

Photo by Karl Hieder—Courtesy Robert Gardner Carpenter Center—Harvard

DETERRENCE. This theme is most often used in current war/peace literature. Those who have faith in deterrence believe that military preparations can make for peace by vastly increasing the costs of war. A would-be aggressor, in a rational calculation of gain and loss, can be made to realize that the costs of warfare outweigh any possible gain. The advocates of deterrence point out that there is no defense against a nuclear war, and consequently our best hope is for a stable, credible deterrent. For a deterrent to be stable it must be invulnerable so that increased effort against it would be futile. Mutual invulnerability would, from this point of view, stabilize the arms race in a balance of terror. This balance would then, presumably, allow conflicts to shift to limited wars, and to an eventual stabilization and finally to reduction of war.

CULTURAL EXCHANGE. War is simply a large scale case of fear of strangers. Such prejudice against foreigners can be dispelled by first-hand contact, and when contacts increase, war becomes less likely. The exchange enthusiasts attempt to stimulate cultural exchange of every kind. Balletomanes can thank them for the visits of the Bolshoi and Kirov Ballets to these shores, and American actors and musicians can thank them for long-term engagements in the world-wide tours of *Porgy and Bess* sponsored by the State Department. Although such variants of cultural exchange are rather new in human experience, certain kinds of exchange—for example, hostages or wives—have been practiced between rivals for millenia.

CULTURAL SELECTIVITY. War is a basic factor in determining the rise and fall of civilizations. No human society exists alone; it lives with other societies and it must react to threats or be subjugated. Weaker peoples may be eliminated by stronger ones, or their social system radically altered. As societies react to the threats they pose to each other, those traits that make for success in warfare tend to outlast those that do not. This theme is sounded (in language not so anthropological) by those who see current international conflicts as a battle for survival between The American Way of Life and Russian and/or Chinese Communism.

Primitive War, Modern Man

Anthropological studies of primitive societies seem quite remote from such pressing questions of peace or war. What can comparisons of primitive military tactics or the tendency to trade women among Hottentots, Andamans, or Iroquois tell us about the invulnerability of hardened missile sites or military uses of space? While the special circumstances of our own generation, our own decade, this year and next, must obviously dominate the thinking of policy makers, an understanding of the direction in which the deeper currents run can help shape policies with a chance of success over the long term. Let us see what the findings of a cross cultural survey (see box, page 16)—examining the warfare patterns of primitive peoples all over the world—can contribute to the quest for peace in the 1960's.

The two major rival hypotheses about the relationship between armaments and warfare are the *arms race* hypothesis, and the *deterrence* hypothesis. The *deterrence* hypothesis holds that to preserve peace one must prepare for war; in other words, that an orientation to war in a society is inversely related to the frequency of its wars. The *arms race* hypothesis holds that preparation for war tends to make war more likely; thus an orientation to war is directly related to the frequency of war.

We tested these hypotheses by studying the selected cultures for several factors:

■ Warlike traits—such as the possession of guns—that seem to indicate an orientation toward warfare.

■ Frequency of warfare. We divided the cultures into two groups—those where warfare is frequent and those where it is not.

■ Correlations between each warlike trait and the frequency of war. If, for example, all forty-eight cultures in this study have guns, and if they all report frequent warfare, we have found a perfect positive correlation between guns and war. This means that (provided there are no errors in our data) whenever we find a society that has guns, we can predict without a qualm that it is plagued with frequent war. If all forty-eight societies should turn out to have guns and none of them report frequent war, we have found a perfect negative correlation. This means that whenever we encounter a society with guns we will be quite sure that it is rarely troubled by war. If all forty-eight units have guns, and half report frequent wars while the other half do not, then there is no correlation at all; finding that a society has guns won't tell us anything, one way or another, about the likelihood of war. The closer a correlation gets to being perfect the greater the likelihood that reasonable conjectures can be made about other societies possessing similar traits.

A Survey of Warfare

A *cross-cultural survey*—which examines and compares several cultures—is the best way to test out any theory about human *culture*.

Culture is, of course, the behavior patterns people learn as part of a social group from others in the group. While culture is found among other animals, only in man is culture a *predominant* factor in governing behavior. Culture consists of millions of behavior patterns. In any one culture, everything goes with everything else. The way John Jones learns to clean his teeth and greet a friend and get married is pretty much the way Tom Brown down the street learns to do these things. So there will be a high correlation between the way all the John Joneses and Tom Browns clean their teeth and the way they get married.

There is no way to study one particular culture in order to see which of the millions of correlated traits included in it are *functionally linked* and which ones are merely unrelated fellow-travelers. For fifty years, many sociologists and anthropologists have *assumed* that traits which seem logically to have a functional link, and which are found together, do in fact have such a link. But the cross-cultural survey is the only tool which can check this assumption against the facts to see if it stands up. One of the most common criticisms of social science in the past fifty years is that it has a large body of carefully collected facts, and it also has a large body of carefully thought through theory—but the two collections have little to do with one another.

Data studies of a single society, however carefully done, cannot test a general theory about human cultures or the societies which human culture organizes, builds, and governs. Only comparative studies of a wide variety of different cultures can scientifically test theories about culture.

Our study, conducted at the Institute for Cross-Cultural Studies and at Northwestern University, is a *search for generalizations about war and culture* that rests upon comparisons of selected characteristics of a limited number of societies around the world. Such study can have something valid to say about *all* cultures only if the societies we examine are truly representative of all human societies. Anthropologists have been observing the many cultures of mankind and recording their findings long enough so that a sort of "culture atlas" of the world's peoples, the Human Relations Area Files, does exist, and is available in libraries. We drew the sample for this study from such an index of the world's cultures.

We included forty-eight societies in the sample—a number small enough to work with and still large enough to yield statistically significant results. Most of the units in the study are primitive tribes. We deliberately eliminated all literate societies (but one) from the sample because of the tendency of literate societies to be very much alike in respect to the military characteristics that interest us in this study. One literate people, the Amhara of northern Abyssinia, is included to represent the type. Geographically, our sample ranges around the world—from the Hottentots and Mongo of Africa to the Chukchi of Siberia, the Gond of India, the Land Dyak of Malaya, the Cheyenne Indians of the American plains, and the Arucanians of Latin America.

A built-in problem in cross-cultural surveys of this kinds arises because societies tend to borrow characteristics from each other. If our calculations show that societies with *frequent warfare* are also societies with a *high degree of military preparedness,* how can we tell whether this correlation is evidence of a relationship based on human nature, or whether it simply means that these societies have picked up both characteristics from their neighbors? (Literate societies borrow so many European characteristics that this is an additional reason for eliminating them from our study entirely.) We tried to guard against this difficulty by testing all the traits in the study for resemblances among neighbors—that is, we asked whether *neighbors* were more likely to share x, y, or z traits than *non-neighbors*. If a correlation occurs that is independent of geographical closeness, it cannot be a simple case of borrowing; it must mean either that the two traits tend to be borrowed together as a pair (which argues some basic relationship between them), or the association arose independently and has nothing to do with borrowing at all. Our *neighbor tests* make us reasonably sure that none of the significant correlations that emerged from this study were based on mere borrowing.

RAOUL NAROLL

These are the warlike traits we finally selected as indications of a military orientation:
- use of fire-and-movement tactics;
- flexibility in the use of surprise tactics;
- multiple expectations of what could be gained by warfare;
- a large number of potential enemies;
- fortifications;
- military preparations other than fortifications;
- boundaries set along the lines of natural obstacles, such as rivers and mountain ranges;
- Western technology, including possession of guns or tools or an expressed interest in firearms;
- expressions of hostility (to test the Freudian theory that if hostility is not expressed within the culture, it will be turned outward in the form of aggression against others).

Some of these traits have subcategories, and nearly all require some additional explanation.

FIRE-AND-MOVEMENT. According to Harry H. Turney-High's book, *Primitive Warfare: Its Practice and Concepts,* the tactic of first firing on the enemy from a distance and then moving in for hand-to-hand combat is a standard doctrine of modern civilized armies and a characteristic that distinguishes primitive from civilized tactics. The systematic use of fire-and-movement in attack requires a higher degree of coordination and control than the use of either projectiles or hand-to-hand combat alone. This kind of combat is more lethal than simpler tactics and warriors must be specially trained to fight this way. We assumed, then, that a group that uses this tactic is more strongly oriented to war than one that does not.

FLEXIBLE SURPRISE TACTICS. In modern warfare, surprise is a basic tactical principle; the attacker tries to strike his enemy unexpectedly whenever he can. However, surprise is not a universally applied military tactic. Some primitive tribes simply line up at extreme missile range and work up from hurling insults to hurling rocks at each other; this tournament-like war usually ends when the first enemy is killed. This kind of combat is a prearranged tryst, like duels under the European *code duello*. In other tribes, however, the warriors will not fight at all unless they can be sure of taking the enemy by surprise. Tribes like this usually send out raiding parties that lurk near the hostile settlements until they can catch their victims unaware. If the victims are alerted, the attackers simply go home.

The most militarily effective attitude toward surprise, of course, is to seek it but not to insist upon it. We held that societies who were capable of this flexible attitude toward surprise tactics had a stronger military orientation than those that held out for surprise alone or those who stuck to tournaments.

MULTIPLE EXPECTATIONS. An anthropologist, as an observer from the outside, probably cannot say with certainty what the causes of primitive warfare are. However, it is possible for him to make a much simpler and very useful set of observations about what the members of a war party

"All warring tribes fight to gain satisfaction for injuries (like murder or witchcraft spells) or to expel a foe from their territory." (A Moennitarri warrior of the North American plains, early nineteenth century)

in a particular culture have in mind when they set out for the attack. This "expectations" approach to primitive warfare was introduced by the anthropologist Quincy Wright in an earlier cross-cultural survey. Wright stated that military expectations in primitive tribes occurred in a certain order, such that the first expectation was always present in warfare; the second was never found without the first, nor the third without the other two, etc.

Our study, like Wright's, found that military expectations did occur in a certain order. The scale they formed ran this way:

1. Revenge and defense. Tribes fight to gain satisfaction for injuries (like murder or witchcraft spells), or to expel a foe from their territory. *All* warring tribes have this expectation.

2. Revenge, defense, and plunder. Tribes may also fight, in addition to the expectation above, for booty of some economic value—cattle, wives, slaves, land, cannibal victims (where the whole body, rather than some ceremonial portion, is consumed for food).

3. Revenge, defense, plunder, and prestige. In addition to both expectations above, warriors will go to battle to prove their military prowess—for instance, to acquire scalps or victims for ceremonial cannibalism.

4. Revenge, defense, plunder, prestige, and political control. The incorporation of the defeated enemy into the political system of the victor becomes an additional goal of warfare. Tribes where all of these expectations are in force, we assumed, are more likely to go to war than tribes where only some of them occur.

MANY POTENTIAL ENEMIES. For each culture unit in the study, we tried to estimate the total number of war-making units which the society might consider to be potential enemies. If a society had more than ten potential enemies, it scored high on this measure; one with less than ten enemies scored low. As this measure actually worked out, the primary contrast was between societies with about five potential enemies and those with more than twenty-five. Our working hypothesis on this point is simply that the larger the number of potential foes, the more likely it is that there will be trouble with at least one of them.

"In the very long run, preparation for war does not make peace more likely." (Detail from a *santos,* a religious effigy from New Mexico.)

MILITARY READINESS. Societies that carry out routine reconnaissance missions, or regularly post sentinels, or have a customary place for warriors to assemble in case of danger have this trait. We consider its presence an indication of a military orientation.

FORTIFICATIONS. Clearly, societies that build fortifications, like fences or man traps, have warfare in mind.

NATURAL OBSTACLES AS BOUNDARIES. We made the working hypothesis that societies that locate their boundaries along the lines of natural obstacles—like rivers or mountain ranges—were more concerned with the possibilities of warfare than societies that did not.

WESTERN TECHNOLOGY. The possession of guns, Western tools, and/or a lively interest in firearms were taken as indications of war orientation.

REPRESSED HOSTILITY. Societies can express their hostility through malicious gossip or quarreling or public ridicule or insults; a society in this study that did none of these things was considered to have a degree of repressed hostility which might find expression in warfare.

Deterrence Theory

Once these traits of military orientation are defined, the next step in the process is to measure the frequency of war in each unit. Using the writings of ethnographers as sources, we considered warfare to be frequent when they used words like "perpetual," "periodic," "annually," "history of wars and conquests," to describe a culture's warfare involvement. Frequent warfare is absent where such reports say that war is "rare," "unusual," "sporadic," and so on. In the absence of more precise, comparable measurements, we were content to assume that the societies which had references to frequent wars fought more often and more intensively than the other societies.

Now we are ready to look for significant correlations. First let us see how the *frequency of war* is related to the characteristics of military orientation which we have defined.

The first conclusions that emerge clearly from these correlations have to do with deterrence. If the deterrence hypothesis were correct, then societies with strong military orientations would have less frequent war. *This study gives no support at all to the deterrence theory.* Very few of the measures of military orientation seem to have any impact, one way or the other, on the frequency of war. Strong negative correlations, which would support the deterrence hypothesis by demonstrating that war frequency decreases as military orientation increases, are completely absent.

The only significant correlations—*multiple expectations, military readiness, forts,* and *hostility*—are positive, and seem to indicate that these military orientations are positively associated with frequent wars. The strongest relationship that shows up is the positive correlation between *war frequency* and *military expectations.* Since that is so, let us

INTERACTION AND COMMUNICATION

also take a look at the relationships between *military expectations* and the other war-orientation traits:

Military Expectations Correlations

Trait	Strong Positive	Moderate Positive	No Relationship
Fire and movement		+	
Many enemies		+	
Military readiness	+		
Forts	+		
Boundaries			0
Technology			0
Hostility			0

Now let us see how the *frequency of war* is related to the characteristics of military orientation which we have defined:

War Frequency Correlations

Trait	Strong Positive	Moderate Positive	No Relationship
Fire and movement			0
Surprise sometimes			0
Multiple expectations	+		
Many enemies			0
Military readiness		+	
Forts		+	
Boundaries			0
Technology			0
Hostility		+	

The measures of warlike orientation most closely associated with *military expectations* seem to be *military readiness* and *fortifications*. That is to say, societies that expect more kinds of satisfactions from successful warfare tend to be societies which fight more frequently and which make more preparation for war. They also tend to be societies with large numbers of *potential enemies,* that use *fire-and-movement* tactics.

What we are saying, in other words, is that these data offer a kind of mild and tentative support for the arms race hypothesis. However, the positive correlations between war frequency and the two armaments measures—*readiness* and *forts*—are not very large, and they could possibly be a chance result. It is also possible that the existence of *military readiness* and *fortifications* are the *result,* and not the cause, of frequent warfare. The *arms race* remains a possible interpretation of this data, if we see all three variables—war frequency, military preparations, and fortifications—as reflections of an underlying war orientation.

We have subjected the notions of *deterrence* and the *arms race* to a cross cultural test; now let us examine the idea that the significance of warfare is its role as an agent of cultural survival.

No single factor plays the dominant role in the selection of traits in cultural evolution; we know that warfare is one of a number of possible trait-spreading mechanisms. The question that concerns us here is not whether warfare explains everything about cultural selection but whether it plays a part of any consequence at all in deciding which traits are retained and which are dropped. What we are asking here, in contemporary terms, is whether the "American Way of Life" or Communism is more likely to survive and possibly spread if the United States or the Soviet Union and/or China are militarily successful.

Territorial Conquest

In this study we measure the effect of warfare on culture in terms of territorial change. There are a number of reasons for using this measure. If we had chosen to use "success" in warfare, we would have run into the difficulty of defining success in different ways for different cultures. In some cultures, the pure emotional satisfaction of expressing hostility seems to be the chief object of war. In others, bringing home trophies is the standard. Modern societies, whose wars are fought by professional military men to gain ends defined by professional statesmen (who are usually military amateurs) define success in war in terms of imposing the will of the victorious nation (that is, the will of that nation's statesmen) upon the people of the defeated nation.

If we stick to territorial changes, our task is simpler. For all societies, defense of tribal territory when challenged is seen as a desirable outcome of war. The opposite possibility—the complete loss of tribal territory—can mean the complete extinction of the culture as a distinct way of life. This was the fate of such enemies of the Iroquois as the Neutrals and the Hurons, for example. In the course of recorded history, many highly influential, civilized cultures have perished utterly—their languages forgotten and their political organizations annihilated: this was the fate of the Sumerians, the ancient Egyptians, the Minoan Cretans, the Hittites.

This study indicates that territorial change is usually accomplished by force of arms. Of the fifty societies which we looked at for data on territorial change, twenty-one reportedly had no change during the period recorded (usually the century preceding colonial conquest). Of the twenty-nine that did have changes in territory, only three experienced the change peacefully (and one of these, the Araucanians, posed so great a military threat to its neighbors that one suspects that intimidation, rather than generosity, was responsible for its territorial accretions).

Territorial change, then, is a reasonable measure of the chances of survival of a culture, and such changes are almost always the result of warfare. We used two measures of territorial change: *growth* and *stability*. Both measures consider the ratio of territory the tribe gained or lost during the period studied to the territory the tribe had at the beginning of the period. The *growth* measure also takes into account the direction of the change—territory gained or lost.

The *growth* measure, by itself, would not be sufficient as a measure of cultural survival. The *stability* measure ignores the direction of change. Since territorial change almost always occurs through war, and since the outcome of a war is a very chancy matter, the society that keeps out of war as much as possible and avoids both gains and losses of territory may be the society most likely to survive.

The significant correlations between measures of war orientation, territorial growth, and territorial instability show several important relationships:

■ Territorial growth has a strong positive correlation with Western technology and a moderate positive correlation with military readiness.

■ Territorial instability has a strong positive correlation with military expectations and also a moderate positive correlation with military readiness.

Thus societies whose territories increase are characterized by Western technology and, to a lesser extent, military readiness. The most plausible explanation is that military preparedness tends to make for territorial expansion. The correlations also show a strong tie between territorial instability and military expectations. Societies which hope for a great deal from warfare are societies whose boundaries are likely to change, one way or another. It is tempting to explain this as a three-link chain of influence, with war frequency leading to increased expectations, and increased expectations leading to instability by making tribal land the stakes of warfare. The results here are equivocal, but they do demonstrate that warfare is an agent of cultural selectivity, and that the notion that we can best preserve our way of life by throwing away our arms is dangerously naive.

There is another naive theory of the causes and cures of warfare that is part of our present-day mythology: the theory that wars are simply a kind of prejudice against strangers, and that therefore we can prevent war by getting to know our enemies better. There are certain obvious difficulties with this proposition: in view of the profound value differences now existing between modern nations, it is quite possible that the better we get to know our enemies the more thoroughly we will dislike them. For the time being, however, we will put aside this possibility and subject the cultural exchange theory to our cross-cultural test.

We found useful data on three measures of peaceful intercourse between peoples: subsidies, trade, and women. A subsidy is a payment that one tribe makes to another for the single purpose of assuring a military alliance. When a weak society is paying out sums to a strong one, we think of the transaction as a tribute the weak people pay for the privilege of being left alone. Perhaps as often, however, the money is paid between nations of equal military strength (money flowed from 18th century England to her continental allies like Frederick the Great of Prussia), or from the strong to the weak (as rivers of foreign aid stream out from the US to her allies in the underdeveloped world). By trade we mean an exchange of goods of any kind—including slaves or wives—between potential enemies. Women—whether they are purchased, wooed, or raped—become part of their husband's household; the exchange of women, therefore, represents the most complete form of cultural contact. In many primitive groups men seek wives in communities which are also their potential military foes.

Our comparisons, regrettably, show no significant relationships at all between the frequency of war and these three measures of peaceful intercourse.

War/Peace Mythology

Our survey of primitive tribes has yielded a number of results that are relevant to current US policy. The study indicates that in the very long run preparation for war does not make peace more likely. It does not seem to make much difference either way, but if it makes any difference at all it is in the direction of making war more likely than peace.

The study shows at the same time that military preparedness in the long run tends to favor territorial growth. Technological innovation seems to be especially effective. This finding supports the common-sense notion that you protect your culture by being prepared to defend it, and is quite incompatible with the position of the unilateral disarmers who claim that a country can best ward off attack by demonstrating its own peaceful intentions. Further study would be necessary to make the results on territorial growth more meaningful. It would be especially useful to identify several types of military preparedness which are substantially unrelated to each other. If territorial growth should prove related to each of these types, the preparedness hypothesis would be very strongly supported indeed.

The findings about military expectations do not have much bearing on current policy, simply because the military expectations of the rival powers today are at their maximum. This is to say that, if war occurs, there appears to be no limit to the kinds of benefits the victor might hope to derive. This is not to deny that both sides to a nuclear exchange might suffer losses far greater than any conceivable gain from victory, but only to state that if one side is clearly victorious in a general war it will not limit its demands upon the survivors of the defeated power.

The findings about peaceful intercourse indicate that it is not realistic to hope that person-to-person programs will do much to ameliorate the international situation. There may well be other reasons amply justifying such exchanges, but this study can offer no support at all for the idea that they lessen the likelihood of war.

Clearly, more creative approaches to the way peace problems can be solved in the second half of the twentieth century are required if our culture, too, is not be become merely a reference point in a future study of warfare.

January-February 1966

Murder, Juries, and the Press

Does sensational reporting lead to verdicts of guilty?

RITA JAMES SIMON

Can newspaper accounts of a murder case prejudice a jury and deny a fair trial to the accused? This is the issue confronting the Supreme Court as it ponders the appeal of Dr. Sam Sheppard in one of the longest and most sensational murder cases in recent history.

In the summer of 1954 the body of a young housewife named Marilyn Sheppard was discovered in a suburban home near Cleveland, Ohio. While the police were gathering evidence in the case, the members of the editorial board of the *Cleveland Press* became convinced that they knew who the murderer was. On July 30 the *Press* ran a banner headline that demanded:

WHY ISN'T SAM SHEPPARD IN JAIL?

Osteopathic physician Sam Sheppard, the victim's husband, was arrested later that same afternoon. Dr. Sheppard's trial was front-page news across the country; daily reports ran in every paper and flickered on every TV screen from coast to coast. A mob of reporters recorded every word for an eager public. Dr. Sheppard was convicted and sentenced to life imprisonment.

From his cell in an Ohio penitentiary, Dr. Sheppard appealed to the Ohio courts again and again to set him free; he claimed that the reportage of his arrest and trial had prejudiced the jurors against him. When his appeal was turned down by the Ohio Supreme Court, Sheppard turned to the federal courts. Ten years after his conviction, US District Court Judge Carl A. Weinman, declaring that "inflammatory" reporting had made Sheppard's trial "a mockery of justice," unlocked the doors of Sheppard's prison. Judge Weinman's view was not shared by his colleagues; in May 1965, the US Court of Appeals in Cincinnati reversed his decision. Sheppard's lawyers appealed to the Supreme Court, and the court has heard the case. Dr. Sam is out of jail pending a decision.

The issue raised by the Sheppard case is not new. The Supreme Court has, in a few cases, reversed convictions where flagrant publicity has clearly prejudiced the jury against the defendant. But the court has been hesitant about making a general statement on the effects of pre-trial news coverage because cases like Sam Sheppard's present a constitutional dilemma; the defendant's guarantee of a fair trial seems to collide with another basic constitutional right—the right of the press to be free of constraint in reporting the news. The British judiciary is convinced that the defendant's rights are the most important consideration; British judges can cite publishers, editors, or agents of a newspaper for contempt if they publish any information about an accused before it is disclosed at his trial.

American newspaper representatives like Alfred Friendly, vice president and associate editor of the *Washington Post,* argue that restrictions on freedom of the press are a greater danger to our liberties than any harm that is or might be created by trial publicity. Sponsors of Senate Bill 290 (which would give federal courts the power to cite for contempt anyone who distributed improper information to the press) insist that the right of an accused to a fair trial must be protected by whatever measures are necessary.

The weighing of the conflicting constitutional values is up to the nine justices. But there is a factual question which ought to be settled before binding legal decisions are made: Are juries really prejudiced by pre-trial news reports? Once a juror has read a news report or seen a TV newscast about a defendant, can he put that information aside and reach a verdict solely on the evidence he hears in court? Or is a juror's verdict indelibly influenced by the reports that bombard him before (and sometimes during) the trial?

My colleagues and I have completed a pilot study in which we conducted a fictional trial to find out how jurors react to newspaper publicity.

First, we wrote two newspaper accounts of the same murder—one as it would be played by a conservative paper like the *New York Times,* the other as the sensational tabloids would handle it. The conservative stories carried a sober account of the murder, as it would run on three successive days, with headlines of modest size (above right):

YOUNG CHICAGO WOMAN KILLED IN APARTMENT

TWO ARRESTED IN SOCIALITE MURDER CASE

NEW EVIDENCE REVEALED IN HYDE CASE

On the sensational stories the headlines (in much larger type, above left) read:

WOMAN SLASHED TO DEATH IN APARTMENT

COPS NAB TWO FOR HYDE KNIFE SLAYING

KNIFE DISCOVERED IN MURDERERS' ROOMS

The sensational stories gave all the gory details of the crime, and revealed the fact that one of the fictional accused, "Fred Kessler," had "a long standing criminal record." The first story mentioned his record; the second reported his release from prison at Joliet in 1957; the third preceded every mention of his name with the phrase "ex-convict." The fictional co-defendant was "Bill Anderson."

For experimental subjects in Champaign and Urbana, Illinois, we turned to the list of registered voters, the source used in most large cities to select people for jury duty. We wrote to every fortieth name on the list, a total of 825 people, describing the problem of trial publicity and asking for the cooperation in our study. We found 97 willing subjects.

At a meeting, we gave the sensational news stories to 51 of our subjects and the conservative clippings to the other 56. When they finished reading, we handed out ballots and asked for a verdict on the guilt or innocence of the accused. The results indicate that people *are* influenced by what they read, and that sensational news coverage has more influence than more sober accounts:

SENSATIONAL	% guilty	% not guilty	% no opinion
Kessler	67	21	12
Anderson	53	33	14
CONSERVATIVE	% guilty	% not guilty	% no opinion
Kessler	37	39	24
Anderson	37	39	24

As these figures indicate, the subjects who read the sensational stories were more likely to believe Kessler guilty than the subjects who saw the conservative account. Subjects who read the conservative stories were more likely to suspend judgment (24 percent had no opinion about the guilt or innocence of either defendant) than those who read sensational accounts (only 12 percent had no opinion about Kessler's guilt, 14 percent about Anderson's). The subjects who read the conservative reports did not differentiate between the two defendants and were less likely to find either of them guilty.

We then conducted the second half of our experiment—and vital changes occurred. Our mock jurors listened to a tape-recording we had made of the "trial" of Fred Kessler and his co-defendant, Bill Anderson. The recording begins with this admonition from the presiding judge:

> Before the trial begins we ask that you lay aside any opinion that you may have formed about the case and that you listen to the testimony and to the attorneys' closing statements with an open mind. The decision that you reach should be based on the evidence presented during the trial—not on the speculation of newspapers.

The "trial" itself began with opening statements from the two attorneys, followed by three witnesses for the prosecution and four for the defense. Since Kessler did not take the stand, there could be no reference during the proceedings to his criminal record. After each attorney made his closing statement, the judge instructed the jurors in the law they were to apply, and told them that if the defendants were found guilty they could receive the death sentence. Once again we asked our jurors to come to individual decisions. (This was not a "verdict" in that the jury did not discuss the trial proceedings.) This was the crucial vote, held in a situation approximating what happens to actual jurors in a real courtroom. Here are the results:

SENSATIONAL	% guilty	% not guilty	% no opinion
Kessler	25	73	2
Anderson	25	73	2
CONSERVATIVE	% guilty	% not guilty	% no opinion
Kessler	22	78	—
Anderson	22	78	—

The most striking finding is that *after they had heard the trial, most of our jurors changed their minds and found the defendants innocent*. This is true regardless of which version of the story the jurors had read before the trial. On the basis of news accounts alone, 67 percent of those who had seen the sensational account were persuaded that Fred Kessler was guilty; after the trial, only 25 percent voted to convict Kessler. These jurors seem to have taken the judge's admonition very seriously. They were able to put out of their minds the material they had read, and to reach a verdict solely on the basis of what they heard at the trial.

Would jurors serving in a real trial do the same?

We believe they would. Our findings gibe with the results of experiments on jury behavior conducted by the University of Chicago Law School a few years ago. As part of a large scale study of the jury system, the Chicago Law School ran an experiment involving automobile negligence actions. The point of the experiment was to see whether juries could disregard (when they were instructed to do so) information they had heard about the insurance status of the people involved in an accident. The accident case was heard by a number of experimental juries, and their deliberations were recorded. The recordings show that jurors instructed to disregard insurance information made noticeably fewer references to the defendant's insurance status than jurors who were not so instructed, and that the references they did make were more likely to be neutral in their implications for the verdict.

There must be a special word of caution about the findings reported in this study. The persons who agreed to participate in it were not representative of the general population. They were primarily upper middle class; about two-thirds of them were business and professional people with a college education. They are not, then, typical of the average jury. They are, however, typical of what is called a "blue-ribbon" jury, and in all fairness we feel entitled to point out that it is a blue-ribbon jury that usually decides cases (like the Sheppard case) that are likely to receive extensive pre-trial publicity.

Our preliminary study indicates that the dangers of pre-trial publicity may have been exaggerated. If these results can be reproduced in a larger sample and in communities of different sizes and in different locations, they would provide strong support for those who warn against the restriction of the freedom of the press to report trial news.

May-June 1966

Sniping—A New Pattern of Violence?

Sniping reports have been distorted by the press, causing misunderstanding by officials and the public

TERRY ANN KNOPF

On July 23, 1968, at 2:15 P.M., Cleveland's Mayor, Carl B. Stokes, who was in Washington, D.C., that day, made what he expected to be a routine telephone call to his office back home. He was told of information from military, F.B.I., and local police intelligence sources indicating that an armed uprising by black militants was scheduled to take place at 8 A.M. the next day. According to the reports, Ahmed Evans, a militant leader who headed a group called the Black Nationalists of New Libya, planned to drive to Detroit that night to secure automatic weapons. There were further reports that Evans' followers had already purchased bandoliers, ammunition pouches, and first-aid kits that same day. Simultaneous uprisings were reportedly being planned for Detroit, Pittsburgh, and Chicago.

At 6 P.M., in response to these reports, several unmarked police cars were assigned to the area of Evans' house. At about 8:20 P.M. a group of armed men, some of whom were wearing bandoliers of ammunition, emerged from the house. Almost at once, an intense gun battle broke out between the police and the armed men, lasting for roughly an hour. A second gun battle between the police and snipers broke out shortly after midnight about 40 blocks away. In the wake of these shoot-outs, sporadic looting and firebombing erupted and continued for several days. By the time the disorder was over, 16,400 National Guardsmen had been mobilized, at least nine persons had been killed (including three policemen), while the property damage was estimated at $1.5 million. Police listed most of their casualties as "shot by sniper."

Immediately, the Cleveland tragedy was described as a deliberate plot against the police and said to signal a new phase in the current course of racial conflict. *The Cleveland Press* (July 24, 1968) compared the violence in Cleveland to guerrilla activity in Saigon and noted: ". . . It didn't seem to be a Watts, or a Detroit, or a Newark. Or even a Hough of two years ago. No, this tragic night seemed to be part of a plan." Thomas A. Johnson writing in *The New York Times* (July 28, 1968) stated: ". . . It marks perhaps the first documented case in recent history of black, armed, and organized violence against the police."

As the notion that police were being "ambushed" took hold in the public's mind, many observers reporting on the events in Cleveland and similar confrontations in other cities, such as Gary, Peoria, Seattle, and York, Pennsylvania, emphasized that the outbreaks had several prominent features in common.

The first was the element of planning. Racial outbursts have traditionally been spontaneous affairs, without organization and without leadership. While no two disorders are similar in every respect, studies conducted in the past have indicated that a riot is a dynamic process that goes through stages of development. John P. Spiegel of Brandeis' Lemberg Center for the Study of Violence, has discerned four stages in the usual sort of rioting: the precipitating event, street confrontation, "Roman holiday," and seige. A sequence of stages is outlined in somewhat similar terms in the section of the Kerner Report on "the riot process." It is significant, however, that neither the Lemberg Center nor the Kerner Commission found any evidence of an organized plan or "conspiracy" in civil disorders prior to 1968. According to the Kerner Report: ". . . The Commission has found no evidence that all or any of the disorders or the incidents that led to them were planned or directed by any organization or group—international, national, or local."

Since the Cleveland shoot-out, however, many observers have suggested that civil disorders are beginning to take a new form, characterized by some degree of planning, organization, and leadership.

The second new feature discerned in many of 1968's summer outbreaks was the attacks on the police. In the past, much of the racial violence that occurred was directed at property rather than persons. Cars were stoned, stores were looted, business establishments were firebombed, and residences, in some instances, were damaged or destroyed. However, since the Cleveland gun battle, there have been suggestions that policemen have become the primary targets of violence. A rising curve of ambushes of the police was noted in the October 7, 1968 issue of the *U.S. News & World Report* which maintained that at least 8 policemen were killed and 47 wounded in such attacks last summer.

Finally, attacks on the police are now said to be *regularly* characterized by hit-and-run sniping. Using either homemade weapons or commercial and military weapons, such as automatics, bands of snipers are pictured initiating guerrilla warfare in our cities.

This view of the changing nature of racial violence

can be found across a broad spectrum of the press, ranging from the moderately liberal *New York Times* to the miltantly rightist *American Opinion*. On August 3, 1968, *The New York Times* suggested in an editorial:

> ... The pattern in 1967 has not proved to be the pattern of 1968. Instead of violence almost haphazardly exploding, it has sometimes been deliberately planned. And while the 1967 disorders served to rip away false facades of racial progress and expose rusting junkyards of broken promises, the 1968 disorders also reveal a festering militancy that prompts some to resort to open warfare.

Shortly afterward (August 14, 1968), *Crime Control Digest,* a biweekly periodical read by many law-enforcement officials across the country, declared:

> The pattern of civil disorders in 1968 has changed from the pattern that prevailed in 1967, and the elaborate U.S. Army, National Guard and police riot control program prepared to meet this year's "long hot summer" will have to be changed if this year's type of civil disturbance is to be prevented or controlled.
>
> This year's riot tactics have featured sniping and hit-and-run attacks on the police, principally by Black Power extremists, but by teen-agers in an increasing number of instances. The type of crimes being committed by the teen-agers and the vast increase in their participation has already brought demands that they be tried and punished as adults.

On September 13, 1968, *Time* took note of an "ominous trend" in the country:

> Violence as a form of Negro protest appears to be changing from the spontaneous combustion of a mob to the premeditated shoot-outs of a far-out few. Many battles have started with well-planned sniping at police.

Predictably, the November 1968 issue of *American Opinion* went beyond the other accounts by linking reported attacks on the police to a Communist plot:

> The opening shots of the Communists' long-planned terror offensive against our local police were fired in Cleveland on the night of July 23, 1968, when the city's Glenville area rattled with the scream of automatic weapons. . . . What happened in Cleveland, alas, was only a beginning.

To further emphasize the point, a large headline crying "terrorism" was included on the cover of the November issue.

Despite its relative lack of objectivity, *American Opinion* is the only publication that has attempted to list sniping incidents. Twenty-five specific instances of attacks on police were cited in the November issue. Virtually every other publication claiming a change in the nature of racial violence pointing to the "scores of American cities" affected and the "many battles" between blacks and the police has confined itself to a few perfunctory examples as evidence. Even when a few examples have been offered, the reporters usually have not attempted to investigate and confirm them.

Without attempting an exhaustive survey, we at the Lemberg Center were able to collect local and national press clippings, as well as wire-service stories, that described 25 separate incidents of racial violence in July and August of last summer. In all these stories, sniping was alleged to have taken place at some point or other in the fracas, and in most of them, the police were alleged to have been the primary targets of the sharpshooters. Often, too, the reports held that evidence had been found of planning on the part of "urban guerrillas," and at times it was claimed that the police had been deliberately ambushed. Needless to say, the specter of the Black Panthers haunts a number of the accounts. Throughout, one finds such phrases as these: "snipers hidden behind bushes . . . ," "isolated sniper fire . . . ," "scattered sniping directed at the police . . . ," "exchange of gunfire between snipers and police . . . ," "snipers atop buildings in the area. . . ." It is small wonder that the rewrite men at *Time* and other national magazines discerned a new and sinister pattern in the events of that summer. Small wonder that many concerned observers are convinced that the country's racial agony has entered a new phase of deliberate covert violence.

Conspirational Planning of Incidents

But how valid is this sometimes conspiratorial, sometimes apocalyptic view? What is the evidence for it, apart from these newspaper accounts?

Our assessment is based on an analysis of newspaper clippings, including a comparison of initial and subsequent reports, local and national press coverage, and on telephone interviews with high-ranking police officials. The selection of police officials was deliberate on our part. In the absence of city or state investigations of most of the incidents, police departments were found to be the best (and in many cases the only) source of information. Moreover, as the reported targets of sniping, police officials understandably had a direct interest in the subject.

Of course, the selection of this group did involve an element of risk. A tendency of some police officials to exaggerate and inflate sniping reports was thought to be unavoidable. We felt, though, that every group involved would have a certain bias and that in the absence of interviewing every important group in the cities, the views of police officials were potentially the most illuminating and therefore the most useful. Our interviews with them aimed at the following points: 1) evidence of planning; 2) the number of snipers; 3) the number of shots fired; 4) affiliation of the sniper or snipers with an organization; 5) statistical breakdowns of police and civilian casualties by sniping; and 6) press coverage of the incident.

As the press reports showed, a central feature in the scheme of those alleging a new pattern involves the notion of planning. Hypothesizing a local (if not national) conspiracy, observers have pictured black militants luring the police to predetermined spots where the policemen become the defenseless victims of an armed attack. No precipitating incident is involved in these cases except perhaps for a false citizen's call.

Despite this view, the information we gathered indicates that at least 17 out of the 25 disorders surveyed (about 70 percent) *did* begin with an identifiable precipitating event (such as an arrest seen by the black community as insulting or unjust) similar to those uncovered for "traditional" disorders. The figure of 70 percent is entirely consistent with the percentage of known precipitating incidents isolated by researchers at the Lemberg Center for past disorders (also about 70 percent).

In Gary, Indiana, the alleged sniping began shortly after two young members of a gang were arrested on charges of rape. In York, Pennsylvania, the violence began after a white man fired a shotgun from his apartment at some blacks on the street. Blacks were reportedly angered upon learning that the police had failed to arrest the gunman. In Peoria, Illinois, police arrested a couple for creating a disturbance in a predominantly black housing-project area. A group of young people then appeared on the scene and began throwing missiles at the police. In Seattle, Washington, a disturbance erupted shortly after a rally was held to protest the arrest of two men at the local Black Panther headquarters. Yet the disorders that followed these incidents are among the most prominently mentioned as examples of planned violence.

Many of the precipitating events were tied to the actions of the police and in some instances they were what the Kerner Commission has referred to as "tension-heightening incidents," meaning that the incident (or the disorder itself) merely crystallized tensions already existing in the community. Shortly before an outbreak in Harvey-Dixmoor, Illinois, on August 6–7, for example, a coroner's jury had ruled that the fatal shooting by police of a young, suspected car thief one month earlier was justifiable homicide. It was the second time in four months that a local policeman had shot a black youth. In Miami, the rally held by blacks shortly before the violence erupted coincided with the Republican National Convention being held about 10 miles away. The crowd was reportedly disappointed when the Reverend Ralph Abernathy and basketball star Wilt Chamberlain failed to appear as announced. In addition, tensions had risen in recent months following increased police canine patrols in the area. Although no immediate precipitating incident was uncovered for the outbreak at Jackson, Michigan on August 5, it is noteworthy that the disorder occurred in front of a Catholic-sponsored center aimed at promoting better race relations, and several weeks earlier, some 30 blacks had attempted to take over the center in the name of "a black group run by black people."

Police guard firemen from "snipers" in Detroit riot.

Let us turn briefly to the eight disorders in which triggering events do not appear to have occurred. Despite the absence of such an incident in the Chicago Heights-East Chicago Heights disorder, Chief of Police Robert A. Stone (East Chicago Heights) and Captain Jack Ziegler (Chicago Heights) indicated that they had no evidence of planning and that the disorder was in all probability spontaneous. In particular, Chief Stone indicated that the participants were individuals rather than members of an organization. The same holds true for the "ambuscade" in Brooklyn, New York, which the district attorney said at the time was the work of the Black Panthers. Although no precipitating event was uncovered, R. Harcourt Dodds, Deputy Commissioner for Legal Matters in the New York City Police Department, indicated there was no evidence of planning by anyone or any group. In Jackson, Michigan, as previously noted, tensions in the community had increased in recent weeks prior to the August disorder over a controversial center which some members of the community thought they should control. Thus the absence of precipitating events in at least three cases does not appear to be significant, least of all as evidence of a deliberate conspiracy to kill.

An assessment of the other five cases is considerably more difficult. In Inkster, Michigan, where four nights of isolated sniper fire were reported in August, Chief of Police James L. Fyke did not identify any precipitating event with the disorder and indicated that the state planned to make a case for conspiracy at a forthcoming trial. On the grounds that the two disorders in his city were under police investigation, Lieutenant Norman H. Judd of the Los Angeles Police Department declined comment on possible triggering events. In San Francisco, Chief of Police Thomas J. Cahill said there was evidence of planning. He said that "a firebomb was ignited and the shots were fired as the police vehicle arrived at the scene."

This brings us to Cleveland and Ahmed Evans, the fifth case in this instance. Because of the dramatic nature of the events and the tremendous amount of attention they received in the national press, any findings concerning Cleveland are of utmost importance. It is significant, therefore, that more recent reports have revealed that the July bloodletting was something less than a planned uprising and that the situation at the time was considerably more complicated than indicated initially.

A series of articles appearing in *The New York Times* is instructive. At the time of the disorder, in an account by Thomas A. Johnson, entitled "This Was Real Revolution," *The New York Times* gave strong hints of a plot against the police: "Early indications here were that a small, angry band of Negro men decided to shoot it out with the police. . . ." The article dwelt upon past statements of Ahmed Evans predicting armed uprisings across the nation on May 9, 1967 (they never materialized), rumors of arms caches across the country, and the revolu-

Fred "Ahmed" Evans who led a small band of militants in a shoot-out with Cleveland police.

WIDE WORLD

tionary talk of black militants. No mention was made of any precipitating event, nor was there any reference to "tension-heightening incidents" in the community at the time.

One month later, in early September, *The New York Times* published the results of its investigation of the disorder. The report was prepared by three newsmen, all of whom had covered the disorder earlier. Their findings shed new light on the case by suggesting that a series of tension-heightening factors were indeed present in the community at the time of the disorder. For one thing, Mayor Stokes attended a meeting with police officials several hours before the first outbreak and felt that the information about a planned uprising was "probably not correct." Ahmed Evans himself was seen, retrospectively, less as the mastermind of a plot than as just another militant. Anthony Ripley of *The New York Times* wrote of him: "Evans, a tall, former Army Ranger who had been dishonorably discharged after striking an officer, was not regarded as a leading black nationalist. He was an amateur astrologer, 40 years old, given more to angry speeches than to action." Numerous grievances in the community—particularly against the police—which had been overlooked at the time of the disorder, were cited later. For example, it was noted that there were only 165 blacks on a police force of more than 2,000 officers, and there was a deep resentment felt by blacks toward their treatment by the police. The reporters also turned up the fact that in 1966 an investigation committee had given a low professional rating to the police department.

Ahmed Evans himself had some more specific grievances, according to Thomas A. Johnson's follow-up article. He noted that Evans had arranged to rent a vacant tavern for the purpose of teaching the manufacture of African-style clothes and carvings to black youths but that the white landlady had changed her mind. He said that Evans had been further angered upon receiving an eviction order from his home. The Ripley article noted that, two hours before the shooting began, Evans said he had been asleep until his associates informed him that police surveillance cars had been stationed in the area. (Evans was accustomed to posting lookouts on top of buildings.) According to Evans, it was then that the group made the decision to arm.

Did the presence of the police in the area serve to trigger the gun battle that followed? What was the role of the civilian tow-truck driver wearing a police-like uniform? Did his hitching up an old pink Cadillac heighten tensions to the breaking point? Were intelligence reports of a plot in error? Why were arms so readily available to the group? What was the group's intention upon emerging from the house? These questions cannot be answered with any degree of absolute certainty. Nevertheless, it is significant that the earliest interpretations appearing in *The New York Times* were greatly modified by the subsequent articles revealing the complexities of the disorder and suggesting it may have been more spontaneous than planned. As Ripley wrote in his September 2 article:

> The Cleveland explosion has been called both an ambush of police and an armed uprising by Negroes. However, the weight of evidence indicates that it was closer to spontaneous combustion.

More recent developments on the controversial Cleveland case deserve mention also. On May 12, 1969, an all-white jury found Ahmed Evans guilty of seven counts of first-degree murder arising out of four slayings during the disorder last July. Evans was sentenced to die in the electric chair on September 22, 1969.

Then, on May 29, 1969, the National Commission on the Causes and Prevention of Violence authorized the release of a report entitled *Shoot-Out in Cleveland; Black Militants and the Police: July 23, 1968* by Louis H. Masotti and Jerome R. Corsi. The report was partially underwritten by the Lemberg Center. Its findings confirmed many of the results of *The Times* investigation and provided additional insights into the case.

Doubt was cast on prior intelligence reports that the Evans group had been assembling an arsenal of handguns and carbines, that Evans planned a trip to Detroit to secure weapons, and that simultaneous outbreaks in other northern cities were planned. ("The truth of these reports was questionable.") Further, it was revealed that these reports came from a single individual and that "other intelligence sources did not corroborate his story." In addition, the Commission report underscored certain provocative actions by the police:

> It was glaringly evident that the police had established a stationary surveillance rather than a moving one. In fact, another surveillance car was facing Ahmed's apartment building from the opposite direction. . . . Both cars contained only white officers; both were in plain view of Ahmed's home. . . . Rightly or wrongly, Ahmed regarded the obvious presence of the surveillance cars over several hours' time as threatening.

The report stressed that "against theories of an ambush or well-planned conspiracy stands the evidence that on Tuesday evening [July 23, 1968] Ahmed was annoyed and apprehensive about the police surveillance."

The Times experience, together with the report of the National Commission on the Causes and Prevention of Violence, strongly suggest that the assumption that the Cleveland disorder was planned is as yet unproved.

It may be significant that 14 out of the 19 police officials who expressed a view on the matter could find no evidence of planning in the disorders in their respective cities. In another instance, the police official said the disorder was planned, but he could offer no evidence in support of his statement. If this and the Cleveland case are added, the number of outbreaks that do not appear to have been planned comes to at least 16 out of 19.

In their assertions that police are now the principal targets of snipers, some observers give the impression that there have been large numbers of police casualties. In most cases, the reports have not been explicit in stating figures. However, as mentioned earlier, *U.S. News & World Report* cited 8 police deaths and 47 police woundings this past summer. In order to assess these reports, we obtained from police officials a breakdown of police casualties as a result of gunfire.

What we learned was that a total of four policemen were killed and that each death was by gunfire. But three of these occurred in one city, Cleveland; the other was in Inkster, Michigan. In other words, in 23 out of 25 cases where sniping was originally reported, no policemen were killed.

Police Casualties

Our total agreed with figures initially taken from local press reports. However, our count of four dead was only half the figure reported in *U.S. News & World Report*. We learned why when we found that the story appearing in that magazine originally came from an Associated Press "roundup," which said that eight policemen had been killed by gunfire since July 1, 1968. But four of these eight cases were in the nature of individual acts of purely criminal—and not racial—violence. On July 2, a Washington, D.C., policeman was killed when he tried to arrest a man on a robbery complaint. A Philadelphia policeman was killed July 15 while investigating a $59 streetcar robbery. On August 5, in San Antonio, a policeman was killed by a 14-year-old boy he had arrested. The youth was a Mexican-American who had been arrested on a drinking charge. And, in Detroit, a policeman was shot to death on August 5 following a domestic quarrel. The circumstances concerning these four cases in no way display the features of a "new pattern" of violence.

The question of how many police *injuries* came from sniper fire is more complicated. A total of 92 policemen were injured, accounting for 14 out of 25 cases. Almost half the injuries—44—came from gunfire. In some instances, our findings showed a downward revision of our earlier information. In Gary, for example, somebody reportedly took a shot at Police Chief James F. Hilton as he cruised the troubled area shortly after the disturbance began. However, when interviewed, Chief Hilton vigorously denied the earlier report. In Peoria, 11 police officers were reportedly injured by shotgun blasts. However, Bernard J. Kennedy, Director of Public Safety, indicated that initial reports "were highly exaggerated" and that only seven officers were actually wounded. In East Point, Georgia, a white policeman had reportedly been injured during the disorder. Yet Acting Police Chief Hugh D. Brown indicated that there were no injuries to the police. In Little Rock, a policeman swore that he had been shot by a sniper. However, Chief of Police R. E. Brians told us that there was no injury and no broken skin. The Chief added that the policeman had been new and was not of the highest caliber. In fact, he is no longer with the department.

In addition, a closer look at the data reveals that the highest figures for numbers of policemen wounded by gunfire are misleading and need to be placed in perspective. Let us examine the three cases with the highest number of injuries: Cleveland with 10 policemen wounded by gunfire; Peoria, with seven; and Harvey-Dixmoor, Illinois, also with seven.

In Peoria, all seven policemen were wounded by the pellets from *a single shotgun blast.* In an interview, Safety Director Kennedy stressed that "none of the injuries incurred were serious." The Harvey-Dixmoor incident was similar. There, five out of the seven injured were also hit by a single shotgun blast. Chief of Police Leroy H. Knapp Jr. informed us that only two or three shots were fired during the entire disorder. (A similar scattering of pellets occurred in St. Paul, where three out of four policemen hit by gunfire received their injuries from one shotgun blast.)

Sniping vs. Accidental Shooting

In Cleveland, almost every injury to a policeman came as a result of gunfire. However, it is not at all clear whether snipers inflicted the damage. In the chaos that accompanies many disorders, shots have sometimes been fired accidentally—by both rioters and policemen. Ripley's September 2 article in *The New York Times* stated the problem very well: "Only by setting the exact position of each man when he was shot, tracing the bullet paths, and locating all other policemen at the scene can a reasonable answer be found." Thus far, no information concerning the circumstances of each casualty in the Cleveland disorder has been disclosed, and this goes for deaths as well as injuries.

Moreover, what applies to Cleveland applies to the other disorders as well. The Little Rock case illustrates the point. Chief of Police Brians verified the shooting of a National Guardsman. However, he also clarified the circumstances of the shooting. He said that during the disorder a group of people gathered on a patio above a courtyard near the area where the National Guard was stationed. One individual, under the influence of alcohol, fired indiscriminantly into the crowd, hitting a guardsman in the foot. Chief Brians added: "He might just as easily have hit a [civil-rights] protestor as a guardsman." What is clear is that the circumstances concerning all casualties need to be clarified so as to avoid faulty inferences and incorrect judgments as much as possible.

Concerning the amount of sniping, there were numerous discrepancies between early and later reports, suggesting that many initial reports were exaggerated.

According to the police officials themselves, other than in the case of Cleveland where 25 to 30 snipers were allegedly involved, there were relatively few snipers. In 15 out of 17 cases where such information was available, police officials said there were three snipers or less. And in 7 out of 17 cases, the officials directly contradicted press reports at the time and said that no snipers were involved!

As for the number of gunshots fired by snipers, the reality, as reported by police, was again a lot less exciting than the newspapers indicated. In 15 out of 18 cases where information was available, "snipers" fired fewer than 10 shots. In 12 out of 18 cases, snipers fired fewer than five. Generally, then, in more than one-quarter of the cases in which sniping was originally reported, later indications were that no sniping had actually occurred.

In Evansville, initial reports indicated that a minimum of eight shots were fired. Yet Assistant Chief of Police Charles M. Gash told us that only one shot was fired.

A more dramatic illustration is found in the case of East Point, Georgia. Although 50 shots were reportedly fired at the time, Acting Chief of Police Hugh Brown informed us that no shots were fired.

In York, 11 persons were wounded in a "gun battle" on the first night. However, it turns out that 10 out of 11 persons were civilians and were injured by shotgun pellets. Only two snipers were involved, and only two to four shots were fired throughout the entire disturbance.

In Waterloo, Iowa, Chief of Police Robert S. Wright acknowledged that shots were fired, but he added: "We wouldn't consider it sniper fire." He told us that there was "no ambush, no concealment of participants, or anything like that." Moreover, he stated that not more than three persons out of a crowd of 50 youths carried weapons and "not a great number of shots were fired." The weapons used were small handguns.

In St. Paul, where 10 shots were reportedly fired at police and four officers were wounded by gunshots, Chief of Police Lester McAuliffe also acknowledged that though there was gunfire, there "wasn't any sniper fire as such."

A similar situation was found in Peoria. Safety Director Kennedy said that the three shots believed fired did not constitute actual sniping.

In Little Rock, Chief Brians discounted reports of widespread sniping and indicated that many "shots" were really firecrackers.

In Gary, early reports were that Chief of Police James Hilton had been fired upon and six persons had been wounded by snipers. Assistant Chief of Police Charles Boone told us that while a few shots might have been "fired in the air," no actual sniping occurred. No one was shot during the disturbance, and no one was injured. Chief Hilton indicated that the fireman who was supposed to have been hit during the outbreak was actually shot by a drunk *prior* to the disorder.

In a few instances, discrepancies between first reports and sober reappraisal can be traced to exaggerations of the policemen themselves. However, most of the discrepancies already cited throughout this report can be attributed to the press—at both the local and national level. In some instances, the early press reports (those appearing at the time of the incident) were so inexplicit as to give the *impression* of a great deal of sniping. In other instances, the early figures given were simply exaggerated. In still other instances, the early reports failed to distinguish between sniper fire and other forms of gunplay.

The Role of the Press

Moreover, the press generally gave far too little attention to the immediate cause or causes of the disturbance. Even in the aftermath of the violence, few attempts were made to verify previous statements or to survey the tensions and grievances rooted in the community. Instead, newspapers in many instances placed an unusually heavy (and at times distorted) emphasis on the most dramatic aspects of the violence, particularly where sniping was concerned.

A look at some of the newspaper headlines during the disorders is most revealing, especially where the "pellet cases" are involved. As mentioned earlier, large numbers of casualties were sustained from the pellets of a single shotgun blast—in Peoria, seven policemen; in Harvey-Dixmoor, five policemen, and in York, 10 civilians were injured in this way; the most commonly cited examples of a "new pattern" of violence. Unfortunately, inaccurate and sensational headlines created an impression of widespread sniping, with the police singled out as the principal targets. A few individual acts of violence were so enlarged as to convey to the reader a series of "bloodbaths." In some cases, an explanation of the circumstances surrounding the injuries was buried in the news story. In other cases, no explanation was given. In still other cases, the number of casualties was exaggerated.

Distorted headlines were found in the local press:
RACE VIOLENCE ERUPTS: DOZEN SHOT IN PEORIA
                        Chicago (Ill.) *Tribune*,
                        July 31, 1968
6 COPS ARE SHOT IN HARVEY STRIFE
                        Chicago *Sun-Times*,
                        August 7, 1968
20 HURT AS NEW VIOLENCE RAKES WEST END AREA
11 FELLED BY GUN FIRE, FOUR FIREMEN INJURED FIGHTING FIVE BLAZES
                        York (Pa.) *Dispatch*,
                        August 5, 1968
These distortions were transmitted on the wire services as well. For example, in Ann Arbor, Michigan, readers were given the following accounts of Peoria and Harvey-Dixmoor in their local newspapers. The first account was based upon a United Press International news dispatch; the second is from an Associated Press dispatch.

10 POLICEMEN SHOT IN PEORIA VIOLENCE
                      By United Press International
                      Ann Arbor (Mich.) *News*,
                      July 30, 1968
Ten policemen were wounded by shotgun blasts today during a four-hour flareup of violence in Peoria, Ill. . . .

EIGHT WOUNDED IN CHICAGO AREA

Ann Arbor News,
August 7, 1968

Harvey, Ill. (AP)—Sporadic gunfire wounded seven policemen and a woman during a disturbance caused by Negro youths, and scores of law enforcement officers moved in early today to secure the troubled area....

Finally, they were repeated in headlines and stories appearing in the national press:

GUNFIRE HITS 11 POLICEMEN IN ILL. VIOLENCE

Washington Post,
July 31, 1968

SHOTGUN ASSAULTS IN PEORIA GHETTO WOUND 9 POLICEMEN

The Law Officer,
Fall, 1968

Chicago—On August 6, in the suburbs of Harvey and Dixmoor, seven policemen and a woman were shot in Negro disturbances which a Cook County undersheriff said bore signs of having been planned.

U.S. News & World Report
August 19, 1968

In all probability, few newspapers or reporters could withstand this type of criticism. Nevertheless, it does seem that the national press bears a special responsibility. Few of the nationally known newspapers and magazines attempted to verify sniping reports coming out of the cities; few were willing to undertake independent investigations of their own; and far too many were overly zealous in their reports of a "trend" based on limited and unconfirmed evidence. Stated very simply: The national press overreacted.

For some time now, many observers (including members of the academic community) have been predicting a change from spontaneous to premeditated outbreaks resembling guerrilla warfare. Their predictions have largely been based upon limited evidence such as unconfirmed reports of arms caches and the defiant, sometimes revolutionary rhetoric of militants.

And then came Cleveland. At the time, the July disorder in that city appeared to fulfill all the predictions—intelligence reports of planning prior to the disorder, intensive sniping directed at the police, the absence of a precipitating incident, and so on. Few people at the time quarreled with the appraisal in *The New York Times* that Cleveland was "perhaps the first documented case" of a planned uprising against the police. Following the events in Cleveland, disorders in which shots may have been fired were immediately suspected to be part of a "wave."

Unwittingly or not, the press has been constructing a scenario on armed uprisings. The story line of this scenario is not totally removed from reality. There *have* been a few shoot-outs with the police, and a handful may have been planned. But no wave of uprisings and no set pattern of murderous conflict have developed—at least not yet. Has the press provided the script for future conspiracies? Why hasn't the scenario been acted out until now? The answers to these questions are by no means certain. What is clear is that the press has critical responsibilities in this area,

for any act of violence easily attracts the attention of the vicarious viewer as well as the participant.

Moreover, in an era when most Americans are informed by radio and television, the press should place far greater emphasis on interpreting, rather than merely reporting, the news. Background pieces on the precipitating events and tension-heightening incidents, more detailed information on the sniper himself, and investigations concerning police and civilian casualties represent fertile areas for the news analyst. To close, here is one concrete example: While four policemen were killed in the violence reviewed in this article, at least 16 civilians were also killed. A report on the circumstances of these deaths might provide some important insights into the disorders.

July-August 1969

SUGGESTED READINGS

The Paranoid Style in American Politics and Other Essays by Richard Hofstadter (New York: Knopf, 1966). A historian looks at the receptiveness of Americans to conspiratorial theories.

Shoot-out in Cleveland; Black Militants and the Police: July 23, 1968. A report of the Civil Violence Research Center by Louis H. Masotti and James J. Corsi (Cleveland, Ohio: Case Western Reserve University, submitted to the National Commission on the Causes and Prevention of Violence, May 16, 1969).

Public Information and Civil Disorders, National League of Cities, Department of Urban Studies (Washington, D.C.: July, 1968) contains recommendations concerning the activities of the news media during civil disorders.

"America as a Mass Society: A Critique" by Daniel Bell, *Commentary* (Vol. 22, July 1956). Bell refutes the sanguine interpretation of modern life as espoused by Fromm, Mannheim, Jaspers, Marcel and others as romantic and irrational, and tries to place "mass society" in a different light.

Symbolic Crusade by Joseph Gusfield (Urbana, Illinois: University of Illinois Press, 1963). A positive view of the relationship between mass society and human personality.

The Image: A Guide to Pseudo-Events in America by Daniel J. Boorstin (New York: Harper and Row, 1964). Constructing reality through public relations, corporate image, opinion research and media fabrication.

Public Opinion by Walter Lippmann (New York: The Free Press, 1949). A classic social-psychological interpretation of political processes.

Language, Thought, and Reality by Benjamin L. Whorf (Cambridge, Mass.: M.I.T. Press, 1967).

The Loom of Language by Frederick Bodmer (New York: Norton, 1944).

Selected Writings in Language, Culture, and Personality by Edward Sapir (Berkeley, Calif.: University of California Press, 1958).

The Medium is the Massage by H. Marshall McLuhan and Quentin Fiore (New York: Random House, 1967). Essays, classic and contemporary, on the nature of language, culture and communication.

Rumors in the Aftermath of the Detroit Riot

MARILYN ROSENTHAL

Every so often a vivid drama captures a vast city population in a special kind of living theater, where the people become both audience and actors. The Boston Strangler had that effect upon the Boston metropolitan area. A similar drama hypnotized Detroit in the winter of 1967–68: its backdrop was the inner city, which lay in ruins from the rioting of the previous June; its principal actors included both public figures and private individuals; its dramatic effect played upon the fear of repeated and more generalized violence; its impact convulsed the entire greater metropolitan area of over four million people; its energy was rumor.

The Detroit rumor drama was built of diffuse elements that swirled subtly into a complex story of many dimensions. Across the stage flashed the immediate events, observed by the normal ambiguity of human intentions and the usual distortions of human understanding. Following the actual events were interpretations and analyses which created a cross fire of printed flyers and articles by white ultraconservatives and right-wingers, black revolutionaries and black militants. There were startling statements on TV programs, sensationalized and irresponsible suburban newspaper exposés, distorted speeches, frightened declarations and backfiring good intentions. This mixed media presentation apparently penetrated the historic memory and the unconscious needs and fears of both black and white. Fearful city and suburban citizens reacted by generating a host of rumors that nearly crippled a major city.

Detroit communcniation had been severely limited by a four-month-old newspaper strike which threatened to continue for several more months. On Thursday, 6 March 1968, Mayor Jerome P. Cavanagh appeared on TV to announce the establishment of a Rumor Control Center housed in the offices of the City Community Relations Commission. He spoke of a city chilled with fear, of psychological damage done to its citizenry, and he urged all citizens to phone the center where, he promised, all stories about the metropolitan area would be checked out, facts established and efforts made to dispel the rumors. The center phone began to ring at 9:00 A.M. the next morning. It continued to ring for almost one month.

While there were rumors in both the black and white communities, I will examine some of those that whites spread and believed. All the major cities in the country were troubled by similar rumors at this time, and perhaps Detroit serves as a case study. What follows is a description of the rumors, the actions they motivated, the events and men generating the rumors, the city's attempts to stop them through the Detroit Rumor Control Center and some ideas that help explain why the rumors were so pervasively and deeply believed.

The Rumors Begin

The first rumor received by the center went like this: Mrs. H. heard from her neighbor who heard from her aunt who heard from a lady in Birmingham [Michigan] who heard from her neighbor who heard from her cleaning lady that the riot was to start on July 1st. The lady in Birmingham had asked her cleaning lady to work on July 1st, and the cleaning woman had responded by saying she could not work on July 1st as this was the day that the riot was to start.

That first day the center received 96 calls; there was to be a day when it would receive 1,600. The calls generally fell into three categories: rumors of irrelevance, rumors of incidents and rumors of fear.

The rumors of irrelevance often included crank calls, questions of gossip and requests for preposterous information. "Is it true the Temptations [a Motown vocal group] are dead?" "I heard the mayor is going around with the WJR weather girl." The staff was instructed to respond to such callers politely but firmly and end conversations as quickly as possible.

The rumors of incidents were stories that quickly gathered around and embellished some actual occurrence. For example, that winter there was a fair amount of disruptive activity in several of the city's high schools and junior highs. Students protested lunchroom conditions and sometimes walked out over accusations of racism and insensitivity to black educational needs. People living near these schools would begin calling in rumors shortly after an incident occurred. As the day ended, the stories became more elaborate and violent. Rumors pictured vicious race rioting, schools burning down, police clubbing or shooting students and teachers. They were all exaggerations, but they typify the pattern in both black and white neighborhoods.

Rumors of Fear

The overwhelming number of rumor calls were of a much less specific nature. The callers seemed to need to have their fears allayed. There was fear of a black invasion of the suburbs; fear that the water systems were going to be blown up or poisoned; fear of violence directed at a specific suburb such as Grosse Pointe or Dearborn; fear that violence would begin on a specific date. "I heard from a man who works in a plant in Livonia that the riots will start on June 20th"; "On July 4th"; "On Easter Sunday." A specific date seemed to give the rumor an air of authenticity.

A rumor that appeared again and again in the center reports concerned the killing of white children. Blacks were going to kidnap and kill a young boy from every subdivision in the suburbs; school buses would be attacked; children would be shot on street corners. In one Jewish neighborhood, the rumor took the quasi-biblical form that a young Jewish male from each street would be shot. Many rumors concerned policemen, and how their families and homes would be attacked and destroyed. It was feared that each policeman's family was to be killed one by one.

By the time the rumors faded away, more than 10,000 calls were recorded, and the great majority of rumor callers were thought to be white. The center developed an elaborate classification system, but one especially frightening rumor defied the usual classifications.

The Castration Rumor

The castration rumor seems to erupt at many times of crisis in history, and it has cross-cultural variants, appearing in Egyptian mythology and elsewhere. While castration rumors were much more frequently heard in whispered private conversation, they did make their way to the center. Although they appear to have had no basis in either fact, incident or statement, they are of such a special, highly charged nature that they must be examined separately.

In essence the rumor was this: A mother and her young son are shopping at a large department store. At one point the boy goes to the lavatory. He is a long time in returning, and the mother asks a floor supervisor to get him. The man discovers the boy lying unconscious on the floor. He has been castrated. Nearby salesclerks recall that several teen-age boys were seen entering the lavatory just before the young boy and leaving shortly before he was discovered.

If the story is told in the white community, the boy is white and the teen-agers are Negro. If it is being told by Negroes, then the mother and the boy are black and the teen-agers white.

The castration story had become a common rumor in the Detroit area by late February 1968. The *Windsor Star,* a Canadian newspaper in wide circulation due to Detroit's newspaper strike, made an abortive attempt to stop this rumor. On 9 March it printed a version of the story adding some brief notes to show how preposterous the rumor was. But the castration rumor was written in such detail, and began the article so realistically, that the effort backfired.

The rumor spead further. Callers reporting the story to the Rumor Control Center after 9 March often said that they had read it as a news story in the *Windsor Star.*

Five years before, the same type of rumor had circulated in many cities around the country, and a Detroit psychiatrist did a study of the phenomenon in 1964. He found the common denominator in the unconscious meaning given to basic mother-son relationship.

Bruce Danto, former director of the city of Detroit's Mental Health Institute, points to the significant elements in the rumor. First, the mother takes her son into a situation that eventually destroys him. The implication here, according to Danto, is that something terrible will happen to young boys the minute they leave the protection of their mother. The age of the boy in the rumor is usually from seven to nine, a time when little boys are coping with Oedipal feelings about their mothers, a time when many have unconscious fears of penis loss. In addition, Danto quotes Freud as saying women as well as men may have fantasies of castration along these lines.

Because of the fear of castration appears during the development of *both* men and women, it might be viewed as an archetype or part of man's collective unconscious. During World War II psychologists collected rumors and subjected them to description and analysis from the Freudian perspective. None of the World War II rumors had any basis in fact either. Rather, according to Marie Bonaparte's *Myths of War,* the rumors were projections of deeply embedded (or archetypal?) emotions that large numbers of people shared and that manifested themselves in times of stress.

In other words, the 1967–68 winter was a time of great racial tension. This tension evoked anxiety in the people of Detroit. The anxiety triggered deep emotional response. Every person is to some extent responsive to castration anxiety, as a current problem or as a vestigial remnant of childhood development. Some in the community experienced this current stress as a spontaneous eruption of castration anxiety manifesting itself in the castration rumor. This was the only explanation of the castration rumor that anyone had to offer.

Barring proof of a specific incident, this explanation would appear convincing. However, one other element can't be neglected: the reality of historic memory. While there may have been no racial incidents of castration in Detroit, old stories of white castration of blacks in the South are not unknown, nor untrue. Individuals may not recall specific cases, but vague memories and hazy recollections of hearing or reading of them linger in the black community's historic memory. So the psychological dynamics suggested by psychiatrists are given added probability as they operate within a context of a plausible historic event.

Obviously, any situation that can resonate the primal anxieties of a whole city, generating rumors of castration and infanticide, must be decidedly dramatic. It was in fact a mixed media show of events, people, TV programs, journalistic reports, attitudes and rumors which kaleidoscopically created the powder keg of Detroit. And as in all good drama, there was a beginning, a middle and an end.

The beginning was in the flames of the Detroit riot of June 1967, and in the background was the newspaper strike. Together they made the city more susceptible to the fear and rumor that nearly strangled it. Such conditions allowed the *Inner City Voice,* "The Voice of Revolution" newspaper, and its right-wing counterpart publications to begin their escalation of rhetoric. An NBC-TV special in September 1967 analyzed this rhetoric, but unfortunately the viewers reacted to the rhetoric and not the analysis. The result was real escalation.

Rumors and Their Mongers

The Patriotic Party. The ultraconservative Patriotic party of Michigan set up a store front in segregated, all-white Dearborn, in early September 1967. Presiding was Jim Freed, a house painter, ex–John Birch Society member, recently Michigan chairman and now national secretary of the Patriotic party. In an office full of George Wallace paraphernalia, Freed speaks sternly to the theme of the House Un-American Activities Committee series of volumes, *World Communist Movement.* He quotes a 1928 statement of the United States Communist party saying that American Negroes would be organized as a vanguard of Communist activity. According to Freed, the black riots are designed to lead to martial law, which leads to UN intervention, which leads to Communist control. "The whole thing could evolve in this direction."

To keep this from happening, Freed's party prepared a red, white and blue flyer. Its three-inch letters screamed "ALARM," and it asked, "Can You Survive the Next Riot?" It told of Negro guerrilla plans for next summer and listed emergency household supplies to stock. "ALARM" reached many people, including blacks. In midwinter, an unidentified black group duplicated its emergency list word for word on its own flyer calling on ghetto residents to "cool it."

The NBC Special. On Friday evening, 15 September 1967, NBC-TV ran a program entitled "Summer '67: What We Learned." Frank McGee and special reporter Daniel P. Moynihan narrated. The Detroit consultant was a young Catholic seminarian, Anthony Locricchio. Set primarily against a backdrop of 1967 Detroit riot shots, the program began with a statement by McGee that "the greatest single need in America today is for communication between blacks and whites." Then, with Moynihan offering interpretive comments, McGee presented a number of interviews with various blacks.

Interviews with two masked Negroes provided the show's dramatic moments. One was a self-styled fire bomber and sniper. The other was introduced as "in the inner circle of black extremists." Their remarks implied the existence of small extremist groups of blacks (and a few whites) who deliberately took advantage of the riot situation to start fires, snipe and encourage more looting. Both spoke of guerrilla plans to blow up sewers and powerplants and to concentrate on "people's lives."

McGee and Moynihan commented on their statements at some length, putting them into context. Moynihan said, "We have seen in this city a cohort of half-educated, half-crazed young people who are planning violence . . . and if they only do half what they say . . . they really can tear the country apart, as we are very clearly involved with the makings of conspiracy . . . we can take away the raw material of their revolution—an enormous, troubled, disorganized agonized lower class." McGee said we must prevent the extremists from dividing us into two hostile camps, "by doing the things that have to be done." It is doubtful that the TV audience heard and understood the explanations. But the dramatic statements were picked up everywhere.

The Conscientious Police Chief. Late in November, Chief Edwin Gleza of suburban Redford Township attended a Michigan Association of Chiefs of Police workshop in Battle Creek. The three-day meetings were of an informational nature concerned with briefings on organized crime and police intelligence. However, one session was devoted to the organizational structure of black extremist groups and used RAM (Revolutionary Action Movement) as an example.

Chief Gleza reacted in a manner unforeseen by the workshop organizers. Through the Redford Chamber of Commerce, he set up an evening meeting with local people in business and industry. The chief took the RAM material most seriously and felt it his duty to pass the information on to local citizens. He informed them of the plans of his police department to protect the town against the possibility of guerrilla activities and suggested means of cooperation. Said Chief Gleza, "I felt that under RAM's stated aims, they [business and industry] could be attacked and they had a right to know."

A suburban newspaper reporter believed the public also had a right to know. An article on the chief's speech soon appeared in the *Observer* newspapers, which serve six communities in the northwest Detroit suburbs. The reports of Chief Gleza's reaction heightened the tension of the rumor drama, and thousands of suburban homes were caught in the grip of fear.

Anthony Locricchio, a 30-year-old former Detroit lawyer who had decided to become a Catholic priest, had gained a reputation as an expert on inner city problems. In early December, he addressed a meeting sponsored by the Saint Clair Shores Human Relations Council and the Christian Mothers Sodality at Saint Lucy Church.

Locricchio described his talk as having a dual purpose: to teach whites to distinguish black "extremists" from black "militants" and to encourage whites to minimize rumors of future black attacks on white suburbs. Personally fearful of backlash against the black community arising out of such rumors, he tried to explain the tactics of extremists, black and white.

The tactic, he said, is to create incidents that polarize moderates and force them to take extreme positions because the planned incidents are such an outrage. Locricchio quoted so-called secret information from a black extremist group to illustrate the tactic of polarization. He said they spoke of forays to white suburbs where white children would be shot. Their plotting led them to the tortuous conclusion that terrorist acts would bring armed whites into the black ghetto and that moderate blacks, seeing this, would be forced into the extremist camp. Locricchio said his speech that night was meant to warn people against reacting emotionally to rumors.

The next day, the *Macomb Daily News* reviewed the speech and headlined the story "Race Expert Tells of Horror Planned by Negro Extremists." The news article related how Locricchio said black extremists would "hit" 50 white suburbs while they set Detroit on fire. It went on to elaborate the details of the attack but neglected to put it into the context that Locricchio said his speech provided. He threatened to sue the Macomb paper. It promised to do a special, two-part series explaining more accurately what he had said. The explanatory articles appeared, but the damage had already been done.

Dramatized by its sensational headline, the story careened violently through the metropolitan area, fed the stories started elsewhere and added to the confusion. Locricchio later ruefully observed, "I was talking about danger to blacks; they [whites] heard danger to whites." His revelation offers a clue to understanding the power of the rumor drama. People hear what they want to hear. The whites needed to hear certain things about the black community. The troublesome habit of distorting reality again made a shambles of objectivity. Why were the whites believing the tales of black violence that composed most of the Detroit rumors?

Dr. Caligari's Cabinet? The "Lou Gordon Show" is reported to reach 100,000 homes in the Detroit area twice weekly. Its host interviews local people on current topics of interest. Gordon describes himself as a local muckraker speaking for the little man, and he often reveals a lack of perspective and depth. His popularity might reflect the widespread desire for simple answers to problems that overwhelm in their complexity.

In January Gordon invited Anthony Locricchio to appear on the show and explain his recent speech. Nothing was clarified. The next week his guests were two black extremists, men whose position in the Negro community is confused and debated, but widely publicized. The two programs, far from being illuminating, fed the voracious, public appetite for stories of black violence. Subtleties, distinctions, elaborations meant nothing, and Gordon's shallow approach served to elicit deceptive, alarming responses. The rumor drama gathered momentum.

Guns in the Newsroom. On 1 February the *Northeast Detroiter,* a newspaper with a circulation of 16,500, headlined an article "Civil War in Detroit's Future." The article was punctuated by boldface subheads such as "Rap Brown—Stokely Carmichael," "Rioters Heavily Armed," "Shoot at White Children" and "Bribe to Rioters." It claimed to cite sources such as Governor George Romney, city officials and the commissioner of the Michigan State Police. It began by describing official preparations being made to combat the anticipated invasion of heavily armed militants. Incredibly, a Lou Gordon speech was quoted to validate the story about plans to shoot "small white children."

The news article harangued the city fathers, accusing them of using "bribery" to prevent rioting: "open housing legislation, civil rights bills, give the Negro money, rebuild his neighborhood with tax-payers money." Homeowners were urged to arm to "make ready for the beginning of the end," because "the dead are expected to total thousands across the nation," and "all we can do is wait." The article was reprinted in their 29 February issue, and the theme reappeared in *Northeast Detroiter* articles during the spring.

Jim Schmidt, the young editor of the *Northeast De-*

troiter, often wears a handgun while at his office. He is perfectly open about it. Moonlighting as a police reporter, he travels with the Detroit police Tactical Mobile Unit. He believes the media have a gentleman's agreement to play down the news of racial tension. Nearly obsessed with the subject of arms and arming, he says that everyone has a right to know that "people here are armed to the teeth. If the militant Negroes plan to riot and snipe, they'd get killed immediately." He's been accused of trying to promote a riot, but he doesn't see it that way.

Donald Lobsinger's "Breakthrough." Donald Lobsinger, founder and leader of a group called Breakthrough, is a physically unprepossessing man preoccupied with thoughts of conspiracy. Like Freed, Lobsinger is convinced the rioting is part of a Communist strategy to undermine the United States. He graduated from the University of Detroit, a Jesuit college, in 1957, with a B.A. in sociology. Self-described as a militant anti-Communist, he was particularly influenced by the writings of a conservative priest, Father Richard Ginder, a Catholic newspaper columnist who wrote "Right or Wrong—The Sunday Visitor."

After college, Lobsinger served in the infantry in Germany for two years. Returning to civilian life, to his parents' home in Dearborn, he became a clerk in the accounting section of the Detroit Department of Parks and Recreation where he is still employed.

In 1959, while on leave from the army, he attended the Communist International Youth Festival in Vienna for several days. He was particularly impressed by the Communists as propagandists, but equally fascinated by the zealous activity of the anti-Communist youth with whom he spent the bulk of his time. He wondered whether American youth and students would be equally committed to opposing Communism. Back home, Lobsinger organized Breakthrough in 1964 "to break through the curtain of silence on the part of the mass news media regarding the extent of Communist influence and activities" in this country.

Breakthrough has distributed masses of flyers, held rallies, demonstrations and counterdemonstrations; they attempted to disrupt a concert of the Soviet Moscow Chamber Orchestra; they picketed Martin Luther King's last Detroit speech and tried to disrupt it. Lobsinger feels his tactics are effective, and he measures his success by the "fierceness of the attacks against us by the Communist and liberal and Left press." He is amazed at being labeled an "extremist, right-wing crackpot," but pleased, too, because "if they take the time to brand you as such, it means that you are important."

During the fall of 1967 at Breakthrough rallies, Lobsinger told his small audiences that the Communists were organizing the current rash of urban violence. He quoted

Bob Benyas PIX

NBC-TV ran a program entitled "Summer '67: What We Learned." Daniel P. Moynihan narrated.

Rap Brown as saying they were merely rehearsals for the violence to come in the not too distant future. When charged with spreading groundless rumors, he replied, "What we have been saying is fact."

Lobsinger viewed the riots as one part of a larger conspiracy to make America socialistic; Mayor Cavanagh and Governor Romney were another part. He feels they deliberately allowed the 1967 riots to spread in order to "make the public accept socialist programs." They are, "One Worlders" who seek a socialist utopia, Lobsinger insists. "Romney, after all, is on the letterhead of the Council on World Tensions."

Breakthrough has also urged whites to arm. Lobsinger is convinced that Communist plans will bring widespread violence to the country in many forms, probably in periodic, guerrilla-like warfare. Local police, National Guard and army units will be so tied down that individual citizens will have to defend themselves. Private arms are the only way to do this, he says. Should white vigilantes invade the inner city ghettos, it would only accelerate the violence and play into Communist hands. Lobsinger's conspiracy is a very complex one.

"The Voice of Revolution." On 20 October the first issue of a monthly radical newspaper appeared in Detroit's black community. Editor John Watson claims the *Inner City Voice* has a circulation of 8,000 to 10,000 distributed through stores, radical bookshops and automobile plants. Watson feels it is read mostly by workers, college and high school students, as well as city officials, police and people like Lobsinger.

Hastily put together, the eight-page newspaper concentrates on police brutality, "honky" prejudice, attacks on Mayor Cavanagh, black revolutionary ideas and activities, black pride and "white fascist" activities. Donald Lobsinger's Breakthrough and Jim Freed's Patriotic party are mentioned frequently. Typical headlines were: "Killer Cops Run Hospital," "Fascists Infiltrate Police," "Free Guns Given With Groceries," "White Invasion Planned," "Brothers Take Care of Whitey," "Violence Must Meet Violence," "Cycle of Depression in Raceland (USA)" and, in their sixth issue, "Detroit's Concentration Camps Waiting for Blacks." Although the information in the concentration camp story was spurious, the sentiments it reflected were widespread, and it became a subject of intense discussion in the black community.

Watson describes himself as a black, Marxist-Leninist admirer of Che Guevara and Regis Debray and proponent of "taking state power from rich white people and giving it to the masses." His thinking incorporates general Marxist theory and one of the many concepts of black power. He puts black power first. "There must be self-determination in the black community where blacks determine policies, tactics, strategies; then they can coalesce with other groups who are doing the same thing."

Watson is sure that the rumors of planned black violence were all in the white community and were intended to arouse whites to attack blacks. The white extremists use his paper for their own propaganda purposes, he feels. "Organizations like the Patriotic party and Fightback [described below] are precipitating talk and action." The police department, which he fears wants to blow up his office, and their hysterical "arms race," fed the rumors. He thought the black community didn't begin reacting to the rumors until February or March when chilling stories began to circulate about threats to the black community.

Locricchio, Watson said authoritatively, didn't know what he was talking about. "Nobody ever said anything about killing white children. There was just general revolutionary discussion of how can you strike back if the white reaction to the black revolution reaches genocidal proportions and blacks have to prove that, in terms of the destruction they are capable of carrying out, white programs of genocide won't be worth it."

Watson and his newspaper exemplify the puzzles surrounding the rhetoric of violence, what David Reisman called rhetorical escalation. The paper violates all conventions of journalism and polite language. Its articles regurgitate centuries of pent-up black rage and frustration. Some stories express bloody revenge fantasies and realities. Although Watson's influence is minimal, his words are horrifying to many whites. To moderate Negroes, he is one of the alienated, embittered black youths who exist on the fringe of the community.

Yet, the leaders of the black community did not dismiss the concentration camp story. Dr. Hubert Locke, a minister and director of religious affairs at Wayne State University, and a special assistant to former Detroit Police Commissioner Ray Girardin, was typical. Locke was willing to dismiss the wild statements of black extremists, because the "so-called battle plans for the cities of people like Carmichael and organizations like RAM make no sense when applied to the suburbs." But he was concerned and unwilling to accept the concentration camp story as mere rumor. Although he shrugged off the *Inner City Voice* story, like Watson he, too, mentioned the book *Concentration Camps,* USA and the provisions under the McCarran Act to reactivate internment camps. "If it happened in Germany with the Jews, it conceivably can happen again. . . . Camps could be used for large numbers of arrested rioters or might be operated if a Fascist spirit, like that of the radical Right, should become dominant in this country." This story, insisted Locke, has a basis in fact, whereas the rumors in the suburbs were entirely without it. (In the spring of 1968, the concentration camp story was treated extensively in a *Look* article.) The rhetoric had escalated again, from rumors of castration and infanticide to rumors of genocide. Fear and anxiety were nearly out of hand.

The Suburban Police Scene

Hubert Locke held that the further away whites were from what was actually going on in the ghettos, the less contact they had with Negroes, the more prone they were to believe even the most fantastic rumors. If fear is any measure of that belief, he was correct, as fear began to run very high in the suburban areas in late winter and early spring. Handgun registrations were up 100 percent to 500 percent above the previous year. In some communities, citizens asked for and received municipally sponsored target practice. The classes in Dearborn received national publicity, and a photograph of women at target practice was printed widely around the country. It also found its way into the March issue of the *Inner City Voice*.

Chief John O'Reilly, head of the Dearborn police department, felt the press had misrepresented the city's gun classes. The newspapers had suggested, he said, that "because Dearborn is a segregated community, it is training its women to shoot in the event of a riot." If the ladies are buying weapons, he felt, they certainly should be instructed in the proper methods and legal implications of their use, which the classes did. He pointed out that the Department of Parks and Recreation had run gun clinics for 15 years. In January, a ladies' service luncheon club had asked the department if they could have gun training after their weekly meetings. The department agreed, advertised this new class and was overwhelmed when it received 600 applications. Chief O'Reilly felt this "reflected apprehension and fear on the part of the general community—fear of general crime in combination with general fear." He dismissed most rumors as too vague to make any sense. Though he didn't predict any kind of trouble in Dearborn during the spring or summer, he was organizing reserve police volunteers as a precautionary measure.

Livonia was the only other community to run city-sponsored gun classes as rumors spread and fear rose. The city ran a total of 13 single-session classes with 25 to 30 in each. The earliest classes enrolled mostly young married men who expressed the desire to set up local vigilante groups. Many came with preconceived ideas about protecting their property and were often jolted when an assistant city attorney would explain the law to them. Older women were often the most vehement in expressing their fear and hate. Many younger women talked about protecting themselves and their children because their husbands were often away on business. One hysterical woman, who found it increasingly difficult to contain herself during a question-and-answer period, finally burst out, "I've got a teen-age daughter, and you know what they want. You know why I'm learning to shoot this gun. Let me tell you, I'm going to use it."

The Livonia Police Department had worked itself into a state of confusion. A department official felt that, in Livonia, only a few rumors were widespread—black snipers would kill a white child on each block, burn shopping centers and poison water supplies. He felt the source of the rumors was "unstable whites . . . and devious colored." He dismissed them as mostly "nonsense" and said they ought to be ignored by the public. "Yet," he continued, "people are restricting their movements, sticking close to home, and handgun registration is up 500 percent in Livonia over last year." The Livonia police switchboard had been jammed with calls about rumors. "We tell people flat out that these rumors are full of hot air," he commented. Then he continued, revealing his overriding ambivalence, "but any Negroes coming down Plymouth Road [a major Livonia thoroughfare] will be shot."

While the police in Redford, Dearborn and Livonia were escalating their rheatoric and mobilizing their communities, police officials in other communities responded to the rumors in a somewhat more restrained fashion. Chief Milton Sackett of Southfield circulated a flyer discrediting the rumors as either groundless or a distorted mingling of fact and fiction. It urged citizens to rely on the police, to remain calm, to refrain from spreading rumors and, above all, *not* to buy guns. "If you feel the need for greater protection in your house—buy a dog." While the flyer was a sober, reasonable communication emphasizing the need to rely on legally constituted agencies in the event of emergency, it assumed that disturbances could take place. The rumors weren't completely discredited in Southfield either.

In the city of Warren, which borders Detroit, Commissioner of Police Walter O'Bee said he had heard only a few rumors, but he was alarmed that handgun registration was 400 percent above normal. He had reinforced his riot squad, had his men study crowd control and was co-operating with the Intelligence Bureaus of other police departments. Although many Negroes work in the plants of Warren, he felt the city had no problems. But trouble might spill over into the city; "minority groups might invade Warren" were his words.

Commissioner O'Bee said the city was not establishing

any gun schools, which, he felt, would only encourage the use of guns. The mayor had issued a statement trying to quiet the rumors. Still, in early April, a Warren businessman held several meetings of a self-protection organization he named Fightback; it received some notoriety, including coverage in the *Inner City Voice*.

Fightback

Ron Portnoy, owner of King's Discount Drugs in Warren, became so agitated by the rumors that he burst into community action on 1 April. He printed and distributed hundreds of flyers headlined "FIGHTBACK!" calling a mass meeting for that evening. Portnoy felt all the rumors were very real. "Younger people are going to cause trouble. The 17- to 23-year-olds. They're being organized and aroused by Carmichael and Brown." He said he had documentary proof that Communist agitators were behind it all. The flyer proclaimed, "The only way to stop them is at the City Limits, before they get to your home and your children. We must not depend on others to protect us, we must do it ourselves."

Fightback was started because Portnoy had complaints. First, "We felt there should be a voice so rioters would know that people in the suburbs are going to resist." He went on, "As an individual, I feel I've lost my voice in local government. The lawmakers are just passing laws for the minorities . . . like civil rights and open housing which is being shoved down our throats at gun point. And this country is being run by people with money, not by the average people anymore." He felt that there had to be a stronger voice for the average white man, and he thought his new organization would provide it.

Portnoy claimed his first meeting drew 600 people, 300 of whom signed up. Chief O'Bee was concerned about Fightback because he felt vigilante groups had no place in the city and that any problems could be handled by the police themselves. "Mr. Portnoy is just very misinformed, and we've had him in here for a long talk." Portnoy complained bitterly that the Warren police were harassing him and intimidating individuals cooperating with Fightback. Whatever the reason, his group faded quickly and never gained a permanent foothold in Warren.

The Role of the Detroit Police

Although not pronounced, a discernible pattern of Rumor Control Center calls revealed that police officers were inadvertently circulating stories. Policemen are men, and naturally they talk to their friends and families. When, for example, police leaves in Detroit were canceled for 21 February—declared Malcom X Day by some black militants—there was a natural pool of people who knew about it. *Northeast Detroiter* editor Jim Schmidt, as a fellow traveler with the Tactical Mobile Unit was one of those who knew. He picked up all sorts of information, quasi information, opinions and attitudes which must have influenced his editorial work. The police department action became the stuff of scores of rumors about what would take place in the city on 21 February.

Former Commissioner Ray Girardin had a great deal to say about the rumors and the Detroit police. His attitudes reflected an honest man agonizing in an overwhelming situation. He tried to see everyone's point of view. On the one hand, "I'm sorry to have to say that many police, without realizing that they carry such authority, do pass on these rumors. The average policeman doesn't stop to weigh what he says." On the other, "A lot of it is just the process of people talking to each other and, without thinking, enlarging on what they have heard."

He found it difficult to answer the question of where all the rumors were coming from, or what they meant. There had been no particular rumors before the Detroit 1967 disturbances, while the Detroit riot in 1943 had been preceded by a violent surge of rumors. He felt that some current rumors were started maliciously and others simply came from nowhere he could put his finger on, like the castration story which mystified him completely. "People on the far right and people on the far left are putting out flyers that duplicate each other. They circulate rumors and scare everybody." But he couldn't help musing, "Is it all being done deliberately to keep the police off balance?"

One rumor frequently heard was that the police themselves would provoke incidents as an excuse to attack Negroes. Girardin reacted emotionally. "Our people are paid to keep peace, but in a group this large, (4,400 men) . . . you'll have people with all sorts of predilections. Our police, as a group, are trying, under extremely difficult conditions, to do the best job possible in law enforcement. . . . This is a rotten, rough job. . . . The average policeman is a pretty confused guy, but he's generally a well-intentioned guy. Some of these people just crack up. We have a Board of Psychiatrists now to review candidates for the force, but our testing hasn't reached the point of refinement yet to filter these guys out."

The Rumors Stop

On the Wednesday before Martin Luther King's assassination, the Rumor Control Center was down to about 40 calls a day. On the Friday after his death until the Tuesday after his funeral, the center switchboard couldn't handle the calls coming in. Callers claimed to have heard from authoritative sources that rioting was going to break out on such and such a day, that trouble was definitely going to start as soon as the troops withdrew from Detroit after the funeral. Mayor Cavanagh and Governor Romney had called out the National Guard Thursday night; they remained until the following Thursday night, keeping order and imposing a nightly curfew.

There was little rioting and looting in Detroit after King's death and few disturbances in Detroit's ghettos after the funeral. Hubert Locke reported that a squad of

Negro leaders had spent literally days on the phone over that period of time, calling all over the Negro community, urging parents to keep their children off the streets and carefully supervised. He feels they were instrumental in keeping the community under control. The presence of the National Guard was apparently reassuring to white suburbanites.

From the week after the funeral through the summer, the Rumor Control Center reported an insignificant number of calls. Donald Lobsinger's Breakthrough and John Watson's *Inner City Voice* continued reading their self-styled scripts, but the vast numbers of urban actors were played out. Why? Did the death of a great black leader hold some subtle significance for white Americans? What was the meaning of this new martyrdom? Both black and white saw the great outpouring of grief, as national television carried little else. Did the wave of genuine sympathy and sorrow constitute a catharsis for white fear and guilt?

There is no question but that the rumors gripped masses of people in the Detroit metropolitan area. In some way (perhaps the reverse of the process that activates fears of castration, infanticide and genocide), Martin Luther King's death and its relatively quiet aftermath in Detroit did provide a catharsis for these fears. In any event, the rumors and the rumor mongers faded away.

Some Final Observations

The summer of 1968 in Detroit was not without incident. Police clashed with the Poor People's Campaign at Cobo Hall. In the fall there was trouble at a policemen's ball and at the George Wallace rally in Detroit. But the dominant rumors of the previous fall, winter and spring did not materialize.

In October of 1968, Mayor Cavanagh cited a variety of factors preventing racial outbreaks during the summer: a national climate of restraint, effective local efforts to provide 30,000 new jobs, the success of the Tigers. He also pointed to wide recognition of the city's ability to mobilize very quickly in response to violence, the city's immediate mobilization after the King assassination being a recent example.

But the rumors left a legacy. Police estimate that there are between 1 million and 1½ million firearms owned privately in Detroit alone. Handgun registration in 1968 was twice what it was in 1966. Several vigilante groups still patrol streets in northwest metropolitan areas.

While speeches, TV shows, flyers and counterflyers provided the media with many of the rumors, these alone cannot account for the intensity of the white response. It is true that there was an overpublicized national rhetoric of black power, confused with isolated cries for black violence. The slogans were not yet clearly defined, and they were, perhaps in part because of this, alarming to large numbers of whites.

Extremists of the Right and Left have always fed on their mutual suspicions, hostilities and rhetoric. Most people, black and white, get caught in between. But the paranoia of the extremists alone does not explain why white suburbanites believed the rumors, bought firearms in unprecedented numbers, attended gun clinics and patrolled their neighborhoods. Dr. Paul Lowinger, a psychiatrist and director of outpatient services at Detroit's Lafayette Clinic, sees the response rooted in white guilt over racism in America. He says the guilt gives rise to a fearful overreaction which permits whites to believe the very worst about what blacks will do Lowinger and other psychiatrists say that the rumors served unconscious needs. Feelings usually hidden or controlled surged to the surface and helped to make the rumors more believable, more urgently spread, vivid enough to act upon. The result was the Detroit rumor drama.

So the actors shouted at each other through the streets of the city, and the echoes reverberated dangerously. The urban drama moved from scene to scene intertwining the natural ambiguity of immediate events, unconscious needs and historical memories. It came to an abrupt end in a catharsis like that of Greek tragedy. A great black leader was killed; his death and sacrifice seemed to drain the emotional intensity and overwhelming fear of whites so that the play was over. The end was a tragic one, but not the tragedy so many Detroiters expected. And, of course, the American racial drama goes on and will continue, for too long, into our increasingly uncertain future.

October 1970

SUGGESTED READINGS

The Psychology of Rumor by Gordon W. Allport and Leo Postman (New York: Holt, Rinehart and Winston, 1947). The fundamental theoretical work in the social psychology of how rumors start, spread, and can be recognized.

Improvised News, A Sociological Study of Rumor by Tomotsu Shibutani (Indianapolis, Indiana: Bobbs-Merrill, 1966). A major work on the nature and function of rumor as a social process, a reaction to the failure of formal information channels. Asks the question, "How do people make up their minds in ambiguous situations?"

The Invasion from Mars by Hadley Cantril (Princeton, New Jersey: Princeton University Press, 1940). A documentary analysis of the panic ensuing from Orson Welles' famous "War of the Worlds" radio drama, significant as a barometer of public attitude toward the media.

"Social Movements" by Herbert Blumer in *Principles of Sociology* edited by Alfred M. Lee (New York: Barnes and Noble, 1955).

The Flow of Information by Melvin L. De Fleur and Otto N. Larsen (New York, Harper, 1958).

Groups in Harmony and Tension by Muzafer and Carolyn W. Sherif (New York: Harper and Row, 1953). An integration of studies on intergroup relations selected from the literature in ethnicity, social psychology and collective behavior. The authors discuss the influences that bring about strain and cooperation both within and between groups.

7 Political Protest & Social Movements

The decade of the 1960s in the industrial nation-states saw the gathering forces of opposition to the status quo erupt into organized resistance to the established social order and into violence against property and people. The appearance of political stability, which many had assumed was the hallmark of highly developed industrial states, was shown to be misleading. Dissatisfaction with inequities within the systems had been covered over or hushed up while countries waged prolonged external wars and engaged in international competition for space and arms superiority. Whatever changes in the institutional arrangements were needed, it was said, would be debated in the halls of legislatures or central committees, adopted into law and enforced by the courts. All causes would have a fair hearing, and a chance at the ballot box was open to everyone.

But the sources of conflict remained largely untouched or ineffectively dealt with. By the nature of the historical and political process of fundamental change, history suggests that they were not likely to be. In the United States, during the first fifty years of the twentieth century, the rights of labor to organize and bargain collectively were secured in bloody combat with factory owners who tarred and feathered union organizers, fired union members, hired scabs to take their jobs, clubbed and shot picketers, and picked up factories and left town when these methods of intimidation failed. Likewise, the extension of voting rights in England during the nineteenth century was achieved by step-by-step combat in the streets as well as in the House of Commons.

One of the myths of American society is the widely held belief that there is a set of values that all Americans share. Although no one can describe these precisely without finding gross exceptions to them, the mere existence of the myth provides dominant socioeconomic groups with a rationale to support their policies and actions. It also provides them with a reason for thinking that there are no basic conflicts of interests and goals that cannot be resolved within the society. Were all groups in agreement on the substance of this core group of values, then the barrier to the solution of apparent conflicts lies in coming to agreement on the means to use, not the ends to achieve. The failure to come to such an agreement, in this view, lies in a failure of communication, not in a contest for control over resources and government. This outlook deflects the issue from the level of political action to an accommodation on the level of human relations. However, it is precisely the transformation of social movements for equality by minority groups into political movements for pre-eminence by these groups that is a characteristic of the 1970s.

The rise of movements of opposition begins with questioning accepted social, political, and economic arrangements and institutions that hitherto have been considered the way things always work and even the right way for them to be organized. Making a living and raising a family ordinarily take up most of a person's time. People act in routine ways which give a pattern of stability to everyday life, even though it is an insecure, chaotic routine. But once the realization dawns that injustice and inequality do not have to be tolerated, the system as it stands is no longer considered legitimate, and demands for immediate change become widespread. Underlying the protest is the chance of success within established society if possible, but beyond that society if necessary.

Mobilization

Dissent, organized opposition, and violent struggle are some of the political tools for changing society. In the long history of the struggle by underclasses, social castes, and colonial subjects, organized political movements have mobilized people to work for the removal of the special social privileges and vested economic interests of the rulers. The mobilization mechanism may be to secure the vote, to widen economic benefits and security, or to promote as fully as possible a government that is run by the people and for their interests. Countermobilization occurs as those in dominant positions or those who feel menaced by an uncertain future, are unwilling to give up their power, or lacking that, their security. Although it has been previously unnecessary to justify the status quo, all available means are now employed to cement loyalty to the system, to discredit dissenters for lack of patriotism, to control the mass media so that the contagion of disruption does not spread, and to use every means, including legal and illegal police power, to stop popular movements of opposition from increasing the scope of their opportunities. In addition to direct coercion is indirect creaming, that is, the absorption of protest within acceptable standards and structures.

The focus of concern and study by sociologists and other social sciences has been greatly affected by the recurrence of radical movements in industrialized countries and liberation movements in the Third World. These concerns are in sharp contrast to their involvement in problems of methodology and theories about systems in equilibrium that were prevalent in the 1940s and 1950s. Under the influence of the critical historical orientations of Karl Marx, Karl Mannheim, and C. Wright Mills, many sociologists turned away from a model of stable society to one of a very different nature. They posited a society with strata of conflicting and competing interests and values, with developing social movements that worked in the long-run direction of social reconstruction. This is a new turn in a conflict-egalitarian model, one that is heavily freighted with a democratic vision of a cooperative, self-governing condition of liberated men.

Challenge and Response

The articles in this section serve two functions: First, each deals with critical sectors of American society that have taken part in social uprisings—the blacks, the poor, the students, the critics of the old politics in the United States. Included also are pieces on the underground resistance in eastern Europe and the revolutionary peasants of North Africa. Second, the articles are analyses of various kinds of responses to social protest by those in control. Robert Blauner gives a critical account of the McCone Commission Report (for which he was a consultant) on the Watts riot in "Whitewash Over Watts." Finding widespread support within the ghetto for the violent outbreak, Blauner claims that the revolt was a crystallization of community identity in a collective expression of unwillingness to accept oppressive rule without fighting back. The people of Watts were particularly expressing

Political Protest & Social Movements

their deep hatred for the police and other representatives of the white majority who operate in the black community "like an army of occupation."

Ellen Kay Trimberger's analysis of the student rebellion at Columbia University is included to exemplify one of a number of such studies of the internal features of disorders on hundreds of American college campuses. In "Why a Rebellion at Columbia Was Inevitable" Trimberger describes the sequence of political negotiations among the parties involved—various factions of students, administration officials, and faculty groups—culminating in the student occupation of university buildings and violent confrontations with the administration, faculty, other students, and finally with the city police who were called in by the university president.

During the last week of August, 1968, the Soviet armed forces invaded Czechoslovakia where they met with an organized and popular resistance. Constantine G. Menges was in the country at the time and describes the tactics used by the resistance forces as well as the political and military devices employed by an occupying force in "Resistance in Czechoslovakia—An Underground in the Open."

Finally, Eric Wolf's article on the "Algerian Peasant Revolt," analyzes one of the six major social and political upheavals of the twentieth century fought with peasant support. These were the Mexican Revolution of 1910, the Russian Revolutions of 1905 and 1917, the Chinese Revolution starting in 1921, the Vietnamese Revolution starting in the World War II period, the Algerian Rebellion of 1954, and the Cuban Revolution of 1958. Although the battle of Algiers is a famous prototype for successful revolutionary action, the final outcome of the revolt was a failure, if measured by how much power the peasant revolutionaries were able to keep.

Often political protest involves polarization not of such "opposites" as the very rich and the very poor, but, in the United States at least, opposition between groups that are proximate to one another. Thus we have strong rivalries between second and third generations of immigrants, between urban blacks and urban poor whites, between Episcopalian bankers and Jewish brokers, and the like. In short, the character of protest is made complex by the patterns of upward mobility. That is why the themes of politics and sociology have crisscrossed to form a new discipline, political sociology. This theme of how classes and races change their political perspectives is illustrated in the work of Seymour M. Lipset and Earl Raab on "The Wallace Whitelash"—a theme that is becoming central in new definitions of class politics in American society.

New Centers of Protest

A major new feature in movements of social and political protest is that they involve groups formerly labeled the *lumpenproletariat,* undesirable and marginal elements in society for whom no political role was predicted (such as welfare mothers and even homosexuals). They have now become central in all protest activities. Similarly, groups which in previous epochs were viewed as bellweathers of revolutionary sentiment, such as a factory workers, have become highly conservative, or least dedicated to established ways of doing things. Thus, a major theoretical innovation illustrated by the articles in this section is how those groups that formerly seemed unlikely candidates for social and political conflict and revolution-making have become vital, while, at the same time, older revolutionary groups have become conservatized as a result of the elaborate process of "making it." It is to these changing features of protest that sociologists have begun giving great attention.

Whitewash Over Watts

The failure of the McCone Commission report

ROBERT BLAUNER

On August 24, 1965, just one week after public order had been restored in the south-central area of Los Angeles known as Watts, Governor Pat Brown of California announced the appointment of an eight-man commission of leading citizens. In his charge to the group (which came to be known as the McCone Commission, after its Chairman, John A. McCone, former head of the CIA), Brown asked it to "prepare an accurate chronology and description of the riots"; to "probe deeply the immediate and underlying causes of the riots"; and finally to "develop recommendations for action designed to prevent a recurrence of these tragic disorders."

For what appears to have been political considerations connected with possible repercussions of the Watts affair on the 1966 gubernatorial campaign, the Commission was given December 1, 1965, as the deadline for the completion of its report. Thus only 100 days were available for a "deep and probing" analysis of the most destructive incidents of racial violence in American history.

In an atmosphere of speed-up that made work on an automobile assembly-line appear leisurely by comparison, the Commission held a series of sixty formal hearings before which eighty sworn witnesses, including city and police officials, leaders and citizens of the white and Negro communities, eventually appeared. It also selected a full-time staff of thirty, primarily lawyers and legal-oriented investigators, to carry out the day-to-day work of assembling data and preparing to write the report. The staff called upon the services of twenty-six consultants (chiefly university professors in the social sciences) for advice and the sub-contracting of research; interviewed ninety persons from the 4,000 arrested; and opened an office in the riot area to receive testimony from Negro citizens. After a total expenditure of $250,000, Commissioner McCone presented the report to Governor Brown in the fanfare of television cameras on December 6.

In view of the conditions under which it was hurried into existence, it should be no surprise that *Violence in the City—An End or a Beginning?* is a slim volume with only eighty-six pages of blown-up type. But the report of the McCone Commission is not only brief, it is sketchy and superficial. Its tone and style are disturbing. There is much glib writing and the approach as well as the format is slick in the manner of our illustrated news weeklies before their recent upgrading. The depth analysis of this fateful outbreak can be read by an average reader in less than an hour —allowing ample time for contemplating the many photographs, both color and black-and-white.

A comparison with the careful and considered report of the Illinois' Governor's Commission which analyzed the 1919 Chicago race riots in a 672-page book *(The Negro in Chicago)* that required three years of planning, research, and writing to produce may well be unfair. But with the considerable budget and the academic sophistication avail-

WIDE WORLD

"For what appears to have been political considerations connected with possible repercussions of the Watts affair on the 1966 gubernatorial campaign, only 100 days were available for an analysis of the most destructive incidents of racial violence in American history." (Governor Brown with the children of Watts.)

The author gratefully acknowledges the aid of Lloyd Street who oriented him to Los Angeles and its Negro community and provided many observations and insights on the Watts rioting.

able today, more was to be expected than the public relations statement presently in our hands.

It is not only the size and style of the McCone document that are disturbing. Its content is disappointing both in its omissions and in underlying political and philosophical perspectives. There is almost nothing in the report that is new or that gives consideration to the unique conditions of Los Angeles life and politics. As Los Angeles councilman Bill Mills commented, most of the material in the report documents conditions in the Negro ghetto that have been common knowledge to sociologists and the informed public for a generation.

More appalling are the report's deeper failures. With a narrow legalistic perspective that approached the riots in terms of the sanctity of law and order, the commissioners were unable (or unwilling) to read any social or political meaning into the August terror. There was no attempt to view the outbreak from the point of view of the Negro poor. The commissioners also play a dangerous game with the thorny problem of responsibility. The Negro community as a whole is absolved from responsibility for the rioting while local and national leaders (civil-rights moderates and extremists alike) are taken to task for inflaming mass discontent and undermining attachments to law and authority. (In his two-page dissenting comment appended to the main report, the Reverend James E. Jones, a Negro commissioner, criticizes the report for attempting "to put a lid on protest.")

In a crude attempt at "horse-trading" in the responsibility market, the positions of the Los Angeles police department and city administrators are consistently protected. In discounting the relevance of police provocation and city policies to the revolt without presenting any facts or evidence, the Commission not only protects powerful interests; it abdicates its mandate to seek out facts and establish as best as it could the objective reality. My most general and serious criticism of the report is this violation of its responsibility to seek truth and its frequent hiding behind opinion and hearsay.

CAUSES OF THE WATTS "REVOLT"

Lurking behind the Watts violence are three basic problems, according to the McCone Commission:
- the widespread unemployment and "idleness" in the Negro ghetto;
- the cultural and educational backwardness of black children that prevents the schools from preparing them for the labor market and integrating them into society.
- the troubled state of police-community relations in the Negro neighborhoods.

EMPLOYMENT. The chapter on employment is forthright in its emphasis on jobs as a central problem and correct in its understanding that male dignity and family responsibility can hardly be expected when men are unable to find steady work. For example: "The most serious immediate problem that faces the Negro in our community is employment—securing and holding a job that provides him an opportunity for livelihood, a chance to earn the means to support himself, and his family, a dignity, and a reason to feel that he is a member of our community in a true and a very real sense." The Commission calls upon federal, state, and city government to create jobs for the Negro and Mexican-American poor. Corporations and labor unions are asked to end discrimination once and for all and to police their progress by keeping careful records on minority employment. Because the Commissioners are convinced that the majority of jobless Los Angeles Negroes are presently un-

"In a crude attempt at 'horse-trading' in the responsibility market, the positions of the Los Angeles police department and city administrators are consistently protected." (Commission chairman John A. McCone (left) and Los Angeles police chief, William H. Parker.)

employable, they call for an expanded and better-coordinated program of job training; they wisely recommend that control of this effort be placed inside the Negro community.

These proposals on employment are worthwhile and necessary but they encourage a deceptive complacency. The report does not probe sufficiently into the depth and seriousness of the problem. There is no consideration of the impact of population trends and technological developments on the availability of jobs, especially for the unskilled, and no willingness to face the escalating employment needs in the rapid expansion of Los Angeles' Negro population. The report is irresponsible because its style and tone convey the impression that its relatively mild and moderate recommendations provide real solutions.

EDUCATION. The treatment of education is the one section of the McCone report that is based on a careful and first-hand study. Kenneth A. Martyn, professor of education at Los Angeles State College, investigated five areas within the Los Angeles City Unified School District as a Commission consultant. Student achievement was compared for four "disadvantaged areas" (of which two were primarily Negro and close to the riot centers) and one "advantaged" area (predominantly white upper-middle class). Average student reading performances in the fifth, eighth, and eleventh grades reveal a consistent backwardness in the lower-class Negro and Mexican districts. The gap is most dramatic at the eighth grade, since by the eleventh many of the poorest "achievers" are already drop-outs. The average student in the white middle class area is in the 79th percentile in reading vocabulary based on national norms; the average students in "Negro" Watts and Avalon are in the 13th and 14th percentiles; the averages in the primarily Mexican areas of Boyle Heights and East Los Angeles are 16 and 17.

Martyn investigated the possibility of discrimination in educational facilities. Some inequalities were found, but hardly enough to explain the systematic backwardness of minority students. The Commission thus locates the problem of Negro school performance in what today is fashionably called "a culturally impoverished environment." Parents have little education and their own background does not foster an orientation toward achievement and learning. Crowded housing conditions are not favorable for disciplined study. And the precariousness of employment and the lack of models of achievement may further dull incentive. In order to break this pattern and "raise the scholastic achievement of the average Negro child up to or perhaps above the present average achievement level in the city," the Commission calls for an intensive infusion of educational resources into the Negro community focusing on three programs: pre-school learning on the model of "Headstart"; the reduction of class size; and the improvement of academic and behavioral counseling.

The McCone report accepts the conventional position that it is the "vicious circular" connection between education and employment that is the crux of the dilemma of the Negro poor. And it places its main bet on education and the future, rather than creating jobs to solve the problems of the present. If the achievement levels of present and future generations of Negro children can be sufficiently raised, they will be motivated to remain in the school system and assimilate the skills and training that will begin reversing this cyclical process. Unfortunately, the middle-class ethos which underlies the Commission's emphasis on future-orientation and achievement is irrelevant to the needs and outlook of the lower-class adult group whose problems of work and training are likely to intensify.

But even with a crash program in education, can the average poor Negro youth be motivated toward achievement and excellence when the condition of his people and community place him in a position of alienation and powerlessness *vis-a-vis* the larger society? What is missing in the report's analysis is a total picture of the Watts community as consistently deprived and disadvantaged in relation to Los Angeles as a whole. Fragmented hints of this picture abound in the report, particularly in the excellent discussion of the woefully inadequate transportation system, but the fragments are never pieced together. If they were, municipal officials would then have to bear some responsibility for permitting this systematic deprivation to persist. By singling out education as the strategic sphere for ameliorative efforts, the Commission aims its biggest guns on the target-area in which the city's hands are relatively "clean" and in which it is relatively easy to suggest that the cultural backgrounds and individual performances of *Negroes themselves* account for a good part of the problem.

THE POLICE ISSUE

If we don't get no good out of this, it will happen again. By good I mean an end to police harassment, and we need jobs. I got eight kids, and I've only worked 10 days this year. I ain't ever been a crook, but if they don't do something, I'm gonna have to *take* something. I don't know how they expect us to live. (Young man in "a striped shirt" quoted by Louise Meriwether, "What the People of Watts Say," *Frontier,* Oct. 1965.)

When a deprived segment of the population breaks out in a violent attack on society and its representatives, the *underlying* causes refer to those long-term elements in its situation that have produced its alienation and despair. *Immediate* causes refer to those more short-run irritants and grievances that have intensified feelings of anger and hatred and focussed them on specific targets. The immediate grievances and conditions that spark illegal violence must have the effect of weakening the oppressed group's normal disposition to accept, at least overtly, the authority structure and legal norms of the society—otherwise mass violence could not erupt. The young Watts Negro quoted above seems to be saying that from his standpoint "jobs" are the underlying cause, "police harassment" the immediate issue. The governor's commission disagrees with his analysis and has its own explanation for the ghetto's sudden loss of attachment to the legal order.

It answers its own question, "Why Los Angeles?" in a way that almost totally relieves the city and county of implication. The rapid migration of Southern Negroes to the city's ghetto serves as their starting point, for these Negroes are unrealistic in expecting that California living will solve all their life-problems. In the context of this "crisis of expectations" Negro frustration and despair were fanned by three "aggravating events in the twelve months prior to the riots":

■ "Publicity given to the glowing promise of the federal poverty program was paralleled by reports of controversy and bickering over the mechanism to handle the program here in Los Angeles, and when the projects did arrive, they did not live up to expectation."

■ "Throughout the nation, unpunished violence and disobedience to law were widely reported, and almost daily there were exhortations, here and elsewhere, to take the most extreme and even illegal remedies to right a wide variety of wrongs, *real and supposed.*"

■ "In addition, many Negroes here felt and *were encour-*

aged to feel that they had been affronted by the passage of Proposition 14—an initiative measure passed by two-thirds of the voters in November 1964 which repealed the Rumford Fair Housing Act and unless modified by the voters or invalidated by the courts will bar any attempt by state or local governments to enact similar laws." (Italics mine.)

The argument is clear. Aside from some blunderings over the anti-poverty war, it was Negro leadership that undermined the commitment of law-abiding black citizens to authority and legal methods of redressing their grievances. What is important is the assumption that the Negro poor's attachment to law and political authority was not weakened by its own experience with police and other official representatives of society, but was instead subverted by an extremist and opportunist leadership. Such an analysis gives the Commission a free field to discount the role of the Los Angeles police and their presence in the ghetto as immediate precipitants of the violence. In short, the Commission has "bought" the line of Chief of Police William Parker who has consistently argued that the riot was a revolt of the criminal and lawless element, prodded on by a Negro leadership which inflamed the Los Angeles black community with the "bugaboo" of "police brutality."

The report devotes a chapter to law enforcement and police-community relations. It takes note of the severe criticism of the police department by many Negro witnesses and frankly admits "the deep and longstanding schism between a substantial portion of the Negro community and the police department." Considering the virtual unanimity in the Negro community concerning police practices as the foremost immediate cause of the outbreak, why did not the Commission seriously investigate the role of law enforcement in the ghetto? The Commission acknowledges that Negro *feelings* of oppressive police action were significant conditions of the rioting. However, it violates its responsibility to truth and impartiality by refusing to examine the factual basis of Negro opinion while stating the beliefs and hearsay of white officers in an aura of established truth:

> ... the police have explained to us the extent to which the conduct of some Negroes when apprehended has required the use of force in making arrests. Example after example has been recited of arrestees, both men and women, becoming violent, struggling to resist arrest, and thus requiring removal by physical force. Other actions, each provocative to the police and each requiring more than normal action by the police in order to make an arrest or to perform other duties, have been described to us.

Precisely the same line is taken with respect to Chief Parker. The Commission duly notes that the outspoken chief is a focal point of criticism and is distrusted by most Negroes. They feel he hates them. Yet the report conveniently omits all rational and objective evidence for such Negro "belief" based on a whole series of public statements made long before the riots. The inference is that Negro belief rests on misinterpretation of fact and paranoid reactions.

However, not only embittered Negro attitudes, but *facts* exist about the police presence in the ghetto—if the Commission would have only looked for them. There was a Youth Opportunities Board study available to the Commission based on intensive interviews with 220 people in the Watts, Willowbrook, and Avalon districts undertaken only two years before the outbreak in this very area. The sample included 70 delinquent and nondelinquent children, 26 parents, and 124 high administrators and lesser personnel of the major agencies in the community (schools, welfare and probation, recreation and youth groups). Attitudes toward the critical agencies of the community were probed, and it was found that of all the "serving institutions" of the larger society greatest hostility was directed toward the police department. A majority of adults as well as children felt that *the behavior of police aggravated the problems of growing up in the Negro community rather than contributed to their solution;* this was in direct contrast to their attitudes toward the schools, the parks, the health services, and the probation officers.

"In discussing the businesses which were looted and burned the Commission concludes (unlike most informed observers) that there was 'no significant correlation between alleged consumer exploitation and the destruction.'"

The real issue has perhaps been muddied by the outcry against "police brutality," the term that Negroes use to sum up their felt sense of grievance against law-enforcement agents. The police liberalization policy of recent years may well have reduced the number of cases of "classic" brutality—beatings, cruel methods of questioning, etc. What the Negro community is presently complaining about when it cries "police brutality" is the more subtle attack on personal dignity that manifests itself in unexplainable questionings and searches, in hostile and insolent attitudes toward groups of young Negroes on the street, or in cars, and in the use of disrespectful and sometimes racist language—in short, what the Watts man quoted above called "police harassment." There is no evidence that this assault on individual self-esteem and dignity has ceased.

Another facet of police brutality is the use of excessive force to control criminal and illegal behavior. Characteristically the Commission passed on its opportunity (and obligation) to assess the use of force by the various law enforcement agencies that put down the August violence, despite its considerable attention to their logistical and coordination problems and the concern of Negroes and liberal groups like the ACLU with what appeared to be unnecessary shootings of looters, including young children.

The police chapter is primarily devoted to the adequacy

". . . The police have explained to us (the McCone Commission) the extent to which the conduct of some Negroes when apprehended has required the use of force in making arrests." (Excerpt from the report.)

of procedures presently available for processing complaints against officer misconduct and to recommendations for improving both them and the general relation between law enforcement and the Negro community. Yet, the demand of Negro leaders and white liberals for an independent civilian review board is described as "clamor"; the proposal is rejected because this device would "endanger the effectiveness of law enforcement." Experience with its use in two cities "has not demonstrated" its "advantages," but characteristically no evidence is given and the cities are not even named. Instead the report advocates the strengthening of the authority of the present Board of Police Commissioners, the civilian heads of the department, and establishment of the new position of Inspector General under the authority of the Chief of Police. The latter "would be responsible for making investigations and recommendations on all citizen complaints." In addition, the police should improve its community relations programs in the ghetto areas and strive to attract more Negroes and Mexicans to careers in law-enforcement.

The Commissioners are aware that "police brutality" has been an issue in all of the Northern Negro riots in recent years and that each began with a police incident. But instead of asking why poor Negroes come to believe that law and authority are not *their* law and their authority, they go on to sermonize:

> Our society is held together by respect for law. A group of officers who represent a tiny fraction of one percent of the population is the thin thread that enforces observance of law by those few who would do otherwise. If police authority is destroyed, if their effectiveness is impaired, and if their determination to use the authority vested in them to preserve a law abiding community is frustrated, all of society will suffer because groups would feel free to disobey the law and inevitably their number would increase. Chaos might easily result.

CHARACTER OF THE WATTS OUTBREAK

There is very little explicit consideration of the character and meaning of the outburst in the McCone Report, in spite of its great concern with causes. The Commission missed an important point of departure by not viewing the Watts violence as a problematic phenomenon, the essence of which needed to be determined through a careful weighing of evidence and through social and political analysis. For this reason the report's implicit assumptions must be inferred because they are introduced in passing and never clearly spelled out.

The analytical perspective is overwhelmingly *riot control* rather than collective or crowd behavior. The attempt of responsible Negro leaders to cool off the mobs is discussed, but the major emphasis is on the tactics used by the various law enforcement agencies. After a fairly thorough discussion of the arrest which set off the events, the Negroes who participated in violence are almost excluded from the story. The very language of the Commission suggests that it has prejudged "the meaning of Watts," even though the debate that has been going on in Negro circles as to the appropriate term of reference suggests that determining the character of these events is a real and difficult question.

On page one of the report, the outbreak is called a "spasm" and "an insensate rage of destruction." Later it is called "an explosion—a *formless, quite senseless,* all but hopeless violent protest" (Italics mine). Only in its discussion of the business targets which were looted and burned does the Commission attempt to locate a meaning or pattern in what the rioters did, and here they conclude—unlike most informed observers—that there was no "significant correlation between alleged consumer exploitation and the destruction."

The legalistic perspective of the Commission and its staff seems to have blocked its sensitivity to the sociological meaning of the riots. When viewed simply as an uprising of the criminal element against law and order (aggravated of course by the more social, economic, and political causes of frustration already discussed), the Commissioners need not look seriously at its human meaning nor need they understand what messages may have been communicated by the rocks, gunfire, and Molotov cocktails. Let us not romanticize the Watts violence. I don't claim that everyone involved and everything done had rational motives. But it is a more humble and scientific attitude to leave the question open and to examine the limited evidence that is available. For the assumption of meaninglessness, the emptying out of content and communication from any set of human actions—*even nonrational violence*—reduces the dignity of the actors involved. In the present context it is a subtle insult to Los Angeles' Negroes. The report ostensibly avoids such an insulting stance by minimizing Negro participation and exculpating the bulk of the community from responsibility from the anti-social outbreak—except of course its leaders who aggravated the underlying tension:

> In the ugliest interval which lasted from Thursday through Saturday, perhaps as many as 10,000 Negroes took to the streets in marauding bands. . . . The entire Negro population of Los Angeles County, about two thirds of whom live in this area (that of the riots), numbers more than 650,000. Observers estimate that only about two percent were involved in the disorder. Nevertheless, this violent fraction, however, minor, has given the face of community relations in Los Angeles a sinister cast.

No evidence is presented for the 2 percent estimate, nor for the total of 10,000 participants on which it is based. We are not told how the Commission defines being "involved in the disorder." A number of distortions are apparently obvious, however. Even if 10,000 were the upper limit, this figure would indicate much more than 2 percent participation. For the Negro curfew area of some 500,000 residents contains many neighborhoods of comfortable middle-class people who were far from the riot center; they should be eliminated from a calculation of the extent of participation in an outbreak of the Negro poor and dispossessed. Second, the total population figures include women, children, and the aged. A more appropriate (and still difficult) question would be the extent of participation of young and mature Negro males in the low-income districts that were the centers of the action.

THE SPIRIT OF REVOLT

Unfortunately, I cannot answer this question precisely, but in view of the Commission's unscientific methodology and dubious deductions there is no reason to accept their view of the participation issue. Consider on this matter Bayard Rustin, who visited Watts with Martin Luther King a few days after the outbreak:

> I could not count heads but reports I have received and my experience with the people leads me to believe that a large percentage of the people living in the Watts area participated. But most of them did not themselves loot and burn but they were on the streets at one time or other. (*New America,* September 17, 1965)

As Rustin suggests, the question is not simply how many engaged in lawless acts. Essential to the meaning of the revolt is the attitude of the "non-participants" toward those who erupted in hate and violence. In the most popular revolutions it is only a small minority that storms the Bastille or dumps tea in Boston Harbor. Only through considering the viewpoints of the "silent mass" is it possible to know whether the Watts riots represented an action of a large segment of Los Angeles Negro poor rather than a cutting loose of a small "violent fraction." Had the McCone Commission done its job, it would have conducted a systematic survey of community opinion to determine the distribution of sentiment in Negro Los Angeles.

My informants reported widespread support within the ghetto for the violent outbreak. Moral approval (as well as active participation) was stronger among youth and among the poor and working-class. Old people and middle-class Negroes were more likely to feel ambivalent and hold back. But there seems to have been at least some participation from all segments of the black community. In the countless interviews and feature stories that appeared in the press and on television, Watts Negroes were more likely to explain and justify the riots rather than to condemn them—certainly the mass media would have little interest in censoring accounts of Negro disapproval. In a statewide public opinion survey conducted in November only 16 percent of the Negroes interviewed attributed the riots to "lack of respect for law and order" in contrast to 36 percent of the whites; "outside agitators" were seen as a most important cause by a scant 7 percent of the Negroes compared to 28 percent of the whites. Seventy-nine percent of the Negro respondents fixed upon "widespread unemployment" and "bad living conditions" as prime causes, compared with only 37 percent of the whites. And months after the rioting a poll conducted by ABC Television found that the proportion of Watts residents who felt that the summer's events had helped the Negroes' cause was twice as much as those who felt it had hurt them.

If the Los Angeles revolt was not simply a "spasm" of lawlessness reflecting the violent inclinations of a minor criminal group, but represented instead the mood and spirit of the low-income Negro community—then we must look more closely at what the crowds were attempting to communicate in their assault upon society.

As the Governor's report correctly notes, the uprising was not organized in advance. Yet it was neither formless nor meaningless. The Negro crowds were expressing more than the blind rage and the anti-white hate epitomized in the "Burn, baby, burn" slogan. They seem to have been announcing an unwillingness to continue to accept indignity and frustration without fighting back. They were particularly communicating their hatred of policemen, firemen, and other representatives of white society who operate in the Negro community "like an army of occupation." They

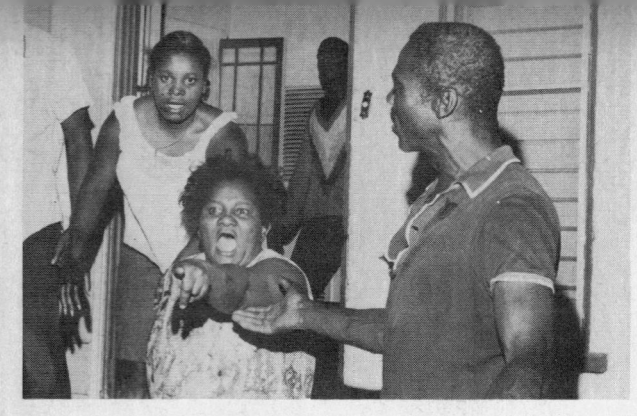

"The Negro crowds were expressing more than blind rage and anti-white hate; they seem to have been announcing an unwillingness to continue to accept indignity and frustration without fighting back."

were asserting a claim to territoriality, an unorganized and rather inchoate attempt to gain control over their community, their "turf." Most of the actions of the rioters appear to have been informed by the desire to clear out an alien presence, white men, rather than to kill them. (People have remarked how few whites were shot considering the degree of sniping and the marksmanship evidenced in accurate hits on automobile lights and other targets.) It was primarily an attack on property, particularly white-owned businesses, and not persons. Why not listen to what people in the crowds were saying as did Charles Hillinger of the *Los Angeles Times* on the night of August 13:

- "White devils, what are you doing in here?"
- "It's too late, white man. You had your chance. Now it's our turn."
- "You created this monster and it's going to consume you. White man, you got a tiger by the tail. You can't hold it. You can't let it go."
- "White man, you started all this the day you brought the first slave to this country."
- "That's the hate that hate produced, white man. This ain't hurting us now. We have nothing to lose. Negroes don't own the buildings. You never did a decent thing in your life for us, white man."

A "NATIVE" UPRISING

Any appraisal of the Watts uprising must be tentative. All the facts are not yet known, and it always takes time to assimilate the full significance of historic and traumatic events. I suggest, however, that it was not primarily a rising of the lawless, despite the high participation of the *lumpenproletariat* and the clearcut attack on law and authority. Neither was it a "conventional race riot" for the Los Angeles terror arose from the initiative of the Negro community and did not fit the simple pattern of whites and blacks engaging in purely racial aggression. And it was not a Los Angeles version of a mass civil rights protest. Its organization was too loose. More important, the guiding impulse was not integration with American society but an attempt to stake out a sphere of control by moving against that society.

Instead my interpretation turns on two points. On the *collective* level the revolt seems to represent the crystallization of community identity through a nationalistic outburst against a society felt as dominating and oppressive. The spirit of the Watts rioters appears similar to that of anti-colonial crowds demonstrating against foreign masters, though in America of course the objective situation and potential power relations are very different. On the *individual* level, participation would seem to have had a special appeal for those young Negroes whose aspirations to be men of dignity are systematically negated by the unavailability of work and the humiliations experienced in contacts with whites. For these young men (and reports indicate that males between the ages of 14 and 30 predominated in the streets), violence permitted expressing their manhood in the American way of fighting back and "getting even"—rather than the passive withdrawal which has been a more characteristic response of the Negro poor.

The gulf between Watts and affluent Los Angeles is disturbingly similar to the cleavage between the lives and interests of "natives" and their colonial masters. The poor Negro's alienation from the institutions and values of the larger society was made clear during the revolt. The sacredness of private property, that unconsciously accepted bulwark of our social arrangements, was rejected; Negroes who looted, apparently without guilt, generally remarked that they were taking things that "really belong" to them anyway. The society's bases of legitimacy and its loci of authority were attacked.

Thus Watts was not simply a racial uprising. Negro police and "responsible" moderate leaders were also the objects of the crowd's anger. Black businessmen who were seen as close to the Negro community were spared damage. From the standpoint of the poor, there was thus an implicit division of the Negro middle-class into those two segments that are found in the colonial situation: a "national bourgeoisie" on the side of liberation and a "native" middle-class that serves as agents for the dominant power arrangements.

Sartre has argued that colonialism reduced the manhood of the peoples it subjected in violating the integrity of indigenous ways of life and in creating the social status of "natives." The condition of slavery in the U.S. and the subsequent history of economic exploitation and second-class citizenship have constituted a similar attack on the manhood of Negro males. The chief contemporary manifestation of this crisis, according to the controversial "Moynihan report," is the precarious position of the man in the lower-class Negro family. The active dominance of the Negro woman and the male's relative passivity and instability are in part a residue of this historical process of manhood reduction; it is of course intimately reinforced by the unavailability of employment and the crisis of authority this brings about in the family. Unable to validate a sense of manly worth in terms of the larger cultural standards of economic responsibility, the lower-class youth orients himself toward the all-male street society whose manhood centers around other values and styles—hip, cool, and soul.

A new generation of Negro militants have created in the civil rights movement a vehicle for the affirmation of their manhood in the political struggle against its systematic negation. But the nonviolent movement which grew up in the South (with its more religiously oriented population, cohesive communities, and clear-cut segregation problems) is not well-adapted to the social condition and psychological temper of the Northern Negro. Unless new possibilities for the expression of initiative, assertiveness, and control are opened, we can expect that violent revolt will become increasingly frequent.

The Watts revolt was also a groping toward community identity. South-central Los Angeles has been a vast Negro ghetto with very amorphous neighborhood and district boundaries, with a glaring lack of leadership and organization. Most of the major civil rights groups were nonexistent in the ghetto; the gap between official Negro spokesman and the poor was even greater than is typical. The word "Watts" itself as a locational reference for the ambiguously-defined district around 103rd and Central had become a stigmatized term among Negroes as well as whites and was rarely used by residents. During the August uprising a reversal in all these tendencies became apparent. The mass action strengthened feeble communal loyalties. The term "Watts" appeared painted on walls and windows as an expression of pride and identity. Youth gangs representing the adjacent neighborhoods of Watts, Willowbrook, and Compton ceased their long standing wars and united to provide a core of organization during the rioting and the subsequent rehabilitation work. Many middle-class blacks saw that their interests could not be severed from those of the ghetto's poor, particularly when their streets and residences were placed within the curfew boundaries drawn by the militia—thus dramatizing the fact of common fate. And since August, a proliferation of community organizing, political action, and civil rights groups have risen up in the Watts area. All these processes—intensified communal bonds, ethnic identity, the hesitant return of the middle-class, and a new sense of pride in place—are graphically summed up in the experience of Stan Saunders, a Watts boy who had moved out of the ghetto to All-American football honors at Whittier College and two years abroad as a Rhodes scholar. His return to Watts two weeks before the revolt may be prototypical:

> At the height of the violence, he found himself joyously speaking the nitty-gritty Negro argot he hadn't used since junior high school, and despite the horrors of the night, this morning he felt a strange pride in Watts. As a riot, he told me, "It was a masterful performance. I sense a change there now, a buzz, and it tickles. For the first time people in Watts feel a pride in being black. I remember, when I first went to Whittier, I worried that if I didn't make it there, if I was rejected, I wouldn't have a place to go back to. Now I can say "I'm from Watts." (*LIFE,* August 27, 1965)

The McCone Commission missed the meaning of the Watts revolt due to the limitations inherent in its perspective. The surface radicalism of its language (in calling for "a new and, we believe, revolutionary attitude toward the problems of the city") cannot belie its basic status-quo orientation. The report advocates "costly and extreme recommendations," and while many of their excellent proposals are indeed costly, they are by no means extreme.

Truly effective proposals would hurt those established institutions and interests that gain from the deprivation of Watts and similar communities—the Commission does not fish in troubled waters. Possibly because they do not want Negroes to control their ethnic neighborhoods, they do not see the relation between community powerlessness and the generalized frustration and alienation which alarms them.

In their approach to the integration of the alienated Negro poor into American society, the Commission is guided by values and assumptions of the white middle-class ethos which are of dubious relevance to the majority of lower-class blacks. Their chief hope for the future is the instillation of achievement motivation in the ghetto poor so that they might embark upon the educational and occupational careers that exemplify the American success story. I am not against middle-class values—but in the immediate critical period ahead "middle-classification" will be effective only with a minority of today's poor.

What is needed—in addition to jobs—is an experimental program for finding innovations that might link the values and social patterns of the Negro lower class with the social and productive needs of the greater society, thus reversing the trend toward alienation. Before the meaningful recommendations can be made that are in line with the enormity of the problem, the sociological and cultural character of the Negro low-income community must be understood. The legalistically-oriented Commission—with its primary commitments to control, law and order, a white-dominated *status quo,* and a middle-class ethic—has not been able to do this.

March-April 1966

SUGGESTED READINGS

To Establish Justice, to Insure Domestic Tranquility: Final Report of the National Commission on the Causes and Prevention of Violence by Milton Eisenhower (New York: Praeger, 1970).

American Violence: A Documentary History, edited by Richard Hofstadter and Michael Wallace (New York: Knopf, 1970).

Violence in America: A Historical and Contemporary Reader, edited by Tom Rose (New York: Random House, 1970). An interesting and useful reader.

Race Riot by Alfred McClung Lee and Norman D. Humphrey (New York: Holt, Rinehart & Winston, 1941) examines the race riot that took place in Detroit in 1941.

Why a Rebellion at Columbia Was Inevitable

ELLEN KAY TRIMBERGER

The student demonstrations at Columbia University in the spring of 1968 caused a very serious institutional crisis—involving the disruption of the university for two months, the arrest of more than 800 students, the injuring of almost 250 students and faculty, and the prospect of continuing conflict. To explain why, one must first understand how the institutional weakness of the university and the politicization of students in recent years led to confrontations between students and the administration.

Starting in 1966, students resorted to direct action against the administration to protest against university policies toward the community and its cooperation with the military, the C.I.A., and the Selective Service. The administrators responded first with concessions, and later with repression, but they failed to re-examine their basic policies—or to make any reforms in the way the university's policies were determined. In fact, the public policies of the university (as opposed to its internal academic issues) were being decided by only a few administrators, after little or no consultation with the faculty, let alone the students.

This combination of a remote and unaccountable administration, a politicized and dissatisfied group of students, and a virtually powerless faculty was explosive. Add to it the unhappiness of the faculty and students over the declining educational quality and reputation of a great university, as well as the absence of effective ways to seek change, and you have a highly overdetermined "revolutionary" situation. (A survey by Allen Barton—"Student and Faculty Response to the Columbia Crisis," Bureau of Applied Social Research, Columbia University, June 1968—found a strong link between student and faculty dissatisfaction with the university and their support of the demonstrators. Thus, 57 percent of the most-dissatisfied faculty and 56 percent of the most-dissatisfied students thought that the sit-ins were justified, compared with only 12 percent of the most-satisfied faculty and 30 percent of the most-satisfied students. In the university as a whole, only 66 percent of the students and only 58 percent of the faculty were satisfied wih Columbia's educational quality.)

Background

For more than 20 years two extremely weak presidents have ruled Columbia, with little contact and rapport with faculty and students. Since the retirement of President Nicholas Murray Butler in 1945 until very recently, Columbia's administration had also been very decentralized. Each school and division had a good deal of academic and administrative autonomy, even to the extent of raising its own funds. What this meant was that the core of the university—the undergraduate colleges and the graduate faculties in arts and sciences —declined, both financially and in educational quality. The pay scales and the teaching loads of these faculties did not stay in line with those of other major universities, and the educational ratings of many of Columbia's famous departments dropped (surveys by Hayward Keniston of the University of Pennsylvania, 1957, and the American Council on Education, 1966).

Several years ago, the Columbia administration launched a massive campaign to stem the university's decline. Their reform plan called for a centralized fund drive, as well as for the physical expansion of the university into Morningside Heights. But these plans for expansion brought Columbia into conflict with the residents of the neighborhood, with city and state officials, and with Harlem leaders (Harlem is next to Morningside Heights, and its residents especially objected to Columbia's plans to build a gymnasium in an adjoining park). Thus Columbia, like other metropolitan universities, was drawn into the urban crisis. But because of its stagnation for the past 20 years, even in construction and in fund-raising, Columbia was in more desperate straits than most other universities, and its officers and trustees were more likely to think not of the public's needs but of the university's narrow self-interest.

At the same time, Columbia students were becoming more and more involved in social-action work with the poor who surround the university. (Since 1966, the largest and most active student organization has been the Citizenship Council, whose 1100 members take part in a variety of community-action projects.) The students' work with the poor brought them into direct opposition to the administration's community policies. Even more important, many students were politicized by the Vietnam war, and became antagonized by the university's contribution to military research.

The students, however, lacked effective channels within the university to express their discontent and to influence administration policy. Student structures are weak at Columbia, and those organizations that have tried to use legitimate channels to reach the administration usually have failed. In Columbia College, the students voted more than six years ago to abolish the student government. The all-university student council is not respected by most students, primarily because it is so powerless. For example, its resolutions in the past two years—on class ranks for the draft, military recruiting on campus, indoor demonstrations, the gym in Morningside Park, and the tuition increase—had no influence on administration policy. Nor did the administration formally or informally consult the student council. In fact, several months before the demonstrations both the president and vice-president of the student council resigned, saying that it was completely ineffective.

Moreover, students were unable to get effective faculty support for their grievances, because of the weakness of faculty organization. At Columbia there is no faculty government. The university council is composed of two elected faculty members from each school, the deans, and a number of administrators, but it is chaired and run by the administration; it meets only three times a year; and it deals almost exclusively with technical and routine matters. Of the arts and sciences faculties, only the small faculty of Columbia College has a formally constituted body that meets often and sometimes takes stands on policy matters. In recent years, a few active and concerned faculty members have used regular committees, or set up ad-hoc ones, to investigate controversial subjects with policy implications. But their reports (in 1967, on student affairs, on reporting class ranks to draft boards, on university civil-rights policies, and on faculty housing) generally were disregarded by the administration. Last year a member of the only standing committee of the university faculty admitted in public that his committee had very little power, and charged: "The present system of government at Columbia is similar to that of Tsar Nicholas II."

Columbia students jeer at police and make the V-for-peace sign. The police had been summoned by Columbia President Kirk in April after 800 students began occupying five university buildings—among them Low Library (background), the administrative building.

The buildings at Columbia were occupied for five days, and the students made themselves comfortable.

Faced with an unresponsive administration and a powerless faculty, student activists turned to direct action. In 1966 and 1967, a coalition of moderate and radical student leaders, with wide undergraduate support, won important concessions from the administration after mass demonstrations and threats to strike. These concessions included:

- a university policy of withholding class ranks from the draft boards;
- the establishment of a special tripartite commission (student, faculty, and administration) to try students who had demonstrated against the C.I.A. Most students saw such a judicial commission as setting a precedent toward greater due process, and as moving away from the traditional methods of student discipline at Columbia, where students were accused, judged, and punished by the dean's office.
- The cancellation of army recruiting on campus and of the annual Naval Reserve Officers Training Corps ceremony.

At the end of the school year in 1967, the student newspaper, *The Columbia Spectator,* wrote (March 17):

"Within the last 12 months, student organizations— enjoying the general sympathy of the student body as a whole—made demands on the university which are of unprecedented nature. And, in turn, the university has given unprecedented response to these demands. The confrontation between the two has developed into what may be a revolution in the role of the student at Columbia. . . . The greatest single phenomenon on the campus in the last 12 months has been the shift to radicalism, the development of the feeling that the usual, slow-moving methods of change are inadequate, and the growing attraction of more forceful action."

But for all the success of student power at Columbia, the administration did nothing to give permanency to the student voice, or to foster reforms in general. The clearest clue to the administration's disinclination to consider reform was President Grayson Kirk's refusal to implement, or even release, the Student Life Report submitted to him in August 1967.

This report was the result of two years of study by five administrators, five faculty members, and five students, all appointed by the president after the first student demonstration in May 1965. Four of the five student members issued a minority report rejecting the majority opinion as "too little and too late." But even the implementation of the majority's recommendations might have been sufficient to prevent the student revolt in April 1968.

The majority recommended that demonstrations inside buildings be allowed as long as they did not disrupt the normal functioning of the university. They proposed the establishment of judicial bodies, composed of students, faculty, and administrators, to impose and review discipline. They also recommended formation of student advisory committees on academic affairs in all departments and schools, and a university tripartite committee on student interests to advise the president.

The four students writing the minority report stated (with what now appears as unusual foresight):

"We believe a tripartite committee on administrative policy should instead be created to decide important matters of non-academic policy, subject to the veto of the president or trustees. It would not make most policy or operating decisions within the university. That is quite properly the responsibility of the administrator. But it should deal with major questions which are of concern to all the elements of the university community. Such recent decisions as whether to involve Columbia in the business of promoting cigarette filters, whether to continue tuition deferment, and where or whether to build a gymnasium and how to allocate its facilities, serve as examples of the scope of the committee. Such matters as the physical expansion of the university, the university's relations with governments, and major policies of student conduct vis-a-vis the rest of the university community would be in the purview of the tripartite committee and its decisions would be policy unless vetoed by the president or trustees."

In September 1967, disregarding this Student Life Report, President Kirk banned all indoor demonstrations. Vice-President David Truman explained, "The administration will not tolerate efforts to make the university an instrument of opposition to the established order." Yet, in order to avoid a free-speech controversy, the administrators later interpreted the rule liberally (and often arbitrarily). They considered two indoor demonstrations early in the year as only "near demonstrations," and the participants were not punished. It was only in early April 1968 that the administration began to enforce the rule. At the same time, the president declined to follow either his own precedent of the year before, or the recommendations of the Student Life majority, by refusing to appoint a tripartite judicial body to try students accused of breaking the rule against indoor demonstrations.

The Great Confrontation

This new ban—following the administration's concessions in 1967 and in the absence of effective channels for student grievances—helped discredit the administration's authority and helped legitimate direct-action tactics in the eyes of the students. Meanwhile, Students for a Democratic Society and other radical groups had formed coalitions with moderate student groups. This was possible because, from March 1967 until Mark Rudd became president in March 1968, S.D.S. was run by moderates, who temporarily rejected direct-action techniques in favor of "research" to expose the administration and "education" to gain the allegiance of moderate students. The student radicals, therefore, had a broad base to mobilize for a student revolt.

In brief, the escalation of confrontation between students and administration from April to June 1968 consisted of:

- a student sit-in at Hamilton Hall, the classroom and administration building of Columbia College, and the detention of a dean for 24 hours;
- the occupation and barricading of five university buildings for five days by about 800 students;
- the administration's calling of 1000 policemen to remove the demonstrators from the buildings, which resulted in the arrest of about 700 students and the injuring of 150 students and faculty;
- a massive strike by 5000 active students;
- the administration's "lock-out" to counter the strike —its canceling of formal classes and exams for the remainder of the school year;
- the start of disciplinary action against the student activists, which led to a second student sit-in at Hamilton Hall;
- the arrest of about 200 more students and the injuring of another 68 in a second police action;
- violence by students during this second police action; and
- the university's suspending of about 75 students.

The occupation of the five buildings and the subsequent student strike mobilized wide student support. Many of the official student leaders supported all of the demands of the occupation forces and even were leaders in the strike. While initially opposed to the barricading of buildings, these moderates saw the confrontation as an opportunity to win the student voice they had so long and fruitlessly sought. As they said later, two days at the barricades would probably accomplish more than years of work through legitimate channels. The moderates' prior use of direct-action techniques also conditioned them to accept more radical tactics.

Throughout the revolt there was solidarity between radical and moderate activists, despite disagreements and tensions. Moderates worked with the radical leaders of the Steering Committee that coordinated the occupation of four of the buildings (the black demonstrators maintained their separate leadership); this coalition continued in the Strike Steering Committee. This solidarity encouraged the moderates to accept the occupation, the demand for amnesty, and the strike.

Later on, the radicals also accepted some of the moderates' stands on tactics and issues—the organization of the Strike Committee along representative lines, and an increased emphasis on the internal restructuring of the university. One reason for the trust between moderates and radicals was their interaction and coalition in former years; but more important was their common alienation from the administration and isolation from the faculty.

As the confrontation escalated, many students previously unaffiliated and politically inactive suddenly became involved, either in support of or in opposition to the sit-in. The strike that followed the police intervention generated more organization and solidarity among students, in the form of "liberated" classes and strike constituencies. In addition, ad-hoc student groups arose to proclaim grievances and make demands for change.

The specific events that propelled increasing numbers of students into confrontation with the administration can now be traced more closely.

In late March of 1968, S.D.S. sponsored a march to President Kirk's office to present a petition signed by 1700 students requesting the university's separation from the Institute of Defense Analyses. The president's response was to put six leaders of S.D.S. on probation for violating his ban on indoor demonstrations. The six students thereupon requested an open hearing before a tripartite judicial board, and were refused. On April 23, S.D.S. held a noon rally to organize a peaceful march into Low Library, the administration building, to present President Kirk with a demand for open hearings for the six students. This march, like the previous one, would deliberately defy the ban on indoor demonstrations. The April rally also repeated demands for the university to cut all ties with I.D.A. and to stop building a gym. Thus, this student movement simultaneously criticized the internal procedures of the university and its public policies.

When the demonstrators reached Low Library, they found the door locked. In much confusion, between 200 and 300 students decided to march to the gym site a few blocks away. After trying to rip down a wire fence and being confronted by police, they returned to campus and voted to sit-in at Hamilton Hall. That night the black students decided to occupy the building by themselves, and asked the whites to leave. Humiliated, white radicals decided spontaneously to break into and occupy the president's office. During the next two days, three additional buildings were occupied. The most militant acts—the detention of the college dean for 24 hours, the occupation of the president's office, and the inspection of his files—alienated many students. On the other hand, moderate students were mobilized by the reorganization of Hamilton Hall under black students and by the occupation of Avery Hall by architecture students and of Fayerweather Hall by graduate social-science students.

After the Student Afro-American Society took over Hamilton Hall it erected barricades at the doors, an act that was to become symbolic of all the "liberated" buildings. This act was probably inspired by the Harlem radicals in the building who were not students. But during the next two days, the course of events inside Hamilton Hall was moderated. The black students became highly organized; they evicted the nonstudents and allowed outsiders (like Rap Brown and Stokely Carmichael) to visit only for a short time; they released the dean; they cleaned the building and maintained it in good condition; they were open to visits and suggestions from professors, city officials, and Negro leaders; and they held numerous negotiations.

The graduate students took over Avery and Fayerweather somewhat haphazardly, but soon became organized. The architecture students had not been political in the past, but recently they had become resentful over university policies toward the community. Earlier in the year, the students and faculty of the School of Architecture had petitioned the administration to reconsider building the gym. Similarly, many of the graduate students in social science had never taken political action before, at least at Columbia, but had become more and more critical of the university's public policies.

Many students soon joined in the occupation of Avery and Fayerweather, and others visited the buildings (through the windows) to discuss the issues and give their support. Most of these students were not radicals and could not have seen themselves doing such a thing two days earlier. These occupations generated feelings of moral exhilaration and solidarity; the buildings were transformed into "communes" where the students engaged in lengthy political discussions.

Failure of Negotiations

Student support of the demonstrations was not limited to those willing to occupy buildings: The *Columbia Spectator* endorsed all the demands of the occupation —the end of university ties with I.D.A., no construction of a gym, the ending of probation for the six students, amnesty for all demonstrators in the occupation, and open hearings for all future disciplinary proceedings. A referendum held by undergraduate honor societies during the occupation, in which 5500 students voted, showed large majorities supporting the goals of the demonstrators, though not their tactics. Ten student leaders, including the president and vice-president of the university student government, came out in support of all the demonstration's demands, including amnesty. They also urged major university reform—including the establishment of faculty-student legislative and judicial bodies. Up to 800 students held vigils to support the rebels. (About 250 students opposed to the sit-ins tried to prevent students and food from reaching the demonstrators holding the president's office.)

After the police action, according to the Barton survey 42 percent of all students (and probably a much larger percentage of the undergraduates) supported a general boycott of all classes. A strike steering committee was formed of about 70 delegates, each representing 70 constitutents. Thus, almost 5000 students were actively organized, and many others boycotted classes. The Strike Committee supported all the original demands of the occupation and went on to demand a restructuring of the university.

The massive and militant student demonstrations immobilized the administration at first, but then were countered by the use of massive police force. The confrontation jarred part of the faculty into a belated, and ultimately unsuccessful, attempt to intervene between the students and the administration.

The great confrontation at Columbia did not lead to a successful negotiation between the students and the administration. In fact, bargaining never really began, for the administration and students could never agree on a basis for negotiation. Indeed, the administration did not seriously seek to negotiate. On the second day of the occupation, the administrators did present a proposal to the black students in Hamilton Hall, but when this was rejected they did not try again. The administration never presented a proposal for negotiating to the white students in the other four buildings. (According to the Barton survey, 50 percent of the faculty and 58 percent of the students thought the administration negotiated too little.)

It was ultimately the organizational weaknesses of Columbia that prevented any effective negotiations.

■ The administration, because of its isolation and lack of supporting structures, became fixated upon upholding its own authority. To negotiate would have accorded some legitimacy to students' grievances, and the administration found this too threatening.

■ The faculty, because of its weak organization and lack of experience in university government, could not counter the administration-student polarization.

The administration made every effort to discredit the demonstrators, but this served only to confirm the views of the most radical students and to strengthen their leadership.

Here were the students sitting in a few "liberated" buildings, with no weapons and with flimsy barricades of furniture, citing slogans of Che Guevara and Mao. But then the administration said that they *were* revolu-

Although about 250 students at Columbia opposed the demonstrations and formed a line to prevent food from reaching the students occupying Low Library, both radicals and moderates supported the revolt.

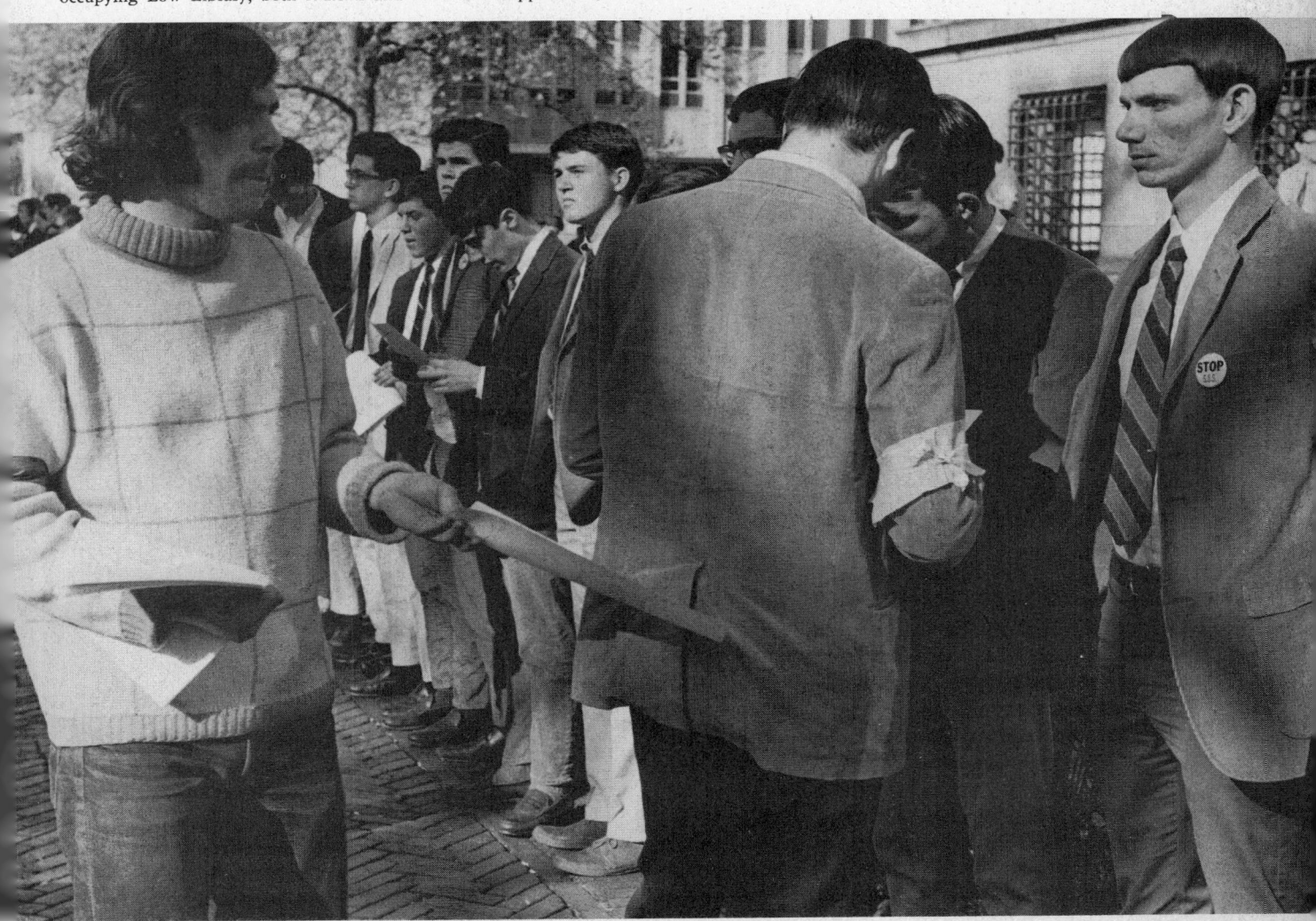

tionaries—"an unscrupulous bunch of revolutionaries out to destroy the university." The students said they would shut down the university; the administration did it for them. Four buildings and a president's office do not constitute a university, but the administration never tried to reschedule classes or to keep the university operating. A radical black leader kept saying that Harlem was marching up to Columbia to burn it down. Immediately the administration closed down the university and then sealed it off. It soon became a standing joke to ask, "When is the community coming?," for not more than 80 to 100 people from Harlem ever showed up.

Here were 800 student demonstrators, supported by all the moderate and legitimate student leaders. But the administration saw only a small minority of radical students organized by outside agitators. Even when Vice-President Truman admitted that there was increasing student support of amnesty, he said it was only because the "students don't understand what the fundamental issue is and they want to get on back to work."

Some of the radicals used vulgar language and obscenities in attacking the administration. Vice-President Truman in turn charged the activists with a "total lack of morality." Personal attacks upon President Kirk were countered with personal attacks upon the radical student leaders. Thus, Vice-President Truman said of Mark Rudd: "He is totally unscrupulous and morally very dangerous. He is an extremely capable, ruthless, cold-blooded guy. He's a combination of a revolutionary and an adolescent having a temper tantrum. . . . It makes me uncomfortable to sit in the same room with him."

The radicals pictured Columbia University, its president and its trustees, as part of the American power structure. And the administrators acted so as to seemingly confirm their dependence upon external groups rather than upon students and faculty. During the crisis, the administrators were isolated from all the students and most of the faculty. They remained cloistered in Low Library, consulting almost exclusively with trustees, Mayor Lindsay, and other outside advisers. The president and vice-president never talked directly and publicly to the demonstrators or to other students. Only once did they meet personally (but secretly) with several of the student leaders.

This approach to the students helped solidify their distrust of the administration and their determination to resist its authority. The issue of amnesty became the focus of distrust between students and administrators. From the first day of the occupation, the students demanded amnesty as a prerequisite to negotiation on the other issues. From the first, the administration refused to consider amnesty.

The student demonstrators sought amnesty as a confirmation of their position. In the words of the Strike Committee:

"Our demand for amnesty implies a specific political point. Our actions are legitimate; it is the laws, and the administration's policies which the laws have been designed to protect, that are illegitimate. It is therefore ridiculous to talk about punishment for students. No one suggests punishment for the administration, who in fact must assume the guilt for the present situation. To consider discipline against the students is thus a political position."

In addition, the activists did not trust the administration to radically change its policies, and therefore they sought to protect the students from even a relatively light punishment, like probation. (A student "on probation" could be suspended for slight infractions during future demonstrations.)

Conversely, the administration saw the granting of any form of amnesty as a capitulation that would undermine its authority. Vice-President Truman said later: "We couldn't give on the amnesty thing at all. Not only would we be destroying the whole position of this university, with that one we'd have been destroying every other university in the country." (It seems that the presidents of Stanford, Northwestern, and France were not listening, for during subsequent weeks they granted amnesty to *their* student rebels.) Hence, during the first days of the occupation the administration told the radical leaders, with great emotion and vehemence, that they would be expelled.

Not only did the administrators refuse amnesty for students, but they also rejected a compromise designed by an ad-hoc faculty group. This faculty group proposed light and equal punishments for all demonstrators, to be imposed by new forms of due process. (The Barton survey found that 78 percent of the students and 69 percent of the faculty believed that all judicial decisions on student discipline should be made in open hearings by a committee of students and faculty.) But the administration twice refused this compromise, and instead resorted to police force.

Twelve hours before using the police the first time in April, President Kirk had accepted the "spirit" of the faculty proposal, but had rejected most of its substance. Among other things, he refused to give up his authority to make the final decision on student discipline; and he refused to agree beforehand to uniform penalties for all the demonstrators. When the students also refused to accept the ad-hoc faculty's compromise, the administration cited the "intransigence" of the demonstrators as justifying their own resort to police force.

Again in May, the president refused to give final authority on discipline to the then-operating Joint Committee on Discipline. After a huge outcry from the faculty, and pressure behind the scenes from both faculty and trustees, he retreated somewhat, but still refused to accept any specific long-range limitations on his authority. The Joint Committee on Discipline also recommended that the university not undertake disciplinary action while criminal charges against certain students were pending in the courts. But one week later the administration called four student leaders to the dean's office for a closed hearing. Most student leaders interpreted these summonses as an attempt to reestablish the former disciplinary procedures behind a thin façade of reform. The four students, therefore, did not appear (both to protect their legal rights in court and to protest the administrators' action), but sent their parents and lawyers instead. This was unacceptable to the administrators, who immediately suspended the four students.

These suspensions seemed deliberately provocative to the demonstrators, and were countered by a second student sit-in. This time the administration announced that it would call the police that same evening, and that anyone arrested would be immediately suspended. Again, the administration, in threatening automatic suspensions, made no reference to the new disciplinary committee or to new judicial procedures. Thus, as the *Columbia Spectator* stated on May 22: "The administration and the strikers yesterday engaged in a test of strength where there was no buffer of faculty intermediaries and no chance of a compromise settlement. Both groups were committed to holding the line against what they regarded as the illegitimate opposition of the other."

There is some evidence that both the administration and the radical student leaders *wanted* the use of the police, at least the first time. The activists believed that the use of the police to clear the buildings would radicalize the campus, and bring many more students and faculty to their side. This did happen after the first police action. (According to the Barton survey, faculty support for the sit-ins increased by 17 percent and student support by 19 percent.) The administration, on the other hand, believed that the police were needed to restore its authority. Vice-President Truman said that "there were only two alternatives: either to give in or to bring in the police."

The result of the police intervention was to create an atmosphere of violence, contempt, and hatred. It was during the second police action that students for the first time became violent—throwing bricks at the police, smashing windows, and perhaps starting fires in several buildings. Apolitical, nonviolent students were enraged at seeing policemen beat their friends, many of whom were only spectators. Apolitical, nonviolent professors were enraged by the burning of a professor's research papers and by fires set in university buildings.

The occupation of Low Library—
before the massive police intervention.

After both police actions, the mood on campus was one of outrage.

Yet the administration maintained its confrontation mentality and became even more committed to a strategy of force and repression. Vice-President Truman commented to the press in May that the most important lesson he had learned from the Columbia crisis was to call the police immediately to oust student demonstrators. In June, President Kirk suspended 75 students for their part in the second sit-in. At the same time, the president continued to maintain that there was nothing fundamentally wrong with the university, and that no positive changes were possible in a crisis

PROTEST AND REBELLION

atmosphere. In response, the student activists—even the moderates—vowed to continue mass action against the university.

The long history of disorganization and withdrawal of the Columbia faculty members prevented them, at first, from taking any stand on the student demonstration. No faculty faction was organized to directly support the students. Nor was there any effectively organized support for the administration. The one attempt by the administration to organize faculty support was to call an unprecedented meeting of the Joint Faculties on Morningside Heights. Two meetings were convened—one right before the first police action and one right after. In both cases, the assembly passed mild, noncommittal statements, which neither condemned nor supported the administration. The meetings were presided over by the president and vice-president, thereby attesting to the faculty's lack of an independent role in university government. Because this body had no independence, no experience, and no leaders, it was unable to seek a solution to the confrontation.

The Faculty Response to Confrontation

During the first part of the crisis, only an ad-hoc faculty group was active. The original organizers of this group included 34 tenured professors, 38 assistant professors, and 84 teachers below that rank. Its membership grew to an active core of about 200. Members of the ad-hoc faculty had many different positions and views on the crisis, but they tended to be more sympathetic to the students than were other faculty members. Many (especially those from Columbia College) had close personal relations with their students, including some of the demonstrators, and some in the past had been among the few faculty activists on university issues. The younger teachers, especially, to a great degree shared the ideals, political frustrations, and disaffection from the university that had propelled the students into the buildings. (Barton's survey of 769 faculty members showed that tenured faculty members were most conservative on all issues, and instructors most favorable to the demonstrations. For example, 12 percent of full professors thought the sit-ins were justified, 38 percent of assistant professors, and 48 percent of lecturers and instructors.) The one purpose that did unite the ad-hoc faculty was a strong stand against the use of the police to resolve the dispute. For five days, members sought a basis for negotiation in order to prevent police action.

From its beginning, the ad-hoc faculty recognized the fierce antagonism between the administration and the demonstrators. And because it had so little active support from the senior faculty and no constitutional status, the ad-hoc group itself was propelled into the politics of confrontation in attempting to persuade the antagonists to accept its efforts at compromise. Its first statement, which shocked many faculty members, made two threats to the administration:

(1) "Should the students be willing to evacuate the buildings on the basis of our proposals, we will not meet classes until the crisis is resolved along these lines."

(2) "Until the crisis is settled, we will stand before the occupied buildings to prevent forcible entry by police or others."

The motive behind these threats was to win credibility from the students and administration, without taking a stand on amnesty. It worked—for a while.

On the third day of the confrontation, Vice-President Truman came to the ad-hoc faculty's meeting to announce that the president had called the police. The faculty present arose in indignation, with shouts of "Shame!" A few of the leaders rushed to the president's office; the rest went and stood in front of the occupied buildings. After several faculty members were physically attacked by a small contingent of policemen seeking entry to the administration building, the president ordered the police to withdraw. He thus granted the ad-hoc faculty a little more time to seek a negotiated settlement.

The ad-hoc faculty, in trying to find a basis for negotiation between the administration and student demonstrators, sought to apply pressure on both sides without itself taking a clear stand on the issues. While strongly disagreeing with the administration's position (and with some of the student actions), the leaders of the ad-hoc faculty never clearly broke with the administration. Nor did they try to organize the senior faculty members and win their active support for the group's proposals. In the Joint Faculties meeting called by the administration, the ad-hoc faculty declined to ask for a vote on its proposal for arbitration. Even though the ad-hoc faculty's leaders believed they could have won a small majority, they did not want to split the faculty, or risk the possibility of being rebuffed by the trustees.

On only one occasion—the day before the first police action—did the ad-hoc faculty try to bolster its posi-

---

SUGGESTED READINGS

Crisis at Columbia: Report of Fact-Finding Commission on Columbia Disturbances (New York: Vintage Books, 1968). The official Cox Commission report on the student revolt at Columbia University.

The Dignity of Youth and Other Atavisms by Edgar Z. Friedenberg (Boston, Mass.: Beacon Press, 1965). A collection of essays about the failure of our high schools. Also included are reviews, by Friedenberg, of important books in the sociology of education.

Divided We Stand: Reflections on the Crisis at Cornell edited by Cushing Strout and David Grossvogel (Garden City, New York: Doubleday, 1970) deals with the issues of student violence and academic freedom.

tion by mobilizing mass support. On that day it obtained 800 faculty and 3000 student signatures, and the support of some city and state political leaders. But these supporters were not an organized constituency that could be mobilized for action. Thus, when both students and administration refused to accept its compromise settlement, the ad-hoc faculty had no alternative plan to check the polarization between administration and students or to block the police action. Even at the zero hour, when both the president and the students had rejected their proposal and they knew that police intervention was imminent, the ad-hoc faculty members could only frantically vote to call on either Governor Rockefeller or Mayor Lindsay to arbitrate the dispute.

It was this reluctance of the faculty to adopt a clear position, rather than trying to find a compromise, that most alienated the student protestors. This was especially true in view of the fact that the faculty institutions were so weak and faculty members had been so inactive in the past. The students did not believe that the ad-hoc faculty could really influence the administration without its taking a stronger stand. Right before the first police intervention, some of the more moderate students occupying Avery and Fayerweather hinted that they were ready to talk about alternatives to complete amnesty, as suggested by the ad-hoc faculty's proposals. But then they decided that they had to stay with the amnesty demand because the ad-hoc faculty did not seem to them to be sufficiently dependable.

The morning after the first police action, the ad-hoc faculty group dissolved in chaos. It was completely alienated by the administration's resort to force. (Many of these faculty members had witnessed the police action and some were injured by the police.) But the group was unable to agree on a common strategy towards the administration. Successive faculty groups also failed to change the administration's stand on discipline and its reliance upon the use of force, nor did they gain the trust and support of the students.

The faculty thus failed to check the escalating polarization and confrontation between students and administration. This failure shocked the faculty into a recognition of the need for fundamental institutional reform.

Restructuring the University

Even before the first police action, some students and faculty members recognized that one result of the conflict would have to be major changes in the university. After the police action, the predominant issue became the restructuring of the university. But student and faculty reformers held different conceptions of how this restructuring would occur and of the ends to be achieved. (The Barton survey found a relatively small difference in answers given by students and faculty on the issues of the crisis, except on items dealing with the relative power of students and faculty in a restructured university. Here the differences were greater than 20 percent.)

Th student activists believed that real change in the university could be obtained and institutionalized only if the crisis continued. Faculty reformers argued that important institutional restructuring could occur only slowly, after careful study in a less stressful atmosphere. The latter envisioned *reform* of the university from above, through the work of a few appointed *committees*. The students desired a *change* from below, through the participation of *constituencies*. Faculty members viewed both the process and results of university reform in *professional* terms; that is, decisions should be made by those with the most relevant expertise. To improve Columbia's educational quality and institutional effectiveness, what was needed, they believed, was a new *rational-legal* organization (more and better committees and courts, and a more progressive administration). The students, on the other hand, wanted the university to divorce itself from existing centers of power and to contribute to the solution of major social and human problems. The students recognized that the professional competence of professors and even administrators would prevail on many technical and academic issues, but they insisted that students as well as faculty must *participate* in setting the university's general public and educational policies.

One incident during the faculty's early efforts at reform illustrates the preference of faculty leaders for change from above by committee, rather than by participatory organization from below—for discussion in private by experts, rather than open deliberation and debate.

In the general outrage after the first police action, the ad-hoc faculty group held an extraordinary meeting. Its steering committee introduced a strong resolution to its members (and to many other faculty members present) that expressed no confidence in the administration and supported the student strike. The resolution obviously would have passed, but during the debate the chairman withdrew the resolution and, along with the steering committee, left the meeting. What happened was that these faculty members began to fear that their resolution was too radical and that it might further polarize the faculty and university community. Later that same day, the leaders of the ad-hoc faculty supported a resolution in the Joint Faculties meeting calling for the establishment of an executive committee of the faculty to propose university reforms. Half of the ad-hoc faculty's leaders were appointed to this committee of 12, and the ad-hoc faculty group was thus dissolved.

The new Executive Committee of the Faculty (in contrast to the ad-hoc faculty group) had ready access to the trustees and enjoyed the confidence of the administration, but it had neither a constituency nor any clear mandate. The ad-hoc faculty had begun, at least, to build a participating constituency. Although the Executive Committee could call meetings of the Joint Faculties, it never did. Its work was done behind closed doors, and as a group it became invisible to most of the campus. During the second police action, and on the arguments over discipline, it publicly supported the administration, and worked only secretly to pressure the president and vice-president to adopt a more conciliatory stand. Such procedures did not gain it the confidence and support of the students.

Moreover, in its first month of work (to the end of the academic year), the Executive Committee failed to formulate any principles for restructuring the university that could have been publicly debated, but simply organized a series of study groups for the summer. Students and faculty were asked to join the paid staff of these committees, but no campaign was undertaken to actively recruit such members. In any case, most concerned students viewed such committees as an inadequate response to the crisis. Even the moderate students most committed to restructuring the university feared being coopted through their participation in such efforts. Another new faculty group, the Independent Faculty, formed out of the remaining 15 leaders of the ad-hoc faculty, also failed to organize a real constituency.

The student organizations pressing for reform were much different. Representation on the Steering Committee to lead the strike was based upon constituencies. Any group of 70 students could elect a member to the Strike Steering Committee. Subsequently, the Steering Committee split, about half of its members withdrawing to form their own organization, Students for a Restructured University. This new organization wanted to give primary emphasis to the internal reform of the university; the Strike Committee was more concerned with political conflicts of the larger society, and with the relationship of the university to these political issues. Both groups continued to support the original demands of the sit-ins, and to vigorously oppose the administration. Both continued to organize students. The two groups also united on special issues, and both remained suspicious of faculty organizations. In addition to these two student groups, caucuses arose in many school and graduate departments to press for educational and institutional reform. This proliferation of student groups backing the reform of the university was in sharp contrast to the lack of faculty participation.

At present, the faculty committees are in extremely weak positions vis-à-vis the administration and trustees. Within the Faculty Executive Committee, there is probably a powerful minority that supports the administration and wants only minimal change. Moreover, the Executive Committee does not have the support of most students. Even more troublesome is the extent of the faculty's division over whether students should take part in university decision-making. About half of the faculty are willing to grant students some decision-making power, according to Barton, but the others favor only regular consultation with them.

It thus seems evident that it is only through organizing constituencies that the faculty committed to reform at Columbia will be able to achieve real change in the university, or even to recreate its basic cohesion. Faculty reform leaders will have to assert organized pressure to gain ascendency and to make sure that new university committees, judicial bodies, and legislative organs are not just appointed from above, but receive general consent. Yet it is still questionable whether faculty leaders will arise and make the attempt. Columbia, therefore, faces more polarization, confrontation, and probably repression.

In Conclusion

It was the great and increasing polarization between administrators, students, and faculty that prevented a solution to the Columbia student revolt. In this polarization the moderate positions were destroyed: Student moderates became radicalized, administration moderates became rigid and conservative, faculty moderates failed in attempts to mediate and became alienated from both sides. The weakness of the moderates was a result of the institutional weaknesses of Columbia— the archaic and isolated nature of administrative authority, the lack of effective faculty and student governments, and the attenuation of faculty-student relations. These institutional weaknesses led to a general lack of administrative and faculty responsiveness to student grievances and to the students' attempt to compel response by dramatic action.

A critical problem of Columbia, then, is to strengthen all components of the university in order to render them more responsive to one another. Even the administration requires strengthening—not, however, apart from students and faculty, but by new links to them. The forging of multiple institutional relations *within* the university can increase the interdependence of students, faculty, and administration, and simultaneously decrease dependence upon external forces (especially for the administration, but also for the faculty and even for the students).

Only then can the university fully develop its own capacities for intellectual and moral excellence, and independently determine its social responsibilities.

Resistance in Czechoslovakia— An Underground in the Open

CONSTANTINE C. MENGES

PRAGUE, AUGUST 28—It was clearly a major surprise to the leaders of the Soviet Union that Czechoslovakia did not dissolve into a state of collapse and confusion after Russia's military invasion and the kidnaping of the principal Czech leaders. Instead, an organized and a popular resistance immediately coalesced. This resistance is a superb achievement. And it may change the political possibilities for Czechoslovakia, for it has—in only seven days—left an indelible imprint upon the country.

The popular resistance avoids violence: It is mainly symbolic. And, in its first phase, it was entirely spontaneous. In the center of Prague, thousands of people parade past the Soviet tanks, wearing the tricolor ribbons of the Czech flag or carrying photos of Dubček, first secretary of the Communist Party, or Svoboda, the country's president, as well as slogans. They avidly read the thousands of wallposters, cartoons, and painted slogans that virtually flood the walls around Wencelas Square. They run eagerly to the couriers distributing the resistance-press papers, and pass any news on from one to another. Thursday, Friday, and Saturday (August 22, 23, and 24), there was a crescendo of community feeling among the people, who thought they were on the brink of another long harsh night.

There is a mutually reinforcing and reinvigorating relationship between the organized resistance and the popular resistance. The popular resistance, along with the total absence of bureaucratic collaboration with the Soviet forces, provides the environment in which the organized resistance has a chance to survive the specially imported KGB agents (secret police) put on their trail. For the popular resistance occupies much of the energy and attention of the occupying troops. It sustains the morale of those in the Czech police, army, and bureaucracy exposed to direct Soviet pressure. And it acts as a warning to potential collaborators—either opportunists, or the few who might have ideological reasons to side with the Soviets—that the situation is still fluid and the Soviets are not guaranteed a victory yet. As long as collaboration is prevented, the bargaining position of the Czech Communist Party is much stronger; there is less chance that the organized resistance can be extirpated; and the Soviets have no anchor for any kind of government except an overt military occupation.

The organized resistance, through the vital clandestine radio transmitters and daily press, informs the people about what is really happening in the country, in both large and small ways, provides leadership and focus for the mass resistance. Its primary tasks are to sustain and facilitate the unity of the Czechoslovak Communist Party and government organs against the occupation, to maintain the population's morale and to give both the political activists and masses the sense that they can and are *doing* something against the Soviets. Information and a sense of some potency are undoubtedly the twin ingredients of enduring morale and cohesion.

The invasion occurred at 10 p.m. on Tuesday, August 20; Dubček learned of it at 11:15 and immediately called a meeting of the CCP Presidium. By 1:30 a.m. the party and government had decided to resist the Soviet action with all means short of violence and to follow a policy of absolute non-collaboration with the occupying powers. Dubček and the Prime Minister returned to their respective offices to wait and were arrested at 4 in the morning. By the same evening, August 21, the free radios and some freedom papers had appeared.

According to all information there had been no plans even of a contingency or exercise nature for resistance against this kind of aggression. But there were apparently some rough guidelines for the key party members including all members of the Party Congress in the event of war with the west. There also were arrangements for military radio communications in wartime which helped in the organization of the mobile and multiple clandestine radio networks.

The radio is the key element because it enables the party and other parts of the organized resistance to function. The best example of this was the calling of the 14th Extraordinary Party Congress on the day following the occupation (Thursday, August 22). The new presidium selected by this congress was more progressive than the one the Soviets feared would have been chosen in September. The entire weight of the CCP moved with near unanimity to Dubček's side (all but 5 to 10 of 1200 delegates). The resolutions denouncing the invasion and supporting the integrity of the party and the government and the explicit refutation of the Soviet pretense of an invitation to save the country from counterrevolution was the most central political event in the invasion's aftermath.

But it was an event only because of the free-radio network. It was the radio that broadcast the resolutions of the party, the composition of the new presidium, and the explicit denunciation of the invasion. The radio made this an event inside Czechoslovakia and outside Czechoslovakia—both equally important for Soviet-Czech bargaining. Had there been no radio, the news would have been suppressed or distorted, and the 14th Congress would not have had the immediate unifying effect it did have.

Without the radio the party might not have been able to organize itself to hold the congress at all, much less so quickly. The radio told the party delegates—in code—that there would be a congress and where. Then, when it was discovered that the Soviets had found out about the meeting and were waiting, the radio told the people to spread the word all over Czechoslovakia that the party delegates should not go to the appointed place but to the nearest large factory, where they would receive further instructions. On Thursday, thousands of people wore signs and wrote posters telling this to the party delegates. These warnings were highly successful and only a few delegates were caught.

On Thursday evening, the free radios announced that they had word that there would be large-scale arrests in the next two nights—and the main victims would be journalists, writers, intellectuals, and other

"The Truth Will Win," is an old Czech slogan that appeared in underground newspapers during the invasion crisis.

political activists. To make the Soviet secret police's work more difficult, the people were asked to take down all street signs and house numbers in Prague. Within hours, thousands in all neighborhoods had practiced this new mode of urban concealment.

From Thursday on, the free radios—through Czech police sources—got hold of the license numbers of the cars used by the Russian police for arresting people. These numbers would be broadcast, and again the people would watch for the numbers and write them on posters to spread the word. Whenever the cars were spotted, they would be surrounded, the prisoners released, the other occupants beaten, and the car destroyed. But after three days the KGB got around this by getting duplicate license numbers of those held by Czech citizens—and increasing the number of cars, using many as decoys. But three important days had been gained to allow people to hide or leave. And the leadership provided by nameless but trusted and admired voices of the free radios, in combination with the people's chance to participate in a directly useful act, had an enormously exhilarating effect on them. Even talking about these efforts was a great tonic to morale.

The Soviets seemed completely unprepared for these rapidly mobile, well-informed radio stations, which entirely overshadowed their own propaganda efforts and, worse, informed the West of what was happening on an hour-to-hour basis. To silence them, teams of KGB were dispatched in Prague, Pilsen, and parts of Slovakia—their methods restricted to the usual secret-police repertory. And on Friday (August 23) the free radio announced that the Soviets were sending in a train packed with jamming equipment. The radio asked the railway workers' union to make sure that the train did not reach its destination, and within hours all over Czechoslovakia the station signs identifying the towns were destroyed or covered up. There were hourly reports from railway-union people saying "All is well," "Train in difficulties," and the like. This was high drama—the radio following the route of its would-be electronic executioners, then announcing toward the end of the next day—"Train lost." On Monday (August 26) the Soviets leapfrogged Czech resistance and flew in jamming and detection equipment by helicopter.

Resistance Papers Have Major Impact

Within one day after the invasion on Thursday, more than a score of freedom-press newspapers were being distributed in all parts of Czechoslovakia. In Prague alone there were at least 14 papers on the streets by Friday (August 23). Most of them were put out by the staffs of the regular party, factory, or commercial newspapers, and they carried the same formats as these papers. Among these are *Vercerni Praha,* organ of the Young Communist Party; *Rude Pravo; Mylady Svet;* and the new and very progressive papers published only since March 1968, *Reporter* and *Student.*

All of these newspapers have taken a fiercely anti-Soviet, anti-invasion position and emphasize their desire for neutrality, self-determination, and the integrity of the party and government. All support Dubček and Svoboda. The papers publish photos of violent acts by occupation troops, of victims, of burning buildings, of various secret Communist Party meetings, and of anti-occupation demonstrations. The whole thrust is toward the mobilization of Czech and world opinion to act against the invaders with all means *short of violence*. The papers relay instructions from the free-radio network to the people and, perhaps most important, keep the population informed about the negotiations between the Czech leaders and Warsaw Pact powers in Moscow. These talks, people feel, will decide the future; but few have any optimism about the outcome.

The papers are usually limited to one to three pages, but—within Prague at least—some circulate in three daily editions. One paper has a verified production of 80,000 per edition, so a circulation of 400,000 for all papers in Prague is a possibility. As of Tuesday, August 27, there was no circulation of any pro-Soviet paper in Czechoslovakia—except for propaganda leaflets dropped by helicopter and burned almost before touching the ground. A pro-Soviet radio station was put into operation almost immediately after the debris from Wednesday's battle for the central-broadcasting facilities had been cleared, but none listen except to mock. The Occupational Command has special radio and sound TV broadcasts in Russian and German and some distribution of *Pravda* and leaflets specifically for the invading armies.

As with the radio stations, the very existence of the resistance papers—in spite of frenetic efforts to destroy them—has a major impact on morale and on the political cohesion of the Czech party and the bureaucracies. To the people, distributing and receiving papers have in themselves become important acts of nonprovocative defiance. Small cars or trucks drive right into Wencelas Square and, under tank gun-barrels, distribute the newspapers, which are eagerly sought by a surging crowd. If the soldiers make any move to capture the distributors the crowd keeps the Russians away with its weight, and the little truck prances off. Distributors on foot, usually teenagers, carried papers openly until Sunday, and went into the main centers of Prague. All people, old and young, police and the Czech army, reach out for the papers in a manifest gesture of support.

By Sunday the occupation was increasingly cracking down on the distributors of the press. The tank guard-

Czechoslovakian students preparing resistance posters at an underground headquarters.

posts over every bridge halted all cars going into central Prague and made thorough searches. Soldiers made more determined efforts to catch the walking distributors and a more clandestine operation resulted—there was, for example, much more passing out of papers on the trams, or to the trams in outlying areas. On Sunday, with the sudden imposition of the bridge checkpoints, the first distributions were made by ambulances and Czech police cars that had not been searched. Again this tangible demonstration of unity—the police giving out the papers, at times under the eyes of the Soviet troops—had its effect on both the Czechs and the Soviets. Parenthetically, the radio reported late Sunday night that, after nightfall, Soviet troops had machine-gunned one police car and several ambulances.

Within 24 hours of the occupation the free radios had become accurately informed in detail about events in every part of Czechoslovakia, the West, and in Moscow—to the extent that information was released. Broadcasting 24 hours a day and concerned solely with the crisis, the radio stations combined morale-boosting exhortations, intense analysis, and the coordination of popular and organized resistance with reporting on all Soviet occupation moves and countermeasures. How was this possible?

The key was the telephone. Informants would call designated relay stations—i.e., a person sitting by a telephone—with any news of interest. The relay person would filter this information (to avoid duplication, for example), then call a telephone watcher at one of the secret radio stations. There would be the usual news-reporting-system checks for accuracy, then an editor would decide what would be broadcast. Closing the internal telephone system would have hurt the newscasts, but also have brought the economy to a standstill, and this the Soviets were not yet ready to do. Tapping and tracing all lines was technically impossible. And informers or prisoners had not yet identified the main radio-telephone hookups being used—which, in any case, were changed almost daily.

For external news, each radio station had two simple portable shortwave sets. One monitor would listen to news from Western sources, and note and collect any items of direct interest. These would then be broadcast. The other monitor followed the Moscow and East German propaganda version of what was happening in Czechoslovakia and would then broadcast a brief resumé of the propaganda line and a refutation if the matter was important or time permitted. Thus two shortwave radios (reception of both West and East without jamming is generally very good in Czechoslovakia) and the telephone, plus informants and 24 hours of coverage, created a far more informed, dense, and faster communication network than is customary even in the most news-saturated Western cities.

This information funnel was used by the resistance *newspapers* in a very simple way. Each press had several shortwave radios and kept a continuous monitor on the various free-radio stations. First priority for publication was any guidance for mass action that the free radios called for—such as the one-hour general strike on Friday, August 23. Next came news about Soviet-Czech talks, and then the rest of the happenings as decided by the various editorial staffs. Virtually the only source of information for the papers, though, was the radio—the clandestine internal stations and, at times, Western stations.

Czechoslovakia has a complex language that few foreigners speak or read. Without interpreters and helpers, finding the documents or even file drawers needed in the secret-police stations, in the military headquarters (emergency plans for radio communication, for instance), and in the party files (addresses, contingency plans) is a much more difficult and time-consuming task. All the more so if fast, last-minute sabotage has produced burned records, facilities in turmoil, and the like.

Prague is an old city with picturesque winding streets that have not yet surrendered to some regular and predictable sequence of numbers. In the older sections, where many writers and intellectuals live or have friends, the house numbering is especially erratic. Take down all street signs and house numbers, destroy all detailed maps of Prague in the tourist and government offices, and *then* let the Soviet secret police hunt for the addresses of their potential victims. There are no scouts, guides, and trailblazers for these colonial masters; they must find their way through the now apparently trackless urban complex alone.

How to Hide a Congress

Where can you hide a large meeting of 1200 people when enemy troops and police know the date and the city and are watching? Where can large supplies of paper, ink, press plates, and forging equipment for identity papers be safely hidden when a city is occupied with only hours of warning? Where can people well-known to the Russian secret police be hidden while they continue working? Where can couriers come and go with ease? Where are telephone lines so numerous that tapping is nearly impossible? The organized Czech resistance found the ingenius answer: in the large industrial factories.

One worker looks like another as thousands stream in and out of the factory's many gates. Large industrial plants are indeed jungles of steel and concrete, with many hiding places only the workers would and could know. The 14th Congress was held in one of Europe's largest industrial complexes; the 1200 delegates easily disappeared in the midst of more than 40,000 workers, and there was enough elbow room to permit films and tape-recording of the proceedings to be made and smuggled out of the country.

Besides all the advantages of scale and complexity that large factories could offer the resistance, there was a double-edged institutional sword waiting in the heavy industrial centers. The Communist Party was always popular with a large minority of workers in heavy industry, and in spite of the party's 20 years of bungling there were still actual as well as nominal supporters in the many cells within the factories. These stood ready to give effective and disciplined assistance to the party leadership. So, after 20 years, the party of the workers found the working class again.

The party cells also had an armed workers-militia in each large factory. Though this total of 7,000 to 10,000 militia could not hold out for long against the armored divisions poured into Czechoslovakia, any Soviet attempt to control entry into the large factories, or to search the premises, would have been possible only after the killing of many, many workers. *That* was the one point where the Czech resistance was determined to threaten violence. And during the first week of occupation the Soviet Union was not prepared to assault the Communist workers' militia. There was also the additional, tacit threat of wholesale sabotage of Czechoslovak heavy industry in the event of a military assault on the factories.

People in Czeckoslovakia ask how long the organized resistance can survive. The radio is the spearhead and also the Achilles' heel—there are well-defined techniques for locating transmitters. There should probably be contingency planning for smuggling out information and for having some of the staff transmit messages from outside the Czech borders.

The press is vulnerable to a shortage of printing supplies as the Soviet control system tightens—its facilities are spread out and separated from the necessary raw materials; road traffic is light and ever more subject to control. Large numbers of foot couriers would give the secret publishing locations away. Perhaps the answer lies in using the presses of the various factory newsletters (several are already in operation). But distribution is again a problem as the distance of the presses from the population increases—though workers could each take 10 to 50 copies home at night for wider distribution.

But perhaps greater than the dangers posed by the hunters bent on liquidating the resistance are the more subtle political techniques the Soviets may use. The organized resistance constitutes a vital element in the political cohesion that is the sole possible bargaining device the Czechs can use with the Soviet Union. As long as the Czechs remain together, the U.S.S.R. can rule only by a military government, or try to quash the unity by stepping up the level of terror and violence, as in fact had occurred in stages from Friday to Tuesday (August 23-27).

A danger seen by many Czechs is that in the next two weeks the U.S.S.R. may use apparent conciliation as a way of dividing the Czech Communist Party and also the organized resistance. A compromise by the Czech leadership, followed by the Soviet Union's violation of its agreements (as is universally expected in Prague), would sacrifice the integrity of the resistance in return for no real tangible gains. And the great fear is that during this interim phase of compromise the

Czech administration and partial cooperation would draw potential Czech collaborators over to the Soviet side, and expose parts of the organized resistance. This would be followed by a renewed Soviet crackdown, on one pretense or another, which this time would swoop down directly on the resistance with far greater success than before. The result would be a government by Soviet power and Czech collaborators.

The Czechs who were so shocked by the Bratislava agreements and the invasion will not accept the above interpretation of Soviet political tactics as the concoction of a "cold warrior" or devil theorist. They know that their strength derives from their unity, and that the most vulnerable point in this unity would be a false compromise that exposed or divided the organized resistance. But the possibility of a genuine agreement need not be excluded; it becomes more probable the longer the Czech leadership and people present a united front.

Whatever the future holds, the courage, the creativity, and the prudence of the organized and the popular resistance have astounded the Soviets, heartened the Czechs, made the progressive elements of the Czech Communist Party even more respected. They also may make the contemplated reversal of history by violence far less harsh than the Soviets hoped.

SANTA MONICA, OCT. 29—On numerous occasions the Western press has carried the headline, "Czechs Give In to USSR." And this "giving in" has in fact often occurred—on paper. The agreements of August 27 represented a Czech promise to bring about the "normalization" required by the Soviet leaders, and so did the agreement of October 5 and the Soviet-Czech military agreement signed at the end of October. During this time, press censorship was restored; the Czech government gave Soviet troops the authority to remain in the country; at Soviet demand, the new governing group of the Czech Communist Party, chosen at the secret congress, was enlarged; and several prominent reformers resigned their government positions.

But more important than the formal concessions made by the Czech leaders has been the reality of their internal policy. The basic strategy of the Czechs seemed to be one of actual surrender to the international-policy demands of the Soviet Union—the stationing of troops in Czechoslovakia, and the slowing down of trade with Western countries—in exchange for the time needed to consolidate an internal policy designed to maintain the essence, if not the visible forms, of the liberalization's key elements.

The "censored" press did in fact avoid the use of several terms the Soviets found objectionable, and several of the most liberal papers did not appear again. Yet the press has published the Czech government's frequent denials of the standard argument of the Soviets that they were invited into the country; it continues to assert that there was and is no counterrevolution in Czechoslovakia; and it has continued to keep the people accurately informed about events in the country. While the Soviets have demanded that many former secret-police officials dismissed by the reform Czech government be returned to power, this has been ignored, and the Minister of the Interior stated on September 10 that the Czech government would continue to guarantee the basic civil liberties of all citizens and would not permit a return to the old secret-police system. And, in the very subtle area of personnel changes within the upper and middle levels of the party and government, it appears that the government has been able to resist pressure to install pro-Soviet officials and Russian advisers.

The duel will go on and the outcome is uncertain. Two major dangers continue to loom. One is that the concessions of the Dubček-Svoboda leadership may split the anti-Soviet political resistance into two groups —because of the reformers' opposition to any compromises. The other is that the Soviets will tire of the minuet of noncompliance and launch a major police action against the key activists—a number they place at 40,000—as soon as the secret police can succeed and the Soviets have the administrative ability to govern the country.

During September and October the popular resistance barely surfaced and the clandestine press and radios barely functioned. Yet it can be assumed that during this time a great deal of planning and preparation has been going on in the event a renewed and full-fledged resistance might be necessary. And this knowledge, combined with the impressive performance of the Czechs so far, must cause the Soviets some anxiety when they consider the consequences of large-scale direct repression. So there is a third possibility: The Czechs continue to work together and to subtly prevent the reestablishment of a police state until the current Soviet policy softens, or until the current Soviet regime is changed or distracted by other, more serious threats.

December 1968

SUGGESTED READINGS

August Twenty-First: The Rape of Czechoslovakia by Colin Chapman (Philadelphia: Lippincott, 1968). On-the-spot descriptions of the invasion of Czechoslovakia and the events that followed as reported by two British journalists.

Intervention: The Causes and Consequences of the Czechoslovakian Invasion by Isaac Levine (New York: McKay, 1969).

Algerian Peasant Revolt

ERIC R. WOLF

France's shattering impact on traditional Algerian society set the terms for the rebellion that broke out in 1954, a rebellion that has been called "the revolution that failed"

Six major social and political upheavals, fought with peasant support, have shaken the world of the twentieth century: The Mexican revolution of 1910, the Russian revolutions of 1905 and 1917, the Chinese revolution which metamorphosed through various phases from 1921 onwards, the Vietnamese revolution which has its roots in the Second World War, the Algerian rebellion of 1954 and the Cuban revolution of 1958. All of these were to some extent based on the participation of rural populations. Here I will concentrate on the Algerian Revolution, but first let me make some general comments to set the story in context.

Romantics to the contrary, it is not easy for a peasantry to engage in sustained rebellion. A peasant's work is more often done alone, on his own land, than in conjunction with his fellow's, and his life is geared to an annual routine and to planning for the year to come. Momentary alterations of routine threaten his ability to take up the routine later. At the same time, however, control of land enables him to retreat into subsistence production if adverse conditions affect their market crop.

Moreover, the peasant's interests—especially among poor peasants—often cross-cut class alignments. Rich and poor may be kinfolk, or a peasant may be at one and at the

This article is excerpted from *Peasant Wars of the Twentieth Century* by Eric R. Wolf, published by Harper and Row. © 1969 Eric R. Wolf.

Photographs by Peter Throckmorton NANCY PALMER

same time owner, renter, sharecropper, laborer for his neighbors and seasonal hand on a nearby plantation. Each different involvement aligns him differently with his fellows and with the outside world. Hence peasants are often merely passive spectators of political struggles or long for the sudden advent of a millennium, without specifying for themselves and their neighbors the many rungs on the staircase to heaven.

If it is true that peasants are slow to rise, then peasant participation in the great rebellions of the twentieth century must obey some special factors that exacerbated the peasant condition. We will not understand that condition unless we keep in mind constantly that it has suffered greatly under the impact of three great crises: the demographic crisis, the ecological crisis and the crisis in power and authority. The demographic crisis is most easily depicted in bare figures, though its root causes remain ill understood. Mexico, for example, had a population of 5.8 million at the beginning of the nineteenth century; in 1910 —at the outbreak of the revolution—it had 16.5 million. Vietnam is estimated to have sustained a population of between 6 and 14 million in 1820; it had 30.5 million inhabitants in 1962. Cuba had 550,000 inhabitants in 1800; by 1953 it had 5.8 million. Algeria had an indigenous population of 10.5 million in 1963, representing a fourfold increase since the beginnings of French occupation in the first part of the nineteenth century.

These population increases coincided with a period in history when land and other resources were increasingly converted into commodities—in the capitalist sense of that word. As commodities they were subjected to the demands of a market which bore only a very indirect relation to the needs of the rural populations. Where, in the past, market behavior had been largely subsidiary to the existential problems of subsistence, now existence and its problems became subsidiary to the market. The alienation of peasant resources proceeded directly through outright seizure or through coercive purchase, as in Mexico, Algeria and Cuba; or it took the form—especially in China and Vietnam—of stepped-up capitalization of rent which resulted in the transfer of resources from those unable to keep up to those able to pay. In addition, capitalist mobilization of resources was reinforced through the pressure of taxation and through increased need for industrially produced commodities on the part of the peasantry itself. All together, however, these various pressures disrupted the precarious ecological balance of peasant society. At the same time as commercialization disrupted rural life, it also created new but unstable ecological niches in industry. Increased instability in the rural area was thus accompanied by a still unstable commitment to industrial work.

Finally, both the demographic and the ecological crisis converged in the crisis of authority. The development of the market produced a rapid circulation of the elite, in which the manipulators of the new free-floating resources —labor bosses, merchants, industrial entrepreneurs—challenged the inherited power of the controllers of fixed social resources, the tribal chief, the mandarin, the landed nobleman. Undisputed and stable claims thus yielded to unstable and disputed claims. This rivalry between primarily political and primarily economic power-holders contained its own dialectic. The imposition of the market mechanism entailed a diminution of social responsibilities for all concerned: the economic entrepreneur did not concern himself with the social cost of his activities; while the traditional power-holder was often too limited in his power to offer assistance or was subject to co-optation by his successful rivals. The advent of the market not only produced a crisis in peasant ecology; it deranged the numerous middle-level ties between center and hinterland, between the urban and the rural sectors. The result was an ever-widening gap between the rulers and the ruled.

Conquest and Colonization

In 1830 an altercation between the Turkish governor of Algeria and the French consul brought French armies to Algiers. At first, France merely established a protectorate, but in 1840 the French government decided on the wholesale conquest and colonization of the entire country— largely in order to divert attention from the growing unpopularity of the regime of Charles X at home. The war was carried on by flying columns with a scorched earth policy of total devastation.

The first effect of the conquest was to deprive the native population of much of their land and to transfer it into the hands of Europeans. Algeria, like most other non-Western areas of the world, had not known the European institution of absolute private property before the advent of the Europeans; rather there existed a complex hierarchy of use rights, with ultimate title to the land being held on the one hand by the bey as ruler and on the other hand by the tribes. In either case, however, the lowliest cultivator could, by investing his labor, maintain his claim to the land and a viable share of its produce; and these rights were heritable.

When in 1863 the French applied Western European concepts of private property in land to Muslim holdings, they destroyed in one blow the entire pyramid of over-rights which had guaranteed the livelihood of the cultivator but which had stood in the way of making land a freely circulating commodity. At the same time it threw all land held by Muslims upon the open market and made it available for purchase or seizure by French colonists. The French had already, as successors to the rights of sovereignty, raised taxes and parceled out the bey's best lands to settlers.

Some Frenchmen foresaw the consequences. Before the institution of private property, one observer noted,

There was at the bottom of that chaos some guarantee

of work, a certain sentiment of equality. With the beginning of individualization it will no longer be the same. Once the land is definitely acquired, inequality begins: on one side the owners, on the other side the proletarians, exactly as in our civilized societies.

The *colon* (French colonial) press, nevertheless, acclaimed the step. *L'Independent* of Constantine, 12 April 1861, wrote:

> Thanks to the constitution of property which proceeds from this, the greater part of Algerian territory passes immediately from the condition of dead value to the state of real value; millions spring from nothing. . . . The countryside will become populated and the cities will witness in their midst the flowering of all aspects of commerce and industry.

The imposition of French norms of private property in land went hand in hand with a program for the dismemberment of the great tribes whose chiefs had been the main supporters and beneficiaries of Turkish rule. The program was so effective that by the time France became involved in World War II the tribe had ceased to exist as a relevant social and political unit within the Algerian polity. When in 1941 the French caretaker government at Vichy took steps to reconstitute the tribes in the interests of improved control, French administrators concurred sadly that the steps taken in 1863 had done their job all too well in ending tribal power once and for all.

The *douars* inhabited by segments of former tribes were not made independent entities in their own right, but organized into larger communes on the French model. Some were communities dominated by Europeans, where the municipal council and mayor were elected by French citizens, and where Muslims were allowed to choose only a fourth of the delegates, even though the Muslim population might constitute the majority; others were mixed communities of Europeans and Muslims headed by a civil administrator and backed by an appointed council of Frenchmen and native chiefs (*caids*); and still others were indigenous communities commanded by a French officer, assisted by a native chief. All Muslims were permitted to use their own customary or Quranic law, but special laws against nonpayment of taxes, political activity against France, public assembly—including pilgrimages and public feasts—without permits, travel without permits, refusal to register births or deaths all singled out the Muslims as a population with special disabilities. The entire edifice of control was capped by making Algeria administratively part of metropolitan France. Assimilation to French cultural norms was set up as an idea, but separation—under conditions of economic, social, political and legal inequality—became the established fact.

Old Bonds Are Broken

The breakup of tribal units and the chiefs' power associated with them, however, produced several unforeseen consequences. It made it impossible for the chiefs to carry out free distributions of grain in time of famine from stores accumulated through gifts and levies paid by their tribal dependents. The law of 1863 also put an end to the distribution of charity by local religious lodges (*zaouias*), drawing supplies from their *habus* properties. These properties had become private lands and were thrown upon the market. Moreover, the new *douars* only rarely renewed the traditional custom of maintaining food reserves in communal silos, which had been supplied by traditional payments. Thus disappeared a set of vital economic defenses, leaving the rural population dependent wholly upon the activities of moneylenders and credit merchants in time of need.

A further paradoxical consequence of tribal fragmentation was the accentuated growth within the *douars* of the councils of tribal notables (*djemaa*). The French recognized these councils in both the mixed and indigenous communes, either granting them considerable autonomy or using them in a consultative capacity, especially in matters of Muslim law. But in the communities dominated by Europeans, theory made no provision for native participation. But here too there also developed a honeycomb of what one French legal expert has called *djemaas occultes* (hidden councils). Both open and hidden councils thereby maintained a tradition of local decision-making and self-management that was to prove of capital importance in aiding the rebel cause in 1954.

French encroachment also produced revolts. The first of these, dating from 1832 to 1847, was led by Abd el Kader. Basing his support on local chiefs in the countryside, the revolt failed; but his distrust of the great families, combined with support of Islam, has caused Algerian nationalists to see in Abd el Kader a forerunner of the populist revolt of the twentieth century. The second revolt, led by a great chieftan, Moqrani, was even shorter lived, 1871–72, and marked the last uprising by a native feudatory. At the same time, however, the prospect of a rebellion in the countryside seems to have haunted numerous Muslim chiefs and merchants sufficiently to cause them to throw in their lot with the French against the rebels. Thus the notables of Constantine on 21 April 1871 addressed themselves to the French authorities in a letter in which, as L. Rinn put it,

> they asked the governor not to confuse them, educated, enlightened people . . . who appreciate with gratitude the protection and justice of France, with the "bedouins" or people of the tribes. . . . [They are] sedentary and literate citizens, who love quiet, peace, tranquility and comfort . . . the "bedouin" will not renounce their traditional conduct, the customs of their mountains, unless they are subjected to severe and energetic repression which fills them with a dread and terror that causes them to fear for their lives. Only force and violence can conquer their nature.

Force and violence were not long in coming. They took the form of punitive expropriations in favor of European colonists, carried out to make the native population pay for the costs of the rebellion. The expropriations were justified by the Superior Government Council in the following words:

> The expropriation is a punishment capable of leaving a permanent trace; a seizure of property well justified by persistent and repeated return to crime will smite the spirit of the guilty sufficiently by subjecting them to an effective repression with consequences which cannot be wiped out. The real employment of expropriation, that is peace; that is blood and ruins avoided in the future . . . political interest, the security of the colony, the civilizing of races who will not come to us until the hope of shaking our domination has disappeared from their minds, a clairvoyant humanity which avoids the disasters of the future by the severity of the present command the maintenance of expropriation and its consequences.

In addition, special punitive levies eight times larger than the annual tax charges were imposed on the rebellious areas and collected through the agency of the chiefs who had remained faithful to the French. The chiefs, said the peasants, "have taken our skin and bones and now they break our bones to eat the marrow." The terrible memory of these years when "justice and truth disappeared," "brother was set against brother" and the chiefs "grew rich through treason" has remained green in Kabyle chants recorded half a century later. It reinforced a permanent ambivalence toward the traditional chiefs and their successors as pro-French intermediaries between the conquerors and the indigenous masses, an ambivalence that was to be of moment in the turmoil leading up to the war of independence.

Envelopment

While the Muslims were thus expropriated and forced to witness the dismemberment of their social framework, Algeria was thrown wide open to European immigration and settlement. The new *colons* were all Frenchmen in name, but only half of them were of direct French origin, drawn mainly from poor, south-central France and—after the French defeat of 1871—from Alsace. The other half was made up primarily of Spaniards and Italians, of Corsicans and Maltese. It was the mixed character of this population which caused the French writer Anatole France to say in 1905 that France had during 70 years fleeced, chased and run to ground the Arabs in order to people Algiers with Italians and Spaniards. At first segregated residentially into separate settlements, they quickly came to make common cause through intermarriage and through common hatred of Arabs. A sense of envelopment and the threat of submersion can be found in the early novels of Albert Camus, himself born and raised in Algeria; and it was this fear which caused the *colons* first to resist any and every effort at reform initiated in metropolitan France, and later to embrace one or another variety of fascism, culminating in their support of the terroristic Organisation de l'Armée Sécrète (OAS) at the end of the war of independence.

The mainstay of *colon* economy, and the mainstay of the Algerian economy as a whole, came to be vineyard cultivation and the production of wine, especially after 1880 when the phylloxera louse destroyed much of French viticulture and France was forced to import much of her wine. Wine exports from Algeria came to form 50 percent of all Algerian exports. The acreage in vineyards more than doubled between 1900 and 1954 at the expense of food crops and pasture. As Michel Launay wrote, "The result is that the vine has displaced and polluted all else: it has chased away the wheat, it has chased away the sheep, it has chased away the forest and the dwarf palm. It has polluted the river where the skins and pips, lees, and refuse are thrown." This was especially true in western Algeria where low rainfall favored the extension of vineyards up to the very limits of the steppe. This area became the center of European rural settlement; nine-tenths of all Algerian vineyards—and thus most of the main cash crop— were in the hands of Europeans. At the same time, vineyard cultivation greatly contributed to social and economic differentiation among the *colons* themselves. Wine production and transport require considerable capital outlays in pressing cellars, vats and other plants and thus favored the ascendancy of the large *colon* over the small who had to rely on him for credit and access to the processing plant. It also placed much of the political control of the colony in the hands of a powerful oligarchy of wine merchants, shippers and bankers.

Many *colons* lost their land and moved to town. By 1954 over three-quarters of a million Europeans, or more than 80 percent of the entire European population, lived in urban centers. Here their occupations mirrored the skewed character of an agrarian country, dependent on one major cash crop, in its relation to an industrial metropolis. Of a total work force of some 300,000 Europeans, 35,000 were skilled workers and 55,000 were listed as unskilled; the remainder worked either in administration or management (close to 50,000) or in services of one kind or another (about 160,000). Most of these were office employees, small traders, caterers and mechanics. Despite these differences, they were as one in defense of their privileges which made the lowest French *colon* the superior of any Arab. Their unity was the product of their common fear of the Muslim majority.

How did that majority react to the changes imposed on it? The revolt of El Moqrani was to be the last major effort at armed resistance until some 80 years later. It was also to be the last major effort, until 1954, of the rural population to take the political initiative. There set in a long period of political inactivity, which only gave way to new political efforts around the time of World War I. Moreover, political activity would be first renewed in the cities, including the cities of France with their newly generated proletariat, before it would spread once again into the rural hinterland. Frantz Fanon, who has analyzed in overly Manichaean terms the conflict between conquerors and conquered, has portrayed their relations as one of continuous and endemic violence. Violence was certainly present during the 83 years between Moqrani's revolt and 1954, but it remained covert rather than overt, quiescent rather than emphatic. This was a period not so much of incubation of the revolution-to-be, but rather of muted changes and adjustments, experiments in social and cultural relations, with attendant advances and retreats. At the same time it was a period marked by shifts in the cognitive and emotional evaluation of different possibilities, rather than by a single-minded ideological rehearsal of things to come.

The Veil

Those Algerians who took any interest in politics and expressed a concern about the relation of Algeria to France oscillated between two main positions; sometimes they held both positions simultaneously, sometimes in quick succession. The defendants of one position called for increased contact with French cultural norms and assimilation to them. Socially, this assimilationism was most congruent with the interests of middle-class professionals of whom there were about 450 in the higher ranks, whose social standing depended on their French education, and who saw in their French degrees a passport to mobility. The other tendency was anti-assimilationist and directed toward an effort to define an Algerian nationality, different from the French and opposed to it. On a behavioral level this tendency manifested itself—even among assimilationists—in an attitude of reserve against foreign encroachment upon the intimate spheres of family life and religion.

Pierre Bourdieu has made the same point in stating that for the Algerians, adherence to traditional forms came to fulfill "essentially a symbolic function; it played the role, objectively, of a language of refusal" and illustrated this point with reference to the traditional custom of veiling of which Frenchmen were especially critical: the veil worn by Muslim women

> is above all a defense of intimacy and a protection against intrusion. And, confusedly, the Europeans have always perceived it as such. By wearing the veil, the Algerian woman creates a situation of non-reciprocity; like a disloyal player, she sees without being seen, without allowing herself to be seen. And it is the entire dominated society which, by means of the veil, refuses reciprocity, which sees, which penetrates, without allowing itself to be seen, regarded, penetrated.

Islam would thus prove to be one of the roots of Algerian nationalism. In the course of the 1920s and 1930s, the attitude of refusal and withdrawal would issue in a new and active movement, founded in an attempt to return to the purity of the Quran. The centers of this Islamic revival lay not in the new French towns of the Mediterranean littoral, but in the old Islamic towns of the hinterland, once the seats of active and well-to-do Islamic traders and entrepreneurs, such as Tlemcen, Nedroma, Constantine, Mila, Tebessa, Sidi Okba, Biskra and Ghardaïa. With the advent of French rule, many of them receded into the background; Constantine and Tlemcen, for instance, once possessed a thriving textile industry which declined under the impact of French competition. It is no accident, as Morizot has pointed out, that Tlemcen—pivot of a religious exodus to Tunisia in 1911—produced Messali Hadj, the first organizer of a nationalist Algerian party, while Constantine gave rise to Ben Badis, the Algerian protagonist of a revived and militant Islam.

Taught by the Islamic schoolmen of Constantine, Sheikh Abd-el-Hamid Ben Badis was to fuse Algerian religious tradition with the innovating influence of the Islamic reform movement of the early twentieth century. In the context of North Africa, this brought the reformers into direct conflict with local forms of Islam, as practiced in numerous religious lodges. These lodges, and the popular religious fraternities built upon them, had acted strongly in support of Abd el Kader during his resistance against the French and remained anti-French until the turn of the century. Thereafter, however, they had come to an accommodation with the French authorities who consciously supported them as convenient means for keeping the social body of Algeria as divided as possible.

The Badissia, as the reform movement came to be known after the name of its principal figure, was antagonistic to the traditional holy men. Instead it asserted the authority of the reformist schoolmen, the *ulema,* and furthered the creation of numerous orthodox schools (*medersas*) in the hinterland. Beginning in the cities, they nevertheless seeded the hinterland with associations of all kinds, including Islamic boy scouts, under the aegis of their slogan: "Arabic is my language, Algeria is my country, Islam is my religion." Their social support in the countryside was provided in the main by the middle-class peasantry and among the small merchants, entrepreneurs and teachers of the rural towns.

Islam's Role

Such an affiliation of independent peasantry with the new urban world by means of religious associations—new organizational forms within the traditional religious matrix—may also have received reinforcement through the stimulus of economic interests. The Badissia strongly opposed the heterodox religious feasts carried on by the holy men and the expenditures associated with them. These expenditures constitute a major drain on a peasantry, and their abolition by a religious reform movement is a common feature in many parts of the world. In many parts of the Andes and Middle America, for instance, it has underwritten conversions to Protestantism in otherwise traditionally Catholic Indian communities. The Badissia also demanded the restoration of the properties of religious foundations seized by the French. As a notable of Aoubelli said to Michel Launay: "Since at the conquest many Muslims gave their property to the habus to save them from annexation by the French, the claim to a return [of these properties] challenged the whole picture of colonial property." In the words of Jacques Berque, the Badissia created a new and Jacobin Islam.

This Jacobin Islam would have especially strong appeal not only to Islamic traders and entrepreneurs of declining towns in the hinterland, but also to the rural class of middling landowners and numerous small traders, as shown in Launay's investigation of the area of Ain-Temuchent in Oran Province. The agricultural workers and the poor peasants in general clung to their traditional holy men and resisted the reformers. And years later it was this same stratum, the middle peasants, in Ain-Temuchent which furnished support for the uprising of 1954: "The organizers of the insurrection were the small holders, not the little proletarianized small holders but the small holders almost able to make ends meet, well-off in comparison with agricultural workers." Moreover, René Delisle is quite correct when he says that "the insurrection of 1954 and the independence of 1962 are thus, in this respect, only the necessary conclusion of the action initiated in 1930 by the reformist Ulemas, restorers of Islam and of Arab tradition."

New Proletariat

If reformist Islam provided one of the sources of Algerian nationalism, the other source lay in the increasing development of an Algerian semiproletariat. This, in turn, was the product of two major causes: the decay of the traditional pattern of Algerian sharecropping, the *khammesat* (from *khammes,* "a fifth"), coupled with the need—especially strong in central Algeria, among the Berber-speaking Kabyles—to supplement a meager agriculture with some other form of employment.

Under the *khammesat,* the sharecropper received not only tools and seed, but also money advances and food, sums which were then subtracted from the final produce. The new French legal codes, however, allowed sharecroppers to abandon their landlords without previous reimbursement of these costs. While the law thus freed the sharecroppers from a form of traditional bondage, it also hastened the decline of sharecropping and the advent of day labor. Previous conditions of servitude had canceled out the variable effects of good and poor years, by standardizing sharecropper duties and rights. Now workers sought positions as sharecroppers during bad years, in order to

Peter Throckmorton NANCY PALMER

Many peasants drifted into the cities where they became a semiproletariat.

Under French rule, the peasants could no longer be sure of anything. Torn from the soil and the protection of traditional chiefs, they fell into an ideological vacuum.

guarantee their livelihood, but abandoned their owners with the advent of a promising year. Shortly after the passage of the law the *qaid* of Heumis testified that

> French law having emancipated the sharecropper, the owners in large numbers preferred not to give them work, for fear of losing their advances. The sharecropper no longer finds work because one does not want to engage him in ways other than by the day.

The result was both an increased number of men looking for work as wage laborers and a reduction in the area previously cultivated. Now, said an old Muslim teacher to Launay, "the agricultural worker cannot be sure of anything." One effect of growing wage labor was therefore the creation of a large floating semiproletariat, which was to bear all the stigmata of a growing economic insecurity.

Yet the growing trend toward wage labor possessed still another face. Increasingly, many areas—but most notably the mountains of Kabylia—began to experience the pressures of population growth on available food resources. French colonization had driven the natives into the barren hinterland, often producing compact and dense settlements in terrain which could not support such numbers. Military pacification and the spread of modern health care further curtailed the Malthusian checks on the population growth. As a result, many Kabyles were forced to seek alternative sources of livelihood outside their mountains.

At the same time, Algerians—and again most especially the Berber-speakers from Kabylia—began to be recruited into the labor force of metropolitan France. World War I witnessed the first massive employment of Algerians in France itself, to replace French laborers called to the colors and now at the front. Between 1915 and 1918 some 76,000 Algerians left to work in French factories. This trend was continued steadily over the years, until in 1950 there were some 600,000 Algerians in the metropolis. This large-scale movement caught up great numbers of Algerians in the forced draft of acculturation. They received their education, as Germaine Tillion has put it, in the "school of the cities." As a result, there developed on French soil a fully fledged Algerian proletariat with strong and enduring ties to the rural Algerian hinterland.

Nationalism and Education

This working-class milieu had two immediate effects. First, it incubated the first modern nationalist Algerian movement, in the formation of the Etoile Nord Africaine in Paris in 1925, in which Messali Hadj became the dominant personality. Left-wing party and trade union activity associated with this experience in urban France provided the migrant workers both with models of organization and with fragments of socialist ideology which they found of use in interpreting the condition of their home-

Peter Throckmorton NANCY PALMER

land. It proved doubly significant, moreover, that—upon their return to Algeria—they could do little to give substance to their aspirations through the *colon*-dominated Socialist and Communist unions and parties of the colony. From the first, the logic of the colonial situation forced them to give their support to nationalist parties, first to the Messalist Parti Populaire Algérien, and later to its more militant successors.

The second consequence of the French experience was that it produced among the Algerian workers in the metropole the realization that an adequate French education constituted a passport to entry into the modern technical civilization. Tillion notes that

> twenty-five years later, one meets certain doctors, certain lawyers, certain professors, certain mathematicians or chemists whose brilliant studies have been paid for during these already long distant years by a father or an elder brother out of his laborer's salary. To achieve this result, the illiterate émigré must have had to deprive himself daily of what in France we call the "vital minimum," and even before he could do that he had to grasp the mechanisms and the values of an alien world, indoctrinate his family, separate his little boy from his mother, and then push him—ardently, patiently, proudly—to the fore.

Both of these trends—the growth of reformist Islam on the one hand, the city ward migration of Algerian workers on the other—were to contribute decisively to the outbreak of the Algerian revolt of 1954. Reformist Islam provided the cultural form for the construction of a new network of social relations between clusters of middle peasants in the countryside and the sons of the urban elite of the hinterland towns. The city ward migration of the Algerian peasantry—most especially that of the Kabyles—not only brought them into contact with industrial and urban patterns of life, but produced a professional class in the course of that migratory experience. Once again networks were forged which linked clusters of peasants in the countryside with spokesmen and representatives in the cities. In studies of prominent Moslems involved in the revolution and its sequel, four features stood out: most were young men, whose formative political experience lay in the years of indecision of the 1930s and 1940s; a disproportionate number, compared to their role in the total population of Algeria, were of Berber origin; many were French-educated; many had served in the French army during World War II. Wholly against the expectations of the French, who had always pursued a policy of keeping the Berbers culturally and politically separate from the Arab population, in order to better divide and rule, the forces generated by a common involvement in processes set up by the French impact itself would bring these disparate groups into fusion.

Death of Assimilationism

Undoubtedly this fusion was speeded up by the events of the period preceding World War II, and the world war itself. As long as there was hope that reform in France could produce greater liberty and autonomy for Muslim Algerians, there also remained some hope that the expectations of both assimilationists and nationalists could be met without the use of force and violence. But as it became increasingly clear—during long years of political prevarication and failure—that no French government capable of instituting reform was likely to emerge, the militant nationalists gained ground, and the tendency toward clandestine operations also gained momentum. To this must be added the impact of domestic trends. Between 1930 and 1954 the number of small Muslim owners decreased by a fifth and the number of day laborers rose by more than a quarter. During World War II and after, harvests were poor, wine production was down and livestock was lost in large numbers.

Even more significant, undoubtedly, were the more proximate causes of a political nature: France suffered a crushing defeat in 1940, revealing her weakness to all who had eyes to see. At the same time, half of the French nation was engaged in fighting the other half in underground operations, sharply raising the level of all-round uncertainty and illegality. The advent of fascism in France strongly supported violence on the part of fascist *colons* against the Algerian population. At the same time, however, Algerians were mobilized in considerable numbers to fight for France, thus both undergoing military training and achieving a level of significant equality with French fellow combatants.

All of this came to a head at Sétif on 1 May 1945. Some 8,000 to 10,000 Muslims had gathered to celebrate the Allied victories in Europe; many came with placards calling for the release from prison of Messali Hadj and for equality between Muslims and Christians. Shots were fired, and a riot ensued which spread to other towns. The riot was fiercely repressed by French air and ground forces, and estimates of Muslims killed vary between 8,000 and 45,000, with 15,000 not an unlikely number. There is little doubt, says the Swiss journalist Charles-Henri Favrod, that "it was these events of 1945 which decided the revolution of 1954." French inability and unwillingness to grant concessions in time spelled the end of the assimilationist cause. This is most clearly exemplified in the person of Ferhat Abbas, long a leader of the assimilationists, who decided in April of 1954 that a party that "fights in favor of a 'revolution by law' can no longer advance. . . ."

Militant and subversive movements increasingly developed among the proletarian nationalists. The Parti Populaire Algérien (PPA), driven underground in 1939, developed in 1947 a paramilitary arm in the MTLD—the Mouvement pour le Triomphe des Libertés Démocratiques. Within the MTLD, in turn, there grew up a secret terrorist society called Organisation Spéciale (OS); by 1949 it had 1,900 members. The founder members of the OS became the members of the Comité Révolutionnaire d'Unité et d'Action (CRUA), which unleashed the revolt of 1954. Not all the members of the PPA, however, were to join in the revolt. On the contrary, the struggle for independence against the French was to be accompanied throughout by a deadly struggle between partisans of the revolt and units derived from Messali Hadj's original PPA. This struggle was to prove especially bloody in metropolitan France, where close to a thousand Muslims died in internecine warfare.

The Revolt Begins

The insurrection broke out on the night of 31 October to 1 November 1954 with some three score incidents of attacks on French garrisons and police stations, ambushes and arson. Although widely scattered, most attacks erupted in eastern Algeria, especially in the mountains of the Aurès. The insurgents were few in number, probably no more than 500, with 300 of them concentrated in the Aurès; and they possessed less than 50 obsolete shotguns.

The Aurès was a logical first base for the revolt. Occupied by Berber-speakers, it has long been a zone of dissidence from any central government. Jacques Soustelle, anthropologist, governor-general of Algeria in 1955 and a leading spokesman and conspirator in the movement for an Algérie Française, was to say:

one sees clearly that the Romans erred in limiting their occupation to the approaches to the mountain, since it

The Berbers of the Aures Mountains supplied many recruits for the guerrilla forces. Here an FLN nurse assists a Berber woman.

remained for centuries the reservoir of uncontrolled forces ready to overflow. Our penetration in the Aurès and Nemenchas has been very weak: we have committed the same error as the Romans, with the same results.

Berber social and political organization resembles an "ordered anarchy"; anthropologists speak of it as unilineal and segmentary. In theory this works as a system of checks and balances as long as the units are more or less stable. Under French rule, however, this ideal balance had been upset. Improved health services had removed the checks on population growth and served to increase the pressure of population against available resources. The spread of money economy and the introduction of new needs—for coffee, sugar, ground grain—undermined traditional patterns of self-sufficiency. Land became a commodity, to be bought and sold. After World War I the migration of men to France initiated a system of monetary remissions in which work in the metropolis underwrote the economy of the mountains. All these trends accentuated competition among men and exacerbated opposition between tribal factions. The rebels adroitly exploited these local feuds, finding allies among one or another local fraction in the mountain area and helping them against their enemies. They also formed bandit groups. In the Aurés they established their first military district (Wilaya I), which remained a rebel bastion throughout the war. At the same time, between November 1954 and mid-March 1956, small determined groups of fighters began hit-and-run raids in other parts of Algeria.

With the advent of the revolt, CRUA became the executive committee of the National Liberation Front (Front de Libération Nationale, or FLN), which was to consist of an External Delegation, based in Cairo, and an Internal Delegation, made up of the military leaders of the revolt in Algiers. These military leaders were to head up six military districts, or *wilayas;* a seventh district would comprise metropolitan France. The total organization headed by the military leaders was to be known as the Army of National Liberation (Armée de Libération Nationale, or ALN). At the core of the army were to be the *mujahidin,* fighters for the faith, who were to be the regulars, surrounded by a fringe of civilian guerrillas, *mussabilin,* and *fidayin,* non-uniformed terrorists and saboteurs. The formal table of organization of the army could not hide the fact, however, that the organizational structure of the FLN represented a compromise solution between the interests of civilian and military leaders. This created a strain that was to be compounded during the war by further conflicts between various military leaders, and between those carrying on the guerrilla war inside the country and those who organized armed units outside. Jean Daniel has said that there existed in the FLN not one organizational pyramid, but a multitude of pyramids, and that "the unity of the FLN was never realized except in situations which forced the multiplicity of pyramids to move in the same direction." Ideologically, too, what held the movement together was a common nationalism. Socialist phraseology appeared occasionally in FLN pronouncements but remained vague enough not to become the rallying cry of any one faction against another until after the advent of Algerian independence.

By April 1956 French sources estimated rebel strength at 8,500 fighters and some 21,000 auxiliaries. Possessed of insufficient troop strength, the French were unable to prevent the westward spread of rebel units along the parallel mountain chains of the Atlas, despite repeated commando raids into the hostile interior. By April 1956, however, French units brought to Algeria from France, Germany and French West Africa augmented French forces to about 250,000 men; conscription was soon to add another 200,000. This increased force permitted a change in French tactics from the use of flying columns to the *quadrillage,* or grid system, in which towns and communication centers were held in strength, while mobile units of paratroopers, volunteers and foreign legionnaires probed the hinterland.

This new tactic did not eliminate the ALN, but it did check its activity in the back country. Toward the end of 1956, the ALN therefore mounted an offensive in the urban centers. Terrorist attacks increased in all cities, but especially in Algiers, where 120 acts took place in December alone. As everyone who has seen *The Battle of Algiers* knows, the ALN had successfully infiltrated the Muslim quarter of the city, the Casbah, with its population of 80,000. Here it had recruited some 4,000 men to its ranks, around a core of *lumpenproletariat,* "hooligans with a pure heart," who were given an opportunity to wash themselves clean of past sins. While the shift to urban terrorism had important psychological effects on the urban population, especially among Muslims who were won to the cause of the ALN in proportion to the inability of the French to protect them, the fact is it proved ineffective militarily. Between February and October 1957, the Tenth Paratroop Division commanded by General Jacques Massu effectively destroyed the terrorist organization in Algiers.

The Battle of Algiers

Checked within the country itself, the ALN was thus forced to seek alternative sources of support, which it found in neighboring Tunisia and Morocco. These two neighboring states, which had achieved independence from France in 1956, permitted the ALN to establish training centers on their soil and recruit new forces from among Algerians both within and without Algeria. By the end of 1957 there were more than 60,000 Algerian refugees in Tunis and 40,000 in Morocco. Recruitment by the ALN for this new "external" army grew apace. By the end of 1957, again it numbered 25,000 troops, while the "internal" forces amounted to only 15,000.

Toward the end of the war, guerrilla action within Algeria had been almost quashed by the French army, effectively reduced to occasional ambushes such as that shown in this photograph.

Yet this shift in ALN tactics also produced a comparable response from the French. By mid-September 1957 the French had constructed along the Moroccan frontier an elaborate barrier of electrified wire, alarm systems, strong points, mine fields and observation posts. A similar barrier was raised on the Tunisian side, thus effectively sealing off the external armies from the internal zone of operations. In 1958 the French also expanded their military effort inside Algeria. Each of the known ALN bases was cordoned off by a "pacified" zone, and attacks were mounted in turn on each of the separate military districts of the ALN. Communication between the districts was effectively destroyed, while all attempts of the ALN to mount battalion-size counterthrusts proved ineffective.

The rebels were therefore forced back once again upon the small-group tactics with which they had begun the insurrection. French military activity was, moreover, supported by a vast effort at relocating the civilian population, thus separating the rebels from possible sources of support. More than 1.8 million people were moved from their homes between 1955 and 1961, while others fled from the zones of military operation into the already overcrowded cities. Finally, the French counterthrust was capped by the employment of psychological warfare, ranging from mass persuasion and the provision of social services by army personnel to forcible indoctrination and torture.

Who "Won"?

The French effort had several consequences for the nationalist camp. It accentuated feuds among the leadership, especially between the leaders of the revolt outside Algeria and the military chieftains in the field. It isolated the military districts from each other and from outside sources of arms and support, curtailing their fighting capacity and reducing them ultimately to the level of petty principalities, at loggerheads with one another over resources, tactics and strategy. At the same time it left untouched the growing "external army" which grew more important for the nationalist leadership as a bargaining point in any final negotiations for peace in direct proportion to the decline of the internal army in both strength and effectiveness. Thus the end of the war was to find the external army under the leadership of Houari Boumédienne as the only intact and organized body of Algerians.

At the same time, the French effort dialectically produced the forces of its own undoing. As the French proved victorious, the hold of the nationalist cause over the minds of Algerians paradoxically grew apace. Some of the reasons for this were internal. The experience of forcible relocation, flight of refugees to the cities, the destruction of agricultural resources, the annihilation of nomadic groups who could no longer mount their migrations—all these pulverized the social relations of traditional society and produced a fearsome ideological vacuum. The conflict itself further polarized French settlers and Muslims, reinforcing their separate identities, which French efforts at psychological warfare exacerbated rather than reduced. At the same time, the costs of the conflict became ever more burdensome. In addition to loss of life and the stresses attendant upon war, the financial cost of the war to France proved huge: 50 billion new francs and $1.7 million in foreign currency spent on arms and attempts to close budgetary deficits.

But the social and political costs of the war were even higher, for it brought into the open a series of hidden conflicts which severely curtailed France's ability to continue the fight. France had not only gone through the defeat and dislocation of World War II; it had just witnessed defeat at the hands of the Vietminh in Vietnam. People were weary of war, all the more so when conscripts were drafted in metropolitan France to fight in Algeria. At the same time, a new financial and technocratic elite hoped for an expansion of French participation in a European common market, in place of continuing the expensive and fruitless colonial wars. On the other side were ranged the intransigent French *colons* in Algeria, who could countenance no peaceable accommodation with the Muslim majority, and a professional army which had returned from Vietnam grimly determined to install military dominance in Algeria and metropolitan France rather than to accept defeat in another guerrilla war.

These segmental conflicts, however, were but symptoms of a larger long-standing conflict between metropolitan and overseas France. As Herbert Lüthy put it,

> The truth of the matter is that the history of the French republic and that of the French colonial empire were impelled by different forces, went their different ways, and seldom met. . . . The empire was something with which the French people had nothing whatever to do, and its story was that of machinations of high finance, the Church, and the military caste, which tirelessly re-erected overseas the Bastilles which had been overthrown in France.

In the course of the Algerian War, these conflicts became manifest in three major episodes. During the first of these de Gaulle came to power to end the Fourth Republic on the shoulders of a threatened army coup d'état in Algiers and *colon* demonstrations (May 1958). The second was an abortive insurrection against de Gaulle, staged by settlers and army leaders in Algiers in January 1960. The third was a revolt of army leaders in Algeria in April 1961, a revolt which was put down and fizzled out after a wave of *colon* terrorism. The government in Paris successfully coped with the threat of instability which emanated from Algeria; but it also decided to end that threat in the future by ridding itself of a colony that had become an economic, military and political liability. The peace negotiations between the French government and the representatives of

Dickey Chapell NANCY PALMER

the Algerian rebels produced a tacit alliance calculated to put an end to the threat to metropolitan France through the sacrifice of the volatile French *colons* and their protofascist military allies. Thus, victory came to the ALN less through its own brave and desperate struggle during 7½ years of war than through the strains which the war had produced in the foundations of the French polity.

The Algerian events are important not only because a small force of guerrillas challenged a large modern army and deprived it of victory, but because it gives rise to two influential theories on warfare involving peasant populations. One is the "theory of revolutionary war," developed and advocated by officers of the French army that fought in Algeria. The other is the theory of colonial revolutions put forward by Frantz Fanon, doctor, propagandist and diplomat for the Algerian liberation movement.

Fanon and Mao

The "theory of revolutionary war" grew out of the bitter experience of the French army in Vietnam. In the wake of that defeat General Lionel-Max Chassin discovered in the writings of Mao Tse-tung the secret of Communist successes: "It is impossible to win a war, especially a civil war, if the people are not on your side." From now on, according to the new theorists, wars would be fought among the masses, for control of the masses, by a mixture of organizational and psychological techniques. The organizational techniques, which they hoped to bor-

Guerrilla bands in the mountains had to survive with very little help from the 200,000 man regular Algerian army, which the French kept out of Algeria by sealing off the Tunisian and Moroccan borders. In the battle of Algiers, the French paratroopers, despite some losses, defeated the terrorists.

row from Mao, relied on the famous *hiérarchies parallèles,* the combination of organizations based on territoriality with functional organizations. With this system "the individual caught in the fine mesh of such a net has no chance whatever of preserving his independence," as Jean Hoggard wrote in *Revue Militaire d'Information.* The psychological techniques were derived, at least in part, from *The Rape of the Masses,* by Serge Chakotin, a book written on the eve of World War II purporting to show democratic Germans how they could defend democracy against Hitler by means of a "violent propaganda" based on the supposed lessons of Pavlovian conditioning.

The processes of organization and psychological conditioning were to go forward simultaneously through army action in *quadrillage,* forcible relocation, interrogation, the occasional use of torture and through military-sponsored social work and psychological persuasion. Such an approach has enormous appeal to military technicians and social scientists who think of their findings primarily as techniques for human control.

The great flaw of this new vision of war—which attained the status of a religion among many French officers involved in the war—lies in its omission of the human middle term in its multiple cultural aspects—economic, social, political and ideological. Assuming Algerians to be like Frenchmen, possessed of identical culture patterns and interest, the military technicians visualized their task simply as one in which organization reproduces the experimental design of the laboratory and simple conditioning provides the experimental subject with a new set of habits, without the simultaneous creation of a new cultural order for which these new habits could be relevant. Certainly one may also question whether simple conditioning suffices to restructure human responses in the desired way; but it does not seem impossible, at least in the future, that some forms of complex conditioning can in fact achieve such a result. It is clear, however, that what was missing from "the theory of revolutionary war" was any vision of real revolution, of a transformation of the environment congruent with new patterns of habit. Under the conditions of colonial warfare, in Algeria as later in Vietnam under American auspices, the theory was emptied of any cultural content to produce simple obedience to naked power imposed from without.

Frantz Fanon's theory, in contrast, preaches the need for colonial peoples to shake off foreign oppression by force and violence, not merely as a military technique, but as an essential psychological precondition to independence. The colony was established by force and is perpetuated by force. The exercise of force against the native strips him of his essential manhood; he can recover his manhood only when he himself uses violence against his oppressor. But the use of violence also has its social aspect. It unifies the people, "binds them together as a whole, since each individual forms a violent link in the great chain, a part of the great organism of violence which has surged upwards in reaction to the settler's violence in the beginning."

No one can read Fanon without being gripped both by his moral passion and by his insight into the mechanisms of aggression and repression which find their expression in personal and group violence. Yet, in an immediate sense, Fanon's thesis is but the antithesis of the position defended by the French colonels. Against their insistence that men can be captured and rendered impotent by organization, he preaches upheaval, dissolution, disorder. Against their use of psychological violence against the native, he preaches violence against the oppressor. But just like the colonels, Fanon pays no attention to the cultural realities of past history, of group relationships, of the shifting and changing alliances and schisms of concrete human beings, caught up in concrete experiences of past and present. His Manichaean world—like the technocratic pseudorevolutionary order of the colonels—is devoid of economy, society, polity and ideolgy and their determinants. In Fanon, violence is not "politics by other means," in Clausewitz's mundane phrase, violence used as a rational technique calculated in terms of particular human interrelationships; it becomes instead a cosmic force needed to cleanse the universe in order to achieve salvation.

A Revolution That Failed

Violence there certainly was in Algeria, and the rural population responded to it. But the appeal to violence was most succesful in Kabylia, where it permitted the hostile tribal sections to compose their segmental conflicts in a common confrontation with an external enemy. The escalation of violence thus permitted the "massing effect" so characteristic of segmentary societies, in which the autonomous segments form larger coalitions proportional to the magnitude of the external threat. Violence in this setting was both cause and effect of a certain social order, not merely a psychologically motivated act in which men took back their manhood from the oppressor who had robbed them of it. Moreover, the French counterthrusts were often singularly undiscriminating in their brutality: violence was frequently a response to military violence visited alike upon men, women and children.

This is not to gainsay Fanon's penetrating insights into the psychological mechanisms of colonial oppression and submission; yet neither the ideology of the colonels nor the ideology of Frantz Fanon could provide us with a guide to an understanding of what happened in Algeria, during the war and after.

The Turkish writer Arslan Humbaraci subtitled his book on Algeria "A Revolution That Failed." The most significant facts about postwar Algeria stem from the defeat of the internal rebellion and the survival of the external army. When the French departed, the external army entered Algeria. The exhausted Kabyle rebels were no match for its military and political might. The departure of 900,000 Frenchmen at the same time vacated numerous positions in government and services, which adherents of the rebellion regarded as rightfully their own. Whatever tenuous bonds between professionals, peasantry and workers survived the crushing of the internal rebellion now became further attenuated as the fortified Algerian middle class reaped the rewards of ten years of effort and joined the Algerian elite. Socialist experiments, initiated by Ahmed Ben Bella, involving self-management of nationalized French agricultural holdings and shops, resulted in over-bureaucratization and a grave decline of production. At the same time, Algeria remained dependent for credits on France, granted in return for continuing rights to oil and gas discovered in the Sahara. Ben Bella's attempt to stem the decline by organizing the FLN into a monolithic party of the Communist type proved unable—on any level—to contain the centrifugal forces created by economic decline, continued dependence on France and the rapid "bourgeoisification" of the new Algerian power-holders. In 1965 the army stepped in in order to stabilize the situation.

Under Houari Boumédienne, Algeria continues to proclaim itself "socialist" but emphasizes that its socialism is "Algerian," and not "imported," and relies for much of its definitions of socialism on the Islamic *ulema*. Nationalized shops have been returned to their owners; banks, foreign trade and heavy industry—never nationalized —continue in private hands; and the regime has expressed itself in favor of foreign private investment. Algeria continues to be strongly dependent on French aid, becoming in effect France's closest "client-state." At the core of the society stands a strong army, officered by a strongly nationalist staff. The mood is nationalist Islamic Algerian. It is the Jacobin Islam of Ben Badis which has ultimately proved victorious.

May 1970

SUGGESTED READINGS—PEASANTS IN THE MODERN WORLD

Sons of the Shaking Earth by Eric R. Wolf (Chicago: University of Chicago Press, 1959) gives an account of the cultural development of Middle America from prehistoric times to the present.

Peasants by Eric R. Wolf (Englewood Cliffs, N.J.: Prentice-Hall, 1966) attempts to generalize about the economic, social and political characteristics of peasantry.

Peasant Nationalism and Communist Power by Chalmers A. Johnson (Stanford, California: Stanford University Press, 1962). An analysis of the peasant-communit alliance in China compared to the situation in Yugoslavia.

Peasants in the Modern World edited by Phillip K. Bock (Albuquerque, New Mexico: University of New Mexico Press, 1969).
Peasants in Cities: Readings in the Anthropology of Urbanization edited by William Margin (Boston: Houghton-Mifflin, 1970). Two recent readers dealing with the peasant as an artifact in industrial society.

Masses in Latin America edited by Irving Louis Horowitz (New York: Oxford University Press, 1970). A collection of essays emphasizing the role of peasants and laborers originally published in *Studies in Comparative International Development*.

Marx Against the Peasant by David Mitrany (Chapel Hill, North Carolina: University of North Carolina Press, 1951). Mitrany investigates the paradox of a doctrine based on proletarian revolution that has consistently come into power on the tide of peasant uprisings.

SUGGESTED READINGS—REVOLUTION

The Urban Guerrilla by Martin Oppenheimer (Chicago, Ill.: Quadrangle Books, 1969). Oppenheimer feels that Establishment repression and neo-colonialism have created a potential for revolution in this country. He examines the forms that revolutionary movements could take and possible tactics of revolutionary leaders.

The Rebel by Albert Camus (New York: Knopf, 1957). A group of essays on revolutionaries and revolutions by the famous existentialist. Camus does not feel that violence can ever be appropriately used.

The Wretched of the Earth by Franz Fanon (New York: Grove Press, 1963). Fanon was a revolutionary during the Algerian revolution. His book states that all of the violence committed by both sides during the revolt stems from the basic crime of imposed rule by France and the violence used to maintain that rule.

Lenin on Politics and Revolution by Vladimir Lenin, edited and introduced by James E. Connor (New York: Pegasus, 1968).

The Polish Peasant in Europe and America by W. I. Thomas and Florian Znaniecki (New York: Alfred Knopf, 1918). A classic study of Polish peasants in the old and new worlds.

Peasant Communism in Southern Italy, by Sidney G. Farrow (New Haven: Yale University Press, 1967).

The Peasant in Nineteenth-Century Russia edited by Wayne D. Vucinich (Stanford, California: Stanford University Press, 1967).

Peasant Renaissance in Yugoslavia by Ruth Trouton (London: Routledge & Paul, 1952).

Peasant Society edited by Jack M. Potter, Mary N. Diaz and George M. Foster (Boston: Little Brown, 1967).

The Little Community by Robert Redfield (Chicago: University of Chicago Press, 1960).

Peasant Society and Culture: An Anthropological Approach to Civilization by Robert Redfield (Chicago: University of Chicago Press, 1956).

Primitive and Peasant Economic Systems by Manning Nash (San Francisco: Chandler, 1966).

Lord and Peasant in Russia, from the Ninth to the Nineteenth Century by Jerome Blum (Princeton: Princeton University Press, 1961).

The Wallace Whitelash

SEYMOUR MARTIN LIPSET &
EARL RAAB

Party factionalism bedevils his cause, but the Wallace movement may be as strong as ever.

The American Independent Party of George C. Wallace brought together in 1968 almost every right-wing extremist group in the country, and undoubtedly recruited many new activists for the rightist cause. Today many of the state parties organized under his aegis have formal legal status and have announced that they intend to nominate candidates for state and local office during the next few years in an effort to build the party. George Wallace himself has sent out a clear signal that he has plans for the future. He has begun to mail the *George Wallace Newsletter* monthly to a mailing list of over one million names which had been assembled during the election. The old address for Wallace activities was Box 1968, Montgomery, Alabama. It is now Box 1972.

The effort to maintain and build the party, however, faces the perennial problem of ideological extremist movements—splits among its supporters. Even during the 1968 campaign, sharp public divisions over local vs. national control occurred in a number of states, usually because complete control over the finances and conduct of the party's work was kept in the hands of coordinators directly appointed by Wallace and responsible to the national headquarters in Montgomery. In some states, two separate organizations existed, both of which endorsed the Wallace candidacy but attacked each other as too radical. Since the 1968 election, two competing national organizations have been created, and again each is attacking the other as extremist.

George Gardner

The group directly linked to Wallace has had two national conventions. The first, held in Dallas in early February, attracted 250 delegates from 44 states and set up a group known as The Association of George C. Wallace Voters. The Dallas meeting was attended by a number of top Wallace aides, including Robert Walter, who represents Wallace in California; Tom Turnipseed, a major figure in the Wallace presidential effort since it started; Dan Smoot, the right-wing radio commentator; and Kent Courtney, the editor of the *Conservative Journal*. The same group met again on May 3 and 4 in Cincinnati, and formally established a new national party to be called The American Party. A Virginian, T. Coleman Andrews, long active on the ultraconservative front, was chosen as chairman. Wallace gave his personal blessing to the new party and its officers. One of his Montgomery aides, Taylor Hardin, who maintains a national office with 20 employees in Montgomery, indicated that the party would have a considerable degree of "central control."

The competing national group met in Louisville on February 22, 1969, and established a new national conservative party to be composed largely of autonomous state parties. As if to emphasize the extent to which it fostered local control, this organization called itself "The National Committee of the Autonomous State Parties, known as the American Independent Party, American Party, Independent Party, Conservative Party, Constitutional Party." This group, or constellation of groups, was united in its opposition to domination by Wallace and his Montgomery aides. Although the former candidate received compliments at the convention, the delegates were much more concerned with building a movement that was not limited to his supporters in 1968. The national chairman of the new group, William K. Shearer of California, editor of the *California Statesman*, had already broken with Wallace during the campaign on the issue of local autonomy. At the Louisville convention, Shearer said:

> Governor Wallace has not shown any interest in a national party apart from a personal party. A candidate properly springs from the party and not the party from the candidate. The party should not be candidate-directed. While we have great respect for Mr. Wallace, we do not think there should be a candidate-directed situation. We want our party to survive regardless of what Mr. Wallace does.

The Shearer group also appears to be more conservative on economic issues than the Wallace-dominated one. During the convention, Wallace was criticized for being "too liberal" for his advocacy during the campaign of extended social security and farm parity prices.

Confederate flags greeted George Wallace when he came to Chicago in 1968.

The leaders of each faction claim that the other includes extremists. Robert Walters attacked Shearer's group as composed of "radicals and opportunists" and as having "a pretty high nut content." Shearer, on the other hand, has said that he finds many in the Wallace-dominated party "not too savory."

The publications of the competing groups indicate that each is supported by viable segments of the 1968 party. The Shearer National Committee, however, is clearly much weaker financially, since the Wallace national group retained a considerable sum from the 1968 campaign for future activities. It is also unlikely that they can attract many Wallace voters against the opposition of the candidate. The competition for support, however, does give each group an immediate function; and both national organizations appear to be busy holding state and local conventions designed to win over those who were involved in the presidential campaign.

It is difficult to tell how much support the American Party retains. Early in 1969 the party ran a candidate in a special election for Congress in Tennessee's Eighth District. Wallace ran first in this district in the presidential race, but the A.I.P. congressional candidate, William Davis, ran a bad second to the Democrat. The A.I.P. secured 16,319 votes (25 percent) in the congressional race, compared to 32,666 for the Democrat and 15,604 for the Republican. Wallace himself took an active part in the campaign, making speeches for Davis, but he was clearly unable to transfer his presidential support to his follower.

While Davis's showing in Tennessee was fairly respectable, another A.I.P. by-election candidate, Victor Cherven, who ran for the state senate in Contra Costa County in California in late March, secured only 329 out of the 146,409 votes cast. Cherven even ran behind two other minor party nominees. In mid-June, in a by-election for a seat in the California assembly from Monterey, an A.I.P. candidate, Alton F. Osborn, also secured an insignificant vote, 188 out of 46,602. The first effort to contest a congressional seat outside the South failed abysmally, when an American Party candidate in a Montana by-election received half of 1 percent of the vote, 509 out of 88,867 ballots on June 25. Election day, November 4, 1969, produced the best evidence of the inability of the Wallace followers to develop viable local parties. In Virginia, a state in which Wallace had secured 322,203 votes or 23.6 percent in 1968, both rightist parties ran candidates for governor. Dr. William Pennington, the gubernatorial nominee of the Andrews-Wallace American Independent Party obtained 7,059 votes, or .8 percent of the total; and Beverly McDowell, who ran on the Conservative Party ticket of the Shearer segment of the movement, did slightly better, with 9,821 votes, or 1.1 percent of the electorate. Pennington's and McDowell's combined total in 1969 only equalled 5 percent of Wallace's vote in Virginia.

But if Wallace's strength cannot be transferred to local and state candidates, most of it still remains with him on the level of national politics. The Gallup Poll, which chronicled George Wallace's rise in popularity through 1967 and 1968, has continued to examine his possible strength in a future presidential contest. In three national surveys in April, July and September, samples of the electorate were asked how they would now vote in a contest between Nixon, Edward Kennedy and Wallace. Nixon appeared to have gained from both parties, as compared with the 43 percent he received in the 1968 election. His support remained consistently high, 52 percent in April, 52 in July, and 53 in September. Kennedy's backing fluctuated more, 33, 36, 31, as contrasted with the 43 percent that Humphrey had secured. Wallace also dropped, securing 10, 9, and 10 percent in the same three polls. Thus, he lost about a quarter of his support during 1969, but still retains a respectable following for a new campaign. Wallace's social base remains comparable to that which backed him in the election, and he remains a major force in the South, where he pulls 25 percent of the choices as compared with 5 percent in the rest of the country.

Who *did* support George Wallace in 1968? A detailed answer to that question will perhaps tell us more than anything else about his chances for the future, as well as about the potentiality of right-wing extremism in America.

Election Results

Election Day results confirmed the basic predictions of the preelection opinion polls. George Wallace secured almost ten million votes, or about 13.5 percent of the total voting electorate. He captured five states with 45 electoral votes, all of them in the Deep South: Mississippi, Georgia, Alabama, Louisiana and Arkansas. With the exception of Arkansas, which had gone to Johnson in 1964, these were the same states Barry Goldwater won in that year. But Wallace lost two states carried by Goldwater—South Carolina, the home state of Nixon's southern leader, the 1948 Dixiecrat candidate Strom Thurmond, and Arizona, Goldwater's home state.

Since the support for Wallace seemingly declined considerably between early October and Election Day, falling from about 21 percent to 13 percent, an analysis of his actual polling strength is obviously important. Fortunately, the Gallup Poll conducted a national survey immediately after the election in which it inquired both how respondents voted, and whether they had supported another candidate earlier in the campaign. The data of this survey were made available by the Gallup Poll for our analysis. They are particularly useful since it would appear that most voters who had supported Wallace, but shifted to another candidate, did report this fact to Gallup interviewers. Thirteen percent indicated they had voted for Wallace, while another 9 percent stated that they had been for him at an earlier stage in the campaign.

From the national results among whites, it is clear that

the data are heavily influenced by the pattern of support in the South. Wallace's voters were most likely to be persons who did not vote in 1964, or who backed Goldwater rather than Johnson. The pattern of an extremist party recruiting heavily from the ranks of nonvoters coincides with the evidence from previous extremist movements both in this country and abroad. Wallace also clearly appealed to those in smaller communities, and his strength was greatest among those with the least education. With respect to income, his backers were more likely to come from the poorer strata than the more well-to-do, although he was slightly weaker among the lowest income class—under $3,000—than among the next highest. He was strongest among those in "service" jobs, a conglomerate which includes police, domestic servants and the military. Of the regular urban occupational classes, his support was highest among

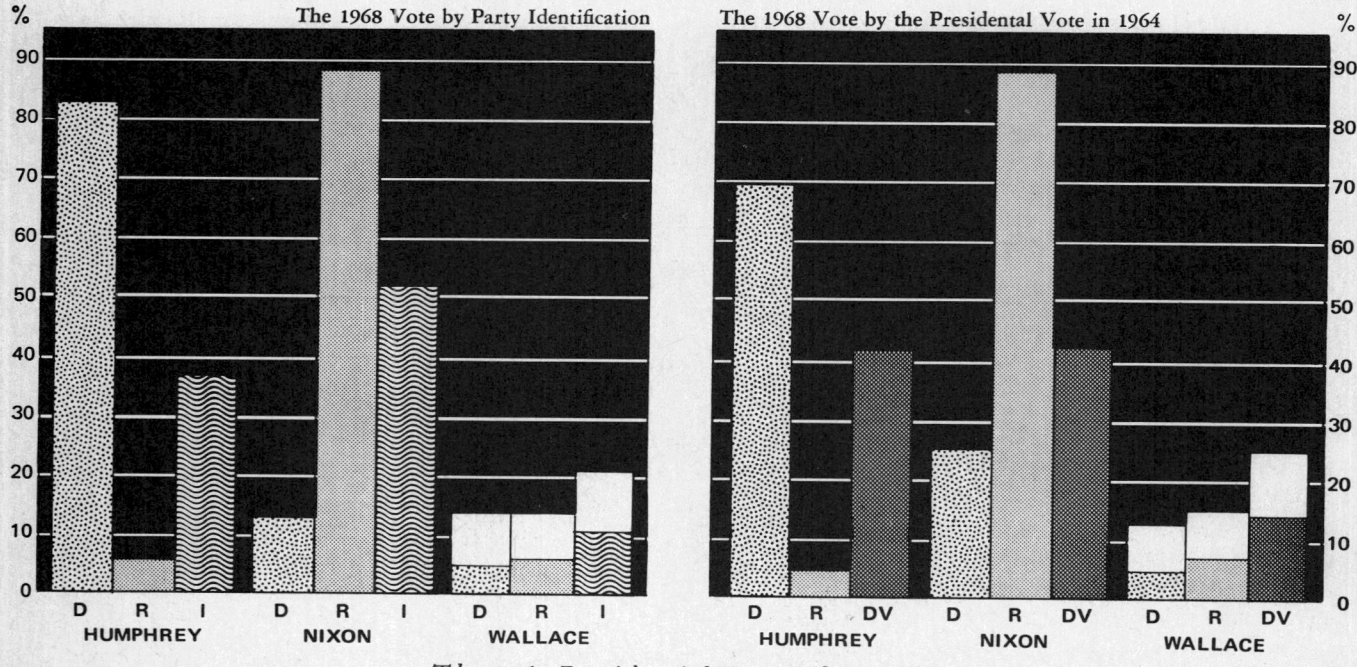

The 1968 Presidential Vote: The Non-South

The 1968 Presidential Vote: The South

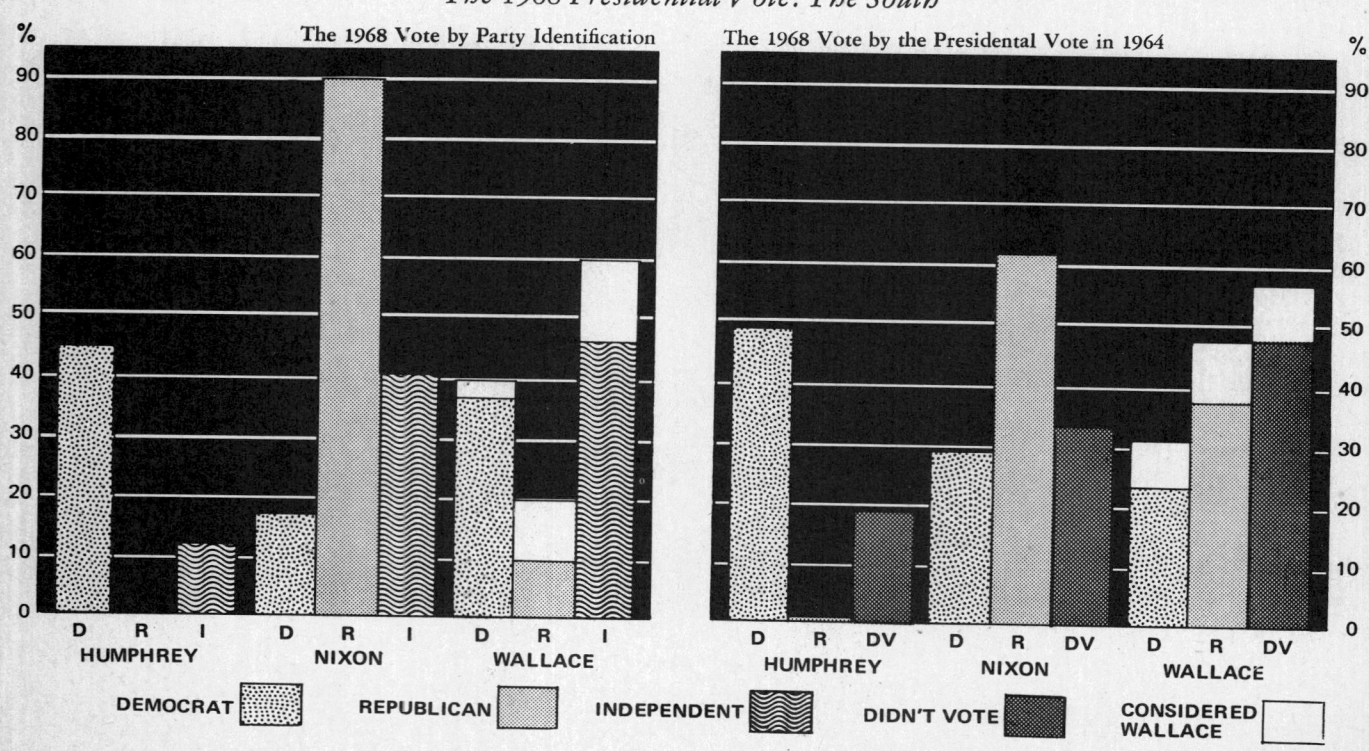

the unskilled, followed by the skilled, white collar workers, those in business and managerial pursuits, and professionals, in that order. The number of farmers voting for Wallace was relatively low, a phenomenon stemming from differences between farmers in the South and in the rest of the country. Among manual workers, Wallace was much weaker with union members than nonunionists.

Voting Patterns

The vote behavior with respect to other factors also corresponds in general to preelection predictions. Wallace was backed more heavily by men than by women, a pattern characteristically associated with radical movements, whether of the left or right. Surprisingly, young voters were more likely to prefer him than middle-aged and older ones, with the partial exception that voters in the 25- to 29-year-old category were a bit more likely to prefer Wallace than the 21- to 24-year-old age group. Religion also served to differentiate: Wallace received a higher proportion of the votes of Protestants than Catholics, a product of his strength in the predominantly Protestant South.

Viewed nationally, however, the pattern of support for Wallace is a bit deceiving since so much of his support was in the South. He carried five southern states and received a substantial vote in all the others, plus the border states. To a considerable extent, his movement in the South took on the character of a "preservatist" defense of southern institutions against the threat from the federal government. In most southern states, it was a major party candidacy. In the rest of the country, however, the Wallace movement was a small radical third party, organized around various extreme right-wing groups. While it obviously gave expression to racial concerns, it also included a number of other varieties of the disaffected. One would expect, therefore, differences in the types of voters to whom he appealed in the different sections. The variation in his support in the two sections is presented in graphs 1-4 and Tables 1 and 2.

The variations between the sections are apparent along a number of dimensions. Northern Wallace voters were more likely to come from the ranks of identified and committed Republicans than were those from the South. Thus in the South, a much larger proportion of people who were identified as Democrats (37 percent) than as Republicans (10 percent) voted for him. Conversely in the North, a slightly larger segment of the Republicans voted for him than did Democrats. This emphasis is reversed, however, with respect to the 1964 vote. In both sections, larger proportions of Goldwater voters opted for Wallace than did Johnson supporters. Relatively, however, he did better among the southern Goldwater voters. The seeming contradiction may be explained by the fact that Wallace did best among "independents," and that there were proportionately many more independents in the South than in the North. Southern independents presumably are people who have opted out of the Democratic party toward the right, many of whom voted for Goldwater in 1964 and Wallace in 1968. His greatest support, both North and South, of course, came from the ranks of those who did not vote in 1964. Almost half of the southern nonvoters in the 1964 election who voted in 1968 chose Wallace.

The effect of the social stratification variables were relatively similar in both parts of the country. In general, the better educated, the more well-to-do, and those in middle-class occupations were less likely to vote for Wallace than voters in the lower echelons.

As far as religion is concerned, nationally Wallace appeared to secure more support among Protestants than Catholics, but a sectional breakdown points up the fact that this was an artifact of the relatively small Catholic population in the South. Outside of the South, Wallace secured more support from Catholics than from Protestants. The pattern appears to be reversed in the South, but the number of Catholics in the sample is too small to sustain a reliable estimate. What is perhaps more significant than the Catholic-Protestant variation is the difference among the Protestant denominations. Wallace's greatest backing, North and South, came from Baptists, followed by "other," presumably mainly fundamentalist sects which have a history of disproportionately backing right-wing groups. Wallace, after all, became the protector of the "southern way of life" and the status of those who bear it, not only for southerners, but for southern migrants to the North. This, apart from education, is one significance of the disproportionate support of Wallace by northern Baptists.

As noted earlier, perhaps the most surprising finding of the polls was the consistent report by Gallup, Harris and the Michigan Survey Research Center that youth, whether defined as 21 to 24 or 21 to 29 years old, were more favorable to the third-party candidate than those in older age groups. Two special surveys of youth opinion also pointed in this direction. One was commissioned by *Fortune* and carried out by the Daniel Yankelovich organization among 718 young people aged 18 to 24 in October 1968. It revealed that among employed youth 25 percent were for Wallace, as compared to 23 for Humphrey, 31 for Nixon and 15 without a choice. Among college students, Wallace received 7 percent of the vote. A secondary analysis of this survey indicated that class and educational level differentiated this youth group as well. Thus 31 percent of young manual workers who were the sons of manual workers were for Wallace, as contrasted with but 6 percent among nonmanuals whose fathers were on the same side of the dividing line. A preelection survey by the Purdue Opinion Poll among a national sample of high school students, reported that Wallace had considerable strength among them as well: 22 percent, backing which came heavily from members of southern, and economically less affluent families.

This "shift to the right" among youth had first been detected among young southerners. Although various surveys had found a pattern of greater youth support for integration in the South during the forties and fifties, by the 1960's this finding had been inverted, according to two

1968 PRESIDENTIAL VOTING IN THE NON-SOUTH BY %

	Humphrey	Nixon	Wallace	Considered Wallace	Total Wallace Symp.
OCCUPATION					
Non-manual	42	53	5	5	10
Manual	49	42	9	13	22
Union family	57	34	9	16	25
Nonunion	39	52	9	8	17
EDUCATION					
Grade school or less	53	40	7	10	17
High school or less	43	49	7	9	17
Some college	43	52	5	4	9
INCOME					
less than $3,000	41	53	5	5	11
$3,000-$6,999	46	44	10	9	19
$7,000-$9,999	42	52	6	11	17
$10,000-$14,999	46	47	6	8	14
$15,000 plus	39	58	3	7	10
RELIGION					
Roman Catholic	53	39	8	9	17
Jewish	87	13	—	3	3
Protestant	34	53	6	10	15
Baptist	33	51	16	10	25
Methodist	32	65	3	10	13
Presbyterian	28	68	5	11	15
Lutheran	43	54	3	6	9
Episcopal	40	61	—	5	5
Others	31	59	9	13	22
SIZE OF PLACE					
Rural	37	56	7	11	20
2,500-49,999	43	52	5	6	11
50,000-499,999	44	51	6	5	10
500,000-999,999	46	45	9	6	16
1,000,000 plus	50	44	7	8	15
AGE					
21-25	54	34	13	7	20
26-29	35	54	11	6	17
30-49	43	49	8	14	22
50 plus	43	53	3	5	8
SEX					
Men	43	48	9	11	20
Women	45	51	5	6	11

1968 PRESIDENTIAL VOTING IN THE SOUTH BY %

	Humphrey	Nixon	Wallace	Considered Wallace	Total Wallace Symp.
OCCUPATION					
Non-manual	22	57	22	14	36
Manual	14	33	53	6	59
Union family	30	30	40	5	45
Nonunion	8	34	58	6	64
EDUCATION					
Grade school or less	23	28	49	8	57
High school or less	21	42	36	11	48
Some college	19	60	21	10	31
INCOME					
less than $3,000	27	30	43	8	51
$3,000-$6,999	18	39	44	5	48
$7,000-$9,999	17	42	42	12	54
$10,000-$14,999	23	63	15	13	28
$15,000 plus	24	62	15	15	29
RELIGION					
Roman Catholic	47	29	24	6	29
Jewish	—	—	—	—	—
Protestant	18	46	36	10	46
Baptist	13	43	45	11	56
Methodist	22	43	35	5	40
Presbyterian	10	76	14	14	29
Lutheran	—	—	—	—	—
Episcopal	—	—	—	—	—
Others	21	25	45	7	52
SIZE OF PLACE					
Rural	17	38	45	4	49
2,500-49,999	21	43	36	8	44
50,000-499,999	23	52	25	9	33
500,000-999,999	31	58	12	3	15
1,000,000 plus	—	—	—	—	—
AGE					
21-25	—	—	—	—	—
26-29	26	37	37	5	42
30-49	14	52	34	8	41
50 plus	26	41	33	10	43
SEX					
Men	24	39	37	11	48
Women	18	51	31	8	39

NORC polls reported by Paul Sheatsley and Herbert Hyman. They suggested that southern youth who grew up amid the tensions produced by the school integration battles reacted more negatively than the preceding generations who had not been exposed to such conflicts during their formative political years. And as the issue of government-enforced integration in the schools and neighborhoods spread to the North, white opinion in central city areas, which are usually inhabited by workers, also took on an increased racist character.

What has happened is that increasing numbers of white young people in the South and in many working-class districts of the North have been exposed in recent years to repeated discussions of the supposed threats to their schools and communities posed by integration. They have been reared in homes and neighborhoods where anti-Negro sentiments became increasingly common. Hence, while the upper-middle-class scions of liberal parents were being radicalized to the left by civil rights and Vietnam war issues, a sizeable segment of southern and northern working-class youth were being radicalized to the right. The consequence of such polarization can be seen in the very different behavior of the two groups in the 1968 election campaign.

The indications that the Wallace movement drew heavily among youth are congruent with the evidence from various studies of youth and student politics that suggests young people are disposed to support the more extreme or idealistic version of the politics dominant within their social strata. In Europe, extremist movements both of the right and left have been more likely to secure the support of the young than the democratic parties of the center. Being less committed to existing institutions and parties than older people, and being less inured to the need to compromise in order to attain political objectives, youth are disproportionately attracted to leaders and movements which promise to resolve basic problems quickly and in an absolute fashion.

So much for those who actually voted for Wallace.

Equally significant are those who supported Wallace in the campaign but didn't vote for him. Presumably many who shifted from Wallace did so because they thought he could not win, not because they would not have liked to see him as president. This is the uneasiness of the "lost vote." There is also the "expressive" factor, the votes in polls which do not count. Casting a straw vote for Wallace was clearly one method of striking a generalized note of dissatisfaction in certain directions. But since total considerations take over in the voting booth, the nature of the defections becomes one way to measure these dissatisfactions in various quarters. On another level, there is the factor of the social reinforcements that may or may not exist in the voter's milieu and are important for the ability of a third-party candidate to hold his base of support under attack.

The Defectors

In general, Wallace lost most heavily among groups and in areas where he was weak to begin with. Individuals in these groups would find less support for their opinions among their acquaintances, and also would be more likely to feel that a Wallace vote was wasted. In the South, however, almost four-fifths of all those who ever considered voting for Wallace did in fact vote for him. In the North, he lost over half of his initial support: only 43 percent of his original supporters cast a ballot for him. Similarly, Baptists and the small "other" Protestant sects were more likely to remain in the Wallace camp than less pro-Wallace religious groups.

There were certain significant differences in the pattern of defections with respect to social stratification. In the South, middle-class supporters of Wallace were much more likely to move away from him as the campaign progressed. He wound up with 90 percent of his preelection support among southern manual workers, and 61 percent among those in nonmanual occupations. In the North, however, Wallace retained a larger proportion of his middle-class backers (52 percent) than of his working-class followers (42 percent).

The data from the Gallup survey suggest, then, that the very extensive campaign of trade union leaders to reduce Wallace support among their membership actually had an effect in the North. Almost two-thirds (64 percent) of northern trade union members who had backed Wallace initially *did not* vote for him, while over half of those southern unionist workers (52 percent) who had been for him earlier voted for him on Election Day. A similar pattern occurred with respect to the two other measures of stratification, education and income. Wallace retained more backing among the better educated and more affluent of his northern supporters, while in the South these groups were much more likely to have defected by Election Day than the less educated and less privileged.

The variations in the class background of the defectors in the different sections of the country may be a function of varying exposures to reinforcing and cross-pressure stimuli in their respective environments. On the whole we would guess that middle-class Wallace supporters in the North came disproportionately from persons previously committed to extreme rightist ideology and affiliations. Wallace's support among the northern middle-class corresponds in size to that given to the John Birch Society in opinion polls. If we assume that most people who were pro-Birch were pro-Wallace, then presumably Wallace did not break out of this relatively small group. And this group, which was heavily involved in a reinforcing environment, could have been expected to stick with him. In the South, on the other hand, he began with considerable middle-class support gained from people who had been behind the effort to create a conservative Republican party in that section. The majority of them had backed Barry Goldwater in 1964. This large group of affluent southern Wallace-ites encompassed many who had not been involved in extremist activities. And it would seem that the efforts of the southern conservative Republicans (headed by Strom Thurmond) to convince them that a vote for Wallace would help Humphrey were effective. Conversely, among northern manual workers, an inclination to vote for Wallace placed men outside the dominant pattern within their class.

Back to the Home Party

Which of the other two candidates the Wallace defectors voted for clearly depended on background. Three-fifths of those who shifted away from Wallace during the campaign ended up voting for Nixon. But those Wallace backers who decided to vote for one of the major party candidates almost invariably reverted to their traditional party affiliation. The pattern is even clearer when southern Democrats are eliminated. Among the 29 northern Democrats in our sample who defected from Wallace, 90 percent voted for Hubert Humphrey. Humphrey recruited from among the less educated and poorer Wallace voters, Nixon from the more affluent and better educated.

The pattern of shifting among the Wallace voters points up our assumption that Wallace appealed to two very different groups: economic conservatives concerned with repudiating the welfare state, and less affluent supporters of the welfare state who were affected by issues of racial integration and "law and order." As some individuals in each of these groups felt motivated to change their vote, they opted for the candidate who presumably stood closer to their basic economic concerns. The data also point up the difficulty of building a new movement encompassing people with highly disparate sentiments and interests.

After specifying what kinds of groups voted for whom, the most interesting question still remains, especially with respect to deviant and extremist political movements such as Wallace's: What creates the differentials within each of

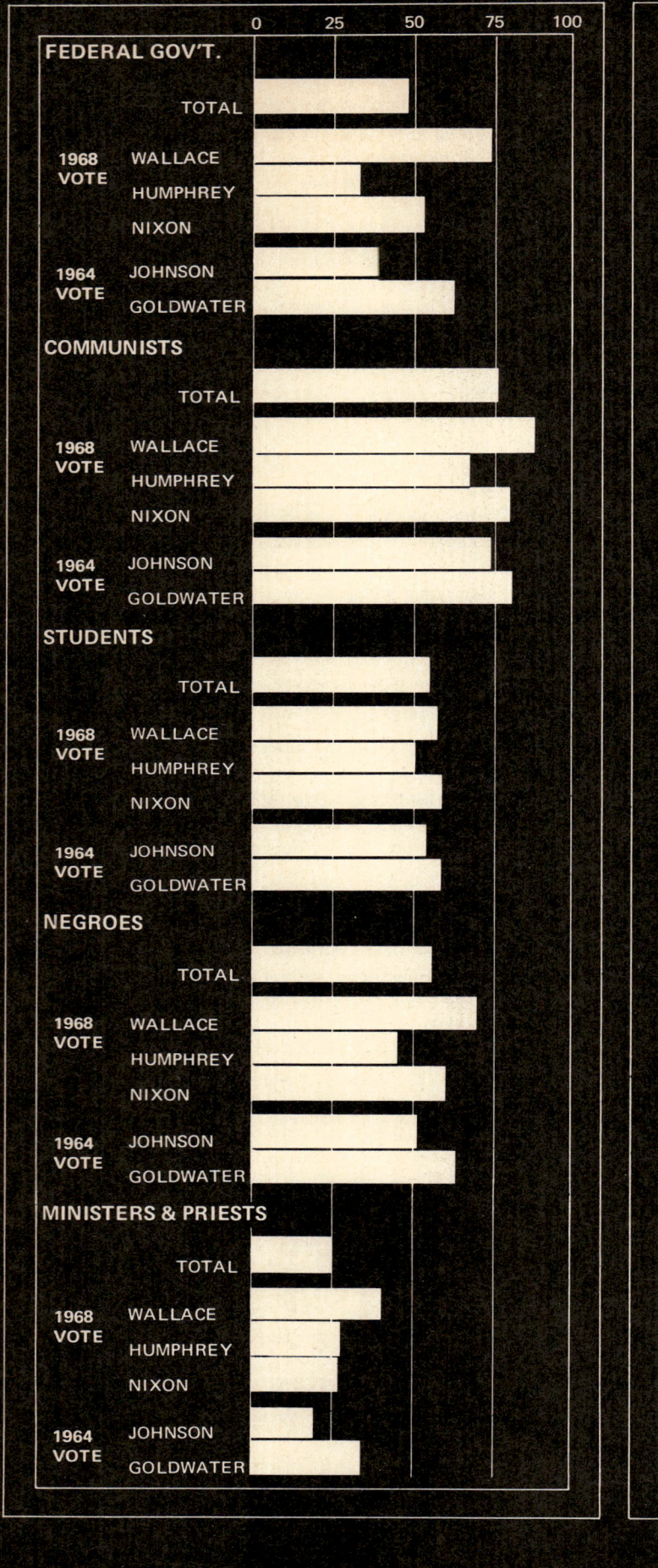

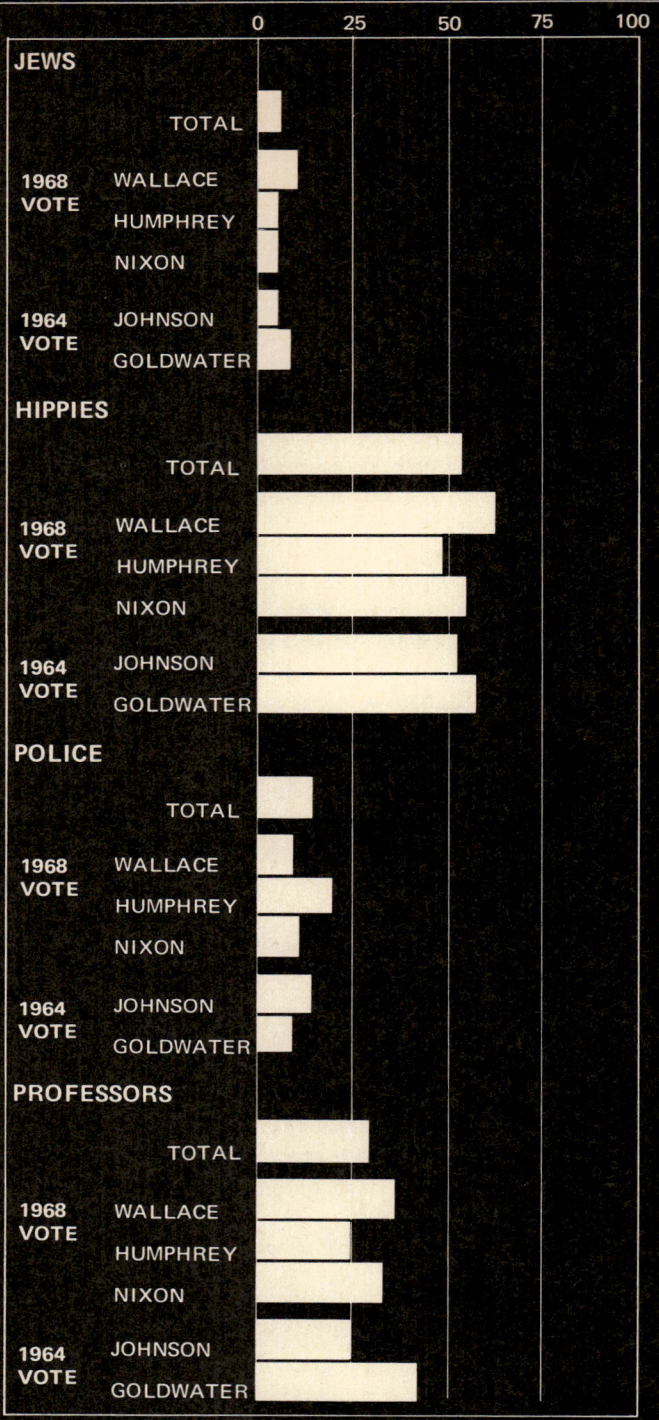

"Which Groups are Responsible for Trouble in the Country?"

1968 and 1964 voters single out "Enemies of the American Way" (by percentage).

FEDERAL GOV'T.
- TOTAL
- 1968 VOTE: WALLACE, HUMPHREY, NIXON
- 1964 VOTE: JOHNSON, GOLDWATER

COMMUNISTS
- TOTAL
- 1968 VOTE: WALLACE, HUMPHREY, NIXON
- 1964 VOTE: JOHNSON, GOLDWATER

STUDENTS
- TOTAL
- 1968 VOTE: WALLACE, HUMPHREY, NIXON
- 1964 VOTE: JOHNSON, GOLDWATER

NEGROES
- TOTAL
- 1968 VOTE: WALLACE, HUMPHREY, NIXON
- 1964 VOTE: JOHNSON, GOLDWATER

MINISTERS & PRIESTS
- TOTAL
- 1968 VOTE: WALLACE, HUMPHREY, NIXON
- 1964 VOTE: JOHNSON, GOLDWATER

JEWS
- TOTAL
- 1968 VOTE: WALLACE, HUMPHREY, NIXON
- 1964 VOTE: JOHNSON, GOLDWATER

HIPPIES
- TOTAL
- 1968 VOTE: WALLACE, HUMPHREY, NIXON
- 1964 VOTE: JOHNSON, GOLDWATER

POLICE
- TOTAL
- 1968 VOTE: WALLACE, HUMPHREY, NIXON
- 1964 VOTE: JOHNSON, GOLDWATER

PROFESSORS
- TOTAL
- 1968 VOTE: WALLACE, HUMPHREY, NIXON
- 1964 VOTE: JOHNSON, GOLDWATER

FEDERAL GOV'T.

		0	25	50	75	100
	TOTAL					
1968 VOTE SOUTH	WALLACE					
	HUMPHREY					
	NIXON					
1968 VOTE NON-SOUTH	WALLACE					
	HUMPHREY					
	NIXON					

COMMUNISTS

		0	25	50	75	100
	TOTAL					
1968 VOTE SOUTH	WALLACE					
	HUMPHREY					
	NIXON					
1968 VOTE NON-SOUTH	WALLACE					
	HUMPHREY					
	NIXON					

STUDENTS

		0	25	50	75	100
	TOTAL					
1968 VOTE SOUTH	WALLACE					
	HUMPHREY					
	NIXON					
1968 VOTE NON-SOUTH	WALLACE					
	HUMPHREY					
	NIXON					

NEGROES

		0	25	50	75	100
	TOTAL					
1968 VOTE SOUTH	WALLACE					
	HUMPHREY					
	NIXON					
1968 VOTE NON-SOUTH	WALLACE					
	HUMPHREY					
	NIXON					

MINISTERS & PRIESTS

		0	25	50	75	100
	TOTAL					
1968 VOTE SOUTH	WALLACE					
	HUMPHREY					
	NIXON					
1968 VOTE NON-SOUTH	WALLACE					
	HUMPHREY					
	NIXON					

JEWS

		0	25	50	75	100
	TOTAL					
1968 VOTE SOUTH	WALLACE					
	HUMPHREY					
	NIXON					
1968 VOTE NON-SOUTH	WALLACE					
	HUMPHREY					
	NIXON					

HIPPIES

		0	25	50	75	100
	TOTAL					
1968 VOTE SOUTH	WALLACE					
	HUMPHREY					
	NIXON					
1968 VOTE NON-SOUTH	WALLACE					
	HUMPHREY					
	NIXON					

POLICE

		0	25	50	75	100
	TOTAL					
1968 VOTE SOUTH	WALLACE					
	HUMPHREY					
	NIXON					
1968 VOTE NON-SOUTH	WALLACE					
	HUMPHREY					
	NIXON					

PROFESSORS

		0	25	50	75	100
	TOTAL					
1968 VOTE SOUTH	WALLACE					
	HUMPHREY					
	NIXON					
1968 VOTE NON-SOUTH	WALLACE					
	HUMPHREY					
	NIXON					

"Which Groups are Responsible for Trouble in the Country?"

Southern and Non-Southern voters in 1968 single out "Enemies of the American Way" (by percentage).

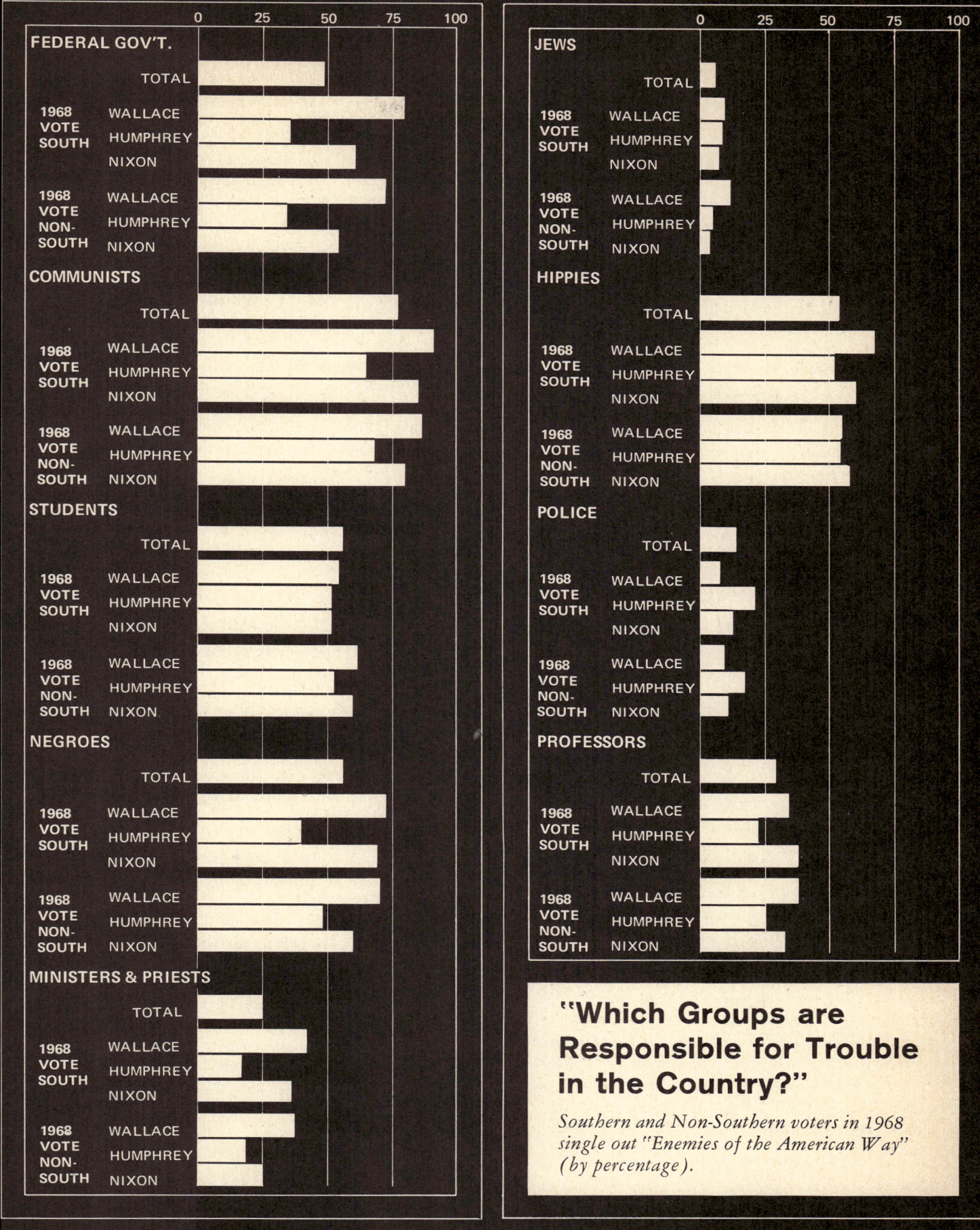

these groups? Why, in other words, do some members of a group vote for a particular candidate, but not others? Quite clearly, members of the same heuristic group or class may vary greatly in their perception of the world, and will therefore differ as to political choice. Since candidates do differ in their ideology and position on particular issues, we should expect that the values of the electorate should help determine which segments of a particular strata end up voting one way or another.

Data collected by the Louis Harris Poll permit us to analyze the connection between political attitudes and voter choice in 1968. The Harris data are derived from a special reanalysis of the results of a number of surveys conducted during the campaign that were prepared by the Harris organization for the American Jewish Committee. Based on 16,915 interviews, it points up consistent variations. The question that best indicated differing political attitudes among those voting for a given candidate was one in the Harris survey that asked, "Which groups are responsible for trouble in the country?" Choices ranged from the federal government to Communists, students, professors, Jews and others. The relevant responses are presented on the preceding pages.

The findings of the Harris organization clearly differentiate the supporters of the different candidates in 1968 and 1964. On most items, the rank order of opinions goes consistently from right to left, from Wallace to Goldwater to Nixon to Johnson to Humphrey. That is, the Wallace supporters show the most right-wing opinions, while the Humphrey ones are most left. As a group those who voted for Goldwater in 1964 are somewhat more "preservatist" than the Nixon supporters in 1968. There is, of course, a considerable overlap. Since none of these items bear on attitudes toward the welfare state, what they attest to is the disdain which rightists feel towards groups identified with social changes they dislike.

The Wallace supporters differ most from the population as a whole with respect to their feelings toward the federal government, Negroes, the Ku Klux Klan, and most surprisingly, "ministers and priests." Although Wallace himself did not devote much attention to attacking the liberal clergy, his followers were seemingly more bothered by their activities than by those of professors. Although the electorate as a whole was inclined to see "students" as a major source of trouble, Wallace backers hardly differed from the supporters of the two other candidates in their feelings. As far as we can judge from these results, they confirm the impression that Wallace appealed strongly to people who identified their distress with changes in race relations, with federal interference, and with changes in religious morality. It is of interest that the Wallace supporters in the South and those in the non-South project essentially the same pattern. The southern differential is very slight with respect to blaming Negroes, still slight but higher in blaming clergymen, and higher yet in blaming the federal government.

Fears that Wallace would convert his following into an extraparliamentary influence on the government and terrorize opponents by taking to the streets—fears based on statements that Wallace himself made during the campaign—have thus far proved unwarranted. Wallace seems largely concerned with maintaining his electoral base for a possible presidential campaign in 1972. The effort to continue control of the party from Montgomery seems to be dedicated to this end.

The Movement in '72

The existence of local electoral parties, even those willing to follow Wallace's lead completely, clearly poses a great problem for him. Wallace's electoral following is evidently much greater than can be mobilized behind the local unknown candidates of the American Party. To maintain the party organizations, they must nominate men for various offices. Yet should such people continue to secure tiny votes, as is likely in most parts of the country, Wallace may find his image as a mass leader severely injured. He seems to recognize this, and though concerned with keeping control over the party organization, he has also stressed the difference between the "movement" and the "party," describing the two as "separate entities" which agree on "purposes and aims." Wallace is emphatic about this: "The *movement* will be here in 1972. The *movement* is solvent and it will be active." Speaking at the Virginia convention of the American Party in mid-July of 1969, he said, "A new party ought to go very slow. It ought to crawl before it walks. It ought to nominate a candidate only if he has a chance to be elected." In Tulsa he again warned his followers to move slowly, if at all, in nominating congressional and local candidates. He argued that if he were elected president in the future he "wouldn't have any trouble getting support from Congress, because most of its [major party] members were for the things he's for."

One aspect of the nonparty "movement" may be the reported expansion of the Citizens Councils of America, whose national headquarters is in Jackson, Mississippi. Its administrator, William J. Simmons, helped direct Wallace's presidential campaign in Mississippi, where he received 65 percent of the vote. In June, 1969, Simmons said:

> There has been no erosion in Wallace strength. Wallace articulates the hopes and views of over 99 percent of our members. This state is not enchanted with Nixon, and Wallace sentiment is very strong indeed.

He also reported that the Council, mainly concerned with the maintenance of segregation in the schools had expanded "as a result of backlash generated by campus riots and better grassroots organizational work." The impetus of the Wallace campaign also had obviously helped. The Citizens Councils remain one reservoir of future organizational strength for Wallace.

Moreover, Wallace has attempted to maintain his ties to other groups whose members had backed him in 1968. The Birch Society's principal campaign during 1969 has been against sex education and pornography; Wallace has devoted a considerable part of his talks during the year to the subject. In addition he publicly embraced for the first time the ultraconservative "Christian Crusade" of Billy James Hargis by attending its annual convention.

In his speeches and *Newsletter* Wallace has retained the same combination of "preservatist" moralism and populist economic issues that characterized his presidential campaign. On the one hand, he continues to emphasize the issues of "law and order," "campus radicalism," "military failures in Vietnam," and "the need for local control of schools." On the other hand, speaking in Tulsa, one of the principal centers of the oil industry, he called for tax reform that would benefit the little man, adding that "the 27½ percent oil depletion allowance ought to be looked into." He argued that we must "shift the [tax] burden to the upper-class millionaires, billionaires and tax-exempt foundations." Since this kind of rhetoric flies in the face of the deep-dyed economic conservatives among his supporters, such as the Birchers, it is clear that Wallace's cafeteria of appeals still suffers from the same sort of contradictions that characterized it in 1968, contradictions, it might be added, which have characterized most other right-wing extremist movements in American history.

Righteous Rightists

Another problem that Wallace faces comes from supporters who want to build an extremist movement, rather than an electoral organization for one man's candidacy. This can be seen in the activities of an autonomous youth organization, the National Youth Alliance, formed by those active in Youth for Wallace. As of September, 1969, the NYA claimed 3,000 dues-paying members recruited from the 15,000-person mailing list of the Youth for Wallace student organizations. The group has a more absolutist and militant character than either adult party, and it is much more unashamedly racist. Members wear an "inequality button" emblazoned with the mathematical symbol of inequality. Among other things, the Alliance advocates "white studies" curricula in colleges and universities. According to its national organizer, Louis T. Byers, "The purpose of these will be to demonstrate the nature of mankind. The equality myth will be exploded forever." In an article describing its objectives the then-national vice-president, Dennis C. McMahon, stated that NYA "is an organization with the determination to liquidate the enemies of the American people on the campus and in the community." The tone of this pro-Wallace youth group sounds closer to that of classic fascism than any statements previously made by Wallace's associates. As McMahon wrote,

The National Youth Alliance is an organization that intends to bury the red front once and for all. . . . The NYA is made up of dedicated self-sacrificing young people who are ready to fight, and die if necessary, for the sacred cause.

. . . Now is the time for the Right Front terror to descend on the wretched liberals. In short, the terror of the Left will be met with the greater terror of the Right. . . .

Tar and feathers will be our answer to the pot pusher and these animals will no longer be allowed to prowl and hunt for the minds of American students.

. . . A bright future full of conquest lies ahead of us . . . Soon the NYA will become a household word and the Left will be forced to cower in the sewers underground as they hear the marching steps of the NYA above them.

The racism of NYA leaders includes approval, if not advocacy, of virulent anti-Semitism. Its national headquarters in Washington distributes literature by Francis Parker Yockey, including his book *Imperium,* which defines Jews, Negroes, Indians and other minorities as "parasites" on the Western world. The five members of its adult advisory board have all been involved in anti-Semitic activities. Two of them, Revilo P. Oliver and Richard B. Cotten, were forced out of the Birch Society because of their overt racist and anti-Semitic views. A third, retired Rear Admiral John Crommelein, ran for president on the anti-Semitic National States Rights Party ticket in 1960; while a fourth, retired Marine Lieutenant General Pedro A. Del Valle, is an officer of the Christian Educational Association, which publishes the overtly anti-Semitic paper *Common Sense.* The fifth member of the board, Austin J. App, former English professor at LaSalle College, is a contributing editor to the anti-Semitic magazine *American Mercury.*

Perhaps most interesting of all the problems that Wallace will have to deal with is the fact that the national chairman of his American Party, T. Coleman Andrews, has publicly advocated the Birch Society's version of that hoary international conspiracy, the historic plot of the Illuminati. The Illuminati, which was an organization of Enlightenment intellectuals formed in Bavaria in 1776, and dissolved according to historical record in 1785, has figured in the conspiratorial theories of assorted American rightwing movements as the insiders behind every effort for religious liberalism, economic and social reform since the 1790s. In recent times, both Father Coughlin, the foremost right-wing extremist of the 1930s, and Robert Welch, the head of the Birch Society, have explained various threats to "the American way" from the French Revolution to the Communist movement, as well as the behavior of most key officials of the government, as reflecting the power of this secret cabal of satanically clever plotters. In a newspaper interview following the establishment of the American party in May, Andrews bluntly announced:

I believe in the conspiratorial theory of History. . . . [The Birch Society has been] responsible, respectable. . . . [R]ecently, the Birch Society has begun to prosper. People are beginning to see that its original theories were right. . . . There is an international conspiracy.

Though George Wallace himself has never publicly stated a belief in the conspiracy of the Illuminati (he prefers to talk about the role of Communists, pseudo-intellectuals and the Council on Foreign Relations) the formal organization of his personally controlled national party is headed by a man who has no such hesitation. On May 26, 1969, Wallace formally sanctioned the American Party as the political arm of the movement and said that if he ran for president again it would be under the American Party's banners.

However, while the pulls towards conspiracy theory and towards ideological racism are evident in the background, the logic of the Wallace-ite movement and its future as a mass movement obviously rest on other foundations. S. M. Miller points out that many had been shocked by "the attraction of George Wallace as a presidential candidate to a large number of union members . . . racism appeared to be rampant in the working class." When the vote came, however, racism seemed to have receded before economic concerns. Their disaffection remains nevertheless. As Miller writes, "About half of American families are above the poverty line but below the adequacy level. This group, neither poor nor affluent, composed not only of blue-collar workers but also of many white-collar workers, is hurting and neglected." It is the members of this group that the Wallace-ite movement must grow on if it is to grow, not out of their ideological racism as much as out of their general sense of neglected decline.

Tempered Extremism

Whether the Wallace movement itself will have returned to full or fuller electoral vigor by 1972 depends on a number of factors which emerge from an examination of America's right-wing extremist past. Determinative—not just for the Wallace movement but for any extremist movement—will be the larger historical circumstances. The disaffection of the white working-class and lower middle-class has been noted; if that disaffection grows, and *at the same time* the pressures of an increasingly disaffected black population increase, the soil will of course be fertile for a George Wallace kind of movement. It is the pressure of the emergent black population that provides an essentially preservatist thrust to the social and economic strains of the vulnerable whites. Whether the major political parties can absorb these concomitant pressures in some pragmatic fashion as they have in the past is another conditional factor, which is also partly dependent on historical development.

Wallace, however, is clearly preparing to use another issue in 1972, the responsibility for American defeat in Vietnam. Like others on the right, he has repeatedly argued that if the U.S. government really wanted to win the war, it could do so easily, given America's enormous superiority in resources and weapons technology. Consequently, the only reason we have not won is political: those who have controlled our strategy consciously do not want to win. But, he argued recently, if it "should be that Washington has committed itself to a policy of American withdrawal, irrespective of reciprocal action on the part of the enemy, in effect acknowledging defeat for our forces, which is inconceivable, we feel that such withdrawal should be swiftly accomplished so that casualty losses may be held to a minimum." And he left on October 30 for a three-week tour of Vietnam and Southeast Asia, announcing that he would run in 1972 if Vietnam were turned over to the Communists "in effect or in substance." Clearly Wallace hopes to run in 1972 on the issue that American boys have died needlessly, that they were stabbed in the back by Lyndon Johnson and Richard Nixon.

In order to do so, however, Wallace must keep his movement alive. As he well recognizes, it is subject to the traditional organizational hazards of such a movement, notably fragmentation, and the ascendancy of overt extremist tendencies that will alienate the more respectable leadership and support. During the year following the election, Wallace has performed as though he understood these hazards well. He has avoided expressions of overt extremism. He has attempted to keep his organization formally separated from the fringe groups and more rabid extremists, even those who were in open support of him. In a letter sent to key Wallace lieutenants around the country, asking about the local leadership that might be involved in the next Wallace campaign, James T. Hardin, administrative assistant to Wallace, carefully emphasized that "perhaps of greatest importance, we would like your opinion as to those who demonstrated neither ability nor capability to work with others and who were, in fact, a detriment to the campaign. . . ."

Whether Wallace can succeed in avoiding the organizational hazards of which he seems aware, and whether historical circumstances will be favorable, is of course problematical. But whether his particular movement survives or not, George Wallace has put together and further revealed the nature of those basic elements which must comprise an effective right-wing extremist movement in America.

December 1969

SUGGESTED READINGS

The Conservative Tradition in American Thought edited by Jay A. Siglend (New York: Putnam, 1964).

A Populist Reader edited by George B. Tindall (New York: Harper and Row, 1966). Two recent anthologies of documents and commentaries elucidating two divergent strains in American political thinking.

The Politics of Mass Society by William Kornhauser (Glencoe, Ill.: The Free Press, 1959).

8 Style & Substance in Sociology

Sociology is one of several disciplines that concerns itself with the study of man and his society. Along with the other social sciences, the biological sciences, and literature and the arts, sociology is committed to increasing our understanding of the human animal living in groups. The special focus of sociology is on man's relations with other men, the enduring social relations that he creates, and the changing form of these social structures. As we have seen earlier in this book, sociologists concentrate their research efforts on groups, associations, communities, institutions, or even societies as a whole. In other words, man in interaction, not man alone, is the essential focus for this discipline, for, although each man lives his own personal life, he has become a human being by his membership in the group that socialized him, and he lives through his years in collectivities of many sizes and sorts. Society would not exist without individuals, but there would be no human beings if there were no social life.

Sociology has turned its attention to the study of group life in a systematic way with the aim of accumulating a body of knowledge about society that is more reliable than the common-sense observations made by people themselves in the course of ordinary living. There is a great deal of current and accumulated wisdom about how society works—some of which is mythical, some of which is dependable and true. It is well to remember, however, as Kenneth E. Boulding points out in his article "Ecology and Environment" that depending entirely on personal experience for understanding the world is dangerous because individuals can sample only a minute part of it. Nevertheless, making precise observations, gathering information from wider sources, and using techniques of scientific measurement, as sociologists attempt to do, should result in less biased and unreliable findings about social life. When sociologists study social life in this way, they also aim to draw out some generalizations from their studies of specific groups that will permit them to support some broader notions about how people interact in comparable situations. These generalizations from empirical data can also contribute to building theories of social life on the basis of tested propositions in which we may feel a good deal of confidence. It should be kept in mind, however, that sociology and the rest of the social sciences are very young disciplines; there is honest disagreement over findings, and the "laws" of social life are not at the stage of discovery equal to that of the physical and biological sciences.

Doing Sociology

The essays by Raymond Mack on "Science as a Frame of Reference" and "Intellectual Strategies and Research Tactics" develop two important themes in sociology. In the first, the characteristics of the scientific method are defined as they are practiced commonly by scientists from all fields of study, whether they be working in the low temperature physicist's underground laboratory, the plant biologist's greenhouse, or the nursery school under observation by a psychologist. The techniques of research done by these scientists may differ radically, but they share a commitment to observing and interpreting what they see as objectively as possible and submitting their findings to correction and retesting by other scientists. As any discipline approaches the ideals of scientific practice more closely, the society in which scientists work makes use of scientific findings in practical ways.

While the sciences share a logical-philosophical frame of reference, they develop special techniques of study appropriate to the things being studied. In his piece on "Intellectual Strategies and Research Tactics" Mack gives an insider's view of how a sociologist goes about tackling a research problem. In the process we are let in on a sociologist's reasoning that underlies the selection of particular research tools. He used a number of them—the study of past and present documents, participant observation, and informal interviews. We see how involved a sociologist becomes, and must become, in the life of the society he is studying in order to arrive at any deeper understanding of it than an ordinary observer. Particularly, we see that he enters the society with well-formulated questions in mind and armed with findings from other studies; these questions, based on knowledge from societies previously studied, serve both as guidelines for observation, propositions to be tested, and the basis for accumulating valid knowledge about society.

Style

Social science has a peculiar difference with respect to the physical and biological sciences in the nature of its subject matter: the objects studied are people who talk back, and who have private lives and group interests that they do not necessarily wish to open up to research. If the people being studied feel that the research findings may not benefit them or might even hurt them, there is no good reason for them to cooperate in giving information—in fact, they may make themselves inaccessible or give misinformation. Hans Toch and Peter Rossi approach this knotty problem of the nature of social-science subject matter from two interrelated, if distinctive, points. In a discussion of the advantages of involving the subjects of the study themselves in the research project, Hans Toch presents a specific and unusual case of bringing the people studied into the study process in his article "The Convict as Researcher." Peter Rossi points out that cooperation between administrators of social-action programs with researchers who are involved in testing the results of their programs is good as long as the findings are positive but deteriorate when they are negative. In a further treatment of the relationship between research workers and their subjects, Herbert C. Kelman questions the ethics of researchers who have neglected to protect the welfare of subjects of experimental investigations in his article "Deception in Social Research."

The research efforts of sociologists are in demand more and more by members of society who seek answers to problems encountered in every area of social life. While some sociologists feel that the discipline should spend its energies upon

Style & Substance in Sociology

becoming scientific by perfecting methodological rigor, another strong movement is underway toward making sociology useful to society. As soon as knowledge is applied to the solution of practical problems or toward the formulation of public policy, the problem of whose interests are being served arises. When such powerful clients as the Department of Defense and the office of the president of the United States employ sociologists to do specific research, we know that established institutions and organizations are making use of sociology in some fashion. Sociologists, however, are sensitive to the possibility that these institutions' definition of their research problems may deflect them from a free and critical appraisal of the established social order. Lee Rainwater and William F. Yancey raise the issue of the practical use of social-science findings in "Black Families and the White House." Irving Louis Horowitz gives an analysis of the contents and implications of a confidential report on how social-science research can benefit the Defense Department in his article "Social Science Yogis and Military Commissars." In his article on the Violence Commission, Jerome Skolnick tries to assess what effects, if any, social scientists on the research staffs of presidential commissions have on the final reports of these commissions.

As the articles in the final section make clear, social science is as much a series of recommendations for action, as it is a reflection on the construction of the social world. Therefore, the policy recommendations provided by sociologists to government officials, health and welfare practitioners, army officers, revolutionaries, and others is at least as important in the evolution of the sociological culture as any specific set of findings. For as these articles also make clear, sociology provides legitimation for policy decisions, whether or not it provides exact scientific statements about the things discussed. Thus, whether black families are in truth substantially matriarchal or not, the assumption that they are provides a source for certain government policies that either reinforce or resist such social structures. Thus, the style of sociology leads directly into the nature of human values—what in a society is worth preserving, and what requires urgent changing.

When all is said and done, then, sociology is not simply a series of methodological exercises, and not even a set of immutable principles that guide men in the study of their society. It is something at once more modest and more ambitious than either methods or principles. That something may be called *style*. It is a way of looking at the world and its problems, whether those problems affect individuals or whole civilizations. It is an alternative to other modes of explaining behavior, such as psychology and biology, or a theory of mind and a theory of instincts. Sociology is therefore as much a way of viewing everyday events as it is the scientific study of those events. There are those who claim that even were the scientific status of sociology completely called into question, the worth of sociology would remain intact, since the "stylistic" aspects as herein understood have a validity in the explanation of behavior that is over and above any theory of verification and evidence.

While one does not have to adopt such an extreme view, or exclude from a purview of explanation the life of the mind or the life of the private self, it is indeed the case that the revolution that sociology has helped establish is directly linked to its ability to explain behavior as a consequence of social conditions and social interactions. In this sense, the style of sociology helps anchor a doctrine of social solutions in the external relations men have to each other and to their institutions, rather than toward changes in personal and private activities. Thus, sociology as a style offers basic guidelines to seek out ways of changing the social system, irrespective of the "immutability" or "malleability" of human nature. For whatever else we have learned from the study of society, it is that it changes much more rapidly than people—and that, in fact, these changes are often the prelude for changes in the human personality and the cultural tradition. This capacity of society to change is both the aim and the opportunity of those dedicated to the study of human societies.

Ecology & Environment

KENNETH E. BOULDING

What can we know and teach about social systems?

Recently I came upon the reassuring news that the year 1910 was a crucial one in human history because this was the year when the medical profession began to do more good than harm. I wonder whether the teaching profession has reached this watershed yet. I am almost certain that government hasn't; every time Congress adjourns I sigh with relief that a damaging process has been temporarily suspended. Yet, as a teacher, I must ask whether I am doing any better.

With respect to doing better than Congress, let that be as it may. But with respect to doing better than past performance, teaching could and must be improved—of this I am sure. My thesis here is that the principal task of education in this day is to convey from one generation to the next a rich image of the total earth, that is, the idea of the earth as a total system.

We can start with the concept of the earth as a series of approximately concentric spheres: the lithosphere, the hydrosphere, the atmosphere, the biosphere and finally the sociosphere, or (more awkwardly) the anthroposphere. This last, of course, is the sphere of man and all his activities, and in our time it increasingly dominates all the others, for good and ill. Thanks to it, the evolution of the elements is now continuing where it seems to have left off four or six billion years ago. Thanks to it, the evolution of life seems on the point of being purposefully altered, as man gets his busy little fingers ever more deeply into the business of genetic programming. This is the kind of world we have to prepare children for.

Toward a Unified Social Science

If we look closely at the various social sciences, it becomes clear that they are all studying the same thing and are all operating at the same systems level. This is not true of all the sciences: the crystallographer studies the world at a different systems level from that of the physiologist and the physiologist from that of the social scientist. But the economist, the political scientist, the anthropologist, the sociologist and the social psychologist, even the historian and the human geographer, are all really studying the same thing, which is the sociosphere, that is, the three billion human beings, all their inputs, outputs, interactions, organizations, communications and transactions.

The different social scientists, of course, study the sociosphere from different points of view. We also carve up the sets of organizations and institutions: economists study banks, anthropologists tribes, political scientists governments, sociologists families and so on. In this matter we should do some trading around. It would be fun to have anthropologists study banking on the ground that bankers are really a savage tribe. The economist has already been moving in on the family, which we call a spending unit. Political scientists have already begun to look at the political structure of the corporation, and the game theorists have even begun to move in on moral philosophy. All this is much to the good, but it has not yet affected our teaching very much, and the way we divide up the field can easily result in a misapprehension by students who do not see that all institutions are part of the totality.

In short, I agree with several observers that we are moving very rapidly toward a unified social science, simply because we are all coming to realize that the sociosphere itself is a unity and offers a single system to be studied. This does not deny the usefulness of such abstractions as economic systems, the international system or the integrative system, which is that aspect of the sociosphere which deals with such matters as status, community, identity, legitimacy, loyalty and love. We must somehow manage to teach the students that all these systems have a certain structure and dynamics of their own, that they also all interact very strongly with each other and that they are all indeed abstractions from a total system of reality.

What I am arguing for is, frankly, a general systems approach to education. But I think of general systems not so much as a body of doctrine as a way of looking at things which permits the perception of the world as a totality and fosters communication among the specialized disciplines.

A system can be defined as anything which is not chaos, and by this definition earth is clearly a system in spite of large random elements. The task of learning is to perceive what is chaos and what is not chaos in the world. It is important both to perceive order where it exists and not to perceive it where it does not, for that leads us into superstition.

The Dynamics of Systems

All real systems are dynamic; that is, they exist in four dimensions, three of space and one of time. What we are trying to do in the learning process is to try to perceive the continuing patterns in this four-dimensional solid. This is really what education is all about.

We cannot of course visualize four dimensions directly. It is very useful, however, to visualize two dimensions of space and one of time. So we visualize the earth going around the sun as a kind of spiral tapeworm, the cross section of which is roughly circular in the plane of space.

There are four easily distinguishable types of pattern in the space-time continuum which correspond to four types of dynamics. The simplest kind is Newtonian celestial mechanics, which really involves the perception of stable relationships between today and tomorrow or between today, tomorrow and the next day. If regularity of this kind persists, we can easily project it into the future as we perceive it in the past. Thus, if we have a stable relationship between today and tomorrow, then if we know the state of the system today we know it tomorrow; and if we know it tomorrow we know it the day after and so on indefinitely into the future. In social systems we have to be careful about such projections however. The astronomer is fortunate in that the planets are moved by extremely well behaved angels, whereas in social systems things are moved by people who are not well behaved, and if our projections are mistaken for predictions we can be led badly astray.

A famous example of projections that were proven false is the projections of the U.S. Bureau of the Census in the middle 1940s according to which the United States would have a stable population of about 180 million by the 1980s. Between 1945 and 1947, however, we had a "system break," in which the basic parameters of the demographic system shifted in such a manner as to give us a much larger rate of population expansion than had been expected. Almost everybody in the 1950s found themselves with much larger numbers of children to educate than they expected. Thus, when constants are not constant, as they frequently are not in social systems, we have to learn to take predictions based on constant parameters with a great deal of reserve.

The Life Cycle Pattern

A second dynamic pattern can be seen in the homely analogy of wallpaper. If we see a wallpaper with a regular pattern, we have a good deal of confidence that the pattern continues under the mirror and behind the furniture or even beyond our field of vision. Similarly, we can see the space-time continuum as a four-dimensional wallpaper in which our field of vision is cut off abruptly at the present. If, however, we perceive the beginnings of past patterns, we may reasonably expect them to be projected into the future.

Perhaps the best example of this principle is the life cycle. Up to now, at any rate, man has shared with all other living creatures a very regular life pattern. A person's age is probably the most important single piece of information we can know about him. If he is one year old we know he will look like a baby, and if he is 90 he will look like an old man. This pattern may, of course, be upset by the growth of biological knowledge in the next generation or so, and we may be in great danger of immortality. This would present the human race with probably the greatest crisis it has ever had to face. Who, for instance, would want to be an assistant professor for 500 years? What makes life tolerable, especially for the young, is death, and if we do away with it, we are in real trouble.

Life cycle patterns are also found in human artifacts, such as automobiles, buildings and so on. The concept is less applicable to social organizations which often have the capacity for self-renewal. Neither organizations nor civilizations are under the necessity of aging, although this does sometimes happen. The fact that people die, however, means that organizations can renew their youth as the old occupants of powerful positions die off and younger occupants take their place. We do not seem to be able to do this with neurons.

Mutation and Selection

A third type of dynamic system is that of evolution and learning. These can be put together because they are essentially the same thing. Even biological evolution is a learning process by which matter is "taught" to form itself into more and more improbable structures as time goes on. Similarly, human learning involves the construction of more and more improbable images in the mind. Both these processes take place by mutation and selection.

One of the difficulties with evolutionary theory is that it is hard to put content into it. It is a beautiful vision, but it has extraordinarily little predictive power. There is a good reason for this, for any dynamic system which has information or knowledge in it as a fundamental element is inherently unpredictable. It has to have what I call fundamental surprise. Thus, if we could predict what we are going to know in 25 years we would know it now, and if we could predict the result of a research project there would be no need to do it and you could not get any money for it.

The Decision System

The fourth dynamic process is of peculiar importance in social systems and might be called the decision system. We can see the movement of the social system through time as a kind of "decision tree" in which we keep coming to decision points where there are a number of possible futures and of which we select only one. Our decisions, however, depend on values, and in man values are almost wholly learned. Instincts are quite literally for the birds. A decision tree, therefore, is a curiously unstable dynamic structure which is hard to predict. Decision theory states that everybody does what he thinks best at the time, which is hard to deny. The tricky problem is how do we learn not only what the real alternatives are, but also what values we place on them. It is true that we move toward what we think are the higher payoffs, but the trick is that we learn what the payoffs are only by moving toward them. The economist tends to assume that decision-making is a maximization process, like getting to the top of a mountain.

Yet, if we had to deduce the mountain from the behavior of people who climb it, which is the theory of revealed preference, the theory becomes dangerously close to the proposition that people do what they do, and it does not require much theory to tell us this, no matter how elegant the mathematical language in which it is wrapped. The situation is even worse than this because in actual decisions we are not climbing a real mountain, but an imaginary mountain, and a mountain, furthermore, which is like a featherbed and falls in as we get to the top of it. We learn to like what we get as well as to get what we like.

One way out of this morass is to look for structures which determine decisions because perhaps they determine the information flows and corrupt or purify information as it flows up through an organization. Lawrence Senesh wrote a delightful poem about cities once, the last verse of which reads, in part, as follows:

If cities will be
Rich, exciting and bold
. . .
For work and for play,
The people who live there
Must make them that way.

I could not help adding a verse to it as I felt that his was a little too Pollyannish. Here is my version:

The reason why cities are ugly and sad
Is not that the people who live there are bad;
It's that most of the people who really decide
What goes on in the city live somewhere outside.

This simple structural fact throws a great deal of light on the whole dynamics of urban decay. At this level we have to admit that we do not know very much, although there do seem to be possibilities of knowing a great deal more in the future.

How does this apply to teaching about social systems?

I have been neglectful of equilibrium systems up to this point simply because a realistic appraisal must regard them as special cases of the general dynamic process. Nevertheless, as a teacher of economics I cannot throw them away because in many cases they are all we have, and in any case they are a useful intellectual steppingstone to an appreciation of a more complex dynamics. Somewhere in the teaching business, therefore, we have to tell people about equilibrium systems, and we can even point to actual phenomena in society and also in the biosphere, perhaps even in the atmosphere, where something like a quasi equilibrium exists. Thus, the notion of ecological equilibrium is a tremendously important concept which we must get over to the student at some point. Here I endorse Alfred Kuhn's theory that ecology is the beginning of wisdom in a great many spheres.

Somewhere in the schools we must get the idea across that society is a great pond, and just as in a fish pond (if it's unpolluted) frogs, vegetation and chemicals all interact to form a reasonably stable equilibrium of populations, so in society we have rough equilibrium at any one moment of interacting populations of criminals, police, auto-

Almost everyone in the 1950s found themselves with more children than had been expected from population predictions.

mobiles, schools, churches, supermarkets, nations, armies, corporations, laws, universities and ideas. The ideal time for formalizing this concept would seem to be in high school algebra when the student is studying simultaneous equations. The essential proposition of ecological equilibrium is that if everything depends on everything else and if there is one equation of equilibrium for each population, we have n-equations and n-unknowns which with a bit of luck may have a solution in which the equilibrium size of each population is consistent with the size of all the others. The fact that ecological systems do exist in nature means that sometimes these equations can be solved. Boulding's first law is that anything which exists is possible. It is surprising how many people do not believe it. There must be some ecological equations, therefore, which have a solution, and this is worked out in the pond and the prairie and the forest and likewise in the city, the nation and the world. Even in the primary grades we could get something of this idea across.

It is a big step from the concept of ecological equilibrium to the concepts of homeostasis and cybernetics by which equilibrium conditions are maintained through a dynamic process. But even in grade school children can understand the thermostat and go on to see that the body regulates many processes in a similar way. Social organizations are similarly full of homeostatic mechanisms by which disruptive change is resisted and role occupants are replaced.

Recently in Poland I saw an example of the homeostatis of beauty. Many ancient buildings in Poland that were destroyed during the war have been rebuilt exactly as they were before; large parts of Warsaw have been rebuilt stone by stone, street by street, house by house, church by church and palace by palace. The Russians did the same thing with Leningrad. Here the image of a city perpetuates itself in society because decisions are made on the basis of an idea of beauty from the past. The astonishing recovery of nations such as Japan and Germany after a destructive war is a good example of how an old equilibrium reasserts itself.

The next concept beyond that of ecological equilibrium and homeostasis is that of ecological succession in which

George Gardner

"What makes life tolerable, especially for the young, is death and if we do away with it, we are in real trouble."

the equilibrium is gradually changed by irreversible movements. This gets us right into the developmental process and into the theory of evolution, both biological and social. Mutation is a process by which new equations are introduced into the ecological system; selection is the process by which these equations result either in a new solution or in a rejection of the new populations. Likewise, in the learning process information put into the old structure of ideas, either coming from outside or generated from within, is a mutation which may be rejected or which may restructure the mind into a new ecological pattern.

We still have a long way to go before we can begin to understand the human learning process even though real progress is being made in this direction. We have even further to go before we can understand the process of education, which is by no means the same thing as learning. One of the things that is most puzzling is why some people survive the educational process and some do not—in the sense that after they have gone through formal education they never seem to learn anything again. The main object of formal education should be to teach people how to continue learning, yet as educators we fall very far short of this idea.

The most depressing experience I ever had as a teacher was while standing one day in the commencement procession at a little college where I was teaching. I overheard one senior say to another, both of them splendid in their caps and gowns, "Well, that is the last time I am ever going to have to crack a book." I almost tore my hair in despair. How often, with our grades and quizzes and exams, assignments and curricula do we destroy the learning process in our attempts at forced feeding?

Priorities in the Social Sciences

I would like to conclude by looking at some possible content areas of high priority in the social sciences which could contribute toward the larger ends we have in view.

My first suggestion as to content is the comparative study of relatively stable cultures, most of which, of course, comes out of anthropology. A good deal of anthropology is at the level of natural history rather than analysis—interesting stories about strange people—but it does at least give the student the idea that there are many ways of doing things besides his own and so opens up worlds of culture beyond his own backyard. It is important for young children to have a feeling that there are a great many ways of doing things. I am convinced that if a thing is worth doing it is worth doing wrong, or at least worth doing in many ways. The curse of the British educational system in which I grew up was the idea that there is a right way to do everything. I have a vivid memory of a British mother at a swimming pool making her children absolutely miserable by saying all the time, "Swim properly, swim properly," while our children just swam cheerfully. The Russians are even worse than the British when it comes to the appalling concept of propriety, for there even ideas have to be "correct." Anthropology undermines propriety because it shows there are many different kinds of stable systems.

Even in complex social systems the student should be able to perceive certain stabilities and capacities for regeneration. Students can be made to see that the recovery of a society after a disaster, the regeneration of a limb of a starfish and even the return of the liquor industry after Prohibition are all examples of similar systems of regeneration and homeostasis. Once we have established the idea that there are stabilities in equilibria we can then go on to dynamics, to developmental systems and into concepts of economic and political development and ideological change.

One of the unfortunate effects of Marxism and the cold war has been a polarization of views on the matter of dialectics. Most Communists cannot admit that there are any non-dialectical systems, and we find it hard to admit that there are dialectical ones. This is disastrous because obviously there are both, and we need to see the total social dynamic process as a complex interaction of dialectical and non-dialectical elements. As a result of our polarization of this matter, both parties have developed unrealistic attitudes towards conflict. The dialecticians idealize it, whereas in this country we tend to suppress it because of our lack of confidence in our ability to manage it. We ought to be able to train people to feel that a well-managed conflict is a beautiful thing and should not be suppressed. On the other hand, a badly managed conflict can be disastrous for all parties. We see this in all areas of social life. It is well-managed conflicts, not the absence of conflicts that make for success in marriage, in industrial relations, and in party politics, and underlie almost all creativity in both art and science. This is something that formal education does not seem to teach very well.

One final question which puzzles me a good deal about formal education is what people should know in the way of plain old facts. General principles are obviously not enough. If you live in California you need to know that Sacramento is the capital, although you may not need to recall immediately what is the capital of Chad. We have never asked ourselves seriously what is the minimum that people need to know in the way of factual material. In the light of the knowledge explosion this question becomes more important all the time, for it becomes almost criminal to teach people things they do not really need to know if this prevents them from learning things they do need to know. On this point I have four very tentative suggestions.

Facts: How Many and What Kind

In the first place, we need to know something about the order of magnitude of the factual world. It is often more important to know orders of magnitude than it is to know about particular details. Thus, people ought to know that in this country agriculture is only 5 percent of the gross national product. We ought to know that the world war industry is equal to the total income of the poorest half of the human race. We ought to know that Japan in recent years has had a rate of economic development of 8 percent per annum per capita, whereas the United States has had about 2½ percent. We ought to have some idea as to what the "real maps" of the world look like. We even ought to know a lot of things that nobody knows, such as the rate at which the real resources of planet earth are being depleted, and the rate at which the basic metabolic processes of the biosphere are being upset. We often stuff students with names and dates and general principles, but there is an intermediate area of orders of magnitude. Even in universities there is an incredible ignorance about the orders of magnitude of the world.

The second point is that it is often more important to know where to find information than to have it in your head. This is one point where my own formal training was sadly deficient. When I was at Oxford, for instance, the catalogue of the Bodleian Library was written in elegant eighteenth-century longhand in enormous and rather inaccessible volumes. This no doubt accounts for the fundamental Oxford principle that it is much easier to think something up than to look it up. In this day and age, however, we must teach people how to search for information. Computers and information retrieval are going to revolutionize the process of search. But in order to use information systems, one must have a certain amount of information to start with.

A third suggestion is that we need to give people factual information—at least on an order-of-magnitude basis—about the shape of the space-time continuum in which they live. This is history-geography, which to my mind should be the same subject, history being only geography in four dimensions. From the point of view of total earth, formal education does a poor job on this, mainly because it is deliberately distorted to create an artificial national image. Thus, students are surprised when they learn that medieval Europe was a peninsula on the edge of the civilized world and that even at the time of the Roman Empire the Han Empire in China was probably superior in knowledge and technology. After about 700 A.D. there is little doubt that the most developed country was China, that Islam was the second layer of development and Europe, the third. In that period most advances in technology started in China and came to Europe by way of Islam. This is not the impression that we produce in our school system, and white Americans, at any rate, ought to know that their European ancestors were by no means top dogs and that in the Middle Ages it would not be wholly unfair to categorize them as slowly emerging hillbillies.

My fourth objective for formal education is to develop a lively appreciation of the nature and necessity of sampling and a distrust of purely personal experience. One of the fatal weaknesses of Deweyism is that while theoretically it emphasized starting from where the student is, in practice it often resulted in an emphasis on *being* where the student is. If where he is is in a backyard at West Lafayette, Indiana, where is that? The really interesting thing is not where you are but where you are not, and the purpose of education is to get you from where you are to where you aren't. This is why a purely empirical bias in the culture can be very dangerous because it results in a bias of the attention toward what exists for one, whereas the things that do not exist for one are much more numerous and perhaps more important. Even in the evolutionary process many of the most interesting things were those which did not survive, and we need to know why they did not.

One of the greatest political problems arises from the tendency of people to generalize from their own personal experience to propositions about society as a whole. Formal education should teach people that their personal experience, important as it is to them, is a very imperfect sample of the totality, and we must give people an idea of *how* to sample this totality. Errors of sampling are even commoner in literature and the arts than they are in the sciences and a widespread understanding of the nature of sampling error might preserve us from the literally deadly seriousness of the cults of youth, radicalism and the avant-garde.

What formal education has to do is to produce people who are fit to be inhabitants of the planet. This has become an urgent necessity because for the first time in human history we have reached the boundaries of our planet and found that it is a small one at that. This generation of young people have to be prepared to live in a very small and crowded spaceship. Otherwise they are going to get a terrible shock when they grow up and discover that we have taught them how to live in a world long gone. The nightmare of the educator is what Veblen called "trained incapacity," and we have to be constantly on the watch that this does not become one of our main products.

March 1970

From *Social Science in the Schools: A Search for Rationale*, edited by Irving Morrissett and W. W. Stevens, Jr., © 1970 by Holt, Rinehart and Winston.

Science as a Frame of Reference

RAYMOND W. MACK

"A social scientist is a man who, if he has two little boys, sends one to Sunday School every Sunday and keeps the other one home as an experimental control group." So runs one of our bits of occupational in-group humor. Would that we more often knew such precision!

The scientific *method* in social science is the same scientific method which underlies the work done in the chemist's laboratory, the zoologist's dissecting room, and the astronomer's observatory. But the *techniques* of gathering information vary from discipline to discipline: the chemist has his Bunsen burner and his watch glass, the zoologist his scalpel and his microscope, the astronomer his radio telescope and his charts. The social scientist has his interview schedule and his questionnaire. For each, the controlled experiment is an ideal seldom achieved but often approximated. For all, the canons of the scientific method are identical.

The unity of the sciences lies in their method. The scientific method is a way of trying to make sense out of the booming, buzzing confusion of the universe. It is an intellectual stance toward information. The scientific method is a set of assumptions about when a fact is a fact. The method provides scientists with a set of guideposts for gathering information and for bringing order to congeries of data.

Persons using the scientific method as a frame of reference operate under three assumptions: (1) that the human senses are the most reliable medium for gathering data; (2) that human reason is the most valid tool for organizing data; and (3) that agreement among a number of competent observers is the best check on the efficiency of the data gathering and organizing process called for in the first two assumptions.

Knowledge is scientific, then, when (1) an observer gathers information through one or more of his senses—sight, hearing, touch, taste, or smell—and (2) uses logic to interpret his information, that is, to relate one fact to another, and (3) other scientists sufficiently well-trained in the observer's specialty to understand what he has done use their sense experience and human reason on the information and arrive at the same conclusion.

When one of these criteria is violated in the search for knowledge, the conclusions are not scientific. Science does not provide us with knowledge about God because, by definition, the supernatural cannot be experienced through human senses. A random collection of facts does not constitute a science because facts do not speak for themselves; human reason must be employed to explain the relationships among facts and among sets of facts.

Scientists often use instruments for collecting information: thermometers, stethoscopes, tape recorders, questionnaires. These are the techniques which vary from discipline to discipline. They are simply aids to implementing the scientific method, which is unvarying. These devices are auxiliaries to the human senses. Scientists use them to bring greater precision to their own sense experience.

But the most refined gauge does not measure anything. A human being does the measuring. The instrument extends the range and sharpens the precision of his observations. A yardstick does not measure, and a Geiger counter does not count: a man does. It is the eye and the ear of the scientist using them that translate their sensitive markings and murmurings into scientific facts.

It is hardly correct, then, to speak of facts as being more or less scientific. A set of observations may be more or less precise, but if they are the product of sense experience logically interpreted and independently verified, they are scientific.

While the method of science is unvarying, the bodies of knowledge accumulated via the scientific method are ever-changing. The scientific method does not change, but the content of a scientific discipline does. This does not necessarily mean that a set of facts is disproved, but often that the gaining of additional information leads to a reinterpretation of what is known. Einstein's theory of relativity does not disprove Newton's scientific facts; it explains more by adding to and reinterpreting Newton's observations.

When a man accepts science as a frame of reference, and uses it in his daily work life, it is bound to have some impact upon his frame of mind. The stereotype which non-scientists hold of the scientist offers a clue to that frame of mind. Laymen often see scientists as cold-blooded skeptics, uninvolved in the values of their culture or the issues of their society, and hard to convince of anything. Like most stereotypes, this one is organized around elements of truth. The scientist is neither as bad as some people think in his lack of capacity for emotional conviction, nor as good as others think in his ability to separate his personal preferences from his objective scholarly conclusions.

But his training and practice do lead a scientist to attempt to separate his own wishes and convictions from the process of observing and interpreting data. The scientific method, with its commitment to sense experience and independent verification, is an attempt to assure complete objectivity. A social scientist, even more than others, should be aware that his own experience and cultural conditioning will influence his choice of research problems. He has learned in his own society a set of rules and preferences and even a way of thinking. That is why he uses the scientific method: as a guard against confusing what he would like to find with what is actually there.

He may not be able to bring his scientific frame of mind to every problem he addresses as a Republican, as a Baptist, as a father, or as a friend, but when he is working, his commitment to the method helps him to get outside himself and his milieu and to see his physical and social environment objectively. In this sense, too, the stereotype is founded on fact: the scientist *at work* is a man alienated from his society. As a citizen, the bacteriologist may loathe the ravages of tuberculosis and want passionately to find a means of preventing the disease. As a citizen, a sociologist may love democratic concepts of justice and deplore the ways in which poverty and racial discrimination cause his society to fall short of its own ideals. But at work, the bacteriologist must measure, not curse, the virulence of the bacillus; the sociologist must invest his work time in analyzing the effectiveness of special interest groups, not in cheerleading.

Calling something science does not make it scientific, of course. Astrology remains more popular than astronomy. Alchemy preceded chemistry, and there were hosts of economic and political philosophers eager to turn the lead of their opinions into the gold of truth long before there were many economists and political scientists using the scientific method to further their understanding of human behavior. There are still people who call themselves social scientists, but who evidence little inclination to subject their pet theories to the hazards of empirical test.

Nonetheless, this century has seen a larger and larger proportion of scholars using the scientific method as a means to the end of learning more about human social behavior. Every year, more students are exposed to science as a frame of reference. The mass media report and comment upon information gathered by observation, interviews, and questionnaires. Political leaders, educators, businessmen, church administrators make policy decisions based upon data gathered by social scientists. The growing acceptance of science as a frame of reference can encourage belief that decision makers may come to feel more at home with science as a frame of mind.

November-December 1964

SUGGESTED READINGS

Method and Measurement in Sociology by Aaron Cicourel (New York: Free Press, 1964) has a good critique of the methods employed by sociologists.

Unobtrusive Measures: Nonreactive Research in the Social Sciences by Eugene V. Webb, Donald T. Campbell, Richard D. Schwartz and Lee Sechrest (Chicago: Rand McNally, 1966) explores a variety of novel research methods. These methods are designed especially to permit the sociologist to study social behavior without influencing it.

Aspects of Scientific Explanation by Carl G. Hempel (New York: Free Press, 1965) is an interesting work on the philosophy of science. It is good background reading for this section.

Collected Papers. 1. The Problem of Social Reality by Alfred Schutz (The Hague: Martinus Nijhoff, 1962). Schutz is one of the philosophers who had an important influence on the ethnomethodological school. Ethnomethodology is principally concerned with investigating and understanding the most basic aspects of social behavior.

Studies in Ethnomethodology by Harold Garfinkel (Englewood Cliffs, N.J.: Prentice Hall, 1967) explains the method and aims of ethnomethodology and presents some case studies.

A Methodology for Social Research by Gideon Sjoberg and Roger Nett (New York: Harper and Row, 1968) presents a theoretical perspective on sociological methods.

Survey Sampling by Leslie Kish (New York: Wiley, 1965) explores the uses the sociologist can derive from sampling.

"Some Methodological Problems of Field Studies" by Morris Zelditch Jr., *American Journal of Sociology* (Vol. 67, March, 1962). A useful discussion of an interesting research technique.

"Problems of Inference and Proof in Participant Observation" by Howard S. Becker, *American Sociological Review* (Vol. 23, Dec. 1958).

Experimenter Effects in Behavioral Research by Robert Rosenthal (New York: Appleton-Century-Crofts, 1966). A psychologist details some of the methodological problems that bias research in all social science fields.

"Interview Techniques and Field Relationships" by Benjamin D. Paul in *Anthropology Today* edited by A. L. Kroeber (Chicago: University of Chicago Press, 1953) gives an anthropological viewpoint on a research technique employed by many sociologists.

"The Participant Observer and Over-Rapport" by S. M. Miller *American Sociological Review,* (Vol. 17, Feb. 1952).

"Interview-Respondent Interaction: A Study of Bias in the Information Interview" by J. Allen Williams *Sociometry* (Vol. 27, Sept. 1964) discusses problems inherent in acquiring information through interviewing.

The Rules of Sociological Method by Emile Durkheim translated by Saul A. Solovay and John H. Mueller, 8th edition (New York: Free Press, 1964) is a classic work on method.

Intellectual Strategies and Research Tactics

RAYMOND W. MACK

Social scientists are perhaps at their most misleading in describing how they do their work. They may be models of objectivity in reporting *what* they find and they will usually work within the canons of scientific method in trying to interpret what their data *mean*. But ask a social scientist *how* he found out, and you are likely to get an outrageous oversimplification.

I know a social scientist who has spent twenty years in learning about factory workers: working in factories himself, observing and interviewing laborers on the job, talking with them casually off the job, studying their personnel records, and reading what other social scientists have written about factory workers. When he was asked how he gathered the data for one of his studies, he replied: "We administered a questionnaire to a random sample of 104 men in one plant." Actually, his conclusions were based upon all the experience I have described. He gathered one set of data with a questionnaire, but he brought to the task of interpreting it all those other sets of data he has acquired as observer, participant observer, interviewer, and reader.

The selection of research techniques is a matter of strategy, not of morals. What is the right way to gather social data? The answer depends on what one is trying to learn about, and on the social setting in which he is trying to find out. Let me use my experience on the Caribbean island of Barbados as an example of what I mean by adopting research techniques to suit the research problem and the research setting.

My involvement with Barbados grew out of my interest in social organization and social classes. As a student of class structure, I have found myself drawn increasingly during the past decade into research on, and analyses of, the role of race in the social structure in the United States.

Having studied and written about race relations in the United States, I thought that I could broaden my perspective and might deepen my insight into the American situation by observing the meaning of race in another society. Reading about Caribbean societies led me to the conclusion that Barbados had experienced enough historical parallels to the American situation to make comparison meaningful and was sufficiently different to make contrast enlightening.

During the two years between my first look at Barbados and the completion of my study, I was able to spend only about six months actually living in Barbados. If one is going to try to achieve some understanding in such a brief period of how a total society is structured, then he must seize every available tool to help accomplish the mission. My work, therefore, cannot be described as solely library research, nor as participant observation, nor as an interview study. I was shamelessly opportunistic in data gathering.

I read 17th century history, 18th century political science, 20th century travel guides, and both daily newspapers in Barbados, the *News* and the *Advocate*. I studied census bulletins, government economic reports, civil lists, and gossip columns. I was a participant observer at dinner parties, at picnics, on the beach, in bars and restaurants, at dances, at cricket matches, and at horse races. I attended House of Assembly meetings and Town Council welfare hearings. I interviewed cane cutters, planters, taxi drivers, refinery owners, cooks, insurance brokers, maids, automobile salesmen, housewives, newspapermen, storekeepers, waiters, real estate speculators, government ministers, schoolteachers, clergymen, hotel owners, airline employees, leisured expatriates, students, radio announcers, civil servants, one shoeshine boy, and the American Vice-Consul. My interviewees included white Barbadians from the "Big Six" families of the island's power structure; Negro Oxford graduates who have achieved enough political power to make the "Big Six" nervous; mulattoes whom an observer accustomed to the rules in the United States would call "Negro," but who are pass-as-white; old-family members chronically in debt after the fashion of South Carolina "genteel poverty"; working class Negroes; and poor whites viewed with contempt by everyone else regardless of race, color, or creed. My data was gathered from no specifiable sample of the universe of Barbadians, but if total immersion is the way to salvation, I showed good faith.

Since my goal was to learn about race and class and their interrelationship, my strategy led me to start at the bottom of the class structure. The tactic of avoiding early contact with members of the power structure was based on the assumption that I could later produce scholarly credentials which would explain lower class associations to upper class people; but if I became identified early with occupants of the seats of power, it would be extremely difficult later to achieve rapport with workers dependent upon the moguls or with middle class people resentful of their exclusion from the inner circle.

So I talked first with taxi drivers, bus conductors, waiters, the baby sitter, the yard man next door, and gradually became involved in a network of informants: I used to work as a dance band musician before retiring into social science and this provided useful entree into the night world of the island. Many of the musicians working in hotels and night clubs had listened to records and become greatly interested in jazz, and I was able to play with them and talk with them after working hours. My preschool children spent hours on the beach, and were good enough to introduce me to the parents of their friends, who spanned the color spectrum and the power pyramid.

Gradually, my network of middle class acquaintances widened. My landlord introduced me to the extension officer of the University of the West Indies. He in turn introduced me to a school principal, a newspaper columnist, and a government officer. The newsman took me to a welfare hearing; the principal introduced me to a police officer.

I learned to capitalize on the Barbadian's enthusiasm for his island, using it as a probing open-ended question. When new acquaintances asked what I was doing there, I answered truthfully that it was a delightful place for my wife and children to vacation, and that I was writing a book on race relations and social class *in the United States*. Almost invariably, a Barbadian would respond to this information with the observation that "If you're interested in race relations and social class, you ought to study Barbados." Whenever and however a Barbadian phrased this sentiment, I replied with questions. Barbados is pretty similar to the United States, isn't it? Yes, I write about social class and race—why? What's unusual about Barbados? Yes, politics has a good deal to do with race relations in the United States; does it here, too?

Such an informal approach to a design for data-gathering has its obvious disadvantages, as does a multiple strategy in the use of field techniques. But I came to the task of analysis and writing with the idea that shuttling from library to observation to interview and back to library had not only equipped me with reliability checks, but had given me insights I might have missed with a more limited armamentarium.

What did I find in Barbados?

When the division of a population according to race is almost the same as the division according to property or income or some other important criterion of social power, race is highly relevant to the boundaries of groups. In Barbados, class differences created and maintained group boundaries. The recent history of Barbados also suggests that, when class boundaries shift rapidly, the boundaries of races also become fluid. The acquisition of political power by nonwhites allowed them to rock the rest of the system.

But this diminishing importance of racial distinctions in Barbados occurred because there were many non-whites eager and able to fill statuses previously held by whites. The insularity and intimacy of the society also made it difficult to pretend that these ambitious, educated, powerful Negroes were not there. In the United States, on the other hand, it is possible for many white people to have little or no contact with Negroes except as their social inferiors: bellboys, boot-blacks, cleaning women, janitors, parking lot attendants, steel mill laborers, and field hands.

SUGGESTED READINGS

The Scientific Approach; Basic Principles of the Scientific Method by Carlo L. Lastrucci (Cambridge, Mass.: Schenkman, 1963) is one of the best treatments of the philosophy of the scientific method.

Science and Common Sense by James B. Conant (New Haven, Conn.: Yale University Press, 1951) is a simplified discussion of the scientific method.

Sociological Work: Method and Substance by Howard S. Becker (Chicago: Aldine, 1970). A fundamental collection of essays on sociological research, with a special emphasis on ethnography and field techniques.

Sociological Methods: A Source Book by Norman K. Denzin (Chicago: Aldine, 1970). A systematic analysis of each of the major strategies employed in sociological research.

The Human Perspective in Sociology by Severyn T. Bruyn (Englewood Cliffs, N. J.: Prentice-Hall, 1966) explores the theory, philosophy, methods and practice of participant-observation.

Sociological Work: Method and Substance edited by Howard S. Becker (Chicago: Aldine, 1970).

"The Methodology of Participant Observation" by Severyn T. Bruyn *Human Organization* (Vol. 22, Fall 1963).

"Problems in Participant Observation" by Morris S. Schwartz and Charlotte Green Schwartz, *American Journal of Sociology* (Vol. 60, Jan. 1955). The authors discuss how anxiety and bias can be sources of distortion in the process of gathering data.

"Participant Observation and the Collection and Interpretation of Data" by Arthur J. Vidich, *American Journal of Sociology* (Vol. 60, Jan. 1955). The social role of the participant observer and the images which respondents have of him have a decisive influence on the character of the data collected.

"The Participant-Observer Technique in Small Communities" by Florence R. Kluckholm, *American Journal of Sociology* (Vol. 46, Nov. 1940).

The Analysis of Social Systems by Harry C. Bredemeier and Richard M. Stephenson (New York: Holt, Rinehart and Winston, 1962). An introductory sociology textbook which employs the systems framework throughout, with a good section on culture from the systems point of view.

Parts and Wholes edited by Daniel Lerner (New York: Free Press, 1963) is a very helpful book for information on systems perspective.

Sociology and Modern Systems Theory by Walter Buckley (Englewood Cliffs, N.J.: Prentice Hall, 1967). This book includes useful criticisms of the systems approach. It is a difficult book, but the first three chapters are worth studying.

A Primer on Social Dynamics: History as Dialectics and Development by Kenneth E. Boulding (New York: The Free Press, 1970). A basic statement on overall patterns in the dynamics of social change.

Modern Systems Research for the Behavioral Scientist by Walter Buchly (Chicago: Aldine, 1968). A basic sourcebook of classic and contemporary article on general systems theory and research.

The Convict as Researcher

HANS TOCH

J. Douglas Grant and I recently concluded a study on the social psychology of violence. In studying violence inside prisons we operated with a resident research staff that combined sophistication, practical experience, and the ability to inspire confidence in our informants. Our group in San Quentin prison, for instance, consisted of six men whose graduate training added up to 83 years of confinement. Their competence to study violence in prisons is obvious since five of them also qualified as subjects.

Our top researcher was an interdisciplinary social scientist for whom I cannot find enough praise. His name is Manuel Rodriguez, and his academic background consists of an eighth grade education, a term in the U. S. Army Supply School, and a short course in automobile repair.

But Rodriguez has other qualifications. Before the age of 18 he was arrested for malicious mischief and assault. Later he was sentenced for such offenses as armed robbery, burglary, firearms possession, narcotic addiction, and drunk driving. (I might confess that since joining us he has been arrested again, this time for driving without a license while engaged in research.)

Rodriguez has spent 15 of his 36 years behind bars, mostly in the California State Prison at San Quentin. As an inmate Rodriguez became interested in our research subject. He describes the beginning of his interest:

> I was assigned to the weight-lifting section of the gymnasium. Most of the more violence-prone inmates come here to blow off steam at one time or another. It is also sort of a refuge where an inmate can get away from the pressures of staff scrutiny and the yards. We try to keep violence nonexistent, if possible, in this section. This was part of my job, although it was not explicit. In many cases—as a peacemaker—I had to convince both would-be combatants that they could retreat without losing face or pride. Most inmates contemplating violence will usually go to a respected member of the prison community for advice on "Shall I kill this guy or not?" I and a friend of mine were two of these persons so respected. When these guys who are straddling the fence between violence and nonviolence came to us we began to actively prescribe nonviolence. . . .

Rodriguez started out as an informed layman, with a completely pragmatic concern with violence. Today he is a sophisticated researcher, and he is an expert on the subject.

His transmutation began in early 1965 when he became a trainee in the New Careers Development Project directed by my collaborator, J. Douglas Grant. This revolutionary program is aimed at converting standard clients of professional services (such as Manuel) into dispensers of professional services—or at least into intermediaries between clients and professionals. Research work seemed one obvious target for this effort. Inmate Rodriguez was thus put to work, during his training period in prison, on the first stage of our study. His work included research design, as well as code construction, interviewing, and coding. After Rodriguez was released on parole, we were happy to hire him as a staff member.

Outside, Rodriguez has acted as our principal interviewer. He has interviewed parolees with violent records and citizens who have assaulted police officers. He is not only a sympathetic and incisive interviewer, but became unusually successful in stimulating interest among potential subjects. He is 5 feet 10 inches tall and weighs 175 pounds. He generally wears shirts that allow an unimpeded view of two arms full of tattoos. In addition, when we began the police assaulter interviews, Manual grew a bushy moustache to make himself look—as he put it—more "subculture." This prop undergirded an invitation to participate that started with the words, "We are not a snitch outfit," but then proceeded to a thoughtful, honest exposition of our objective.

We have tried to blur the line between the observer and the observed. Each of our interviewees is invited to sit down with us to conceptualize the data obtained from him. Each one is asked to help find common denominators in the particulars obtained in the interview. Each one gets the same opportunity we do to play scientist and becomes a minor partner in our enterprise. We obtain some material of extraordinary sophistication from these nonprofessional collaborators.

Results and Rapport

Why do we choose to rely on these nonprofessionals? How do they serve us better than the usual research associates and assistants with the conventional technical and academic credentials?

First, and most obviously, the empirical reason: They bring us better results. They are able to establish trust where we are not, to get data that we could not get, and to obtain it in the subjects' own language. I think I can best illustrate this advantage by excerpting a brief passage out of one of our prison interviews. The respondent here is a seasoned inmate whose reputation is solidly based on a long record of violent involvements. The interviewer is one of our nonprofessional researchers—another inmate:

Q: Was it the next day that you were going through the kitchen line and that he approached you and said he was coming down and wanted his stuff, and you better be there with it?
A: He said he was coming to get me, and I better be ready. The inference was—Was I going to be ready?
Q: So you went back to the kitchen and got a shank [knife] and then went to your pad. Now this dude who was doing the talking to you now, this is the one who you were playing coon can [a card game] with? The next morning one of the dudes approached you?
A: The next morning. The same dude. When I came out of my cell in the wing this guy approached me. He lived in the wing.
Q: What is his message?
A: His message is just a play, and they were playing a pat hand. It wasn't anything different from the day before. I told him. . . .

This excerpt fits into a standardized interview schedule that was designed to tease out sequences of interpersonal events leading to violence. But it also is a snatch of conversation between two persons discussing a subject of mutual interest in the most natural and appropriate language possible. In this type of interaction, data collection occurs with no constraint, and without translations designed to please or to educate the researcher.

Another advantage to be obtained in the use of nonprofessionals is the benefit of their unique perspective in data interpretation. A well-chosen lay researcher can often be in a position to correct naive inferences by less experienced professionals. In one dramatic experience one of my research partners, inmate Hallinan of San Quentin, chided me (in writing) for drawing a hasty and incorrect conclusion from an interview we had conducted:

Your interpretation seems to be influenced by the subject's storied loquaciousness rather than the incidents themselves. Is the subject's behavior, as he claims, the result of his being an Indian leader, and having to intercede in their behalf, or is it because of his need to establish a personal reputation as a prison tough guy? I choose the latter interpretation; an interpretation based on how the subject has behaved, not how he thinks he has behaved. . . .

An Indian functions within the rigid framework of rules. "There are family codes, tribal codes, and Indian laws," is how he puts it. But there is also . . . a joint code that he is well aware of: "The cons have their own rules, and one of them is that they step on the weak." . . .

The first incident that the subject becomes involved in is the rat-packing of an Indian child molester in order to ostracize and punish the molester, and also to solidify his position among the low-riders. So, rather than being a leader of these Indians, he is using his Indian blood to further his own ends. He wants to be a tough con, someone to be feared and respected. "The new guys that come in, no one knows about them." "Once you get a reputation you have to protect it." The above statements, and others similar in nature, were made by the subject during the course of the interview. [Their] significance is self-evident.

How does the subject go about building a reputation? As he says, fighting for home boys, and interceding for other Indians? No. Of the ten incidents—actually nine, because No. 1 and No. 9 are the same—No. 6 no violence occurred; No. 2 involved helping a friend, although the details were vague; No. 7 was a fight of his own making; No. 9 he was attacked; and No. 10 was the rat-packing incident. The remaining four involved custody. He was proudest of No. 8. In regards to this incident the following dialogue occurred:

Q: Do you think this incident helped your reputation?
A: It sure as hell did. I knocked down the Captain.
Q: How did you feel just before you knocked him down?
A: Like a big man.
Q: During?
A: I sure am doing it right this time.

The subject is also proud of the fact that at one time he had spat on the warden. . . . Obviously the subject feels that these things scare people. . . .

The word circulates that he has fought with the "bulls," implying that he will jump on a convict with little provocation. The facts are never pursued, but accepted prima facie, because those who pass on these rumors and exaggerations are the very ones who are most impressed by them. The rumor returns and the subject begins to believe his own yard reputation. . . .

Our subject has completed the building of his reputation, petty though it is, and now he and his low-rider friends can observe and honor it. Not that the cons on the yard do, but the subject feels that they do, and this is all that really matters. If anything he is tolerated, not respected and feared as he would like.

It is obvious that inmate Hallinan is not only furnishing me with a lesson in perspective, but is also demonstrating that he can compete with professionals in his methodological acumen and his ability to vividly summarize and communicate research conclusions. And although this analysis is unusually literate, because inmate Hallinan has invested much prison time in creative writing courses, much can be learned even from our most unlettered collaborators.

There is another aspect to the use of nonprofessionals which relates to a less tangible and more general advantage. Most social researchers sense some difficulty in the

SOCIAL SCIENCE METHODS AND VIEWPOINTS

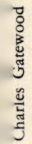

initial approach to subject populations of vastly different backgrounds from our own. Some of us react at this juncture with an elaborate process of ingratiation or "gaining of rapport" in which we, and the research, are presented in the (presumably) best light. This posturing is often transparently insincere and always wasteful. Worse, it usually achieves merely a wary and delicate stalemate, during which only a hit-and-run raid for data is possible before the subjects discover what has happened to them.

Avoiding Exploitation

During rare moments of honesty, we may admit that even when we induce subjects to cooperate, our dealings with them are seldom the exciting adventure we tell our students about. I say this because I suspect that the real problem is not one of communication and social distance at all—it may have nothing to do with habits or dress or the use of most vivid vocabulary. It may be that our subjects understand us only too well—that what we ask is unreasonable and unfair. After all, at best we are supplicants, and at worst, invaders demanding booty of captive audiences. In return for a vague promise or a modest remuneration we expect a fellow human being to bare his soul or to make controversial and potentially incriminating statements. The "communication" is one way—the researcher maintains his position as an "objective" recipient of non-reciprocated information.

We also make our informant aware that we are not interested in him as a person but as a "subject"—a representative of a type, or a case, or an item in a sample. He knows this because he knows who he is and who we are. He knows that he is being approached because he is the inhabitant of a ghetto or a prison, because he is a "consumer," or because he acts as an informer. And he knows that his aims are being subordinated to our own. How can he share our objectives, after all, if he cannot even see the results of the efforts in which he has participated?

I speak with considerable humility here, because I almost once again made the mistake of taking my Viennese accent and my parochial concerns into prison cells and police stations, expecting to secure frank answers to prying questions. I have done this sort of thing often in the past. This strategy strikes me now not only as naive but as offensive.

Therefore, Grant and I followed an alternative course in our violence project, such as I have briefly described. This has supplied us with linkage across cultural gaps, with highly motivated informants, with substantive expertise, with heightened analytic power, and with the feeling that we have been fair.

I shall not pretend that these benefits are automatic and free of risk. Like professional researchers, nonprofessional participants in research must be selected with care. Unintelligent or completely illiterate persons would be of limited use, as would social isolates. A cynical, exploitive, or immature outlook can create a poor prospect for programs that have the usual training resources. This is also true of rigidly held preconceptions, though to a lesser extent.

On the other hand, too close attention to selection criteria may produce a staff of quasi-professional nonprofessionals—which is also bad. They may be rejected by the subjects and even be considered a species of Uncle Tom. Not being trusted, they may have relatively limited useful knowledge or insight, contribute little, discover they are marginal members of the team, develop poor motivation.

Even careful selection will not altogether eliminate these possibilities. The nonprofessional must get training that is not only directly related to research but also can provide him with incentives, support, and a meaningful self-concept. Some of this training may be of the sort routinely encountered in graduate schools; some may be more characteristic of social movements. The nonprofessional researcher must be, in a sense, a *convert*. He must acquire a new role, a new set of values, and new models and friends while remaining in close touch with his old associates. The professional merely places others under the microscope; but the nonprofessional must convert his own life experiences into data. While the rest of us can view research as a job, the nonprofessional must see the involvement as a mission or a crusade—or he will have trouble doing it at all.

What training then should these nonprofessionals get? First, research indoctrination, in the purest sense of the word, that aims directly at awakening curiosity and at the desire to reach latent meanings or patterns. It must try to inculcate suspicion of the unrepresentative and unique and a phobia against premature interpretation. Obviously, it must also provide tools—intensive practical instruction in the use of steps to be employed, including interviewing techniques, content analysis, survey problems, and data processing. This training must not only include general background information and acquaintance with the content of the research but also self-corrective and social skill training of the kind necessary to work with sensitive groups.

But the most critical challenge is ours. Will we treat the trained nonprofessional as a partner and colleague and respect his integrity and abilities? We must preserve the nature of our own contribution; but we must also be prepared to become members of our own team.

Nonprofessionals, if given the opportunity, can help us shape ideas, formulate designs, and analyze results. We should continue to provide intellectual discipline and a sense of perspective. For the rest, we may find ourselves in the unaccustomed position of being students to spirited and able teachers—and the benefits will be reflected in the quality of research, as well as in the resolution of ethical dilemmas that currently often leave social researchers with a bitter taste in the mouth.

September 1967

Evaluating Social Action Programs

PETER ROSSI

We are today groping for new and presumably better treatments for a variety of social ills and have enough wealth to correct some of the obvious faults of our society. But, ironically, no matter how heavy our consciences now, we can no longer expect reforms to produce massive results. We have passed the stage of easy solutions. To borrow a parallel from medicine, we can much more easily and decisively reduce death and illness by bringing safe water to a backward land than by trying to get Americans to stop smoking.

Similarly with social ills. Provide schools and teachers to all children and illiteracy goes down dramatically; but to achieve a level of education high enough to assure everyone a good job is a lot more difficult. Diminishing returns set in: The more we have done in the past, the more difficult it becomes to add new benefits. Partly this is because so much has already been achieved; partly because in the past we have not had to deal so much with individual motivation. Almost everyone has enough motivation to learn to read; it takes a lot more to learn a specialized skill.

In short, massive results will not occur, and new social treatments are going to be increasingly expensive in time and money. Practitioners and policy-makers are apprehensive; they want evaluations of program effectiveness, but they are afraid of what might be shown.

Take Project Head Start. Everyone would agree that universal schooling for children has been a huge success—compared to no schooling or schooling only for those who can pay. But poor children are still behind and need help. And a preschool program for them can never make as much change as universal schooling did.

Effective make-up treatment must be expensive. Each trainee at a Job Corps camp costs somewhere between $5,000 and $10,000 a year, as compared to considerably less than $1,000 a year in the usual public high school. Yet Job Corps training is not five to ten times as effective.

Also, the less the effect, the greater is the measurement precision needed to demonstrate its existence—so in evaluation too it will cost more to reveal less.

But if social scientists are pessimistic about results, operators of programs tend to be quite optimistic, at least when facing congressional appropriations committees. Claims made in public are usually much higher than any results we can reasonably expect. So the interests and actions of the program administrators themselves tend to undermine good evaluation.

Finally, controlled experiments—the most desirable model—are not frequently used in evaluation. There is not a single piece of evaluation research being carried out on any of the major programs of the war on poverty that closely follows the controlled experiment model.

The Power of Wishful Thinking

The will to believe that their programs are effective is understandably strong among administrators. As long as the results are positive (or at least not negative), relations between practitioners and researchers are cordial and even effusive. But what if the results are negative?

A few years ago the National Opinion Research Center undertook research on the effects of fellowships and scholarships on graduate study in arts and sciences. The learned societies that sponsored the research sincerely believed that such aids were immensely helpful to graduate students and that heavily supported fields were able to attract better students. The results turned out to be equivocal. First, financial support did not seem to have much to do with selecting a field for study. Second, it did not appear that good students were held back by lack of fellowships or scholarships. The committed ones always found some way to get their PhD's, often relying on their spouses for help.

The first reaction of the sponsors was to attack the study's methodology—leading to the coining of the aphorism that the first defense of an outraged sponsor was methodological criticism. Policy remained unaffected: Sponsors are still asking more and more federal help for graduate students on the grounds that it allows more to go into graduate study, and also spreads talent better among the various fields.

Another example of the power of wishful thinking has to do with the relationship between class size and learning. It is an article of faith among educators that the smaller the class per teacher, the greater the learning experience. Research on this question goes back to the very beginnings of empirical research in educational social science in the early 1920's. There has scarcely been a year since without several dissertations and theses on this topic, as well as larger researches by mature scholars—over 200 of them. The latest was done by James Coleman in his nationwide study for the Office of Education under the Civil Rights Act of 1964. Results? *By and large, class size has no effect on learning by students, with the possible exception of the language arts.*

What effect did all this have on policy? Virtually none. Almost every proposal for better education calls for reduced class size. Even researchers themselves have been apologetic, pointing out how they *might* have erred.

I do not know of any action program that has been put out of business by evaluation research, unless evaluation itself was meant to be the hatchet. Why? Mainly because practitioners (and sometimes researchers) never seriously consider the possibility that results *might* come out negative or insignificant. When a research finding shows that a program is ineffective, and the research director has failed to plan for this eventuality, then the impact can be so devastating that it becomes more comforting to deny the worth of the negative evaluation than to reorganize one's planning.

Getting the Results You Want

Given unlimited resources, it is possible to make some dent in almost any problem. Even the most sodden wretch on skid row can be brought to a semblance of respectability (provided he is not too physically deteriorated) by intensive, and expensive, handling. But there is not sufficient manpower or resources to lead each single skid row inhabitant back to respectability, even briefly.

Many action programs resemble the intensive treatment model. They are bound to produce *some* results, but they cannot be put into large-scale operation.

Note the distinction between "impact" and "coverage." The *impact* of a technique is its ability to produce changes in each situation to which it is applied, while *coverage* of a technique is its ability to be applied to a large number of cases. Thus, face-to-face persuasion has high impact, but its coverage is relatively slight. In contrast, bus and subway posters may have low impact but high coverage.

An extremely effective technique is one that has both high impact and high coverage. Perhaps the best examples can be found in medicine. Immunizing vaccines are inexpensive, easy to administer, and very effective in certain diseases. It does not seem likely, however, that we will find vaccines, or measures resembling them in impact and coverage, for modern social ills. It is a mistake, therefore, to discard out of hand programs which have low impact but the potentiality of high coverage. Programs which show small positive results on evaluation but can be generalized to reach large numbers of people can, in the long run, have an extremely significant cumulative effect.

The Control Group Problem

The scientific integrity of a controlled experiment depends on whether the experimenter can determine which subjects go to the experimental and which to the control groups and whether these allocations are unbiased. But there are many distorting influences.

First, political. Practitioners are extremely reluctant to give the experimenters enough power. For example, to evaluate the worth of a manpower retraining program properly, the potential trainees must be separated into experimental and control groups, and then checked for contrasts after the training. This means that some of them, otherwise qualified, are arbitrarily barred from training. Public agencies are extremely reluctant to authorize such discrimination.

In part, this problem arises because researchers have not sufficiently analyzed what a "control" experience is. A control group need not be deprived of all training—of a chance of any help—merely that type of help.

A placebo treatment for a job retraining program might be designed to help men get jobs that do not involve retraining, and over which the training program should demonstrate some advantage.

Even in the best circumstances, with the best sponsors, controlled experiments can run into a number of booby traps. There was the well-designed evaluation research that could not raise enough volunteers for either experimental or control groups. So the experimenter opted to fill only the experimental groups, abandoning all attempts at proper control.

Or there was the research on the effectiveness of certain means of reaching poor families with birth control information, contaminated by the city health department setting up birth control clinics in areas designated as controls!

Or there is the continuing risk in long-range evaluations that the world will change the control group almost as fast as the experiment changes the experimental group. For instance, David Wilner and his associates undertook to evaluate the effects of public housing in Baltimore when general improvement in housing was on the upswing, and by the end of the period the difference in housing quality between experimental and control groups was minor.

In sum, it is not easy either to get the freedom to undertake properly controlled experiments or to do them when that consent is obtained.

Strategy for Good Evaluation Research

A number of lessons can be drawn to help devise proper evaluation research.

First, most of us are still a long way from full commitment to the outcomes of evaluation research. It is part of the researcher's responsibility to impress on the practitioner that in most cases results are slight and that there is more than an off-chance that they will be unfavorable. What to do about this probability must be worked out in advance; otherwise the research may turn out to be a fatuous exercise.

Second, how can we devise ways of using controlled experiments in evaluation? As noted, political obstacles and our nonsterile world make uncontaminated controls difficult and rare.

Since there is such a high likelihood of small effects, we need very powerful research designs to get clear results. This takes money. But wouldn't it be worthwhile to set up such powerful designs to evaluate *several* items simultaneously, so that the outcome would be more useful for setting policy? For instance, wouldn't it be better to run an evaluation on several types of Job Corps camps simultaneously, comparing them one with the other, rather than comparing one with the Job Corps in general? Such a differential study would give more and better information than a gross evaluation.

If controlled experiments—the desirable model—are used so rarely, what *is* being used? Most frequently quasi-experiments so constructed that some biases do affect the control groups, or correlational designs in which persons getting some sort of treatment are contrasted with others not treated—with relevant characteristics being controlled statistically.

How bad are such "soft" evaluational techniques, particularly correlational designs? When can they be employed with confidence?

First, it seems to me that when massive effects are expected or desired, soft techniques are almost as good as subtle and precise ones. If what is desired, for instance, is complete remission of all symptoms in all persons treated, then a control group is hardly necessary. If a birth control method is judged effective only if all chance of conception is eliminated, then the research design can be very simple. All that needs to be done is administer the technique and then check for any births (or conceptions) thereafter. If effectiveness is defined as fewer births, the design should be more complicated and requires control groups.

The obverse also holds. If a treatment shows no effects with a soft method, then it is highly unlikely that a very precise evaluation will show more than very slight effects. Thus, if children in an ordinary Head Start program show no gain in learning compared to those who do not participate (initial learning held constant), then it is not likely that a controlled experiment, with children randomly assigned to experimental and control groups, is going to show dramatic differences either.

This means that it is worthwhile to consider soft methods as the first stage in evaluation research, discarding treatments that show no effects and retaining more effective ones to be tested with more powerful, controlled designs.

Although checking for possible correlations after the event may introduce biases, such designs are extremely useful in investigating long-term effects. It may be impossible to show a direct laboratory relationship between cigarette smoking and lung cancer, but the long-term correlation between the two, even if not pure enough for the purist, can hardly be ignored. Similarly, though NORC's study of the effect of Catholic education on adults may have selection biases too subtle for us to detect, we still know a great deal about what results might be expected, even if we could manage a controlled experiment for a generation. The net differences between parochial school Catholics and public school Catholics are so slight that we now know that parochial schools are not an effective device for inculcating religious beliefs.

From all these considerations, a useful strategy for evaluational research seems to emerge:

■ A RECONNAISANCE PHASE—a rough screening in which the soft and the correlational designs filter out those programs worthwhile investigating further;

■ AN EXPERIMENTAL PHASE—in which powerful controlled experiments are used to evaluate the relative effectiveness of a variety of those programs already demonstrated to be worth pursuing.

June 1967

SUGGESTED READINGS

Research Methods in Social Relations by Claire Selltiz, Marie Jahoda, Morton Deutsch, and Stuart Cook (New York: Holt, Rinehart and Winston, 2nd edition, 1959) is a good text on research methods. Is especially useful for students who have never before studied research methods.

Knowledge for What? by Robert Lynd (Princeton, N.J.: Princeton University Press, 1939). An excellent book on the relationship between scientist and society.

The Servants of Power by Loren Baritz (Middletown, Conn.: Wesleyan University Press, 1960) shows how social scientists are used by industrialists to further industry's ends.

"The Behavioral Scientist and Social Responsibility: No Place to Hide," by Leonard Krasner, *Journal of Social Issues* (Vol. 21, April 1965) focuses on psychologists but can easily be applied to sociologists as well.

The Relevance of Sociology edited by Jack D. Douglas (New York: Appleton-Century-Crofts, 1970) discusses the relationship between knowledge and its use and how it should be used.

Field Work: An Introduction to the Social Sciences by Buford H. Junker (Chicago: University of Chicago Press, 1960) explores a variety of research techniques used by sociologists.

Sociologists at Work edited by Philip Hammond (New York: Basic Books, 1964).

Ethics, Politics and Social Research by Gideon Sjoberg (Cambridge, Mass.: Schenkman, 1967).

"The Informant in Quantitative Research" by Donald T. Campbell *American Journal of Sociology* (Vol. 60, no. 4, Jan. 1955, pp. 339-342). The anthropological use of the informant is distinguished from the social survey method.

The Sociology of Research by Gunnar Boalt (Carbondale and Edwardsville, So. Ill.: Southern Ill. Univ. Press, 1969) proposes a way to measure the values of the social scientist as the values impinge on the research process.

Deception in Social Research

Experiments can be harmful to human subjects when scientists don't tell the whole truth

HERBERT C. KELMAN

In order to advance the understanding of human behavior, psychologists regularly use human beings as subjects in a wide variety of experiments. In many of these experiments, the subject is kept in the dark or misinformed about the true purpose of the experiment. Sometimes the deception exposes him to embarrassing, disturbing, or potentially harmful experiences that he had not bargained for.

There is generally a good reason for the use of deception. Many of the phenomena that the psychologist wishes to study would be altered if the subject knew the purpose of the experiment—if he knew, for example, what psychological processes the experimenter is trying to activate and what reactions he is hoping to observe. And yet the use of deception, even when it is done for a scientifically valid reason, poses ethical questions.

These questions are fairly obvious when the deception has potentially harmful consequences for the subject; they are more subtle, but nonetheless important, even in experiments where there is little danger of harmful effects. The issue is: How can we strike a proper balance between the interests of science and the considerate treatment of people who make themselves available as the raw material of research?

The problem of deception has taken on increasingly serious proportions in recent years as its use has become almost a standard feature in psychological experiments. Deception has been turned into a game, often played with great skill and virtuosity. A considerable amount of creativity and ingenuity by social psychologists is given to the development of increasingly elaborate deception situations.

For example, the potentially harmful effects of deception are dramatized in some recent studies of obedience. One volunteer was "smiling and confident" when he entered the laboratory. "Within 20 minutes," the experimenter reported, "he was reduced to a twitching, stuttering wreck, who was rapidly approaching a point of nervous collapse." What caused him to become a "wreck" was an experiment in which subjects were led to believe that they were participating in a learning study. They were instructed to administer increasingly severe shocks to another person, who after a while began to protest vehemently. In fact, of course, the "victim" was an accomplice of the experimenter and did not receive any real shocks. But in some cases, the experimenter instructed the subject to continue to "shock" the "victim" up to the maximum level, which the subject believed to be extremely painful when the victim writhed in pain and pounded his head against the wall.

Not surprisingly, both obedient and defiant (those who refused to administer shocks) subjects exhibited a great

SOCIAL SCIENCE METHODS AND VIEWPOINTS

deal of stress. And there is surely good reason to believe that at least some of the obedient subjects came away from this experience with lowered self-esteem, realizing that they yielded to authority to the point of inflicting extreme pain on a fellow human being. The fact that, in the experimenter's words, they had "an opportunity to learn something of importance about themselves, and more generally, about the conditions of human action" is beside the point.

If this were a lesson *from life,* it would constitute an instructive confrontation and provide a valuable insight. But do researchers, for purposes of experimentation, have the right to provide such potentially disturbing insights to subjects who do not know that this is what they volunteered for?

And yet, this same research illustrates the complexity of the issues raised by the use of deception. These studies of obedience have produced significant and challenging findings which have posed some basic questions about human behavior and social life. Without deception, this line of investigation could probably not have been pursued.

A GENERATION OF DECEIVERS

It is easy to view the situation with alarm, but it is much more difficult to formulate an unambiguous position on this problem. As a working experimental social psychologist, I know that there are good reasons for using deception in many experiments. There are many significant problems, like the study of obedience, that probably cannot be investigated without the use of deception—at least, given the present level of development of our experimental techniques. Thus, researchers are always confronted with a conflict of values. If they regard the acquisition of scientific knowledge about human behavior as a positive value, and if an experiment using deception constitutes a significant contribution to such knowledge which could not be achieved by other means, then it is difficult to rule out the experiment unequivocally. The question is not simply whether or not to use deception, but whether the amount and type of deception are justified by the significance of the study and the unavailability of alternative procedures.

What concerns me most, then, is not so much that deception is used, but that it is used without question. I sometimes feel that a whole generation of psychologists now in training will not know there is any other way of doing experiments. Too often deception is used, not as a last resort, but as a matter of course. The attitude seems to be: If you can deceive, why tell the truth?

What are some of the major problems posed by the use of this dangerously doubled-edged tool? There are three areas to consider:
- the ethical implications;
- the real effectiveness of deception;
- the implications for the future of psycho-social research in our society.

ETHICAL IMPLICATIONS. Ethical problems of a rather obvious nature arise in those experiments in which deception has potentially harmful consequences for the subject. For example, a brilliant experiment was recently designed to observe the effects of threat on group solidarity and the need for strong leadership. In this study (one of the very rare examples of an experiment conducted in a natural setting) independent food merchants in a number of Dutch towns were brought together for group meetings and informed that a large organization would soon open a chain of supermarkets in the Netherlands. In a "high threat" condition, the subjects were told that their towns would probably be selected as sites for such markets, which would cause a considerable drop in their business. On the advice of the executives of the shopkeepers' organizations who had helped to arrange the group meetings, the investigators never revealed, even after the experiment was over, that the supermarket threat was a fiction.

I have been worried about those Dutch merchants ever since I first heard about this study. Did some of them go out of business in anticipation of the heavy competition? Do some of them have an anxiety reaction every time they see a bulldozer? Chances are that they soon forgot about this threat (unless, of course, supermarkets actually did move into town) and that it became just one of the many little moments of anxiety that occur in every shopkeeper's life. But do investigators have the right to add to life's little anxieties and to risk the possibility of more extensive anxiety purely for the purposes of such experiments?

Two other recent studies provide further example of potentially harmful effects arising from the use of deception. In one set of studies, male college students were led to believe that they had been homosexually aroused by photographs of men. In the other study, subjects of both sexes were given disturbing information about their levels of masculinity or femininity, presumably based on an elaborate series of psychological tests they had taken. In all of these studies, the deception was explained to the subjects at the end of the experiment. One wonders, however, whether this explanation removes the possibility of harmful effects. For many persons in this age group, sexual identity is a live and sensitive issue, and the self-doubts generated by this laboratory experience could linger.

What about the less obvious cases, in which there is little danger of harmful effects? Serious ethical issues are also raised by such deception per se, and the kind of use of human beings that it implies. In other inter-human relationships, most psychologists would never think of doing the things that they do to their subjects—exposing them to lies and tricks, deliberately misleading them, and making promises or giving assurances that they intend to disregard. They would view such behavior as a violation of the respect to which all fellow humans are entitled. Yet they seem to forget that the experimenter-subject relationship—whatever else it is—is a *real* inter-human relationship, in which the experimenter has a responsibility towards the subject as another human being whose dignity he must respect. The difference between the experimenter's behavior in everyday life and his behavior in the laboratory is so marked that one wonders why there has been so little concern with this problem.

The broader ethical problem of the very use of deception becomes even more important when we view it in the present-day historical context. We are living in an age of mass societies, in which the transformation of man into an object, to be manipulated at will, occurs on a mass scale, in a systematic way, and under the aegis of specialized institutions deliberately assigned to this task. In institutionalizing the use of deception in psychological experiments we are contributing to a historical trend that threatens the values most of us cherish.

METHODOLOGICAL IMPLICATIONS. I have increasing doubts about the effectiveness of deception as a method for social research.

A basic assumption in the use of deception is that a subject's awareness of what the experimenter is really trying to find out would affect the subject's behavior in such a way that the experimenter could not draw valid conclusions from it. For example, if the experimenter is interested in studying the effects of failure on conformity, he must create a situation in which subjects actually feel that they have failed, and in which they can be kept unaware of his interest in observing conformity. In short, it is important to keep the subjects naive about the purposes of the experiment so that they can respond spontaneously.

How long, however, will it be possible to find naive subjects? Among college students it is already very difficult. They may not know the exact purposes of the particular experiment in which they are participating, but many of them know that it is *not* what the experimenter says it is. As one subject pithily put it, "Psychologists always lie!"

There are, of course, other sources of human subjects that have not been tapped, but even here it is only a matter of time until word about psychological experiments gets around and sophistication increases. Whether or not a subject knows the true purpose of the experiment, if he does not believe what the experimenter tells him, then he is likely to make an effort to figure out the purpose of the experiment and to act accordingly. This may lead him to do what he thinks the experimenter wants him to do. Conversely, if he resents the experimenter's attempt to deceive him, he may try to throw a monkey wrench into the works. Whichever course the subject uses, however, he is operating in terms of his own conception of the nature of the situation, rather than in terms of the conception that the experimenter is trying to induce. In short, the experimenter can no longer assume that the conditions that he is trying to create are the ones that actually define the situation for the subject. Thus, the use of deception, while it is designed to give the experimenter control over the subject's perceptions and motivations, may actually produce an unspecifiable mixture of intended and unintended stimuli that make it difficult to know just what the subject is responding to. Therefore, is there any future in the use of deception?

IMPLICATIONS FOR THE FUTURE. My third main concern about the use of deception is that, from a long-range point of view, there is obviously something self-defeating about it. As experiments of this kind continue, potential subjects become more and more sophisticated, and scientists become less and less able to meet the conditions that their experimental procedures require. Moreover, potential subjects become increasingly distrustful, and future relations between subjects and experimenters upon which successful research depends are likely to be undermined. Thus, we are confronted with the anomalous circumstance that, the more this research is carried on, the more difficult and questionable it becomes.

The use of deception also involves a contradiction between experimental procedures and the long-range aims of scientists and teachers. In order to be able to carry out experiments, they are concerned with maintaining the naiveté of the population from which they draw subjects. This perfectly understandable desire to keep procedures secret go counter to the traditional desire of the scientist and teacher to inform and enlighten the public. For the long run, it even suggests the possible emergence of a special class, in possession of secret knowledge—a possibility that is clearly antagonistic to the principle of open communication to which scientists and intellectuals are so fervently committed.

ENRICHMENT THROUGH EXPERIMENT

If my concerns about the use of deception are justified—and I think that they are—what are some of the ways they can be dealt with? I would like to suggest two basic remedies:

■ exploring ways of counteracting and minimizing the negative efforts of deception;

■ giving careful attention to the development of new experimental techniques that can dispense with the use of deception altogether.

In those experiments in which deception could have harmful effects, there is an obvious requirement to build protections into every phase of the process. Subjects must be selected in a way that will exclude individuals who are especially vulnerable; the potentially harmful manipulation (such as the induction of stress) must be kept at a moderate level of intensity; the experimenter must be sensitive to danger signals in the reactions of his subjects and be prepared to deal with crises when they arise; and, at the conclusion of the session, the experimenter must take time, not only to reassure the subject, but also to help him work through his feelings about the experience to whatever degree may be required.

In general, a good principle to follow is that a subject ought not to leave the laboratory with greater anxiety or lower self-esteem than he came with. I would go beyond it to argue that the subject should in some positive way be enriched by the experience—he should come away from it with the feeling that he has learned something, understood something, or grown in some way. And this adds special importance to the kind of feedback—about what was really being done—that is given to the subject at the end of the experimental session.

This post-experimental feedback is also the primary way of counteracting negative effects in those experiments in which the issue is deception as such, rather than possible threats to the subject's well-being. If the subject is deceived, then he must be given a full and detailed explanation of what has been done and of the reasons for doing it. It is not enough to give the subject perfunctory feedback. These explanations should be meaningful and instructive for the subject and helpful in rebuilding his relationship with the experimenter. I feel very strongly that, to accomplish these purposes, the experimenter must keep the feedback itself inviolate and under no circumstance give the subject false feedback, or pretend to be giving him feedback while in fact introducing another experimental manipulation.

THE CASE FOR COOPERATION

My second suggestion is that scientists invest some of the creativity and ingenuity now being devoted to the construction of elaborate deceptions to the search for alternative experimental techniques that do not rely on the use of deception. They would be based on the principle of eliciting the subject's positive motivations to contribute to the experimental enterprise. They would draw on the subject's active participation and involvement in the proceedings and encourage him to cooperate in making the experiment a success by conscientiously taking the roles and carrying out the tasks that the experimenter assigns to him. In short, the kind of techniques I have in mind would be designed to involve the subject as an active participant in a joint effort with the experimenter.

Perhaps the most promising sources of alternative experimental approaches are procedures using some sort of role-playing—that is, procedures in which the experimenter asks the subject to act *as though* he were in a certain situation rather than actually creating that situation experimentally as a "real" one. I have been impressed, for example, with the role-playing that I have observed in the Inter-Nation Simulation, a laboratory procedure in which the subjects take the roles of decision-makers of various nations. This situation seems to create a high level of emotional involvement and to elicit motivations that have a real-life quality to them.

In general, the results of role-playing experiments have been very encouraging. Despite the fact that they know it is all make-believe, subjects usually react realistically to the experimental stimuli, and these reactions follow an orderly pattern.

There are other types of procedure, in addition to role-playing, that are worth exploring. For example, it may be possible to conduct more experiments in a natural non-laboratory setting in which, with the full cooperation of the subjects, specific experimental variations are introduced. The advantages of dealing with motivations at a real-life level of intensity might well outweigh the disadvantages of subjects' knowing the general purpose of the experiment. A much simpler alternative, also worth exploring, would be for experimenters to inform the subjects at the beginning of a laboratory experiment that they will not receive full information about what is going on, but ask them to suspend judgment until the experiment is over.

Whatever alternative approaches are tried, there is no doubt that they will have their own problems and complexities. Procedures effective for some purposes may be quite ineffective for others, and it may well turn out that for certain kinds of problems there is no adequate substitute for the use of deception. But there *are* alternative procedures that, for many purposes, may be as effective or even more effective than procedures built on deception.

These approaches often involve a radically changed set of assumptions about the role of the subject in the experiment: *the subject's motivation to cooperate is utilized rather than by-passed.* These new procedures may even call for increasing the sophistication of potential subjects, rather than maintaining their naiveté.

THE WHITE HOUSE

Black Families and the White House

"Perhaps most important—its influence radiating to every part of life—is the breakdown of the Negro family structure."

Lyndon B. Johnson
Howard University, June 4, 1965

George Gardner

Black Families and The White House

The political implications of the Moynihan Report controversy

LEE RAINWATER
WILLIAM L. YANCEY

"So, unless we work to strengthen the family, to create conditions under which most parents will stay together—all the rest: schools and playgrounds, public assistance and private concern, will never be enough to cut completely the circle of despair and deprivation."

Lyndon B. Johnson, Howard University, June 4, 1965

Lyndon Johnson's speech at Howard University was remarkable for its eloquence and for its insights into the basic plight of Negro Americans. It seemed to signal an important shift in the stance of federal government toward civil rights issues. The "next and more profound stage" of the civil rights struggle would go beyond legal protection of *rights,* to providing the *resources* for Negro Americans to turn freedom into an equal life. The emphasis was on the social and economic factors of jobs, housing, education, community and *family life.* Despite the voracious appetite of the federal government for social science findings and consultation, it was unique to find a social science perspective—developed over three decades of economic, sociological, and psychological research on "the Negro problem"—so central to a major presidential address.

But the President's speech also signaled the beginning of a major public controversy over the now-famous report by Daniel Patrick Moynihan—*The Negro Family: The Case for National Action.* At the time of the speech the report was still confidential ("for official use only") and the President undoubtedly did not know he was creating a storm center. In view of the deep rifts the Moynihan report caused in government, and between the administration and the civil rights movement, it is amazing that President Johnson was never directly embroiled in the controversy and never became a target for the animosities it unleashed.

The report on the Negro family had been completed in March, 1965, by Moynihan, Assistant Secretary of Labor, in collaboration with two members of his staff, Paul Barton and Ellen Broderick. It expressed Moynihan's views on bringing Negro Americans into full participation in the society. It also reflected his belief that government should make greater use of the social sciences on policy making.

Presidential assistant Richard N. Goodwin and Moynihan had drafted the speech, at the President's direction, on the night of June 3 and into the early hours of June 4. The speech was the first public expression of a budding White House strategy—now seemingly discarded as too expensive—to "leap frog" the civil rights movement instead of always merely reacting to it.

Before the speech was given, however, approval was sought and obtained from three civil rights leaders—Martin Luther King, Jr., Roy Wilkins, and Whitney Young.

Robert Carter, general counsel of the NAACP said of of the speech: "The President had an amazing comprehension of the barriers that are present in our society to Negroes' progress, and an amazing comprehension of the debilitation that results from slum living. He also demonstrated that he understood the problems of translating abstract generalities into a specific program."

Yet, by the following October, Moynihan and his report (but not the President's speech) were under heavy attack—from anonymous layers of the federal government, in the inner councils of some civil rights groups, by some social scientists, and finally, in public meetings and in the press. By the time of the White House Conference "To Fulfill These Rights" in November—called for by the President in the Howard University speech—the controversy over the Moynihan report and Negro family stability was so hot that it was blamed by some high administration figures for making the conference a "total disaster."

The events from completion of the Moynihan report in March to the conference in November dramatize not only the complexities of formulating national policy, but also the political implications of social science information. As with so many policy matters, the attitudes and actions of a small number of people determined the course of major national events.

Moynihan's Strategy

The Moynihan report is clearly not an article prepared for a learned journal, nor an ordinary position paper prepared by a political executive. Rather, it is a hybrid which seeks on the one hand to present certain social science facts and at the same time to argue a particular and rather unusual policy position. As such, it reflects some of the intellectual difficulties of each of the elements that go into making the hybrid, and some additional ones that come from the combination of the two approaches.

Daniel Patrick Moynihan joined the New Frontier in 1961 as special assistant to Secretary of Labor Goldberg and by 1963 was appointed Assistant Secretary of Labor. He was one of a new breed of public servants, the social scientist-politicos, who combine in their backgrounds both social science training and experience and full-time involvement in political activity. A PhD in political science, he had also attended the London School of Economics. From 1955 to 1959 he had worked as an assistant to Governor Harriman of New York; from 1959 to 1961 he had been the director of the New York State Government Research Project at Syracuse University.

Cabinet officers and their assistants stand between the "presidential government" and the "permanent government" of civil servants and appointed officials who serve for longer periods of time than the elected administration. In addition to the normal privileges of his office, Moynihan had a close personal relationship with the White House staff. Both his political experience and his personal conception of public service pointed him very strongly in the direction of the "presidential government." Moynihan had been a member of the four-man team that drew up the original War on Poverty proposal (the others were Sargent Shriver, Adam Yarmolinsky, and James Sundquist). He had been particularly concerned to strengthen the employment aspects of the program.

The office which Moynihan held is of crucial importance for understanding the report and the controversy. The report was written from the standpoint of a member of the "presidential government" who has the right to suggest policy of a sweeping nature. Only such a person would have been able to write a report relatively free of the long review process typical of government reports, to speak directly and on a relatively equal footing with the White House staff, and to resist the counter-pressures that would come from other departments that might feel the report had policy implications inimicable to their programs.

The Challenge of Family Welfare

Although Moynihan strongly believed that modern government can formulate policies and programs to deal with problems before there is a surge of popular demand or even well-formulated political pressure, he had strong doubts that the range of federal activity designed to cope with problems of poverty was likely to be effective.

Increasingly, he had come to feel that the idea of family welfare offered (1) the possibility for a focus in working out social and economic problems, and (2) a standard to evaluate how successful the programs were. Thus, he told a conference on poverty at Berkeley, in February, 1965:

We are beginning to see something of the relation of unemployment to family structure. . . . The next great social issue raised in America ought to be the question of how to insure a decent family income and a decent family setting for the working people of America, as we have already done—and as a result of no inconsiderable intervention of the federal government—for middle class Americans.

Earlier Moynihan had thought he sensed some tendency by administration officials to think the Civil Rights Act of 1964 had solved a good part of the civil rights problem. He was concerned with the credence given public opinion polls showing that a majority of Negroes in Harlem felt the Civil Rights Act would make a "very great difference"

in their lives. The sharp contrast between this optimistic mood and the depressing figures on social and economic status disturbed him. Late in November of 1964 he decided to write a report on the Negro family for internal use in the government:

I woke up a couple of nights later (that is, after one such conversation with a highly placed optimist) at four o'clock in the morning and felt I had to write a paper about the Negro family to explain to the fellows how there was a problem more difficult than they knew and also to explain some of the issues of unemployment and housing in terms that would be new enough and shocking enough that they would say, "Well, we can't let this sort of thing go on. We've got to do something."

He organized a small working staff and through them began to collect government statistics that in one way or another had bearing on the problem. In March the document was formally cleared by Secretary of Labor Wirtz.

Moynihan was writing for a very small, primarily White House, audience. He wanted the highest levels of the administration to adopt the view that family welfare provided a central point of reference in evaluating the effectiveness of programs dealing with disadvantaged groups. He looked to a broader redefinition of the civil rights issue by the government as a whole.

While the document was to be an unusual one for government policy papers, it must at least have some kinship with them. Therefore, there was heavy emphasis on government statistics, since these are the "authoritative data" with which high level officials are accustomed to working. Though it sought to present a complex argument, the document must be short and sharply focused.

Although early in his planning Moynihan had thought of suggesting solutions as well as defining a problem, he finally determined not to include any reference to solutions in the report in order to force his readers to pay attention to the problem itself.

Thus, in April and May the report was distributed to only a few persons within the Department of Labor and the White House; as time went on, particularly as the reputation of the report spread within the administration and demands for it increased, distribution grew wider.

Having discussed the report with members of the White House staff, Moynihan prepared a memorandum for the President summarizing its findings and adding seven steps "as a start" toward developing programs for Negro Americans. On May 4, 1965, Secretary Wirtz forwarded the memorandum to the White House, indicating that it was the work of Moynihan, and endorsing his analysis and recommendations.

The memorandum summarized the main points of the report itself and went on to suggest two directions for action proposals, one involving administrative actions, and the other involving programs. In the area of administrative action Moynihan suggested:

The Report and Its Critics

The Report Said...

At the heart of the deterioration of the fabric of Negro society is the deterioration of the Negro family.... There is considerable evidence that the Negro community is in fact dividing between a stable middle class group... and an increasingly disorganized and disadvantaged lower class group. ... This paper is not, obviously, directed to the first group.

Nearly a quarter of urban Negro marriages are dissolved. Nearly one-quarter of Negro births are now illegitimate. Almost one-fourth of Negro families are headed by females. Only a minority of Negro children reach the age of 18 having lived all their lives with both their parents.

The breakdown of the Negro family has led to a startling increase in welfare dependency.

THE ROOTS OF THE PROBLEM
   SLAVERY.... "the most awful the world has ever known."
   THE RECONSTRUCTION.... At the time of emancipation Negro women were already "accustomed to playing the dominant role in family and marriage relations" and that this role persisted in the decades of rural life that followed.
   URBANIZATION. In every index of family pathology—divorce, separation, and desertion, female family head, children in broken homes, and illegitimacy—the contrast between urban and rural environment for Negro families is unmistakable.
   UNEMPLOYMENT AND POVERTY. *Negro unemployment,* with the exception of a few years during World War II and the Korean War, *has continued at disaster levels for 35 years.* ... When jobs were reasonably plentiful ... the Negro family became stronger and more stable. As jobs became more difficult to find, the stability of the family became more and more difficult to maintain.
   THE WAGE SYSTEM. Between 1960 and 1963, median non-white family income slipped ... to 53 percent of white income.

THE TANGLE OF PATHOLOGY
   ... There is no one Negro problem. There is no one solution. Nevertheless, at the center of the tangle of pathology is the weakness of the family structure.
   MATRIARCHY. A fundamental fact of Negro American family life is the often reversed roles of husband and wife.
   DELINQUENCY AND CRIME. The overwhelming number of offenses committed by Negroes are directed toward other Negroes: the cost of crime to the Negro community is a combination of that to the criminal and to the victim.
   THE ARMED FORCES. The ultimate mark of inadequate preparation for life is the failure rate on the Armed Forces mental test.... A grown young man who cannot pass this test is in trouble. Fifty-six percent of Negroes fail it.

THE CASE FOR NATIONAL ACTION
The object of this study has been to define a problem, rather than propose solutions to it.... Three centuries of injustice have brought about deep-seated structural distortions in the life of the Negro American. At this point, the present tangle of pathology is capable of perpetuating itself without assistance from the white world. The cycle can be broken only if these distortions are set right.

The policy of the United States should be to bring the Negro American to full and equal sharing in the responsibilities and rewards of citizenship. To this end, the programs of the Federal Government bearing on this objective shall be designed to have the effect, directly or indirectly, of enhancing the stability and resources of the Negro American family.

The Critics Responded...

It draws dangerously inexact conclusions from weak and insufficient data; encourages (no doubt unintentionally) a new form of subtle racism that might be termed "Savage Discovery," and seduces the reader into believing that it is not racism and discrimination but the weaknesses and defects of the Negro himself that account for his present status.

The all-time favorite "savage" is the promiscuous mother who produces a litter of illegitimate brats in order to profit from AFDC. Other triumphs of savage discovery are the child who cannot read because, it is said, his parents never talk to him, and the "untenantable" Negro family....
William Ryan, The Nation, Nov. 22, 1965

The errors of the report ... have already produced quite damaging political consequences. They have led to facile "explanations" of the urban riots of 1964-65, and continue—clearly contrary to the intention of its authors—to provide ammunition to those who would deny ... real equality of opportunity.

The report is much more optimistic about the employment situation among Negroes than are other observers. The crucial factor is income level, which Herman Miller, one of our most competent authorities on income statistics, believes is actually worsening rather than getting better among Negroes....

The method of analyzing family data by color instead of by income level results in an alarmist picture of differences between white and Negro family structures. Other more careful studies by Hylan Lewis ... allow for income differential and reach much more sober conclusions.
Benjamin F. Payton, Christianity and Crisis, Dec. 13, 1965

The Moynihan report does not offer any recommendations to implement its policy proposal, arguing that the problem must be defined properly first in order to prevent the hasty development of programs that do not address themselves to the basic problem. While this argument was perhaps justified as long as the report remained confidential, it may have some negative consequences now that the contents have been released to the press.

This possibility is enhanced by the potential conflict between the two major themes of the report, that Negroes must be given real equality, and that, because of the deterioration of the family, they are presently incapable of achieving it. The amount of space gives to the latter theme, and the obvious sensationality of the data make it possible that the handicaps of the Negro population will receive more attention than Moynihan's forthright appeal for an equality of outcomes.
Herbert Gans, Commonweal, Oct. 15, 1965

The family and family behavior among Negroes show great range and variability; *especially overlooked and underrated is the diversity among* low income Negro families. When these are overlooked for any reason, there is danger that the depreciated, and *probably more dramatic and threatening, characteristics of a small segment of the population may be imputed to an entire population.*
Hylan Lewis, Agenda paper, White House Planning Conference

■ Appointment of a working party to review every relevant program of the federal program to determine whether it operated to strengthen families or to weaken them.
■ Establishment of a Negro information center to bring together data on Negroes and develop methods for measuring success or failure in solving Negro problems.

In terms of program Moynihan emphasized the following points:
■ Employment for Negro men—"we must not rest until every able-bodied Negro male is working."
■ Adequate family housing, particularly in the suburbs and away from the ghetto.
■ Family planning services.
■ Redesigning women's jobs so that men can fill them.
■ Programs to counter the underrepresentation of Negroes in the armed forces because of failure to pass armed forces tests.

It is not clear to us to what extent the President himself attended to the arguments developed in the report and related memoranda. But he was at least sufficiently impressed to encourage his staff to work with Moynihan on the Howard University speech and on preliminary plans for informal meetings in the White House with social scientists and for the fall conference.

Opposition in the Permanent Government

There is an inherent tension between "presidential government" and "permanent government" because lower-level civil servants remain in their jobs when top-level men are shuffled by changes in administration.

Although one of the strongest (but only implicit) rules in the civil service is that one should not directly criticize his presidentially-appointed superiors, criticisms of the Moynihan report occurred first within the government (in fact, in his own Department of Labor) rather than in the civil rights movement or among social scientists who consulted to the government.

The criticisms made by "permanent government" people in the Department of Labor were not that the data were inaccurate, but rather that the selection of data was not in accord with their understanding of the situation. They felt that Moynihan did not include enough comparisons with whites (using economic and educational controls), that he did not include any data contradicting his conclusions, and that the conclusions themselves were not cautious enough. This is a common difference of perspective between presidential appointees and the "permanent government."

In this case, Moynihan made a self-conscious *political* judgment to deal exhaustively with ways in which the Negro situation was getting *worse*, not better. He felt the

"Negro unemployment, with the exception of a few years during World War II and the Korean War, has continued at disaster levels for 35 years." (*The Negro Family: The Case for National Action*, page 20.)

Dennis Porter

SOCIAL SCIENCE AND PUBLIC POLICY

administration should be informed of the dangers inherent in the social transformation taking place—with Negro expectations rising faster than improvement in conditions.

Some senior members of the "permanent government" supported Moynihan's analysis as both scientifically adequate and politically relevant. However, none of these senior experts were brought into the various planning activities abortively initiated during the summer of 1965; in short, the potential "permanent government" support for the thesis was not mobilized.

Though "permanent government" critics believed Moynihan's use of data was inappropriate, the rules of the game were that they could not engage in blatant, public criticism.

Solutions to this general dilemma must take subtle forms. In the case of the Moynihan report, three traditional strategies were used by the "permanent government":

■ conversation, rumors, and verbal analysis—communicated where it will do the most good;

■ going outside of government to obtain support from autonomous people who may criticize with impunity;

■ writing an independent document which clearly contradicts the report but is not a direct polemic.

Getting "The Word"

It was through informal communication networks that "the word" first went out about the report—in hallway talks, at meetings, at lunches, on the telephone, and at parties.

Whenever the President makes a speech people in the government start thinking to themselves, "What are the implications of the speech for me, for my responsibilities? What was he really trying to say, what's behind it all?"

Soon after the President's speech there was a good deal of conversation in the cocktail circuit to the effect that the Moynihan report provided "the real story" for what the President was trying to get at. Thus one government civil rights official told us, "Late in June all sorts of people started telling me that in order to really understand the President's Howard speech you had to have read the Moynihan report and that it was a very powerful document. So I began to wonder, what is in this Moynihan report?"

In government, those most directly concerned with civil rights—the President's Council on Equal Opportunities and the Civil Rights Commission—were not consulted before the speech and neither had received copies of the Moynihan report at that time. Wiley Branton, director of the Council on Equal Opportunities became concerned about the implications of the report. At pre-planning sessions for the White House Conference Branton spoke out against the use of the phrase "the Negro family." "(It) struck me in a psychologically bad way," he said. "I didn't like the way it was being used."

It was, of course, quite embarrassing for government civil rights experts to be told by persons outside the government about the Moynihan report, but even more embarrassing when they were unable to answer the questions raised by civil rights leaders. The atmosphere of secrecy and tight security built around the report no doubt added to the developing uneasiness in the movement.

In the civil rights network there was little concern with the report's technical adequacy. However, there was considerable fear that its emphasis on the Negro family might be used to blame Negroes for their own troubles. There was also fear that the report might lead to programs designed to deal directly with family problems rather than with more basic changes in discriminatory patterns or socio-economic deprivation. Anxiety was heightened because, for two months, the Moynihan report was unavailable to key people in the civil rights network.

Finally, a more ominous and directly personal note crept into the bundle of ideas that became "the word." It was suggested that Moynihan was really "anti-Negro," a "subtle racist," an apologist for the white power structure. He seemed to fit the specifications for the newest villain of the civil rights movement, "the white liberal." As the controversy spread outside of government, this view gained ground—particularly among those who did not know Moynihan, and those most unsympathetic to his emphasis on socio-economic rather than anti-discrimination measures. The fact that Moynihan had few contacts with the civil rights movement made such attributions easy—he was an unknown quantity.

By its very existence (as well as its contents) Moynihan's report on the Negro family seemed an attack on the welfare establishment's approach to Negro problems. Its implicit message was that they had not cared enough to really understand the problem.

The welfare establishment (Health, Education, and Welfare; Labor Department; Office of Economic Opportunity) is in a very difficult position because it knows how inadequate the national social welfare program is, but must also defend it against political attacks. Further, the welfare establishment has acquiesced to subtle and blatant discrimination and inadequate labor and welfare services to Negroes. Its orientation is to perfect existing programs while the Moynihan report stated that current federal programs were inadequate and new ones must be developed.

The strategies of the two groups meshed but for quite different reasons—for the welfare establishment the report was too "alarmist," for the civil rights groups it was too "optimistic."

It should be noted that the Moynihan controversy developed through the informal communication channels of the government and into the larger community of those who deal with the government *because no effective counter pressures were brought to bear by the "presidential government."* Moynihan had left the government in July and was involved in a political campaign as candidate for president of the City Council in New York. The White House had not cut down on the speculation by developing initiatives which would point out its direction for the future.

The fact that the report existed and was being considered in high places slowly became public over the summer and the early fall. The first fairly full summaries of the report came in mid-July and early August. Finally, after the Watts riots newspaper articles began to draw on the report's contents.

The effect of press coverage of the Moynihan report was to subtly exaggerate the already dramatic and sensational aspects of Moynihan's presentation and considerably deepen the impression that the report dealt almost exclusively with the "pathology" and "instability" of the family as the cause of Negro problems. Most of the distortion was the inevitable result of the way the press handles "social problem" reporting. The press has a tendency to think in terms of what is wrong with individuals rather than institutions, and to concentrate on personal experiences and suffering, rather than on the more impersonal forces which lie behind personal experience. In only a few cases did the press treatment grind an overtly conservative ideological axe (particularly articles by syndicated columnists Mary McGrory, Roland Evans and Robert Novak, and Richard Wilson).

From the beginning, in the background stories on the President's speech, two somewhat contradictory themes appeared that were to plague the Moynihan thesis in the coming months:

■ In a *New York Times* story of June 5, "White House sources" are quoted to the effect that the Howard speech was the first major presidential civil rights statement conceived independently of the direct pressure of racial crisis. Johnson's target was "The whole nation and the total social and economic plight of its Negro citizens." Further —and erroneously—the speech was said to have been under study for about two months and that "much consultation with civil rights leaders and experts in the social sciences went into its preparation." The following day the *Times* editorialized: "The cures for the social afflictions that hold the Negro in thrall lie in public and private programs that make the present War on Poverty . . . seem incredibly puny. In the absence of much more massive action to engender full employment, clear the slums and make more schooling available to more people, the chief effect of these programs may be to confront the United States with problems not unlike those of the 'revolutions of rising expectations' in Africa and Asia."

■ On the other hand, the *Washington Star's* Mary McGrory (an influential columnist with good access to the White House), also drawing on "White House aides," told quite a different story. McGrory's story said that in the speech "President Johnson suggested that the time had come for (Negroes) to come to grips with their own worst problem, 'the breakdown of Negro family.'" *Self-improvement* was to be the key to the announced next stage in civil rights. Miss McGrory quoted his aides as saying that the President was determined "that the unprecedented White House Conference he has called for next fall will not turn into a seminar for relieving old woes and grievances or generate only new demands for help from the federal government." Rather he hoped Negroes would find solutions of their own.

We have been unable to determine how the two differing themes originated in the White House. We lean to the interpretation that two different sets of people were saying different things, rather than the possibility that one source was telling two stories.

The Report Made Public

On July 17 John D. Pomfret of the *New York Times* received the first White House authorization to read and write about the contents of the report but not to describe its authorship. He was told to attribute the report to a "White House study group" which was said to be "laying the groundwork for a massive attempt to revive the structure of the Negro family." *This* was said to be the key to the next phase in achievement of Negro equality.

Pomfret's selections from the report gave a somewhat distorted impression of its content. There was a full presentation of statements concerning Negro family disorganization including quotations that "the fundamental problem" was that of family structure and that "the fundamental source of weakness of the Negro community is the deterioration of the Negro family." The report's section on the roots of the problem, however, was completely ignored so that there was no real discussion of the effects of unemployment, low income, urbanization, or past history. The article noted that the administration was convinced that it must take the lead and no longer work as a broker for proposals put forward by pressure groups.

Pomfret's article apparently triggered a decision by the White House, in consultation with the Labor Department,

---

SUGGESTED READINGS

Blackways of Kent by Hylan Lewis (Chapel Hill, N. C.: Univ. of North Carolina Press, 1965). Lewis became an accepted member of a southern black community and wrote this report on his observations.

A Study of Slum Culture by Oscar Lewis (New York: Random House, 1968). The author provides information on the housing, education, occupations, income and patterns of migration of the Puerto Ricans in New York.

On Understanding Poverty; Perspectives from the Social Sciences by Daniel Patrick Moynihan (New York: Basic Books, 1969).

The Uneasy-Partnership: Social Science and the Federal Government in the Twentieth Century by Gene M. Lyons (New York: Russell Sage Foundation, 1969) treats the interaction between the government and social scientists in this century. It provides a good history of the development and problems of the social sciences.

Social Class and Social Policy by S. M. Miller and Frank Riessman (New York: Basic Books, 1968). The authors suggest that poverty is relative to time and place, and that a wide variety of factors have to be analyzed to determine poverty levels for any given area.

to release the report to those who requested it. Within a week Labor had placed an order with the Government Printing Office for 500 copies. No special consideration seems to have been given this decision; it just seemed a good idea.

As the controversy grew a series of preparatory meetings for the conference were held in the White House during the month of July. At these meetings social experts presented their views to a group of about 10 White House assistants and staff members. The experts came in one at a time, so that each man gave his own views, but without an opportunity for exchange with any of the other experts. Those called to the White House included a distinguished list of social scientists—Professors Talcott Parsons, Erik Erikson, Kenneth Clark, Robert Coles, Thomas Pettigrew, Urie Bronfenbrenner, and James Wilson.

Although at the time the Voting Rights Bill was signed in July, the President had asked James Farmer, John Lewis, Roy Wilkins, and A. Philip Randolph for their suggestions, no real planning was underway. For a number of reasons the planning staff was not appointed until early October. Yet press coverage of pre-planning sessions at the White House made it appear that actual planning was going on; and civil rights leaders were growing painfully aware that they had not been invited.

Then, on August 9, just before the Watts outbreak the full report was summarized by *Newsweek* in a two-page article, "The New Crisis: the Negro Family," which provided a full summary of the report's main points and three charts. For the first time, Moynihan is listed as "among the authors" of the report, although the White House apparently still preferred that the report be identified as its product. The report "set off a quiet revolution in the basic White House approach to the continuing American dilemma of race." *Newsweek* was aware of the touchiness of the issue: "The Negro family problem was scarcely news to social scientists. But its very intimacy has excluded it from the public dialogue of civil rights; it reaches too deep into white prejudices and Negro sensitivities."

On August 18, by far the most influential news story connecting the report with the post-riot atmosphere appeared. This was Roland Evans and Robert Novak's column "Inside Report" which was headlined simply: "The Moynihan Report." The article purported to tell the facts of an intense debate within the administration on how to handle the Moynihan report—"a much-suppressed, much-leaked Labor Department document which strips away usual equivocations and exposes the ugly truth about the big city Negro's plight." The report was said to bring up a taboo subject: preferential treatment for Negroes. The writers went on to say that Moynihan began working on his report because he was deeply disturbed by the big city riots of the summer of 1964. Their "inside" view of how Moynihan came to write the report continued: "He wondered, for instance, why in a time of decreasing unemployment, the plight of the urban Negro was getting worse—not better. His answer, a 78-page report (based largely on unexciting census bureau statistics), revealed the breakdown of the Negro family. He showed that broken homes, illegitimacy, and female-oriented homes were central to big city Negro problems."

This column seems to have been tremendously influential in the negative reaction to the report which was then beginning to build outside of the government. Readers in Washington and New York could find their worst fears confirmed in the column. The government was seriously entertaining a wild report which placed the causes of ghetto problems on the Negro family and not on unemployment or other institutional sources of deprivation.

In this context of presumably authoritative inside information, the statement that in a time of decreasing unemployment the plight of the urban Negro was getting worse because of the breakdown of the Negro family was highly incendiary, misleading, and highly disturbing to those in the civil rights field. From the Evans and Novak column it would be impossible to tell that the brunt of Moynihan's argument was that underemployment and related poverty produced family breakdown. In short, the Evans and Novak column neatly reflected the growing pall over the report—the emphasis on the riots, on a controversy about a sensitive issue, and the isolation of the Negro family as a problem divorced from more traditional issues of employment, housing, education, poverty.

New Meaning in Watts

Thus after Watts the report was also used to explain the riots. We have in our files 11 articles relating the Moynihan report or the breakdown of the Negro family to the Watts riot. Because of the newspaper coverage, the Moynihan report was taken as the government's explanation for the riots.

Watts gave the Moynihan report new meaning. It is difficult to say which of these two groups was more shaken by the riots. Members of the civil rights organizations have told us that the government was shaken and that they themselves were not. On the other hand, members of government have pointed their finger in the opposite direction. The question of who was more disturbed is of little importance in that it is clear that Watts renewed the convictions of both that something new must be done.

The urban Negro was in direct conflict with "law and order." The riot meant, for the Johnson Administration, that the poverty program had done little to solve the problems of the urban poor. (The fact that little money had been spent in the Watts area did in fact save the administration some embarrassment over the success or failure of the poverty program.)

Watts made explicit the failure of the movement. "Civil rights organizations have failed," commented James Farmer,

National Director of CORE just after Watts; "No one had any roots in the ghetto." And Bayard Rustin said, "We must hold ourselves responsible for not reaching them." Thus Watts made clear the alienation of the urban Negro from the civil rights movement.

One can readily imagine the uneasiness that had developed in the civil rights organizations by the time of Watts. They had been brought into the White House separately and lackadaisically, but not with the academicians who, according to the newspapers, were having a major role in the planning of the White House Conference. In addition to this, there were constant references to a report on the Negro family that was evidently having a great influence on the administration. But they thought the report was still an internal document and not available to them.

With no official word from Washington concerning the report's relationship to the White House Conference, other than previous newsleaks, and copies of the report only beginning to be available, controversy over the Moynihan report developed in a vacuum.

The "secret" or "public" status of the document during August and September is a strange issue indeed. No official announcement as to the report's availability or "declassification" was made; the press routinely referred to it as "still secret." Yet, beginning in mid-August the Labor Department began filling requests as they came in, limiting orders to one per customer because of the demand. (It should be noted that once the document was assigned a GPO number and a sales price it was in the public domain; why the newsmen who had these copies continued to refer to it as "still unreleased" is a mystery.)

By the end of September GPO had delivered over 2000 copies to Labor, more than half of which had been distributed to government officials (including heavy demand from Capitol Hill), the press and assorted individuals, voluntary organizations, and academics. By mid-1966, GPO had printed 72,133 copies of the report and sold 48,520 copies.

Several government civil rights experts warned the White House, with increasing urgency, that civil rights leaders were becoming greatly concerned at the newspaper and rumor-mill statements that the conference would be "about the family." The White House, however, seemed to believe that civil rights organizations had been adequately informed about the contents of the conference and there was no need for special communications or clarifying press releases. As one outside observer commented, "They just didn't work on their problem, even after they were told about it."

The early concern stimulated by newspaper versions of the report is reflected in a letter written on August 27, by sociologist Herbert Gans to Richard Goodwin of the White House staff. Gans wrote:

I think the emphasis (on family difficulties) is all to the good, if not overdone. There is a danger, however, that it may result in a wave of social work and psychiatric solutions intended to change the Negro female-based family to a middle class type. Such solutions could deflect attention away from the economic causes of the Negro problem.

Another event added to the growing concern within the civil rights movement. It took place aboard the presidential yacht, the *Honey Fitz,* on September 15.

Vice-President Humphrey decided to get together with civil rights leaders informally to foster better communications between the government and the movement. The Vice-President's staff arranged an afternoon ride on the *Honey Fitz* and invited several leaders of the civil rights movement including Clarence Mitchell of the Washington NAACP, Floyd McKissick of CORE, Whitney Young, Martin Luther King, Andrew Young of the SCLC along with the Vice-President, Wiley Branton, and several of the Vice-President's staff.

Accounts of the boat ride are not consistent, but one thing is clear—it did not turn out to be the relaxing evening on the Potomac expected by the Vice-President. Instead, "they almost turned the boat over." An argument began over enforcement of the voting rights bill.

But another matter intruded. One of the Vice-President's staff attempted to answer the demands of McKissick and Mitchell for more registrars with the question, *"What about this Moynihan report; the problem is more than just getting people registered to vote?"* Civil rights leaders replied, "Let's get back to the specific issue of *now!*" As McKissick explained to us: "Many of the students in the South had made personal sacrifice in order to get people out to vote. But when we did this, when we got masses to go, there were no registrars. That made us waste a whole damn summer of work. Then they go and turn to the Moynihan report."

Although we have no indication that the boat ride had a direct relationship to the coming White House Conference, it was one of the few communications between the government and civil rights organizations during September. The implication of the boat ride conversation seemed clear to the civil rights leaders. The administration was using the Moynihan report as its excuse for not moving more rapidly on the implementation of laws.

The Rumors Develop

By early October several major criticisms of the report had developed. First, the report seemed to overlook the problem of discrimination and place the blame for Negroes' deprivations on the Negro community rather than the white community, and thus was used to justify the status quo. It might be used by Southern racists to support the racist doctrine that the Negro is inferior and segregation must be maintained. It could be used by politicians as an excuse to halt further government efforts in the area of civil rights—the government had used it on the *Honey Fitz* to parry the civil rights leaders' attack on the Justice Department for not sending more federal voting registrars. Finally the report apparently was to be at the center of the White House Conference "To Fulfill These Rights."

By October, the White House silence concerning rumors seemed a reversal of the Howard speech—the report that "caused" the President to call for additional bold steps in civil rights and urban poverty seemed now to become the government's excuse to do nothing but achieve consensus.

Floyd McKissick, the new director of CORE, said of the report: "My major criticism of the report is that it assumes that middle class American values are the correct ones for everyone in America. Just because Moynihan believes in these values doesn't mean that they are the best."

Clarence Mitchell of the Washington office of the NAACP objected to the report because it "implied that it was necessary for the improvement of the Negro community to come from within."

Bayard Rustin criticized the report by saying, "It left people with the view that this was a complete and perfectly true picture of the Negro families. But then it gave no suggestions for corrective measures. Second, the report accentuated or exaggerated the negative. One important point that must be made is what may seem to be a disease to the white middle class may be a healthy adaptation to the Negro lower class. Finally, we must talk about the poor family, not simply the Negro family. Poverty is a problem. It is amazing to me that Negro families exist at all."

But others saw it another way. Many persons in the movement agreed with Robert Carter of the NAACP who said: "I could not understand the great shock that people were expressing over the report. Moynihan, it seemed to me, was making a comment on the results of discrimination in our society. It's an old story and not a startling discovery and not new. These things that he points out—the pathologies of the ghetto—are a result of discrimination."

Then Carter added a very perceptive comment, "The real costs of doing what must be done in order to improve the structure of the Negro family are great. My question is, is the administration really prepared to do these things? President Johnson's speech was not an artificial abstraction; the problem is whether or not he is now willing to carry out what he said he would do."

Norman Hill of the AFL-CIO, and previously national program chairman for CORE, said, "I liked the report. It told me that wide economic changes in the social structure were needed in order to solve these problems. Nevertheless, I can understand the defensiveness of civil rights activists. There are things that are in the report that could well create problems for them."

Whitney Young said, "My book, *To Be Equal,* identifies the same pathologies in the Negro ghetto. I think that the title *The Negro Family* was tragic . . . it has stigmatized an entire group of people when the majority of that group of people do not fall into the category of the Negro family that Moynihan describes. Also one can't talk about the pathologies of Negroes without talking about the pathologies of white society. If Negroes are sick socially, then whites are sick morally."

Martin Luther King, in a speech made on October 29, in Westchester County, New York, synthesized civil rights reactions to the Moynihan report succinctly with the state-

"Almost one-fourth of Negro families are headed by females. Only a minority of Negro children reach the age of 18 having lived all their lives with both parents." *(The Negro Family: The Case for National Action,* page 9.)

George Gardner

ment, "As public awareness (of the breakdown of the Negro family) increases there will be dangers and opportunities. The opportunity will be to deal fully rather than haphazardly with the problem as a whole—to see it as a social catastrophe and meet it as other disasters are met with an adequacy of resources. The danger will be that problems will be attributed to innate Negro weaknesses and used to justify neglect and rationalize oppression."

Civil rights leaders held a meeting in New York in mid-September where they decided they must get into the conference planning. When representatives went to Washington, they discovered for themselves there was no planning to get into.

Finally, on October 4 the President announced the dates of the coming conference, November 15 and 16. Final arrangements for the conference began with six weeks to go. There was no continuity between this burst of activity in the fall and the earlier summer meetings with social scientists except for the fact that some White House staff members were involved in both.

Vietnam Complications

It is difficult to understand why the White House allowed this hiatus to develop and why they refused to effectively deny that this conference was about the family. Perhaps it was because they considerably underestimated the complex intellectual and human relations task involved; certainly it was because Watts took up so much of the energy of those who were involved in the planning. And as one top government official observed: "You know, there are fewer than 20 men in the government who can really get something new done; with Vietnam building up they just had to drop this other thing." A highly placed expert on the civil rights movement reported that he was called to the White House in July to discuss the conference with the President and his staff, but when he arrived nobody could see him because they were tied up on Vietnam problems.

One close observer of Washington civil rights events has called this sequence of events an example of the "benign Machiavellianism" of the Johnson administration. It appears that failure to treat the conference as the important event it had first seemed served several functions. First of all, it strongly disorganized the civil rights forces who in the end managed to bring about a show of unity only in opposition to the Moynihan report, *not in effective demands on the administration.*

For a government that wanted to move vigorously on social and economic reform to benefit Negroes, the Moynihan *report* provided a strong justification. For a government that wanted to "cool it," to avoid action that could no longer be afforded without having to take the blame for inaction, the Moynihan *controversy* provided an ideal distraction. The President and his aides could relax. A civil rights strategy of "getting Moynihan" would obviously distract from "getting" the White House in the sense of either pressing for expanded federal commitments, or protesting the lack of action.

Of the considerable disorganization in the administration's handling of the conference planning, one high government source said to us, "There was no one in charge of the conference. Someone suggested to put the conference off until the spring, but they said they couldn't do this because the President had said in his speech that there would be a fall conference. So someone suggested they could set the date in the fall and make it a planning session."

It must also be remembered that the President is a person who has the habit of delaying decisions and does not like other people to get him in trouble. Some say he sensed that the White House Conference was getting out of control in two ways. First, it was possible for the conference to become a forum on Vietnam since civil rights leaders had joined the critics of government policy in Vietnam. Second, the White House apparently began to be concerned about progress the conference might develop; would the conference come up with recommendations that the administration was unwilling or unable to carry out?

Until the latter part of September it was widely believed that the conference was going to focus on the family. At two meetings in October the civil rights people were fully brought into the planning. They were made to understand that the conference would have eight panels, only one dealing with the family (a decision made in July). Further, the family panel would center on the paper written by sociologist Hylan Lewis—a non-Moynihan approach. There were still some objections to any discussion of the family, but White House representatives insisted that at least this much of the Moynihan thesis be retained.

In the middle of October CORE met with its recently formed research advisory staff made up of social scientists such as Herbert Gans, S. M. Miller, and Frank Riessman. Since it was understood that Lewis' family paper would not be "Moynihanian," CORE adopted the strategy of developing its own social-science-based proposals and foregoing an attack on Moynihan.

The Protestant Council Critique

During the early fall there was a parallel development which increased the controversy over the Moynihan report. Those involved—the church-race groups of the Protestant Council of the City of New York and the National Council of Churches—were not close enough to the networks between civil rights and government to slow down when the civil rights organizations changed strategy and began to neglect the Moynihan thesis.

The church's involvement in the Moynihan controversy was spearheaded by Dr. Benjamin Payton who in the summer of 1965 was Director of the Office of Religion and Race of the Protestant Council. (Since that time he has been promoted to the job vacated by Robert Spike, Director of the National Council of Churches' Commission on Religion and Race.) Payton became concerned about the Moynihan report when he read John Pomfret's article in the *New York Times* (July 17). He began writing his critique of the Moynihan report during Moynihan's campaign in New York, but he delayed releasing his critique until after the New York primary on September 14. Payton worked very closely with Mrs. Anna Hedgeman of the National Council of Churches who was running against Moynihan in the New York primary. (Both lost.)

Payton mailed several hundred copies of the critique, including some "to persons I knew in universities. I wanted sociological critiques of the Moynihan report done as soon as possible." His paper was a vigorous attack on the report, combining his views with those of William Ryan, with an effort to substitute "metropolitics" for "family stability" as the important issue. (See page 8.) One is left with the impression that his quarrel was with the public image of the Moynihan report rather than the report itself.

On November 9, under the leadership of Dr. Payton's office, a New York Pre-White House Conference meeting of approximately 100 leaders of New York civic, religious, and civil rights organizations, resolved: *"It is our position that the question of family stability be stricken entirely from the agenda and be approached through an economic and urban analysis of the needs in the critical area of jobs, housing, and quality integrated education."* (Italics ours.)

Whatever the motivation and/or lack of communication with civil rights leaders who were already taking another course, it is clear that the Protestant Council's involvement in the Moynihan controversy sustained the issue after most civil rights leaders were willing to let it die.

Negro women also objected to the implications of the report. Parts of the report were the target of Mary Keyserling's (director of the Women's Bureau of the Department of Labor) speech to the Conference of Negro Women held in Washington November 11. The women criticized the report for several reasons. It implied that the matrifocal family was itself pathological, rather than being a means of adapting to the slums. The report did not give credit to the strength of the matrifocal family. Finally, Moynihan had implied that Negro women were overemployed and should be taken out of their jobs to open up the labor market for men.

Confrontation at the Conference

The conference planners were in an extremely ticklish position. Too vigorous a repudiation of Moynihan could be taken as a criticism of the President; no repudiation could be seen as part of a government plot to "do in" the movement. The report was so controversial that it was an embarrassment to all concerned.

At the opening session of the conference Berl Bernhard, its executive director, amused the participants by saying, "I want you to know that I have been reliably informed that no such person as Daniel Patrick Moynihan exists."

In order to head off direct intrusion of the controversy into the conference proceedings, its planners chose the organizer of the family session very carefully. He had to be a man who was trusted by civil rights groups, who could not be considered tainted by the brush of "subtle racism." The planners chose Hylan Lewis, professor of sociology at Howard University, a man with a distinguished record of research into Negro family life. Civil rights activists were reassured by this choice, and understood that the tone of his agenda paper would be, if anything, anti-Moynihan.

The agenda paper for the family panel represented a careful attempt to shed light on the situation of Negro families, particularly poor Negro families, and to discuss some of the issues without fanning the controversy.

Though it did not contain any direct attack on the Moynihan report or its main thesis, the agenda paper was inevitably read and reported as a critical response to the report. The *Washington Post* reported that it "challenges the main thrust of the Moynihan report."

The family panel discussion concentrated quite heavily on the necessity for employment, income maintenance, and education programs to provide sources of family stability for poor Negroes, as well as for poor whites.

The emphasis on "social work approaches" to family stability, so feared by critics of the report, was a distinctly minor theme in the sessions. Much of the discussion echoed Moynihan's criticisms of the welfare bureaucracy.

Moynihan was a participant in the family panel. But he felt so compromised by the controversy that he spoke only three times.

During the second day, however, someone gave Moynihan a copy of Payton's critique and he read it quickly. Late in the morning session, Moynihan rose to speak directly to Payton on "a point of personal privilege." Moynihan expressed difficulty in believing that Payton had read his report. He asked the assembled group, "Do you see that the object of this report was not to say that jobs don't matter, but rather that jobs matter in the most fundamental way? . . . (and that) we can measure our success or failure as a society, not in terms of the gross national product, not in terms of income level . . . but in the health, and the living, loving reality of the family in our society."

Payton was unwilling to accept Moynihan's explanation. He noted Moynihan's statement that the deterioration of the Negro family is "the fundamental source of weakness of the Negro community at the present time." Payton felt that this added up to a view "that the Negro family is now probably so pathological that even the provision of jobs won't do it." Because of these errors "conclusions have become very widespread which have done the Negro community a fundamental harm." The confrontation was dramatic, but did little to clarify matters.

The intrusion of the controversy was picked up by the press ("Moynihan Conspicuously Ignored: The Non-Person at The Conference"), and became part of a general administration attempt to discredit and downgrade its accomplishments. Thus, Evans and Novak, in a column headlined, "Civil Rights Disaster," wrote that "one high policy maker in the administration grumbled bitterly that the Negro leadership knows only how to put its hand out to Uncle Sam." The *New York Times* observed that the administration was displeased that the subject of the family was rejected or ignored—"it's back to the drafting board at the White House."

'Can Do' Conference in June

At the full-scale White House Conference "To Fulfill These Rights" in June Moynihan was present, but his paper on the Negro family had been consigned to oblivion. There were no copies available at the conference.

Evidently the decision to remove the topic of the Negro family from the agenda of the White House Conference was made sometime in the early part of the year, *before* the President appointed the council for the June conference. *No copies of the Moynihan report were made available to the council.* As Clifford Alexander of the White House staff firmly stated, "The family is not an action topic for a 'cando' conference."

This change was not welcomed by all. Dorothy Height, president of the National Council for Negro Women said at a press conference on the first morning of the conference that "Those of us who are aware of the problems of the Negro family look to this conference with the hope that something will be done about the family in the ghetto."

But the subject of the Negro family was rarely broached. Roy Wilkins explained that "The Negro community resents, without logic, the efforts to focus attention on the Negro family, as if it were a moral criticism of themselves. They regard it as a diversionary matter to the real issues—housing, employment, job training, and justice."

Political Uses of Social Science

The most significant question raised by the Moynihan report has to do with *the establishment of an independent federal government stance with respect to the situation of the Negro American.* The government's attempt to lead rather than follow in the civil rights struggle is meaningful only if the government puts forward a program. It was quite clear that an effective program will require major federal expenditures; the more intimately the administration officials understand the problems Moynihan put on their desks the clearer it will become to them that the back wages due the Negro community dwarf any current domestic program.

Whether the government assumes an independent role or not, a very real question is raised concerning the adequacy of the presently existing liaison mechanisms between the federal government and the civil rights organizations. The government, probably at the White House level, needs much more extensive liaison with the civil rights movement than it now has but it probably will not tolerate this until it is ready to make some major permanent commitment in this area.

The central issue raised by the Moynihan report for the government-social science relationship is that of the political use of social science findings. The suitable criteria for evaluating a persuasive document are not that all the i's are dotted, but that the persuasive document selects crucial issues with which to deal and that it presents these crucial issues in such a way that they do not directly contradict or go counter to a fuller and more balanced intellectual understanding of what is being dealt with.

Having said this, however, we must look at some of the dangers involved in such a persuasive document. The greatest danger is that the sharply focused persuasive argument can be taken as presenting the "whole truth." If the policy generating process stops with that one document, or if the document comes to be used for purposes other than that for which it was designed, then the danger of unconstructive uses is considerably increased.

The most central issue in the civil rights organizations and social science area has to do with the extent to which private organizations like those of the civil rights movement have the resources to make use of social science information in pursuit of their policy goals. As Melvin Webber has observed: information represents political and economic capital, "information like money, yields power to those who have it."

If the federal government ever actually succeeds in establishing an independent role in the civil rights area, failure to make extensive and sophisticated use of the social sciences will put the civil rights movement at a very great competitive disadvantage in bringing to bear countervailing power and proposals.

In their pursuit of adequate comprehension of the reality of the lives of Negro Americans and the forces which play on them, social scientists are likely to come increasingly into conflict with established and preferred views on the part of highly varied white power groups on the one hand, and civil rights groups on the other. They have the task, then, of guarding their autonomy against the pressures of all of these groups which may wish to dictate the nature of the problems considered, the findings developed, and the implications drawn.

Further, social science as a whole, as well as the individual social scientist, has a responsibility not only to study significant problems and to report findings and policy implications accurately, but also to be sensitive to the way these findings are used, particularly to whether or not they are used in ways that seem illegitimate given the findings. Social science has a responsibility in this way to monitor the persuasive or technical applications of social science and to comment upon these uses in a vigorous and meaningful way.

Social Science Yogis & Military Commissars

An analysis of the contents and implications of a confidential report on how social science research can benefit the Defense Department

IRVING LOUIS HOROWITZ

"The bonds between the government and the universities are . . . an arrangement of convenience, providing the government with politically usable knowledge and the university with badly needed funds." The speaker of these words, Senator J. William Fulbright, went on to warn that such alliances may endanger the universities, may bring about "the surrender of independence, the neglect of teaching, and the distortion of scholarship." Many other distinguished Americans are worried by the growing number of alliances between the military and the university.

The Setting

Instead of the expected disclaimers and denials from university officials, however, in recent months these men—from both the administrative and academic sides —have rushed to take up any slack in doing secret research on campus, asking that the number of projects they are already handling be increased. Arwin A. Dougal, assistant director of the Pentagon's office for research and engineering, has indicated that while some major universities are gravely concerned about academic research for military ends, most universities realize how important "classified research" is to the national security. Indeed, Dougal has said that many professors involved in secret research actually try to retain their security clearances when their projects are completed. Rather than disengaging themselves, they, like many university leaders, are eager to participate to an even greater extent.

Symptomatic of the ever-tightening bond between the military and the social scientist is a "confidential," 53-page document entitled *Report of the Panel on Defense Social and Behavioral Sciences*. It was the offspring of a summer 1967 meeting, in Williamstown, Mass., of members of the Defense Science Board of the National Academy of Sciences. This board is the highest-ranking science advisory group of the Defense Department. The meeting's purpose: to discuss which social-science research could be of most use to the Department of Defense (DoD).

The *Report of the Panel on Defense Social and Behavioral Sciences* throws a good deal of light on current relations between the national government and the social sciences. Unlike Project Camelot, the abortive academic-military project to investigate counterinsurgency potentials in the Third World, this Report was not inspired by government contractual requests. It is the work of leading social scientists who have been closely connected with federal research. Unlike *Report from Iron Mountain,* this Report can hardly be described as a humanistic hoax. The authors are known, the purpose of the Report explicit, and the consequences clearly appreciated by all concerned. What we have in this Report is a collective statement by eminent social scientists, a statement that can easily be read as the ominous conversion of social science into a service industry of the Pentagon.

Most of the scholars who prepared this Report have one striking similarity—they have powerful and simultaneous academic and government linkages. They move casually and easily from university to federal affiliation —and back again to the university.

The panel's chairman, S. Rains Wallace, the exception, is president of the American Institutes of Research, a nonprofit organization that does research under contract for government agencies, including the DoD.

Gene M. Lyons, who is executive secretary of the Advisory Committee on Government Programs in the Behavioral Sciences of the National Research Council (affiliated with the National Academy of Sciences), is also a professor at Dartmouth College. (He maintains, however, that he attended only one day of the meeting, and as an observer only.)

Peter Dorner, functioning through the Executive Office of the President on the Council of Economic Advisers, is also a professor of economics at the Land Tenure Center of the University of Wisconsin.

Eugene Webb, listed as a professor at Stanford University, is now serving a term as a member of the Institute for Defense Analysis, specifically, its science and technology division.

Other panel members—Harold Guetzkow of Northwestern University; Michael Pearce of the RAND Corporation; anthropologist A. Kimball Romney of Harvard University; and Roger Russell, formerly of Indiana University and now Vice-Chancellor for Academic Affairs at the University of California (Irvine) —also shift back and forth between the polity and the academy. It is plain, then, that these men have penetrated the political world more deeply than members of past project-dominated research activities.

In addition to this similarity, nearly all of these social scientists have had overseas experience, and are intimately connected with federal use of social science for foreign-area research. Yet, as in the case of Camelot, this common experience does not seem to produce any strong ideological unanimity. The men range from relatively conservative political theorists to avowed pacifists. This underscores the fact that patriotism and professional purpose tend to supersede the political viewpoints or credos these men may adhere to.

The Report

The Report closely follows the memorandum that John S. Foster Jr., director of Defense Research and Engineering of the Department of Defense, issued to the chairman of the panel. Foster's marching orders to the panel members requested that they consider basically four topics: "high-payoff" areas in research and development—"areas of social and behavioral science research in which it would be reasonable to expect great payoffs over the next three to ten years"; research to solve manpower problems; Project THEMIS, a DoD project for upgrading the scientific and engineering capabilities of various academic institutions so they can do better research for the Defense Department; and, finally, broad-ranging government-university relationships.

Before commenting on the Report, let me provide a summary of its findings and recommendations.

To begin with, the Report urges increased effort and funding for research on manpower, in all its aspects; for research on organization studies; for research on decision-making; for increasing the understanding of problems in foreign areas; and for research on man and his physical environment.

■ Under "Manpower," we read, among other things:
"In order to make full use of the opportunities provided by Project 100,000 [to make soldiers out of rehabilitated juvenile delinquents] both for the military and for the national economy, we recommend that fully adequate funds be invested to cover all aspects of the military and subsequent civilian experience of the individuals involved."

■ Under "Organization Studies":
"Research on style of leadership and improved meth-

Soldiers ready to buck crowds at the march on the Pentagon, 1967.

ods of training for leadership should be revitalized."
- Under "Decision-Making":

"Techniques for the improvement of items which might assist in forecasting alliances, neutralities, hostile activities, etc., and for use in tactical decision-making need to be expanded, applied, and tested in the real world."
- Under "Understanding of Operational Problems in Foreign Areas":

"Despite the difficulties attendant upon research in foreign areas, it must be explicitly recognized that the missions of the DoD cannot be successfully performed in the absence of information on (a) socio-cultural patterns in various areas including beliefs, values, motivations, etc.; (b) the social organization of troops, including political, religious, and economic; (c) the effect of change and innovation upon socio-cultural patterns and socio-cultural organization of groups; (d) study and evaluation of action programs initiated by U.S. or foreign agencies in under-developed countries.

"Solid, precise, comparative, and current empirical data developed in a programmatic rather than diffuse and opportunistic fashion are urgently needed for many areas of the world. This goal should be pursued by: (a) multidisciplinary research teams; (b) series of field studies in relevant countries; (c) strong representation of quantitative and analytic skills; (d) a broad empirical data base."
- Under "Man and His Physical Environment":

"Continuing and additional research are needed on the effect of special physical and psychological environments upon performance and on possibilities for the enhancement of performance through a better understanding of man's sensory and motor output mechanisms, the development of artificial systems which will aid performance, and the search for drugs or foods which may enhance it."
- Under "Methodology":

"We recommend increased emphasis upon research in behavioral-science methodology. While this is basic to all of the areas listed above, it needs to be recognized as worthy of investment in its own right. The systematic observation of the many quasi-experimental situations which occur in everyday military activities must be made possible if we are to learn from experience. We recommend that a capability be established in one or more suitable in-house laboratories to address the question of how the logistical problems of such observation can be solved."
- On government-university relations:

"There is disagreement concerning the involvement of first-rate academic groups in behavioral science research relevant to long-term DoD needs. The task statement implies that DoD has not been successful in enlisting the interest and service of an eminent group of behavioral scientists in most of the areas relevant to it. This panel does not concur. We therefore recommend that the [National Academy of Sciences] Panel on Behavioral and Social Sciences be asked to address this problem and to determine whether, in fact, an acceptable proportion of first-rate academic workers are involved in DoD behavioral-science research."

"More high-quality scientists could probably be interested in DoD problems if DoD would more

Alliances between the universities and the government, Senator Fulbright has said, may bring about "the surrender of independence, the neglect of teaching, and the distortion of scholarship."

Hugh Rodgers

Why the DoD is No. 1

The Department of Defense (DoD) is the most sought-after and frequently-found sponsor of social-science research. And the DoD is sought and found by the social scientists, not, as is often imagined, the other way around. Customarily, military men provide only grudging acceptance of any need for behavioral research.

There are four distinct reasons why the DoD is sponsoring more and more social-science research.

■ First, money. In fiscal 1968, Congressional appropriations for research and development amount to the monumental sum of $14,971.4 million. Of this, an incredible $13,243.0 million, or about 85 percent, is distributed among three agencies whose primary concern is the military system: the Atomic Energy Commission, the National Aeronautics and Space Administration, and the DoD. The figure for the DoD alone is $6680.0 million. This means that a single federal agency commands nearly two-fifths of the government research dollar. So it is easy to see why so much effort and energy is expended by social scientists trying to capture some of the monies the DoD can experiment with. As bees flock to honey, men flock to money—particularly in an era when costly data-processing and data-gathering strain the conventional sources of financing.

■ Second, the protection that research has when done for the DoD. I am referring to the blanket and indiscriminate way in which Congressional appropriations are made for both basic and applied research. Policy-linked social scientists operate under an umbrella of the secrecy established by the DoD's research agencies. Reasons of security ward off harassment by Congressional committees. Attacks over supposed misallocation of funds and resources—undergone by the National Institutes of Health at the hands of the committee headed by Rep. L.H. Fountain of North Carolina—are spared those academics with Defense Department funding.

This dispensation is strikingly illustrated by the fact that DoD allocations for research and development are not itemized the way allocations are for Health, Education, and Welfare. This auditing cover allows for even more experimenting in DoD spending than its already swollen funds might indicate. Such a *carte blanche* situation probably places far less of a strain on social scientists than would be the case if they worked for other agencies. In the world of research, power provides the illusion of freedom.

■ Third, the relatively blank-check Congressional approach to DoD funds, and the security umbrella of the auditing system, provide social scientists with unlimited resources. DoD allocations are not broken down into sub-agencies, nor are any of their specialized activities or services checked—unlike the usual scrutiny directed at other agencies.

That this fact has not gone entirely unnoticed is shown by the Congressional demand that as of 1968 the DoD be called to account on an appropriation budget.

■ Fourth, the DoD's connection with the "national security" —which protects the DoD and those who work for it— offers great temptations to social researchers interested in the "big news." For it enables the DoD not only to outspend such agencies as the National Science Foundation in university-based activities, but to penetrate areas of non-Defense research that are central only to the social-science researcher. Programs to support juvenile-delinquency research (Project 100,000) and others to upgrade academic institutions (Project THEMIS) are sponsored by the DoD rather than by the Office of Economic Opportunity, and not simply because of their disproportionate fundings. Just as important is the legitimation the DoD can provide for policy-oriented researchers in sensitive areas.

These are the main reasons why many social-science researchers are now enlisting the support of the DoD in their activities—despite the negative publicity surrounding Project Camelot and other such fallen angels.   I.L.H.

---

frequently state its research needs in terms which are meaningful to the investigator rather than to the military.... Publicity concerning the distinguished behavioral scientists who have long-term commitments to the DoD should be disseminated as a way of reassuring younger scientists and improving our research image."

The Panelists

Why did these distinguished social scientists accept the assignment from the DoD? Most of them seemed particularly intrigued by the chance to address important issues. They view the work done by the DoD in such areas as racially segregated housing, or the rehabilitation of juvenile delinquents through military participation, as fascinating illustrations of how social science can settle social issues. It is curious how this thirst for the application of social science led the panelists to ignore the *prima facie* fact that the DoD is in the defense business, and that therefore it inevitably tends to assign high priority to military potential and effectiveness. Further, the question of what is important is continually linked to matters of relevance to the DoD. In this way, the question of professional autonomy is transformed into one of patriotic responsibility.

In general, the idealism of social scientists participating in DoD-sponsored research stems from their profound belief in the rectifiability of federal shortcomings, as well as in the perfectibility of society through the use of social science. Despite the obviousness of the point, what these social scientists forget is that the federal government as well as its agencies is limited by historical and geopolitical circumstances. It is committed to managing cumbersome, overgrown committees and data-gathering agencies. It is committed to a status quo merely for the sake of rational functioning. It can only tinker with innovating ideas. Thus federal agencies will limit investigation simply to what

George Gardner

In its typically dry language, the Report notes: "Exposure to conditions to which man is not normally adjusted, 'environmental stresses,' produce compensatory modifications of behavior." Here, as part of a training program for army medics, a serviceman wears a plastic band that depicts his intestines spilling out of a deep abdominal wound.

is immediately useful not out of choice, but from necessity.

The social scientist often imagines he is a policy formulator, an innovating designer. Because of the cumbersome operations of government, he will be frustrated in realizing this self-image and be reduced to one more instrumental agent. His designing mentality, his strain toward perfecting, will appear unrealistic in the light of what he can do. He gets caught up in theoryless applications to immediacy, surrenders the value of confronting men with an image of what *can be,* and simply accepts what others declare *must be.* Thus, what the social scientist knows comes down to what the Defense Department under present circumstances can use.

Although the initiative for this Report came from the social scientists, the DoD provided the structure and direction of its content. To a remarkable degree, the study group accepted DoD premises.

For example, the two major assumptions that influenced its thinking are stated baldly. First, since the DoD's job now embraces new responsibilities, its proper role becomes as much to wage "peacefare" as warfare. Peacefare is spelled out as pacification of total populations, as well as a role in the ideological battle between East and West. Toward such ends, it is maintained, social science can play a vital part.

Nowhere in the document is the possibility considered that the DoD ought not to be in many of these activities—that perhaps the division of labor has placed too great an emphasis upon this one agency of government at the expense of all others. Nor is it anywhere made clear that similar types of educational and antipoverty programs the DoD is engaged in are already under way in other branches of government—that DoD activities might be duplicating and needlessly multiplying the efforts of the Department of Health, Education and Welfare or the National Science Foundation.

The second explicit assumption the group makes is that hardware alone will not win modern wars; Manpower is needed, too. Here the panelists see social science as providing data on the dynamics of cultural change and a framework for the needs and attitudes of other people.

But here, too, there is a remarkable absence of any consideration of the sort of "manpower" deployed in foreign environments; or of the differing responses of overseas peoples to such manpower. The foreign role of the U.S. Defense Department is simply taken as a given, a datum to be exploited for the display of social science information. In this sense, U.S. difficulties with foreign military activities can be interpreted as a mere misunderstanding of the nature of a problem. Expertise and objectivity can then be called upon where a policy design is lacking or failing. Thus even the DoD can mask policy shortcomings behind the fact of a previously inadequate supply of data. In this way, the credibility gap gets converted into a mechanical informational gap. Which is exactly what is done in the Report. All efforts, in other words, are bent to maximizing social science participation rather than to minimizing international conflict.

Still a third assumption of the panel participants— one that is not acknowledged—is that their professional autonomy will not be seriously jeopardized by the very fact of their dependence upon the DoD. Indeed, many scholars seem to have abandoned their primary research interests for the secondary ones that can be funded. And the main responsibility for this shift lies not with the DoD but with the social-science professions and the scholarly community at large.

As one panel member ironically noted, in response to my questionnaire, the position of the DoD is an unhappy reflection of university demands that individual scholars and university presidents pay for expanding university overhead and enlarge graduate programs—rather than any insistence by federal agencies that the nature of social science be transformed. Another panel member indicated that, whatever dishonor may exist in the present relationships between social science and the DoD, the main charge would have to be leveled at the professoriat, rather than at the funding agencies. And while this assignment of priorities in terms of who is responsible for the present era of ill will and mistrust can be easily overdone, and lead to a form of higher apologetics in which there is mutual accusation by the social scientists and government policy-makers, it does seem clear that the simplistic idea that the evil government corrupts the good social scientist is not only an exaggeration but, more often, a deliberate misrepresentation.

The Findings

Reexamining the specific findings of first section of the Report, "High Payoff Research in Development Areas," leaves no doubt that the panelists mean by "high payoff" those potential rewards to be netted by the DoD, rather than advantages to be gained by social scientists. This is made explicit in the section on "Manpower," in which the main issues are contended to concern problems of improving the performance of soldiers equipped with high-level technology. It is in this connection that the panelists heartily approve of Project 100,000. Although (with the exception of two panelists) there is a special cloudiness as to the nature of Project 100,000, the panelists have no doubt that the employment of delinquents in this fashion makes the best use of marginal manpower for a "tremendous payoff" for the future efficiency of the defense establishment.

A number of the Report's recommendations amount to little more than the repetition of basic organizational shibboleths. But even at this level, special problems seem to arise. There is confusion in the minds of the panelists, or at least throughout the Report that they prepared, about what constitutes internal DoD functions as opposed to those belonging to general military functions. The phrase "military establishment" functions as an umbrella disguising this ambiguity. Not only is the relationship between a civilian-led DoD and a "military establishment" unresolved, but beyond that the panelists appear willing to discount the organizational intermingling of the DoD with other governmental agencies—such as the Census Bureau, the Department of Labor, and the Department of Health, Education, and Welfare.

This leads to a tacit acceptance of DoD organizational colonialism. Not only is the DoD urged to be on the lookout for other agencies' collecting similar data and doing similar sorts of analyses, but also an explicit request that the DoD exert a special effort to use the work of outside agencies is included. On behalf of "cooperation," there exists the risk of invasion of privacy, and other dangers encountered when any single department functions as a total system incorporating the findings of other sub-units.

The Report contends that those parts of the armed services responsible for developing basic knowledge about decision-making have done their work well. It is interesting that no examples are given. Moreover, the military and civilian personnel who provide support for decision-making within the military establishment are said to have a rare opportunity to contribute to this steadily-improving use of sound decision-making models for areas like material procurement for frontline battle medical services. Nothing is said about the nature of the conflict to be resolved, or the values employed in such decisions.

While several members of the panel, in response to the questionnaire of mine, indicated that they held this Report to be an indirect resolution of problems raised by Project Camelot, the formulations used in this Report are similar to those used in the Camelot study concerning overseas research.

The Report states: "Comparative organizational work should not be done only within civilian groups such as large-scale building and construction consortia and worldwide airlines systems, but also within foreign military establishments." In Project Camelot, the same desire for military information was paramount. Curiously, no attention is given to whether, in fact, this is a high-payoff research area; or if it is, how this work is to be done without threatening the sovereignty of other nations. In other words, although the Report superficially is dedicated to the principle of maximum use of social science, this principle is not brought into play at the critical point. The ambiguities and doubts raised by previous DoD incursions into the area of foreign social research remain intact and are in no way even partially resolved.

The panelists are dedicated to the principle of high-payoff research, but appear to be disquietingly convinced that this is equivalent to whatever the members of the panel themselves are doing, or whatever their professional specialties are. Thus a high-payoff research area becomes the study of isolation upon individual and group behavior; or the area of simulation of field experiences that the military may encounter; or the study of behavior under conditions of ionizing radiation. It is not incidental that in each instance the panelists themselves have been largely engaged in such kinds of work. One is left with the distinct impression that a larger number of panelists would have yielded only a larger number of "high-payoff" areas, rather than an integrated framework of needs. This leads to a general suspicion that the Report is much more self-serving than a simple review of its propositions indicates.

The references to methodology again raise the specter of Camelot, since it is evident that no general methodology is demonstrated in the Report itself and no genuine innovations are formulated for future methodological directions. There is no discussion of the kind of methodology likely to yield meaningful prediction. Instead, the DoD is simply notified of the correctness of its own biases. We are told that "predictive indicators of a conflict or revolutionary overthrow are examples of the type of data which can gain from control applications." No illustrations of the success of such predictors is given. The purpose turns out to be not so much prediction as control of revolutionary outbreaks. This, then, constitutes the core methodological message of the Report.

Project THEMIS

As for Project THEMIS, designed to upgrade scientific and engineering performances at colleges and universities for the benefit of the Defense Department, the project titles at the institutions already selected do not furnish enough information to assess the actual nature of the research. A proposal of more than $1.1 million for research into "chemical compounds containing highly electro-negative elements" was turned down by the dean of faculties at Portland State College.

Said he: "I know what the proposal was talking about. It could very easily be interpreted as a proposal involving biological warfare. The proposal could be construed as committing the university to biological warfare."

Among the universities now contracted for Project THEMIS work is the University of Utah, with the project title "Chemistry of Combustion." Newspaper accounts during the summer of 1967 indicated clearly that this project was aimed at improving missile fuels. Additional illustrations could be given, but the point is clear: Project THEMIS is what it claims to be, a program to involve universities in research useful to the Defense Department.

The panelists assure us that "DoD has been singularly successful at enlisting the interest and services of an eminent group of behavioral scientists in most of the areas relevant to it." They go on to say that, indeed, "the management of behavioral science research in the military department should be complimented for long-term success in building the image of DoD as a good and challenging environment in which to do both basic and applied research." No names are cited to indicate that there are eminent clusters of behavioral scientists working in the DoD. Nor is there an indication whether "the eminent men" connected with DoD are in fact remotely connected as part-time consultants (like the panelists themselves) or intimately connected with basic work for the government. And even though Foster's letter indicates that there is a problem of recruitment and government-university relations, the panel simply dismisses this as insignificant. Yet members go on to note that the DoD image is perhaps more tarnished than they would like to think; that, for example, the Civil Service Commission discriminates against the behavioral scientist with respect to appointments, and that it is hard to persuade behavioral scientists that the DoD provides a supportive environment for them. Despite the censure of the Civil Service Commission, it is claimed that

---

SUGGESTED READINGS

Right and Wrong in Foreign Policy by James Eayrs (Toronto: University of Toronto Press, 1966). A discussion of morality, foreign policy and social science and the extent to which overlapping of the three occurs.

Policy-Making in Britain edited by Richard Rose (London: Macmillan, 1969) is a comprehensive book of readings which covers the diverse factors that determine the course of public policy. Political scientists, journalists and civil servants, as well as sociologists have contributed to the reader.

The Uses and Abuses of Social Science: Behavioral Science and National Policy Making edited by Irving Louis Horowitz (New Brunswick, N.J.: *Trans*-action Books, E. P. Dutton & Co., 1971).

Social Science and National Policy edited by Fred R. Harris (Chicago: Aldine, 1970).

the DoD has not been as attractive and as successful in social-science recruitment as we were earlier led to believe.

More damaging, perhaps, is the allegation of the panelists that quality control of research at universities is not in any way superior to that exercised within other research sources, such as the DoD. They tend to see "quality control" as something unrelated to university autonomy and its implications for objectivity. Lest there be any ambiguity on this point, they go on to indicate in an extraordinary series of unsupported allegations that the difficulty is not one of social-science autonomy versus the political requirements of any agency of government, but rather one of bad public relations—which is in turn mostly blamed on "Representatives of Civilian Professional Organizations" who lack a clear picture of DoD requirements and yet testify before Congressional committees, which in turn are backed up by social and behavioral scientists who regard such DoD activities as a threat to academic freedom and scientific integrity, and who "are usually ignorant of the work actually being performed under DoD's aegis."

The specific committee hearings referred to are nowhere indicated. Certainly, the various hearings on such proposed measures as a national social science foundation, or on social accounting, do exhibit the highest amount of professional integrity and concern. It might be that DoD intellectuals are concerned precisely over the non-policy research features of such proposed legislation.

Finally, the panelists offer a gentle slap on the wrist to defense research managers who allegedly lack the time to address themselves to these kinds of problems. In short and in sum, the Report ignores questions having to do with social science autonomy as if these were products of misperceptions to be resolved by good will and better public relations between the DoD and the Academy. That such conclusions should be reached by a set of panelists, half of whom are highly placed in academic life, indicates the degree to which closing the gap between the academy and the polity has paradoxically broken down the political capabilities of social science by weakening its autonomous basis.

The panelists have enough firmness of mind to make two unsolicited comments. But the nature of the comments reveals the flabbiness that results from the tendency of social scientists to conceive of their sciences as service activities rather than as scientific activities. They urge, first, that more work be done in the area of potential high-payoff fields of investigation that might have been overlooked in their own Report, given the short time they had available in preparing it. They further urge the establishment of a continuous group with time to examine other areas in greater depth and to discuss them more deliberately, so that high-payoff areas can be teased out and presented for cost considerations. In other words, the unsolicited comments suggest mechanisms for improving these kinds of recommendations and making them permanent. They do not consider whether the nature of social science requirements might be unfit for the bureaucratic specifications of Foster's originating letter.

Advise and Dissent

In some ways, the very tension between social scientists and policy-makers provided each group with a reality test against which basic ideas could be formulated about policy issues. But the very demand for a coalescence of the two, whether in the name of "significant" research or as a straight patriotic obligation, has the effect of corrupting social science and impoverishing policy options.

The question that the Report raises with terrible forcefulness is not so much about the relationship between pure and applied research, but about what the character of application is to be. Applied research is clearly here to stay and is probably the most forceful, singular novel element in American social science in contrast to its European background. What is at stake, however, is a highly refined concept of application that removes theoretical considerations of the character and balance of social forces and private interests from the purview of application. The design of the future replaces the analysis of the present in our "new utopian" world.

The panelists simply do not entertain the possibility that the social world is a behavioral "field" in which decisions have to be made between political goals no less than means. Reports cannot "depoliticalize" social action to such an extent that consequences do not follow and implicit choices are not favored. Innovation without a political goal simply assumes that operations leading to a change from one state to another are a value. The Report does not raise, much less favor, significant political changes in the operations of the DoD; and its innovative efforts are circumscribed to improving rather than to changing. However, efficiency is a limited use of applicability because it assumes rather than tests the adequacy of the social system.

The era of good feelings between the federal government and social science, which characterized the period between the outbreak of World War II and extended through the assassination of President John F. Kennedy, no longer exists. In its place seems to be the era of tight money. The future of "nonprofit" research corporations tied to the DoD is being severely impeded from both sides. Universities such as Pennsylvania, the University of California, and Princeton have taken a hard look at academic involvement in classified research for the Pentagon. Princeton, with its huge stake in international-relations programming, is even considering cancelling its sponsorship of a key research arm, the Institute for Defense Analysis. On the other side, many of the "hard" engineering types have continued to press their doubts as to the usefulness of software research. And this barrage of criticism finds welcome support among high military officers who would just as soon cancel social science projects as carry out their implications.

With respect to the panelists, it must be said that a number of them have indicated their own doubts about the Report. One of the participants has correctly pointed out that the Report has not yet been accepted by the DoD, nor have the findings or the recommendations been endorsed by the National Academy of Sciences. Another member claimed that his main reason for accepting the invitation to serve on the panel was to argue against the Defense Department's involving universities in operations such as Project Camelot. He went on to point out that his mission was unsuccessful, since he obviously did not influence the other panelists.

A third panelist points out that the Camelot type of issue was not, to his recollection at least, a criterion in any discussion of the topics. Yet he strongly disclaims his own participation as well as membership in the National Academy of Science Advisory Committee on Government Programs in the Behavioral Sciences. He also indicates that his panel had nothing but an administrative connection with the National Academy of Sciences, and he, too, seems to indicate that he had an ancillary advisory role rather than an integrated preparatory role.

Trying to gauge the accuracy with which the final Report represented a true consensus of the panelists proved most difficult. While most panelists, with hedging qualifications, agreed that the Report reflected an accurate appraisal of their own views, the question of the actual writeup of the document brought forth a far from consistent response. One panelist claims that "all members contributed to the basic draft of the Report. Each assumed responsibility for composing a section, all of which were then reviewed by the panel as a whole." Another panelist declared his participation only "as an observer," and that he was not involved in any final writeup. Yet a third panelist disclaimed any connection with preparing the Report.

A final, and still different, version was stated as follows: "The report was written by members of the committee and the overall editing and bringing-together responsibility was undertaken by Rains Wallace. One or two members of the committee were assigned to specific topics and drafts were prepared at Williamstown. These went to Wallace, who organized them, did some editing, and sent them back to us. Each person responded and the final version was then prepared by Wallace." In other words, the actual authorship of a document that was released "in confidence" over the names of some of America's most

According to the Report, a question "especially tractable" to behavioral-science research is: "What organizational forms . . . are conducive to more rational and informed military decisions, both at a tactical and strategic level?" A May Day parade in Moscow.

distinguished social scientists is either the work of all and the responsibility of none, or perhaps—as is more likely the case—the work of one or two people and the responsibility of all.

F.A.R. vs DoD

The issuance, even in semi-private form, of this Report reveals the existence of a wide gap between the thinking of the two chief departments involved in sensitive research and in research in foreign areas—namely, the Department of Defense and the Department of State. Indeed, the issuance of this Report is likely to exacerbate the feelings of high officials in the State Department that the Defense Department position represents an encroachment.

The memorandum issued in December 1967 by the Department of State's Foreign Area Research Coordination group (F.A.R.), in which it set forth foreign-area research guidelines, represents a direct rebuke or, at the very least, a serious challenge to the orientation that the Report of the Defense Science Board represents. It is a high point in federal recognition that real problems do exist.

The F.A.R. Report is broken into two different sections with seven propositions in each section. First, under Guidelines for Research Contract Relations Between Government and Universities, are the following:

(1) The government has the responsibility for avoiding actions that would call into question the integrity of American academic institutions as centers of independent teaching and research.

(2) Government research support should always be acknowledged by sponsor, university, and researcher.

(3) Government-supported contract research should, in process and results, ideally be unclassified, but given the practical needs of the nation in the modern world, some portion may be subject to classification. In this case the balance between making work public or classified should lean whenever possible toward making it public.

(4) Agencies should encourage open publication of contract research results.

(5) Government agencies that contract with university researchers should consider designing their projects so as to advance knowledge as well as to meet the immediate policy or action needs.

(6) Government agencies have the obligation of informing the potential researcher of the needs that the research should help meet, and of any special conditions associated with the research contract, and generally of the agency's expectations concerning the research and the researcher.

(7) The government should continue to seek research of the highest possible quality in its contract program.

A second set of seven recommendations is listed under Guidelines for the Conduct of Foreign Area Research Under Government Contract, and these too bear very directly on the panel Report and do so most critically and tellingly.

(1) The government should take special steps to ensure that the parties with which it contracts have the highest qualifications for carrying out research overseas.

(2) The government should work to avert or minimize adverse foreign reactions to its contract research programs conducted overseas.

(3) When a project involves research abroad, it is particularly important that both the supporting agency and the researcher openly acknowledge the auspices and financing of research projects.

(4) The government should under certain circumstances ascertain that the research is acceptable to the host government before proceeding on the research.

(5) The government should encourage cooperation with foreign scholars in its contract research program.

(6) Government agencies should continue to coordinate their foreign-area research programs to eliminate duplication and overloading of any one geographical area.

(7) Government agencies should cooperate with academic associations on problems of foreign-area research.

This set of recommendations (with allowances made for the circumstances of their issuance) unquestionably represents the most enlightened position yet taken by a federal agency on the question of the relationship between social science and practical politics. These sets of recommendations not only stand as ethical criteria for the federal government's relationship to social scientists, but—even more decisively—represent a rebuke to precisely the sort of militarization of social science implicit in the panel Report. The reassertion by a major federal policy-making agency of the worth to the government of social science autonomy represented the first significant recognition by a federal agency that Project Camelot was the consequence, not the cause, of the present strains in social science-federal bureaucracy relationships.

May 1968

The Violence Commission

JEROME H. SKOLNICK

Internal Politics and Public Policy

The 1960s are already infamous for assassinations, crime in the streets, student rebellion, black militancy, wars of liberation, law and order—and national commissions. We had the Warren Commission, the Crime Commission, the Riot Commission and the Violence Commission; and the point about them was that they were among the major responses of government to the social dislocations of the decade. Millions of people followed the work of these commissions with interest and gave at least summary attention to their reports. Social scientists were also interested in commissions, though skeptical about their value. Most would probably agree with Sidney and Beatrice Webb's description of Royal Commissions, "These bodies are seldom designed for scientific research; they are primarily political organs, with political objects."

I share this view, yet I have worked with three commissions, albeit under very special arrangements guaranteeing freedom of publication. The discussion that follows is partly analytical and partly autobiographical, especially where I discuss my work as director of the task force on "Violent Aspects of Protest and Confrontation" for the Violence Commission. If the autobiography stands out, that is because I did not participate in commissions to observe them. I studied the phenomena at issue—crime, police, protest and confrontation—not commissions. Still, my experience may be helpful in understanding commission structures, processes and dilemmas.

Constituencies

Commissions have three functioning groups: commissioners, the executive staff, the research staff, with overlapping but distinctive interests.

Andrew Kopkind has recently written that President Lyndon B. Johnson chose the 11 commissioners for his National Advisory Commission on Civil Disorders because of their remarkable qualities of predictable moderation. The Violence Commission, chaired by Dr. Milton Eisenhower, was perhaps even more predictably "moderate" than the Riot Commission. It included a member of the southern and congressional establishment, Congressman Hale Boggs;

Archbishop, now Cardinal, Terence J. Cooke, Francis Cardinal Spellman's successor; Ambassador Patricia Harris, standing for both the political woman and the Negro establishment; Senator Philip A. Hart, Democrat of Michigan, associated with the liberal establishment in the Senate; Judge A. Leon Higginbotham, a Negro and a federal judge from Philadelphia; Eric Hoffer, the president's favorite philosopher, presenting the backlash voice of the American workingman; Senator Roman Hruska, Republican of Nebraska, a leading right-wing Republican; and Albert E. Jenner, Jr., prominent in the American Bar Association and in Chicago legal affairs. In addition, there was Republican Congressman William M. McCulloch of Ohio, who had served on the Kerner Commission and was the only overlapping member of both commissions. In response to criticisms that the Riot Commission contained no social scientists, Dr. W. Walter Menninger was appointed, although he is a practicing psychiatrist and not a social scientist. Finally, there were Judge Ernest W. McFarland, the man whom Lyndon Baines Johnson had replaced in the House of Representatives, and another Texan, Leon Jaworski, a close personal adviser to the president and a prominent and conservative lawyer.

Obviously, the commissioners themselves cannot perform the investigative and analytical work of the commission. Commissioners are chosen because apparently they represent various economic and political interests, not because they have distinguished themselves as scholars or experts. In fact, they do not "represent" anyone. What they best mirror is a chief executive's conception of pluralist America.

Moreover, even if a commissioner should have the ability to do the research, he or she usually has other demands on their time. Inevitably, then, the staff of the commission does the work—all of the leg work and the research and most of the writing of the final report, with, of course, the commission's approval.

The staffs of both the Riot Commission and the Violence Commission were similar. The executive staff, working out of Washington, was charged with getting the research and writing job done and with organizing the time of the commission. In each case, the director of the executive staff was a leading Washington attorney who had ties with the Johnson administration, David Ginsburg for the Riot Commission, Lloyd Cutler for the Violence Commission. Moreover, younger attorneys were named as their closest associates.

There had been considerable friction in the Riot Commission between the research staff and the executive staff, as well as between both and the commissioners. According to Andrew Kopkind, the social scientists under Research Director Robert Shellow drafted a document called "The Harvest of American Racism" which went further than most top staff officials thought prudent in charging that racism permeated American institutions. "Harvest" characterized the riots as the first step in a developing black revolution in which Negroes will feel, as the draft put it, that "it is legitimate and necessary to use violence against the social order. A truly revolutionary spirit has begun to take hold . . . and unwillingness to compromise or wait any longer, to risk death rather than have their people continue in a subordinate status." According to Kopkind, both Ginsburg and Victor Palmieri, his deputy director, admitted that they were appalled when they read "Harvest." Shortly after its submission many of the 120 investigators and social scientists were "released" from the commission staff in December 1967 (on public grounds that money was needed to pursue the war in Vietnam). But Kopkind says that there is every reason to believe that the "releasing" was done by Palmieri (with Ginsburg's concurrence) because of the failure of Shellow's group to produce an "acceptable" analytical section. The commissioners themselves are reported to have known little of the firing or of the controversy surrounding it but were persuaded by Ginsburg to go along with it.

I tell this story only because it bears on the central question of what effects, if any, informed researchers and writers can have on the final reports of commissions, the public face they turn to the world. Kopkind, for example, argues that the "Harvest" incident proves that the *Kerner Report* would have been "liberal" regardless of events preceding its final writing. He concludes, "The structure of the Commission and the context in which it operated suggest that its tone could have hardly been other than 'liberal.' The finished product almost exactly reproduced the ideological sense given it by President Johnson more than half a year earlier. The choice of Commissioners, staff, consultants and contractors led in the same direction." Yet that outcome is not at all evident from the rest of Kopkind's analysis, which argues, for example, that the commissioners were selected for their predictable moderation, that one commissioner, Charles Thornton, attempted to torpedo the report just before its launching and that the findings of the report were patently offensive to President Johnson. It is at least arguable that the "liberalism" of the final report was not inevitable, that it might have been far more on the conservative side of "moderate" and that the "Harvest" document had something to do with moving it to the Left.

The Eisenhower Violence Commission

When Senator Robert F. Kennedy was assassinated and the president appointed yet another commission, many observers were suspicious. Was this the only response that Washington could give to domestic tragedy? Even the press gave the Violence Commission unfavorable publicity. The commissioners seemed even more conservative than the riot commissioners. Some considered the commission a devious plot by President Johnson to reverse or smudge the interpretation of civil disorders offered by the Riot Commission.

Furthermore, what could the Violence Commission say that hadn't already been said by the Riot Commission? The distinction between civil disorder and violence was not, and still isn't, self-evident. Moreover, because of the flap over the firing of the social scientists on the Kerner Commission, many of that community were deeply and understandably dubious about the possibility of doing an intellectually respectable job under commission auspices.

The executive staff saw this problem and coped with it, first, by establishing the position of research director, so that social scientists (James F. Short, Jr., jointly with Marvin Wolfgang, as it turned out) occupied a place in the hierarchy of the executive staff, a club usually limited to corporation lawyers. Authority still rested with the executive director, but the research directors performed four important functions; they initiated the commission policy of independent task forces with freedom of publication; they helped select the social science staff; they served as liaison between the social scientists, the executive staff and the commissioners; and they served as good critics and colleagues.

Furthermore, they promoted another departure from Kerner Commission practice, namely that social scientists and lawyers are the co-directors of task forces.

Some additional comments are warranted here because organizational structures and rules may seriously influence intellectual autonomy. University social scientists with little legal or governmental experience may assume that freedom to write and publish follows from well-intentioned assurances of future support. Yet as one experienced man with whom I shared a panel recently put it: "He who glitters may one day be hung."

The social scientist must understand the ways he can be hung and protect himself accordingly. First, his materials can be used and distorted. Second, his name can be used, but his material and advice ignored. This is particularly possible when social scientists hold highranking but relatively powerless titles on the commission. Ultimately, they are placed in the dilemma of seeming to endorse the final product. (In the Violence Commission, for example, the names of James F. Short, Jr., and Marvin Wolfgang seemingly "endorse" the scholarly merit of the final report. In addition, the presence of a recognized social science staff does the same. To this extent, we were all "co-opted," since none of us, including Short and Wolfgang, were responsible for the final report.) Third, he may experience subtle (sometimes not so subtle) pressures to shape or present his findings in favored directions. Finally, his work may be suppressed.

In general, one receives maximum protection with a *written* contract guaranteeing freedom of publication. Beyond that, however, experienced Washington hands can be quite charming—which holds its own dangers for one's intellectual independence.

From the very beginning, the executive staff expressed some doubts about the ultimate impact the commission's own report would have on public policy, or even the shape it would take. Recall that this was the summer of 1968,

following the assassination of Senator Kennedy and before the national conventions of both parties. Who could foretell what future event would have what future impact on national politics? Who could, with confidence, predict the nominees for the presidency, the victor and his attitude toward the commission?

Task Force Reports

Like the able corporation lawyers they are, the executive staff came up with a prudent primary goal, a set of books called *Task Force Reports,* which they hoped could be a solid contribution to understanding the causes and prevention of violence in America. I call this goal prudent because it set a standard that was at least possible in theory. From these studies, it was felt, the commission would write its own report; the initial idea was to have each task force report provide the materials for a summary chapter for the commission report.

Modest as this plan was, it soon ran into difficulty. Commissions are usually run at a gallop. With all the best intentions and resources in the world, it is virtually impossible to complete eight books of high quality in five months, particularly when no central vision controls the research and writing. Our own report, *The Politics of Protest,* was completed on time, but we worked under enormous pressure. Still, we had several advantages.

First, a shared perspective among key staff members contributed to a fairly consistent analysis. We shared a deep skepticism about counterinsurgency views of civil disorder as a form of "deviant" pathology that needed to be stamped out as quickly as possible. On the contrary, we assumed that insurgents might conceivably be as rational as public servants. Our approach was influenced, first, by subjectivist and naturalistic perspectives in sociology, which lead one, for instance, to take into account both the point of view of the black rioter and to assume his sanity, and to assume as well the sanity of the policeman and the white militant. Second, we were influenced by revisionist histories of America, which see her as a more tumultuous and violent nation than conventional histories have taught us to believe. Finally, we were influenced by social historical critiques of the theory of collective behavior, which interpret seemingly irrational acts on the part of rioters as forms of primitive political activity, and by an emphasis upon social history in understanding such collective behavior as student protest, rather than upon analysis of "variables."

Another advantage in favor of our task force was that our headquarters was at the Center for the Study of Law and Society at Berkeley. This kept us away from the time-consuming crises of Washington, although the tie-line kept us in daily touch with events there. In addition, the center and the Berkeley campus offered a critical mass of resources that probably could not be duplicated anywhere else. Our location, then, combined with my status as independent contractor with the commission, offered a degree of independence unavailable to the other task force directors. For example, the staff members of our task force were not required to have a White House security clearance.

Finally, the staff was far from unhappy about working for a national commission. Those involved, regardless of expressions of skepticism, were not opposed to making a contribution to a national understanding of the issues involved. My contract with the government, and its contract with me, assured the staff that its best understanding of the issues would be made public.

Given time limitations, it was impossible to undertake the original research one would need for a large-scale social science project. My inclination, shared by the research directors and the executive staff, was to recruit a staff experienced in research on the areas under study. We saw the five-month period as an opportunity to summarize findings rather than to undertake original investigation.

We did, however, conduct original interviews with black militants and with police. As can be imagined, these interviews were not easily obtained. For black militants our interviewer was a man with extensive connections, but who stipulated that he would interview only if we agreed to listen to and not transcribe the tapes and make no notations of who was being interviewed. The interviews substantiated much that we suspected and served to sharpen our analytical outlook. Similarly, the interviews we held with policemen—conducted, incidentally, by a former policeman—served to fill gaps in our thesis that the police were becoming an increasingly politicized force in the United States.

I should also add that our emphasis on social history and political analysis seemed to violate some of the expectations of some portions of our audience.

Audiences and Hearings

The Politics of Protest staff worked with three audiences in mind. First, we were concerned with trying to persuade the commissioners of the validity of our findings and the validity of our analysis. They were our primary audience. Our second was the general public, an audience we had little confidence in being able to influence except, perhaps, through persuading the commissioners. Most reports have a limited readership—and *The Politics of Protest* isn't exactly *The Love Machine*. So our third audience was the academic community and the media representatives. In the long run, the university had to be our major audience, since the report is scholarly and the media treated with publication as news, quickly displaced by other stories.

The audience for the hearings was both the commissioners and the general public. Several members of the executive staff believed that one reason the Kerner Commission failed to gain public acceptance was its failure to educate the public along the way. The "predictably moderate" commissioners had been emotionally moved in the hearings, especially by representatives of the black communities of

Hiroji Kubota MAGNUM

"Eric Hoffer was an exemplary witness..." UPI

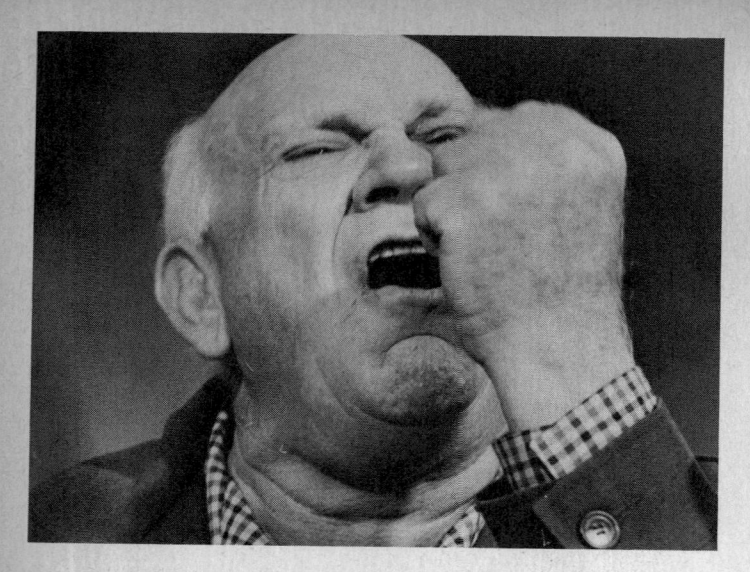

America, but the public had never been allowed to hear this testimony. Consequently, the Violence Commission hearings were made public, and each task force was given three days for hearings.

Hearings are a form of theater. Conclusions must be presented to evoke an emotional response in both the commissioners and the wider television audience. In this respect, the planners of the hearings can be likened to the author and director of a play with strategy substituting for plot. Yet strategies can and do go awry, and so the outcome of the play is not determined, nor can one guarantee whether the effect on the audience will be tragedic or comedic.

A staff tries to get across a point of view on the subject matter. At the same time, however, it is also expected to be "objective," that is, lacking a point of view. The expectation is that staff and commissioners will walk along fresh roads together, reaching similar conclusions. This expectation derives from the image of a trial. Such an adjudicatory model must, however, be largely fictional. The "judges," the commissioners, already have strong views and political interests, though they are supposed to be neutral. The staff, too, is supposed to lack opinions, even though it was selected because of prior knowledge.

Since strategy substitutes for plot, there really are only three possible outcomes. The play may be a flop, that is, the staff perspective is not communicated; or the perspective is communicated, but unemotional so as to merely make a record; or emotional engagement is achieved. Here social science as theater reaches its ultimate art.

Commissioners are used to hearings, are used to testimony and probably cannot be moved in any new direction unless emotionally engaged. Commissioners are culturally deprived by the privatized life of the man of power. Whatever may have been their former backgrounds, commissioners are now the establishment. They may be driven to and from work, belong to private clubs and remain out of touch with the realities of the urban and political worlds they are assumed to understand. They are both protected and deprived by social privilege.

Moreover, their usual mode of analysis is legalistic and rationalistic. Not intellectuals, they are decision makers interested in protecting the record. Furthermore, they are committed to the prevailing social, economic and political structures, although they will consider reforms of these structures and may well be brought to see contradictions within them. In addition, they are affiliated with certain political and social interests. Consequently, there are practical limits to the possibilities of persuading any of them to a novel position.

The public is another audience for the hearings, but there are also constraints on teaching the public. All that "public hearings" means is that the media are present, not the mass of the public, and the media reports only the most dramatic messages. Also, commissioners themselves become part of the cast. The TV will register an exchange between a witness and a commissioner. So a strategist (director) must anticipate what that exchange might be.

Finally, the presence of the press alters the atmosphere of the hearing room. We held mostly public hearings and some hearings in executive session. With the television cameras and the radio people and the newspaper people present, the commissioners were stiff and formal. When the press left, the commissioners visibly relaxed.

Given these conditions, how does one go about casting? First, we tried to present witnesses who represented a variety of points of view. That was elementary. But within that framework we had to decide: what kinds of witnesses representing what kinds of points of view will bring the most enlightened position with the greatest effect both on the commissioners and on the general public?

There are practical limitations in hearings. Obviously, it may not be possible to get the witness you want, or to get him for a particular day. Ira Heyman, general counsel, and I were given three days for hearings to discuss the antiwar and student movements, black militancy and the responses of the social order. This was not enough time for any of these topics to be adequately discussed. The one day of hearings on black militancy was especially inadequate, although undoubtedly the most exciting. It was also the most difficult to arrange, the most trying and the most rewarding.

Hoffer vs. the Black

First, there was some question as to whether any well-known black militant would have anything to do with the Violence Commission. Even if he should want to, anybody who stepped forward to represent the militant black community could be charged with playing a "personality" game and disavowed as representing even a segment of the black community. After much thought, we decided on Huey P. Newton, minister of defense of the Black Panther party, as a widely acceptable representative of black militancy. He was willing to cooperate, politically minded and seeking opportunity to present his point of view.

Herman Blake, an assistant professor of sociology at

A. Leon Higginbotham offered a dignified censure of Hoffer. UPI

the University of California at Santa Cruz, joined me in interviewing Newton and was to present the interview to the commissioners. Although Blake would not officially be representing the Panthers, Newton knew him, knew of his work and trusted him to make an accurate analysis of the tape of the interview that was to be played to the commission.

As it turned out, there was no problem at all. Both Blake and I, in Charles Garry's presence, interviewed Newton in the Alameda County Courthouse Jail, where he was being held while standing trial for the alleged murder of an Oakland policeman.

The Newton tape, and Blake's testimony, produced an emotionally charged confrontation between Blake and Eric Hoffer and a dignified censure of Hoffer by Judge Higginbotham, vice-chairman of the commission.

Mr. Hoffer: I tell you there is rage among the Negroes on the waterfront. It is at the meetings when they get together. Suddenly they are repeating a ritual. A text. You are repeating it. Now I have . . . I don't know of these people, where they were brought up. All my life I was poor and I didn't live better than any Negro ever lived, I can tell you. When I was out picking cotton in the valley the Negroes were eating better than I did, lived in better houses, they had more schooling than I did . . .

Mr. Blake: Have you ever been called a nigger?

Mr. Hoffer: Let me finish it. By the way, the first man in the U.S. I think who wrote about the need to create a Negro community was in 1964 when I . . .

Mr. Blake: Why do you stop calling it a community then?

Mr. Hoffer: I say that you have to build a community. You have to build a community and you are not . . .

Mr. Blake: We can't build a community with white people like you around telling us we can't be what we are.

Mr. Hoffer: You are not going to build it by rage. You are going to build it by working together.

Mr. Blake: You are defining it.

Mr. Hoffer: They haven't raised one blade of grass. They haven't raised one brick.

Mr. Blake: We been throwing them, baby, because you been out there stopping them from laying bricks and raising grass.

Judge Higginbotham: Mr. Chairman . . .

Dr. Eisenhower: Mr. Blake . . .

Mr. Jenner: Would you do me a personal favor and stay for a moment, Mr. Blake?

Judge Higginbotham: Mr. Chairman, if I may, I feel compelled because I trust that this Commission will not let statements go in the record which are such blatant demonstrations of factual ignorance that I am obliged to note on the record how totally in error Mr. Hoffer is on the most elementary data.

The McCone Commission, headed by the former director of Central Intelligence, who I assume while he may not be the philosopher which Mr. Hoffer is, that he is at least as perceptive and more factually accurate. The McCone Commission pointed out that in Watts, California, you had unemployment which ran as high as 30 and 40 percent. Sometimes 50 percent among youth. It pointed out in great detail [that] in the Watts area you had the highest percent of substandard housing any place in L.A.

If my colleague, Mr. Hoffer, who I would like to be able to call distinguished, would take time out to read the data of the McCone Report, which is not challenged by anyone, based on government statistics, at least the first portion of his analysis would be demonstrated to be totally inaccurate, and I am willing, as a black man, to state that what I am amazed at is—that with the total bigotry, patent, extensive among men who can reach fame in this country —[not] that there has been as little unity as there has been. It is surprising that there has been as much.

I think that Mr. Hoffer's statements are indicative of the great racist pathology in our country and that his views are those which represent the mass of people in this country. I think that what Toynbee said that civilizations are destroyed from within, that his comments are classic examples of proving that.

Dr. Eisenhower: Mr. Blake, only because we have two other distinguished persons to testify this afternoon, I am going to conclude this part of our testimony. I want you to know that I personally had some questions to ask you but my good friend Judge Higginbotham asked precisely the questions in his part that I had intended to do. So on behalf of the Commission I thank you for your willingness to come, for your candor, for being with us and I accept the sincerity and truth of what you said to us.

Mr. Blake: Thank you.

That day, I think it is fair to say, was the most emotional day of the hearings for the Violence Commission. Eric Hoffer was an exemplary witness for the depth of racism existing in this country. No wealth of statistics could have conveyed as well to the other commissioners and to the public in general what racism meant to the black man.

Yet Hoffer is also a popular public figure. Moreover, only a minute or so of the hearings was shown on national television. There, Hoffer was seen shouting at a bearded black man in a dashiki. It is doubtful that much enlightenment was achieved by the televising of that exchange. I believe that in the long run the reports themselves will have a far greater impact than the TV time allocated to the hearings.

A first draft of *The Politics of Protest* was sent off to the executive staff of the commission on 27 December 1968, approximately five months after the initial phone call from Washington. They received the report with mixed feelings. They were, I know, impressed with the magnitude and quality of the report, but it violated the kinds of expectations they had about commission reports. We were clearly less concerned about "balance" and "tempered" language than we were about analytical soundness, consistency and clarity. Some of the commissioners were described to me as "climbing the walls as they read it." And this did not make an easy situation for the executive staff. They suggested in January that it be toned down, and I did *not* tell them to go to hell. I listened carefully to their suggestions and accepted most of them concerning language and tone. But I did not alter the analysis in any of the chapters. I.F. Stone was later to call our analysis "Brilliant and indispensable," and a *Chicago Tribune* editorial ranked it alongside the *Walker Report* as "garbage."

The Impact of Commission Reports

Since the report was published, I have often been asked the question: Of what use is all this? Does it actually contribute to public policy? My answer is, I don't know. *The Politics of Protest* apparently made little impact on the commission itself. It was cited only once in the final report of the commission, and then out of context. But the book has been given considerable publicity, has been widely and favorably reviewed and has been widely adopted for classroom use. The major audience for *The Politics of Protest* will probably be the sociology and political science class, although more than most books on this subject it will find its way into the hands of decision makers.

The Politics of Protest will also provide an alternative analysis to the main report of the Violence Commission. Naturally, we think our analysis is more pointed, more consistent, more scholarly and more directed to the historical causes of American violence than the commission's own report, which adopts a managerial, counterinsurgency perspective that looks to symptoms rather than causes. But history will tell. Reports sponsored by commissions are ultimately intellectual documents subject to the criticism that any book or investigation might receive.

Yet they are something more as well. Despite the increasing tendency among radicals and intellectuals to challenge the usefulness and integrity of commission reports, they do tend to create an interest over and above that of similar work by individual scholars. One can even point to a series of commission reports that have had an enormous impact—those used by Karl Marx in developing his critique of capitalist production. Without the narrative provided by these commissions, Marx's *Capital* would have been a much more abstract and predictably obscure document and simply would not have attracted the readership it did. Marx himself, in his preface to *Capital*, offers an accolade to these investigative commissions.

Commission reports, whatever their analytical strictures, defects or omissions, come to have a special standing within the *political* community. If a social scientist or a journalist gathers "facts" concerning a particular institution, and these facts are presented in such a way as to offer a harshly critical appraisal of that social institution, the gathering and the analysis of such facts may be called "muckraking." But if the same or a similar set of facts is found by a commission, it may be seen as a series of startling and respectable social findings.

And herein lies the essential dilemma posed by the commission form of inquiry. On the one hand, we find a set of high-status commissioners whose name on a document will tend to legitimize the descriptions found therein; and on the other hand, precisely because of the political character of the commissioners, the report will be "balanced" or "inconsistent" depending on who is making the judgment. A commission, upon hearing one expert testify (correctly) that there is darkness outside and another testify (incorrectly) that the sun is shining will typically conclude that it is cloudy.

Nevertheless, whatever facts are gathered and are presented to the public, they are in the public domain. No set of facts is subject only to one interpretation and analysis. Surely it was not in the minds of the commissioners of inquiry in nineteenth-century England to provide the factual underpinning for a Marxist critique of capitalist production. Yet, there was no way to stop it. So my point is simply this: to the extent that a commission of inquiry develops facts, it necessarily has done something of social value. Its interpretations can be challenged. How those facts and how those interpretations will be met and used depends upon the integrity and ability of the intellectual community.

October 1970

SUGGESTED READINGS

The Rise and Fall of Project Camelot: Studies in the Relationship Between Social Science and Practical Politics by Irving Louis Horowitz (Cambridge, Massachusetts: MIT Press, 1967).

Social Research and Social Policy edited by Howard E. Freeman (Englewood Cliffs, N.J.: Prentice-Hall, 1969).

Notes on Authors

ALTMAN, IRWIN (*"Together in Isolation"*), is adjunct professor of social psychology at American University and research psychologist with the Naval Medical Research Institute. He is co-author with J. E. McGrath, of *Small Group Research* (1965).

BARON, HAROLD M. (*"Black Powerlessness in Chicago"*), is a research associate at the Center for Urban Affairs, Northwestern University, and — under a grant from the Russell Sage Foundation — is writing a book on the institutional bases of urban racism. He was formerly the research director of the Chicago Urban League.

BECKER, HOWARD S. (*"The Culture of Civility"*), is professor of sociology at Northwestern University and author of *Outsiders: Studies in the Sociology of Deviance*; editor of *The Other Side*, and *Campus Power Struggles*, and co-author of *Making the Grade: The Academic Side of College Life* with Blanche Geer and Everett C. Hughes.

BENNETT, JOHN W. (*"Communal Bretheren of the Great Plains"*), is professor of anthropology at Washington University, where he is also senior fellow of the Center for the Biology of Natural Systems. Current research interests center on social and technical change, human ecology and agrarian development. He has done extensive study in Japan, Israel, Taiwan, Canada and the United States and he has written many books.

BENNIS, WARREN G. (*"Beyond Bureaucracy"*), is a social psychologist, formerly Provost of the Faculty of Social Sciences and Administration, State University of New York at Buffalo. Among his recent works are *Changing Organizations, The Temporary Society*, and *Organization Development: Its Nature, Origins and Prospects*.

BENSMAN, JOSEPH (*"Classical Music and the Status Game"*), is associate professor of sociology at City College of the City University of New York. His most recent book is *Dollars and Sense: Ideologies, Ethics and the Meaning of Work in Profit and Non-Profit-Making Agencies*. Other works include *The Third American Revolution* and an expanded version of *Small Town in a Mass Society* (both with A. J. Vidich).

BERG, IVAR (*"Rich Man's Qualifications for Poor Man's Jobs"*), is professor of sociology and associate dean of faculties at the Columbia University Graduate School of Business. His books include *Educational Credentials for Jobs in a Democratic Society*, and *Sociology and the Business Establishment*, with David Rogers.

BERK, RICHARD (*"White Institutions and Black Rage"*), lecturer in sociology at Goucher College, is currently studying the relation of black militancy and civil disorders to the actions of city officials and major institutions. He has conducted research on politics and the poor, and is now finishing a study of ghetto retail merchants.

BLAUNER, ROBERT (*"Whitewash over Watts"*), associate professor of sociology at the University of California at Berkeley, wrote *Alienation and Freedom: The Factory Worker and His Industry* (University of Chicago Press, 1964). He has conducted a study of Negroes and other American ethnic groups, with special emphasis on manhood. He was a consultant to the McCone Commission.

BOESEL, DAVID (*"White Institutions and Black Rage"*), research associate with the Group for Research on Social Policy at Johns Hopkins University and analyst for the Kerner Commission, is now completing his study on the ghetto riots for the department of government at Cornell University.

BOSERUP, ANDERS (*"The Politics of Protracted Conflict"*), has done research on ethnic conflicts at the Institute for Peace and Conflict Research in Copenhagen, Denmark. In addition to his work on Northern Ireland, he is conducting a study of the language conflict in Belgium. He is a member of the Committee of Experts of the Danish Government Committee on Security Policy.

BOULDING, KENNETH E. (*"Ecology and Environment"*), professor of economics at the University of Colorado, is a past president of the American Economics Association and the International Peace Research Society, and former director of the Center for Conflict Resolution at the University of Michigan. He is the author of many books in the social sciences on conflict and future planning, including *The Meaning of the Twentieth Century, The Impact of the Social Sciences, Conflict and Defense*, and *Economics as a Science*.

BRIGGS, JEAN (*"Kapluna Daughter: Living with Eskimos"*), is associate professor in the department of sociology and anthropology of the Memorial University of Newfoundland and research associate of a project entitled Identity and Modernity in the East Arctic. Her research of Eskimo emotional patterns is an extension of that reported in her book *Never in Anger* (Cambridge: Harvard University Press, 1970).

BRONFENBRENNER, MARTIN (*"The Japanese Howdunit"*), is chairman of the economics department at the Graduate School of Industrial Administration, Carnegie-Mellon University in Pittsburgh. Aside from Japan, his research interests center on the economic theory of income distribution and monetary policy.

BROWNING, HARLEY L. ("*Timing of Our Lives*"), is associate professor of sociology at the University of Texas at Austin and director of the Population Research Center. His major research interests are the modernization process, particularly urbanization and internal migration in Latin America and explorations in social demography.

CHRISTIE, NILS ("*The Scandinavian Hangover*"), is professor of criminology at the Institute of Criminology and Criminal Law of the University of Oslo, Norway. He has been in the U.S. with a Rockefeller Foundation fellowship to the Center for the Study of Law and Society and the University of California, Berkeley.

CLOWARD, RICHARD A. ("*Advocacy in the Ghetto*"), professor of social work at Columbia University, was a founder of Mobilization for Youth and is its director of research. Cloward is co-author with Lloyd Ohlin of *Delinquency and Opportunity* which won the award of the International Society of Criminology in 1965.

COATES, CHARLES H. ("*America's New Officer Corps*"), a professional military man, graduated from West Point in 1924. Following retirement from the military Col. Coates returned to studies, receiving a Ph.D. in sociology in 1955. He is on the faculty of the University of Maryland. Coates is senior author of *Military Sociology: A Study of American Military Institutions and Military Life*.

CRESSEY, DONALD R. ("*The Respectable Criminal*"), dean of the College of Letters and Science and professor of sociology at the University of California at Santa Barbara, is author of *Other People's Money* and *Theft of a Nation*. He has also written extensively on prisons and law enforcement.

DAVIS, FRED ("*Why All of Us May Be Hippies Someday*"), is professor of sociology at the University of California, San Francisco. He is the author of *Passage Through Crisis, Polio Victims and Their Families* and the editor of *The Nursing Profession, Five Sociological Essays*. He is presently conducting research in the areas of youth culture and the spontaneous termination of deviant careers.

DE FRIESE, GORDON H. ("*Open Occupancy — What Whites Say, What They Do*"), is assistant professor of sociology at Cornell University. His research interests are in work-role alienation among white-collar and professional workers, and institutional dependency within the military.

DRYFOOS, ROBERT J., JR. ("*Two Tactics for Ethnic Survival — Eskimo and Indian*"), is assistant professor of anthropology at Southern Connecticut State College. The data for this article was obtained under two field-work training grants provided by the National Institute of Mental Health and administered by the Department of Anthropology of the University of North Carolina at Chapel Hill.

EIDSON, BETTYE K. ("*White Institutions and Black Rage*"), is associate professor of sociology at the University of Michigan. She previously worked at the Bureau of Social Science Research and has conducted research on government programs for the unemployed as well as study of community structure and conflict in 15 United States cities.

ELMAN, RICHARD M. ("*Advocacy in the Ghetto*"), is a free-lance writer who was formerly research assistant at the Columbia University School of Social Work Research Center. Among his many publications are *The Poorhouse State* and *The Speculators*.

FISHER, A. D. ("*Whites Rites Versus Indian Rights*"), is associate professor of anthropology and educational foundations at the University of Alberta, in Canada. He is co-editor with Roger Owen and James J. F. Deetz of *The North American Indians: A Source Book*, and he has contributed articles about Canada's Indians to a number of Canadian journals.

FLACKS, RICHARD ("*Young Intelligentsia in Revolt*"), is associate professor of sociology at the University of California in Santa Barbara. He has done considerable research and writing on the student movement and the New Left. He was a founder of the Students for a Democratic Society.

FORD, W. SCOTT JR. ("*Open Occupancy — What Whites Say, What They Do*"), is assistant professor of sociology at the Institute for Social Research, Florida State University, Tallahassee. His interests are community studies, urban sociology, and race relations.

GAGNON, JOHN ("*The Decline and Fall of the Small Town*" and "*Psychosexual Development*"), is an associate professor in the department of sociology at the State University of New York, Stony Brook. His work is in the areas of criminology, deviant behavior, youth, the community, and marriage and the family. Among his books are *Sex Offenders: An Analysis of Types*, with Paul H. Gebhard, Cornelia V. Christenson, and Nardell B. Pomeroy, and *Sexual Deviance: A Reader*, edited with William Simon.

GARBARINO, MERWYN S. ("*Seminole Girl*"), is assistant professor of anthropology at the University of Illinois at Chicago Circle. She is also a fieldworker in the Welfare and Family Services Department of the American Indian Center in Chicago. Until she began working at the Indian Center, she was engaged in research on the Florida Seminole at Big Cypress Reservation.

GERRARD, NATHAN L. ("*The Serpent Handling Religions of West Virginia*"), is professor and chairman of the department of sociology, Morris Harvey College, Charleston, W. Va. He has maintained continuous and intimate contact with a serpent-handling church for the last seven years. His study was supported by the Wenner-Gren Foundation and the National Institute of Mental Health. His research interests include the cultural and social patterns of the "hollows," the communities of non-farm rural poor in West Virginia.

GROVES, W. EUGENE ("*White Institutions and Black Rage*"), a member of the group for Research on Social Policy at Johns Hopkins University, is presently conducting a detailed analysis of policing in the ghetto, and with Peter H. Rossi is planning to survey the social conflict arising from drug use on college campuses.

GUTMAN, HERBERT G. ("*Industrial Invasion of the Village Green*"), associate professor of history at the State University of New York at Buffalo, has published numerous articles on labor and social history and is completing two books: *American Labor Thought: The Mind of the Worker, 1860-1900*, and *The Shock of American Industrialization*.

HANDEL, GERALD ("*The Working Classes—Old and New*"), is associate professor of sociology and director of the Social Research Laboratory of the City College of the City University of New York. Among his publications are *Family World* and *Workingman's Wife* which he co-authored.

HAYTHORN, WILLIAM W. ("*Together in Isolation*"), a social psychologist, is director of the behavioral sciences department of the Naval Medical Research Institute. He heads a program of research on the effects of isolation and confinement of small groups.

HOROWITZ, IRVING LOUIS ("*The Culture of Civility*" and "*Social Science Yogis and Military Commissars*"), is chairman of the department of sociology of Livingston College at Rutgers University, director of Studies in Comparative International Development there, and editor-in-chief of *Trans*-action magazine. Among his major books are *The Rise and Fall of Project Camelot, Professing Sociology, The War Game, Three Worlds of Development* and *Radicalism and the Revolt against Reason*.

HORTON, JOHN ("*Time and Cool People*"), assistant professor of sociology at the University of California at Los Angeles, has written in the areas of political sociology and sociological theory. He is continuing his research on time and social structure and is writing a book on ideological assumptions in current studies of social problems.

HOWARD, JOHN R. ("*The Making of a Black Muslim*"), is associate professor of sociology at Livingston College, Rutgers University. He co-edited *Where It's At: Radical Perspectives in Sociology* and co-authored *Life Styles in the Black Ghetto*. He is currently doing research on structural supports for black mobility.

KELMAN, HERBERT C. ("*Deception in Social Research*"), is professor of psychology and research psychologist at the Center for Research on Conflict Resolution at the University of Michigan. Kelman's recent books are *A Time to Speak: on Human Values and Social Research* and *Cross-National Encounters: The Personal Impact of an Exchange Program for Broadcasters*.

KIESLER, CHARLES A. ("*Conformity and Commitment*"), associate professor of psychology at Yale, is chairman of the interdisciplinary honors major in culture and behavior. His research interests are in experimental social psychology, attitude change, and interpersonal influence and group effects on the individual. He has published books on *Conformity* (1969) and on *Attitude Change* (1969) with other authors.

KNOPF, TERRY ANN ("*Sniping—A New Pattern of Violence*"), a research associate at the Lemberg Center for the Study of Violence, Brandeis University, is in charge of the Center's Riot Data Clearinghouse, a research and service division. She is the author of a recent work on security patrols entitled *Youth Patrols: An Experiment in Community Participation*. This article was drawn from the Center's publication *Riot Data Review* (March, 1969) which she also authored.

LESLIE, CHARLES ("*Modern India's Ancient Medicine*"), is professor of anthropology and chairman of the University College department of anthropology at New York University. Besides continuing research on medical revivalism, he is editing a volume on Asian films and popular cultures.

LEWY, GUENTER ("*The Future of the Islamic Religion*"), is professor of government at the University of Massachusetts at Amherst. He is the author of *The Catholic Church and Nazi Germany* (1964). A longer version of this article on Islam appears in *Political Theory and Social Change* (1967), edited by David Spitz.

LIPSET, SEYMOUR MARTIN ("*The Wallace Whitelash*"), is professor of government and social relations at Harvard. He has authored or co-authored many books including *Agrarian Socialism, Union Democracy, Social Mobility in Industrial Society, Political Man, The First New Nation* and *Revolution and Counter-Revolution*.

LONG, NORTON E. ("*Private Initiative in the 'Great Society'*"), is director of the Center of Community and Metropolitan Studies at the University of Missouri—St. Louis. Author of *The Polity*. Long served as a federal price and housing administrator from 1942 to 1948. From 1961 to 1963 he was staff consultant to the governor of Illinois.

LYMAN, STANFORD H. ("*Red Guard on Grant Avenue*"), associate professor of sociology and social psychology at the University of Nevada, was born and reared in San Francisco where he became familiar with Chinatown. Together with Marvin B. Scott he is the author of *Sociology of the Absurd* and *Agony and Ecstasy: Notes on Student Revolution*. An anthology of his writings appears in *The Oriental in the West*, will soon be published.

MACK, RAYMOND W. ("*Science as a Frame of Reference*" and "*Intellectual Strategies and Research Tactics*"), is chairman of the department of sociology at Northwestern University and Director of the Center for Urban Affairs. Among his books are *Sociology and Social Life*, with Kimball Young, *Race, Class and Power, Transforming America: Patterns of Social Change*, and most recently, *Our Children's Burden: School Desegregation in Ten American Communities*.

MENGES, CONSTANTINE C. ("*Resistance in Czechoslavakia–An Underground in the Open*"), a political scientist, has been with RAND Corporation since 1967. Previously as a resident consultant, he undertook a study of Colombian financial institutions. His recent principal field of research has been in Latin American political economy.

MILLER, WALTER B. ("*The Corner Gang Boys Get Married*"), an anthropologist, is a research associate at the Joint Center for Urban Studies at M.I.T. and Harvard and a member of the Subcommittee on Research of the National Manpower Advisory Committee. This article is taken from his forthcoming book on city gangs.

MORRIS, MARIAN GENNARIA ("*Psychological Miscarriage: An End to Mother Love*"), has graduate degrees in both nursing and social work and was research associate at Hahnemann Medical College and Hospital in Philadelphia. At Children's Hospital of Los Angeles, Department of Psychiatry, she has done work on abusive parents.

MOSKOS, CHARLES C., JR. ("*Why Men Fight*"), is professor and chairman of the department of sociology at Northwestern University. Awarded a Faculty Research Fellowship by the Ford Foundation 1969-70, he observed United Nations peacekeeping operations in Cypress. His book *The American Enlisted Man* was published recently.

MOTZ, ANNABELLE B. ("*The Family as a Company of Players*"), is professor of sociology at American University, Washington, D.C. She is the author of articles that reflect her research interest in social psychology, social organization, and family living.

NAGEL, STUART S. ("*The Tipped Scales of American Justice*"), associate professor of political science at the University of Illinois, has served as assistant counsel to the Senate Judiciary Committee. A more detailed account of this article appears in his book, *The Legal Process from a Behavioral Perspective* (Dorsey, 1969).

NAROLL, RAOUL ("*Does Military Deterrence Deter?*"), is professor of anthropology, sociology, and political science at Northwestern University. The study described in this article was part of Project Michaelson, a social science research project supported by the US Navy as part of the Polaris submarine development program.

PLATH, DAVID W. ("*A Case of Ostracism and Its Unusual Aftermath*"), is associate professor of anthropology at the University of Illinois. His principal research is on Japan's response to modernization, in which he has dealt with patterns of work and leisure, revitalization movements and utopian communities.

RAAB, EARL ("*The Wallace Whitelash*"), is director of the Jewish Community Relations Council of San Francisco. He has taught at San Francisco State College and the University of California at Berkeley. He co-authored *Major Social Problems*, and with Lipset, he wrote *Prejudice and Society*. This article is taken from their book, *The Politics of Unreason: Right-Wing Extremism in America, 1790-1970*, one of a series of studies sponsored by the Anti-Defamation League.

RAINWATER, LEE ("*The Working Classes—Old and New*" and "*Black Families and the White House*"), is professor of sociology in the Department of Sociology and John F. Kennedy School of Government at Harvard University and senior editor of *Trans*-action. His major works include *Behind Ghetto Walls: Black Families in a Federal Slum, And the Poor Get Children: Sex, Contraception and Family Planning in the Working Class, Family Design: Marital Sexuality, Family Size and Contraception, Moynihan Report and the Politics of Controversy* (with William Yancey), and *Workingman's Wife: Her Personality, World and Life Styles*.

ROGLER, LLOYD H. ("*A Better Life: Notes from Puerto Rico*"), professor of sociology at Case Western Reserve University, is studying urbanization in Latin America. Born and raised in Puerto Rico, he is also interested in the psychiatric aspects of Puerto Rican family life in the United States and in the slums of Puerto Rico. His book on this subject, written with August B. Hollingshead, is *Trapped: Families and Schizophrenia*.

ROSE, PETER I. ("*Outsiders in Britain*"), is professor and chairman of the department of sociology and anthropology at Smith College and director of the Social Science Research Center. He is the author of *They and We, The Study of Society, The Ghetto and Beyond*, and *The Subject Is Race*, a study of the teaching of race relations in US colleges.

ROSEN, LAWRENCE ("*I Divorce Thee*"), is an assistant professor of anthropology at the University of Illinois. He spent two years in Morocco and is now working on a monograph of the social organization of a Moroccan city.

ROSENTHAL, MARILYN ("*Rumors in the Aftermath of the Detroit Riot*"), is a doctoral student in the American Culture Program at the University of Michigan. A former lecturer in the English department at Eastern Michigan University, she is interested in various aspects of mass culture and behavior.

ROSSI, PETER ("*White Institutions and Black Rage*" and "*Evaluating Social Action Programs*"), formerly director of the University of Chicago's National Opinion Research Center, is chairman of the department of social relations at Johns Hopkins University and director of the Group for Research on Social Policy. His recent books include *The Education of Catholic Americans* (with A. M. Greeley) and *The New Media and Education* (with B. Biddle).

ROTH, JULIUS ("*Who's Complaining?*"), is professor of sociology at the University of California at Davis. His main research interests have been relationships between patients and staff in hospitals and the careers of college students. Among his published works is *Timetables: Structuring the Passage of Time in Hospital Treatment and Other Careers*.

SCHIFF, LAWRENCE F. ("*Dynamic Young Fogies—Rebels on the Right*"), is director of Psychological Research of the Adolescent Service of Boston State Hospital where his research is on individual change and the effect of social environment on the individual. As a psychologist with the Psychiatric Home Treatment Service, he participated in a pioneering venture in community psychiatry in which psychotic patients were treated at home.

SCOTT, JOHN FINLEY ("*Sororities and the Husband Game*"), is associate professor of sociology at the University of California, Davis. His published articles deal with kinship in complex societies and the role of norms in sociological theory. This article is based on his paper, "The American College Sorority: Its Role in Class and Ethnic Endogamy," published in the *American Sociological Review*.

SENNETT, RICHARD ("*Genteel Backlash: Chicago 1886*"), assistant professor of sociology at Brandeis University and a fellow of the Cambridge Institute, is director of the Urban Family Study, a project exploring changes in white working-class family life. He is the author of *Families Against the City: Middle Class Homes of Industrial Chicago* and the *Uses of Disorder: Personal Identity and City Life*.

SHILOH, AILON ("*Sanctuary or Prison—Responses to Life in a Mental Hospital*"), is professor of anthropology in public health at the Graduate School of Public Health at the University of Pittsburgh. A medical anthropologist with many years of experience in the Middle East, Africa and the United States, he is author of *Studies in Human Sexual Behavior: The American Scene* and *Alternatives to Doomsday*.

SIMMON, GEOFFREY ("*Hippie in College—From Teeny-Boppers To Drug Freaks*"), is a graduate student in sociology at Michigan State University. His interest in youth cultures has been heightened by his past participation in and increasingly informed observation of the hippie subculture.

SIMON, RITA JAMES ("*Murder, Juries, and the Press*"), is professor and head of the department of sociology at the University of Illinois. A member of the Institute of Communications Research, she is author of the book *The Jury and the Plea of Insanity, As We Saw the Thirties* and *Readings in the Sociology of Law*.

SIMON, WILLIAM ("*The Decline and Fall of the Small Town*" and "*Psychosexual Development*"), is program supervisor in sociology and anthropology at the Institute for Juvenile Research in Chicago. At the Institute for Sex Research at Indiana University, he collaborated with John H. Gagnon in the preparation of many articles on sexual behavior. With Gagnon and Paul H. Gebhard, he wrote *A Technical Report on the Marginal Tabulations of the Institute for Sex Research*.

SKOLNICK, JEROME ("*The Violence Commission*"), is professor at the University of California at Berkeley School of Criminology and research sociologist at the Center for the Study of Law and Society there. He was director of the Task Force on Violent Aspects of Protest and Confrontation of the National Commission on the Causes and Prevention of Violence, and published a book on *The Politics of Protest*.

STRAUSS, ANSELM L. ("*Healing by Negotiation*"), is professor of sociology and chairman of the graduate program in sociology at the University of California Medical Center in San Francisco. He is the author of many books on problems of health care and treatment and issues surrounding the medical profession. He is co-author of *Time for Dying, The Professional Scientist, Boys in White, Psychiatric Professions and Ideologies,* and *Awareness of Dying: A Study of Social Interaction*.

SUDNOW, DAVID ("*Dead on Arrival*"), is assistant professor of sociology at the University of California at Irvine. He has done research on the social organization of hospitals and of the legal profession, and now is doing film research on people's nonverbal interactions.

TOCH, HANS ("*The Convict As Researcher*"), is professor of psychology at Michigan State University. He edited *Legal and Criminal Psychology* and is the author of *The Social Psychology of Social Movements*. This article is based on research done with J. D. Grant for a book on violence.

TOMASSON, RICHARD F. ("*Religion Is Irrelevant in Sweden*"), is professor and chairman of the department of sociology at the University of New Mexico. His book *Sweden: Prototype of Modern Society* contains a more detailed version of his article, which also appeared in *Social Compass* (No. 6, 1968). He is currently studying the modernization of Iceland.

TRIMBERGER, ELLEN KAY ("*Why a Rebellion at Columbia Was Inevitable*"), is assistant professor of sociology at Queens College of the City University of New York. She has made a comparative study of elite modernization in Japan and Turkey.

TROUT, GRAFTON ("*Hippies in College—From Teeny Boppers to Drug Freaks*"), is assistant professor of sociology at Michigan State University. His specialization is urban sociology and social deviance and change.

WEISS, MELFORD S. ("*Rebirth in the Airborne*"), is assistant professor of anthropology at Sacramento State College in California. His current research interests include a study of Chinese communities in America.

WEISS, ROBERT S. ("*The Fund of Sociability*"), is a lecturer in sociology in the Department of Psychiatry of the Harvard Medical School, working in its Laboratory of Community Psychiatry. His research interests centers on problems in social psychology and research methods.

WHYTE, MARTIN K. ("*Rural Russia Today*"), is research associate at the Center for Chinese Studies at the University of Michigan. He has done research on political study groups in schools, factories, offices, rural communes and corrective labor camps in China.

WILDAVSKY, AARON ("*The Two Presidencies*"), is professor of political science and chairman of the department at the University of California, Berkeley. He received a grant from the Social Science Research Council in 1965 for a study of the presidency in public opinion and has published extensively on the American presidency. He is the author, with Nelson Polsby, of *Presidential Elections* (1964).

WILLIAMS, WALTER ("*Cleveland's Crisis Ghetto*"), is deputy director of the Center for Priority Analysis, National Planning Association. His current interests include investigating how modern analytical techniques can be used to develop relevant data for social policy. Formerly at the Office of Economic Opportunity, he was primarily concerned there with income maintenance and manpower, particularly in the urban ghetto.

WOLF, ERIC R. ("*Algerian Peasant Revolt*"), is professor of anthropology at the University of Michigan. Author of *Sons of the Shaking Earth* and *Peasant Wars of the Twentieth Century* and many other works, he has recently done field research in the Italian Alps in German-speaking and Italian-speaking villages.

YANCEY, WILLIAM L. ("*Black Families and the White House*"), is assistant professor of sociology and director of the Urban and Regional Development Center at Vanderbilt University. He is co-author with Lee Rainwater of the *Moynihan Report and the Politics of Controversy*.

Name Index

Abbas, Ferhat, 464
Abernathy, Ralph, 413
Abu-Bekr, 314
Adams, Henry, 388
Adams, Robert, 388–89
Aitov, A., 32–3
Alexander, Clifford, 521
Alger, Horatio, 179, 295
Alkan, Charles H. V., 244
Allen, Francis A., 233
Altman, Irwin, 360, 367
Andrews, T. Coleman, 472, 481
App, Austin J., 481
Aries, Phillippe, 294–5
Arnett, Peter, 391
Asch, Solomon, 93

Bacon, Warren, 345
Banfield, Edward, 346
Baran, Paul, 255
Barclay, Dorothy, 161
Baron, Harold M., 299, 340
Barr, Sherman, 377, 381
Barton, Allen, 440, 445–50
Barton, Paul, 510
Becker, Howard S., 158, 209
Beers, Clifford W., 98
Beethoven, Ludwig van, 244
Belknap, Ivan, 98
Ben Badis, Abd-el-Hamid, 461, 470
Ben Bella, Ahmed, 470
Bennett, John W., 1, 4, 12
Bennis, Warren, 91, 143
Bensman, Joseph, 222, 241
Berg, Ivar, 300, 353
Berk, Richard, 258
Berque, Jacques, 462
Bhore, Joseph, 78
Birch, John, 182
Birnbaum, Ezra, 383
Blake, Herman, 536–7

Blake, R. R., 145
Blos, Peter, 181
Blauner, Robert, 430, 432
Blumer, Herbert, 126
Bockoven, J. Sanbourne, 102
Boesel, David, 223, 258
Boggs, Hale, 532
Bonaparte, Marie, 421
Boone, Charles, 417
Boserup, Anders, 222, 248
Boulding, Kenneth E., 483, 486
Boumédienne, Houari, 467, 470
Bourdieu, Pierre, 461
Branton, Wiley, 514, 517
Brians, R. E., 416–7
Bridges, Harry, 211
Briggs, Jean L., 3, 44
Brockway, Fenner, 270–1
Broderick, Ellen, 510
Bronfenbrenner, Martin, 4, 65
Bronfenbrenner, Urie, 516
Brown, Esther L., 102
Brown, Hugh D., 416–7
Brown, Pat, 432
Brown, Rap, 423, 425, 427, 444
Browning, Harley, 91, 137
Browning, Rufus C., 277–8
Bryde, John F., 267
Buckley, Benjamin, 387
Buckley, Louis, 129
Buckley, Warden, 389
Buckley, William F., 181
Burke, Kenneth, 170
Butcher, James, 326
Butler, Nicholas Murray, 440
Byers, Louis T., 481
Byrd, Richard E., 367
Byrnes, James, 338

Cahill, Thomas J., 414

Campbell, Angus, 260, 264
Campbell, Clarence, 89
Camus, Albert, 460
Carmichael, Stokely, 423–5, 427, 444
Carnegie, Andrew, 390
Carter, Robert, 510, 518
Catherine the Great, Empress of Russia, 13
Cavanagh, Jerome P., 419, 425, 427–8
Cawelti, John, 295
Cervantes, Lucius F., 267
Chakotin, Serge, 469
Chamberlain, Wilt, 413
Chaplin, Charles, 144
Chassin, Lionel-Max, 468
Cherven, Victor, 473
Chiang Kai-shek, 125
Chin, John Yehall, 119
Chopra, R. N., 78
Choy, J. K., 124
Christie, Nils, 4, 61
Clark, Kenneth B., 263, 516
Clausewitz, Karl von, 470
Cleaver, Eldridge, 211
Clinard, Marshall B., 219
Cloward, Richard A., 136, 267, 361, 376
Coates, Charles H., 224, 276
Coles, Robert, 516
Collver, Andrew, 139
Comte, Auguste, 89
Connolly, James, 251, 253–4
Cooke, Terence J., 533
Cooke, Watts, 387
Cooley, Charles Horton, 89
Corbin, Lee H., 93
Corsi, Jerome R., 415
Cotten, Richard B., 481
Coughlin, Edward, 481
Courtney, Kent, 472
Cressey, Donald R., 158, 221
Crommelein, John, 481

Cromwell, Olvier, 80
Cutler, Lloyd, 533

Daley, Richard, 215
Daniel, Jean, 466
Danto, Bruce, 421
Darwin, Charles, 1
Davis, Fred, 5, 80
Davis, Rennard, 340
Davis, William, 473
Dawson, William, 346
Deakin, Nicholas, 273–4
Debray, Régis, 425
De Fleur, Melvin L., 372–3
De Friese, Gordon H., 360, 372
De Gaulle, Charles, 24, 467
Delisle, René, 462
Del Valle, Pedro A., 481
De Salvo, James, 93
Dewey, John, 160, 273
Dexter, Lewis A., 335
Dickens, Charles, 1, 139
Dodds, R. Harcourt, 414
Doerr, Paul L., 277
Dorner, Peter, 523
Dorosh, Efim, 29
Dougal, Arwin A., 522
Dreiser, Theodore, 287
Drucker, Peter, 146
Dryfoos, Robert J., Jr., 3, 57
Dubcek, Alexander, 451–3, 456
Du Bois, W. E. B., 274
Duchal, A. S., 32
Dulles, John Foster, 339
Dutschke, Rudi, 193

Eddy, Elizabeth, 152
Eidson, Bettye, 258
Einstein, Albert, 493
Eisenhower, Dwight D., 186, 332, 335–7, 339

Eisenhower, Milton, 532, 537
Ellison, Ralph, 81
Elman, Richard M., 361, 376
Erikson, Erik H., 169, 178,
    181, 183, 516
Evans, Ahmed, 411, 414–5
Evans, Roland, 515–6, 521

Fanon, Frantz, 461, 468–70
Farmer, James, 516
Farrell, James F., 287
Fass, Horst, 391
Favrod, Charles-Henri, 464
Fisher, A. D., 223, 266
Fitch, Robert, 249
Flacks, Richard, 157, 185
Fogelson, Robert M., 263
Fomin, V. 33
Ford, W. Scott, 360, 372
Foster, John S., Jr., 523
Fountain, L. H., 525
Fourastie, Jean, 138
France, Anatole, 347, 460
Frazier, E. Franklin, 115
Frederick the Great,
    King of Prussia, 408
Freed, Jim, 422, 424–5
Freedman, Marcia, 354
Freud, Sigmund, 72, 160,
    169–70, 176, 295, 421
Friedenberg, Edgar, 182
Friedmann, Eugene A., 205
Friendly, Alfred, 409
Fuchs, Estelle, 261
Fulbright, J. William, 522
Fullilove, C. W., 113
Fyke, James L., 414

Gagnon, John H., 1, 18, 156,
    169
Galilei, Galileo, 93
Gandhi, Mohandas K., 75
Gans, Herbert, 512, 517, 519
Garbarino, Merwyn S., 224,
    280
Garry, Charles, 537
Gash, Charles M., 417
Gerrard, Nathan L., 299, 325
Gibbon, Edward, 143
Gibbon, Peter, 252, 254
Ginder, Richard, 424
Ginsburg, David, 533
Girardin, Ray, 425, 427
Gitlin, Todd, 188
Glass, Ruth, 273
Gleza, Edwin, 422–3
Goffman, Erving, 98–9,
    101–2, 159
Goldberg, Arthur, 510
Goldberg, David, 141
Goldwater, Barry, 178, 181,
    332, 473–5, 477–8, 489
Goodwin, Richard N., 510,
    517
Gordon, Lou, 423
Gordon, Milton, 275
Grant, J. Douglas, 497, 499

Gray, J. Glenn, 393
Green, Mrs. Wendell, 345
Greenblatt, Milton, 102
Gregory, Dick, 382
Griffiths, Peter, 271
Groves, W. Eugene, 258
Guetzkow, Harold, 523
Guevara, Ernesto (Che),
    425, 445
Gustafsson, Berndt, 319–20
Gustav Vasa, King of Sweden,
    322
Gustav III, King of Sweden,
    323
Gutman, Herbert G., 361
    385

Hadj, Messali, 461, 463–4
Handel, Gerald, 222, 246
Hardin, James T., 482
Hardin, Taylor, 472
Hargis, Billy James, 481
Harriman, Averell, 511
Harris, Patricia, 533
Hart, Philip A., 533
Hatcher, Richard D., 263
Havighurst, Robert J., 205,
    268
Haythorn, William, 360,
    367
Head, F. H., 288
Heckscher, Gunnar, 322
Hedgeman, Anna, 520
Height, Dorothy, 521
Heilbroner, Robert, 82
Hendry, Jean, 60
Henry, Jules, 41, 369
Hensley, George Went, 325
Heyman, Ira, 536
Hiestand, Dale, 358
Higginbotham, A. Leon, 533,
    537
Hill, Norman, 518
Hill, Robert D., 263
Hillinger, Charles, 438
Hilton, James F., 416–7
Hing, Alex, 118
Hitler, Adolf, 469
Hobart, Garrett A., 389
Hobsbawm, E. J., 115
Hoffer, Eric, 533, 536–8
Hofstadter, Richard, 295
Hoggard, Jean, 469
Hoover, Herbert, 182
Hoover, J. Edgar, 126
Horowitz, Irving Louis, 158,
    209, 485, 522
Horton, John, 3, 35
Howard, John R., 90, 106
Hruska, Roman, 533
Hum, Foo, 124
Humbaraci, Arslan, 470
Humphrey, Hubert H., 473–9,
    517
Huntington, Samuel P., 335–7
Huxley, Aldous, 84
Hyman, Herbert, 476

Il'iashenko, F., 33
Isaacs, Harold, 273

Jackson, Andrew, 280
Jackson, Henry, 335
Janowitz, Morris, 276–8,
    393
Jaworski, Leon, 533
Jenner, Albert E., Jr., 533
Johnson, Ellis, 145
Johnson, Lyndon B., 42, 215,
    332, 334–5, 339, 398,
    474–5, 478, 480, 482, 510,
    515–6, 518–9, 532–3
Johnson, Thomas A., 411, 414
Johnson, W. H., 170
Jones, James, 393
Jones, James E., 433
Jones, LeRoi, 211
Judd, Norman H., 414

Kader, Abd el, 459, 461
Kafka, Franz, 143
Kagan, Jerome, 172
Kaplan, Bert, 17
Kelman, Herbert C., 484, 504
Keniston, Hayward, 440
Kennedy, Bernard J. 416–7
Kennedy, Edward, 473
Kennedy, John F., 228, 332–3,
    338–9, 529
Kennedy, Robert F., 533–4
Kerner, Otto, 533
Kerr, Clark, 147
Keyserling, Mary, 520
Khalid, Khalid Muhammad,
    316
Khan, Ayub, 317
Kiesler, Charles A., 90, 92
Kiesler, Sara, 93, 95
King, Martin Luther, Jr., 424,
    427–8, 437, 510, 517–9
Kinsey, Alfred, 172
Kipling, Rudyard, 274
Kirk, Grayson, 442–4, 446–7
Kluckhohn, Clyde, 4
Kluckhohn, Florence, 84
Knapp, Leroy H., Jr., 416
Knopf, Terry Ann, 362, 411
Kopkind, Andrew, 532–3
Kreisler, Joseph, 376–77, 381
Kuznetsov, Anatoly, 33

Lai, Denny, 116
Lal, Kaviraj Kunja, 74
Landers, Ann, 217
Lane, Robert E., 219
Lantz, Herman, 18
Larkin, James, 253–4
Launay, Michel, 460, 462–3
Leavitt, Harold, 147
Lee, Lim P., 116
Lenin, Vladimir I., 68
Leslie, Charles, 4, 70
Lewis, Hylan, 512, 519–20
Lewis, John, 516

Lewis, Oscar, 17
Lewy, Guenter, 299, 314
Liang, Dapien, 124
Liebow, Elliot, 136, 259
Lindsay, John V., 446, 449
Linn, Lawrence S., 373
Lipset, Seymour Martin, 39,
    335, 431, 471
Little, Kenneth, 273
Little, Roger, 396
Lobsinger, Donald, 424–5,
    428
Locke, Hubert, 425–6, 427
Locricchio, Anthony, 422–5
Long, Norton E., 300, 347
Lowinger, Paul, 428
Lüthy, Herbert, 467
Lyman, Stanford M., 90, 113
Lyons, Gene M., 523

McAuliffe, Lester, 417
McCarthy, Joseph R., 126
McClelland, David, 146
McCone, John A., 432, 537
McCulloch, William M., 533
McDonnell, Joseph P., 388–9
McDowell, Beverly, 473
McFarland, Ernest W., 533
McGee, Frank, 422–3
McGrory, Mary, 515
McKinley, William G., 389
McKissick, Floyd, 517–8
McMahon, Dennis C., 481
McNamara, Robert S., 338–9
Mack, Raymond, 483–4, 493,
    495
Mahler, Gustav, 244
Mailer, Norman, 393
Maine, Henry, 304
Malcolm X, 42, 106, 427
Mannheim, Karl, 268, 430
Mansergh, Nicholas, 253
Mao Tse-tung, 119, 126,
    445, 468–9
Marcuse, Herbert, 147
Marshall, S. L. A., 393
Martyn, Kenneth A., 433–4
Marvin, Lee, 400
Marx, Karl, 28, 72, 75, 79, 86,
    185, 222, 388–9, 430, 538
Maslow, Abraham, 176
Mason, Philip, 275
Masotti, Louis H., 415
Massu, Jacques, 466
Masters, Virginia, 170
Maurois, André, 1
Mayo, Elton, 145
Mead, Margaret, 142
Mechanic, David, 149
Menges, Constantine G., 431,
    451
Menninger, W. Walter, 533
Meredith, James, 382
Meriweather, Louise, 434
Michael, Donald, 83
Miller, Herman, 510
Miller, S. M., 480, 519

Miller, Walter B., 90, 96, 157
Mills, Bill, 433
Mills, C. Wright, 276–8, 430
Mitchell, Clarence, 517–8
Mohammed, 314–5
Moore, Bill, 117
Moqrani, El, 459–61
Morris, Marian Gennaria, 156, 163
Moses, Robert, 349
Moskos, Charles C., Jr., 361, 391
Moss, Howard, 172
Motz, Annabelle B., 156, 159
Moynihan, Daniel Patrick, 422–3, 510–521
Mukhopadhyaya, Girindranath, 74
Murray, Arthur, 84
Mutsuhito, Emperor of Japan, 65

Nagel, Stuart S., 221, 233
Naguib, Mohammed, 316
Naroll, Raoul, 361, 402
Nasser, Gamal A., 316–7
Newton, Huey P., 536–7
Newton, Isaac, 493
Nicholas II, Czar of Russia, 13, 441
Nixon, Richard M., 473–80, 482
Nkrumah, Kwame, 249
Novak, Robert, 515–6, 521
Noyes, John Humphrey, 11

O'Bee, Walter, 426–7
Ohkawa, Kazushi, 65
Ohlin, Lloyd E., 136, 267
Oliver, Revilo P., 481
Omar, 314
Oppenheimer, Mary, 249
O'Reilly, John, 426
Orshansky, Mollie, 130
Orwell, George, 84, 233
Osborn, Alton F., 473
Ozaki, Masutarō, 6–11
Ozarin, Lucy, 98

Paine, Thomas, 316
Paisley, Ian, 254, 256
Pallak, Michael, 93, 95
Palmer, Potter, 287
Palmieri, Victor, 533
Parker, Seymour, 268–9
Parker, William, 435
Parsons, Albert, 288–9
Parsons, Talcott, 175, 294, 516
Pasteur, Louis, 67
Payton, Benjamin F., 512, 519–20
Pearce, Michael, 523
Pennington, William, 473
Pettigrew, Thomas, 516
Plath, David W., 1, 6

Plaut, Thomas, 17
Pomfret, John D., 515, 520
Portnoy, Ron, 427

Raab, Earl, 431, 471
Radcliffe-Brown, A. R., 305
Radford, William, 335
Rafferty, Max, 210–1
Rainwater, Lee, 222, 246, 484–5, 510
Rand, Ayn, 181–2
Randolph, A. Philip, 516
Ray, Charles, 268–9
Rheingold, Joseph, 174
Richmond, A. H., 273
Riesman, David, 83
Riessman, Frank, 519
Rinn, L., 459
Ripley, Anthony, 414–6
Robinson, James, 335–6
Rockefeller, Nelson A., 449
Rodriguez, Manuel, 497
Rogler, Lloyd H., 298, 310
Romney, A. Kimball, 523
Romney, George, 424–5, 428
Roosevelt, Franklin D., 332
Rose, Peter I., 223, 270
Rosen, Lawrence, 298, 301
Rosenthal, Marilyn, 362, 419
Rossi, Peter, 258, 484, 501
Roth, Julius, 91, 150
Rothstein, Richard, 340
Rousseau, Jean-Jacques, 316
Rubenfeld, Seymour, 267
Rudd, Mark, 443, 446
Rusk, Dean, 338
Russell, Roger, 523
Rustin, Bayard, 437, 517–8
Ryan, Joan, 268–9
Ryan, William, 512, 520

Sackett, Milton, 426
Sakumura, J., 93
Sartre, Jean-Paul, 438
Saunders, Stan, 439
Schiff, Lawrence F., 157, 178
Schlesinger, Arthur, Jr., 333, 338
Schmidt, Jim, 423, 427
Schofield, William, 326
Schuman, Howard, 260, 264
Schumpeter, Joseph A., 144
Scott, John Finley, 298, 305
Sennett, Richard, 224, 287
Sharma, Pandit Hari Prapanna, 78
Shearer, William K., 472–3
Sheatsley, Paul, 476
Shellow, Robert, 533
Sheppard, Marilyn, 409
Sheppard, Sam, 409–10
Shiloh, Ailon, 90, 98
Shils, Edward, 393
Short, James F., 534
Shriver, Sargent, 511
Shubkin, V., 34

Simmon, Geoffrey, 158, 206
Simmons, William J., 480
Simon, Rita James, 362, 409
Simon, William, 1, 18, 156, 169
Simons, Menno, 16
Skolnick, Jerome, 485, 532
Smith, Adam, 65–6, 183
Smoot, Dan, 472
Snell, Amos J., 291
Sommer, Robert, 150
Soustelle, Jacques, 464
Sparer, Edward, 378
Spellman, Francis, 533
Spencer, Herbert, 4, 390
Spiegel, John P., 411
Spies, August, 288–9
Spike, Robert, 519
Spindler, George, 269
Stalin, Joseph, 29, 336
Stendahl, 394
Stokes, Carl, 263, 411, 414
Stone, I. F., 538
Stone, Robert A., 414
Stouffer, Samuel, 393
Strauss, Anselm, 360, 364
Stulman, Harriet, 340
Sudnow, David, 221, 225
Sugihara, Yoshie, 6
Sukarno, Achmed, 67
Sumner, William Graham, 5
Sundquist, James, 511
Sun Yat Sen, 125
Sutherland, Edwin H., 216
Svoboda, Ludwig, 451–3, 456
Sweezy, Paul, 255

Tati, Jacques, 144
Tegnér, Esaias, 324
Telemann, Georg P., 244
Tellegen, Auke, 326
Thackeray, William, 296
Theobald, Robert, 83
Thernstrom, Stephan, 294
Thornton, Charles, 533
Thurmond, Strom, 473, 477
Tilak, Lokamanya, 76
Tillion, Germaine, 463
Tingsten, Herbert, 319
Toch, Hans, 484, 497
Tolstoy, Leo, 165, 394
Tomasson, Richard F., 299, 318
Tone, Wolfe, 252–3
Trimberger, Ellen Kay, 431, 440
Trout, Grafton, 158, 206
Truman, David, 443, 446–8
Truman, Harry S., 332, 336–9
Tsien Hwue-shen, 126
Turney-High, Harry H., 405
Turnipseed, Tom, 472
Tuttle, Socrates, 389
Tylor, Edward, 1

Udall, Stewart, 333
Usman, Muhammad, 77

Vandenberg, Arthur H., 335
Van Gennep, Arnold, 195
Veblen, Thorstein, 67, 159–60
Volpe, John, 123
Voltaire, F., 316

Walker, Daniel, 538
Wallace, George C., 192, 422, 428, 471–82
Wallace, S. Rains, 523, 530
Walters, Robert, 472–3
Washington, Booker T., 123
Watson, John, 425–6, 428
Wax, Murray, 267
Wax, Rosalie, 267
Wayne, John, 400
Webb, Beatrice, 532
Webb, Eugene, 523
Webb, Sidney, 532
Webber, Melvin, 521
Weber, Max, 39, 82, 143–4, 160, 222
Weinman, Carl A., 409
Weiss, Melford S., 157, 194
Weiss, Robert S., 158, 198
Weisskopf, Walter, 82
Welch, Robert, 481
Westie, Frank R., 372–3
Wharton, Edith, 296
Whyte, Martin K., 3, 28
Wildavsky, Aaron, 299, 332
Wiley, George, 382
Wilkins, Roy, 510, 516, 521
Williams, Walter, 91, 127
Willis, Benjamin, 345
Wilner, David, 502
Wilson, Harold, 254, 271
Wilson, James Q., 343, 346, 516
Wilson, Richard, 515
Wirt, Anne, 326
Wirtz, Willard, 146, 511
Wolcott, Harry, 269
Wolf, Eric, 431, 457
Wolfgang, Marvin, 534
Wong, Ken, 116
Wong, Mason, 124
Wong, Stan, 119
Woo, George, 118–20
Wright, Frank Lloyd, 295
Wright, Quincy, 405
Wright, Robert S., 417

Yancey, William F., 485, 510
Yankelovich, Daniel, 475
Yarmolinsky, Adam, 511
Yashin, A., 32
Yockey, Francis Parker, 481
York, Richard H., 102
Young, Andrew, 517
Young, Whitney, 510, 517–8

Zanna, Mark, 93
Ziegler, Jack, 414
Zimmer, Heinrich, 71

Subject Index

accommodation: limits of, 213–5; and peace, 213–5
adolescence: and conservatism, 178–83; psychosexual behavior in, 172–5; and search for identity, 178–83
Advocate (Barbados), 496
Africa (*see* Ghana *and* Third World)
African Systems of Kinship and Marriage (Radcliffe-Brown), 305
Age of Innocence (Wharton), 296
alcoholism, in Scandinavia, 61–4
Algeria: assimilation in, 464; education in, 463–4; nationalism in, 463–4; peasant revolt in 457–70
alienation, in India, 72–4
American Mercury, 481
American Opinion, 412
American Sociological Review, 372
American Soldier, The (Stouffer et al.), 393–4
Amish, 12–3, 16
Anabaptists, 16; Amish, 12–3, 16; Hutterians, 12–7; Mennonites, 16
Animal Farm (Orwell), 233
Ann Arbor News, 417–8
applied research, and political goals, 529–31
arms race, and war, 402–4
asceticism, and Black Muslims, 106–7, 109–12
assimilation, in Algeria, 464
Asylums (Goffman), 98
attitudes: vs. behavior, 372–5; toward education, 246–7
Autobiography (Wright), 295

backlash, and the Haymarket riots (Chicago, 1886), 287–96
Battle of Algiers, The, 466

behavior: vs. attitudes, 372–5; collective, 419–28; psychosexual, 169–77; public vs. private, 372–5; and social pressure, 372–5
bilingualism, and education, 269
Black Muslims, 106–12; and asceticism, 106–7, 109–12; and deviance, 106–7, 109–12
blacks (*see also* Black Muslims, ethnic groups *and* ghetto): and the distribution of wealth, 304–52; and exclusion from government, 340–6; and exclusion from private institutions, 341–3; and family structure, 510–21; and job opportunities, 259–60, 340–6; marginality of, 340–52; in political parties, 262–4; powerlessness of, 340–6; street culture of, 35–42; vs. whites, 258–65, 270–5, 340–6, 372–5
Blue Book (Birch), 182
bourgeoisie (*see also* middle class), Third World, 249–50
bureaucracy, 143–54; effectiveness of, 143–7; and industrialization, 143–7; and welfare, 377–84
Business Week, 246

California Statesman, 472
Capital (Marx), 538
capitalism, 347–52; and the distribution of wealth, 347–52; in Japan, 65–9
caste, 223–4, 225–57; features in open societies, 223–4, 258–75
Castle (Kafka), 143
Catholicism (*see also* religion), vs. Protestantism in Ireland, 248–57
census (Cleveland, 1965), 127–36
Centuries of Childhood (Aries), 294
Chicago, black powerlessness, 340–6

Chicago Sun-Times, 417
Chicago Tribune, 290–1, 417, 538
childhood, socialization, 155–6, 159–77
Chinatown (San Francisco), 113–26; discrimination against, 125–6; power structure, 120–5; rebellion in, 113–26; Red Guards, 113–26
Chinese-Americans (*see also* Chinatown), in San Francisco, 113–26
Christianity and Crisis, 512
civil rights (*see* justice)
class (*see also* stratification), 222–4, 225–57; and death, 225–32; definition of, 222; and family patterns, 247; intellectuals as a, 185–6; and justice, 235–6; middle, 159–62, 246–7, 305–9; working, 246–7
Cleveland: census (1965), 127–36; ghetto, 127–36; riots, 127
Cleveland Press, 409, 411
collective farms (*see also* communal living), USSR, 28–34
colonialism: British (in Ireland), 248–50; French (in Algeria), 458–9; and Third World, 249–50
Columbia Spectator, 442, 444, 447
Columbia University, and rebellion, 440–50
Common Defense, The (Huntington), 336
Common Sense, 481
Commonweal, 512
communal living (*see also* Anabaptists *and* collective farms), 6–17; Amish, 12–3, 16; Hutterites, 12–7
communication (*see also* interaction *and* mass communications), 359–61; collective, 419–28; definition of, 359; overload, 363
community (*see also* small town): leadership, 25–7; status, 241–5; urban, 113–42
Concentration Camps, U.S.A. (Allen), 426
conflict, 376–401; ethnic, 250–1; interpersonal, 367–71; Protestant-Catholic (Ireland), 248–57
conformity, 92–5; definitions of, 92–3; middle-class, 159–62; price of, 162
Congress and Foreign Policy-Making (Robinson), 336
Congress and the Nation (Congressional Quarterly Service), 333
consensus, normative, 5
conservatism, 178–83, 471–82; and adolescence, 178–83; and resistance to change, 385–6
Conservative Journal, 472
Contemporary Psychology, 366
courts (*see also* juries *and* justice), and crime, 409–10
crime: and courts, 409–10; and the press, 409–10; white-collar, 216–9
Crime Control Digest, 412
culture, 1–87; vs. biology, 1; commonalities of, 2; definition of, 1, 5, 404; Eskimo, 44–56; street, 35–42; and subcultures, 2, 35–42, 80–7; and time, 39; variations in, 35–64; and war, 403–8
Culture Against Man (Henry), 369
custodial ethic, 98–9, 102, 104–5
Czechoslovakia, resistance in, 451–6

death: and hospital decision-making, 225–32; and life cycle, 137–42; and social class, 225–32
dehumanization, of motherhood, 163–8
Delinquency and Opportunity (Cloward and Ohlin), 136, 267
democracy: and deviance, 213–5; price of, 213
Department of Defense: vs. Department of State, 531; uses of social science, 522–31
Department of State, vs. Department of Defense, 531
deterrence, military theory of, 402–8
Detroit, riots, 419–28
development (*see also* industrialization, progress *and* Third World): in Japan, 65–9; and life expectancy, 137–42; models, 69; policies, 67–9; psychosexual, 169–77; small-town, 18–27
deviance (*see also* rebellion), 80–7; and Black Muslims, 106–12; and democracy, 213–5; in San Francisco, 209–15 and socialization, 209–19; tolerance of, 209–15
discrimination (*see also* prejudice), against ethnic groups, 125–6, 223–4, 258–75
dissatisfaction: and complaint, 150–4; individual reactions to, 150–4; options to, 150–4
divorce (*see also* marriage), Moslem, 301–4
Dropout: Causes and Cures, The (Cervantes), 267
drugs: and hippies, 80, 206–8; socialization into, 206–8
Dutchman (Jones), 211
ecology, 486–92
economy, 300, 347–58; in Japan, 65–9; private initiative, 347–52
education: in Algeria, 463–4; and bilingualism, 269; and job performance, 353–58; and the military, 277; and mobility, 224, 280–6; opportunities for Indians, 266–9; as ritual, 268; systems approach, 487–92; working- vs. middle-class attitudes, 246–7
elite: military, 276–8; in Ulster (Ireland), 248–9
endogamy, definition of, 308
England (*see* Great Britain)
environment (*see* ecology)
equality (*see* discrimination, justice *and* stratification)
Eros and Civilization (Marcuse), 147
Eskimo, 44–60; ethnic survival of, 57–60; norms, 44–56
ethics, in social science research, 504–8
ethnic groups (*see also* race), 113–26, 280–6; conflict between, 250–1; discrimination against, 125–6, 223–4, 258–75; tactics for survival, 57–60, 125–6
exogamy, definition of, 308

faculty, response to Columbia rebellion, 448–9
family (*see also* marriage), 297–313; black, 510–21; and class, 247; in India, 139; middle-class, 159–62; and mobility, 310–3; in Puerto Rico, 310–3; role-playing, 159–62; in rural USSR, 29–32; and socialization, 159–68; welfare, 511, 513; working-class, 247
Family of Outcasts (Rubenfeld), 267
folkways, definition of, 5
Fortune, 475
Frontier, 434

gangs (*see* street corner gangs)
George Wallace Newsletter, 471, 481
German Ideology, The (Marx) 86
Ghana (*see also* Third World), polity, 249
ghetto (*see also* blacks): Chinatown (San Francisco), 120; Cleveland, 127–36; merchants, 260–1; police harassment techniques, 264–5; and riots, 430–9; socioeconomic polarization in, 127; street culture in, 35–42; teachers, 261; welfare, 261–2, 376–84
goals: of applied research, 529–31; in a street culture, 41–2
government (*see also* Department of Defense, Department of State *and* polity), and exclusion of blacks, 340–6
Great Britain: and colonialism in Ireland, 248–50; racial discrimination in, 270–5
Great Society: and the distribution of wealth, 347–52; private initiative in, 347–52; suburbia, 348–9
groups (*see also* ethnic groups), 88–112; conformity to, 92–5; corner gang, 96–7; definition of, 88–9; influence on individual behavior, 374–5; primary vs. secondary, 89–90

Haight-Ashbury (*see also* San Francisco), 80–7
Haymarket riots (Chicago, 1886), 287–96; and backlash, 287–96; and police, 289–91
hedonism: hippie, 206; religious, 328–31
hippies, 5, 80–7; and drugs, 80, 206–8; future of, 86–7; and hedonism, 206; and normative order, 80–7; politicized, 206–8
hospitals: negotiation in, 364–6; and stratification of death, 225–32
Hutterian Brethren, 12–7
hypergamy, definition of, 308
hypogamy, definition of, 308

identity: and Indians, 269; search for, 178–83
Imperium (Yockey), 481
Indépendent, L' (Constantine, Algiers), 459
India (*see also* Third World): alienation in, 72–4; family in, 139; life expectancy in, 137, 139; medicine in, 70–9; revivalism in, 70–9; tradition in, 70–9
Indian: and bilingualism, 269; educational opportunities for, 266–9; ethnic survival of, 57–60; identity, 269; mobility, 280–6; vs. white, 266–9
industrialization (*see also* development *and* progress): and bureaucracy, 143–7; early patterns, 385–90; in Paterson (N.J.), 386–90
Inner City Voice, 422, 425–8
institutions, 297–358; economic, 65–9, 300, 347–58; family, 29–32, 139, 159–68, 247, 301–13, 510–21; political, 332–46; religious, 29–32, 248–57, 314–31; "total," 98–105; white, 258–65, 340–6
intellectuals, as a class, 185–6
intelligentsia: definition of, 185; growth of, 185; and radicalism, 185–93; and youths, 185–93
interaction (*see also* communication), 359–75; collective, 419–28; conflict vs. cooperation, 376–401; in isolation, 367–71; patterns, 88–9, 364–75; primary vs. secondary, 89–90; symbolic, 359–61; white-black, 372–5

internalization, of norms, 155–7, 159–77
intolerance (*see also* prejudice), 250–1
Ireland (*see also* Third World *and* Ulster): British colonialism in, 248–50; religious divisions in, 248–57
Irish Question, The (Mansergh), 253
isolation: and interaction, 367–71; and personality, 367–71; and psychological pairing, 367–71

Japan: communal living in, 6–11; development in, 65–9
jobs (*see also* work): and blacks, 259–60, 340–6; and education, 353–8
Journal of Social Issues, 181
juries (*see also* courts *and* justice): and mass communications, 409–10; press influence on, 409–10
justice (*see also* courts, discrimination, juries *and* polity), 224; and class, 235–6, 238; federal vs. state, 239; and legitimacy, 299; North vs. South, 238–9; and race, 236–8; and sex, 236, 238; in the United States, 233–9; urban vs. rural, 238–9

"Kerner Report," 223, 411, 533–4
kinship, in rural USSR, 29–32

Labor Standard, 388–9
Labour in Irish History (Connolly), 251
Law Officer, The, 418
leadership, small-town, 25–7
learning, psychosexual behavior, 169–77
left-wing (*see* radicalism)
legitimacy, and polity, 299
leisure, and work, 147
Life, 439
life cycle: and death, 137–42; and life expectancy, 137–42
life expectancy: in India, 137, 139; and marriage, 141–2; in Mexico, 137; social consequences of, 137–42
life styles, working- vs. middle-class, 246–7
Look, 426
Los Angeles Times, 438
Love Machine, The (Susann), 535
lumpenproletariat, 431

McCarran Act, 426
"McCone Report," 430–9, 537
Macomb Daily News, 423
marginality, black, 340–6
marriage (*see also* divorce *and* family), 297–8; and corner gang boys, 96–7; and life expectancy, 141–2; middle class, 305–9; Moslem, 301–4; and sexual intercourse, 177; terminology, 308
Marxism, and race prejudice theory, 250
mass communications (*see also* press): and juries, 409–10; and news distortion, 411–8; and rumor, 419–28
mass media (*see* mass communications)
mental hospitals: and mental illness, 98–105; as "total" institutions, 98–105
mental illness, 98–105; and custodial ethic, 98–9, 102, 104–5; and mental hospitals, 98–105

methods: and deception, 504–8; involving subject participation, 497–9; scientific, 493–5; of social science research, 483–7, 493, 495–6, 501–3; and techniques, 493
Mexico, life expectancy in, 137
middle class (*see also* bourgeoisie): attitudes toward education, 246–7; conformity, 159–62; family, 159–62, 247; marriage, 305–9
military: deterrence, 402–8; and education, 277; elite, 276–8; takeovers in Third World, 249; and upward mobility, 276–8; urban origins of, 277–8; uses of social science, 522–31
minorities (*see* ethnic groups)
mobility, 223–4, 276–96; and education, 224, 280–6; and family roles, 310–3; Indian, 280–6; and military careers, 276–8
mobilization, political, 430–82
models, for development, 69
moral order (*see also* mores), 5; challenge to, 80–7
mores (*see also* norms): definition of, 5; violations of, 5, 80–7
mortality, control of, 137–42
Moslem (*see also* Black Muslims): marriage and divorce, 301–4; religion, 314–7
motherhood, dehumanization of, 163–8
motivation, in war, 391–401
"Moynihan Report," 510–21; critics of, 512
Muhammad Speaks, 106
Mylady Svet (Prague), 453
Myths of War (Bonaparte), 422

Nation, The, 512
National Commission on the Causes and Prevention of Violence (*see* "Skolnick Report")
nationalism, in Algeria, 463–4
National Review, 181
negotiation: at Columbia University, 444–8; and hospitals, 364–6
Negroes (*see* blacks)
Negro Family: The Case for National Action, The (Moynihan) (*see* "Moynihan Report")
Negro in Chicago, The (Park and Burgess), 432
Negro Politics (Wilson), 346
New America, 437
New Left, 185, 188–93
New Left Review, 252
News (Barbados), 496
New Society, 275
Newsweek, 516
New York Sun, 386
New York Times, 228, 411–2, 414–6, 418, 515, 520–1
norms (*see also* mores), 6–34; and consensus, 5; Eskimo, 44–56; internalization of, 155–7, 159–77; rural USSR, 29–32
North: and justice, 238–9; and 1968 presidential elections, 473–7
Northeast Detroiter, 423–4, 427
Observer, 423

old age, and loss of primary relations, 198–205
On Adolescence (Blos), 181
ostracism, 6–9, 11

Passing On: The Social Organization of Dying (Sudnow), 226
Paterson (N.J.), history of industrialization in, 386–90
peace, and accommodation, 213–5
peasant, revolt, 457–70
People of Coaltown, The (Lantz), 18
personality, and isolation, 367–71
Personality in a Communal Society (Kaplan and Plaut), 17
pluralism, 272–5
police: and Detroit riot, 426–7; and ghetto harassment techniques, 264–5; and Haymarket riots (Chicago, 1886), 289–91; and Watts riot, 434–6
policies (*see also* public policy), for development, 67–9
policy-making, and exclusion of blacks, 343–6
political parties (*see also* polity), and blacks, 262–4
Politics of Protest, The (Skolnick) (*see also* "Skolnick Report"), 534–5, 538
polity (*see also* government *and* justice), 299–300; black powerlessness, 340–6; Ghana, 249; and power, 322–46; presidency, 332–9; Ulster (Ireland), 248–57
polygyny, definition of, 308
populism, urban, 118–20
poverty: and the distribution of wealth, 340–52; and welfare, 376–84
power (*see also* powerlessness), 222–4; of American presidency, 332–9; in Chinatown (San Francisco), 120–5; definition of, 222; legal vs. socioeconomic, 301–4; political, 322–46; of the powerless, 148–9
Power Elite, The (Mills), 276
powerlessness: black, 340–6; power of, 148–9
Pravda (USSR), 453
prejudice (*see also* discrimination), racial, 250, 270–5
Presentation of Self in Everyday Life, The (Goffman), 159
presidency (*see also* polity), 332–9; and 1968 elections—North vs. South, 473–7; power of, 332–9
press (*see also* mass communications): distortions and public opinion, 411–8; influence on juries, 409–10; and rumor, 419–28
prestige, within status communities, 241–5
primary groups: corner gang, 96–7; definition of, 89–90; and old age, 198–205; vs. secondary groups, 89–90
Primitive Warfare: Its Practice and Concepts (Turney-High), 405
private initiative (*see* capitalism)
Professional Soldier, The (Janowitz), 276
progress (*see also* development *and* industrialization), and revivalism, 70–2
proletariat (*see* working class)
protest (*see also* dissatisfaction *and* rebellion): in Czechoslovakia, 451–6; political, 429–70
Protestantism (*see also* religion), vs. Catholicism in Ireland, 248–57
psychological pairing, and isolation, 367–71

public opinion: and the press, 411–8; and rumor, 419–28
public policy (*see also* "Moynihan Report"), and social science, 510–38
Puerto Rico, family roles in, 310–3

Quotations from Chairman Mao Tse-tung (Mao Tse-tung), 117

race (*see also* ethnic groups): and justice, 236–8; prejudice, 250; relations, 223–4, 258–75, 280–6
racism (*see* race)
radicalism: and intelligentsia, 185–93; youth, 185
Rape of the Masses, The (Chakotin), 469
rebellion (*see also* deviance, protest *and* riots), 429–70; in Chinatown, 113–26; at Columbia University, 440–50; of intelligentsia, 185–93; peasant, 457–70; right-wing, 178–83
Red Guards (San Francisco), 113–26; and populism, 118–20
religion (*see also* Anabaptists, Black Muslims, Catholicism *and* Protestantism), 298–300, 314–31; divisions in Ireland, 248–57; and hedonism, 328–31; institutionalization of, 314–24; Moslem, 314–7; in rural USSR, 29–32; serpent-handling, 325–31; in Sweden, 318–24
Reporter (Prague), 453
Report from Iron Mountain (Lewin), 523
Report of the Panel on Defense, Social and Behavioral Sciences (Defense Science Board of the National Academy of Sciences), 523
research: applied, 529–31; ethics in, 504–8; methods, 483–7, 493–6, 501–3; pure, 529; techniques, 493, 495–6
revivalism: in India, 70–9; and progress, 70–2
Revue Militaire d'Information, 469
right-wing (*see* conservatism)
"Riot Commission," 263–5
riots (*see also* rebellion): Cleveland, 127; Commission, 263–5; Detroit, 419–28; Haymarket (Chicago, 1886), 287–96; and police, 426–7, 434–6; Watts, 430–9
rites: and education, 268; of passage, 194–7, 268
role-playing (*see also* roles), family, 159–62
roles: family, 310–3; psychosexual, 169–77
Rude Pravo (Prague), 453
rumor, 419–28; and mass media, 419–28; and the press, 419–28; and public opinion, 419–28
rural: USSR, 28–34; vs. urban justice, 238–9
Russia (*see* USSR)

San Francisco (*see also* Haight-Ashbury), 80–7; Chinese-Americans, 113–26; deviance in, 209–15
San Francisco Chronicle, 210
Scandinavia (*see also* Sweden), alcoholism in, 61–4
science, as frame of reference, 493–5
secondary groups: definition of, 89–90; vs. primary groups, 89–90
self, and socialization, 155–7, 159–77
serpent-handling religions, 325–31
sex, and justice, 236, 238

sexual intercourse, and stratification, 176–7
Sister Carrie (Dreiser), 287
"Skolnick Report," 532–8
small town (*see also* community): decline of, 18–27; development, 18–27; leadership, 25
social action, and social science, 501–3
social change, 65–87; resistance to, 26–7, 70–9
social class (*see* class)
social evolution (*see also* progress), 4; and prediction, 488
Social Forces, 373
socialization, 155–219; adult, 178–205; definition of, 155–7; deviant, 209–19; into drugs, 206–8; early, 155–6, 159–77; and emergence of self, 155–7, 159–77; through the family, 159–68; political, 178–93
social mobility (*see* mobility)
social movements, 429–82; Black Muslims, 106–12; conservative, 178–83, 471–82; hippies, 80–7, 206–8
social organization, 88–154; and bureaucracy, 143–54; definition of, 8; and social groups, 88–112; and urban communities, 113–42
social pressure, and behavior, 372–5
social science, 483–5; applied research in, 529–31; methods, 483–7, 493, 495–6, 501–3; military uses of, 522–31; priorities, 490–2; and public policy, 510–38; and social action, 501–3; techniques, 493, 495–6; trends, 484
social stratification (*see* stratification)
social workers, 261–2
Soul on Ice (Cleaver), 211
South: Democratic party in, 250; and justice, 238–9; and 1968 presidential elections, 473–7
stagnation, in rural USSR, 32–4
status, 221–4; communities, 241–5; and the professional musician, 241–5
status communities, prestige within, 241–5
stratification (*see also* class), 221–96; of death, 225–32; of justice, 233–9; open vs. closed, 223–96; and sexual intercourse, 176–7
street corner gangs, and marriage, 96–7
street culture, 35–42
Student (Prague), 453
student movement, 185, 187–93
Students for a Democratic Society (SDS), 188–9
subculture, 2; hippie, 80–7, 206–8; of street people, 35–42
suburbia, in the Great Society, 348–9
Supplemental Studies (Fogelson and Hill), 263
Sweden, religion in, 318–24

Tally's Corner (Liebow), 136, 259
teachers, ghetto, 261
techniques, research, 493, 495–6
Theory of the Leisure Class, The (Veblen), 159
Third World (*see also* development): bourgeoisie, 249–50, and colonialism, 249–50; military takeovers, 249; political instability, 249–50
time: and culture, 39; in a street culture, 38–41
Time, 412–3

To Be Equal (Young), 518
tolerance, of deviance, 209–15
"total institution" (*see also* mental hospitals), 98–105
trade unions, and exclusions of blacks, 342–4
tradition: in India, 70–9; in rural USSR, 29–32; and the working class, 246–7
Trans-action, 335, 508
trials (*see* justice)

Ulster (*see also* Ireland *and* Third World): elite, 248–9; polity, 248–57; religious divisions in, 248–57
Ulster Protestant (Ireland), 250
USSR, rural, 28–34
United States, justice, 233–9
U.S. News & World Report, 411, 416, 418
urban: communities, 113–42; origins of military, 277–8; populism, 118–20; vs. rural justice, 238–9; status communities, 241–5

Vanity Fair (Thackeray), 296
Vercerni Praha (Prague), 453
Vietnam war (*see also* war), and soldiers' motivations, 391–401
violence (*see also* war): Commission, 532–8; patterns of, 411–8; sniping, 411–8
Violence in the City—An End or a Beginning? (McCone Commission) (*see also* "McCone Report"), 432

"Walker Report," 538
Wall Street Journal, 345
war (*see also* Vietnam war *and* violence): and arms race, 402–4; and cultural exchange, 402–3; and cultural selectivity, 402–3; and culture, 403–8; and deterrence, 402–8; and primitive societies, 403–8; and soldiers' motivations, 391–401; Vietnam, 391–401
Washington Post, 409, 418, 520
Washington Star, 515
Watts riot, 430–9; and the "Moynihan Report," 516–7
wealth, distribution of, 340–52
welfare, 261–2; and bureaucracy, 377–84; and the "Moynihan Report," 511, 513
West Virginia, serpent-handling religions, 325–31
whites: vs. blacks, 258–65, 270–5, 340–6, 372–5; vs. Indians, 266–9
Windsor Star (Canada), 421
work (*see also* jobs), vs. leisure, 147
working class, 246–7; in Algeria, 462–3; attitudes toward education, 246–7; family, 247; life styles, 246–7; traditional vs. modern, 246–7
World Communist Movement (House Un-American Activities Committee), 422

York Dispatch (Pa.), 417
youth: and intelligentsia, 185–93; radical, 185

DATE DUE		
APR 30 1980		
JUN 30 1982		

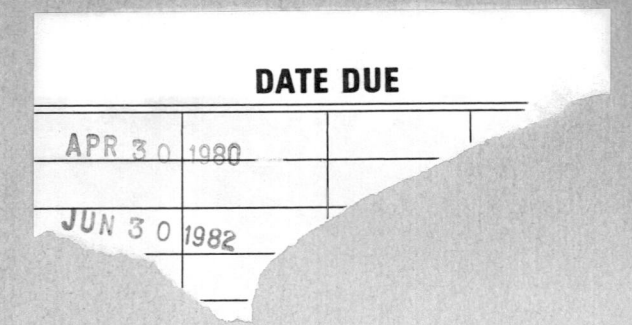